# Let me hear from you...

A teacher or textbook writer is like someone who plants seeds and hopes they will grow. I would like to hear from you about the results. Did your interest in psychology blossom and flourish? What did you like best or least? Frequently students, having a fresh approach to the field, suggest excellent new ideas or notice contradictions and problems that even their professors have overlooked.

*You may tear out this form, fold it, and mail it.*

School: _____ Your instructor's name: _____

1. How did this book affect you? Was it interesting, useful, thought-provoking?

   _____

   _____

   _____

   _____

2. Do you have suggestions for what I should add or change in the next edition? (For example, did you find any particular section difficult or confusing?)

   _____

   _____

   _____

   _____

3. Here is a place for any additional comments:

   _____

   _____

   _____

   _____

*Optional:*

Your name: _____

Address: _____

Email address: _____

Date: _____

May the publisher quote you in publicity for the text?     _____ yes     _____ no

Thanks!

*James W. Kalat*

FOLD HERE

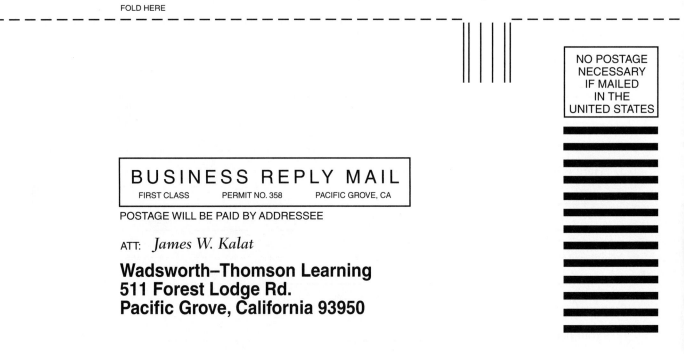

NO POSTAGE
NECESSARY
IF MAILED
IN THE
UNITED STATES

BUSINESS REPLY MAIL

FIRST CLASS          PERMIT NO. 358          PACIFIC GROVE, CA

POSTAGE WILL BE PAID BY ADDRESSEE

ATT: *James W. Kalat*

**Wadsworth–Thomson Learning**
**511 Forest Lodge Rd.**
**Pacific Grove, California 93950**

FOLD HERE

# INTRODUCTION TO

# Psychology

INTRODUCTION TO

# Psychology

## SIXTH EDITION

**James W. Kalat**

*North Carolina State University*

**WADSWORTH**

™

**THOMSON LEARNING**

Australia • Canada • Mexico • Singapore • Spain • United Kingdom • United States

**WADSWORTH**

**THOMSON LEARNING** ™

Psychology Publisher: *Vicki Knight*
Development Editor: *Penelope Sky*
Assistant Editor: *Jennifer Wilkinson*
Editorial Assistant: *Dan Moneypenny*
Marketing Manager: *Marc Linsenman*
Marketing Assistant: *Megan Hansen*
Production Editor: *Kirk Bomont*
Production Service: *Nancy Shammas, New Leaf Publishing Services*
Manuscript Editor: *Frank Hubert*

Permissions Editor: *Mary Kay Polsemen*
Art Editor: *Kathy Joneson*
Illustrations: *Precision Graphics*
Photo Researcher: *Meyers Photo-Art*
Interior Design: *Ellen Pettengell*
Cover Design: *Roy R. Neuhaus*
Cover Image: *Robert Everts/Stone Images*
Print Buyer: *Kris Waller*
Typesetting: *GTS Graphics, Inc.*
Printing and Binding: *R. R. Donnelley & Sons/Willard*

*For more information about this or any other Wadsworth product, contact:*
WADSWORTH–THOMSON LEARNING
511 Forest Lodge Road
Pacific Grove, CA 93950 USA
www.wadsworth.com
1-800-423-0563 (Thomson Learning Academic Resource Center)

*For permission to use material from this work, contact us by:*
Web:   www.thomsonrights.com
Fax:    1-800-730-2215
Phone: 1-800-730-2214

Printed in the United States of America

10   9   8   7   6   5   4   3   2   1

**Library of Congress Cataloging-in-Publication Data**

Kalat, James W.
   Introduction to psychology / James W. Kalat. — 6th ed.
      p. cm.
   Includes bibliographical references and index.
   ISBN 0-534-53988-2
   1. Psychology.   I. Title
BF121.K26 2001
150—dc21                              2001035226

*To My Family*

# About the Author

JAMES W. KALAT (rhymes with ballot) is Professor of Psychology at North Carolina State University, where he teaches courses in introduction to psychology and biological psychology. Born in 1946, he received an AB degree summa cum laude from Duke University in 1968 and a PhD in psychology from the University of Pennsylvania in 1971. He is also the author of *Biological Psychology* (7th ed.) (Belmont, CA: Wadsworth, 2001). In addition to textbooks, he has written journal articles on taste-aversion learning, the teaching of psychology, and other topics. A remarried widower, he has three children, two stepchildren, and two grandchildren.

# Brief Contents

# Contents

**CHAPTER 3**

# Biological Psychology

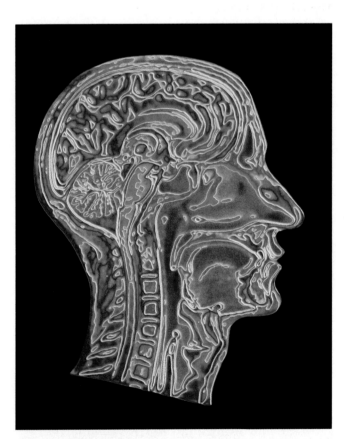

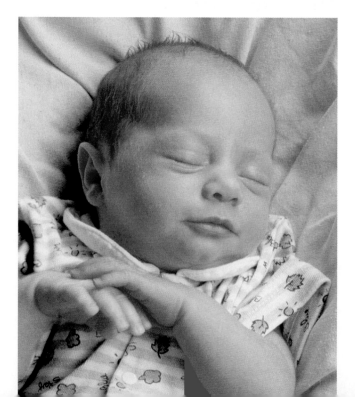

**CHAPTER 6**

# Learning

## CHAPTER 7
# Memory

## CHAPTER 8
# Cognition and Language

# CHAPTER 9
# Intelligence and Its Measurement

## CHAPTER 10
# Human Development

## CHAPTER 11
# Motivation

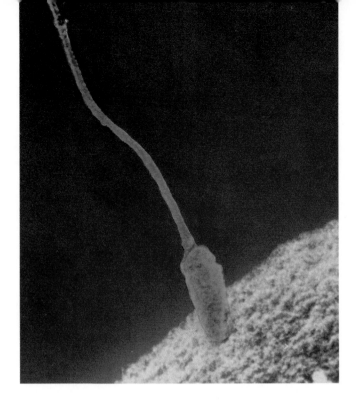

# CHAPTER 12

# Emotions, Health Psychology, and Stress

## CHAPTER 16
# Specific Disorders and Treatments

# Preface to the Instructor

What can we expect students to remember from a course years after it ends? I am sure I have forgotten most of the facts I learned in college, and I suspect the same is true for you and for most of our students. Mastery of facts should not be the goal of education anyway. I hope the field of psychology will continue to progress so that many of the facts we now teach will be supplanted by new research in future decades.

Ideally, a course in psychology or a textbook about it should accomplish two goals. The first is to instill a love of learning, so that our graduates will keep up with new developments in the field, so that they continue to update their education. I fantasize that some of my former students occasionally pick up a copy of *Scientific American, American Scientist, Cerebrum,* or some other good magazine and read articles about psychological research. The second goal is to teach the skills of evaluating evidence and questioning assertions, so that if students do read or hear about a new discovery in psychology (or any related field), they will ask the right questions and draw the appropriate conclusions (or lack of them).

I do not believe that a textbook can instill the habit of questioning assertions merely through boxes labeled "Critical Thinking." In the past I have avoided even using that phrase, because I consider it overused and misused. In this edition I have yielded and you will see the phrase here and there. Regardless of terminology, I have tried to model the habit of critical thinking—evaluating the evidence—throughout the text. My goal is to help students learn to ask their own questions, distinguish between good and weak evidence and, ultimately, appreciate the excitement of psychological inquiry.

## What's New in the Sixth Edition

The Table of Contents for this edition is similar to the last edition, except that I have merged the first and second modules of Chapter 13, "Personality." The information in the text has been greatly updated, however. The sixth edition contains more than 500 references that are new since 1997, about half of them from 2000 or 2001. Every chapter has been reorganized, with new material added and old material clarified. Many figures and photographs have been revised or replaced. Throughout the text you can find many new Concept Checks, Try It Yourself exercises, and What's the Evidence sections. See, for example, page 299 for a new Try It Yourself exercise on overconfidence.

Here are a few examples of new content:

*Chapter 1:* A time line of major events in psychology and concurrent fields.

*Chapter 2:* A new example of a nonreplicable phenomenon: the much-ballyhooed "Mozart effect"; new examples of how the wording of a survey question influences the results; new discussion with example of why before-and-after studies can be misleading.

*Chapter 3:* New research on changes in brain anatomy due to experience, including the growth of new neurons under some conditions; fascinating new study showing that people with left-hemisphere brain damage are better than other people at identifying when someone is lying.

*Chapter 4:* A new description of Dobelle's work that enables people with damaged eyes to see, using a camera that sends information directly to the brain; a discussion of phantom limb, noting recent research that has completely changed our understanding; brightness contrast, with wonderful new figure. (Don't take my word for it that it's wonderful; check it yourself on page 139.)

*Chapter 5:* New evidence that memories of something just learned become strengthened during sleep; expanded and reorganized treatment of dreaming; new research on narcolepsy.

*Chapter 6:* New material on classical conditioning as a timed response, further supporting the idea that a conditioned response prepares for the unconditioned stimulus.

*Chapter 7:* Much revised and expanded treatment of the role of attention in working memory; fascinating new example of implicit memory: Brain-damaged amnesic patients, after playing Tetris for 7 hours, don't remember playing the game, but nevertheless visualize little falling blocks as they fall asleep.

*Chapter 8* is the most interactive chapter in the book. It has 22 Try It Yourself exercises, 17 Concept Checks, and 4 A Step Further exercises. For example, note the new demonstration of a different version of the Stroop effect: When you see the name of a color written in an incongruent color, such as the word RED written in blue, it's easier to *say* "red," but it's easier to *point* to a blue patch.

New section noting that the evolution of language ability is not just a consequence of overall intelligence: People with Williams syndrome have normal or good language development despite mental retardation in most other areas.

Comment on the fact that deaf children who don't learn sign language while young learn it only with difficulty later. This observation is our best evidence for a critical period of human language learning.

*Chapter 9:* Expanded treatment of the Flynn effect, the tendency for raw performance on IQ tests to improve with each generation; new evidence that IQ and school achievement have increased in African Americans since about 1970, cutting by ⅓ the gap between African Americans and European Americans.

*Chapter 10:* New explanation of fetal alcohol syndrome; new example showing that even three-year-olds sometimes distinguish between appearance and reality, depending on how they are tested; completely rewritten section on death and dying, introducing terror-management theory; rewritten material on family influences, strengthening the emphasis on evaluation of evidence; expanded and clarified criticism of most birth order studies (another example of critical evaluation of the evidence); new section on gender and self-esteem, noting problems of measurement.

*Chapter 11:* Compared to other countries, Americans eat a more healthful diet but worry more that it's unhealthful.

*Chapter 12:* Major expansion of the section on happiness, including the hot new research topic "positive psychology" which is used to pursue the theme of evaluating evidence.

*Chapter 13:* Revised and clarified criticisms of the Big Five personality traits; interesting new finding that scores on anxiety tests have gradually increased over the decades, for uncertain reasons; expanded and updated criticisms of projective techniques.

*Chapter 14:* Updated and expanded discussion of the relationship between attractiveness and good genes; revised, updated, and expanded discussion of men's and women's preferences in their partners; brief new section about marriage counseling; revised and updated account of the Prisoner's dilemma.

*Chapter 15:* Clarified criticisms of *DSM-IV;* new examples of the difficulty of preventing mental disorders.

*Chapter 16:* New research on panic disorder leads to a revised interpretation of its causes and treatment; discussion of St. John's wort as an antidepressant, including the fascinating side effect that it activates a liver enzyme that breaks down other medications; note that prevalence of schizophrenia has declined worldwide since the mid-1900s for no known reason.

# Teaching and Learning Supplements

A number of important supplements accompany the text. Nancy Melucci of Santa Monica College prepared a very thorough and creative Instructor's Resource Guide that includes suggestions for class demonstrations and lecture material; it also contains possible answers to the "Step Further" questions. The Study Guide, by Pamela Brouillard of Texas A & M, Corpus Christi, provides various study aids, including practice test items and an ESL component. A bank of test items has been prepared by Pamela Brouillard and Mark Hartlaub, both from Texas A & M, Corpus Christi. That bank is also available on computer disc. Note that many of the items have already been class tested and the display indicates the percent correct and point biserial for students at N. C. State University. Note also that the test item bank includes a special file of items that cut across chapters, intended for a comprehensive final exam.

Other supplements for the text include transparencies (0-534-53995-5), PsychLink (0-534-58025-4), CNN videos, WebTutor Advantage, the PsychLink CD, and PsychNow! online.

In addition, you and your students will also have access to the *Kalat Sixth Edition* section of the Wadsworth Psychology Study Center at http://psychology.wadsworth.com. This is a convenient place to communicate with students and other instructors, pick up pedagogical tips, lecture ideas, and other instruction aids, and find pertinent resources among annotated lists of Internet links, organized by the subject areas covered in the book. Students can use the *Kalat Sixth Edition* site to test and enhance their understanding of the text through chapter-by-chapter interactive tutorial quizzes and practice tests.

# Acknowledgments

An author needs self-confidence bordering on arrogance just to begin the job of writing a textbook and, to complete it, the humility to accept criticism of favorite ideas and carefully written prose. A great many people provided helpful suggestions that made this a far better text than it would have been without them.

In preparing this edition, I was fortunate to work with very skilled and dedicated people. Vicki Knight, my acquisitions editor, provided consistent encouragement, friendship, support, and wise advice. Penelope Sky, my developmental editor, was the guiding force behind the illustrations, from identifying what needed to be depicted to selecting photos and revising drawings. She also provided detailed comments on certain content points, especially in the final two chapters. Jennifer Wilkinson did a tireless job of supervising all the supplements. Kirk Bomont was meticulous in shepherding the book into production. Frank Hubert was one of the quickest and most cooperative copy editors I have dealt with in my two decades of textbook writing. Nancy Shammas did a marvelous job of supervising the production and keeping everyone on schedule, a most complicated task with a book such as this. Precision Graphics, which managed the art development, and Ellen Pettengell, who designed the interior, and Roy Neuhaus who created the cover, had the patience and artistic judgment to counterbalance their very nonartistic author. Mary Kay Polsemen accomplished the nearly impossible task of managing all the permissions requests. Marc Linsenman planned and executed the marketing strategies. Joan Murie, the photo researcher, found an amazing variety of images. To each of these, my thanks and congratulations.

My wife, Jo Ellen Kalat, not only provided support and encouragement, but also listened to my attempts to explain concepts and offered many helpful suggestions and questions. My colleagues at North Carolina State University provided me with encouragement, ideas, and free advice. I thank Larry Upton particularly for his extensive and insightful comments. I also received helpful advice from Lynne Baker-Ward, Amy Halberstadt, and Bob Pond.

I would like to single out for special praise Michelle N. Shiota, University of California–Berkeley, and Stavros Valenti, Hofstra University, for their detailed and insightful comments. The following people reviewed all or part of the book, and I thank them for their help: Cynthia Bane, Denison University; Gregory Buchanan, Beloit College; Karen Couture, Keene State College; Susan Field, Georgian Court College; Deborah Frisch, University of Oregon; Rick Fry, Youngstown State University; Richard Harris, Kansas State University; Debra Hollister, Valencia Community College; Charles Huffman, James Madison University; Lisa Jordan, University of Maryland; Jon Kahane, Springfield College; Chris Layne, University of Toledo; Chantal Levesque, University of Rochester; Steve Madigan, University of Southern California; Don Marzolf, Louisiana State University; Beth Neal-Beliveau, Indiana University–Purdue University at Indianapolis; Wendy Palmquist, Plymouth State College; Elizabeth Parks, Kennesaw State University; Mark Samuels, New Mexico Institute of Mining and Technology; Whitney Sweeney, Beloit College; Alan Swinkels, St. Edward's University; Donald Walter, University of Wisconsin–Parkside; Jeffrey Weatherly, University of North Dakota; and Jay Wright, Washington State University.

I also thank the following for their helpful comments and suggestions: G. William Domhoff, University of California, Santa Cruz; Lynn Friedman, Carnegie Mellon University; Kristen Kling, St. Cloud State University; Richard Pisacreta, Ferris State University; R. B. Lotto and Dale Purves, Duke University; Ruth Schiller, Normandale Community College; and Kathleen Vohs, Case Western Reserve University.

A great many students who read the previous edition sent me letters with helpful comments and suggestions. I especially thank Catherine Heither, Normandale Community College; Naomi Huber, N. C. State University; and Futoshi Kobayashi, University of Texas at Austin.

*James Kalat*

# Preface to the Student

Welcome to introductory psychology! I hope you will enjoy reading this text as much as I enjoyed writing it. When you finish, I hope you will fill out the comments page at the back of the book, cut the page out, and mail it to the publisher, who will pass it along to me. Please include a return address.

The first time I taught introductory psychology, several students complained that the book we were using was interesting to read but impossible to study. What they meant was that they had trouble finding and remembering the main points. I have tried to make this book interesting, clear, and as easy to study as possible.

Each chapter is divided into two or more modules, so that you can study one section at a time. Each chapter begins with a table of contents, to alert you to the topics ahead. At the end of each module is a summary of important points, with page references. If a point is unfamiliar you should reread the appropriate text. At the end of each chapter you will find suggestions for further reading, a list of Internet sites to explore, and a list of important terms.

When an important term first appears in the text, it is highlighted in **boldface** and defined in *italics*. All these terms reappear in alphabetic order (with definitions) at the end of the chapter and in the Glossary/Subject Index (with definitions) at the end of the book. You might want to find the Glossary/Subject Index right now and familiarize yourself with it. Note that for each term there is both a definition and a page reference.

I sometimes meet students who think they have mastered the course because they have memorized all the definitions. They are mistaken. You do need to understand the words, but don't waste time memorizing definitions. It is better to use each word in a sentence or list some examples for each term.

At various points in the text are Concept Checks, questions that ask you to use or apply the information you just read. Try to answer each of them, and then turn to the indicated page to check your answer. If your answer is incorrect, you might want to reread the section.

You will also find an occasional passage marked A Step Further. Here you are required to go beyond the text discussion. In many cases there are several reasonable answers. I hope you will think about these questions, perhaps talk about them with fellow students, and maybe ask your instructor's opinion.

I have included in the text a number of items marked Try It Yourself. Some of these require a fair amount of time, but most can be done with little or no equipment in just a minute or two. You will understand and remember the text far better if you do try these exercises. In some cases you will understand the text *only* if you try them. I recall test questions I asked my own students that were answered correctly by almost everyone who tried a particular Try It Yourself exercise, and missed by almost everyone else. A word to the wise . . .

On the inside covers, note the Theme Index, which directs you to pages where Critical Thinking exercises appear in the text, as well as the influences of gender and culture on behavior. In the back of the book you will also find a list of all the references cited in the text, in case you want to check something for more details.

You can enhance your knowledge with the optional Study Guide that accompanies this text. If your book store does not stock it, you can ask them to order a copy. The ISBN is 0-534-53990-4. You can also go to http://psychology.wadsworth.com where example test items (not as many as the Study Guide) and other helpful resources are available.

Now I'll answer a few of the questions often asked by students.

**Do you have any useful suggestions for improving study habits?** Whenever students ask me why they did badly on the latest test, I ask, "When did you read the assignment?" Some answer, "Well, I didn't exactly read *all* of the assignment," or "I read it the night before the test." If you want to learn the material well, I recommend reading the text before the lecture, reviewing it again within a day after the lecture, and quickly going over it again a few days later. Then reread the textbook assignments and your lecture notes before any test. Memory researchers have clearly established that you will understand and remember something better by studying it several times over several days than by spending the same amount of time all at once. Also, of course, the more total time you spend studying, the better.

When you study, don't just read the text: Stop and think about it. The more actively you use the material, the better you will remember it. One way to improve your studying is to read by the SPAR method: **S**urvey, **P**rocess meaningfully, **A**sk questions, **R**eview.

*Survey:* Know what to expect so that you can focus on the main points. When you start a chapter, first look over the outline to get a preview of the contents. Before starting a new module, turn to the end and read the summary.

*Process meaningfully:* Read the chapter carefully, stopping to think from time to time. Tell your roommate something you learned. Think about how you might apply a concept to a real-life situation. Pause when you come to the Concept Checks and try to answer them. Do the Try It Yourself exercises. Try to monitor how well you understand the text and adjust your reading accordingly. Good readers read quickly through easy, familiar content but slowly through difficult material.

*Ask questions:* When you finish the chapter, try to anticipate what you might be asked later. You can use questions in the Study Guide or compose your own. Write out the questions and think about them, but do not answer them yet.

*Review:* Pause for a few hours or more. Now return to your questions and try to answer them. Check your answers against the text or the answers in the Study Guide. Reinforcing your memory a day or two after you first read the chapter will help you retain the material longer and deepen your understanding. If you study the same material several times at lengthy intervals, you increase your chance of remembering it long after the course is over.

**Is it worthwhile to buy and use the Study Guide?**
The Study Guide is designed for students who would like help studying, remembering the material, or answering multiple-choice questions. It is most useful to freshmen and students who have had trouble with similar courses in the past. The correct answers to multiple-choice questions are included, as well as explanations of why they are correct. You can work through each chapter of the Study Guide in one or two hours. The Study Guide can help if you are willing to spend enough time with it in addition to reading the text.

**What do those parentheses mean, as in "(Newstead & Makinen, 1997)"? Am I supposed to remember the names and dates?** Psychologists generally cite references not in footnotes but in parentheses. "(Newstead & Makinen, 1997)" refers to an article written by Newstead and Makinen, published in 1997. All the references cited in the text are listed in alphabetical order (by the authors' last names) in the References section at the back of the book.

You will also notice a few citations that include two dates separated by a slash, such as "(Wundt, 1862/1961)." This means that Wundt's document was originally published in 1862 and was republished in 1961. (In this case, Wundt's original work was in German and the 1961 version was an English translation.)

No one expects you to memorize the parenthetical source citations. They are provided so you can look up the source of a statement and check it for further information. A few names *are* worth remembering, however. For instance, you will read about such famous people as B. F. Skinner, Jean Piaget, and Sigmund Freud. Names that are important to remember are emphasized in the discussion, not enclosed in parentheses.

**Can you help me read and understand graphs?** The graphs in this book are easy to follow. Just take a minute

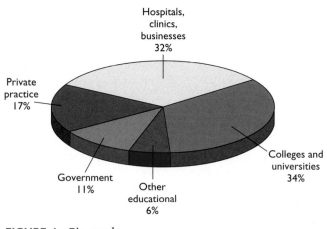

FIGURE 1   Pie graph

or so to study them carefully. You will encounter four kinds: pie graphs, bar graphs, line graphs, and scatter plots. Let's look at each kind.

*Pie graphs* show how a whole is divided into parts. Figure 1 shows that more than one-third of all psychologists take a starting job with a college or some other educational institution. Another one-fifth to one-fourth of psychologists work in independent practice. The total circle represents 100% of all psychologists.

*Line graphs* show how one variable is related to another variable. In Figure 2, you see that 80% of people correctly remembered a set of letters—such as HOZDF—after a 3-second delay. As the delay time increased, the percentage of people remembering the letters declined sharply.

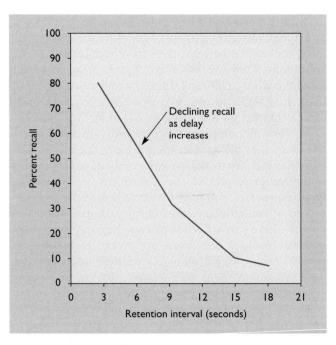

FIGURE 2   Line graph

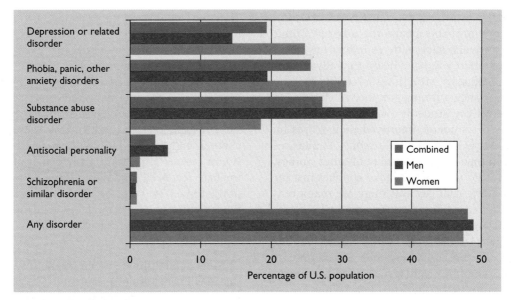

**FIGURE 3** Bar graph

*Bar graphs* show how often events fall into one category or another. Figure 3 shows how many adults in the United States suffer from certain psychological disorders. The length of the bars indicates the frequency of particular disorders.

*Scatter plots* are similar to line graphs, with this difference: A line graph shows averages, whereas a scatter plot shows individual data points. By looking at a scatter plot, we can see how much variation occurs among individuals.

To prepare a scatter plot, we make two observations about each individual. In Figure 4, each student is represented by one point. If you take that point and scan down to the *x*-axis, you find that student's SAT score. If you then scan across to the *y*-axis, you find that student's grade average for the freshman year. A scatter plot shows whether two variables are closely or only loosely related.

**We may have to take multiple-choice tests on this material. How can I do better on those tests?**

1. Read each statement carefully. Do not choose the first answer that looks correct; first make sure that the other answers are wrong. If two answers seem reasonable, decide which of the two is better.

2. If you don't know the correct answer, make an educated guess. Start by eliminating any answer that you know cannot be right. An answer that includes absolute words such as *always* or *never* is probably wrong. (Psychologists occasionally make an absolute statement. For example, "People *never* see anything in complete darkness." However, such absolutes are rare.) Also eliminate any answer that includes unfamiliar terms. If you don't remember ever hearing of something, it probably is not the right answer.

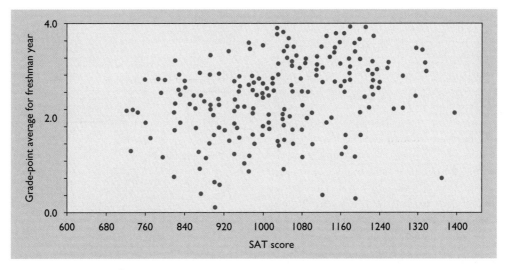

**FIGURE 4** Scatter plot

3. After you finish a test, check your answers and rethink them. You have probably heard the advice, "Don't change your answers; stick with your first impulse." No matter how often you have heard that advice, it is wrong. J. J. Johnston (1975) tested it by looking through answer sheets from a number of classes. He found that of all the students who changed one or more answers, 71 students improved their scores by doing so and only 31 lowered their scores. Similar results have been reported in a number of other studies. I do not mean that you should make changes just for the sake of making changes. But there are many reasons why your reconsidered answer might be better than the first. Sometimes when you read the questions that appear later in a test, one of them may remind you of something that helps you correct an earlier answer. Sometimes you reread a question and realize that you misunderstood it the first time.

Why, then, do so many students (and professors) believe that it is a mistake to change an answer? Think of what happens when you get a test paper back. When you look it over, which items do you examine most carefully?

The ones you got wrong, of course. You may notice three items that you originally answered correctly and then changed. You may overlook the five other items you changed from wrong to right.

If you want to practice your multiple-choice skills, try your hand at the interactive tutorial quizzes available at the *Kalat Sixth Edition* Web site; once again, the address is http://psychology.wadsworth.com. These quizzes, one per chapter, go hand-in-hand with the material in this book. If you answer a question incorrectly online, you get immediate feedback guiding you to a better understanding of the topic. The Web site also includes discussion boards where you can exchange ideas with other readers, and Internet links where you can learn more about certain topics.

Most of all, I hope you enjoy the text. I have included the liveliest examples I can find. My goal is not just to teach you some facts, but to encourage a love of learning so that you will read more and educate yourself about psychology long after your course is over.

*James Kalat*

# INTRODUCTION TO

# Psychology

# What Is Psychology?

CHAPTER 1

**I**f you are like most students, you start off assuming that just about everything you read in your textbooks and everything your professors tell you must be true. But what if it isn't? Just suppose that a group of impostors has replaced the faculty of your college. They pretend to know what they are talking about and they all vouch for one another's competence, but in fact they are all totally unqualified. They have managed to find textbooks that support their own prejudices, but the information in the textbooks is all wrong too. If that happened, how would you know?

As long as we are entertaining such skeptical thoughts, why limit ourselves to colleges? When you read an advice column in the newspaper or read a book about how to invest money or listen to a political commentator, how do you know who has the right answers and who is an impostor?

The answer is that *none* of us has the right answers all of the time. Even professors, textbook authors, advice columnists, politicians, and "experts" of all sorts have strong reasons for some beliefs and weak reasons for others, and sometimes they think they have strong reasons only to find out to their embarrassment that they were wrong. I don't mean to imply that you should start disbelieving everything you read or hear. But you should insist that people tell you the reasons for their conclusions. Don't be satisfied with, "Take my word for it." Ask for the evidence, and then you can draw your own conclusions. You still might not be right, but if you make a mistake, at least it will be your own mistake and not someone else's.

*You have just encountered the theme of this book: Evaluate the evidence.* You have heard and you will continue to hear all sorts of claims concerning psychology. Some are valid, some are wrong, some are partly valid under certain conditions, and some are so vague that we cannot even imagine what it would mean for them to be right or wrong. When you finish this book, you will be in a better position to examine evidence and to judge for yourself which claims to take seriously.

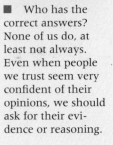

■ Who has the correct answers? None of us do, at least not always. Even when people we trust seem very confident of their opinions, we should ask for their evidence or reasoning.

# The Goals of Psychologists

*What is psychology?*

*What are its major philosophical questions—the ones that motivate research and form the basis for persistent controversies?*

*What are the various areas of psychology, and what do various kinds of psychologists do?*

*Would it make sense to major in psychology?*

The term *psychology* derives from the Greek roots *psyche,* meaning "soul" or "mind," and *logos,* meaning "word"; thus, psychology is literally the study of the mind or soul. In its early days of the late 1800s and early 1900s, psychology was defined as the scientific study of the mind. Around 1920 psychologists became disenchanted with the idea of studying the mind. First, mind is something private and not easily available to scientific study. Second, talking about "the mind" implies that mind is a thing with an independent existence. Most researchers consider mind a process, more like a fire than like the piece of wood that is undergoing the fire. At any rate, through the middle 1900s psychologists defined their field as the study of behavior. Behavior is clearly observable and suitable for scientific study. However, frankly, people care about what they see, hear, and think, not just about what they do. When you look at this optical illusion

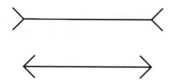

and say that the horizontal part of the top line looks longer than that of the bottom line (although really it isn't), we want to know why it *looks* longer to you, not just why you *said* it looks longer. So, for a compromise, let's define **psychology** as *the systematic study of behavior and experience.* The word *experience* lets us discuss your perceptions, images, and so forth without any implications of a mind that exists independently of your body.

Almost everyone tries to understand why people act the way they do, and every culture has developed a "folk psychology" to try to explain people's feelings and actions. Much of folk psychology is correct, or at least close enough to be useful much of the time, and common

sense is more accurate about psychology than it is about, say, physics. But your common sense is probably not the same as that of another person, especially someone from a different culture, and when we carefully evaluate our commonsense ideas, we find that some are correct, some are not, and some are partly but not entirely correct. Let's try a few questions about psychology. Choose one answer for each item:

1. Typically, we use only 10% of our brains.
   true     uncertain     false
2. Alcoholism is a disease.
   true     uncertain     false
3. A drink of alcohol kills about 5000 brain cells.
   true     uncertain     false
4. People will not do anything under hypnosis that they would refuse to do otherwise.
   true     uncertain     false
5. People often dream they are flying, but they never dream they hit the ground. If you did dream you hit the ground, you would die.
   true     uncertain     false
6. If you want to change people's behavior, first you have to change their attitudes.
   true     uncertain     false
7. A polygraph test can reveal whether or not a person is telling the truth.
   true     uncertain     false
8. Acts of violence are more common on nights of a full moon.
   true     uncertain     false
9. After finishing a test, you should:
   **a.** go back, rethink your answers, and consider changing some of them.
   **b.** stick with your first impulse.
10. Infants can recognize their own mother's voice on the day of birth.
    true     uncertain     false

Done? Okay, now I'll give you what I consider the correct answers:

1. **Typically, we use only 10% of our brains.** *False.* I have heard this saying many times, and you probably have too. Does it mean that you could lose 90% of your brain and still do what you do now? If so, it's obviously false. Does it mean that only 10% of your brain cells are active at any time? If so, again it's false. Granted, each of us could probably do much more

5

with our brains than we are doing now, but that doesn't mean we use only part of our brains. I'm a poor athlete, but that's not because I use only 10% of my muscles. I use them all, just not very skillfully.

2. **Alcoholism is a disease.** Here the best answer is *uncertain*! It depends on what you mean by "disease." In some ways alcoholism is like a medical disease and in some ways not, and much dispute remains about whether alcoholism should be treated by medical doctors. We consider this issue further in Chapter 15.

3. **A drink of alcohol kills about 5000 brain cells.** Again, the best answer is *uncertain*. The next time you hear someone say that an alcoholic drink kills some number of brain cells, ask, "Who counted?" We do know that people who drink enormous amounts of alcohol over many years lose many brain cells, but most of those people aren't getting enough vitamins or proteins in their diets, and the nutritional deficiencies are probably responsible for much of the brain damage.

4. **People will not do anything under hypnosis that they would refuse to do otherwise.** Again, the best answer is *uncertain*. Researchers have found that hypnotized people will sometimes do some very odd things, sometimes even dangerous things, but so do people who are not hypnotized, especially if they know they are in an experiment. That is, it's hard to find anything that we are sure people would "refuse to do otherwise"! Chapter 5 elaborates on this point.

5. **People often dream they are flying, but they never dream they hit the ground. If you did dream you hit the ground, you would die.** If this were true, how would anyone know? At best this statement is *uncertain*, but I have met some people who say they have dreamt they hit the ground (and they survived), so let's call this one *false*.

6. **If you want to change people's behavior, first you have to change their attitudes.** *False*. As we'll see in Chapter 16, sometimes it's pretty easy to change people's behavior, and after their behavior changes, their attitudes change to match the behavior.

7. **A polygraph test can reveal whether or not a person is telling the truth.** *It depends*. ("It depends" is frequently a good answer in psychology.) Here it depends on how much accuracy you expect from the test. A polygraph is right more often than it's wrong, but it is far from perfect, and it frequently makes the error of saying that an honest person is lying. Chapter 12 goes into more detail.

8. **Acts of violence are more common on nights of a full moon.** *False*. Although many people believe this statement, research studies have consistently failed to support it.

9. **After finishing a test, you should: (a) go back, rethink your answers, and consider changing some of them or (b) stick with your first impulse.** *Go back and consider changing your answers.* If you missed this one, you should go back and read the Preface to the Student.

10. **Infants can recognize their own mother's voice on the day of birth.** *True*. After all those false or uncertain statements, I thought I should give you one that's true. It probably doesn't sound like it would be true, and you might wonder how anyone could know. If you can't contain your curiosity, look ahead to Chapter 10.

Note that in several cases the best answer was "uncertain" or "it depends." People should never be afraid to say "I don't know." In psychology you should get used to the idea that many questions are unanswered and that some answers apply only under limited circumstances. Also note the range of questions we just considered, from brain mechanisms to attitudes to treatment of alcoholism. You can consider this little quiz to be a preview of some of the breadth of psychology. Psychologists want to understand why we think and act the way we do—and that task is a big one.

# Major Philosophical Issues in Psychology

Many psychological concerns date back to the philosophers of ancient Greece. Although psychology has moved away from philosophy in its methods, it continues to be motivated by some of the same issues. Three of the most profound questions are free will versus determinism, the mind-brain problem, and the nature-nurture issue.

## *Free Will Versus Determinism*

Beginning with the Renaissance period in Europe, people began to look for scientific explanations for the phenomena they observed. One of the key points of this scientific revolution was a shift toward seeking the *immediate* causes of an event (what led to what) instead of the *final* causes (the ultimate purpose of the event in an overall plan). That is, scientists acted on the basis of **determinism,** *the assumption that everything that happens has a cause, or determinant, in the observable world*.

Is the same true for human behavior? We are, after all, part of the physical world, and our brains are made of the same kinds of chemicals as anything else in the world. According to the *determinist* assumption of human behavior, everything we do has a cause (Figure 1.1).

Clearly, many of the causes lie within us. A person walking down a mountainside is not like a rock that is bouncing down the same mountainside. The claim of psychological determinism is that, even when you make complicated decisions about how to get down a mountain safely, your decision is a product of the combined influence of your genetics, your past experiences, and the current environment. Just as an engineer can design a robot to consider information and make appropriate decisions, your genes and your experiences have programmed you to make appropriate decisions. (You did not design or program yourself.)

Logically, the opposite of determinism should be *indeterminism,* the idea that events happen randomly. Few people, however, find that view appealing. Opponents of determinism instead defend **free will,** generally defined as the *belief that behavior is caused by a person's independent decisions.* But what are "independent decisions"? Determinism agrees that the individual makes decisions but points out that a robot does too. It is often unclear how the free will idea differs from determinism. To be really different from determinism, the free will position would have to hold that someone's "independent decisions" are independent from the physics and chemistry of the body.

The test of determinism is ultimately empirical: If everything we do has a cause, our behavior should be predictable. Is it?

In some cases behavior is easy to predict. For example, if you hear a sudden, unexpected, extremely loud noise, what will you do? I can predict easily: Unless you are deaf or comatose, you will tense your muscles. I can even predict which muscles will become tense and almost exactly *when* they will become tense.

In other cases psychologists' predictions are more like those of a meteorologist. A meteorologist who wants to predict tomorrow's weather for some city will want to know the location and terrain of that city, today's weather in and around that city, and so forth. Even with all that information, the meteorologist will predict something such as, "High temperature in the low 30s, low temperature around 20, and a 10% chance of precipitation." The lack of precision and occasional errors do not mean that the weather has a free will, just that it is subject to so many small influences that no one can predict it with complete accuracy.

Similarly, a psychologist trying to predict whether you will commit an act of criminal violence in the next year will want to know as much as possible about your past behavior, that of your friends and family, your current health, your genetics, where you live, and a great deal more. Even

**FIGURE 1.1** Behavior is guided by external forces, such as waves, and by forces within the individual. According to the determinist view, even those internal forces follow physical laws.

with all that information, the psychologist's predictions will be less accurate than a meteorologist's weather predictions.

Determinists are unembarrassed; after all, human behavior is subject to far more influences than the weather is, including some that are hard to measure. Still, we can make better predictions than psychologists used to, and with continued increases in knowledge, we can expect still greater improvements. A free will advocate who rejects determinism would insist that predictions of behavior could *never* become accurate, even with *complete* information about the person and the situation. To that idea, a determinist replies that the only way to find out is to try.

Let's note an important point here: The assumption that behaviors have observable causes seems to work, and anyone planning to do research on behavior is almost forced to start with this assumption. Still, to be honest, it is merely an assumption, not a certainty.

**A STEP FURTHER**
*Determinism*

What kind of evidence, if any, would support the concept of free will? To support the concept of free will, one would need to demonstrate that no conceivable theory could make correct predictions about some aspect of behavior. Should a psychologist who believes in free will conduct the same kind of research that determinists conduct, a different kind, or no research at all?

## The Mind-Brain Problem

Everything we experience or do depends on the physics and chemistry of the nervous system. What, then, is the role of the mind? In fact, what, if anything, *is* the mind? The *philosophical question of how experience is related to the brain* is the **mind-brain problem** (or mind-body problem). In a universe composed of matter and energy, why is there such a thing as a conscious mind? One view, called **dualism,** holds that *the mind is separate from the brain but somehow controls the brain and therefore the rest of the body.* The problem is that dualism contradicts the law of conservation of matter and energy, one of the cornerstones of physics. According to that law, the only way to influence any matter or energy, such as the matter and energy that compose your brain, is to act on it with other matter or energy. That is, if the mind isn't composed of matter and energy, it can't *do* anything. For that reason nearly all brain researchers favor **monism,** *the view that conscious experience is inseparable from the physical brain.* That is, either the mind is something the brain produces (perhaps accidentally) or mind and brain activity are just two terms for the same thing.

As you can imagine, the mind-brain problem is a thorny philosophical issue, but it does lend itself to research. Research can determine links between brain activity, on the one hand, and behavior and experience, on the other hand. For example, consider Figure 1.2. A technique called positron-emission tomography (PET) enables investigators to measure the amount of activity in different parts of the brain at various times. The photos in Figure 1.2 show brain activity while a person is engaged in nine different tasks. Red indicates the highest degree of brain activity, followed by yellow, green, and blue. As

you can see, the various tasks increase activity in different brain areas, although all areas show some activity at all times (Phelps & Mazziotta, 1985).

Data such as these show a close relationship between brain activity and psychological events. You might well ask: Did the brain activity cause the thoughts, or did the thoughts cause the brain activity? Most brain researchers reply that neither brain activity nor mental activity "causes" the other; rather, brain activity and mental activity are the same thing (see Dennett, 1991).

Even if we accept this position, we are still far from understanding the mind-brain relationship. Is mental activity associated with all brain activity or just certain types? Why does conscious experience exist at all? Could a brain get along without it?

Research studies are not about to resolve the mind-brain problem and put philosophers out of business. But research results do constrain the types of philosophical answers that we can seriously consider. The hope of learning more about the mind-brain relationship is one of the ultimate goals for many psychologists, especially those whose work we shall study in Chapters 3 and 4.

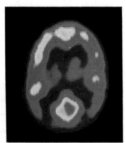

Resting state

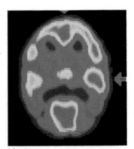

Music

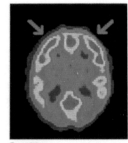

Cognitive

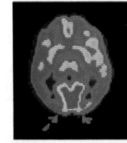

Visual

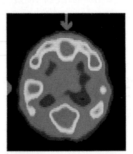

Language

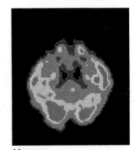

Memory

**FIGURE 1.2** PET scans show the brain activity of normal people engaged in different activities. Left column: Brain activity with no special stimulation, while passively watching something or listening to something. Center column: Brain activity while listening to music, language, or both. Right column: Brain activity during performance of a cognitive task, an auditory memory task, and the task of moving the fingers of the right hand. Red indicates the highest activity, followed by yellow, green, and blue. Arrows indicate the most active areas. (Courtesy of Michael E. Phelps and John C. Mazziotta, University of California, Los Angeles, School of Medicine)

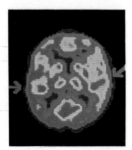

Auditory

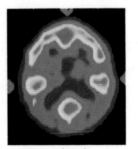

Language and music

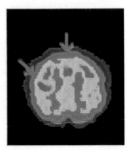

Motor

**A STEP FURTHER**
*Mind and Brain*

One way to think about the mind-brain relationship is to ask whether something other than a brain—a computer, for example—could have a mind. How would we know?

What if we built a computer that could perform all the intellectual functions that humans perform? Could we then decide that the computer is conscious, as human beings are?

## The Nature-Nurture Issue

Why do most little boys spend more time than little girls do with toy guns and trucks and less time with dolls? Are such behavioral differences mostly the result of genetic differences between boys and girls, or are they mostly the result of differences in how society treats boys and girls?

Alcohol abuse is a big problem in some cultures and a rare one in others. Are these differences entirely a matter of social custom, or do genes influence alcohol use also?

Certain psychological disorders are more common in large cities than in small towns and in the countryside. Does life in crowded cities somehow cause psychological disorders? Or do people develop such disorders because of a genetic predisposition and then move to big cities in search of jobs, housing, and welfare services?

Each of these questions is related to the **nature-nurture issue** (Figure 1.3): *How do differences in behavior relate to differences in heredity and environment?* The nature-nurture issue shows up from time to time in practically all fields of psychology, and it seldom has a simple answer.

**A STEP FURTHER**
*Nature and Nurture*

Suppose researchers found that alcohol abuse is uncommon in Turkey because of Turkey's strict legal sanctions against alcohol use. Should we then assume that the differences in alcohol use among other countries is also due to nongenetic causes?

## What Psychologists Do

We have considered some major philosophical issues related to the entire field of psychology. However, psychologists usually deal with smaller, more answerable questions.

Psychology is an academic, nonmedical discipline that includes many branches and specialties, ranging from the helping professions to research on learning, memory, and brain functions. The educational requirements for becoming a psychologist vary from one country to another (Newstead & Makinen, 1997). In the United States and Canada, a psychologist starts with a bachelor's degree (usually after 4 years of college) and then probably a PhD

FIGURE 1.3 Why do different children develop different interests? They may have had different hereditary tendencies, but they have also experienced different environmental influences. Separating the roles of nature and nurture can be difficult.

degree (at least another 4 or 5 years, sometimes much more). Some people practice psychology with a master's degree (intermediate between a bachelor's and a doctorate), and others have a PsyD (doctor of psychology) degree, which generally requires less research experience than a PhD. Any psychologist specializes in a particular branch of psychology, such as experimental, developmental, clinical, or industrial.

Psychologists work in many occupational settings, as shown in Figure 1.4 (Chamberlin, 2000). The most common settings are colleges and universities, private practice, hospitals and mental health clinics, and government agencies.

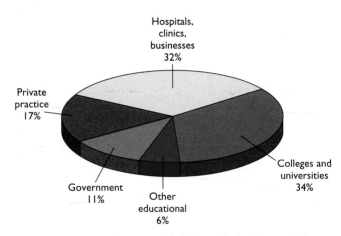

**FIGURE 1.4** More than one third of psychologists work in academic institutions; the remainder find positions in a variety of settings. (Based on data of Chamberlin, 2000)

## Psychologists in Teaching and Research

Many psychologists who are not clinical psychologists have positions in colleges and universities where they teach and do research that will, they hope, lead to a greater understanding of behavior and experience and perhaps have useful applications. A small percentage of psychologists work in full-time research institutions. Here we preview a few major categories of psychological research.

### Biological Psychology

A **biopsychologist** (or **behavioral neuroscientist**) *tries to explain behavior in terms of biological factors, such as electrical and chemical activities in the nervous system, the effects of drugs and hormones, genetics, and evolutionary pressures.* For example, the evidence suggests that certain genes influence the probability that someone will develop schizophrenia, depression, or alcoholism. However, the behavioral outcome depends on experiences as well as genetics.

Biopsychologists also study the effects of brain damage. Brain damage can result from such things as a sharp blow to the head, a ruptured blood vessel in the brain, an interruption of oxygen supply, prolonged malnutrition, or exposure to toxic chemicals. The effects of brain damage on behavior vary enormously depending on the location and extent of the damage.

People have long known that various drugs can alter behavior. For example, opiates (e.g., heroin or morphine) generally make people quiet, passive, and insensitive to pain. Amphetamines and cocaine stimulate increased activity in most people. Biopsychologists try to understand how drugs affect the brain. They have found that most drugs that affect behavior do so by altering the chemical communication between one neuron and another at junctions called *synapses.*

So, according to biopsychologists, why are people different from each other? There are many reasons: People are born with different genes. They develop slightly different brains and different hormonal patterns. Some

have suffered brain damage. Some are under the influence of drugs or of nutritional deficiencies that affect the brain. Anything that affects the body, especially the brain, will also affect behavior.

### Learning and Motivation

The research field of **learning and motivation** studies *how behavior depends on the outcomes of past behaviors and on current motivations.*

How often we engage in any particular behavior depends on the results of engaging in that behavior in the past. For example, you undoubtedly have a friend whose interests differ from yours. One of you likes dancing, and the other likes painting. Or one likes to play the guitar, and the other is active in political causes. The one who likes dancing may have received praise for dancing or may experience some good bodily sensations while dancing. The one who enjoys painting may once have tripped while dancing, and therefore sought something else to do. The details vary from one person to another, but our current behavior depends on our past learning.

Researchers in this field (most of whom call themselves *behaviorists*) study how the consequences of an action modify future behavior. For example, do frequent payoffs (money, praise, etc.) produce the same results as less frequent or less predictable rewards? If someone were expecting a large payoff and instead got a smaller payoff, what would be the effect compared to someone who was used to a smaller payoff? What are the effects of punishment? Notice the theoretical orientation: The behaviorist studies what the person *does* as a result of the consequences of past actions, not what the person *thinks.* Because of this emphasis on actions instead of thoughts, behaviorists can conduct many of their studies on nonhuman animals.

### Cognitive Psychology

**Cognition** refers to *thinking and acquiring knowledge.* A **cognitive psychologist** *studies those processes.* (The root *cogn-* also shows up in the word *recognize,* which literally means "to know again.") As a rule cognitive psychologists do not simply ask people to describe their thought processes. (If people understood their own thoughts that well, there would be less need for psychologists.) Cognitive psychologists conduct experiments to infer what people know, how they came to know it, and how they use their knowledge to solve new problems. Some cognitive psychologists develop and test computer models of how people think.

One typical question for a cognitive psychologist is: What do experts know or do that sets them apart from other people? One possible distinction is simply that the expert knows more facts. Consider a subject on which you are an expert: how to find your way around your college campus. A fellow student asks you, "How do I get from here to the biology building?" To answer, you can draw on the knowledge you share with the other student: "Go over toward the library. Then cut behind the library, between the library and the math building. The biology building will be right in front of you." That communication was effective because you and the other student shared a good deal of knowledge about the campus. Contrast the situation when you communicate with a visitor to the campus who knows almost nothing. You say, "Go over toward the library . . . " "Wait, where's the library?" "Well, go out this door, make a right, go to the next street . . . " Someone with little or no previous knowledge will need detailed and extensive instructions (Isaacs & Clark, 1987).

Another distinction between the expert and the non-expert is that the expert knows which details are important. For example, someone might look at a group of birds on a beach and say, "Hey, look at all the seagulls." An expert bird watcher identifies them as three gull species and two tern species. The inexperienced bird watcher replies, "Oh, I see. Some of them have darker feathers than others." The expert answers, "No, the ones with darker feathers are just younger. To tell one species from the other, you have to check the color of the beak, the color of the legs, the size of the bird, the color of the eye ring . . . " The expert knows what to look for—what is relevant and what is not (Murphy & Medin, 1985).

### Developmental Psychology

**Developmental psychologists** *study the behavioral capacities typical of different ages and how behavior changes with age,* "from womb to tomb." In a typical study, developmental psychologists examine a particular behavior across a certain age span, such as language from age 2 to age 4 or the speed of solving intellectual tasks from age 60 to age 80. The first question is: What do people do at one age that they do *not* do at another age? The second question is: Why? Was the change due to a biological process, to changes in experience, or to a complex combination of

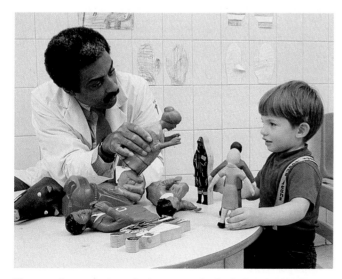

■ Developmental psychologists study the behavioral differences among people of different ages.

both? Developmental psychologists frequently need to address the nature-nurture issue that we mentioned earlier.

### Social Psychology

**Social psychologists** *study how an individual influences other people and is influenced by others.* When we are with other people, we tend to take our cues from them about what we should do. Suppose you arrive at a party and notice that the other guests are walking around, talking, and helping themselves to snacks. You do the same. When you go to a religious service or an art museum, you again notice how other people are acting and conform your behavior to theirs.

Certainly, if you had grown up in a different country, you would have developed vastly different customs. Even within a given culture, though, individuals acquire different behaviors because of the people around them. If you had made friends with a different set of people in high school, you might be a much different person today. According to social psychologists, people are also heavily influenced by other people's expectations. For example, parents often intentionally or unintentionally convey expectations that boys will be more competitive and girls will be more cooperative or that teenagers will be immature and that 25-year-olds will be responsible. At least to some extent, people's behavior tends to live up to—or down to—the expectations of others. Social psychologists study such influences.

### CONCEPT CHECK

1. **a.** Of the kinds of psychological research just described—biological psychology, learning and motivation, cognitive psychology, developmental psychology, and social psychology—which field concentrates most on children?
   **b.** Which is most concerned with how people behave in groups?
   **c.** Which concentrates most on thought and knowledge?
   **d.** Which is most interested in the effects of brain damage?
   **e.** Which is most concerned with studying the effect of a reward on future behavior? (Check your answers on page 16).

## Service Providers to Individuals

When most people hear the term *psychologist*, they first think of *clinical psychologists*, who constitute one type of **psychotherapist,** *specialists in helping people with psychological problems.* Those problems range from depression and substance abuse to marriage conflicts, difficulties making decisions, or even the mere feeling that "I should be getting more out of life." Some clinical psychologists are college professors and researchers, but most are full-time private practitioners.

It is important to distinguish among several types of therapists. The term *therapist* itself has no precise meaning and in many places even untrained, unlicensed people can hang out a shingle and call themselves therapists. Four of the main kinds of service providers for mentally troubled people are clinical psychologists, psychiatrists, social workers, and counseling psychologists.

## Clinical Psychology

**Clinical psychologists** *have an advanced degree in psychology, with a specialty in understanding and helping people with psychological problems.* Most have a PhD, which requires research training and the completion of a substantial research dissertation. Also, as part of their training, they undergo at least 1 year of supervised clinical work called an *internship.* Clinical psychologists can base their work on any of various theoretical viewpoints, which we shall explore in later chapters. They try, in one way or another, to understand why a person is having difficulties and then to help that person become more successful and make better choices.

## Psychiatry

**Psychiatry** is a *branch of medicine that deals with emotional disturbances.* To become a psychiatrist, a student first earns an MD degree and then takes an additional 4 years of residency training in psychiatry. Psychiatrists and clinical psychologists provide similar services for most clients: They listen, ask questions, and try to help. Psychiatrists, however, are medical doctors and can therefore prescribe drugs, such as tranquilizers and antidepressants, whereas psychologists cannot.

Does psychiatrists' ability to prescribe drugs give them an advantage over psychologists? Sometimes, but not always. Ours is an overmedicated society. Some psychiatrists habitually treat anxiety and depression with drugs, whereas a psychologist tries to treat problems by changing the person's way of living. Some psychologists favor a change in the law that would permit them to take some extra training to gain the right to prescribe drugs. Others fear that gaining prescription privileges would mean losing psychologists' distinctive focus on talking extensively with their clients (Hayes & Helby, 1996). Prescription privileges will probably remain a controversial topic.

## Some Other Therapy Providers

Several other kinds of professionals also provide help and counsel. Psychiatric nurses and clinical social workers have an undergraduate or master's degree in nursing or social work plus additional training in the care of emotionally troubled people. **Psychoanalysts** are *psychotherapists who rely heavily on the theories and methods pioneered by the early 20th-century Viennese physician Sigmund Freud and later developed by a number of others.* Freud and his followers attempted to infer the hidden, unconscious, symbolic meaning behind people's words and actions, and in various ways psychoanalysts today continue that effort. There is some question about who may rightly call themselves psychoanalysts.

Some people apply the term to any psychotherapist who attempts to uncover unconscious thoughts and feelings, perhaps even including followers of Carl Jung or other theorists who broke away from Freud in significant ways. Others apply the term only to graduates of a 6- to 8-year program at an institute of psychoanalysis. Those institutes admit only people who are already either psychiatrists or clinical psychologists. Thus, people completing psychoanalytic training will be at least in their late 30s.

**Counseling psychologists** *help people with educational, vocational, marriage, health-related, and other decisions.* A counseling psychologist has a doctorate degree (PhD, PsyD, or EdD) with supervised experience in counseling. The activities of a counseling psychologist overlap those of a clinical psychologist, but with a different emphasis. Whereas a clinical psychologist deals mostly with anxiety, depression, and other emotional distress, a counseling psychologist deals mostly with important life decisions and family or career readjustments, which, admittedly, can cause anxiety or depression! Counseling psychologists work in educational institutions, mental health centers, rehabilitation agencies, businesses, and private practice.

Table 1.1 compares various types of psychotherapists.

## CONCEPT CHECK

**2.** Can psychoanalysts prescribe drugs? (Check your answer on page 16.)

**TABLE 1.1 Clinical Psychologists and Other Psychotherapists**

| Type of Therapist | Education |
| --- | --- |
| *Clinical psychologist* | PhD with clinical emphasis, or PsyD plus internship. Total of generally 5+ years after undergraduate degree. |
| *Psychiatrist* | MD plus psychiatric residency. Total of 8 years after undergraduate degree. |
| *Psychoanalyst* | Psychiatry or clinical psychology plus 6–8 years in a psychoanalytic institute. Others who rely on Freud's methods also call themselves psychoanalysts. |
| *Psychiatric nurse* | From 2-year (AA) degree to master's degree, plus supervised experience. |
| *Clinical social worker* | Master's degree plus 2 years of supervised experience. Total of at least 4 years after undergraduate degree. |
| *Counseling psychologist* | PhD, PsyD, or EdD plus supervised experience in counseling. |

## Service Providers to Organizations

Psychologists also work in business, industry, and school systems in some capacities that might be unfamiliar to you, doing things you might not think of as psychology. The job prospects in these fields have been good, however, and you might find these fields interesting. Let's explore these fields in detail here, because they do not have whole chapters devoted to them later, as do areas such as developmental and social psychology.

### Industrial/Organizational Psychology

*The psychological study of people at work* is known as **industrial/organizational psychology.** It deals with such issues as matching the right person with the right job, training people for jobs, developing work teams, determining salaries and bonuses, planning an organizational structure, and organizing the workplace so that workers will be both productive and satisfied. I/O psychologists study the behavior of both the individual and the organization, including the impact of economic conditions and governmental regulations.

Here's an example of a concern for industrial/organizational psychologists (Campion & Thayer, 1989): A company that manufactures complex electronic equipment needed to publish reference and repair manuals for its products. The engineers who designed the devices could not devote the necessary time to write the manuals, and none of them were skilled writers anyway. So the company hired a technical writer to prepare the manuals, but after a year she received an unsatisfactory performance rating. The manuals she wrote contained too many technical errors; besides that, she was constantly complaining.

The writer countered that, when she asked various engineers in the company to check her manuals or to explain technical details to her, they were always too busy. She found her job complicated and frustrating; her office was badly lit, noisy, and overheated, and her chair was uncomfortable. Whenever she mentioned any of these problems, however, she was told that she "complained too much."

In a situation such as this, an industrial/organizational psychologist can help the company to evaluate the possible solutions. First, the problem might be employee selection; maybe the company hired the wrong person for this job. If so, they should fire the current writer and hire someone who is an expert on electrical engineering, who is also an outstanding writer, and who *likes* a badly lit, noisy, overheated, uncomfortable office. However, if the company cannot find or afford such a person, then it needs to improve the working conditions and provide the current employee with more training or more help with the technical aspects of the job.

As this example shows, when a company blames its workers for doing a poor job, I/O psychologists often discover that the real problem lies with the job itself. In other cases, however, the problem does lie with the workers. In such cases the I/O psychologist tries to improve the company's method of selecting employees, such as identifying useful cognitive tests (similar to the tests students take in school), personality tests, improved interviews, biographical inventories, and so forth.

**A STEP FURTHER**
*I/O Psychology*

I/O psychologists usually consult with business and industry, but suppose they were called on to help a university where certain professors had complained that "the students are too lazy and stupid to understand the lectures." How might the I/O psychologists react?

### Ergonomics

Some years ago, my son Sam, who was then about 16 years old, turned to me as he was rushing out the door and asked me to turn off his stereo. I went to the stereo in his room and tried to find an on–off switch or a power switch. No such luck. I looked in vain for the manual. Finally, in desperation, I had to unplug the stereo.

Learning to operate our increasingly complex machinery is one of the perennial struggles of modern life. Sometimes the consequences can be serious. Imagine an airplane pilot who intends to lower the landing wheels and instead raises the wing flaps. Or a worker in a nuclear power plant who fails to notice a warning signal.

In one field of psychology, an **ergonomist,** or **human factors specialist,** *attempts to facilitate the operation of machinery so that the average person can use it as efficiently and as safely as possible.* The term *ergonomics* is derived from Greek roots meaning "laws of work." Ergonomics was

■ Ergonomists help redesign machines to make them easier and safer to use. An ergonomist uses principles of both engineering and psychology.

first used in military settings, where complex technologies sometimes required soldiers to spot nearly invisible targets, to understand speech through deafening noise, to track objects in three dimensions while using two hands, and to make life-or-death decisions in a split second. The military turned to psychologists to determine what skills their personnel could master and to redesign the tasks to fit those skills.

Ergonomists soon applied their experience not only to business and industry but also to everyday devices. As Donald Norman (1988) pointed out, many intelligent and educated people find themselves unable to use all the features on a camera, a microwave oven, or a videocassette recorder; some even have trouble setting the time on a digital watch.

When designing machinery, ergonomists emphasize the **principle of compatibility,** *the concept that people's built-in or learned expectations enable them to learn certain procedures more easily than other procedures.* For example, it is easier for us to learn that a burst of loud noise means danger than to learn that a particular melody means danger. Similarly, we expect to turn a knob clockwise to move something to the right and counterclockwise to move something to the left (as we do when steering a car). These examples may seem obvious, but in many cases ergonomists must do trial-and-error research to find the best way to set up the controls for a new device.

At some universities the ergonomics program is part of the psychology department; at others it is part of engineering; at still others it is administered jointly by both departments. Regardless of who administers the program, ergonomics necessarily combines features of psychology, engineering, and computer science.

### School Psychology

A great many children have academic problems at one time or another. Some children simply have trouble sitting still or paying attention. Others get into trouble for misbehavior. Others have specialized problems with reading, spelling, arithmetic, or other academic skills. Some have distractions in their home life that prevent them from concentrating on their studies. Other children, because of their special gifts or talents, master their schoolwork faster than most children and become bored. They, too, need special attention.

**School psychologists** are *specialists in the psychological condition of students,* usually in kindergarten through 12th grade. The role of school psychologists varies substantially depending on the psychologists themselves, their education, and the school system. Broadly speaking, school psychologists identify the educational needs of children, devise a plan to meet those needs, and then either implement the plan themselves or advise teachers how to implement it.

School psychology can be taught in a psychology department, a branch of the department of education, or a department of educational psychology. In some countries it is possible to practice school psychology with only a bachelor's degree. In the United States the minimum is usually a master's degree, but job opportunities are much greater for people with a doctorate degree, and a doctorate may become necessary in the future. Job opportunities in school psychology have been strong and are continuing to grow. Most school psychologists work for a school system; others work for mental health clinics, guidance centers, and other institutions.

Table 1.2 summarizes some of the major fields of psychology, including several that have not been discussed.

# Should You Major in Psychology?

Can you get a job if you major in psychology? Psychology is one of the most popular majors in the United States, Canada, and Europe. So if psychology majors cannot get jobs, a huge number of people are going to be in trouble!

The bad news is that very few jobs specifically advertise for college graduates with a bachelor's degree in psychology. The good news is that an enormous variety of jobs are available for graduates with a bachelor's degree, not specifying any major. Therefore, if you get a degree in psychology, you will compete with history majors, English majors, astronomy majors, phys ed majors, and others for jobs in government, business, and industry. According to one survey, only 20 to 25% of people who graduated with a degree in psychology took a job closely related to psychology, such as personnel work or social services (Borden & Rajecki, 2000). Still, many of them took very good jobs, even if they were not exactly psychology jobs.

Even if you get a job that seems remote from psychology, your psychology courses will have taught you a good deal about how to evaluate evidence, organize and write papers, handle statistics, listen carefully to what people say, understand and respect cultural differences, and so forth. In short, a psychology major can provide a useful background for many occupations.

Psychology also provides a good background for people entering professional schools. Many students major in psychology and then apply to medical school, law school, divinity school, or other programs. Find out what coursework is expected for the professional program of your choice and then compare the coursework required for a psychology major. You will probably find that the psychology major is compatible with your professional preparation.

If you want a career as a psychologist, you should aspire to an advanced degree, preferably a doctorate. A doctorate will qualify you to apply for positions as a college

**TABLE 1.2** Some Major Specializations in Psychology

| Specialization | General Interest | Example of Specific Interest or Research Topic |
|---|---|---|
| *Biopsychologist* | Relationship between brain and behavior | What body signals indicate hunger and satiety? |
| *Clinical psychologist* | Emotional difficulties | How can people be helped to overcome severe anxiety? |
| *Community psychologist* | Organizations and social structures | Would improved job opportunities decrease certain types of psychological distress? |
| *Counseling psychologist* | Helping people to make important decisions and to achieve their potential | Should this person consider changing careers? |
| *Developmental psychologist* | Changes in behavior as people grow older | At what age can a child first distinguish between appearance and reality? |
| *Educational psychologist* | Improvement of learning in school | What is the best way to test a student's knowledge? |
| *Environmental psychologist* | The influence of noise, heat, crowding, and other environmental conditions on human behavior | How can a building be designed to maximize the comfort and productivity of the people who use it? |
| *Ergonomist* | Communication between person and machine | How can an airplane cockpit be redesigned to increase safety? |
| *Experimental psychologist* | Sensation, perception, learning, thinking, memory | Do people have several kinds of learning? Do they have several kinds of memory? |
| *Industrial/ organizational psychologist* | People at work, production efficiency | Should jobs be made simple and foolproof or interesting and challenging? |
| *Personality psychologist* | Personality differences | Why are certain people shy and others gregarious? |
| *Psychometrician* | Measurement of intelligence, personality, and interests | How fair are current IQ tests? Can we devise better tests? |
| *School psychologist* | Problems that affect schoolchildren | How should the school handle a child who regularly disrupts the classroom? |
| *Social psychologist* | Group behavior, social influences | What methods of persuasion are most effective for changing attitudes? |

professor or, depending on your area of specialization, jobs in hospitals, clinics, private practice, school systems, or research. An increasing percentage of doctorate-level psychologists now work in business, industry, and the military doing research related to practical problems. If you are a first- or second-year college student now, it will probably take you another 8 years or more to get a doctorate, and no one can accurately predict the job market that far into the future. Frankly, psychology is not the right career for someone who is just looking for a safe, secure way to make a living. It is for those whose excitement about the field draws them irresistibly to it.

The types of people majoring in psychology have become more diverse over the years. In its early days, around 1900, psychology was more open to women than most other academic disciplines, but even so, the opportunities for women were limited

**FIGURE 1.5** Mary Calkins, one of the first prominent women in U.S. psychology.

(Milar, 2000). Mary Calkins (Figure 1.5), an early memory researcher, was described as the best graduate student the Harvard psychology department had had to that point, but she was denied a PhD because Harvard insisted on its tradition of granting degrees to men only (Scarborough & Furomoto, 1987). She did, however, serve as president of the American Psychological Association, as did Margaret Washburn, another important woman in the early days of psychology.

Today, by contrast, women receive about two thirds of the psychology PhDs in North America and most of those in Europe also (Newstead & Makinen, 1997; Sanderson & Dugoni, 1999). In some subfields such as developmental psychology, women receive as much as 80% of the new PhD degrees. Women are about as likely as men to assume leadership in the major psychological organizations and editorship of the major journals.

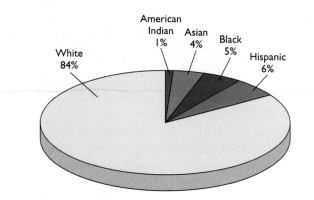

**FIGURE 1.6** New psychology PhDs by race/ethnicity in 1999.

Minorities constitute a growing percentage of psychologists, although the total number is still small. Figure 1.6 shows the distribution for PhD degrees in psychology granted in 1996 in the United States (Sanderson & Dugoni, 1999). Universities have been actively seeking more applications from minorities who are interested in graduate studies.

## IN CLOSING

### Types of Psychologists

An experimental psychology researcher, a clinical psychologist, an ergonomist, and an industrial/organizational psychologist are all psychologists, even though their daily activities have little in common. What does unite psychologists is a dedication to progress through research.

I have oversimplified this discussion of the various psychological approaches in several ways. First, biological psychology, cognitive psychology, social psychology, and the other fields all have their own specialized interests and questions, but they also constitute different ways of approaching many of the same questions. Furthermore, the various approaches overlap significantly. Nearly all psychologists combine insights and information gained from a variety of approaches. To understand why one person differs from another, psychologists combine information about biology, learning experiences, social influences, and much more.

As we proceed through this book, we shall consider one type of behavior at a time and, generally, one approach at a time. That is simply a necessity; we cannot talk intelligently about all kinds of psychological processes at once. But bear in mind that all these processes do ultimately fit together; what you do at any given moment depends on your biology, your past experiences, your social setting, your emotions, and a great deal more.

## Summary

The page number after an item indicates where the topic is first discussed.

- *What is psychology?* Psychology is the systematic study of behavior and experience. Psychologists deal with both theoretical and practical questions. (page 5)
- *Determinism/free will.* Determinism is the view that everything that occurs, including human behavior, has a physical cause. That view is difficult to reconcile with the conviction that humans have free will—that we deliberately, consciously decide what to do. (page 6)
- *Mind-brain.* The mind-brain problem is the question of how conscious experience is related to the activity of the brain. (page 7)
- *Nature-nurture.* Behavior depends on both nature (heredity) and nurture (environment). Psychologists try to determine the influence of those two factors on differences in behavior. The relative contributions of nature and nurture vary from one behavior to another. (page 9)
- *Research fields in psychology.* Psychology as an academic field has many subfields, including biological psychology, learning and motivation, cognitive psychology, developmental psychology, and social psychology. (page 10)
- *Psychology versus psychiatry.* Clinical psychologists have either a PhD, PsyD, or master's degree; psychiatrists are medical doctors. Both clinical psychologists and psychiatrists treat people with emotional problems, but only psychiatrists can prescribe drugs and other medical treatments. Counseling psychologists help people deal with difficult decisions; they sometimes but less often also deal with psychological disorders. (page 12)
- *Service providers to organizations.* Nonclinical fields of application include industrial/organizational psychology, ergonomics, and school psychology. (page 13)
- *Job prospects.* People with a bachelor's degree in psychology enter a wide variety of careers or continue their education in professional schools. Those with a doctorate in psychology have additional possibilities depending on their area of specialization. In psychology, as in any other field, job prospects can change between the start and finish of one's education. (page 14)

## Answers to Concept Checks

1. **a.** Developmental psychology. **b.** Social psychology. **c.** Cognitive psychology. **d.** Biological psychology. **e.** Learning and motivation. (page 11)
2. Most psychoanalysts can prescribe drugs because most are psychiatrists, and psychiatrists are medical doctors. However, psychoanalysts who are psychologists are not medical doctors and therefore cannot prescribe drugs. (page 12)

# Psychology Then and Now

*How did psychology get started?*

*What were the interests of psychologists in the early days?*

*How has psychology changed over the years?*

Imagine yourself as a young scholar in about 1880. Enthusiastic about the new scientific approach in psychology, you have decided to become a psychologist yourself. Like other early psychologists, you have a background in either biology or philosophy. You are determined to apply the scientific methods of biology to the problems of philosophy.

So far, so good. But what questions will you address? A good research question is both important and answerable. In 1880 how would you decide which questions are important? You cannot get research ideas from a psychological journal, because the first issue won't be published until next year. (And incidentally, it will be all in German.) You cannot follow in the tradition of previous researchers, because there haven't *been* any previous researchers. You are on your own.

Furthermore, in the late 1800s and early 1900s, psychologists were not yet sure which questions were answerable. Sometimes they are still unsure: Should we try to study the nature of human consciousness, or should we skip conscious experience and instead concentrate on describing what people actually do? Many of the changes that have occurred during the history of psychology have been changes in investigators' decision about answerable research questions.

In the next several pages, we shall explore some of these changes in psychological research questions, including projects that dominated psychology for a while and then faded from interest. We shall discuss additional historical developments in later chapters. Figure 1.7 outlines some major historical events inside and outside psychology.

## The Early Era

At least since Aristotle (384–322 B.C.), philosophers and fiction writers have debated why people act the way they do, why they have the experiences they do, and why one person is different from another. Without discounting the importance of these great thinkers, several 19th-century scholars wondered whether a scientific approach would be fruitful. They were impressed by the great strides made in physics, chemistry, and biology; they believed that similar progress could be made in psychology if evidence were collected and evaluated scientifically.

## Wilhelm Wundt and the First Psychological Laboratory

The origin of psychology as we now know it is generally dated to 1879, when medical doctor and sensory researcher Wilhelm Wundt (pronounced "voont") set up the first psychology laboratory in Leipzig, Germany. Wundt and others had conducted psychological experiments before, but this was the first time anyone had established a laboratory exclusively for psychological research. Wundt's interests were broad, ranging from the physiology of the sense organs to cultural differences in behavior, with emphases on motivation, voluntary control, and cognitive processes (Zehr, 2000).

One of Wundt's fundamental questions was: What are the components of experience, or mind? He proposed that experience is composed of elements and compounds, like those of chemistry. Psychology's elements were, he maintained, sensations and feelings (Wundt, 1896/1902).[1] So at any particular moment, you might experience the taste of a fine meal, the sound of good music, and a certain degree of pleasure. These would merge into a single experience (a compound), but that experience would still include the separate elements. Furthermore, Wundt maintained, your experience is partly under your voluntary control; you can shift your attention from one element to another and get a different experience.

Wundt's question about the components of experience was a philosophical one, and some of his opinions about the elements of the mind resembled the writings of philosophers before him. But Wundt, unlike the others, tried to test his statements by collecting data. He presented various kinds of lights, textures, and sounds and asked subjects to report the intensity and quality of their sensations. That is, he asked them to **introspect**—*to look within themselves*. He measured the changes in people's experiences as he changed the stimuli.

---

[1] A reference containing a slash, such as this one, refers to a book originally published in the first year (1896) and reprinted in the second year (1902).

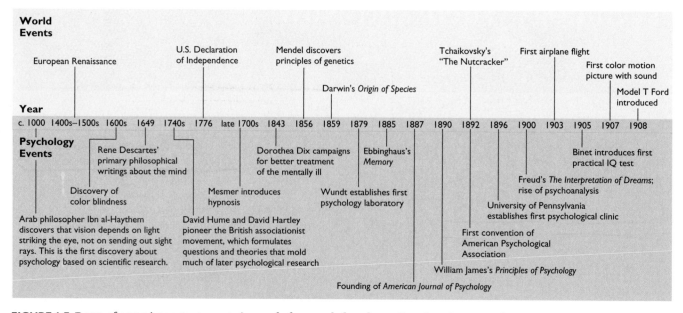

**World Events**

European Renaissance | U.S. Declaration of Independence | Mendel discovers principles of genetics | Tchaikovsky's "The Nutcracker" | First airplane flight | First color motion picture with sound | Model T Ford introduced

Darwin's *Origin of Species*

**Year**

c. 1000  1400s–1500s  1600s  1649  1740s  1776  late 1700s  1843  1856  1859  1879  1885  1887  1890  1892  1896  1900  1903  1905  1907  1908

**Psychology Events**

Rene Descartes' primary philosophical writings about the mind

Dorothea Dix campaigns for better treatment of the mentally ill

Ebbinghaus's *Memory*

Binet introduces first practical IQ test

Discovery of color blindness

Mesmer introduces hypnosis

Wundt establishes first psychology laboratory

Freud's *The Interpretation of Dreams*; rise of psychoanalysis

University of Pennsylvania establishes first psychological clinic

Arab philosopher Ibn al-Haythem discovers that vision depends on light striking the eye, not on sending out sight rays. This is the first discovery about psychology based on scientific research.

David Hume and David Hartley pioneer the British associationist movement, which formulates questions and theories that mold much of later psychological research.

First convention of American Psychological Association

William James's *Principles of Psychology*

Founding of *American Journal of Psychology*

**FIGURE 1.7** Dates of some important events in psychology and elsewhere. (Based partly on Dewsbury (2000a).

Wundt also demonstrated that it was possible to conduct meaningful psychological experiments. For example, in one of his earliest studies, he set up a pendulum that struck metal balls and made a sound at two points on its swing (points b and d in Figure 1.8). People would watch the pendulum and determine where it appeared to be when they heard the sound. Often, the pendulum appeared to be slightly in front of or behind the ball when people heard the strike. The apparent position of the pendulum at the time of the sound differed from its actual position by an average of 1/8 of a second (Wundt, 1862/1961). Apparently, the time we think we see or hear something is not the same as when the event occurred. Wundt's interpretation was that a person needs about 1/8 of a second to shift attention

**FIGURE 1.8** (Left) In one of Wilhelm Wundt's earliest experiments, the pendulum struck the metal balls (b and d), making a sound each time. To an observer, however, the ball appeared to be somewhere else at the time of the sound, generally the distance that it would travel in about 1/8 of a second. Wundt inferred that a person needs about 1/8 of a second to shift attention from one stimulus to another. (Right) The Walt Disney studios rediscovered Wundt's observation decades later: The character's mouth movements seem to be in synchrony with the sounds if the movements precede the sounds by 1/8 to 1/6 of a second.

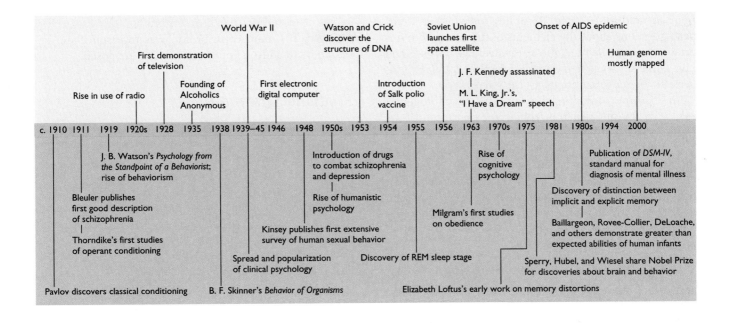

from one stimulus to another. (The same idea has been re-discovered in other contexts, as we shall see in Chapter 8.)

Wundt and his students were prolific investigators; the brief treatment here does not do him justice. He wrote more than 50,000 pages about his research, but his most lasting impact came from setting the precedent of studying psychological questions by collecting scientific data.

## Edward Titchener and Structuralism

At first, most of the world's psychologists received their education from Wilhelm Wundt himself. One of Wundt's students, Edward Titchener, came to the United States in 1892 as a psychology professor at Cornell University. Like Wundt, Titchener believed that the main question of psychology was the nature of mental experiences.

Titchener (1910) typically presented a stimulus and asked his subject to analyze it into its separate features—for example, to look at a lemon and describe its yellowness, its brightness, its shape, and so forth. He called his approach **structuralism,** *an attempt to describe the structures that compose the mind,* particularly sensations, feelings, and images. Later researchers were more interested in what those elements *do* (their functions).

If you asked psychologists today whether they thought Titchener correctly described the structures of the mind, you would probably get blank looks or shoulder shrugs. After Titchener died in 1927, psychologists virtually abandoned his research methods and even his questions. Why? Remember that a good scientific question is both

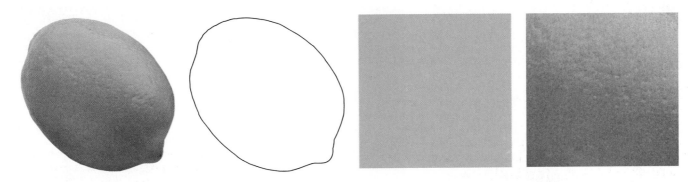

■   Edward Titchener asked subjects to describe their sensations. For example, they might describe their sensation of shape, their sensation of color, and their sensation of texture while looking at a lemon. Titchener had no way to check the accuracy of these reports, however, so later psychologists abandoned his methods.

important and answerable. Regardless of whether Titchener's questions about the elements of the mind were important, the more he tried, the less answerable they seemed to be. Quite simply, when observers described their experiences, Titchener could not check their accuracy.

For example, imagine you are the psychologist: I look at a lemon and tell you my experience of its brightness is totally separate from my experience of its yellowness. How do you know whether I am lying to you, telling you what I think you want me to say, or even deceiving myself? Other psychologists' frustration with this approach eventually turned many of them against studying the mind and toward studying observable behaviors.

## William James and Functionalism

Almost simultaneously with the work of Wundt and Titchener, Harvard University's William James articulated some of the major issues of psychology and won eventual recognition as the founder of American psychology. James's book *The Principles of Psychology* (James, 1890) defined the questions that dominated psychology for years afterward and even to some extent today.

James had little patience for either Wundt's or Titchener's search for the elements of the mind. He focused on the actions that the mind *performs* rather than the ideas that the mind *has*. That is, instead of trying to isolate the elements of consciousness, he preferred *to learn how the mind produces useful behaviors*. For this reason we call his approach **functionalism.** He suggested the following examples of good psychological questions (James, 1890):

- How can people strengthen good habits?
- Can someone attend to more than one item at a time?
- How do people recognize that they have seen something before?
- How does an intention lead to action?

James proposed possible answers but did little research of his own. His main contribution was to inspire later researchers to address the questions that he posed.

## Studying Sensation

One of early psychologists' main research topics was the relationship between physical stimuli and psychological sensations. To a large extent, the study of sensation *was* psychology. The first English-language textbook of the "new" scientifically based psychology devoted almost half of its pages to a discussion of the senses and the related topic of attention (Scripture, 1907). By the 1930s standard psychology textbooks devoted less than 20% of their pages to these topics (Woodworth, 1934), and today, it is down to about 5–10%.

Why were early psychologists so interested in sensation? One reason was philosophical: They wanted to understand mental experience, and experience is composed mostly if not entirely of sensations. The other reason was strategic: A scientific psychology had to begin with answerable questions, and many questions about sensation are indeed answerable.

Early psychologists discovered that what we see, hear, and otherwise sense is not the same as what is actually there. For example, the *perceived* intensity of a stimulus is not directly proportional to the *actual* physical intensity of the stimulus: That is, a light that is twice as intense as another light does not look twice as bright. Figure 1.9 shows the relationship between the intensity of light and its perceived brightness. *The mathematical description of the relationship between the physical properties of a stimulus and its perceived properties* is called the **psychophysical function** because it relates psychology to physics. Such research demonstrated that, at least in the study of sensation, scientific methods can provide nonobvious answers to psychological questions.

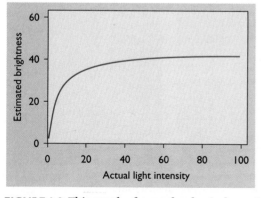

**FIGURE 1.9** This graph of a psychophysical event shows the perceived intensity of light versus its physical intensity. When a light becomes twice as intense physically, it does not seem twice as bright. (Adapted from Stevens, 1961)

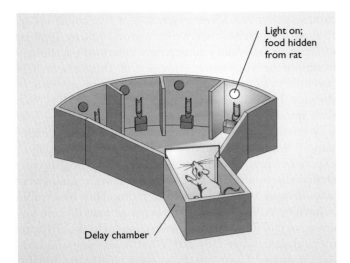

FIGURE 1.10 One of the tasks used by early comparative psychologists to assess animal intelligence tested the delayed-response problem. A stimulus was presented and a delay ensued; then the animal was expected to respond to the re-membered stimulus. Variations on this delayed-response task are still used today.

FIGURE 1.11 Another task popular among early comparative psychologists was the detour problem. An animal needed to first go away from the food in order to move toward it.

## Darwin and the Study of Animal Intelligence

Charles Darwin's theory of evolution by natural selection (Darwin, 1859, 1871) had an enormous impact not only on biology but also on psychology. Darwin argued that humans and other species share a remote common ancestor. This proposal implied that each species had evolved specializations adapted to different ways of life, but it also implied that all vertebrate species had many basic features in common. It further implied that nonhuman animals should exhibit varying degrees of human characteristics, including intelligence.

Presuming that we accept this last implication, what should psychologists do about it? Some early **comparative psychologists,** *specialists who compare different animal species,* did something that seemed more reasonable at first than it did later: They set out to measure animal intelligence. They apparently imagined that they could rank-order animals from the smartest to the dullest. Toward that goal, they set various species to such tasks as the delayed-response problem and the detour problem. In the *delayed-response problem,* an animal was given a signal indicating where it could find food. Then the signal was removed and the animal was restrained for a while (Figure 1.10) to see how long it could remember the signal. In the *detour problem,* an animal was separated from food by a barrier (Figure 1.11) to see whether it would take a detour away from the food in order to get to it.

However, measuring animal intelligence turned out to be more difficult than it sounded. Too often a species

seemed dull-witted on one task but brilliant on another. For example, zebras are generally slow to learn to approach one pattern instead of another for food, unless the patterns happen to be narrow stripes versus wide stripes, in which case they suddenly excel (Giebel, 1958) (see Figure 1.12). If rats are trained to look for food under the object that looks different from the others, they fail miserably, but if the task is to choose the object that *smells* different from the others, rats learn quickly (Langworthy & Jennings, 1972). With humans, too, it is possible to do well on one task but not another, but the discrepancy is even more extreme among species.

FIGURE 1.12 Zebras learn rapidly when they have to compare stripe patterns (Giebel, 1958). How "smart" a species is perceived to be depends in part on what ability or skill is being tested.

Eventually, psychologists realized that the relative intelligence of nonhuman animals was a complicated and probably meaningless question. Some researchers today hesitate even to say that monkeys are more intelligent than frogs (Macphail, 1985), preferring instead to talk about which particular abilities are better developed in one species or another.

## Measuring Human Intelligence

While some psychologists studied animal intelligence, others pursued human intelligence. Francis Galton, a cousin of Charles Darwin, was among the first to try to measure intelligence and to ask whether intellectual variations were based on heredity. Galton was fascinated with trying to measure almost everything (Hergenhahn, 1992). For example, he invented the weather map, measured degrees of boredom during lectures, suggested the use of fingerprints to identify individuals, and—in the name of science—attempted to measure the beauty of women in different countries.

In an effort to determine the role of heredity in human achievement, Galton (1869/1978) examined whether the sons of famous and accomplished men tended to become eminent themselves. (Women in 19th-century England had little opportunity for fame.) Galton found that the sons of judges, writers, politicians, and other noted men had a high probability of similar accomplishment themselves. He attributed this edge to heredity. (I'll leave this one for you to judge: Did he have adequate evidence for his conclusion? If the sons of famous men become famous themselves, is heredity the only explanation?)

Galton also tried to measure intelligence, but the tests he developed—measuring simple sensory and motor skills—were unsatisfactory. In 1905 a French researcher, Alfred Binet, devised the first useful intelligence test, which we shall discuss further in Chapter 9. At this point just note that the idea of testing intelligence became popular in the United States and other Western countries. Psychologists, inspired by the popularity of intelligence tests, later developed tests of personality, interests, and other psychological characteristics. Also note that measuring human intelligence faces some of the same problems as animal intelligence: People have a great many intelligent abilities, and it is possible to be highly adept at one and not another.

## The Rise of Behaviorism

Earlier in this chapter, I casually defined psychology as "the systematic study of behavior and experience." For a substantial period of psychology's history, most experimental psychologists would have objected to the words "and experience." Some psychologists still object today, though less strenuously. From about 1920 to 1960 or 1970, most laboratory researchers described psychology as simply the study of behavior, period. These researchers had little to say about minds, experiences, or anything of the sort. (According to one quip, psychologists had "lost their minds.")

What did psychologists have against the study of experience? Recall the failure of Titchener's effort to analyze experience into its components. Most psychologists concluded that questions about the mind were unanswerable. Instead, they addressed questions about observable behaviors: What do people and other animals do, and under what circumstances? How do changes in the environment change what they do? What is learning and how does it occur? These questions were clearly meaningful and answerable, although the answers might be complex.

## John B. Watson

We can regard John B. Watson as the founder of **behaviorism,** *a field of psychology that concentrates on observable, measurable behaviors and not on mental processes.* Watson was not the first behaviorist—it is uncertain who was the first—but he systematized the approach, popularized it, and stated its goals and assumptions (Watson, 1919, 1925). Here are two quotes from Watson:

> Psychology as the behaviorist views it is a purely objective experimental branch of natural science. Its theoretical goal is the prediction and control of behavior. (Watson, 1913, p. 158)

> The goal of psychological study is the ascertaining of such data and laws that, given the stimulus, psychology can predict what the response will be; or, on the other hand, given the response, it can specify the nature of the effective stimulus. (Watson, 1919, p. 10)

## Studies of Learning

Inspired by Watson, many researchers set out to study animal behavior, especially animal learning. One advantage of studying nonhuman animals is that the researcher can control the animals' diet, waking-sleeping schedule, and other life experiences far more completely than with humans. The other supposed advantage was that nonhuman learning might be simpler to understand. Many psychologists optimistically expected to discover simple, basic laws of behavior comparable to Newton's laws of physics. Many believed that behavioral laws would be more or less the same from one species to another, so they studied animals, especially rats. By 1950 well over half of all psychological studies on animals used rats as subjects (Beach, 1950).

Researchers simplified their task by not only concentrating on just a few species but also by focusing on just a

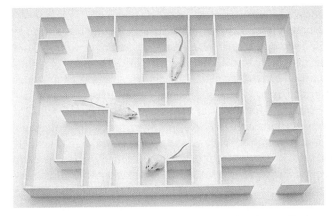

■ Early behaviorists studied rats in mazes, hoping to find general laws of behavior. As they discovered that this apparently simple behavior was very complicated, their interest declined and they turned to other topics.

few examples of learning, such as maze learning. One highly influential Yale psychologist, Clark Hull, was very explicit about what he considered an important psychological question: "One of the most persistently baffling problems which confronts modern psychologists is the finding of an adequate explanation of the phenomena of maze learning" (Hull, 1932, p. 25). Would you list that topic today as one of the most important things you would like to understand in psychology?

As research progressed, however, psychologists found that even the behavior of a rat in a maze was far more complicated than they had expected. As a result, the kinds of maze studies that were popular in the 1950s are a rarity today. Just as psychologists of the 1920s abandoned Titchener's structuralist approach to the mind, later psychologists abandoned the hope that studying a few simple situations would lead to a discovery of universal principles of behavior.

## From Freud to Modern Clinical Psychology

In the early 1900s, clinical psychology was a small field devoted largely to visual, auditory, movement, and memory disorders (Routh, 2000). The treatment of psychological disorders (or mental illness) was mostly the province of psychiatry, a branch of medicine, and of other doctors who were more influenced by neurophysiology than by experimental psychology (Taylor, 2000). The Austrian psychiatrist Sigmund Freud revolutionized and popularized psychotherapy with his methods of analyzing patients' dreams and memories. He tried to trace current behavior to early childhood experiences, including sexual fantasies. We shall examine Freud's theories in much

more detail in Chapter 13. Freud's influence was strong, and by the mid-1900s, most psychiatrists in the United States and Europe were following his methods, at least in part.

During World War II more people wanted therapy, especially soldiers traumatized by war experiences. Because psychiatrists could not keep up with the need, psychologists began providing therapy. Clinical psychology became a much more popular field and much more similar to psychiatry (except without the license to prescribe drugs). New methods of psychotherapy arose, and research began to differentiate between more and less effective methods. Today Freud's methods are far less popular than they used to be, and other methods have taken their place, as we shall see in Chapters 15 and 16. Some therapists rely on selective use of rewards and other principles of learning, whereas others attempt to alter people's thoughts, especially how they interpret their successes and failures. *Humanistic psychologists* rely mostly on listening, encouraging people to explore their feelings, and providing a supportive atmosphere of unconditional positive regard. The underlying belief is that people have the inherent capacity to solve their problems for themselves.

## More Recent Trends in Psychology

The rest of this book will focus on the current era in psychology, with occasional flashbacks to the history of particular topics. Psychology today is an extremely diverse field, ranging from the study of simple visual processes to interventions intended to change whole communities or societies.

Recall that some of the earliest psychological researchers wanted to study the mind, experience, and consciousness, but the introspective methods of Titchener seemed to lead nowhere. Still today, many people believe that a study of consciousness or self is futile (Horgan, 1999). On the other hand, since the mid-1960s, cognitive psychology (the study of thought and knowledge) has become more prominent within psychology, largely at the expense of the behavioral emphasis (Robins, Gosling, & Craik, 1999). Researchers of today rely much less on introspection than did those of the early 1900s. Instead of asking people about their thoughts, they carefully measure the accuracy and speed of responses under various circumstances to infer what people know and how they use their knowledge. They also use brain scans to determine what happens when and where in the brain while someone is solving a problem or answering a question. Cognitive psychologists study human information processing in much the same way they would the information processing of a computer.

New fields of application have also arisen. For example, health psychologists study how people's health is influenced by their behaviors, such as smoking, drinking, sexual activities, exercise, diet, and reactions to stress. They also try to help people change their behaviors to promote better health. Forensic psychologists apply their knowledge in courts of law, dealing with such questions as "Is this defendant mentally competent to stand trial?" and "How accurate is eyewitness testimony likely to be under the circumstances of this case?" Sports psychologists apply psychological principles to helping athletes set goals, train, concentrate their efforts during a contest, and so forth.

Psychologists today have also broadened their scope to include more of human diversity. In an earlier era, psychological researchers seeking general laws or principles of behavior often assumed that they could discover these by studying rats, pigeons, or any other convenient species. When they studied humans, they generally limited themselves to convenient samples, such as college students. That strategy is justifiable for certain purposes. For example, all vertebrate species have eyes that operate on the same basic principles, so for many purposes a researcher could study the eyes of any individual, even any species. In other cases, however, the choice of partici-

widowed or divorced women the same age (Yip, 1998). So before we draw any conclusions about the relationship between marriage and suicide, we have to note that it is not an invariant automatic relationship; it has something to do with the status of married people of a particular age and gender in a particular culture.

For another example, Sigmund Freud proposed that an important point of a young boy's psychological development is ambivalence (mixed positive and negative feelings) toward his father, because the boy has romantic feelings toward his mother and sees the father as a competitor. That idea had problems enough in applying to European or American culture, but a study of other cultures damages it further: In some cultures the father is merely the mother's lover, whereas the mother's brother (the child's uncle) is the one who raises and disciplines the child. In those cultures boys develop ambivalent feelings toward the uncle (who is definitely not a romantic competitor for the mother), not toward the father (Segal, Lonner, & Berry, 1998). In this example a study of other cultures helps to illuminate certain aspects of our own behavior.

Similarly, when studying any aspect of human social behavior, psychologists should compare the results from different cultures and various ethnic groups to see what is a fixed part of human nature and what is not. **Cross-cultural study,** *research that compares people from various cultures,* have become increasingly influential in psychology.

What will psychology be like in the future? We don't know, of course, but we assume it will reflect the changing needs of humanity. A few likely trends are foreseeable. During the 1900s advances in medicine enabled people to live longer, while advances in technology enabled them to build homes (and shopping centers) where there used to be forests and wetlands, heat and cool their homes, travel by car or plane to distant locations, and buy and discard enormous numbers of products. In short, we are quickly destroying our environment, using up natural resources, and polluting our air

■ We can learn much about what is or is not a stable feature of human nature by comparing people of different cultures.

pants can be critical. For example, a great many studies have shown married people are less likely to commit suicide than are unmarried people. But then additional studies found an exception: In Hong Kong married women over age 60 have a higher suicide rate than do

and water. Sooner or later it will become necessary either to decrease the population or to decrease the average person's use of resources (Howard, 2000). Convincing people to change their behavior is partly a political matter, but likely it will also be partly a task for psychologists.

## *Psychology Through the Years*

Throughout the early years of psychology, many psychologists went down blind alleys, devoting enormous efforts to projects that produced disappointing results. Not all the efforts of early psychologists were fruitless, though; in later chapters you will encounter some classic studies that have withstood the test of time. Still, if psychologists of the past spent countless years on fashionable projects, only to decide later that their efforts were misguided, how do we know that many psychologists aren't on the wrong track right now?

The answer is that we don't. Thousands of psychologists are engaged in various kinds of research, and chances are, many of them are working on projects that will never accomplish much. As you read through later chapters, you are welcome to entertain doubts. Maybe some psychologists' questions are not as simple as they seem; perhaps some of their answers are not very solid; perhaps you can think of a better way to approach certain topics.

In short, psychologists do not have all the answers. But that is not a reason for despair. Much like a rat in a maze, researchers make progress by trial and error. They pose a question, try a particular research method, and find out what happens. Sometimes the results are fascinating and rich in practical consequences; sometimes they turn out to be puzzling or inconclusive. If one study after another proves disappointing, psychologists either look for a new method or else they change the question they are asking. By abandoning unsuccessful approaches, they eventually find the way to better questions and better answers.

## Summary

- *Choice of research questions.* During the history of psychology, researchers have several times changed their opinions about what constitutes an interesting, important, answerable question. (page 17)

- *First experiments.* In 1879 Wilhelm Wundt established the first laboratory devoted to psychological research. He demonstrated the possibility of psychological experimentation. (page 17)
- *Limits of self-observation.* One of Wundt's students, Edward Titchener, attempted to analyze the elements of mental experience, relying on people's own observations. Other psychologists became discouraged with this approach. (page 19)
- *The founding of American psychology.* William James, generally considered the founder of American psychology, focused attention on how the mind guides useful behavior rather than on the contents of the mind. By doing so James paved the way for the rise of behaviorism. (page 20)
- *Early sensory research.* In the early days of psychology, many researchers concentrated on studies of the senses, partly because they were more likely to find definite answers on this topic than on other topics. (page 20)
- *Darwin's influence.* Charles Darwin's theory of evolution by natural selection influenced psychology in many ways; it prompted some prominent early psychologists to compare the intelligence of different species. That question turned out to be more complicated than anyone had expected. (page 21)
- *Intelligence testing.* The measurement of human intelligence was one concern of early psychologists that has persisted through the years. (page 22)
- *The era of behaviorist dominance.* As psychologists became discouraged with their attempts to analyze the mind, they turned to behaviorism. For many years psychological researchers concentrated on behavior, especially animal learning, to the virtual exclusion of mental experience. (page 22)
- *Maze learning.* Clark Hull exerted great influence for a number of years. Eventually, his approach became less popular because rats in mazes did not seem to generate simple or general answers to major questions. (page 23)
- *Psychological research today.* Today, psychologists study a wide variety of topics. Still, we cannot be certain that we are not currently going down some blind alleys, just as many psychologists did before us. (page 23)

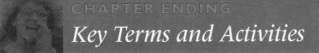
CHAPTER ENDING
## *Key Terms and Activities*

## Key Terms

You can check the page listed for a complete description of a term. You can also check the glossary/index at the end of the text for a definition of a given term, or you can download a list of all the terms and their definitions for any chapter at this Web site:

http://psychology.wadsworth.com/

**behaviorism:** a field of psychology that concentrates on observable, measurable behaviors and not on mental processes (page 22)

**biopsychologist** (or **behavioral neuroscientist**): a specialist who tries to explain behavior in terms of biological factors, such as electrical and chemical activities in the nervous system, the effects of drugs and hormones, genetics, and evolutionary pressures (page 10)

**clinical psychologist:** someone with an advanced degree in psychology, with a specialization in understanding and helping people with psychological problems (page 12)

**cognition:** thinking and acquiring knowledge (page 10)

**cognitive psychologist:** a specialist who studies thought processes and the acquisition of knowledge (page 10)

**comparative psychologist:** a specialist who compares different animal species (page 21)

**cross-cultural studies:** research studies that compare people from various cultures (page 24)

**counseling psychologist:** someone trained to help people with educational, vocational, marriage, health-related, and other decisions (page 12)

**determinism:** the assumption that all behavior has a cause, or *determinant,* in the observable world (page 6)

**developmental psychologist:** a specialist who studies the behavioral capacities of different ages and how behavior changes with age (page 11)

**dualism:** view that the mind is separate from the brain (page 7)

**ergonomist** (or **human factors specialist**)**:** a psychologist with engineering skills who works to facilitate the operation of machinery so that the average user can use it as efficiently and as safely as possible (page 13)

**free will:** the doctrine that behavior is caused by a person's independent decisions, not by external determinants (page 7)

**functionalism:** an attempt to understand how mental processes produce useful behaviors (page 20)

**industrial/organizational psychology:** the study of people at work (page 13)

**introspection:** looking within oneself (page 17)

**learning and motivation:** study of how behavior depends on the outcomes of past behaviors and on current motivations (page 10)

**mind-brain problem:** the philosophical question of how the conscious mind is related to the physical nervous system, including the brain (page 7)

**monism:** view that consciousness is inseparable from the physical brain (page 8)

**nature-nurture issue:** the question of the relative roles played by heredity (nature) and environment (nurture) in determining differences in behavior (page 9)

**principle of compatibility:** the concept that people's built-in or learned expectations enable them to learn certain procedures more easily than others (page 14)

**psychiatry:** a branch of medicine that deals with emotional disturbances (page 12)

**psychoanalyst:** a psychotherapist who relies heavily on the theories of Sigmund Freud (page 12)

**psychology:** the systematic study of behavior and experience (page 5)

**psychophysical function:** the mathematical description of the relationship between the physical properties of a stimulus and its perceived properties (page 20)

**psychotherapist:** a specialist who provides help for people with psychological problems (page 11)

**school psychologist:** a specialist in the psychological condition of students (page 14)

**social psychologist:** a specialist who studies how an individual influences others and is influenced by other people (page 11)

**structuralism:** an attempt to describe the structures that compose the mind (page 19)

## Suggestions for Further Reading

Scarborough, E., & Furomoto, L. (1987). *Untold lives: The first generation of American women psychologists.* New York: Columbia University Press. A rich account of history and biography.

Sechenov, I. (1965). *Reflexes of the brain.* Cambridge, MA: MIT Press. (Original work published 1863) One of the first attempts to deal with behavior scientifically and still one of the clearest statements of the argument for determinism in human behavior.

## Web/Technology Resources

Careers in Psychology

**www.drlynnfriedman.com/**

Clinical psychologist Lynn Friedman offers advice on majoring in psychology, going to graduate school, and starting a career.

Psychological Science Agenda

**www.apa.org/psa/**

*Psychological Science Agenda,* the newsletter of the American Psychological Association Science Directorate, carried a series of articles written by people working in interesting and unusual nonacademic careers. Among the careers: research in the public sector, highway safety research, market research and consulting, acquisition and sponsoring editor, director of education and research, human factors and user interface design, trial consultant, and executive search consultant. The APA Science Directorate now sponsors a Personal Stories of Nonacademic Careers Web page (www.apa.org/science/psa.html) that lists most of these and others.

## HistPsyc Headlines Pages

**www.unb.ca/web/units/psych/likely/headlines/**

David Likely, at the University of New Brunswick, produced the HistPsyc Headlines Pages, which provide a history of important events related to psychology from 1650 to 1959, plus links to related sites. He has also developed several on-line study aids for students interested in the history of psychology that are available from his home page at www.unb.ca_/web/units/psych/likely/psyc4053.htm.

## Today in the History of Psychology

**www.cwu.edu/~warren/today.html**

Warren Street, at Central Washington University, offers a sample of events in the history of psychology for every day of the year. Pick a date, any date (as they say), from the History of Psychology Calendar and see what happened on that date. The APA sponsors this site, which is based on Street's book, *A Chronology of Noteworthy Events in American Psychology.*

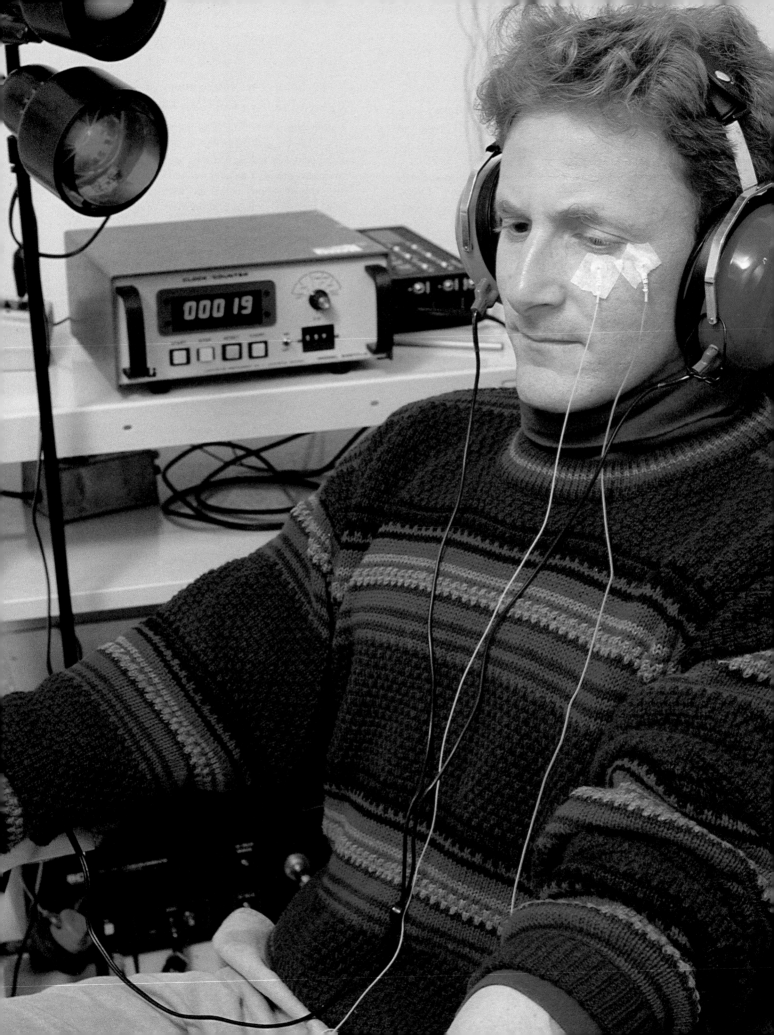

# Scientific Methods in Psychology

**2**

**CHAPTER**

couple of years ago, I was watching a Discovery Channel nature documentary about elephants. After the narrator discussed the enormous amount of food elephants eat, he started on their digestive system. He commented that the average elephant passes enough gas in a day to propel a car for 20 miles (32 km). I thought, "Wow, isn't that an amazing fact!" and I told a couple of other people about it.

A while later I started to think, "Wait a minute. *Who measured that? And how?!* Did some people really attach a balloon to an elephant's rear end and collect gas for 24 hours? And then put it into a car to see how far they could make the car go? Was that a full-sized car or an economy car? City traffic or highway? How do they know they measured a typical elephant? Maybe they chose an extra gassy one. Did they determine the mean for a broad sample of elephants?"

The more I thought about it, the more I realized that the documentary makers couldn't possibly have adequate evidence for their claim about propelling a car on elephant gas.

"Oh, well," you might say. "What difference does it make?" You're right; it doesn't matter much. However, my point is not to ridicule the makers of this documentary but to ridicule *me*. Remember, I said I told two people about this claim before I started to doubt it. For decades I have been teaching students to question assertions, evaluate the evidence, think critically, and so forth, and here I was, uncritically accepting a silly statement about elephants and even telling other people, who for all I know, may have gone on to tell other people who told still other people until someday it might become part of our folklore: "*They say* that you can propel a car 20 miles on a day's worth of elephant gas!"

The point is that all of us—myself included—need to discipline ourselves to question the evidence behind new claims, especially the interesting or exciting claims that we would most like to believe. This chapter concerns the evaluation of evidence in psychology.

# Thinking Critically About Science and the Evaluation of Evidence

*How do scientists evaluate theories?*

*Why are most scientists so skeptical of new theories and claims that seem to contradict our current understanding?*

You will sometimes hear nonscientists say that something has been "scientifically proved." Most scientists themselves avoid the word *proved*, except when they are talking about a mathematical proof. Repeated observations can make a conclusion extremely probable, but the word *prove* sounds a little too final.

Scientists generally agree on how to evaluate theories, and that feature distinguishes science from many other human endeavors. For example, what evidence can you imagine that would cause you to change your religious beliefs? What about your political affiliation? Most people find it difficult to imagine a fact that would change their opinions. In contrast, two scientists who favor different theories can usually imagine evidence that would decide the issue one way or the other. In that sense psychologists (most psychologists, anyway) follow the scientific method. Obviously, our knowledge of psychology is much less impressive than that of physics, chemistry, and biology. But like physicists, chemists, and biologists, psychologists do generally agree on what constitutes good evidence and what does not.

**A STEP FURTHER**
*Scientific Thinking*

If people interested in ethics agreed with one another about how to evaluate theories, could they make progress comparable to that of scientists? Could theologians?

## Steps for Gathering and Evaluating Evidence

*Above all, scientists want to know the evidence behind a given claim.* In psychology as in other fields, students should learn to question assertions and ask for the evidence behind a given claim.

The word *science* derives from a Latin word meaning "knowledge." The simplest route to knowledge is careful observation, and much of science consists of recording observations. We also gain scientific knowledge by testing **hypotheses,** which are *testable predictions of what will happen under certain conditions.* Research designed to test hypotheses goes through the series of steps described in the following four paragraphs (see also Figure 2.1). Articles in scientific publications generally follow this sequence, too. In each of the remaining chapters of this book, you will find an example of a psychological study described in a section entitled "What's the Evidence?" Here the examples concern the possible relationship between televised violence and aggressive behavior.

### Hypothesis

A hypothesis can be based on a larger theory. For example, "if our understanding of social influence is correct, then children who watch a great deal of violence will themselves become more violent." In other cases the hypothesis is the product of preliminary observations. For example, someone who notices several

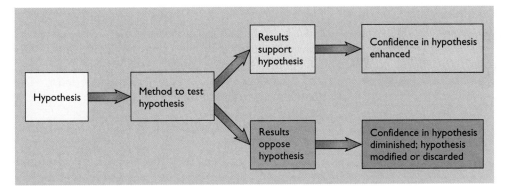

**FIGURE 2.1** A hypothesis leads to predictions. An experimental method tests those predictions; a confirmation of a prediction supports the hypothesis; a disconfirmation indicates a need to revise or discard the hypothesis. Conclusions remain tentative, especially after only one experiment. Most scientists avoid saying that their results "prove" a conclusion.

aggressive children who watch violent television programs might suggest a hypothesis that links violent programs to violent behavior.

## Method

Any hypothesis could be tested in many ways. To test the effects of violent television shows, one possibility would be to measure how much time various children watch violence on television and relate that amount of time to a measure of their violent behavior. However, even if the relationship appeared strong, the results would not demonstrate cause and effect. (Maybe watching violence provokes violence, but it is also possible that children who are already violent prefer violent programs.) Another approach would be to ask one group of children to watch one set of programs and another group to watch a different set of programs and then record behavioral differences between the groups.

## Results

Fundamental to any research is measuring the outcome. A phenomenon such as "violent behavior" can be especially tricky to measure. (How do we decide what is *real* violence and what is just playfulness? Do threats count? Does verbal abuse?) It is important for an investigator to follow clear rules for making measurements. After making the measurements, the investigator must determine whether the results are impressive enough to call for an explanation. For example, if someone found that children who watched violent television programs committed only 1% more aggressive acts than children watching other programs, the results may represent nothing more than chance fluctuations or at most a very small influence of the programs. A larger effect, using a large and diverse sample of children, would justify a stronger conclusion.

## Interpretation

The final task is to determine what the results mean. If they clearly contradict the hypothesis, researchers should either abandon or modify the original hypothesis. (Maybe it applies only to certain kinds of people or only under certain circumstances.) If the results match the prediction, investigators gain confidence in their hypothesis, but they should not necessarily accept it. Even though the results fit the hypothesis, they might fit other hypotheses as well. Because almost any study has limitations, the ultimate conclusion can come only from the results of many studies.

# Replicability

Most scientific researchers are scrupulously honest in reporting their results. Distortions of data are rare and scandalous. Despite their habit of honesty, scientists do not accept the statement "trust me" or "take my word for it." Anyone who reports a result in a scientific article also re-

ports the methods in enough detail that someone else could repeat the study, and those who doubt the result are invited to do so. If they get the same results, they presumably will be convinced. But if they cannot, they should reject the original finding and base no theory upon it. **Replicable results** are *those that anyone can obtain, at least approximate, by following the same procedures,* and scientific progress is based only on replicable results.

Let's consider an example of a nonreplicable result. In 1993 a team of researchers had several groups of young people listen to a Mozart sonata, a "relaxation tape," or silence and then take some psychological tests. They reported that the people who listened to Mozart performed better than the others on one test of spatial reasoning (Rauscher, Shaw, & Ky, 1993). Their implication was that listening to complex nonrepetitive music might be good for brain functioning.

Wouldn't it be great if we could increase people's intelligence that easily? The government of the state of Georgia considered giving every newborn baby a recording of Mozart's music at state expense. The classical radio station in my hometown sometimes introduces Mozart compositions with an announcement that listening to them might improve the listener's intelligence.

Unfortunately, the effect has not been replicable. Several other studies using virtually the same method as the original one found either no difference or a trivially small difference between the Mozart listeners and the other groups (Chabris, 1999; Steele, Bass, & Crook, 1999). One study found some improvement after listening to Mozart, but also after listening to Schubert or listening to a story. The researchers suggested that the improvement was due simply to being relaxed before taking the test (Nantais & Schellenberg, 1999).

So, what conclusion should we draw? The answer is, when the results are inconsistent, we draw no conclusions at all. Maybe the original result was a coincidence, and performances had nothing to do with the music. Or maybe either the original investigators or the later ones had some hidden flaw in their research. Or maybe listening to Mozart really does raise intellectual performance, but only under some limited set of circumstances. Maybe . . . who knows? The point is, until or unless someone finds conditions under which the phenomenon is replicable (consistently repeatable), we should not take it seriously. This rule may seem unduly harsh, but it is our best defense against error.

Sometimes, however, an effect is small but real. For example, many studies have compared unprovoked aggressive behavior in men and women. Many but not all studies find that men are more aggressive, and the size of the effect varies from one study to another. Despite this variation, we do not regard the sex difference in aggressive behavior as unreplicable. Rather, our interpretation is that a small sex difference competes with many other influences on aggressive behavior. If we combine the results of many studies, we can get an approximate measure of the size of the effect. A **meta-analysis** *combines the results of many studies and analyzes them as though they were all one very large study.* One meta-analysis concluded that men are indeed more likely than women to engage in unprovoked violence (Bettencourt & Miller, 1996). In most cases a meta-analysis will also determine which variations in procedure increase or decrease the effects.

## Criteria for Evaluating Scientific Theories

After investigators collect mounds of evidence and identify the replicable findings, what do they do with the results? One goal of scientific research is to establish **theories,** *comprehensive explanations of observable events.* A good theory starts with as few assumptions as possible and leads to as many predictions as possible. In that way it reduces the amount of information we must remember. For example, according to the *law of effect* (to be discussed in Chapter 6), if a human or any other animal makes a response that is consistently followed by a reinforcer (e.g., food to a hungry person or water to a thirsty one), then the future probability of that response will increase. This principle summarizes results achieved for many species, many responses, and many reinforcers; we don't have to learn the results separately for each situation.

When we are confronted with several competing theories, we must evaluate them to decide which is the best. First, consider what is wrong with this theory: "George does poorly in school because he has a learning disability." How do we know he has a learning disability? Well, we know because he does poorly in school. As you can see, this is no explanation. If someone has separate evidence for a learning disability (like a brain scan or something else measured independently from school performance), then it's a possible explanation. Any good theory *should predict new observations.* It gets no credit for "predicting" something that we already knew.

Second, consider what is wrong with this theory: "People who are under too much stress will fail to achieve their full potential." I won't argue that the statement is wrong, but it is too vague to be useful. We don't know how much stress is "too much" for a given individual, and there is no way to measure a person's "full potential." The more precise a theory's predictions, the better. One way of saying this is that a theory should be **falsifiable.** What scientists mean by *falsifiable* is that *the theory makes sufficiently precise predictions that we can at least imagine evidence that would contradict the theory (if we in fact obtained such evidence).* Of course, if someone actually obtained evidence that contradicted the predictions, then the theory would be falsifi-*ed.* A falsified theory is useless. Falsifi-*able* is different; it does not mean that the theory has been shown to be wrong, just that, if it *were* wrong, we could demon-

strate it to be wrong (Figure 2.2). "Too much stress prevents someone from reaching full potential" is not falsifiable because it is hard to imagine a result that would contradict it. Here is an example of a falsifiable statement: "Vision occurs after light stimulates the eyes." It is falsifiable because we can imagine evidence that would contradict it. If an eyeless person could see, or if anyone could see in complete darkness, then we would know the theory was false. The fact that no one has ever found such results is impressive support in favor of the statement.

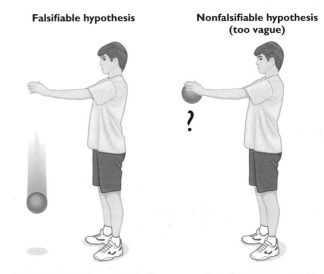

**Falsifiable hypothesis**

**Nonfalsifiable hypothesis (too vague)**

?

An object dropped near the Earth's surface will fall at a rate of 980.665 cm/sec², slowed slightly by air resistance.

If an object is dropped, something interesting will happen.

**FIGURE 2.2** A good theory makes precise (falsifiable) predictions.

Now consider what is wrong with this statement: "I did not wake up on time today, so I must have been kidnapped by aliens." The problem here is that we can easily conceive of a simpler explanation for the fact that someone overslept. Given a choice between an exciting, surprising explanation and a commonplace, even boring explanation that fits the same results, scientists favor the commonplace explanation. This preference for simple explanations, known as the *principle of parsimony* (literally, *stinginess*), is central to scientific thinking, so we shall examine it in detail in the following section.

## CONCEPT CHECK

1. Identify each of the following theories as either falsifiable or not falsifiable:
   a. Other things being equal, people need a longer time to memorize a longer list of words than a shorter list.
   b. Some people have supernatural powers that science cannot explain.

c. Children who suffer any kind of frustration during the 1st year of life will eventually develop emotional difficulties. (Check your answers on page 38.)

**A STEP FURTHER**
*Falsifiability*

Is the theory that "there is intelligent life elsewhere in the universe" falsifiable? Is the theory that "there is *no* intelligent life elsewhere in the universe" falsifiable? When it is impractical to test a theory, should we compromise our usual rules about falsifiability?

# Parsimony and Degrees of Open-Mindedness

According to the principle of **parsimony** (also known as *Occam's razor*), *scientists prefer the theory that explains the results using the simplest assumptions.* In other words, whenever possible, scientists explain new observations in familiar terms, using theories that they have already accepted. A theory that makes radically new assumptions is acceptable only after a complete failure to explain the results in a simpler way.

Parsimony is a conservative tendency: It tells us to adhere as much as possible to what we already believe. Science is therefore a very conservative—that is, cautious—enterprise. You might protest: "Shouldn't we remain open-minded to new possibilities?"

Yes, if open-mindedness means a willingness to consider proper evidence, but not if it means the assumption that "anything has as much chance of being true as anything else." Your degree of open-mindedness should depend on the strength of the evidence and logic supporting your current opinion. Consider two examples:

*Visitors from outer space.* I personally doubt that visitors from other planets have ever landed on Earth, and I doubt that they ever will. (If you want to get from one solar system to another in years instead of millennia, you need to travel close to the speed of light. At that speed a collision with even a dust particle would be catastrophic.) Still, I know my conclusions are based on uncertain assumptions about the technology and biology of alien life forms, so I am relatively open-minded to new evidence. If I saw weird-looking beings stepping out of an odd-looking spacecraft, I would consider the parsimonious possibility that some Earthling had staged a hoax, but I can imagine evidence that would change my opinion.

*Perpetual motion machines.* A "perpetual motion machine" is one that generates more energy than it uses. For centuries people have attempted and failed to develop such a machine. (Figure 2.3 shows one example.) The U.S. Patent Office is officially closed-minded on this issue, refusing even to consider patent applications for such machines, because a perpetual motion machine violates the second law of thermodynamics. According to that law, within a closed system, entropy can never decrease. A more casual statement of the law is that any work wastes some energy; you have to bring energy into a system to accomplish any work. Therefore, we need to keep adding energy to a machine to keep it going. The second law of thermodynamics is supported by an enormous amount of data plus logical arguments about why it must be true. Could it be wrong? Well, maybe, but I recommend only the slightest amount of open-mindedness here. If someone shows you what appears to be a perpetual motion machine, look carefully for a hidden battery or other power source—that is, some simple, parsimonious explanation. A claim as extraordinary as a perpetual motion machine requires extraordinary evidence.

What does all this discussion have to do with psychology? Sometimes people claim spectacular results that would seem to be impossible according to everything we know or think we know. Although it is only fair to examine the evidence behind such claims, it is also reasonable to maintain a skeptical attitude and to look as closely as possible for a simple, parsimonious explanation of the results. Let us consider two more examples.

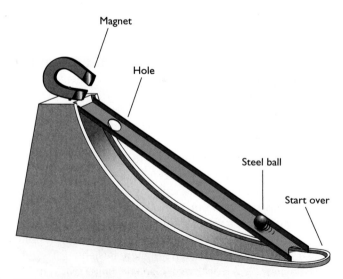

**FIGURE 2.3** A proposed perpetual motion machine: The magnet pulls the metal ball up the inclined plane. When the ball reaches the top, it falls through the hole and returns to its starting point, from which the magnet will again pull it up. Can you see why this device is sure to fail? (See answer A on page 39.)

## Applying Parsimony: Clever Hans, the Amazing Horse

Early in the 20th century, Mr. von Osten, a German mathematics teacher, set out to prove that his horse, Hans, had great intellectual abilities, particularly in arithmetic (Figure 2.4). To teach Hans arithmetic, he first showed him a single object, said "one," and lifted Hans's foot once. Then he raised Hans's foot twice for two objects and so on. Eventually, when von Osten presented a group of objects, Hans learned to tap his foot by himself, and with practice he managed to tap the correct number of times. With more practice it was no longer necessary for Hans to see the objects. Von Osten would just call out a number, and Hans would tap the appropriate number of times.

**FIGURE 2.4** Clever Hans and his owner, Mr. von Osten, demonstrated that the horse could answer complex mathematical questions with great accuracy. The question was, "How?" (After Pfungst, 1911, in Fernald, 1984)

Mr. von Osten moved on to addition and then to subtraction, multiplication, and division. Hans caught on quickly, soon responding with 90–95% accuracy. Then von Osten began touring Germany; he asked questions and Hans tapped out the answers. Hans's abilities grew until he could add fractions, convert fractions to decimals or vice versa, do simple algebra, tell time to the minute, and give the values of all German coins. Using a letter-to-number code, he could spell out the names of objects and even identify musical notes such as B-flat. (Evidently, Hans had perfect pitch.) He responded correctly even when questions were put to him by people other than von Osten, in unfamiliar places, with von Osten nowhere in sight.

Given this evidence, many people were ready to believe that Hans had great intellectual powers. But others sought a more parsimonious explanation. Enter Oskar Pfungst. Pfungst (1911) discovered that Hans could not answer a question correctly unless the questioner had calculated the answer first. Evidently, the horse was some-

how getting the answers from the questioner. Next Pfungst learned that, when the questioner stood in plain sight, Hans's accuracy was 90% or better, but when he could not see the questioner, his answers were almost always wrong.

Eventually, Pfungst observed that anyone who asked Hans a question would lean forward to watch Hans's foot. Hans had simply learned to start tapping whenever someone stood next to his right forefoot and leaned forward. As soon as Hans had given the correct number of taps, the questioner would give a slight upward jerk of the head and change facial expression in anticipation that this might be the last tap. (Even skeptical scientists who tested Hans did this involuntarily. After all, they thought, wouldn't it be exciting if Hans got it right?) Hans simply continued tapping until he received that cue.

In short, Hans was indeed a clever horse, but we do not believe that he understood mathematics. Note that Pfungst did not prove, and no one needed to prove, that Hans *didn't* understand mathematics. Pfungst merely demonstrated that he could explain Hans's behavior in the simple, parsimonious terms of responses to facial expressions, and therefore, no one needed to assume that Hans had any more complicated abilities. The same principle applies for psychology in general: If we can find a simple explanation for some result, we prefer it to an explanation that requires new assumptions. Any extraordinary claim requires extraordinary evidence.

# An Exercise About Parsimony

Simonton (1977) reported that classical music composers who became famous early in life died younger, on the average, than composers who became famous late in life. One interpretation is that highly creative people "burn themselves out" quickly. Maybe so, but can you think of a simpler, more parsimonious explanation? After you try, check answer B on page 39 for the author's suggestion.

## Applying Parsimony: Extrasensory Perception

One controversial topic in psychology is **extrasensory perception (ESP)**. Supporters of extrasensory perception *claim that certain people can acquire information without using any sense organ and without receiving any form of physical energy*. These people claim, for instance, that a person gifted with ESP can identify another person's thoughts (via telepathy) even when the two are separated by a thick lead barrier that would block the transmission of almost any form of energy. They also claim that people with telepathic powers can identify thoughts just as accurately from a distance of 1000 kilometers as from an adjacent room, in apparent violation of the inverse-square law of physics.

Master magician Lance Burton can make people and animals seem to suddenly appear, disappear, float in the air, or do other things that we know are impossible. Even if we don't know how he accomplishes these feats, we take it for granted that they are magic tricks, based on methods of misleading the audience. Other performers claim their amazing results depend on psychic powers. A more parsimonious explanation is that their feats, like Burton's, depend on misleading the audience.

Some ESP supporters also claim that certain people can perceive inanimate objects that are hidden from sight (clairvoyance), predict the future (precognition), and influence such physical events as a roll of dice by sheer mental concentration (psychokinesis). In other words they claim it is possible to gain information or to influence physical events without receiving or transmitting any physical energy. A conclusive demonstration of any of these claims would require us not only to overhaul some major concepts in psychology,

but also to discard the most fundamental tenets of physics.

What evidence is there for ESP?

## Anecdotes

One kind of evidence consists of anecdotes—people's reports of isolated events. Someone has a dream or a hunch that comes true or says something, and someone else says, "I was just thinking exactly the same thing!" Such experiences may seem impressive when they occur, but they are meaningless as scientific evidence. First, consider the possibility of coincidence. Of all the hunches and dreams that people have, some are bound to come true eventually by pure chance. Second, people tend to remember and talk about the hunches and dreams that *do* come true and to forget the others. They hardly ever say, "Strangest thing! I had a dream, but then nothing like it actually happened!" Third, people often exaggerate the coincidences that occur, both in their own memories and in the retelling. We could evaluate anecdotal evidence only if people recorded their hunches and dreams before the predicted events and then determined how many unlikely predictions actually came to pass.

 Sometime you might try keeping track of psychics' predictions in tabloid newspapers for the new year. By the end of the year, how many came true? How many would you expect to come true just by chance? (The latter number is, of course, difficult to estimate.)

You may have heard of the "prophet Nostradamus," a 16th-century French writer who allegedly predicted many events of later centuries. Figure 2.5 presents four samples of his writings. No one knows what his predictions mean until *after* the predicted events happen. After something

1. The great man will be struck down in the day by a thunderbolt. An evil deed, foretold by the bearer of a petition. According to the prediction another falls at night time. Conflict at Reims, London, and pestilence in Tuscany.

2. When the fish that travels over both land and sea is cast up on to the shore by a great wave, its shape foreign, smooth, and frightful. From the sea the enemies soon reach the walls.

3. The bird of prey flying to the left, before battle is joined with the French, he makes preparations. Some will regard him as good, others bad or uncertain. The weaker party will regard him as a good omen.

4. Shortly afterwards, not a very long interval, a great tumult will be raised by land and sea. The naval battles will be greater than ever. Fires, creatures which will make more tumult.

**FIGURE 2.5** According to the followers of Nostradamus, each of these statements is a specific prophecy of a 20th-century event (Cheetham, 1973). Can you figure out what the prophecies mean? Compare your answers to answer C on page 39. The prophecies of Nostradamus are so vague that no one knows what they mean until after the predicted event. Consequently, they are not really predictions and also not testable.

happens, people imaginatively reinterpret his writings to fit the event. (His predictions are not falsifiable.)

## CONCEPT CHECK

**2.** How could someone scientifically evaluate the accuracy of Nostradamus's predictions? (Check your answer on page 39.)

## *Professional Psychics*

Various stage performers claim to read other people's minds and to perform other psychic feats. Two of the most famous are Uri Geller and The Amazing Kreskin. Actually, Kreskin has consistently denied doing anything supernatural; he prefers to talk of his "extremely sensitive," rather than "extrasensory," perception (Kreskin, 1991). Still, part of Kreskin's success as a performer comes from allowing people to believe he has mental powers that defy explanation, and his performances are similar to those of people who do call themselves psychics.

 After carefully observing Geller, Kreskin, and others, David Marks and Richard Kammann (1980) concluded that these performers exhibited the same kinds of deception commonly employed in magic acts. For example, Kreskin sometimes begins his act by asking the audience to read his mind. Let's try to duplicate this trick right now: Try to read my mind. I am thinking of a number between 1 and 50. Both digits are odd numbers, but they are not the same. For example, it could be 15 but it could not be 11. (These are the instructions Kreskin gives.) Have you chosen a number? Please do.

All right, my number was 37. Did you think of 37? If not, how about 35? You see, I started to think 35 and then changed my mind, so you might have got 35.

Probably about half of my readers successfully "read my mind." If you were one of them, are you impressed? Don't be. At first, it seemed that you had a lot of numbers to choose from (1 to 50), but by the end of the instructions, you had only a few. The first digit had to be 1 or 3, and the second had to be 1, 3, 5, 7, or 9. You had to eliminate 11 and 33 because both digits are the same, and you probably eliminated 15 because I cited it as a possible example. That leaves only seven possibilities. Most people like to stay far away from the example given and tend to avoid the highest and lowest possible choices. That leaves 37 as the most likely choice and 35 as the second most likely.

Second act: Kreskin asks the audience to write down something they are thinking about while he walks along the aisles talking. Then, back on stage, he "reads people's minds." He might say something like, "Someone is thinking about his mother . . ." In any large crowd, someone is bound to stand up and shout, "Yes, that's me. You read my mind!" On occasion he describes something that someone has written out in great detail. That person generally turns out to be someone sitting along the aisle where Kreskin was walking.

After a variety of other tricks (see Marks & Kammann, 1980), Kreskin goes backstage while the local mayor or some other dignitary hides Kreskin's paycheck somewhere in the audience. Then Kreskin comes back, walks up and down the aisles and across the rows, and eventually shouts, "The check is here!" The rule is that if he guesses wrong, then he does not get paid. (He hardly ever misses.)

This is an impressive trick, and even more impressive if you're part of the audience. How does he do it? Very simply, it is a Clever Hans trick. Kreskin studies people's faces. Most people want him to find the check, so they get more excited as he gets close to it and more disappointed or distressed if he moves away. In effect they are saying, "Now you're getting closer" and "Now you're moving away." At last he closes in on the check.

We can also explain the performances of many other stage performers in terms of simple tricks and illusions. Of course, someone always objects, "Well, maybe so. But there's this other guy you haven't investigated yet. Maybe he really does possess psychic powers." Well, maybe. But until there is solid evidence to the contrary, it is simpler (more parsimonious) to assume that other performers are also using illusion and deception.

## *Experiments*

Because stage performances and anecdotal events always take place under uncontrolled conditions, we cannot determine the probability of coincidence or the possibility of deception. Laboratory experiments provide the only evidence about ESP worth serious consideration.

For example, consider the *ganzfeld* procedure (from German words meaning "entire field"). A "sender" is given a photo or film, selected at random from four possibilities, and a "receiver" in another room is asked to describe the sender's thoughts and images. Typically, the receiver wears half Ping-Pong balls over the eyes and listens to static noise through earphones to minimize normal stimuli that might overpower the presumably weaker extrasensory stimuli (Figure 2.6). Later a judge examines a transcript of what the receiver said and compares it to the four photos or films, determining which one it matches most closely. On the average it should match the target about one in four times. If a receiver "hits" more often than one in four, we can calculate the probability of accidentally doing that well. (ESP researchers, or parapsychologists, use a variety of other experimental procedures, but in each case the goal is to determine whether someone can gain more information than could be explained by chance without using his or her senses.)

Over the decades ESP researchers reported many apparent examples of telepathy or clairvoyance, none of which were replicable under well-controlled conditions. In the case of the ganzfeld studies, one review reported that 6 of the 10 laboratories using this method found

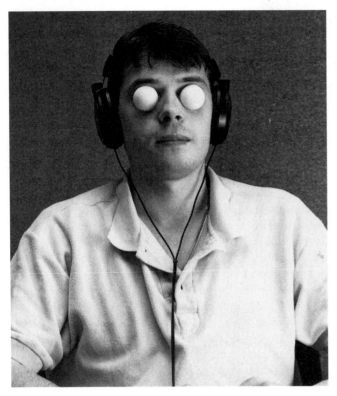

**FIGURE 2.6** In the ganzfeld procedure, a "receiver," who is deprived of most normal sensory information, tries to describe the photo or film that a "sender" is examining.

positive results (Bem & Honorton, 1994); the authors suggested that here was, at last, a replicable phenomenon. However, since then 14 studies from 7 laboratories failed to find evidence that the receiver chose the target stimulus any more often than one would expect by chance (Milton & Wiseman, 1999). In short, the ganzfeld phenomenon is nonreplicable, just like all previous claims of ESP.

The lack of replicability is one major reason to be skeptical of ESP. But there is another more fundamental reason: parsimony. If someone claims to have a horse that does mathematics or if a person claims to be able to read the mind of someone in another room, we should search thoroughly for a simpler explanation and adopt a radically new explanation only if the evidence compels us to do so. Even then we cannot accept a new explanation until someone specifies it clearly. Saying that some result demonstrates "an amazing ability that science cannot explain" does not constitute an explanation.

### IN CLOSING
## Scientific Thinking in Psychology

What have we learned about science in general? Science does not deal with proof or certainty. All scientific conclusions are tentative and are subject to revision. The history of any scientific field contains examples of theories that were once widely accepted and were later revised. Nevertheless, this tentativeness does not imply a willingness to abandon well-established theories in the face of any apparently contradictory evidence.

Scientists always prefer the most parsimonious theory. They abandon accepted theories and assumptions only when better theories and assumptions become available. Scientists closely scrutinize any claim that violates the rule of parsimony. Before they will accept any such claim, they insist that it be supported by replicable experiments that rule out simpler explanations.

## Summary

- *Scientific approach to psychology.* Although psychology does not possess the same wealth of knowledge as other sciences, it shares with other scientific fields a commitment to scientific methods, including a set of criteria for evaluating theories. (page 31)
- *Steps in a scientific study.* A scientific study goes through the following sequence of steps: hypothesis, methods, results, interpretation. Because almost any study is subject to more than one possible interpretation, we base our conclusions on a pattern of results from many studies. The results of a given study are taken seriously only if other investigators can replicate them. (page 31)
- *Criteria for evaluating theories.* A good theory agrees with observations and leads to correct predictions of new information. It leads to predictions precise enough that we can state what results would or would not contradict them. All else being equal, scientists prefer the theory that relies on simpler assumptions. (page 33)
- *Skepticism about extrasensory perception.* Claims of the existence of extrasensory perception are scrutinized very cautiously because the evidence reported so far has been unreplicable and because the scientific approach includes a search for parsimonious explanations. (page 35)

## Answers to Concept Checks

**1. a.** Falsifiable. If researchers found that people could memorize short lists faster or equally as fast as longer lists, their result would contradict the theory. The statement is *falsifiable* (in principle) but has not been *falsified* by actual data. **b.** Not falsifiable. Even if researchers could scientifically explain every action of every person they had ever tested, the possibility would remain that some untested people have unexplainable powers. (Can you restate the theory so that it is falsifiable?) **c.** Probably not falsifiable, unless someone can specify a reliable method to determine whether a child has suffered "frustration" and a reliable way to determine whether someone has emotional difficulties. As stated, the theory is too vague to be scientifically useful. (page 33)

2. To evaluate Nostradamus's predictions, we would need to ask someone to tell us precisely what his predictions mean before the events they supposedly predict had transpired. Then we would ask someone else to estimate the likelihood of those events. Eventually, we would compare the accuracy of the predictions to the advance estimates of their probability. That is, we should be impressed with seemingly correct predictions only if our observers had rated these events "unlikely" before they occurred. (page 37)

## Answers to Other Questions in the Module

a. Any magnet strong enough to pull the metal ball up the inclined plane would not release the ball when it reached the hole at the top. (page 34)

b. Some of the people who become famous while young will die young and some will die old, as with any other population of people. But those who become famous late in life will *all* be old when they die! Therefore, it is almost necessary that those who become famous when young will, on the average, die younger than those who became famous when old. (page 35)

c. The prophecies of Nostradamus (see page 36), as interpreted by Cheetham (1973), refer to the following: (1) the assassinations of John F. Kennedy and Robert F. Kennedy, (2) Polaris ballistic missiles shot from submarines, (3) Hitler's invasion of France, and (4) World War II.

# Conducting Psychological Research

*How do psychological researchers study processes that are difficult to define?*

*How do they design their research, and what special problems can arise?*

*How do researchers confront the ethical problems of conducting research using both human and nonhuman species?*

A radio talk show once featured two psychologists as guests. The first argued that day care was bad for children, because she had seen in her clinical practice many clients who had been left in day care as children and grew up to be sadly disturbed adults. The second psychologist, researcher Sandra Scarr (1997), pointed out that the clinician had no way of knowing about the children left in day care who became healthy, well-adjusted adults. (Such people seldom consult a therapist.) Scarr then described the eight best research studies, concerning thousands of children in four countries, each of which found no evidence that day care produced any long-term undesirable consequences.

Which conclusion would you draw? I hope you would conclude that day care is okay for children. To Scarr's dismay, however, the people who called in to the program seemed just as convinced by the anecdotes of disturbed people as by the extensive research studies, and several callers described anecdotes of their own.

Psychology, like any other field, can make progress only by distinguishing between good evidence and weak evidence. Furthermore, psychological research can be tricky; sometimes even a careful investigation runs into unexpected difficulties. In this module we shall consider some of the special problems encountered when applying scientific methods to psychological phenomena.

## General Principles

The primary goal of this module is not to prepare you to conduct psychological research, but to help you be an intelligent interpreter of research. When you hear about some new study, you should be able to ask pertinent questions to decide how good the evidence is and what conclusion (if any) it justifies.

## Definitions of Psychological Terms

Suppose a physicist asks you to measure the effect of temperature on the length of an iron bar. You ask, "What do we really mean by temperature and length?" The physicist might reply, "Don't worry about it. Just measure the length with this ruler and measure the temperature with this thermometer. What I mean by length is the measurement you get with the ruler, and what I mean by temperature is the reading on the thermometer."

We need the same strategy in psychology. If we want to measure the effect of hunger on students' ability to concentrate, we could spend hours attempting to define what hunger and concentration really are, or we could say, "Let's measure hunger by the hours since the last meal and concentration by the length of time that the student continues reading without stopping to do something else."

By doing so we would be relying on an **operational definition,** *a definition that specifies the operations (or procedures) used to produce or measure something, a way to give it a numerical value.* An operational definition is not the same as a dictionary definition. You might object that "time since the last meal" is not what you really mean by *hunger.* You would be right, but the reading on a thermometer isn't what temperature *really* is either. An operational definition enables us to get on with research, and it enables one researcher to repeat another's research and obtain similar results.

Suppose that someone wants to investigate whether children who watch violence on television are likely to behave aggressively themselves. In this case the investigator needs operational definitions for *televised violence* and *aggressive behavior.* For example, the investigator might define *televised violence* as "the number of acts shown or described in which one person injures another." According to this definition, a 20-minute stalking scene would count as much as a quick attack, and a murder shown on screen would be equivalent to one about which the characters just talk. An unsuccessful attempt to injure someone would not count as violence at all, and verbal insults probably wouldn't count either. This definition might prove to be unsatisfactory, but at least it states how one investigator measures violence.

Similarly, the investigator needs an operational definition of *aggressive behavior.* To define it as "the number of acts of assault or murder committed within 24 hours after watching a particular television program" would be an operational definition but not a very useful one because (we hope) almost everyone would have a score of zero. A better operational definition of *aggressive behavior* specifies more likely acts. For example, the experimenter might place a large plastic doll in front of a young child and record how often the child punches it.

Let's take one more example: What is love? Never mind what it *really* is. If we want to study it, we need to measure it, and therefore, we need an operational definition. One possibility would be "how many hours you are willing to spend with another person who asked you to stay nearby."

## CONCEPT CHECK

3. Which of the following is an operational definition of intelligence?
   a. the ability to comprehend relationships,
   b. a score on an IQ test,
   c. the ability to survive in the real world, or
   d. the product of the cerebral cortex of the brain. What would you propose as an operational definition of friendliness? (Check your answer on page 54.)

## Population Samples

The **population** *is the entire group of individuals to be considered.* Researchers generally wish to draw conclusions that apply to a large population, such as all 3-year-olds or all people with depression or even all human beings. Because it is not practical to examine everyone, researchers study a small number of people, a *sample,* and assume that what is true of the sample applies to the whole population. For example, pollsters ask 1000 or so voters which candidate they plan to vote for and then project the probable result for the whole city, state, or country. (Of course, in a close election, the prediction can go wrong, especially if the ballot is confusing, as was apparently the case in some parts of Florida in the election of 2000.)

In some cases almost any sample is satisfactory. For example, early investigators established that the eyes, ears, and other sense organs operate on the same principles for all people (with obvious exceptions such as those with visual or hearing impairments). Indeed, the main principles are the same even in other animal species. Similarly, some of the principles of learning, memory, hunger, thirst, sleep, and so forth are similar enough among all people that an investigator can do further research with almost any group—students in an introductory psychology class, for example. We refer to *a group chosen because of its ease of study* as a **convenience sample.**

Even with fairly simple behaviors, we can add to our understanding by studying a more diverse sample, however. For example, we can establish general principles about sleep by studying college students, or even a group of laboratory rats, but those studies will not tell us how age differences affect sleep or about the effects of depression on sleep. With other issues a convenience sample becomes increasingly inappropriate. If you wanted to study world political attitudes, clearly you couldn't draw general conclusions after interviewing students on one college campus.

To conduct a meaningful study of a behavior that varies significantly among people, we need either a representative sample or a random sample of the population. A **representative sample** *closely resembles the population in its percentage of males and females, Blacks and Whites, young and old, city dwellers and farmers, or whatever other characteristics are likely to affect the results.* To get a representative sample of the people in a given region, an investigator would first determine what percentage of the residents belong to each category and then select people to match those percentages. Unfortunately, a sample that is representative with regard to one set of characteristics might not be representative of other characteristics, such as religion or education.

In a **random sample,** *every individual in the population has an equal chance of being selected.* For example, to produce a random sample of Toronto residents, an investigator might select a certain number of city blocks at random from a Toronto map, randomly select one house from each of those blocks, and then randomly choose one person from each of those households. A random sample of 1000 people or so is likely to resemble the whole population, but it is difficult to get a random sample. We can choose people randomly, but not everyone we choose agrees to participate. Survey researchers usually try hard to get a random sample; researchers doing experiments, however, almost always use volunteers. Imagine that I advertise a study on the effects of marijuana on behavior. Who would be most likely to volunteer? Probably not a random sample. Such limitations are not a cause for despair, but a researcher who cannot get a random or representative sample should state the conclusions cautiously, making it clear that the results may not apply to a broader population.

What if we want to draw generalizations about all humans, not just those in one country? If you imagine trying to get a random or representative sample of all the people on the planet, you will quickly realize the impracticality. Nevertheless, although we cannot expect to study people from all cultures, it can be useful to study **cross-cultural samples,** *groups of people from at least two cultures,* preferably cultures as different as possible. For example, consider a few questions about human nature: Do people learn facial expressions of emotions or do certain emotions have a built-in facial expression? Is a financially prosperous society necessarily a happy society?

Are people biologically predisposed to marriage? If we find differences in a behavior across cultures, we know the behavior is learned instead of built in. If the behavior is the same across cultures, then it may be part of our biological heritage.

Cross-cultural sampling is difficult, however (Matsumoto, 1994). Obvious problems include the expense, language barriers, and convincing members of another culture to answer personal questions and cooperate with unfamiliar kinds of tests. Also, imagine trying to compare "typical" sexual behaviors between two countries. There may be so much diversity within each country that the comparison between two countries becomes almost meaningless.

■ A psychological researcher can test generalizations about human behavior by comparing people from different cultures.

# CONCEPT CHECK

4. Suppose I compare the interests and abilities of male and female students at my university. If I find a consistent difference, can I assume that it represents a difference between men and women in general? (Obviously, the answer is no, or else I would not have asked the question.) Why not? (Check your answer on page 55.)

## Experimenter Bias and Blind Studies

When experimenters record their data, sometimes they have trouble separating what they see from what they expect to see. For example, students in one psychology class were told that they would watch a person engage in a difficult hand-eye coordination task before and after drinking alcohol. The person was in fact drinking only apple juice and performed equally well before and after drinking. Nevertheless, most of the students reported seeing a sharp deterioration in his performance (M. D. Goldstein, Hopkins, & Strube, 1994).

**Experimenter bias** is *the tendency of an experimenter unintentionally to distort the procedures or results of an experiment based on the expected outcome of the study.* The distortion is unintentional, and the experimenter may even be trying to avoid it. Imagine that you, as a psychological investigator, are testing the hypothesis that left-handed children are more creative than right-handed children. (I don't know why you would be testing this silly hypothe-

sis, but just suppose you are.) If the results support your hypothesis, you can expect to get your results published and you will be well on your way to becoming a famous psychologist. Now you watch a left-handed child do something that seems slightly creative. You are not sure whether to count it or not. You want to be fair. You don't want your hypothesis to influence your decision about whether to consider the act creative. Just try to ignore your hypothesis.

To overcome the potential source of error in an investigator's bias, psychologists prefer to use a **blind observer**—that is, *an observer who can record data without knowing what the researcher has predicted.* For example, we might ask someone to record creative acts by a group of children, without any hint that we are interested in the effects of handedness. Because blind observers do not know what hypothesis is being tested, they can record their observations more fairly.

Ideally, the experimenter will conceal the procedure from the participants as well. For example, suppose experimenters gave one group of children a pill that was supposed to increase their creativity. If those children knew the prediction, maybe they would act more creatively just because they knew they were expected to do so. Or maybe the children not taking the pill would pout about not getting it and therefore not do much. The best solution, therefore, is to give the drug to one group and a **placebo** (*a pill with no known pharmacological effects*) to another group, without telling the children which pill they are taking or what results the experi-

**TABLE 2.1** Single-Blind and Double-Blind Studies

| Who is aware of which subjects are in which group? | | | |
|---|---|---|---|
| | **Observer** | **Subjects** | **Experimenter Who Organized the Study** |
| *Single-blind* | aware | unaware | aware |
| *Single-blind* | unaware | aware | aware |
| *Double-blind* | unaware | unaware | aware |

menter expects. The advantage of this kind of study is that the two groups will not behave differently because of their expectations.

*A study in which either the observer or the participants are unaware of which participants received which treatment* is called a **single-blind study** (Table 2.1). *A study in which both the observer and the participants are unaware* is known as a **double-blind study.** Of course, the experimenter who organized the study would need to keep records of which participants received which procedure. (A study in which *everyone* loses track of the procedure is known jokingly as "triple blind.")

# Observational Research Designs

The general principles that we just discussed apply to many kinds of research. Psychologists use various methods of investigation, and each has its own advantages and disadvantages. Most research in any field starts with description: What happens and under what circumstances? Astronomers deal almost entirely with observational data; most other scientific fields, including psychology, start with observational data and proceed, when possible, to experiments. Let's first examine several kinds of observational studies. Later we shall consider experiments, which have a much greater ability to illuminate cause-and-effect relationships.

## Naturalistic Observations

A **naturalistic observation** is *a careful examination of what many people or nonhuman animals do under more or less natural conditions.* For example, biologist Jane Goodall (1971) spent years observing chimpanzees in the wild, recording their food habits, their social interactions, their gestures, and their whole way of life (Figure 2.7).

Similarly, psychologists sometimes try to observe human behavior "as an outsider." A psychologist might observe what happens when two unacquainted people get on an elevator together: Do they stand close or far apart? Do they speak? Do they look toward each other or away? Does it matter whether the people are two men, two women, or a man and a woman? Do Japanese people act the same as Brazilians? A psychologist might also record the behaviors of 6-month-old children, expert crossword puzzle solvers, depressed patients, or any other type of people. After all, the first step toward understanding people is to know what they do.

## Case Histories

Some rare conditions are psychologically fascinating. For example, some people have amazingly good memories or amazingly poor memories. People with Williams syndrome are mentally retarded in many ways but have impressive language abilities (Bellugi, Wang, & Jernigan, 1994). A psychologist who encounters someone with a rare condition may report a **case history,** *a thorough description of the unusual person.* A case history often relies on naturalistic observation; we distinguish it because it focuses on a single individual.

A case history may include information about the person's medical condition, family background, unusual experiences, current behavior, and ability to perform

**FIGURE 2.7** In a naturalistic study, observers record the behavior of people or other species in their natural settings. Here noted biologist Jane Goodall records her observations on chimpanzees. By patiently staying with the chimps, Goodall gradually won their trust and learned to recognize individual animals. In this manner she was able to add enormously to our understanding of chimpanzees' natural way of life.

various tasks—in short, anything that the investigator thinks might be interesting or important. A case history is more than just an anecdote. An anecdote is a report of an experience that may not have been carefully recorded, such as "I had a hunch and it came true." A case history is potentially replicable by anyone who has the chance to study the same individual or a similar individual again.

A case history is well suited to exploring an unusual person; however, it does not tell us whether that person is typical of others with the same condition. Ideally, a series of case histories can reveal a pattern and encourage investigators to conduct other kinds of follow-up research.

## Surveys

A **survey** is *a study of the prevalence of certain beliefs, attitudes, or behaviors, based on people's responses to specific questions.* Surveys are widespread in Western society. In fact, no matter what your occupation, at some time you will probably conduct a survey of your employees, your customers, your students, your neighbors, or fellow members of an organization you have joined. You will also frequently read survey results in the newspaper or hear them reported on television. Thus, you should be aware of some of the difficulties of survey research and understand that survey results can be misleading.

### Sampling

Getting a truly random or representative sample is a prerequisite for any kind of serious research—and particularly with surveys. In 1936 the *Literary Digest* mailed 10 million postcards, asking people their choice for president of the United States. Of the 2 million responses, 57% preferred the Republican candidate, Alfred Landon. Landon later lost by a wide margin to the Democratic candidate, Franklin Roosevelt. The problem was that the *Literary Digest* had selected names from the telephone book and automobile registration lists. In 1936, at the end of the Great Depression, most poor people were Democrats, and very few of them owned telephones or cars.

### The Competence of Those Being Interviewed

When you answer a survey, do you carefully think about your answer to every question, or do you answer some of them impulsively? In one 1997 survey, only 45% of the respondents said they believed in the existence of intelligent life on other planets. However, a few questions later on the survey, 82% said they believed the U.S. government was "hiding evidence of intelligent life in space" (Emery, 1997). Did 37% of the people *really* think that the U.S. government is hiding evidence of something that doesn't exist? More likely, I submit, they were answering without much thought.

 Here's another example: Which of the following programs would you most like to see on television reruns? Rate your choices from highest (1) to lowest (10). (Please fill in your answers, either in the text or on a separate sheet of paper, before continuing to the next paragraph.)

___ *South Park*     ___ *Xena, Warrior Princess*
___ *Thirtysomething*     ___ *The X-Files*
___ *Cheers*     ___ *Teletubbies*
___ *Seinfeld*     ___ *Space Doctor*
___ *I Love Lucy*     ___ *Homicide*

When I conducted this survey with my own students at North Carolina State University, nearly all did exactly what I asked—they gave every program a rating, including *Space Doctor*, a program that never existed. More than two thirds rated it either seventh, eighth, or ninth—it usually beat *Teletubbies*—but more than 10% rated it in the top five, and a few ranked it as their top choice.

They did nothing wrong, of course. I asked them to rank all of the programs and they did. The fault, if there is one, lies with anyone who interprets such survey results as if they represented informed opinions. This exercise demonstrates that most people will express opinions even when they have no idea what they are talking about. (The same is true of political surveys.)

### The Wording of the Questions

 Let's start with a little demonstration. Please answer these three questions:

**1.** Overall, how successful do you think you have been in life so far? (Circle one.)

−5   −4   −3   −2   −1   0   +1   +2   +3   +4   +5

**2.** How often do you get headaches, backaches, toothaches, and muscle pains? (Circle one.)

| almost never | a few times a year | once or twice a month | more than twice a month |

**3.** Your college has just received a huge contribution which it can spend any way it chooses. The administration has decided to poll students and faculty for their opinions. What percentage should it reserve for the following purposes? (Percentages should add to 100%.)

Improvements to buildings     _____ %
All other purposes     _____ %

Now cover up those answers and reply to these similar questions:

**4.** Overall, how successful do you think you have been in life so far? (Circle one.)

0   1   2   3   4   5   6   7   8   9   10

**5.** How often do you get headaches, backaches, toothaches, and muscle pains? (Circle one.)

| less than twice a month | more than twice a month but less than once a day |
| about once a day | several times a day |

**6.** Your college has just received a huge contribution which it can spend any way it chooses. The administration has decided to poll students and faculty for their opinions. What percentage should it reserve for the following purposes? (Percentages should add to 100%.)

| | |
|---|---|
| Financial aid for needy students | _____ % |
| Increased faculty salaries | _____ % |
| Additions to the library | _____ % |
| Better parking facilities | _____ % |
| Improvements to buildings | _____ % |
| Increased campus security | _____ % |
| All other purposes | _____ % |

On questions such as these, people answer differently based on the choices available (Schwarz, 1999). (You may not have, if you thought about your answers to the first three questions while you were answering the next three.) Most people rate their success higher on a −5 to +5 scale (i.e., closer to the highest possible) than they do on a 0 to 10 scale. On a question about aches and pains, most people pick an answer in the middle of whatever the scale is. So if "more than twice a month" is the highest answer, they report aches less than twice a month. But if "less than twice a month" is the lowest answer, they report aches more than that often. On the question about spending the money, most people feel obligated to devote some money to everything on the list, and many people divide it almost equally among the choices. If "improvements to buildings" is the only option listed, the average student (in my classes) offers that option about 40% of the money. If it has to compete against five other choices (plus "all other purposes"), then buildings get only about 15% of the money. (Students generally vote the largest share to "financial aid for needy students.")

A different example: Visitors to the London Zoo were shown a set of photos of endangered animals and asked to rank them from the one most worthy of conservation efforts to the one with the least priority. Some visitors were given just the photos; others got the names also. Some of the names made a big difference. One unattractive little insect was ranked 53rd out of a possible 57 without its name, but with its name—British wortbiter cricket—it rose to 26th. (It was the only animal with "British" as part of its name.) One monkey was already a respectable 18th without its name, but rose to 6th with its name, "Diana monkey," apparently because the name reminded people of Princess Diana. "Royal python" and "Rothschild's mynah" also profited by having their names read, but "Red faced black spider monkey" and "Strawberry poison frog" declined when people knew their names (Carvell, Inglis, Mace, & Purvis, 1998).

The point of all this is simple: People's answers to any question depend on the exact phrasing of the question. So the next time you hear that "38% of the people surveyed replied that . . . ," ask how the question was worded. Even a slightly different wording could yield a different percentage.

**Surveyor Biases**

Sometimes a survey is sponsored by an organization that words the questions to encourage the answers they hope to receive. Here is an example: According to a 1993 survey, 92% of high school boys and 98% of high school girls claimed to have been victims of sexual harassment (Shogren, 1993). Shocking, isn't it? However, the survey defined sexual harassment by a long list of acts ranging from serious offenses (e.g., having someone rip your clothes off in public) to minor annoyances. For example, if someone wrote sexual graffiti on the rest room wall and you found it offensive, you could consider yourself sexually harassed. If you tried to make yourself look sexually attractive (as most teenagers do, right?) and then attracted a suggestive stare from someone you *didn't* want to attract, that stare would count as sexual harassment.

Sexual harassment is, of course, a serious problem, but a survey that combines major and minor offenses provides no useful information. Figure 2.8 shows a fictional survey very similar to those that various organizations send out. Whenever the questions are written to suggest one "correct" answer, you can safely assume that the organization is more interested in soliciting support than in knowing your honest opinions.

## Correlational Studies

Another type of research is a correlational study. A **correlation** is *a measure of the relationship between two variables.* (A variable is anything that can differ among individuals in some measurable way. Height and weight are variables; so are years of education and reading speed.) A **correlational study** is *a procedure in which investigators measure the correlation between two variables without controlling either of them.* For example, investigators have observed that students who attend class regularly generally receive better test scores than do those who frequently miss class (Cavell & Woehr, 1994). This statement highlights a relationship between two variables—class attendance and test scores. The investigator simply measured these variables without attempting to influence anything.

A survey can be considered a correlational study if the interviewers compare two or more groups. For example, the interviewers might compare the beliefs of men and women or those of young people and old people. The interviewer could thereby measure a relationship between one variable (sex or age) and another (beliefs).

**The Correlation Coefficient**

Some correlations are stronger than others. For example, we would probably find a strong positive correlation between hours per week spent reading novels and scores on a vocabulary test. We would observe a lower correlation between hours spent reading novels and scores on a chemistry test.

The standard way to measure the strength of a correlation is known as a **correlation coefficient,** *a mathematical*

### Survey on Behalf of the Litterers' Society

1. Prior to reading the enclosed letter, were you aware of how little damage litter does to the environment, or how much money the government wastes in an effort to harass innocent citizens who happen to drop a little bit of litter now and then?

    _____ yes    _____ no

2. Do you agree that moderate, responsible littering is one of the rights we should expect in a free society?

    _____ yes    _____ no    _____ undecided

3. Are you in favor of having the government use your tax dollars to arrest and persecute people whose only "crime" is littering?

    _____ yes    _____ no    _____ undecided

4. Do you see a need for an educational campaign to inform the public about the good that littering contributes to *natural* recycling?

    _____ yes    _____ no    _____ undecided

5. Are you outraged that shortsighted do-gooders would pass extremely restrictive, punitive laws against littering, merely to advance their own political careers?

    _____ yes    _____ no    _____ undecided

6. Do you support the noble attempts of the Litterers' Society to fight against excessive and unnecessary regulations, and will you support the Society with your generous donation?

    _____ Yes! Enclosed is my        _____ Sorry, I can't afford a
    generous donation!                          contribution at this time.

**FIGURE 2.8** An example of how to bias a survey. This imaginary survey for an imaginary society has a style of questions similar to those found in many surveys sponsored by actual political and social organizations. The request for a donation is a reliable clue that the organization is not really seeking your opinion and will probably not even bother to tabulate the results.

estimate of the relationship between two variables. *The coefficent can range from +1 to −1.* A correlation coefficient indicates how accurately we can use a measurement of one variable to predict another. A correlation coefficient of +1, for ex-

ample, means that as one variable increases, the other increases also. A correlation coefficient of −1 means that as one variable increases, the other decreases. A correlation of either +1 or −1 enables us to make perfect predictions of one variable from measurements of the other one. (In psychology you probably will never encounter a perfect +1 or −1 correlation coefficient.) A negative correlation is just as useful as a positive correlation and can indicate just as strong a relationship. For example, the more often people practice golf, the lower their golf scores, so golf practice is negatively correlated with scores.

A 0 correlation indicates that measurements of one variable have no linear relationship to measurements of the other one. That is, as one variable goes up, the other does not consistently go up or down. A 0 or very low correlation arises either when two variables really are unrelated or when one or both of them are poorly measured. (If something is inaccurately measured, we can hardly expect something else to predict it accurately.)

Figure 2.9 shows hypothetical (fictitious) data demonstrating how grades on a final exam in psychology might

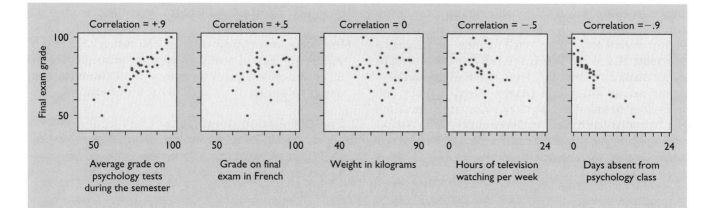

**FIGURE 2.9** In a scatterplot each dot represents data for one person; for example, each point in the center graph tells us one person's weight and that person's grade on the psychology final exam, in this case using hypothetical data. A positive correlation indicates that, as one variable increases, the other generally does also. A negative correlation indicates that, as one variable increases, the other generally decreases. The closer a correlation coefficient is to +1 or −1, the stronger the relationship.

correlate with five other variables. (This kind of graph is called a scatterplot. Each dot represents the measurements of two variables for one person.) Grades on a psychology final exam correlate strongly with grades on the previous tests in psychology, less strongly with grades on the French final exam, not at all with the person's weight, and negatively with the amount of time spent watching television and the number of times the student was absent from class. Note that a correlation of +.9 is almost a straight ascending line; a correlation of −.9 is close to a straight descending line.

## CONCEPT CHECKS

5. Identify each of these as a positive, zero, or negative correlation:
   a. The more crowded a neighborhood, the lower the income.
   b. People's telephone numbers have no relationship to their IQ scores.
   c. People who awaken frequently during the night are more likely than other people to feel depressed.
6. Which indicates a stronger relationship between two variables, a +.50 correlation or a −.75 correlation?
7. A newly developed test of self-esteem is found to correlate very poorly (near 0) with measures of happiness. Why might that be? (Check your answers on page 55.)

### Illusory Correlations

Casual observation often misleads us about a possible correlation. For example, years ago a drug company marketed the drug Bendectin to relieve morning sickness in pregnant women. After a few women who had taken the drug had babies with birth defects, widespread publicity blamed the drug. Thereafter, women who took the drug and had babies with birth defects blamed the drug. Actually, only 2–3% of the women taking the drug had babies with birth defects—the same as the percentage among women not taking the drug. When people expect to see a connection between two events (such as Bendectin and birth defects), they remember the cases that support the connection and disregard the exceptions, thus perceiving an **illusory correlation,** *an apparent relationship based on casual observations of unrelated or weakly related events.* Many social stereotypes are examples of illusory correlations.

As another example of an illusory correlation, consider the widely held belief that a full moon affects human behavior. For hundreds of years, many people have believed that crime and various kinds of mental disturbance are more common under a full moon than at other times. In fact, the term *lunacy* (from the Latin word *luna,* meaning "moon") originally meant mental illness caused by the full moon. Some police officers report that they receive more calls on nights with a full moon, and hospital workers report more emergency cases on such nights. Those reports, however, are based on what people recall rather than on carefully analyzed data. James Rotton and I. W. Kelly (1985) examined all available data relating crime, mental illness, and other phenomena to the phases of the moon. They concluded that the phase of the moon has either no effect at all on human behavior or so little effect that we cannot measure it.

Why then does this belief persist? We do not know when or how it first arose. (It may have been true many years ago, before the onset of artificial lights.) But we can guess why it persists. Suppose, for example, you are working at a hospital. You expect to handle more emergencies on a night with a full moon than at other times. Sooner or later, on a full-moon night, you encounter an unusually high number of accidents, assaults, and suicide attempts. You say, "See? There was a full moon and people went crazy!" You will remember that night for a long time and disregard the other full-moon nights when nothing special happened, as well as nights without a full moon when you were swamped with emergency cases.

■ People's expectations and faulty memories produce illusory correlations, such as between the full moon and abnormal behavior.

### Correlation and Causation

A correlation tells us whether two variables are related to each other and, if so, how strongly. It does not tell us *why* they are related, and a correlational study does not justify a cause-and-effect conclusion. For example, there is a strong positive correlation between the number of books people own about chess and how good they are at playing chess. Does owning chess books cause someone to become a good chess player? Of course not. Does being a good chess player cause someone to buy chess books? Not exactly. Rather, people who start to like chess buy chess books, which help them improve their game. As they get better, they become even more interested, buy more books, and get even better at the game. But neither the chess books nor the skill actually causes the other.

"Then what good is a correlation?" you might ask. The simplest answer is that correlations help us make useful predictions. If your friend has just challenged you to a game of chess, you can quickly scan your friend's bookshelves and estimate your chances of winning.

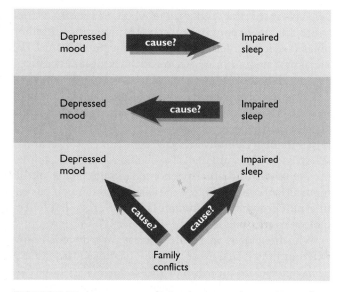

**FIGURE 2.10** A strong correlation between depression and impaired sleep does not tell us whether depression interferes with sleep, poor sleep leads to depression, or whether another problem leads to both depression and sleep problems.

Here are two more examples to illustrate why we cannot draw conclusions regarding cause and effect from correlational data (see also Figure 2.10):

• *Unmarried men are more likely than married men to spend time in a mental hospital or prison.* That is, for men marriage is negatively correlated with mental illness and criminal activity. Does the correlation mean that marriage leads to mental health and good social adjustment? Or does it mean that the men in mental hospitals and prisons are unlikely to marry? (Both explanations could, of course, be valid.)

• *People who engage in regular exercise tend not to feel depressed.* This correlation could indicate that exercise helps decrease the chance of depression. It could also mean that nondepressed people exercise more than depressed people do. And it could also reflect the fact that being young, healthy, and employed increases one's probability of exercising and also decreases one's probability of depression.

To repeat: A correlation does not tell us about causation. To determine causation, an investigator needs to manipulate one of the variables directly, through a research design known as an *experiment.* When an investigator manipulates one variable and then observes corresponding changes in another variable, a conclusion about causation can

be justified, presuming, of course, that the experiment is well designed.

## CONCEPT CHECK

**8.** Suppose we find a .8 correlation between students' reported interest in psychology and their grades on a psychology test. What conclusion can we draw? (Check your answer on page 55.)

## Experiments

An **experiment** is *a study in which the investigator manipulates at least one variable while measuring at least one other variable.* A before-and-after study can be an experiment, but it is generally not the best kind. Consider this example: Researchers give a rat a saccharin-flavored solution to drink for 15 minutes. They remove the solution, wait 30 minutes, and then inject the rat with a chemical that causes nausea. The next day they offer it the saccharin solution again and note that the rat does not drink it. Evidently, the rat blamed its illness on what it drank and now avoids that taste. Right? Well, maybe, but maybe the rat is still so sick the next day that it can't drink. (In fact, maybe the rat is dead. Did anyone check?) There have been better experiments on this question, as we shall see in Chapter 6, and rats (and others) really do avoid tastes that are followed by illness. The point here is that a before-and-after study is hard to interpret; behavior can change over time for reasons other than the one we wish to study.

A better design is to compare two groups: The investigator assembles a suitable sample of people or animals, divides them randomly into two groups, and then conducts some procedure with one group and not the other. Someone, preferably a blind observer, records the behavior of the two groups. If the behavior of the two groups differs in some consistent way, then the difference is probably the result of the experimental procedure. Table 2.2 contrasts experiments with observational studies. We now take it for granted that all experimental

**TABLE 2.2 Comparision of Five Methods of Research**

| Observational Studies | |
|---|---|
| *Case Study* | Detailed description of single individual; suitable for studying rare conditions. |
| *Naturalistic Observation* | Description of behavior under natural conditions; particularly valuable method when it is unethical or impractical to conduct laboratory investigations. |
| *Survey* | Study of attitudes, beliefs, or behaviors based on answers to questions. |
| *Correlation* | Description of the relationship between two variables that the investigator measures but does not control; determines whether two variables are closely related but does not address questions of cause and effect. |
| *Experiment* | Determination of the effect of an independent variable (controlled by the investigator) on the dependent variable (that being measured); the only method that can inform us about cause and effect. |

research follows this format, but in fact, experiments comparing one group against another were rare before 1900 and became common in psychology before they did in medicine and other research fields (Dehue, 2000).

I shall describe psychological experiments and some of their special difficulties. To illustrate, let's use the example of experiments conducted to determine whether watching violent television programs leads to an increase in aggressive behavior.

ONCEPT CHECK

9. You read a description of an unsatisfactory before-and-after study of rats getting sick after drinking a saccharin solution. Propose a better experiment using an experimental group and a control group. (Check your answer on page 55.)

## Independent Variables and Dependent Variables

An experiment is an attempt to measure the effect of changes in one variable on one or more other variable(s). The **independent variable** is *the item that an experimenter* changes *or controls—for example, the amount of violent television that people are permitted to watch.* The **dependent variable** is *the item that an experimenter* measures *to determine how it was affected.* In our example the experimenter measures the amount of aggressive behavior that the participants exhibit. You can think of the independent variable as the cause and the dependent variable as the effect (see Figure 2.11).

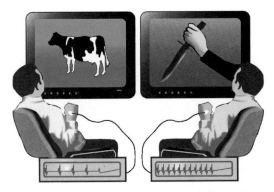

FIGURE 2.11 An experimenter manipulates the independent variable (in this case the programs people watch) so that two or more groups experience different treatments. Then the experimenter measures the dependent variable (in this case pulse rate) to see how the independent variable affected it.

ONCEPT CHECK

10. An instructor wants to find out whether the frequency of testing in an introductory psychology class has any effect on students' final exam performance. The instructor gives weekly tests in one class, just three tests in a second class, and only a single midterm exam in the third class. All three classes are given the same final exam, and the instructor then compares their performances. Identify the independent variable and the dependent variable. (Check your answers on page 55.)

## Experimental Group, Control Group, and Random Assignment

An **experimental group** *receives the treatment that an experiment is designed to test.* In our example the experimental group would watch televised violence. The **control group** is *a set of individuals treated in the same way as the experimental group except for the procedure that the experiment is designed to test.* People in the control group would watch only nonviolent television programs (Figure 2.12). (The type of television program is the independent variable; the resulting behavior is the dependent variable.)

In principle this procedure sounds easy, although difficulties arise in practice. For example, if we are studying a group of teenagers with a history of violent behavior, it may be difficult to find nonviolent programs that hold their attention. As their attention wanders, those who were watching the nonviolent programs start picking fights with one another, and suddenly, the results of the experiment look very odd indeed.

Suppose we conduct a study inviting young people to watch either violent or nonviolent programs, and then we discover that those who watched violent programs act more aggressively. What conclusion could we draw? None, of course. Those who chose to watch violence were probably different from those who chose the nonviolent programs. Any good experiment has **random assignment** of participants to groups: *The experimenter uses a chance procedure, such as drawing names out of a hat, to make sure that every participant has the same probability as any other participant of being assigned to a given group.*

Consider another example: We set up a rack of cages and put each rat in a cage by itself. The rack has five rows of six cages each, numbered from 1 in the upper left-hand corner to 30 in the lower right. Regardless of the procedures we use, we find that the rats with higher cage numbers are more aggressive than those with lower numbers. Why?

We might first guess that the difference has to do with location. The rats in the cages with high numbers are farthest from the lights and closest to the floor. They get fed last each day. To test the influence of these factors, we move some of the cages to different positions in the rack, leaving each rat in its own cage. To our surprise, the rats in cages 26–30 are still more aggressive than those in cages 1–5. Why? (How could they possibly know which number is on their cage, and even if they did know, why would they care?)

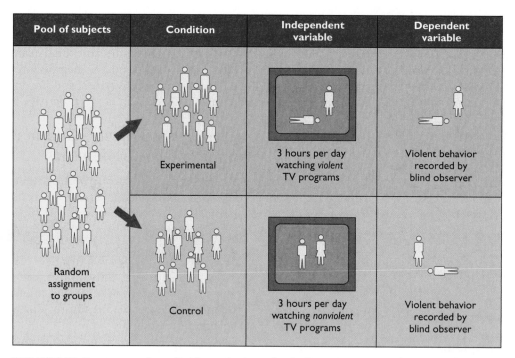

| Pool of subjects | Condition | Independent variable | Dependent variable |
|---|---|---|---|
| Random assignment to groups | Experimental | 3 hours per day watching *violent* TV programs | Violent behavior recorded by blind observer |
| | Control | 3 hours per day watching *nonviolent* TV programs | Violent behavior recorded by blind observer |

**FIGURE 2.12** Once researchers decide on the hypothesis they want to test, they must design the experiment. These procedures test the effects of watching televised violence. An appropriate, accurate method of measurement is essential.

The answer concerns how rats get assigned to cages. When an investigator buys a shipment of rats, which one goes into cage 1? The one that is easiest to catch! Which ones go into the last few cages? The vicious, ornery little critters that put up the greatest fight. The rats in the last few cages were more aggressive from the start.

The point is that, even when using rats, an experimenter must assign individuals at random to the experimental group and the control group. This advice is even more important with humans.

■ Even rats must be assigned to groups randomly.

**WHAT'S THE EVIDENCE?**
*Televised Violence and Aggressive Behavior*

We have talked in general terms about research on the effects of televised violence. Let's consider some actual examples.

Some of the evidence comes from correlational studies. For example, people who watch a great deal of televised violence are more likely than other people to engage in aggressive behavior (National Institute of Mental Health, 1982). However, the meaning is not clear. Does watching violence make people aggressive, or do aggressive people like to watch violence? To examine a possible cause-and-effect relationship, we must conduct experiments.

**HYPOTHESIS** Boys who watch violent television programs will engage in more acts of aggression than will boys who spend the same amount of time watching nonviolent programs. (The researchers focused on boys because boys tend to be more aggressive than girls.)

**METHOD** The experimenters chose to study male juvenile delinquents in an institution (Parke, Berkowitz, Leyens, West, & Sebastian, 1977). The disadvantage of this choice was that the conclusions might apply only to a limited group. The advantage was that the experimenters could control the choice of television programs (the independent variable).

The boys in the study were randomly assigned to two cottages. Those in one cottage watched violent films on five consecutive nights; those in the other cottage watched nonviolent films. Throughout the study period, blind observers (who didn't know to which cottage each boy was assigned) recorded incidents of aggressive behavior by each boy. On the sixth day, each boy was put into an experimental setting where he was given the opportunity at certain times to press a button that, he thought, would deliver an electric shock to another boy. (In fact, no shocks were given.) The experimenters recorded the frequency and intensity of shocks that each boy tried to deliver (the dependent variable).

**RESULTS**   Compared to the boys who had watched nonviolent films, those who had watched the violent films engaged in more acts of aggression and pressed the button to deliver more frequent and more intense electric shocks.

**INTERPRETATION**   At least in this study, watching violent films did lead to increased violence. As with most studies, however, this one had limitations. The boys in this experiment were not representative of boys in general, much less of people in general. Moreover, we cannot assume that we would get similar results with different violent films or different methods of measuring aggressive behavior.

---

The only way to get around the limitations of a given experiment is to conduct additional experiments, using different samples of people, different films, and different measures of aggressive behavior. Many such experiments have been conducted, and most have found that watching violent films increases aggressive behavior, slightly and temporarily. However, it also increases nonviolent types of antisocial, uncooperative behavior, so the viewers are not just copying the actions on the film. One possibility is that experimenters who show violent films imply that they don't disapprove of such things; the viewers conclude that they can probably get away with some misbehaviors without being punished (Felson, 1996). That is, watching violence may remove some inhibitions rather than actually cause aggressive behavior.

The controversy about the effects of watching violence is an old one and sure to persist. In the 1930s and 1940s, people worried about whether listening to crime programs on the radio was harmful to young people (Dennis, 1998), and way back in the time of Plato and Aristotle, people worried whether it was dangerous for children to listen to certain kinds of storytellers (Murray, 1998). Today, many people worry about dangerous video games and Internet sites as well as television and movies. The technology changes, but the question stays the same.

## Demand Characteristics

Research on human behavior poses some thorny problems because people who know they are part of an experiment figure out, or think they have figured out, what is going to happen in the experiment. Their expectations can influence behavior enough to overwhelm the effects of whatever the experimenter is actually doing.

To illustrate: In some well-known studies on sensory deprivation that were popular in the 1950s, people were placed in an apparatus that minimizes vision, hearing, touch, and other sensory stimulation. Within hours many participants reported hallucinations, anxiety, and difficulty concentrating. Now suppose you have heard about these studies, and you agree to participate in an experiment described as a study of "meaning deprivation." The experimenter asks you about your medical history and then asks you to sign a form agreeing not to sue if you have a bad experience. You see an "emergency tray" containing medicines and instruments, which the experimenter assures you is there "just as a precaution." Now you enter an "isolation chamber," which is actually an ordinary room with two chairs, a desk, a window, a mirror, a sandwich, and a glass of water. You are going to be left there for 4 hours. You are shown a microphone which you can use to report any hallucinations or other distorted experiences and a "panic button" you can press for escape if the discomfort becomes unbearable.

Staying in a room by yourself for a few hours should hardly be a traumatic experience. But all the preparations suggested that terrible things were about to happen, so when this study was actually conducted, several students reported that they were hallucinating "multicolored spots on the wall," that "the walls of the room are starting to waver," or that "the objects on the desk are becoming animated and moving about" (Figure 2.13). Some complained of anxiety, restlessness, difficulty concentrating, and spatial disorientation. One pressed the panic button to demand release (Orne & Scheibe, 1964).

Students in a control group were led to the same room, but they were not shown the "emergency tray," were not asked to sign a release form, and were given no other indication that anything unusual was likely to happen. They, in fact, reported no unusual experiences.

Sensory deprivation probably does influence behavior. But as this experiment illustrates, we must carefully distinguish between the effects of the independent variable and the effects of what the participants expect from the experiment. Martin Orne (1969) defined **demand characteristics** as *cues that tell a participant what is expected of him or her and what the experimenter hopes to find.* In a sense demand characteristics set up *self-fulfilling prophecies.* That is, when designing an experiment, the experimenter has a certain expectation in mind and then inadvertently conveys that expectation to the participants, influencing them to behave as expected. To eliminate demand characteristics, many experimenters take

a                                                                          b

**FIGURE 2.13** (a) In experiments on sensory deprivation, a person who is deprived of most sensory stimulation becomes disoriented, loses track of time, and reports hallucinations. But do these results partly reflect the person's expectation of having distorted experiences? (b) In one experiment students were placed in a normal room after undergoing various procedures designed to make them expect a dreadful experience. Many reported hallucinations and distress.

elaborate steps to conceal the purpose of the experiment. A double-blind study serves the purpose: If two groups share the same expectations but behave differently because of the treatment they receive, then the differences in behavior are presumably not the result of their expectations.

## CONCEPT CHECK

11. Which of the following would an experimenter try to minimize or avoid?
    falsifiability, independent variables, dependent variables, blind observers, demand characteristics
    (Check your answers on page 55.)

# Ethical Considerations in Research

In any experiment psychologists manipulate a variable to determine how it affects behavior. Perhaps you object to the idea of someone trying to alter your behavior. If so, consider that every time you talk to people you are trying to alter their behavior at least slightly. Most experiments in psychology are no more disruptive than a conversation.

Still, some experiments do raise ethical issues. Psychologists are seriously concerned about the ethical issues that arise both in the experiments they conduct with humans and in those they conduct with animals.

## Ethical Concerns with Humans

Earlier in this chapter, I discussed experiments on the effects of televised violence. If psychologists believed that watching violent programs might really transform viewers into murderers, then it would be unethical to conduct experiments to find out for sure. It would also be unethical to perform procedures likely to cause significant pain or embarrassment or to exert any other harmful effects.

The central ethical principle is that experiments should include only procedures that people would agree to experience. No one should leave a study muttering, "If I had known what was going to happen, I never would have agreed to participate." To maintain high ethical standards for the conduct of experiments, psychologists ask prospective participants to give their **informed consent** before proceeding, *a statement that they have been told what to expect and that they agree to continue*. When experimenters post a sign-up sheet asking for volunteers, or at the start of the experiment itself, they explain what will happen—that the participants will receive electric shocks or they will be asked to drink concentrated sugar water or whatever. They also inform the participants of their right to withdraw from the study at any time if they find it too disagreeable. Informed consent sounds like a simple principle, and usually it is. However, special problems arise with research on children, with mentally retarded people or anyone else who may not understand the proposed procedure (Bonnie, 1997), and with severely depressed people, who may have lost interest in their own well-being (Elliott, 1997). In such cases researchers either consult the person's guardian or nearest relative or simply decide not to proceed.

Experiments conducted at a college or at any other reputable institution must first be approved by an institutional review board. Such a committee judges whether the proposed studies include procedures for informed consent and whether they safeguard each participant's confidentiality. The committee also tries to prevent risky procedures. For example, the committee would not approve a proposal to use large doses of cocaine, even if some people were eager to give their informed consent.

The committee also judges procedures in which investigators want to deceive participants temporarily to hide the purpose of the study. For example, suppose researchers want to test whether it is difficult to persuade people who know someone is trying to persuade them, presumably because they put up defenses. The researchers want to use two groups of people—one group that has been informed of the upcoming persuasion and one that does not know what to expect. The second group might even be misinformed about the intent of the study. Most people see little objection to this temporary deception, but the institutional committee would have to review the procedures and give its permission before the study could proceed.

Finally, the American Psychological Association, or APA (1982), publishes a booklet detailing the proper ethical treatment of volunteers in experiments. Any member who disregards these principles may be censured or expelled from membership in the APA.

## Ethical Concerns with Animals

Much psychological research requires the use of human participants. However, animal research can help us understand basic processes, such as how nerves work, how the eyes and ears work, the functions of sleep, and the effects of rewards and punishments on the rates of behaviors (Figure 2.14). Researchers are especially likely to turn to animals if they want to control aspects of life that people will not let them control (e.g., who mates with whom), if they want to study behavior continuously over months or years (longer than people are willing to participate), or if the research poses health risks. Animal research has long been essential for preliminary testing of most new drugs, surgical procedures, and methods of relieving pain. People with untreatable illnesses argue that they have the right "to hope for cures or relief from suffering through research using animals" (Feeney, 1987). Even outside the medical field, much of our current knowledge in psychology either began with animal research or made use of animal studies at some point.

Nevertheless, some people oppose much or all of animal research. Animals, after all, cannot give informed consent. Some animal-rights supporters insist that ani-

mals should have the same rights as humans, that keeping animals (even pets) in cages is nothing short of slavery, and that killing any animal is murder. Others oppose some kinds of research but are willing to compromise about others. Psychologists, too, vary in their attitudes. Most support animal research in general, but almost all would draw a line somewhere separating acceptable research from unacceptable (Plous, 1996). Naturally, different psychologists draw that line at different places.

In this debate, as in so many other political controversies, one common tactic is for each side to criticize the most extreme actions of its opponents. For example, animal-rights advocates point to studies that exposed monkeys or puppies to painful procedures that seem hard to justify. On the other hand, researchers point to protesters who have distorted facts, vandalized laboratories, and even threatened to kill researchers and their children—and in one case, oddly enough, threatened to kill the researcher's pet dog. Some protesters have even stated that they would oppose the use of any AIDS medication if its discovery came from research with animals.

Unfortunately, when both sides concentrate on criticizing their most extreme opponents, they trivialize the real issues and make points of agreement harder to find. One fairly thorough study by a relatively unbiased outsider concluded that the truth is messy: Some research is painful to the animals *and* nevertheless valuable for advancing our understanding of important scientific or medical issues in ways that we could not otherwise achieve (Blum, 1994). In other words we cannot remain innocent of harming animals and still make the scientific and medical progress that we value.

**FIGURE 2.14** A mirror mounted on a young owl's head enables investigators to track the owl's head movements and thereby to discover how it localizes sounds with one ear plugged. The findings may help researchers understand how blind people use their hearing to compensate for visual loss. An experiment such as this subjects the animal to only a minor inconvenience. Some experiments, however, inflict pain or discomfort and are therefore more likely to raise ethical objections.

If we cannot simply choose between progress and protecting animals, we must find a compromise. Professional organizations such as the Neuroscience Society and the American Psychological Association publish guidelines for the proper use of animals in research. Colleges and other research institutions maintain laboratory animal care committees to ensure that laboratory animals are treated humanely, that their pain and discomfort are kept to a minimum, and that experimenters consider alternatives before they impose potentially painful procedures on animals. Because such committees must deal with competing values, their decisions are never beyond dispute. How can we determine in advance whether the value of the expected experimental results (which are hard to predict) will outweigh the pain the animals will endure (which is hard to measure)? As is so often the case with ethical decisions, reasonable arguments can be raised on both sides of the question, and no compromise is fully satisfactory.

## IN CLOSING
### Psychological Research

I mentioned at the beginning of this chapter that scientists avoid the word *prove*. Psychologists certainly do. (The joke is that psychology courses don't have true-false tests, just maybe-perhaps tests.) The most complex, and therefore most interesting, aspects of human behavior are products of genetics, a lifetime of experiences, and countless current influences. Given the practical and ethical limitations, it might seem that the whole idea of psychological research is doomed from the start. However, largely because of these difficulties, many psychologists have been highly inventive in designing complex ways to isolate the effects of certain influences. A single study rarely answers a question decisively, but many studies can converge to increase our total understanding.

## Summary

- *Operational definitions.* For many purposes psychologists prefer operational definitions, which state how to measure a given phenomenon or how to produce it. (page 40)
- *Sampling.* Psychologists hope to draw conclusions that apply to a large population and not just to the small sample they have studied, so they try to select a sample that resembles the total population. They may select either a representative sample or a random sample. To apply the results to people worldwide, they need a cross-cultural sample. (page 41)
- *Experimenter bias and blind observers.* An experimenter's expectations can influence the interpretations of behavior and the recording of data. To ensure objectivity,

investigators use blind observers, who do not know what results are expected. In a double-blind study, neither the observer nor the participants know the researcher's predictions. (page 42)
- *Naturalistic observations.* Naturalistic observations provide descriptions of humans or other species under natural conditions. (page 43)
- *Case histories.* A case history is a detailed research study of a single individual, generally someone with unusual characteristics. (page 43)
- *Surveys.* A survey is a report of people's answers on a questionnaire. It is easy to conduct a survey and, unfortunately, very easy to conduct one badly. (page 44)
- *Correlations.* A correlational study is a study of the relationship between variables that are outside the investigator's control. The strength of this relationship is measured by a correlation coefficient, which ranges from 0 (no relationship) to plus or minus 1 (a perfect relationship). (page 45)
- *Illusory correlations.* Beware of illusory correlations—relationships that people think they observe between variables after mere casual observation. (page 47)
- *Inferring causation.* A correlational study will not uncover cause-and-effect relationships, but an experiment can. (page 47)
- *Experiments.* Experiments are studies in which the investigator manipulates one variable to determine its effect on another variable. The manipulated variable is the independent variable. Changes in the independent variable may lead to changes in the dependent variable, the one the experimenter measures. (page 48)
- *Random assignment.* An experimenter should randomly assign individuals to form experimental and control groups. That is, all individuals should have an equal probability of being chosen for the experimental group. (page 49)
- *Demand characteristics.* Cues that inform participants of the expected results are called demand characteristics. Skillful experimenters try to minimize demand characteristics. (page 51)
- *Ethics of experimentation.* Experimentation on either humans or animals raises ethical questions. Psychologists try to minimize risk to their participants, but they cannot avoid making difficult ethical decisions. (page 52)

## Answers to Concept Checks

**3.** A score on an IQ test is an operational definition of intelligence. (Whether it is a particularly good definition is another question.) None of the other definitions tells us how to measure or produce intelligence. Many operational definitions are possible for "friendliness," such as "the number of people that someone speaks to within 24 hours." You can probably think of a better operational definition. Remember that an operational definition specifies a clear method of measurement. (page 41)

4. Clearly not. It is unlikely that the men at a given college are typical of men in general or that the women are typical of women in general. Moreover, at some colleges the men are atypical in some respects and the women atypical in different ways. (page 42)

5. **a.** Negative correlation between crowdedness and income. **b.** Zero correlation between telephone scores and IQ. **c.** Positive correlation between wakenings and depression. (page 47)

6. The −.75 correlation indicates a stronger relationship—that is, a greater accuracy of predicting one variable based on measurements of the other. A negative correlation is just as useful as a positive one. (page 47)

7. One possibility is that happiness is unrelated to self-esteem. Another, perhaps more likely, possibility is that we have used an inaccurate measurement of either self-esteem or happiness or both. Correlations are necessarily low if one of the measurements is inaccurate. (page 47)

8. We can conclude only that, if we know either someone's interest level or test score, we can predict the other with reasonably high accuracy. We *cannot* conclude that an interest in psychology will help someone to learn the material or that doing well on psychology tests increases someone's interest in the material. Both conclusions may well be true, but a correlational study cannot demonstrate a cause-and-effect relationship. (page 48)

9. Here's one possibility: The experimental group of rats drinks saccharin and later is made sick. The control group drinks nothing but is made sick. Perhaps another control group drinks saccharin and is not made sick. The next day all groups are offered a choice between saccharin and water. If the first group learned an association between saccharin and illness, it should show the lowest saccharin preference. (page 49)

10. The independent variable is the frequency of tests during the semester. The dependent variable is the students' performance on the final exam. (page 49)

11. Of these, only demand characteristics are to be avoided. If you did not remember that falsifiability is a good feature of a theory, check page 33. Every experiment must have at least one independent variable (what the experimenter controls) and at least one dependent variable (what the experimenter measures). However, a study with many independent or dependent variables might become too complicated. Blind observers provide an advantage. (page 52)

# Measuring and Analyzing Results

*How can the "average" results in a study be described?*

*How can we describe the variations among individuals?*

*How can a researcher determine whether the results reflect a consistent trend, or whether these results could have arisen just by chance?*

Some years ago a television program about the alleged dangers of playing the game Dungeons and Dragons reported 28 known cases of D&D players who had committed suicide. Alarming, right?

Not necessarily. At that time at least 3 million young people played the game regularly. The reported suicide rate among D&D players—28 per 3 million—was considerably *less* than the suicide rate among teenagers in general.

So do these results mean that playing D&D *prevents* suicide? Hardly. The 28 reported cases are probably an incomplete count of all suicides by D&D players. Besides, the correlation between playing D&D and committing suicide, regardless of its direction and magnitude, could not possibly tell us about cause and effect. Maybe the kinds of young people who play D&D are simply different from those who do not.

Then what conclusion should we draw from these data? *None at all.* Sometimes, as in this case, the data are meaningless. Even when the data are potentially meaningful, people sometimes present them in a confusing or misleading manner (Figure 2.15). Let's consider some proper ways of analyzing and interpreting results.

## Descriptive Statistics

To explain the meaning of a study, an investigator must summarize the results in an orderly fashion. When a re-

searcher observes the behavior of 100 people, we have no interest in hearing all the details about every person. We want to know the general trends or averages. We might also want to know whether most people were similar to the average or whether they varied a great deal. An investigator presents the answers to those questions through **descriptive statistics,** which are *mathematical summaries of results,* such as measures of the average and the amount of variation. The correlation coefficient, discussed earlier in this chapter, is one kind of descriptive statistic.

## Measurements of the Central Score

There are three ways of representing the central score: mean, median, and mode. The **mean** is *the sum of all the scores divided by the total number of scores.* (Generally, when people say "average," they refer to the mean.) For example, the mean of 2, 10, and 3 is 5 (15 ÷ 3). The mean is especially useful if the scores approximate the **normal distribution** (or normal curve), *a symmetrical frequency of scores clustered around the mean.* A normal distribution is often described as a bell-shaped curve. For example, if we measure how long it takes 30 students to memorize a poem, these times will probably follow a pattern similar to the normal distribution.

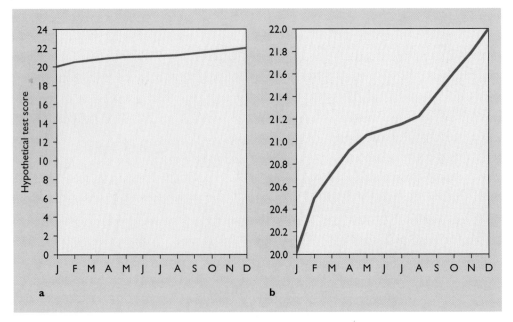

**FIGURE 2.15** Why statistics can be misleading: Both of these graphs present the same data, an increase from 20 to 22 over 1 year's time. But by ranging only from 20 to 22 (rather than from 0 to 22), graph (b) makes that increase look much more dramatic. (After Huff, 1954)

The mean can be misleading, however, if the distribution is far from normal. For example, one survey asked people how many sex partners they hoped to have, ideally, over the next 30 years. The mean for women was 2.8 and the mean for men was 64.3 (Miller & Fishkin, 1997). But those results are extremely misleading. Almost two thirds of women and about half of men replied "1." That is, they hoped for a loving monogamous relationship with one partner. Most of the rest replied with other small numbers (2 or 3 or a few more), but a few men replied in the hundreds, thousands, or even tens of thousands. I have repeated this survey with my own classes, and I find that an occasional man even uses scientific notation such as $3.5 \times 10^5$. (Others give nonnumerical answers such as "as many as possible" or "all of them.") If we average in even one or two huge numbers with a large number of small ones, we can get a mean such as 64.3, which is not at all typical of people's answers.

When the population distribution is extremely abnormal, we can better represent the typical individual with the median instead of the mean. To determine the **median,** *we arrange all the scores in order from the highest score to the lowest score. The middle score is the median.* For example, if the scores are 2, 10, and 3, the median is 3. In the survey just mentioned, the median for *both* women and men was that they hoped for one sex partner the rest of their lives. In short, a few extreme scores greatly affect the mean but have little effect on the median.

The third way to represent the central score is the **mode,** *the score that occurs most frequently.* For example, in the distribution of scores 2, 2, 3, 4, and 10, the mode is 2. The mode is seldom useful except under special circumstances. Suppose we surveyed a sample of students at a college about how much they study and gathered the results shown in Figure 2.16. Half of the

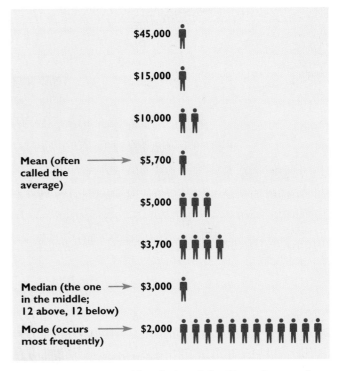

**FIGURE 2.17** The monthly salaries of the 25 employees of company X, showing the mean, median, and mode. (After Huff, 1954)

students study a great deal, and half of them study very little. The mean for this distribution is 4.28 hours per day, a very misleading figure because all the students study either much more or much less than that. The median is no better as a representation of these results: Because we have an even number of students, there is no middle score. We could take a figure midway between the two scores nearest the middle, but in this case those scores are 2 and 7, so we would compute a median of 4.5, again a very misleading figure. A distribution like this is called a *bimodal distribution* (one with two common scores); the researcher might simply describe the two modes and not even mention the mean or the median.

To summarize: Roughly speaking, the mean is what most people intend when they say "average." The median is the middle score after the scores are ranked from highest to lowest; the mode is the most common score (Figure 2.17).

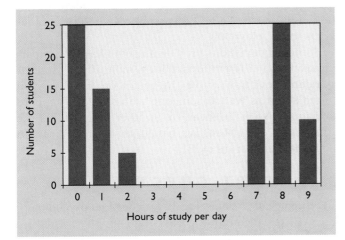

**FIGURE 2.16** Results of an imaginary survey of study habits at one college. This college apparently has two groups of students—those who study as hard as they can and those who find other things to do. In this case both the mean and the median are misleading. This distribution is bimodal; its two modes are 0 and 8.

## CONCEPT CHECK

12. **a.** For the following distribution of scores, determine the mean, the median, and the mode: 5, 2, 2, 2, 8, 3, 1, 6, 7.
    **b.** Determine the mean, median, and mode for this distribution: 5, 2, 2, 2, 35, 3, 1, 6, 7. (Check your answers on page 60.)

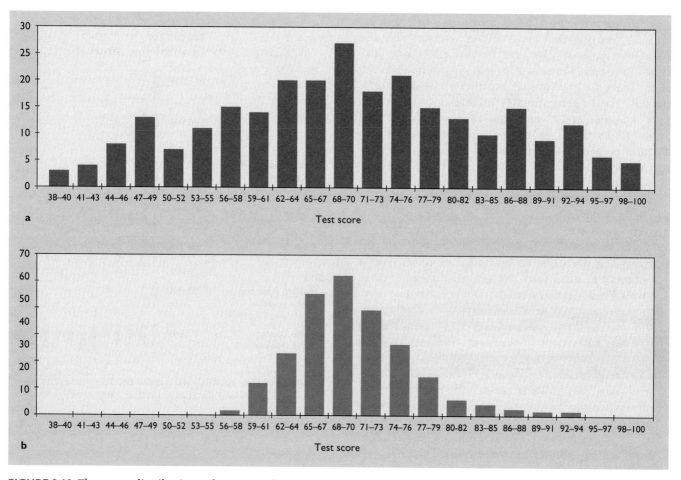

**FIGURE 2.18** These two distributions of test scores have the same mean but different variances and different standard deviations.

## Measures of Variation

Figure 2.18 shows two distributions of test scores. Suppose that these represent scores on two introductory psychology tests. Both tests have the same mean, 70, but different distributions. If you had a score of 80, you would beat only 75% of the other students on the first test, but with the same score you would beat 95% on the second test.

To describe the difference between Figure 2.18a and b, we need a measurement of the variation (or spread) around the mean. The simplest such measurement is the **range** of a distribution, *a statement of the highest and lowest scores.* The range in Figure 2.18a is 39 to 100, and in Figure 2.18b it is 58 to 92.

The range is a simple calculation, but it is not very useful because it reflects only the extremes. Statisticians need to know whether most of the scores are clustered close to the mean or scattered widely. The most useful measure is the **standard deviation (SD),** *a measurement of the amount of variation among scores in a normal distribution.* In the appendix to this chapter, you will find a formula for calculating the standard deviation. For present purposes you can simply remember that when the scores are closely clustered near the mean, the standard deviation is small; when the scores are more widely scattered, the standard deviation is large.

As Figure 2.19 shows, the Scholastic Assessment Test (SAT) was designed to produce a mean of 500 and a standard deviation of 100. Of all people taking the test, 68% score within 1 standard deviation above or below the mean (400–600); 95% score within 2 standard deviations (300–700). Only 2.5% score above 700; another 2.5% score below 300.

Standard deviations provide a useful way of comparing scores on different tests. For example, if you scored 1 standard deviation above the mean on the SAT, you tested about as well as someone who scored 1 standard deviation above the mean on another test, such as the American College Test. We would say that both of you had a deviation score of +1.

## CONCEPT CHECK

13. Suppose that you score 80 on your first psychology test. The mean for the class is 70, and the standard deviation is 5. On the second test, you receive a score of 90. This time the mean for the class is also 70, but the standard deviation is 20. Compared to the other students in your class, did your performance improve, deteriorate, or stay the same? (Check your answer on page 61.)

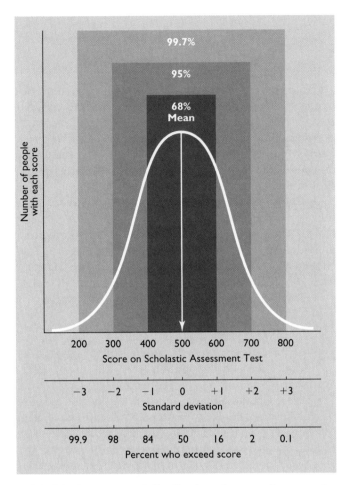

**FIGURE 2.19** In a normal distribution of scores, the amount of variation from the mean can be measured in standard deviations. In this example scores between 400 and 600 are said to be within 1 standard deviation from the mean; scores between 300 and 700 are within 2 standard deviations.

# Evaluating Results: Inferential Statistics

Suppose researchers conducted a study comparing two kinds of therapy for helping people to quit smoking cigarettes. At the end of 6 weeks of therapy, people who have been punished for smoking average 7.5 cigarettes per day, whereas those who have been rewarded for *not* smoking average 6.5 cigarettes per day. Presuming that the smokers were randomly assigned to the two groups and that the study was properly conducted, is this the kind of difference that might easily arise by chance? Or should we take this difference seriously and recommend that all therapists use rewards and not punishment?

To answer this question, we obviously need to know more than just the numbers 7.5 and 6.5. How many smokers were in the study? (10 in each group? 100? 1000?) And how much variation occurred within each group? Are most people's behaviors close to the group means, or are there a few extreme scores that distort the averages?

One way to deal with these issues is to present the means and 95% confidence intervals for each, as shown in Figure 2.20. The **95% confidence interval** is *the range within which the true population mean lies, with 95% certainty.* "Wait a minute," you protest. "We already know the means: 7.5 and 6.5. Aren't those the *true* population means?" No, those are the means for particular samples of the population. Someone who studies another group of smokers may not get quite the same results. What we care about is the mean for all smokers. It is impractical to measure that mean, but if we know the sample mean, the size of the sample, and the standard deviation, we can estimate whether the sample mean is likely to be close to the population mean. Figure 2.20 presents two possibilities. In part a the 95% confidence intervals are small; in other words the standard deviations were small, the samples were large, and the sample means are almost certainly close to the true population means. In part b the confidence intervals are larger, so the numbers 7.5 and 6.5 are just rough approximations of the true population means. Presenting data with confidence intervals can enable readers to decide for themselves how large and impressive the difference is between two groups (Hunter, 1997; Loftus, 1996).

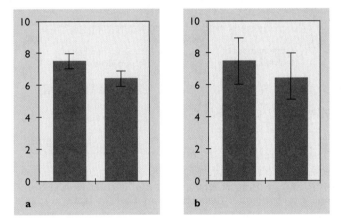

**FIGURE 2.20** The vertical lines indicate 95% confidence intervals. The pair of graphs in part a indicate that the true mean has a 95% chance of falling within a very narrow range. The graphs in b indicate a wider range and therefore suggest less certainty that reward is a more effective therapy than punishment.

A 95% confidence interval is one kind of **inferential statistic,** which is a *statement about a large population based on an inference from a small sample.* One alternative to the 95% confidence interval is a test that determines the probability that purely chance variation would achieve a difference as large as the observed one. For example, if we compared two groups of smokers who were actually treated the same way, what would be the chance that the groups would differ by as much as the difference between 7.5 and 6.5? The result is summarized by a *p* (as in *probability)* value. For example, **p < .05** indicates that *the probability that randomly generated results would resemble the observed results is less than 5%.* The smaller the *p* value, the more impressive the results. The usual agreement is that, if *p* is less than .05, researchers consider the results to be **statistically significant** or **statistically reliable**—that is, *unlikely to have arisen by chance.* A more cautious researcher might consider the results to be significant or reliable only if *p* were less than .01 or even .001. The appendix at the end of this chapter gives an example of a statistical test that can be used to determine a *p* value. Statistical significance depends on three factors: the size of the difference between the groups, the number of research participants in each group, and the amount of variation among individuals within each group (Figure 2.21).

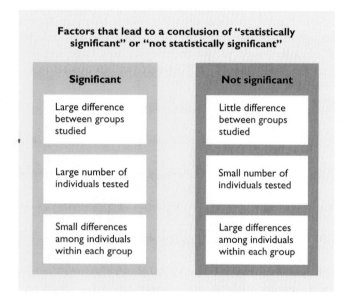

**Factors that lead to a conclusion of "statistically significant" or "not statistically significant"**

| Significant | Not significant |
|---|---|
| Large difference between groups studied | Little difference between groups studied |
| Large number of individuals tested | Small number of individuals tested |
| Small differences among individuals within each group | Large differences among individuals within each group |

**FIGURE 2.21** Researchers say that results are *statistically significant* if they calculate that chance variations in data would be unlikely to produce a difference between groups as large as the one that the researchers actually observed.

## CONCEPT CHECK

14. Should we be more impressed with results when the 95% confidence intervals are large or small? Should we be more impressed if the *p* value is large or small? (Check your answer on page 61.)

Examining the statistics is only the first step toward drawing a conclusion. To say that an experiment has statistically reliable results means only that we would be unlikely to get such results merely by chance. If not by chance, then how? At that point psychologists use their knowledge to try to determine the most likely interpretation of the results.

# Statistics and Conclusions

Sometimes psychological researchers get consistent, dependable effects, and they do not even have to consider statistics: Turn out the lights in a sealed room; people will no longer be able to see. Add sugar to your iced tea; it tastes sweet. The bigger the effect, the less we need to rely on complicated statistical tests. We pay more attention to statistics when we measure smaller effects: Does a change in the wording alter people's responses to a survey? Does the use of an electronic study guide improve students' test scores? Does family therapy provide better results than individual therapy to treat alcohol and drug abuse? Psychologists frequently deal with small, fragile effects and therefore need a solid understanding of statistics.

## Summary

* *Mean, median, and mode.* One way of presenting the central score of a distribution is via the mean, determined by adding all the scores and dividing by the number of individuals. Another way is the median, which is the middle score after all the scores have been arranged from highest to lowest. The mode is the score that occurs most frequently. (page 56)
* *Standard deviation (SD).* To indicate whether most scores are clustered close to the mean or whether they are spread out, psychologists report the range of scores, called the standard deviation. If we know that a given score is a certain number of standard deviations above or below the mean, then we can determine what percentage of other scores it exceeds. (page 58)
* *Inferential statistics.* Inferential statistics are attempts to deduce the properties of a large population based on the results from a small sample of that population. (page 59)
* *Probability of chance results.* The most common use of inferential statistics is to calculate the probability that a given research result could have arisen by chance. That probability is low if the difference between the two groups is large, if the variability within each group is small, and if the number of individuals in each group is large. (page 59)
* *Statistical significance.* When psychologists say $p < .05$, they mean that the probability that accidental fluctuations could produce the kind of results they obtained is less than 5%. They generally set a standard of 5% or less. If the results meet that standard, they are then said to be statistically significant or reliable. (page 60)

## Answers to Concept Checks

**12. a.** Mean = 4; median = 3; mode = 2. **b.** Mean = 7; median = 3; mode = 2. Note that changing just one number in the distribution from 8 to 35 greatly altered the mean without affecting the median or the mode. (page 57)

13. Even though your score rose from 80 on the first test to 90 on the second, your performance actually deteriorated in comparison to other students' scores. A score of 80 on the first test was 2 standard deviations above the mean, better than 98% of all other students.

A 90 on the second test was only 1 standard deviation above the mean, a score that beats only 84% of the other students. (page 58)

14. In both cases smaller. A small 95% confidence interval indicates high confidence in the results. A small *p* value indicates a low probability of getting such a large difference merely by chance. (page 60)

## CHAPTER ENDING
# Key Terms and Activities

## Key Terms

**95% confidence interval:** the range within which the true population mean lies, with 95% certainty (page 59)

**blind observer:** an observer who can record data without knowing what the researcher has predicted (page 42)

**case history:** a thorough description of a single individual, including information on both past experiences and current behavior (page 43)

**control group:** a group treated in the same way as the experimental group except for the procedure that the experiment is designed to test (page 49)

**convenience sample:** a group chosen because of its ease of study (page 41)

**correlation:** a measure of the relationship between two variables, which are both outside the investigator's control (page 45)

**correlation coefficient:** a mathematical estimate of the relationship between two variables, ranging from +1 (perfect positive relationship) to 0 (no linear relationship) to −1 (perfect negative relationship) (page 45)

**correlational study:** a procedure in which investigators measure the correlation between two variables without controlling either of them (page 45)

**cross-cultural samples:** groups of people from at least two cultures (page 41)

**demand characteristics:** cues that tell a subject what is expected of him or her and what the experimenter hopes to find (page 51)

**dependent variable:** the item that an experimenter measures to determine how changes in the independent variable affect it (page 49)

**descriptive statistics:** mathematical summaries of results such as measures of the average and the amount of variation (page 56)

**double-blind study:** a study in which neither the observer nor the subjects know which subjects received which treatment (page 43)

**experiment:** a study in which the investigator manipulates at least one variable while measuring at least one other variable (page 48)

**experimental group:** the group that receives the treatment that an experiment is designed to test (page 49)

**experimenter bias:** the tendency of an experimenter to unintentionally distort procedures or results, based on the experimenter's own expectations of the outcome of the study (page 42)

**extrasensory perception (ESP):** the alleged ability of certain people to acquire information without using any sense organ and without receiving any form of energy (page 35)

**falsifiable:** (with reference to a theory) making sufficiently precise predictions that we can at least imagine evidence that would contradict the theory (if anyone had obtained such evidence) (page 33)

**hypothesis:** a testable prediction of what will happen under certain conditions (page 31)

**illusory correlation:** an apparent relationship based on casual observations of unrelated or weakly related events (page 47)

**independent variable:** in an experiment, the item that an experimenter manipulates to determine how it affects the dependent variable (page 49)

**inferential statistics:** statements about large populations based on inferences from small samples (page 59)

**informed consent:** a subject's agreement to take part in an experiment after being told what to expect (page 52)

**mean:** the sum of all the scores reported in a study divided by the number of scores (page 56)

**median:** the middle score in a list of scores arranged from highest to lowest (page 57)

**meta-analysis:** a procedure that combines the results of many studies and analyzes them as though they were all one very large study (page 33)

**mode:** the score that occurs most frequently in a distribution of scores (page 57)

**naturalistic observation:** a careful examination of what many people or nonhuman animals do under natural conditions (page 43)

**normal distribution** (or **normal curve**): a symmetrical frequency of scores clustered around the mean (page 56)

**operational definition:** a definition that specifies the operations (or procedures) used to produce or measure something, a way to give it a numerical value (page 40)

***p* < .05:** an expression meaning that the probability of accidentally achieving results similar to the reported results is less than 5% (page 60)

**parsimony:** (literally, stinginess) scientists' preference for the theory that explains the results using the simplest assumptions (page 34)

**placebo:** an inactive pill that has no known pharmacological effect on the subjects in an experiment (page 42)

**population:** the entire group of individuals to be considered (page 41)

**random assignment:** a chance procedure for assigning subjects to groups so that every subject has the same probability as any other subject of being assigned to a particular group (page 49)

**random sample:** a group of people picked in random fashion, so that every individual in the population has an equal chance of being selected (page 41)

**range:** a statement of the highest and lowest scores in a distribution of scores (page 58)

**replicable result:** a result that can be repeated (at least approximately) by any competent investigator who follows the same procedures used in the original study (page 32)

**representative sample:** a selection of the population chosen to match the entire population with regard to specific variables (page 41)

**single-blind study:** a study in which either the observer or the subjects are unaware of which subjects received which treatment (page 43)

**standard deviation (SD):** a measurement of the amount of variation among scores in a normal distribution (page 58)

**statistically significant (or statistically reliable) results:** effects that have a low probability of having arisen by chance (page 60)

**survey:** a study of the prevalence of certain beliefs, attitudes, or behaviors, based on people's responses to specific questions (page 44)

**theory:** a comprehensive explanation of observable events (page 33)

## Suggestions for Further Reading

Martin, D. (1996). *Doing psychology experiments* (4th ed.). Pacific Grove, CA: Brooks/Cole. A discussion of all aspects of research, including methods of conducting research and statistical analyses of results.

Stanovich, K. E. (2001). *How to think straight about psychology* (6th ed.). Boston: Allyn & Bacon. An excellent discussion of how to evaluate evidence in psychology and how to avoid pitfalls.

# Web/Technology Resources

## HyperText Psychology_BASICS

**www.science.wayne.edu/~wpoff/basics.html**

This site walks you through the basics of research: social science methods; field studies, surveys, and experiments; and the use of statistics in interpreting results.

## Center for Social Research Methods

**trochim.human.cornell.edu/**

Bill Trochim of Cornell University offers Knowledge Base, an interactive on-line textbook for an introductory course in research methods. The site includes links to other Web sites devoted to social research and research methods; an on-line statistical adviser to help you select the appropriate statistical test for your data; common research design exercises; several full-length research papers; and more for the budding researcher.

## Statistical Assessment Service (STATS)

**www.stats.org/**

Here you'll learn how statistical and quantitative information and research are represented (and misrepresented) by the media and how journalists can learn to convey such material more accurately and effectively. The *Vital STATS* newsletter and STATS Spotlight include many interesting articles; Dubious Data Awards provide hilarious reading about the misuse of statistics; Newsclips are more serious examples of mangled and misunderstood data.

## Psychological Research Opportunities

**www.apa.org/science/infostu.html**

The American Psychological Association provides information about opportunities for students to help in the conduct of research.

## APPENDIX TO CHAPTER 2
# *Statistical Calculations*

This appendix shows you how to calculate a few of the statistics mentioned in Chapter 2. It is intended primarily to satisfy your curiosity. Ask your instructor whether you should use this appendix for any other purpose.

## Standard Deviation

To determine the standard deviation (SD):

1. Determine the mean of the scores.
2. Subtract the mean from each of the individual scores.
3. Square each of those results, add the squares together, and divide by the total number of scores.

The result is called the *variance*. The standard deviation is the square root of the variance. Here is an example:

| Individual scores | Each score minus the mean | Difference squared |
|---|---|---|
| 12.5 | −2.5 | 6.25 |
| 17.0 | +2.0 | 4.00 |
| 11.0 | −4.0 | 16.00 |
| 14.5 | −0.5 | 0.25 |
| 16.0 | +1.0 | 1.00 |
| 16.5 | +1.5 | 2.25 |
| 17.5 | +2.5 | 6.25 |
| 105 | | 36.00 |

The mean is 15.0 (the sum of the first column, divided by 7). The variance is 5.143 (the sum of the third column, divided by 7). The standard deviation is 2.268 (the square root of 5.143).

## A Typical Statistical Test: The *t*-Test

Statistical tests are available to suit different kinds of data. Suppose we test many people's memory twice, once on a day when they are well rested and once after a night of little or no sleep. Imagine that scores on this test range from 0 to 25. For each person we determine the difference between performance on the 2 days. For example:

| Well-rested performance | Nonrested performance | Difference |
|---|---|---|
| 17 | 14 | +3 |
| 23 | 14 | +9 |
| 15 | 18 | −3 |
| 25 | 24 | +1 |
| 21 | 16 | +5 |
| 19 | 17 | +2 |
| 22 | 14 | +8 |
| 24 | 19 | +5 |
| | | 30 |

We then determine $X_D$, the mean of the differences ($30 \div 8 = 3.75$) and $\sigma$, the standard deviation of the differences (3.63). We enter those into this formula for $t$, along with $N$, the number of people tested (which is 8):

$$t = \frac{X_D}{\sigma/\sqrt{N-1}} = \frac{3.75}{3.63/2.64} = 2.73$$

The larger the value of $t$, the less likely that the difference between the two groups is due to chance. The value of $t$ will be high if the difference between the two scores ($X_D$) is large, if the standard deviation ($\sigma$) is small relative to the mean, and if the number of individuals ($N$) is large. Statistics books contain tables to show the likelihood of a given $t$ value. In this case, with a group of eight people and a $t$ value of 2.73, $p < .05$. That is, the probability of getting such a large difference between the two sets of scores by chance (if sleeplessness really had no effect on performance) is less than 5%.

## Correlation Coefficients

To determine the correlation coefficient, we designate one of the variables $x$ and the other one $y$. We obtain pairs of measures, $x_i$ and $y_i$. Then we use the following formula:

$$r = \frac{[(\Sigma x_i y_i) - n \cdot x \cdot y]}{n \cdot sx \cdot sy}$$

In this formula ($\Sigma x_i y_i$) is the sum of the products of $x$ and $y$. For each pair of observations ($x$, $y$), we multiply $x$ times $y$ and then add together all the products. The term $n \cdot \bar{x} \cdot \bar{y}$ means $n$ (the number of pairs) times the mean of $x$ times the mean of $y$. The denominator, $n \cdot sx \cdot sy$ means $n$ times the standard deviation of $x$ times the standard deviation of $y$.

## Web/Technology Resources

Introductory Statistics: Concepts, Models, and Applications

**www.psychstat.smsu.edu/introbook/sbk00.htm**

You can read an entire statistics textbook by David W. Stockburger, Southwest Missouri State University, on the Web or download it, free!

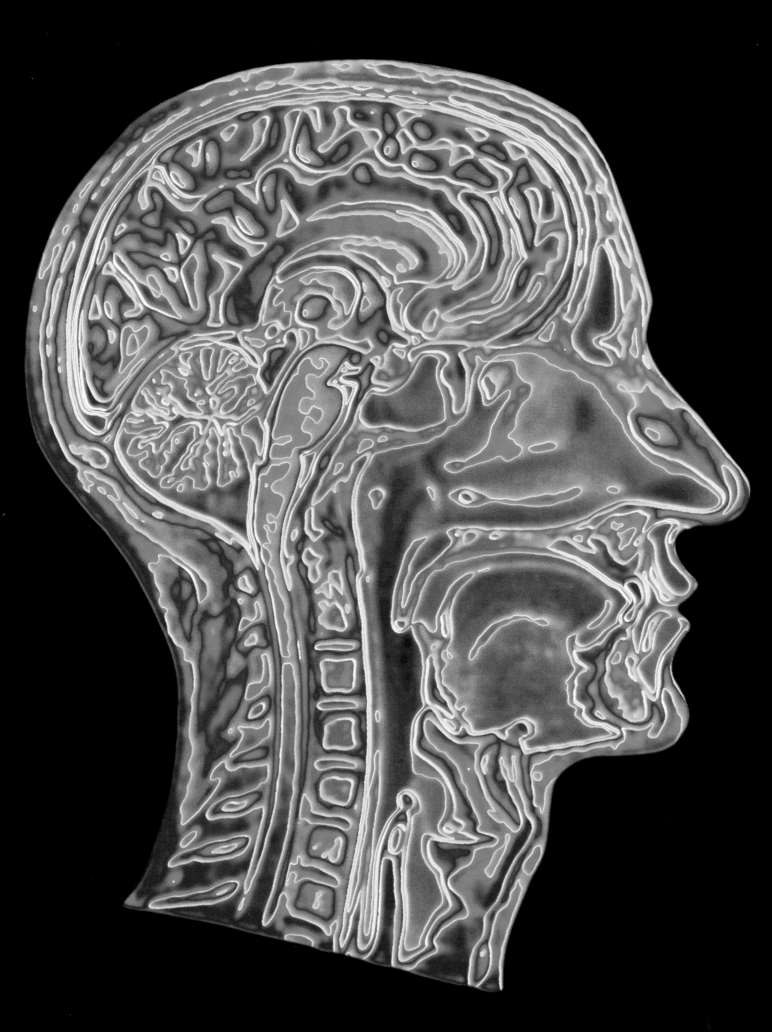

# Biological Psychology

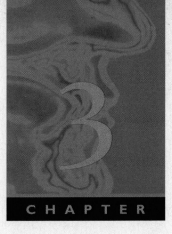

**CHAPTER 3**

It is easy to look at a human brain, which weighs only 1.2 to 1.4 kg (2.5 to 3 pounds), and marvel at its abilities. Some brains are even more compact. A bee's brain (if you want to call it that) is so small that you would need a microscope to find it. And yet the complexity of bee behavior would put a $1 million computer to shame. A bee flies around until it locates flowers, finds food in the flowers, evades predators, finds its way back to the hive, and then does a dance that tells other bees where it found the food. When necessary, it also takes care of the queen bee, protects the hive against intruders, and so forth. Not bad for a microscopic brain.

What does it feel like to be a bee? Does it feel like anything? We don't know. In fact, you and I cannot get inside each other's heads either. We can only infer each other's experiences, but never know them directly.

Researchers necessarily proceed piecemeal, first answering the easiest questions. We now know a great deal about how nerves work, how brains record sensory experiences, and the effects of various kinds of brain

■ A bee has amazingly complex behavior, but we have no way to get inside the bee's experience to know what (if anything) it feels like to be a bee.

damage. What we understand least is why brain activity produces experience at all. (Philosopher David Chalmers calls this "the hard problem.") We have much evidence indicating genetic influences on behavior, but in most cases we know little about how the genes exert their effects. Progress in brain research has been enormous, but we can be just as easily awed by how much we know or how much we have yet to learn.

Will we someday understand nerves well enough to "read the mind" of a bee or even to decide whether a bee has experiences at all? We cannot say, but the fascination of the mind-brain question motivates many researchers to tireless efforts. This chapter discusses genes, nerve cells, and the functions of different brain areas. Module 5.3 later in the text discusses the effects of drugs on the brain and behavior.

# Genes and Behavior

*How do heredity and evolution influence behavior?*

Monozygotic (identical) twins share all their genes in common, as opposed to dizygotic (fraternal) twins who share only half their genes. One pair of monozygotic twins who were separated at birth and reared in different western Ohio cities were reunited in adulthood (Figure 3.1). They quickly discovered that they had a great deal in common: Both had been named Jim by their adoptive parents. Each liked carpentry and drafting, had built a bench around a tree in his yard, and worked as a deputy sheriff. They both chewed their fingernails, gained weight at the same age, smoked the same brand of cigarettes, drove Chevrolets, and took their vacations in western Florida. Each married a woman named Linda and then divorced her and married a woman named Betty. One had a son named James Alan and the other a son named James Allen; both had a pet dog named Toy. Undoubtedly, some of these similarities are mere coincidences. Lots of people drive Chevrolets, for example, and many people from western Ohio vacation in western Florida. It's hard to believe that they had genes causing them to marry a Linda and divorce her to marry a Betty. (If either had been adopted by a family in Afghanistan, they would have had trouble finding either a Linda or a Betty. And did the Lindas and Bettys have genes that attracted them to men named Jim?)

All right, but we go on to other monozygotic twins separated at birth. One pair of women each wore rings on seven fingers. A pair of men discovered that they used the same brands of toothpaste, shaving lotion, hair tonic, and cigarettes. When they sent each other a birthday present, their presents crossed in the mail and each discovered that he had received exactly the same present he had sent. Another pair reported that whenever they went to the beach, they waded into the water backward and only up to their knees (Lykken, McGue, Tellegen, & Bouchard, 1992).

The list of bizarre coincidences goes on, but they are after all anecdotes and therefore hard to evaluate scientifically. Stronger evidence comes from studies that examined up to 100 pairs of twins who were reared in separate homes and then reunited as adults. (Finding such twins is a dauntingly difficult task.) Researchers performed multiple tests on the twins, some of whom were monozygotic and others dizygotic. The monozygotic twins resembled each other more than did the dizygotic pairs with regard to hobbies, vocational interests, consumption of coffee and fruit juices, preference for awakening early in the morning or staying up late at night, answers on personality tests, and support of right-wing beliefs (DiLalla, Carey, Gottesman, & Bouchard, 1996; Hur, Bouchard, & Eckert, 1998; Hur, Bouchard, & Lykken, 1998; Lykken, Bouchard, McGue, & Tellegen, 1993; McCourt, Bouchard, Lykken, Tellegen, & Keyes, 1999). In short, genetic factors have a surprisingly large influence on a wide range of behaviors.

Psychologists would like to know exactly how genes influence development, which aspects of environment are also important, and how genes and environment combine their influences.

FIGURE 3.1 Identical twins Jim Lewis and Jim Springer were separated at birth, reared in separate cities of western Ohio, and reunited in adulthood. Like many identical twins who were reunited after growing up separately, they discovered that they shared a long list of detailed similarities.

Let's first take a quick survey of genes and what they do. Then we shall explore in more detail the application of genetics to human behavior. At the end of this module, we shall consider the evolution of behavior.

## Genetic Principles

If you have already studied genetics in a biology class, much of this discussion will be a review. Skim anything you already know and concentrate on the unfamiliar material.

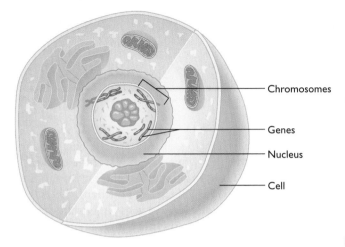

**FIGURE 3.2** Genes are sections of chromosomes in the nuclei of cells. (Scale is exaggerated for illustration purposes.)

genes for eye color, two for hair color, and so forth. (The exception: Men have one X chromosome and one Y chromosome and therefore have unpaired genes on their X and Y chromosomes.) *If both genes of a pair are the same,* you are **homozygous** (HO-mo-ZI-gus) for that gene. *If the two genes are different,* you are **heterozygous** (HET-er-o-ZI-gus) for that gene (Figure 3.5). (A *zygote* is a fertilized egg. *Homozygous* means that the egg—or other cell—has the same gene on both chromosomes.)

If you have one gene for brown eyes and one for blue eyes, you will have brown eyes. The gene for brown eyes is considered a **dominant gene** because *it exerts evident effects even if someone is heterozygous for that gene;* a **recessive gene** *shows its effects only in the homozygous condition.* Very few behavioral differences in hu-

Nearly every plant or animal cell (with a few exceptions, such as a red blood cell) contains a nucleus, which includes *strands of hereditary material* called **chromosomes** (Figure 3.2). Chromosomes provide the chemical basis of heredity. Humans have 23 pairs of chromosomes in each cell of the body, except egg or sperm cells, which have 23 unpaired chromosomes. At fertilization the 23 chromosomes in the egg cell combine with the 23 in the sperm to form the 23 pairs that will characterize the new person (Figure 3.3).

*Sections along each chromosome* are known as **genes,** *which control the chemical reactions that direct the individual's development,* for example, determining whether one becomes a tall dark-haired woman or a short blond man. Genes exert these effects by controlling the body's chemistry: Genes are composed of a chemical called DNA, which controls the production of another chemical called RNA, which in turn controls the production of proteins. These proteins either become part of the body's structure or control the rates of chemical reactions in the body. So genes exert their effects by a long, complex route (Figure 3.4).

Any cell that has a pair of chromosomes also has a pair of each gene, one on each chromosome. You have two

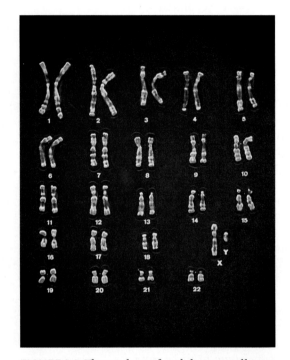

**FIGURE 3.3** The nucleus of each human cell contains 46 chromosomes, 23 from the sperm and 23 from the ovum, united in pairs.

■ Albinos occur in many species, always because of a recessive gene. (a) Striped skunk. (b) American alligator. (c) Mockingbird.

**FIGURE 3.4** The genes, composed of DNA, control the production of RNA, which in turn controls the production of proteins. Proteins form many structures of the body (e.g., muscles); they also control the rate of many chemical reactions (e.g., digestion).

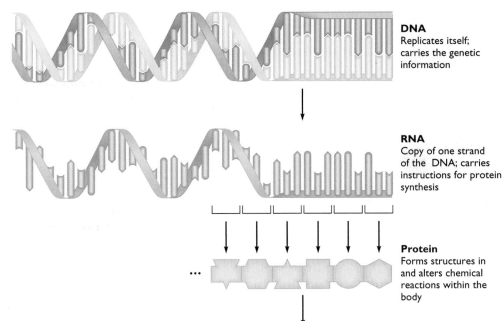

**DNA**
Replicates itself; carries the genetic information

**RNA**
Copy of one strand of the DNA; carries instructions for protein synthesis

**Protein**
Forms structures in and alters chemical reactions within the body

Physical appearance and abilities

mans depend on a single gene. One example, admittedly not a very important one, is the ability to curl the tongue lengthwise (Figure 3.6). The gene enabling tongue curling is dominant, so if you have this gene, you can curl your tongue. If you are homozygous for the noncurling gene, you must struggle through life without this ability.

A person who is heterozygous for a particular gene will show the effects of the dominant gene but can still pass on the recessive gene to a son or daughter. For example, two parents who are heterozygous for the tongue-curling gene will both be able to curl their tongues, but they could each pass a recessive gene to their child, who would then lack this ability.

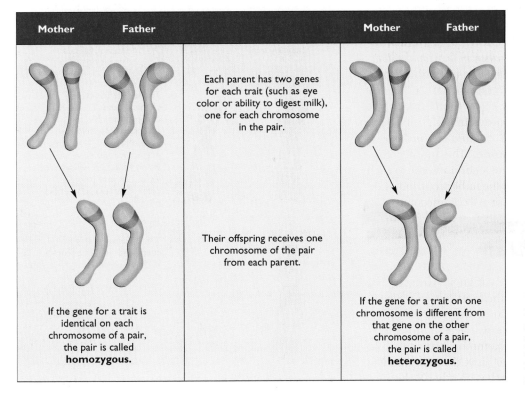

| Mother | Father | | Mother | Father |

Each parent has two genes for each trait (such as eye color or ability to digest milk), one for each chromosome in the pair.

Their offspring receives one chromosome of the pair from each parent.

If the gene for a trait is identical on each chromosome of a pair, the pair is called **homozygous.**

If the gene for a trait on one chromosome is different from that gene on the other chromosome of a pair, the pair is called **heterozygous.**

**FIGURE 3.5** In a pair of homozygous chromosomes, the gene for a given trait is identical on both chromosomes. In a heterozygous pair, the chromosomes contain different genes for a trait.

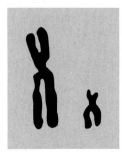

FIGURE 3.6 This figure depicts the ability to curl the tongue lengthwise as an example of a behavior that depends on a single gene. The gene that enables you to curl your tongue is a dominant gene, indicated by a triangle here. The square refers to a recessive gene for the inability to curl the tongue.

In the diagram:
- △ (Gene from mother) ☐ (Gene from father) = **heterozygous** (dominant and recessive; dominant gene prevails, so you can curl tongue)
- ☐ △ = **heterozygous** (recessive and dominant; dominant gene prevails, so you can curl tongue)
- △ △ = **homozygous** (dominant and dominant; no contest: you can curl tongue)
- ☐ ☐ = **homozygous** (recessive and recessive; no contest: you *cannot* curl tongue)

## CONCEPT CHECK

1. Suppose you can curl your tongue but your sister cannot. Are you homozygous or heterozygous for the tongue-curling gene, or is it impossible to say? What about your sister?
2. If two parents cannot curl their tongues, what can you predict about their children? (Check your answers on page 77.)

## Sex-Linked and Sex-Limited Genes

*One pair of human chromosomes* is known as **sex chromosomes** because they *determine whether an individual will develop as a male or as a female.* There are two types of sex chromosomes, known as X and Y (Figure 3.7). *A female has two* **X chromosomes** *in each cell; a male has one X chromosome and one* **Y chromosome.** The mother contributes one X chromosome to each child, and the father contributes either an X or a Y chromosome.

*Genes located on the X chromosome are known as* X-linked or **sex-linked genes.** An X-linked recessive gene shows its effects more often in men than in women. For example, the most common type of colorblindness depends on an X-linked recessive gene and is therefore more common in men than in women. A man with that gene on his X chromosome will definitely be colorblind because he has no other X chromosome. His Y chromosome contains neither the gene for col-

FIGURE 3.7 An electron micrograph of X and Y chromosomes shows the difference in length. (From Ruch, 1984)

orblindness nor the gene for normal color vision. A woman with the color-blindness gene has a second X chromosome, which probably contains a dominant gene for normal color vision. If so, she will have normal color vision herself but could transmit the colorblindness gene to any of her children (Figure 3.8).

Genetically controlled differences between the sexes do not necessarily depend on sex-linked genes. For example, adult men generally have deeper voices and more facial hair than women do. Those characteristics are controlled by genes that are present in both sexes but activated by men's hormones. Similarly, the genes controlling breast development are present in both sexes but activated by women's hormones. **Sex-limited genes** are *those that affect one sex more strongly than the other, even though both sexes have the genes*.

Why do most boys fight more than girls do? We don't know, but if genes are responsible, they are probably sex-*limited* genes rather than sex-*linked* genes. Male hormones may activate certain genes that promote aggressive behavior; we have no evidence suggesting an X-linked or Y-linked gene for aggressive behavior.

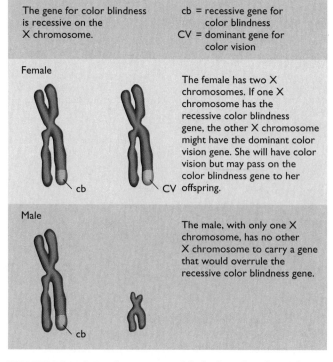

The gene for color blindness is recessive on the X chromosome.

cb = recessive gene for color blindness
CV = dominant gene for color vision

**Female**

The female has two X chromosomes. If one X chromosome has the recessive color blindness gene, the other X chromosome might have the dominant color vision gene. She will have color vision but may pass on the color blindness gene to her offspring.

**Male**

The male, with only one X chromosome, has no other X chromosome to carry a gene that would overrule the recessive color blindness gene.

FIGURE 3.8 Why males are more likely than females to be colorblind.

**3.** Suppose a colorblind man marries a woman who is homozygous for normal color vision. What sort of color vision will their children have? (Check your answer on page 77.)

## *Identifying and Localizing Genes*

Modern technology enables researchers to identify and localize the genes responsible for certain conditions. For example, researchers have located several genes that increase the risk of Alzheimer's disease (a condition associated with progressive memory loss) and genes that lead to several other diseases. You could (for a price) have someone examine your chromosomes and tell you which diseases you are likely to get. As research progresses, chromosomal tests may be able to tell you more and more about yourself and your probable future.

How much would you want to know? Your answer probably depends on what you could do with the information. For example, learning that you were predisposed to alcoholism might lead you to take precautions, such as not joining a fraternity or sorority with a reputation for heavy drinking. On the other hand, learning that you were likely to develop Alzheimer's disease in old age would do you less good because you wouldn't know what to do about it. Still, identifying the genes that predispose people to Alzheimer's disease may lead researchers to a better understanding of the disease and ultimately to methods of prevention or treatment.

Identifying risk genes poses some possible harms as well. Conceivably, employers or insurance companies could someday require genetic tests of all applicants and then discriminate against anyone whose test indicated a likelihood of developing a serious disorder. At present no employers or insurance companies seem interested in such a policy.

## *Estimating Heritability in Humans*

The ability to curl your tongue lengthwise is an oddity because it apparently depends entirely on a single gene. Huntington's disease (a condition marked by tremors, loss of muscle control, and eventual deficits in memory and judgment) is also associated with a single gene: If you have that gene, you will almost certainly get the disease (unless you die of something else first), and if you don't have the gene, you cannot get the disease, as far as we know. In fact, an examination of your chromosomes could tell you not only whether you will get the disease but also, if so, approximately *when* you will get it (Brinkmann, Mezei, Theilmann, Almqvist, & Hayden, 1997). We could name a few other examples of single-gene determinants of behavior, but not many.

Most behaviors develop through complex influences of many genes and environmental influences. You will occasionally hear someone ask whether a behavior (e.g., alcoholism) depends on heredity or environment. That question is meaningless, because obviously, every behavior depends on both heredity and environment. (Take away either your heredity or your environment and there is no "you" left!) However, a small change in wording makes the question meaningful: Does a given *difference* in behavior (e.g., the difference between an alcoholic and a nonalcoholic) depend more on *differences* in heredity or *differences* in environment? That is, if we want to predict whether more people in group A or group B will become alcoholics, how well could we succeed if we knew their heredity, and how well if we knew their environment?

The answer to a question like this is summarized by the term **heritability,** *an estimate of the variance within a population that is due to heredity.* Heritability ranges from 1, indicating that all variance is due to heredity, to 0, indicating that none of it is. For example, tongue curling has a heritability of almost 1. (It would be exactly 1 except that an injury to the tongue muscles could prevent tongue curling.)

For an example of a condition with 0 heritability, consider which language someone speaks. If you want to predict whether a child will speak English, Greek, or Bengali, you should ask which language is spoken by the child's parents and in the community. Examining the child's genes will not help.

Nearly all behaviors have a heritability between 0 and 1. To estimate the heritability of a behavior, researchers rely on the following types of evidence (Segal, 1993):

• Do **monozygotic** *(identical; literally, "one-egg")* **twins** resemble each other more closely than **dizygotic** *(fraternal; literally, "two-egg")* **twins** do (Figure 3.9)? Monozygotic twins have identical heredities; dizygotic twins resemble each other genetically only as much as a brother and sister do. If dizygotic twins resemble each other in some behavior as much as monozygotic twins do, then genetic differences are *not* important for the variations in that behavior. If monozygotic twins resemble each other more than dizygotic twins do, a genetic influence is a likely explanation, but not the only one. Most monozygotic twins share a single amniote before birth, whereas all dizygotic twins have separate amniotes (Figure 3.10). Therefore, monozygotic twins have more similarities in prenatal influences than do dizygotic twins, and what appears to be evidence for a genetic influence might also reflect similarity in prenatal environment (Phelps, Davis, & Schartz, 1997).

• Do twins who are adopted by separate families and reared apart resemble each other more closely than we would expect for unrelated people? If so, again genetic similarity is a likely explanation, although another possibility is that the twins were both influenced by their *prenatal* (before-birth) environment—that is, their mother's eating, drinking, and smoking habits, her age, and so forth.

• To what extent do adopted children resemble their adoptive and biological parents? If children who are adopted in infancy closely resemble their biological parents in some re-

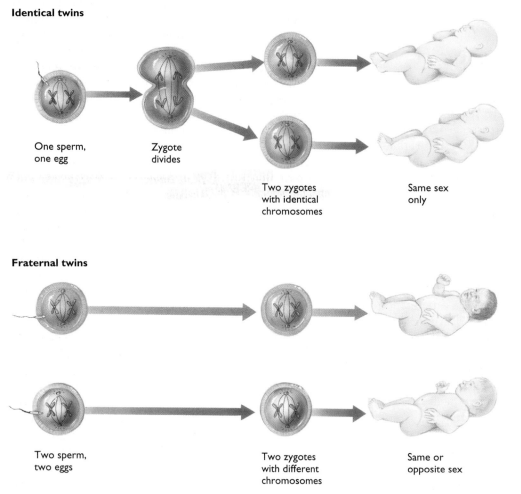

**Identical twins**

One sperm, one egg → Zygote divides → Two zygotes with identical chromosomes → Same sex only

**Fraternal twins**

Two sperm, two eggs → Two zygotes with different chromosomes → Same or opposite sex

**FIGURE 3.9** Identical (monozygotic) twins develop from the same fertilized egg. Fraternal (dizygotic) twins grow from two eggs fertilized by two different sperm.

gard, that resemblance probably reflects a genetic influence, although again we should consider prenatal influences. A low correlation with the adoptive parents can also be misleading. Recall from Chapter 2 what a correlation means: Two variables are highly correlated if we can use measurements of one to predict the other accurately. Imagine trying to predict which adopted children will become alcoholics by examining the alcohol habits of their adoptive parents. You can't make much of a prediction because adoption agencies almost never let alcoholics adopt children. But the lack of correlation between adopted child and adoptive parent in this case underestimates how big a difference the family environment could make (Stoolmiller, 1999).

What is my point? Simply: Much evidence supports a genetic contribution to variations in almost all behaviors, but we should try to evaluate the evidence behind any claim. Most of our evidence does not distinguish clearly between the effects of genetics and prenatal environment.

**FIGURE 3.10** All dizygotic (fraternal) twins develop with separate amniotes and therefore separate blood supplies. Most monozygotic (identical) twins develop with a single amniote and therefore always have the same blood supply, the same hormone levels, and so forth. Some of the similarities seen between monozygotic twins may be due to their similar prenatal environments.

a    b

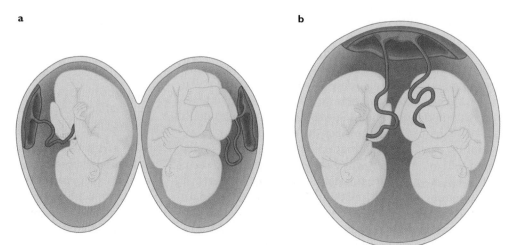

## CONCEPT CHECK

**4.** If our society changed so that an equally good environment was provided for all children, would the heritability of behaviors increase or decrease? (Check your answer on page 77.)

# Direct and Indirect Influences

Based on studies of twins and adopted children, researchers have found at least moderate heritability for a wide variety of behaviors and conditions, including some

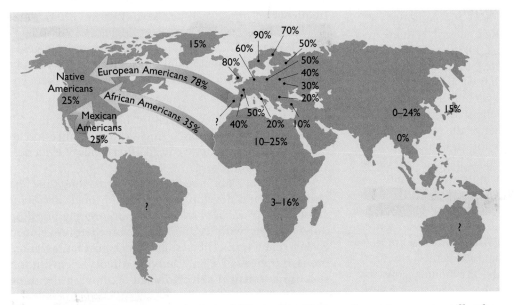

**FIGURE 3.11** Adult humans vary in their ability to digest lactose, the main sugar in milk. The numbers in this figure refer to the percentage of each population's adults that can easily digest lactose. In Asian countries and other locations where most adults cannot digest lactose, cooks seldom use dairy products. (Based on Flatz, 1987, and Rozin & Pelchat, 1988)

surprises. Adopted children have been shown to resemble their birth parents with regard to how much time they spend watching television (Plomin, Corley, DeFries, & Fulker, 1990). Monozygotic twins reared apart resemble each other in their religious devoutness (Waller, Kojetin, Bouchard, Lykken, & Tellegen, 1990). (Their religious affiliation, however, depends on the adoptive family. There is no gene for Presbyterian.) How could variations in such complicated behaviors depend on genetic differences? (Imagining a role for prenatal environment is even more difficult in these cases.)

Genes can influence behaviors indirectly, without necessarily altering brain structure or chemistry. For example, a gene that tends to make someone active and restless will probably interfere with behaviors that require sitting still, such as watching television or attending religious services. For another example, a gene that makes you tall will increase your probability of playing basketball, and if you spend more time playing basketball, you will probably spend less time playing chess, writing poetry, and so forth.

Or consider dietary choices: Most Asian adults, including Americans of Asian ancestry, seldom drink milk. Within other ethnic groups, some adults enjoy milk and others do not. Part of the variation in dairy consumption is under the control of genes that control the body's ability to digest *lactose,* the sugar in milk.

Almost all infants of any ethnic group can digest lactose. As they grow older, most Asian children and many non-Asian children lose the ability to digest it. (They lose that ability even if they drink milk frequently. The loss depends on genes.) They can still enjoy a little milk, and more readily enjoy cheese and yogurt and other easy-to-digest dairy products, but they can get gas and cramps from too much milk or ice cream (Flatz, 1987; Rozin & Pelchat, 1988). Figure 3.11 shows how the ability to digest dairy products varies from one part of the world to another. The point is that a gene can affect behavior by altering chemical reactions outside the brain itself.

Another result: A study of thousands of Australian twins found that monozygotic twins resembled each other more closely than dizygotic twins did with regard to age of first sexual intercourse (Dunne et al., 1997). How might a gene possibly influence age of starting sexual activity? First, obviously genes don't override the environment. If some of these twins had been adopted into a Bedouin Arab society, where boys and girls are not permitted to play together or to intermingle in any way before marriage, whatever genes influenced the Australians would have had no effect on their age of starting sexual activities. Still, how could a gene influence age at first sexual intercourse? We can imagine several possibilities:

- Genes influence rate of maturation: Those who begin puberty early will have more opportunities for early sex than those who enter it late.
- Genes influence secretion of sex hormones: Young people with higher hormonal levels probably have a stronger sex drive.
- Genes influence physical appearance: More attractive individuals have more opportunities for sexual activity. Some may refuse those opportunities, but the availability of those opportunities will have some influence, on the average.

Note that this third possibility implies that a gene can affect your behavior by influencing how other people react to you. This example underscores the difficulty of separating genetic influences from environmental influences. If you have a gene that affects your appearance and your appearance influences other people's behavior, then the gene has influenced your behavior. If you had an identical twin who was reared in a separate environment, both of you would no doubt share some similar behaviors, and those similarities would count as evidence for heritability of the behavior, even though the gene would have no influence except as a result of the environment (Gottlieb, 2000).

## Heredity and the Environment

You might sometimes hear someone say, "I hope researchers never conclude that . . . [fill in the blank: intelligence, depression, alcoholism, etc.] is under genetic control, because if it is, that means that we can't do anything about it." Nonsense. The fact that genetic differences have a major influence says nothing about whether an environmental intervention might change the results. For example, even if you have genes for straight hair, your health, your diet, and your grooming habits might cause you to have straight hair, curly hair, or no hair at all.

Here is another example: **Phenylketonuria (PKU)** is *an inherited condition that, if untreated, leads to mental retardation.* (The condition depends on a recessive gene. About 2% of people with European or Asian ancestry are heterozygous carriers for this gene, and the gene is absent in African populations.) People who are homozygous for PKU lack the chemical reactions that break down a substance called *phenylalanine,* a common constituent of proteins, into other chemicals. On an ordinary diet, an affected child will accumulate phenylalanine in the brain and become mentally retarded; however, an affected person who follows a diet low in phenylalanine can be intellectually normal. (It's a difficult diet that requires avoiding all proteins and substituting an expensive formula containing all the amino acids except phenylalanine.) Thus, an environmental intervention (here a controlled diet) can greatly influence a condition that is known to be under genetic control.

# Evolution and Behavior

Our genes are a product of evolution. Given what we know about genes, we can infer that evolution *must* occur and must have been occurring for as long as genetics and reproduction have been as they are today. The argument, based on the ideas of English naturalist Charles Darwin (1859), is as follows:

**1.** The genes that an organism inherits from its parents strongly influence its characteristics. In short, like begets like. Most children look somewhat like their parents, for example.

**2.** On occasion genetic variations will cause an organism to differ from its parents. Such variations may arise from recombinations of genes (some from one parent and some from the other) or from **mutations,** *random changes in the structure of genes.* Recombinations and mutations alter the appearance or activity of the organism. Most mutations are disadvantageous, although an occasional mutation will give an individual an advantage in coping with some situations.

**3.** If individuals with a certain gene or gene combination reproduce more successfully than others do, the genes that confer an advantage will spread. Over many generations the frequency of those genes will increase while the frequency of others will decrease (Weiner, 1994). Such *changes in the gene frequencies of a species* constitute **evolution.** We know that mutations sometimes occur in genes and that an occasional mutation can lead to greater success in reproduction, so we can logically deduce that evolution *must* occur.

This argument does not tell us, however, whether all forms of life evolved from a single common ancestor. To deal with that question, we need other kinds of evidence, such as the fossil record.[1]

Animal and plant breeders discovered a long time ago that they could develop new strains through **artificial selection,** or *selective breeding.* By purposefully breeding only animals with certain traits, breeders developed cocker spaniels, racehorses, and chickens that lay enormous numbers of eggs. Darwin's theory of evolution stated that **natural selection** can accomplish the same results as selective breeding. If, in nature, *individuals with certain genetically controlled characteristics reproduce more successfully than others do, then future generations will come to resemble those individuals more and more.*

Some people assume, mistakenly, that evolution means "the survival of the fittest," but what matters most in evolution is not survival but *reproduction* (Figure 3.12). Someone who lives 100 years without having a child has failed to spread his or her genes. Someone who has five healthy children before dying at age 30 is a big success in evolutionary terms.

A gene that increases someone's chance of surviving long enough to reproduce will be favored over a gene that causes death in infancy. But genes that have no influence on the individual's survival can also be favored. For example, a gene that makes an individual more successful at attracting mates would certainly be favored, as

---

[1] "What about creation science?" you may ask. Creation scientists argue that certain observations are hard to explain in terms of natural selection; however, no one has yet found evidence supporting the alternative view that life began suddenly in more or less its present form. It is fair to admit that biologists do not know everything about how evolution operates, but the points that biologists dispute are the details, not the fundamental concept of natural selection.

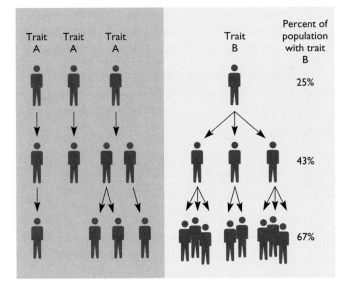

**FIGURE 3.12** What's important for evolution is reproduction, not survival. Here the population starts with three people carrying trait A and one with trait B. The person with B and his or her descendants produce more children, on the average, than people with A do. Consequently, the genes controlling trait B will increase in prevalence from one generation to the next.

would a gene that makes someone more successful at protecting his or her offspring or other close relatives.

## CONCEPT CHECK

5. Infertile worker bees are sisters of the queen bee, which lays all the eggs. In comparison with species in which all individuals are fertile, would you expect worker bees to be more likely or less likely to risk their lives to defend their sister? Would you expect a queen bee to be more or less likely than a worker bee to risk her life?
(Check your answers on page 77.)

Occasionally, people say something like "every generation our little toes get smaller and smaller because we don't use them," or "through evolution, we will gradually get rid of the human appendix because we don't need it." Such statements reflect a misunderstanding. We do not add, change, or lose genes because of the way we use some part of the body. The only way that people could evolve a smaller little toe

would be if people with genes for smaller than average little toes reproduced more than other people.

Another common misunderstanding: Evolution does not necessarily mean long-term improvement. (Darwin himself didn't like the term *evolution* and seldom used it, because it implied improvement. He preferred "descent with modification.") A gene will spread within a population if those who currently have that gene reproduce more than others do. The result could be a population that succeeds well in its current environment but is ill-adapted when the environment changes.

Evolution adapts the behavior of an animal as well as its anatomy to its way of life. One classic example is the mating behavior of the kittiwake, a member of the gull family (Tinbergen, 1958). Kittiwakes, unlike other gulls, nest on narrow ledges of steep cliffs (Figure 3.13). Because there are only so many suitable ledges, kittiwakes fight ferociously to claim territories. By contrast, herring gulls, which nest on the ground, rarely fight over territory, because for them one nesting site is about as good as any other. Kittiwakes use mud to build a hard nest with a barrier to prevent their eggs from rolling off the ledge. Herring gulls make no such effort. Kittiwakes ignore passing eagles and hawks, which cannot land on the kittiwakes' tiny ledges; herring gulls, by contrast, are terrorized by predatory birds. When kittiwake chicks hatch, they remain virtually motionless until they are old enough to fly. The advantage of this behavioral tendency is clear: A chick that takes even a step or two may fall off the ledge. Herring gull chicks, in contrast, begin to wander out of their nest long before they can fly.

Each of these kittiwake behaviors is well adapted to life on a narrow ledge. But have these behaviors been built into the animal by evolution, or are they learned anew by each individual? In the rare cases when kittiwakes nest on the ground, the chicks remain motionless anyway, even though they are in no danger of falling. If the egg of a herring gull is placed in a kittiwake's nest, the kittiwakes accept the foreign egg and care for the chick after it hatches. But the chick invariably takes a few steps and falls to its death. Evidently, a chick's tendency to move or not is unlearned and presumably a product of evolutionary influences. On the other hand, we don't really know why kittiwakes ignore passing eagles and hawks. Maybe they have evolved fearlessness toward these predators, but maybe they have simply learned that they are safe on their ledges.

**FIGURE 3.13** The nesting behavior of kittiwakes is superbly adapted for their survival. For example, the parents build a mud barrier on the edge of the nest, and the young remain motionless until they are able to fly.

# Sociobiology

**Sociobiology** is *a field that tries to relate the social behaviors of a species to its biology, particularly to its evolutionary history.* According to sociobiologists, an animal interacts with others of its species in a particular way because similar behaviors in past generations have increased the probability of survival and mating. That is, individuals with a genetic tendency to engage in these social behaviors passed on their genes; individuals that behaved another way were less successful at passing on their genes.

## Animal Examples

Sociobiologists try to understand how various social behaviors may have helped animals to survive and reproduce. Here are two examples:

• Lions generally live in prides made up of one adult male, several adult females, and their young. If a new male succeeds in driving off the old male, he is likely to kill all the young. Why? Female lions are not sexually receptive while they are nursing their young. By killing the young, the new male brings the females into sexual receptivity and increases the likelihood of spreading his genes (E. O. Wilson, 1975).

• In a species of bird called reed buntings, a male–female pair will stick together fairly closely, although many females also occasionally mate with neighboring males. Males help with incubating the eggs and taking care of the young; however, some males help more than others do. Researchers have found that females that engage in a large number of "extramarital affairs" with neighboring males elicit the least help from their male partners (Dixon, Ross, O'Malley, & Burke, 1994). One interpretation is that a male vigorously helps raise the young only if he is likely to be their father. An alternative (more feminist) possibility is that a female is loyal to a male only if he helps with the young. In either case we do not assume that the birds understand why they behave as they do. It is just that those who behaved this way in previous generations passed on their genes, and now their descendants behave the same way.

## Human Sociobiology

The capacity for human social behavior is no doubt the product of our evolutionary history, but any specific behavior is also the product of our experiences within a culture. Consider one example and note the difficulty of drawing a conclusion: Men are more likely than women are to seek multiple sexual partners. A sociobiological interpretation is that a man who impregnates several women is spreading his genes, whereas a woman with multiple sexual partners can't get pregnant more often than a woman with one partner. Moreover, a woman with multiple partners might have trouble getting any

one of them to help her rear the children. Therefore, the sociobiologists say, we may have evolved some sex-limited genes that increase males' interest or decrease females' interest in multiple partners (Buss, 1994).

All of this is plausible, and yet there are some problems. One is that we know little about the life of ancient humans. Maybe a woman with multiple sex partners would get a little help from all of them, after all. A second problem is the difficulty of separating evolutionary influences from learned influences. In cultures throughout the world, some men (not all) seek multiple sex partners, whereas fewer women do, but that cross-cultural similarity doesn't necessarily indicate an evolved genetic influence. For example, people in all the world's cultures also believe that two plus two equals four, but we don't conclude that people have a gene for two plus two. We shall return to this issue in the section in Chapter 14.

## IN CLOSING
## Genes, Evolution, and Behavior

Many people object to the whole idea of behavior genetics. "How could a simple molecule such as a gene or a protein control something as complex as mood, extraversion, sexual orientation, intelligence, or criminality?" The reply is, consider an even simpler molecule: Think what enormous effects the alcohol molecule can have. The analogy between genes and alcohol illustrates an important point: Alcohol molecules, even in large quantities, do not *force* anyone to stagger, say stupid things, commit acts of violence, or anything else. The behavior depends on everything else in the nervous system on which the alcohol is acting. Similarly, no gene by itself forces any behavior. The actual outcome depends on a multitude of influences, including past experiences, current circumstances, and other genes. To say that genes influence behaviors is not at all to say that they determine the behaviors or that the environment is unimportant. In fact, understanding how the genes exert their effects may give researchers their best clue about which environmental interventions might be effective for modifying the behavior.

## Summary

• *Genes.* Genes, which are segments of chromosomes, control heredity. Because chromosomes come in pairs, every person has two of each gene, one received from the father and one from the mother. The sex chromosomes are an exception; each male has one Y chromosome and one unpaired X chromosome. (page 68)

• *Dominant and recessive genes.* A dominant gene exerts its effects even in people who have only one dominant gene, but people must have two of a recessive gene, one on each chromosome, to show its effects. (page 68)

- *Sex-linked and sex-limited genes.* Genes on the X chromosome are sex linked. A sex-linked recessive gene will show its effects more frequently in males than in females. A sex-limited gene is present in both sexes, but it exerts its effects more strongly in one than in the other. (page 70)
- *Identifying and localizing genes.* Researchers have located the gene responsible for Huntington's disease, and they are trying to identify and localize as many other human genes as possible. Identifying people's behavioral tendencies and risks by examining their genes offers the potential for significant benefits and also for possible misuse. (page 71)
- *Evidence for genetic influences.* Researchers determine the contribution of genes to human behavior by studying whether monozygotic twins resemble each other more than dizygotic twins do, by comparing monozygotic twins reared in separate environments, and by examining how adopted children resemble their biological parents and their adoptive parents. However, none of these lines of evidence fully separates genetic influences from prenatal environment's influences. (page 71)
- *How genes affect behavior.* Genes apparently affect an amazing variety of behaviors, often indirectly, by influencing some aspect of the body that in turn influences behavior. (page 73)
- *Influence of the environment on gene expression.* It is possible for a behavior that reflects a genetic influence to be highly modified by a change in the environment. (page 74)
- *Evolution.* Evolution by natural selection is a logical necessity, given the principles of heredity and the fact that individuals with certain genes leave more offspring than do individuals with other genes. (page 74)
- *Sociobiology.* Sociobiologists try to explain social behaviors in terms of the survival and reproductive advantages of those behaviors. To interpret human behavior in such terms, one must carefully distinguish behaviors that are part of human nature from those that are highly dependent on culture and individual experience. In many cases we simply do not know enough yet to make that distinction. (page 76)

## Answers to Concept Checks

1. It is impossible to say whether you are homozygous or heterozygous for the tongue-curling gene. Because it is a dominant gene, it produces the same effects in both the homozygous and heterozygous conditions. Your sister, however, must be homozygous for the noncurling gene. (page 70)
2. Because both of the parents must be homozygous for the inability to curl their tongues, they can transmit only "noncurler" genes, and their children will be noncurlers also. (page 70)
3. The woman will pass a dominant gene for normal color vision to all her children, so they will all have normal color vision. The man will pass a gene for deficient color vision on his X chromosome; the daughters will therefore be carriers for colorblindness. (page 71)
4. If all children had equally supportive environments, the heritability of behaviors would *increase*. Remember, heritability refers to how much of the difference among people is due to hereditary variation. If the environment is practically the same for all, then environmental variation cannot account for much of the variation in behavior. Whatever behavioral variation still occurs would be due mostly to hereditary variation. (Note one implication: Any estimate of heritability applies only to a given population. In another population the heritability could be much different.) (page 73)
5. Because the infertile worker bees cannot reproduce, the only way they can pass on their genes is by helping the queen bee. Consequently, they will sacrifice their own lives to defend the queen. They will also risk their lives to defend other workers in the hive because these workers also try to defend the queen. The queen, however, will do little to defend a worker because doing so would not increase her probability of reproducing. (page 75)

# Neurons and Behavior

*Can we explain our experiences and our behavior in terms of the actions of single cells in the nervous system?*

One highly productive strategy in science is *reductionism*—the attempt to explain complex phenomena by reducing them to combinations of simpler components. Biologists explain breathing, blood circulation, and metabolism in terms of chemical reactions and physical forces. Chemists explain chemical reactions in terms of the properties of the elements and their atoms. Physicists explain the properties of the atom in terms of a few fundamental forces.

How well does reductionism apply to psychology? Can we explain human behavior and experience in terms of chemical and electrical events in the brain? The only way to find out is to try. Here we explore efforts to explain behavior based on single cells of the nervous system.

## Nervous System Cells

You experience your "self" as a single entity that senses, thinks, and remembers. And yet neuroscientists have found that the nervous system responsible for your experiences consists of an enormous number of separate cells. The brain processes information in **neurons** (NOO-rons), or *nerve cells*. Many of the neurons in the human nervous system are extremely small; the best current estimate is that the nervous system contains nearly 100 billion neurons (R. W. Williams & Herrup, 1988), as shown in Figure 3.14. The nervous system also contains another kind of cells called **glia** (GLEE-uh), *which support the neurons in many ways such as by insulating them and by removing waste products*. The glia are about one tenth of the size of neurons but about 10 times more numerous.

Until the early 1900s, many researchers thought it likely that all the neurons physically merged so that the tip of each neuron actually joined the next neuron. We now know that each neuron remains separate from the others. How do so many separate neurons and glia combine forces to produce the single stream of experiences that is you? The secret is communication. Each neuron receives information and transmits it to other cells by conducting electrochemical impulses. Sensory neurons carry information from the sense organs to the central nervous system; neurons there process the information,

compare it to past information, and exchange information with other neurons until ultimately some of them send commands to the muscles and glands. A rapid exchange of information enables about 100 billion neurons to produce a single functioning system.

To understand our nervous system, we must first understand the properties of both the individual neurons and the connections among them. Neurons have a variety of shapes, depending on whether they receive information from a few sources or from many and whether they send impulses over a short distance or over a long distance (Figure 3.15).

A neuron consists of three parts—a cell body, dendrites, and an axon (Figure 3.16). The **cell body** *contains the nucleus* of the cell. The **dendrites** (from a Greek word meaning "tree") are *widely branching structures that receive transmissions from other neurons*. The **axon** is a *single, long, thin, straight fiber with branches near its tip*. Some vertebrate axons are covered with *myelin*, an insulating sheath that speeds up the transmission of impulses along an axon. As a rule an axon transmits information to other cells, and the dendrites or cell body of each cell receives that information. That information can be either excitatory or inhibitory; that is, it can increase or decrease the

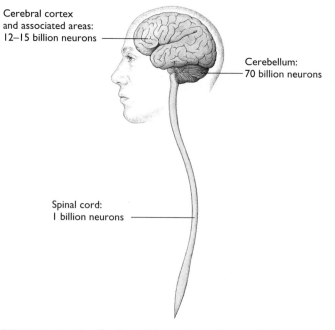

Cerebral cortex
and associated areas:
12–15 billion neurons

Cerebellum:
70 billion neurons

Spinal cord:
1 billion neurons

**FIGURE 3.14** Distribution of the estimated 83–86 billion neurons in the adult human central nervous system. (Based on data of R. W. Williams & Herrup, 1988)

**FIGURE 3.15** Neurons, which vary enormously in shape, consist of a cell body and branched attachments called axons (coded blue for easy identification) and dendrites. The neurons in (a) and (b) receive input from many sources, the neuron in (c) from only a few sources, and the neuron in (d) from an intermediate number of sources. The sensory neurons (e), carry messages from sensory receptors to the brain or spinal cord. Inset: Electron micrograph showing cell bodies in brown and axons and dendrites in green. The color was added artificially; electron micrographs are made by reflecting electron beams, not light, and therefore they show no color.

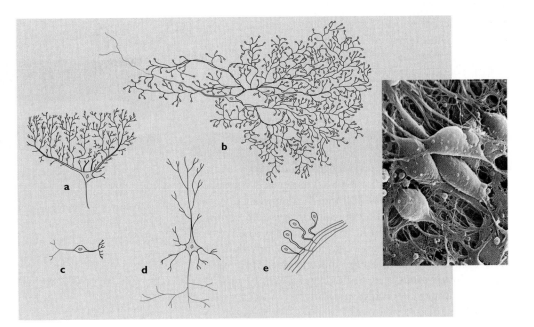

probability that the next cell will send a message of its own. Inhibitory messages are important for many purposes. For example, during a period of painful stimulation, your brain has mechanisms to inhibit further sensation of pain.

At one time researchers believed that neurons had a fixed anatomy. We now know that it is constantly growing new branches to its dendrites and axons and losing old branches. Those changes are particularly prominent in animals (including people) that have had

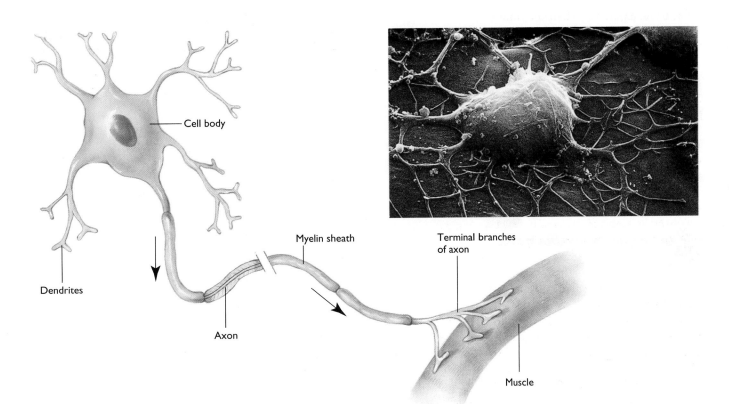

**FIGURE 3.16** The generalized structure of a motor neuron shows the dendrites, the branching structures that receive transmissions from other neurons, and the axon, a single, long, thin, straight fiber with branches near its tip. Axons range in length from 1 millimeter to more than 1 meter and carry information to other cells. Inset: A photomicrograph of a neuron.

new and challenging experiences (Greenough, 1975; Jacobs, Schall, & Scheibel, 1993; Woolf, Zinnerman, & Johnson, 1999).

Until recently researchers also believed that all neurons form before birth or early after it, so that beyond early infancy one could only lose neurons and never gain new ones. That belief was not entirely correct. Nearly all neurons form very early in life, but in a few brain areas, it is possible for *undifferentiated cells called* **stem cells** to develop into additional neurons, even in humans (Eriksson et al., 1998). That process is stimulated after certain kinds of brain damage, so the development of new neurons may sometimes help compensate for the loss of old ones (Magavi, Leavitt, & Macklis, 2000). It is worth emphasizing, however, that new neurons form slowly, sporadically, and only in certain brain areas and under certain conditions. It is not a simple matter like growing new skin cells or blood cells.

## The Action Potential

Imagine what would happen if axons conveyed information by electrical conduction: Because axons are made of poorly conducting materials, electrical impulses would weaken rapidly as they traveled toward your brain. The farther from your brain some information started, the less you would feel it. Short people would feel a pinch on their toes more intensely than tall people would . . . if indeed either felt their toes at all.

Instead, axons convey information by a special combination of electrical and chemical processes called an **action potential,** *an excitation that travels along an axon at a constant strength, no matter how far it must travel.* An action potential is a yes/no or on/off message, like a standard light switch. (Most switches don't let you make the light dimmer or brighter. It's either on or off.) This principle is known as the *all-or-none law.*

The advantage of an action potential over simple electrical conduction is that action potentials from distant places like your toes reach your brain at full strength. The disadvantage is that action potentials are slower than electrical conduction. Your knowledge of what is happening to your toes is always about a twentieth of a second out of date. Fortunately, that delay is seldom a problem.

Here is a quick outline of how the action potential works:

**1.** When the axon is not stimulated, its membrane has a **resting potential**, *an electrical polarization across the membrane (or covering) of an axon, with a negative charge inside the axon.* A typical value is -70 millivolts on the inside relative to the outside. The resting potential is maintained by a mechanism called the sodium-potassium pump, which pumps sodium ions (with a +1 charge) out of the axon while pumping into it a smaller number of potassium ions (also with a +1 charge). The result is that the outside has more positive charges (see Figure 3.17). Sodium is concentrated mostly outside the cell and potassium inside, but they can cross back and forth only at special "gates," and those gates are closed.

**2.** Excitation of some portion of the membrane (normally because of a message from another cell) opens some sodium gates on the membrane to allow sodium ions to enter the axon (Figure 3.18). As they enter they drive the charge inside the cell to a slightly positive charge. This sudden, large increase in positive charge within the axon is the action potential.

**3.** After the sodium gates have been open for barely an instant, they snap shut. Then potassium gates open to allow potassium ions to leave the axon. The potassium ions each carry a positive charge, so their exit drives the inside of the axon back to its original resting potential (Figure 3.19b).

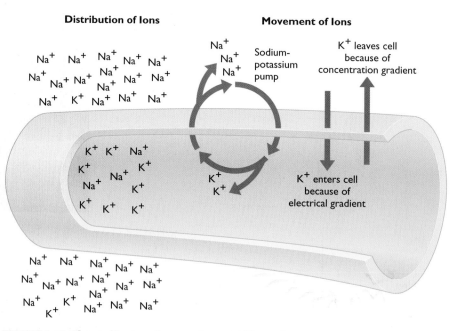

**FIGURE 3.17 The sodium and potassium gradients for a resting membrane** Sodium ions are concentrated outside the neuron; potassium ions are concentrated inside. However, because the body has far more sodium than potassium, the total number of positive charges is greater outside the cell than inside. Protein and chloride ions (not shown) bear negative charges inside the cell. At rest, very few sodium ions cross the membrane except by the sodium-potassium pump. Potassium tends to flow into the cell because of an electrical gradient, and tends to flow out because of the concentration gradient.

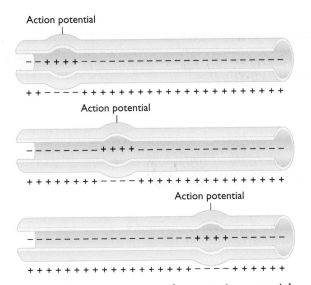

FIGURE 3.18 Ion movements conduct an action potential along an axon. At each point along the membrane, sodium ions enter the axon and alter the distribution of positive and negative charges. As each point along the membrane returns to its original state, the action potential flows to the next point.

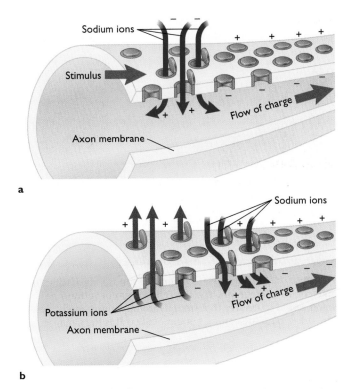

FIGURE 3.19 (a) During an action potential, sodium gates in the neuron membrane open, and sodium ions enter the axon, bringing a positive charge with them. (b) After an action potential occurs at one point along the axon, the sodium gates close at that point and open at the next point along the axon. When the sodium gates close, potassium gates open, and potassium ions flow out of the axon, carrying a positive charge with them. (Modified from Starr & Taggart, 1992)

**4.** Eventually, the sodium-potassium pump removes the invading sodium ions and recaptures the escaping potassium ions.

You will recall that the axon does not conduct like an electrical wire. The action potential travels down the axon like a wave of energy, and the stimulation at each point excites the next point along the axon. You could imagine it like a fire burning along a string: The fire at each point ignites the next point, which in turn ignites the next point. That is, after sodium ions cross at one point along an axon, some of them diffuse to the neighboring portion of the axon and thereby excite that part of the membrane enough to open its own sodium gates. Therefore, the action potential spreads to this next area and so on down the axon, as shown in Figure 3.19. In this manner the action potential remains equally strong all the way to the end of the axon.

Now all of this information is clearly important to investigators of the nervous system, but why should a psychology student care? First, it explains why sensations on points on your fingers and toes do not fade away by the time they reach your brain. Second, an understanding of action potentials is one step toward understanding the communication between one neuron and the next. Third, certain drugs operate by blocking action potentials. For example, anesthetic drugs (e.g., Novocain) silence neurons by clogging the sodium gates. When your dentist drills a tooth, the receptors in your tooth send out the message "Pain! Pain! Pain!" But that message does not get through to the brain, because a shot of Novocain has blocked the sodium gates and thereby halted the sensory messages.

## C ONCEPT CHECK

**6.** If a mouse and a giraffe both get pinched on the toes at the same time, which will respond faster? Why? (Check your answer on page 86.)

## Synapses

Communication between one neuron and the next is not like transmission along an axon. At a **synapse** (SIN-aps), *the specialized junction between one neuron and another* (Figure 3.20), *a neuron releases a chemical that either excites or inhibits the next neuron.* That is, the chemical can make the next neuron either more or less likely to produce an action potential. The events at synapses are central to everything that your brain does because the synapses are where each neuron receives information.

A typical axon has several branches, each ending with a little bulge called a *presynaptic ending,* or **terminal bouton**

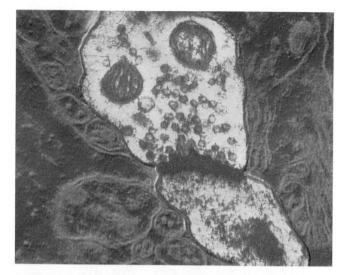

**FIGURE 3.20** This synapse is magnified thousands of times in an electron micrograph. The top cell (shown in yellow) has small round structures that store neurotransmitter molecules. The thick, dark area at the bottom of the cell is the synapse.

(or **button**), as shown in Figure 3.21. When an action potential reaches the terminal bouton, it causes the release of molecules of a **neurotransmitter,** *a chemical that has been stored in the neuron and that can activate receptors of other neurons* (Figure 3.21). Different neurons use different chemicals as their neurotransmitters, but each neuron releases the same chemical or combination of chemicals from all branches of its axon (Eccles, 1986). The neurotransmitter molecules diffuse across a narrow gap to the **postsynaptic neuron,** *the neuron on the receiving end of the synapse.* There the neurotransmitter molecules attach to receptors on the neuron's dendrites or cell body (or for special purposes on the tip of its axon). The neural communication process is summarized in Figure 3.22.

Depending on the neurotransmitter and the type of receptor, the attachment can either excite or inhibit the postsynaptic neuron. That neuron produces an action

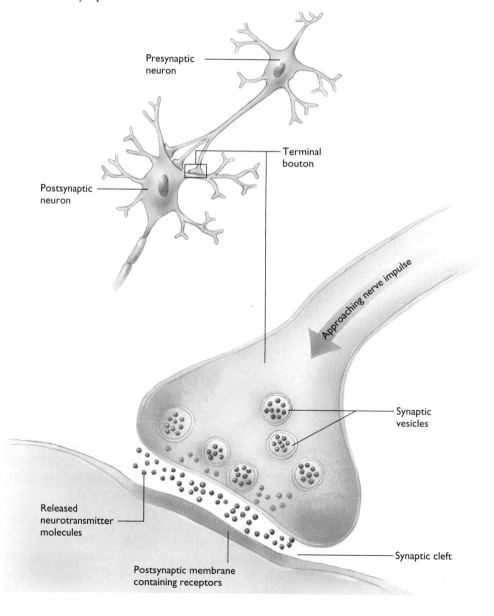

**FIGURE 3.21** The synapse is the junction of the presynaptic (message-sending) cell and the postsynaptic (message-receiving) cell. At the end of the presynaptic axon is the terminal bouton (or button), which contains many molecules of the neurotransmitter, ready for release.

Presynaptic neuron

Postsynaptic neuron

Terminal bouton

Approaching nerve impulse

Synaptic vesicles

Released neurotransmitter molecules

Postsynaptic membrane containing receptors

Synaptic cleft

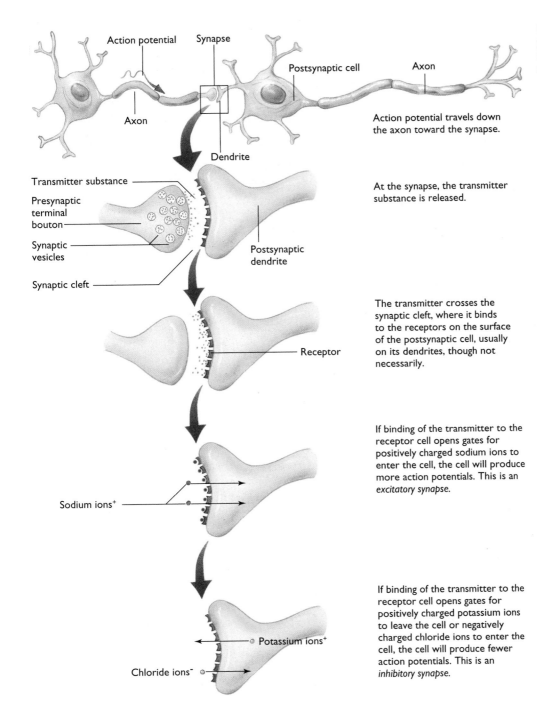

**FIGURE 3.22** The complex process of neural communication actually takes only 1–2 milliseconds.

Action potential travels down the axon toward the synapse.

At the synapse, the transmitter substance is released.

The transmitter crosses the synaptic cleft, where it binds to the receptors on the surface of the postsynaptic cell, usually on its dendrites, though not necessarily.

If binding of the transmitter to the receptor cell opens gates for positively charged sodium ions to enter the cell, the cell will produce more action potentials. This is an *excitatory synapse.*

If binding of the transmitter to the receptor cell opens gates for positively charged potassium ions to leave the cell or negatively charged chloride ions to enter the cell, the cell will produce fewer action potentials. This is an *inhibitory synapse.*

potential of its own if the total amount of excitation at any moment outweighs the total amount of inhibition, coming from a variety of synapses. The process resembles making a decision: When you are trying to decide whether to do something, you weigh all the pluses and minuses and act if the pluses are stronger.

Inhibition is not the absence of excitation; it is like stepping on the brakes. For example, when a pinch on your foot causes you to raise it, thus contracting one set of muscles, inhibitory synapses in your spinal cord block activity in the muscles that would move your leg the opposite direction. Those inhibitory synapses prevent mes-

sages from trying to raise your leg and extend it at the same time.

After a neurotransmitter excites or inhibits a receptor, it separates from the receptor, terminating the message. From that point on, the fate of the receptor molecule varies. It could become reabsorbed by the axon that released it (through a process called *reuptake)*; it could diffuse away, get metabolized, and eventually show up in the blood or urine; or it could bounce around for a moment, return to the postsynaptic receptor, and reexcite it. Many antidepressant drugs act by blocking reuptake and therefore prolonging the effects of one transmitter or another.

# CONCEPT CHECK

7. Under some conditions the axons and dendrites of a neuron increase their branching. How will that affect the number of synapses present?
8. Dopamine is a neurotransmitter that inhibits postsynaptic neurons. If a drug were injected to prevent dopamine from attaching to its receptors, what would happen to the postsynaptic neuron? (Check your answers on page 86.)

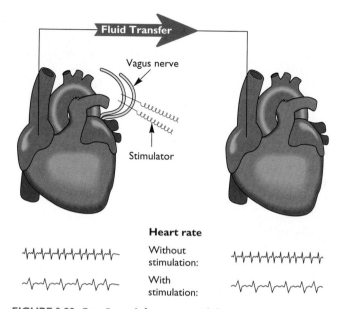

**FIGURE 3.23** Otto Loewi demonstrated that axons release chemicals that can affect other cells. Using a frog, he electrically stimulated a set of axons known to decrease the heart rate. Then he collected some fluid from around the heart and transferred it to the surface of another frog's heart. When that heart slowed its beat, Loewi concluded that the axons in the first heart must have released a chemical that slows the heart rate.

**WHAT'S THE EVIDENCE?**
*Neurons Communicate Chemically*

You have just learned that neurons communicate by releasing chemicals at synapses. Perhaps you are perfectly content to take my word for it and go on with something else. Still, it is advisable to pause and contemplate the evidence responsible for an important conclusion.

Today, neuroscientists have a wealth of evidence that neurons release chemicals at synapses. They can radioactively trace where chemicals go and what happens when they get there; they also can inject purified chemicals at a synapse and use extremely fine electrodes to measure the response of the postsynaptic neuron. But scientists of the 1920s had no fancy equipment, and still they managed to establish that neurons communicate with chemicals. Otto Loewi conducted a simple, clever experiment, as he later described in his autobiography (Loewi, 1960).

**HYPOTHESIS** If a neuron releases chemicals, an investigator should be able to collect some of those chemicals, transfer them from one animal to another, and thereby get the second animal to do what the first animal had been doing. Loewi had no method of collecting chemicals released within the brain itself, so he worked with axons communicating with the heart muscle. (The communication between a neuron and a muscle is similar to that between neurons.)

**METHOD** Loewi began by electrically stimulating some axons connected to a frog's heart. These particular axons slowed down the heart rate. As he continued to stimulate those axons, he collected some of the fluid on and around that heart and transferred it to the heart of a second frog.

**RESULTS** When Loewi transferred the fluid from the first frog's heart, the second frog's heart rate also slowed (Figure 3.23).

**INTERPRETATION** Evidently, the stimulated axons had released a chemical that slows heart rate. At least in this case, neurons send messages by releasing chemicals.

Loewi eventually won a Nobel Prize in physiology for this and related experiments. Even outstanding experiments have limitations, however. In this case the main limitation was the uncertainty about whether the conclusion applied only to frog hearts or whether it applied to all communication by neurons. Answering *that* question required enormous efforts and much more elaborate equipment. (The answer is that *most* communication by neurons depends on chemicals; a few synapses use electrical communication.)

# Neurotransmitters and Behavior

The use of drugs that affect neurotransmitters has already revolutionized psychiatry, and understanding the role of those neurotransmitters could potentially revolutionize our theoretical understanding of psychology. The brain has dozens of neurotransmitters, and each activates many kinds of receptors. For example, serotonin activates at least 15 kinds, probably more (Roth, Lopez, & Kroeze, 2000). Each receptor type controls somewhat different aspects of behavior. For example, serotonin type 3 receptors are responsible for nausea, and this fact makes it possible to develop drugs that block nausea without much effect on any other aspect of behavior (Perez, 1995).

Any drug that increases or decreases the activity of a particular type of receptor produces specific effects on behavior. One is tempted, therefore, to guess that any unusual behavior is due to an excess or deficiency of some

■   Former boxing champion Muhammad Ali developed symptoms of Parkinson's disease, presumably because of blows to his head.

kind of synaptic activity. One example that apparently fits this hypothesis is **Parkinson's disease,** *a condition that affects about 1% of people over the age of 50. The main symptoms are difficulty in initiating voluntary movement, slowness of movement, tremors, rigidity, and depressed mood.* All of these symptoms can be traced to a gradual decay of one pathway of axons that release the neurotransmitter **dopamine** (DOPE-uh-meen), *a chemical that promotes activity levels and facilitates movement* (Figure 3.24). One common treatment is the drug L-dopa, which enters the brain, where neurons convert it into dopamine. The effective-

ness of this treatment for most people with mild cases of Parkinson's disease supports our beliefs about the link between the transmitter and the disease.

An example that shows more of the difficulty of interpreting results is **attention deficit disorder (ADD),** *a condition marked by impulsive behavior and short attention span.* ADD is usually treated with amphetamine or methylphenidate (Ritalin), and researchers know how those drugs work: Both drugs prevent presynaptic neurons from reabsorbing (and thus recycling) the neurotransmitters dopamine and serotonin after releasing them (Volkow et al., 1998). Amphetamine also increases the release of dopamine (Giros, Jaber, Jones, Wightman, & Caron, 1996). So both drugs prolong the activity of dopamine and serotonin at their synaptic receptors. It might seem, therefore, that the underlying problem in ADD is either a deficiency of those transmitters or an abnormality of their receptors. However, most people with ADD have normal dopamine release and receptors, and many people with abnormal dopamine receptors do not have ADD (Faraone & Biederman, 1998; Swanson et al., 2000). Perhaps understanding the drugs that relieve the problem doesn't tell us what caused the problem. One study found that methylphenidate improves attention even for normal healthy children, who presumably have normal dopamine activity (Zahn, Rapoport, & Thompson, 1980).

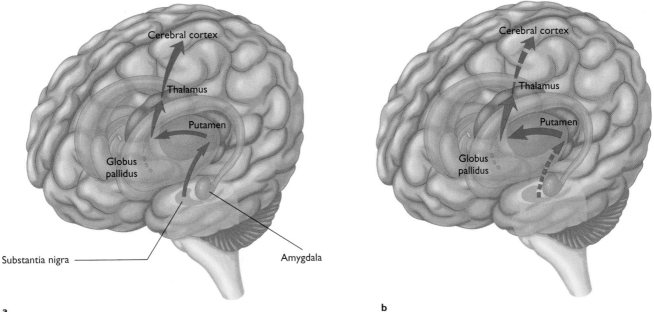

a                                                                                                  b

**FIGURE 3.24** With Parkinson's disease, axons from the substantia nigra gradually die. (a) Normal brain. (b) Brain of person with Parkinson's disease. Green = excitatory path; red = inhibitory.

As we shall see in Chapter 16, drugs that alleviate depression and schizophrenia also act on dopamine and serotonin synapses, but again we are not yet sure that the cause of depression or schizophrenia has any close relationship to either transmitter. My overall point is *not* that the transmitters are irrelevant to behavioral disorders—far from it—but just that each transmitter is part of a complex overall system. We still have much to learn about the relationship between the elements of the nervous system and their behavioral outcomes.

## CONCEPT CHECK

9. People suffering from certain disorders are given haloperidol, a drug that blocks activity at dopamine synapses. How would haloperidol affect someone with Parkinson's disease? (Check your answer on this page.)

### IN CLOSING

## Neurons And Behavior

Here is an imperfect analogy for the nervous system: At U.S. high school or college football games, one section of the stands is sometimes set aside for fans holding large cards. When their leader calls out a signal, such as "16," each of them holds up the appropriate card. If you were one of the fans, your card 16 might be all red, providing no clue about what the overall message might be. But the pattern provided by a few hundred fans might spell "Go, State." The message of neurons is a little like that because the activity or inactivity of any cell or synapse is part of a large overall pattern. The analogy is imperfect because the card message tells something to viewers on the other side of the field, whereas nothing reads the message of the neurons, except for the neurons themselves. However, the analogy works in some regards: Each neuron conveys a message that means nothing by itself but becomes part of an important message in context. Also, a mistake by one cardholder or one neuron is not too costly, and the overall message still gets through. Only a systematic mistake by a whole group of individuals (neurons) could destroy or garble the message.

## Summary

- *Neuron structure.* A neuron, or nerve cell, consists of a cell body, dendrites, and an axon. The axon conveys information to other neurons. (page 78)
- *The action potential.* Information is conveyed along an axon by an action potential, which is regenerated without loss of strength at each point along the axon. (page 80)
- *Mechanism of the action potential.* An action potential depends on the entry of sodium into the axon. Anything that blocks this flow will block the action potential. (page 80)
- *How neurons communicate.* A neuron communicates with another neuron by releasing a chemical called a neurotransmitter at a specialized junction called a synapse. A neurotransmitter can either excite or inhibit the next neuron. (page 81)
- *Neurotransmitters and behavioral disorders.* An excess or a deficit of a particular neurotransmitter can lead to abnormal behavior, such as that exhibited by people suffering from Parkinson's disease. However, understanding what happens at some kind of synapse is far removed from understanding the entire behavior pattern. (page 84)

## Answers to Concept Checks

6. The mouse will react faster because the action potentials have a shorter distance to travel in the mouse's nervous system than in the giraffe's. (page 81)
7. Increased branching of the axons and dendrites will increase the number of synapses. (page 84)
8. Under the influence of a drug that prevents dopamine from attaching to its receptors, the postsynaptic neuron will receive less inhibition than usual. If we presume that the neuron continues to receive a certain amount of excitation, it will then produce action potentials more frequently than usual. (page 84)
9. Haloperidol would increase the severity of Parkinson's disease. In fact, large doses of haloperidol can induce symptoms of Parkinson's disease in anyone. (page 86)

# The Nervous System and Behavior

*Does a person who loses part of the brain also lose part of the mind?*

Why should psychologists care about the organization of the brain and the effects of brain damage? There are both practical and theoretical reasons.

A practical reason is that they need to distinguish between people who act strangely because of bad experiences and people who act strangely because of a brain disorder. To do so, psychologists need to recognize possible symptoms of brain damage.

A theoretical reason is that the study of brain damage helps to explain the organization of behavior. In some manner behavior must be made up of component parts,

but what are they? Is behavior composed of ideas? Sensations? Movements? Personality characteristics? And how do the various components combine to produce the overall pattern? One way to answer such questions is to examine brain-damaged people—people who have lost parts of their mental processing.

Another theoretical reason is that studying the brain sheds light on the mind-brain relationship discussed in Chapter 1. According to brain researchers, the mind *is* brain activity. To take away part of your brain is to take away part of your mind. All the examples in this module are relevant to that position.

## The Major Divisions of the Nervous System

Psychologists and biologists distinguish between the central nervous system and the peripheral nervous system. The **central nervous system** consists of *the brain and the spinal cord*. The central nervous system communicates with the rest of the body by the **peripheral nervous system,** which is composed of *bundles of axons between the spinal cord and the rest of the body*. The *peripheral nerves that communicate with the skin and muscles* are collectively called the **somatic nervous system.** Those that control the heart, stomach, and other organs are called the *autonomic nervous system*. Figure 3.25 summarizes these major divisions of the nervous system.

Early in its embryological development, the central nervous system of vertebrates, including humans, is a tube with three lumps, as shown in Figure 3.26. Those lumps develop into the *forebrain*, the *midbrain*, and the *hindbrain*; the rest of

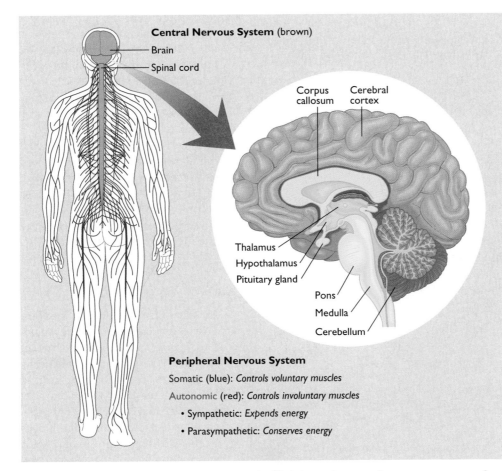

**Central Nervous System** (brown)
- Brain
- Spinal cord

Corpus callosum
Cerebral cortex

Thalamus
Hypothalamus
Pituitary gland

Pons
Medulla
Cerebellum

**Peripheral Nervous System**

Somatic (blue): *Controls voluntary muscles*

Autonomic (red): *Controls involuntary muscles*
- Sympathetic: *Expends energy*
- Parasympathetic: *Conserves energy*

**FIGURE 3.25** The nervous system has two major divisions: the central nervous system and the peripheral nervous system. Each of these has major subdivisions, as shown.

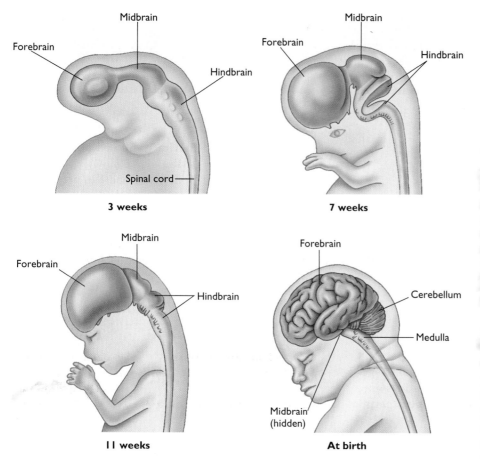

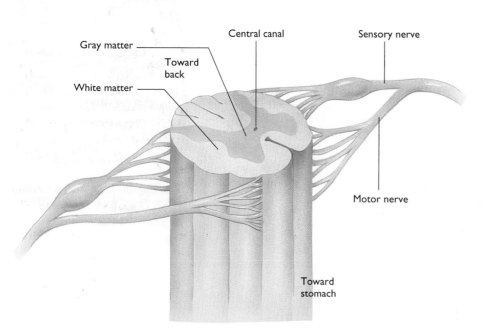

**3 weeks**

**7 weeks**

**11 weeks**

**At birth**

**FIGURE 3.26** The human brain begins development as three lumps. By birth the forebrain has grown much larger than either the midbrain or the hindbrain, although all three structures perform essential functions.

**FIGURE 3.27** The spinal cord receives sensory information from all parts of the body except the head. Motor nerves in the spinal cord send messages to control the muscles and glands.

the tube develops into the spinal cord. The forebrain, which contains the cerebral cortex and other structures, is by far the dominant portion of the brain in mammals, especially in humans.

## The Spinal Cord

The **spinal cord** *communicates with the body below the level of the head by means of sensory neurons and motor neurons* (Figure 3.27). The **sensory neurons** *carry information about touch, pain, and other senses from the periphery of the body to the spinal cord.* The **motor neurons** *transmit impulses from the central nervous system to the muscles and glands.*

The spinal cord serves both reflexive and voluntary behavior. A **reflex** is a *rapid, automatic response to a stimulus.* For example, suppose you put your hand on a hot stove. Stimulation of pain receptors in your finger sends messages along sensory neurons; within the spinal cord, these neurons send messages via interneurons to motor neurons, which then send impulses to the muscles that jerk your hand away from the hot stove.

The spinal cord is also necessary for voluntary behaviors. Every nonreflexive movement requires a message from the brain to the spinal cord and from the spinal cord to the muscles. People who have suffered damage to the spinal cord become paralyzed from that point down, although reflexes such as the knee-jerk reflex will remain.

## The Autonomic Nervous System

The **autonomic nervous system,** closely associated with the spinal cord, *controls the internal organs such as the heart.* The term *autonomic* means involuntary or automatic, in the sense that we have little voluntary control of it. We are generally unaware of its activity, although it does receive information from, and sends information to, the brain and the spinal cord.

The autonomic nervous system consists of two parts: (a) The *sympathetic nervous system*, controlled by a chain of neurons lying just outside the spinal cord, increases heart rate and breathing rate and readies the body for vigorous fight-or-flight activities. (b) The *parasympathetic nervous system*, controlled by neurons at the very top and very bottom levels of the spinal cord, decreases heart rate, increases digestive activities, and in general promotes activities of the body that take place during rest (Figure 3.28). We shall return to this topic in more detail in the discussion of emotions (Chapter 12).

**Sympathetic system**
uses much energy

- Pupils open
- Saliva decreases
- Pulse quickens
- Sweat increases
- Stomach less active
- Epinephrine (adrenaline) secreted

**Parasympathetic system**
conserves energy

- Pupils constrict
- Saliva flows
- Pulse slows
- Stomach churns

**FIGURE 3.28** The sympathetic nervous system prepares the body for brief bouts of vigorous activity; the parasympathetic nervous system promotes digestion and other nonemergency functions. Although both systems are active at all times, the balance can shift from a predominance of one to a predominance of the other.

## The Endocrine System

Although the endocrine system is not part of the nervous system, it is closely related to it, especially to the autonomic nervous system. Messages from the nervous system control the release of hormones from the endocrine system, and many hormones alter brain activity.

The **endocrine system** is *a set of glands that produce hormones and release them into the blood*. Figure 3.29 shows some of the major endocrine glands. **Hormones** are *chemicals released by glands and conveyed via the blood to other*

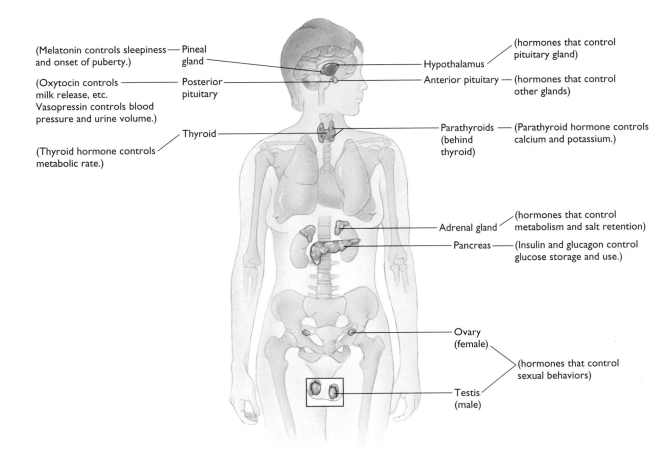

(Melatonin controls sleepiness and onset of puberty.) — Pineal gland

(Oxytocin controls milk release, etc. Vasopressin controls blood pressure and urine volume.) — Posterior pituitary

(Thyroid hormone controls metabolic rate.) — Thyroid

Hypothalamus — (hormones that control pituitary gland)

Anterior pituitary — (hormones that control other glands)

Parathyroids (behind thyroid) — (Parathyroid hormone controls calcium and potassium.)

Adrenal gland — (hormones that control metabolism and salt retention)

Pancreas — (Insulin and glucagon control glucose storage and use.)

Ovary (female)

Testis (male) — (hormones that control sexual behaviors)

**FIGURE 3.29** Glands in the endocrine system produce hormones and release them into the bloodstream. This shows only some of the endocrine glands and some of their most abundant hormones.

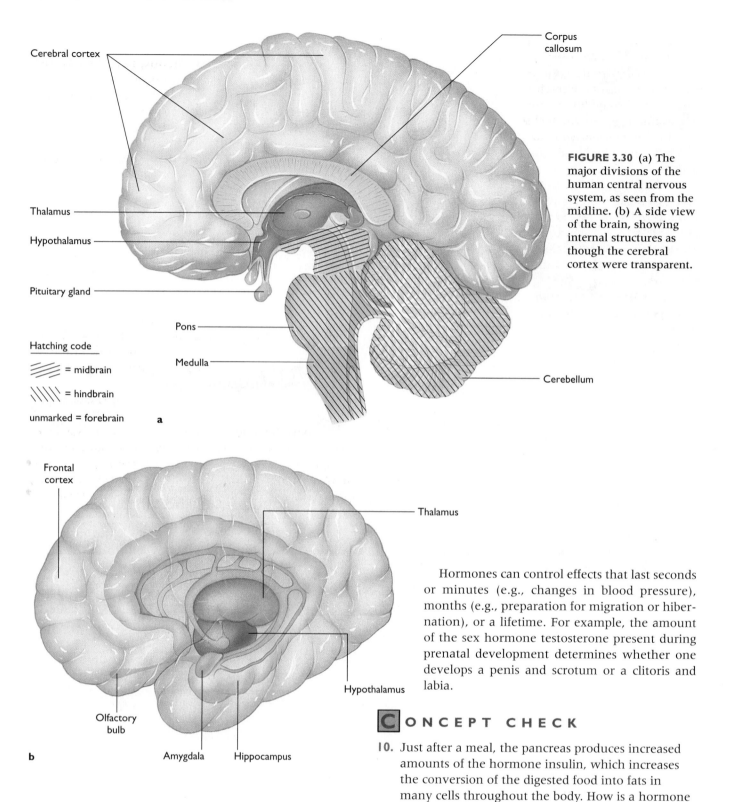

Cerebral cortex

Corpus callosum

Thalamus

Hypothalamus

Pituitary gland

Hatching code

///// = midbrain

\\\\\ = hindbrain

unmarked = forebrain

a

Pons

Medulla

Cerebellum

**FIGURE 3.30** (a) The major divisions of the human central nervous system, as seen from the midline. (b) A side view of the brain, showing internal structures as though the cerebral cortex were transparent.

Frontal cortex

Thalamus

b

Olfactory bulb

Amygdala    Hippocampus

Hypothalamus

*body parts, where they alter activity.* Hormones' effects on the nervous system resemble those of neurotransmitters, and many chemicals act as both hormones and neurotransmitters. The difference is that a neurotransmitter is released immediately adjacent to a synapse. When the same chemical is used as a hormone, it is released into the blood, which diffuses it throughout the body.

Hormones can control effects that last seconds or minutes (e.g., changes in blood pressure), months (e.g., preparation for migration or hibernation), or a lifetime. For example, the amount of the sex hormone testosterone present during prenatal development determines whether one develops a penis and scrotum or a clitoris and labia.

## CONCEPT CHECK

**10.** Just after a meal, the pancreas produces increased amounts of the hormone insulin, which increases the conversion of the digested food into fats in many cells throughout the body. How is a hormone more effective for this purpose than a neurotransmitter would be? (Check your answer on page 101.)

## Between the Spinal Cord and the Forebrain

Above the spinal cord, we find the hindbrain, the midbrain, and the forebrain, which includes the cerebral cortex (see Figure 3.30). Information passing between the spinal cord and the cerebral cortex (in either direction) travels through other structures on the way. In some cases that route is simple. For example, the primary motor area of the cerebral cortex sends axons that simply pass through to the spinal cord. For a more complex example, when you feel something with your fingers, the axons from your touch receptors send information to the spinal cord, which relays it to cells in the medulla (part of the hindbrain), which relay it to cells in the midbrain, which in turn relay it to cells in the thalamus (in the forebrain), which then relay it to part of the cerebral cortex. When I mention "relaying" information, I do not mean that the cells merely take the information and pass it along. They combine and contrast it with other information and change it in various ways.

Furthermore, structures along the way have functions of their own. The **medulla** and **pons,** *structures in the hindbrain* (Figure 3.30), receive sensory input from the head (taste, hearing, touch sensations on the scalp) and send impulses for motor control of the head (e.g., chewing, swallowing, and breathing). They also have axons that control breathing and heart rate, so damage here is life-threatening.

The medulla, pons, and midbrain also contain the *reticular formation* and several other systems that send messages throughout the forebrain to regulate its arousal (Young & Pigott, 1999). A malfunction in these systems, depending on its nature and location, can render someone either persistently sleepy or persistently aroused.

The **cerebellum** (Latin for "little brain"), *another part of the hindbrain,* is important for any behavior that requires aim or timing, such as tapping out a rhythm, judging which of two visual stimuli is moving faster, and judging whether the delay between one pair of sounds is shorter or longer than the delay between another pair (Ivry & Diener, 1991; Keele & Ivry, 1990). The cerebellum also helps control shifts of attention from one stimulus to another (Townsend et al., 1999), so its effects are far more widespread than the "balance and coordination" that older textbooks used to attribute to the cerebellum.

In later chapters we shall return to examine some of the forebrain structures that you see in Figure 3.30. The hippocampus is a key topic in the memory section (Chapter 7), and the hypothalamus and amygdala are important for emotional and motivated behaviors (Chapters 11 and 12).

 **C** ONCEPT CHECK

**11.** People who have become intoxicated on alcohol have slow, slurred speech and cannot walk a straight line. From these observations which part of the brain would you guess that the alcohol has most greatly impaired? (Check your answer on page 101.)

## *The Forebrain*

The forebrain consists of two **hemispheres,** *the left and the right halves* (Figure 3.31). Each hemisphere is responsible for sensation and motor control on the opposite side of the body. (Why does each hemisphere control the opposite side instead of its own side? People have speculated, but no one knows.)

The *outer covering of the forebrain,* known as the **cerebral cortex,** is especially prominent in humans. You have probably heard people talk about "having a lot of gray matter." The cerebral cortex in the forebrain is *gray matter;* it contains a great many cell bodies, which are grayer than the axons. The interior of the forebrain beneath the cerebral cortex contains huge numbers of axons, many of them covered with *myelin,* a white insulation. You can see areas of gray matter and white matter in Figure 3.32.

For the sake of convenience, we describe the cortex in terms of four *lobes*—occipital, parietal, temporal, and frontal, as shown in Figure 3.33. The **occipital lobe,** *at the rear of the head, is specialized for vision*. Different areas within (and outside) the occipital lobe contribute to different aspects of vision, such as shape, color, and motion.

The **parietal lobe,** *just anterior (forward) from the occipital lobe, is specialized for the body senses, including touch, pain, temperature, and awareness of the location of body parts.* The **primary somatosensory** (body-sensory) **cortex,** *a strip in the anterior portion of the parietal lobe, has neurons sensitive to*

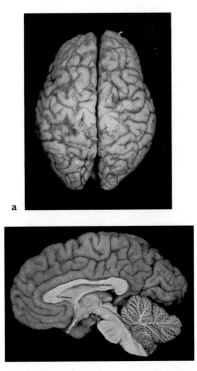

**FIGURE 3.31** The human cerebral cortex: (a) left and right hemispheres; (b) inside view of a complete hemisphere. The folds greatly extend the brain's surface area.

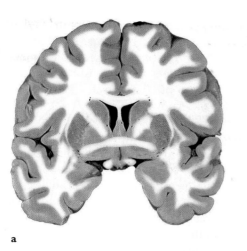
a

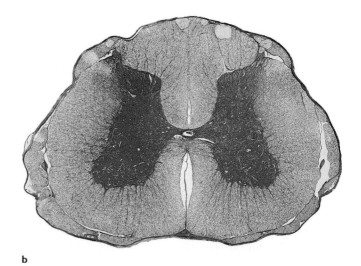
b

**FIGURE 3.32** (a) This cross section of a human brain shows the distinction between gray matter (composed mostly of cell bodies and dendrites) and white matter (composed almost entirely of axons). Myelin, a fatty sheath that surrounds many axons, makes the white matter white. (b) The H-shaped structure in the center is gray matter, composed largely of cell bodies. The surrounding white matter consists of axons. The axons are in organized tracts; some carry information from the brain and higher levels of the spinal cord downward, while others carry information from lower levels upward. *(Source: Manfred Kage/Peter Arnold, Inc.)*

*touch in different body areas,* as shown in Figure 3.34. Note that in Figure 3.34a larger areas are devoted to touch in the more sensitive parts of the body, such as the lips and hands, than to less sensitive areas, such as the abdomen and the back. Damage to any part of the somatosensory cortex will impair sensation from the corresponding part of the body.

Damage in the right parietal lobe (see Figure 3.33) leads to a fascinating phenomenon—**neglect** *(disregard)* of the left side of the body and the left side of the world. Someone with such damage may read only the right side of a page, draw only the right side of an object (Heilman, 1979) (see Figure 3.35), and put clothing on only the right side of the body, insisting that the left half belongs to someone else.

If you were to tickle such a person simultaneously on the left and right sides of either wrist, he or she would report the sensation on the right side of that wrist, ignoring the sensation on the left side. Now turn the person's hand upside down and repeat the experiment. He or she reports

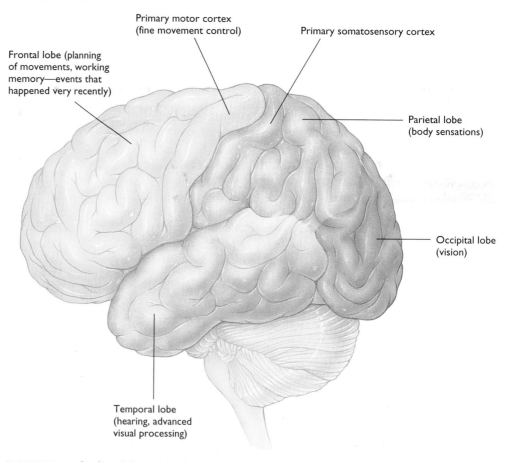

**FIGURE 3.33** The four lobes of the human cerebral cortex, with indications of some of their major functions.

Primary motor cortex (fine movement control)

Primary somatosensory cortex

Frontal lobe (planning of movements, working memory—events that happened very recently)

Parietal lobe (body sensations)

Occipital lobe (vision)

Temporal lobe (hearing, advanced visual processing)

the sensation on what has *now* become the right side of the hand, as illustrated in Figure 3.36 (Moscovitch & Behrmann, 1994). That is, the impairment is not a loss of sensation from one part of the body; it is a loss of attention.

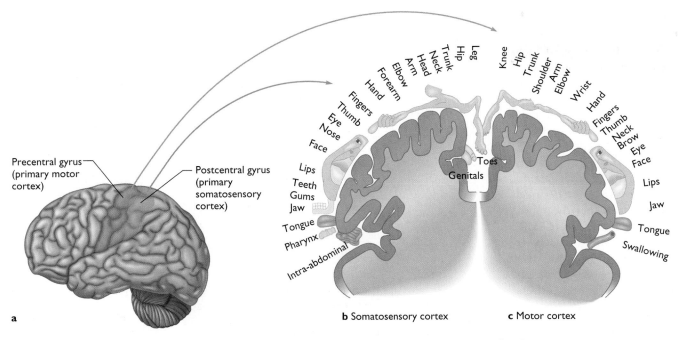

**FIGURE 3.34** (a) Locations of the primary somatosensory cortex and the primary motor cortex. (b) The primary somatosensory cortex and (c) the primary motor cortex, illustrating which part of the body each brain area controls. Larger areas of the cortex are devoted to body parts that need to be controlled with great precision, such as the face and hands. The figure shows the left primary somatosensory cortex, which receives information from the right side of the body, and the right primary motor cortex, which controls the muscles on the left side of the body. (b and c after Penfield & Rasmussen, 1950)

The **temporal lobe** of each hemisphere, *located toward the left and right sides of the head, is the main processing area for hearing and some of the complex aspects of vision,* such as face recognition and motion detection. One area in the temporal lobe of the left hemisphere is important for language comprehension. Damage centered here impairs people's ability to understand what other people are saying; they also have trouble remembering the names of objects. The structure of neurons and their connections are different in the left and right hemispheres, and presumably those differences prepare the left hemisphere for language functions (Galuske, Schlote, Bratzke, & Singer, 2000).

Other parts of the temporal lobe are critical for certain aspects of emotion. The *amygdala* (Figure 3.30) is a subcortical structure within the temporal lobe, richly

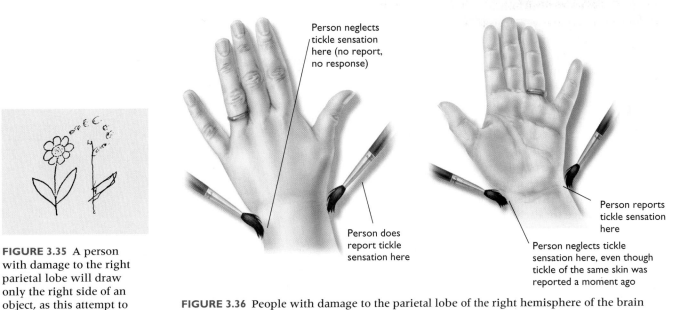

**FIGURE 3.35** A person with damage to the right parietal lobe will draw only the right side of an object, as this attempt to copy a picture of a flower shows. (From Heilman & Valenstein, 1993)

**FIGURE 3.36** People with damage to the parietal lobe of the right hemisphere of the brain neglect (ignore) stimuli on the left side of either wrist. After the hand is rotated to a new position, the patient ignores what is now on the left, even though he or she attended to the same skin in the previous position. That is, the problem is one of attention, not of simple sensation.

connected to both cortical and other subcortical areas. People with damage to the amygdala have almost no fear or anxiety (LaBar, LeDoux, Spencer, & Phelps, 1995). Most people remember emotionally distressing events better than neutral events, but those with damage to the amygdala do not, presumably because they do not feel the emotional distress (Cahill, Babinsky, Markowitsch, & McGaugh, 1995). They can neither recognize facial expressions of fear in others nor imagine what a frightened face would look like (Adolphs, Tranel, Damasio, & Damasio, 1995).

The **frontal lobe,** *at the anterior (forward) pole of the brain,* includes the **primary motor cortex,** *a structure that is important for the control of fine movements,* such as moving one finger at a time. As with the primary somatosensory cortex, each area of the primary motor cortex controls a different part of the body, and larger areas are devoted to precise movements of the tongue and fingers than to, say, the shoulder and elbow muscles. The *anterior sections of the frontal lobe,* called the **prefrontal cortex,** contribute to the organization and planning of movements and to certain aspects of memory. Indeed, planning a movement depends on memory. Recall, for example, the delayed-response task (page 21): The individual must remember a signal during a delay and then make the appropriate movement. Certain areas in the left frontal lobe are essential for human language.

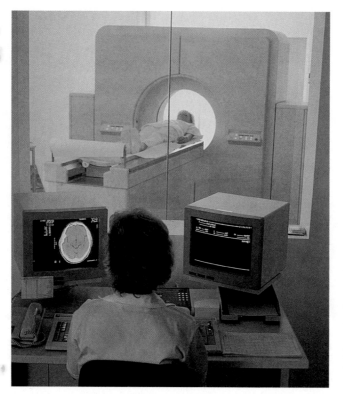

**FIGURE 3.37** To form a CAT scan, a person's head must lie motionless while x-rays pass through it from one angle after another. The result is a detailed representation of the brain's anatomy.

e. poor performance on a delayed-response task, indicating difficulty remembering what has just happened. (Check your answers on page 101.)

## Brain Scans

How do we know that these brain areas have the functions that I have described? For many years nearly all the evidence came from observations of brain damage. Researchers can now supplement such evidence with modern techniques that measure brain activity as it happens. One technique is **computerized axial tomography (CT** or **CAT),** *which passes x-rays through the head of someone who has a dye in the blood to increase contrast between fluids and brain cells* (see Figure 3.37). The x-rays are recorded by detectors on the other side of the head. After x-rays are recorded at each angle through 180°, the information is processed by a computer, which generates an image like the one in Figure 3.38. CAT scans provide excellent detail about brain anatomy, including areas of tumor growth or other abnormalities. However, they do not indicate brain activity.

## CONCEPT CHECK

12. The following five people are known to have suffered damage to the cerebral cortex. From their behavioral symptoms, determine the probable location of the damage for each person:
    a. impaired perception of the left half of the body and a tendency to ignore the left half of the body and the left half of the world
    b. impaired hearing and some changes in emotional experience
    c. inability to make fine movements with the right hand
    d. loss of vision in the left visual field

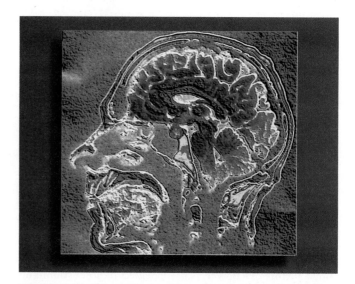

**FIGURE 3.38** This CAT scan shows the anatomy of a living human brain.

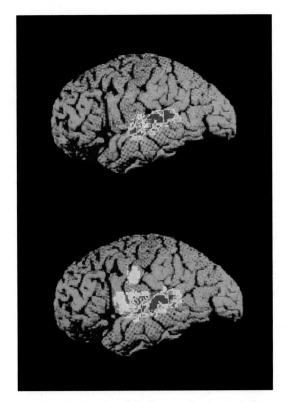

**FIGURE 3.39** A PET scan of the human brain. Red shows areas of most-increased activity during some task, yellow shows areas of next most-increased activity.

Another method does tell us about brain activity: **Positron-emission tomography (PET)** *provides a high-resolution image of brain activity by recording radioactivity emitted from injected chemicals* (Phelps & Mazziotta, 1985). First someone receives an injection of a radioactively labeled compound such as glucose. Glucose, a simple sugar which is the brain's main fuel (almost its only fuel), is absorbed mainly in the most active brain areas. Therefore, radioactivity comes primarily from those areas. Detectors around the head record the amount of radioactivity coming from each part of the brain and send that information to a computer, which generates an image such as the one in Figure 3.39. Red indicates areas of greatest activity, followed by yellow, green, and blue. PET scans can show changes in activity from minute to minute, with much detail in the image. However, the procedure is expensive and it requires exposing the brain to radioactivity, a risky process if it is repeated several times.

Another technique is **functional magnetic resonance imaging (fMRI),** which *uses magnetic detectors outside the head to measure the amounts of hemoglobin with and without oxygen in different parts of the brain* (J. D. Cohen, Noll, & Schneider, 1993). (Adding or removing oxygen changes the response of hemoglobin to a magnetic field.) Highly active brain areas use much oxygen and therefore decrease the oxygen bound to hemoglobin in the blood. The fMRI technique thus shows which brain areas are currently more active than others, as in Figure 3.40.

Brain scans are a potentially powerful research tool, but designing a good study and interpreting the results can be difficult. For example, suppose we want to determine which brain areas are important for recent memory. We record activity while someone is engaged in a memory task and compare that activity to times when the person is doing. . . what? Doing nothing? That comparison wouldn't work; the memory task presumably includes sensory stimuli, motor responses, attention, and other processes besides memory. Researchers must design a

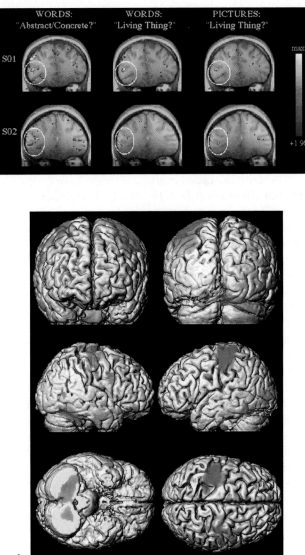

**FIGURE 3.40** (a) This brain scan was made with functional magnetic resonance imaging (fMRI). Participants looked at words or pictures and judged whether each item was abstract or concrete, living or nonliving. Yellow shows the areas most activated by this judgment; red shows areas less strongly activated. (From Wagner, Desmond, Demb, Glover, & Gabrieli, 1997. Photo courtesy of Anthony D. Wagner) (b) **Motor activation.** A male volunteer, using his dominant right hand, was either rotating a small cylinder or resting in alternating 30-second intervals during a 5-minute fMRI scan, yielding six perspectives in which motor areas of the left brain are highlighted.

comparison task that requires attention to the same sensory stimuli, the same hand movements, and so forth as the memory task. Many researchers have cleverly designed suitable comparison tasks (e.g., Rowe, Toni, Josephs, Frackowiak, & Passingham, 2000), but in many cases it is quite difficult to do so.

## A STEP FURTHER:
### *Testing Psychological Processes*

Suppose you want to determine which brain areas are active during recent memory. Try to design some task that requires memory and a comparison task that is similar in every other way except for the memory requirement.

## Effects of Experience on Brain Structure

The drawing in Figure 3.25 shows "the human nervous system." We do not need to specify whose nervous system because the gross structure is about the same from one person to another anywhere in the world. The detailed anatomy does vary, however, and some of these variations depend on people's experiences.

A good example is the effect of musical training. Figure 3.34a shows how the somatosensory cortex represents different parts of the body. One area, for example, represents the fingers, and researchers have measured the average amount of cortex devoted to the fingers. The results are different, however, for people who have played a violin since childhood. Nearly all violinists hold the bow with the right hand and finger the strings with the left hand. The result of many years of practice is that the amount of sensory cortex devoted to the left hand becomes about twice as large as usual (Elbert, Pantev, Wienbruch, Rockstroh, & Taub, 1995).

Many children have *absolute pitch,* or "perfect pitch," the ability to hear a note and identify it as B-flat, C-sharp, or whatever. Fewer than 1 person in 10,000 retains that ability into adulthood, and those few are people who began piano, voice, or other musical lessons in early childhood and continued practicing from then on (Takeuchi & Hulse, 1993). For those who maintain absolute pitch, one area of the temporal lobe of the cerebral cortex is significantly larger than normal (Schlaug, Jäncke, Huang, & Steinmetz, 1995).

Could adult experience also change brain structure? Surprisingly, yes. One study using brain scans found that London taxi drivers had a larger posterior hippocampus than other people do on average, and that the longer they had been taxi drivers, the larger was their posterior hippocampus (Maguire et al., 2000). The posterior hippocampus is essential for spatial memory, and apparently, the extensive use of spatial memory by taxi drivers had caused growth in this area.

The general point is that our brain anatomy is not fixed at birth. Unusual or prolonged experiences can modify the structure of the brain to improve its performance. However, the brain changes are specific to the task. People who practice music have brain changes that help them with music, whereas people who drive taxis have brain changes that improve spatial memory. We have no evidence that using your brain is like exercising your muscles to "bulk them up." That is, practicing a mental skill prepares your brain to be better at that skill and anything else that is closely related, but it doesn't improve overall ability on unrelated tasks.

## The "Binding Problem"

As researchers answered certain questions about brain function, a new one arose: One part of your brain is responsible for hearing, another for touch, several other areas for various aspects of vision, and so forth, and those areas have few if any direct connections with one another. So how do you get the experience of being a single "self"? If you shake a baby's toy rattle, how do you know that what you feel, what you see, and what you hear are all the same object? *The question of how separate brain areas combine forces to produce a unified perception of a single object* is called the **binding problem.**

A naive explanation would be that all the various parts of the brain funnel their information to a "little person in the head" who puts it all together. Although no one takes that concept seriously, the underlying idea is hard to abandon, and brain researchers have sometimes imagined a "master area" of the brain that would serve the same purpose, integrating all the information and making decisions.

Research on the cerebral cortex, however, has found no master area or central processor. Few neurons receive a combination of visual and auditory information or visual and touch information.

In fact, the mystery deepens: Even in vision, different brain areas process different aspects of the stimulus. Figure 3.41 illustrates three major visual pathways in the human cerebral cortex. The point of this figure is to illustrate the idea of separate pathways, not their exact locations.

A person who suffers damage in the *primary visual cortex* (area V1) becomes blind in part or all of the visual field. However, someone with damage to the inferior temporal cortex can still see, but cannot recognize complex shapes. Sometimes the deficit is quite limited; after damage to one small area, people suffer **faceblindness,** *a specific inability to recognize people by their faces.* Such a person can see faces well enough to say, "He is almost bald, has a somewhat thin face, and dark eyes," but can't identify who it is. The brain area responsible for faces is also active for expert recognition of other items—for exam-

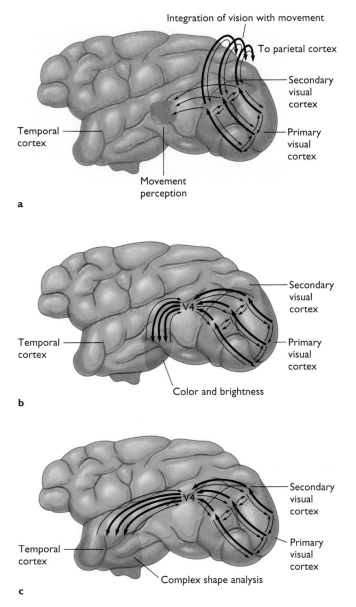

**FIGURE 3.41** Three major visual pathways in the cerebral cortex: (a) One path is responsible for movement perception; (b) a second path deals with color and brightness; (c) the third path provides analysis of complex shapes. Because the three paths are largely independent of one another, brain damage can impair one aspect of visual perception without blocking the others. These drawings show the cortex of monkeys, the most common species for such research.

ple, it becomes active when bird experts identify birds, car experts identify cars, or dog show judges watch dogs (Tarr & Gauthier, 2000). People with faceblindness can still read, however, so the problem is not just a matter of seeing details (Farah, Wilson, Drain, & Tanaka, 1998).

People with damage to parts of the color pathway lose an ability called **color constancy,** which is *the ability to continue recognizing colors even after a change in lighting.* For example, when you wear green-tinted glasses, you can still recognize which objects are white, yellow, and so forth. People with certain kinds of brain damage would see everything in shades of green (Zeki, 1980, 1983).

Damage in a third pathway produces a very surprising deficit: **motionblindness,** *trouble identifying the movement of objects* (Marcar, Zihl, & Cowey, 1997). One such patient found that she could not safely cross a road because she could not see which cars were moving or how fast. She had trouble pouring coffee into a cup because she could not see the liquid level gradually rising in the cup. (Eventually, she would stop when she saw coffee all over the table.) For most of us, it is difficult to imagine what the world must look like to a motionblind person. It might be like living in a world with only strobe lights shining once every few seconds, except that these people experience no blackouts in their perception.

In short, different parts of your cerebral cortex specialize in different aspects of vision, just as different areas control hearing, touch, and so forth. How do we bind stimuli together? No one knows, but we do know that binding occurs only for precisely simultaneous events. Have you ever watched a film or television show in which the soundtrack is slightly ahead of or behind the picture? If so, you immediately knew that the sound wasn't coming from the performers on screen. You get the same experience if you watch a foreign-language film that was poorly dubbed. However, when you watch a ventriloquist, the motion of the dummy's mouth simultaneous with the sound causes you to perceive the sound as coming from the dummy. One hypothesis is that simultaneous high-frequency brain waves in different brain areas are responsible for binding a

■ We hear the sound as coming from the dummy's mouth only if sound and movements are synchronized. In general, binding depends on simultaneity of two kinds of stimuli.

stimulus together (Rodriguez et al., 1999; Roelfsema, Engel, König, & Singer, 1997). Still, that hypothesis leaves many questions unanswered, such as the basic one of *how* simultaneous activity in separate brain areas could combine to produce a unified, bound experience. At this point the binding problem is unanswered. Its great appeal is that it appears to be one way of phrasing the mind-brain problem (from Chapter 1) that research might succeed in explaining.

## The Corpus Callosum and the Split-Brain Phenomenon

What would happen if the two hemispheres of your brain could not communicate with each other? Such a situation does arise after damage to the **corpus callosum,** *a set of axons connecting the two hemispheres* (Figure 3.42). Several other sets of axons also connect the two hemispheres (Banich, 1998), but they convey much less information. Corpus callosum damage prevents someone from comparing sights seen on one side of their world to those on the other side and from comparing something felt with one hand to something in the other. In effect the person no longer has one cerebral cortex but two half-cortexes side by side, and maybe even two separate spheres of consciousness.

Occasionally, brain surgeons cut the corpus callosum in an effort to relieve **epilepsy,** *a condition in which neurons somewhere in the brain emit abnormal rhythmic, spontaneous impulses.* Depending on where the abnormal impulses start and where they spread, epilepsy can produce varied effects. Most people with epilepsy respond well to antiepileptic drugs and live normal lives. A few, however, continue to have frequent major seizures that prevent them from working, going to school, or living a normal life. When all else fails, surgeons sometimes recommend cutting the corpus callosum. The original idea was that epileptic seizures would be limited to one hemisphere and therefore would be less incapacitating.

The operation was more successful than expected. Not only are the

**a**   Corpus callosum

**b**

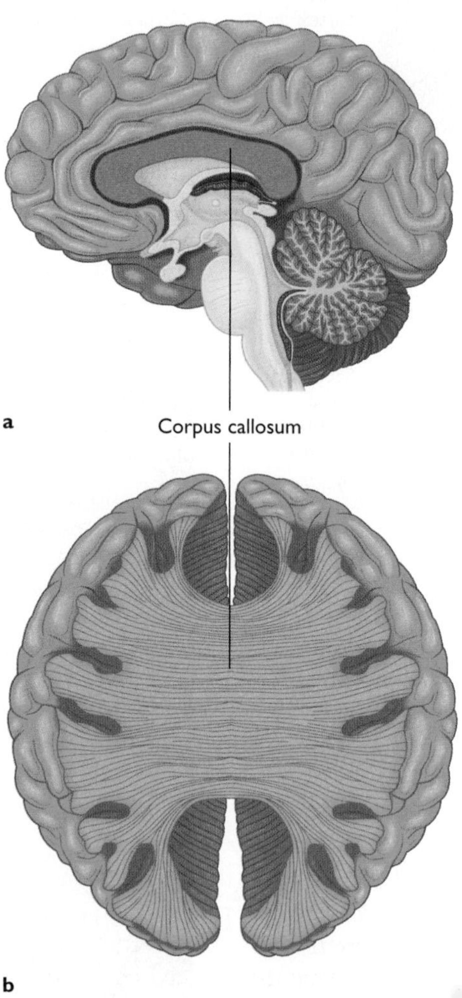

**FIGURE 3.42** The corpus callosum is a large set of axons that convey information between the two hemispheres of the cerebral cortex. (a) A midline view showing the location of the corpus callosum. (b) A horizontal section showing how each axon of the corpus callosum links one spot in the left hemisphere to a corresponding spot in the right hemisphere.

seizures limited to one side of the body, but they also become less frequent. A possible explanation is that the operation interrupts the feedback loop between the two hemispheres that allows an epileptic seizure to echo back and forth. However, although these split-brain patients resume a normal life, they have some interesting behavioral side effects. Before I can discuss these, we need to consider some anatomy.

### Connections Between the Eyes and the Brain

*Note: This section presents a concept that is contrary to most people's expectations, and the left-right-right-left connections can be confusing. So please read carefully!*

Because each hemisphere of the brain controls the muscles on the opposite side of the body, each half of the brain needs to see the opposite side of the world. This does *not* mean that your left hemisphere sees with the right eye or that your right hemisphere sees with the left eye.

 Convince yourself: Close one eye, then open it and close the other. Note that you see almost the same view with both eyes. You see each half of the world with part of your left eye and part of your right eye.

Figure 3.43, which shows the human visual system, warrants careful study. Light from each half of the world strikes receptors on the opposite side of *each* retina. (The retina is the lining in the back of each eye. The retina is lined with receptors.) Information from the left half of each retina travels via the *optic nerves* to the left hemisphere of the cerebral cortex; information from the right half of each retina travels via the optic nerves to the right hemisphere.

Here is one way to remember this material: *Light from each side of the world strikes the opposite side of the retina. The brain is connected to the eyes so that each hemisphere sees the opposite side of the world.* If you remember those two statements, you should be able to deduce that each hemisphere is connected to the half of each retina *on the same side,* as shown in Figure 3.43. You might also draw the diagram for yourself.

What about the very center of the retina? The cells in a thin strip

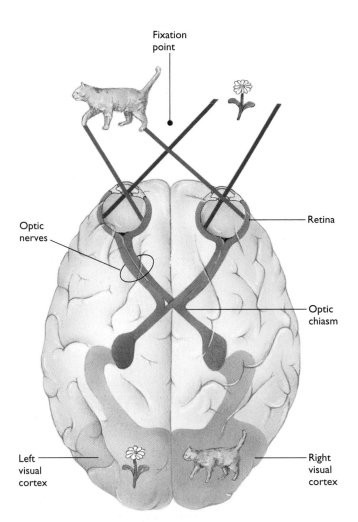

**FIGURE 3.43** In the human visual system (viewed here from above), light from either half of the world crosses through the pupils to strike the opposite side of each retina. Axons from the left half of each retina travel to the left hemisphere of the brain; axons from the right half of each retina travel to the right hemisphere of the brain.

down the center of each retina send axons to both sides of the brain.

## Effects of Severing the Corpus Callosum

For almost all right-handed people and about 60% of left-handed people, parts of the left hemisphere control speech. For most other left-handers, both hemispheres control speech. Complete right-hemisphere control of speech is uncommon. The right hemisphere is critical for understanding the emotional aspects of speech, however, as we shall see later.

Assuming you have left-hemisphere control of speech, can you talk about something you feel with the left hand or see in the left visual field? Yes, easily, if your brain is intact: The information enters your right hemisphere, but then passes quickly across the corpus callosum to your left hemisphere.

The result is different if the corpus callosum is severed. When a woman with a severed corpus callosum touches different things with her two hands, she can describe only what she feels with the right hand because the information from the left hand goes to the right (nonspeech) hemisphere (Nebes, 1974; Sperry, 1967). If she is given several choices and is asked to point to what her left hand has just felt, she points to it correctly. . . with her left hand. In fact, she may point correctly with her left hand while saying, "I have no idea what it was. I didn't feel anything." Evidently, the right hemisphere can understand the instructions and answer with the hand it controls, but it cannot talk.

Now consider what happens when she sees something (Figure 3.44). Ordinarily, she moves her eyes and sees the same thing in both hemispheres. In the laboratory, however, researchers can restrict information to one side of the brain by presenting information faster than the eyes can move. The woman in Figure 3.44 focuses her eyes on a point in the middle of the screen. The investigator flashes a word such as *hatband* on the screen for a split second, too briefly for an eye movement. When asked what she saw, she replies, "band," which is what the left hemisphere saw. (Information from the right side, you will recall, goes to the left side of each retina and from there to the left hemisphere.) If she is asked what *kind* of band it might be, she will be puzzled: "I don't know. Jazz band? Rubber band?" However, if she is asked to use the left hand to point at what she saw, she points to a hat (which the right hemisphere saw).

Split-brain people get along reasonably well with common behaviors such as walking or even tying shoes because well-practiced behaviors don't need much input from the cerebral cortex anyway. The problem comes with unfamiliar behaviors. Two split-brain people were asked "pretend you're threading a needle" and "pretend you're attaching a fishhook to a line." Both behaviors require both hands, and in fact, the movements are very similar. The person who had frequently threaded a needle before the operation had no trouble with threading a needle, but couldn't show how to attach a fishhook. Another person who had previously attached many fishhooks but never used a sewing needle had exactly the opposite results (Franz, Waldie, & Smith, 2000).

In special circumstances the two hemispheres find clever ways to cooperate. In one experiment a split-brain person was looking at pictures flashed on a screen, as in Figure 3.44a. He could seldom name the objects flashed in the left visual field, but after some delay, he could name simple shapes. Here is how he did it: After seeing the object in the left visual field (with the right hemisphere), he let his eyes move around the room. (Both hemispheres control the eye muscles.) When the right hemisphere saw something with the same shape as the object it had just seen, it would stop moving the eyes. The left hemisphere just waited for the eyes to stop moving and then called out the shape of the object it saw.

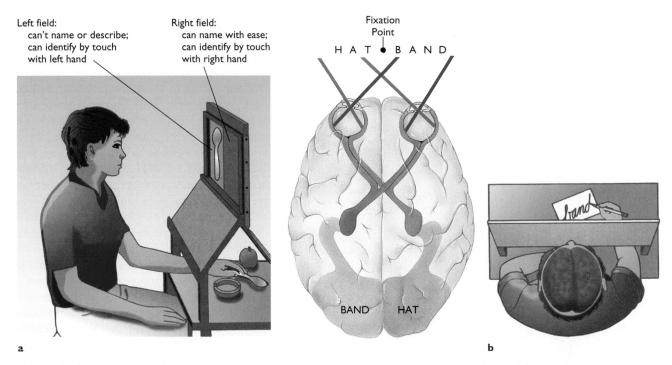

**FIGURE 3.44** (a) A woman with a severed corpus callosum cannot name something she sees in her left visual field but can find the corresponding object with her right hand. (b) When the word *hatband* is flashed on a screen, a woman with a split brain can report only what her left hemisphere saw, *band*. However, with her left hand she can point to a hat, which is what the right hemisphere saw.

## CONCEPT CHECK

13. Information coming to the left hemisphere of the brain comes from which part of the retinas?
14. After damage to the corpus callosum, a person can describe some of what he or she sees, but not all. Where must the person see something in order to describe it in words? One eye or the other? One half of the retina? One visual field or the other? (Check your answers on page 101.)

What does the right hemisphere do? It does not speak, but it understands both spoken and written language, especially with short words and simple grammar. It is especially important for understanding the emotional content of speech; people with right-hemisphere damage often can't tell when a speaker is being sarcastic and frequently don't understand jokes (Beeman & Chiarello, 1998). The right hemisphere is also better than the left for recognizing and understanding facial expressions (Stone, Nisenson, Eliassen, & Gazzaniga, 1996) and for tasks that are hard to put into words, such as drawing pictures or arranging puzzle pieces.

Let me describe an interesting study. It will seem that I am changing the subject, but later you will see that I am not. People in this study watched a videotape that showed each of ten people speaking twice. In one speech they described themselves completely honestly and in the other case they told nothing but lies. Do you think you could tell when someone was telling the truth? The average for MIT undergraduates was 47% correct, slightly *less* than they should have done by random guessing. Other groups did about equally badly, except for one group that managed to get 60% correct. (That's still not great, but it's better than anyone else did.) Guess who were these people who could tell lies from truth? They were people with left-hemisphere brain damage! They could understand almost nothing of what people were saying, so they relied entirely on gestures and facial expressions—which the right hemisphere is quite good at understanding (Etcoff, Ekman, Magee, & Frank, 2000).

Split-brain surgery is rare. We study such patients not because you are likely to encounter one but because they teach us something about brain organization: Although we cannot fully explain our experience of a unified consciousness, we see that it depends on communication across brain areas. If communication between the two hemispheres is lost, then each hemisphere becomes partly independent of the other.

Before closing this section, I want to caution you about a common misunderstanding. The left hemisphere is specialized for language and the right hemisphere for emotional perception and complex visual-spatial tasks. Some writers have gone beyond this generalization to claim that the left hemisphere is logical and the right hemisphere is creative, so logical people are left-brained and creative people are right-brained. Some have even suggested that we could all become more creative if we could find a way to exercise the right hemisphere.

In fact, although certain tasks activate one hemisphere more than the other, no task relies on just one hemisphere. What's the evidence that some people are left brained or that others are right brained? We have *no* evidence, except in the rare cases of people who have had damage to one hemisphere or the other. Nevertheless, the hypothesis is popular. Some people who think illogically excuse themselves by saying "I'm a right-brained person," with the implication that *because* they are illogical, *therefore* they are creative!

## IN CLOSING

## *Brain and Self*

This module has included examples of split-brain people, people who neglect the left half of the body, people who lose the ability to recognize faces, and so on. I hope you found these examples interesting, but beyond that, the main point is that the brain is full of separate systems with separate specializations. A small area of brain damage can impair one ability while having little effect on others.

Here's another way of stating this conclusion, with greater emphasis on the philosophical implications: Your self consists of many separate abilities, and it is possible to lose one of them independently of the others. Furthermore, if you lose part of your brain, you also lose part of your capacity for behavior and experience. As far as we can tell, brain activity and mind are inseparable; we cannot have one without the other.

## Summary

* *Central and peripheral nervous systems.* The central nervous system consists of the brain (forebrain, midbrain, and hindbrain) and the spinal cord. The peripheral nervous system consists of nerves that communicate between the central nervous system and the rest of the body. (page 87)
* *Autonomic nervous system and endocrine system.* The autonomic nervous system controls the body's organs, preparing them for emergency activities or for vegetative activities. The endocrine system consists of organs that release hormones into the blood. (page 88)
* *The central nervous system.* Information passing between the cerebral cortex and the spinal cord goes through several intervening structures such as the midbrain and medulla. The intervening structures have important functions of their own. (page 90)
* *The cerebral cortex.* The four lobes of the cerebral cortex and their primary functions are: occipital lobe, vision; temporal lobe, hearing and some aspects of vision; parietal lobe, body sensations; frontal lobe, movement and preparation for movement. Damage in the cere-

bral cortex can produce specialized deficits, depending on the location of damage. (page 90)
* *Imaging brain activity.* Modern technology enables researchers to develop images showing the structure and activity of various brain areas in living, unanesthetized people. (page 94)
* *Experience and brain structure.* The anatomy of the nervous system is constantly in flux in small ways. Extensive practice of a behavior can modify brain structure, especially if the practice begins early in life. (page 96)
* *The binding problem.* Brain researchers cannot yet explain how we develop a unified experience of an object, even though our registers of hearing, touch, vision, and so forth occur in different brain areas that do not connect directly to one another. Even different aspects of vision depend on different brain areas so that it is possible to lose face recognition or motion perception without impairing other aspects of vision. (page 96)
* *Corpus callosum.* The corpus callosum is a set of axons through which the left and right hemispheres of the cortex communicate. If the corpus callosum is damaged, information that reaches one hemisphere cannot be shared with the other. (page 98)
* *Connections from eyes to brain.* In humans information from the *left* visual field strikes the *right* half of both retinas, from which it is sent to the *right* hemisphere of the brain. Information from the *right* visual field strikes the *left* half of both retinas, from which it is sent to the *left* hemisphere. (page 98)
* *Split-brain patients.* The left hemisphere is specialized for language in most people, so split-brain people can describe information only if it enters the left hemisphere. Because of the lack of direct communication between the left and right hemispheres in split-brain patients, such people show signs of having separate fields of awareness. (page 99)

## Answers to Concept Checks

**10.** The storage of fats takes place at many sites throughout the body. A hormone diffuses throughout the body; a neurotransmitter exerts its effects only on the neurons immediately adjacent to where it was released. (page 90)
**11.** Although alcohol impairs activity throughout the brain, one of the first areas to show a substantial effect is the cerebellum. The typical symptoms of alcohol intoxication are also symptoms of impairment to the cerebellum. (page 91)
**12.** a. right parietal lobe; b. temporal lobe; c. primary motor cortex of the left frontal lobe; d. right occipital lobe; e. prefrontal cortex. (page 94)
**13.** The left hemisphere receives input from the left half of each retina. (page 100)
**14.** To describe something, a person must see it with the left half of the retina of either eye. The left half of the retina sees the right visual field. (page 100).

## Key Terms

**action potential:** an excitation that travels along an axon at a constant strength, no matter how far it must travel (page 80)

**artificial selection:** the purposeful breeding, by humans, of animals with certain traits, also known as selective breeding (page 74)

**attention deficit disorder (ADD):** a condition marked by impulsive behavior and short attention span (page 85)

**autonomic nervous system:** system of neurons that controls the internal organs such as the heart (page 88)

**axon** a single, long, thin, straight fiber that transmits information from a neuron to other neurons or to muscle cells (page 78)

**binding problem:** the question of how separate brain areas combine forces to produce a unified perception of a single object (page 96)

**cell body:** the part of the neuron that contains the nucleus of the cell (page 78)

**central nervous system:** the brain and the spinal cord (page 87)

**cerebellum:** (Latin for "little brain") a hindbrain structure that is active in the control of movement, especially for complex, rapid motor skills and behaviors that require precise timing (page 91)

**cerebral cortex:** the outer surface of the forebrain (page 91)

**chromosome:** strand of hereditary material found in the nucleus of a cell (page 68)

**color constancy:** the ability to continue recognizing colors even after a change in lighting (page 97)

**computerized axial tomography (CT or CAT):** a procedure to measure brain activity as it happens in which x-rays pass through the head of someone who has a dye in the blood to increase contrast between fluids and brain cells (page 94)

**corpus callosum:** a large set of axons connecting the left and right hemispheres of the cerebral cortex and thus enabling the two hemispheres to communicate with each other (page 98)

**dendrite:** one of the widely branching structures of a neuron that receive transmissions from other neurons (page 78)

**dizygotic twins:** (literally, "two-egg" twins) fraternal twins who develop from two eggs fertilized by two different sperm. Dizygotic twins are no more closely related than are any other children born to the same parents (page 71)

**dominant gene:** a gene that will exert evident effects on development even in a person who is heterozygous for that gene (page 68)

**dopamine:** a neurotransmitter that promotes activity levels and facilitates movement (page 85)

**endocrine system:** a set of glands that produce hormones and release them into the bloodstream (page 89)

**epilepsy:** a condition characterized by abnormal rhythmic activity of brain neurons (page 98)

**evolution:** changes in the gene frequencies of a species (page 74)

**faceblindness:** impairment of the ability to recognize faces, despite otherwise satisfactory vision (page 96)

**frontal lobe:** a portion of each cerebral hemisphere at the anterior pole, with sections that control movement and certain aspects of memory (page 94)

**functional magnetic resonance imaging (fMRI):** a technique that uses magnetic detectors outside the head to measure the amounts of hemoglobin, with and without oxygen, in different parts of the brain and thereby provides an indication of current activity levels in various brain areas (page 95)

**gene:** a segment of a chromosome that controls chemical reactions that ultimately direct the development of the organism (page 68)

**glia:** a cell of the nervous system that insulates neurons, removes waste materials (such as dead cells), and performs other supportive functions (page 78)

**hemisphere:** the left or right half of the brain; each hemisphere is responsible for sensation and motor control on the opposite side of the body (page 91)

**heritability:** an estimate of the variance within a population that is due to heredity (page 71)

**heterozygous:** having different genes on a pair of chromosomes (page 68)

**homozygous:** having the same gene on both members of a pair of chromosomes (page 68)

**hormone:** a chemical released by glands and conveyed by the blood to other parts of the body, where it alters activity (page 89)

**medulla:** a structure that is located in the hindbrain and is an elaboration of the spinal cord; controls many muscles in the head and several life-preserving functions, such as breathing (page 91)

**monozygotic twins:** (literally, "one-egg" twins) identical twins who develop from the same fertilized egg (page 71)

**motionblindness:** impaired ability to detect motion in visual perception, despite otherwise satisfactory vision (page 97)

**motor neuron:** a neuron that transmits impulses from the central nervous system to the muscles or glands (page 88)

**mutation:** a random change in the structure of a gene (page 74)

**natural selection:** the tendency, in nature, of individuals with certain genetically controlled characteristics to reproduce more successfully than others do; future generations will come to resemble those individuals more and more (page 74)

**neglect:** the tendency to ignore stimuli on one side of the body or one side of the world (page 92)

**neuron:** a cell of the nervous system that receives information and transmits it to other cells by conducting electrochemical impulses (page 78)

**neurotransmitter:** a chemical that is stored in the terminal of an axon and that, when released, activates receptors of other neurons (page 82)

**occipital lobe:** the rear portion of each cerebral hemisphere, critical for vision (page 91)

**parietal lobe:** a portion of each cerebral hemisphere; the main receiving area for the sense of touch and for the awareness of one's own body (page 91)

**Parkinson's disease:** a condition that affects about 1% of people over the age of 50. The main symptoms are difficulty in initiating voluntary movement, slowness of movement, tremors, rigidity, and depressed mood (page 85)

**peripheral nervous system:** the bundles of axons that convey messages between the spinal cord and the rest of the body (page 87)

**phenylketonuria (PKU):** an inherited disorder in which a person lacks the chemical reactions that convert a nutrient called phenylalanine into other chemicals; unless the diet is carefully controlled, the affected person will become mentally retarded (page 74)

**pons:** a structure adjacent to the medulla that receives sensory input from the head and controls many muscles in the head (page 91)

**positron-emission tomography (PET):** provides a high-resolution image of brain activity by recording radioactivity emitted from injected chemicals (page 95)

**postsynaptic neuron:** a neuron on the receiving end of a synapse (page 82)

**prefrontal cortex:** an area in the anterior portion of the frontal lobes, critical for planning movements and for certain aspects of memory (page 94)

**primary motor cortex:** a strip in the posterior (rear) part of the frontal cortex that controls fine movements, such as hand and finger movements (page 94)

**primary somatosensory cortex:** a strip in the anterior (forward) part of the parietal lobe that receives most touch sensations and other information about the body (page 91)

**recessive gene:** a gene that will affect development only in a person who is homozygous for that gene (page 98)

**reflex:** a rapid, automatic response to a stimulus (page 88)

**resting potential:** electrical polarization that ordinarily occurs across the membrane of an axon that is not undergoing an action potential (page 80)

**sensory neuron:** a neuron that carries information about touch, pain, and other senses from the periphery of the body to the spinal cord (page 88)

**sex chromosomes:** the pair of chromosomes that determine whether an individual will develop as a female or as a male (page 70)

**sex-limited gene:** a gene that affects one sex more strongly than the other, even though both sexes have the gene (page 70)

**sex-linked gene:** a gene located on the X chromosome (page 70)

**sociobiology:** a field that tries to relate the social behaviors of a species to its biology, particularly to its evolutionary history (page 76)

**somatic nervous system:** peripheral nerves that communicate with the skin and muscles (page 87)

**spinal cord:** that part of the central nervous system that communicates with sensory neurons and motor neurons below the level of the head (page 88)

**stem cells:** undifferentiated cells (page 80)

**synapse:** the specialized junction between one neuron and another; at this point, one neuron releases a neurotransmitter, which either excites or inhibits the next neuron (page 81)

**temporal lobe:** a portion of each cerebral hemisphere; the main processing area for hearing, complex aspects of vision, and certain aspects of emotional behavior (page 93)

**terminal bouton** (or **button**): a bulge at the end of an axon from which the axon releases a chemical called a neurotransmitter (page 81)

**X chromosome:** a sex chromosome; females have two per cell and males have only one (page 70)

**Y chromosome:** a sex chromosome; males have one per cell and females have none (page 70)

## Suggestions for Further Reading

Kalat, J. W. (2001). *Biological psychology* (7th ed.). Belmont, CA: Wadsworth. Chapters 1 through 4 deal with the material discussed in this chapter in more detail.

Klawans, H. L. (1996). *Why Michael couldn't hit*. New York: Freeman. Informative and entertaining account of how the rise and fall of various sports heroes relates to what we know about the brain.

Plomin, R., & Crabbe, J. (2000). DNA. *Psychological Bulletin, 126*, 806–828. Review of the role of genetics in psychology.

## Web/Technology Resources

Human Genome Project

**www.ornl.gov/TechResources/Human_Genome/home.html**

This is the definitive site for understanding the Human Genome Project, from the basic science to ethical, legal, and social considerations to the latest discoveries.

M.M.M. Brain Tour: Building Blocks

**suhep.phy.syr.edu/courses/modules/MM/Biology/biology2.html**

Good illustrations and very readable text lead you through this tour of neurons, neurotransmitters, and neural organization, produced by the Mind and Machine MODULE team at Syracuse University.

## A Brief Tour of the Brain

**suhep.phy.syr.edu/courses/modules/MM/Biology/biology.html**

Scientists at Syracuse University review the structure and functions of the brain and its parts, right down to the neurons; includes illustrations and very readable text.

## The Whole Brain Atlas

**www.med.harvard.edu/AANLIB/home.html**

Stunning photographs of both normal and abnormal brains.

## Brain Scans

**www.biophysics.mcw.edu**

Click on various links to see images and movies of the three-dimensional structure of the brain.

## BrainPoke!

**www.wlu.edu/~web/bp/brainpk.html**

Tell the surgeon where to poke the brain. See the effect. Does the effect match your expectations?

## The L.A. Times Brain Page

**www.latimes.com/HOME/NEWS/SCIENCE/REPORTS/_THEBRAIN/**

The *L.A. Times* Brain Page has one of the more impressive pages you will see on the Web. Note the background of the page itself. You will find several interesting brain facts, articles, and links on this page.

# Sensation and Perception

**4**

CHAPTER

**W**hen my son Sam was 8 years old, he asked me, "If we went to some other planet, would we see different colors?" He did not mean just a new mixture of familiar colors. He meant colors that were as different from familiar colors as yellow is from red or blue. I told him that would be impossible, and I tried to explain why.

No matter where we go in outer space, no matter what unfamiliar objects or atmospheres we might encounter, we could never experience a color or a sound or any other sensation that would be fundamentally different from what we experience on Earth. Different combinations, perhaps. But fundamentally different sensory experiences, no.

Three years later, Sam told me he was wondering whether people who look at the same thing are all having the same experience: When different people look at something and call it "green," how can we know whether they are all seeing the same "green"? I agreed that there is no way of knowing for sure.

Why am I certain that colors on a different planet would look the same as they do here on Earth and yet uncertain whether colors look the same to different people here? The answer may be obvious to you. If not, I hope it will be after you have read this chapter.

**Sensation** is the *conversion of energy from the environment into a pattern of response by the nervous system*. It is the registration of information. **Perception** is *the interpretation of that information*. For example, light rays striking your eyes give rise to sensation. When you conclude from that sensation, "I see my roommate," you are expressing your perception. (In practice the distinction between sensation and perception is often difficult to make.)

■ No matter how exotic some other planet might be, it could not have colors we do not have here. The reason is that our eyes can see only certain wavelengths of light, and color is the experience our brains create from those wavelengths.

# Vision

*How do our eyes convert light energy into something that we can experience?*

*How do we perceive colors?*

We live in a world full of **stimuli**—*energies that affect what we do*. Our eyes, ears, and other sensory organs are packed with **receptors**—*specialized cells that convert environmental energies into signals for the nervous system*. We see, hear, and so forth because stimuli activate receptors, which in turn send messages to the brain, which eventually uses this information to guide our behavior.

You have probably already been given this account in a science class in high school, perhaps even in elementary school. But did you believe it? Evidently, not everyone does. One survey posed the questions, "When we look at someone or something, does anything such as rays, waves, or energy go out of our eyes? into our eyes?" Among first graders (about age 6), 49% answered (incorrectly) that energy went out of the eyes, and 54% answered that energy came into the eyes. (It was possible to say *yes* to both.) Among college students, 33% said that energy went out of the eyes; 88% said that energy came in (Winer & Cottrell, 1996).

The idea that the eyes send out sight rays is hardly the only widespread misconception about vision. We are often led astray because we imagine that what we see is simply a copy of the outside world, but it is not. For example, color is not a property of objects; it is something your brain creates in response to light of different wavelengths. Brightness is not the same thing as the intensity of the light. (Light that is twice as intense does not appear twice as bright.) Our experiences *translate* the stimuli of the outside world into very different representations.

## The Detection of Light

What we call *light* is just one part of the electromagnetic spectrum. As Figure 4.1 shows, the **electromagnetic spectrum** is *the continuum of all the frequencies of radiated energy*—from gamma rays and x-rays, which have very short wavelengths, through ultraviolet, visible light, and infrared to radio and TV transmissions, which have very long wavelengths.

What makes "visible light" visible? The answer is our receptors, which are equipped to respond to wavelengths

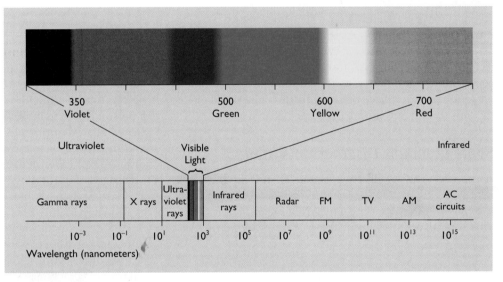

**FIGURE 4.1** Visible light, what human eyes can see, is only a small part of the entire electromagnetic spectrum. While experimenting with prisms, Isaac Newton discovered that white light is a mixture of all colors, and color is a property of light. A carrot looks orange because it reflects orange light and absorbs all the other colors.

from 400 to 700 nanometers (nm). With different receptors we might see a different range of wavelengths. Some species—bees, for example—respond to wavelengths shorter than 350 nm, which are invisible to humans.

## The Structure of the Eye

When we see an object, light reflected from that object passes through the **pupil**, an *adjustable opening in the eye through which light enters*. The **iris** is the *colored structure on the surface of the eye, surrounding the pupil*. It is the structure we describe when we say someone has brown, green, or blue eyes. When the light is dim, muscles open the pupil to let in more light. When the light is bright, muscles narrow the pupil.

After light passes through the pupil, it travels through the *vitreous humor* (a clear jellylike substance) and strikes the retina at the back of the eyeball. The **retina** is a *layer of visual receptors covering the back surface of the eyeball* (Figure 4.2). As light passes through the eye, the cornea and the lens focus the light on the retina as shown.

The **cornea,** *a rigid transparent structure on the outer surface of the eyeball,* always focuses light in the same way. The **lens** is a *flexible structure that can vary in thickness,* enabling the eye to **accommodate,** that is, *to adjust its focus for objects at different distances.* When we look at a distant object, for example, our eye muscles relax and let the lens become thinner and flatter, as shown in Figure 4.3a. When we look at a close object, our eye muscles tighten and make the lens thicker and rounder (Figure 4.3b).

## Some Common Disorders of Vision

As people grow older, they gradually develop **presbyopia,** *decreased flexibility of the lens and therefore inability to focus on nearby objects.* (The Greek root *presby* means "old." This root also shows up in the word *presbyterian,* which

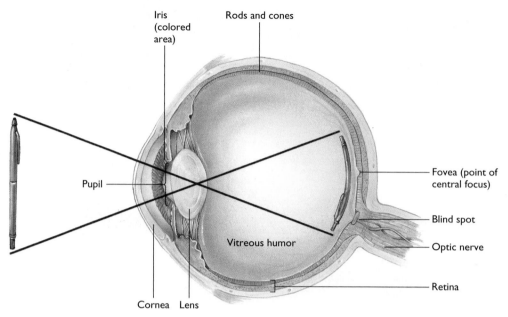

FIGURE 4.2 The lens gets its name from Latin for *lentil,* referring to its shape—an appropriate choice, as this cross section of the eye shows. The names of other parts of the eye also refer to their appearance.

means "governed by the elders.") Many people's eyes are not quite spherical. A person whose eyeballs are elongated, as shown in Figure 4.4a, can focus well on nearby objects but has difficulty focusing on distant objects. Such a person is said to be *nearsighted,* or to have **myopia** (mi-O-pee-ah). About half of all 20-year-olds are nearsighted and must wear glasses or contact lenses to see well at a distance. An older person with both myopia and presbyopia needs bifocal glasses to help with both near focus and distant focus. A person whose eyeballs are flattened, as shown in Figure 4.4b, has **hyperopia,** or *farsightedness.* Such a person can focus well on distant objects but has difficulty focusing on close objects.

Two other common visual disorders are glaucoma and cataracts. **Glaucoma** is a *condition characterized by increased pressure within the eyeball;* the result can be damage to the optic nerve and therefore a progressive loss of peripheral vision ("tunnel vision"). A **cataract** is a *disorder in which the lens becomes cloudy.* People with severe cataracts can have the lens surgically removed and replaced with a contact lens. Because the normal lens filters out more blue and ultraviolet light than other light, people with artificial lenses sometimes report seeing blue more clearly and distinctly than they ever had before (Davenport & Foley, 1979). They do, however, suffer increased risk of damage to the retina from ultraviolet light.

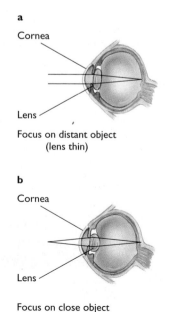

FIGURE 4.3 The flexible, transparent lens changes shape so that objects (a) far and (b) near can come into focus. The lens bends entering light rays so that they fall on the retina. In old age the lens becomes rigid, and people find it harder to focus on nearby objects.

**a**
Cornea

Lens

Focus on distant object
(lens thin)

**b**
Cornea

Lens

Focus on close object
(lens thick)

## CONCEPT CHECK

1. Suppose you have normal vision and you try on a pair of glasses made for a person with myopia. How will the glasses affect your vision? (Check your answer on page 121.)

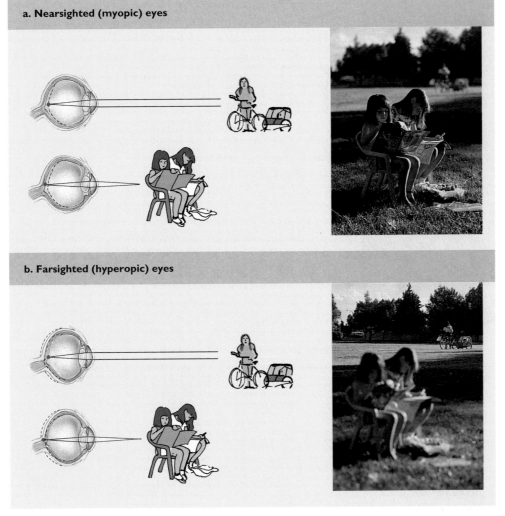

a. Nearsighted (myopic) eyes

b. Farsighted (hyperopic) eyes

**FIGURE 4.4** The structure of (a) nearsighted and (b) farsighted eyes distorts vision. Because the nearsighted eye is elongated, light from a distant object focuses in front of the retina. Because the farsighted eye is flattened, light from a nearby object focuses behind the retina. (The dashed line shows the position of the normal retina in each case.)

## The Visual Receptors

The visual receptors of the eye, specialized neurons in the retina at the back of the eyeball, are so sensitive to light that they are capable of responding to a single photon, the smallest possible quantity of light. There are two types of visual receptors: cones and rods, which differ in appearance, as Figure 4.5 shows, and in function. The **cones** are *receptors adapted for color vision, daytime vision, and detailed vision*. The **rods** are *receptors adapted for vision in dim light*.

About 5–10% of all the visual receptors in the human retina are cones. Most birds have at least that high a proportion of cones and correspondingly have good color vision. Species that are active mostly at night—rats and mice, for example—have mostly rods, and thus good perception in faint light.

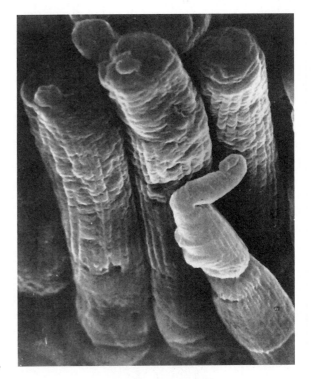

**FIGURE 4.5** Rods and cones seen through a scanning electron micrograph. The rods, which number over 120 million in humans, help us see in dim light. The 6 million cones in the retina can distinguish gradations of color in bright light; they enable us to see that roses are red, magenta, ruby, carmine, cherry, vermilion, scarlet, and crimson—not to mention pink, yellow, orange, and white.

**FIGURE 4.6** The consequence of having receptors mostly on the top of the retina: Birds of prey, such as these owlets, can see down much more clearly than they can see up. In flight that arrangement is helpful. On the ground they have to turn their heads almost upside down to see above them.

The proportion of cones is highest toward the center of the retina. The **fovea** (FOE-vee-uh), *the central area of the human retina*, is adapted for highly detailed vision (see Figure 4.2). Of all retinal areas, the fovea has the greatest density of receptors; also, more of the cerebral cortex is devoted to analyzing input from the fovea than input from other areas. If you want to see something in detail, such as letters of the alphabet, you focus it on the fovea.

Hawks, owls, and other predatory birds have a greater density of receptors on the top of the retina (for looking down) than on the bottom of the retina (for looking up). When these birds are flying, this arrangement enables them to see the ground beneath them in detail. When they are on the ground, however, they have trouble seeing above themselves (Figure 4.6).

The fovea consists solely of cones (Figure 4.2). Away from the fovea, the proportion of cones drops sharply. For that reason you are colorblind in the far periphery of your eye.

 Try this experiment: Hold several pens or pencils of different colors behind your back. (Any objects will work as long as they have about the same size and shape and approximately the same brightness.) Pick one at random without looking at it. Hold it behind your head and bring it very slowly into your field of vision. When you just barely begin to see it, you will probably not be able to tell what color it is. (If glaucoma or another medical problem has impaired your peripheral vision, you will have to bring the object closer to your fovea before you can see it at all, and then you will see its color at once.)

The rods are more effective than the cones for detecting dim light for two reasons: First, a rod is slightly more responsive to faint stimulation than a cone is. Second, the rods pool their resources. Only a few cones converge their messages onto the next cell in the visual system, whereas many rods converge their messages. In the far periphery of the retina, more than 100 rods send messages to the next cell (see Figure 4.7). Table 4.1 summarizes some of the key differences between rods and cones.

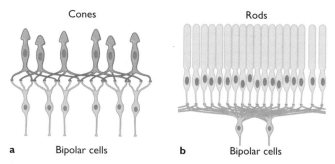

**FIGURE 4.7** Because so many rods converge their input into the next layer of the visual system, known as bipolar cells, even a small amount of light falling on the rods can stimulate the bipolar cells. Thus, the periphery of the retina, with many rods, has good perception of faint light. However, because bipolars in the periphery get input from so many receptors, they have only imprecise information about the location and shape of objects.

**TABLE 4.1** Differences Between Rods and Cones

|  | Rods | Cones |
|---|---|---|
| *Shape* | Nearly cylindrical | Tapered at one end |
| *Prevalence in human retina* | 90–95% | 5–10% |
| *Greatest incidence by species* | In species that are active at night | In birds, primates, and other species that are active during the day |
| *Area of the retina* | Toward the periphery | Toward the fovea |
| *Contribution to color vision* | No direct contribution | Critical for color vision |
| *Response to dim light* | Strong | Weak |
| *Contribution to perception in detail* | Little | Much |

# CONCEPT CHECK

**2.** Why is it easier to see a faint star in the sky if you look slightly to the side of the star instead of straight at it? (Check your answer on page 121.)

## Dark Adaptation

Suppose you go into a basement at night trying to find your flashlight. The only light bulb in the basement is burned out. A little moonlight comes through the basement windows, but not much. At first you can hardly see anything. A minute or two later, you are beginning to see well enough to find your way around, and eventually you can see well enough to find the flashlight. This *gradual improvement in the ability to see in dim light* is called **dark adaptation.**

The mechanism behind dark adaptation is this: Exposure to light causes a chemical change in certain molecules called *retinaldehydes,* thereby stimulating the visual receptors. (Retinaldehydes are derived from vitamin A.) Under normal (moderate) light, the receptors *regenerate* (rebuild) the retinaldehydes about as fast as the light is altering them, and the person maintains about a constant level of visual sensitivity. In darkness or very dim light, however, the receptors can regenerate their molecules without interruption, so the person gradually becomes better able to detect faint lights.

The cones and rods adapt to the dark at different rates. During the day our vision ordinarily relies overwhelmingly on cones. When we enter a dark place, our cones regenerate their retinaldehydes faster than the rods do, but by the time the rods finish their regeneration, they are far more sensitive to faint light than the cones are. At that point we are seeing mostly with rods.

Here is how a psychologist demonstrates this process of dark adaptation (E. B. Goldstein, 1989): You are taken into a room that is completely dark except for one tiny flashing light. You have a knob that controls the intensity of the light; you are told to make the light so dim that you can barely see it. Over the course of 3 or 4 minutes, you will gradually decrease the intensity of the light, as shown in Figure 4.8a. Note that a decrease in the intensity of the light indicates an increase in the sensitivity of your eyes. If you stare straight at the point of light, your results will demonstrate the adaptation of your cones to the dim light. (You have been focusing the light on your fovea, which has no rods.)

Now the psychologist repeats the study with one change in procedure: You are told to stare at a very faint light while another light flashes somewhat to the side of the fovea, where it stimulates both rods and cones. You turn a control knob until the flashing light in the periphery is just barely visible. (Figure 4.8b shows the results.) During the first 7 to 10 minutes, the results are the same as before. But then your rods become more sensitive than your cones, and you begin to see even fainter lights. Your rods continue to adapt to the dark over the next 20 minutes or so.

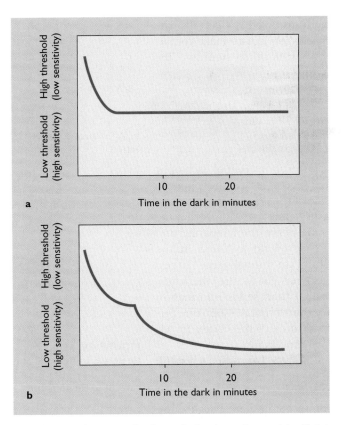

**FIGURE 4.8** These graphs show dark adaptation to (a) a light you stare at directly, using only cones, and (b) a light in your peripheral vision, which you see with both cones and rods. (Based on E. B. Goldstein, 1989)

If you would like to demonstrate dark adaptation for yourself without any apparatus, try this: On a dark night, with only slight amounts of light coming through your windows, turn on a light in your room. Close one eye and cover it tightly with your hand for a few minutes. By the end of that time, your covered eye will be adapted to the dark and your open eye will be adapted to the light. Next turn off your light and then open both eyes. You will see well with your dark-adapted eye and poorly with the light-adapted eye.

# CONCEPT CHECK

**3.** You may have heard people say that cats can see in the dark. Is that possible?

**4.** After you have thoroughly adapted to extremely dim light, will you see more objects in your fovea or in the periphery of your eye? (Check your answers on page 121.)

## The Visual Pathway

If you or I were designing an eye, we would probably run the axons of the cones and rods straight to the brain. Nature chose a different method. The visual receptors send their impulses *away from* the brain, toward the center of the eye, where they make synaptic contacts with other neurons called bipolar cells. The *bipolar cells* in turn make contact with still other neurons, the **ganglion cells,** which are *neurons that receive their input from the bipolar cells.* The *axons from the ganglion cells join to form* the **optic nerve,** *which turns around and exits the eye,* as Figures 4.2 and 4.9 show. Half of each optic nerve crosses to the opposite side of the brain at the optic chiasm (KI-az-m). Axons from the optic nerve then separate and go to several locations in the brain. In humans the largest number go to the thalamus, which then sends information to the occipital lobe, the primary area of the cortex for visual processing.

The *area where the optic nerve exits the retina* is called the **blind spot.** There is no room for receptors here because the exiting axons take up all the space. Ordinarily, you are unaware of your blind spot.

 To illustrate, cover your left eye and stare at the center of Figure 4.10; then slowly move the page forward and backward. When your eye is about 25–30 cm (10–12 inches) away from the page, the lion disappears because it falls into your blind spot. In its place you perceive a continuation of the circle.

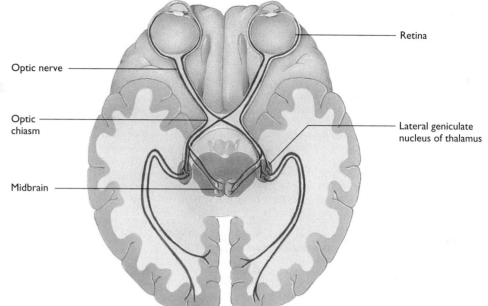

**FIGURE 4.9** Axons from cells in the retina depart the eye at the blind spot and form the optic nerve. In humans about half the axons in the optic nerve cross to the opposite side of the brain at the optic chiasm. Some optic nerve axons carry information to the midbrain; others carry it to the thalamus, which relays information to the cerebral cortex.

**FIGURE 4.10** Close your left eye and focus your right eye on the animal trainer. Move the page toward your eyes and away from them, until you find the point where the lion on the right disappears. At that point the lion is focused on the blind spot of your retina, where you have no receptors. What you see there is not a blank spot but a continuation of the circle.

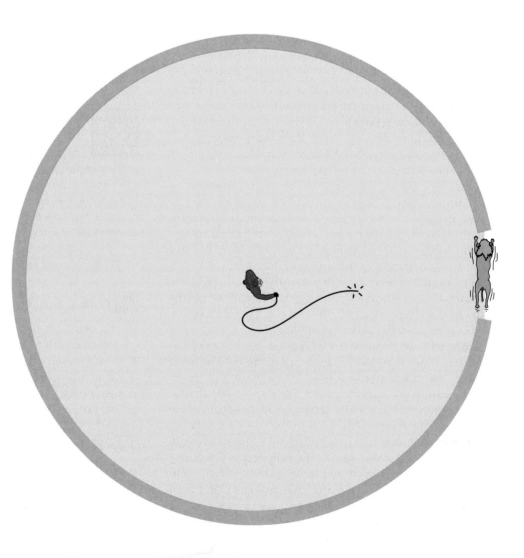

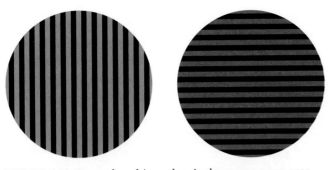

**FIGURE 4.11** To produce binocular rivalry, move your eyes toward the page until the two circles seem to merge. You will alternate between seeing red lines and green lines.

Information from the left and right eyes remains separate until it reaches the visual cortex. Each cell in the visual cortex receives input from one part of the left retina and a corresponding part of the right retina—that is, two retinal areas that ordinarily focus on the same point in space. Under normal conditions the input coming from the left retina is almost the same as that coming from the right retina, and the two effects summate. However, examine Figure 4.11 to see what happens if the retinal images conflict.

 Move your eyes so close to the page that the two circles seem to merge. You have some neurons in your visual cortex that respond to vertical lines. When you merge the two circles, those cells are getting stimulated by one pattern and inhibited by the other (Logothetis, Leopold, & Sheinberg, 1996). For a short while, the stimulation dominates but then for a while the inhibition dominates. Meanwhile, inhibition and stimulation are also alternating for cells that respond to horizontal lines. The net effect is that you see green lines, then red lines, then green lines again, and so forth. The *alternation between seeing the pattern in the left retina and the pattern in the right retina* is known as **binocular rivalry.**

We become aware of visual information after it reaches the cerebral cortex. Someone who has intact eyes but a damaged visual cortex is blind and even loses visual imagery. However, someone with damaged eyes and an intact brain can at least imagine visual scenes. One laboratory has developed a way to bypass damaged eyes and send visual information directly to the brain. As shown in Figure 4.12, a camera attached to a blind person's sunglasses sends messages to a computer which then sends messages to electrodes that stimulate appropriate spots in the person's visual cortex (Dobelle, 2000). After hours of practice, such people can see well enough to find their way around, to identify simple shapes, and to count how many fingers someone holds up. The goal is a more elaborate array of electrodes that might be more useful than a guide dog without being much more expensive.

## Color Vision

As Figure 4.1 shows, different colors of light correspond to different wavelengths of electromagnetic energy. (White light consists of an equal mixture of all the visible wavelengths.) How does the visual system convert these wavelengths into our perception of color? The process begins with three kinds of cones, which respond to different wavelengths of light. Later cells in the visual path code this wavelength information in terms of pairs of opposites—roughly, red versus green, yellow versus blue, and white versus black. Finally, cells in the cerebral cortex compare the input from various parts of the visual field to synthesize a color experience for each object. We shall examine these three stages in turn.

### *The Trichromatic Theory*

Thomas Young was an English physician of the 1700s who, among other accomplishments, helped to decode the Rosetta stone (making it possible to understand Egyptian hieroglyphics), introduced the modern concept of energy, revived and popularized the wave theory of light, and offered the first theory about how people perceive color. His theory, elaborated and modified by Hermann von Helmholtz in the 1800s, came to be known as the

**FIGURE 4.12** William Dobelle has developed an apparatus that takes an image from a camera attached to a blind person's sunglasses, transforms it by a computer, and sends a message to electrodes in the visual cortex. By this means someone with damaged eyes regains some vision.

**trichromatic theory** or the **Young-Helmholtz theory.** It is called *trichromatic* because it claims that our receptors respond to three primary colors. In modern terms we say that *color vision depends on the relative rate of response by three types of cones.* Each type of cone is most sensitive to a particular range of light wavelengths (Figure 4.13). One type is most sensitive to short wavelengths (which we generally see as blue), another to medium wavelengths (seen as green), and another to long wavelengths (red). Each wavelength prompts varying levels of activity in the three types of cones. So, for example, green light excites mostly the medium-wavelength cones, red light excites mostly the long-wavelength cones, and yellow light excites the medium-wavelength and long-wavelength cones about equally. Every wavelength of light produces its own distinct ratio of responses by the three kinds of cones. White light excites all three kinds of cones equally.

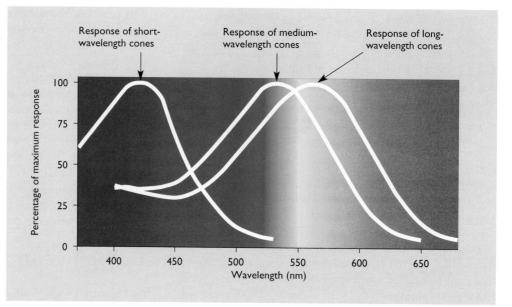

**FIGURE 4.13** Sensitivity of three types of cones to different wavelengths of light. (Based on data of Bowmaker & Dartnall, 1980)

Young and Helmholtz proposed their theory long before experiments confirmed the existence of these three types of cones (Wald, 1968). They relied entirely on a behavioral observation: Observers can take three different colors of light and then, by mixing them in various proportions, match all other colors of light. (Note that mixing light of different colors is not the same as mixing paints of different colors. Mixing yellow and blue *paints* produces green; mixing yellow and blue *lights* produces white.)

The short-wavelength cones, which respond most strongly to blue, are less numerous than the other two types of cones, especially in the fovea. Consequently, a tiny blue point may look black. For the retina to detect blueness, the blue must extend over a moderately large area.

 Figure 4.14 illustrates this effect. Count the red spots and then the blue spots. Then stand farther away and count the spots again. You will probably see as many red spots as before but fewer blue spots.

**FIGURE 4.14** Blue spots look black unless they cover a sizable area. Count the red dots; then count the blue dots. Try again while standing farther from the page.

# CONCEPT CHECK

5. According to the trichromatic theory, how does our nervous system tell the difference between bright yellow–green and dim yellow–green light? (Check your answer on page 121.)

## The Opponent-Process Theory

Young and Helmholtz were right about how many cones we have, but our perception of color has some complicated features that the trichromatic theory cannot easily handle. For example, four colors, not three, *seem* to most people to be primary or basic: red, green, yellow, and blue. Yellow simply does not seem like a mixture of reddish and greenish experiences, nor is green a yellowish blue. Furthermore, if you stare at an object of one color, say, red, and then look away, you see a colored afterimage—in this case green. Each color appears to have an opposite, and there is no obvious reason why it should, according to the trichromatic theory.

For these reasons, a 19th-century scientist, Ewald Hering, proposed the **opponent-process theory** of color vision: *We perceive color not in terms of independent colors but in terms of a system of paired opposites—red versus green, yellow versus blue, and white versus black.* This idea is best explained in terms of an example.

 Stare at the white dot near the center of the Figure 4.15 for a minute or so under a bright light without moving your eyes or your head. Then look at a plain white or gray background. *Do this now.*

When you looked away, you saw the *Mona Lisa* in her normal coloration. After staring at something blue, you get a yellow afterimage. Similarly, after staring at yellow,

FIGURE 4.15 Use this image to see the negative afterimages of opposite colors, which rebound after sufficient stimulation. Stare at the white dot for a minute or more; then focus on a white background.

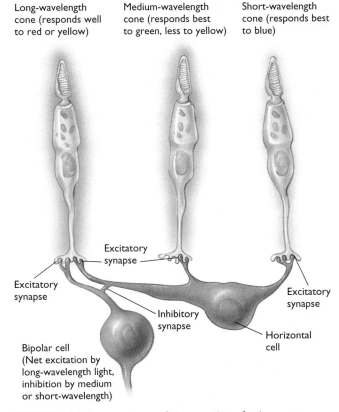

FIGURE 4.16 One way to explain negative afterimages: Long-wavelength ("red") light produces net excitation in this bipolar cell. Medium- or short-wavelength light produces inhibition. Because short-wavelength cones are scarce, such a cell as this one is mostly inhibited by medium-wavelength ("green") light. When the bipolar cell is excited, it produces a perception of red. But when it is fatigued, it responds less than usual, as if it were being inhibited, and therefore yields a perception of green.

you see blue; after red, you see green; after green, you see red; after white, black; and after black, white. These *experiences of one color after the removal of another* are called **negative afterimages.**

We can explain these negative afterimages in terms of excitation and inhibition of neurons in the visual system. For example, consider the bipolar cell in Figure 4.16. It receives an excitatory synaptic message from the long-wavelength cone (responding to light we usually see as red), and it is most strongly inhibited by the medium-wavelength cone (corresponding to green). So in fact, anything that makes this cell increase its response produces a red sensation and anything that decreases its response produces a green sensation. After a period of prolonged excitation, when the stimulus is removed, the now fatigued cell becomes less active than usual, just as if it were being inhibited. Therefore, it yields a green sensation. Similarly, other bipolar cells are excited by green and inhibited by red or excited by blue and inhibited by yellow.

This mechanism of excitation and inhibition is found in bipolar cells and also in ganglion cells and several other types of cells in the visual system (DeValois & Jacobs, 1968; Engel, 1999). Which type is actually responsible for the color perception, including the negative color after-

images? Simply, we don't know. Many cell types contribute in different ways, but where we actually become conscious of the sensation is a difficult question.

# CONCEPT CHECK

6. How would the bipolar cell in Figure 4.16 respond to yellow light? Why?
7. The negative afterimage that you created by staring at Figure 4.15 may seem to move against the background. Why doesn't it stay in one place? (Check your answers on page 121.)

## The Retinex Theory

The opponent-process theory, though it accounts for many phenomena of color vision, overlooks an important one. Suppose you look at a large white screen illuminated entirely with green light in an otherwise dark room. How would you know whether this is a white screen illuminated with green light or a green screen illuminated with

**FIGURE 4.17** Despite the green and red filters used in producing the center and right-hand photographs, you can still identify the colors of the objects in the photos. The effect would be much more convincing if you were actually on location, looking at this scene through tinted glasses. Here each photo is surrounded by the white page, which sets an effective standard. Your ability to identify the color of an object, despite changes in the light striking the environment, is called color constancy.

white light? Or a blue screen illuminated with yellow light? (Actually, the possibilities go on and on.) The answer is, you wouldn't know. But now someone wearing a brown shirt and blue jeans stands in front of the screen. Suddenly, you see the shirt as brown, the jeans as blue, and the screen as white, even though all the objects are reflecting more green light than anything else. The point is that we do not ordinarily perceive the color of an object in isolation. We perceive color by comparing the light an object reflects to the light that other objects in the scene reflect. As a result we can perceive blue jeans as blue and bananas as yellow regardless of the type of light. This *tendency of an object to appear nearly the same color under a variety of lighting conditions* is called **color constancy** (see Figure 4.17).

In response to such observations, Edwin Land (the inventor of the Polaroid Land Camera) proposed the **retinex theory.** According to this theory, *we perceive color through the cerebral cortex's comparison of various retinal patterns* (Figure 4.18). (*Retinex* is a combination of the words *retina* and *cortex.*) The cerebral cortex compares the patterns of light coming from different areas of the retina and synthesizes a color perception for each area (Land, Hubel, Livingstone, Perry, & Burns, 1983; Land & McCann, 1971).

The strongest evidence for this theory comes from brain-damaged patients. Damage to one region of the cortex destroys color constancy (Zeki, 1993; Zeki, McKeefry, Bartels, & Frackowiak, 1998). To a person with such brain damage, an object that looks orange under one light looks red under another and yellow, greenish, or even white under still other lights. As the retinex theory predicts, the phenomenon of color constancy depends on the activity of the cerebral cortex.

In the 1800s the trichromatic theory and the opponent-process theory were considered rival theories, but vision researchers today consider both of them, as well as the retinex theory, to be correct statements that happen to address different aspects of vision. The trichro-

matic theory is certainly correct in stating that human color vision starts with three kinds of cones. The opponent-process theory explains how the bipolar cells and later cells organize color information. The retinex theory adds the final touch, noting that the cerebral cortex compares color information from various parts of the visual field.

**A STEP FURTHER**
*Color Afterimages*

If you stare for a minute at a small green object on a white background and then look away, you will see a red afterimage. But if you stare at a green wall nearby so that you see nothing but green in all directions, then when you look away you do not see a red afterimage. Why not?

## Colorblindness

For a long time, people apparently assumed that anyone with normal vision could see and recognize colors (Fletcher & Voke, 1985). Then during the 1600s, the phenomenon of colorblindness (or color deficiency) was unambiguously recognized. Here was the first clue that color vision is a function of our eyes and brains, and not just of the light itself.

The total inability to distinguish one color from another is extremely rare, except as a result of brain damage. However, about 4% of all people are partly colorblind. Investigators believe that most cases of colorblindness result from either the absence of one of the three types of cones or a decreased responsiveness by one type (Fletcher & Voke, 1985). People with a deficiency of the medium-wavelength cones are relatively insensitive to medium-wavelength (green) light (Boynton, 1988).

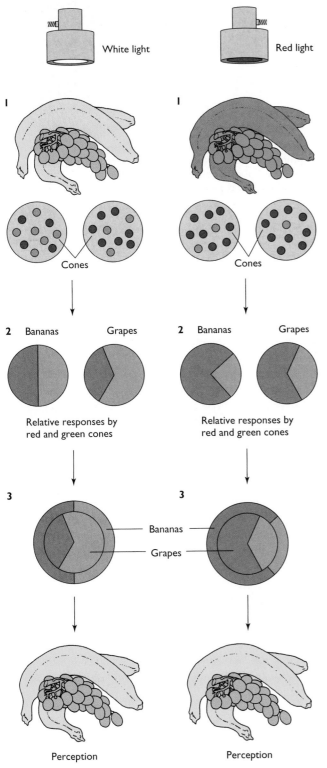

**FIGURE 4.18** When bananas and grapes reflect red light, they excite a higher percentage of long-wavelength (red) cones than usual. According to the retinex theory, brain cells determine the red-green percentage for each fruit. Then cells in the visual cortex divide the "red-greenness" of the bananas by the "red-greenness" of the grapes to produce color sensations. In red and white light, the ratios between the fruits are nearly constant.

The most common type of colorblindness is sometimes known as **red-green colorblindness.** People with red-green colorblindness *have difficulty distinguishing red from green and either red or green from yellow.* Actually, red-green colorblindness has two forms: *protanopia* and *deuteranopia.* People with protanopia lack long-wavelength cones; people with deuteranopia lack medium-wavelength cones. People with the rare *yellow-blue colorblindness* (also known as *tritanopia*) have trouble distinguishing yellows and blues. They are believed to lack short-wavelength cones.

 Figure 4.19 gives a crude but usually satisfactory test for red-green colorblindness. What do you see in each part of the figure? (To interpret your answers, refer to answer A on page 121.)

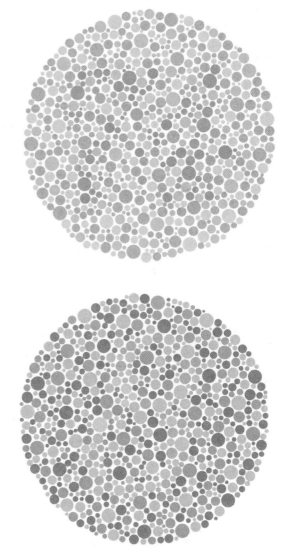

**FIGURE 4.19** These items provide an informal test for red-green blindness, an inherited condition that mostly affects men. What do you see? Compare your answers to answer A on page 121.

How does the world look to colorblind people? Their descriptions use all the usual color words: Roses are red, violets are blue, bananas are yellow, grass is green. But their answers do not mean that they perceive colors the same as other people do. Can they tell us what a "red" rose actually looks like? In most cases no. Certain rare individuals, however, are red-green colorblind in one eye but have normal vision in the other eye. Because they know what the color words really mean (from experience with their normal eye), they can tell us what their colorblind eye sees. They say that objects that look red or green to the normal eye look yellow or yellow-gray to the colorblind eye (Marriott, 1976).

If you have normal color vision, Figure 4.20 will show you what it is like to be red-green color-blind. First, cover part b, a typical item from a colorblindness test, and stare at part a, a red field, under a bright light for about a minute. (The brighter the light and the longer you stare, the greater the effect will be.) Then look at part b. Staring at the red field has fatigued your red cones, so you will now have only a weak sensation of red. As the red cones recover, you will see part b normally.

Now stare at part c, a green field, for about a minute and look at part b again. Because you have fatigued your green cones, the figure in b will stand out even more strongly than usual. In fact, certain red-green colorblind people may be able to see the number in b only after staring at c. (Refer to answer B on page 121.)

**A STEP FURTHER**
*Color Experiences*

In the introduction to this chapter, I suggested that we would see no new colors on another planet and that we cannot be certain that different people on Earth really have the same color experiences. Now try to explain the reasons behind those statements.

**IN CLOSING**
*How We See*

Before there were any people or other color-sighted animals, was there any color on Earth? *No.* There was light, to be sure, and different objects reflected different wave-

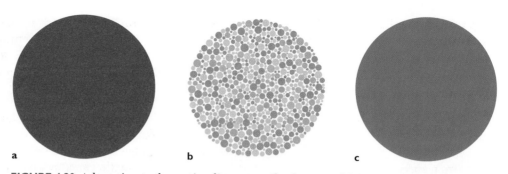

**FIGURE 4.20** Adaptation to these stimuli temporarily alters sensitivity to reds and greens. First, stare at pattern (a) under bright light for about a minute and then look at (b). What do you see? Next stare at (c) for a minute and look at (b) again. Now what do you see? Compare your answer to answer B on page 121.

lengths of light, but color exists only in brains, not in the objects themselves. Our vision is not just a copy of the outside world; it is a construction that enables us to interact with the world to our benefit.

To many readers vision and our other senses seem more complicated than some of the later topics in this book, such as emotion. To some extent sensation may really be more complicated than emotion, but the apparent difference in complexity exists partly because researchers have learned so much more about the senses. The more we learn about any topic, the more sophisticated questions we can ask. The complexity of what we now know about vision is a tribute to many generations of researchers.

## Summary

- *Common misconceptions.* The eyes do not send out "sight rays," nor does the brain build little copies of the stimuli it senses. It converts or translates sensory stimuli into an arbitrary code that represents the information. (page 109)

- *Focus.* The cornea and lens focus the light that enters through the pupil of the eye. If the eye is not spherical or if the lens is not flexible, corrective lenses may be needed. (page 110)

- *Cones and rods.* The retina contains two kinds of receptors: cones and rods. Cones are specialized for detailed vision and color perception. Rods detect dim light. (page 111)

- *Blind spot.* The blind spot is the area of the retina through which the optic nerve exits; this area has no visual receptors and is therefore blind. (page 114)

- *Binocular rivalry.* Under normal circumstances the two retinas receive similar information patterns and provide the brain with information for three-dimensional perception. If the two retinas receive incompatible patterns, we experience a competition in which one pattern or the other dominates at any given moment. (page 115)

- *Color vision.* Color vision depends on three types of cones, each most sensitive to a particular range of light wavelengths. The cones transmit messages so that the bipolar and ganglion cells in the visual system are excited by light of one color and inhibited by light of the opposite color. Then the cerebral cortex compares the responses from different parts of the retina to determine the color of light coming from each area of the visual field. (page 115)

- *Colorblindness.* Complete colorblindness is rare. Certain people have difficulty distinguishing reds from greens; in rare cases some have difficulty distinguishing yellows from blues. (page 118)

## Answers to Concept Checks

1. If your vision is normal, then wearing glasses intended for a myopic person will make your vision blurry. Such glasses alter the light as though they were bringing the object closer to the viewer. Unless the glasses are very strong, you may not notice much difference when you are looking at distant objects because you can adjust the lens of your eyes to compensate for what the glasses do. However, nearby objects will appear blurry in spite of the best compensations that the lenses of your eyes can make. (page 110)

2. The center of the retina consists entirely of cones. If you look slightly to the side, the light falls on an area of the retina that consists partly of rods, which are more sensitive to faint light. (page 113)

3. As do people, cats can adapt well to dim light. No animal, however, can see in complete darkness. Vision is the detection of light that strikes the eye. (Similarly, the x-ray vision attributed to the comic book character Superman is impossible. Even if he could send out x-rays, he would not see anything unless those x-rays bounced off an object and back into his eyes.) (page 113)

4. You will see more objects in the periphery of your eye. The fovea contains only cones, which cannot become as sensitive as the rods do in the periphery. (page 113)

5. Although bright yellow-green and dim yellow-green light would evoke the same ratio of activity by the three cone types, the total amount of activity would be greater for the bright yellow-green light. (page 116)

6. The bipolar cell would be almost unaffected by yellow light. Yellow light would stimulate the long-wavelength cone, which excites the bipolar cell, but it would stimulate the medium-wavelength cone, which inhibits the bipolar cell, about equally. (page 117)

7. The afterimage is on your eye, not on the background. When you try to focus on a different part of the afterimage, you move your eyes and the afterimage moves with them. (page 117)

## Answers to Other Questions in the Module

A. In Figure 4.19a a person with normal color vision sees the numeral 74; in Figure 4.19b the numeral 8.

B. In Figure 4.20b you should see the numeral 29. After you have stared at the red circle in part a, the 29 in b may look less distinct than usual, as though you were red-green colorblind. After staring at the green circle, the 29 may be even *more* distinct than usual. If you do not see either of these effects at once, try again, but this time stare at a or c a little longer *and* continue staring at b a little longer. The effect does not appear immediately, only after a few seconds.

# The Nonvisual Senses

*How do hearing, the vestibular sense, skin senses, pain, taste, and olfaction work?*

Consider these common expressions:

I *see* what you mean.
I *feel* sympathy toward your plight.
I am deeply *touched* by everyone's support and concern.
The Senate will *hold* hearings on the budget proposal.
She is a person of great *taste*.
He was *dizzy* with success.
The policies of this company *stink*.
That *sounds* like a good job offer.

Each sentence expresses an idea in terms of sensation, though we know that these terms are not meant to be taken literally. If you compliment people on their "fine taste," you are not referring to their tongues.

The broad, metaphorical use of terms of sensation is not accidental. Our thinking and brain activity deal mostly, if not entirely, with sensory stimuli. Perhaps you doubt that assertion: "What about abstract concepts?" you might object. "Sometimes I think about numbers, time, love, justice, and all sorts of other nonsensory concepts." Yes, but how did you learn those concepts? Didn't you learn numbers by counting objects you could see or touch? Didn't you learn about time by observing changes in sensory stimuli? Didn't you learn about love and justice from specific events that you saw, heard, and felt? Could you explain any abstract concept without referring to something you detect through your senses?

We have already considered how we detect light. Now let's discuss how we detect sounds, head tilt, skin stimulation, and chemicals.

## Hearing

The mammalian ear converts sound waves into mechanical displacements that a row of receptor cells can detect. **Sound waves** are *vibrations of the air or of another medium.* They vary in both frequency and amplitude (Figure 4.21). The frequency of a sound wave is the number of *cycles (vibrations) that it goes through per second,* designated **hertz (Hz)**. **Pitch** is a *perception closely related to frequency.* We perceive a high-frequency sound wave as high

pitched and a low-frequency sound as low pitched. **Loudness** is a *perception that depends on the amplitude of sound waves*—that is, their intensity. Other things being equal, the greater the amplitude of a sound, the louder it sounds to us. Because pitch and loudness are psychological experiences, however, they are influenced by factors other than the physical frequency and amplitude of sound waves. For example, tones of different frequencies may not sound equally loud, even though they have the same physical amplitude.

The ear, a complicated organ, converts relatively weak sound waves into more intense waves of pressure in the *fluid-filled canals of the snail-shaped organ* called the **cochlea** (KOCK-lee-uh), *which contains the receptors for hearing* (Figure 4.22). When sound waves strike the eardrum, they cause it to vibrate. The eardrum is connected to three tiny bones: the hammer, the anvil, and the stirrup (also known by their Latin names: malleus, incus, and stapes). As the weak vibrations of the large eardrum travel through these

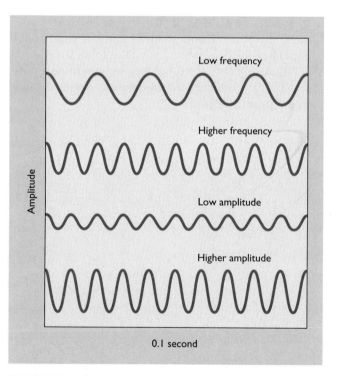

**FIGURE 4.21** The period (time) between the peaks of a sound wave determines the frequency of the sound; we experience frequencies as different pitches. The vertical range, or amplitude, of a wave determines the sound's intensity and loudness.

Surgery can sometimes correct conduction deafness by removing whatever is obstructing the bones' movement. Someone with conduction deafness can still hear his or her own voice because it is conducted through the skull bones to the cochlea, bypassing the eardrum altogether. The other type of hearing loss is **nerve deafness,** which *results from damage to the cochlea, the hair cells, or the auditory nerve.* Nerve deafness can result from heredity, disease, or prolonged exposure to loud noises. Surgery cannot correct nerve deafness. Hearing aids can compensate for hearing loss in most people with either type of deafness (Moore, 1989). Hearing aids merely increase the intensity of the sound, however, so they are of little help in cases of severe nerve deafness.

Many people have hearing impairments for only certain frequencies. For example, people with damage to certain parts of the cochlea have trouble hearing high frequencies or medium-range frequencies. Modern hearing aids can be adjusted to intensify only the frequencies that a given person has trouble hearing.

## Pitch Perception

Adult humans can hear sound waves from about 15–20 hertz to about 15,000–20,000 Hz (cycles per second). The low frequencies are perceived as low pitch; the high frequencies are perceived as high pitch, but frequency is not the same as pitch. (For example, doubling the frequency doesn't make the pitch seem twice as high; it makes it one octave higher.) The upper limit of hearing declines with age and also after exposure to loud noises. Thus, children hear higher frequencies than adults do.

We hear pitch by different mechanisms at different frequencies. At low frequencies (up to about 100 Hz), *a sound wave through the fluid of the cochlea vibrates all the hair cells, which produce action potentials in synchrony with the sound waves.* This is the **frequency principle.** For example, a sound with a frequency of 50 Hz makes each hair cell send the brain 50 impulses per second.

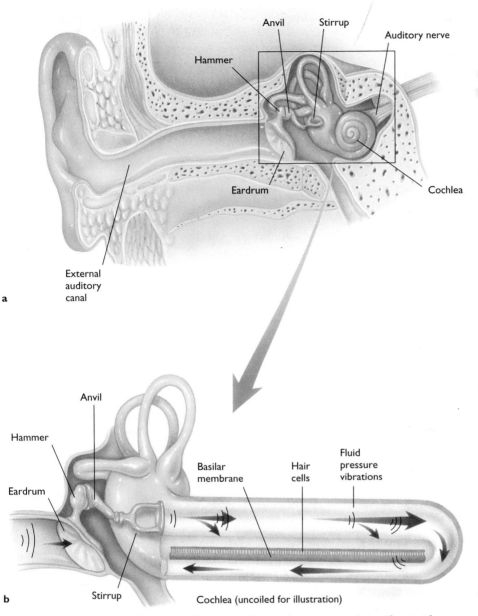

**FIGURE 4.22** When sound waves strike the eardrum (a), they cause it to vibrate. The eardrum is connected to three tiny bones—the hammer, anvil, and stirrup—that convert the sound wave into a series of strong vibrations in the fluid-filled cochlea (b). Those vibrations displace the hair cells along the basilar membrane in the cochlea, which is aptly named after the Greek word for *snail.* Here the dimensions of the cochlea have been changed to make the general principles clear.

bones, they are transformed into stronger vibrations of the much smaller stirrup. The stirrup in turn transmits the vibrations to the fluid-filled cochlea, where the vibrations displace hair cells along the basilar membrane in the cochlea. These hair cells, which act much like touch receptors on the skin, are connected to neurons whose axons form the auditory nerve. The auditory nerve transmits impulses to the brain areas responsible for hearing.

People can lose hearing in two ways. One is **conduction deafness,** which *results when the bones connected to the eardrum fail to transmit sound waves properly to the cochlea.*

■ Hearing is the sensing of vibrations. Evelyn Glennie, profoundly deaf since childhood, has become a famous percussionist. Although she cannot hear her music, she detects the vibrations through her stocking feet.

Beyond about 100 Hz, hair cells cannot keep pace. (A neuron never fires more than about 1000 action potentials per second, and it cannot maintain that rate for long.) Even so, each sound wave excites at least a few hair cells, and *groups of them, volleys, respond to each vibration by producing an action potential* (Rose, Brugge, Anderson, & Hind, 1967). This is known as the **volley principle.** Thus, a tone at 1000 Hz might send 1000 impulses to the brain per second, even though no single neuron was firing that rapidly. Volleys can keep up with most speech and music sounds up to about 4000 Hz. (The highest note on a piano is 4224 Hz.)

At still higher frequencies, we must rely on a different mechanism. At each point along the cochlea, the hair cells are tuned resonators that vibrate only for sound waves of a particular frequency. That is, *the highest-frequency sounds vibrate hair cells near the stirrup end and lower-frequency sounds (down to about 100–200 Hz) vi-*

brate hair cells at points farther along the membrane (Warren, 1999). This is the **place principle.** Note that tones less than about 100 Hz excite all the hair cells equally, and we hear them by the frequency principle. We identify tones from 100 to 4000 Hz by a combination of the volley principle and the place principle. Beyond 4000 Hz we identify tones just by the place principle. Figure 4.23 summarizes the three principles of pitch perception.

## CONCEPT CHECK

8. Suppose a mouse emits a soft high-frequency squeak in a room full of people. Which kinds of people are least likely to hear the squeak?
9. When hair cells at one point along the basilar membrane produce 50 impulses per second, we hear a tone at 5000 Hz. What do we hear when the same hair cells produce 100 impulses per second? (Check your answers on page 134.)

## Localization of Sounds

What you hear is actually a stimulus in your ear, but you experience the sound as "out there," and you can generally estimate its approximate place of origin. How do you do that?

The auditory system determines the direction of a source of sound by comparing the messages coming from the two ears. If a sound is coming from a source directly in front, the messages will arrive at the two ears simultaneously with equal loudness. If it comes from the left, however, it will arrive at the left ear slightly before the right ear, and it will be louder in the left ear (Figure 4.24). You do not hear separate sounds; it seems like one sound coming from the left. The difference between the messages in the two ears indicates how far the sound source is to the left or right.

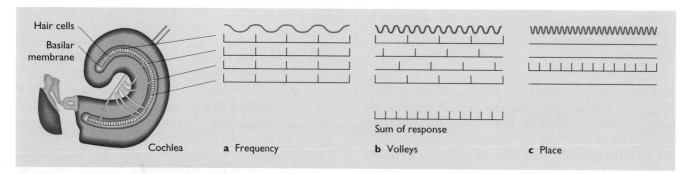

**FIGURE 4.23** The auditory system responds differently to low-, medium-, and high-frequency tones. (a) At low frequencies hair cells at many points along the basilar membrane produce impulses in synchrony with the sound waves. (b) At medium frequencies different cells produce impulses in synchrony with different sound waves, but the group as a whole still produces one or more impulses for each wave. (c) At high frequencies only one point along the basilar membrane vibrates; hair cells at other locations remain still.

**FIGURE 4.24** The stereophonic hearing of our ears enables us to determine where a sound is coming from. The ear located closest to the sound will receive the sound waves first. A change of less than one ten-thousandth of 1 second can alter our perception of the location of a sound source.

## CONCEPT CHECK

**10.** Why is it difficult to tell whether a sound is coming from directly in front of or directly behind you?

**11.** If someone who needs hearing aids in both ears wears one in only the left ear, what will be the effect on sound localization?

**12.** Suppose you are listening to a monaural (nonstereo) radio. Can the station play sounds that you will localize as coming from different directions, such as left, center, and right? Can it play sounds that you will localize as coming from different distances? Why or why not? (Check your answers on page 134.)

## The Vestibular Sense

In the inner ear on each side of the head, adjacent to the structures responsible for hearing, is a structure called the *vestibule*. The **vestibular sense** that it controls *tells us the direction of tilt and amount of acceleration of the head and the position of the head with respect to gravity.* It plays a key role in posture and balance and is responsible for the sensations we experience when we are riding on a roller coaster or sitting in an airplane during takeoff.

The vestibular sense also enables us to keep our eyes fixated on a target when our head is moving. When you walk down the street, you can keep your eyes fixated on a distant street sign, even though your head is bobbing up

The auditory system can also detect the approximate distance of a sound source. If a sound grows louder, you interpret it as coming closer. If two sounds differ in pitch, you assume the one with more high-frequency tones is closer. (Low-frequency tones carry better over distance, so if you can hear a high-frequency tone, its source is probably close.) However, loudness and frequency tell you only the *relative* distances of sound sources, not the *absolute* distance. The only cue for absolute distance is the amount of reverberation (Mershon & King, 1975). In a closed room, you first hear the sound waves coming directly from the source and a little later the waves that reflected off the walls, floor, ceiling, or other objects. If you hear many reflected sounds (echoes), you judge the source of the sound to be far away. In a noisy room, the echoes are hard to hear, so people have trouble localizing sound sources; because they hear few echoes, all sounds seem nearby (McMurtry & Mershon, 1985).

■ The vestibular sense plays a key role in posture and balance as it reports the position of the head.

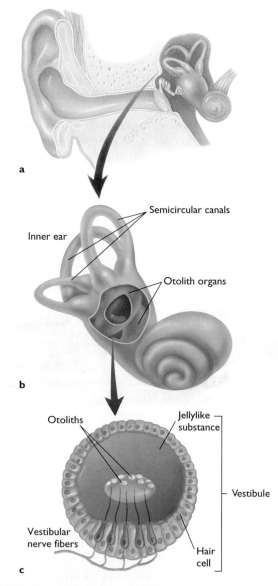

Semicircular canals

Inner ear

Otolith organs

b

Otoliths

Jellylike substance

Vestibule

Vestibular nerve fibers

Hair cell

c

**FIGURE 4.25** (a) Location of and (b) structures of the vestibule. (c) Moving your head or body displaces hair cells that report the tilt of your head and the direction and acceleration of movement.

and down. The vestibular sense detects each head movement and controls the movement of your eyes to compensate for it.

 To illustrate: Try to read this page while you are jiggling the book up and down and from side to side, keeping your head steady. Then hold the book steady and move your head up and down and from side to side. You probably will find it much easier to read when you are moving your head than when you are jiggling the book. The reason is that your vestibular sense keeps your eyes fixated on the print during head movements. People who have suffered injury to their vestibular sense report that their vision is blurry while they are walking. To read street signs, they must come to a stop.

The vestibular system is composed of three semicircular canals, oriented in three separate directions, and two otolith organs (Figure 4.25b). The *semicircular canals* are lined with hair cells and filled with a jellylike substance. When the body accelerates in any direction, the jellylike substance in the corresponding semicircular canal pushes against the hair cells, which send messages to the brain. The two *otolith organs* shown in Figure 4.25b also contain hair cells (Figure 4.25c), which lie next to the *otoliths* (calcium carbonate particles). Depending on which way the head tilts, the particles excite different sets of hair cells. The otolith organs report the direction of gravity and therefore which way is up.

If the otoliths provide unreliable information, we can use vision instead. For astronauts in the zero-gravity environment of outer space, the otoliths cannot distinguish up from down; indeed, the up–down dimension is almost meaningless. Instead, they learn to rely entirely on visual signals, such as distance and direction to the walls of the ship (Lackner, 1993).

## The Cutaneous Senses

What we commonly think of as the sense of touch actually consists of several partly independent senses: pressure on the skin, warmth, cold, pain, vibration, movement across the skin, and stretch of the skin. These sensations depend on several kinds of receptors, as Figure 4.26 shows (Iggo & Andres, 1982). A pinprick on the skin feels different from a light touch, and both feel different from a burn, because each excites different receptors. Collectively, these sensations are known as the **cutaneous senses,** meaning the *skin senses*. Although they are most prominent in the skin, we also have them in our

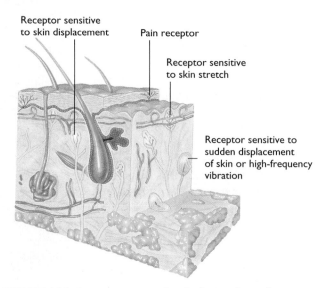

Receptor sensitive to skin displacement

Pain receptor

Receptor sensitive to skin stretch

Receptor sensitive to sudden displacement of skin or high-frequency vibration

**FIGURE 4.26** Cutaneous sensation is the product of many kinds of receptors, each sensitive to a particular kind of information.

internal organs, enabling us to feel internal pain, pressure, and temperature. Therefore, the cutaneous senses are sometimes known by the broader term *somatosensory system*, meaning *body-sensory system*.

On the fingertips, the lips, and other highly sensitive areas of skin, the receptors are densely packed, whereas they are more widely scattered on the back and other less sensitive areas. Similarly, more of the cerebral cortex is devoted to sensation from the lips and fingers than the less sensitive areas. If you ask someone to place an object in your hand (e.g., a pencil or a spoon) without showing it to you or telling you what it is, you can probably identify the object just by feeling it. You would probably fail to identify a more complicated or less familiar object, such as a scale model of the Eiffel Tower, however. With extensive practice, you could improve your ability to identify objects by touch. Participants in one study felt raised-line drawings, such as those in Figure 4.27, without seeing them. Some of the participants were sighted; some were blind since birth; and some had become blind later in life. Most sighted people found it very difficult to identify what the drawings represented, presumably because they had little practice at paying close attention to touch. People blind since birth also did poorly, but for a different reason: A raised-line drawing of an umbrella makes little sense to someone who has never seen a drawing of the object. (Feeling an umbrella in three dimensions isn't much like seeing a drawing in two.) In contrast, people who had lost their vision later in life could identify the objects well (Heller, 1989). They had the advantage of previous experience with visual drawings plus years of close attention to touch.

Tickle is another kind of cutaneous sensation. Have you ever wondered why you can't tickle yourself? Actually, you can, a little, but it's not the same as when someone else tickles you. The reason is that when you are about to touch yourself, certain parts of your brain build up an anticipation response that is quite similar to the result of the actual stimulation (Carlsson, Petrovic, Skare,

**FIGURE 4.27** Sighted and blind subjects felt these raised-line drawings and tried to identify what they represented. Most sighted subjects and subjects blind since birth found the task very difficult and seldom answered correctly. Subjects who had become blind later in life performed much better (Heller, 1989).

Petersson, & Ingvar, 2000). That is, when you try to tickle yourself, the sensation comes as no surprise.

## Pain

Pain receptors are simple, bare nerve endings that send messages to the spinal cord. The experience of pain, however, is a complicated mixture of sensation (the information about tissue damage) and emotion (the unpleasant reaction). The sensory and emotional qualities are governed by different brain areas (Craig, Bushnell, Zhang, & Blomqvist, 1994; Fernandez & Turk, 1992). Telling people to expect pain or distracting them from the pain can greatly change the emotional response without changing the sensation itself (Ploghaus et al., 1999).

### The Gate Theory of Pain

You visit a physician because of severe pain, but as soon as the physician tells you the problem is nothing to worry about, the pain starts to subside. Have you ever had such an experience? Pain can increase or decrease greatly just because of expectations. Recall the term *placebo* from Chapter 2: A placebo is a drug or other procedure that has no important effects other than those that result from people's expectations; researchers ordinarily give placebos to control groups. However, placebos sometimes produce such large effects that they have become a research topic on their own. Consider the following: In one experiment college students had a smelly brownish liquid rubbed onto the one finger. It was in fact just a placebo, but they were told that it was a painkiller. Then they were given a painful pinch stimulus to that finger and a finger of the other hand. They consistently reported less pain on the finger with the placebo (Montgomery & Kirsch, 1996). How placebos work is far from clear, but these results eliminate mere relaxation, which would presumably affect both hands equally.

Think about the various times you have had cuts or other minor injuries. You probably could relieve the pain by massaging the skin near the cut or applying either cold packs or hot packs (Rollman, 1991). However, when you have had a sunburn, even a light touch on the sunburned area became excruciatingly painful (Devor, 1996). A variety of processes can either increase or decrease the pain caused by a particular injury.

Because of observations such as these, Ronald Melzack and P. D. Wall (1965) proposed the **gate theory** of pain, the idea that *pain messages must pass through a gate, presumably in the spinal cord, that can block the messages.* For example, rubbing the surrounding skin sends inhibitory messages to the spinal cord, closing the pain gates. Pleasant or distracting events also send inhibitory messages. The gate can also enhance the pain messages; for example, inflamed skin (after sunburn, for example) increases sensitivity of the spinal cord neurons so that almost any stimulation becomes painful (Malmberg, Chen, Tonegawa, & Basbaum, 1997). In short, the activities of the rest of the nervous system can facilitate or inhibit the transmission of pain messages (Figure 4.28).

single position for hours without growing uncomfortable, thereby damaging their bones and tendons (Comings & Amromin, 1974).

Although it would be a mistake to rid ourselves of pain altogether, we would like to limit it. One way is to provide distraction. For example, surgery patients in a room with a pleasant view complain less about pain, take less painkilling medicine, and recover faster than do patients in a windowless room or a room with a poor view (Ulrich, 1984).

Several other methods depend on medications. *Pain stimuli cause the nervous system to release a neurotransmitter,* called **substance P,** for intense pains and another transmitter, glutamate, for all pains including mild ones. Mice that lack substance P receptors react to all painful stimuli as if they were mild (DeFelipe et al., 1998). Another set of neurons release **endorphins,** *neurotransmitters that inhibit the release of substance P and thereby weaken pain sensations* (Pert & Snyder, 1973; Reichling, Kwiat, & Basbaum, 1988) (see Figure 4.29). The term *endorphin* is a combination of the terms *endogenous* (self-produced) and *morphine.* The drug morphine, which stimulates endorphin synapses, has long been known for its ability to inhibit dull, lingering pains. Endorphins are also released by pleasant experiences, such as sexual activity or thrilling music (A. Goldstein, 1980). (That effect may help to explain why a pleasant view helps to ease postsurgical pain.) In short, endorphins are a powerful method of closing pain gates.

Paradoxically, another method of decreasing pain begins by inducing it. The *chemical* **capsaicin** *stimulates receptors that respond to painful heat* (Caterina, Rosen, Tominaga, Brake, & Julius, 1999) and thereby *causes the release of substance P.* Injecting capsaicin or rubbing it on the skin produces a temporary burning sensation (Yarsh, Farb, Leeman, & Jessell, 1979). However, because capsaicin releases substance P faster than the neurons can resynthesize it, after the burning sensation subsides, the result is a fairly long-lasting decrease in pain sensitivity. Several skin creams intended for the relief of aching muscles contain capsaicin. (Don't rub them on right before you go to bed. They produce a burning sensation before they relieve the muscle pain.)

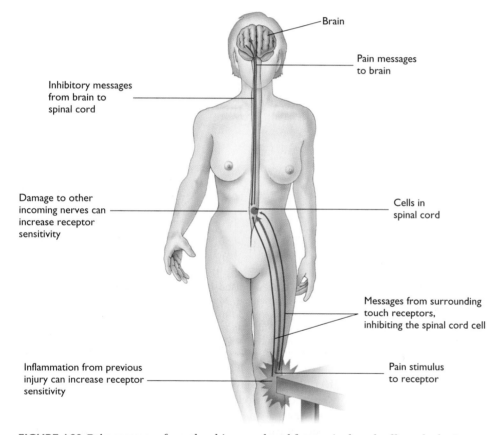

**FIGURE 4.28** Pain messages from the skin are relayed from spinal cord cells to the brain. According to the gate theory of pain, those spinal cord cells serve as a gate that can block or enhance the signal. The proposed neural circuitry is simplified in this diagram. Green lines indicate axons with excitatory inputs; red lines indicate axons with inhibitory inputs.

## Mechanisms of Decreasing Pain

Some people are completely insensitive to pain. Before you start to envy them, consider: they often burn themselves by picking up hot objects, scald their tongues on hot coffee, cut themselves without realizing it, and bite their tongues hard, even biting off the tip. They sit in a

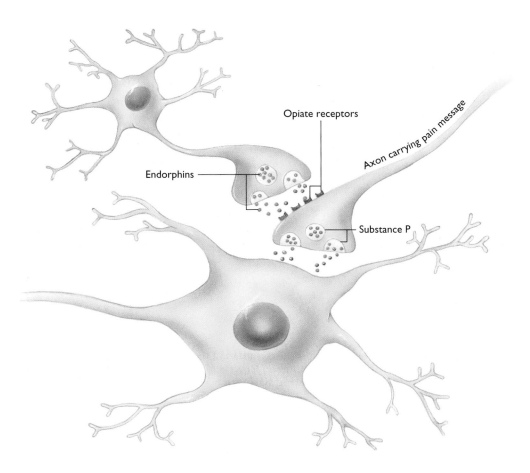

**FIGURE 4.29** Substance P is the neurotransmitter most responsible for pain sensations. Endorphins are neurotransmitters that block the release of substance P, thereby decreasing pain sensations. Opiates decrease pain by mimicking the effects of endorphins.

Opiate receptors

Axon carrying pain message

Endorphins

Substance P

Jalapeños and other hot peppers contain capsaicin. The reason that they taste hot is that their capsaicin releases enough substance P from the tongue to cause a stinging, hot sensation.

## CONCEPT CHECK

13. Naloxone, a drug used as an antidote for an overdose of morphine, is known to block the endorphin synapses. How could we use naloxone to determine whether a pleasant stimulus releases endorphins?
14. Psychologist Linda Bartoshuk recommends candies containing moderate amounts of jalapeño peppers as a treatment for people with pain in the mouth. Why? (Check your answers on page 134.)

## Phantom Limbs

A particularly fascinating phenomenon is the **phantom limb,** *a continuing sensation of an amputated body part.* For example, someone might report occasional feelings of touch, tingling, or pain from an amputated hand, arm, leg, foot, or any other amputated part. The phantom sensation might last only days or weeks after the amputation, but it sometimes lasts years or even a lifetime (Ramachandran & Hirstein, 1998).

Physicians and psychologists have long wondered about the cause of phantom sensations. Some believed it was an emotional reaction, and others believed it began with irritation of nerves at the stump where the amputation occurred. Research in the 1990s established that the problem lies within the brain.

In the last chapter, Figure 3.34 shows how each part of the somatosensory cortex gets its input from a different body area. Figure 4.30a repeats part of that illustration. Part b shows what happens immediately after an amputation of the hand: The hand area of the cortex becomes inactive because the axons from the hand are inactive. (You might think of the neurons in the face area of the cortex as "widows" that have lost their old partners and are signaling their eagerness for new partners.) As time passes, axons from the face, which ordinarily excite only the face area of the cortex, form (or strengthen) branches to the hand area of the cortex. So any stimulation of the face continues to excite the face area but now also excites the hand area. When it stimulates the hand area, it produces a hand experience—in other words a phantom limb (Flor et al., 1995; Ramachandran & Blakeslee, 1998).

One way is known to relieve phantom sensations: Amputees who learn to use an artificial limb gradually lose their phantoms (Lotze et al., 1999). Evidently, the hand

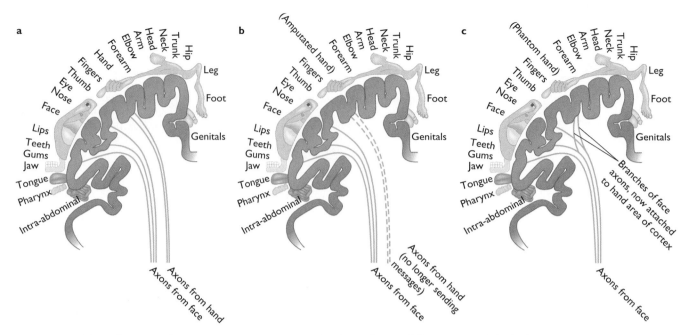

**FIGURE 4.30** (a) Each area in the somatosensory cortex gets its input from a different part of the body. (b) If one body part, such as the hand, is amputated, its part of the cortex no longer gets its normal input. (c) However, the axons from a neighboring area, such as the face, can branch out to excite the vacated area or strengthen existing synapses. Now any stimulation of the face will excite both the face area and the hand area. But when it stimulates the hand area, it feels like the hand, not the face.

and arm areas of their cortex start feeling the artificial limb (!), and this sensation displaces the abnormal sensation coming from the face. To many researchers, it came as a surprise that the nervous system can act this way.

 **C ONCEPT CHECK**

15. A phantom hand sensation is greater at some times than others. When should it be strongest? (Check your answer on page 134.)

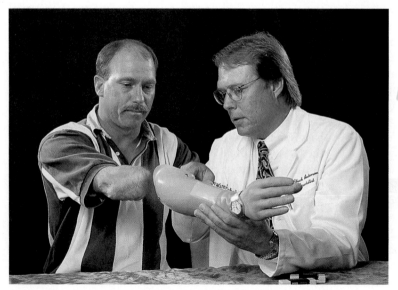

■ After an amputee gains experience using an artificial limb, phantom limb sensations fade or disappear altogether.

# The Chemical Senses: Taste and Olfaction

Many textbooks on sensation ignore taste and olfaction or mention them only briefly. If rats or raccoons wrote sensation textbooks, however, they would probably devote as much coverage to taste and olfaction as they would to hearing and mention vision only briefly. Many invertebrates have no vision or hearing at all, surviving with only chemical senses and touch.

## Taste

Vision and hearing enable humans to find food and water, to avoid danger, to keep our balance, and to find suitable mates. The sense of **taste,** which *detects chemicals on the tongue,* serves just one function: It governs our eating and drinking.

The *taste receptors are* in the **taste buds,** *located in the folds on the surface of the tongue,* almost exclusively along the outside edge of the tongue in adults (Figure 4.31). (Children's taste buds are more widely scattered.)

 Try this demonstration (based on Bartoshuk, 1991): Soak something small (a cotton swab will do) in sugar water, salt water, or vinegar. Then touch it to the center of your tongue, not too far back. You will feel it but taste nothing. Then slowly move the soaked

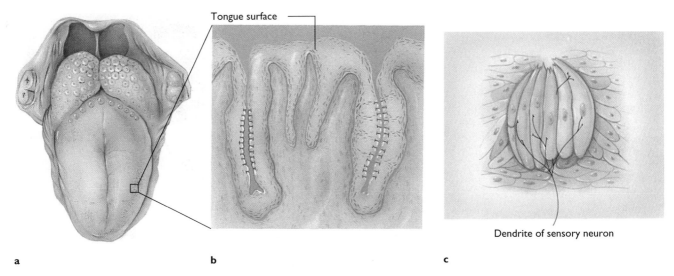

Tongue surface

Dendrite of sensory neuron

a                    b                    c

**FIGURE 4.31** (a) The tongue is a powerful muscle used for speaking and eating. Taste buds, which react to chemicals dissolved in saliva, are located along the edge of the tongue in adult humans but are more widely distributed in children. (b) A cross section through part of the surface of the tongue showing taste buds. (c) A cross section of one taste bud. Each taste bud has about 50 receptor cells within it.

substance toward the side or front of your tongue. Suddenly, you taste it.

If you go in the other direction (first touching the side of the tongue and then moving toward the center), you will continue to taste the substance even when it reaches the center of your tongue. The explanation is not that you suddenly grew new taste buds. Rather, your taste buds tell you nothing about location. Once you have stimulated any taste buds, you will continue tasting the substance, but the taste receptors do not tell you *where* you are tasting the substance. If you now stimulate *touch* receptors elsewhere on your tongue, your brain interprets the taste perception as coming from the spot you are touching, even though the taste sensation is in fact coming from somewhere else.

## Different Types of Taste Receptors

Researchers now have a reasonably clear understanding of how taste receptors work (Lindemann, 1996). Traditionally, Western cultures have talked about four primary tastes: sweet, sour, salty, and bitter. However, the taste of monosodium glutamate (MSG), common in many Asian cuisines, cannot be fully described in terms of those four primaries (Kurihara & Kashiwayanagi, 1998; Schiffman & Erickson, 1971), and researchers have found a taste receptor specific to MSG (Chaudhari, Landin, & Roper, 2000). So it may be better to talk about five primary tastes. English has never had a word for the taste of MSG (similar to the taste of unsalted chicken soup), so researchers have adopted the Japanese word *umami.*

Bitter taste is hard to explain because such diverse chemicals taste bitter. About the only thing they have in common is that most bitter substances are poisonous or at least harmful in large amounts. How could such diverse chemicals all excite the same receptor? The answer

is that they don't. We have a large number of different bitter receptors—probably in the dozens—each sensitive to different types of chemicals (Matsunami, Montmayeur, & Buck, 2000). Any chemical that excites any of these receptors produces the same bitter sensation.

## Individual Differences

Researchers in the 1930s discovered that the chemical phenothiocarbamide (PTC) tasted bitter to some people but was tasteless to others. The difference depends on a single gene; people with two recessive genes are insensitive to PTC. Decades later, additional research found that people insensitive to PTC, called *nontasters,* have fewer taste buds than other people, and have less than the usual sensitivity to other tastes as well. Another group of people, called *supertasters,* have more than the usual number of taste buds, again for genetic reasons, and detect most tastes extremely strongly. Most supertasters dislike black coffee, black breads, hot peppers, sour fruits such as grapefruit, and strong-tasting vegetables such as radishes and Brussels sprouts (Bartoshuk, Duffy, Lucchina, Prutkin, & Fast, 1998; Drewnowski, Henderson, Short, & Barratt-Fornell, 1998). They also tend to be content with smaller portions of food, and most of them are relatively thin. In short, genes can affect food intake by altering taste receptors.

## Olfaction

**Olfaction** is the *sense of smell.* The olfactory receptors, located on the mucous membrane in the rear air passages of the nose (Figure 4.32), detect the presence of certain airborne molecules. Chemically, these receptors are much like synaptic receptors, except that they are stimulated by chemicals from the environment instead of

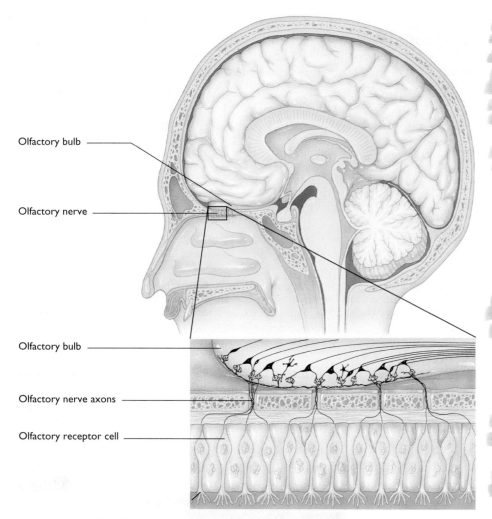

Olfactory bulb

Olfactory nerve

Olfactory bulb

Olfactory nerve axons

Olfactory receptor cell

**FIGURE 4.32** The olfactory receptor cells lining the nasal cavity send information to the olfactory bulb in the brain. There are at least 100 types of receptors with specialized responses to airborne chemicals.

research put the number at several hundred, whereas mice have about 1000 (Mombaerts, 1999). Each olfactory receptor has only a single receptor protein, enabling it to detect only a small group of closely related chemicals (Serizawa et al., 2000). Such extreme specificity is rare in the body; the only other example is the immune system. We do not yet know exactly how the brain makes sense of hundreds of channels of olfactory information (Figure 4.33).

Olfaction is particularly important for food selection. Neurons in the prefrontal cortex receive both taste and olfactory information, producing the combined sensation that we call *flavor*. These cells also receive input that indicates hunger, and they respond vigorously to the flavor of a food only when the individual is hungry (Rolls, 1997).

Olfaction also serves social functions, especially in nonhuman mammals that identify one another by means of **pheromones,** which are *chemicals they release into the environment*. Nearly all nonhuman mammals rely on pheromones for

chemicals released by other neurons. The axons of the olfactory receptors form the olfactory tract, which extends to the olfactory bulbs at the base of the brain.

How many kinds of olfactory receptors do we have? Until 1991 researchers had virtually no idea. In principle researchers could determine the number of receptor types with behavioral data. With color vision, for example, the researchers of the 1800s established that people can mix three colors of light in various amounts to match any other color. Therefore, even before the technology existed to examine the cones in the retina, researchers had reason to believe that the retina had three kinds of cones. Regarding olfaction, however, no one reported such behavioral results. Can people match all possible odors by mixing appropriate amounts of three, four, seven, or ten primary odors, or what?

Perhaps it is just as well that no one spent a lifetime trying to find out. Linda Buck and Richard Axel (1991) used modern biochemical technology to demonstrate that the nose has at least 100 types of olfactory receptors, and later

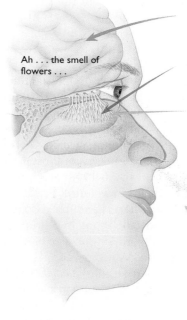

Ah . . . the smell of flowers . . .

3. The spatial and temporal pattern of nerve impulses represents the stimulus in some meaningful way.

2. Receptors convert the energy of a chemical reaction into action potentials.

1. Stimulus molecules attach to receptors.

Odorant molecules

**FIGURE 4.33** Olfaction, like any other sensory system, converts physical energy into a complex pattern of brain activity.

sexual communication. For example, a female dog in her fertile and sexually responsive time of year emits pheromones that attract every male in the neighborhood that isn't chained down or locked up. Pheromones act primarily on the vomeronasal organ, a set of receptors near, but separate from, the standard olfactory receptors (Monti-Bloch, Jennings-White, Dolberg, & Berliner, 1994). Each of those receptors responds to one and only one chemical, and they respond to it even at extremely low concentrations (Leinders-Zufall et al., 2000).

Humans prefer *not* to recognize one another by smell. The deodorant and perfume industries exist for the sole purpose of removing and covering up human odors. But perhaps we respond to pheromones anyway, unconsciously. For example, young women who are in frequent contact, such as roommates in a college dormitory, tend to synchronize their menstrual cycles, probably as a result of pheromones they secrete (McClintock, 1971). One study examined women in Bedouin Arab families. The advantages of studying that culture are that the mother and sisters within a family have extensive daily contact, unmarried women have almost no contact with men, and very few women use oral contraceptives. Thus, pheromones have a maximum opportunity to show their effects. The results showed that the women in most families were at least partly synchronized; they might not begin to menstruate on exactly the same day, but they were close (Weller & Weller, 1997).

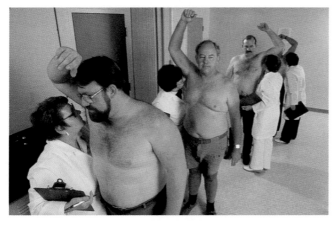

■ Professional deodorant tester: That's a career option you probably never even considered. U.S. industries spend millions of dollars to eliminate the kinds of personal odors that are essential to other mammalian species.

IN CLOSING
### Sensory Systems

The world as experienced by a bat (which can hear frequencies of 100,000 Hz) or a dog (which can discriminate among odors that you and I would never notice) or a mouse (which depends on its whiskers when exploring the world) is in many ways a different world from the one that people experience. The function of our senses is not to tell us about everything in the world, but to alert us to the information we are most likely to use, given our way of life.

## Summary

* *Pitch.* At low frequencies of sound, we identify pitch by the frequency of vibrations of hair cells. At intermediate frequencies, we identify pitch by volleys of responses from many neurons. At high frequencies, we identify pitch by the location where the hair cells vibrate. (page 122)

* *Localizing sounds.* We localize the source of a sound by detecting differences in the time and loudness of the sounds our two ears receive. We localize the distance of a sound source mostly by the amount of reverberation, or echoes, following the main sound. (page 124)

* *Vestibular system.* The vestibular system tells us about the movement of the head and its position with respect to gravity. It enables us to keep our eyes fixated on an object while the rest of our body is in motion. (page 125)

* *Cutaneous receptors.* We experience many types of sensation on the skin, each dependent on different receptors. The fingertips, lips, and face have especially rich supplies of such receptors. (page 126)

* *Pain.* The experience of pain can be greatly inhibited or enhanced by other simultaneous experiences, including touch to surrounding skin or the person's expectations. Pain depends largely on stimulation of neurons that are sensitive to the neurotransmitter substance P, which can be inhibited by endorphins. (page 127)

* *Phantom limbs.* After an amputation the corresponding portion of the somatosensory cortex stops receiving its normal input. Soon axons from neighboring cortical areas form branches that start exciting the silenced areas of cortex. When they receive the new input, they react the old way, producing a phantom sensation. (page 129)

* *Taste receptors.* Even before researchers identified the taste receptors, they knew that there must be at least four kinds because certain procedures affect one taste quality (e.g., sweetness) without affecting the others. An adult human has taste receptors only along the edges of the tongue. (page 130)

* *Olfactory receptors.* The olfactory system—the sense of smell—depends on at least 100 types of receptors, each with its own special sensitivity. Olfaction is important for many behaviors, including food selection and (especially in nonhuman mammals) identification of potential mates. (page 131)

# Answers to Concept Checks

8. Obviously, the people farthest from the mouse are least likely to hear it. In addition, older people would be less likely than young people are to hear the squeak because the ability to hear high frequencies declines in old age. Another group unlikely to hear the squeak are those who have had repeated exposure to loud noises. For this reason you should avoid attending loud rock concerts and listening to recorded music played at a loud volume. You could damage your hearing in the long run, even if you do not realize it now. (page 124)

9. We still hear a tone at 5000 Hz, but it is louder than before. For high-frequency tones, the pitch we hear depends on which hair cells are most active, not how many impulses per second they fire. (page 124)

10. We localize sounds by comparing the input into the left ear with the input into the right ear. If a sound comes from straight ahead or from directly behind us (or from straight above or below), the input into the left ear will be identical with the input into the right ear. (page 125)

11. Sounds will be louder in the left ear than in the right, and therefore, they may seem to be coming from the left side even when they aren't. (However, a sound from the right will still strike the right ear before the left, so time of arrival at the two ears will compete against the relative loudness.) (page 125)

12. Various sounds from the radio cannot seem to come from different directions because your localization of the direction of a sound depends on a comparison between the responses of the two ears. However, the radio can play sounds that seem to come from different distances because distance localization does not depend on a difference between the ears. It depends on the amount of reverberation, loudness, and high-frequency tones, all of which can be varied with a single speaker. Consequently, the radio can easily give an impression of people walking toward you or away from you, but not of people walking left to right or right to left. (page 125)

13. First determine how much the pleasant stimulus decreases the experience of pain for several people. Then give half of them naloxone and half of them a placebo. Again measure how much the pleasant stimulus decreases the pain. If the pleasant stimulus decreases pain by releasing endorphins, then naloxone should impair its painkilling effects. (page 129)

14. The capsaicin in the jalapeño peppers will release substance P faster than it can be resynthesized, thus decreasing the later sensitivity to pain in the mouth. (page 129)

15. The phantom hand sensation should be strongest when something is rubbing against the face. (page 130)

# The Interpretation of Sensory Information

*What is the relationship between the real world and the way we perceive it?*

*Why are we sometimes wrong about what we think we see?*

No doubt you have heard people say that "a picture is worth a thousand words." If so, what is one one-thousandth of a picture worth? One word? Often, it is not worth even that.

Printed photographs, such as the one on page 106, are composed of a great many dots. Ordinarily, you will be aware of only the overall patterns and objects, but if you magnify a photo, as in Figure 4.34, you can see the individual dots. Although one dot by itself tells us almost nothing, the pattern of dots as a whole constitutes a meaningful picture.

Actually, our vision is like this all the time. Your retina is composed of about 126 million rods and cones, each of which sees one dot of the visual field. What you perceive is not dots, however, but lines, curves, and complex objects. In a variety of ways, your nervous system starts with an array of details and extracts the meaningful information.

## Perception of Minimal Stimuli

Some of the very earliest psychological researchers asked, "What is the weakest sound, the weakest light, the weakest touch, and so forth that a person can detect?" They assumed that this question would be easy to answer and a good starting point for further research. As is often the case, however, a question that appeared simple soon became more complicated.

### Sensory Thresholds and Signal Detection

In a typical experiment to determine the threshold of hearing—that is, the minimum intensity at which humans can detect sound—participants are presented with tones of varying intensity in random order, including some trials with no tone at all. Each time, the participants are asked to say whether they heard a tone. Figure 4.35 presents typical results. Notice that no sharp line separates sounds that people can hear from sounds they cannot. Researchers therefore define a **sensory threshold** as the *intensity at which a given individual can detect a stimulus 50% of the time*. Note, however, that anyone will sometimes report stimuli below the threshold or fail to report stimuli above the threshold.

FIGURE 4.34 Although this photograph is composed entirely of dots, we see objects and patterns. The principles at work in our perception of this photograph are at work in all our perceptions.

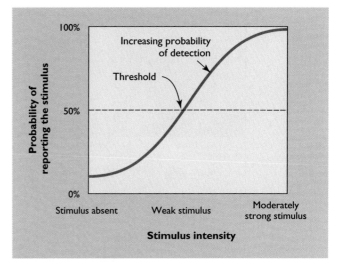

FIGURE 4.35 Typical results of an experiment to measure a sensory threshold. There is no sharp boundary between stimuli that you can perceive and stimuli that you cannot perceive.

Your threshold can change drastically from one time to another. For example, if you have been outdoors on a bright, sunny day and you now walk into a movie theater, you will have trouble seeing the seats at first. After a few minutes, your threshold drops (i.e., your sensitivity increases) and you can see the seats well. Your threshold would drop still further in a completely darkened room. The *sensory threshold at the time of maximum sensitivity* is called the **absolute threshold.**

When people try to detect weak stimuli, they can be correct in two ways: reporting a stimulus when it is present (a "hit") and reporting no stimulus when it is absent (a "correct rejection"). They can also be wrong in two ways: failing to detect a stimulus (a "miss") and detecting a stimulus when none was present (a "false alarm"). Figure 4.36 outlines these possibilities.

**Signal-detection theory** is the *study of people's tendencies to make hits, correct rejections, misses, and false alarms* (Green & Swets, 1966). (Psychologists borrowed signal-detection theory from engineering, where this system is applied to such matters as detecting radio signals in the presence of interfering noise.) In signal-detection studies, we compare responses for stimulus-present and stimulus-absent trials. For example, suppose that someone reports a stimulus present on 80% of the trials when we present it. That statistic tells us very little by itself, unless we know how often the person said it was present on trials when it was not. If he or she also said "present" on 80% of trials with no stimulus, then the person was not actually detecting anything at all—just guessing "yes" most of the time. We would be more impressed if

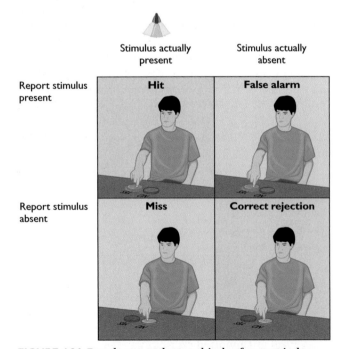

**FIGURE 4.36 People can make two kinds of correct judgments (green backgrounds) and two kinds of errors (red backgrounds). Someone who too readily reports the stimulus present would get many hits, but also many false alarms.**

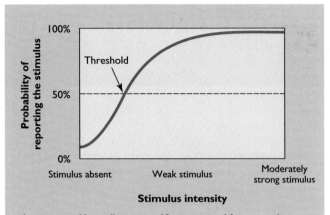

Instructions: You will receive a 10-cent reward for correctly reporting that a light is present. You will be penalized 1 cent for reporting that a light is present when it is not.

a

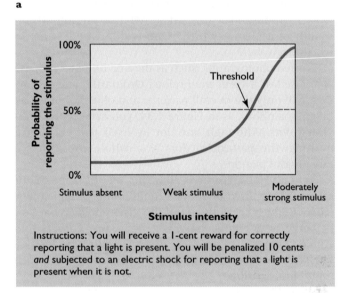

Instructions: You will receive a 1-cent reward for correctly reporting that a light is present. You will be penalized 10 cents *and* subjected to an electric shock for reporting that a light is present when it is not.

b

**FIGURE 4.37 Results of experiments to measure a sensory threshold using two different sets of instructions.**

the person seldom reported the stimulus present when it was absent.

In a signal-detection experiment, people's responses depend on their willingness to risk a miss or a false alarm. (When in doubt, they have to risk one or the other.) Suppose you are the participant and I tell you that you will receive a 10-cent reward every time you correctly report that a light is present, but you will be fined 1 cent for saying "yes" if a light was not present. The lights are extremely faint, and sometimes you are not sure whether you saw one or not. When you are not sure, you will probably guess "yes," and the results will resemble those in Figure 4.37a. Then I change the rules: You will receive a 1-cent reward for correctly reporting the presence of a light, but you will suffer a 10-cent penalty and an electrical shock if you report a light when none was present. Now you will say "yes" only if you are certain you saw a light, and the results will look like those in Figure 4.37b.

In short, people's answers depend on the instructions they receive and the strategies they use, not just what their senses tell them.

People can become cautious about false alarms for other reasons, too. In one experiment participants were asked to try to read words that were flashed on a screen for just a split second. They performed well when ordinary words such as *river* or *peach* were shown. For emotionally loaded words such as *penis* or *bitch*, however, they generally said they were not sure what they saw. Psychologists have suggested several explanations for such results (e.g., G. S. Blum & Barbour, 1979); one likely possibility is that participants hesitate to blurt out an emotionally charged word unless they are certain they are right.

The signal-detection approach is useful in many settings that are remote from a vision or hearing laboratory. For example, if someone uses a personality test to identify people suffering from depression, it is important to evaluate both the number and kinds of errors that the test makes. A "miss" would be a failure to identify a depressed person. A "false alarm" would be calling someone depressed who in fact is not. Depending on the consequences of failing to treat someone who needs help or of providing treatment to someone who doesn't need it, we might be more willing to make one kind of mistake than the other. The legal system is also a signal-detection situation. When we evaluate the suitability of any kind of evidence—DNA matching, lie detector tests, eyewitness testimony, and so forth—the key questions are how often this kind of evidence would label a guilty person as innocent (a miss) and how often it might lead to the conviction of an innocent person (a false alarm). In the legal system, most people are much more willing to accept misses than false alarms. (That is, we reject any evidence that is likely to convict an innocent person.)

## CONCEPT CHECK

16. Suppose we find that nearly all alcoholics and drug abusers have a particular pattern of brain waves. Can we now look for that pattern of brain waves and use it to identify people with an alcohol or drug problem? (Check your answer on page 154.)

## Subliminal Perception

You have probably heard of **subliminal perception,** the idea that *a stimulus can influence our behavior even when it is presented so faintly or briefly or along with such strong distractors that we do not perceive it consciously.* (*Limen* is Latin for "threshold"; thus, subliminal means "below the threshold.") Some people claim that subliminal perception can powerfully manipulate human behavior.

Are such claims plausible? The first problem is to define *subliminal.* When psychologists refer to a "subliminal stimulus," they generally mean "a stimulus that someone did not consciously detect on a given occasion." However,

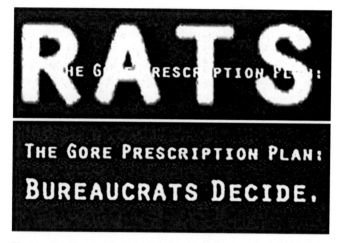

■ During the 2000 U.S. presidential campaign, one television ad attacking Al Gore had the RATS portion of BUREAUCRATS on the screen for one frame. A subliminal message may or may not have been intended, but researchers find little or no effect from subliminal messages.

how do we know whether someone detected a stimulus? We ask, of course. But a reply that "I did not see" the stimulus could mean "I saw nothing," "I'm unsure what I saw," or "I forget what I saw." Therefore, the results are sometimes difficult to interpret.

## What Subliminal Perception Cannot Do

Many years ago claims were made that subliminal messages could control people's buying habits. For example, an unscrupulous theater owner might insert a single frame reading "EAT POPCORN" in the middle of a film. Customers who were not consciously aware of the message could not resist it, so they would flock to the concession stand to buy popcorn. Despite many tests of this claim, no one found any evidence to support it (Bornstein, 1989).

Another claim is that certain rock recordings contain "satanic" messages that were recorded backward and superimposed on the songs. Some people allege that listeners unconsciously perceive these messages and then turn to drugs or devil worship. The issue for psychologists is whether people who hear a backward message can understand it and whether it influences their behavior. Psychologists have recorded various messages (nothing satanic) and asked people to listen to them played backward. So far, no one listening to the backward messages has been able to discern what they would sound like played forward, and listening to them has not influenced anyone's behavior in any detectable way (Vokey & Read, 1985). In other words, even if certain music does contain messages recorded backward, we have no reason to believe that the messages influence anyone.

A third unsupported claim: Many bookstores and music stores sell "subliminal audiotapes" that claim they can help you to improve your memory, quit smoking, lose weight, raise your self-esteem, and so forth. In one study psychologists asked more than 200 volunteers to listen to a popular brand of audiotape. But they intentionally mislabeled some of the tapes. That is, some tapes with self-esteem messages were labeled "memory tapes" and some tapes with memory messages were labeled "self-esteem tapes." After 1 month of listening, most who *thought* they were listening to self-esteem tapes said they had greatly improved their self-esteem; those who *thought* they were listening to memory tapes said their memory had greatly improved. What they were *actually* hearing made no difference. In other words whatever memory improvement occurred was a result of people's expectations, not the tapes themselves (Greenwald, Spangenberg, Pratkanis, & Eskanazi, 1991).

### What Subliminal Perception Can Do

Subliminal messages *cannot* give people a sudden urge to buy something, do something, or change their behavior in any major way. What they *can* do is more subtle.

Suppose people watch a series of pictures flashed on a screen, each for just a split second. In one study people could identify only 13.5% of the objects shown, and if they were forced to guess on the others, they were only rarely correct, so when they said they didn't know, they really didn't. However, if a picture that they couldn't identify was shown again later in the same series (after 15–20 other pictures), their accuracy jumped to 34.5% (Bar & Biederman, 1998). That is, seeing an object once, even though they couldn't recognize it, unconsciously or subliminally "primed" them to see the object better later.

A brief subliminal exposure to an emotional message sometimes produces an emotional response. In one study undergraduate students showed mild signs of nervousness or discomfort after viewing a very brief presentation of the message NO ONE LOVES ME but not after viewing the unemotional message NO ONE LIFTS IT (Masling, Bornstein, Poynton, Reid, & Katkin, 1991).

Similarly, people in one study viewed a happy, neutral, or angry face flashed on a screen for less than 1/30 of a second, followed immediately by a neutral face. Under these conditions no one reports seeing a happy or angry face, and even if asked to guess, people do no better than chance. However, when they see a happy face, they

slightly and briefly move their facial muscles in the direction of a smile; after seeing an angry face, they tense their muscles slightly and briefly in the direction of a frown (Dimberg, Thunberg, & Elmehed, 2000).

The fact that subliminal perception affects behavior at all is theoretically interesting. It shows that we are not consciously aware of all the information we process or all the events that influence us (Greenwald & Draine, 1997). However, the effects of subliminal perception are smaller than some people hope and other people fear.

## Perception and the Recognition of Patterns

How do you know what you're looking at? Take what seems like a very simple example: When you look at something, how does your brain decide how bright it is? We might guess that the answer would be simply that the more intense the light, the greater the activity of the receptors in the retina, therefore the greater the activity sent to your brain, and therefore the brighter the appearance. Exceptions abound, however, and produce the phenomenon of **brightness contrast,** *an increase or decrease in an object's apparent brightness because of the effects of objects around it.* Consider Figure 4.38. Compare the pink bars in the middle left section to those in the middle right. I assume the ones on the right look darker—perhaps much darker—but in fact, they are the same. Then examine Figure 4.39.

**FIGURE 4.38** Because pink bars appear to lie above the dark bars on the left and below them on the right, we see a contrast between pink and dark red on the left, pink and white on the right. Therefore, we see the pink bars on the right as darker, even though they are actually the same shade as the others.

 Compare the little square in the center of the upper face of the cube to the one in the center of the front face. The one on the top face looks brown, whereas the one on the front face looks yellow or orange. Amazingly, they are physically the same (Lotto & Purves, 1999). Don't believe it? Cover everything on the page except those two squares and then compare them.

If two spots on the page reflect light the same way, why don't we see them the same? Apparently, when the brain sees something, it uses its past experience to calculate how that pattern of light probably was generated (Lotto & Purves, 1999). In Figure 4.39 the context clearly indicates that the top face is in bright light whereas the front face is in a shadow. The square you

**FIGURE 4.39** The little squares in the center of the top and front faces of the left cube look very different but they are physically identical. The cube on the right has those same squares, but the context has been removed. Try covering everything on the left cube except the two central squares, or fold the page so you can match the squares of the right cube with those of the left. (From Lotto & Purves, 1999)

see in the top face is seen as a dark object, brown in color. The square you see in the front face is rather bright considering that it's in a shadow, and therefore, it looks yellow or orange.

Similarly, in Figure 4.38 we see what appears to be a partly clear white bar covering the center of the left half of the grid, and the pink bars look very light. The corresponding section to the right also has pink bars, but these appear to be under the red bars and on top of a white background; here the pink looks much darker. As you will have guessed by now, the pink bars on the left are actually the same brightness and color as those on the right.

## C ONCEPT CHECK

17. Of the three theories of color vision discussed earlier in this chapter (trichromatic, opponent-process, and retinex), which one best accounts for your perception of Figure 4.39? (Check your answer on page 155.)

If just perceiving brightness is that complicated, you can imagine how hard it is to explain something like face recognition. People are amazingly good at recognizing faces, though inept at explaining how they do it. When you someday attend your 25th high school reunion, you will probably recognize many people despite major changes in their appearance.

 Can you match the high school photos in Figure 4.40 with the photos of the same people as they looked 25 years later? Probably not, but other people who had attended that high school suc-

ceeded with a respectable 49% accuracy (Bruck, Cavanaugh, & Ceci, 1991).

To some extent we recognize faces by unusual characteristics—a peculiar shape of nose, a characteristic mouth, or especially thick eyebrows—but it is easier to recognize a whole face than a nose, mouth, or any other part of a face. People with certain kinds of brain damage are unable to recognize faces in spite of being able to read and recognize many kinds of objects (Farah, 1992). People with other kinds of brain damage can recognize faces normally but cannot recognize simple objects such as coffee cups or read even short words (Moscovitch, Winocur, & Behrmann, 1997). Particular parts of the cerebral cortex are more active when people look at faces than when they look at other complex patterns, such as flowers, and many psychologists believe that the brain has a special "module" devoted specifically to face recognition (Kanwisher, 2000). Curiously, autistic children are poor at recognizing faces, and when they look at a face, it does not excite the brain area that is responsible for face recognition in other people (Schultz et al., 2000). Evidently, they don't treat faces as something special; they react to faces as they do to any other object.

The rest of us recognize faces as a whole, not just by specific features such as the eyes and nose. To illustrate, consider Figure 4.41. You probably will identify the two faces immediately as those of Bill Clinton and Al Gore. But now look more closely: The faces were digitally manipulated via computer so that they are exactly alike—about halfway between Clinton's real face and Gore's (Sinha & Poggio, 1996). You recognize the two faces

**FIGURE 4.40** High school photos and the same people 25 years later. Can you match the photos in the two sets? (Check answer C on page 155.) (From Bruck, Cavanaugh, & Ceci, 1991)

High-school photos

a    b    c    d    e

25 years later

1    2    3    4    5

6    7    8    9    10

**FIGURE 4.41** Can you easily recognize these faces as Bill Clinton and Al Gore? Note that the faces themselves have been altered to be identical. We recognize the individuals partly by facial features, but also partly by hair, head size, shape, and even the overall context of the picture.

partly by hair, head shape, relative height, and so forth. Now try Figure 4.42. Who is that? Note how the false hair makes the face hard to recognize. In short, face recognition depends partly on eyes, nose, and other features, but also partly on the overall context.

## The Feature-Detector Approach

Even explaining how we recognize a simple letter of the alphabet is difficult enough. According to one explanation, we begin recognition by breaking a complex stimulus into its component parts. For example, when we look at a letter of the alphabet, *specialized neurons* in the visual cortex, called **feature detectors,** *respond to the presence of certain simple features, such as lines and angles.* That is, one neuron in your visual cortex might become active only when you are looking at a horizontal line in a particular location. That feature detector would be detecting the feature "horizontal line." Other neurons might detect horizontal lines in other locations, vertical lines, and so forth.

Feature detectors certainly cannot provide the whole explanation for how we perceive letters, much less faces.

FIGURE 4.42 Who is this? We recognize people partly by hair as well as facial features. If you're not sure who it is, check answer D, page 155.

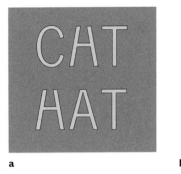 

a                                    b

FIGURE 4.43 We perceive elements differently depending on their context. In (a) the A in CAT is the same as the H in HAT, but we perceive them differently. In (b) the central character can appear to be a B or the number 13, depending on whether we read horizontally or vertically. (Part b from Kim, 1989)

For example, we perceive the words in Figure 4.43a as CAT and HAT, even though the A in CAT is identical to the H in HAT, and therefore, both of them stimulate the same feature detectors. Likewise, the character in the center of 4.43b can be read as either the letter B or the number 13. Feature detectors are essential in the early stages of visual perception, but the perception of a complex pattern requires more than just feature detectors.

**WHAT'S THE EVIDENCE?**
*Feature Detectors in the Human Visual System*

We can easily imagine feature detectors in the human brain, and we can imagine all kinds of properties for them. But what evidence do we have for their existence?

We have two kinds of evidence: one from laboratory animals and one from humans.

**EXPERIMENT I**

**HYPOTHESIS**   Neurons in the visual cortex of cats and monkeys will respond specifically when light strikes the retina in a particular pattern.

**METHOD**   Two pioneers in the study of the visual cortex, David Hubel and Torsten Wiesel (1981 Nobel Prize winners in physiology and medicine), inserted thin electrodes into cells of the occipital cortex of cats and monkeys and then recorded the activity of those cells when various light patterns struck the animals' retinas. At first they used mere points of light; later they tried lines (Figure 4.44).

**RESULTS**   They found that each cell responds best in the presence of a particular stimulus (Hubel & Wiesel, 1968). Some cells become active only when a vertical bar of light strikes a given portion of the retina. Others become active only when a horizontal bar strikes the retina. In other words such cells appear to act as feature detectors.

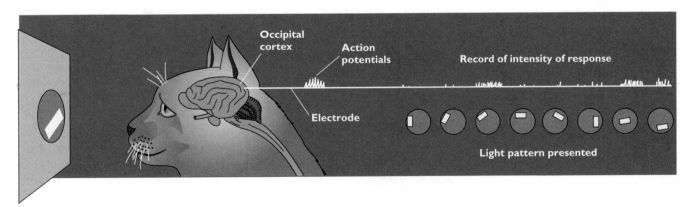

FIGURE 4.44 Hubel and Wiesel implanted electrodes to record the activity of neurons in the occipital cortex of a cat. Then they compared the responses evoked by various patterns of light and darkness on the retina. In most cases a neuron responded vigorously when a portion of the retina saw a bar of light oriented at a particular angle. When the angle of the bar changed, that cell became silent but another cell responded.

In later experiments Hubel and Wiesel and other investigators found cells that respond to other kinds of features, such as movement in a particular direction.

**INTERPRETATION** Hubel and Wiesel reported feature-detector neurons in both cats and monkeys. If the organization of the occipital cortex is similar in species as distantly related as cats and monkeys, it is likely (though not certain) to be similar in humans as well.

A second line of evidence is based on the following reasoning: If the human cortex does contain feature-detector cells, one type of cell should become fatigued after we stare for a time at the features that excite it. When we look away, we should see an aftereffect created by the inactivity of that type of cell. (Recall the negative afterimage in color vision, as shown by Figure 4.15.)

One example of this phenomenon is the **waterfall illusion:** *If you stare at a waterfall for a minute or more and then turn your eyes to some nearby cliffs, the cliffs will appear to flow upward.* By staring at the waterfall, you fatigue the neurons that respond to downward motion. When you look away, those neurons become inactive, but others that respond to upward motion continue their normal activity. Even though the motionless cliffs stimulate those neurons only weakly, the stimulation is enough to produce an illusion of upward motion.

For another example, here is a demonstration that you can perform yourself.

**EXPERIMENT 2**

**HYPOTHESIS** After you stare at one set of vertical lines, you will fatigue the feature detectors that respond to lines of a particular width. If you then look at lines slightly wider or narrower than the original ones, they will appear to be even wider or narrower than they really are.

 **METHOD** Cover the right half of Figure 4.45 and stare at the little rectangle in the middle of the left half for at least 1 minute. (Staring for a longer time will increase the effect.) Do not stare at just one point; move your focus around within the rectangle. Then look at the square in the center of the right part of the figure and compare the spacing between the lines of the top and bottom gratings (Blakemore & Sutton, 1969).

**RESULTS** What did you perceive in the right half of the figure? People generally report that the top lines look narrower than they really are and the bottom lines look wider.

**INTERPRETATION** Staring at the left part of the figure fatigues one set of cells sensitive to wide lines in the top part of the figure and another set sensitive to narrow lines in the bottom part. Then, when you look at lines of medium width, the fatigued cells become inactive. Therefore, your perception is dominated by cells sensitive to narrower lines in the top part and to wider lines in the bottom part.

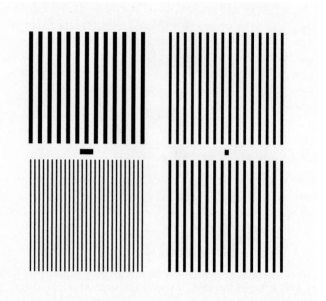

**FIGURE 4.45** Use this display to fatigue your feature detectors and create an afterimage. Follow the directions in Experiment 2. (From Blakemore & Sutton, 1969)

To summarize, we have two types of evidence for the existence of visual feature detectors: (a) The brains of other species contain cells with the properties of feature detectors, and (b) after staring at certain patterns, we see aftereffects that can be explained as fatigue of feature-detector cells in the brain.

The research just described was only the start of an enormous amount of activity by laboratories throughout the world; later results have led to revised views of what the earlier results mean. For example, even though certain neurons respond better to a single vertical line

than to points or lines of other orientations, the vertical line may not be the best stimulus for exciting those neurons. Most respond even more strongly to a sine-wave grating of lines:

Thus, the feature that such cells detect is probably more complex than just a line. Furthermore, because each cell responds to stimuli as different as a line and a group of lines, obviously no one cell provides an unambiguous message about what someone is seeing at any moment. The perception emerges from the pattern of activity of a large population of neurons (H. C. Hughes, Nozawa, & Kitterle, 1996).

One important point about scientific advances: A single line of evidence—even excellent, Nobel Prize-winning evidence—seldom provides the final answer to any question. We should always look for multiple ways to test a hypothesis; even if several kinds of evidence support a conclusion, a great many unanswered questions can still remain.

## Do Feature Detectors Explain Perception?

The neurons I have been describing are active during the early stages of visual processing. Do we simply add up the responses of a great many feature detectors so that the sum of enough feature detectors constitutes your perception of, say, your psychology professor's face? No, brain researchers doubt that the responses of simple horizontal- or vertical-line feature detectors equal our conscious visual experience (He, Cavanagh, & Intiligator, 1996). Rather, they are just a preliminary step in a complex set of visual processes occupying most of the brain.

To illustrate why simple feature detectors alone cannot explain perception, consider Figure 4.46. Parts a and b are composed of small geometric forms. Although we might guess that part a is made up of segments of a three-dimensional cube, we do not *see* the cube. Part b hardly even suggests a cube. In parts c and d, the added lines provide a context that enables us to see the cube. In part e, the deletion of short lines from a enables us to *see* imaginary lines that provide the same context. In c, d, and e, we have perceptually organized a meaningful pattern that goes well beyond the sum of the individual lines taken one at a time.

Similarly, in Figure 4.47a we see a series of meaningless patches. In Figure 4.47b the addition of some black glop immediately enables us to perceive these same patches as the word *psychology* (Bregman, 1981). We can perceive the letters in part b only by imposing an active interpretation on the pattern.

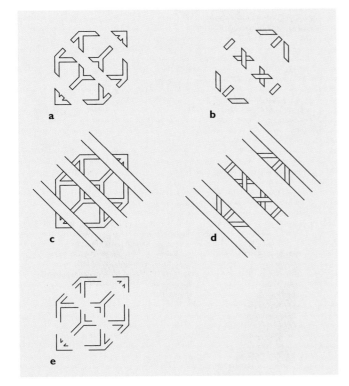

**FIGURE 4.46** (a) and (b) appear to be arrays of flat objects. Introducing a context of overlapping lines causes a cube to emerge in (c), (d), and (e). (From Kanizsa, 1979)

## Gestalt Psychology

Figure 4.48, which we see as the overall shape of an airplane, is a photo of several hundred people. Out of context one person is no more a piece of an airplane than a piece of anything else; the plane is the overall pattern, not the sum of the parts. Recall also Figure 4.34 from earlier in this chapter: The photograph is composed entirely of dots, but we perceive a pattern of objects, not just a collection of dots.

Such observations derive from **Gestalt psychology,** a field that focuses on our ability to perceive overall patterns. *Gestalt* (geh-SHTALT) is a German word that has no exact English equivalent, although "configuration" and "pattern" come close. The founders of Gestalt

**FIGURE 4.47** Why is the word "psychology" easier to read in (b) than in (a)? (After Bregman, 1981)

**FIGURE 4.48** According to Gestalt psychology, the whole is different from the sum of its parts. Here we perceive an assembly of several hundred people as an airplane.

psychology rejected the idea that a perception can be broken down into its component parts. If a melody is broken up into individual notes, the melody is lost. Their slogan was, "The whole is different from the sum of its parts."

According to Gestalt psychologists, visual perception is an active creation, not just the adding up of lines, dots, or other pieces. We considered examples of this principle in Figures 4.45 and 4.46. Here are some further examples.

Figure 4.49 shows a photo and a drawing of two animals. As you look at these pictures, you may see the animals almost at once, or you may see meaningless black and white patches from which you suddenly organize the perception of animals. (If you give up, check answer E on page 155.) To perceive the animals, you must separate **figure and ground**—that is, you must distinguish the *object from the background.* Ordinarily, you make that distinction almost instantly; and only in special cases such as this one, do you become aware of the process.

Figure 4.50 contains five **reversible figures,** *stimuli that can be perceived in more than one way.* In effect we test hypotheses: "Is this the front of the object or is that the front? Is the object facing left or right? Is this section the foreground or the background?" In Figure 4.50 part a is called the *Necker cube,* after the psychologist who first called attention to it. Which is the front face of the cube? If you look long enough, you will see it two ways. You can see part b either as a vase or as two profiles. In part c, with a little imagination, you might see a woman's face or a man

a

b

**FIGURE 4.49** Do you see an animal in each picture? If not, check answer E on page 155. (Part b from Dallenbach, 1951)

**FIGURE 4.50** Reversible figures: (a) The Necker cube. Which is the front face? (b) Faces or a vase. (c) Sax player and woman's face ("Sara Nader"). (d) An old woman or a young woman. (e) A face or what? (Part c from Shepard, 1990; part d from Boring, 1930)

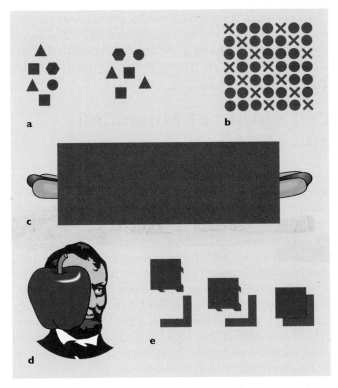

**FIGURE 4.51** Gestalt principles of (a) proximity, (b) similarity, (c) continuation, (d) closure, and (e) good figure.

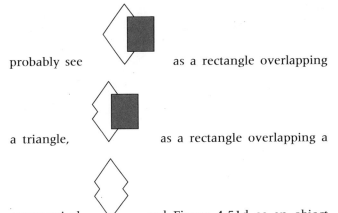

probably see ⬦▮ as a rectangle overlapping a triangle, ⬦▮ as a rectangle overlapping a symmetrical ⬦, and Figure 4.51d as an object overlapping a complete, familiar face.

Of course, the principle of closure is similar to that of continuation. With a complicated pattern, however, closure takes into account more than just a continuation of the lines. For example, in Figure 4.51c you fill in the gaps to perceive one long hot dog. With some additional context, you would probably perceive the same pattern as two shorter hot dogs:

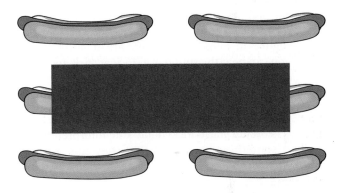

Finally, we tend to perceive a **good figure**—*a simple, symmetrical figure.* As a rule simple and symmetrical figures are more likely to occur in nature than irregular figures.

If you see ⬭⬭, it is more likely to be composed of one ellipse overlapping another than to be composed of ◗ and ◖ meeting at exactly the right point. In Figure 4.51e, even after we see that the right-hand drawing is a green backward L overlapping part of an irregular object, we continue to perceive it as a red square overlapping a green square. In Figure 4.52a we perceive a white pie piece overlapping three ovals (Singh, Hoffman, & Albert, 1999). That perception is so convincing that you may have to look carefully to persuade yourself that there is no line establishing a border for the pie piece. However, if we tilt the black objects slightly, as in Figure 4.52b, the illusion of something lying on top of them disappears. We "see" the overlapping object only if it is symmetrical, a good figure.

blowing a horn. (If you need help, check answer F on page 155.) Part d shows both an old woman and a young woman. Almost everyone sees one or the other immediately, but many people lock into one perception so tightly that they cannot see the other one. Part e was drawn by an 8-year-old girl who intended it as the picture of a face. Can you find another possibility? (If you have trouble with parts d or e, check answers G and H on page 155.) Overall, the point of the reversible figures is that we perceive by imposing order on an array, not just by adding up lines and points.

The Gestalt psychologists described some principles of how we organize perceptions into meaningful wholes, as illustrated in Figure 4.51. **Proximity** is the *tendency to perceive objects that are close together as belonging to a group.* The objects in part a form two groups because of their proximity. The *tendency to perceive objects that resemble each other as forming a group* is called **similarity.** The objects in b group into Xs and Os because of similarity. When lines are interrupted, as in c, we may perceive **continuation,** *a filling in of the gaps.* You probably perceive this illustration as a rectangle covering the center of one very elongated hot dog.

When a familiar figure is interrupted, we perceive a **closure** of the figure—that is, *we imagine the rest of the figure.* The figure we imagine completes what we already see in a way that is simple, symmetrical, or consistent with our past experience (Shimaya, 1997). For example, you

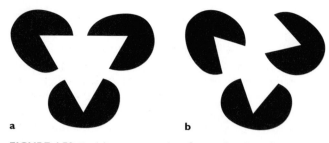

**FIGURE 4.52** In (a) we see a triangle overlapping three irregular ovals. We see it because triangles are "good figures" and symmetrical. If we tilt the ovals, as in (b), they appear as irregular objects, not as objects with something on top of them. (From Singh, Hoffman, & Albert, 1999)

# CONCEPT CHECK

18. Which of the Gestalt principles were operating in your perception of Figures 4.46 and 4.47? (Check your answers on page 155.)

## Gestalt Principles in Hearing

The perceptual organization principles of Gestalt psychology apply to hearing as well as to vision. There are reversible figures in sound, just as there are in vision. For instance, you can hear the sound of a clock as "tick, tock, tick, tock" or as "tock, tick, tock, tick." You can hear your windshield wipers going "dunga, dunga" or "gadung, gadung."

As with visual reversible figures, people occasionally get so locked into one interpretation of something they hear that they have trouble hearing it any other way. For example, read this sentence to a friend: "The matadors fish on Friday." Pause long enough to make sure your friend has understood the sentence. Then say: "The cat on the mat adores fish on Friday." If you read the second sentence normally, without pausing between mat and adores, your friend is likely to be puzzled: "Huh? The cat on the matadors . . .?" Had you not just read the first sentence, your friend would have easily understood the second sentence.

## Feature Detectors and Gestalt Psychology

The Gestalt approach to perception does not conflict with the feature-detector approach as much as it might seem. The feature-detector approach describes the first stages of perception—how the brain takes individual points of light and connects them into lines and then into more complex features. According to the feature-detector approach, the brain says, "I see these points here, here, and here, so there must be a line. I see a line here and another line connecting with it here, so there must be a letter L."

The Gestalt approach describes how we combine visual input with our knowledge and expectations. According to the Gestalt interpretation, the brain says, "I see what looks like a circle, so the missing piece must be part of a circle too."

Which view is correct? Both, of course. Our perception must assemble the individual points of light or bits of sound, but once it forms a tentative interpretation of the pattern, it uses that interpretation to organize or reorganize the information.

# Perception of Movement and Depth

As an automobile drives away from us, its image on the retina grows smaller, yet we perceive it as moving, not as shrinking. That perception illustrates **visual constancy**—our *tendency to perceive objects as keeping their shape, size, and color, even though what actually strikes our retina changes from time to time*. Figure 4.53 shows examples of two visual constancies: shape constancy and size constancy. Constancies depend on our familiarity with objects and on our ability to estimate distances and angles of view. For example, we know that a door is still rectangular even when we view it from an odd angle. But to recognize that an object keeps its shape and size, we have to perceive movement or changes in distance or angle. How do we do so?

## Perception of Movement

It is common sense to assume that anyone who can see a rabbit should be able to see its size, shape, color, and its direction and speed of movement. In this case our common sense is wrong. You already know that some people are colorblind and therefore cannot see the rabbit's color. Also, as mentioned briefly in Chapter 3, some people are motionblind, and therefore, their ability to see the rabbit's movement is impaired. Motionblindness results from damage to a small area in the temporal lobe of the cortex (Zihl, von Cramon, & Mai, 1983). This rare condition illustrates a major point: The visual system of the brain has separate pathways to analyze different aspects of what we see. One pathway analyzes shape, another analyzes color, and yet another analyzes movement (Zeki, 1993).

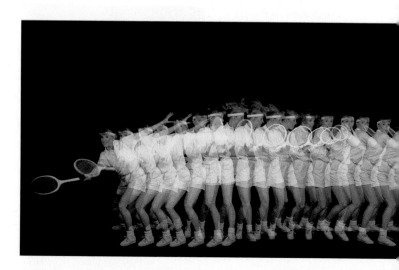

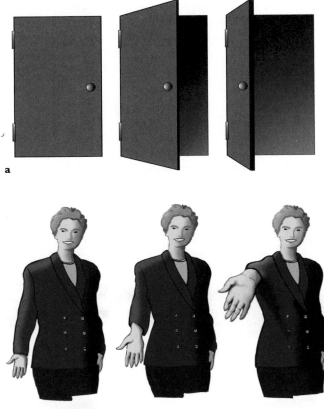

a

b

**FIGURE 4.53** (a) Shape constancy: We perceive all three doors as rectangles. (b) Size constancy: We perceive all three hands as equal in size.

 The detection of motion in the visual world raises some interesting issues, including how we distinguish between our own movement and the movement of objects. Try this simple demonstration: Hold an object in front of your eyes and then move it to the right. Now hold the object in front of your eyes and move your eyes to the left. The image of the object moves across your retina in the same way, regardless of whether you move the object or move your eyes. Yet you perceive the object as moving in one case but not in the other. Why?

The object does not appear to move when you move your eyes for two reasons. One reason is that the vestibular system constantly keeps the visual areas of the brain informed of movements of your head. When your brain knows that your eyes have moved to the left, it interprets a change in what you see as being a result of that movement. One man with a rare kind of brain damage was unable to connect his eye movements with his perceptions. Whenever he moved his eyes, he perceived the world as moving. Whenever he watched moving objects or watched anything while he himself moved, he became dizzy and nauseated (Haarmeier, Thier, Repnow, & Petersen, 1997).

The second reason that the object does not appear to move is that we perceive motion when an object moves *relative to the background* (Gibson, 1968). For example, when you walk forward, stationary objects in your environment move across your retina. If something fails to move across your retina, you perceive it as moving in the same direction as you are.

What do we perceive when an object is stationary and the background is moving? That seldom happens, but when it does, we may *incorrectly perceive the object as moving against a stationary background,* a phenomenon called **induced movement.** For example, when you watch clouds moving slowly across the moon from left to right, you sometimes perceive the clouds as a stationary background and the moon as an object moving from right to left. Induced movement is a form of *apparent movement,* as opposed to *real movement.*

I have already mentioned the waterfall illusion (page 142) as an example of apparent movement. Another example is **stroboscopic movement,** an *illusion of movement created by a rapid succession of stationary images.* When a scene is flashed on a screen and is followed a split second later by a second scene slightly different from the first, you perceive the objects as having moved smoothly from their location in the first scene to their location in the second scene (Figure 4.54). Motion pictures are actually a series of still photos flashed on the screen.

We also experience an *illusion of movement created when two or more stationary lights separated by a short distance blink on and off at regular intervals.* Your brain creates the sense of motion in what is called the **phi effect.** You may have noticed signs in front of restaurants or motels that make use of this effect. As the lights

**FIGURE 4.54** A movie consists of a series of still photographs flickering at 86,400 per hour. You perceive moving objects, however, not a series of stills. Here you see a series of stills spread out in space instead of time.

blink on and off, the arrow seems to be moving and inviting you to come inside.

Our ability to detect visual movement played an interesting role in the history of astronomy. In 1930 Clyde Tombaugh was searching the skies for a possible undiscovered planet beyond Neptune. He photographed each region of the sky twice, several days apart. A planet, unlike a star, moves from one photo to the next. However, how would he find one tiny dot that moved among all the countless unmoving dots in the sky? He put each pair of photos on a machine that would flip back and forth between one photo and the other. When he came to the correct pair of photos, the machine flipped back and forth between them, and he immediately noticed the one moving dot (Tombaugh, 1980). We now know that little dot as the planet Pluto (Figure 4.55).

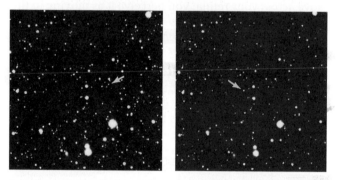

**FIGURE 4.55** Clyde Tombaugh used movement perception to discover the planet Pluto. He photographed each area of the sky twice, several days apart. Then he used a machine to flip back and forth between the two photos of each pair. When he came to one part of the sky, he immediately noticed one dot that moved between the two photos. That dot was the planet Pluto.

## Depth Perception

Although we live in a world of three dimensions, our retinas are in effect two-dimensional surfaces. **Depth perception,** our *perception of distance,* enables us to experience the world in three dimensions. This perception depends on several factors.

 One factor is **retinal disparity**—*the difference in the apparent position of an object as seen by the left and right retinas.* Try this: Hold one finger at arm's length. Focus on it with one eye and then with the other. Note that the apparent position of your finger shifts with respect to the background. Now hold your finger closer to your face and repeat the experiment. Notice that the apparent position of your finger shifts even more. The discrepancy between the slightly different views the two eyes see becomes greater as the object comes closer. We use the amount of discrepancy to gauge distance.

A second cue for depth perception is the **convergence** of our eyes—that is, the *degree to which they turn in to focus on a close object* (Figure 4.56). When you focus on a distant object, your eyes are looking in almost parallel directions.

**FIGURE 4.56** Convergence of the eyes as a cue to distance. The more this viewer must converge her eyes toward each other in order to focus on an object, the closer the object must be.

When you focus on something close, your eyes turn in; you can sense the tension of your eye muscles. The more the muscles pull, the closer the object must be.

Retinal disparity and convergence are called **binocular cues** because they *depend on the action of both eyes.* **Monocular cues** enable a person to *judge depth and distance effectively with just one eye,* or when both eyes see the same image, as they do when you look at a picture. Several monocular cues help us judge the approximate distance of objects, such as those in Figure 4.57.

*Object size:* Other things being equal, an object close to us produces a larger image than does one that is farther away. This cue is useful only if we already know the

**FIGURE 4.57** We judge depth and distance in a photograph using monocular cues (those that would work even with just one eye): (a) Closer objects occupy more space on the retina (or in the photograph) than do distant objects of the same type. (b) Nearer objects show more detail. (c) Closer objects overlap certain distant objects. (d) Objects in the foreground look sharper than objects do on the horizon.

**FIGURE 4.58** Which animal is the hunter attacking? Most readers of this text, using monocular cues to distance, will reply that the hunter is attacking the deer. However, many African subjects thought he was attacking a baby elephant. Evidently, the tendency to use monocular cues to distance depends on experience with photographs and drawings; the African subjects were from cultures with little such experience. (From Hudson, 1960)

*Accommodation:* The lens of the eye *accommodates*—that is, it changes shape—to focus on nearby objects, and your brain detects that change and thereby infers the distance to an object. Accommodation could help tell you how far away the photograph itself is, although it provides no information about the relative distances of objects in the photograph.

The ability to use these monocular cues to interpret an illustration depends partly on our experience with photographs and drawings. For example, in the two drawings of Figure 4.58, does it appear to you that the hunter is aiming his spear at the deer? When these drawings were shown to people of certain African cultures that create much sculpture but little drawing, many people said the hunter was aiming at a baby elephant (Hudson, 1960). This comparison illustrates that people have to learn how to use monocular cues to judge depth in drawings.

Another monocular cue helps us to perceive depth when we are looking at a three-dimensional scene, though it does not help us when we are looking at a photograph. When we are moving—riding along in a car, for example—close objects seem to pass by swiftly, although distant objects seem to pass by very slowly. *The faster an object passes by, the closer it must be.* That principle is **motion parallax.**

approximate actual size of the objects. For example, the jogger in the photo produces a larger image than do any of the houses, which we know are actually larger. So we see the jogger as closer. The rocks and hills, however, actually differ in size, so the relative sizes of their images do not tell us their distance.

*Linear perspective:* As parallel lines stretch out toward the horizon, they come closer and closer together. Examine the road in Figure 4.57. At the bottom of the photo (close to the viewer), the edges of the road are far apart; at greater distances they come together.

*Detail:* We see nearby objects, such as the jogger, in some detail. More distant objects are increasingly hazy and less detailed.

*Interposition:* A nearby object interrupts our view of a more distant object. Interposition tells us the distances of telephone poles relative to other objects.

*Texture gradient:* Notice the distance between one telephone pole and the next. At greater distances the poles come closer and closer together. The "packed together" appearance of objects gives us another cue to their approximate distance.

*Shadows:* Shadows help us gauge sizes as well as relative locations of objects.

■ If you were a passenger on this train, the ground beside the tracks would appear to pass by more quickly than the more distant elements in the landscape. In this photo's version of motion parallax, the ground is blurred and more distant objects are crisp.

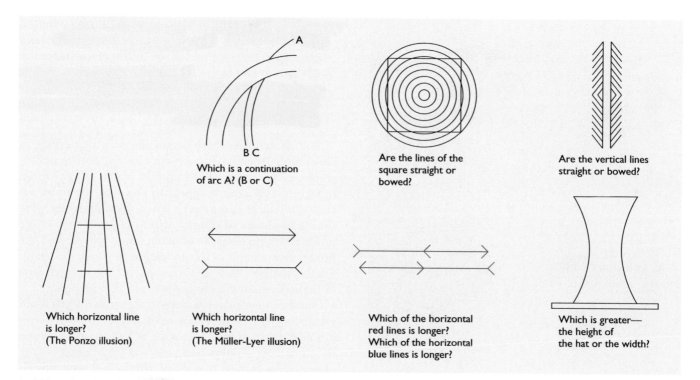

**FIGURE 4.59** Many paintings rely on an optical illusion, but we are more aware of the illusion in geometric figures. (Check your answers with a ruler and a compass.)

ONCEPT CHECK

19. Which monocular cues to depth are available in Figure 4.58?
20. With three-dimensional photography, cameras take two views of the same scene from different locations through lenses with different color filters or with different polarized-light filters. The two views are then superimposed. The viewer looks at the composite view through special glasses so that one eye sees the view taken with one camera and the other eye sees the view taken with the other camera. Which depth cue is at work here? (Check your answers on page 155.)

a single explanation for all optical illusions. (Remember the principle of parsimony from Chapter 2.) They can explain many, though not all, optical illusions from the relationship between size perception and depth perception.

## The Relationship Between Depth Perception and Size Perception

If you can estimate the size of an object, you can deduce its distance. If you can estimate its distance, you can deduce its size. Figure 4.60 shows that a given image on the retina may represent either a small, close object or a large, distant object.

## Optical Illusions

Many people claim to have seen ghosts, flying saucers, the Loch Ness monster, Bigfoot, or people floating in the air. Maybe they are lying, maybe they did see something extraordinary, or maybe they saw something ordinary but misinterpreted it. An **optical illusion** is a *misinterpretation of a visual stimulus.* Figure 4.59 shows a few examples. Psychologists would like to develop

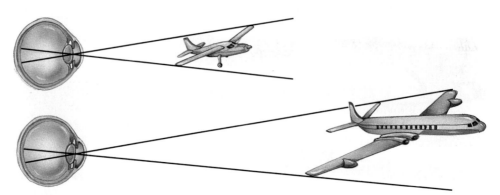

**FIGURE 4.60** The trade-off between size and distance: A given image on the retina can indicate either a small, close object or a large, distant object.

Watch what happens when you take a single image and change its apparent distance: Stare at Figure 4.15 again to form a negative afterimage. First examine the afterimage while you are looking at the wall across the room. Then look at the afterimage against the palm of your hand. Suddenly, the image becomes smaller. As you move your hand backward and forward, you can make the apparent size change.

In the real world, we can usually estimate the size and distance of objects. When you walk along the street, for instance, you never wonder whether the people you see are giants far away or miniature people a few centimeters away. However, when you have fewer cues about the size or distance of an object, you can become confused (Figure 4.61). I once saw an airplane overhead and was unsure whether it was a small, remote-controlled toy airplane or a distant, full-size airplane. Airplanes come in many sizes, and the sky has few cues to distance.

A similar issue arises in reported sightings of UFOs. When people see an unfamiliar object in the sky, they can easily misjudge its distance. If they overestimate its distance, they also will overestimate its size and speed.

FIGURE 4.61 Because fish come in many sizes, we can estimate the size of a fish only if we know how far away it is or if we can compare its size to other nearby objects. See what happens when you cover the man and then cover the hand.

What does all this have to do with optical illusions? Whenever we misjudge distance, we misjudge size as well. For example, Figure 4.62a shows people in the Ames room (named for its designer, Adelbert Ames). The room is designed to look like a normal rectangular room, though its true dimensions are as shown in Figure 4.62b. The right corner is much closer than the left corner. The two young women are actually the same height. If we eliminated all the background cues, we would correctly perceive the women as being the same size but at different distances. However, the apparently rectangular room provides such powerful (though misleading) cues to distance that the women appear to differ greatly in height.

Even a two-dimensional drawing on a flat surface can offer cues that lead to erroneous depth perception. People who have had much experience with photos and drawings tend to interpret two-dimensional drawings as if they were three-dimensional. Figure 4.63 shows a bewildering two-prong/three-prong device and a round staircase that seems to run uphill all the way clockwise or downhill all the way counterclockwise. Both drawings puzzle us because we try to interpret them as three-dimensional objects.

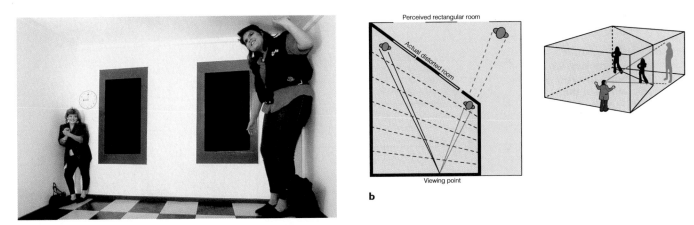

FIGURE 4.62 The Ames room is a study in deceptive perception, designed to be viewed through a peephole with one eye. (a) Both of these people are actually the same height. We are so accustomed to rooms with right angles that we can't imagine how this apparently ordinary room creates this optical illusion. (b) This diagram shows the positions of the people in the Ames room and demonstrates how the illusion of distance is created. (Part b from Wilson et al., 1964)

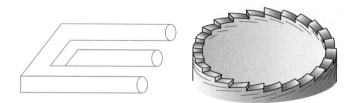

**FIGURE 4.63** These two-dimensional drawings puzzle us because we try to interpret them as three-dimensional objects.

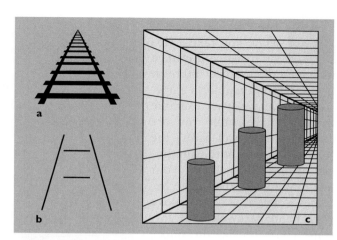

**FIGURE 4.64** Many optical illusions depend on misjudging distances. In part (b) the top line looks longer because the perspective, suggesting railroad tracks like part (a), implies a difference in distance. In part (c) the jar on the right seems larger because the context makes it appear farther away.

In Figure 4.64a, we interpret the railroad track as heading into the distance. Similarly, because the background cues in part b suggest that the upper line is farther away than the lower line, we perceive the upper line as being larger. The same is true of the right-hand cylinder in part c. Recall from Figure 4.60 that when two objects produce the same-size image on the retina, we perceive the more distant one as larger. In short, by perceiving two-dimensional representations as if they were three-dimensional, we misjudge distance and consequently misjudge size. When we are somehow misled by the cues that ordinarily ensure constancy in size and shape, we experience an optical illusion (Day, 1972).

We can experience an *auditory illusion* by a similar principle: If we misestimate the distance to a sound source, we will misestimate the intensity of the sound. In one study experimenters misled students about the distance of a sound by using the **visual capture effect,** the *tendency to hear a sound as coming from a visually prominent source.* (You experience this effect when you "hear" a voice coming from a ventriloquist's dummy or from a movie or television screen.) The experimenters had an unchanging sound source that the students never saw, plus a silent "dummy loudspeaker" that moved. The students thought they heard the sound coming from the dummy loudspeaker, regardless of where the experimenters placed it. When the loudspeaker was far away, most students said the sound was louder than when the

speaker was close (Mershon, Desaulniers, Kiefer, Amerson, & Mills, 1981). Remember, the actual sound was the same in all cases. When people thought they heard such a sound from a greater distance, they interpreted it as being more intense.

## Cross-Cultural Differences in Seeing Optical Illusions

For most of us, the Müller-Lyer illusion is quite convincing (see Figure 4.65). According to one attempt at explaining this illusion, the lines with outward-facing arrowheads (on the left in Figure 4.65) appear larger because they resemble the edges of the back of a building; the lines with inward-facing arrowheads resemble the front of a building (see Figure 4.66). If we perceive one line (a) as being closer than the other line (b), we are likely to interpret the closer one as shorter.

**FIGURE 4.65** The Müller-Lyer illusion: Ignoring (or trying to ignore) the arrowheads, which of the horizontal lines on the left is the same length as the horizontal line at the right? (Check answer I on page 155.) For most people in the United States, Canada, and Europe, this is a strong and convincing illusion. The illusion is present but apparently weaker for many people from less technological societies.

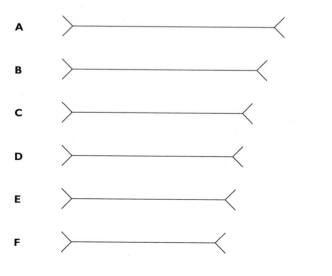

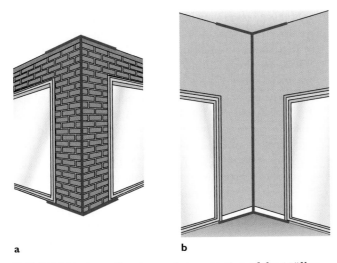

**FIGURE 4.66** According to one interpretation of the Müller-Lyer illusion, inward-facing arrowheads make a line appear shorter because they make the line resemble the front of a building (as in a), but outward-facing arrowheads make the line resemble the back of a building (as in b). If we interpret the line with inward-facing arrowheads as closer, we will also interpret the line as shorter.

For several reasons this explanation is not altogether convincing, but it did lead to the interesting prediction that the Müller-Lyer illusion might be stronger in cultures that have experience with rooms and buildings and weaker in cultures that build circular huts or that live in other rural environments. The illusion might also depend on people's experience with drawings of objects.

To test this hypothesis, researchers showed participants stimuli similar to those in Figure 4.65 and determined which of the horizontal lines with outward arrows appeared the same length as the line with inward arrows. They found that the illusion was stronger for people who lived in cities and weaker for forest dwellers (Segall, Campbell, & Herskovits, 1966) and Zambian farm dwellers (V. M. Stewart, 1973). Even the forest and farm dwellers did see the illusion, however; the difference was merely how large an illusion they saw. Furthermore, children generally experienced a larger illusion than adults did, indicating that the ability to see the illusion does not require extensive visual experience.

Clearly, the results indicate a cultural influence, but they do not necessarily indicate a cultural difference in depth perception. All the testing was done with drawings on paper, and the differences among cultures probably reflect differences in experience with interpreting two-dimensional drawings (Montello, 1995).

## The Moon Illusion

To most people, the *moon close to the horizon appears about 30% larger than it appears when it is higher in the sky*. This **moon illusion** is so convincing that some people have tried to explain it by referring to the bending of light rays by the atmosphere or another physical phenomenon. The explanation, however, must depend on the observer, not the light rays. If you actually measure the moon image with navigational or photographic equipment, you will find that it is the same size at the horizon as it is higher in the sky. For example, Figure 4.67 shows the moon at two positions in the sky; you can measure the two images to demonstrate that they are really the same size. (The atmosphere's bending of light rays makes the moon look orange near the horizon, but it does not increase the size of the image.) However, photographs cannot capture the full strength of the moon illusion as we see it in real life. In Figure 4.67 (or any similar pair of photos), the moon looks almost the same at each position; in the actual night sky, though, the moon looks enormous at the horizon.

One possible explanation is that the vast terrain between the viewer and the horizon provides a basis for size comparison. When you see the moon at the horizon, you can compare it to the other objects you see at the horizon, all of which look tiny. By contrast the moon looks large. When you see the moon high in the sky, however, it is surrounded only by the vast, featureless sky, so in contrast the moon appears relatively small (Baird, 1982; Restle, 1970).

A second possible explanation is that the terrain between the viewer and the horizon gives an impression of great distance. When the moon is high in the sky, we have no basis to judge distance, and perhaps we thus unconsciously see the overhead moon as closer than the moon is at the horizon. If we see the "horizon moon" as

**FIGURE 4.67** Ordinarily, the moon looks much larger at the horizon than it does overhead. In photographs this illusion disappears, completely or almost completely but the photographs do serve to demonstrate that the physical image of the moon is the same in both cases. The moon illusion requires a psychological explanation, not a physical one.

more distant, we will perceive it as larger (Kaufman & Rock, 1989; Rock & Kaufman, 1962). This explanation is appealing because it relates the moon illusion to our misperceptions of distance, a factor already accepted as important for many other illusions.

Many psychologists are not satisfied with this explanation, however, mostly because they are not convinced that the horizon moon looks farther away than the overhead moon. If we ask people which looks farther away, many say they are not sure. If we insist on an answer, most say the horizon moon looks *closer,* contradicting the theory. Some psychologists reply that the situation is complicated: We unconsciously perceive the horizon as farther away; consequently, we perceive the horizon moon as very large; then, because of the perceived large size of the horizon moon, we secondarily and consciously perceive it as closer (as people report), although we continue to unconsciously perceive it as farther away (Rock & Kaufman, 1962).

One major message arises from work on optical illusions and indeed from all the research on visual perception: What we perceive is not the same as what is "out there." Our visual system does an amazing job of providing us with useful information about the world around us, but under unusual circumstances we can be very wrong about what we think we see.

## IN CLOSING
## *Making Sense Out of Sensory Information*

You have probably heard the expression, "Seeing is believing." The saying is true in many ways, including that what you believe influences what you see. Perception is not just a matter of adding up all the events striking the retina; we look for what we expect to see, we impose order on haphazard patterns, we see three dimensions in two-dimensional drawings, and we see optical illusions. Everything we have experienced in the past, everything that we know (or think that we know) influences what we perceive today.

## Summary

- *Perception of minimal stimuli.* There is no sharp dividing line between sensory stimuli that can be perceived and sensory stimuli that cannot be perceived. (page 135)
- *Signal detection.* To determine how accurately someone can detect a signal or how accurately a test diagnoses a condition, we need to consider not only the ratio of hits to misses when the stimulus is present, but also the ratio of false alarms to correct rejections when the stimulus is absent. (page 136)

- *Subliminal perception.* Under some circumstances a weak stimulus that we do not consciously identify can influence our behavior, at least weakly or briefly. However, the evidence does not support claims of powerful, irresistible effects. (page 137)
- *Face recognition.* People are amazingly good at recognizing faces, partly by individual features such as eyes or nose, but also partly by the overall pattern, head size and shape, and the context. (page 139)
- *Detection of simple visual features.* In the first stages of the process of perception, feature-detector cells identify lines, points, and simple movement. Feature detectors cannot account for many of the active, interpretive aspects of perception, however. (page 140)
- *Perception of organized wholes.* According to Gestalt psychologists, we perceive an organized whole by identifying similarities and continuous patterns across a large area of the visual field. (page 143)
- *Visual constancies.* We ordinarily perceive the shape, size, and color of objects as constant, even though the pattern of light striking the retina varies from time to time. (page 146)
- *Motion perception.* We perceive an object as moving if it moves relative to its background. We can generally distinguish between an object that is actually moving and a similar pattern of retinal stimulation that results from our own movement. (page 146)
- *Depth perception.* To perceive depth, we use the retinal discrepancy between the views that our two eyes see. We also use other cues that are just as effective with one eye as with two. People need some experience with photos or drawings before they can use depth cues to interpret sizes and distances in the drawings. (page 148)
- *Optical illusions.* Many, but not all, optical illusions result from interpreting a two-dimensional display as three-dimensional or from other faulty estimates of depth. (page 150)
- *The size-distance relationship.* Our estimate of an object's size depends on our estimate of its distance from us. If we overestimate its distance, we will also overestimate its size. (page 150)

## Answers to Concept Checks

**16.** We have been told the "hit" rate, but we cannot evaluate it unless we also know the "false alarm" rate. That is, how many people without any alcohol or drug problem have this same pattern of brain waves? If that percentage is large, the test is useless. The smaller that percentage is, the better. (page 137)

**17.** The retinex theory is the only one that accounts for your perception of Figure 4.39. According to the retinex theory, your cortex compares your input in various parts of the retina to synthesize a perception of each part based on the whole context. (page 139)

**18.** In Figure 4.46 continuation, closure, and perhaps good figure; in Figure 4.47 closure. (page 146)

19. Object size is a cue that the elephant (usually larger than a deer) must be far away. Interposition is a cue in part a; the deer overlaps a hill that overlaps the hill with the elephant. Linear perspective is a cue in part b. (page 150)
20. Retinal disparity. (page 150)

## Answers to Other Questions in the Module

**C.** a. 7. b. 1. c. 5. d. 9. e. 4.
**D.**

**E.**

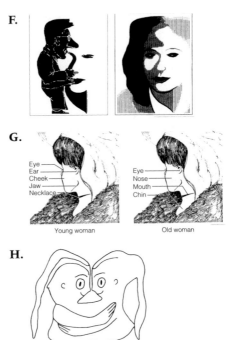

**F.**

**G.**

Eye
Ear
Cheek
Jaw
Necklace

Young woman

Eye
Nose
Mouth
Chin

Old woman

**H.**

**I.** Line d is the same length as the one on the right. (Check it with a ruler.)

---

## CHAPTER ENDING
### Key Terms and Activities

## Key Terms

**absolute threshold:** the sensory threshold at a time of maximum sensitivity  (page 136)

**accommodation of the lens:** adjustment of the thickness of the lens to focus on objects at different distances  (page 110)

**binocular cues:** visual cues that depend on the action of both eyes  (page 148)

**binocular rivalry:** alteration between seeing the pattern in the left retina and the pattern in the right retina  (page 115)

**blind spot:** the area where the optic nerve exits the retina  (page 114)

**brightness contrast:** an increase or decrease in an object's apparent brightness because of the effects of objects around it  (page 138)

**capsaicin:** a chemical that stimulates the release of substance P  (page 128)

**cataract:** a disorder in which the lens of the eye becomes cloudy  (page 110)

**closure:** in Gestalt psychology, the tendency to imagine the rest of an incomplete, familiar figure  (page 145)

**cochlea:** the snail-shaped, fluid-filled structure that contains the receptors for hearing  (page 122)

**color constancy:** the tendency of an object to appear nearly the same color under a variety of lighting conditions  (page 118)

**conduction deafness:** hearing loss that results when the bones connected to the eardrum fail to transmit sound waves properly to the cochlea  (page 123)

**cone:** the type of visual receptor that is adapted for color vision, daytime vision, and detailed vision  (page 111)

**continuation:** in Gestalt psychology, the tendency to fill in the gaps in an interrupted line  (page 145)

**convergence:** the degree to which the eyes turn in to focus on a close object  (page 148)

**cornea:** a rigid, transparent structure on the surface of the eyeball  (page 110)

**cutaneous senses:** the skin senses, including pressure on the skin, warmth, cold, pain, vibration, movement across the skin, and stretch of the skin  (page 126)

**dark adaptation:** a gradual improvement in the ability to see in dim light (page 113)

**depth perception:** the perception of distance, which enables us to experience the world in three dimensions (page 148)

**electromagnetic spectrum:** the continuum of all the frequencies of radiated energy (page 109)

**endorphin:** any of the neurotransmitters that decrease the perception of pain (page 128)

**feature detector:** a neuron in the visual system of the brain that responds to the presence of a certain simple feature, such as a horizontal line (page 140)

**figure and ground:** an object and its background (page 144)

**fovea:** the central part of the retina that has a greater density of receptors, especially cones, than any other part of the retina (page 112)

**frequency principle:** identification of pitch by the frequency of action potentials in neurons along the basilar membrane of the cochlea, synchronized with the frequency of sound waves (page 123)

**ganglion cells:** neurons in the eye that receive input from bipolar cells, which in turn receive their input from the visual receptors (page 114)

**gate theory:** the proposal that pain messages must pass through a gate, probably in the spinal cord, that can block these messages (page 128)

**Gestalt psychology:** an approach to psychology that seeks to explain how we perceive overall patterns (page 143)

**glaucoma:** a condition characterized by increased pressure within the eyeball, resulting in damage to the optic nerve and therefore a loss of vision (page 110)

**good figure:** in Gestalt psychology, the tendency to perceive simple, symmetrical figures (page 145)

**hertz (Hz):** a unit of frequency representing one cycle (vibration) per second (page 122)

**hyperopia:** farsightedness; the inability to focus on nearby objects (page 110)

**induced movement:** a perception that an object is moving and the background is stationary when in fact the object is stationary and the background is moving (page 147)

**iris:** the colored structure on the surface of the eye, surrounding the pupil (page 109)

**lens:** a flexible structure that can vary its thickness to enable the eye to focus on objects at different distances (page 110)

**loudness:** a perception that depends on the amplitude of a sound wave (page 122)

**monocular cues:** visual cues that are just as effective with one eye as with both (page 148)

**moon illusion:** the apparent difference between the size of the moon at the horizon and its size when viewed higher in the sky (page 153)

**motion parallax:** the apparently swift motion of objects close to a moving observer and the apparently slow motion of objects farther away (page 149)

**myopia:** nearsightedness; the inability to focus on distant objects (page 110)

**negative afterimage:** a color that a person sees after staring at its opposite color for a while (page 117)

**nerve deafness:** hearing loss that results from damage to the cochlea, the hair cells, or the auditory nerve (page 123)

**olfaction:** the sense of smell; the detection of chemicals in contact with the membranes inside the nose (page 131)

**opponent-process theory:** the theory that we perceive color in terms of a system of paired opposites: red versus green, yellow versus blue, and white versus black (page 116)

**optic nerve:** a set of axons that extend from the ganglion cells of the eye to the thalamus and several other areas of the brain (page 114)

**optical illusion:** a misinterpretation of a visual stimulus as being larger or smaller, or straighter or more curved, than it really is (page 150)

**perception:** the interpretation of sensory information (page 108)

**phantom limb:** continuing sensation of an amputated body part (page 129)

**pheromone:** an odorous chemical, released by an animal, that changes how other members of the species respond to that animal socially (page 132)

**phi effect:** the illusion of movement created when two or more stationary lights separated by a short distance flash on and off at regular intervals (page 147)

**pitch:** a perception closely related to the frequency of sound waves (page 122)

**place principle:** identification of pitch by determining which auditory neurons, coming from which part of the basilar membrane, are most active (page 124)

**presbyopia:** decreased flexibility of the lens and therefore inability to focus on nearby objects (page 110)

**proximity:** in Gestalt psychology, the tendency to perceive objects that are close together as belonging to a group (page 145)

**pupil:** the adjustable opening in the eye through which light enters (page 109)

**receptor:** a specialized cell that converts environmental energies into signals for the nervous system (page 109)

**red-green colorblindness:** impaired ability to distinguish red from green and either red or green from yellow (page 119)

**retina:** a layer of visual receptors covering the back surface of the eyeball (page 110)

**retinal disparity:** the difference in the apparent position of an object as seen by the left and right retinas (page 148)

**retinex theory:** the theory that color perception results from the cerebral cortex's comparison of various retinal patterns (page 118)

**reversible figure:** a stimulus that you can perceive in more than one way (page 144)

**rod:** the type of visual receptor that is adapted for vision in dim light (page 111)

**sensation:** the conversion of energy from the environment into a pattern of response by the nervous system (page 108)

**sensory threshold:** the intensity at which a given individual can detect a sensory stimulus 50% of the time; a low threshold indicates the ability to detect faint stimuli (page 135)

**signal-detection theory:** the study of people's tendencies to make hits, correct rejections, misses, and false alarms (page 136)

**similarity:** in Gestalt psychology, the tendency to perceive objects that resemble each other as belonging to a group (page 145)

**sound waves:** vibrations of the air or of another medium (page 122)

**stimulus:** energy in the environment that affects what we do (page 109)

**stroboscopic movement:** an illusion of movement created by a rapid succession of stationary images (page 147)

**subliminal perception:** the ability of a stimulus to influence our behavior even when it is presented so faintly or briefly or along with such strong distractors that we do not perceive it consciously (page 137)

**substance P:** a neurotransmitter responsible for much of the transmission of pain information in the nervous system (page 128)

**taste:** the sensory system that responds to chemicals on the tongue (page 130)

**taste bud:** the site of the taste receptors, located in one of the folds on the surface of the tongue (page 130)

**trichromatic theory** (or **Young-Helmholtz theory**): the theory that color vision depends on the relative rate of response of three types of cones (page 116)

**vestibular sense:** a specialized sense that detects the direction of tilt and amount of acceleration of the head and the position of the head with respect to gravity (page 125)

**visual capture effect:** the tendency to localize a sound as coming from a prominent visual feature (such as a loudspeaker or a ventriloquist's dummy) (page 152)

**visual constancy:** the tendency to perceive objects as unchanging in shape, size, and color, despite variations in what actually reaches the retina (page 146)

**volley principle:** identification of pitch by groups of hair cells responding to each vibration by producing an action potential (page 124)

**waterfall illusion:** a phenomenon in which prolonged staring at a waterfall and then looking at nearby cliffs causes those cliffs to appear to flow upward (page 142)

# Suggestions for Further Reading

Hubel, D. H. (1988). *Eye, brain, and vision.* New York: Scientific American Library. A treatment by an investigator who shared the Nobel Prize in physiology and medicine for his research on the physiology of vision.

Ramachandran, V. S., & Blakeslee, S. (1998). *Phantoms in the brain.* New York: Morrow. Fascinating explanation of phantom limbs and related phenomena.

Rock, I. (1984). *Perception.* New York: Scientific American Books. Includes discussions of visual constancies, illusions, motion perception, and the relationship between perception and art.

Warren, R. M. (1999). *Auditory perception: A new analysis and synthesis.* Cambridge, England: Cambridge University Press. Superb treatment of hearing, with a CD-ROM disk that includes demonstrations of auditory phenomena.

# Web/Technology Resources

## More Illusions

**www.exploratorium.edu/exhibits**

Here are wonderful illusions, both visual and auditory. Enjoy.

## Seeing, Hearing, and Smelling

**www.hhmi.org/senses/**

Elaborate psychological and medical information, courtesy of the Howard Hughes Medical Institute.

## Smells and Flavors

**http://www.leffingwell.com/**

Rich source of information about olfaction, ranging from the chemistry of perfumes to the olfactory receptors and how our brains handle olfaction.

## Hearing

**http://www.iurc.montp.inserm.fr/cric/audition/english/start.htm**

Detailed treatment of the auditory system with excellent graphics.

## Perception & Action Projects

**george.arc.nasa.gov/PBA_Group/html/open.html**

NASA has posted demonstrations of perceptual illusions and examples of behavioral adaptation by Malcolm M. Cohen.

## Reverse Speech Home Page

**www.reversespeech.com/**

You've heard that particular recordings contain hidden messages that can be heard only if the material is played backward. One person had the time and patience to research such claims. You will need the RealAudio plug-in, available for free at www.realaudio.com/products/player/index.html. Can you provide a better explanation for the reversed messages?

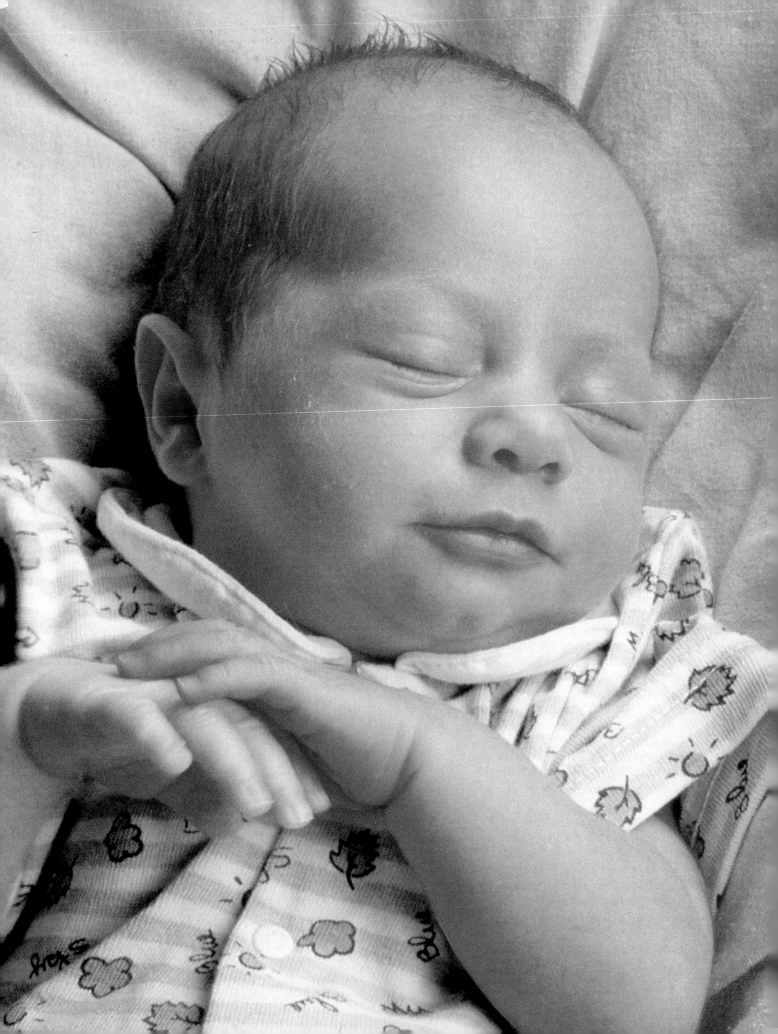

# States
# of Consciousness

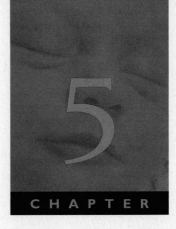

5

CHAPTER

uring an *absence seizure*, a kind of epilepsy, people stare blankly for a while. Occasionally, they then do something more complex, such as walking down the hall, entering another room, and sitting down on a chair. Within a minute they "snap out of it," look around, and wonder where they are and what they have been doing. They report no memory of the episode, as if their minds had been "absent" (Damasio, 1999). Were they really unconscious during that period? Either some surprisingly complex behaviors can happen without consciousness, or it is possible to be conscious without storing any memories. In either case it appears that consciousness occurs in different kinds and degrees.

Consciousness is a fascinating topic, but it is also one of the most difficult phenomena to investigate (J. D. Cohen & Schooler, 1997). Does consciousness depend on certain brain areas or processes more than others? Is it really unitary, or do many brain areas each have their own "pieces" of consciousness? Which nonhuman animals (if any) are conscious? What about preverbal children? Newborns? Fetuses in the middle of pregnancy? People with brain damage? Computers?

Some psychologists regard

■ Sleep and dreams are an alteration of consciousness. People who have trouble sleeping at night are likely to have difficulties the next day.

these questions as answerable; others do not. The main problem is that consciousness, being an internal experience, can be observed by oneself but not by others. As William James (1892/1961, p. 19) said about consciousness, "Its meaning we know so long as no one asks us to define it." The best we can do scientifically is to examine procedures that seem to alter consciousness, such as sleep and dreams, hypnosis, and drugs.

# Sleep and Dreams

*Why do we sleep?*

*What accounts for the content of our dreams?*

Ground squirrels hibernate during the winter, a time when they would have trouble finding food. The females awaken in spring as soon as food becomes available. The males also need to awaken in time to eat, but they have another concern as well: The females are ready to mate as soon as they come out of their winter burrows, and each female mates only once a year. Any male who awakens later than the females pays for his extra rest by missing his only mating opportunity for the *entire year.* So males don't take any chances; they all awaken from hibernation a full week before the females do. And then they sit around waiting . . . with no females, nothing to eat, and little to do except fight with one another (French, 1988).

The point is that animals have evolved internal timing mechanisms to prepare their behavior for predictable needs. Male ground squirrels have a mechanism that awakens them from hibernation while the air is still cold and well before food is available. They awaken not in response to their current situation but in preparation for what will happen a few days later. Similarly, most migrating birds start south in the fall well before their northern homes become inhospitable.

Humans also have built-in timing mechanisms. We do not have an annual mechanism for migration or hibernation, but we do have mechanisms to prepare us for activity during the day and for sleep during the night.

## Our Circadian Rhythms

Humans and other highly visual animals are active during the day and inactive at night (Figure 5.1). Rats, mice, and other less visual animals are active at night and inactive during the day. Each species generates a **circadian rhythm,** a *rhythm of activity and inactivity lasting about 1 day.* (The term *circadian* comes from the Latin roots *circa* and *dies,* meaning "about a day.") The rising and setting of the sun provide cues to reset our rhythm each day; in an environment with no cues for time, most people will generate a waking–sleeping rhythm lasting a little longer than 24 hours. The best current estimate is about 24.2 hours (Czeisler et al., 1999), although the exact length varies depending on the brightness and timing of light (Campbell, 2000).

One of the earliest demonstrations of humans' circadian rhythms was a study of two people who spent a few weeks in a remote part of Mammoth Caves in Kentucky (Kleitman, 1963). For 24 hours per day, the temperature

FIGURE 5.1 The rising and setting of the sun do not directly produce our daily rhythm of wakefulness and sleepiness, but they synchronize that rhythm. We adjust our internally generated cycles so that we feel alert during the day and sleepy at night.

was a constant 12° Celsius (54° F), and the relative humidity was 100%. They saw no light except from lamps that they controlled themselves, and they heard no noises except their own. Any decisions about when to sleep and when to awaken had to come from within, not from the environment. Yet they went to sleep and awoke at about the same time every day.

Sleepiness and alertness depend strongly on one's position within the circadian rhythm. If you have ever gone all night without sleep—as most college students do at one time or another—you probably grew very sleepy between about 2 and 5 A.M. But if you were still awake at 7 or 8 A.M., you began feeling less sleepy, not more. You became more alert because of your circadian rhythm, even though your sleep deprivation had continued.

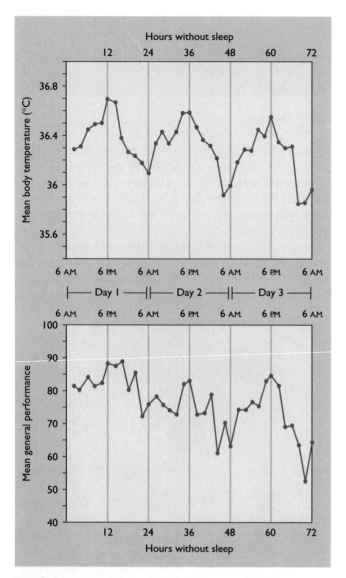

**FIGURE 5.2** Cumulative effects of three nights without sleep: Both body temperature and logical reasoning decrease each night and increase the next morning. They also deteriorate from one day to the next. (From Babkoff, Caspy, Mikulincer, & Sing, 1991)

In one study volunteers went without sleep for three nights. An experimenter periodically took their temperature and measured their performance on logical reasoning tasks. Both temperature and logical reasoning declined during the first night and then increased the next morning. During the second and third nights, temperature and reasoning decreased more than they had the first night, but they increased again the next day (Figure 5.2). Thus, sleep deprivation produces a pattern of progressive deterioration superimposed on the normal circadian cycle of rising and falling body temperature and alertness (Babkoff, Caspy, Mikulincer, & Sing, 1991). In short, sleepiness apparently depends partly on how long one has gone without sleep and partly on the time of day (i.e., one's circadian rhythm).

## Morning People and Evening People

Our circadian rhythms do not affect us all in exactly the same way. "Morning people" awaken early and full of energy, doing their best work before noon; "evening people" take longer to warm up in the morning (literally as well as figuratively) and do their best work in the afternoon or evening (Horne, Brass, & Pettitt, 1980). Most people are pretty consistent, and you probably know whether you are a morning person, evening person, or somewhere in between.

The morning person/evening person distinction is particularly relevant for research on aging. Most young adults are either evening people or neutral (about equally alert at all times), whereas nearly all people over age 65 are morning people. For many years researchers reported substantial declines in memory with older people. But who did most of this research? Graduate students. How old are graduate students? Most are in their 20s. What time do graduate students choose to conduct their research? Late afternoon or evening, a fine time for young graduate students but not for 65-year-olds. Researchers in one study compared the memories of young adults (18–22 years old) and older adults (66–78 years old) at different times of day. Early in the morning, the older adults did just as well as the younger ones. However, as the day went on, the younger adults either remained steady or improved, whereas the older adults deteriorated steadily (May, Hasher, & Stoltzfus, 1993). Figure 5.3 shows the results of this study.

Incidentally, the relationship between age and morning or evening arousal is apparently not something specific to our culture or even our species. Young rats are about equally able to perform difficult tasks at all times of day, but aged rats do best shortly after they wake up and then deteriorate as the day goes on (Winocur & Hasher, 1999).

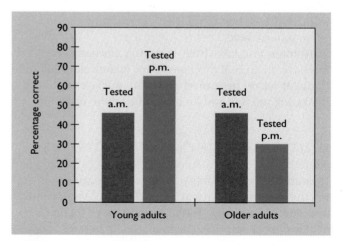

**FIGURE 5.3** If tested early in the morning, older people perform as well as younger people on memory tasks. As the day progresses, young people improve and older people deteriorate.

**A STEP FURTHER**
*Morning and Evening People*

Are most college classes offered in the early morning or late afternoon? Is that because *you* want to take them at that time or because your aging professors want to schedule them then?

## Shifting Sleep Schedules

Ordinarily, the light of early morning resets the body's clock each day to keep it in synchrony with the outside world. If you travel across time zones, the light in your new location will eventually reset your clock to the new time, but until it does, your internal rhythms will be out of phase with your new environment. For example, if you travel from California to France, it will be 7 A.M. (time to get up) when your body says it is 10 P.M. (not quite bedtime). You will experience **jet lag,** *a period of discomfort and inefficiency while your internal clock is out of phase with your new surroundings.* You will gradually adjust to the new schedule, but some people adjust faster than others.

**FIGURE 5.4  People traveling east suffer more serious jet lag than people traveling west.**

Most people find it easier to adjust when flying west, where they go to bed later, than flying east, where they go to bed earlier. Thus, east-coast people adjust to west-coast time more easily than west-coast people adjust to east-coast time (Figure 5.4). International pilots, who must constantly adjust to different schedules, develop a variety of techniques to combat fatigue, such as napping, conserving energy, and drinking coffee (Petrie & Dawson, 1997).

It is possible to have an experience like jet lag without leaving town. Suppose you stay up late on Friday night and wake up late on Saturday morning. (Many readers will not find this scenario difficult to imagine.) Then you stay up late again on Saturday and wake up late on Sunday. By Monday morning, when it is time to awaken for school or work, your circadian rhythm has reset, so even though the clock on your table says 7 A.M., your internal clock thinks you are somewhere west and the time is about 5 A.M.

Companies that want to keep their factories going nonstop run three work shifts, such as midnight–8 A.M., 8 A.M.–4 P.M., and 4 P.M.–midnight. Because few people want to work regularly on the "graveyard shift" (mid-

night–8 A.M.), many companies rotate their workers among the three shifts. Suppose that you worked the 8 A.M.–4 P.M. shift today but tomorrow you are scheduled for midnight–8 A.M. You can't get to sleep at 4 in the afternoon, so you show up for work without having slept. You are likely to make many mistakes during the night, and by the time you are ready to drive home the next morning, your coordination and judgment will be as badly impaired as if you were legally drunk (Dawson & Reid, 1997). Even people who work the night shift month after month may continue feeling groggy on the job and sleeping fitfully during the day.

There are two ways for employers to ease the burden on their workers: First, when they transfer workers from one shift to another, they should transfer workers to a *later* shift, not an earlier shift (Czeisler, Moore-Ede, & Coleman, 1982) (Figure 5.5). That is, someone working the 8 A.M.–4 P.M. shift should switch to the 4 P.M.–midnight shift (equivalent to traveling west) instead of the midnight–8 A.M. shift (equivalent to traveling east).

Second, employers can help workers adjust to the night shift by providing bright lights to mimic sunlight. In one study young men exposed to very bright lights at night adjusted well to working at night and sleeping during the day. Within 6 days their circadian rhythms had shifted to the new schedule. Another group of men who worked the same schedule under dimmer lights showed no indications of altering their circadian rhythms (Czeisler et al., 1990).

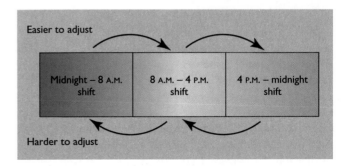

**FIGURE 5.5  The graveyard shift is aptly named—serious industrial accidents usually occur at night, when workers are least alert. Night-shift jobs providing emergency services are essential. But few people want to work permanently at night, so workers rotate among three shifts. As in jet lag, the direction of change is critical. Moving forward—clockwise—is easier than going backward.**

## CONCEPT CHECK

1. Suppose you are the president of Consolidated Generic Products in the United States. You are negotiating a difficult business deal with someone from the opposite side of the world. Should you prefer a meeting place in Europe or on an island in the Pacific Ocean? (Check your answer on page 176.)

**A STEP FURTHER**
*Sleep Cycles*

Imagine someone who cannot get to sleep until 3 A.M.; for months she has been trying to get to bed earlier but failing. What advice would you offer? (Hint: Remember that our internal clocks can shift more easily to a later time than to an earlier time.)

## Brain Mechanisms of Circadian Rhythms

The circadian rhythm of sleep and wakefulness is generated by a tiny structure at the base of the brain known as the *suprachiasmatic nucleus*. If that area of the brain is damaged, the body's activity cycles become erratic (Rusak, 1977). If cells from that area are kept alive outside the body, they generate a circadian rhythm on their own (Earnest, Liang, Ratcliff, & Cassone, 1999; Inouye & Kawamura, 1979). In short, this brain area is the body's clock (see Figure 5.6).

The suprachiasmatic nucleus exerts its control partly by regulating the pineal gland's secretions of the hormone *melatonin*, which induces drowsiness. Ordinarily, the human pineal gland starts increasing its release of melatonin at about 8 to 10 P.M., so people find it easy to fall asleep about 2 or 3 hours later. If you take a melatonin pill in the evening, you will notice little if any effect because you were already producing increased melatonin at that time. However, if you have just flown a few time zones east and want to get to bed in a couple of hours, but you're not sleepy yet, then a melatonin pill can be helpful indeed (Deacon & Arendt, 1996).

## CONCEPT CHECK

2. Suppose you are required to work the midnight–8 A.M. shift, and you would like to go to sleep at 4 P.M. in order to be well-rested before starting work. Would a melatonin pill help? If so, when should you take it? (Check your answer on page 176.)

# Why We Sleep

We would not have been born with a mechanism that forces us to sleep for 8 hours or so out of every 24 unless sleep did us some good. But what good does sleep do? Scientists have proposed two theories.

## The Repair and Restoration Theory

According to the **repair and restoration theory,** *the purpose of sleep is to enable the body to recover from the exertions of the day.* We undeniably need sleep, and we suffer if we do not get it. If you are not doing well in school or if you are frequently ill, one possibility you should consider is that you are not getting enough sleep. Sleep deprivation leads to impaired concentration, irritability, and impaired functioning of the immune system (Dement, 1972; Everson, 1995; Rechtschaffen & Bergmann, 1995). Driving while sleep deprived is just as dangerous as driving drunk, and many of the worst industrial accidents can be traced to people who were working while sleepy (Dement & Vaughan, 1999).

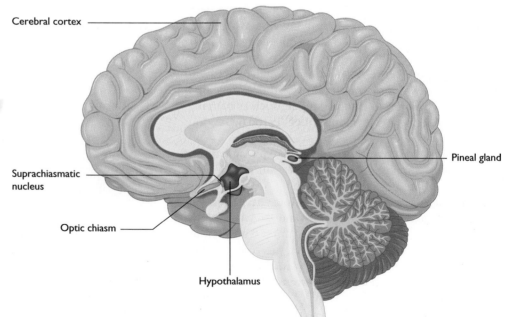

**FIGURE 5.6** The suprachiasmatic nucleus, a small area at the base of the brain, produces the circadian rhythm. Information from the optic nerves resets the circadian rhythm but is not necessary for its generation. Cells in the suprachiasmatic nucleus can generate approximately a 24-hour rhythm of activity on their own, even if they are separated from the rest of the body.

However, most of the restorative functions that occur during sleep—such as digestion and protein synthesis—also occur during quiet waking periods. That is, we do need sleep, but it is possible to imagine evolving the ability to do all the necessary restorative functions without setting aside a part of the day for sleep. The following list highlights facts that the repair and restoration theory has trouble explaining:

• People need only a little more sleep after a day of extreme physical or mental activity than after a day of inactivity (Horne & Minard, 1985).

• Some people get by with much less than the "normal" 7.5 to 8 hours of sleep per day. One extreme case was a healthy 70-year-old woman who slept only about 1 hour each night (Meddis, Pearson, & Langford, 1973).

• Some people fare better than we would have expected after a week or more of sleep deprivation (Figure 5.7). In 1965 a San Diego high school student, Randy Gardner, stayed awake for 264 hours and 12 minutes—11 days—

FIGURE 5.7 Even near the end of Randy Gardner's 264 consecutive hours without sleep, he was able to perform tasks requiring strength and skill. Here observers dutifully record his every move.

in a project for a high school science fair. Gardner suffered no serious psychological consequences (Dement, 1972). On the last night, he played about 100 arcade games against sleep researcher William Dement and won every game. Just before the end of the 264 hours, he held a television press conference and handled himself well. He then slept for 14 hours and 40 minutes and awoke refreshed.

If a torturer prevented you from sleeping for the next 11 days, would you do as well as Randy Gardner? Probably not, for two reasons: First, Gardner knew he could quit if necessary. A sense of control makes any experience less stressful. Second, people vary in their ability to tolerate sleep deprivation. We heard about Gardner only because he tolerated it so well. We have no idea how many other people tried to deprive themselves of sleep for many days but gave up.

The summary evaluation of the repair and restoration theory is that the body does do some restoration during sleep, and sleep deprivation *is* harmful. However, each of us has an urge to sleep, even a need to sleep, at a certain time of day, regardless of how active or inactive we have been during the day. Also, no one so far has identified a repair process that occurs during sleep that could not occur at other times. Therefore, it is possible that sleep serves other functions as well.

## The Evolutionary, or Energy-Conservation, Theory

Sleep is a way of conserving energy. If we built a solar-powered robot to explore another planet, we would probably program it to shut down most of its activities at night. According to the **evolutionary,** or **energy-conservation, theory of sleep,** *evolution equipped us with a regular pattern of sleeping and waking for the same reason—to conserve fuel and to prevent us from walking into dangers* (Kleitman, 1963; Webb, 1979). Humans and other highly visual species are relatively inefficient at night. Throughout our evolutionary history, until the invention of electric lights, most nighttime activities were wasteful and dangerous. By sleeping we could decrease our energy use by 10 to 25%. When food is scarce, people either sleep more or lower their body temperature more than usual, thus conserving even more energy (Berger & Phillips, 1995).

However, sleep protects us only from the sort of trouble we might walk into; it does not protect us from trouble that comes looking for us! So we sleep well in a familiar, safe place; but we sleep lightly when we fear that burglars will break into the house or that bears will nose into our tent. Animals in danger of being attacked during sleep rouse quickly at any noise. Many birds spend part of the night with one eye open and one hemisphere semiawake. Birds that are surrounded by others of their species sleep more soundly—presumably secure that the others will squawk if they spot danger. However, a bird at the end of the line spends much of the night with one eye open (Rattenborg, Lima, & Amlaner, 1999) (see Figure 5.8).

The evolutionary theory accounts well for differences in sleep among species (Campbell & Tobler, 1984). For example, why do cats sleep so much and horses so little? First, cats can afford to have long periods of inactivity because they eat one or two large meals per day; horses

**FIGURE 5.8** Many birds sleep with one eye open, unless they are sitting next to another bird that might be keeping watch. Humans, too, sleep less well if they are in an unfamiliar or possibly dangerous place.

need to spend most of the day grazing. Second, cats are seldom attacked while they sleep, whereas horses must always be ready to run away (Figure 5.9). (Woody Allen once said, "The lion and the calf shall lie down together, but the calf won't get much sleep.")

Which of these two theories regarding sleep is correct? To a large degree, both are. Supporters of the repair and restoration theory concede that the timing and even the amount of sleep depend on when the animal is least efficient. Supporters of the evolutionary theory concede that, during the time that evolution has set aside for an animal to conserve energy, the animal takes that opportunity to perform repair and restoration functions.

## Stages of Sleep

In the mid-1950s, American and French researchers independently discovered a stage of sleep called *paradoxical sleep* or **rapid eye movement (REM) sleep** (Dement & Kleitman, 1957a, 1957b; Jouvet, Michel, & Courjon, 1959). *During this stage of sleep, the sleeper's eyes move rapidly back and forth under the closed lids.* (All other stages of sleep are known as non-REM, or NREM, sleep.) A paradox is an apparent contradiction; REM sleep is sometimes called paradoxical because it is light in some ways and deep in others. It is light because the brain is active and the body's heart rate, breathing rate, and temperature fluctuate substantially (Parmeggiani, 1982). It is deep because the large muscles of the body that control posture and locomotion are deeply relaxed. Indeed, the nerves to those muscles are virtually paralyzed at this time. REM also has some features that are hard to classify as deep or light, such as penis erections and vaginal lubrication.

William Dement's early research indicated that people who were awakened during REM sleep usually reported they had been dreaming, but people who were awakened during any other period seldom reported dreaming. So at first REM sleep was thought to be almost synonymous with dreaming. Later research has weakened that link, however. Adults who are awakened during REM sleep

**FIGURE 5.9** Sleep time for mammals varies widely. Animals that are rarely attacked sleep a lot; those in danger of attack sleep only a few hours. Diet also relates to sleep. (Based on data from Zepelin & Rechtschaffen, 1974)

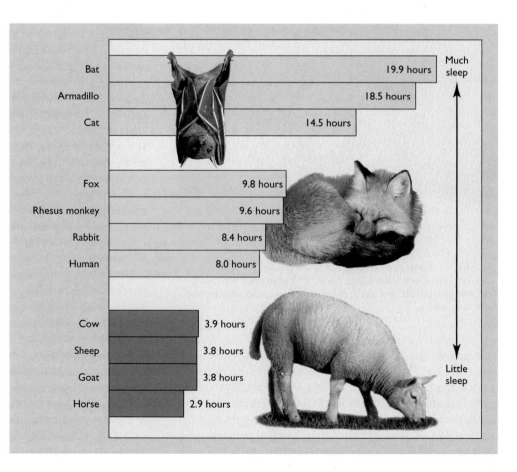

report dreams about 85–90% of the time, whereas those awakened during NREM sleep report dreams on 50–60% of occasions (Foulkes, 1999). REM dreams are on the average more complicated and more visual, but not always. People sometimes have complex, highly visual dreams during NREM sleep also, especially toward the end of the night. Furthermore, some brain-damaged people have REM sleep but no dreams, and others have dreams but no REM sleep (Solms, 1997). Thus, REM intensifies brain activity, but many researchers now doubt that it causes dreams (Domhoff, 1999).

## Sleep Cycles During the Night

Sleep researchers distinguish among stages of sleep by recording brain waves with electrodes attached to the scalp (Figure 5.10). *A device* called an **electroencephalograph (EEG)** *measures and amplifies slight electrical changes on the scalp that reflect patterns of activity in the brain.* Sleep researchers *combine an EEG measure with a simultaneous measure of eye movements to produce a* **polysomnograph** (literally, "many-sleep measure") as shown in Figure 5.11. Upon falling asleep one enters non-REM stage 1, when the eyes are nearly motionless and the EEG shows many short, choppy waves, as shown in Figure 5.11a. These small waves indicate a fair amount of brain activity, with brain cells firing out of synchrony with one another. Because they are out of synchrony, their activities nearly cancel each other out, like people in a crowd talking at the same time.

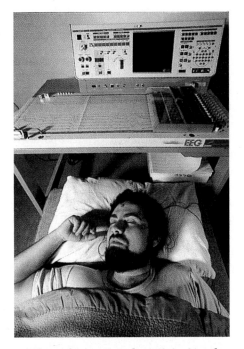

**FIGURE 5.10** Electrodes monitor the activity in a sleeper's brain, and an EEG then records and displays brain-wave patterns.

As sleep continues a person progresses into non-REM stages 2, 3, and 4, as shown in Figure 5.11b–e. These stages are most easily distinguished by the number of long, slow waves; stage 1 has the fewest, and stage 4 has the most. These large waves indicate *decreased* brain activity. They grow larger from one stage to the next because the brain has little stimulation, so the little activity that does occur drives many neurons in synchrony. (Note that the eyes remain mostly inactive in each of these stages.)

After stage 4 a sleeper gradually moves back through stages 3 and 2. After stage 2, however, the sleeper enters REM sleep, not stage 1. That is, REM sleep replaces most of stage 1 except for the first episode of the night. In Figure 5.11f the EEG in REM sleep resembles that of stage 1, but the eyes are moving more extensively and more regularly than they do during other stages. At the end of REM sleep, the sleeper cycles through stages 2, 3, 4 and then back to 3, 2, and REM again. In a healthy young adult, each cycle lasts 90 to 100 minutes on average. As shown in Figure 5.12, the cycles continue throughout the night, but as the night progresses, the duration of stages 3 and 4 gets shorter and the duration of REM and stage 2 increases. Figure 5.12 represents sleep under quiet, undisturbed conditions; someone who sleeps in an uncomfortable room will have many awakenings and very little stage 3 or 4 sleep (Velluti, 1997).

## Sleep Stages and Dreaming

The interest in REM sleep prompted sleep investigators to awaken people during REM sleep and ask for dream reports in an attempt to answer some very basic questions. For example, does everyone dream? Adults who claim they do not dream have been taken into the laboratory and attached to a polysomnograph, which revealed normal periods of REM sleep. When these people were awakened during a REM period, they usually reported dreaming (to their own surprise). Apparently, they dream normally but forget their dreams quickly. However, children younger than 5 years old seldom report dreams, even if awakened during REM sleep (Foulkes, 1999).

Another question: How long do dreams last? William Dement and Edward Wolpert (1958) awakened people after REM periods of various durations and asked them to describe their dreams. Someone awakened after 1 minute of REM sleep would usually tell a brief story; a person awakened after 5 minutes of REM sleep would usually tell a story about 5 times as long, and so on. Evidently, dreams take place in "real time." That is, a dream is not over in a split second; if a dream seemed to last several minutes, it probably did.

 **C** ONCEPT CHECK

**3.** Is dreaming more common toward the end of the night's sleep or toward the beginning? (Check your answer on page 176.)

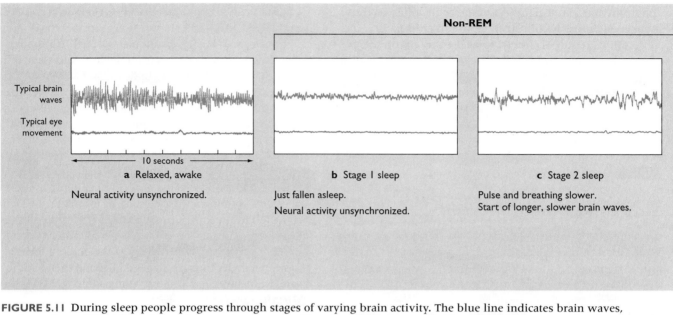

**FIGURE 5.11** During sleep people progress through stages of varying brain activity. The blue line indicates brain waves, as shown by an EEG. The red line shows eye movements. Note that REM sleep resembles stage 1 sleep except for the addition of rapid eye movements. (Courtesy of T. E. Le Vere)

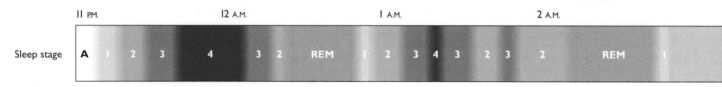

**FIGURE 5.12** This fairly typical sleeper had five cycles of REM and non-REM sleep and awakened (A) briefly three times during the night. Note that stage 4 occupies much time early in the night but less later; REM sleep becomes more and more prevalent as the night progresses. (From Dement, 1972)

## The Functions of REM Sleep

Given that people spend 20–25% of an average night in REM sleep, it presumably serves an important function, but what? The most direct way to approach this question is to deprive people of REM sleep and study how this deprivation affects their health or behavior.

In one study William Dement (1960) monitored the sleep of eight young men for seven consecutive nights and awakened them for a few minutes whenever their EEG and eye movements indicated the onset of REM sleep. He awakened the members of a control group equally often but at random times so that he did not necessarily interrupt their REM sleep. Over the course of 1 week, Dement found it harder and harder to prevent REM sleep in the experimental group . . . and harder to keep them from quitting the experiment. On the first night, the average participant had to be awakened 12 times; by the seventh night, 26 times. During the day REM-deprived participants experienced anxiety, irritability, and impaired concentration. On the eighth night, all were permitted to sleep without interruption. Most showed a "REM rebound," spending 29% of the night in REM sleep compared with 19% before the experiment began. People in the control group, who had not been deprived of REM sleep, showed no such REM rebound.

So evidently, REM sleep does satisfy a need, and the body will work to catch up on at least some of the REM sleep it has missed. However, in this and related studies, the effects of REM deprivation were not catastrophic, so the question of why we need REM sleep remained.

A second approach is to determine which people get more REM sleep than others. One clear pattern is that infants get more REM sleep than children and children more than adults. From that observation many researchers have inferred that REM sleep serves a function that is more acute in younger people. Maybe so, but maybe not. Infants not only get more REM sleep but also more total sleep (Figure 5.13). If we compare species, we find that the species that get the most sleep (e.g., cats) also generally have the greatest percentage of REM sleep. Among adult humans those who sleep 9 or more hours per night spend a large percentage of that time in REM sleep; those who sleep 6 hours or less also get less REM sleep. In short, those who sleep the most spend the greatest percentage of that time in REM. It is as though a certain amount of *non*-REM sleep is necessary each night, and additional amounts of REM sleep can be added if sleep continues long enough (Horne, 1988).

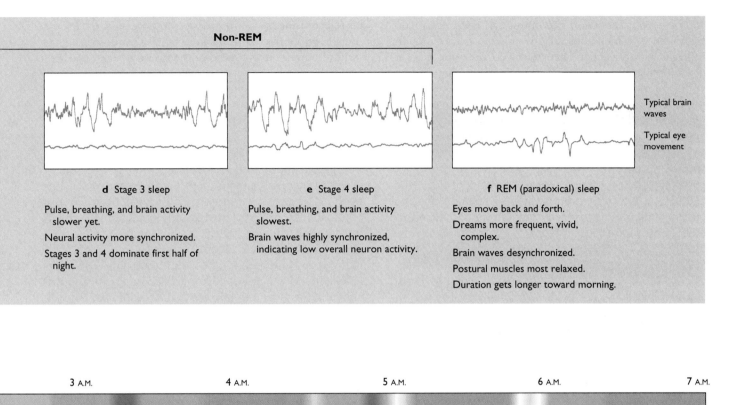

**Non-REM**

Typical brain waves

Typical eye movement

**d** Stage 3 sleep

Pulse, breathing, and brain activity slower yet.

Neural activity more synchronized.

Stages 3 and 4 dominate first half of night.

**e** Stage 4 sleep

Pulse, breathing, and brain activity slowest.

Brain waves highly synchronized, indicating low overall neuron activity.

**f** REM (paradoxical) sleep

Eyes move back and forth.

Dreams more frequent, vivid, complex.

Brain waves desynchronized.

Postural muscles most relaxed.

Duration gets longer toward morning.

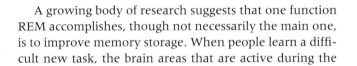

A growing body of research suggests that one function REM accomplishes, though not necessarily the main one, is to improve memory storage. When people learn a difficult new task, the brain areas that are active during the learning also become more active than usual during REM sleep that night (Maquet et al., 2000). When people learn something and then get tested the following day, their performance usually improves, but only if they got at least 6 hours of sleep and a mixture of REM and NREM sleep (Stickgold, Whidbee, Schirmer, Patel, & Hobson, 2000). REM sleep appears to be particularly important for storing memories of motor skills, as opposed to verbal information (Plihal & Born, 1997).

Still, the fact that REM sleep helps to consolidate memories does not necessarily indicate that memory storage is its original or primary function. For example, what are the uses of computers? For most people the answers would include e-mail, Internet use, writing papers, and playing video games.

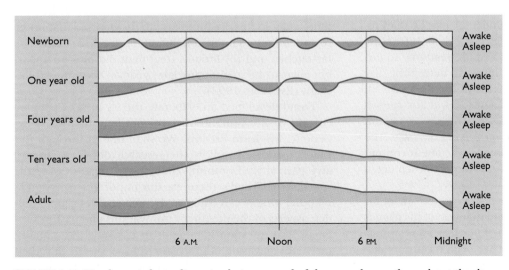

**FIGURE 5.13** Newborns' sleep alternates between wakefulness and naps throughout the day. Within a few months, infants consolidate most of their sleep into one longer period at night, although they continue having one or two naps during the day. As people grow older, the amount of sleep per day decreases. (Based on Kleitman, 1963)

But the *original* function of computers was only to do mathematical calculations; all the other uses came later. Similarly, REM has been around at least since the days of the earliest mammals and birds; its original function might not be the one we notice most prominently today. One speculation is that its original function was simply to move the eyes around after prolonged sleep. The corneas of the eyes (see Figure 4.2) usually get most of their oxygen directly from the air; they also get some from the fluid behind them. During sleep the eyelids are shut, and they no longer get oxygen from the air. After several hours of sleep, the fluid behind the cornea can become so stagnant that the cornea would get little oxygen from that source either, unless the eyes shook back and forth to get the fluid moving. REM is, in fact, more common after prolonged sleep and more common in species with large eyes, for whom stagnation of the fluid is most likely to be a problem. It is therefore plausible that REM evolved originally as a means of getting oxygen to the corneas (Maurice, 1998).

## The Content of Our Dreams

*Even a saint is not responsible for what happens in his dreams.*

—St. Thomas Aquinas

What do we dream about and why? People once believed that dreams foretold the future. Occasionally, of course, they do—either by coincidence or because the dreamer had a reason to expect some outcome. Today, psychologists do not expect dreams to tell us about the future, but some do look to dreams to tell us something about the dreamer. Even that effort is controversial, however; how much we can learn about people from their dreams is far from certain.

### Freud's Approach

The Austrian physician and founder of psychoanalysis, Sigmund Freud, maintained that dreams reveal the dreamer's unconscious thoughts and motivations. To understand a dream, he said, one must determine the dreamer's associations to each detail of the dream. Each dream has a **manifest content**—*the content that appears on the surface*—and a **latent content**—*the hidden content that is represented symbolically in the actual experience*. The only way a psychoanalyst can discover the latent content is to understand the dreamer's associations to each detail of the manifest content.

To illustrate, Freud (1900/1955) interpreted one of his own dreams, in which he dreamed that one of his friends was his uncle. He worked out the following associations: Both this friend and another one had been recommended for an appointment as professor at the university. Both had been turned down, probably because they were Jews. Freud himself had been recently recommended for the same appointment, but he feared that he too would

be rejected for the same reason. Freud's only uncle had once been convicted of illegal business dealings. Freud's father had said, however, that the uncle was not bad, but just a simpleton.

What was the relationship between the two friends and the uncle? One of the friends was in Freud's judgment a bit simpleminded. The other had once been accused of sexual misconduct, although he was not convicted. By linking these two friends to his uncle, Freud interpreted the dream as meaning, "Maybe they didn't get the university appointment because one was a simpleton (like my uncle) and the other was regarded as a criminal (like my uncle). If so, my being Jewish might not stop me from getting the appointment."

Freud's approach to dream analysis became popular for many years, although it is now on the decline. The problem lies in how to test it. We can talk about the meaning of a dream just as we can talk about the meaning of a novel, but in both cases the interpretation is subjective and arguable, not scientific. That is, the interpretations are not falsifiable, in the sense described in Chapter 2.

In some cases, such as the dream just described, Freud's interpretation is at least plausible. In other cases it is less so. One of his most famous dream analyses concerned a man who reported remembering a dream from when he was 4 years old (!) in which he saw six or seven white dogs with large tails sitting motionless in a tree outside his window. (The actual dream was of spitz dogs, although Freud's writings always described them as wolves.) After a laborious line of reasoning, Freud concluded that the child had dreamed about his parents in their bed clothes (presumably white, which is why the dogs or wolves were white). The motionless dogs represented the opposite—frantic (sexual) activity. The big tails also represented their opposite—the boy's fear of having his penis cut off. In short, said Freud, the boy had dreamed about watching his parents have sex . . . doggystyle. Decades later researchers actually located the man who had told this dream to Freud. He reported that (a) he regarded Freud's interpretation of his dream as extremely far-fetched and (b) Freud's treatment did him no apparent good, as he spent many later years in continued treatment (Esterson, 1993).

Freud developed an elaborate theory of how people's current wishes combine with memories of their early experiences to form dreams. We shall not go through this theory because, frankly, the research does not support any part of it (Domhoff, 2000). Still, regardless of the specifics of Freud's theories, the important question is whether *anyone* can listen to dreams and determine hidden aspects of the dreamer's motivations and past experience. That question is difficult to answer. Undoubtedly, many therapists do offer dream interpretations that their clients find meaningful. The problem is that because we have no way to check the accuracy of the interpretation, there is a serious risk of going astray with confident but misleading analyses.

# CONCEPT CHECK

**4.** A popular paperback purports to tell you what your dreams mean. The author says that every element of a dream has a symbolic meaning—in many cases a sexual meaning. A ballpoint pen represents a penis, for example, and walking up a flight of stairs represents sexual arousal. Would Freud agree or disagree with the author of this book? (Check your answer on page 176.)

## The Activation-Synthesis Theory

An important contemporary theory relates dream content to spontaneous activity that arises in the brain during REM sleep. According to the **activation-synthesis theory of dreams,** *input arising from the pons (see Figure 4.30) activates the brain during REM sleep. The cortex takes that more or less random activity plus whatever stimuli are striking the sense organs and does its best to synthesize a story to make sense of all this activity* (Hobson & McCarley, 1977). The activation-synthesis theory does not necessarily imply that our dreams are meaningless. Even if they begin with more or less random activity in various brain areas, the dreamer's interpretations of this activity depend on his or her personality, motivations, and previous experiences. Still, Freud saw the meaning as the cause of the dream; in the activation-synthesis theory, the meaning occurs only as a by-product of other processes.

Many kinds of dreams do appear to relate to the spontaneous activity of the brain during REM sleep. For a most basic example, input from the pons activates the visual areas of the brain during REM sleep, especially during the first minutes of a REM period, and nearly all dreams include visual content (Amzica & Steriade, 1996). Also, many people occasionally dream of flying or falling, probably because the vestibular system detects the body's horizontal position and the brain interprets this sensation as floating or flying (Hobson & McCarley, 1977; Velluti, 1997).

Have you ever dreamed that you are trying to walk or run away but you cannot move? One explanation is that the major postural muscles are really paralyzed during REM sleep. Thus, your brain could send messages telling your muscles to move but then receive sensory feedback indicating that they have not moved at all.

The main problem with the activation-synthesis theory is that it does not make clear, testable predictions. For example, people almost always sleep horizontally but only occasionally dream of flying or falling. Why not always? Our muscles are always paralyzed during REM sleep. Why don't we always dream that we can't move? *After* a dream the activation-synthesis theory can provide explanations, but it offers only vague predictions of who will dream about what and when. Recall from Chapter 2 that a good theory should be falsifiable; it should make

clear, precise predictions. The one prediction the theory makes is that sounds and other stimuli in the room might be incorporated into the dream, but in fact, few dreams have an apparent connection to any stimulation present at the time.

## The Neurocognitive Theory

Another alternative, the **neurocognitive theory,** *treats dreams as just another example of thinking, except that they occur under special conditions* (Domhoff, 2001; Foulkes, 1999; Solms, 2000). Those conditions include:

- persisting activity of the cortex
- great reduction of sensory stimulation, including reduced activity in the primary sensory areas of the brain
- loss of voluntary self-control of thinking

The result is that the brain is active enough to engage in imagination, but the images are not overridden by sensory information or intentional control. According to this theory, REM sleep is not necessary for dreaming, although the arousal associated with REM tends to intensify dreams. The arousal of emotional areas of the brain, especially in the temporal lobe, adds an emotional content to many dreams (Maquet et al., 1996).

Researchers working within this framework have attempted simply to describe people's dreams. David Foulkes (1999) found that the ability to dream requires a fair amount of cognitive maturity. Even infants have a great deal of REM sleep, but a child younger than 5 years old who is awakened during REM sleep very seldom reports any experience that we could call a dream. It is hard to know whether young children don't have dreams or just can't report them. However, even somewhat older children report dreams in fewer than half of their REM awakenings, and at those ages only children with strong visual-spatial abilities (e.g., the ability to solve puzzles) often report clear dreams. Evidently, the stronger one's imagination during wakefulness, the greater the chance of dreaming when asleep. The dreams that young children report are mostly of unmoving images. Table 5.1 outlines stages of the development of dreaming in children.

Studies of adult dreams find that they are seldom either bland or bizarre, and most dreams deal with content similar to what people have been thinking about (Domhoff, 1996; Hall & Van de Castle, 1966). For example, preteens seldom dream about the opposite sex, but teenagers do (Strauch & Lederbogen, 1999). Blind people frequently dream about difficulties in locomotion or transportation (Hurovitz, Dunn, Domhoff, & Fiss, 1999). In one study young adults checked off from a list the topics (e.g., marriage, family, friends, and hobbies) those that were "concerns" to them and others that were matters of indifference. Then they reported their dreams over three nights. They frequently dreamed of the concerns and very rarely of the nonconcerns. If the experimenter suggested, right before bedtime, that they try to dream about a certain topic, suggesting that they dream about one of their concerns increased that type of dream still further, but suggesting a dream about a topic of little interest had no effect (Nikles, Brecht, Klinger, & Bursell, 1998). There are some exceptions, however, to the rule that we dream about what we do or care about in waking life: People rarely dream about reading, writing, using a computer, or watching television (Schredl, 2000). Of course, even when awake, most of us don't often fantasize about those activities.

 You might try keeping a dream diary and checking the content of your dreams. Do you in fact dream mostly about the topics that you think about or fantasize about while you are awake?

For adult dreamers in the United States—and apparently in other countries, too, according to more limited data—one common dream theme is "things that could go wrong." People often dream of falling, being chased, being naked in public, or being unable to do something they need to do. The most common emotion in adult dreams is apprehension or fear; dreams include more misfortune than good fortune; and the dreamer is more often the victim of aggression than the cause of it (Domhoff, 1996; Hall & Van de Castle, 1966). People occasionally awaken with disappointment that it was only a dream, but more often they awaken with relief. Curiously, 11- to 13-year-olds have more happy dreams than people of any other age (Foulkes, 1999).

Many other questions about dreaming remain unanswerable, however. For example, how accurately do we remember our dreams? Well, how would we find out? With real events we can compare people's memories to what actually happened, but we have no way to compare reported dreams to the originals. Or consider this apparently simple question: Do we dream in color? The fact that people ask this question reveals why it is difficult to answer: They ask because they do not remember whether their dreams were in color. But how could an investigator determine whether people dream in color except by asking them to remember? The best evidence we have is that, when people are awakened during REM sleep, when their recall should be as sharp as possible, they report color at least half of the time (Herman,

**TABLE 5.1 Stages in the Development of Dreaming in Children**

| | Age | | |
|---|---|---|---|
| | 3–5 years | 5–7 years | 7–9 years |
| Frequency of dream reports if awakened during REM sleep | 15%, and many of these reports are questionable | 31% | 43% |
| Median length of dream report | 14 words | 41 words | 72 words |
| Dream content | A single motionless image; many reports of animals, almost none about the self, almost no emotions | A simple event with some motion; almost none about the self doing anything | More complex stories; self is active in many; mostly happy with some fear |

Based on Foulkes, 1999

Roffwarg, & Tauber, 1968; Padgham, 1975). This result does not necessarily mean that their other dreams are in black and white; it may mean only that the colors in those dreams were not memorable.

You might wonder whether blind people have visual dreams. The answer depends on when someone became blind. People who became blind after about age 5 to 7 continue to have visual dreams, and some have them quite often. However, people who were born blind or who became blind in early childhood have no visual imagery in their dreams; instead, they dream of sounds, touch, smells, and taste (Hurovitz et al., 1999). Sighted people only rarely dream of smells or tastes (Zadra, Nielsen, & Donderi, 1998).

## CONCEPT CHECK

5. Recall the man who remembered dreaming at age 4 about dogs sitting motionless in a tree. Freud interpreted the motionlessness as a symbolic representation of its opposite, intense activity. Given what we now know about children's dreams, what other explanation could you offer? (To answer this question, we shall assume that an adult can accurately remember what he dreamed at age 4!) (Check your answer on page 176.)

# Abnormalities of Sleep

Comedian Steven Wright says that someone asked him, "Did you sleep well last night?" He replied, "No, I made a few mistakes."

We laugh because sleep isn't the kind of activity on which a person makes mistakes; sleep just happens. Sometimes, however, sleep doesn't happen or it happens at the wrong time or it does not seem restful or we have bad dreams. We would not call these unpleasant experiences "mistakes," but in one way or another, our sleep is not what we wanted it to be.

■ These comic strips represent actual dreams as described to the artist. Dreams often mix possible with impossible events and frequently explore the theme of "things that could go wrong."

## Insomnia

*Insomnia* literally means "lack of sleep." However, we cannot usefully define insomnia in terms of the number of hours of sleep. Some people feel well rested after fewer than 6 hours of sleep per night; others feel poorly rested after 9 hours. A complaint of **insomnia** indicates that *the person feels poorly rested the next day.* By this definition about one third of all adults have occasional insomnia and about one tenth have serious or chronic insomnia (Lilie & Rosenberg, 1990). Most of those with serious insomnia have other medical or psychological disorders as well, such as anxiety disorders or depression (Ohayon, 1997).

People sometimes have trouble sleeping because of noise, worries, indigestion, uncomfortable temperatures, use of alcohol or caffeine, and other miscellaneous problems. Overuse of tranquilizers can also cause insomnia. That statement may be surprising because people often take tranquilizers as a way of *relieving* insomnia. The problem is that no pill will exert its effects for exactly the period of time that someone wants to sleep. Some tranquilizers produce brief effects that wear off before morning, so the person awakens early (Kales, Soldatos, Bixler, & Kales, 1983). Others have effects that last too long, so the person remains sleepy for a prolonged part of the next day. Moreover, people who use tranquilizers as sleeping pills may come to depend on them so that they cannot sleep without them (Kales, Scharf, & Kales, 1978).

Most people with insomnia suffer from a variety of other complaints and disorders, including tension, depression, personality disturbances, loss of energy, and increases in body temperature and metabolism. Does the lack of sleep *cause* these other problems? Maybe, maybe not; the fact that people with insomnia also tend to have other problems is merely a correlation, and a correlation does not demonstrate causation.

How might we determine whether insomnia leads to these other problems? Here is a clever experiment that addresses this issue (Bonnet & Arand, 1996).

**HYPOTHESIS**  A previously normal person who is forced to sleep only as long as someone with insomnia and at the same times will develop a similar pattern of medical and psychological abnormalities.

**METHOD**  Experimenters identified ten adults with insomnia, who were defined as people who, for at least the last year, on more nights than not, took at least 45 minutes to get to sleep and awoke for at least an hour during the night. The experimenters then advertised for volunteers who had no sleeping problems. For each person with insomnia, they matched one volunteer of the same gender and approximately the same age and weight. For seven nights the experimenters monitored the sleep of

■ Insomnia is identified not by how many hours one sleeps at night but by how sleepy the person is the following day.

the people with insomnia. Whenever one of them went to sleep, the volunteer partner was allowed to go to sleep. When the person with insomnia woke up, the matched volunteer was awakened also. Thus, each volunteer awoke and went to sleep at the same times as one person with insomnia. This kind of design is known as a *yoked control experiment* because each participant in one group is "yoked" to one person in the other group. At various times during the week, each person was given a variety of medical and psychological tests.

**RESULTS** Table 5.2 summarizes the results.

**INTERPRETATION** After 1 week of enforced insomnia, the normal people had less vigor, so we may conclude that lack of sleep decreases pep and energy. In other regards, however, the week of enforced insomnia produced either no effect or effects opposite to those found in people suffering from chronic insomnia. We

conclude, therefore, that sleep deprivation by itself does not cause tension, depression, personality disturbances, or increases in body temperature or metabolic rate. Instead, many people develop insomnia because of nervous system disorders that also lead to tension, depression, high body temperature, and so forth.

## Sleep Apnea

Among the many possible causes of insomnia, one is known as *sleep apnea* (AP-nee-uh). *Apnea* means "no breathing." Many people have either irregular breathing or occasional periods of 10 seconds or so without breathing during their sleep. People with **sleep apnea,** however, may *fail to breathe for a minute or longer and then wake up gasping for breath.* When these people do manage to breathe during their sleep, they generally snore. They may lie in bed for 8 to 10 hours per night but actually sleep less than half that time. During the following day, they are likely to feel sleepy and they may have headaches.

Many people with sleep apnea are obese—especially obese middle-aged or older men who are unable to find a sleeping position that lets them breathe easily (Mezzanotte, Tangel, & White, 1992). Others have brain abnormalities, especially in the medulla, that interfere with their breathing during sleep.

## Narcolepsy

People who experience *sudden attacks of extreme, even irresistible, sleepiness in the middle of the day* are said to have **narcolepsy.** Such people may also experience sudden attacks of muscle weakness or paralysis. Sometimes they have vivid dreamlike experiences while awake. Each of these symptoms could be interpreted as a sudden intrusion of REM sleep into the waking period of the day (Guilleminault, Heinzer, Mignot, & Black, 1998).

Most people with narcolepsy have no relatives with similar problems. Narcolepsy also occurs in dogs, for whom it has a strong genetic basis. Researchers who located the gene responsible for narcolepsy in dogs discovered that it controls the brain receptors for a chemical called *hypocretin* or *orexin* (Lin et al., 1999). Other researchers found that preventing production of that chemical can cause narcolepsy in mice, who do not ordinarily get it (Chemelli et al., 1999). If you have never heard of hypocretin or orexin, don't feel bad. Not much is known about this chemical, except that it is almost completely limited to one small part of the brain (the

**TABLE 5.2 Results of Insomnia Experiment**

| | People with Insomnia | Normal People after 1 Week of Enforced Insomnia |
|---|---|---|
| *Tension* | More tense than most people | Decreased tension |
| *Mood* | Depressed | Not depressed |
| *Vigor* | Low | Low |
| *Personality* | Disturbed in several ways | Normal |
| *Estimate of own sleep* | Underestimate amount of sleep | Correctly estimate amount of sleep |
| *Body temperature* | Higher than normal | Lower than normal |
| *Metabolic rate* | Higher than normal | Lower than normal |

lateral hypothalamus). The best guess is that human narcolepsy is also caused by some lack of production or sensitivity to that chemical, probably not for genetic reasons. Focusing on this chemical should speed the search for better treatments for narcolepsy and perhaps also for insomnia and other sleep disorders.

## Sleep Talking, Sleepwalking, Nightmares, and Night Terrors

Many people, whether or not they suffer from insomnia, nevertheless have unsettling experiences during their sleep. Sleep talking is the most common and least troublesome. Most people talk in their sleep more often than they realize because they do not remember sleep talking themselves and usually no one else is awake to hear them. Sleep talking occurs with about equal probability in REM and non-REM sleep. It can range from a single indistinct word or grunt to a clearly articulated paragraph. Sleep talkers sometimes pause between utterances, as if they were carrying on a conversation with someone else. In fact, it is possible to engage some sleep talkers in a dialogue. Sleep talking is nothing to worry about. It is not related to any mental or emotional disorder, and sleep talkers rarely say anything that they would be embarrassed to say when awake.

Sleepwalking tends to run (walk?) in families. True sleepwalking occurs mostly in children during stage 4 sleep and lasts fewer than 15 minutes. Few children hurt themselves when sleepwalking, and most children outgrow it (Dement, 1972). A person who appears to be sleepwalking may really be awake but confused. You have no doubt heard people say that you should never awaken a sleepwalker. This is another of those misconceptions, like "we use only 10% of our brain," in which people are quoting each other, each person confident that the others know what he or she is talking about. In fact, sleep researchers report that waking a sleepwalker is neither dangerous nor harmful, although the person may indeed be disoriented and confused (Moorcroft, 1993).

Other concerns include nightmares and night terrors. A nightmare is an unpleasant dream, but a dream nevertheless. A night terror, however, is a state of extreme panic, including a heart rate three times the normal rate. Night terrors occur during stage 3 or stage 4 sleep but never during REM sleep. They are fairly common in young children and less common in adults (Salzarulo & Chevalier, 1983).

## Leg Movements While Trying to Sleep

Have you ever lain in bed, trying to fall asleep, when suddenly one of your legs kicked? An occasional leg jerk while trying to fall asleep is a common experience and no cause for concern. In contrast, some people have pro-

longed "creepy-crawly" sensations in their legs, accompanied by repetitive leg movements strong enough to awaken the person, especially during the first half of the night (Moorcroft, 1993). This condition, known as **periodic limb movement disorder** (or more informally, as restless leg syndrome), is a common cause of poor sleep in people over the age of 50. Sufferers can stop the leg kicks by standing and walking, but by doing so they of course interrupt their sleep. The causes of this disorder are unknown, and the best advice is to avoid factors that can make the condition worse—such as caffeine, stress, or fatigue. Tranquilizers suppress these leg movements in some people (Schenck & Mahowald, 1996).

## CONCEPT CHECK

**6.** Why would it be unlikely, if not impossible, for sleepwalking to occur during REM sleep? (Check your answer on page 176.)

## Hypersomnia

Finally, consider a disorder that is the opposite of insomnia: A small number of people suffer from **hypersomnia,** *excessive but unrefreshing sleep.* In a typical case, the person sleeps 8 or 9 hours per day during the week, plus an afternoon nap, and then "catches up" by sleeping 18, 20, even 22 hours per day on weekends. Even after this much sleep, the person has trouble awakening and feels confused and poorly rested. In some cases the disorder can be traced to a history of head trauma, viral infection, or mood disorder, but in many cases the cause is unknown (Bassetti & Aldrich, 1997).

## If You Have Trouble Sleeping . . .

Insomnia can be a brief, minor annoyance or a sign of a potentially serious disorder. If you experience persistent difficulties, consult a physician, but for occasional or minor insomnia, you can try a few things yourself (Hauri, 1982; Lilie & Rosenberg, 1990):

- Try to associate your bed with sleeping, not with lying awake. If you find that you just can't get to sleep, get up, do something else, and return to bed when you start to feel sleepy.
- Try to keep a regular schedule of when you go to bed and when you wake up each day.
- Avoid caffeine, nicotine, and other stimulants, especially in the evenings.
- Avoid habitual use of alcohol or sleeping pills. (Either may help you get to sleep occasionally, but they become counterproductive after repeated use. Also, alcohol decreases REM sleep.)
- Keep your bedroom cool and quiet.
- Get a consistent amount of exercise daily, but don't exercise shortly before bedtime.

■ One recommended strategy if you have trouble sleeping: Don't just lie in bed worrying about your lack of sleep. Get up, do something else, and try going back to sleep later.

## IN CLOSING
## *The Mysteries of Sleep and Dreams*

Sleep and dreams are unlike wakefulness in some ways, but they are not a state of complete unconsciousness. For example, a parent will awaken at the sound of a child softly crying. The brain is never completely off duty, never completely relaxed.

Although our understanding of sleep and dreams continues to grow, several major questions remain. Even such basic issues as the function of REM sleep remain in doubt. People have long found their dreams a source of wonder, and researchers continue to find much of interest and mystery.

## Summary

* *Circadian rhythms.* Sleepiness depends on the time of day. Even in an unchanging environment, people become sleepy in cycles of approximately 24 hours. (page 161)
* *Theories about our need for sleep.* Several repair and restoration functions take place during sleep. Sleep also serves to conserve energy at times of relative inefficiency. (page 164)
* *Sleep stages.* During sleep people cycle through sleep stages 1 through 4 and back through stages 3 and 2 to 1 again. The cycle beginning and ending with stage 1 lasts about 90 to 100 minutes. (page 166)
* *REM sleep.* A special stage known as REM sleep replaces many of the stage-1 periods. REM sleep is characterized by rapid eye movements, a high level of brain activity, and relaxed muscles. People usually dream during this stage but can dream in other stages also. The function of REM sleep is still uncertain. (page 166)
* *The content of dreams.* Freud proposed that dreams are the product of unconscious wishes. The activation-synthesis theory claims that dreams are an accidental by-product of random arousal during REM sleep. The neurocognitive theory states that dreaming is just another example of thinking, except that it occurs under conditions of low sensory input and no voluntary control of thinking. (page 170)
* *Insomnia.* Insomnia—subjectively unsatisfactory sleep—can result from many influences, including a biological rhythm that is out of phase with the outside world, sleep apnea, narcolepsy, overuse of sleeping pills, and periodic limb movement disorder. (page 173)

## Answers to Concept Checks

1. You should prefer to schedule the meeting on a Pacific island so that you will travel west and the other person will travel east. (page 164)
2. Try a melatonin pill 2 or 3 hours before your desired bedtime—in this case about 1 to 2 p.m. (page 164)
3. REM sleep and dreaming are more common toward the end of the night's sleep. (page 167)
4. Freud would disagree with the premise of this book. Freud believed that the symbolism of dream elements differed from one person to another; it was necessary to ask the dreamer to describe his or her associations to each element. (page 171)
5. Before age 5 almost all the dreams that children report are of stationary images; they apparently almost never dream of anything moving. (page 172)
6. During REM sleep, the major postural muscles of the body are completely relaxed. (page 175)

# Hypnosis

*What can hypnosis do?*

*What are its limitations?*

*Truth is nothing but a path traced between errors.*[*]

—Franz Anton Mesmer

If a hypnotist told you that you were 4 years old and you suddenly starting acting like a 4-year-old, we would say that you are a good hypnotic subject. If the hypnotist said that you see your cousin sitting in the empty chair in front of you, and you agreed that you see her, then again we would remark on the depth of your hypnotism.

But what if you had *not* been hypnotized and you suddenly started acting like a 4-year-old or insisted that you saw someone in that empty chair? In this case psychologists would suspect that you were suffering from a serious psychological disorder. Hypnosis induces a temporary state that is sometimes bizarre; no wonder we find it so fascinating.

**Hypnosis** is *a condition of increased suggestibility that occurs in the context of a special hypnotist–subject relationship.* The term *hypnosis* comes from Hypnos, the Greek god of sleep, although the similarity between hypnosis and sleep is superficial. People in both states close their eyes and lose initiative, and hypnotized people, like dreamers, accept contradictory information without protest. Hypnotized people, however, can walk around and respond to objects and events in the real world. Also, their EEG is like that of waking people, not sleepers (Rainville et al., 1999).

Hypnosis was first practiced by an Austrian philosopher and physician, Franz Anton Mesmer (1734–1815). When treating certain medical problems, Mesmer would pass a magnet back and forth across the patient's body to redirect the flow of blood, nerve activity, and certain undefined "fluids." Some patients reported dramatic benefits. Later, Mesmer discovered that he could dispense with the magnet and use only his hand. From this observation you or I would conclude that magnetism was unimportant and that the phenomenon was related to the power of suggestion. Mesmer, however, drew the quirky conclusion that he did not need a magnet because *he himself* was a magnet. With that claim he gave us the term "animal magnetism."

In his later years, Mesmer grew even more peculiar. After his death, others studied "animal magnetism" or "Mesmerism," eventually calling it "hypnotism." But by that time, many physicians and scientists associated hypnosis with eccentrics, charlatans, and other practitioners of hocus-pocus. Even today, some stage performers use hypnosis for entertainment. We should carefully distinguish the exaggerated claims from the legitimate use of hypnosis by licensed therapists.

## Ways of Inducing Hypnosis

Mesmer thought hypnosis was a power that emanated from his own body. If so, only special people could hypnotize others. Today, we believe that becoming a successful hypnotist requires practice but no unusual powers or personality.

■ Although Mesmer is often depicted as irresistibly controlling people, psychologists now recognize that hypnosis reflects a willingness by the hypnotized person.

---

[*]Does this sound profound? Or is it nonsense? Mesmer said many things that sound profound at first, but the more we think about them, the less sense they make.

**FIGURE 5.14** A hypnotist induces hypnosis by repeating suggestions, relying on the hypnotized person's cooperation and willingness to accept suggestions. No one can force hypnosis on an unwilling person.

The first step toward being hypnotized is simply agreeing to give it a try. Contrary to what you may have seen in the movies or on television, no one can hypnotize an uncooperative person. The hypnotist tells you, for example, to sit down and relax, and you do so because you would like to experience hypnosis. The whole point of hypnosis is doing what the hypnotist suggests, and by sitting down and relaxing, you are already starting to follow suggestions.

A hypnotist might then monotonously repeat something like, "You are starting to fall asleep. Your eyelids are getting heavy. Your eyelids are getting very heavy. They are starting to close. You are falling into a deep, deep sleep" (Figure 5.14). In another technique (Udolf, 1981), the hypnotist suggests, "After you go under hypnosis, your arm will begin to rise automatically." (Some people, eager for the hypnosis to succeed, shoot their arm up immediately and have to be told, "No, not yet. Just relax; that will happen later.") Then the hypnotist encourages you to relax and suggests that your arm is starting to feel lighter, as if it were tied to a helium balloon. Later the hypnotist suggests that your arm is beginning to feel a little strange and is beginning to twitch. The timing of this suggestion is important, because when people stand or sit in one position long enough, their limbs really do begin to feel strange and twitch. If the hypno-

tist's suggestion comes at just the right moment, you think, "Wow, that's right. My arm does feel a little strange. This is really starting to work!" Believing that you are being hypnotized is a big step toward actually being hypnotized.

# The Uses and Limitations of Hypnosis

Hypnosis can produce relaxation, concentration, temporary changes in behavior, and sometimes, changes that persist beyond the end of the hypnotic state. A "deeply" hypnotized person will follow many of the hypnotist's suggestions. There is no evidence, however, that hypnosis gives people any new physical or mental abilities.

## What Hypnosis Can Do

One well-established effect of hypnosis is to inhibit pain. Some people can undergo medical or dental surgery with just hypnosis and no anesthesia (Figure 5.15). Hypnosis is particularly helpful for people who react unfavorably to anesthetic drugs and those who have developed a tolerance for painkilling opiates.

Recall from Chapter 4 that pain has both sensory and emotional components. Hypnosis alters mostly the emotional components. Even when a hypnotized person says that he or she feels no pain, the heart rate and blood pressure still shoot up as much as they do in nonhypnotized people (Hilgard, 1973). Under hypnotic suggestion to feel no unpleasantness, a person subjected to painful stimuli will have high arousal in the parietal cortex areas responsive to body sensations but not in the frontal cortex areas responsive to unpleasant emotions (Rainville, Duncan, Price, Carrier, & Bushnell, 1997) (see Figure 5.16).

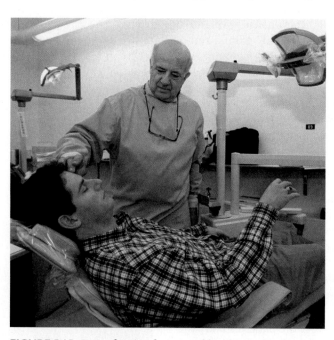

**FIGURE 5.15** Some dentists have used hypnosis as a means of relieving pain, even for tooth extractions, root canal surgery, and other seriously painful procedures.

Another potentially constructive use of hypnosis is the **posthypnotic suggestion,** *a suggestion to do or experience something particular after coming out of hypnosis.* For example, people who are told to forget what happened during hypnosis often do forget, although careful testing can reveal that the memory is not completely obliterated (David, Brown, Pojoga, & David, 2000). People also re-

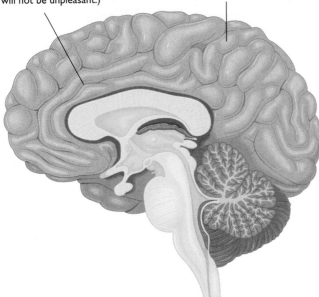

Area of frontal cortex responsive to emotional distress. (Activity decreased by hypnotic suggestion that stimulus will not be unpleasant.)

Area of parietal cortex responsive to painful stimulation

**FIGURE 5.16** Hypnotic suggestions to experience less pain can decrease the emotional intensity but generally have less effect on the sensation itself. The hypnotic suggestion that a stimulus will not be unpleasant decreases activity in the frontal cortex areas associated with emotional distress but has little effect on the sensory cortex.

spond to posthypnotic suggestions to change their behavior. In one study adults already known to be easily hypnotized were randomly assigned to different groups. One group was handed a stack of 120 addressed stamped postcards and asked (without being hypnotized) to mail one back each day until they exhausted the stack. Another group was given a posthypnotic suggestion to mail one card per day. The nonhypnotized group actually mailed back more cards, but they reported the experience differently. The nonhypnotized people said they had to remind themselves each day to mail a card. Those given the posthypnotic suggestion said they never made a deliberate effort, but the idea of mailing a card just "popped into mind" and then they felt a sudden compulsion to mail one (Barnier & McConkey, 1998).

Posthypnotic suggestions can help people change bad habits, *if* they have already agreed that they wish to. For example, posthypnotic suggestions have helped people give up tobacco, lose weight, stop nail-biting, become more sexually responsive, and stop having night terrors (Kihlstrom, 1979; Udolf, 1981). The effects of a single hypnotic suggestion wear off over time, but repeated suggestions can extend the effect. In one study people were taught to use repeated self-hypnosis to quit cigarette smoking. Almost one fourth of the participants managed to quit smoking for at least the next 2 years (Spiegel, Frischholz, Fleiss, & Spiegel, 1993)—a pretty good result for a habit that is notoriously difficult to break.

## Distortions of Perception Under Hypnosis

A few people report visual or auditory **hallucinations** *(sensory experiences not corresponding to reality)* under hypnosis, and many report touch hallucinations after suggestions such as "your nose itches" or "your left hand feels numb" (Udolf, 1981). When hypnotized people report hallucinations, are they telling the truth or are they just saying what the hypnotist wants them to say?

At least in some cases, people's reports are correct. In one study researchers performed brain scans while people listened to sounds, imagined sounds, or hallucinated them under hypnotic suggestion. The hypnotic suggestion activated some of the same brain areas as actual sounds did, but imagining sounds did not activate those areas (Szechtman, Woody, Bowers, & Nahmias, 1998). Evidently, hypnotic hallucinations are more like real experiences than like imagination.

However, when hypnotized people claim that they don't see or hear something, careful testing can demonstrate that the information did register at least in some ways. In one study people who were highly susceptible to hypnosis looked at the optical illusion shown in Figure 5.17a. Like other people, they reported that the top horizontal line looked longer than the bottom horizontal line. Then they were hypnotized and told not to see the radiating lines but to see only the two horizontal ones. Those who said that they no longer saw the radiating lines still perceived the top line as longer than the bottom one (R. J. Miller, Hennessy, & Leibowitz, 1973). If the radiating lines had truly disappeared, then they would have seen something like Figure 5.17b, where the horizontal lines look equal. So these people did see the radiating lines, at least at some level, even though they reported that they did not.

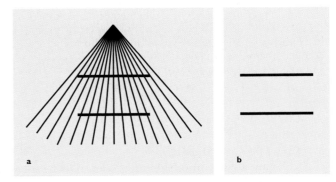

**FIGURE 5.17** Horizontal lines of equal length in (a) the Ponzo illusion and (b) without the optical illusion. Researchers employ such visual stimuli to determine how hypnosis may alter sensory perception.

## What Hypnosis Cannot Do

Most of the spectacular claims made for the power of hypnotic suggestion turn out to be less impressive on closer scrutiny. For instance, people under hypnosis can become as stiff as a board so that they can balance their head and neck on one chair and their feet on another chair and even allow someone to stand on their body (Figure 5.18)! Amazing? Not really. You can probably do the same without hypnosis. It's easier than it looks. (I do not recommend that you invite someone to stand on you. Someone who does not balance correctly could injure you.)

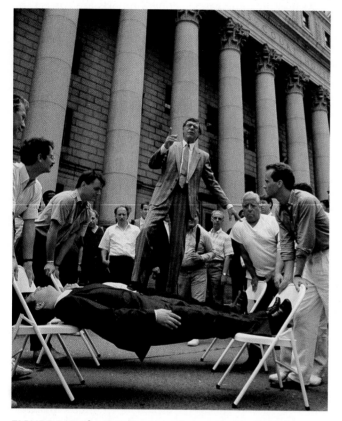

**FIGURE 5.18** The U.S. Supreme Court ruled in 1987 that criminal defendants may testify about details they recalled under hypnosis. Its decision sparked this protest by the magician known as The Amazing Kreskin, who borrowed a stunt usually used to demonstrate the power of hypnosis—standing on a person suspended between two chairs.

Many people have attempted to use hypnosis to enhance memory. For example, a distressed person tells a psychotherapist, "I don't know why I have such troubles. Maybe I had some really bad experience when I was much younger, but I just can't remember." Or a witness to a crime says, "I saw the culprit for a second or two, but now I can't give you a good description." Therapists and police officers have sometimes turned to hypnotism in the hope of uncovering hidden memories. However, hypnotized people are highly suggestible. Even when they are given an innocent suggestion such as "you will remember more than you told us before," many hypnotized people respond with new but incorrect information. Let's consider one typical study.

## WHAT'S THE EVIDENCE?
*Hypnosis and Memory*

The design of this study and many like it is simple: The experimenter presents a large array of material, tests people's memory of it, and then retests some people under hypnosis and other people without hypnosis to see how the hypnosis changes their memory (Dywan & Bowers, 1983).

**HYPOTHESIS** People will remember some of the material without hypnosis and then will remember more of it after hypnosis.

**METHOD** Fifty-four people looked at a series of 60 slides of black-and-white drawings of simple objects (such as pencil, hammer, or bicycle), presented one every 3.5 seconds. Then they were given a sheet with 60 blank spaces and asked to recall as many of the items as possible. The slides were presented a second and third time, and after each session, the participants had another chance to recall items. Each day for the next week, they again wrote a list of all the items they could remember (but without seeing the slides again). Finally, a week after the original slide sessions, they returned to the laboratory. Half of them (selected at random) were hypnotized and the others were just told to relax; then all were asked to recall as many of the drawings as possible.

**RESULTS** Figure 5.19 shows the means for the two groups. The hypnotized people did report some new memories that they had not recalled before and more than the nonhypnotized group did. However, both groups reported more incorrect items than correct items, and the hypnotized group reported more incorrect items than the nonhypnotized group did.

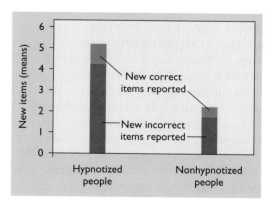

**FIGURE 5.19** Items recalled 1 week after viewing a series of slides and *not* recalled before that. Hypnosis did increase people's recall of items they had not recalled before. However, most of the new "memories" they confidently reported were incorrect. (Modified from Dywan & Bowers, 1983)

**INTERPRETATION** These results show no evidence that hypnosis improves memory. Rather, it may decrease people's usual hesitance about reporting uncertain or doubtful memories. It may also cause people to confuse imagination with reality.

You might note that this study is an example of the signal-detection issue discussed in Chapter 4 (page 136): A reported new memory is a "hit," but the number of hits, by itself, is useless information unless we also know the number of "false alarms"—reported memories that are incorrect.

Many other studies have produced similar conclusions: Hypnosis sometimes does increase the number of correct items recalled, but it also increases the number of incorrect items recalled, and people who have been hypnotized continue to report both the correct and incorrect items with high confidence, even after the hypnotic session (Steblay & Bothwell, 1994). Typically, hypnotized people are more confident than nonhypnotized people in both their correct and incorrect reports (Fligstein, Barabasz, Barabasz, Trevisan, & Warner, 1998).

In response to such findings, a panel appointed by the American Medical Association (1986) recommended that courts of law should refuse to admit any testimony that was elicited under hypnosis, although hypnosis might occasionally be used as an investigative tool if all else fails. (For example, if a hypnotized witness reports a license plate number, and the police track down the car and find blood on it, the blood is certainly admissible evidence, even if the hypnotized report is not. Success stories of that type are rare.)

However, professional hypnotists have objected to having their work rejected by the courts, and some judges do admit hypnotically induced testimony, provided that the hypnotic session was fully recorded so that opposing attorneys could watch it. The result is sometimes, shall we say, questionable. In one case a truck crashed into a car in an intersection, killing the driver and seriously wounding a passenger in the backseat, whose head injury left him dazed and confused at the time and unable to remember anything afterward. Three eyewitnesses testified, and the police agreed, that the car had entered the intersection on a red light and that the truckdriver was not to blame. *After* the backseat passenger collected damages from the driver's insurance company, and almost 2 years after the accident, he contacted a hypnotist to help him remember more of how the accident happened. Under hypnosis he reported that just before the accident he leaned forward and saw that the light was green, thus implying that the accident was the truckdriver's fault. Although it is extremely doubtful that hypnosis could reinstate a 2-year-old memory of an event that caused head injury and confusion, the judge ruled that because the hypnotic session had been carefully recorded, it could be admitted as evidence. A few days later, the truck company settled the suit for hundreds of thousands of dollars (Karlin, 1997).

An even more doubtful claim is that hypnosis can help people recall their early childhood. A hypnotist might say, "You are getting younger. It is now the year . . . ; now it is . . . ; now you are only 6 years old." A hypnotized person may act like a young child, playing with teddy bears and blankets (Nash, Johnson, & Tipton, 1979). But is he or she reliving early experiences? Evidently not.

**1.** The childhood "memories," such as the names of friends and teachers and the details of birthday parties, are generally inaccurate, according to records that parents or others have kept (Nash, 1987).

**2.** Someone who has presumably regressed under hypnosis to early childhood retains spelling and other skills learned later in life. When asked to draw a picture, he or she does not draw as children draw but as adults imagine that children draw (Orne, 1951) (see Figure 5.20).

**3.** Hypnotized subjects will respond just as well to suggestions that they are growing older as to suggestions that they are growing

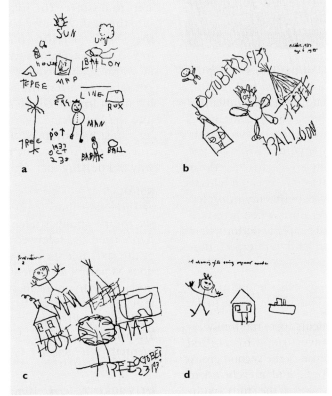

**FIGURE 5.20** Regression or role playing? One person made drawing (a) at age 6 and the other three drawings (b, c, & d) as a college student under hypnosis. While under hypnosis the person was asked to regress to age 6. The drawings created while under hypnosis are not like drawings done in childhood. Orne (1951) concluded that the hypnotized students played the role of a 6-year-old and drew as they thought a child would.

younger. They give as convincing a performance of being an older person as of being a younger person (Rubenstein & Newman, 1954). Because their reports of the future can only be imagination, we should assume the same for their past.

You may even encounter the astounding claim that hypnosis can help someone to recall memories from a previous life. Hypnotized young people who claim to be recollecting a previous life most often describe the life of someone similar to themselves and married to someone remarkably similar to their current boyfriend or girlfriend. If they are asked whether their country (in their past life) is at war or what kind of money is in use, their guesses are seldom correct (Spanos, 1987–1988).

## CONCEPT CHECK

7. List two practical uses of hypnosis that the evidence supports and one that it does not. (Check your answer on page 185.)

■ Will hypnotized people do anything that they would otherwise refuse to do? The problem with answering that question is that nonhypnotized people will sometimes perform some strange and dangerous acts, either because an experimenter asked them to or on their own.

## WHAT'S THE EVIDENCE?
### *Hypnosis and Risky Acts*

Most hypnotists agree about one of the limits of hypnosis: "You don't have to worry," a hypnotist will reassure you. "People will not do anything under hypnosis that they would ordinarily refuse to do." That reassurance is an important strategy in getting you to agree to hypnosis. But is it true? And how would anyone know? Do you suppose that hypnotists frequently ask clients to perform criminal or immoral acts and meet with repeated refusals and then report these unethical experiments in professional journals? Not likely. Furthermore, when investigators have in fact asked hypnotized people to perform dangerous acts, the results have been hard to interpret. Here is one example.

**HYPOTHESIS** Hypnotized people will sometimes perform acts that nonhypnotized people would refuse to do.

**METHOD** Eighteen college students were randomly assigned to three groups. The investigator hypnotized those in one group, instructed those in the second group to pretend they were hypnotized, and merely asked those in the third group to participate in the study (without even mentioning hypnosis). All students were then asked to perform three acts: First, they were told to go to a box in a corner of the room and pick up a poisonous snake. The snake really was poisonous. Anyone who got too close to the snake was restrained at the last moment. Second, the hypnotist poured some highly concentrated, fuming nitric acid into a large container and distinctly stated that it was nitric acid. To dispel any doubts, he

threw a coin into the acid and let the students watch it start to dissolve. The hypnotist then told them to reach into the acid with bare hands and remove the coin. Here there was no last-second restraint. Anyone who followed the instructions was told to wash his or her hands in warm soapy water immediately afterward. (Today's ethical procedures would prevent this study.) Third, the hypnotist instructed the student to throw the nitric acid into the face of the hypnotist's assistant. Unnoticed, the hypnotist had swapped the container of nitric acid for a container of water, but the hypnotized person had no way of knowing that.

**RESULTS** Five of the six hypnotized students followed all three directions (Orne & Evans, 1965). Moreover, the six control-group students who were pretending to be hypnotized also followed all three commands! So did two of the six students who were just told to take these actions as part of an experiment, with no mention of hypnosis. (Nonhypnotized subjects did, however, hesitate much longer than the hypnotized subjects.)

Why would people do such extraordinary things? They explained that they simply trusted the experimenter: "If he tells me to do something, it can't really be dangerous."

**INTERPRETATION** Hypnotized people *will* do some strange and dangerous acts. However, nonhypnotized people will do them also, at least when they know they are participating in an experiment conducted by someone they regard as reputable.

In short, we simply do not have adequate evidence to decide whether people under hypnosis will do anything that they would utterly refuse to do otherwise because it is hard to find anything that people will refuse to do!

There is a message here about the importance of control groups: We cannot simply imagine what people would do without hypnosis, or any other procedure, we need to test people to see what they would do.

# Is Hypnosis an Altered State of Consciousness?

If a hypnotist tells you, "Your hand is rising; you can do nothing to stop it," your hand might indeed rise. If you were later asked why, you might reply (as many do) that you lost control over your own behavior. Still, you were not a puppet. Was the act voluntary, involuntary, or something in between?

At one extreme, some psychologists regard hypnosis as a special state of consciousness characterized by greatly increased suggestibility. At the other extreme, some psychologists emphasize the similarities between hypnosis and normal wakeful consciousness, especially that hypnotized people are aware of their surroundings and their own behaviors. Most psychologists take intermediate positions, noting that hypnotized people are neither "faking it" nor under the control of the hypnotist. That is, hypnosis is a special state in some ways but not others (Kirsch & Lynn, 1998). For example, most people who are highly hypnotizable are also highly responsive to suggestions without hypnosis, but a few people are suggestible under hypnosis but not without it (Braffman & Kirsch, 1999).

One way to determine whether hypnosis is a special state of consciousness is to find out whether unhypnotized people can do everything that hypnotized people do. That is, if you agreed to pretend that you were hypnotized, could you act exactly like a hypnotized person?

## How Well Can a Nonhypnotized Person Pretend to Be Hypnotized?

In several experiments some college students were hypnotized while others were told to pretend they were hypnotized. An experienced hypnotist then examined them and tried to determine which ones were really hypnotized.

Fooling the hypnotist turned out to be easier than expected. The pretenders were able to tolerate sharp pain without flinching and could pretend to recall old memories. They made their bodies as stiff as a board and lay rigid between two chairs. When standing people were told to sit down, they did so immediately (as hypnotized people do) without first checking to make sure there was a chair behind them (Orne, 1959, 1979). When told to experience anger or another emotion, they exhibited physiological changes such as increased heart rate and sweating, just as hypnotized people do (Damaser, Shor, & Orne, 1963). Not even highly experienced hypnotists could accurately identify the pretenders.

However, a few differences between the hypnotized people and pretenders did emerge (Orne, 1979). The pretenders failed to match some of the behaviors of hypnotized people—not because they couldn't do them but because they did not know how a hypnotized subject would act. For instance, when the hypnotist suggested, "You see Professor Schmaltz sitting in that chair," people in both groups reported seeing the professor. Some of the hypnotized subjects, however, said they were puzzled. "How is it that I see the professor there, but I can also see the entire chair?" Pretenders never reported seeing this "double reality."

At that point in the experiment, Professor Schmaltz actually walked into the room. "Who is that entering the room?" asked the hypnotist. The pretenders would either say they saw no one, or they would identify Schmaltz as someone else. The hypnotized subjects would say, "That's Professor Schmaltz." Some then said that they were confused by seeing the same person in two places at the same time. For some of them, the hallucinated professor faded at that moment, whereas others continued to accept the double image.

One study reported a way to distinguish hypnotized people from pretenders that succeeds more than 90% of the time. But it might not be the way you would expect. Simply ask people a few questions, such as how deeply hypnotized they thought they were, how relaxed they were, and whether they were aware of anything in the room other than what the hypnotist suggested they attend to. People who rate themselves as "extremely" hypnotized, "extremely" relaxed, and so forth are almost always pretenders. Those who rate themselves as only mildly influenced were the ones who were hypnotized (Martin & Lynn, 1996).

So, what is our conclusion? Is hypnosis an altered state, or are hypnotized people just playing a role? Apparently, unhypnotized people playing the role of "hypnotized people" can mimic just about any effect of hypnosis, that they know about it. However, the fact that unhypnotized role-players can copy hypnotized people does not mean that hypnosis is "nothing but" role-playing (Hilgard, 1971). The effects that role-players learn to imitate happen spontaneously for the hypnotized people.

## CONCEPT CHECK

8. Does hypnosis give people the power to do anything they could not do otherwise? Does it cause them to do anything they would be unwilling to do otherwise? (Check your answers on page 185.)

## Faked Hypnosis by a Criminal Defendant

In 1979 Kenneth Bianchi was arrested for raping and strangling two women. He was suspected of being the "Hillside strangler" who had been terrorizing the Los Angeles area with similar rapes and stranglings. While he

**FIGURE 5.21** Kenneth Bianchi, accused of being the Hillside strangler, pleaded not guilty on the grounds that he had a "multiple personality" and that his evil second personality was responsible for the crimes. Psychiatrist Martin Orne, however, persuaded the court that Bianchi was faking his second personality and, indeed, that he was only pretending to be hypnotized.

was awaiting trial, a psychiatrist hypnotized him and claimed to uncover a second personality, "Steve Walker," who had first appeared when Bianchi was 9 years old and who had, Bianchi said, actually committed the crimes. Bianchi pleaded not guilty by reason of insanity.

But was Bianchi really insane or was he faking the second personality and, indeed, only pretending to be hypnotized (Figure 5.21)? Six psychiatrists were asked to examine Bianchi. One of them was Martin Orne, the psychiatrist who had conducted the research on whether college students could effectively pretend to be hypnotized. He knew how difficult it was to detect pretenders, but his earlier research had also taught him a few tricks. At first the six psychiatrists were divided about whether Bianchi was really insane or merely faking. Eventually, Orne convinced them that Bianchi was faking, based on the following evidence (Orne, Dinges, & Orne, 1984):

• Bianchi behaved in ways that were not typical of hypnotized people. For example, when Orne suggested that someone was sitting in an empty chair, Bianchi not only claimed to see that person but even reached out to shake hands! Orne concluded that Bianchi was trying too hard to prove that he was hypnotized.

• In one hypnosis session, Bianchi's "Steve" personality tore the filter tip off a cigarette. After the hypnosis was over, the "Ken" personality expressed amazement and said he couldn't imagine who might have torn the filter tip off. This

episode might suggest that Bianchi had completely forgotten his experience under hypnosis. However, Orne observed that Bianchi did exactly the same thing with three other hypnotists. Again, Bianchi was apparently trying to convince everyone that he had been deeply hypnotized.

• At one point Orne told Bianchi that he doubted Bianchi was a true case of multiple personality because "real" multiple personalities have three personalities, not just two. (This statement is not true; Orne just wanted to see what would happen.) Later that day Bianchi developed a third personality.

By uncovering these facts, Orne exposed Bianchi's pretense. Bianchi agreed to plead guilty in return for the state's dropping its request for the death penalty. He also stopped claiming to have multiple personalities. In short, it is possible, but not easy, to distinguish between hypnotized people and those who are only pretending.

# Meditation: In Some Ways Like Hypnosis

Hypnosis is not the only method of inducing a relaxed and possibly altered state of consciousness. **Meditation,** *a method of inducing a calm, relaxed state through the use of special techniques,* follows a tradition that has been practiced in various parts of the world for thousands of years. For example, one may sit quietly while repeating a meaningless sound (e.g., "om") for 15 to 20 minutes twice a day. The point is "to empty one's mind"—that is, to expel all the worries, troubles, and doubts that otherwise intrude into our thoughts. In that respect meditation has some similarities to the relaxed, passive state of hypnosis. However, it includes no hypnotist or suggestions.

■ Meditation excludes the worries and concerns of the day and thereby induces a calm, relaxed state.

Many studies document that meditation decreases physiological arousal, as measured by heart rate, breathing rate, blood pressure, EEG patterns, and so forth (e.g., Travis & Wallace, 1999). Those benefits do not necessarily confirm the claims that meditation performs a special transcendental or spiritual function, however. Most studies that have compared meditation with relaxation have found little or no difference in results between the two groups (Holmes, 1987). The point is not that meditation is useless, but only that it is one of several ways to relax, and relaxation of any kind is helpful. As with hypnosis, it is important to separate the real phenomenon from the exaggerated claims.

## IN CLOSING
### *The Nature of Hypnosis*

Researchers have still not reached a consensus on exactly what hypnosis is. They do agree on a few general points, however: Hypnosis is not just faking or pretending to be hypnotized, and it does not give people mental or physical powers that they otherwise lack. Hypnosis merely enables people to relax, concentrate, and follow suggestions better than they usually do. Be skeptical of anyone who claims much more than that for hypnosis.

## Summary

* *Nature of hypnosis.* Hypnosis is a condition of increased suggestibility that occurs in the context of a special hypnotist–subject relationship. Psychologists try to distinguish the genuine phenomenon, which deserves serious study, from exaggerated claims. (page 177)
* *Hypnosis induction.* To induce hypnosis, a hypnotist asks a person to concentrate and then makes repetitive suggestions. The first steps toward being hypnotized are the willingness to be hypnotized and the belief that one is becoming hypnotized. (page 177)
* *Uses.* Hypnosis can alleviate pain, and through posthypnotic suggestion, it can help people combat bad habits. (page 178)
* *Sensory distortions.* Hypnosis can induce hallucinations and other sensory distortions. However, when hypnotized people are told not to see something, even when they claim not to see it, enough aspects of the information get through to the brain to influence other perceptions. (page 179)
* *Nonuses.* Hypnosis does not give people special strength or unusual powers. Most of the new "memories" evoked under hypnosis are false. (page 179)
* *Uncertain limits.* Although many hypnotists insist that hypnotized people will not do anything that they would refuse to do when not hypnotized, there is little solid evidence to back up this claim. (page 182)
* *Hypnosis as an altered state.* Controversy continues about whether hypnosis is a special state of consciousness and, indeed, what we mean by an altered state. (page 183)
* *Meditation.* Meditation can induce a relaxed condition that one might regard as an altered state of consciousness. (page 184)

## Answers to Concept Checks

**7.** Supported by the evidence: Hypnosis can decrease pain, and posthypnotic suggestions can help people break bad habits. Not supported: Hypnosis does not improve people's memories. (Neither does it give them added strength.) (page 182)

**8.** No evidence indicates that hypnosis empowers people to do anything they could not do otherwise if sufficiently motivated. That is, people pretending to be hypnotized can mimic all the things hypnotized people do, and the only exceptions are things that the imitators did not know about. As to whether hypnosis can make people do something they would ordinarily refuse to do, we simply do not know. In certain experiments hypnotized people have done some strange things, such as attempting to pick up a poisonous snake or putting their hand into a vat of concentrated acid. However, nonhypnotized people did, too. It is hard to find an act that people will refuse to do, especially if they know they are in an experiment. (page 183)

# 5.3 Drugs and Their Effects

*What experiences do abused drugs produce?*

*Why do people experiment with such drugs?*

Many people incorrectly assume that any drug they receive from a physician or pharmacy must be safe. In fact, almost any drug is dangerous in large doses or after extensive use. Furthermore, many abused drugs—including amphetamines, morphine, and even cocaine—have legitimate medical uses. The dividing line between "good" and "bad" drugs is a blurry one that depends more on the quantities and the reasons for their use than it does on the chemistry of the drugs themselves.

The abuse of alcohol and other drugs is a widespread problem, which we shall consider in Chapter 16. Here our focus is on the experiences associated with common drugs of abuse. In the study of drug effects, it is more difficult than usual to separate fact from fiction. Many people who are trying to discourage drug use have made such strong claims about the harms of drug use that some people stop believing the warnings. At the opposite extreme, many people who defend their own use of drugs have seriously understated the dangers. As with other topics, we should be skeptical of claims that go beyond the evidence.

## A Survey of Abused Drugs and Their Effects

Some abused drugs, such as alcohol and opiates, have predominantly calming effects. Others, such as amphetamines and cocaine, are known for their stimulating effects. Still others, such as LSD, produce hallucinations. What do they have in common that would account for their tendency to be abused? Nearly all abused or addictive drugs increase the activity at

dopamine synapses in the brain, especially at particular types of dopamine receptors known as types $D_2$, $D_3$, and $D_4$ (Maldonado et al., 1997). They can do so by a variety of means, including increased release of dopamine, blocking the mechanisms that remove dopamine from the synapse after its release, stimulating neurons that release dopamine, or inhibiting neurons that inhibit release of dopamine. The addictive actions of dopamine (and therefore of abused drugs) depend largely on a tiny brain area called the *nucleus accumbens,* apparently a central area for attention and perhaps habit formation (Berridge & Robinson, 1998). Figure 5.22 shows the location of the nucleus accumbens. Table 5.3 lists some of the commonly abused drugs and their most prominent effects.

However, we should not expect to find all the answers to addiction in the chemistry of the drugs. People can also become addicted to gambling and even to some extent videogame playing, even though these addictions do not include any "substance." Videogame playing, and presumably gambling as well, can increase the release of

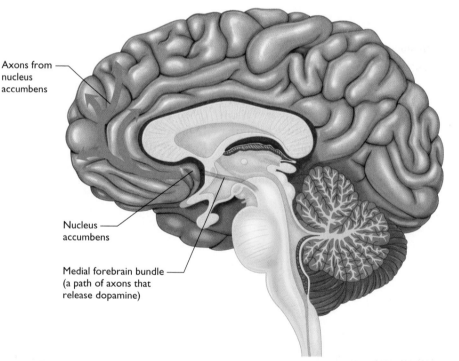

Axons from nucleus accumbens

Nucleus accumbens

Medial forebrain bundle (a path of axons that release dopamine)

**FIGURE 5.22** The nucleus accumbens is a small brain area that is critical for the motivating effects of many experiences, including drugs, food, and sex. Most abused drugs increase the activity of dopamine, an inhibitory transmitter in this area. Other abused drugs, such as PCP, inhibit the activity of glutamate, an excitatory transmitter here. That is, a *decrease* in output by the nucleus accumbens is important for the effects of abused drugs and other motivating experiences.

**TABLE 5.3**  Commonly Abused Drugs and Their Effects

| Drug Category | Effects on the Nervous System | Effects on Behavior |
|---|---|---|
| *Stimulants* | | |
| Amphetamine | Increases release of dopamine and decreases reuptake, prolonging effects | Increases energy and alertness |
| Cocaine | Decreases reuptake of dopamine, prolonging effects | Increases energy and alertness |
| Methylphenidate (Ritalin) | Decreases reuptake of dopamine, but with slower onset and offset than cocaine | Increases alertness; much milder withdrawal effects than cocaine |
| Caffeine | Blocks a chemical that inhibits glutamate synapses | Increases energy and alertness |
| Nicotine | Stimulates some acetylcholine synapses; stimulates some neurons that release dopamine | Increases arousal; abstention by a habitual smoker produces tension and depression |
| *Depressants* | | |
| Alcohol | Facilitates effects of GABA, an inhibitory neurotransmitter | Relaxation, reduced inhibitions, impaired memory and judgment |
| Benzodiazepine tranquilizers | Facilitates effects of GABA, an inhibitory neurotransmitter | Relaxation, decreased anxiety, sleepiness |
| *Narcotics* | | |
| Morphine, heroin, other opiates | Stimulate endorphin synapses | Decreases pain; withdrawal from interest in real world; unpleasant withdrawal effects during abstention |
| Marijuana | Excites anandamide and 2-DG receptors | Decreases pain and nausea; intensification of some sensory experiences; distorted sense of time |
| *Hallucinogens* | | |
| LSD | Stimulates serotonin type 2 receptors at inappropriate times | Hallucinations, sensory distortions |
| MDMA ("ecstasy") | Stimulates neurons that release dopamine; at higher doses also stimulates neurons that release serotonin | At low doses increases arousal; at higher doses hallucinations; can damage or destroy axons |
| Phencyclidine (PCP or "angel dust") | Inhibits one type of glutamate receptor | Intoxication, slurred speech; at higher doses hallucinations, thought disorder, impaired memory and emotions |

dopamine in the nucleus accumbens *in those people who develop a strong habit* (Koepp et al., 1998). An addiction is in the person, not in the drug.

## Stimulants

**Stimulants** are *drugs that boost energy, heighten alertness, increase activity, and produce a pleasant feeling.* Two powerful stimulants are amphetamine and cocaine. Methylphenidate (Ritalin) is another drug with the same type of effects, but it acts more slowly. Decades ago, physicians accidentally discovered that stimulant drugs help some

children with attention deficits to focus their attention better. To this day, the explanation is uncertain.

Amphetamine increases the release of dopamine in the brain (Giros, Jaber, Jones, Wightman, & Caron, 1996). Amphetamine, cocaine, and methylphenidate all prevent neurons from reabsorbing the dopamine they have released; they thereby prolong the effects of the dopamine (Volkow, Wang, & Fowler, 1997; Volkow, Wang, Fowler et al., 1998). Because each of these drugs also increases the activity at norepinephrine and serotonin synapses, their effects on behavior are complex and far-reaching, including increases in heart rate, blood

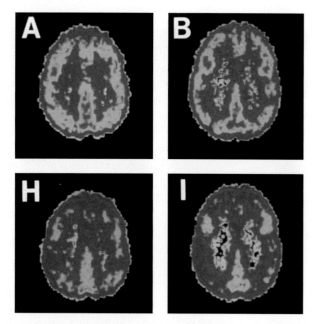

**FIGURE 5.23** "Your brain on drugs." Parts A and B show the activity of a normal brain in horizontal section, as measured by PET scans. Parts H and I show activity of the same brain under the influence of cocaine. Red indicates the highest amount of activity, followed by yellow, green, and blue. Note that cocaine has decreased the amount of activity in the brain.

**FIGURE 5.24** Because crack is smoked, it reaches the brain in 8 seconds, much faster than other forms of cocaine. All else being equal, the faster that a drug reaches the brain, the more intense the experience will be and the greater the probability of addiction.

pressure, and body temperature. Cocaine has additional anesthetic (sensation-blocking) effects similar to the effects of novocaine and lidocaine.

We regard cocaine as a stimulant because it increases heart rate, makes people excited and alert, and interferes with their sleep. However, cocaine actually *decreases* the overall activity within the brain (London et al., 1990). That effect may seem to contradict the statement that cocaine prolongs the activity of a couple of neurotransmitters; however, those transmitters are predominantly inhibitory transmitters. Thus, by increasing dopamine and norepinephrine activity, cocaine decreases the activity of many brain neurons (Figure 5.23).

If cocaine decreases the activity of neurons, you might ask, how does it act as a stimulant for behavior? The brain is a complicated organ that often operates on the principle of double negatives: Cocaine decreases the activity of neurons which were, in turn, acting to inhibit still other neurons. By inhibiting an inhibitor, cocaine has the net effect of stimulating the final behavioral outcome.

Cocaine has long been available in the powdery form of cocaine hydrochloride, a chemical that can be sniffed. It produces mostly stimulant effects that increase gradually over a few minutes and then decline gradually over about half an hour. It also anesthetizes the nostrils and can in some cases damage the lungs. Sniffed cocaine hydrochloride is only occasionally habit-forming.

Before 1985 the only way to get a more intense effect from cocaine hydrochloride was to treat it with ether to convert it into *freebase cocaine*—cocaine with the hydrochloride removed. Smoking freebase cocaine enables a high percentage of it to enter the body rapidly and thereby enter the brain rapidly. The faster a drug enters the brain, the more intense the resulting experience will be.

The drug known as *crack cocaine* first became available in 1985. Crack is cocaine that has already been converted into freebase rocks, ready to be smoked (Brower & Anglin, 1987; Kozel & Adams, 1986) (see Figure 5.24). It is called "crack" because it makes popping noises when smoked. Crack produces a rush of potent effects within just a few seconds, much faster than other forms of cocaine. The effects are generally described as pleasant, although some people report intense anxiety instead, and other people suffer heart attacks or other severe medical complications. Long-term use can lead to a sore throat, mental confusion, lung diseases, and other serious problems.

Because crack cocaine enters the brain so rapidly, it can become powerfully habit-forming, although the habit forms gradually over 2 to 4 years, so frequent users may lull themselves into a false sense of security: "I can take it or leave it" (Gawin, 1991). During periods of using the drug, the drug experience itself becomes the focus of so much attention that the person neglects usual activities such as eating, sleeping, going to work, or taking care of family members.

Because selling crack is so lucrative, rival gangs in large cities compete with each other to control the sales. The resulting violence has created a problem for society that goes far beyond the direct harm done by the drug itself.

Coffee, tea, and many soft drinks contain caffeine, which is also a stimulant, though less powerful and less dangerous than amphetamine or cocaine. Habitual coffee drinkers can become dependent on it, and abstaining from it can cause headaches and drowsiness (Hughes et al., 1991). Surgical patients sometimes report distress that people assume stems from the operation but really is a result of caffeine withdrawal.

Tobacco cigarettes deliver nicotine, which stimulates acetylcholine receptors, thereby increasing wakefulness and arousal. Some of those acetylcholine receptors stimulate neurons that increase the release of dopamine in the nucleus accumbens (Pich et al., 1997). Thus, nicotine's effects overlap those of amphetamines, cocaine, and other addictive drugs.

Although nicotine is generally classed as a stimulant, most smokers say it relaxes them. The research points to an explanation for this paradox. As people smoke more and more, their stress levels and tension *increase,* and habitual smokers experience greater stress levels than nonsmokers. However, a habitual smoker who goes even a short time between cigarettes begins to feel withdrawal symptoms, including nervousness and unhappy mood. Smoking another cigarette relieves the withdrawal symptoms and restores the usual mood, which is slightly tense but not as bad as the withdrawal state (Parrott, 1999). Quitting altogether would lead to a temporary unpleasant withdrawal state, and to an eventual state of reduced stress. We shall consider cigarette addiction again in Chapter 16.

ONCEPT CHECK

9. A drug called AMPT (alpha-methyl-para-tyrosine) prevents the body from making the transmitter dopamine. If someone took a large dose of AMPT, how would it affect that person's later responsiveness to cocaine, amphetamine, or methylphenidate? (Check your answer on page 193.)

## Depressants

**Depressants** *are drugs that predominantly decrease arousal.* Two common types of depressants are alcohol and tranquilizers.

When archeologists unearthed a Neolithic village in Iran's Zagros Mountains, they found a jar that had been constructed about 5500–5400 B.C., one of the oldest hu-

man-made crafts ever found (Figure 5.25). Inside the jar, especially at the bottom, the archeologists found a yellowish residue. They were curious to know what the jar had held, so they sent some of the residue for chemical analysis. The unambiguous answer came back: The jar had been a wine vessel (McGovern, Glusker, Exner, & Voigt, 1996).

Clearly, human use of alcohol is a tradition that has stood the test of time. **Alcohol** is a *class of molecules that includes methanol, ethanol, propyl alcohol (rubbing alcohol), and others. Ethanol is the type that people drink;* the others are toxic if consumed. Alcohol acts primarily as a relaxant. Moderate use of alcohol serves as a tension reducer, a relaxant. In greater amounts it can increase aggressive and risk-taking behaviors, mainly by depressing the fears and anxieties that ordinarily inhibit such activities.

Excessive use can damage the liver and other organs, aggravate or prolong many medical conditions, and impair memory and motor control. A woman who drinks alcohol during pregnancy risks impairing her baby's brain development, health, and appearance (see Chapter 10).

Alcohol abuse is a worldwide problem, although it is more common in some populations than others. Within the United States, alcohol abuse is more common among Native Americans than among other ethnic groups and least common among those of Asian ancestry. The reasons are not well understood, but it is not true (as many have supposed) that Native Americans get drunk more easily than others. If anything, they are *less* affected than others by moderate amounts of alcohol (Garcia-Andrade, Wall, & Ehlers, 1997). Whatever the explanation, the ethnic differences are worth taking seriously; many ob-

**FIGURE 5.25** This jar, dated about 5500–5400 B.C., is one of the oldest human crafts ever found. It was used for storing wine.

servers believe that differences in alcohol use constitute a major reason for ethnic differences in life span (Rivers, 1994).

Another type of depressant drugs, **tranquilizers,** *help people to relax and to fall asleep; they can also decrease muscle tension and suppress epileptic seizures.* Barbiturates, once a common type of tranquilizer, proved to be highly habit-forming and life-threatening in large doses. Today, the most common tranquilizers are chemicals called *benzodiazepines,* which include the drugs diazepam (Valium) and alprazolam (Xanax). Benzodiazepines can also be habit-forming, although less so than barbiturates. Thousands of tons of these pills are taken every year in the United States.

Benzodiazepines exert their calming effects by facilitating transmission at synapses that use the neurotransmitter GABA. Alcohol facilitates transmission at the same synapses, though by a different mechanism (Sudzak et al., 1986). Taking alcohol and tranquilizers together can be dangerous because together they increase GABA transmission so profoundly that they suppress the brain areas that control breathing and heartbeat.

One benzodiazepine drug, flunitrazepam, has attracted attention as the "date rape drug." Flunitrazepam (called "roofie") dissolves quickly in water; it has no color, odor, or taste; and it can therefore be easily slipped into a woman's drink without her realizing it. The effects of this drug, like those of other tranquilizers, include drowsiness, poor muscle coordination, and memory impairment—

■ After California legalized marijuana for medical uses, many clubs and stores opened for the sale and distribution of the drug.

including impaired ability to describe the attack later (Anglin, Spears, & Hutson, 1997; Woods & Winger, 1997). A hospital that suspects a woman has been given flunitrazepam can run a simple urine test to determine the presence of this drug.

## Narcotics

**Narcotics** *are drugs that produce drowsiness, insensitivity to pain, and decreased responsiveness to events.* The classic examples of narcotics, **opiates,** *are either natural drugs derived from the opium poppy or synthetic drugs with a chemical structure similar to that of natural opiates.* An opiate drug makes people feel happy, warm, and content, with little anxiety or pain. However, the person will experience

nausea and will tend to ignore the real world. Once the drug has left the brain, the affected synapses become understimulated, and the user then enters withdrawal. Elation gives way to anxiety, pain, and hyperresponsiveness to sounds and other stimuli.

Morphine (named after Morpheus, the Greek god of dreams) has important medical use as a painkiller. When used for that purpose, morphine is almost never habit-forming. Here is an important point: No drug is automatically habit-forming. The probability of abuse or habit formation depends largely on why people are taking the drug.

Opiate drugs such as morphine, heroin, methadone, and codeine bind to a specific set of neurotransmitter receptors in the brain (Pert & Snyder, 1973). The discovery of neurotransmitter receptors prompted neuroscientists to look for naturally occurring brain chemicals that bind to those receptors because it hardly seemed likely that evolution would equip us with receptors to respond just to extracts of the opium poppy. Researchers found that the brain produces several chemicals, called **endorphins,** that *bind to the opiate receptors* (Hughes et al., 1975), as mentioned in Chapter 4. Endorphins serve to inhibit chronic pain. They also inhibit neurons that inhibit the release of dopamine (North, 1992); by this double negative, they increase dopamine release and therefore produce reinforcing effects.

Marijuana (*cannabis*) is also generally classified as a narcotic because it induces drowsiness. Beyond that one fact, however, it is not much like the opiates. Marijuana's effects include an intensification of sensory experiences and the illusion that time is passing very slowly (Weil, Zinberg, & Nelson, 1968). It has possible medical uses such as reducing pressure in the eyes in an attempt to relieve glaucoma, a common cause of blindness. It also reduces nausea, acts as a weak painkiller, and suppresses tremors. However, legal restrictions have limited medical research on marijuana.

Although people are aware of marijuana's effects for no more than 2 or 3 hours after using it, it dissolves in the fats of the body, so traces of it can be found for weeks after the drug has been used (Dackis, Pottash, Annitto, & Gold, 1982). One consequence is that someone can "test positive" for marijuana use long after quitting it.

The literature on marijuana has not always been a model of excellent science. One of the arguments emphasizing the dangers of marijuana is that many users are criminals, mentally ill, or otherwise disreputable people. Would you accept that evidence as indicating the dangers of marijuana? I hope not. As stated in Chapter 2, correlation does not demonstrate causation. Does marijuana lead to criminality and mental illness, or do criminality and mental illness increase people's interest in marijuana (and other substances)? Both hypotheses are plausible. Some have also attacked marijuana as a "gateway drug" on the grounds that many people who eventually use heroin or cocaine started with marijuana. True, but before using marijuana, most had also used alcohol and tobacco, experimented with risky sexual behaviors, and so on. It is not clear that using marijuana is a more important a step than any of the other experiences.

On the other hand, marijuana use does pose risks. Frequent marijuana smoking increases the risk of lung cancer. Many users experience impaired learning and memory (L.L. Miller & Branconnier, 1983). Animal research indicates that marijuana smoke can temporarily shrink the dendrites of brain neurons (Westlake et al., 1991).

The active ingredient in marijuana is THC, or tetrahydrocannabinol, which attaches to receptors that are abundant throughout the brain (Herkenham, Lynn, deCosta, & Richfield, 1991), especially in the hippocampus (an important brain area for memory) and brain areas important for the control of movement (Herkenham et al., 1990). The presence of those receptors implies that the brain produces some THC-like chemical of its own. Researchers first discovered a brain chemical that they named *anandamide* (from *ananda*, the Sanskrit word for "bliss") that attaches to the same receptors as THC (Devane et al., 1992). However, the brain does not have much anandamide. A more prevalent compound that attaches to the same receptors has the not very catchy name *sn*-2 arachidonylglycerol, abbreviated 2-AG (Stella, Schweitzer, & Piomelli, 1997). At this point no one knows what anandamide or 2-AG does in the body. Curiously, chocolate also contains

**FIGURE 5.26** Tablas, or yarn paintings, created by members of the Huichol tribe (Mexico), evoke the beautiful lights, vivid colors, and "peculiar creatures" experienced after the people eat the hallucinogenic peyote cactus in highly ritualized ceremonies.

chemicals that probably attach to the THC receptors (diTomaso, Beltramo, & Piomelli, 1996). So people who say that they are "addicted to chocolate" may be more literally correct than they had supposed.

The research on THC receptors helps to explain why people frequently die of an overdose of opiates, but rarely of marijuana: Opiate receptors are densely located in the medulla and other brain areas that control heart rate and breathing, whereas these same areas have very few THC receptors (Herkenham et al., 1990). So even large doses of marijuana are unlikely to stop the heartbeat or breathing.

## Hallucinogens

*Drugs that induce sensory distortions* are called **hallucinogens** (Jacobs, 1987). Most of these drugs are derived from certain mushrooms or other plants; some are manufactured. Hallucinogenic drugs such as LSD intensify sensations and can sometimes produce a dreamlike state or an intense mystical experience. Peyote, a hallucinogen derived from a cactus plant, has a long history of use in Native American religious ceremonies. (Figure 5.26)

LSD attaches mainly to one kind of brain receptor sensitive to the neurotransmitter serotonin (Jacobs, 1987). It stimulates those receptors at irregular times and prevents the brain's neurotransmitters from stimulating the receptors at the normal times. We have an interesting gap in our knowledge at this point: We know that LSD's disruption of certain kinds of serotonin receptors leads to hallucinogenic experiences, but we do not understand how altering those receptors leads to the resulting experiences.

The drug MDMA (methylenedioxymethamphetamine), better known as "ecstasy," produces stimulant effects similar to amphetamine at low doses and hallucinogenic effects similar to LSD at higher doses. Of all abused drugs, this is the one for which the evidence is strongest that it produces brain damage. Use of this drug stimulates dopamine and serotonin axons, thus producing the stimulant and hallucinogenic effects, but in the process damages or destroys those axons (McCann, Lowe, & Ricaurte, 1997).

Figure 5.27 diagrams the effects of several drugs.

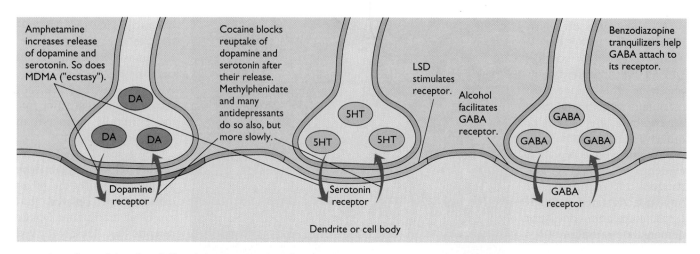

**FIGURE 5.27** Both legal and illegal drugs operate at the synapses. Drugs can increase the release of neurotransmitters, block their reuptake, or directly stimulate or block their receptors.

# Chronic Drug Effects

Initially, any drug produces some presumably desirable effect such as excitement, relaxation, or a distortion of experience. As the drug leaves the brain and the effects wear off, the person experiences **withdrawal effects,** which are generally *the opposite of the initial effects.* For example, a few hours after taking cocaine or amphetamine, someone becomes inactive and depressed. Furthermore, after someone has taken a drug repeatedly, its effects grow weaker and weaker, unless the person increases the dosage. This *decrease in effect* is called **tolerance.** Drug users often seek the drug partly to combat the withdrawal effects, increasing their dosage to compensate for the tolerance. That is, withdrawal effects and tolerance tend to promote increased use of a drug.

## Drug Withdrawal

When habitual users suddenly stop using a drug, they gradually enter a state of withdrawal. With alcohol the typical withdrawal symptoms are sweating, nausea, sleeplessness, and in severe cases hallucinations and seizures (Mello & Mendelson, 1978). With opiate drugs the typical withdrawal symptoms are anxiety, restlessness, loss of appetite, vomiting, diarrhea, sweating, and gagging (Mansky, 1978). People who quit using tranquilizers can experience sleeplessness and nervousness. Someone who *feels compelled to use a drug to reduce unpleasant withdrawal symptoms* is said to have a **physical dependence** on the drug.

We distinguish between physical dependence and **psychological dependence,** which is a *strong repetitive desire for something without any accompanying physical symptoms of withdrawal.* For example, habitual gamblers have a psychological dependence on placing bets, even though they can abstain from gambling without under-

going anything like the effects of "cold turkey" heroin withdrawal. A psychological dependence can be extremely insistent, and in many cases it is pointless to try to decide whether someone's dependence is physical or psychological. (For example, the withdrawal effects for someone who quits using cocaine include mostly "psychological" effects such as a lack of pleasure, with only fairly brief physiological effects. So is the dependence physiological or psychological?)

## Drug Tolerance

People who take a drug repeatedly develop a tolerance to its effects. To achieve the desired high, drug users must steadily increase the dose. Some longtime users inject three or four times more heroin or morphine into their veins than it would take to kill a nonuser.

What brings about drug tolerance? It may result in part from automatic chemical changes that occur in cells throughout the body to counteract the drug's effects (Baker & Tiffany, 1985). It may also result in part from psychological causes. For example, alcohol impairs the coordination of rats as well as that of humans. If rats are simply injected with alcohol every day for 24 days, they show no apparent tolerance for alcohol, as indicated by a coordination test given on the last day. However, if their coordination is tested after each of the 24 injections, each test session offers the rats an opportunity to practice their coordination, so their performance steadily improves (Wenger, Tiffany, Bombardier, Nicholls, & Woods, 1981). In other words, by practicing coordination while under the influence of alcohol, the rats develop a tolerance to alcohol. Similarly, people who use stimulant drugs as appetite suppressants start to develop a tolerance to the effects after a few meals. We shall discuss drug tolerance in more detail in the next chapter.

# CONCEPT CHECK

10. People who use stimulant drugs as appetite suppressants ordinarily develop a tolerance. How could they prevent the development of this tolerance? (Check your answer on this page.)

## Drugs and Awareness

If you were to change a few of a computer's connections at random, you could produce an "altered state," which would almost certainly not be an improvement. Giving drugs to a human brain is a little like changing the connections of a computer, and almost any drug at least temporarily impairs brain functioning somehow, even if the drug is used under medical supervision and accomplishes some good along with the bad. By examining both the desirable and undesirable effects of drugs on the brain, we can gain greater insight into the brain's normal processes and functions.

One message of this chapter is that altered states of consciousness are not vast alterations. Dreaming is much like other thinking, and people usually dream about the same topics they fantasize about when awake. Hypnosis makes people more suggestible, but the effects are usually mild. Drugs also alter behavior, but the result depends on the person's personality as well as the nature of the drug itself. Even an "altered" consciousness has much in common with your normal state.

## Summary

* *Stimulants.* Stimulant drugs such as amphetamines and cocaine increase activity levels and pleasure. Compared to other forms of cocaine, crack produces more rapid effects on behavior, greater risk of addiction, and greater risk of damage to the heart and other organs. (page 186)
* *Alcohol.* Alcohol, the most widely abused drug in our society, relaxes people and relieves their inhibitions. It can also impair judgment and reasoning. (page 189)

* *Tranquilizers.* Benzodiazepine tranquilizers, widely used to relieve anxiety, also can relax muscles and promote sleep. (page 190)
* *Opiates.* Opiate drugs bind to endorphin receptors in the nervous system. The immediate effect of opiates is pleasure and relief from pain. (page 190)
* *Marijuana.* Marijuana's active compound, THC, acts on abundant receptors, found mostly in the hippocampus and certain brain areas important for the control of movement. Because the medulla has few THC receptors, a large dose of marijuana is seldom fatal. (page 190)
* *Hallucinogens.* Hallucinogens induce sensory distortions. LSD acts at one type of serotonin synapse; we do not yet know why activity at that type of synapse should produce these effects. MDMA produces stimulant effects at low doses, hallucinogenic effects at higher doses, and a risk of brain damage. (page 191)
* *Withdrawal.* After using a drug, the user enters a rebound state known as withdrawal. Drug users often crave drugs as a way of decreasing their withdrawal symptoms. (page 192)
* *Tolerance.* People who use certain drugs repeatedly become less and less sensitive to them over time. (page 192)

## Answers to Concept Checks

9. Someone who took AMPT would become much less responsive than usual to amphetamine, cocaine, or methylphenidate. These drugs increase the release of dopamine or prolong its effects, but if the neurons haven't been able to make dopamine, they cannot release it. (page 189)
10. Instead of taking a pill just before a meal, people should take it between meals, when they are not planning to eat right away, or when they plan to skip a meal altogether. If they eat right after taking a pill, they soon develop a tolerance to its appetite-suppressing effects. However, even if they follow the advice to take the pills between meals, most people are not likely to lose weight in the long run. After their appetite is suppressed for a while, they are likely to experience increased appetite later. (page 193)

# Key Terms and Activities

## Terms

**activation-synthesis theory of dreams:** the theory that parts of the brain are spontaneously activated during REM sleep and that a dream is the brain's attempt to synthesize these sensations into a coherent pattern (page 171)

**alcohol:** a class of molecules that includes methanol, ethanol, propyl alcohol (rubbing alcohol), and others (page 189)

**circadian rhythm:** a rhythm of activity and inactivity lasting approximately one day (page 161)

**depressant:** drugs that predominantly decrease arousal (page 189)

**electroencephalograph (EEG):** a device that measures and amplifies slight electrical changes on the scalp that reflect brain activity (page 167)

**endorphins:** chemicals produced by the brain that have effects resembling those of opiates (page 190)

**evolutionary theory** (or **energy-conservation theory) of sleep:** the theory that sleep evolved primarily as a means of forcing animals to conserve their energy when they are relatively inefficient (page 165)

**hallucination:** a sensory experience not corresponding to reality, such as seeing or hearing something that is not present or failing to see or hear something that is present (page 179)

**hallucinogens:** drugs that induce sensory distortions (page 191)

**hypersomnia:** excessive but unrefreshing sleep (page 175)

**hypnosis:** a condition of increased suggestibility that occurs in the context of a special hypnotist-subject relationship (page 177)

**insomnia:** failure to get enough sleep at night in order to feel well rested the next day (page 173)

**jet lag:** the discomfort and inefficiency that travelers experience in a new time zone because their internal clocks are out of phase with the light-dark cycle of their new environment (page 163)

**latent content:** the hidden content that is represented symbolically in a dream experience, according to Freud (page 170)

**manifest content:** the content that appears on the surface of a dream, according to Freud (page 170)

**meditation:** a method of inducing a calm, relaxed state through the use of special techniques (page 184)

**narcolepsy:** a condition characterized by suddenly falling asleep, or at least feeling very sleepy, during the day (page 174)

**narcotics:** drugs that produce drowsiness, insensitivity to pain, and decreased responsiveness to events (page 190)

**neurocognitive theory:** approach that treats dreams as just another example of thinking, except that they occur under special conditions (page 171)

**opiates:** either drugs derived from the opium poppy or synthetic drugs that produce effects similar to those of opium derivatives (page 190)

**periodic limb movement disorder:** a condition occurring during sleep, marked by unpleasant sensations in the legs and many repetitive leg movements strong enough to interrupt sleep (page 175)

**physical dependence:** a condition whereby a habitual drug user is driven to seek the drug to escape or avoid the unpleasant withdrawal effects that occur during abstention from the drug (page 192)

**polysomnograph:** a device that measures sleep stages using a combination of EEG and eye-movement records (page 167)

**posthypnotic suggestion:** a suggestion made to hypnotized subjects that they will do or experience something particular after coming out of hypnosis (page 178)

**psychological dependence:** a strong repetitive desire for something without any physical symptoms of withdrawal (page 192)

**rapid eye movement (REM) sleep:** a stage of sleep characterized by rapid eye movements, a high level of brain activity, and deep relaxation of the postural muscles; also known as paradoxical sleep (page 166)

**repair and restoration theory:** the theory that the purpose of sleep is to enable the body to recover from the exertions of the day (page 164)

**sleep apnea:** a condition causing a person to have trouble breathing while asleep (page 174)

**stimulants:** drugs that boost energy, heighten alertness, increase activity, and produce a pleasant feeling (page 186)

**tolerance:** the weakened effect of a drug after repeated use (page 192)

**tranquilizers:** drugs that help people to relax (page 190)

**withdrawal effects:** experiences that occur as a result of the removal of a drug from the brain (page 192)

## Suggestions for Further Reading

Dement, W. C. (1992). *The sleepwatchers.* Stanford, CA: Stanford Alumni Association. An account by one of the founders of sleep research.

Moorcroft, W. (1993). *Sleep, dreaming, and sleep disorders: An introduction* (2nd ed.). Lanham, MD: University Press of America. An excellent review of research on many aspects of sleep and dreams.

Rhue, J. W., Lynn, S. J., & Kirsch, I. (Eds.). (1993). *Handbook of clinical hypnosis.* Washington, DC: American Psychological Association. A collection of articles, mostly about the uses of hypnosis for treating psychological disorders.

Rivers, P. C. (1994). *Alcohol and human behavior.* Upper Saddle River, NJ: Prentice Hall. Covers all aspects of alcohol use from its effects on physiology to its role in society and culture.

## Web/Technology Resources

### Sleep Disorders

**www. asda.org/default.htm**

Learn more about sleep disorders and treatment.

### Dream Research

**www.dreamresearch.net**

The best scientific work on the content of dreams.

### Sleep Research

**www.sleepfoundation.org/**

Links to all kinds of information about sleep.

### Web of Addictions

**www.well.com/user/woa/**

Andrew L. Homer and Dick Dillon provide factual information about alcohol and other abused drugs. Fact sheets and other material are arranged by drug, with links to Net resources related to addictions, in-depth information on special topics, and a list of places to get help with addictions.

### National Clearinghouse for Alcohol and Drug Information

**www.health.org/newsroom/**

News reports about drug and alcohol abuse, with links to many other sites.

# Learning

CHAPTER 6

**L**earning is a change in behavior as a result of experience. Suppose we set up a simple experiment on animal learning. We put a monkey midway between a green wall and a red wall. If it approaches the green wall, we give it a few raisins; if it approaches the red wall, it gets nothing. After a few trials, the monkey always approaches the green wall. After it has made the correct choice, say, 12 times in a row, we are satisfied that the monkey has learned something.

Now imagine the same experiment with an alligator. We use the same procedure as with the monkey, but we get different results. The alligator strains our patience, sitting for hours at a time without approaching either wall. When it finally moves, it is as likely to approach one wall as the other. After hundreds of trials, *we* have learned something: not to go into the alligator-training business! But we see little evidence that the alligator has learned anything.

Should we conclude that alligators are slow learners? Not necessarily. Maybe they are just not hungry. Maybe they can't see the difference between red and green. Maybe they learn but also forget quickly, so they cannot put together a long streak of consecutive correct approaches. To decide for sure about alligators' learning, we would need to test them under other conditions.

Similar problems arise when we evaluate human learning. If little Joey is having academic troubles, should we consider him a "slow learner"? Not necessarily. Like the alligator, Joey may not be sufficiently motivated, or he may have trouble seeing or hearing. Maybe he is distracted by his emotional troubles at home. (That's a possibility we probably wouldn't consider with the alligator.)

Psychologists have spent an enormous amount of time studying learning. One of their main discoveries is how important it is to consider all the influences that might interfere with learned performance. Psychologists have developed and polished many of their skills by conducting experiments on learning.

This chapter is about the procedures that produce changes in behavior—why you lick your lips at the sight of tasty food, why you turn away from a food that once made you sick, why you get nervous if a police car starts to follow you, and why you shudder at the sight of a ferocious person with a chain saw. This chapter is also about why you work harder at some tasks than at others and why you sometimes persevere for so long before giving up. Chapter 7 deals with memories. Obviously, any change in behavior implies some sort of memory, and any memory implies previous learning. Still, the study of learning is based on a different research tradition from that of memory.

■ Understanding how an animal learns or why it fails to learn requires careful testing of all the factors that can influence behavior.

# Behaviorism

*How and why did the behaviorist viewpoint arise?*
*What is its enduring message?*

Different kinds of psychologists disagree about the primary goals of psychology. For example, in later chapters we shall encounter *humanistic psychologists,* who are mainly interested in people's personal experiences and values. Here we discuss **behaviorists,** *psychologists who insist that psychologists should study only observable, measurable behaviors, not mental processes.* The discussion of behaviorism will lead us into a discussion of learning, a field of research that behaviorists have traditionally dominated.

The term *behaviorist* applies to theorists and researchers with quite a range of views (O'Donohue & Kitchener, 1999). Two major categories are *methodological behaviorists* and *radical behaviorists.* **Methodological behaviorists** *study only the events that they can measure and observe*—in other words the environment and the individual's actions—*but they sometimes use those observations to make inferences about internal events* (Day & Moore, 1995). For example, depriving an animal of food, presenting it with very appealing food, or making it exercise will increase the probability that the animal will eat food, work for food, and so forth. From such observations a psychologist can infer an **intervening variable,** *something that we cannot directly observe but that links a variety of procedures to a variety of possible responses.* In this case the intervening variable is *hunger:*

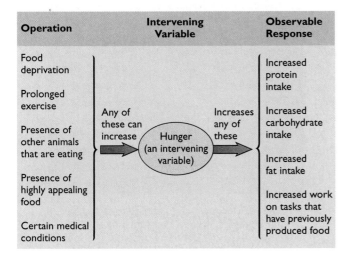

| Operation | Intervening Variable | Observable Response |
|---|---|---|
| Food deprivation | | Increased protein intake |
| Prolonged exercise | | |
| Presence of other animals that are eating | Any of these can increase → Hunger (an intervening variable) → Increases any of these | Increased carbohydrate intake |
| Presence of highly appealing food | | Increased fat intake |
| Certain medical conditions | | Increased work on tasks that have previously produced food |

Similarly, one could use other kinds of observations to infer other intervening variables, such as thirst, sex drive, anger, fear, and so forth. Note that any of these intervening variables is inferred from behavior, never observed directly.

The important point is that a methodological behaviorist will use such terms only after anchoring them firmly to observable procedures and responses—that is, after giving them a clear operational definition (as discussed in Chapter 2). Most psychological researchers are methodological behaviorists, even if they do not use that term.

## A STEP FURTHER
### Intervening Variables

Choose an intervening variable, such as fear or anger, and describe what measurements you could use to infer it. In the process do you in fact establish an operational definition?

**Radical behaviorists** do not deny that private events such as hunger or fear exist, and they agree that it is possible to study the circumstances that cause people to *say,* "I am hungry," "I am frightened," and so forth. The distinguishing feature of radical behaviorists is that they *deny that hunger, fear, or any other internal, private event causes behavior* (Moore, 1995). For example, they would say if food deprivation leads to hunger and hunger leads to eating, why not just say that food deprivation leads to eating? What do we gain by introducing the word *hunger?* According to radical behaviorists, any internal state is caused by an event in the environment (or by the individual's genetics), and therefore, the ultimate cause of any behavior lies in the observable events that led up to the behavior, not the internal states.

According to this point of view, most discussions of mental events are just sloppy language. For example, as B. F. Skinner (1990) argued, when you say, "I *intend* to . . . ," what you really mean is "I am about to . . . " or "In situations like this, I usually . . . " or "This is in the preliminary stages of happening . . . ." That is, any statement about intentions or mental experiences can be converted into a description of behavior.

■ Behaviorists agree that all psychological investigations should be based on behavioral observations. A methodological behaviorist might use observations of, say, facial expressions to make inferences about such processes as "sadness." A radical behaviorist, however, would study the facial expressions themselves, but not as a means of inferring something else.

## The Rise of Behaviorism

Behaviorism can be clearly understood only within the historical context in which it arose. During the early 1900s, one highly influential group within psychology, the *structuralists* (see Chapter 1), studied thoughts and ideas by asking people to describe their own experiences. The early behaviorists were, to a large extent, protesting against structuralism. Behaviorists insisted that it is useless to ask people to report their own private experiences. For example, if someone says, "My idea of roundness is stronger than my idea of color," we have no way to check the accuracy of the report. We are not even certain what it means. If psychology is to be a scientific enterprise, behaviorists insisted, it must deal with only observable, measurable events—that is, behaviors and the environment.

To avoid any mention of the mind, thoughts, or knowledge, some behaviorists went to the opposite extreme. One of the forerunners of behaviorism, Jacques Loeb (1918/1973), argued that much of animal behavior, and perhaps human behavior as well, could be described in terms of simple responses to simple stimuli—for example, approaching light, turning away from strong smells, clinging to hard surfaces, walking toward or away from moisture, and so forth (see Figure 6.1). Complex behavior, he surmised, is just the result of adding together many changes of speed and direction elicited by various stimuli. Loeb's view of behavior was an example

of **stimulus–response psychology,** *the attempt to explain behavior in terms of how each stimulus triggers a response.*

Although the term *stimulus–response psychology* was appropriate for Loeb, it is an inaccurate and misleading description of the behaviorists of today. Behaviorists do not believe that we can point to a simple stimulus to explain every action. Behavior is a product of not only the current stimuli but also the history of stimuli and responses and their outcomes, plus the internal state of the organism, such as wakefulness or sleepiness (Staddon, 1999).

If behaviorists are to deal successfully with complex behaviors, they must be able to explain changes in behavior. The behaviorist movement became the heir to a tradition of animal learning research that had begun for quite different reasons. Charles Darwin's theory of evolution by natural selection inspired many early psychologists to study animal learning and intelligence (Dewsbury, 2000b). At first those psychologists were interested in comparing the intelligence of various species. By about 1930, however, most psychologists had lost interest in that topic because it seemed unanswerable. (In many cases a species that seemed more intelligent on one task seemed less intelligent on another.) Nevertheless, the behaviorists carried forth the tradition of experiments on animal learning, although they asked different questions. If nonhumans learn in more or less the same way as

**FIGURE 6.1** Jacques Loeb, an early student of animal behavior, argued that much or all of invertebrate behavior could be described as responses to simple stimuli, such as approaching light, turning away from light, or moving opposite to the direction of gravity.

humans do, behaviorists reasoned, then it should be possible to discover the basic laws of learning by studying the behavior of a convenient laboratory animal, such as a pigeon or a rat. This enterprise was most ambitious and optimistic; its goal was no less than to determine the basic laws of behavior, analogous to the laws of physics. Most of the rest of this chapter will deal with behaviorists' research about learning.

# The Assumptions of Behaviorism

Behaviorists make several assumptions, including determinism, the ineffectiveness of mental explanations, and the power of the environment to select behaviors (Moore, 1995). Let's consider each of these points.

## Determinism

Behaviorists assume that we live in a universe of cause and effect; in other words they assume *determinism,* as described in Chapter 1. Given that our behavior is part of the universe, it too must have causes that can be understood through scientific methods. That is, behavior follows laws, and if we determine those laws and then learn enough about any individual's genetics, past experiences, and current influences, we could predict that individual's behavior. (Of course, just as it is impractical to predict the weather completely, there will always be some practical limits to how thoroughly we can predict behavior.)

One example of a behavioral law is that an individual will increase the rate of any behavior that leads to food. Behaviorists seek more and more detailed laws of behavior, and they test their understanding by trying to predict or control behavior.

## The Ineffectiveness of Mental Explanations

In everyday life we commonly explain our behaviors in terms of their motivations or emotions or our mental state. However, behaviorists insist that such statements explain nothing:

**Q.** Why did she yell at that man?
**A.** She yelled because she was angry.
**Q.** How do you know she was angry?
**A.** We can tell she was angry because she was yelling.

Clearly, references to mental states risk luring us into circular reasoning. To avoid mental explanations, behaviorists either avoid mental terms altogether or use them very cautiously. B. F. Skinner, the most famous and influ-

ential behaviorist, resisted using even apparently harmless words such as *hide* because they imply an intention (L. D. Smith, 1995). Skinner preferred simply to describe what the individuals *did,* instead of guessing what they were *trying* to do.

The same insistence on description is central to both the British and American legal systems: A witness is asked, "What did you see and hear?" An acceptable answer would be, "The defendant was sweating and trembling, and his voice was wavering." It would be unacceptable to say, "The defendant was nervous and worried" because such a statement requires an inference that the witness is not entitled to make. (Of course, the judge or jury might draw an inference.)

## The Power of the Environment to Mold Behavior

Behaviors produce outcomes. Eating your carrots has one kind of outcome; insulting your roommate has another. The kind of outcome determines how often the behavior will occur in the future. In effect our environment selects successful behaviors, much as evolution selects successful animals.

■ Behaviorists emphasize the role of experience in determining our actions—both our current experience and our past experiences in similar situations.

Behaviorists have sometimes been accused of believing that the environment controls practically all aspects of behavior. The most extreme statement of environmental determinism came from John B. Watson, one of the founders of behaviorism, who said, "Give me a dozen healthy infants, well-formed, and my own specified world to bring them up in and I'll guarantee to take any one at random and train him to become any type of specialist I might select—doctor, lawyer, artist, merchant-chief, and yes, even beggar-man thief—regardless of his talents, penchants, tendencies, abilities, vocations, and race of his ancestors" (Watson, 1925, p. 82).

Watson admitted that his statement was an exaggeration. He defended himself by saying that many other people had similarly exaggerated the role of heredity in molding behavior. Today, few psychologists would claim that variations in behavior depend entirely on the environment (or that they depend entirely on heredity, for that matter). Although behaviorists do not deny the importance of heredity, they do not generally emphasize it. Their research focuses on how the environment selects one behavior over another, and their explanations of individual differences concentrate on how different people's behaviors emerge from different learning histories.

## IN CLOSING
### Behaviorism as Method and Viewpoint

Some behaviorists take more extreme positions than others do. The same could be said for liberals, conservatives, environmentalists, vegetarians, or advocates of any other theoretical position. Just as politicians often attack their opponents by exaggerating their most extreme positions, some psychologists dismiss behaviorism by attacking the extreme statements of John Watson, Jacques Loeb, or other early behaviorists. Others abandon behaviorism because they want to investigate knowledge, imagination, or other internal processes, and they find behaviorist procedures and terminology too limiting.

Many students quickly dismiss behaviorism also because, at least at first glance, it seems so ridiculous: "What do you *mean*, my thoughts and beliefs and emotions don't cause my behavior?!" The behaviorists' reply is, "Exactly right. Your thoughts and other internal states do not cause your behavior because events in your present and past environment caused those thoughts. The events that caused the thoughts are therefore the real causes of your behavior, and psychologists should spend their time trying to understand the influence of the events, not trying to analyze your thoughts."

Don't be too quick to agree or disagree. Just contemplate this: If you believe that your thoughts or other internal states cause behaviors *independently* of your previous experiences, what evidence could you provide to support your claim?

## Summary

- *Range of positions among behaviorists.* Behaviorists insist that psychologists should study behaviors and their relation to observable features of the environment. Methodological behaviorists use these observations to draw inferences about internal states. Radical behaviorists insist that internal states are of little scientific use and that they do not control behavior. The causes of the internal states themselves, as well as of the behaviors, lie in the environment. (page 199)
- *The origins of behaviorism.* Behaviorism began in part as a protest against structuralists, who asked people to describe their own mental processes. Behaviorists insisted that the structuralist approach was futile and that psychologists should study observable behaviors. (page 200)
- *Behaviorists' interest in learning.* Before the rise of the behaviorist movement, other psychologists had studied animal intelligence. Behaviorists adapted some of the methods used in previous studies but changed the questions, concentrating on the basic mechanisms of learning. (page 200)
- *Behaviorists' assumptions.* Behaviorists assume that all behaviors have causes (determinism), that mental explanations are unhelpful, and that the environment acts to select effective behaviors and suppress ineffective ones. (page 201)

# Classical Conditioning

*When we learn a relationship between two stimuli, what happens?*

*Do we start responding to one stimulus as if it were the other?*

*Or do we learn how to use information from one stimulus to predict something about the other?*

You are sitting in your room when your roommate flicks a switch on the stereo. Your experience has been that the stereo is set to a deafening level, and flicking that switch has always led to a startle response. You flinch, not because of the sound of the switch itself, but because of what it predicts.

Certain aspects of our behavior consist of learned responses to signals. However, even apparently simple responses to simple stimuli no longer seem as simple as they once did. Psychologists' efforts to discover what takes place during learning have led them to conduct thousands of experiments, many of them on nonhumans. For certain kinds of learning, such as birdsong learning, the results depend heavily on which species is being studied, but for many other kinds of learning, the similarities among species are more impressive than the differences. In some ways it is easier to study rats or pigeons than humans because a researcher can better control what and when they eat and many other variables likely to influence performance.

## Pavlov and Classical Conditioning

Aristotle explained falling objects by saying that objects sought the ground, which was their natural resting place. Later explanations of falling objects, first by Newton and then by Einstein, eliminated the "seeking" and explained falling objects in purely mathematical terms.

The behaviorists tried to do the same for learning. If a cat claws at the refrigerator and meows, you might say that it "expects" food or "knows" food is in the refrigerator, but behaviorists would not. Behaviorists around 1920 instead sought simple mechanical explanations.

Therefore, the mood of the time was ready for the simple theories of Ivan P. Pavlov, a Russian physiologist who had won a Nobel Prize in physiology in 1904 for his research on digestion. As Pavlov continued his research, one day he noticed that a dog would salivate or secrete stomach juices as soon as it saw the lab worker who ordinarily fed the dogs. Because this secretion undoubtedly depended on the dog's previous experiences, Pavlov called it a "psychological" secretion. Pavlov enlisted the help of other specialists, who then discovered that "teasing" a dog with the sight of food produced salivation that was as predictable and automatic as any reflex. Pavlov adopted the term *conditional reflex,* implying that he only *conditionally* (or tentatively) accepted it as a reflex (Todes, 1997). However, the term has usually been translated into English as *conditioned reflex,* which has different connotations.

## Pavlov's Procedures

Pavlov guessed that animals are born with certain *automatic connections*—we call them **unconditioned** (or *unconditional*) **reflexes**—*between a stimulus such as food and a response such as secreting digestive juices.* He conjectured that

■ Ivan P. Pavlov (with the white beard) with students and an experimental dog. Pavlov focused on limited aspects of the dog's behavior—mostly salivation—and devised some apparently simple principles to describe that behavior.

animals acquire new reflexes by transferring a response from one stimulus to another. For example, if a neutral stimulus (e.g., a buzzer) always preceded food, an animal might begin to respond to the buzzer as it responds to food. Thus, the buzzer would also elicit digestive secretions. The *process by which an organism learns a new association between two paired stimuli—a neutral stimulus and one that already evokes a reflexive response—*has come to be known as **classical conditioning,** or **Pavlovian conditioning.** (It is called classical because it has been known and studied for a long time.)

Pavlov used an experimental setup like the one in Figure 6.2 (Goodwin, 1991). First, he selected dogs with a moderate degree of arousal. (Highly excitable dogs would not hold still long enough, and highly inhibited dogs would fall asleep.) Then he attached a tube to one of the salivary ducts in the dog's mouth to measure salivation. He could have measured stomach secretions, but it was easier to measure salivation.

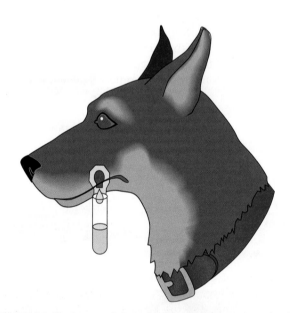

**FIGURE 6.2** Pavlov used dogs for his experiments on classical conditioning and salivation. The experimenter can ring a buzzer (CS), present food (UCS), and measure the responses (CR and UCR). Pavlov himself collected saliva with a simple measuring pouch attached to the dog's cheek; his later colleagues used a more complex device.

Pavlov found that, whenever he gave a dog food, saliva flowed in the dog's mouth. The food → salivation connection was automatic, requiring no training. Pavlov called the food the unconditioned stimulus, and he called the salivation the unconditioned response. The **unconditioned stimulus (UCS)** is *an event that consistently, automatically elicits an unconditioned response,* and the **unconditioned response (UCR)** is *an action that the unconditioned stimulus automatically elicits.*

Next Pavlov introduced a new stimulus, such as a metronome. Upon hearing the metronome, the dog lifted

its ears and looked around but did not salivate, so the metronome was a neutral stimulus with regard to salivation. Pavlov sounded the metronome a couple of seconds before giving food to the dog. After a few pairings of the metronome with food, the dog began to salivate as soon as it heard the metronome (Pavlov, 1927/1960).

We call the metronome the **conditioned stimulus (CS)** because the dog's *response to it depended on the preceding conditions—*that is, the pairing of the CS with the UCS. The salivation that followed the sounding of the metronome was the **conditioned response (CR).** The conditioned response is simply *whatever response the conditioned stimulus begins to elicit as a result of the conditioning (training) procedure.* In Pavlov's experiment and in many others, the conditioned response closely resembles the unconditioned response, but in some cases it is quite different. At the start of the conditioning procedure, the conditioned stimulus does *not* elicit a conditioned response. After conditioning, it does.

To summarize: The *unconditioned stimulus* (UCS), such as food or shock, automatically elicits the *unconditioned response* (UCR), such as salivating or tensing the muscles. A neutral stimulus, such as a tone or metronome, that is paired with the UCS becomes a *conditioned stimulus* (CS). At first this neutral stimulus elicits either no response or some irrelevant response, such as just looking around. After some number of pairings of the CS with the UCS, the conditioned stimulus elicits the *conditioned response* (CR). Figure 6.3 diagrams these relationships.

Here are some other examples of classical conditioning:

- You hear a tone and then you get a puff of air to your eyes. After a few repetitions, hearing the tone makes you blink your eyes.

  Unconditioned stimulus, → Unconditioned response,
  UCS (air puff)        UCR (blinking eyes)
  Conditioned stimulus, → Conditioned response,
  CS (tone)             CR (blinking eyes)

- Your alarm clock makes a faint clicking sound a couple of seconds before the alarm goes off. At first the click by itself does not awaken you, but the alarm does. After a week or so, however, you awaken as soon as you hear the click.

  Unconditioned stimulus, → Unconditioned response,
  UCS (alarm)           UCR (awakening)
  Conditioned stimulus, → Conditioned response,
  CS (clicking)         CR (awakening)

- You hear the sound of a dentist's drill shortly before the unpleasant experience of the drill on your teeth. From then on the sound of a dentist's drill arouses anxiety.

  Unconditioned stimulus, → Unconditioned response,
  UCS (drill on your    UCR (tensing your
  teeth)                muscles)
  Conditioned stimulus, → Conditioned response,
  CS (drill sound)      CR (tensing your
                        muscles)

**At first,**

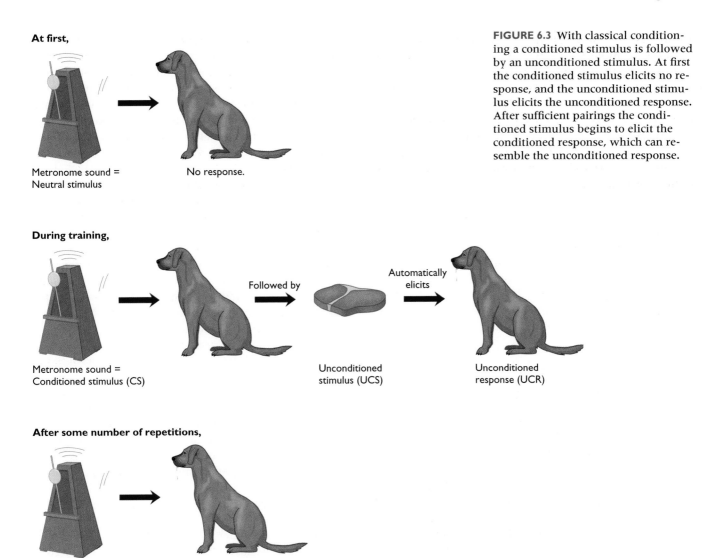

Metronome sound =
Neutral stimulus

No response.

**During training,**

Metronome sound =
Conditioned stimulus (CS)

Followed by

Unconditioned
stimulus (UCS)

Automatically
elicits

Unconditioned
response (UCR)

**After some number of repetitions,**

Metronome sound =
Conditioned stimulus (CS)

Conditioned
response (CR)

**FIGURE 6.3** With classical conditioning a conditioned stimulus is followed by an unconditioned stimulus. At first the conditioned stimulus elicits no response, and the unconditioned stimulus elicits the unconditioned response. After sufficient pairings the conditioned stimulus begins to elicit the conditioned response, which can resemble the unconditioned response.

- When your partner is in a romantic mood, he or she puts on some special cologne or perfume and turns on soft music. When in a grouchy mood, he or she scowls, indicating readiness for a quarrel.

  Unconditioned stimulus, UCS (receptive partner) → Unconditioned response, UCR (romantic activities)

  Conditioned stimulus, CS (nice smell, soft music) → Conditioned response, CR (ready for romance)

  Unconditioned stimulus, UCS (grouchy partner) → Unconditioned response, UCR (arguments)

  Conditioned stimulus, CS (scowling expression) → Conditioned response, CR (readiness for a fight)

Note the usefulness of classical conditioning in each case: It prepares an individual for likely events.

The unconditioned stimulus can be almost any stimulus that evokes an automatic response. The conditioned stimulus can be almost any detectable stimulus—a light, a sound, the cessation of a light or sound, a smell, and so on. Even a mental image can be a conditioned stimulus. Psychologists in general and behaviorists in particular are not sure what a mental image really is, but the effects can be strong. For example, many cancer patients who have had repeated chemotherapy treatments become nauseated when they imagine the building where they received treatment (Dadds, Bovbjerg, Redd, & Cutmore, 1997).

 Try this: Form an image of a lemon, a nice fresh juicy one. You cut it into slices and then suck on a slice of it. And then another slice. Imagine that sour taste. As you imagine the lemon, do you notice yourself salivating?

All else being equal, conditioning occurs more rapidly if the conditioned stimulus is unfamiliar. For example, if you heard a tone 1000 times (followed by nothing) and then started hearing the tone followed by a puff of air to your left eye, you would be slow to show signs of conditioning. Similarly, imagine two people who are bitten by a snake. One has never been close to a snake before; the other has spent years tending snakes at the zoo. You can guess which one will develop a fear of snakes.

All else being equal, conditioning is also facilitated when people are aware of the connection between the CS and UCS. (Presumably, the same is true for nonhumans, but how could we check?) If people are told that they are about to receive a series of trials in which a brief tone will be followed by a puff of air to the eyes, they condition faster than without the instructions. If the tones and air puffs are presented when people are highly distracted with other tasks, they are slow to condition (Clark & Squire, 1999). So classical conditioning is in that way similar to other kinds of learning and memory.

We shall start by discussing mostly laboratory studies but later come to an application of classical conditioning to the human phenomenon of drug tolerance. In Chapter 16 we shall consider the role of classical conditioning in the development of phobias.

 ONCEPT CHECK

1. At the start of training, the CS elicits ___ and the UCS elicits ___. After many repetitions of the CS followed by the UCS, the CS elicits ___ and the UCS elicits ___.
2. A nursing mother consistently responds to her baby's crying by putting the baby to her breast. The baby's sucking causes the release of milk. Within a few days, as soon as the mother hears the baby crying, the milk starts to flow, even before she puts the baby to her breast. What is the conditioned stimulus? The conditioned response? The unconditioned stimulus? The unconditioned response? (Check your answers on page 212.)

## The Phenomena of Classical Conditioning

The *process that establishes or strengthens a conditioned response* is known as **acquisition.** Figure 6.4 shows how the strength of a conditioned response increases after pairings of the conditioned and unconditioned stimuli. Acquisition is not the end of the story, however, because any response that can be learned can also be unlearned.

Once Pavlov had demonstrated how classical conditioning occurs, inquisitive psychologists wondered what would happen after various changes were made in the procedures. Their investigations, prompted by practical concerns, theoretical concerns, or simple curiosity, have extended our knowledge of classical conditioning. Here are a few of the main phenomena.

### Extinction

Suppose I sound a buzzer and then blow a puff of air into your eyes. After a few repetitions, you will start to close your eyes as soon as you hear the buzzer (Figure 6.5). Now I sound the buzzer repeatedly without the puff of air. What do you do?

You will blink your eyes the first time and perhaps the second and third times, but before long you will stop. This decrease of the conditioned response is called **extinction** (see Figure 6.4). *To extinguish a classically conditioned response, repeatedly present the conditioned stimulus (CS) without the unconditioned stimulus (UCS).* That is, acquisition of a response (CR) occurs if the CS predicts the UCS; extinction occurs if the CS no longer predicts the UCS.

Extinction is not the same as forgetting. Both weaken a learned response, but they arise in different ways. Forgetting occurs when we have no opportunity to practice a certain behavior over a period of time. Extinction occurs as the result of a specific experience—the presentation of the conditioned stimulus without the unconditioned stimulus.

Extinction does not erase the original connection between the CS and the UCS. You might think of acquisition as learning to do something and extinction as learning to inhibit the response. For example, suppose you have gone through original learning in which a tone regularly preceded a puff of air to your eyes. You learned to blink your eyes at the tone. Then you went through an extinction process in which you heard the tone many times but received no air puffs. You extinguished, so the tone no longer elicited a blink. Now, without warning, you get another puff of air to your eyes. As a result, the next time you hear the tone, you will blink your eyes. Extinction inhibited your response to the CS (here, the tone), but a sudden puff of air weakens that inhibition (Bouton, 1994).

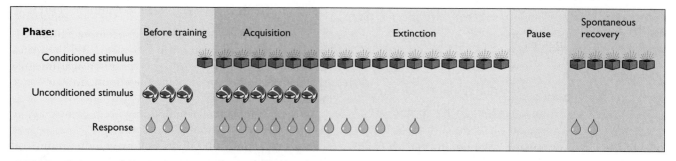

**FIGURE 6.4** Phases of classical conditioning: Classical conditioning proceeds through several phases, depending on the time of presentation of the two stimuli. If the conditioned stimulus regularly precedes the unconditioned stimulus, acquisition occurs. If the conditioned stimulus is presented by itself, extinction occurs. A pause after extinction yields a brief spontaneous recovery.

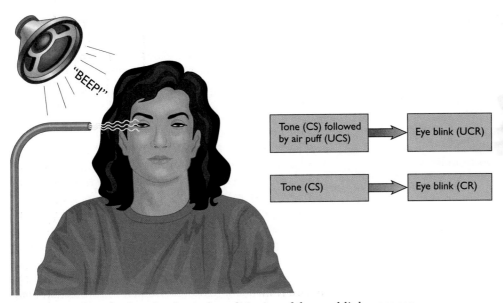

**FIGURE 6.5** The procedure for classical conditioning of the eye-blink response.

Tone (CS) followed by air puff (UCS) → Eye blink (UCR)

Tone (CS) → Eye blink (CR)

## Spontaneous Recovery

Suppose you are in a classical conditioning experiment. At first, you repeatedly hear a buzzer sound (CS) which is always followed by a puff of air to your eyes (UCS). Then the buzzer stops predicting an air puff, and after a few trials, your response to the buzzer extinguishes. Now suppose you just sit there for a long time with nothing happening and then suddenly you hear another buzzer sound. What do you suppose you will do? Chances are that you will blink your eyes at least slightly. **Spontaneous recovery** refers to this *temporary return of an extinguished response after a delay* (see Figure 6.4). Spontaneous recovery requires no additional CS–UCS pairings

Why does spontaneous recovery take place? Think of it this way: At first the buzzer predicted a puff of air to your eyes, and then it didn't. You behaved in accordance with the more recent experiences. Hours later neither experience is much more recent than the other, and the effects of the original acquisition are almost as strong as those of extinction.

## CONCEPT CHECK

**3.** In Pavlov's experiment on conditioned salivation in response to a buzzer, what procedure could you use to produce extinction? What procedure could you use to produce spontaneous recovery? (Check your answers on page 212.)

## Stimulus Generalization

Suppose your alarm clock makes a faint clicking sound (CS) a few seconds before the alarm (UCS), and you have learned to awaken as soon as you hear the click. What if you now buy a new alarm clock? It makes a different clicking sound before the alarm goes off. Will the click awaken you?

It probably will. The closer the sound of the new click is to the original one, the more likely you are to respond by awakening (Figure 6.6). **Stimulus generalization** is the *extension of a conditioned response from the training stimulus to similar stimuli.*

This definition may sound pretty straightforward, but in fact, psychologists find it difficult to specify exactly what "similar" means (Pearce, 1994). For example, if you hear a clicking sound somewhere other than in your bedroom or at a time other than your usual awakening time, it may be ineffective. So your response at any moment depends on how similar the total configuration of stimuli is to the set on which you were trained, and that similarity is hard to measure.

## Discrimination

Suppose your alarm clock makes one kind of click when the alarm is about to ring but occasionally makes a different kind of click at other times. Eventually, you will learn to **discriminate** between these two clicks: You will *respond differently to the two stimuli because they predicted different outcomes.* You will awaken when you hear one click but not when you hear the other. Similarly, you learn that one bell signals that it is time for class to start, and a different bell signals a fire.

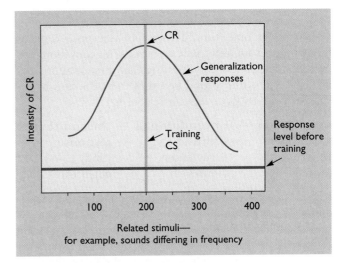

**FIGURE 6.6** Stimulus generalization is the process of extending a learned response to new stimuli that resemble the one used in training. As a rule a stimulus similar to the training stimulus elicits a strong response; a less similar stimulus elicits a weaker response.

**A STEP FURTHER**
*Discrimination*

We can easily determine how well human subjects discriminate between two stimuli. We can simply ask, "Which note has the higher pitch?" or "Which light is brighter?" How could we determine how well a nonhuman can discriminate between two stimuli?

# Drug Tolerance as an Example of Classical Conditioning

Classical conditioning occurs in many laboratory settings; it also occurs in the outside world, sometimes in surprising ways. One such example is **drug tolerance:** *Users of certain drugs experience progressively weaker effects after taking the drugs repeatedly.* Consequently, the users crave ever larger amounts of the drug.

Drug tolerance depends partly on classical conditioning. Consider: When drug users inject themselves with morphine or heroin, the drug injection procedure is an elaborate stimulus that includes the time, place, and so forth as well as the needle injection itself. This total stimulus reliably predicts a second stimulus, the drug's entry into the brain, which triggers a variety of body defenses against its effects—for example, changes in hormone secretions, heart rate, and breathing rate.

| First stimulus | → | Second stimulus | → | Automatic response |
|---|---|---|---|---|
| (Injection procedure) | | (Drug enters brain) | | (Body's defenses) |

Whenever one stimulus predicts a second stimulus that produces an automatic response, the conditions are present for classical conditioning. The first stimulus becomes the CS, the second becomes the UCS, and its response is the UCR. So we can relabel as follows:

| Conditioned stimulus | → | Unconditioned stimulus | → | Unconditioned response |
|---|---|---|---|---|
| (Injection procedure) | | (Drug enters brain) | | (Body's defenses) |

If conditioning occurs here, what would be the consequences? Suppose the CS (drug injection) produces a CR that resembles the UCR (the body's defenses against the drug). The result is that as soon as the person starts injecting the drug, before it even enters the body, the body is already mobilizing its defenses against the drug. Therefore, the drug will have less effect. In other words the body develops tolerance. Shepard Siegel (1977, 1983)

has confirmed that classical conditioning occurs during drug injections. That is, after many drug injections, the injection procedure by itself evokes the body's antidrug defenses:

| Conditioned stimulus | → | Conditioned response |
|---|---|---|
| (Injection procedure) | | (Body's defenses) |

One prediction that he tested was as follows: If the injection procedure serves as a conditioned stimulus, then the body's defense reactions should be strongest if the drug is administered in the usual way, in the usual location, with as many familiar stimuli as possible. (The whole experience constitutes the conditioned stimulus.) The evidence strongly supports this prediction for a variety of drugs (Marin, Perez, Duero, & Ramirez, 1999; Siegel, 1983). For example, a rat that is repeatedly injected with alcohol gets better and better at maintaining its balance while intoxicated. But if it is now tested in the presence of loud sounds and strobe lights, its balance suffers. Conversely, if it had practiced its balance while intoxicated in the presence of loud sounds and strobe lights, its balance suffers if it is tested *without* those stimuli (Larson & Siegel, 1998).

Why do some people die of a drug overdose that is no larger than the dose they normally tolerate? They probably took the fatal overdose in an unfamiliar setting. For example, someone who is accustomed to taking a drug at home in the evening could suffer a fatal reaction from taking it at a friend's house in the morning. Because the new setting did not serve as a CS, it failed to trigger the usual drug tolerance.

## CONCEPT CHECK

4. When an individual develops tolerance to the effects of a drug injection, what are the conditioned stimulus, the unconditioned stimulus, the conditioned response, and the unconditioned response?
5. Within the classical-conditioning interpretation of drug tolerance, what procedure should extinguish tolerance? (Check your answers on page 212.)

# Explanations of Classical Conditioning

What is classical conditioning, really? As is often the case, the process appeared at first to be fairly simple, but later investigation found it to be a more complex and indeed more interesting phenomenon.

## Pavlov's Explanation

Pavlov believed that, for classical conditioning to occur, the conditioned stimulus and the unconditioned stimulus must be close together in time, with the conditioned stimulus occurring first. In the following sketches, read time left to right:

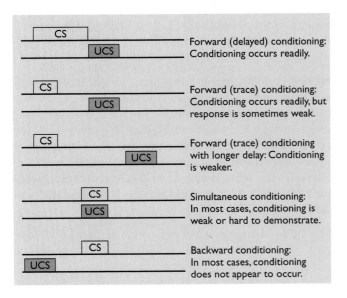

| | |
|---|---|
| CS / UCS | Forward (delayed) conditioning: Conditioning occurs readily. |
| CS / UCS | Forward (trace) conditioning: Conditioning occurs readily, but response is sometimes weak. |
| CS / UCS | Forward (trace) conditioning with longer delay: Conditioning is weaker. |
| CS / UCS | Simultaneous conditioning: In most cases, conditioning is weak or hard to demonstrate. |
| CS / UCS | Backward conditioning: In most cases, conditioning does not appear to occur. |

Conditioning occurs most readily with forward conditioning, with the CS and UCS close in time. *Nearness in time* is called **temporal contiguity.** Ordinarily, the conditioned stimulus is presented first, followed by the unconditioned stimulus. In some cases the conditioned stimulus (e.g., a buzzer) continues until the presentation of the unconditioned stimulus (delayed conditioning); in other cases the conditioned stimulus stops noticeably before the unconditioned stimulus starts (trace conditioning). Generally, delayed conditioning produces stronger effects than trace conditioning. In either case, however, the delay is short between the start of one stimulus and the start of the other. All else being equal, the longer the delay between the CS and the UCS, the weaker the conditioning.

Pavlov proposed a neurological theory, assuming that every stimulus excites a specific area of the brain. A buzzer excites a "buzzer center," and meat excites a "meat center." Exciting both centers at the same time establishes and strengthens a connection between them. From then on, any excitation of the buzzer center (CS) also excites the meat center (UCS) and evokes salivation (Figure 6.7).

Pavlov's theory was appealing because it offered a simple mechanical explanation of learning, even though he had no evidence for the existence of CS centers or UCS centers, much less connections between them. Later evidence has demonstrated the need for a different explanation, however.

## *A Signal, Not Just a Transfer of Responses*

According to Pavlov's view of classical conditioning, an animal comes to respond to the conditioned stimulus as if it were the unconditioned stimulus. That is, the animal simply transfers a response from the UCS to the CS. With his results that interpretation was reasonable; the conditioned response and the unconditioned response were both salivation. However, in some situations the conditioned and unconditioned responses are quite different. For example, a shock (UCS) causes rats to jump and shriek, but a conditioned stimulus predicting the shock makes rats freeze in position. They do not react to the conditioned stimulus as if it were a shock but as a signal of danger. In short, the conditioned response prepares the individual for the unconditioned stimulus.

Consider also the effects of a delay between CS and UCS. In trace conditioning the CS stops noticeably before the start of the UCS. Conditioning is often slow under this procedure and the response can be weak, but when

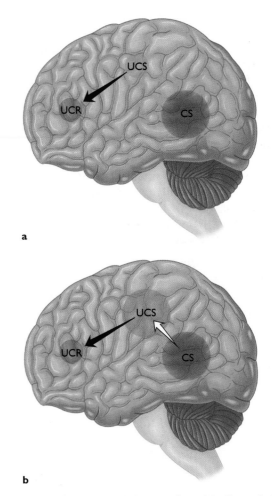

**FIGURE 6.7** Pavlov believed that conditioning depended on temporal contiguity: (a) At the start of conditioning, activity in the UCS center automatically causes activation of the UCR center. At this time activity of the CS center does not affect the UCS center. (b) After sufficient pairings of the CS and UCS, their simultaneous activity causes the growth of a connection between the CS and UCS centers. Afterward, activity in the CS center will flow to the UCS center and therefore excite the UCR center.

it does occur, it starts at about the same time as the UCS. For example, if the delay between CS and UCS is 1 second, the CR occurs about 1 second after the CS. If the CS–UCS delay is 2 seconds, the CR occurs 2 seconds after the CS and so forth. Clearly, the animal is timing its response. The animal isn't treating the CS as if it were the UCS; it is using the CS as a way to prepare for the UCS (Gallistel & Gibbon, 2000).

Under most conditions backward conditioning (UCS first, then CS) produces no responses. Should we conclude that the animal doesn't learn any connection between the two stimuli? No. A better explanation is that a CS after the UCS doesn't give the animal any chance to make a preparatory response. By the time it gets the CS, it is already too late (Gallistel & Gibbon, 2000). Appropriately, researchers have found that classical conditioning depends on the cerebellum, a brain area that is known to be essential for any kind of carefully timed responding (Tracy, Thompson, Krupa, & Thompson, 1998; Woodruff-Pak, Papka, & Ivry, 1996).

**WHAT'S THE EVIDENCE?**
*Contiguity Alone or Contingency*

Contrary to what Pavlov believed, temporal contiguity is not always sufficient to establish classical conditioning. We shall consider two highly influential experiments.

**EXPERIMENT 1**

**HYPOTHESES**  For this study we compare two hypotheses: The contiguity hypothesis is that pairing a new stimulus repeatedly with a shock will produce a conditioned response to that stimulus. The contingency hypothesis is that conditioning to this stimulus will fail if another stimulus already predicted the shock.

**METHOD**  With one group of rats, a light (CS) was repeatedly followed by a shock (UCS) until the rats showed a clear, consistent response to the light. With a second group, a tone (CS) was followed by the shock until the rats consistently responded to the tone. Then both groups experienced the light and the tone simultaneously, followed by the same shock. Later the experimenter tested the rats' reactions to the light and the tone presented separately (Kamin, 1969) (see Figure 6.8).

**RESULTS**  After pairing of the combined light-plus-tone with shock, rats continued to respond as before to whichever stimulus they had originally associated with shock (light for one group, tone for the other). However, they responded very weakly to the new added stimulus. That is, even though the new stimulus was always followed by the shock, animals developed little response to it. These results demonstrate the **blocking effect:** *The previously established association to one stimulus blocks the formation of an association to the added stimulus.*

**INTERPRETATION**  If temporal contiguity were the only factor responsible for learning, the rats should have

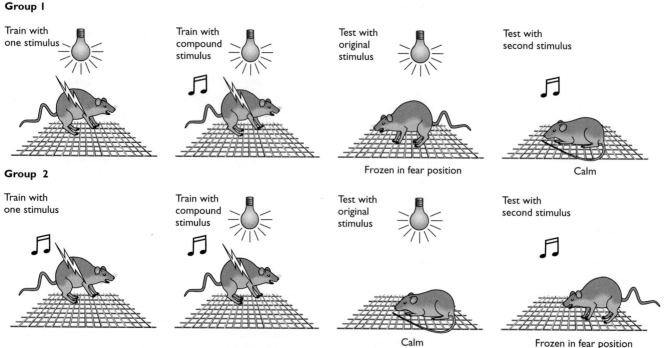

**FIGURE 6.8** In Kamin's experiment each rat first learned to associate either light or sound with shock. Then it received a compound of both light and sound followed by shock. Even after many pairings, each rat continued to show fear of its old stimulus (the one that already predicted shock). The rats showed little response to the new stimulus.

learned a strong response to both the light and the tone, because both were presented just before the shock. The failure of the rats to learn a response to the new stimulus indicates that conditioning depends on more than just presenting two stimuli together in time; the first stimulus must be informative or predictive of the second stimulus.

## EXPERIMENT 2

**HYPOTHESES**   Again we compare two hypotheses. According to the contiguity hypothesis, conditioning will occur whenever a CS is consistently followed by a UCS. According to the contingency hypothesis, conditioning will occur if the UCS is likely after the CS *and unlikely without the CS.*

**METHOD**   For rats in Group 1, conditioned stimulus and unconditioned stimulus were presented in the sequence shown at the top of Figure 6.9. The horizontal line represents time; the vertical arrows represent times of stimuli presentation. For rats in Group 2, the two stimuli were presented in the sequence shown at the bottom of Figure 6.9. In both cases every presentation of the conditioned stimulus immediately preceded a presentation of the unconditioned stimulus. But in the second case, the unconditioned stimulus occurred frequently both in the presence and in the absence of the conditioned stimulus; therefore, the CS was a poor predictor of the UCS (Rescorla, 1968, 1988).

**RESULTS**   Rats receiving the first sequence of stimuli developed a strong response to the conditioned stimulus. Those receiving the second sequence of stimuli developed little or no response (Rescorla, 1968, 1988).

**INTERPRETATION**   Although both groups of rats received the same number of CS–UCS pairings, one group learned a response to the CS and the other group did not. Evidently, *animals (including humans) associate a conditioned stimulus with an unconditioned stimulus only when the CS predicts the occurrence of the UCS.* If the conditioned stimulus immediately precedes the unconditioned stimulus but provides no new information, it is ineffective for conditioning.

# CONCEPT CHECK

6. If temporal contiguity were the only factor responsible for classical conditioning, what result should the experimenters have obtained in Experiment 2?

7. Suppose you have already learned to flinch when you hear the sound of a dentist's drill because of the association between that sound and forthcoming pain. Now your dentist turns on some soothing background music at the same time as the drill. That is, the background music is paired with the pain just as much as the drill sound is. Will you learn to flinch at the sound of that background music if it is presented by itself? (Check your answers on page 212.)

## Conditioning, Contiguity, and Contingency

A conditioned response develops only if there is a **contingency** (*predictability*)—that is, only if the UCS is more likely after the CS than it would be otherwise. Classical conditioning has therefore been compared to scientific

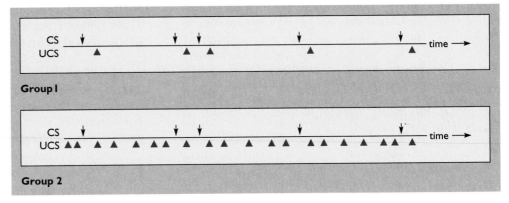

**FIGURE 6.9** In Rescorla's experiment the CS was always followed by the UCS in both groups. However, Group 2 received the UCS so frequently at other times that the CS was not a useful predictor. Group 1 developed a strong conditioned response to the CS; Group 2 did not.

reasoning (Denniston, Miller, & Matute, 1996): The learner discovers which event predicts which outcome.

However, we should not imagine that a rat literally calculates the probability of a shock after a tone versus the probability of a shock during a period without a tone (Papini & Bitterman, 1990). Indeed, there is no reason to assume that the animal is "thinking" about these events at all. Even in humans it is possible to produce conditioning when people are not consciously aware of the stimuli. In one study people looked at photos of faces presented "subliminally" (briefly, followed by an interfering stimulus). One of the photos was always followed by shock. Even after people developed a conditioned response to that photo, though, they could not describe it. And when they finally got a good long look at the photo, they described it as unfamiliar (Parra, Esteves, Flykt, & Öhman, 1997).

Therefore, when we say that the results of classical conditioning are *like* scientific reasoning, we mean that both produce an outcome that depends on contingencies, or predictabilities. The underlying mechanisms do not require deep thinking; they might only be combinations of relatively simple processes.

## IN CLOSING

## *Classical Conditioning Is More Than Drooling Dogs*

People sometimes use the term "Pavlovian" to mean simple, mechanical, robotlike behavior. But Pavlovian or classical conditioning is not a mark of stupidity: It is a way of responding to relationships among events, a way of preparing us for what is likely to happen. Classical conditioning requires processing a fair amount of information.

Classical conditioning is important for some aspects of our behavior but less important for others. It alters our motivational or emotional reactions to stimuli, our "gut feelings"—including responses related to fear, preparations for eating, preparations for a drug injection, and so forth. But it does not control walking toward or away from various stimuli. That is, classical conditioning might tell us to be afraid, but it does not tell us how to avoid the frightening item. It might tell us to salivate in preparation for eating, but it does not tell us how to find food. Other types of learning can answer these other questions, as we shall see later in this chapter.

## Summary

* *Classical conditioning.* Ivan Pavlov discovered classical conditioning, the process by which an organism learns a new association between two stimuli that have been paired with each other—a neutral stimulus (the conditioned stimulus) and one that initially evokes a reflexive response (the unconditioned stimulus). The organism displays this association by responding in a new way (the conditioned response) to the conditioned stimulus. (page 203)

* *Extinction.* After classical conditioning has established a conditioned response to a stimulus, the response can be extinguished by repeatedly presenting that stimulus by itself. (page 206)

* *Spontaneous recovery.* If the conditioned stimulus is not presented at all for some time after extinction and is then presented again, the conditioned response may return to some degree. That return is called spontaneous recovery. (page 207)

* *Stimulus generalization.* An individual who learns to respond to one stimulus will respond similarly to similar stimuli. However, it is difficult to specify how we should measure similarity. (page 207)

* *Discrimination.* If one stimulus is followed by an unconditioned stimulus and another similar stimulus is not, the individual will come to discriminate between these two stimuli. (page 207)

* *Drug tolerance.* Drug tolerance is partly a form of classical conditioning in which the drug administration procedure comes to evoke defensive responses by the body. (page 208)

* *Temporal contiguity versus contingency.* Pavlov believed that temporal contiguity between two stimuli caused classical conditioning. Later studies indicate that conditioning depends also on contingency, or the extent to which the occurrence of the first stimulus predicts the occurrence of the second. (page 208)

## Answers to Concept Checks

1. No response (or at least nothing of interest) . . . the UCR . . . the CR . . . still the UCR. (page 206)
2. The conditioned stimulus is the baby's crying. The unconditioned stimulus is the baby's sucking at the breast. Both the conditioned response and the unconditioned response are the release of milk. Many nursing mothers experience this classically conditioned reflex. (page 206)
3. To bring about extinction, present the buzzer repeatedly without presenting any food. To bring about spontaneous recovery, first bring about extinction; then wait hours or days and present the buzzer again. (page 207)
4. The conditioned stimulus is the injection procedure. The unconditioned stimulus is the entry of the drug into the brain. Both the conditioned response and the unconditioned response are the body's defenses against the drug. (page 208)
5. To extinguish tolerance, present the injection procedure (conditioned stimulus) without injecting the drug (unconditioned stimulus). Instead, inject just water or salt water. Shepard Siegel (1977) demonstrated that repeated injections of salt water do reduce tolerance to morphine in rats. (page 208)
6. If temporal contiguity were the only factor responsible for classical conditioning, the rats exposed to the first sequence of stimuli should have responded just as those exposed to the second sequence of stimuli. In both cases the CS was always followed by the UCS. (page 211)
7. No, you will not learn to flinch at the sound of the background music. Because the drill sound already predicted the pain, the new stimulus is uninformative and will not be strongly associated with the pain. Your results will be an example of the blocking effect. (page 211)

# Operant Conditioning

*How do the consequences of our behaviors affect future behaviors?*

Sometimes a very simple idea can be amazingly powerful. Consider democracy, for example: What could be simpler than the idea that every person gets one vote? Or consider the idea of natural selection, an extremely simple concept that brings order to an enormous array of biological facts that would otherwise seem unrelated. In this module we shall consider the idea that behaviors become more likely or less likely because of their consequences. In other words we either repeat a behavior or cease doing it, depending on the outcome. This simple, even obvious, idea is quite powerful.

## Thorndike and Operant Conditioning

Shortly before Pavlov performed his innovative experiments, Edward L. Thorndike (1911/1970), a Harvard graduate student, had begun training some cats in a basement. Saying that earlier experiments had dealt only with animal intelligence, never with animal stupidity, he devised a simple behavioristic explanation of learning.

Thorndike put cats into puzzle boxes (Figure 6.10) from which they could escape by pressing a lever, pulling

a string, or tilting a pole. Sometimes he placed food outside the box. (Usually, though, cats worked just to escape from the box.) The cats learned to make whatever response opened the box. Thorndike discovered that they learned faster if the response opened the box immediately; any delay would impair learning.

When a cat had to tilt a pole to escape from the box, it would first paw or gnaw at the door, scratch the walls, or pace back and forth. Eventually, it would bump against the pole by accident and the door would open. The next time, the cat would go through the same repertoire of behaviors but might bump against the pole a little sooner. Over many trials the time it took the cat to escape grew shorter, in a gradual and irregular fashion. Figure 6.11 shows a learning curve to represent this behavior. A *learning curve* is a graph of the changes in behavior that occur over successive trials in a learning experiment.

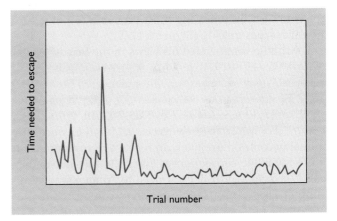

**FIGURE 6.11** Trial and error or insight? As the data from one of Thorndike's experiments show, the time that a cat needs to escape from a puzzle box gradually grows shorter, but in an irregular manner. Thorndike concluded that the cat did not at any point "suddenly get the idea." Instead, reinforcement gradually increased the probability of the successful behavior.

Had the cat "figured out" how to escape? Had it come to "understand" the connection between bumping against the pole and opening the door? No, said Thorndike. If the cat had gained some new insight at some point, he explained, its speed of escaping would have suddenly increased at that time. Instead, the cat's performance improved slowly, gradually, and inconsistently. One could not designate at which point the cat understood.

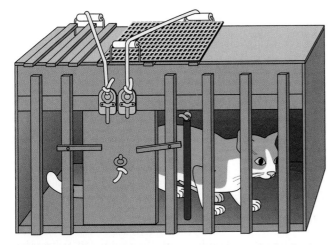

**FIGURE 6.10** Each of Thorndike's puzzle boxes had a device that could open it. Here tilting the pole will open the door. (Based on Thorndike, 1911/1970)

Thorndike concluded that learning occurs only when certain behaviors are strengthened at the expense of others. An animal enters a given situation with a certain repertoire of responses such as pawing the door, scratching the walls, pacing, and so forth (labeled $R_1$, $R_2$, $R_3$, . . . in Figure 6.12). First, the animal engages in its most probable response for this situation ($R_1$ in the figure). If nothing special happens, it proceeds to other responses, eventually reaching a lower-probability response that opens the door—for example, bumping against the pole ($R_7$ in the figure). The opening of the door serves as a reinforcement.

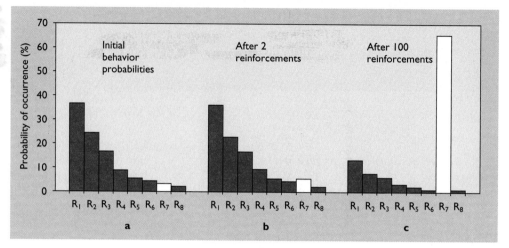

**FIGURE 6.12** According to Thorndike, a cat starts with a large set of potential behaviors in a given situation. When one of these, such as pushing at a pole, leads to reinforcement, the future probability of that behavior increases. We do not need to assume that the cat understands what it is doing or why.

A **reinforcement** is *an event that increases the future probability of the most recent response*. Thorndike said that it "stamps in," or strengthens, the response. The next time Thorndike's cat is in the puzzle box, it has a slightly higher probability of bumping the lever; after each succeeding reinforcement, the probability will go up another notch until it becomes the most probable response and the cat escapes quickly (Figure 6.12c).

Thorndike summarized his views in the **law of effect** (Thorndike, 1911/1970, p. 244): *"Of several responses made to the same situation, those which are accompanied or closely followed by satisfaction to the animal will, other things being equal, be more firmly connected with the situation, so that, when it recurs, they will be more likely to recur."* In other words the animal becomes more likely to repeat the responses that led to favorable consequences even if it does not understand why. In fact, it doesn't need to "understand" anything at all. A fairly simple machine could produce responses at random and then repeat the ones that led to reinforcement.

Thorndike revolutionized the study of animal learning, substituting experimentation for the collection of anecdotes. He also demonstrated the possibility of simple explanations for apparently complex behaviors (Dewsbury, 1998). On the negative side, he led researchers to study animals in contrived laboratory situations unrelated to the animals' normal way of life or evolutionary history (Galef, 1998).

The kind of learning that Thorndike studied is known as **operant conditioning** (because the subject *operates* on the environment to produce an outcome) or **instrumental conditioning** (because the subject's behavior is *instrumental* in producing the outcome). Operant or instrumental conditioning is *the process of chang-*

*ing behavior by following a response with reinforcement*. The defining difference between operant conditioning and classical conditioning is one of procedure: *In operant conditioning the subject's behavior determines an outcome and is affected by that outcome. In classical conditioning the subject's behavior has no effect on the outcome (the presentation of either the CS or the UCS).*

In general the two kinds of conditioning also differ in the behaviors they affect. That is, classical conditioning applies primarily to **visceral responses** (i.e., *responses of the internal organs*), such as salivation and digestion, whereas operant conditioning applies primarily to **skeletal responses** (i.e., *movements of leg muscles, arm muscles, etc.*). However, this distinction sometimes breaks down. For example, if a tone is consistently followed by an electric shock (a classical-conditioning procedure), the tone will make the animal freeze in position (a skeletal response) as well as increase its heart rate (a visceral response).

## CONCEPT CHECK

8. When I ring a bell, an animal sits up on its hind legs and drools; then I give it some food. Is the animal's behavior an example of classical conditioning or operant conditioning?

   So far, you do not have enough information to answer the question. What else would you need to know before you could answer? (Check your answer on page 225.)

## *Extinction, Generalization, Discrimination, and Discriminative Stimuli*

No doubt you are familiar with the saying, "If at first you don't succeed, try, try again." Better advice is, "Try again,

**TABLE 6.1** Comparison of Classical Conditioning and Operant Conditioning

|  | Classical Conditioning | Operant Conditioning |
|---|---|---|
| *Terminology* | CS, UCS, CR, UCR | Response, reinforcement |
| *Subject's behavior* | Does not control UCS | Controls reinforcement |
| *Paired during acquisition* | Two stimuli (CS and UCS) | Response and reinforcement (in the presence of certain stimuli) |
| *Responses studied* | Mostly visceral (internal organs) | Mostly skeletal (movements) |
| *Extinction procedure* | CS without UCS | Response without reinforcement |

but differently!" If you try repeatedly but never succeed, you may be doing something wrong.

In operant conditioning **extinction** *occurs if responses stop producing reinforcements.* For example, you were once in the habit of asking your roommate to join you for supper. The last five times you asked, your roommate said no, so you stop asking. In classical conditioning extinction is achieved by presenting the CS without the UCS. Table 6.1 compares operant conditioning and classical conditioning.

You will recall the phenomena of stimulus generalization and discrimination in classical conditioning. Similar phenomena occur in operant conditioning. Someone who receives reinforcement for a particular response to a certain stimulus will probably make the same response in the presence of a similar stimulus. *The more similar a new stimulus is to the original reinforced stimulus, the more strongly the subject is likely to respond.* This phenomenon is known as **stimulus generalization.** For example, you might reach for the turn signal in a rented car in the same place you would find it in your own car.

Someone who is *reinforced for responding to one stimulus and not for responding to another stimulus* will come to **discriminate** between them and *will respond more vigorously to one than to the other.* For example, you walk toward a parked car that you think is yours, but then you realize it is not. After several such experiences, you learn to identify your own car from a distance.

A *stimulus that indicates which response is appropriate or inappropriate* is called a **discriminative stimulus.** A great deal of our behavior is governed by discriminative stimuli. For example, you do not simply learn to talk in class or be quiet in class; you learn to talk in class when the professor encourages discussion and you learn to be quiet when the professor lectures. Similarly, you learn to drive fast on some streets and slow where the signs indicate a lower speed limit. Throughout your day one stimulus after another signals which behaviors will or will not be reinforced. *The ability of a stimulus to encourage some responses and discourage others* is known as **stimulus control.**

## Why Are Certain Responses Learned More Easily Than Others?

Thorndike's cats learned to push and pull various devices in their efforts to escape from his puzzle boxes. But when Thorndike tried to teach them to scratch or lick themselves to receive the same reinforcement, they learned very slowly and performed inconsistently. Why?

One possible reason is **belongingness,** the *concept that certain stimuli "belong" together or that a given response is more readily associated with certain outcomes than with others.* Belongingness is an idea that Thorndike himself suggested, although psychologists neglected it for decades, preferring to believe that animals could just as easily associate almost any stimulus with any response. Eventually, psychologists revived the concept of belongingness, also sometimes known as "preparedness" (Seligman, 1970). For example, dogs can readily learn that a sound coming from one location means "raise your left leg," and a sound coming from another location means "raise your right leg." But it takes them virtually forever to learn that a ticking metronome means raise the left leg and a buzzer means raise the right leg (Dobrzecka, Szwejkowska, & Konorski, 1966) (see Figure 6.13).

Presumably, Thorndike's cats were slow to associate scratching themselves with escaping from a box because the two activities do not "belong" together. (Cats evolved the ability to learn "what leads to what" in the real world, and scratching oneself seldom opens doors in the real world.) But there is another possible explanation for why cats have trouble learning to scratch themselves for reinforcement: Perhaps a cat will scratch itself only when it itches (Charlton, 1983).

 Consider what would happen if you knew that you could win a large prize if you finished first in a rapid swallowing contest. (Why not? People compete at everything else.) You quickly swallow once, twice, maybe three times, but each successive swallow gets harder and harder. (Go ahead and try it.) Some behaviors are just not easy to produce in large quantities.

**FIGURE 6.13** According to Thorndike's principle of belongingness, some items are easy to associate with each other because they "belong" together; others do not. For example, dogs easily learn to use the direction of a sound as a signal for which leg to raise, but they have trouble using the type of sound as a signal for which leg to raise.

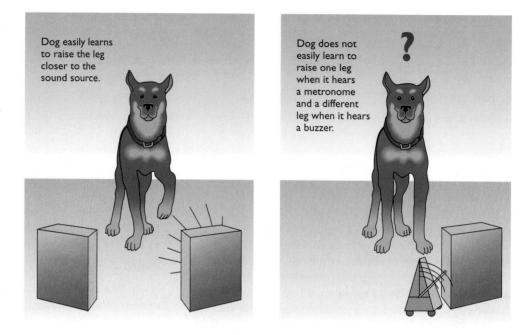

# B. F. Skinner and the Shaping of Responses

The most influential radical behaviorist, B. F. Skinner (1904–1990), demonstrated many uses of operant conditioning. Skinner was an ardent practitioner of parsimony (Chapter 2), always seeking simple explanations in terms of reinforcement histories rather than more complex mental processes.

One problem confronting any student of behavior is how to define a response. For example, imagine watching a group of children and trying to count "aggressive behaviors." What is an aggressive act and what isn't? Psychologists studying intelligence, emotion, or personality spend much of their time trying to find the best method of measurement. Even simple food-getting or shock-escaping responses are hard to define and measure. Skinner dispensed with the arguments (Zuriff, 1995): He set up a box, called an *operant-conditioning chamber* (or *Skinner box,* a term that Skinner himself never used), in which a rat presses a lever or a pigeon pecks an illuminated disk, or "key," to receive food (Figure 6.14). He then operationally defined the response as anything that the animal did to depress the lever or key. So if the rat pressed the lever with its snout instead of its paw, the response still counted; if the pigeon batted the key with its wing instead of pecking it with its beak, it still counted. The behavior was defined by its outcome, not by muscle movements.

Does that definition make sense? Skinner's reply was that it did because it led to consistent results in his experiments. Many other researchers agreed, and Skinner's procedures became standard in many laboratories. When deciding how to define a term (e.g., *response*), the best

**FIGURE 6.14** B. F. Skinner examines one of his laboratory animals in an operant-conditioning chamber, or "Skinner box." When the light above the bar is on, pressing the bar is reinforced. A food pellet rolls out of the storage device (left) and down the tube into the cage.

definition is the most useful one, the one that produces the clearest results.

## Shaping Behavior

Suppose you want to train a rat to press a lever. If you simply put the rat in a box and wait, the rat might never press it. To avoid interminable waits, Skinner introduced a powerful technique, called **shaping,** for *establishing a new response by reinforcing successive approximations to it.*

To *shape* a rat to press a lever, you might begin by reinforcing the rat for standing up, a common behavior in rats. Soon the rat receives a few reinforcements and begins standing up more frequently. Now you change the rules, giving food only when the rat stands up while facing the lever. Soon it spends much of its time standing up and facing the lever. (It extinguishes its behavior of standing and facing in any other direction because those responses are not reinforced.) Next you provide reinforcement only when the rat faces the correct direction while standing in the half of the cage nearest the lever. You gradually move the boundary, and the rat moves closer to the lever. Then the rat must touch the lever and, finally, apply weight to it. Through a series of short, easy steps, you might shape the rat to press a lever in a matter of minutes. Similarly, education is a kind of shaping procedure: First, your parents or teachers praise you for counting your fingers; later, you must add and subtract to earn their congratulations; step by step, your tasks get more complex, until you are doing calculus.

## Chaining Behavior

To produce complex sequences of behavior, psychologists use a procedure called **chaining.** Assume that you want to train an animal, perhaps a guide dog or a show horse, to go through a sequence of actions in a particular order. You could *chain* the behaviors, *reinforcing each one with the opportunity to engage in the next behavior.* That is, first the animal learns the final behavior for a reinforcement; then it learns the next to last behavior, which is reinforced by the opportunity to perform the final behavior. And so on.

For example, a rat might first be placed on the top platform in Figure 6.15, where it eats food. Then it is placed on the intermediate platform with a ladder in place leading to the top platform. The rat learns to climb the ladder. After it has done so repeatedly, it is placed again on the intermediate platform, but this time the ladder is not present. It must learn to pull a string to raise the ladder so that it can climb to the top platform. Finally, the

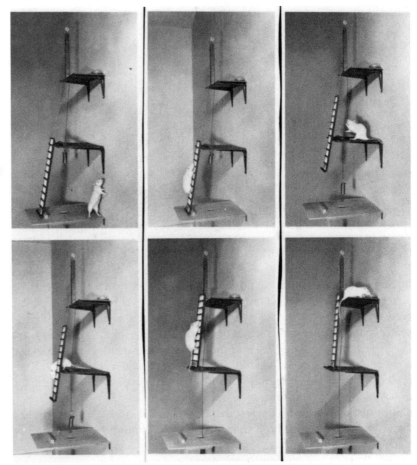

**FIGURE 6.15** Chaining is a procedure in which the reinforcement for one behavior is the opportunity to engage in the next behavior. To reach food on the top platform, this rat must climb a ladder and pull a string to raise the ladder so that it can climb up again. Behavior chains longer than this can be sustained by reinforcement at the end of the chain.

rat is placed on the bottom platform. It now has to learn to climb the ladder to the intermediate platform, pull a string to raise the ladder, and then climb the ladder again. For each response in the chain, the reinforcement is the opportunity to engage in the next behavior; the final response leads to food.

Humans learn to make chains of responses, too. First, you learned to eat with a fork and spoon. Later, you learned to put your own food on the plate before eating. Eventually, you learned to plan a menu, go to the store, buy the ingredients, cook the meal, put it on the plate, and then eat it. Each behavior is reinforced by the opportunity to engage in the next behavior.

To show how effective shaping and chaining can be, Skinner performed this demonstration: First, he trained a rat to go to the center of a cage. Then he trained it to do so only when he was playing a certain piece of music. Then he trained it to wait for the music, go to the center of the cage, and sit up on its hind legs. Step by step, Skinner eventually trained the rat to wait for the music (which happened to be the "Star-Spangled Banner"), move to the center of the cage, sit up on its hind legs, put its claws on a string next to a pole, pull the string to hoist a flag, and then salute the flag. Only then did the rat get its reinforcement. Needless to say, a display of patriotism is not part of a rat's usual repertoire of behavior.

# Increasing and Decreasing the Frequency of Responses

Nearly all of our behavior is governed by its consequences. Investigators of operant conditioning try to determine in detail how those consequences exert their effects.

## Reinforcement and Punishment

Recall that *reinforcement* is an event that increases the probability that a response will be repeated. A **punishment** is *an event that decreases the probability of a response*. A reinforcement can be either the presentation of an item such as food or the removal or avoidance of an item such as pain. A punishment can be either the presentation of an item such as pain or the removal of an item such as food.

Other things being equal, an immediate reinforcement is more effective than a delayed one. Which would you prefer, $500 now or a promise of $1000 three years from now? People vary enormously in their willingness to delay gratification. Some would prefer even a very small immediate reward to $1000 three years from now (Simpson & Vuchinich, 2000). Generally, children would prefer a small reward now to a larger one later. As people grow older, they become more and more likely to choose the delayed but larger reward (Green, Myerson, & Ostraszewski, 1999).

Immediate punishments are effective for almost anyone, but people vary in how much they are deterred by a delayed punishment. Law enforcement almost always provides delayed punishments. A thief gains an immediate reinforcement and faces a delayed, uncertain punishment. As is obvious from the crime rate, the threat does not deter everyone. Much of the variation in people's behavior in such matters as honesty can be described in terms of their responses to immediate and delayed reinforcements and immediate and delayed punishments.

In one famous experiment on punishment, B. F. Skinner (1938) first trained food-deprived rats to press a bar to get food and then stopped reinforcing their bar presses—an extinction procedure. For the first 10 minutes of extinction, some rats not only failed to get food but had the bar slap their paws every time they pressed it. They temporarily suppressed their bar-pressing, but in the long run, they made as many presses as did the rats that never received any punishment.

Skinner concluded that punishment was ineffective, except for temporarily suppressing behavior. That conclusion, however, is an overstatement (Staddon, 1993). A better conclusion would have been that punishment does not greatly weaken a response if the individual has no other response available. Skinner's rats were food deprived and had no other way to seek food. Similarly, if

someone shocked you for breathing, you would not stop breathing, not because you were a slow learner, but because you had no alternative.

Punishment can backfire in several ways. For example, a parent who spanks a child for nervous fidgeting may find that the spanking makes the child even more nervous and fidgety. Nevertheless, a quick, consistent, mild punishment can be informative and helpful. For example, if you want to teach your 3-year-old daughter not to put her hand on the stove, a stern, sharp "NO!" can be effective, especially if it is accompanied by an explanation.

## CONCEPT CHECK

**9.** The U.S. government imposes strict punishments for selling illegal drugs. Based on what you have just read, why are those punishments ineffective for many people? (Check your answer on page 226.)

Reinforcements are events that strengthen behaviors and punishments are events that weaken them, but psychologists draw additional distinctions, as shown in Table 6.2. Note that the entries in the upper left and lower right of the table are both types of reinforcement; either gaining food or preventing pain will *increase* the behavior. The items in the upper right and lower left are types of punishment; either preventing food or gaining pain will *decrease* the behavior. Food and pain are, of course, just examples; many kinds of events serve as reinforcers or punishers.

Let's go through these terms and procedures carefully. **Positive reinforcement** is the *presentation of an event that strengthens or increases the likelihood of a behavior.* A typical example is working for money or food.

Punishment occurs when a response is followed by an event such as pain; the result is to decrease the frequency of that response. For example, you put your hand on a hot stove and burn yourself, or you insult someone who then slaps you. Punishment is also called **passive avoidance learning** because *the individual learns to avoid some outcome by being passive* (e.g., by *not* putting your hand on the stove or by *not* insulting people).

**Omission training** occurs *when the omission of the response produces reinforcement.* Therefore, producing the response also leads to a lack of reinforcement. For example, "If you make one more snotty remark, you will get no dessert!" Omitting the snotty remark is reinforced with dessert; producing the response leads to a lack of dessert. (This procedure is occasionally called *negative punishment* to indicate that the response is punished by the absence of a reinforcer.)

Finally, **active avoidance learning** or **escape learning** occurs if the *responses lead to escape from or avoidance of something unpleasant.* One therefore learns to make the response, even though it is followed by nothing happening. Examples are learning to come indoors when a storm is brewing (to avoid getting wet) and learning to get out of the way when you hear a driver blowing a horn (to avoid getting hit). Because the *response is reinforced by the absence*

**TABLE 6.2 Four Categories of Operant Conditioning**

| | Food, etc. | | Pain, etc. | |
|---|---|---|---|---|
| Behavior gains it | **Positive reinforcement**<br><br>Example: "If you clean your room, I'll take you out for a pizza tonight."<br><br>Consequence: Behavior (cleaning room) *increases* in frequency | | **Punishment** or **passive avoidance**<br><br>Example: "If you insult me, I'll slap you!"<br><br>Consequence: Behavior (insulting someone) *decreases* in frequency | |
| Behavior prevents it | **Omission training**<br><br>(also called punishment or negative punishment)<br><br>Example: "If you hit your little brother again, you'll get no dessert tonight!"<br><br>Consequence: Behavior (hitting) *decreases* in frequency | | **Active avoidance** or **escape learning**<br><br>(also called negative reinforcement)<br><br>Example: "If you carry an umbrella today, you can avoid getting wet."<br><br>Consequence: Behavior (carrying umbrella) *increases* in frequency | |

*of a painful event,* escape or avoidance learning is also sometimes called *negative reinforcement.* Note that a negative reinforcement is *not* a punishment; it is reinforcement (strengthening) by the *absence* of something that would have occurred. The terms "escape learning" and "avoidance learning" are less confusing than the term "negative reinforcement" (see Kimble, 1993), but you should understand all of these terms.

In summary, responses are increased by gaining something like food (positive reinforcement) or avoiding something like pain (escape or avoidance training or negative reinforcement). Responses are decreased by receiving pain (punishment) or by losing a chance for food or the like (omission training).

■ Being penalized for fighting is an effective use of punishment. The punishment is quick and consistent, and a player has other behaviors available that avoid punishment.

# CONCEPT CHECK

10. Identify each of the following examples, using the terms shown in Table 6.2:
    a. Your employer gives you bonus pay for working overtime.
    b. You learn to stop playing your accordion at 5 A.M. because your roommate threatens to kill you if you do it again.
    c. You turn off a dripping faucet, ending the "drip drip drip" sound.
    d. You drink less beer than you once did because you feel sick after drinking more than one glass.
    e. Your swimming coach says you cannot go to the next swim meet (which you were looking forward to) because you broke a training rule.
    f. Because you drive recklessly, you temporarily lose the privilege of driving the family car.
    g. You stay away from some fellow students who are coughing and sneezing because you do not want to catch whatever illness they have. (Check your answers on page 226.)

## A STEP FURTHER
### Using Reinforcement

Your local school board proposes to improve class attendance by lowering the grades of any student who misses a certain number of classes. Might the board achieve the same goal more effectively by using positive reinforcement?

■ Lucy Pearson (left) has collected over 110,000 hubcaps. Jim Hambrick (right) collects Superman items. Many people develop strong but apparently impractical motivations.

## What Constitutes Reinforcement?

With operant conditioning a response becomes more common because it is followed by a reinforcer. But what is a reinforcer? It is "something that increases the probability of the preceding response." So far, we are just going around in circles. It would be helpful to specify the basis of reinforcement, so we would know better how to reinforce a child for studying or how to reinforce a worker for doing a job well.

Thorndike suggested a trial-and-error approach to finding reinforcers: We could simply try a number of likely reinforcers to see what works. If some event serves as a reinforcer for one behavior, it will also serve as a reinforcer for others. That approach is, however, theoretically unsatisfactory. *Why* is food reinforcing, for example?

Many reinforcers satisfy biological needs, such as hunger, but not all are biologically useful. For example, saccharin, a sweet but biologically useless chemical, can be a reinforcer. We may be tempted to say that reinforcement is a pleasant event, but pleasure isn't easy to define either. Besides, many people who spend long hours gambling or using drugs show few signs of pleasure (Berridge & Robinson, 1995). Also consider how hard you work to get a decent grade in a course, and how little actual pleasure you feel when you finally get it. So reinforcement is not identical to pleasure.

David Premack (1965) proposed a simple rule: *The opportunity to engage in frequent behavior* (e.g., eating) *will be a reinforcer for any less-frequent behavior* (e.g., lever pressing). This relationship is known as the **Premack principle.** Thus, for example, if you ordinarily spend more time reading than watching television, someone could increase your television watching by reinforcing you with books. For someone else it might be possible to reinforce reading with opportunities to watch television. In short, a given opportunity may or may not be a reinforcer depending on the individual and the response to be reinforced.

The limitation of the Premack principle is that we are sometimes reinforced by opportunities for uncommon behaviors. For example, if we watched how often people did various acts, we might not guess that someone who almost never had sex would be strongly reinforced by an opportunity for sex. For another example, how much time do you spend clipping your toenails during an average week? Almost none? Still, if you are badly overdue for clipping them, an opportunity to do so would be reinforcing. So the key is not how often you do something, but whether you have recently been doing it less often than you would like. According to the **disequilibrium principle** of reinforcement, *each of us has a normal, or "equilibrium," state in which we divide our time among various activities in some preferred way, and if we are removed from that state, a return to it will be reinforcing* (Farmer-Dougan, 1998; Timberlake & Farmer-Dougan, 1991). You might think of it like the graphs in Figure 6.16: Initially, a teenager eats 100 cookies per week and loads the dishwasher once (part a). Then the parents establish a reinforcement contingency of 5 cookies for loading the dishwasher and no cookies at other times. Behavior must now lie somewhere along the line in part b. The teen starts loading the dishwasher more often than before, as shown in part c. Note that an opportunity for the deprived behavior (cookie eating) has reinforced the other behavior.

## CONCEPT CHECK

11. Anorexia nervosa is a condition in which someone who is obsessed with weight loss refuses to eat enough to survive. Suppose you want to use positive reinforcement to encourage more eating. According to the disequilibrium principle, how should you begin? (Check your answer on page 226.)

### Unconditioned and Conditioned Reinforcement

Food and drink are reinforcers for virtually everyone, even the very young, but money is a reinforcer only for

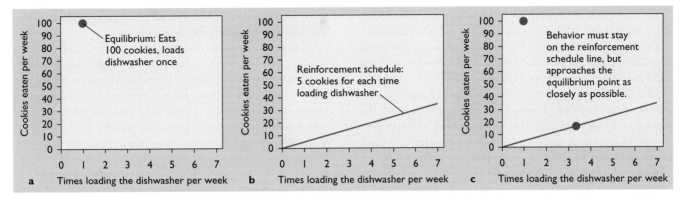

**FIGURE 6.16** This teenager's equilibrium state, or spontaneous behavior, is to eat 100 cookies per week and load the dishwasher once (a). The parents establish a reinforcement contingency of 5 cookies for loading the dishwasher (b). As shown in (c), the teen must remain on the line established in (b), but will gravitate toward the point closet to the equilibrium point.

those who have learned how to use it. Psychologists therefore distinguish between **unconditioned reinforcers,** *which are reinforcing because of their own properties,* and **conditioned reinforcers,** *which became reinforcing because of their previous association with an unconditioned reinforcer.* Food and water are unconditioned reinforcers. Coins and bills (conditioned reinforcers) become reinforcing because they can be exchanged for food or other unconditioned reinforcers. A student learns that good grades will win the approval of parents and teachers; an employee learns that increased sales will win the approval of an employer. We spend most of our time working for conditioned reinforcers. (Don't confuse these terms with conditioned and unconditioned *stimuli* or *responses,* which re-

fer to classical conditioning. Reinforcers are elements of operant conditioning.)

### Reinforcement as Learning What Leads to What

Thorndike, you will recall, believed that reinforcement strengthens the response that preceded it. According to that strictly mechanical view of reinforcement, any animal or person who receives reinforcement simply engages in the response more frequently, without necessarily understanding *why* and, in fact, without necessarily understanding anything at all.

According to another view, individuals learn what leads to what (Tolman, 1932). A rat may learn that running down an alley leads to food. Having learned that, the rat does not automatically go running down the alley all the time. It runs down the alley only when it needs food.

For example, suppose an animal wanders through a maze and receives something it does not need, such as food just after it has eaten a meal. After the rat's next few meals, we test it in the maze again, and each time it wanders through at about the same speed. Now we test it one more time, but this time when it's hungry. Suddenly, the rat scurries through the maze, indicating that it had learned more than it had previously shown (Tolman & Honzik, 1930). This procedure is known as *latent learning* because what is learned is at first *latent* (not apparent to the observer). Latent learning is generally taken as evidence that the animal learns what leads to what; it doesn't just increase response tendencies.

Another example: A rat is reinforced with sugar water for making response A and is reinforced with food pellets for making response B. After both responses have become well established, the rat is made ill after consuming, say, the sugar water. Now, when given the opportunity to make either response, the rat makes mostly response B. Evidently, the original training did not only increase two responses; the rat learned which response produced which outcome (Colwill, 1993).

So, what exactly does a rat or any other species learn during operant conditioning? It learns the probability

■ Many conditioned reinforcers are surprisingly powerful. Consider, for example, how hard some first-graders will work for a little gold star that the teacher pastes on an assignment.

of various outcomes after each possible response and in the presence of various stimuli. That is, it forms both response-reinforcement and stimulus-reinforcement associations. It is influenced both by the recent and the previous histories of reinforcements (Dragoi & Staddon, 1999). Operant conditioning doesn't just change the response probabilities; it changes the meaning of the stimuli and the meaning of the responses (DeGrandpre, 2000). In short, to account for all the results, we have to assume that an animal keeps track of quite a lot.

## Schedules of Reinforcement

The simplest procedure in operant conditioning is to provide reinforcement every time the correct response occurs. **Continuous reinforcement** refers to *reinforcement for every correct response.* As you know, not every response in the real world leads to reinforcement.

*Reinforcement for some responses and not for others* is known as **intermittent reinforcement.** We behave differently when we know that only some of our responses will be reinforced. Psychologists have investigated the effects of many **schedules of reinforcement,** which are *rules or procedures for the delivery of reinforcement.* Four schedules for delivery of intermittent reinforcement are fixed ratio, fixed interval, variable ratio, and variable interval (see Table 6.3). A ratio schedule provides reinforcements depending on the number of responses. An interval schedule provides reinforcements depending on the timing of responses.

**TABLE 6.3 Some Schedules of Reinforcement**

| Type | Description |
| --- | --- |
| Continuous | Reinforcement for every response of the correct type |
| Fixed ratio | Reinforcement following completion of a specific number of responses |
| Variable ratio | Reinforcement for an unpredictable number of responses that varies around a mean value |
| Fixed interval | Reinforcement for the first response that follows a given delay since the previous reinforcement |
| Variable interval | Reinforcement for the first response that follows an unpredictable delay (varying around a mean value) since the previous reinforcement |

### Fixed-Ratio Schedule

A **fixed-ratio schedule** *provides a reinforcement only after a certain (fixed) number of correct responses have been made*— after every 5th response, for example. Some animals continue responding even with a schedule that reinforces only every 100th or 200th response. We see similar behavior among pieceworkers in a factory whose pay de-

pends on how many pieces they turn out or among fruit pickers who get paid by the bushel.

The response rate for a fixed-ratio schedule tends to be rapid and steady. However, if the schedule requires a large number of responses for reinforcement, there may be a temporary interruption after each reinforced response. For example, if you have just completed 10 calculus problems, you may pause briefly before starting your French assignment; after completing 100 problems, you would pause even longer.

### Variable-Ratio Schedule

A **variable-ratio schedule** is similar to a fixed-ratio schedule except that *reinforcement is provided after a variable number of correct responses.* For example, reinforcement may come after an average of 5 responses, but sometimes comes after as few as 1 or 2 and sometimes after 20 or more responses. Variable-ratio schedules generate steady response rates. Gambling is reinforced on a variable-ratio schedule because the gambler receives payment on an irregular basis for some responses and not for others.

Variable-ratio schedules occur in everyday life whenever each response has about an equal probability of success. For example, when you apply for a job, you might or might not get it. The more times you apply, the better your chances, but you cannot predict how many applications you need to submit before you get a job offer.

### Fixed-Interval Schedule

A **fixed-interval schedule** *provides reinforcement for the first response made after a specific time interval.* For instance, an animal might get food for only the first response it makes after each 2-minute interval. Then it would have to wait another 2 minutes before another response would be effective. Animals (including humans) on such a schedule usually learn to pause after each reinforcement and begin to respond again only as the end of the time interval approaches.

Checking your mailbox is an example of behavior on a fixed-interval schedule. If your mail is delivered at about 3 P.M., you will get no reinforcement for checking your mailbox at 2 P.M. If you are eagerly awaiting an important letter, you might begin to check around 2:30 and continue checking every few minutes until it arrives.

### Variable-Interval Schedule

In a **variable-interval schedule,** *reinforcement is available after a variable amount of time has elapsed.* For example, reinforcement may come for the first response after 2 minutes, then for the first response after 7 seconds, then for the first response after 3 minutes 20 seconds, and so forth. There is no way to know how much time will pass before the next response is reinforced. Consequently, responses on a variable-interval schedule occur at a slow but steady rate. For example, you phone your best friend and hear a busy signal. You don't know how soon your friend will hang up, so you try again every few minutes.

Stargazing is another example of a response that is reinforced on a variable-interval schedule. The reinforcement for stargazing—seeing a comet, for example—appears at irregular, unpredictable intervals. Consequently, both professional and amateur astronomers scan the skies regularly.

### Extinction of Responses Reinforced on Different Schedules

Suppose Sarah has found an interesting e-mail message two or three times every day since she entered college, but Donna has found one only once every few days. Now without any notice or warning, the e-mail server stops delivering anything to either of them. Which one will continue checking her e-mail longer?

Donna will continue longer, even though Sarah has had more reinforcements. Extinction of responses is almost always slower after a schedule of intermittent reinforcement (either a ratio schedule or an interval schedule) than after a schedule of continuous reinforcement (reinforcement for every response). One explanation is that the lack of reinforcement is nothing new for someone who has been responding for intermittent reinforcement. Someone who has had continuous reinforcement can immediately notice the change.

 **ONCEPT CHECK**

12. Identify which schedule of reinforcement applies to each of the following examples:
    **a.** You attend every new movie that appears at your local theater; you find most of them dull (not reinforcing) but really enjoy about one fourth of them.
    **b.** You occasionally check your e-mail to find out whether you have any new messages.
    **c.** You tune your television set to an all-news cable channel, and you look up from your studies to check the sports scores every 30 minutes.
13. Stargazing in the hope of finding a comet was cited as an example of a variable-interval schedule. Why is it *not* an example of a variable ratio?
14. A novice gambler and a longtime gambler both lose 20 bets in a row. Which one is more likely to continue betting? Why? (Check your answers on page 226.)

# Applications of Operant Conditioning

Although operant conditioning arose from purely theoretical concerns, it has a long history of applications. Here are four examples.

## *Animal Training*

Most animal acts are based on training methods similar to Skinner's. To induce an animal to perform a trick, the trainer first trains it to perform a simple act that is similar to its natural behavior. Then the trainer shapes the animal to perform more complex behaviors. Most animal trainers rely on positive reinforcement and seldom use punishment.

During World War II, Skinner proposed a military application of his training methods (Skinner, 1960). The military was having trouble designing a guidance system for its air-to-ground missiles. It needed an apparatus that could recognize a target and guide a missile toward it but that was compact enough to leave room for explosives. Skinner taught pigeons to recognize a target and peck in its direction. If pigeons were placed in the nose cone of a missile, the direction of their pecking would guide the missile to the target. Skinner demonstrated that pigeons would do the job cheaply and accurately while taking very little space, but the military laughed off the whole idea.

a                                                      b

■   The high-tech hope of robots handling housekeeping chores has yet to materialize, but in the meantime, simian aides—trained monkeys—are helping the disabled. (a) Monkeys are proving useful for indoor tasks for people with limited mobility. (b) This monkey is being trained to retrieve objects identified with a laser beam. Such training relies on shaping behavior Skinner style—building a new response by reinforcing sequential approximations to it.

## Persuasion

How could you persuade someone to do something that he or she did not want to do? To use an extreme example, how could you convince a prisoner of war to cooperate with the enemy?

The best way is to start by reinforcing a slight degree of cooperation and then working up to the goal, little by little. This principle has been applied by people who had probably never heard of B. F. Skinner, positive reinforcement, or shaping. During the Korean War, the Chinese Communists forwarded some of the letters written home by prisoners of war but intercepted others. (The prisoners could tell from the replies which letters had been forwarded.) The prisoners began to suspect that they would have better luck getting their letters through if they said something mildly favorable about their captors. So from time to time, they would include a brief remark that the Communists were not really so bad, that certain aspects of the Chinese system seemed to work pretty well, or that they hoped the war would end soon.

After a while the Chinese captors devised essay contests; the soldier who wrote the best essay (in the captors' opinion) would win a little extra food or some other privilege. Most of the winning essays contained a statement or two that complimented the Communists on a minor matter or admitted that "the United States is not perfect."

Gradually, more and more soldiers started to include such statements in their essays. Occasionally, the Chinese might ask one of them, "You said the United States is not perfect. We wonder whether you could tell us some of the ways in which it is not perfect, so that we can better understand your system." Then they would ask the soldiers who had cooperated to read aloud their lists of what was wrong with the United States, and so on. Gradually, without torture or coercion and with only modest reinforcements, the Chinese induced prisoners to make public statements denouncing the United States, to make false confessions, to inform on fellow prisoners, and even to reveal military secrets (Cialdini, 1993).

The point is clear: Whether we want to get rats to salute the flag or soldiers to denounce it, the most effective training technique is to start with easy behaviors, reinforce those behaviors, and then shape gradually more complex behaviors.

## Applied Behavior Analysis/ Behavior Modification

In one way or another, people are almost constantly trying to influence other people's behavior. Psychologists have developed influence procedures based on operant conditioning.

In **applied behavior analysis,** also known as **behavior modification,** a *psychologist first determines the reinforcers that sustain an unwanted behavior and then tries to al-* *ter that behavior by reducing the reinforcements for the unwanted behavior and providing suitable reinforcers for more acceptable behaviors.* For example, consider the use of safety belts in cars. Many adults still do not habitually wear safety belts despite repeated reminders that seat belts save lives and despite state laws that fine people for failure to wear belts.

One approach is to reinforce people for wearing safety belts. Many companies have monitored their employees while entering or leaving the parking lot and given prizes for wearing safety belts. Typical prizes are a dollar, a meal coupon, a T-shirt, or a lottery ticket. The results have consistently shown a marked increase in the number of people wearing safety belts (Hagenzieker, Bijleveld, & Davidse, 1997).

Another example: People in the United States and many other countries spend much of their time at desks, in cars, or on the sofa despite warnings that inactivity puts them at risk for obesity, diabetes, heart disease, and so forth. How could we influence people to exercise more? In one study college students spent hours in a room with a stationary bicycle and several other choices of inactive behaviors. Most students spent little or no time on the bicycle *unless* riding it turned on a videotaped movie, a video game, or another highly preferred opportunity (Saelens & Epstein, 1999). This type of reinforcement has been used to get obese children to exercise more (Goldfield, Kalakanis, Ernst, & Epstein, 2000).

## CONCEPT CHECK

15. Of the procedures characterized in Table 6.2, which one applies to laws that penalize people for not wearing seat belts? Which one applies to giving prizes to people who do wear seat belts? (Check your answers on page 226.)

## Breaking Bad Habits

Some people learn to conquer their own bad habits by means of reinforcements. Nathan Azrin and Robert Nunn (1973) recommend this three-step method:

1. Become more aware of your bad habit. Interrupt the behavior and isolate it from the chain of normal activities. Then you might imagine an association between the behavior and something repulsive. For example, to break a nail-biting habit, imagine your fingernails covered with sewage.
2. If no one else will reinforce you for making progress, provide your own reinforcements. For example, buy yourself a special treat after you have abandoned your bad habit for a certain period of time.
3. Do something incompatible with the offending habit. For example, if you have a nervous habit of hunching up your shoulders, practice depressing your shoulders.

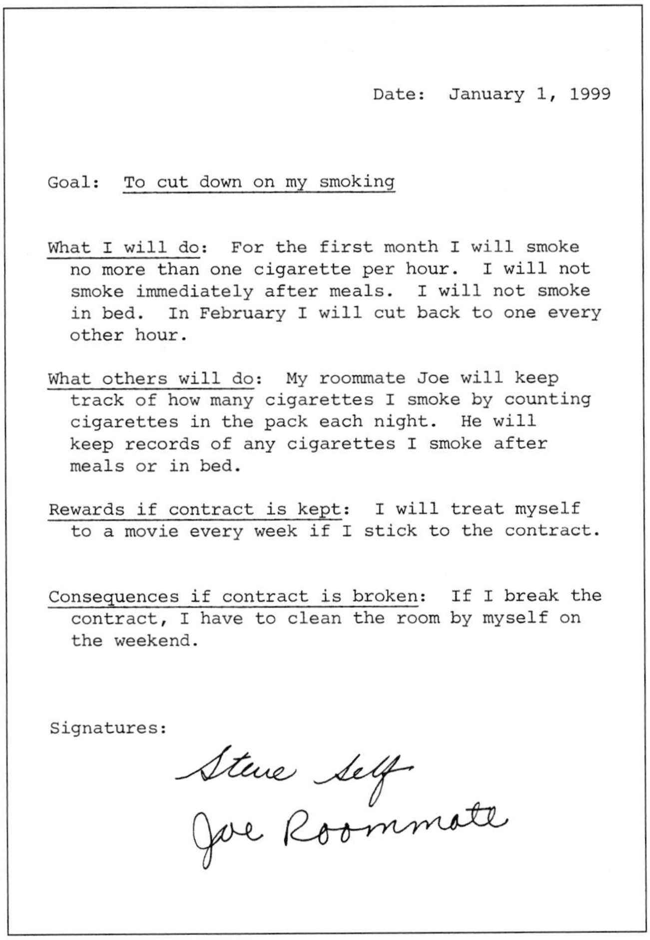

```
                                    Date:  January 1, 1999


Goal:  To cut down on my smoking


What I will do:  For the first month I will smoke
  no more than one cigarette per hour.  I will not
  smoke immediately after meals.  I will not smoke
  in bed.  In February I will cut back to one every
  other hour.

What others will do:  My roommate Joe will keep
  track of how many cigarettes I smoke by counting
  cigarettes in the pack each night.  He will
  keep records of any cigarettes I smoke after
  meals or in bed.

Rewards if contract is kept:  I will treat myself
  to a movie every week if I stick to the contract.


Consequences if contract is broken:  If I break the
  contract, I have to clean the room by myself on
  the weekend.



Signatures:
                 Steve Self
                 Joe Roommate
```

**FIGURE 6.17** Sometimes people try to change their own behavior by setting up a system of reinforcements and punishments.

Figure 6.17 shows an example of a college student setting up a list of reinforcements and punishments to support his goal of decreasing his smoking. If he successfully limited his smoking, he would treat himself to a movie. If he broke his vow, he would have to clean the room by himself on the weekend. Many people set up similar patterns of reinforcement and punishment for themselves, generally without a written contract. If you decide to try this approach, set clear goals, choose realistic reinforcers, and keep track of your successes and failures.

## IN CLOSING

### Operant Conditioning and Human Behavior

Suppose one of your instructors announced that everyone in the class would receive the same grade at the end of the course, regardless of performance on tests and papers. Would you study hard in that course? Probably not. Or suppose your employer said that all raises and pro-

motions would be made at random, with no regard to how well you do your job. Would you continue working as hard as possible? Not likely. Do not take it as an insult that some aspects of your behavior resemble that of a pigeon or a rat in a Skinner box. For any organism to survive, its behavior must increase or decrease depending on its consequences. That is the main point of operant conditioning.

## Summary

- *Reinforcement.* Edward Thorndike introduced the concept of reinforcement. A reinforcement increases the probability that the preceding response will be repeated. (page 213)
- *Operant conditioning.* Operant conditioning is the process of controlling the rate of a behavior through its consequences. (page 214)
- *Extinction.* In operant conditioning a response becomes extinguished if it is no longer followed by reinforcement. (page 215)
- *Shaping.* Shaping is a technique for training subjects to perform difficult acts by reinforcing them for successive approximations to the desired behavior. (page 216)
- *Reinforcement and punishment.* Behaviors can be reinforced (strengthened) by presenting favorable events or by omitting unfavorable events. Behaviors can be punished (suppressed) by presenting unfavorable events or by omitting favorable events. (page 218)
- *The nature of reinforcement.* The opportunity to engage in a more probable behavior will reinforce a less probable behavior. Something that an individual can exchange for a reinforcer becomes a reinforcer itself. (page 220)
- *Learning what leads to what.* Animals (and people) learn which reinforcement is associated with which behavior. Their frequency of repeating a given behavior depends on their motivation to receive the reinforcement at the moment. (page 221)
- *Schedules of reinforcement.* The frequency and timing of a response depend on the schedule of reinforcement. In a ratio schedule of reinforcement, an individual is given reinforcement after a fixed or variable number of responses. In an interval schedule of reinforcement, an individual is given reinforcement after a fixed or variable period of time. (page 222)
- *Applications.* People have applied operant conditioning to animal training, persuasion, applied behavior analysis, and the breaking of bad habits. (page 223)

## Answers to Concept Checks

**8.** You would need to know whether the bell was always followed by food (classical conditioning) or whether food was presented only if the animal sat up on its hind legs (operant conditioning). (page 214)

9. To be effective, punishments must be quick and consistent. Punishments for drug dealing are neither quick nor consistent. Furthermore, punishment most effectively suppresses a response when the individual has alternative responses that can gain reinforcements. Many people who gain enormous profits by selling drugs would have no alternative legal way to gain similar profits. (page 218)

10. **a.** positive reinforcement; **b.** punishment or passive avoidance; **c.** escape learning or negative reinforcement; **d.** punishment or passive avoidance; **e.** omission training or negative punishment; **f.** omission training or negative punishment; **g.** avoidance learning or negative reinforcement. (page 219)

11. Begin by determining how this person spends his or her time—for example, exercising, reading, watching television, visiting with friends. Then determine something that he or she has recently not had much opportunity to do. Activities for which one has only limited opportunities become good reinforcers. (page 221)

12. **a.** variable ratio. (You will be reinforced for about one fourth of your entries to the theater but on an irregular basis.) **b.** variable interval. (The messages appear at unpredictable times, so your responses are reinforced at unpredictable intervals.) **c.** fixed interval. (page 223)

13. In a variable-ratio schedule, the number of responses matters but the timing does not. If you have already checked the stars tonight and found no comets, checking three more times tonight will probably be fruitless. Checking at a later date gives you a better chance. (page 223)

14. The habitual gambler will continue longer because he or she has a history of being reinforced for gambling on a variable-ratio schedule, which retards extinction. (For the same reason, an alcoholic who has had both good experiences and bad experiences while drunk is likely to keep on drinking even after several consecutive bad experiences.) (page 223)

15. If you think of "not wearing seat belts" as a behavior, then penalizing people for that behavior is a punishment. If (more reasonably) you think of wearing seat belts as the behavior to be changed, wearing seat belts is a way of avoiding punishment, and the example is therefore one of avoidance behavior or negative reinforcement. Giving prizes to people who agree to wear seat belts is an example of positive reinforcement. (page 224)

# Other Kinds of Learning

*What kinds of learning do not fit neatly into the categories of classical or operant conditioning? What are the special features of these kinds of learning?*

*How do we learn from the successes and failures of others without trying every response ourselves?*

Operant and classical conditioning both depend on an association between a first event (response or CS) and a second event (reinforcement or UCS). The main difference is that in operant conditioning the first event is something the individual does, whereas in classical conditioning the first event is a stimulus presented from the outside. It might seem that all possible examples of learning would fall into either of these two categories; several, however, are difficult to classify or require another category altogether.

## Conditioned Taste Aversions

First, suppose an experimenter repeatedly presents a light followed by a shock. After a few pairings, the animal in the experiment shows an increased heart rate whenever it sees that light. Which kind of learning is this?

Second, suppose the experimenter turns on the light and then waits to see what the animal does. If (and only if) it looks toward the light, it gets a shock. Before long the animal consistently turns away from the light. Which kind of learning is this?

The first is classical conditioning; the second is operant. But now consider a third experiment: The experimenter turns on a light. The animal looks toward it. Then it gets a shock. Now suppose *on the very next trial* and from then on, the animal avoids the light. What kind of learn-

ing took place? It's hard to say. Did the light itself predict the shock (as in classical conditioning) or did the animal's response to the light (looking at it) produce the shock (as in operant conditioning)? When learning occurs reliably after just one pairing, it is difficult to distinguish between classical and operant conditioning.

One kind of learning that does occur reliably after a single trial is an *association between eating something and getting sick*, which we call **conditioned taste aversion,** first documented by John Garcia and his colleagues (Garcia, Ervin, & Koelling, 1966). This kind of learning shows some special features, including strong learning despite delays of minutes or hours. For example: A rat is drinking a saccharin solution, which it has never tasted before. Saccharin tastes sweet, and in small amounts it is neither healthful nor harmful. After the rat has drunk for a few minutes, the experimenter removes the bottle, waits minutes or even hours, and then injects a small amount of poison, thus making the rat moderately ill. The experimenter then waits a day or longer to let the rat recover and offers it a choice between the saccharin solution and unflavored water. The rat will strongly prefer the unflavored water (Garcia, et al., 1966). In contrast, rats that have not been poisoned, or that have been poisoned after drinking something else, strongly prefer the saccharin solution to plain water. Evidently, the first group of rats have learned a connection between taste and illness, in spite of the long delay and their having experienced the pairing only once. In many other cases of either classical or operant conditioning, learning is greatest with a 1- or 2-second delay between the events to be associated and hard to demonstrate at all with delays over 20 seconds (Kimble, 1961).

An animal that learns a conditioned taste aversion to a particular food treats that food as if it were foul tasting (Figure 6.18) (Garcia, 1990). Some ranchers in the western United States have used this type of learning to deter

**FIGURE 6.18** This coyote previously fell ill after eating sheep meat containing a mild dose of lithium salts. Now it reacts toward both live and dead sheep as it would toward bad-tasting food.

coyotes from eating sheep. They offer the coyotes sheep meat containing low levels of lithium salts or similar poisons. Afterward, the coyotes no longer attack sheep and act as if sheep meat tasted bad. This technique has the advantage of protecting the ranchers' sheep without killing the coyotes, which are a threatened species.

Conditioned taste aversions are special in another regard as well: Recall that an animal can associate something it ate with getting ill hours later. No doubt the animal had many other experiences between its meal and the illness, so why didn't it associate the illness with something else instead? The answer is that animals are predisposed to associate illness mostly with what they eat. In one classic experiment (Garcia & Koelling, 1966), rats were allowed to drink saccharin-flavored water from tubes that were set up so that, whenever the rats licked the water, a bright light flashed and a loud noise sounded. Some of the rats were exposed to x-rays (which can induce nausea) while they drank. Others were given electric shocks to their feet 2 seconds after they had begun to drink. After the training was complete, each rat was tested separately with a tube of saccharin-flavored water and a tube of unflavored water that produced lights and noises. (Figure 6.19 illustrates this experiment.)

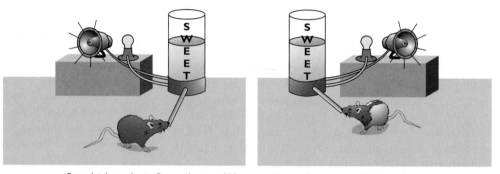

Rats drink saccharin-flavored water. Whenever they make contact with the tube, they turn on a bright light and a noisy buzzer.

Then

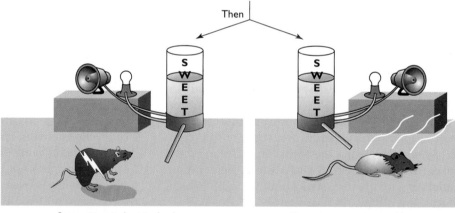

Some rats get electric shock.

Some rats are nauseated by x-rays.

Next day: Rats are given a choice between a tube of saccharin-flavored water and a tube of unflavored water hooked up to the light and the buzzer.

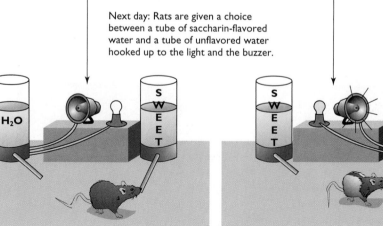

**FIGURE 6.19** An experiment by Garcia and Koelling (1966): Rats "blame" tastes for their illness and lights and sounds for their pain.

Rats that had been shocked avoid the tube with the lights and noises.

Rats that had been nauseated by x-rays avoid the saccharin-flavored water.

The rats that had been exposed to x-rays avoided only the flavored water. The rats that had received shocks while drinking avoided only the tube that produced lights and noises. Evidently, rats (and other species) have a built-in predisposition to associate illness mostly with what they have eaten or drunk and to associate skin pain mostly with what they have seen or heard. (The predisposition to associate illness with food is an example of preparedness, mentioned earlier in this chapter.) Such predispositions are presumably beneficial because foods are more likely to cause internal events, and lights and sounds are more likely to signal external events.

One problem remains with all of this: I have described associations between food and "illness," but some drugs that make the animal very ill produce only weak learned aversions, and some procedures such as x-rays that hardly make the animal ill at all (and produce only slight nausea in humans) produce powerful aversions to recently eaten foods. In one experiment rats learned an aversion to a food because they ran in a running wheel after eating (Nakajima, Hayashi, & Kato, 2000). The running may have produced motion sickness, but the rats did run voluntarily. Frankly, we do not well understand what experiences produce learned aversions.

ONCEPT CHECK

16. Name the unusual features of conditioned taste aversions. (Check your answer on page 233.)

## Birdsong Learning

Birdsongs brighten the day for people who hear them, but they are earnest business for the birds themselves. For most species only males sing, and they sing only in spring, the mating season. As a rule a song indicates, "Here I am. I am a male of species _____ . If you're a female of my species, please come closer. If you're a male of my species and you can hear me, you're too close. If I find you, I'll attack." (Among the delights of birdsongs are the exceptions to the rule. Mockingbirds copy all the songs they hear and defend their territory against intruders of all species—sometimes even squirrels, cats, people, and automobiles. Carolina wrens sing male-and-female duets throughout the year. But on to more relevant matters.)

If you were to rear an infant songbird in isolation from others of its species, would it develop a normal song on its own? Maybe or maybe not, depending on its species. Some species have to learn their song. For example, in several sparrow species, a male develops a normal song only if he hears the song of his own species. He *learns most readily* during a **sensitive period** *early in life*. The duration of that period varies among species but generally ends by fall, when the adult males stop singing. The young bird learns better from a live tutor, such as his fa-

ther, than from a tape-recorded song in a laboratory (Baptista & Petrinovich, 1984; Marler & Peters, 1987, 1988). It will not learn at all from the song of another species. Evidently, a fledgling sparrow is equipped with mechanisms to produce approximately the right song and ways of identifying which songs to imitate (Marler, 1997).

Birdsong learning resembles human language learning in that both take place in a social context, both occur most easily in early life, both start with babbling and gradually improve, and both deteriorate gradually if the individual becomes deaf later (Brainard & Doupe, 2000). Song learning differs, however, from standard examples of classical and operant conditioning. During the sensitive period, the infant bird just listens. We cannot call the song he hears an unconditioned stimulus because it elicits no apparent response. At no time in this sensitive period does the bird receive any apparent reinforcement. Nevertheless, he learns a representation of how his song should sound, even though we cannot classify this learning as either classical or operant. The following spring, when the bird starts to sing, we see a trial-and-error process with a strange form of operant conditioning. At first his song is a disorganized mixture of sounds, somewhat like a babbling human infant. As time passes he eliminates some sounds and rearranges others until he matches the songs he heard the previous summer (Marler & Peters, 1981, 1982).

The point is that the principles of learning vary from one situation to another. If a situation poses special problems (e.g., food selection, song learning in birds, probably language learning in humans), we can expect to find that species have evolved their own special ways of learning (Rozin & Kalat, 1971).

■ A male white-crowned sparrow learns his song in the first months of life but does not begin to sing it until the next year.

# C ONCEPT CHECK

**17.** What aspects of birdsong learning set it apart from classical and operant conditioning? (Check your answers on page 233.)

# Social Learning

According to the **social-learning approach** (Bandura, 1977, 1986), *we learn about many behaviors before we try them the first time. Much learning, especially in humans, results from observing the behaviors of others and from imagining the consequences of our own behavior.* For example, if you want to learn how to swim, paint pictures, play bridge, or drive a car, you *could* try to learn strictly by trial and error, but you would probably start by watching someone who has already learned. When you eventually try the task yourself, your attempt will be subject to reinforcement and punishment; therefore, it falls into the general realm of operant conditioning, but you will be facilitated by your observations of others. Thus, it is useful to examine social learning as a special case.

■ A Japanese toilet is a hole in the ground with no seat. Western visitors usually have to ask how to use it. (You squat.)

■ According to the social-learning approach, we learn many behaviors by observing what others do, imitating behaviors that are reinforced, and avoiding behaviors that are punished. This girl is being blessed by the temple elephant. Others who are watching may later imitate her example.

Although psychologists speak of "social-learning theory," it is not a theory in the sense described in Chapter 2. The social-learning approach is more a point of view or a field of emphasis focusing on the effects of observation, imitation, setting goals, and self-reinforcement. In this sense much of human behavior depends on social learning; after all, most school learning is an attempt to learn from the experiences of other people.

## Modeling and Imitation

If you visit another country, especially one with customs very different from your own, you may find yourself bewildered about things you used to take for granted. Ordering food in a restaurant is not done the way you did it back home; paying for the meal is done differently, too. A hand gesture such as is considered friendly in some countries but rude and vulgar in others. Americans visiting Japan often have trouble understanding how to use the baths and toilets. With effort you can learn foreign customs either because someone explains them to you or because you watch and copy. We say that you *model* your behavior after others or *imitate* others. On a smaller scale, you also use modeling or imitation to learn the customs of a religious organization, a fraternity or sorority, a new place of employment, or any other group you join.

Albert Bandura, Dorothea Ross, and Sheila Ross (1963) studied the role of imitation for learning aggressive behavior. They asked two groups of children to watch films in which an adult or a cartoon character violently attacked an inflated "Bobo" doll. Another group watched a film in which the characters did not attack the doll. They then left the children in a room with a Bobo doll. Only the children who had watched films with attacks on the doll attacked the doll themselves, using

 A child will mimic an adult's behavior even when neither one is reinforced for the behavior. This girl attacks a doll after seeing a film of a woman hitting it. People who witness violent behavior, including violence at home, may be more prone than others to turn to violent behavior themselves.

many of the same movements they had just seen. The clear implication is that children copy the aggressive behavior they have seen in others.

Is the same true for adolescents and adults? This issue warrants our concern because many popular movies include so much violence. As you read in Chapter 2, the available evidence does not demonstrate that watching violence on television or in movies necessarily causes violent behavior. However, some individuals are more highly influenced than others; some viewers (especially adolescents with a history of violent behavior) identify closely with an extremely violent character in a film. Others may be strongly influenced by a film because it resembles an event they have witnessed in their own lives. Many cases have been reported in which people have reenacted scenes they had just seen in a film (S. Snyder, 1991).

### CONCEPT CHECK

18. Many people complain that they cannot find much difference between the two major political parties in the United States because so many American politicians campaign using similar styles and take similar stands on the issues. Explain this observation in terms of social learning. (Check your answer on page 233.)

## Vicarious Reinforcement and Punishment

Six months ago, your best friend quit a job with Consolidated Generic Products to open a restaurant. Now you are considering quitting your job and opening your own restaurant. How do you decide what to do?

You would probably start by asking how successful your friend has been. You do not automatically imitate someone's behavior, even someone you admire. Rather, you imitate behavior that has been reinforcing for that person. In other words you learn by **vicarious reinforcement** or **punishment**—that is, by *substituting someone else's experience for your own.*

Whenever a new business venture succeeds, other companies try to follow the same course. For example, the first few successful Internet companies were followed by a horde of imitators. When a venture fails, other companies try to learn the reasons for that failure to avoid making the same mistakes. When a sports team wins consistently, other teams copy its style of play. And when a television program wins high ratings, other producers are sure to present look-alikes the following year.

**A STEP FURTHER**
*Vicarious Learning*

Might vicarious learning lead to a certain monotony of behavior and contribute to the lack of variety in the television programs and movies that are offered to the public? How can we learn vicariously without becoming just like everyone else?

In many cases vicarious punishment seems to affect behavior less than vicarious reinforcement does. We are bombarded by reminders that failure to wear seat belts will lead to injury or death, and yet many of us fail to buckle up. Despite widespread publicity about the consequences of driving while intoxicated, using addictive drugs, or engaging in unsafe sex, many people ignore the dangers. Even the death penalty, an extreme example of vicarious punishment, does not demonstrably lower the murder rate.

Why does vicarious punishment so frequently produce weak effects? One explanation is that, to be influenced, we must identify with the person who is receiving a vicarious reinforcement or punishment. Most of us think of ourselves as successful people; we see someone who is getting punished as a "loser" and therefore "not like us." Thus, we continue to ignore the dangers.

## Self-Efficacy in Social Learning

We mostly imitate people we regard as successful and would like to resemble. Advertisers, keenly aware of this tendency, feature endorsements from people consumers are likely to admire. Cereal and candy advertisements feature happy, healthy children; soft-drink ads feature attractive young adults; ads for luxury cars feature people who look wealthy.

So, when you watch an Olympic diver win a gold medal for a superb display of physical control, do you then go out and try to imitate those dives? Probably not, simply because you doubt you can duplicate the diver's performance. People imitate someone else's behavior only if they have a sense of **self-efficacy**—*the perception*

■ We tend to imitate the actions of successful people, but only if we feel self-efficacy, a belief that we could perform the task well.

*that they themselves could perform the task successfully.* You observe your past successes and failures, compare yourself to the successful person, and estimate your chance of success. Studies of workers find that the most productive people are consistently those who report high self-efficacy, or confidence in their ability (Stajkovic & Luthans, 1998).

 Can we conclude from these data that self-efficacy improves workers' performance? Why or why not? Check Answer A on page 233 for the author's suggestion.

Don't focus too closely on the "self" in self-efficacy. Sometimes people know that they cannot do much themselves but gain confidence in what they can do with a group effort (Bandura, 2000). Even a group can have a feeling of efficacy or nonefficacy; a group with confidence in its abilities accomplishes much more than a group with doubts.

■ We acquire a sense of self-efficacy mostly through our own successes but also partly by watching and identifying with role models.

## Self-Reinforcement and Self-Punishment in Social Learning

We learn by observing others who are doing what we would like to do. If our sense of self-efficacy is strong enough, we try to imitate their behavior. But actually succeeding often requires prolonged efforts. People typically set a goal for themselves and monitor their progress toward that goal. They even provide reinforcement or punishment for themselves, just as if they were training someone else. They say to themselves, "If I finish this math assignment on time, I'll treat myself to a movie and a new magazine. If I don't finish on time, I'll make myself clean the stove and the sink." (Self-punishments are usually pretty mild and seldom imposed.)

People who have never learned to use self-reinforcement can be taught to do so. Donald Meichenbaum and Joseph Goodman (1971) worked with a group of elementary school children who acted impulsively, blurted out answers, and failed to consider the consequences of their actions. To encourage them to set appropriate goals for themselves and to practice self-reinforcement in achieving them, Meichenbaum and Goodman taught the children to talk to themselves while working on a task. For example, a child might say, "Okay, what do I have to do? You want me to copy the picture. . . . Okay, draw the line down, down, good; then to the right, that's it; now down some more and to the left. Good, I'm doing fine so far. Remember, go slowly. Now back up again. No, I was supposed to go down. That's okay. Just erase the line carefully. . . ." After only four training sessions, the children had learned to pause before answering questions, and they were answering more questions correctly.

Unfortunately, self-reinforcement and self-punishment do not always succeed. One psychologist, Ron Ash (1986), tried to teach himself to stop smoking by means of punishment. He decided to smoke only while he was reading *Psychological Bulletin* and other highly respected but tedious publications. By associating smoking with boredom, he hoped to eliminate his desire to smoke. Two months later he was smoking as much as ever, but he was starting to *enjoy* reading *Psychological Bulletin*!

## IN CLOSING
## *Why We Do What We Do*

Almost everything you have done today was a learned behavior—from getting dressed and combing your hair this morning to reading this chapter right now. In fact, you probably would have trouble listing many things you have done today that were not learned. Even your bad habits are examples of learning.

One point that I hope has emerged in this chapter is that learning takes many forms. Classically conditioned salivation, operantly conditioned movements, conditioned taste aversions, and socially learned behaviors occur under diverse circumstances. The underlying mechanisms in the brain may or may not be the same, but at a descriptive level, these types of learning differ in some important ways. In short, your behavior is subject to a wide variety of learned influences.

## Summary

- *Conditioned taste aversions.* Animals, including people, learn to avoid foods, especially unfamiliar ones, if they become ill afterward. This type of learning occurs reliably after a single pairing, even with a delay of hours between the food and the illness. Animals are predisposed to associate illness with what they eat or drink, not with other events. (page 227)
- *Birdsong learning.* Infant birds of some species must hear their songs during a sensitive period in the first few months of life if they are to develop a fully normal song the following spring. During the early learning, the bird makes no apparent response and receives no apparent reinforcement. (page 229)
- *Learning by observation.* We learn much by observing what other people do and what consequences they experience. (page 230)
- *What we imitate.* We tend to imitate behaviors that have led to reinforcement for other people. We are less consistent in avoiding behaviors that have led to punishment. (page 231)

- *Whom we imitate.* We are more likely to imitate the actions of people we admire and people with whom we identify. (page 231)
- *Self-efficacy.* Whether we decide to imitate a behavior that has led to reinforcement for others depends on whether we believe we are capable of duplicating that behavior. (page 231)
- *Self-reinforcement and self-punishment.* Once people have decided to try to imitate a certain behavior, they set goals for themselves and may even provide their own reinforcements and punishments. (page 232)

## Answers to Concept Checks

**16.** Conditioned taste aversions develop after a single trial despite delays of minutes or hours between food and illness—a longer delay than any that could produce rapid learning in any other situation psychologists have studied. Also, animals are predisposed to associate foods and not other events with illnesses. (page 229)
**17.** The most distinctive feature is that birdsong learning occurs during a time when the learner makes no apparent response and receives no apparent reinforcement. Also, at least in certain sparrow species, birdsong learning occurs most readily during an early sensitive period, and the bird is capable of learning its own species' song but not the song of another species. (page 230)
**18.** One reason that most American politicians run similar campaigns and take similar stands is that they all tend to copy the same models—candidates who have won elections in the past. Another reason is that they all pay attention to the same public opinion polls. (page 231)

## Answer to Other Question in the Module

**A.** No. Finding that people with high self-efficacy are also highly productive is a correlational result, and correlation does not demonstrate causation. It is possible that high self-efficacy improves performance, but it is equally possible that a history of successful performance improves self-efficacy. It is also possible, of course, that both are true. (page 232)

## Key Terms

**acquisition:** the process by which a conditioned response is established or strengthened (page 206)

**active avoidance learning:** learning to make a response to avoid an event such as shock (page 218)

**applied behavior analysis (or behavior modification):** a procedure for determining the reinforcers that sustain an unwanted behavior and then reducing the reinforcements for the unwanted behavior and providing suitable reinforcers for more acceptable behaviors (page 224)

**behaviorist:** a psychologist who insists that psychologists should study only observable, measurable behaviors, not mental processes (page 199)

**belongingness:** the concept that certain stimuli are readily associated with each other and that certain responses are readily associated with certain outcomes (page 215)

**blocking effect:** the tendency of a previously established association to one stimulus to block the formation of an association to an added stimulus (page 210)

**chaining:** a procedure for developing a sequence of behaviors in which the reinforcement for one response is the opportunity to engage in the next response (page 217)

**classical conditioning (or Pavlovian conditioning):** the process by which an organism learns a new association between two paired stimuli—a neutral stimulus and one that already evokes a reflexive response (page 204)

**conditioned reinforcer:** an event that becomes reinforcing because it has previously been associated with an unconditioned reinforcer (page 221)

**conditioned response (CR):** whatever response the conditioned stimulus begins to elicit as a result of the conditioning procedure (page 204)

**conditioned stimulus (CS):** a stimulus that comes to evoke a particular response after being paired with the unconditioned stimulus (page 204)

**conditioned taste aversion:** the tendency to avoid eating a substance that has been followed by illness when it was eaten in the past (page 227)

**contingency:** the prediction of one stimulus from the presence of another (page 211)

**continuous reinforcement:** reinforcement for every correct response (page 222)

**discrimination:** (1) in classical conditioning making different responses to different stimuli that have been followed by different outcomes (page 207); (2) in operant conditioning learning to respond in one way to one stimulus and in a different way to another stimulus (page 215)

**discriminative stimulus:** stimulus that indicates on which occasion a response will produce a certain consequence (page 215)

**disequilibrium principle:** the principle that an opportunity to engage in any deprived activity will be a reinforcer because it restores equilibrium (page 220)

**drug tolerance:** the progressively weaker effects of a drug after repeated use (page 208)

**escape learning:** learning to escape from an event such as shock (page 218)

**extinction:** (1) in classical conditioning (page 206) the dying out of the conditioned response after repeated presentations of the conditioned stimulus without the unconditioned stimulus; (2) in operant conditioning the weakening of a response after a period without reinforcement (page 215)

**fixed-interval schedule:** a rule for delivering reinforcement for the first response that the subject makes after a specified period of time has passed (page 222)

**fixed-ratio schedule:** a rule for delivering reinforcement only after the subject has made a specific number of correct responses (page 222)

**intermittent reinforcement:** reinforcement for some responses and not for others (page 222)

**intervening variable:** something that we infer without directly observing it and that links a variety of procedures to a variety of possible responses (page 199)

**law of effect:** Thorndike's theory that a response followed by favorable consequences becomes more probable and a response followed by unfavorable consequences becomes less probable (page 214)

**methodological behaviorist:** a psychologist who studies only measurable, observable events but sometimes uses those observations to make inferences about internal events (page 199)

**omission training:** learning to suppress a behavior that would lead to the omission of an event such as food (page 218)

**operant conditioning (or instrumental conditioning):** the process of changing behavior by following a response with reinforcement (page 214)

**passive avoidance learning:** learning to avoid an outcome such as shock by being passive—that is, by inhibiting a response that would lead to the outcome (page 218)

**positive reinforcement:** strengthening a behavior through the presentation of an event such as food (page 218)

**Premack principle:** the principle that the opportunity to engage in a frequent behavior will reinforce a less frequent behavior (page 220)

**punishment:** an event that decreases the probability that a response will be repeated (page 218)

**radical behaviorist:** a behaviorist who denies that internal, private events are causes of behavior (page 199)

**reinforcement:** an event that increases the future probability of the most recent response  (page 214)

**schedule of reinforcement:** a rule or procedure linking the pattern of responses to the reinforcements  (page 222)

**self-efficacy:** the perception of one's own ability to perform a task successfully  (page 231)

**sensitive period:** a time early in life during which some kind of learning occurs most readily  (page 229)

**shaping:** a technique for establishing a new response by reinforcing successive approximations  (page 217)

**skeletal responses:** movements of the muscles that move the limbs, trunk, and head  (page 214)

**social-learning approach:** the view that people learn by observing and imitating the behavior of others and by imagining the consequences of their own behavior  (page 230)

**spontaneous recovery:** the temporary return of an extinguished response after a delay  (page 207)

**stimulus control:** the ability of a stimulus to encourage some responses and discourage others  (page 215)

**stimulus generalization:** (1) in classical conditioning the extension of a conditioned response from the training stimulus to similar stimuli  (page 207); (2) in operant conditioning the tendency to make a similar response to a stimulus that resembles one that has already been associated with reinforcement  (page 215)

**stimulus–response psychology:** a field that attempts to explain behavior in terms of how each stimulus triggers a response  (page 200)

**temporal contiguity:** nearness in time  (page 209)

**unconditioned reflex:** an automatic connection between a stimulus and a response  (page 203)

**unconditioned reinforcer:** an event that is reinforcing because of its own properties  (page 221)

**unconditioned response (UCR):** an automatic response to an unconditioned stimulus  (page 204)

**unconditioned stimulus (UCS):** a stimulus that automatically elicits an unconditioned response (page 204)

**variable-interval schedule:** a rule for delivering reinforcement after varying amounts of time  (page 222)

**variable-ratio schedule:** a rule for delivering reinforcement after varying numbers of correct responses  (page 222)

**vicarious reinforcement (or vicarious punishment):** observed reinforcement or punishment experienced by someone else  (page 231)

**visceral responses:** activities of the internal organs  (page 214)

## Suggestions for Further Reading

Bandura, A. (1986). *Social foundations of thought and action.* Upper Saddle River, NJ: Prentice Hall. A review of social learning by its most influential investigator.

O'Donohue, W., & Kitchener, R. (1999). *Handbook of behaviorism.* San Diego, CA: Academic Press. Collection of chapters by contemporary behaviorists surveying the range of research and theory in this field.

Rescorla, R. A. (1988). Pavlovian conditioning: It's not what you think it is. *American Psychologist, 43,* 151–160. A theoretical review by an investigator who has contributed significantly to changing views of classical conditioning.

Staddon, J. (1993). *Behaviorism.* London: Duckworth. A critique of both the strengths and weaknesses of Skinner's views.

## Web/Technology Resources

### Positive Reinforcement

**server.bmod.athabascau.ca/html/prtut/reinpair.htm**

Lyle K. Grant of Athabasca University helps students understand what does and what does not constitute positive reinforcement. Be sure you understand the examples before you begin the practice exercise.

### Dr. P's Dog Training

**www.uwsp.edu/acad/psych/dog/dog.htm**

Mark Plonsky of the University of Wisconsin discusses obedience competition, K9 training, assistance dogs, and working dogs, and offers lots of general information.

### Animal Training at Sea World

**www.seaworld.org/animal_training/atcontents.html**

Sea World trainers use operant conditioning principles with performing animals. The discussion covers primary and conditioned reinforcers, shaping, observational learning, and other principles.

### Behaviorism

**http://www.biozentrum.uni-Wuerzburg.de/genetics/ behavior/learning/behaviorism.html**

A history of pioneering research in behaviorism and operant conditioning.

### Operant Conditioning

**snycorva.cortland.edu/~ANDERSMD/OPER/operant. html**

This site offers a basic introduction to the key concepts involved in operant conditioning.

### Albert Bandura

**www.ship.edu/~cgboeree/bandura.html**

C. George Boeree of Shippensburg University provides a short biography of Albert Bandura, describes early research in social learning, and defines many key terms and concepts.

# Memory

7

CHAPTER

**S**uppose I offer you—for a price—an opportunity to do absolutely anything you want for 1 day. You will not be limited by any of the usual constraints on what is possible. You can travel in a flash from one place to another, visiting as many places as you wish, even in outer space. You can travel forward and backward through time, finding out what the future holds and witnessing the great events of history or even prehistoric times. (You will not be able to alter history.) Anything you want to do—just name it and it is yours. Furthermore, I guarantee your safety: No matter where you choose to go or what you choose to do, you will not get hurt.

How much would you be willing to pay for this once in a lifetime opportunity? Oh, yes, I should mention, there is one catch. When the day is over, you will forget everything that happened, completely. Any notes or photos will vanish. And anyone else who takes part in your special day will forget it, too.

Now how much would you be willing to pay? Much less, no doubt, and perhaps nothing. Living without remembering is hardly living at all: Our memories are almost the same as our selves.

■ With a suitable reminder you will find that you remember some events quite distinctly, even after a long delay. Other memories, however, are lost or distorted.

# Types of Memory

*Do we have different kinds of memory?*

*Why did some of the early experiments on memory give misleading results?*

John Horton Conway, a Princeton University mathematics professor, is an accomplished mathematician, magician, game theorist, and computer programmer who is also known for his impressive memory. For example, he has memorized the names of all the stars visible in the northern hemisphere. As he told one interviewer (Seife, 1994, p. 13): "I like knowing things. When a constellation is covered up by a cloud, I predict where the stars will be when the cloud moves away. I really get a feeling of power—knowing what will happen is almost like making it happen." He can also recite poetry that he learned as a child but has not thought about since then. He memorized π to 1000 decimal places and persuaded his wife to learn it too. They take long, romantic walks during which he recites a few places of π, then she says a few, then he says a few.

■ Professor Conway is a brilliant mathematician with an excellent memory for most matters, but he has trouble remembering his colleagues' names.

So, Conway has an outstanding memory, right? Yes, except that during the 20 years he spent at Cambridge University, he never did learn the names of all his colleagues in the math department (Seife, 1994). Perhaps the concept of good memory versus bad memory is flawed. Psychologists' early research assumed we could study any one example of memory and learn the principles that applied to all memory. Eventually, they discovered the limitations of that approach and began to distinguish among different kinds of memory.

## Early Studies of Memory and Their Limitations

If you have an important test on Wednesday morning, how much do you study on Tuesday night? Some professors advise their students against last-minute cramming, and students occasionally misinterpret that advice to mean that last-minute *reviewing* is useless. (I met one student who proudly told me that he didn't study at all the day before a test. He seemed puzzled by his mediocre grades.) What professors mean is that you should study as you go, not wait until the last night to start. But even if you take this advice, a last-minute refresher does help.

A few years ago, someone wrote a proposal for a book called *How to Study in College,* offering the opposite advice: Students should postpone their studying until the last possible moment, because if they studied earlier, they would forget it all. If you have ever waited until the night before a test to start your study, you *know* this advice is bad. So how could its author, a college professor who had read some research on memory, have come to such a faulty conclusion? And what evidence refutes it?

### Ebbinghaus's Pioneering Studies of Memory

The German psychologist Hermann Ebbinghaus (1850–1909) founded the experimental study of memory. Previous researchers had asked people to describe their memories, but they had no way to know whether people's reports were correct. Ebbinghaus conducted his research by teaching new material and then measuring memory of it after various delays. To make sure that the material to be memorized would be unfamiliar, Ebbinghaus invented *nonsense syllables,* meaningless three-letter combinations such as GAK or VUB. He wrote out 2300 such syllables, assembled them in random lists (Figure 7.1), and then set out to study memorization. He had no cooperative introductory psychology students to enlist for his study, nor friends who would volunteer to memorize lists of nonsense syllables, so

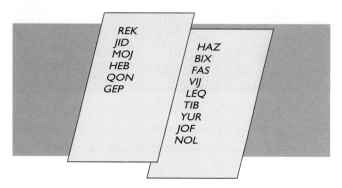

**FIGURE 7.1** Hermann Ebbinghaus pioneered the scientific study of memory by observing his own capacity for memorizing lists of nonsense syllables.

he ran all the tests on himself. Over a period of about 6 years, he memorized thousands of lists of nonsense syllables. (He was either very dedicated to his science or uncommonly tolerant of boredom.)

In one experiment Ebbinghaus memorized several lists of 13 nonsense syllables each and tested his memory after various delays. The results appear in Figure 7.2. On the average he forgot more than half of each list within an hour and still more after that. This study is what moved that text author to recommend that you do your studying immediately before any test. After all, earlier study will be forgotten.

Of course, if you believe this conclusion, then you should also decide that education is pointless. If you will forget most of what you learn within 24 hours, how much will you remember by the time you graduate or a few years later? So unless the whole idea of education is fundamentally flawed, Ebbinghaus's results must not apply to all memory.

## Role of Interference

Suppose we repeat Ebbinghaus's experiment, but instead of conducting all the studies on one person, we persuade many college students to learn a list of nonsense syllables, testing some of them after short delays and some after long delays. The top line of Figure 7.2 shows the results of one such study: Most students still remember most of the nonsense syllables 24 hours after learning them (Koppenaal, 1963).

Why do you suppose most college students remember a list so much better than Ebbinghaus did? You may be tempted to say that college students are very intelligent. True, no doubt, but Ebbinghaus was no dummy either. Or you might suggest that college students have had "so much practice at memorizing nonsense." (Sorry if you think so.) But Ebbinghaus had memorized a lot of nonsense himself. In fact, the problem was that poor Hermann Ebbinghaus had memorized *too much* nonsense— thousands of lists of syllables (Figure 7.3). When anyone memorizes large amounts of similar material, the memory becomes a bit like a room cluttered with many similar items. Learning vast amounts of information does not prevent new learning (any more than a cluttered room stops you from bringing in still more clutter), but it increases the risk of confusing old items with new ones.

If you learn several sets of related materials, the old interferes with the new and the new interferes with the

**FIGURE 7.3** Ebbinghaus could learn new lists of nonsense syllables, but he forgot them quickly because of interference from all the previous lists he had learned. People who memorize many similar lists start to confuse them with one another.

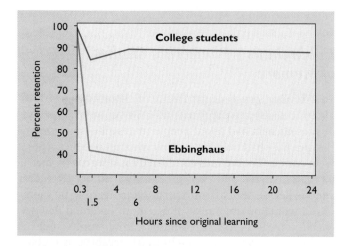

**FIGURE 7.2** Blue line: Recall of lists of syllables by Ebbinghaus (1913) after delays of various lengths. Red line: Recall of lists by college students after delays of various lengths (based on Koppenaal, 1963). Ebbinghaus learned as fast as other people but forgot faster.

old. The *old materials increase forgetting of the new materials* through **proactive interference** (acting forward in time); the *new materials increase forgetting of the old materials* through **retroactive interference** (acting backward in time).

Figure 7.4 shows the difference between these two kinds of interference. Interference accounts for a great deal of our everyday forgetting. You may forget where you parked your car at the local shopping mall because of proactive interference from all the previous times you parked in the same lot. You may forget the French vocabulary list that you studied 3 weeks ago because of retroactive interference from other French words you have studied since then.

The application of this idea to Ebbinghaus is simple: Because he had memorized so many lists of syllables, he had massive proactive interference and forgot new lists unusually quickly. Therefore, the results he collected on himself are misleading if they are applied to anyone else. The moral of the story: When you want to memorize something, beware of studying anything else very similar to it. (Studying unrelated material poses no problem.) Another implication: Don't put too much faith in research based on just one person.

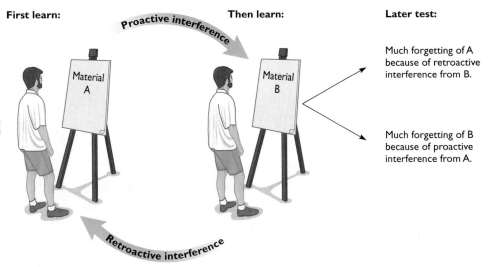

**First learn:**

Material A

**Proactive interference**

**Then learn:**

Material B

**Retroactive interference**

**Later test:**

Much forgetting of A because of retroactive interference from B.

Much forgetting of B because of proactive interference from A.

**FIGURE 7.4** When someone learns two similar sets of materials, each interferes with the other. The old interferes with the new by proactive interference; the new interferes with the old by retroactive interference.

You are likely to recall *ryr* because it is different from the others. If the syllable *kak* had been printed in large purple letters, you would probably remember that one, too.

Similarly, we tend to remember unusual people and those with unusual names. If you meet several men of ordinary appearance with similar names, like John Stevens, Steve Johnson, and Joe Stevenson, it may take a long time to get their names straight. You will more quickly remember a 7-foot-tall, redheaded man named Stinky Rockefeller. *The tendency to remember unusual items better than more common items* is known as the **von Restorff effect,** after the psychologist who first demonstrated it (von Restorff, 1933).

## CONCEPT CHECK

1. Professor Tryhard learns the names of his students every semester. After several years he learns them as quickly as ever but forgets them faster. Does he forget because of retroactive interference or proactive interference?

2. Remember the concept of spontaneous recovery from Chapter 6, page 207? Can you explain it in terms of proactive interference? (Original learning comes first. Extinction—that is, learning not to respond—comes second. What would happen if the first interfered with the second?) (Check your answers on page 249.)

## Distinctiveness

Even with nonsense syllables, we tend to remember distinctive or unusual material. Read the following list and then recall immediately, in any order, as many items as you can:

gak, kug, geg, kig, kag, ryr, gug, guk, kak, kuk, gek

## Dependence of Memory on the Method of Testing

Ebbinghaus tested his memory by requiring himself to state all the syllables without any hints. Might his method have underestimated his memory? For example, most of us occasionally find ourselves unable to remember someone's name or the formula for the volume of a sphere or some other fact that we once knew. Still, we know we haven't forgotten it altogether.

How well you appear to remember something depends on how someone tests you. The simplest method for the tester (but not for the person tested) is to ask for **free recall.** To recall something is *to produce a response, as you do on essay tests or short-answer tests*. For instance, if I ask you, "Please name all the children in your third-grade class," you will probably not name very many, partly because you confuse the names of the children in your third-grade class with those you knew in other grades. (Remember the influence of proactive and retroactive interference.)

You will do better with **cued recall,** a method in which you *receive significant hints about the material.* For example, I might show you a photograph of all the children in your third-grade class (Figure 7.5), or I might give you a list of their initials. Try this: Cover the right side of Table 7.1 with a piece of paper and try to identify the authors of each book on the left. (This method is recall.) Then uncover the right side, revealing each author's initials, and try again. (This method is cued recall.)

With **recognition,** a third method of testing memory, someone is asked to *identify the correct item from several choices.* People usually recognize more items than they can recall. For example, I might give you a list of 60 names and ask you to check off the correct names of children in your third-grade class. Multiple-choice tests use the recognition method.

A fourth method, the **savings,** or **relearning, method,** detects weak memories *by comparing how fast someone relearns something as opposed to learning something new.* Suppose you cannot name some of the children in your third-grade class (recall method) and cannot even pick out their names from a list of choices (recognition method). If I presented you with the correct list of names, you probably would learn it faster than you would learn an unfamiliar list of names. In other words you save time when you relearn material that you learned in the past. The amount of time saved (time needed for original learning minus the time for relearning) is a measure of memory.

**FIGURE 7.5** Can you recall the names of the students in your third-grade class? Trying to remember without any hints is *recall.* Using a photo or a list of initials is *cued recall.* If you tried to choose the correct names from a list, you would be engaged in *recognition.* If you compared how fast you relearned the correct names and how fast you learned another list, you would be using the *savings* (or *relearning*) method.

An overall conclusion: We respect Ebbinghaus as the pioneer who started scientific memory research. However, many memories are remembered far longer and better than Ebbinghaus's results implied. His memory was impaired by proactive interference and by dealing with meaningless and nondistinctive information.

## CONCEPT CHECK

3. Each of the following is an example of one method of testing memory. Identify each method.
   a. Although you thought you had completely forgotten your high school French, you do much better in your college French course than your roommate, who never had French in high school.
   b. You don't have a telephone directory and are trying to remember the phone number of the local pizza parlor.
   c. After witnessing a robbery, you have trouble describing the thief. The police show you several photographs and ask whether any of them was the robber.
   d. Your friend asks, "What's the name of our chemistry lab instructor? I think it's Julie or Judy something." (Check your answers on page 249.)

# The Information-Processing View of Memory

If you type at a computer, the computer shows three kinds of memory. First, if you type letters faster than they can appear on the screen, the computer will store a few letters in a temporary buffer until it can display them. (Many comput-

**TABLE 7.1 The Difference Between Recall and Cued Recall**

*Instructions:* First try to identify the author of each book listed in the left column while covering the right column (recall method). Then expose the right column, which gives each author's initials, and try again (cued recall).

| Book | Author |
| --- | --- |
| *Moby Dick* | H.M. |
| *Emma* and *Pride and Prejudice* | J.A. |
| Hercule Poirot stories | A.C. |
| Sherlock Holmes stories | A.C.D. |
| *I Know Why the Caged Bird Sings* | M.A. |
| *War and Peace* | L.T. |
| This book | J.K. |
| *Canterbury Tales* | G.C. |
| *The Origin of Species* | C.D. |
| *Gone with the Wind* | M.M. |
| *Les Miserables* | V.H. |

(For answers, see page 250, answer A.)

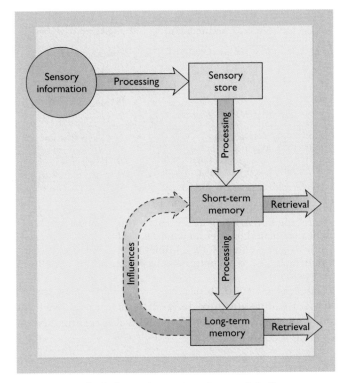

**FIGURE 7.6** The information-processing model of memory resembles a computer's memory system, including temporary and permanent memory.

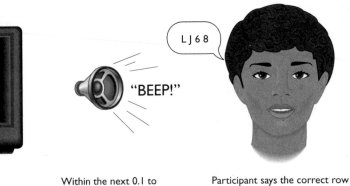

■   A bolt of lightning flashes through the sky for a split second, but you can visualize it in detail for a short time afterward. That image is held momentarily in your sensory store.

## The Sensory Store

 Try this: Close your eyes and turn your head so that you face toward something you haven't been looking at for the last few minutes. Then blink your eyes open and shut as quickly as possible. Immediately after that moment, you will have the impression that you can still "see in your mind's eye" a great deal of detail from what you just saw. However, if you try to describe all that detail, you will not do so well, mainly because the visual image fades faster than you can describe it. (It fades even faster if you look at something else instead of keeping your eyes shut.)

This *very brief storage of sensory information* is called the **sensory store,** also sometimes known as iconic memory. George Sperling (1960) found a way to demonstrate it experimentally. He flashed an array like the one shown in Figure 7.7 onto a screen for 50 milliseconds. When he asked viewers to report what they saw, he found that they could recall a mean of only about four items. If he had

ers today display so fast that you don't see this effect, but it was apparent on older models.) Second, the material you have written not yet saved to a disk is in random access memory (RAM). This material is vulnerable, as you learned if the power ever went off while you were writing something. Finally, you can save something to a disk. A hard disk or set of floppy disks can store vastly more information than RAM and is far less vulnerable. True, you could damage your disks but not as easily as you could turn off your RAM.

According to the **information-processing model** of memory, human memory is much like that of a computer: *Information enters the system, is processed and coded in various ways, and is then stored* (Figure 7.6). According to a popular version of this model, information first enters a sensory store (like the computer's buffer). Some of that information is stored in short-term memory (like RAM), and some of short-term memory is transferred into long-term memory (like a hard drive). Eventually, a cue from the environment causes the system to retrieve information from storage (Atkinson & Shiffrin, 1968). We shall examine each portion of this model.

Stimulus array flashed on screen for 0.05 seconds

Within the next 0.1 to 0.3 seconds, high, medium, or low tone signals indicate which row to say

Participant says the correct row

**FIGURE 7.7** George Sperling (1960) flashed arrays like this on a screen for 50 milliseconds. After the display went off, a signal told the viewer which row to recite.

stopped his experiment at that point, he might have concluded that viewers stored only a little of the array.

Sperling, however, surmised that the sensory store was probably fading while people were reporting their memories. So he told viewers he would ask them to report only one row of the array, a different row each time. After flashing an array on the screen, he immediately used a high, medium, or low tone to signal which row to recall. Most people could name all of the items in whichever row he indicated. Evidently, the whole array was briefly available to memory. When he waited for even 1 second before signaling which row to recall, though, recall was much worse. That is, for the sensory store, "use it or lose it," and you had better use it fast.

Is the sensory store really memory, or is it perception? It is a little of both. Not everything falls neatly into our human-made categories.

|  | Sensory store | Short-term memory | Long-term memory |
|---|---|---|---|
| Capacity | Whatever you see or hear at one instant | 7 ± 2 items in healthy adults | Vast, uncountable |
| Duration | Fraction of a second | About 20 seconds if not rehearsed | Perhaps a lifetime |
| Example | You see something for an instant, and then someone asks you to recall one detail | You look up a telephone number, remember it long enough to dial it | You remember the house where you lived when you were 7 years old |

**FIGURE 7.8** After about 1 second, you can no longer recall information from the sensory store. Short-term memories can be recalled up to about 20 seconds without rehearsal—much longer if you continually rehearse them. Long-term memories decline somewhat, especially at first, but you may be able to retrieve them for a lifetime. Your address from years ago is probably in your long-term memory and will continue to be for the rest of your life.

## CONCEPT CHECK

4. Would viewers probably remember as many items if Sperling had flashed pictures of objects instead of numbers and letters? (Check your answer on page 249)

**A STEP FURTHER**
*Sensory Storage*

Sperling demonstrated the capacity of the sensory store for visual information. How could you demonstrate the capacity of the sensory store for auditory information?

## Short-Term Memory and Long-Term Memory

Of all the vast information that passes through our sensory store, only a small amount catches our attention enough to be stored and processed. Of that information, some gets stored permanently and some fades away. According to the traditional version of information-processing theory, we distinguish between **short-term memory,** *temporary storage of the information that someone has just experienced,* and **long-term memory,** *a relatively permanent store of mostly meaningful information.* For example, while you are playing tennis, your memory of the current score is in your short-term memory; you know it now but you won't remember it later. Your memory for the rules of tennis are

in your long-term memory. Figure 7.8 compares the sensory store and short- and long-term memory. Short-term and long-term memory differ in several regards, as we shall now consider.

### Dependence on Retrieval Cues

If you try to recall a telephone number that you heard just seconds ago, presumably stored in your short-term memory, you recall it easily or not at all. You don't need reminders or hints, and if you have forgotten it, no hint or reminder will do you much good. In contrast, when you store something in long-term memory, you need a *retrieval cue* (or reminder) to find it later. For example, if someone asks you what *demand characteristics* are, you might say you have no idea. Then the person says, "I think they have something to do with research methods in psychology." Still you don't remember. "Do you remember something about an experiment in which people were really in an ordinary room, but they thought they were in sensory deprivation, so they reported hallucinations and panic and . . ." Suddenly, it all comes back to you and you remember the concept.

### Differences in Capacity

The capacity of long-term memory is so vast that we cannot easily measure it. Unlike computers, people do not fill their memories so full that they have no room for something new. (Of course, also unlike computers, people are constantly dumping some of their memories.) Short-term memory, in contrast, has a small capacity. Read each of the following sequences of letters and then look away and try to repeat them from memory. Or read each aloud and ask a friend to repeat it.

E H G P H

J R O Z N Q

S R B W R C N

M P D I W F B S

Z Y B P I A F M O

B O J F K F L T R C

X U G J D P F S V C L

FIGURE 7.9 Short-term memory is like a handful of eggs; it can hold only a limited number of items at a time.

Most normal adults can repeat a list of approximately seven letters, numbers, or words. Some people can remember eight or nine; others, only five or six. George Miller (1956) referred to the short-term memory capacity as "the magical number seven, plus or minus two." When people try to repeat a longer list, however, they may fail to remember even the first seven items. It is somewhat like trying to hold objects in one hand: If you try to hold too many, you drop them all (Figure 7.9).

The limit of seven can be increased or decreased a little. First, we can remember more short words than long words. Bilingual Welsh-English children can repeat a longer list of numbers in English than in Welsh (Ellis & Hennelley, 1980). The reason is that Welsh numbers are harder to pronounce—such as *pedwar* (5) and *chwech* (7). Similarly, it is easier to repeat a long list of numbers in Chinese than in German, again because the Chinese words are shorter (Lüer et al., 1998).

 Second, remember the problem of interference. One reason it is difficult to remember more than about seven numbers is that each number on the list interferes with other numbers on the list. Here are three lists of eight items each. If you have a cooperative roommate or friend, you might try reading the three lists to see which one is easiest to remember:

| 4 | 9 | 5 | 1 | 3 | 0 | 8 | 6 |
| 2 | 4 | 1 | 9 | 3 | hen | cow | pig |
| goose | cat | ox | pig | sheep | horse | dog | cow |

Most people do best with the second list, mixing numbers and one-syllable words (Young & Supa, 1941). Items of two kinds produce less interference with one another than a long list of just numbers or just animals.

Finally, people can best use their approximately seven-item capacity by making those items as large as possible.

For example, consider this string of letters:

Z I T H E R S

If you store that string as seven separate letters, you have already filled your seven-item capacity. However, if you think of it as two words, ZIT and HERS, you have used just two units and have five left. Or you might think of it as one word, ZITHERS, and have six units left. That is, you store more information if you can organize it into familiar *chunks*, or *meaningful units*. **Chunking** *is the process of grouping digits or letters into meaningful sequences* (see Figure 7.10).

With practice people can learn to recognize larger and larger chunks of numbers. One college student volunteered for a lengthy experiment (Ericsson, Chase, & Faloon, 1980). At the start he could repeat about seven digits at a time, the same as most people. Over a year and a half, working 3 to 5 hours per week, he gradually improved until he could repeat 80 digits, as shown in Figure 7.11, by using extraordinary strategies for chunking. He was a competitive runner, so he might store the sequence "3492..." as "3 minutes, 49.2 seconds, a near world-record time for running a mile." He might store the next set of numbers as a good time for running a kilometer, a mediocre marathon time, or a date in history. With practice he started recognizing larger and larger chunks. However, when he was tested on his ability to remember a list of letters, his performance was only average because he had not developed any chunking strategies for letters.

Chunking for short-term memory also helps us form long-term memories. With enough practice you could

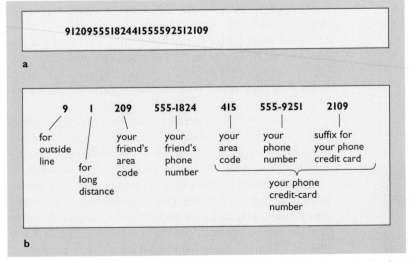

FIGURE 7.10 We overcome the limits of short-term memory through chunking. You probably could not remember the 26-digit number in (a), but by breaking it up into a series of chunks, you can remember it and dial the number correctly.

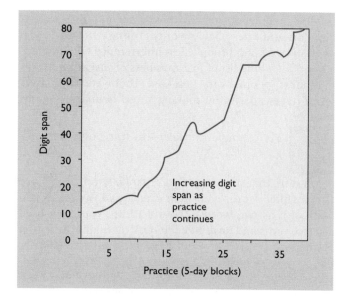

**FIGURE 7.11** Most people can repeat a list of about seven numbers. One college student gradually increased his ability to repeat a list of numbers over 18 months of practice. With practice he greatly expanded his short-term memory for digits but not for letters or words. (From Ericsson, Chase, & Faloon, 1980)

memorize the telephone number 18002255288, but it is easier to remember it as the chunks 1-800-CALL ATT.

## Decay of Short-Term Memories Over Time

People can forget long-term memories, but the mere passage of time (decay) does not necessarily weaken a well-established long-term memory. For example, if you hear a song you learned as a child but haven't heard since, you can recognize it immediately and sing along. Harry Bahrick (1984) tested people who had studied Spanish in school anywhere from 1 to 50 years previously. People who had studied it 1 or 2 years ago remembered more than those who had studied it 3 to 6 years ago, but beyond 6 years the retention appeared to be stable (Figure 7.12). In other words we do not completely forget old memories even if we seldom use them.

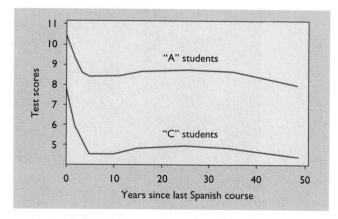

**FIGURE 7.12** Spanish vocabulary as measured by a recognition test shows a rapid decline in the first few years but then long-term stability. (From Bahrick, 1984)

In contrast, short-term memories disappear unless people continually rehearse them or unless they are sufficiently meaningful to get stored quickly into long-term memory. Lloyd Peterson and Margaret Peterson (1959) demonstrated the decay of short-term memory with a classic experiment that you can easily repeat if you coax a friend to cooperate. First, read aloud a meaningless sequence of letters, such as HOZDF. Then wait 10 seconds and ask your friend to repeat it. It is an easy task because your friend rehearsed those letters during the delay.

Forgetting will occur within seconds, however, if you prevent rehearsal. Say "I am going to read you a list of letters, such as HOZDF. Then I'm going to tell you a number, such as 231. When you hear the number, begin counting backward by threes: 231, 228, 225, 222, 219, and so on. When I tell you to stop, I'll ask you to repeat the sequence of letters." Record your data as in Table 7.2.

**TABLE 7.2**

| Letter Sequence | Starting Number | Delay in Seconds | Correct Recall? |
|---|---|---|---|
| BKLRE | 712 | 5 | |
| ZIWOJ | 380 | 10 | |
| CNVIU | 416 | 15 | |
| DSJGT | 289 | 20 | |
| NFMXS | 601 | 25 | |

 Try this experiment with several friends and compute the percentage of those who recalled the letters correctly after various delays. Figure 7.13 gives Peterson and Peterson's results. Note that only about 10% of their subjects could recall the letters correctly after 18 seconds. In other words, if we fail to rehearse something, a short-term memory will generally decay within 20 seconds or less.

However, people can hold short-term memories longer if they are more meaningful, and the results are quite different with extremely meaningful content. If you ask people to memorize "there is a poisonous snake under your chair," they will remember it well no matter how long they count backward by threes. Highly meaningful material enters long-term memory quickly.

Furthermore, Peterson and Peterson's experiment does not demonstrate an absolute distinction between short-term and long-term memory. Let's reconsider the demonstration: You read the letters BKLRE, asked someone to count backward by threes for 5 seconds, and then probably found that the person could recall the letters. After two more trials, you came to DSJGT and a 20-second delay, and the person probably could not recall it. But DSJGT was the fourth trial, potentially subject to a fair amount of proactive interference. Suppose you try this with another

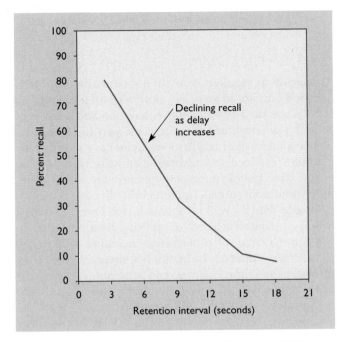

**FIGURE 7.13** In a study by Peterson and Peterson (1959), people remembered a set of letters well after a short delay, but their memory faded greatly over 20 seconds if they were prevented from rehearsing during that time.

volunteer, but now you *start* with DSJGT and a 20-second delay. Your new volunteer will probably remember DSJGT (Keppel & Underwood, 1962). Evidently, the forgetting of items stored in short-term memory depends partly on interference, as it does with long-term memory.

## CONCEPT CHECK

5. Name one way in which short-term memory and long-term memory are evidently different and one way in which they are similar. (Check your answers on page 250.)

### The Transfer from Short-Term Memory to Long-Term Memory

For many years psychologists thought of short-term memory and long-term memory as separate stages: Information first enters short-term memory and stays there for a while. If rehearsal kept it there long enough, it would **consolidate** to *form a long-term memory* (Figure 7.14).

But how long is long enough? There is no biological constant here. If someone tells you "you got an A on the test" or "you got the job you wanted," you store that information rapidly into long-term memory. If you try to memorize a long list of nonsense syllables, you need to work at it for vastly longer. Psychologists today are convinced that the time something stays in short-term memory has little or nothing to do with the formation of a long-term memory. Consolidation requires emotional

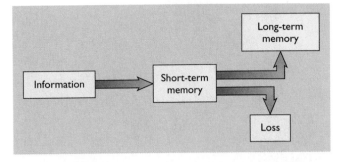

**FIGURE 7.14** According to the original conception of the relationship between short-term and long-term memory, if a short-term memory is rehearsed long enough, it becomes a long-term memory; without consolidation it is lost. This view is now considered oversimplified.

arousal, processing of the meaning, and development of connections with other stored memories. We shall return to this point in the next module.

## Working Memory

The original concept was that short-term memory is the way we store something just long enough to build a long-term storage. Today, researchers reconceptualize temporary memory storage as the information you are working with at the moment, regardless of whether you ever store it as a more permanent memory. Indeed, we frequently deal with information that we would not want to store permanently. While you are playing basketball, for example, you remember the score, the time left in the game, which player you are guarding, what strategy your team is using, how many fouls you have, and so forth. Even if you held all that information through a long time-out, or even the halftime break, it eventually becomes obsolete and you replace it with new information.

To emphasize this different perspective, researchers speak of *working* memory instead of short-term memory. **Working memory** is *a system for processing or working with current information*. It is almost synonymous with someone's current sphere of attention. Working memory includes at least three major components (Baddeley & Hitch, 1994):

• *A phonological loop,* which stores and rehearses speech information. The phonological loop, similar to the traditional view of short-term memory, enables us to repeat seven or so items immediately after hearing them. It is probably essential for anyone first learning a language (Baddeley, Gathercole, & Papagno, 1998). It is also essential for understanding a long sentence; you have to remember the words at the start of the sentence long enough to connect them to the words at the end.

• *A visuospatial sketchpad,* which stores and manipulates visual and spatial information, providing for vision what the phonological loop provides for speech (Luck & Vogel,

■ Kutbidin Atamkulov travels from one Central Asian village to another singing from memory the tale of the Kirghiz hero, Manas. The song, which lasts 3 hours, has been passed from master to student for centuries. Human memory can hold an amazing amount of information.

1997). You would use this process for recognizing pictures or for imagining what an object looks like from another angle.

Researchers distinguish between the phonological and visuospatial stores because you can do an auditory word task and a visuospatial task at the same time without much interference, but not two auditory tasks or two visuospatial tasks (Baddeley & Hitch, 1974; Hale, Myerson, Rhee, Weiss, & Abrams, 1996). People may have additional stores for touch, smell, and taste, but so far researchers have concentrated mostly on the auditory and visual stores.

• *A central executive,* which governs shifts of attention. The hallmark of good working memory is the ability to shift attention as needed between two or more tasks. Recall the basketball example from a moment ago: When you shift back and forth between offense and defense, you have different items to remember. Or imagine a hospital nurse who has to keep track of the needs of several patients, sometimes interrupting the treatment of one patient to take care of an emergency and then returning to complete the interrupted task.

Here are a couple of demonstrations of attentional factors or central executive processes. First, I might read you a list of words such as *maple, elm, oak, hemlock, chestnut, birch, sycamore, pine, redwood, walnut, dogwood, hickory.* After each word you are supposed to say the *previous* word. So after I say "maple, elm," you should say "maple." Then I say "oak" and you reply "elm." If you do well on that task, I make it a step more difficult: You should repeat what I said *two* words ago. So you wait for "maple, elm, oak," and reply "maple." Then I say "hemlock" and you reply "elm." Note how you need to shift back and forth between listening to the new word and repeating something from memory.

Second example: I flash on the screen a simple arithmetic question and a word, such as

Is (2 × 3) + 1 = 8? spring

As quickly as possible, you should read the arithmetic question, answer it *yes* or *no,* and then say the word. As soon as you do, I display another question and word. I repeat this a few times and then ask you to say all the words you saw in order. To do well you have to shift your attention between the arithmetic and the words. Some people have trouble remembering even two words under these conditions; others can remember five or six.

People who do well on this task (who are considered to have a "high capacity" of working memory) also do well on a variety of other tasks, including intelligence tests (Engle, Tuholski, Laughlin, & Conway, 1999). They do better than most other people at naming as many animals as possible in 10 minutes and at learning several consecutive word lists without confusing one with another—that is, they minimize the effects of proactive interference. Interestingly, if people have to perform an additional constantly distracting task, such as tapping a rhythm with their fingers, everyone's performance suffers, but those with the best working memory suffer the most (Kane & Engle, 2000; Rosen & Engle, 1997). They still perform better than people with less working memory, but not by as much as usual. Of course, one reason is that those with poor working memory weren't doing well anyway, so they had less room to get worse. Another explanation is that people with good working memory usually do well because they direct their attention to the important aspects of the task. With a constant distractor, they lose that advantage.

## CONCEPT CHECK

6. Some students like to listen to music while studying. Is the music likely to help or impair their study? (What might the answer depend on?) (Check your answer on page 250.)

## Other Memory Distinctions

Later in this chapter, we shall encounter the distinction between declarative memories and procedural memories. A *declarative memory* is the ability to state a fact; a *procedural memory* is a skill, a memory of how to do something. Certain kinds of brain damage impair declarative memory without damaging procedural memories. That is, a man who forgets his address and telephone number may nevertheless remember how to tie his shoes and how to ride a bicycle.

Psychologists also find it useful to distinguish between two kinds of long-term declarative memory—**semantic memory,** *memory of general principles,* and **episodic memory,** *memory for specific events in a person's life, gener-*

*ally including details of when and where they happened* (Tulving, 1989). For example, your memory of the rules of tennis is a semantic memory; your memory of the most recent time you played tennis is an episodic memory. Your memory of the periodic table of chemistry is a semantic memory; your recollection of breaking a test tube in a chemistry lab is an episodic memory.

Episodic memories are in many cases more fragile than semantic memories. For example, people sometimes remember a statement they have heard (a semantic memory) but forget when, where, and from whom they heard it (an episodic memory). That phenomenon is known as **source amnesia,** *remembering the content but not the context of learning it.* Because of source amnesia, people sometimes confuse reliable information with the unreliable: "Did I hear this idea from my professor or was it on *South Park*? Did I read about brain transplants in *Scientific American* or in the *National Enquirer?*" As a result you might dismiss an idea at first ("Oh, that's just a rumor!" or "Oh, that's just my nutty roommate's idea!") but later remember the idea, forget where you heard it, and start to take it seriously (Johnson, Hashtroudi, & Lindsay, 1993; Riccio, 1994). For this reason we experience the *sleeper effect* discussed in Chapter 14—minimal influence at first from a weak source, but sometimes increased persuasion later.

## CONCEPT CHECK

7. Is your memory of your current mailing address a semantic memory or an episodic memory? What about your memories of the day you moved to your current address? (Check your answers on page 250.)

### IN CLOSING
## Varieties of Memory

Although researchers still disagree with one another on many points about memory, they do agree about what memory is *not*: Memory is not a single store into which we simply dump things and later take them out. When Ebbinghaus conducted his studies of memory in the late 1800s, he thought he was measuring the properties of memory, period. We now know that the properties of memory depend on the type of material being memorized, the individual's experience with similar materials, the method of testing, and the recency of the event. Memory is not one process, but many.

## Summary

- **Ebbinghaus's approach.** Hermann Ebbinghaus pioneered the experimental study of memory by testing his own ability to memorize and retain lists of non-

sense syllables. Although the general principles he reported were valid, his measurements of the speed of learning and forgetting do not apply to all memory. (page 239)
- **Variations in memory strength.** People remember material best if they have minimal interference from similar materials, if the material is distinctive, and if the method of testing is capable of detecting a weak memory. (page 240)
- **The information-processing model.** Psychologists distinguish among various types of memory. According to the information-processing model of memory, information first enters a sensory store, then becomes a short-term memory and finally a long-term memory. (page 242)
- **Memory capacity.** Short-term memory has a capacity of only about seven items in normal adults, although chunking can enable us to store much information in each item. Long-term memory has a very large, not easily measured capacity. (page 244)
- **Weaknesses of the traditional information-processing model.** Contrary to what psychologists once believed, how long an item remains in short-term memory is a poor predictor of whether it will enter long-term memory. (page 247)
- **Working memory.** As an alternative to the traditional description of short-term memory, most current researchers identify working memory as a system for storing and processing several kinds of current information. The distinctive feature of good working memory is the ability to shift attention back and forth among several tasks as necessary. (page 247)
- **Semantic and episodic memories.** An additional distinction can be drawn between semantic memories (memories of general principles) and episodic memories (memories of personal experiences). In most cases episodic memories are more fragile and more easily lost or distorted. (page 248)

## Answers to Concept Checks

1. It is due to proactive interference—interference from memories learned earlier. Much of the difficulty of retrieving long-term memories is due to proactive interference. (page 241)
2. First, the subject learns the response; second, the subject learns the extinction of the response. If the first learning proactively interferes with the later learning, spontaneous recovery will result. (page 241)
3. **a.** savings; **b.** recall; **c.** recognition; **d.** cued recall. (page 242)
4. If we assume that it would take longer to name objects than numbers or letters, people would probably name fewer. The longer it takes for people to answer, the more their sensory store fades. (page 244)

5. Short-term memory has a limited capacity of about seven items in normal adults, whereas long-term memory has an extremely large capacity (difficult to estimate). Both short-term memory and long-term memories are more rapidly forgotten in the presence of interference. (page 247)

6. If the music requires any attention at all or evokes any response, such as occasionally singing along, it will impair attention. The difference will be most noticeable for the best students. However, background music with no words and no tendency to evoke responses is probably a slight benefit if it prevents the student from noticing other sounds that might be more distracting. (page 248)

7. Your memory of your current address is a semantic memory. Your memory of the events of moving day is an episodic memory. (page 249)

## Answer to Other Questions in the Module

A. Hermann Melville, Jane Austen, Agatha Christie, Arthur Conan Doyle, Maya Angelou, Leo Tolstoy, James Kalat, Geoffrey Chaucer, Charles Darwin, Margaret Mitchell, Victor Hugo. (page 242)

# Memory Improvement

*How can we improve our memories?*

There you are, sitting in class taking a geography test, unable to remember the major rivers of Africa. You remember reviewing that section in your book last night; you even remember that it was on the upper left side of the page, and there was a diagram to the right. You even remember the cappuccino you were sipping as you were studying. And the time was 9:30 P.M. You just don't remember the names of the rivers.

Why do we sometimes remember so much useless information while forgetting what we need to know? And how can we improve our memory? The short answer is, to improve your memory, improve the way you store the material in the first place. The rest of this module elaborates on this point.

## The Influence of Emotional Arousal

People usually remember emotionally arousing events. Chances are you vividly remember your first day of college, your first kiss, the time your team won the big game, and times when you were extremely frightened or extremely

■ Do you remember the first time you saw a comet? Most people recall emotionally arousing events, sometimes in great detail, although not always accurately.

excited. You forget most of the countless unexciting events of your life. Think about this: Of all the high school and college courses you have taken, which were the most interesting or exciting to you? And which ones do you remember most clearly? Are they the same courses?

The effects of arousal on memory have been known for centuries. In England in the early 1600s, when people sold land, they did not yet have the custom of recording the sale on paper. (Paper was expensive and most people were illiterate anyway.) Instead, residents of the area would gather together in a ceremony; someone announced the sale and instructed everyone to remember it. Of all those present, whose ability to remember the sale was most important? The children, because they would live the longest. And of all those present, who were least interested? Right, again, it's the children. To increase the chances that the children would remember, the adults would kick them while telling them about the business deal. (Avoiding such abuse is just another of the many benefits of literacy.)

Although emotional intensity increases the vividness and intensity of a memory, unfortunately it does not guarantee the memory's accuracy. Many people report "flashbulb" memories of where they were, what they were doing, or even the weather at the time they heard shocking news, such as the assassination of a political leader. One investigator asked English people to remember the moment they first heard about the Hillsborough football disaster, when a stampede of fans trying to enter the stadium crushed 95 people to death. Many people claimed to have clear recollections of the moment when they first heard the news. However, when the same people were reinterviewed, the "clear, vivid" memories they later reported were not always the same as what they reported originally (D. B. Wright, 1993). Thus, emotionally charged memories are subject to distortion, just as other memories are.

Why are emotionally arousing events generally so memorable? The physiological explanation is that emotional arousal increases the release of the hormones cortisol and epinephrine (adrenaline) from the adrenal gland. Some of the cortisol gets to the brain. The epinephrine does not, but it stimulates peripheral nerves that extend into the brain. The net effect is increased excitation of certain brain areas that enhance memory storage, including an area called the *amygdala* (Cahill & McGaugh, 1998; Williams, Men, Clayton, & Gold, 1998). After damage to the amygdala, people can still learn, but they don't remember emotionally exciting events any better than ordinary ones (LaBar & Phelps, 1998).

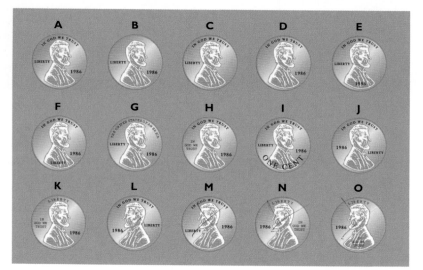

## CONCEPT CHECK

8. Most people with posttraumatic stress disorder have lower than normal levels of cortisol. What would you predict about their memory? (Check your answer on page 257)

# Meaningful Storage and Levels of Processing

If you want to memorize something, such as a definition, you might try repeating it many times. Other things being equal, repetition does aid memory, but other things are seldom equal, and repetition without careful attention is a poor way to learn.

**FIGURE 7.15** Can you spot the genuine penny among 14 fakes? (Based on Nickerson & Adams, 1979) If you're not sure (and you don't have a penny with you), check answer B on page 257.

To illustrate: Examine Figure 7.15, which shows a real U.S. penny and 14 fakes. If you live in the United States, you have seen pennies countless times, but can you now identify the real one? Most U.S. citizens cannot (Nickerson & Adams, 1979). (If you do not have a penny in your pocket, check answer B on page 257. If you are not from the United States, try drawing the front and back of a common coin in your own country.) In short, mere repetition, such as looking at a coin many times, does not guarantee a strong memory.

According to the **levels-of-processing principle** (Craik & Lockhart, 1972), *how easily we can retrieve a memory depends on the number and types of associations we form.* When you read something—this chapter, for example—you might simply read over the words, giving them little thought. In that case you have engaged in shallow pro-

cessing, and you will remember little or nothing at test time. Alternatively, you might stop and think about various points that you read, relate them to your own experiences, and think of your own examples of the principles discussed. The more ways you think about the material, the deeper your processing is and the more easily you will remember it later. Table 7.3 summarizes this model.

As an example, imagine several groups of students who study a list of words in several ways. One group simply reads the list over and over, and a second counts the letters in each word. Both procedures produce superficial processing and poor recall later. A third group tries to think of a synonym for each word or tries to use each word in a sentence. As the students think about the words, they store them at a deeper level of processing, so they will recall them better than the first two groups. Students in the fourth group try to relate each word to themselves: "How does this apply to me? What experiences do I remember that relate to this word?" This group does even better than the third group. For a while psychologists thought that relating words to yourself produces a special kind of strengthening, but later research found equally strong memories in students who tried to relate each word to

■ Most actors prepare for a play by spending much time thinking about the meaning of what they say (a deep level of processing) and spending only a little time simply repeating the words (a shallow level of processing).

**TABLE 7.3 Levels-of-Processing Model of Memory**

| Superficial processing | Simply repeat the material to be remembered: "Hawk, Oriole, Tiger, Timberwolf, Blue Jay, Bull." |
|---|---|
| Deeper processing | Think about each item. Note that two start with T and two with B. |
| Still deeper processing | Note that three are birds and three are mammals. Also, three are major league baseball teams and three are NBA basketball teams. Use whichever associations means the most to you. |

their mothers (Symons & Johnson, 1997). The conclusion is that memory grows stronger when people elaborate and organize the material and relate it to whatever they know and care about. Because doing so requires attention and effort, absolutely any kind of distraction interferes with storing new memories (Fernandes & Moscovitch, 2000).

You can improve your level of processing in two ways (Einstein & Hunt, 1980; McDaniel, Einstein, & Lollis, 1988): First, you can think about the items on the list one by one. Second, you can look for relationships among the items. You might notice, for example, that the list consists of five animals, six foods, four methods of transportation, and five objects made of wood. One of the skills we gain through education is learning to organize material in this way. According to one study of the Kpelle people in West Africa, teenage children who had gone to school organized a list of words into categories, such as foods, types of clothing, and hunting materials. Unschooled children did not sort the list into categories and generally did not remember the words very well (Scribner, 1974).

## CONCEPT CHECK

9. Many of the best students in a course (those who get the best grades) read the assigned text chapters more slowly than average. Why?
10. Most actors and public speakers who have to memorize lengthy passages spend little time simply repeating the words and more time thinking about them. Why? (Check your answers on page 257.)

## The Timing of Study Sessions

Researchers have known since the time of Ebbinghaus that the timing of study greatly influences recall. If you read a list of 20 words and try to recall them, you will best remember *the items at the beginning and end of the list.* That tendency, known as the **serial-order effect,** includes two aspects: The *primacy effect* is the tendency to remember well the first items. It is partly explained by the fact that you could rehearse the first few items by themselves without any proactive interference from previous items. The *recency effect* is the tendency to remember well the final items. One reason is that the final items are not subject to retroactive interference.

Recency is important not just for remembering items on a list, but for remembering almost anything. If you try to list all the people you have ever dated or all the times you have been to the beach or all the movies you have ever seen or any other series of events, you will probably include the most recent one.

Because recency improves memory, it is helpful to review material shortly before any test. But what about original learning? Should you study something all at once, perhaps the day before the test, or would it be better to study a little at a time over a longer period?

Psychologists' answer here is clear: Spread out your study. Imagine yourself in the following study: A three-letter combination appears on a computer screen. It might be a word like BUG or an unpronounceable, meaningless combination like FXH. You are instructed to study it for as long as you want—absolutely no rush—until you are sure you will be able to recall it later. There will be 27 such three-letter combinations. Take your time with each one. Don't proceed until you are sure you have learned it well, then press the key to go on to the next item. At the end, theoretically you should get them all correct. However, when this study was actually conducted, the average student recalled only 49% of them (Nelson & Leonesio, 1988). Two conclusions follow: (1) People are often poor judges of how well they have learned something. While you are staring at something, you may have a vivid short-term memory and a strong conviction that you will remember it later, but you may be wrong (Maki & Serra, 1992; Weaver & Kelemen, 1997). (2) Just studying something once is seldom effective, even if you study it very hard that one time. Students would have done better if they could have gone through the list once, paused, gone through it again, rested again, reviewed, and so forth.

Furthermore, refreshers spread out over a long time are an excellent way to strengthen a memory. Psychologist Harry Bahrick and members of his family studied foreign-language vocabulary, varying the frequency of study. Some had a study session every 2 weeks; others studied the same number of hours but spread out over longer times, such as once every 8 weeks. The result: More frequent study led to

■ People need to monitor their understanding of a text to decide whether to continue studying or whether they already understand it well enough. Most readers have trouble making that judgment correctly.

**FIGURE 7.16** According to the principle of encoding specificity, the way we code a word during original learning determines which cues will remind us of that word later. For example, when you hear the word *queen*, you may think of that word in any of several ways. If you think of *queen bee*, then the cue *playing card* will not remind you of it later. If you think of the *queen of England*, then *chess piece* will not be a good reminder.

faster learning, but less frequent study led to better long-term retention, as measured years later (Bahrick, Bahrick, Bahrick, & Bahrick, 1993).

Results of many other studies confirm the same general principle: If you want to remember something in the long term, you should study and review under varying conditions with substantial intervals between study sessions (Schmidt & Bjork, 1992). *One systematic way to organize your study* is the **SPAR method:**

**S**urvey. Get an overview of what the passage is about. Scan through it; look at the boldface headings; try to understand the organization or goals of the passage.

**P**rocess meaningfully. Read the material carefully. Think about how you could use the ideas or how they relate to other things you have read. Evaluate the strengths and weaknesses of the argument. The more actively you think about what you read, the better you will remember the material.

**A**sk questions. If the text provides questions, like the Concept Checks in this text, try to answer them. Then pretend you are the instructor; write the questions you would ask on a test and answer them yourself. In the process you will discover which sections of the passage you need to reread.

**R**eview. Wait a day or so and then retest your knowledge. Spreading out your study over time increases your ability to remember it over the long term.

## CONCEPT CHECK

11. If you want to do well on the final exam in this course, what should you do now—review this chapter or review the first three chapters in the book? (Check your answers on page 257.)

# The Use of Special Coding Strategies

A librarian who places a new book on the shelf also enters some information into the retrieval system so that anyone who knows the title, author, or topic can find the book. Similarly, when you store a memory, you store it in terms of **retrieval cues,** *associated information that might help you regain the memory later*. We shall examine two illustrations of retrieval cues: the encoding specificity principle and the use of mnemonic devices.

## Encoding Specificity

When you learn something, the associations you form at the time can remind you of the material later. According to the **encoding specificity principle** (Tulving & Thomson, 1973), *the associations you form at the time of learning will be the most effective retrieval cues* (Figure 7.16). In fact, everything happening to you at that time becomes a potential retrieval cue for later.

 Here is an example (modified from Thieman, 1984). First, read the pairs of words (in psychological jargon *paired associates*) in Table 7.4a. Then turn to Table 7.4b on page 256. For each of the words on that list, try to recall a related word on the list you just read. *Do this now.* (The answers are on page 257, answer C.)

**TABLE 7.4a**

| |
|---|
| Clergyman—Cardinal |
| Trinket—Charm |
| Social event—Ball |
| Shrubbery—Bush |
| Inches—Feet |
| Take a test—Pass |
| Weather—Fair |
| Geometry—Plane |
| Tennis—Racket |
| Stone—Rock |
| Magic—Spell |
| Envelope—Seal |
| Cashiers—Checkers |

Most people find this task difficult. Because they initially coded the word *cardinal* as a type of clergyman, for example, they do not think of it when they see the retrieval cue *bird*. If they had thought of it as a bird, then *clergyman* would not have been a good reminder.

The principle of encoding specificity extends to other aspects of experience at the time of storage. When animals learn something in one location, they often forget it if tested in another (Bouton, Nelson, & Rosas, 1999). Chances are, some of the information you think you have forgotten from high school or earlier would come back if you returned to the room where you learned it.

In one study college students who were fluent in both English and Russian were given a list of words such as *summer, birthday, doctor, newborn,* and *contest,* some in English and some in Russian. For each word they were asked to describe any related event they remembered. In response to Russian words, they recalled mostly events that happened when they were speaking Russian. In response to English words, they recalled mostly events when they were speaking English (Marian & Neisser, 2000).

Another example: If you experience something while you are in a particular mood, you are somewhat more likely to think of it again when you are in the same mood (Bower, 1994). For example, when you are sad, you remember even small details from other times you were sad. After your mood improves, you will find it more difficult to remember those same events, and pretending to be sad won't help (Eich & Macaulay, 2000).

If you learn something while under the influence of a drug, such as a tranquilizer, you will probably remember it more easily when you take that drug again than at other times. **State-dependent memory** is *the tendency to remember something better if your body is in the same condition during recall as it was during the original learning.* State-dependent memory is usually a small effect, but it can be seen if an experimenter measures carefully.

The encoding specificity principle has a couple of clear implications. First, if you want to remember something at a particular time and place, make your study conditions as similar as possible to the conditions when you will try to remember the material. Everything that is present at the time of study is a potential retrieval cue. You might even study in the same room where you will take a test, at approximately the same time of day. On the other hand, if you want to remember the material for life, under a wide variety of conditions, then you should vary your study habits. Study the material at many times, in many places, and think about it in many ways. The more associations you form, the more retrieval cues will help you recall the information later.

A parachute lets you coast down slowly, like the parasympathetic nervous system.

### CONCEPT CHECK

**12.** A section earlier in this module (page 253) recommended spreading out your study over a long time instead of doing it all at one sitting. How does that advice fit with the encoding specificity principle? (Check your answer on page 257.)

## Mnemonic Devices

If you needed to memorize something lengthy and not especially exciting—for example, a list of all the bones in the body—how would you do it? One effective strategy is to attach systematic retrieval cues to each term so that you can remind yourself of the terms when you need them.

A **mnemonic device** is *any memory aid that is based on encoding each item in a special way.* The word *mnemonic* (nee-MAHN-ik) comes from a Greek root meaning "memory." (The same root appears in the word *amnesia,* "lack of memory.")

Mnemonic devices come in many varieties. Some are simple, such as thinking up a little saying that reminds you of each item to be remembered, such as "Every Good Boy Does Fine" to remember the notes EGBDF on the musical staff. If you have to remember the functions of various brain areas, you might try links like the ones shown in Figure 7.17 (Carney & Levin, 1998).

If the symphony excites you, it arouses your sympathetic nervous system.

**FIGURE 7.17** A simple mnemonic device is to think of a short story or image that will remind you of what you need to remember. Here you might think of images to help remember functions of different brain areas.

Suppose you had to memorize a list of Nobel Peace Prize winners (Figure 7.18). You might try making up a little story: "Dun (Dunant) passed (Passy) the Duke (Ducommun) of Gob (Gobat) some cream (Cremer). That made him internally ILL (Institute of International Law). He suited (von Suttner) up with some roses (Roosevelt) and spent some money (Moneta) on a Renault (Renault) . . ." You'd still have to study the names, but your story might help.

Nobel Peace Prize Winners

| | |
|---|---|
| 1901 | H. Dunant and F. Passy |
| 1902 | E. Ducommun and A. Gobat |
| 1903 | Sir W. R. Cremer |
| 1904 | Institute of International Law |
| 1905 | Baroness von Suttner |
| 1906 | T. Roosevelt |
| 1907 | E. T. Moneta and L. Renault |
| 1908 | K. P. Arnoldson and F. Bajer |
| 1909 | A. M. F. Beernaert and Baron d'Estournelles de Constant |

| | |
|---|---|
| 1990 | M. Gorbachev |
| 1991 | A. S. Suu Kyi |
| 1992 | Rigoberta Menchú |
| 1993 | Nelson Mandela and Frederik W. de Klerk |
| 1994 | Yasir Arafat, Yitzhak Rabin, and Shimon Peres |
| 1995 | Joseph Rotblat and Pugwash Conferences on Science and World Affairs |
| 1996 | Carlos Felipe Ximenes Belo and José Ramos-Horta |
| 1997 | Jody Williams and International Committee to Ban Landmines |
| 1998 | John Hume and David Trimble |
| 1999 | Doctors Without Borders |
| 2000 | Kim Dae Jung |

**FIGURE 7.18** A list of Nobel Peace Prize winners: Mnemonic devices can be useful when people try to memorize long lists like this one.

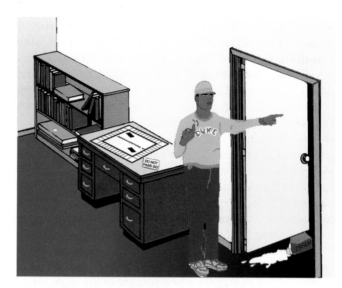

**FIGURE 7.19** The method of loci is one of the oldest mnemonic devices. First, learn a list of places, such as "my desk, the door of my room, the corridor, . . ." Then link each of these places to the items on a list of words or names, such as a list of the names of Nobel Peace Prize winners.

Another effective mnemonic device is the **method of loci** (method of places). *First, you memorize a series of places, and then you use a vivid image to associate each of these locations with something you want to remember.* For example, you might start by memorizing every location along the route from your dormitory room to, say, your psychology classroom. Then you link the locations, in order, to the names.

Suppose the first three locations you pass are the desk in your room, the door to your room, and the corridor. You should first form a mental image linking the first pair of Nobel Peace Prize winners, Dunant and Passy, to the first location, your desk. You might imagine a Monopoly game board on your desk, with a big sign "DO NOT (Dunant) PASS (Passy) GO." Then you link the second pair of names to the second location, your door: A DUKE student (as in Ducommun) is standing at the door, giving confusing signals. He says "DO COME IN (Ducommun)" and "GO BACK (Gobat)." Then you link the corridor to Cremer, perhaps by imagining someone has spilled CREAM (Cremer) all over the floor (Figure 7.19). You continue in this manner until you have linked every name to a location. Now, if you can remember all those locations in order and if you have good visual images for each one, you will be able to recite the list of Nobel Peace Prize winners.

A similar device is the **peg method.** *You start by memorizing a list of objects, such as "One is a bun, two is a shoe, three is a tree, . . ." Then you form mental images to link the names with these peg words,* just as you would with the method of loci. For example, for number one, "I ate a BUN at the DUNE PASS (Dunant, Passy)," imagining *dune pass* as a passageway between sand dunes. Later, you use all your peg words to help you remember the list of names. To use mnemonic devices well, you need to be clever and resourceful in producing images. (What image can you devise for Nobel Peace Prize winner Mikhail Gorbachev?)

How useful are elaborate mnemonic devices? Learning to use mnemonics takes some time and effort, but the rewards are substantial for someone who wants to memorize long lists. Some people find mnemonics useful for remembering people's names. (For example, you might remember someone named Harry Moore by picturing

**TABLE 7.4b**

*Instructions:* For each of these words, write a related word that you remember from the *second column* of the list in Table 7.4a

Exhibition—

Animal—

Part of Body—

Transportation—

Football—

Crime—

U.S. politician—

Music—

Personality—

Write—

Bird—

Board game—

Sports—

him as "more hairy" than everyone else.) Few people find mnemonics useful for everyday tasks such as remembering where you parked your car, but mnemonics can be helpful in their proper place.

## IN CLOSING
## Improving Our Memory

We often speak of "storing" and "retrieving" memories as if we were putting items on a shelf and then taking them off. For some purposes this analogy is satisfactory, but don't take it too seriously. The more you know about something and the more interested you become, the easier it is to establish new memories and find them when you need them. It is as though putting a certain kind of item on your "shelf" makes it easier to add more items of the same kind.

## Summary

- **Emotional arousal.** Emotionally exciting events tend to be remembered vividly, if not always accurately. (page 251)
- **Levels-of-processing principle.** According to the levels-of-processing principle, a memory becomes stronger (and easier to recall) if we think about the meaning of the material and relate it to other material. (page 252)
- **Timing of study.** If you study all at one time, you cannot be sure how much you have learned and how much you will forget. It is best to spread out the study, and the more you spread it out, the longer you are likely to remember it. (page 253)
- **Encoding specificity.** When we form a memory, we store it with links to the way we thought about it at that time. When we try to recall the memory, a cue is most effective if it is similar to the links we formed at the time of storage. (page 254)
- **Mnemonics.** Specialized techniques for establishing systematic retrieval cues can help people remember ordered lists of names or terms. (page 255)

## Answers to Concept Checks

8. Because of the lower cortisol levels, they should have trouble storing memories and therefore report frequent memory lapses. (page 252)
9. Students who read slowly and frequently pause to think about the meaning of the material are engaging in deep processing and are likely to remember the material well, probably better than those who read through the material quickly. (page 253)
10. Simply repeating the words would produce a shallow level of processing and poor retention. A more efficient means of memorizing is to spend most of one's

time thinking about the meaning of the speech and only a little time memorizing the words. (page 253)

11. To prepare well for the final exam, you should review all the material at irregular intervals. Thus, you might profit by skimming over Chapters 2 and 3 right now. Of course, if you have a test on Chapter 7 in a day or two, your goal is different and your strategy should be different. (page 254)
12. If you study all at one sitting, the memory will be encoded specifically to the time and place of that study, the other things you are thinking about at that moment, and other temporary details. If you study at several times, the memory will attach to a greater variety of retrieval cues instead of being specific to just one set. (page 255)

## Answers to Other Questions in the Module

**B.** The correct coin is A. (page 252)
**C.** (page 256)
Exhibition—Fair
Animal—Seal
Part of body—Feet
Transportation—Plane
Football—Pass
Crime—Racket
U.S. politician—Bush
Music—Rock
Personality—Charm
Write—Spell
Bird—Cardinal
Board game—Checkers
Sports—Ball

# Memory Loss

Suppose you defied all the advice given to computer owners and passed your computer through a powerful magnetic field. Chances are you would erase its memory completely, but suppose you found that you had erased just the text files and not the graphics files. Or suppose the old memories were intact but you could no longer store new ones. From the damage you would find hints about how your computer's memory works.

The same is true of human memory. Various kinds of brain damage impair one kind of memory and not another, enabling us to draw inferences about how memory is organized.

## Normal Forgetting

Pick your favorite type of meal. I'm going to imagine that you said pizza, but substitute whatever else you wish. If you try to list all the pizza meals you can remember, you will probably start with several recent ones and then add some especially interesting or unusual meals from long ago. Any very old memories you can still recall now will probably stay with you indefinitely. That is, most memories fade rapidly, but the longer you have held onto one, the less it fades. The overall trend of memory and forgetting looks approximately as shown in the following diagram (Rubin & Wenzel, 1996). The family of curves shows that the rate of forgetting varies among individuals and even among situations for a given individual. Nevertheless, the shape of the curve is consistent.

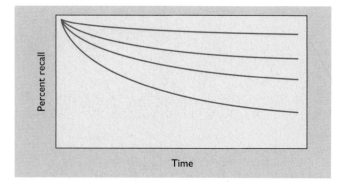

Why do we forget? Let us review the possibilities already discussed in this chapter. One explanation is interference. For example, sports fans will forget most of the details of games they saw last year, largely because of interference from memories of other games before and since.

■ Bob Williams was one of 40 aging former paratroopers who reenacted his parachute jump on the 50th anniversary of D day. Ordinarily, we forget most events from 50 years ago. However, this was a very distinctive, emotionally arousing event, followed by very few other experiences that were similar enough to produce interference. Returning to the scene of the original jump provides contextual cues that would help to retrieve the memory.

A second possibility is that memory traces gradually decay, like old photographs that fade in the sunlight. The effects of decay and interference are difficult to disentangle experimentally. That is, during any delay a memory is subject to the effects of both time and interference from other experiences. Nevertheless, researchers have considered decay a likely explanation of forgetting from working memory or short-term memory, and we can demonstrate the decay just by distracting people for a few seconds and noting how much they forget. It is not clear that long-term memories decay because we retain many long-term memories for events we haven't thought about in years.

A third possible explanation is that memories seem to be forgotten because we no longer have the appropriate retrieval cues. For example, if you learned certain facts in an eighth-grade geography class, the retrieval cues included the context—when and where you learned them (the classroom, the city, the other students around you). If you try to remember these facts years later, you no longer have the contextual cues to help remind you. Sometimes, if people return to the place where they learned something (at least in their imagination), they remember information they thought they had forgotten.

You are, of course, most likely to forget anything that you did not pay attention to when it happened. Sometimes you can attend to some aspects of the information and not others and therefore remember only certain parts. For example, people often remember an idea and forget where they heard it—the phenomenon of source amnesia, as mentioned on page 249. Have you ever told someone a joke or perhaps a bit of gossip only to have that person say, "Yes, I was the one who told *you* that"? In one experiment students sat in a group trying to think of solutions to a problem. A week later each student was asked separately to think of new solutions. Many of them offered, as their own "original" idea, something that they had heard another student suggest the previous week (Marsh, Landau, & Hicks, 1997). They had simply forgotten where they got the idea. The result is unintentional plagiarism: More often than we realize, we claim an idea to be new, not remembering that we first heard it from someone else.

# CONCEPT CHECK

13. List three common reasons for forgetting and specify which one applies more to short-term than long-term memory. (Check your answers on page 265)

# Amnesia After Brain Damage

In contrast to normal forgetting, **amnesia** is a *severe loss or deterioration of memory.* Even in the most severe cases, people don't forget everything they ever learned. For example, they don't forget how to walk and talk or how to eat at the table. The specific deficits of amnesic patients tell us much about the distinctions among the various types of memory. We shall consider amnesia based on several types of brain damage, plus amnesia of infancy and old age.

## Hippocampal Damage

In 1953 a man with the initials H. M. was subjected to unusual brain surgery in an attempt to control his severe epilepsy. Unresponsive to antiepileptic drugs, H. M. had suffered severe seizures almost every day. In desperation surgeons removed most of his **hippocampus,** *a large forebrain structure in the interior of the temporal lobe* (Figure 7.20), where they believed his epileptic seizures were originating. They also removed some surrounding brain areas. At the time researchers had not studied hippocampal damage in any species and they did not know what to expect.

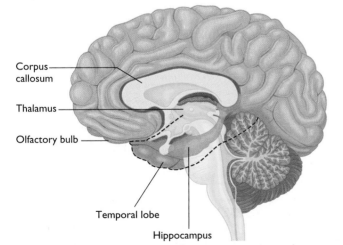
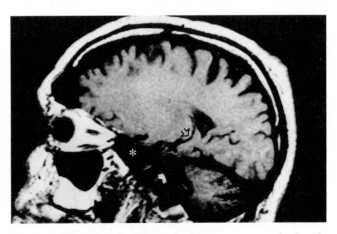

**FIGURE 7.20** (a) The hippocampus is a large subcortical structure of the brain. (b) After damage to the hippocampus and related structures, patient H. M. had great difficulty storing new long-term memories. The photo shows a scan of the brain of H. M. formed by magnetic resonance imaging. The asterisk indicates the area from which the hippocampus is missing. The arrow indicates a portion of the hippocampus that is preserved. (Photo courtesy of Suzanne Corkin and David Amaral)

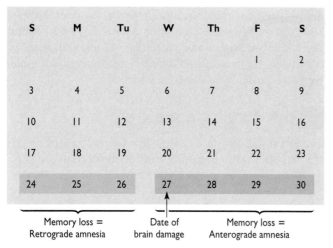

| S | M | Tu | W | Th | F | S |
|---|---|----|---|----|---|---|
|   |   |    |   |    | 1 | 2 |
| 3 | 4 | 5  | 6 | 7  | 8 | 9 |
| 10 | 11 | 12 | 13 | 14 | 15 | 16 |
| 17 | 18 | 19 | 20 | 21 | 22 | 23 |
| 24 | 25 | 26 | 27 | 28 | 29 | 30 |

Memory loss = Retrograde amnesia     Date of brain damage     Memory loss = Anterograde amnesia

**FIGURE 7.21** Retrograde amnesia is loss of memory for events in a certain period *before* brain damage or another trauma. Anterograde amnesia is difficulty forming new memories *after* some trauma.

The results of the surgery were favorable in a few regards. H. M.'s epileptic seizures decreased in frequency and severity. His personality and intellect remained the same; in fact, his IQ score increased slightly, presumably because of the decreased epileptic interference.

However, he suffered such severe memory problems that later physicians would never attempt the same surgery again (Corkin, 1984; Milner, 1959). H. M. suffered a massive **anterograde** (ANT-eh-ro-grade) **amnesia,** *inability to store new long-term memories.* For years after the operation, he cited the year as 1953 and his own age as 27. Later he took wild guesses (Corkin, 1984). He would read the same issue of a magazine repeatedly without realizing that he had read it before. He could not even remember where he had lived. He also suffered a moderate **retrograde amnesia,** *loss of memory for events that occurred shortly before the brain damage* (see Figure 7.21). That is, he had some trouble recalling events that had happened within the last 1 to 3 years before the operation, although he could recall older

events. People who suffer a head injury with loss of consciousness generally have retrograde amnesia for the events leading up to the injury.

H. M. could form normal short-term memories, such as repeating a brief list of items, and if he was permitted to rehearse them without distraction, he could even retain the list of items for several minutes. He could also learn new skills, as we shall see in a moment.

Like Rip van Winkle (the story character who slept for 20 years and awakened to a vastly changed world), H. M. became more and more out of date with each passing year (Gabrieli, Cohen, & Corkin, 1988; M. L. Smith, 1988). He did not recognize the names or faces of people who became famous after the mid-1950s. He could not name the president of the United States even when Ronald Reagan was president, though he remembered Reagan as an actor prior to 1953. He did not understand the meaning of words that had entered the English language after the time of his surgery. For example, he guessed that *biodegradable* means "two grades," that *soul food* means "forgiveness," and that a *closet queen* might be "a moth." For H. M. watching the evening news was like visiting another planet.

In spite of H. M.'s massive memory difficulties, he can still acquire and retain new skills. We refer to *skill retention* as **procedural memory,** in contrast to **declarative memory,** *the ability to recall factual information.* For example, H. M. has learned to read material written in mirror fashion (N. J. Cohen & Squire, 1980):

*with the words reversed like this*

Although H. M. has learned to read mirror writing, he does not remember having learned it. He has also learned a simple finger maze, and he has learned the correct solution to the Tower of Hanoi puzzle, shown in Figure 7.22 (N. J. Cohen, Eichenbaum, Deacedo, & Corkin, 1985). He does not *remember* learning these skills, however. He claims that he has never seen any of these tasks before, and he is always a bit surprised by his success.

The results for H. M. led researchers to study people who accidentally suffered damage to the hippocampus, as

**FIGURE 7.22** In the Tower of Hanoi puzzle, the task is to transfer all the disks to another peg, while moving only one at a time and never placing a larger disk onto a smaller disk. Patient H. M. learned the correct strategy and retained it from one test period to another, although he did not remember ever seeing the task before. That is, he showed procedural memory but not declarative memory.

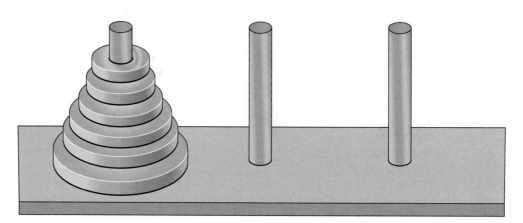

well as laboratory animals with similar damage. At this point researchers are still not agreed on exactly how the hippocampus contributes to memory, but these patterns seem clear:

- The hippocampus is important for storing episodic and some semantic memories for retrieval later.
- Other things being equal, the more difficult a memory task, the more likely it depends on the hippocampus (Reed & Squire, 1999).
- The hippocampus is important for remembering details. One man with hippocampal damage could sketch the general layout of his home neighborhood but could not identify photos of houses and other landmarks within the neighborhood (Rosenbaum et al., 2000).

## *Frontal-Lobe Damage*

Amnesia can also arise after damage to the frontal lobes, especially the prefrontal cortex (see Figure 7.20). Because the frontal lobes receive a great deal of input from the hippocampus, the symptoms of frontal-lobe damage overlap those of hippocampal damage. However, frontal-lobe damage produces some special memory impairments of its own.

Frontal-lobe damage can be the result of a stroke, trauma to the head, or **Korsakoff's syndrome,** *a condition caused by a prolonged deficiency of vitamin B$_1$, usually as a result of chronic alcoholism.* This vitamin deficiency leads to a loss or shrinkage of neurons in many parts of the brain, especially the prefrontal cortex and parts of the thalamus. Patients suffer multiple impairments of memory, apathy, and confusion (Squire, Amaral, & Press, 1990). Patients with Korsakoff's syndrome suffer severe retrograde amnesia, generally covering most events beginning about 15 years before the onset of their illness (Squire, Haist, & Shimamura, 1989). They also suffer from anterograde amnesia. If given a long list of words to remember, they temporarily remember the words at the end of the list, but they forget those at the beginning (Stuss et al., 1994). A few minutes later, they forget even the words at the end.

Such patients have particular difficulty remembering when and where various events took place (Shimamura, Janowsky, & Squire, 1990). For example, if asked what they ate this morning or what they did last night, they give a confident but wrong answer, although it may have been true at some previous time.

Patients with frontal-lobe damage, whatever the cause, have a characteristic pattern of answering questions with a bewildering mixture of correct information, out-of-date information, and wild guesses. Their guesses, or **confabulations,** are apparent *attempts to fill in the gaps in their memory.* Other people confabulate, too, when they cannot quite remember something that they believe they should (Moscovitch, 1995), but people with frontal-lobe

damage confabulate in self-contradictory or preposterous ways, as the following example illustrates (Moscovitch, 1989, pp. 135–136):

**PSYCHOLOGIST:** How old are you?
**PATIENT:** I'm 40, 42, pardon me, 62.
**PSYCHOLOGIST:** Are you married or single?
**PATIENT:** Married.
**PSYCHOLOGIST:** How long have you been married?
**PATIENT:** About 4 months.
**PSYCHOLOGIST:** What's your wife's name?
**PATIENT:** Martha.
**PSYCHOLOGIST:** How many children do you have?
**PATIENT:** Four. (He laughs.) Not bad for 4 months.
**PSYCHOLOGIST:** How old are your children?
**PATIENT:** The eldest is 32; his name is Bob. And the youngest is 22; his name is Joe.
**PSYCHOLOGIST:** How did you get these children in 4 months?
**PATIENT:** They're adopted.
**PSYCHOLOGIST:** Who adopted them?
**PATIENT:** Martha and I.
**PSYCHOLOGIST:** Immediately after you got married you wanted to adopt these older children?
**PATIENT:** Before we were married we adopted one of them, two of them. The eldest girl Brenda and Bob, and Joe and Dina since we were married.
**PSYCHOLOGIST:** Does it all sound a little strange to you, what you are saying?
**PATIENT:** I think it is a little strange.
**PSYCHOLOGIST:** I think when I looked at your record it said that you've been married for over 30 years. Does that sound more reasonable to you if I told you that?
**PATIENT:** No.
**PSYCHOLOGIST:** Do you really believe that you have been married for 4 months?
**PATIENT:** Yes.

Why do these patients confabulate? According to Morris Moscovitch (1992), the frontal lobes are necessary for *working with memory,* the strategies we use to reconstruct memories that we cannot immediately recall. For example, if someone asks you who Romeo's girlfriend was or whether helium is a gas or a liquid, you can probably answer at once without much effort or concern. But if you are asked what is the farthest north that you have ever traveled or what was the most recent time you saw a modern art exhibit, your answer will require effort and reasoning. People with frontal-lobe damage have difficulty inferring what must have happened in their past, so they make unlikely guesses.

## *Implicit Memory in Amnesic Patients*

Brain damage can produce defects in some aspects of memory but not in others. For example, H. M. and many other people with amnesia have poor factual memories but easily acquire new procedural memories. Moreover, they show evidence of memories if they are tested in a special way (Reber, 1997). The kinds of memory tests we have considered so far—recall, recognition, and so forth—have been tests of **explicit memory**—*a person who states the answer regards it as coming from his or her memory.* For example, to the question "Who is your psychology instructor?" you would have to state the name or choose it from a list of choices. In contrast to such explicit or direct tests of memory, a test of **implicit** or *indirect* **memory** *does not require any awareness that one is using memory.* Implicit memory can be unconscious, like driving a car, in which the driver remembers skills but does not ordinarily think about them (Willingham & Goedert-Eschmann, 1999). A test of implicit memory does not even ask you to remember anything. Someone might say a word such as *pardon* and later give you part of the word, such as *par___* or *_ard_* and ask you to fill in letters to make any word that comes to mind. Table 7.5 contrasts explicit and implicit memory tests.

 Before we proceed try the demonstration below: Here you see some three-letter combinations. Add letters to form each of these into an English word:

BEL_____

HEL_____

CON_____

TRA_____

MOD_____

DEF_____

You could have thought of any number of words—the dictionary lists well over 100 familiar CON— words alone. Did you happen to write any of the following: *below, helium, concern* or *consider* or *contrast, travel, modern, defect*? Each of these words appeared in the three paragraphs before this demonstration. Reading or hearing a word temporarily *primes* that word and increases the chance that you will use it yourself (Graf & Mandler, 1984; Schacter, 1987). If you wrote any of these words, you probably did not realize you were using your memory, and if I had asked you to use your memory explicitly ("Please write everything you can remember from the last three paragraphs"), you still might not have included any of these words.

Brain-damaged amnesic patients show relatively normal priming despite deficits in explicit memory. For example, one brain-damaged patient heard lists of words. Sometimes he was given pairs of words and asked to guess which one was on the list—for example, *concern* or *contest, travel* or *tractor, modern* or *modify.* This task asked for explicit memory, and he guessed correctly only half the time. However, when he was given three-letter stems and asked to complete each stem with any word that came to mind, he wrote the words that were on the list—for example, CON-cern, TRA-vel, MOD-ern. Despite this normal implicit memory, even after 40 sessions of such tests, he says he does not recognize the psychologist testing him and does not remember being tested before (Hamann & Squire, 1997).

**TABLE 7.5  Several Ways to Test Memory**

|  | Description | Example |
|---|---|---|
| *Recall* | You are asked to say what you remember. | Name the Seven Dwarfs. |
| *Cued recall* | You are given significant hints to help you remember. | Name the Seven Dwarfs. Hint: One was always smiling, one was smart, one never talked, one always seemed to have a cold . . . . |
| *Recognition* | You are asked to choose the correct item from among several items. | Which of the following were among the Seven Dwarfs: Sneezy, Sleazy, Dopey, Dippy, Hippy, Happy? |
| *Savings (relearning)* | You are asked to relearn something: If it takes you less time than when you first learned that material, some memory has persisted. | Try memorizing this list: Sleepy, Sneezy, Doc, Dopey, Grumpy, Happy, Bashful. Can you memorize it faster than this list: Sleazy, Snoopy, Duke, Dippy, Gripey, Hippy, Blushy? |
| *Implicit memory* | You are asked to generate words, without necessarily regarding them as memories. | You hear the story "Snow White and the Seven Dwarfs." A while later you are asked to fill in these blanks to make any words that come to mind:<br>___ L ___   ___ P ___<br>___ N ___   ___ Z ___<br>___ ___ C<br>___ O ___ E ___<br>___ R ___   ___ P ___<br>___   ___ P P ___<br>___ A ___ H ___ U ___ |

Another example: Researchers asked some young adults who had never before played the video game Tetris (Figure 7.23) to play it for 7 hours over 3 days. On the third night, they went to sleep in the laboratory, and just as they were about to fall asleep, the researchers aroused them and asked what they were experiencing. Most said they were imagining little Tetris blocks moving and falling. Brain-damaged amnesic patients also reported seeing them, although they didn't know what they were! They didn't remember playing the game (Stickgold, Malia, Maguire, Roddenberry, & O'Connor, 2000). One patient said he saw "images that are turned on their side. I don't know what they are from. I wish I could remember, but they are like blocks."

Studies of amnesic patients highlight the differences between declarative and procedural memories, between explicit and implicit memories, and between the ability to recall old memories and the ability to store new memories. The phenomenon of implicit memory demonstrates that a memory can influence behavior even if someone is not consciously aware of it.

**FIGURE 7.23** People who spend many hours playing the game Tetris report seeing images of Tetris blocks, especially as they are falling asleep. So do people with severe amnesia, even though they don't remember playing the game. (Courtesy of Blue Planet Software, Inc. Tetris © Elorg 1987–2002.)

## CONCEPT CHECK

14. **a.** Is remembering how to tie your shoes a procedural memory or a declarative memory?
    **b.** You remember an event that happened to you the first day of high school. Is that a procedural or a declarative memory?
15. Which of the following is an example of implicit memory?
    **a.** You read a chapter about Central America and then try to answer some practice questions about it. Although you cannot answer questions in the format "name the capital of Honduras," you do answer most of the multiple-choice items correctly.
    **b.** Two people near you are talking about Tibet, and you are not paying attention. After they leave, someone asks you what they had been talking about and you reply that you have no idea. A few minutes later, you spontaneously comment, "I wonder what's going on in Tibet these days."
16. Which kinds of memory are most impaired in H. M. and frontal-lobe patients? Which kinds are least impaired? (Check your answers on page 265.)

## Infant Amnesia

Most adults remember only a few events, if any, from before age 5. They can report events that they "know" happened because someone told them, but knowing that something happened is different from remembering it (Bruce, Dolan, & Phillips-Grant, 2000). However, most people clearly remember many events from beyond age 5 or 6. The *relative lack of early declarative memories,* known as **infant amnesia** or **childhood amnesia,** is difficult to explain (Howe & Courage, 1997). It arises in spite of the fact that young children do form long-term memories. A typical 4-year-old can accurately describe experiences from ages 3, 2, and even earlier such as birthday parties, holiday celebrations, and visits to grandparents (Bauer, 1996). However, within a few more years, almost all of those early memories fade away.

So far, none of psychologists' explanations of infant amnesia is convincing. Sigmund Freud's theory was that infant memories are hidden or repressed because of the emotional traumas of infancy. However, he offered no evidence for this claim nor for his belief that a therapist could accurately reaccess those memories.

■ People retain many procedural memories from early childhood, such as how to eat with chopsticks or a fork and spoon, but they forget nearly all the specific events from that time of their lives.

Another possibility is that early memories are nonverbal and later memories are verbal. The drawback to this hypothesis is that 4- and 5-year-olds (who clearly rely on language) do remember events from ages 2 and 3.

Another theory is that infant amnesia is related to the immaturity of the hippocampus (Moscovitch, 1985). The hippocampus is indeed slow to mature, and young children perform poorly on the kinds of memory that depend on the hippocampus (Overman, Pate, Moore, & Peuster, 1996). However, the hippocampus is evidently mature enough for a 4-year-old to remember events from age 2. So why can't a 10- or 20-year-old remember those same events or even events from age 4?

Still another proposal is that a permanent memory of an experience requires the "sense of self" that develops between ages 3 and 4 (Howe & Courage, 1993). One difficulty is that rats and pigeons develop long-lasting memories. Do we really want to assume that they have a "sense of self"?

Possibly, infant amnesia relates in part to the idea of encoding specificity, mentioned earlier (page 254). If we learn something in one location or in one physiological condition or while thinking about a particular idea, it is easier to remember it if we are again in the same location, physiological condition, and so forth. Maybe we forget our early years just because we are in a different place, a different physiological condition, and almost a different body. We just don't have enough of the right retrieval cues to find those infant memories.

At this point none of these hypotheses is well established. The best conclusion is that infant amnesia is simply not yet understood.

# Amnesia of Old Age

Some older people suffer from Alzheimer's disease or other degenerative conditions that gradually destroy brain cells and thereby impair attention and memory. But what about the memory of healthy older people? Years ago psychologists tended to overstate the memory loss of old age because they compared the average younger people of their era with the average older people. The younger generation had advantages of better nutrition, health care, and education than the older generation ever had. Later, better research, which followed a given set of individuals over the years, found that most healthy people show little decline of memory in old age (Schaie, 1994).

On the average older adults show only mild deficits on the simplest memory tasks but greater deficits on more complex tasks (Babcock & Salthouse, 1990; Salthouse, Mitchell, Skovronek, & Babcock, 1989). If given a short narrative to remember, older adults on the average remember the central points of the narrative almost as well as younger adults, but they forget the odd and irrelevant details (Hess, Donley, & Vandermaas, 1989). Their memory also deteriorates more than that of young adults in the presence of distractions, such as trying to do two tasks at once (Einstein, McDaniel, Smith, & Shaw, 1998). That is, the attentional aspect of their working memory has weakened.

Some old people deteriorate mentally more than others, and we would all like to know how to increase our chances of remaining alert and productive in old age. One study found that professors at the University of California, Berkeley, deteriorated less in old age than did other people in the same region (Shimamura, Berry, Mangels, Rusting, & Jurica, 1995). The suggestion is that intellectual activity helps to protect the brain against deterioration, but we cannot draw that conclusion with confidence; it is also possible that the kinds of people least likely to deteriorate in old age are the ones most likely to pursue intellectual activities from youth on.

## IN CLOSING
### Why Do We Forget?

The most spectacular types of memory loss are clearly pathological, as a result of brain damage. Most of the forgetting that normal people do, however, is a product of mechanisms that are usually adaptive. Memories fade over time (partly because of interference from other events), but after all, something that happened many years ago is probably less relevant now and maybe not worth remembering. We forget many events because we did not attend to them closely at the time they happened, but an event not worth attending to is probably not worth remembering forever. Sometimes we have a "tip of the tongue" experience in which we know something but cannot think of it at the time. That experience may be the price we pay for the ability to think of one thing and block out others; sometimes the mechanism causes us temporarily to block out something we wanted. In short, some degree of memory loss is normal and probably even healthy (Schacter, 1999). If you could remember everything that ever happened to you, and none of those memories faded for even a moment, you might not like the results.

## Summary

- **Normal forgetting.** Forgetting depends partly on interference from related memories. At least for memories of very recent events, passive decay also contributes to forgetting. We also have trouble remembering when we do not have adequate retrieval cues. (page 258)
- **Amnesia after damage to the hippocampus.** H. M. and other patients with damage to the hippocampus have great difficulty storing new declarative memories, although they form normal procedural and implicit memories. (page 259)

- **Korsakoff's syndrome and other damage to the frontal lobes.** After suffering damage to the frontal lobes, people make illogical inferences about their past and therefore make odd confabulations. (page 261)
- **Lessons from amnesia.** Studies of brain-damaged people demonstrate the value of distinguishing among different types of memory, such as declarative and procedural or explicit and implicit. (page 263)
- **Infant amnesia.** Most people remember little from early childhood, even though preschoolers have clear recollections of experiences that happened months or even years ago. So far, psychologists have no convincing theory to explain the loss of early memories. (page 263)
- **Loss of memory in old age.** Most older people suffer some loss of memory, especially for details. Their memory falters especially in the presence of a distraction. (page 264)

## Answers to Concept Checks

**13.** Interference, decay (mostly short-term memory), and unavailability of necessary retrieval cues. (page 259)
**14.** Remembering how to tie your shoes is a procedural memory. Remembering the first day of school is a declarative memory. (page 263)
**15.** Item b is an example of implicit memory. Both recall and recognition are examples of explicit memory. (page 263)
**16.** With H. M. and other amnesic patients, declarative memories are the most impaired and procedural memories are the least impaired. (page 263)

# Memory as Reconstruction

Some years ago a college woman was violently raped by a man she didn't know. As she realized she had no escape, she concentrated on memorizing everything about her attacker so she could use it against him later. She tricked him into turning on the lights. She stared at his eyes, his hair, his thin mustache; she listened carefully to his voice. As soon as he left, she hurried to the police station where she went through a book of photos. She confidently identified one photo. Later she identified him again in a lineup of six similar-looking men. She testified in court that she was sure he was the rapist. She had never been more sure of anything in her life. The defendant had no alibi for his whereabouts at the time of the crime, and he previously had been arrested for sexual assault. The jury convicted him, and the judge sentenced him to life in prison.

Eleven years later a detective had to inform the woman that a DNA test, unavailable at the time of the crime, had now demonstrated conclusively that the man she said had raped her could not have been guilty. The test instead implicated another man of similar appearance (O'Neill, 2000) (see Figure 7.24).

Distortions of memory are common even over short times and become even greater over a delay (Schmolck, Buffalo, & Squire, 2000). We study memory distortions partly to learn how much, and under what circumstances, we can trust eyewitness reports. We also study them for what they tell us about how memory normally works.

## Reconstructing Past Events

If you try to recall something you did some time ago, you will start with the details that you remember clearly and **reconstruct** the rest to fill in the gaps: *During an original experience, we construct a memory. When we try to retrieve that memory, we reconstruct an account based partly on surviving memories and partly on our expectations of what must have happened.* For example, you might recall studying in the library three nights ago. With a little effort, you might remember where you sat, what you were reading, who sat next to you, and where you went for a snack afterward. Within weeks or months, you probably will forget that evening. However, if you happen to fall in love with the person who sat next to you, that chance meeting will become a lifetime memory. Still, when you try to recall it, you will remember some details and have to fill in the others. You might remember where you went for a

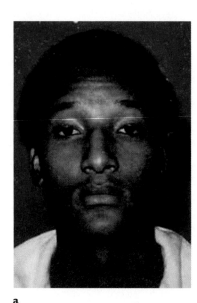

**FIGURE 7.24** Ronald Cotton (a) served 11 years in prison for rape based on the testimony of the victim. A later DNA test demonstrated that the actual perpetrator was Bobby Poole (b). Even clear and confident memories can be distorted.

a                    b

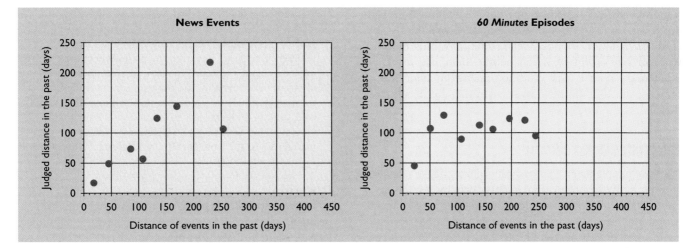

**FIGURE 7.25** People who followed the news and regularly watched the television program *60 Minutes* could estimate the time of various news events but guessed almost randomly about when they saw various *60 Minutes* episodes, except those from the most recent 2 months. (From Friedman & Huttenlocher, 1997)

snack, but if you wanted to recall the book you were reading, you would have to reason it out: "Let's see, that semester I was taking a chemistry course that took a lot of study, so maybe I was reading a chemistry book. No, wait, I remember. When we went out to eat, we talked about politics. So maybe I was reading my political science text."

We also depend on inferences to reconstruct the times of various memories. In one study investigators located 82 adults who consistently kept up with the news and routinely watched the television program *60 Minutes*. They asked each participant to estimate the approximate dates of various news events and of various *60 Minutes* episodes. The results: People could recall the approximate dates of most news events, but not the dates of *60 Minutes* episodes, except for the most recent ones (Friedman & Huttenlocher, 1997) (see Figure 7.25). The reason for this difference is that news stories have a logical order and connections to other events. With *60 Minutes* episodes, however, we have no way to guess the date except by how "fresh" the memory seems, and that impression is evidently not very useful. The important conclusion is that most of our memories from long ago do not have time tags attached to them. If we try to guess when something happened, we usually rely on logical inferences.

## Reconstruction and Inference in List Memory

 Try this demonstration: Read the words in list A once; then turn away from the list, pause for a few seconds, and write as many of the words as you can remember. Repeat the same procedure for lists B and C. *(Please do this now, before reading the following paragraph.)*

| List A | List B | List C |
|--------|--------|--------|
| bed | candy | fade |
| rest | sour | fame |
| awake | sugar | face |
| tired | dessert | fake |
| dream | salty | date |
| wake | taste | hate |
| snooze | flavor | late |
| blanket | bitter | mate |
| doze | cookies | rate |
| slumber | fruits | |
| snore | chocolate | |
| nap | yummy | |

After you have written out your lists, check how many you got right. If you missed several of them, you are normal. The point of this demonstration is not how many you got right, but whether you included *sleep* on the first list, *sweet* on the second, or *fate* on the third. Many people include one or more of these words (which were not on the lists), and some do so with great confidence (Deese, 1959). Apparently, while learning the individual words, people also learn the gist of what they are all about, and from that they reconstruct a memory of another word that the list implied. This powerful effect occurs under a wide variety of conditions, even if people are warned about it before they hear the list (Roediger & McDermott, 2000). Evidently, even when we are just trying to remember a list of words, we reconstruct or infer what "must have" been on the list. (We do not rely on such inferences for short or well-learned lists.)

If you did include *sleep, sweet,* or *fate,* don't worry. Your error is not a sign of a bad memory; in fact, people with really bad memories *don't* make this kind of error (Schacter, Verfaellie, Anes, & Racine, 1998). They don't remember the words that *were* on the list and therefore don't use them to infer related words. If you did not include *sleep, sweet,* or *fate,* well . . . actually, this demonstration works better when people hear the list than when they read it. Try reading the lists to your roommate or another friend and see whether he or she "remembers" the implied words.

## Reconstructing Stories

Suppose people listen to a story about a teenager's day, including a mixture of normal events (watching television) and oddities (clutching a teddy bear and parking a bicycle in the kitchen). Which would people remember better—the normal events or the oddities? You might predict that they would remember the unusual and distinctive events, and you would be right—*if* people are tested while their memory is still strong. However, if we wait long enough for people to start to forget the story, they reconstruct a more typical day for the teenager, recalling the normal events, omitting the unlikely ones, and adding some likely events that the story did not mention, such as "the teenager went to school in the morning." In short, the less certain people's memories are, the more they rely on their expectations (Heit, 1993; Maki, 1990).

In a study that highlights the role of expectations, U.S. and Mexican adults tried to recall three stories. Some were given U.S. versions of the stories; others were given Mexican versions. (For example, in the "going out on a date" story, the Mexican version had the man's sister go along as a chaperone.) On the average, U.S. participants remembered the U.S. versions better, whereas the Mexicans remembered the Mexican versions better (R. J. Harris, Schoen, & Hensley, 1992).

## CONCEPT CHECK

**17.** If you studied a list such as "candy, sour, sugar, dessert, salty, taste . . . " thoroughly instead of hearing it just once, would you be more likely or less likely to include "sweet," which wasn't on the list? Why? (Check your answers on page 273.)

## Hindsight Bias

Let's try another demonstration. First read the following paragraph and then answer the question that follows:

For some years after the arrival of Hastings as governor-general of India, the consolidation of British power involved serious war. The first of these wars took place on the northern frontier of Bengal where the British were faced by the plundering raids of the Gurkas of Nepal. Attempts had been made to stop the raids by an exchange of lands, but the Gurkas would not give up their claims to country under British control, and Hastings decided to deal with them once and for all. The campaign began in November, 1814. It

was not glorious. The Gurkas were only some 12,000 strong; but they were brave fighters, fighting in territory well-suited to their raiding tactics. The older British commanders were used to war in the plains where the enemy ran away from a resolute attack. In the mountains of Nepal it was not easy even to find the enemy. The troops and transport animals suffered from the extremes of heat and cold, and the officers learned caution only after sharp reverses. Major-General Sir D. Octerlony was the one commander to escape from these minor defeats. (Woodward, 1938, pp. 383–384)

**Question**

In light of the information in this passage, what was the probability of each of the four possible outcomes listed below? (The probabilities should total 100%.)

**a.** a British victory          10 %
**b.** a Gurka victory          80 %
**c.** military stalemate with no peace settlement    5 %
**d.** military stalemate with a peace settlement    5 %

Note that each of these possible outcomes seems possible, given the facts as stated. Now that you have made your estimates of the probabilities, I can tell you what really happened: The two sides reached a military stalemate without any settlement. The British had the advantages of superior numbers and superior equipment, but the Gurkas knew the territory and refused to give up, so battles continued indecisively for years.

Now that you know the outcome, would you like to revise your estimates of the probabilities? Perhaps if you reread the paragraph, you will decide that you had overestimated the probabilities of some outcomes and underestimated others.

Subjects in one experiment read the preceding passage about the British and the Gurkas. Some were told which outcome "actually occurred" (although some were misinformed); all were then asked to estimate the probabilities of the four possible outcomes. Each group listed a high estimated probability for the "actual" outcome they had been given (Fischhoff, 1975). That is, once they knew what "really" happened (or incorrectly *thought* they knew), they reinterpreted the information to make that outcome seem likely, or perhaps even unavoidable (Figure 7.26). The subjects' behavior illustrates **hindsight bias,** *the tendency to mold our recollection of the past to fit how events later turned out.* Something happens and we then say, "I *knew* that was going to happen!" (Oh, incidentally, I lied about the outcome of the British–Gurkas war. Actually, the British won. Would you like to reevaluate your estimates *again*?)

Examples of hindsight bias are abundant and sometimes costly. In one study students watched a videotape of a crime and then examined photos of five possible suspects. Although the actual criminal was *not* one of the suspects shown, every student picked someone from the array as the probable culprit. At that point some were told (falsely), "Good, you identified the actual suspect,"

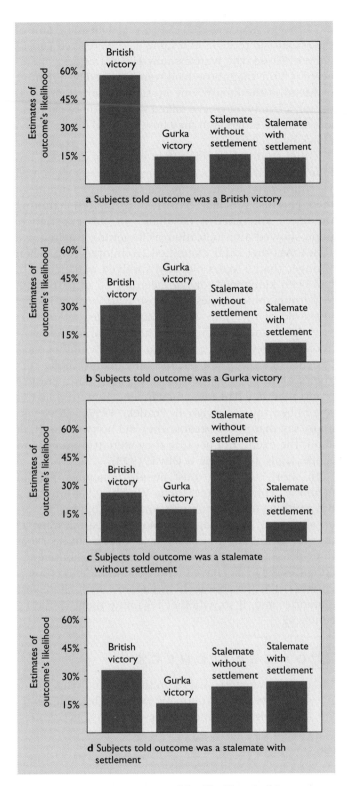

**FIGURE 7.26** Mean estimates of the likelihood of four outcomes varied depending on what each group was told about the "actual" outcome. Those who thought the British had won said that under the circumstances the British had a very high probability of victory. Those who thought the Gurkas had won said that was the most likely outcome under the circumstances, and so forth. (Based on data of Fischhoff, 1975)

and then all were asked how confident they were about their judgment. Those who were told that they were right said that they were quite confident (Wells & Bradfield, 1999). Because of studies like this one, the U.S. Justice Department has made recommendations that police investigators avoid any hint about which member of a lineup the police actually suspect (Wells et al., 2000).

In another study college students were asked to choose between two possible roommates or blind dates based on lists of information about them. A few minutes after they chose, they had already forgotten some of the information, and when asked to describe the two possible choices, they remembered the person they had chosen far more favorably than the original information justified (Mather, Shafir, & Johnson, 2000).

Hindsight bias is pervasive, but not altogether irrational. Frequently, when we are making a decision or prediction, we receive a huge array of information, and we are not sure which parts are relevant or important and which items might even be wrong. When we get the final outcome, we quite reasonably conclude that information that had pointed in that direction was more relevant, more important, and maybe even more correct than information that had pointed in some other direction. Paying attention to the facts consistent with the final outcome might be a good strategy in preparing for the future (Hoffrage, Hertwig, & Gigerenzer, 2000).

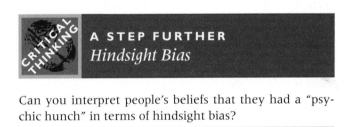

**A STEP FURTHER**
*Hindsight Bias*

Can you interpret people's beliefs that they had a "psychic hunch" in terms of hindsight bias?

# The "False Memory" Controversy

Occasionally, someone tells a therapist about vague unpleasant feelings, and the therapist replies, "Symptoms like yours are usually found among people who were abused, especially sexually abused, in childhood. Do you think you were?" If the client says *yes,* or if the client says *no* and the therapist accepts *no* for an answer, then no controversy arises. However, an occasional eager therapist persists: "The fact that you can't remember doesn't mean that it didn't happen. It may have been so painful that you repressed it." The therapist may then recommend hypnosis, repeated attempts to remember, or other techniques. Several sessions later the client may say, "It's starting to come back to me. . . . I think I do remember. . . ." *Reports of long-lost memories, prompted by clinical techniques,* are known as **recovered memories**.

Sexual abuse in childhood does occur, and no one knows how often. Some abused children do develop long-lasting psychological scars. But when people claim to recover long-forgotten memories, how trustworthy are their reports? Some reports are bizarre. In one case two sisters accused their father of raping them many times, both vaginally and anally; bringing his friends over on Friday nights to rape them; and forcing them to participate in satanic rituals that included cannibalism, the slaughter of babies, and so forth (L. Wright, 1994). The sisters had not remembered any of these events until they spoke with a therapist. In another case a group of 3- and 4-year-old children, after urgings from a therapist, accused their Sunday school teacher of sexually abusing them with a curling iron, forcing them to drink blood and urine, hanging them upside down from a chandelier, dunking them in toilets, and killing an elephant and a giraffe during Sunday school class (M. Gardner, 1994). In neither case was there any physical evidence to support the claims, such as scarred tissues or giraffe bones.

Recovered-memory claims are usually not so bizarre, but their accuracy is hard to gauge. If a 30-year-old woman claims that her father sexually abused her when she was 10, that she had not told anyone about it at the time, and in fact had forgotten it until now, how could anyone check her accuracy? One might consult old school records for any mention of physical and emotional scars, but even the best of such records are incomplete. Psychological researchers can, however, address these questions: When people have abusive experiences, are they likely to forget them for years? And is it possible to persuade someone to "remember" an event that never actually happened just by suggesting it?

## Memory for Traumatic Events

Sigmund Freud, whom we shall consider more fully in Chapter 13, introduced the term **repression** as *the process of moving a memory, motivation, or emotion from the conscious mind to the unconscious mind.* Although many therapists continue to use the concept of repression, the research on memory and forgetting has not clearly supported it (Holmes, 1990). Controlled experiments designed to demonstrate repression have produced small effects that are subject to alternative explanations.

Do people forget traumatic events? It depends. (Almost always a good answer in psychology.) Here it depends on the age of the person at the time of the event, the reaction of other family members, and perhaps the type of event. In one study investigators identified 206 girls who had been brought to a hospital emergency ward because of sexual assault at ages 1 to 12 years. Years later the investigators interviewed 129 of them, who were now adults. Of those 129, 38% did not recall the sexual assault, although many of them openly described other personal, embarrassing, or traumatic experiences (L. M. Williams, 1994). Age was a factor, but not a perfect pre-

dictor. Some who were less than 6 years old at the time of the assault did recall it, and some who were aged 7 to 12 did not. Those who were assaulted by a stranger remembered it more than those who were attacked by a relative or friend of the family. One possible explanation is that the girl's family may have talked with her more about an attack by a stranger and may have avoided discussing an attack by a relative.

Other studies have identified victims of disasters and followed their memory over time. One study examined 16 children who had witnessed the murder of one of their parents. All had recurring nightmares, haunting thoughts, and painful flashbacks of the experience; none showed any indication of forgetting (Malmquist, 1986). Another study examined 20 children who, when younger than 5 years old, had survived a plane crash, had been kidnapped, or had been forced to participate in pornographic movies. Of those who were at least 3 years old at the time, six of nine recalled the events years later, and the other three had partial memories—in contrast to the poor recall of most early childhood experiences (Terr, 1988). On the other hand, many survivors of wars, fires, earthquakes, and plane crashes report that they had some time in life when they did not remember them (Arrigo & Pezdek, 1997). However, many say that it was because they did not *want* to think about the event, not because they were truly unable to (Pope, Hudson, Bodkin, & Oliva, 1998).

In short, although most people remember painful memories, some do forget them. Whether that forgetting has anything to do with repression is far from certain; after all, people forget happy memories at least as often as they forget unhappy ones. The point does seem clear that some people who do not remember any early abusive experiences did in fact have them. What is far less certain is whether it is possible to help people regain those lost memories and, if so, whether regaining them would be beneficial.

## CONCEPT CHECK

18. Based on material earlier in this chapter, why should we expect traumatic events to be remembered better than most other events? (Check your answer on page 273.)

### WHAT'S THE EVIDENCE?
*Suggestions and False Memories*

As mentioned earlier, some therapists have tried to help clients recover lost memories. Critics of that approach have suggested that a therapist who repeatedly urges a client to recall certain memories can unintentionally implant a **false memory,** *a report that someone believes to* *be a memory but that does not correspond to real events* (Lindsay & Read, 1994; Loftus, 1993). Researchers cannot determine whether a particular report of recovered memory was true or false, but they can test how easy it is to implant a false memory. We shall examine three representative experiments.

### EXPERIMENT 1

**HYPOTHESIS**  If people are asked questions that suggest or presuppose a certain fact, many people will later report remembering that "fact," even if it never happened.

**METHOD**  Elizabeth Loftus (1975) asked two groups of students to watch a videotape of an automobile accident. Then she asked one group but not the other, "Did you see the children getting on the school bus?" In fact, the videotape did not show a school bus. A week later, she asked both groups 20 new questions about the accident, including this one: "Did you see a school bus in the film?"

**RESULTS**  Of the first group (those who were asked about seeing children get on a school bus), 26% reported that they had seen a school bus; of the second group, only 6% said they had seen a school bus.

**INTERPRETATION**  The question "Did you see the children getting on the school bus?" presupposes that there *was* a school bus in the film. Some of the students who heard that question reconstructed what happened by combining what they actually saw with what they believed might reasonably have happened and what someone (the researcher) had suggested to them afterward.

### EXPERIMENT 2

The first experiment demonstrated that a suggestion can distort memories of something that people watched. But could a suggestion also distort a personal memory or even implant a memory of an experience that never really occurred?

**HYPOTHESIS**  If people are told about a childhood event by people they trust, they will come to remember it as something they experienced, even if in fact they did not.

**METHOD**  The participants, aged 18 to 53, were told that the study concerned their memories of childhood. Each participant was given four paragraphs, and each paragraph described a different event. Three of the events had actually happened. (The experimenters had contacted parents to get descriptions of childhood events.) A fourth event was a plausible story about getting lost, which had not happened. An example for one Vietnamese woman: "You, your Mom, Tien, and Tuan, all went to the Bremerton Kmart. You must have been 5 years old at the time. Your Mom gave each of you some money to get a blueberry ICEE. You ran ahead to get into the line first, and somehow lost your way in the store. Tien found you crying to an elderly Chinese woman. You three then went together to get an ICEE."

After reading the four paragraphs, each participant was asked to write whatever additional details he or she could remember of the event. Participants were asked to try again 1 week later and then again after another week.

**RESULTS**  Of 24 participants 6 reported remembering the suggested (false) event. Participants generally described the false memories in fewer words than the correct memories, but some did provide a fair amount of additional detail. The woman in the foregoing example said, "I vaguely remember walking around Kmart crying and looking for Tien and Tuan. I thought I was lost forever. I went to the shoe department, because we always spent a lot of time there. I went to the handkerchief place because we were there last. I circled all over the store it seemed 10 times. I just remember walking around crying. I do not remember the Chinese woman, or the ICEE (but it would be raspberry ICEE if I was getting an ICEE) part. I don't even remember being found" (Loftus, Feldman, & Dashiell, 1995).

**INTERPRETATION**  A simple suggestion can provoke some people to recall a personal experience in moderate detail, even though the event never happened. Granted, the suggestion influenced fewer than half of the people tested, and most of them reported only vague memories. Still, the researchers achieved this effect after only a single brief suggestion.

### EXPERIMENT 3

Defenders of the concept of recovered memories are not impressed with false memories such as being lost at a Kmart. Even if this woman was not lost at Kmart at age 5, she was probably lost somewhere, sometime. Implanting a false memory of such a likely event does not demonstrate that one could implant a false memory of, say, childhood sexual abuse.

To this criticism, researchers reply that it would be unethical to try to implant memories of something traumatic. However, it is possible to compare the difficulty of implanting a memory of a likely event or an unlikely one.

**HYPOTHESIS**  When adults hear a suggestion about a childhood religious experience, they will be more likely to accept it and claim to remember if it pertains to the kind of ceremony they practice in their own religion. They will probably not accept a suggestion about a ceremony from another religion.

**METHOD**  The experimenters began by contacting the mothers of 29 Roman Catholic and 22 Jewish teenage girls. All actively practiced their religion through childhood and into the present. The mothers provided descriptions of events (not necessarily religious) that happened to their daughters at about age 8.

The experimenters told each girl five brief episodes and asked them to provide any additional details they could remember. Three of these were real events as described by the mothers. Another one was a false event that would be plausible to the Catholic girls but not to the Jewish girls:

taking Communion and returning to the wrong seat. The other was a false event that should be plausible to the Jews but not to the Catholics: conducting Friday night prayers before sunset and dropping the bread.

**RESULTS** Most girls remembered all three of the correct events and provided additional information. Here are the results for the false events (Pezdek, Finger, & Hodge, 1997):

|  | Recalled neither | Recalled the Catholic event | Recalled the Jewish event | Recalled both |
|---|---|---|---|---|
| Catholic girls (total of 29) | 19 | 7 | 1 | 2 |
| Jewish girls (total of 22) | 19 | 0 | 3 | 0 |

**INTERPRETATION** As predicted, it was easier to implant plausible than implausible memories, but three of the Catholic girls did report false memories corresponding to a Jewish ceremony. Evidently, it is easier to implant a false memory of an event similar to one's actual experiences, but there is no sharp line between implantable and nonimplantable memories.

So, what conclusion should we draw about the possibility of implanting false memories of sexual abuse and the like? The experiments described here are examples of many others that follow the same pattern: Researchers offer normal, untroubled people one or more repetitions of some suggestion of a nontraumatic event. The more repetitions, the bigger the effect on producing reports of false memories (Zaragoza & Mitchell, 1996).

The false memories people report in these experiments are, of course, quite different from some clinical patients' elaborate reports of years of sexual abuse. Ethically, researchers could not attempt to implant traumatic memories; the best they can do is demonstrate the plausibility that prolonged suggestions, perhaps accompanied by hypnosis or other techniques, could produce even bigger effects. Furthermore, some people are more vulnerable to suggestion than others are, and there is some evidence that people who were, or think they were, sexually abused in childhood are especially susceptible to suggestion (Bremner, Shobe, & Kihlstrom, 2000; Clancy, Schacter, McNally, & Pitman, 2000). Finally, to those who say the laboratory evidence is indecisive, the retort is that almost no cases of recovered memories are accompanied by *any* evidence of accuracy.

On the other hand, people do sometimes remember something they haven't thought about in years, and we cannot assume that all cases of recovered memories are totally false (Pope, 1996). The main conclusion is that a memory report in response to suggestions, especially repeated suggestions, is suspect. It may or may not be correct. Anyone interviewing someone about possible traumatic events should tread carefully, avoiding suggestions. Furthermore, any claim of recovering a long-forgotten memory should be treated as only a hypothesis that might lead to other evidence, not as solid evidence in itself.

## Children as Eyewitnesses

Finally, what about children who are witnesses or victims of a crime? Young children forget rapidly and sometimes confuse fantasy with reality. How reliable are they as witnesses?

Research here can be tricky. No ethical researcher would abuse children to see how well they could recall the events or tell children they had been abused to see whether they would report false memories. The best approach yet found is to ask children to report events of a medical or dental examination, where a stranger or near stranger probes various parts of a child's body. How well can the child report what happened?

In a series of such studies, researchers found that children as young as 3 years old report accurately under proper conditions. The youngest children, in the 3- to 5-year range, volunteer very little in response to an invitation to "tell me what happened." However, they do answer correctly to specific questions, such as "Did the doctor shine a light in your eyes?" We might worry that the children were responding to suggestions or agreeing to whatever someone asked them. However, they almost always responded *no* to questions about acts that did not happen, such as "Did the doctor cut your hair?" Children's accuracy was reasonably good even 6 weeks after the physical exam (Baker-Ward, Gordon, Ornstein, Larus, & Clubb, 1993). Undeniably, of course, it is possible to get children to report elaborate false memories with a little extra prodding (Ceci, 1995).

Several factors influence the accuracy of children's reports:

- **The delay between event and questioning.** If 4- to 6-year-old children are asked about an event that did *not* occur in the most recent physical exam, but usually does, they correctly deny it if they are asked within 6 weeks, but by 12 weeks they are likely to report it. Evidently, they start to confuse the most recent exam with the usual exam (Ornstein et al., 1998).

- **The understandability of the questions.** If I asked you whether you have ever seen anyone imbosk a lecythus, I assume you would either say "I don't know" or ask me to explain. However, 3-year-olds seldom do. (They are probably accustomed to not understanding.) When questions are stated very simply, most 3-year-olds answer correctly. If the questions are just slightly confusing, most 3-year-olds habitually answer "yes" (Imhoff & Baker-Ward, 1999).

- **Repetition of the question.** If a 3-year-old is asked the same question twice within a single interview, he or she is likely to answer differently the second time (Poole & White, 1993). Evidently, the child assumes that if someone is asking that question again, the first answer must have been wrong. However, asking the question every few days helps the child remember, and that persistence is important if a child has to testify in court at a later date (Poole & White, 1995).

- **Use of doll props.** Young children have a limited vocabulary, and we might imagine that their reports are limited by their inability to describe many events. Some psychologists try to help them by providing them with anatomically detailed dolls and asking them to act out what happened. This idea sounds reasonable, but when researchers ask children to act out a doctor's exam (where we know what actually happened), they act out many events that did not happen (Greenhoot, Ornstein, Gordon, & Baker-Ward, 1999).

The general recommendations for children's eyewitness testimony are simple: If a child is asked simple questions in a nonthreatening atmosphere, without suggestions or pressure and reasonably soon after the event, even children as young as 3 can be believable (Ceci & Bruck, 1993).

## A STEP FURTHER
### Unlikely Memory Reports

Some people claim to have been abducted by aliens from another planet. Presuming that they are not deliberately lying to get attention, that they are not mentally ill, and that they were not in fact abducted by aliens, how might we explain their reports?

## IN CLOSING
### Memories True, False, and Uncertain

At the end of the last module, I noted that forgetting is not altogether a mistake; it is the outcome of processes that are usually adaptive, such as selective attention and discarding old, probably useless information. Memory distortions are also the product of a mechanism that is ordinarily useful—our ability to use reason and logic to fill in the gaps of our memories (Schacter, 1999). Still, it is wise for us all to remember that what seems like a clear memory is sometimes mistaken.

HE: We met at nine.
SHE: We met at eight.
HE: I was on time.
SHE: No, you were late.
HE: —Ah, yes! I remember it well. We dined with friends.
SHE: We dined alone.
HE: A tenor sang.
SHE: A baritone.
HE: —Ah, yes! I remember it well. That dazzling April moon!
SHE: —There was none that night. And the month was June.
HE: That's right! That's right!
SHE: —It warms my heart to know that you remember still the way you do.
HE: Ah, yes! I remember it well.

—"I Remember It Well" from the musical *Gigi* by Alan Jay Lerner and Frederick Loewe

## Summary

- **Reconstruction.** When remembering stories or events from their own lives, people recall some of the facts and fill in the gaps based on logical inferences of what must have happened. They rely particularly heavily on inferences when they are uncertain about their memory of the events. (page 266)
- **Reconstructions from a word list.** If people read or hear a list of related words and try to recall them, they are likely to include closely related words that were not on the list. (page 267)
- **Hindsight bias.** People often revise their memories of what they previously expected, saying that how events turned out was what they had expected all along. (page 268)
- **False memory debate.** Some therapists have used hypnosis or very suggestive lines of questioning to try to help people remember painful experiences. Some of the reported memories include extreme or bizarre events that people claim they experienced long ago but did not remember until much later. It is important to try to distinguish actual cases of abuse from false memories that depend on suggestion. (page 269)
- **Children as eyewitnesses.** Even children 3 to 5 years old can correctly report events if they are asked simple questions without pressure soon after the event. (page 272)

## Answers to Concept Checks

17. You would be less likely to add a word not on the list. We rely on inferences mostly when the actual memory is weak. (page 268)
18. Any emotionally arousing event stimulates cortisol release and in other ways activates the amygdala, a brain area that helps store memories. (page 270; see also page 251)

CHAPTER ENDING:
# Key Terms and Activities

## Key Terms

**amnesia:** severe loss or deterioration of memory (page 259)

**anterograde amnesia:** the inability to store new long-term memories (page 260)

**chunking:** the process of grouping digits or letters into meaningful sequences (page 245)

**confabulations:** guesses made by amnesic patients to fill in the gaps in their memory (page 261)

**consolidation:** the formation and strengthening of long-term memories (page 247)

**cued recall:** a method of testing memory by asking someone to remember a certain item after being given a hint (page 242)

**declarative memory:** recall of factual information (page 260)

**encoding specificity principle:** the tendency for the associations formed at the time of learning to be more effective retrieval cues than other associations (page 254)

**episodic memory:** memory for specific events in a person's life (page 248)

**explicit memory:** a memory that a person can state, generally recognizing that it is the correct answer (page 262)

**false memory:** a report that someone believes to be a memory but that does not actually correspond to real events (page 270)

**free recall:** a method of testing memory by asking someone to produce a certain item (such as a word) without substantial hints, as on an essay or short-answer test (page 241)

**hindsight bias:** the tendency to mold our recollection of the past to fit how events later turned out (page 268)

**hippocampus:** a forebrain structure in the interior of the temporal lobe that is important for storing certain kinds of memory (page 259)

**implicit memory** a memory that influences behavior without requiring conscious recognition that one is using a memory (page 262)

**infant amnesia (or childhood amnesia):** a relative lack of declarative memories from early in life (page 263)

**information-processing model:** the view that information is processed, coded, and stored in various ways in human memory as it is in a computer (page 243)

**Korsakoff's syndrome:** a condition caused by a prolonged deficiency of vitamin $B_1$, which results in both retrograde amnesia and anterograde amnesia (page 261)

**levels-of-processing principle:** the concept that the number and types of associations established during learning determines the ease of later retrieval of a memory (page 252)

**long-term memory:** a relatively permanent store of information (page 244)

**method of loci:** a mnemonic device that calls for linking the items on a list with a memorized list of places (page 256)

**mnemonic device:** any memory aid that is based on encoding each item in a special way (page 255)

**peg method:** a mnemonic device in which a person first memorizes a list of objects and then forms mental images linking those objects ("peg words") to a list of names to be memorized (page 256)

**proactive interference:** the hindrance that an older memory produces on a newer one (page 241)

**procedural memory:** retention of learned skills (page 260)

**recognition:** a method of testing memory by asking someone to choose the correct item from a set of alternatives (page 242)

**reconstruction** putting together an account of past events, based partly on memories and partly on expectations of what must have happened (page 266)

**recovered memory:** a report of a long-lost memory, prompted by clinical techniques (page 269)

**repression:** according to Freudian theory, the process of moving a memory, motivation, or emotion from the conscious mind to the unconscious mind (page 270)

**retrieval cue:** information associated with remembered material, which can be useful for helping to recall that material (page 254)

**retroactive interference:** the impairment that a newer memory produces on an older one (page 241)

**retrograde amnesia:** loss of memory for events that occurred before the brain damage (page 260)

**savings method (or relearning method):** a method of testing memory by measuring how much faster someone can relearn something than learn something for the first time (page 242)

**semantic memory:** memory of general principles (page 248)

**sensory store:** a very brief storage of sensory information (page 243)

**serial-order effect:** the tendency to remember the items near the beginning and end of a list better than those in the middle (page 253)

**short-term memory:** a temporary storage of a limited amount of information (page 244)

**source amnesia:** remembering content but not the context of learning it (page 249)

**SPAR method:** a systematic way to monitor and improve understanding of a text by surveying, processing meaningfully, asking questions, and reviewing  (page 254)

**state-dependent memory:** the tendency to remember something better if your body is in the same condition during recall as it was during the original learning  (page 255)

**von Restorff effect:** the tendency to remember distinctive or unusual items on a list better than other items  (page 241)

**working memory:** a system that processes and works with current information, including three components—a central executive, a phonological loop, and a visuospatial sketchpad  (page 247)

## Suggestions for Further Reading

Cermak, L. S. (1975). *Improving your memory.* New York: McGraw-Hill. A lively book about mnemonic devices and other ways to improve memory.

Schacter, D. L. (1996). *Searching for memory.* New York: Basic Books. Discusses current theories and research in an accessible manner.

## Web/Technology Resources

The Magic Number Seven, Plus or Minus Two

**www.well.com/user/smalin/miller.html**

This is George Miller's classic article about the limits of short-term memory, complete with graphs and references, as it originally appeared in the *Psychological Review* in 1956.

Memory Techniques and Mnemonics.

**www.demon.co.uk/mindtool/memory.html**

MindTools offers commercial software designed to improve memory and more than 25 free articles about memory and how to improve it, stress management, time management, and other topics.

Amnesia

**www.slc.edu/~ebj/fys/student_pages/amnesia.html**

This site includes links to several kinds of information about memory loss.

American Psychological Association: Memory

**www.apa.org/**

The home page of the American Psychological Association has a "What Are You Looking For?" blank. Type "memory" and you will get a listing of recent research findings.

# Cognition and Language

8

CHAPTER

onsider the statement, "This sentence is false." Is the statement itself true or false? Declaring the statement to be true agrees with its own assessment that it is false. But declaring it to be false would make its assessment correct.

A sentence about itself, called a *self-referential* sentence, can be utterly confusing, like the one above. It can also be true (e.g., "This sentence consists of six words"), false ("Anyone who reads this sentence will be transported suddenly to the planet Neptune"), untestable ("Whenever no one is reading this sentence, it changes into the passive voice"), or amusing ("This sentence no verb" or "This sentence sofa includes an unnecessary word").

In this chapter you will be asked to think about thinking, talk about talking, and read about reading. Doing so is self-referential, and if you try to "think about what you are thinking now," you can easily go into a confusing loop similar to the one in "This sentence is false." For that reason, among many others, psychological researchers focus as much as possible on results obtained from carefully controlled experiments, not just on what people say they think about their own thought processes.

■ Cognitive psychology studies how people think and what they know.

# Thinking and Mental Processing

*What are concepts and attention? How can we measure them?*

**Cognition** means *thinking, gaining knowledge, and dealing with knowledge.* Cognitive psychologists study how people think, how they acquire knowledge, what they know, how they imagine, and how they solve problems. They also deal with how people organize their thoughts into language and communicate with others.

Perhaps it seems that cognitive psychology should be trivially simple. "If you want to find out what people think or what they know, why not just ask them?" Sometimes psychologists can and do ask them; however, in many cases people are not fully aware of their own thought processes (Kihlstrom, Barnhardt, & Tataryn, 1992). Recall, for example, implicit memory as discussed in Chapter 7: Sometimes you see or hear something that influences your behavior without your realizing it. Similarly, we sometimes solve a problem without knowing how we did it.

Cognitive psychology increased in popularity after the introduction and popularization of computers. Although brains and computers do not work the same way, computers provide a valuable way of modeling theories of cognitive processes. A researcher may say, "Imagine that cognitive processes work as follows. . . . Now let's program a computer to go through those same steps in the same order. If we then give the computer the same information that a human has, will it draw the same conclusions and make the same errors as a human?" In short, computer modeling provides a way to test theories of cognition. Today, cognitive psychology uses a variety of methods to measure mental processes and to test theories about what we know and how we know it.

## Categorization

An ancient Greek philosopher once wrote that we can never step into the same river twice. In a sense, of course, he was right; everything is constantly changing. However, we generally find it useful to think of the Nile as the same river from one time to another. It also suits our purposes to use "river" as a general concept to describe the Nile, the Amazon, the Mississippi, and thousands of oth-

ers, despite their differences. Thinking with categories is enormously useful. Labeling something with the category "poisonous mushroom" doesn't mean that it is identical to other items in that category, but it does share important properties with them.

We often take our categories for granted, as if our own way of categorizing objects is the only way possible, but in fact, there are many ways, some more useful than others (Figure 8.1). To understand thinking, we need to understand categorizing.

### Categorization by Prototypes

Do we look up our concepts in a mental dictionary to determine their meaning? We do in some cases only. For example, we think of the term *bachelor* as an unmarried male. Because we would not ordinarily apply the term bachelor to a 3-year-old boy or to a Catholic priest, we might refine the definition to "a male who has not married but could decide to." That definition pretty well explains the concept.

Few concepts can be so clearly defined, however. Try defining *country music,* for example. Also, imagine a man who loses one hair from his head. Is he now bald? Of course not. Then he loses one more hair, then another and another. Eventually, he *is* bald, so was there some point at which losing one hair made him bald? We are forced to that absurdity only if we insist on using baldness as a yes/no category. (The same issue arises in abnormal psychology. We would like to classify everyone as depressed or not depressed, schizophrenic or not, and alcoholic or not, but marginal cases are common.)

According to Eleanor Rosch (1978; Rosch & Mervis, 1975), many categories are defined by *familiar or typical examples* called **prototypes.** According to the categorization by prototypes approach, we decide whether an object belongs to a category by determining how well it resembles the prototypical members of that category, so an item can be a good or weak example of a category.

For example, we define the category "vehicle" by examples: *car, bus, train, airplane, boat, truck.* Other objects are also vehicles to the extent that they resemble the examples. Is a *blimp* also a vehicle? What about an *elevator* or *water skis*? Even if you say "yes," you are likely to pause, and the speed of your answer is a pretty good measure of how well the example fits the concept of vehicle. The main point of Rosch's prototype approach is that category membership can be a matter of degree.

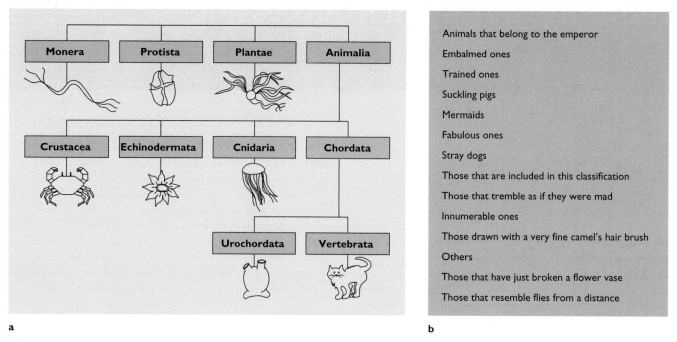

| Animals that belong to the emperor |
| Embalmed ones |
| Trained ones |
| Suckling pigs |
| Mermaids |
| Fabulous ones |
| Stray dogs |
| Those that are included in this classification |
| Those that tremble as if they were mad |
| Innumerable ones |
| Those drawn with a very fine camel's hair brush |
| Others |
| Those that have just broken a flower vase |
| Those that resemble flies from a distance |

a                           b

**FIGURE 8.1** (a) A much-abridged chart of the current scientific classification of the animal kingdom. (b) An alleged listing from an ancient Chinese encyclopedia—actually the product of someone's imagination (Rosch, 1978). The point is that some methods of categorizing are better than others.

However, it is difficult to apply the prototype approach to all human categories (Fodor, 1998). For example, we can talk and think about "bug-eyed monsters from outer space" without ever encountering a single prototype of that category.

## Cross-Cultural Studies of Concepts

When you and I use the same terms—river, vehicle, free will, or anything else—do we really have the same concepts? To take a specific example, do people of different cultures have the same concepts of colors? We can translate some word as meaning *red* or *green*, but how do we know whether the words in two languages really mean the same thing? Here we are asking about the universality of human thinking. One idea is that all human eyes (except those with colorblindness) identify the same "best" red, and therefore, people of all cultures will identify the same wavelength as the best example of red, even if they have different words for it or even if they have no words at all for colors. The other idea is that color concepts are arbitrary, that the words we use influence our thinking, and some other culture's main color names might correspond to hues that you or I would call reddish-orange or greenish-blue or anything at all.

You might suppose that this question would be easy to answer. In fact, as you will see, it is not, and in general cross-cultural research is challenging.

### WHAT'S THE EVIDENCE?
*Color Recognition and Memory by People of Different Cultures*

The English language uses an enormous number of names for colors. If you have any doubt, take a look at a box of crayons or wander through a paint store. Some less technological societies, however, have only a few color names, and the Dani people of New Guinea have only two color words in their language, meaning *dark* and *light*. Eleanor Rosch Heider (1972), however, suggested that even the Dani might react to prototypical reds, greens, blues, and so forth much the same as people who have names for those colors.

**HYPOTHESIS** Certain "focal" colors stand out as the best examples of colors. People of all cultures, even the Dani, will be able to recognize and remember these colors more easily than others.

**METHOD** Heider showed each participant a small chip of color, sometimes a "focal color" such as a typical red, sometimes a "boundary color" that was close to one of the focal colors but not a good example of it, and sometimes an "internominal color" that most people in every culture have trouble naming. Figure 8.2 shows examples. After 5 seconds she took it away, waited 30 seconds, and then showed an array of 160 colors varying in hue and brightness. She asked which of these colors matched the

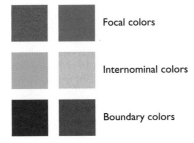

Focal colors

Internominal colors

Boundary colors

**FIGURE 8.2** Elizabeth Rosch Heider asked people to look at a color sample, such as one of these, remember it for 30 seconds, and then pick it out from an array of 160 choices. Her hypothesis was that people would remember more accurately the focal colors than the boundary or internominal colors.

one shown 30 seconds ago. Heider collected data from U.S. college students and people from the Dani culture.

**RESULTS** Both the U.S. college students and the Dani people remembered the focal colors more correctly than the other colors, even though the Dani had no words for any of the colors. Here are the means:

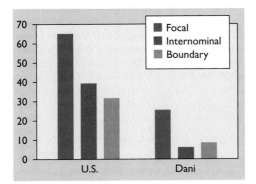

**INTERPRETATION** Yes, the results fit the predictions as both groups remembered the focal colors better than the others. However, we have to hesitate about drawing a firm conclusion because the Dani had low accuracy on all the items. It would be misleading to say that they perceive and remember colors the same as U.S. students.

Later experimenters repeated the same procedure with a different culture from New Guinea, the Berinmo, who have only five color words, corresponding roughly to white, black, red, yellow-orange, and green-blue (Roberson, Davies, & Davidoff, 2000). They too appeared to remember the focal colors better than the others. However, their focal colors weren't quite the same as ours. For example, their idea of the best example of green-blue wouldn't strike Americans as a focal color. Furthermore, researchers noticed an interesting reason why they seemed to remember focal colors better: Regardless of what color was shown, on the memory test the Berinmo usually pointed to one of

the focal colors. So the results say more about response biases than memory.

Drawing a conclusion is therefore difficult. Do people throughout the world really have the same color concepts? The results are ambiguous, and we should probably say "we aren't sure." It may be that people of different cultures have similar concepts, but those who have a word for a concept define it more precisely.

## Conceptual Networks

Choose any concept and try to think about just that and nothing else for 20 seconds. You will find the task difficult because almost anything reminds you of something else. In fact, thinking about something means relating it to a network of similar concepts; you *can't* think about something entirely by itself.

When you think about some concept, for example *bird*, you link it to a hierarchy of more specific terms, such as *sparrow*, and more general terms, such as *animals*:

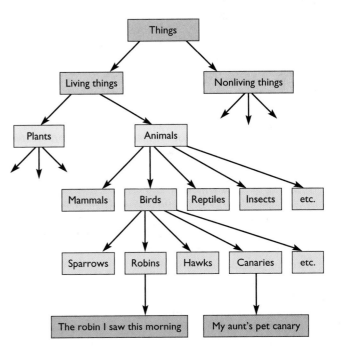

Researchers can demonstrate the reality of this kind of hierarchy by measuring the delay for people to answer various questions (A. M. Collins & Quillian, 1969, 1970). Answer the following true/false questions as quickly as possible:

Canaries are yellow.
Canaries sing.
Canaries lay eggs.
Canaries have feathers.
Canaries have skin.

Presumably you answered "true" to all five items, but you may have answered some faster than others. Most people answer fastest on the *yellow* and *sing* items, slightly slower on the *eggs* and *feathers* items, and still slower on the *skin* item. Why? It is because yellowness and singing are distinctive characteristics of canaries. You probably do not think of eggs or feathers as specific features of canaries; instead you reason (quickly), "Canaries are birds, and birds lay eggs. So canaries must lay eggs." Skin is not a particularly distinctive feature of birds, so you have to reason, "Canaries are birds and birds are animals. Animals have skin, so canaries must have skin."

Even though this way of categorizing things delays you slightly in answering whether canaries have skin, it saves you enormous time and effort overall. When you learn some new fact about birds or animals in general, you don't have to learn it again separately for every individual species. Reasoning in terms of categories and subcategories simplifies our memory.

# CONCEPT CHECK

1. Which would take longer to answer: whether fashion models wear the latest fashions or whether fashion models sometimes get sick? Why? (Check your answers on page 290.)

We also link a word or concept to other concepts that relate to it in a variety of ways. Figure 8.3 shows a possible network of conceptual links for one person (A. M. Collins & Loftus, 1975). The links, of course, vary from person to person and from moment to moment. Suppose this network describes your own concepts. *When you hear about or think about one of the concepts shown in this figure, exciting that concept will activate, or prime, the concepts linked to it* (A. M. Collins & Loftus, 1975). This process is called **spreading activation.** As a result of spreading activation, thinking of one concept primes you to think of its related concepts. For example, if you hear the word *gun* or see a picture of one, you are primed to think of words like *attack* or *murder* (Anderson, Benjamin, & Bartholow, 1998), whereas if you hear *flower*, you are primed to think of a word like *rose*. To be primed means that you might think of the word spontaneously, or you might recognize it faster if it were flashed briefly on a screen or spoken very softly. Spreading activation can also combine concepts from two sources. For example, if you hear the words *flower* and *red*, you have an even higher probability of thinking of the word *rose*. Priming is important during reading. When you come to a difficult word that you barely know, you find it easier to understand if the preceding sentences were about closely related concepts (Plaut & Booth, 2000). In effect, they provide hints about the meaning of the new word.

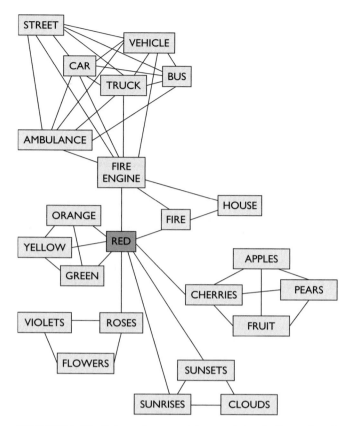

**FIGURE 8.3** We link each concept to a variety of other related concepts. Any stimulus that activates one of these concepts will also partly activate (or "prime") the ones that are linked to it. (From A. M. Collins & Loftus, 1975)

 Here is an illustration that can be explained in terms of a spreading activation model. Quickly answer each of the following questions (or ask someone else):

1. How many animals of each kind did Moses take on the ark?
2. What was the famous saying uttered by Louis Armstrong when he first set foot on the moon?
3. Some people pronounce St. Louis "saint loo-iss" and some pronounce it "saint loo-ee." How would you pronounce the capital city of Kentucky?

The answers are in the footnote on this page.[1] Many people miss these questions and are then embarrassed (or angry!) afterward. Figure 8.4 offers an explanation in terms of spreading activation (Shafto & MacKay, 2000): The question activates a series of sounds and concepts that are linked to one another and to other items. The

---

[1]Answers: 1. None. Moses didn't have an ark; Noah did. 2. Louis Armstrong never set foot on the moon; it was Neil Armstrong. 3. The right pronunciation of the capital of Kentucky is "frank-furt." (Not "loo-ee-ville"!)

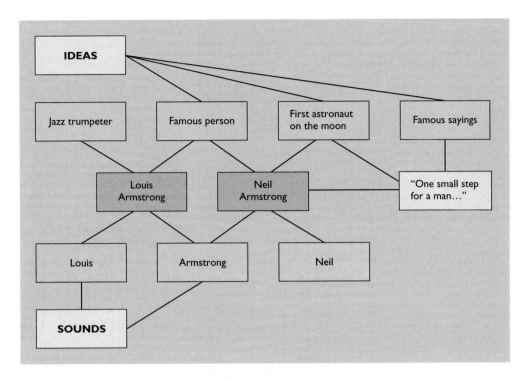

**FIGURE 8.4** According to one explanation, the word *Armstrong* and the ideas *astronaut, first person on the moon,* and *famous sayings* all activate the linked saying "One small step for a man . . ." Even the word *Louis* contributes because both Louis Armstrong and Neil Armstrong were famous people.

sound *Armstrong* and the ideas *first astronaut on the moon* and *famous sayings* are all linked to "One small step for a man . . ." Even the name *Louis Armstrong* is loosely linked to *Neil Armstrong* because both are famous people. (You probably would not respond the same way to a question about "What was the famous line uttered by Jennifer Armstrong . . . ?") The combined effect of all these influences automatically triggers the answer, "One small step for a man . . ."

## CONCEPT CHECK

2. Suppose someone says "cardinal" and then flashes the word *bird* on a screen very briefly. Some viewers identify the word correctly, suggesting priming, and some do not. Considering both priming and the encoding specificity idea from Chapter 7, how might you explain why some people and not others identified the word *bird*? (Check your answer on page 290.)

## Attention

Suppose you have just heard the word *flower* and now you see a picture of many objects, including a flower. One consequence of priming is that you will automatically pay more attention than usual to that flower picture, unless you are for some reason fighting the impulse. In short, whatever you have just seen or heard influences your attention and perception. Attention is guided by many other factors too, some of them automatic and some that you can guide deliberately.

## *Preattentive and Attentive Processes*

I once watched an unusual costume contest. People were told to dress so distinctively that their friends or family could find them as quickly as possible in a crowd. The winner was a young man who stood there on the stage stark naked. Although I concede that he earned the prize, there is a problem with this contest: The most distinctive clothing (or lack of it) depends on what everyone else is wearing. A naked man would be easy to spot in a shopping mall, but less so on a beach and still less so at a nudist colony.

 The point is that something unusual or different will get your attention automatically, but finding something that is surrounded by similar objects will require a long, patient search. For example, look at Figure 8.5. In both part a and part b, find the circle that is intersected by a vertical line.

You probably spotted the vertical line in b about as quickly as the vertical line in a, even though b has far more distracters (circles without lines) (Treisman & Souther, 1985). Apparently, people examine all the circles *in parallel*. That is, you can look at all the circles at once and you don't have to check them one by one. Finding the line relies on a **preattentive process**—*a procedure for extracting information automatically and simultaneously across a large portion of the visual field* (Enns & Rensink, 1990).

Now look at Figure 8.6. Each part contains several pentagons, most of them pointing upward. Find the one pentagon in each part that points downward.

Most people take longer to find the pentagon pointing down in part b than in part a because part b contains more distracters. The more distracters, the longer it takes

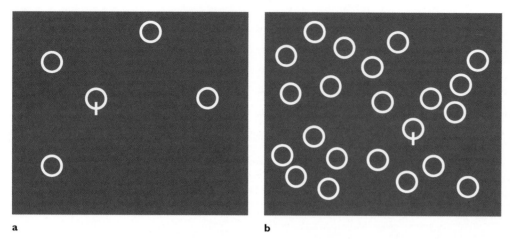

**a**                                    **b**

FIGURE 8.5 Demonstration of preattentive processes: Find the vertical line in each part. Most people find it about equally fast in both parts.

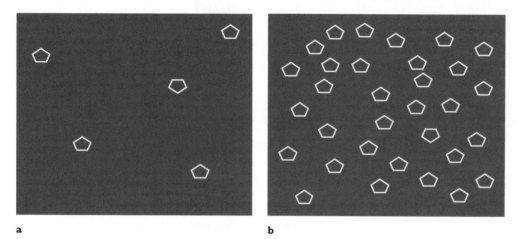

**a**                                    **b**

FIGURE 8.6 Demonstration of attentive processes: Find the pentagon pointing down in each part. Most people take longer to find it in part b.

to find the pentagon that is different; you had to turn your attention to one pentagon at a time until you found the correct one. In contrast to the preceding example, this task requires an **attentive process**—*a procedure that considers only one part of the visual field at a time.* An attentive process is ordinarily a *serial* process because a person must attend to each part one after another in a series.

 Here is another example of an apparently automatic process: Read the following instructions and then examine Figure 8.7:

Notice the blocks of color at the top of the figure. Scanning from left to right, give the name of each color as fast as you can. Then notice the nonsense syllables printed in different colors in the center of the figure. Don't try to pronounce them; just say the color of each one as fast as possible. Then turn to the real words at the bottom. Don't read them; quickly state the color in which each one is printed.

Most people find it very difficult to ignore the words at the bottom of the figure. After all of your years of reading, you can hardly bring yourself to look at **RED** and say

"**green.**" *The tendency to read the word, instead of saying the color of ink as instructed,* is known as the **Stroop effect,** after the psychologist who discovered it.

 The Stroop effect is not easy to explain. One explanation we can discard is the idea that words always take priority over colors. Try the following: Go back to Figure 8.7 and notice the red, green, blue, and yellow patches at the four corners. This time, instead of saying anything, point to the correct color patch. First, try pointing to the color patch corresponding to the color of the ink; that is, when you come to **RED,** point to the blue patch in the lower left. Then try it again but point to the color corresponding to the meaning of the word. That is, when you come to **RED,** point to the red patch in the upper left. Try it now.

You probably found it much harder to point to the patch that matches the word meaning than the one matching the color of the ink (Durgin, 2000). Here is a possible explanation: When you are speaking, you are primed to read the words you see, but when you are pointing, you are more primed to attend to something nonverbal, such as ink color. In either case one response dominates, perhaps automatically, and it will interfere with the less dominant response.

## CONCEPT CHECK

**3.** Suppose you are in a field full of brownish bushes and one brown rabbit that is not moving. If you want to find the rabbit, will you rely on attentive or preattentive processes? What if the field has many stationary rabbits and one that is hopping? Will you then find it by attentive or preattentive processes? (Check your answers on page 290.)

## Shifting Attention

Sometimes you can do two things at once, especially if one of them is a routine task such as driving your car down a familiar road. In fact, a great deal of what we do

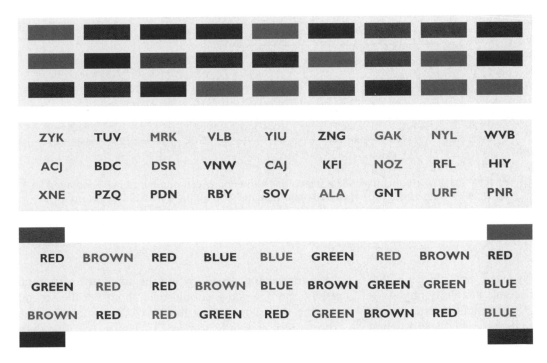

**FIGURE 8.7** Read (left to right) the color of the ink in each part. Try to ignore the words themselves. Your difficulty on the lowest part illustrates the Stroop effect.

requires little attention. When people advise you to "pay careful attention to everything you do," they are giving terrible advice. Careful attention requires effort, and the less attention you need to pay to some routine task, the more you will have available for something more difficult (Bargh & Chartrand, 1999).

 Here is a quick demonstration of your ability to shift attention: Focus your eyes on the x in the middle of the following display. Then, *without moving your eyes*, shift your attention around the circle, identifying one letter after another.

```
            B
    K               J

  S         x         W

     T            G
          N
```

Note the effort you need to shift your attention. Psychologists have found that whenever you intentionally direct your attention to one stimulus, you lose attention to everything else. Each of us has a "perceptual bottleneck." That is, you can attend to only one stimulus or group of related stimuli at one time (Pashler, 1994).

One demonstration of this principle is **negative priming:** *If you see two objects (call them A and B) and attend to just one of them (A), you will temporarily find it difficult to identify the other (B).* Note this contrast: Priming means that after you have just seen something you find it easier to recognize the same thing or something related. Negative priming means that after ignoring something it is more difficult to recognize it.

 Still, the idea of negative priming won't make much sense in the abstract, so examine this demonstration: For each pair of words in the following display, read aloud the word in **green** and ignore the one in **red.** Do so as quickly as possible:

On the average, people respond slightly slower when the correct answer is the word they ignored on the previous pair. For example, after they see "BOARD/TABLE" and say "table" and then look at "TIGER/BOARD," they are slightly delayed on saying "board" (Tipper, 1985). The delay is only slight, however, so you probably were not aware of it in your own behavior. Here is one way of explaining negative priming: When you saw BOARD immediately after ignoring BOARD, you have to exert some effort to direct your attention to it (Milliken, Joordens, Merikle, & Seiffert, 1998).

A related phenomenon is called the **attentional blink:** *During a brief time after perceiving one stimulus, it is difficult to attend to something else.* Just as a blink of the eyes prevents you from seeing anything for a split second, the attentional blink prevents you from attending to something.

For example, consider the display in Figure 8.8. Participants watched a screen that briefly displayed two letters, one in green and one in red. A nonsense pattern followed to make the identification more difficult. If the two letters appeared on the screen simultaneously, participants could identify both of them with reasonable accuracy. However, if one letter preceded the other, participants named the first one correctly but had more trouble with the second.

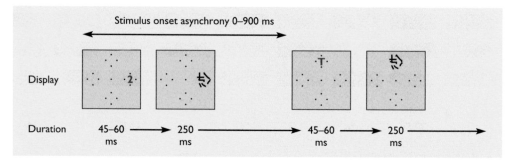

FIGURE 8.8 Participants watched a screen that showed a green number (2 or 5) and a red letter (L or T). Sometimes they appeared simultaneously, sometimes with a delay of up to 900 milliseconds between them. Immediately after each stimulus disappeared, an interfering pattern took its place. The results demonstrated interference from the first stimulus upon the second stimulus. (Modified from Duncan, Ward, & Shapiro, 1994)

The interference was especially severe with a delay of 200 milliseconds (ms) but still noticeable at a delay of 600 ms (Duncan, Ward, & Shapiro, 1994). Similar results occur with words and many other kinds of stimuli (Visser, Bischof, & DiLollo, 1999). One exception: You might not notice most words if they are presented during the attentional blink, but you do notice your own name (K. L. Shapiro, Caldwell, & Sorensen, 1997). Again, the overall conclusion is that after you have directed your attention to one item, you need time and effort to shift it somewhere else.

## CONCEPT CHECK

4. Suppose you are playing a video game and you see two signals, about a quarter-second apart, telling you to do two things. You respond to the first one but not to the second. Why? (Check your answer on page 290.)

### A STEP FURTHER
*The Attentional Blink*

When you read or listen to someone talk, one word or syllable follows another with very short delays. Why doesn't the attentional blink stop you from hearing or reading some of the words?

## *Practical Applications of Attention Research*

Much of intelligent behavior depends on successfully managing your attention. People who are highly distractible, as in attention deficit disorder, have trouble completing a task. Those who focus attention and fail to shift it, as in autism, may fail to respond to something important.

Imagine yourself as an ergonomist (human factors psychologist) designing a piece of machinery that has to include warning signals. When the apparatus is running safely, the first gauge should read about 70, the second 40, the third 30, and the fourth 10. You might arrange the gauges as in the top row of Figure 8.9, but then the person reading the gauges would have to check each one separately, through an attentional process. Note how the bottom row of Figure 8.9 simplifies the process: All the gauges are arranged so that the safe range is on the right. Now someone can glance at the display and notice anything that is out of position through a preattentive process.

Very complex tasks overload almost anyone's attention span. For example, Figure 8.10 shows a small part of the control room of the Three Mile Island nuclear power plant as it looked before a nearly disastrous accident in 1979. You notice immediately the enormous number of knobs and gauges for what is, after all, a complicated system. What you cannot see in the picture is that, in certain cases, the knob controlling something and the gauge measuring it were in different places. After the 1979 accident, ergonomists helped redesign the plant to make it easier to control.

## Mental Imagery

Imagine your room, either at home or at college. Imagine the layout of bed, desk, chairs, and so forth. Is the image you form similar to vision? You may believe the answer is obviously *yes*, but we should not rely on people's self-reports. After all, people sometimes insist that they have a clear mental image of some object but then find that they cannot correctly answer simple questions about it.

 To illustrate, imagine a simple cube balanced with one point (corner) on the table and the opposite point straight up. Imagine that you are holding the highest point with one finger. Now, with a finger of the opposite hand, point to all the remaining corners of the cube. How many corners do you touch?

**FIGURE 8.9** Each gauge represents a measurement of a different variable in a machine, such as an airplane. The top row shows one way of presenting the information. The operator must check each gauge one at a time to find out whether the reading is within the safe range for that variable. The bottom row shows the information represented in a way that is easier to read. The safe range for each variable is rotated to the same visual position. At a glance the operator can detect any reading outside the safe zone.

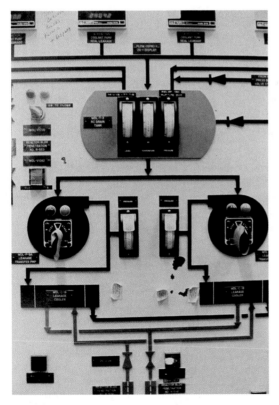

**FIGURE 8.10** The Three Mile Island TMI-2 nuclear power plant had a complex and confusing control system, a small portion of which is shown here. Some of the important gauges were not easily visible to the operators, some of the gauges were poorly labeled, and many of the alarm signals had ambiguous meanings. The nuclear plant currently in operation at Three Mile Island has a much simpler and clearer operating system.

You probably will say that you answered this question by "picturing" a cube in your mind as if you were actually seeing it. However, most people answer the question incorrectly, and few get it right quickly (Hinton, 1979). (Check answer A on page 290.)

So our mental images are sometimes wrong. Further, it is not obvious that we need mental images to answer visual or spatial questions. Computers answer questions quite accurately without drawing little pictures inside themselves. Can we demonstrate that mental images are at least sometimes useful and that they have some of the properties we ordinarily associate with vision? Answering this question was one of the early triumphs of experimental research in cognitive psychology.

**WHAT'S THE EVIDENCE?**
*Mental Imagery*

Roger Shepard and Jacqueline Metzler (1971) conducted a classic study of how humans solve visual problems. They reasoned that if people actually visualize mental images, then the time it takes them to rotate a mental image should be similar to the time needed to rotate a real object.

**HYPOTHESIS** When people have to rotate a mental image to answer a question, the farther they have to rotate it, the longer it will take them to answer the question.

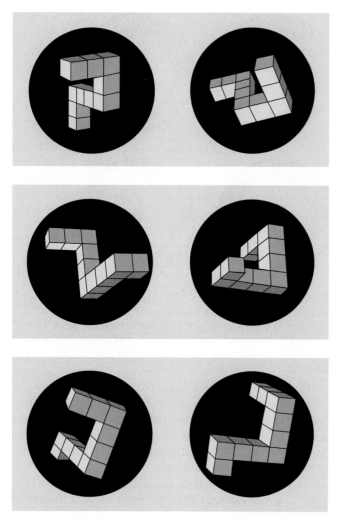

**FIGURE 8.11** Examples of pairs of drawings used in an experiment by Shepard and Metzler (1971). Do the drawings for each pair represent the same object being rotated, or are they different objects? (See answer B on page 290.)

**METHOD** The experimenters showed participants pairs of two-dimensional drawings of three-dimensional objects, as in Figure 8.11, and asked whether the drawings in each pair represented the same object rotated in different directions or whether they represented different objects. (Try to answer this question yourself before reading further. Then check answer B on page 290.)

People answered by pulling one lever to indicate *same* and another lever to indicate *different.* When the correct answer was *same,* someone might determine that answer by rotating a mental image of the first picture until it matched the second. If so, the delay should depend on how far the image had to be rotated.

**RESULTS** Participants answered almost 97% of the items correctly. Their delays before answering *different* were generally longer and less consistent than those for answering *same,* as is generally the case. The interesting point was their delays in answering *same* items. As predicted, their reaction time for responding *same* depended

on the angular difference in orientation between the two views. For example, if the first image of a pair had to be rotated 30 degrees to match the second image, people needed a certain amount of time to pull the *same* lever. If one image had to be rotated 60 degrees to match the other, people took twice as long to pull the lever. In other words people reacted as if they were watching a little model of the object rotate in their head; the more the object needed to be rotated, the longer they took to determine the answer.

**INTERPRETATION** Viewing a mental image is at least partly like real vision.

Whenever possible, researchers try to test a hypothesis in different ways because even an excellent experiment may have some hidden flaw. One study found that, while people were imagining moving objects, their eyes moved almost the same way as when they were actually looking at the same objects (Brandt & Stark, 1997). Another study found that while people were imagining rotating an object, activity increased in most of the same brain areas they would use if they were handling the object (Richter et al., 2000). So at least in this case, common sense appears correct: When we imagine a moving object, it is as if we are seeing something moving inside our heads.

**A STEP FURTHER**
*Mental Imagery*

Some people report that they have auditory images as well as visual images. They "hear" words or songs "in their head." What kind of evidence would we need to test this claim?

## Using Mental Images: Cognitive Maps

You are staying at a hotel in an unfamiliar city. You walk a few blocks to go to a museum, then a few blocks in another direction to get to a restaurant, and still later a few more blocks in another direction to a theater. After the performance how do you return to your hotel? Do you retrace all of your steps? Can you find a shorter route? Or do you give up and hail a cab?

If you can find your way back, you use a **cognitive map,** *a mental image of a spatial arrangement.* One way to measure the accuracy of people's cognitive maps is to test how well they can find the route from one place to another. Another way is to ask them to draw maps. The errors people make in their maps follow some interesting patterns. First, they tend to remember street angles as being close to 90 degrees, even when they are not (Moar & Bower, 1983). We can easily understand that error. For

**FIGURE 8.12** Logical versus actual: location of Reno and Los Angeles. Most people imagine that Los Angeles is farther west because California is west of Nevada.

practical purposes all we need to remember is "go three blocks and turn left" or "go two blocks and turn right"; we do not burden our memory by recalling "turn 72 degrees to the right."

Second, people generally imagine geographic areas as being neatly arranged north to south and east to west (Stevens & Coupe, 1978; B. Tversky, 1981). Try to answer these questions, for example: Which city is farther west—Reno, Nevada, or Los Angeles, California? And which is farther north—Philadelphia, Pennsylvania, or Rome, Italy? Most people reason that, because California is west of Nevada, Los Angeles is "obviously" west of Reno. (Figure 8.12 shows the true positions.) Rome is in southern Europe, and Philadelphia is in the northern United States; therefore, Philadelphia should be north of Rome, right? In fact, Rome is north of Philadelphia.

You now see the differences between a cognitive map and a real map: Cognitive maps, like other mental images, highlight some details, distort some, and omit others. Nevertheless, they are accurate enough for most practical purposes.

### IN CLOSING
## Inferences About Thinking

We cannot observe people's concepts, images, attention, or other cognitions. Nevertheless, psychologists infer these processes and others from the results of the kinds of experiments you have been reading about. Drawing inferences is a time-honored way of doing science: Physicists describe the properties of electrons and quarks; astronomers estimate the age of the universe; biologists reconstruct the probable structure of dinosaurs and other species long since extinct. When dealing with unobservables—whether it be attention processes or quarks—we should remember that any one line of evidence is tentative. The conclusions never become certain, but they become stronger if we find many kinds of studies, using different methods, whose results point in the same direction.

## Summary

- **Categorization.** People use many categories that are hard to define; we determine whether something fits the category by how closely it resembles familiar examples. Many items are marginal examples of a category, so we cannot insist on a yes/no decision. (page 279)
- **Cross-cultural studies of concepts.** Cross-cultural research is difficult. Studies of color concepts in cultures where people have few terms for colors have found ambiguous results. Those people remembered focal colors better than other colors, but they didn't remember any of the colors well, and they appear to have followed the strategy of guessing the bright focal colors regardless of what they saw. (page 280)
- **Conceptual networks.** We store representations of words or concepts with links to related concepts. Hearing or thinking about one concept will temporarily prime the linked concepts, and hearing several concepts can strongly prime another. Sometimes the result is that we answer a question impulsively (like the one about how many animals Moses took on the ark) even when we know better. (page 281)
- **Attentive and preattentive processes.** We notice some items—such as a straight line among circles or a moving object among stationary ones—almost at once, or preattentively, in spite of many potential distracters. Noticing other less distinct items requires more careful attention to one possible target after another. (page 283)
- **Automatic attention.** Sometimes it is difficult to avoid attending to certain stimuli; for example, it is difficult to state the color of the ink in which words are written while ignoring the words themselves (especially if they are color names). (page 284)
- **Shifting attention.** If you attend to one stimulus and ignore another one, you are temporarily impeded if you need to attend to the one you have ignored. Also, during a split second after attending to any stimulus, it is difficult to register a second stimulus. This period is called the attentional blink. (page 284)
- **Mental imagery.** Mental images resemble vision in certain respects. For example, the time required to answer questions about a rotating object depends on how far the object would actually rotate between one position and another. (page 286)
- **Cognitive maps.** People learn to find their way by using cognitive maps, but they make certain consistent errors in these maps, such as remembering all turns as being close to 90-degree angles. (page 288)

## Answers to Concept Checks

1. It would take longer to answer whether fashion models sometimes get sick. Wearing the latest fashions is a distinctive feature of fashion models; becoming ill is not. To answer the second question, you have to reason that models are people, and people sometimes get sick. (page 282)

2. People who heard "cardinal" and thought of it as a bird would have spreading activation to prime the word *bird*. However, other people who thought of "cardinal" as an officer in the Catholic church would have spreading activation to prime a very different set of words, and not *bird*. (page 283)

3. Finding a motionless brown rabbit in a field full of brown objects will require attentive processes, but you could use preattentive processes to find a hopping rabbit in a field where nothing else is moving. (For this reason small animals in danger of predation stay motionless when they can.) (page 284)

4. The second signal arrived during the attentional blink while you were still processing the first stimulus. (page 286)

## Answers to Other Questions in the Module

A. The cube has six (*not* four) remaining corners. (page 287)

B. The objects in pair a are the same; in b they are the same; and in c they are different. (page 288)

# Problem Solving, Expertise, and Error

*What is required to become an expert?*

*What are some common errors of thinking?*

On a college physics exam, a student was once asked how to use a barometer to determine the height of a building. He answered that he would tie a long string to the barometer, go to the top of the building, and carefully lower the barometer until it reached the ground. Then he would cut the string and measure its length.

When the professor marked this answer incorrect, the student asked why. "Well," said the professor, "your method would work, but it's not the method I wanted you to use." When the student objected, the professor offered as a compromise to let him try again.

"All right," the student said. "Take the barometer to the top of the building, drop it, and measure the time it takes to hit the ground. Then, from the formula for the speed of a falling object, using the gravitational constant, calculate the height of the building."

"Hmmm," replied the professor. "That too would work. And it does make use of physical principles. But it still isn't the answer I had in mind. Can you think of another way?"

"Another way? Sure," he replied. "Place the barometer next to the building on a sunny day. Measure the height of the barometer and the length of its shadow. Also measure the length of the building's shadow. Then use the formula

$$\frac{\text{height of barometer}}{\text{length of barometer's shadow}} = \frac{\text{height of building}}{\text{length of building's shadow}}$$

The professor was becoming more and more impressed, but he was still reluctant to give credit, so the student persisted with another method: "Measure the barometer's height. Then walk up the stairs of the building, marking it off in units of the barometer's height. At the top take the number of barometer units and multiply by the height of the barometer to get the height of the building."

The professor sighed: "Just give me one more way—any other way—and I'll give you credit, even if it's not the answer I wanted."

"Really?" asked the student with a smile. "Any other way?"

"Yes, any other way."

"All right," said the student. "Go to the man who owns the building and say, 'Hey, buddy, if you tell me how tall this building is, I'll give you this cool barometer!'"

Whenever we face a new problem, we must devise a new solution instead of relying on a memorized or practiced solution. Sometimes people develop creative, imaginative solutions, like the ones that the physics student proposed. Sometimes they offer less imaginative but reasonable solutions or something quite illogical or no solution at all. Psychologists study problem-solving behavior partly to understand the thought processes behind it and partly to look for ways to help people reason more effectively.

■ How would you carry 98 water bottles—all at one time, with no wheelbarrow or truck? When faced with a new problem, sometimes people find a novel and effective solution, and sometimes they do not.

## Expertise

People vary in their performance on problem-solving and decision-making tasks. In the barometer story just described, we would probably talk about the student's creativity; in other cases we might talk of expertise. In either case some people seem more able than others to find feasible solutions.

Expert performance in music, art, athletics, and other fields can be extremely impressive. An expert crossword puzzle solver not only completes *The New York Times* Sunday crossword—an amazing feat in itself—but tries to make it more interesting by racing against someone else. An expert bird watcher can look at a blurry photo and identify not only the species of bird but also the subspecies, sex, age, and summer or winter plumage.

An expert bridge player will say something like, "It was obvious from the bidding that East had to have the king of diamonds, so obviously it was better to try for an endplay than a finesse." (And a casual bridge player like me wonders "Huh?")

## Practice Makes (Nearly) Perfect

Confronted by such amazing skills, it is tempting to assume that experts were born with a special talent. Not so, say psychologists who have studied expertise (Ericsson & Charness, 1994; Ericsson, Krampe, & Tesch-Römer, 1993). Expertise emerges only after years of concentrated practice. For fields ranging from chess to sports to violin playing, the rule is that expertise requires about 10 years of concentrated practice. Why have the Russians long dominated world chess competitions? Do they have a special talent for chess? A more parsimonious explanation is that more Russians play chess and begin younger than people in other countries. In general, researchers find that if you know how many people in a given country play chess, you can predict fairly accurately how good is the country's best player (Charness & Gerchak, 1996).

Hungarian author Laszlo Polgar set out to demonstrate his conviction that almost anyone can become an expert at something with sufficient effort. He allowed his three young daughters to explore several fields; when they showed an interest in chess, he devoted enormous efforts to nurturing their chess skills. Today, all three daughters are outstanding chess players. One of them, Judit Polgar, reached grand master status about 10 years after she started studying the game (Figure 8.13).

Similarly, most of the world's best violinists began playing violin in early childhood and continued practicing 3 to 4 hours a day throughout their lives. The top performers in any field spend many hours practicing in addition to their public performances. Thus, an expert violinist practices the most difficult passages; a tennis player spends hours working on backhand shots; a golfer works on chip shots. Practice is even more effective if a coach is present to provide extra feedback.

Some researchers have argued that becoming an expert depends *entirely* on practice and is independent of any inborn talents or predispositions. That claim is almost certainly an overstatement (H. Gardner, 1995). If ten people began developing a skill at exactly the same age and practiced for exactly the same amount of time for the same number of years, would they all reach exactly the same level of expertise? Probably not. At a minimum let's admit the obvious: Someone with genes for being short and slow will not become an expert basketball player, and someone born blind will not become an expert photographer. Furthermore, in any field those who show early success are most likely to devote the necessary effort to achieve expertise. The main point, however, is that many years of work are necessary to achieve expertise at anything.

**FIGURE 8.13** Judit Polgar confirmed her father's confidence that prolonged effort could make her an expert in her chosen field, chess. By reaching the status of grand master at age 15 years and 5 months, she beat Bobby Fisher's previous record for being the youngest.

So does all this research mean that *you* could become an expert at something? Well, if you have waited until college age to start a skill as competitive as chess, violin, or basketball, you are very late; nearly all the great performers in those fields started young. Still, you have a choice among many other fields not dominated by child prodigies. However, do not underestimate the necessary effort and sacrifice. For Judit Polgar to become a grand master at chess, she devoted about 8 hours a day to chess from age 5 to 15. She did not go to public school and she missed most of the usual childhood activities. If you want to excel in any field, you have to commit yourself to an enormous effort.

## Expert Pattern Recognition

What exactly do experts do that other people do not? One important characteristic is that experts can look at a pattern and recognize its important features quickly. Much of the research deals with chess because we can accurately identify the experts in chess. In a typical experiment (de Groot, 1966), people were shown pieces on a chessboard, as in Figure 8.14, for 5 seconds. Then they were asked to recall the positions of all the pieces. When the pieces were arranged as they might occur in an actual game, expert players recalled 91% of the positions,

a                          b

**FIGURE 8.14** Pieces arranged on a chessboard as they might actually occur in a game (a) and in a random manner (b). Master chess players can memorize the realistic pattern much better than average players can, but they are no better than average at memorizing the random pattern.

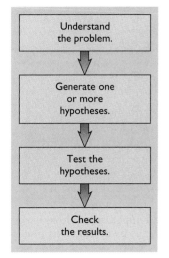

**FIGURE 8.15** The four steps to solving a problem.

whereas novices recalled only 41%. When the pieces were arranged randomly, however, the expert players did no better than the novices. That is, on the average, expert chess players don't have greater overall memory or intelligence; they have simply learned to recognize the common chessboard patterns.

Further evidence for this conclusion includes the fact that the top-level grand master chess players can play simultaneous games against six or so other opponents and play almost as well as if they were facing only one (Gobet & Simon, 1996). Simultaneous play offers little opportunity for planning many moves ahead; in simultaneous play one must rely on quickly recognizing a pattern and knowing what is a good move for that situation.

Chess is the best studied example, but not the only one. In a wide variety of areas from bird identification to reading x-rays to judging gymnastic competitions, experts recognize key patterns that other observers overlook (Murphy & Medin, 1985; Ste-Marie, 1999). They also know the difference between relevant and irrelevant information (Proffitt, Coley, & Medin, 2000).

# Problem Solving

Generally, we go through four phases when we set about solving a problem (Polya, 1957): (a) understanding the problem, (b) generating one or more hypotheses, (c) testing the hypotheses, and (d) checking the result (Figure 8.15). A scientist goes through those four phases when approaching a new, complex phenomenon, and you would probably go through them when trying to assemble a bicycle that came with confusing instructions. We shall discuss these four phases of problem solving in detail.

## *Understanding and Simplifying a Problem*

Sometimes the main key to solving a problem is simply recognizing it. For years airport terminals listed incoming and outgoing flights in order of time, starting with the

ones just completed or about to take place. You can imagine the struggle to find your flight: You might remember that it was supposed to depart somewhere between 10 and 10:30, but you didn't remember exactly when (and planes seldom leave exactly on time anyway), so you would have to sort through listings of many irrelevant flights to find the one you wanted. Eventually, someone recognized this situation as a problem: People look for "the flight to San Jose," not "the flight at 10:27." Then airports quickly switched to listing flights by locations (Figure 8.16).

In other cases we recognize a problem but don't know how to solve it. Often, the best strategy is to start with a simpler version of the problem. For example, here is what may appear to be a difficult, even impossible, problem:

> A professor hands back students' test papers at random. On the average, how many students will accidentally receive their own paper?

Note that the problem does not specify how many students are in the class. At first, you may not know how to approach the problem, but see what happens if you start with simpler cases: How many students will get their own paper back if there is only one student in the class? One, of course. What if there are two students? There is a 50% chance that both will get their own paper back and a 50% chance that neither will. On the average one student will get the correct paper. What if there are three students? Each student then has one chance in three of getting his or her own paper. A one-third chance times three students means that on the average one student will get the correct paper. Already the pattern is clear: If there are $n$ students, each student has one chance in $n$ of getting his or her own paper back. No matter how many students are in the class, on the average one student will get his or her own paper back.

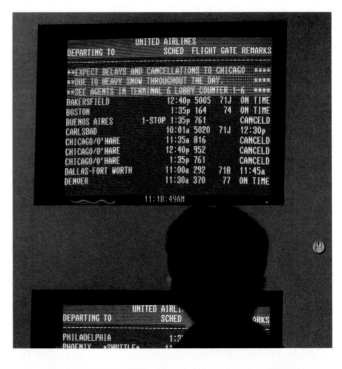

**FIGURE 8.16** Switching airport terminal displays from listings by times (the old way) to listings by destinations (the new way) took little effort and had clear advantages. Sometimes solving a problem is easy after people identify the problem.

## *Generating Hypotheses*

After you have simplified a problem as much as possible, you need to generate *hypotheses*—preliminary interpretations that you can evaluate or test. In some cases you can generate a complete list of possibilities and test them all. For example, suppose you want to connect your television set to a pair of stereo amplifiers, a VCR, and a DVD player, but you have lost the instruction manuals. You have several cables to attach, and each device has input and output channels. You could simply connect the cables by trial and error, testing every possibility until you find one that works. *A mechanical, repetitive procedure for solving a problem* is called an **algorithm.** Testing every possible hypothesis is one example of an algorithm. The rules for alphabetizing a list are another example. You can also learn an algorithm for how to win, or at least tie, every time you play tic-tac-toe.

In many situations, however, the possible hypotheses are too numerous or ill-defined to apply any algorithm. Consider the question, "What should I do with my life?" You could not possibly consider every possible choice. **Heuristics** are *strategies for simplifying a problem or for guiding an investigation.* For the question about your future, you might restrict your attention to a few possible careers and then learn whatever you can about them.

To illustrate the contrast between algorithms and heuristics, consider chess. At a typical point in a game of chess, a player has about 25 legal moves, and the opponent has about 25 legal replies to each of them. To choose your best move by an algorithm, you would consider each of your possible moves, each of your opponent's possible replies, each of your next moves, and so forth, as many moves ahead as possible. Finally, you would select

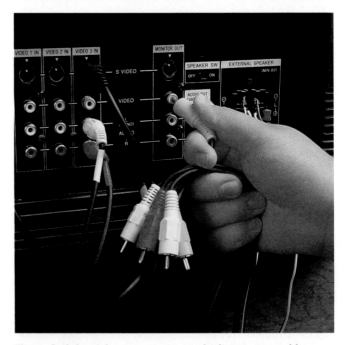

■ To find the right way to connect the lines, you could use the simple algorithm of trying every possible combination, one after the other.

the move that gives you the best result, assuming that your opponent made the best possible reply at each point. This algorithm, however, will overburden your memory, so you simplify it with heuristics: On each move, you select just a few possible moves for serious consideration, aided by your recognition of similar positions you have faced in past games. You consider just a few of your opponent's likely responses, a few of your possible next moves, and so forth.

**FIGURE 8.17** In the Chinese game Go, opponents alternate placing their markers on a 19 × 19 grid, attempting to arrange their own pieces in a safe arrangement or to surround opposing pieces that are not in safe arrangements. For this game an algorithm of imagining every possible move and then every possible reply would be extremely inefficient; effective strategies require heuristics to restrict the moves under consideration.

Unlike humans, the best chess-playing computers do rely on algorithms to test every possible move. The Deep Blue computer program that beat Garry Kasparov, the best human player, did so by considering every possible move and every possible reply, at least 14 or 15 moves ahead (Mechner, 1998). The computer succeeded because it can consider 200 million positions per second (and remember the outcomes). It did use a few simple heuristics, such as favorably evaluating any move that helped control the center of the board, but given the power of its algorithms, it didn't need all the heuristics that a human player develops.

However, in the game of Go (Figure 8.17), which has a 19 × 19 grid and very complex strategies, each player has an average of about 250 possible moves, for each of which the opponent would have 250 possible replies. Whereas Deep Blue can run its algorithm to find the best possible chess move in 3 minutes, a computer would need an estimated 70 years to complete a comparable algorithm for Go! When Deep Blue beat Kasparov, the best available computer program for Go was at the level of a beginner (Mechner, 1998). Even if we assume that computers will continue to get faster and more powerful, programming a computer to win at Go will probably require developing good heuristics—in effect, programming it to think more like a human.

## CONCEPT CHECK

5. Suppose you are a traveling salesperson. You must start from your home city, visit each of several other cities, and then return home. Your task is to find the shortest route. What would be the appropriate algorithm? What would be a possible heuristic for simplifying the problem? (Check your answers on page 308.)

## Testing Hypotheses and Checking the Results

If you think you have solved a problem, test your idea to see whether it will work. Many people who think they have a great idea never bother to try it out, even on a small scale. One inventor applied for a patent on the "perpetual motion machine" shown in Figure 8.18. Rubber balls, being lighter than water, rise in a column of water and flow over the top. The balls are heavier than air, so they then fall, thus moving a belt and thereby generating energy. At the bottom they reenter the water column. Do you see why this system could never work? You would if you tried to build it. (Check answer C on page 308.)

Even if you can't physically check your idea, you can stop to consider whether it is realistic. One article published in 1927 claimed that a deer botfly has a speed of 800 miles per hour (almost 1300 kilometers per hour). Some books and Internet sources to this day list that speed as the record for the fastest species on earth. You and I may never be in a position to measure a deer botfly's speed, but we can consider the likelihood that an insect flies faster than most jet airplanes. One physicist calculated that an object moving that fast would generate more than enough air pressure to squash the fly. If you were struck by a fly at that speed it would be like getting shot with a bullet. And to sustain that speed, the fly would need so much energy that it would have to eat 1.5 times its weight in food *per second* (May, 1999).

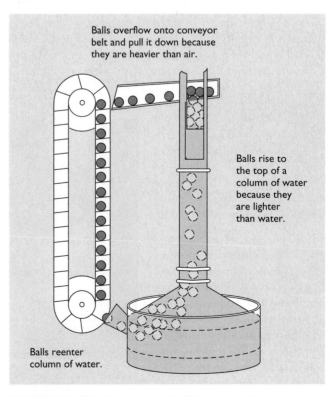

**FIGURE 8.18** What is wrong with this perpetual motion machine?

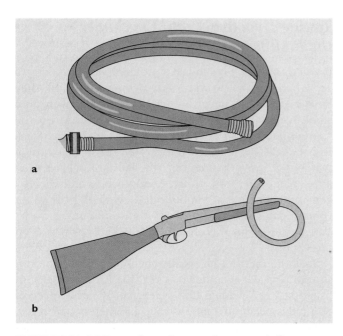

**FIGURE 8.19** (a) Draw the trajectory of water as it flows out of a coiled garden hose. (b) Draw the trajectory of a bullet as it leaves a coiled gun barrel.

## Generalizing Solutions to Similar Problems

You might imagine that people who had just solved one problem would quickly recognize how to solve a similar problem. Sometimes they do, but usually they do not. Many people who understand probability fail to apply the laws of probability to real-life situations (Nisbett, Fong, Lehman, & Cheng, 1987). For example, most people who flipped a coin and got ten consecutive heads would not expect more than five heads out of the next ten flips. But after the same people watch a basketball team win ten consecutive games, they are surprised if the team wins only seven or eight of its next ten. The basketball situation is not exactly the same as coin flipping, but it does have some similarities: A long winning streak depends partly on skill, but also partly on chance.

 In other situations as well, people who have solved one problem correctly fail to solve a similar problem, unless someone explains the similarity (Gick & Holyoak, 1980). For example, Figure 8.19a shows a coiled garden hose. When the water spurts out, what path will it take? (Draw

it.) Figure 8.19b shows a curved gun barrel. When the bullet comes out, what path will it take? (Draw it.)

Almost everyone draws the water coming out of the garden hose in a straight path. Even after doing so, however, many people draw a bullet coming out of a gun in a curved path, as if the bullet remembered the curved path it had just taken (Kaiser, Jonides, & Alexander, 1986). The physics is the same in both situations: Except for the effects of gravity, both the water and the bullet will follow a straight path.

Here is another chance to take a scientific principle that you probably have been taught and apply it to a new problem: Suppose you plug in a refrigerator in the middle of a well-insulated, airtight room, and then you open the refrigerator door all the way. Will the net effect of the refrigerator heat the room, cool it, or make no difference? Before reading further, try answering this question and then check your answer against answer D on page 308.

The correct answer to this question depends on a couple of facts you probably know: One is that refrigerators don't "create coldness"; they just transfer heat from one place to another. The other is the principle of entropy: Every machine has less than perfect efficiency. That is, to operate a machine, you have to bring energy (and therefore heat) into the system. Still, even if you learned those facts in a high school science class, you probably had trouble applying them to a new question.

Why do we sometimes use our solution to an old problem as a guide to solving a new one (as in Figure 8.20), but sometimes not? It is easier to generalize a solution after we have seen several examples of it; after just one example, we think of the solution in just that context (Gick & Holyoak, 1983). There is a general point here that will arise again in Chapter 10: A concept isn't something you either have or don't have. You can have it to a greater or

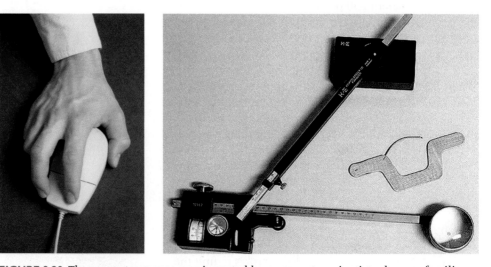

**FIGURE 8.20** The computer mouse was invented by a computer scientist who was familiar with an engineering device called a planimeter that he believed could be modified for use with computers. Such insights are unusual; most people do not generalize a solution from one task to another.

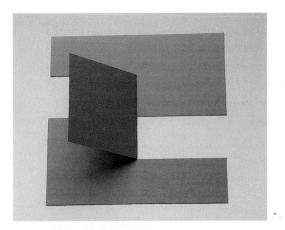

**FIGURE 8.21**  This object was made by cutting and folding an ordinary piece of cardboard, with nothing left over. How was it done?

lesser degree (Siegler, 2000). If you practice a concept in many ways, you increase your ability to apply it to a new situation.

# Special Features of Insight Problems

Some of the problems we have been discussing are "insight" problems or "aha!" problems, in which the correct answer occurs to you suddenly or not at all. Here is an example (M. Gardner, 1978): Figure 8.21 shows an object that was made by cutting and bending an ordinary piece of cardboard. How was it made? If you think you know, take a piece of paper and try to make it yourself. (The solution is on page 308, answer E.)

## *Sudden or Gradual Insights?*

Solving insight problems differs from solving, say, algebra problems. Most people can look at an algebra problem and rather accurately predict how quickly they will solve it, if at all. As they work on it, they can estimate how close they are to a solution. With insight problems, however, people often have no idea whether or not they are about to solve the problem (Metcalfe & Wiebe, 1987).

Does the answer really come as suddenly as it seems? If you were groping your way around in a dark room, you would have no idea how soon you were going to find the door, but nevertheless you were making progress. You would have learned much about the room, including where the door was *not*.

So maybe people are making progress without realizing it on insight problems. To test this possibility, psychologists gave students problems with the following form:

The following three words are all associated with one other word. What is that word?
**color    numbers    oil**

In this case the correct answer is *paint.* As with other insight questions, participants said the answer came to them suddenly if at all and that they did not know when they were about to think of it. Then the experimenters gave the students paired sets of three words each, like those shown here in Sets 1 and 2, to examine for 12 seconds. In each pair one set had a correct answer (like *paint* in the example just given). The other set had no correct answer. Students were asked to generate a correct answer if they could, but if not, at least to guess which set had a correct answer. Examples:

**Set 1**
**playing    credit    report**    *or*    **still    pages    music**

**Set 2**
**town    root    car**    *or*    **ticket    shop    broker**

(You can check your answers on page 309, answer F.)

The main result: Even when students did not know the correct answer, they usually guessed correctly which set had an answer (Bowers, Regehr, Balthazard, & Parker, 1990). Even when they said they had "no confidence" in their guesses, they were still right more often than not. In short, insight solutions are not as sudden as they seem; people often make progress without realizing it.

## *The Characteristics of Creativity*

Why are some people more creative than others? Creativity is not the same as expertise. An expert gymnast goes through the same motions every time, and an expert chess player may use the same strategy in game after

■  Creative problem solving, evident in this temporary bridge made of old railroad cars, has two elements: novelty and social value.

■ Howard Gardner studied the lives of seven highly creative people, including political and spiritual leader Mahatma Gandhi and dance pioneer Martha Graham, to find the features that promote creativity.

game, but a writer, composer, or painter who kept doing the same thing again and again would not be considered creative. One hallmark of creative people is a willingness to take risks. For example, many great opera composers followed one of their top successes with another opera that was a complete failure. Expert performers reach the point where they can be sure their next performance will be a success, but creative producers are never sure about their next creation (Simonton, 2000a).

Creative writers, composers, and scientists have certain features in common, such as nonconformity, risk-taking, willingness to tolerate rejection, openness to new experiences, and at least moderate intelligence (Simonton, 2000b). However, it is misleading to talk about "creative people" as if certain people are creative in everything they do. People have to know a field well before they can make creative contributions to it. That is, don't expect a creative poet to offer creative solutions to an auto-mechanics problem.

Howard Gardner (1993) studied creativity by examining the lives of seven 20th-century people who are widely regarded as creative in very different fields: Sigmund Freud (psychology), Albert Einstein (physics), Pablo Picasso (painting), Igor Stravinsky (musical composition), T. S. Eliot (poetry), Martha Graham (dance), and Mahatma Gandhi (political resistance and spirituality). Gardner found a few patterns that these people had in common, including the following:

• They lived and worked in an atmosphere of moderate tension, sensing that the old ways of doing things are not quite right.
• They all had enough background in their fields to feel self-confident but not so much experience that they became trapped into traditional habits. It is difficult for someone who has been a success in a field for many years to suddenly look at things in a new way.

• During a period early in life, each relied heavily on one or a few close friends for advice and encouragement. The advice helped them polish their ideas, and the encouragement helped them persist in the face of criticism.
• Each threw him- or herself wholeheartedly into the work, sacrificing any possibility of a well-rounded life. Each had a very limited family life and strained relationships with other people. Even Gandhi, a famous advocate for love and justice, loved people in the abstract but had trouble developing close relationships with real, live people.

Creative careers, however, are extremely variable (Simonton, 1997). As a rule poets are recognized for their greatness early in life, generally in their 20s, whereas the greatest, most creative historians seldom do their best work before their 40s or 50s. Within any field some people start early and quit early and others bloom late. Some—such as Bach, Picasso, and Edison—produce enormous quantities of good work, whereas others produce only one or two great works.

## CONCEPT CHECK

**6.** Great creative poets die younger on the average than equally recognized historians. Why? (Hint: Imagine the distribution of ages at death for both groups.) (Check your answer on page 308.)

# Common Errors in Human Cognition

Although we humans pride ourselves on our intelligence and our ability to solve problems, we sometimes make embarrassing mistakes. For decades college professors have been talking about the importance of **critical thinking,** *the careful evaluation of evidence for and against any conclusion.* However, even the sincerest advocates of critical thinking sometimes find that they have been repeating nonsense that they should have questioned. For example, I myself used to repeat the rumors—only I didn't know they were rumors; I thought they were facts—that "glass flows as a very slow liquid," that "when the lemming population gets very high, some of them jump off cliffs," and that "Thomas Crapper invented the flush toilet." I later learned that all of these statements were nonsense. (The story about Thomas Crapper was started by Wallace Reyburn, who wrote the book *Flushed with Pride,* a partly true, partly fictitious biography of Crapper. Thomas Crapper was a real person, but he was just a plumber who built and installed toilets. Everyone might have continued to believe Reyburn's hoax if he hadn't followed it with another book, *Bust Up,* allegedly the biography of Otto Titzling, the inventor of the bra! Crapper was at least a real person, whereas Titzling was a figment of Reyburn's imagination.)

Why do intelligent people sometimes come to false conclusions or accept conclusions without adequate evidence? The reasons are many; here we shall consider just a few.

## Overconfidence

 Let's start with a demonstration. Ten questions follow. Few people know any of the answers exactly, but I'm asking for only an approximation. For each question, answer with a 90% confidence range; that is, give a range within which you are 90% sure the correct answer lies. For example, consider this question:

In the 2000 summer Olympics in Sydney, Australia, how many silver medals did China win?

You reason that China is a large country with many athletes, so you would be surprised if they won fewer than, say, 5 silver medals. But the total number of Olympic events isn't huge, so you also would be surprised if they won more than 25. So you guess "5-25." If so, you would be right because China won 16 silver medals. Okay, that's the idea. Now fill in your answers:

**Your estimate (as a 90% confidence range)**
1. How old was Martin Luther King, Jr., at the time of his death? ____
2. How long is the Nile River? (in miles or kilometers) ____
3. How many countries belong to OPEC? ____
4. How many books are in the Old Testament? ____
5. What is the diameter of the moon? (in miles or kilometers) ____
6. What is the weight of an empty Boeing 747? (in pounds or kilograms) ____
7. In what year was Mozart born? ____
8. What is the gestation period of an Asian elephant? (in days) ____
9. How far is London from Tokyo? (in miles or kilometers) ____
10. What is the deepest known point in the ocean? (in feet or meters) ____

Now turn to answer G on page 309 to check your answers (Plous, 1993). How many of your ranges included the correct answer?

Because you said you were 90% confident of each answer, you should be right on about nine of ten answers. However, very few people get that many correct. Most, in fact, miss more than half of the items. That is, they were **overconfident;** *they believed their answers were more accurate than they actually were.*

Although most people are overconfident about their answers to difficult questions, they are on the average *underconfident* about *easy* questions, mainly because it is hard to be overconfident when your answers are entirely correct (Erev, Wallsten, & Budescu, 1994; Juslin, Winman, & Olsson, 2000). For example, suppose we ask people to predict whether the world will have at least one hurricane next year, and nearly all answer *yes.* Now we ask them to state their confidence on a 0 to 100% scale. At least one hurricane is a virtual certainty, so if even a few people express less than 100% confidence, their average shows underconfidence.

People are especially likely to be overconfident about their own accomplishments. For example, at the beginning of each semester, most students (even poor students) estimate that they will get mostly As and Bs (Prohaska, 1994) (see Figure 8.22). Most students also overestimate the grades they *already* received, reporting slightly higher grades than they actually got (Bahrick, Hall, & Berger, 1996). Similarly, most athletes and

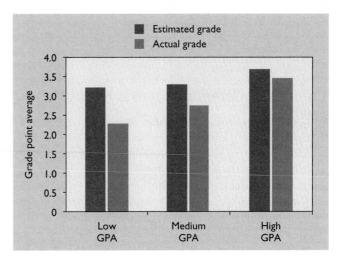

**FIGURE 8.22** At the beginning of a semester, undergraduates in an advanced psychology course estimated their probable semester grade. Students with low, medium, or high grade-point averages generally predicted that they would get an **A or a B.** The best students were slightly overpredicting their success; the worst students were greatly overpredicting. (Based on data of Prohaska, 1994)

coaches predict they will perform better this season than last season, and most people entering a contest think they have a better than average chance of winning.

Philip Tetlock (1994) conducted a study of government officials and consultants, foreign policy professors, newspaper columnists, and others who make their living by analyzing and predicting world events. He asked them to predict some events in U.S. and world politics over the next several years—such as what would happen in Korea, the Middle East, Eastern Europe, and Cuba—and to state their confidence in these predictions (such as 70%). Five years later, he checked their accuracy. He found that most of the experts' confident predictions had poor accuracy. The few experts who had moderately accurate predictions shared these characteristics:

- They showed no strong political leaning. (Experts who were consistently conservative or liberal were wrong as often as they were right.)
- They relied on complex information, instead of arguing by analogy to one historical pattern.
- They were not too sure of themselves. That is, the people most likely to be right were those who admitted they might be wrong.

Of all the people who make a career of predicting, weathercasters are among the most accurate. Although we tend to remember their errors, when meteorologists foretell a "70% chance of rain," it rains close to 70% of the time. One advantage of weathercasting over, say, predicting human behavior is that meteorologists get day-by-day feedback on their predictions. When they are wrong, they have to admit they were wrong and then try to understand why.

## CONCEPT CHECK

7. Although most students overestimate what their grades will be next semester, the best students don't. Why not? (Check your answer on page 308.)

## Premature Commitment to a Hypothesis

 Sometimes we make mistakes because we commit ourselves prematurely to a hypothesis and ignore other possibilities. For example, examine the poorly focused photo in Figure 8.23a and guess what it depicts. Then see Figures 8.23b and 8.23c on the following pages. Most people find that seeing the extremely out-of-focus photo makes it harder to identify the items in the better focused photo. When they saw the first photo, they formed a hypothesis, probably a wrong one, which interfered with correct perception of the later photo (Bruner & Potter, 1964).

Peter Wason (1960) asked students to discover a certain rule he had in mind for generating sequences of numbers. One example of the numbers the rule might generate, he explained, was "2, 4, 6." He told the students

that they could ask about other sequences, and he would tell them whether or not those sequences fit his rule. As soon as they thought they had enough evidence, they could guess the rule.

Most students started by asking, "8, 10, 12?" When told "yes," they proceeded with "14, 16, 18?" Each time, they were told, "Yes, that sequence fits the rule." Soon most of them guessed, "The rule is three consecutive even numbers."

"No," came the reply. "That is not the rule." Many students persisted, trying "20, 22, 24?" "26, 28, 30?" "250, 252, 254?" Eventually, they would say, "Three even numbers in which the second is two more than the first and the third is two more than the second." Again, they were told that the guess was wrong. "But how can it be wrong?" they complained. "It always works!"

The rule Wason had in mind was, "Any three positive numbers of increasing magnitude." For instance, 1, 2, 3, would be acceptable, and so would 21, 25, 24601. Where many students went wrong was in testing only the cases that fit their hypothesis, ignoring other possibilities.

 One special case of premature commitment to a hypothesis is the phenomenon of **functional fixedness,** *the tendency to adhere to a single approach to a problem or a single way of using an item.* Here are three examples:

**1.** You are provided with a candle, a box of matches, some thumbtacks, and a tiny piece of string that is shorter than the width of the candle, as shown in Figure 8.24. Using no other equipment, find a way to mount the candle to the wall so that it could be lit.

**2.** Consider an array of nine dots:

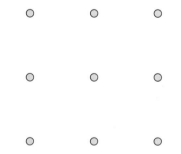

Connect all nine dots with a series of connected straight lines, such that the end of one line is the start of the next. For example, one way would be:

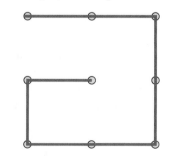

But use the fewest lines possible.

**3.** There are some students in a room. All but two of them are psychology majors, all but two are chemistry majors, and all but two are history majors. How many students are in the room, and what are their majors? (If your first impulse is to say "two of each," try it out: It doesn't work.) Now here's the interesting part: There are two possible solutions. After you have found one solution, discard it and find another. After you have either found solutions to these questions or given up, check answer H on page 309. (Solve these problems before reading further.)

**FIGURE 8.24** You are provided with a candle, a box of matches, some thumbtacks, and a tiny piece of string. What is the best way, using no other equipment, to attach the candle to a wall?

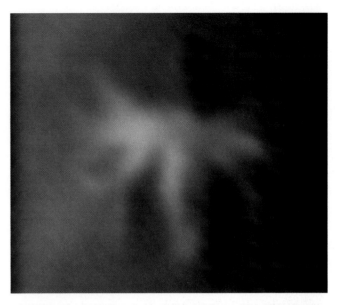

**FIGURE 8.23a** People who form a hypothesis based on the first photo look at succeeding photos to find evidence that they are right. Because their first guess is generally wrong, they don't do as well as people who look at the later photos before making any preliminary guesses. Try to guess what this shows. Then examine parts (b) and (c) on pages 303 and 305.

Question 1 was difficult because most people think of the matchbox as simply a container for matches, not as a potential tool on its own. The box is "functionally fixed" for one way of using it. Question 2 was difficult because most people assume that the lines must remain within the area defined by the nine dots. Question 3 has a double difficulty: It is difficult to think of even one solution, and after thinking of it, it is hard to abandon it to think of an entirely different approach.

## *The Representativeness Heuristic and Base-Rate Information*

Perhaps you have heard the saying: "If something looks like a duck, waddles like a duck, and quacks like a duck, chances are it's a duck." This saying is an example of the **representativeness heuristic,** *the tendency to assume that, if an item is similar to members of a particular category, it is probably a member of that category itself.*

Although the assumption is usually correct, it can lead us astray if we are dealing with something rare. For example, suppose you see something that looks, walks, and sounds like an Eskimo curlew. Is it therefore an Eskimo curlew? Not likely. Eskimo curlews are believed to be extinct; chances are you saw some other similar bird.

When we must decide whether something belongs in category A or category B—for example, an Eskimo curlew versus another bird—we should consider how

much it resembles the two categories and also how common the two categories are. The issue of commonness is known as **base-rate information**—that is, *data about the frequency or probability of a given item.*

People frequently overlook base-rate information and follow only the representativeness heuristic. As a result they identify something as a member of an uncommon category, disregarding the more likely category. For example, consider the following question (modified from Kahneman & Tversky, 1973):

> Psychologists have interviewed 30 engineers and 70 lawyers. One of them, Jack, is a 45-year-old married man with four children. He is generally conservative, cautious, and ambitious. He shows no interest in political and social issues and spends most of his free time on home carpentry, sailing, and solving mathematical puzzles. What is the probability that Jack is one of the 30 engineers in the sample of 100?

Most people estimate a rather high probability—perhaps 80 or 90%—because the description sounds more representative of engineers than lawyers. That estimate isn't really wrong, as we have no logical way to determine the true probability. The interesting point is that if some people are told the sample included 30 engineers and 70 lawyers, and others are told it included 70 engineers and 30 lawyers, both groups make about the same estimate for Jack (Kahneman & Tversky, 1973). Certainly, the base-rate information should have some influence.

Here is another example of overreliance on the representativeness heuristic. Read the following description and then answer the questions following it:

> Linda was a philosophy major. She is 31, bright, outspoken, and concerned about issues of discrimination and social justice.

Now what would you estimate is the probability that Linda is a bank teller? What is the probability that she is a *feminist* bank teller? (Answer before you read on.)

The true probabilities, which are hard to estimate, are not the point. The interesting result is that most people estimate a higher probability that Linda is a *feminist* bank teller than the probability that she is a bank teller (A. Tversky & Kahneman, 1983). However, she could clearly not be a feminist bank teller without being a bank teller. Apparently, people regard this description as fairly typical for a feminist and therefore also for a feminist bank teller (or feminist anything else) but do not regard the description as typical for bank tellers in general (Shafir, Smith, & Osherson, 1990). Because of the representativeness heuristic, people overestimate the probability that Linda is a feminist bank teller.

# CONCEPT CHECK

8. A device was built to protect airplanes by detecting explosives that people might have in their luggage. The device detects 95% of bombs and has a false alarm (saying there is a bomb when there is none) only 5% of the time. Is this device good enough to use? (Hint: Think about the base-rate probability of the presence of a bomb.) (Check your answer on page 308.)

## *The Availability Heuristic*

When we are asked how common something is, we generally start by trying to think of examples. Try this question: In the English language, are there more words that start with *k* or more words with *k* as the third letter? Most people guess that more words start with *k*. They start by trying to think of words that start with *k*: "king, kitchen, kangaroo, key, knowledge, . . ." Those were pretty easy. Then they try to think of words with *k* as the third letter: "ask, ink, . . . uh . . ." They rely on the **availability heuristic,** *the strategy of assuming that how easily one can remember examples of some kind of event indicates how common the event itself is* (Table 8.1). Because it is easier to think of words that start with *k* than words with *k* as the third letter, people assume that more words start with *k*. In fact, however, many more words have *k* as the third letter.

The availability heuristic leads to illusory correlations, as we saw in Chapter 2. Someone asks, "Do people act strange on nights with a full moon?" If you have expected people to act strange on such nights, it is easy to remember times when they acted strange. It is harder to remember times when people did *not* act strange.

Because the news media tend to emphasize the spectacular, our use of the availability heuristic leads us to overestimate some dangers and underestimate others. For example, would you guess that more people die from tornadoes or from lightning? From diabetes or homicide? Stomach cancer or automobile accidents? A tornado that kills 10 people gets national publicity, whereas a bolt of lightning that kills one person may not even make the local television news show. Therefore, we hear about tornado deaths much more often than lightning deaths and assume they are more common, although in fact more people are killed by lightning. Similarly, diabetes and stomach cancer kill far more people than homicide or automobile accidents but get far less publicity. If you guessed that homicide and automobile accidents kill more, probably you were using the availability heuristic based on news reports (Ruscio, 2000).

The reason we follow the representativeness heuristic and availability heuristic is that most of the time they give us correct or nearly correct answers. After all, some-

**TABLE 8.1 The Representativeness Heuristic and the Availability Heuristic**

| | A tendency To Assume That | Leads Us Astray When | Example of Erroneous Assumption |
|---|---|---|---|
| *Representativeness heuristic* | Any item that resembles members of a particular category is probably itself a member of that category. | An item resembles members of a rare category. | You see something that looks the way you imagine a UFO would look so you decide it is a UFO. |
| *Availability heuristic* | How easily we can think of examples of a category indicates how many examples really exist. | One kind of example is easier to think of than another is. | You remember more newspaper reports of airline crashes than of car crashes, so you assume that air crashes are more common than car crashes. |

thing that looks, walks, and sounds like a duck usually is a duck, and the items you easily remember usually *are* plentiful. In some situations, however, we cannot settle for being usually or approximately right. For example, imagine a physician deciding whether or not to treat someone for cancer, or a crew deciding whether an airplane is safe enough to fly, or a psychologist recommending whether to release a patient from a mental hospital. In each case an accurate decision is important and errors could be costly, maybe even disastrous. To make the decisions, people need to consider many types of information and weigh each one appropriately. To decide whether to treat someone for cancer, a physician needs to consider the patient's symptoms, many aspects of an x-ray, several other diagnostic tests, the patient's age, any history of cancer in other family members, and so forth. None of those types of information is 100% valid, some are more important than others, and the results of one test might influence the relative importance of another. In such cases humans almost invariably fall back on simple heuristics instead of accurately weighting each kind of evidence. The best solution is to feed all the information into a computer, give it the algorithms to weigh all the evidence appropriately, and let it make a recommendation. In a wide variety of situations, computers have demonstrated great advantages over human decision makers (Swets, Dawes, & Monahan, 2000).

## Framing Questions

If we were truly logical beings, we would give the same answer to a question no matter how it was worded. In fact, most people give different answers to the same question when it is phrased different ways.

For example, you have recently been appointed head of the Public Health Service. A new contagious disease has been detected, and you must choose between two plans of action. If you do nothing, 600 people will die. If you adopt plan A, you will save the lives of 200 people. If you adopt plan B, there is a 33% chance that you will save all 600 and a 67% chance that you will save no one. *Choose plan A or B before reading further.*

Now another contagious disease breaks out; again you must choose between two plans. If you adopt plan C, 400 people will die. If you adopt plan D, there is a 33% chance that no one will die and a 67% chance that 600 will die. *Choose plan C or D now.*

Figure 8.25 shows the results for more than 150 people. Most chose A over B and D over C. However, note that plan A is exactly the same as C (200 live, 400 die), and plan B is exactly the same as D. Why then did so many people choose both A and D? The reason, according to Tversky and Kahneman, is that most people avoid taking a risk to gain something (like saving lives)

**FIGURE 8.23b**

but willingly take a risk to avoid loss (like not letting people die). *The tendency to answer a question differently when it is framed (phrased) differently* is called the **framing effect.**

Here is another example, dealing with money instead of lives. Which would you rather have?

**W.** a gain of $240 or
**X.** a 25% chance to win $1000

Now you need to make another decision. You have just received an outright gift of $1000, but you must choose between two unpleasant alternatives:

**Y.** a loss of $750 or
**Z.** a 75% chance of losing the entire $1000 (a 25% chance of losing nothing)

Tversky and Kahneman (1981) found that 84% of all people chose W (the no-risk sure gain), whereas 87% chose Z (taking a risk to avoid losing money). Note that W is actually $10 less than choice Y and that X is the same as Z. Again, most people are more willing to take a risk to avoid losing something than they are to gain something.

The framing effect has consequences for persuasion. Suppose you want to encourage people to wear seat belts, exercise, take vitamins, quit smoking cigarettes, or practice "safe sex." Should you say, "If you do this, you will probably live longer"? Or should you say, "If you don't do this, you will probably die sooner?" The results may vary from case to case, but the point is that we cannot assume that the "live longer" and "die sooner" messages will yield the same results (Rothman & Salovey, 1997). How we frame a question changes the way people respond to it.

**FIGURE 8.25** When Amos Tversky and Daniel Kahneman (1981) offered these choices to more than 150 people, 72% chose A over B, and 78% chose D over C. However, plan A is exactly the same as plan C (200 live, 400 die), and plan B is exactly the same as plan D. Why then did so many people choose both A and D? The reason, according to Tversky and Kahneman, is that most people avoid taking a risk when a question is phrased in terms of gain, but they are willing to accept a risk when the question is phrased in terms of loss.

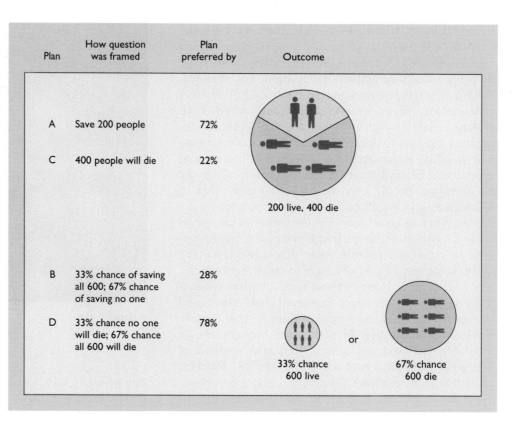

| Plan | How question was framed | Plan preferred by | Outcome |
|------|--------------------------|-------------------|---------|
| A | Save 200 people | 72% | |
| C | 400 people will die | 22% | 200 live, 400 die |
| B | 33% chance of saving all 600; 67% chance of saving no one | 28% | |
| D | 33% chance no one will die; 67% chance all 600 will die | 78% | 33% chance 600 live / or / 67% chance 600 die |

# CONCEPT CHECKS

9. Someone says, "More than 90% of all college students like to watch late-late-night television, whereas only 20% of older adults do. Therefore, more watchers of late-late-night television are college students." What error in thinking has this person made?

10. Someone tells me that if I say "abracadabra" every morning, I will stay healthy. I say it daily and, sure enough, I stay healthy. I conclude that saying this magic word really does ensure health. What error of thinking have I made?

11. Which of the following offers by your professor would probably be more persuasive? a. "If you do this extra project, there's a small chance I will add some points to your grade." b. "I'm going to penalize this whole class for being inattentive today, but if you do this extra project, there's a chance I won't subtract anything from your grade." (Check your answers on page 308.)

## The Sunk Cost Effect

The sunk cost effect is a special case of the framing effect, but before I define it, let's illustrate with some examples:

- You have bought a $100 plane ticket to Wonderfulville and a $200 ticket to Marvelousville. Too late, you realize that they are both for the same weekend. Both tickets are nonrefundable. You think you might prefer Wonderfulville, but you paid more for the ticket to Marvelousville. Where will you decide to go?

- Months ago you bought a $35 ticket to a football game, but now it's the day of the game and the weather is miserably cold. You wish you hadn't bought the ticket, but there it is. Do you go to the game?

Many people say they would go to Marvelousville instead of Wonderfulville because the Marvelousville ticket was more expensive and they don't want to waste the money. Many also say they will go to the football game in the bad weather, again because they don't want to waste the money. These examples illustrate the **sunk cost effect,** *the willingness to do something we wouldn't otherwise choose to do because of money or effort already spent* (Arkes & Ayton, 1999). This tendency arises in many situations. A company or government invests vast amounts of money in some new project, and eventually realizes that the project is a mistake, but doesn't want to cancel it for fear of wasting all the money already spent. A professional sports team gives someone a huge signing bonus, and later finds the player's performance disappointing, but keeps using that player anyway to avoid wasting the money. Curiously, young children never show this effect. The fact that they have already wasted much time or money doesn't induce them to waste still more. No one has ever demonstrated the sunk cost effect in nonhuman animals either, in spite of repeated efforts (Arkes & Ay-

**TABLE 8.2** Expected Winnings on a $1 Decco Ticket (a California Lottery Game)

| Probablity | × | Payoff | = | Expected Value |
|---|---|---|---|---|
| .9573084 | × | $0 | = | $0.000 |
| .040404 | × | $5 | = | $0.202 |
| .0022409 | × | $50 | = | $0.112 |
| .0000467 | × | $5,000 | = | $0.233 |
| Total 1.0 | | | | $0.547 |

Note: Someone who purchases a $1 ticket, has more than a 95% chance of winning nothing, slightly more than a 4% chance of winning $5, and so forth. Overall, the person should expect to receive about 55 cents back for the $1. No one actually receives the 55 cents for a single ticket; but that should be the average payoff after someone has bought many Decco tickets.

**FIGURE 8.23c**

ton, 1999). Apparently, you have to be fairly intelligent to do something this stupid.

# Learning, Memory, Cognition, and the Psychology of Gambling

Suppose your professor asks everyone in class to hand in $10 and then keeps half of it and awards the rest to one of the students, chosen at random. Presuming you were not the winner of the money, would you encourage your professor to repeat this exercise every week from now on?

State lotteries operate much like this example. Table 8.2 illustrates the odds for one state lottery game. Gambling casinos offer much better odds, keeping less than 5% of the gambled money, as compared to the state government's 50%. In either case the great majority of bettors are going to lose money.

Gambling has been a common human behavior throughout history and throughout the world. Here we shall focus on why people make apparently illogical bets, because some of the answers illustrate principles of learning, memory, and thinking as discussed in the last three chapters.

## Overestimation of Control

Rationally, you should not spend $1 on a 1 in 20,000 chance of winning $5000 in a lottery. However, we tend to believe that our actions control our outcomes and therefore that highly skillful people (like you and me, right?) can succeed where other people have failed (Matute, 1996; S. C. Thompson, Armstrong, & Thomas, 1998). Usually, of course, our actions do control outcomes; games of pure chance are the exception (Figure 8.26).

Giving people some illusion of control increases their willingness to gamble. In one study people were given a chance to buy $1 lottery tickets for a $50 prize (Langer, 1975). Some of them were simply handed a ticket; others were permitted to choose their own ticket. Those who chose their own ticket thought they had a better chance of winning. Days later, all the ticket-holders were asked whether they were willing to sell their ticket to someone else. Those who had chosen their own tickets were much less willing to sell, and some refused to sell for less than the full $50 they expected to win!

**FIGURE 8.26** Even with slot machines, many gamblers believe their skill in pulling the handle can influence their results.

## People's Affinity for Long-Shot Bets

 Which would you rather have:

- $100,000 for sure or a 10% chance of winning $1 million?
- $10,000 or a 1% chance at $1 million?
- $1000 or a 0.1% chance at $1 million?
- $100 or a 0.01% chance at $1 million?
- $10 or a 0.001% chance at $1 million?
- $1 or a 0.0001% chance at $1 million?

If you are like most people, you chose the $100,000 over a 10% chance at a million and $10,000 over a 1% chance. But at some point, you switched from the sure profit to the gamble. Especially if the sure profit is $10 or less, most people prefer a chance at winning a million. In fact, almost half of college students said they would forego $10 to have even one chance in a million of winning a million—a gamble of very bad odds (Rachlin, Siegel, & Cross, 1994). A later study, using an Internet sample of thousands of people from 44 countries, confirmed this tendency to prefer a long-shot bet over a sure but small gain (Birnbaum, 1999), so it is not something unique to one culture.

Why do people prefer a slim chance at $1 million to a sure but small gain? First, for most people $10 does not sound like much. Oh, sure, you would rather have $10 than not have it, but another $10 is not going to raise your standard of living. A million dollars would. Furthermore, although you understand the difference between a 10% chance and a 1% chance, it is hard to grasp the difference between a 0.001% chance and a 0.0001% or even a 0.000001% chance. Beyond a certain point, they all blur together and we think, "Someone is going to win, and it might be me." Finally, the extreme unlikeliness of winning may be part of the appeal: People report more pleasure from a surprising gain than from one they expected (Mellers, Schwartz, Ho, & Ritov, 1997). That is, a surprising gambling win is a bigger thrill than your paycheck at work or the money you knew your aunt would send on your birthday.

## Schedules of Reinforcement

Any gambler wins some bets and loses some. The effect is similar to a variable-ratio schedule, as discussed in Chapter 6, but not exactly the same. (In a variable-ratio schedule, an unpredictable number of responses eventually lead to reinforcement. In gambling it is possible to keep betting forever without winning.) Intermittent schedules of reinforcement lead to continued responding, even during a long period without reinforcement.

Howard Rachlin (1990) suggested that gamblers evaluate their success at the end of a string of bets that ends in a win. For example, suppose at the horse races one day you lose six bets and then win one. If your bet on the winner pays more than the amount you lost on the first six bets, then you don't count your progress as "six losses, one win," but as one overall win.

Now imagine a man who buys tickets in a state lottery. Every year he spends hundreds of dollars, maybe thousands, without winning anything. Does he give up? If so, he must admit that all he had invested was a loss. If he continues to buy tickets, he maintains the hope of eventually hitting the jackpot, winning more than enough to make up for all the money he lost. One single payoff could make the whole string of bets a net win. (You could also regard prolonged betting as an example of the sunk cost effect.)

## Vicarious Reinforcement and Punishment

Recall from the discussion of social-learning theory that people learn what to do and what to avoid by observing what happens to others. Recall also that vicarious reinforcement is usually more effective than vicarious punishment.

State governments encourage people to buy lottery tickets (because they raise money for the government), so they focus publicity on people who win a big jackpot (Figure 8.27). You often see news reports showing some instant multimillionaire delirious with excitement. (The state hopes that this vicarious reinforcement will induce you to buy lottery tickets.) You seldom see reports about the millions of people who lost money.

**FIGURE 8.27** States that sponsor lotteries provide publicity and an exciting atmosphere for each big payoff. They hope that this publicity will provide vicarious reinforcement to encourage other people to buy lottery tickets. They do not publicize all the people who lost money on the lottery.

## The Influence of Heuristics

Using the availability heuristic, people assume that, if they can easily recall examples of an event, the event must be common. You can see how this combines forces with vicarious reinforcement. Someone who sees a big lottery winner on television almost every week remembers many such examples and therefore overestimates the likelihood of winning the lottery.

## Self-Esteem

Many gamblers have an additional reason for gambling that is more emotional than logical: They want to beat their opponent. Many habitual gamblers' self-esteem is tied to being "winners," and they like to make that point by winning someone else's money (Peck, 1986). Consequently, someone who has been losing at a poker game will sometimes bet wildly and foolishly in an effort to catch up.

■ Gambling occurs in almost every culture that has possessions and money. Here Egyptians place bets at a racetrack.

In summary, we have the following explanations for why some people continue to gamble despite consistent losses:

- They believe that by skillful play they can increase their probability of winning a game of chance.
- If the potential prize is large, people act as if they do not understand the difference between a small chance of winning and an *extremely* small chance of winning.
- They can continue through a long losing streak if the (imagined) eventual payoff would be large enough to recover all their losses.
- They remember seeing or hearing about many people who have won big jackpots. They thus receive vicarious reinforcement for gambling, and they overestimate the probability of winning.
- They are so eager to beat an opponent that they will take risks they know to be foolish.

Similar explanations apply to the gambles that people take in everyday life. If you drink and drive, or date someone who mistreated you in the past, you are taking a gamble. People take such risks for some of the same reasons just described.

A general point is that people usually have multiple reasons for their behavior. People do not gamble for just one reason any more than you went to college for just one reason. A second general point is that the principles of learning, memory, and cognition do not apply to separate domains; we can apply all of those principles to a single behavior, such as gambling.

**A STEP FURTHER**
*Framing a Question*

Recall the discussion on page 303 about how the phrasing of a question influences people's answers. For example, most people will take more risks to avoid a loss than to increase a gain. Can you use this principle to explain why many gamblers on a losing streak will continue betting, sometimes increasing their bets? Is there a different way to think about the situation to decrease the temptation to continue gambling?

IN CLOSING

## Successful and Unsuccessful Problem Solving

In this module we have considered the best and worst of human thinking—expertise and error. Experts polish their skills through extensive practice. Of course, all of us have to make decisions about topics in which we are far from being experts, and we cannot expect ourselves to make perfect decisions. However, without insisting on perfection we can at least hold ourselves to the standard of not doing anything foolish. We often make mistakes even when we have enough information, time, and skill to make a better decision. Perhaps if we become more aware of common errors, we can be more alert to avoid them.

## Summary

- **Becoming an expert.** Experts are made, not born. Becoming an expert requires years of practice and effort. (page 291)
- **Expert pattern recognition.** Experts recognize and memorize familiar and meaningful patterns more rapidly than less experienced people do. (page 292)

- **Steps for solving a problem.** People take four steps to solve a problem: understanding the problem, generating hypotheses, testing the hypotheses, and checking the result. (page 293)
- **Algorithms and heuristics.** People solve problems by using algorithms (repetitive means of checking every possibility) or heuristics (ways of simplifying the problem to get a reasonable solution). (page 294)
- **Generalizing.** People who have learned how to solve a problem often fail to apply that solution to a similar problem. (page 296)
- **Insight.** With insight problems people have trouble estimating how close they are to a solution. However, they may be making more progress than they realize. (page 297)
- **Creativity.** Creative people work in a field in which they have knowledge and self-confidence; no one is creative in all fields. Many highly creative people go through a period in which they rely on a small group of friends, perhaps just one, for support and encouragement. They dedicate their lives to their work, often to the exclusion of all else. (page 297)
- **Critical thinking.** Even people who try conscientiously to evaluate the evidence for every claim sometimes find themselves repeating a nonsensical statement that they know they should have doubted. (page 298)
- **Reasons for errors.** People tend to be overconfident about their own judgments, especially on difficult questions. Other common mistakes in human reasoning include premature commitment to a hypothesis, overreliance on the representativeness heuristic and the availability heuristic, altering answers depending on the phrasing of the question, and doing something unpleasant to avoid admitting one has wasted money or effort. (page 299)
- **Reasons for gambling.** Gambling illustrates the combined influences of learning, memory, and cognition. Many people make bad bets because they overestimate their control, because they are insensitive to the difference between a small chance and an extremely small chance of winning, and because they hear more about winners than losers. Some people gamble as a way of improving their self-esteem. (page 305)

## Answers to Concept Checks

5. An algorithm would check each possible route: For your home city (H) and three other cities (1, 2, and 3), the possible routes would be H-1-2-3-H, H-1-3-2-H, and H-2-1-3-H. (Three other routes that you could generate would be the mirror images of these

three and therefore are not necessary to consider.) As the number of cities increases, the number of possible routes rises rapidly. If you had to visit ten cities, your algorithm would have to consider almost 2 million routes. One possible heuristic would be to consider only those routes that led you from any city to one of the two cities closest to it. (page 295)

6. Because many poets are recognized for their greatness while they are still young, it is possible to be a great poet and die young. Most historians are in their 40s or later when they do their first outstanding work; therefore, it is almost impossible to be recognized as a great historian and die young. (page 298)

7. It is like the statement that we can't be overconfident when we are completely correct. The best students will in fact probably get excellent grades next semester. They can't overestimate their success, at least not by much. (page 300)

8. A false-alarm rate of 5% is far too high. Imagine a plane with 100 passengers, each checking two bags. Of the 200 probably innocent bags, this device will identify 5%—that is, 10 bags—as containing a bomb! Speer (1989) estimated that this device (which the Federal Aviation Administration actually considered using) would have 5 million false alarms for every bomb it found. (page 302)

9. Failure to consider the base rate: 20% of all older adults is a larger number than 90% of all college students. (page 304)

10. Premature commitment to one hypothesis without testing the hypothesis that one could stay healthy without the magic words. (page 304)

11. Probably b. People are generally more willing to take a risk to avoid losing something than to gain something. (page 304)

## Answers to Other Questions in the Module

C. The water in the tube would leak out of the hole in the bottom. Any membrane heavy enough to keep the water in would also keep the rubber balls out. (page 295)

D. The refrigerator will heat the room. The amount of heat coming out the back of the refrigerator will be greater than the amount of cooling coming from the front. (page 296)

E. This illustration at the top of the next page shows how to cut and fold an ordinary piece of paper or cardboard to match the figure, with nothing left over. (page 297)

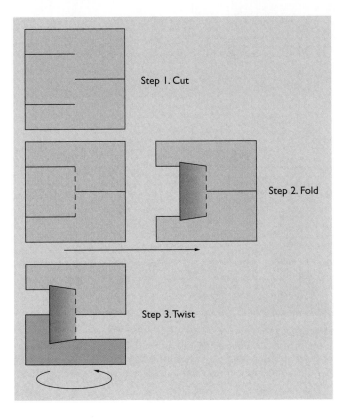

Step 1. Cut

Step 2. Fold

Step 3. Twist

(2) The dots can be connected with four lines:

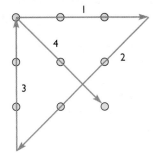

(3) One answer is three students: one psychology major, one chemistry major, and one history major. The other possibility is two students who are majoring in something else—music, for example. (If there are two music majors, all but two of them are indeed majoring in psychology etc.) (pages 300–301)

**F.** Set 1: The words *playing, credit,* and *report* are all associated with *card.* Set 2: The words *ticket, shop,* and *broker* are all associated with *pawn.* (page 297)

**G.** (1) 39 years. (2) 4187 miles, or 6738 kilometers. (3) 13 countries. (4) 39 books. (5) 2160 miles, or 3476 kilometers. (6) 390,000 pounds, or 177,000 kilograms. (7) 1756. (8) 645 days. (9) 5959 miles, or 9590 kilometers. (10) 36,198 feet, or 11,033 meters. (page 299)

**H.** (1) The best way to attach the candle to the wall is to dump the matches from the box and thumbtack the bottom of the box to the wall, as shown in this picture. The tiny piece of string is irrelevant.

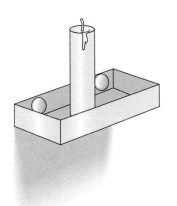

# Language

Language is an extremely versatile system. Other species have various ways of exchanging signals, but only human languages have the property of **productivity,** *the ability to express new ideas.* Every day we say and hear a few stock sentences, such as "Nice weather we're having," or "I can't find my keys," but we also say and hear sentences that no one has ever said before.

You might ask, "How do you know that no one has ever said that sentence before?!" Well, of course, no one can be certain that a particular sentence is new, but we can be confident that many sentences are new (without specifying which ones) just because of the enormous number of possible ways to rearrange words. Imagine trying this exercise (but don't really try it unless you have a vast amount of spare time): Pick a sentence of more than ten words from any book you choose. How long would you need to keep reading, in that book or any other, until you found exactly the same sentence again?

In short, we do not memorize all the sentences we will ever use. Instead, we learn rules for making sentences and interpreting other people's sentences. The famous linguist Noam Chomsky (1980) has described those rules as a **transformational grammar,** which is *a system for converting a deep structure into a surface structure.* The deep structure is the underlying logic or meaning of a sentence. The surface structure is the sequence of words as they are actually spoken or written (Figure 8.28). According to this theory, whenever we speak we transform the deep structure of the language into a surface structure. Two surface structures can resemble each other without representing the same deep structure, or conversely, they can represent the same deep structure without resembling each other.

For example, "John is easy to please" has the same deep structure as "pleasing John is easy" and "it is easy to please John." These sentences all represent the same underlying idea.

In contrast, consider the sentence, "Never threaten someone with a chain saw." The surface structure of that sentence maps into two quite different deep structures. One means that you should not use a chain saw to threaten someone. The other means you should not threaten someone who has a chain saw.

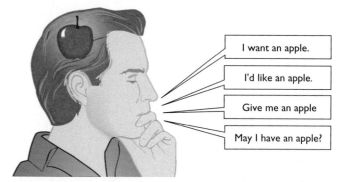

**FIGURE 8.28** According to transformational grammar, we can transform a sentence with a given surface structure into any of several other sentences with different surface structures. All of them represent the same deep structure, which is the underlying logic of the sentence.

The productivity of language enables humans to communicate and elaborate on ideas to a far greater extent than any other species can. Language researcher Terrence Deacon describes a brief talk about language that he presented to his 8-year-old son's elementary school class. One child asked whether other animals have their own languages. Deacon explained that other species have methods of communication, but none has a flexible system similar to human language. The child persisted, asking whether other animals had at least a *simple* language, perhaps one with only a few words and short sentences. No, he replied, they do not have even a simple language.

Then another child asked, "Why not?" (Deacon, 1997, p. 12). Deacon paused. And then paused some more. Why not, indeed. He realized that this 8-year-old had asked a profound question. If language is so extremely useful to humans, why haven't other species evolved at least a little of it?

Language comes easily to humans in contrast to nonhumans, which learn only a little language at best, despite psychologists' best efforts at teaching. Evidently, humans are highly specialized for language learning.

## Precursors to Language in Nonhumans

One way to examine humans' specialization for language is to determine how far other species could progress toward language with sufficient training. Beginning in the

1920s, several psychologists reared chimpanzees in their homes and tried to teach them to talk. The chimpanzees learned many human habits (Figure 8.29) but understood only a little of language. Later Allen Gardner and Beatrice Gardner (1969) taught a chimpanzee named Washoe to use the sign language of the American deaf (Ameslan). Sign language is closer to the hand gestures that chimpanzees use naturally and does not require human voice sounds, for which chimpanzee vocal tracts are poorly adapted. Washoe eventually learned the symbols for about 100 words.

However, Washoe and other chimpanzees trained in this way used their symbols almost exclusively to make requests, not to describe and rarely in new, original combinations (Pate & Rumbaugh, 1983; Terrace, Petitto, Sanders, & Bever, 1979; C. R. Thompson & Church, 1980). By contrast a human child with a vocabulary of 100 words or so starts linking them into many original combinations and short sentences.

The results have been different, however, for another chimpanzee species, *Pan paniscus,* sometimes known as the pygmy chimpanzee (a misleading term because these

a

b

c

d

FIGURE 8.29 Speaking is physically impossible for chimpanzees, but some psychologists have tried to teach them to communicate by using gestures or symbols. (a) One of the Premacks' chimps arranges plastic chips to make a "sentence" request for food. (b) Viki in her human home, helping with the housework. After years with the Hayeses, she could make only a few sounds similar to English words. (c) Kanzi, a bonobo, presses symbols to indicate words. Among the primates bonobos have shown the most promising ability to acquire language. (d) A chimp signing *toothbrush*. (e) Roger Fouts with Alley the chimp, who is signing *lizard*.

e

**FIGURE 8.30** Kanzi, a bonobo, points to answers on a board in response to questions he hears through earphones. Experimenter Rose Sevcik sits with him but does not hear the questions, so she cannot intentionally or accidentally signal the correct answer.

animals are almost as large as common chimpanzees) and sometimes known as the bonobo. Bonobos' social behavior resembles that of humans in several regards: Males and females form strong attachments; females are sexually responsive throughout the month, not just during their fertile period; males contribute to infant care; and adults often share food with one another.

Several bonobos have used symbols in impressive ways. First, they occasionally use the symbols to name and describe objects that they are not requesting. Second, they sometimes use the symbols to describe past events. (One with a cut on his hand explained that his mother had bit him.) Third, they frequently make original, creative requests, such as asking one person to chase another. A couple of bonobos seem to comprehend symbols about as well as a 2- to 2½-year-old child understands language (Savage-Rumbaugh et al., 1993).

A couple of bonobos have also shown considerable understanding of spoken English, even following odd spoken commands such as "bite your ball" and "take the vacuum cleaner outside" (Savage-Rumbaugh, 1990; Savage-Rumbaugh, Sevcik, Brakke, & Rumbaugh, 1992). They even passed the test of responding to commands issued over earphones, used to eliminate the possibility of unintentional "Clever Hans"-type signals, as discussed in Chapter 2 (Figure 8.30).

The explanation for this impressive success probably pertains partly to species differences: Perhaps bonobos have greater language capacities than common chimpanzees. Another part of the explanation may pertain to the method of training: Learning by observation and imitation probably promotes better understanding than

the formal training methods that were used in previous studies (Savage-Rumbaugh et al., 1992). Finally, the bonobos began their language experience early in life. Humans apparently have a sensitive period for easy language acquisition early in life, and the same may be true for bonobos.

## CONCEPT CHECK

12. Based on the studies with bonobos, can you offer advice about how to teach language to children with impaired language learning? (Check your answer on page 323.)

# Human Specializations for Learning Language

Is the glass half full or half empty? Should we be impressed that bonobos understand language almost as well as a 2½-year-old child or wonder why they do not progress further? Humans are clearly specialized to learn language in a way that no other species can.

## Language and General Intelligence

Did we evolve language just as an accidental by-product of evolving big brains and great intelligence? The idea sounds appealing, but several observations argue strongly against it. Dolphins and whales have larger brains than humans have but do not develop language. (Yes, they communicate, but not in a flexible system resembling human language.) Some people with massive brain damage have less total brain mass than a chimpanzee but continue to speak and understand language. Also, there is a study of people in one family, all having a particular gene, who develop normal intelligence but have a serious deficiency of language (Fisher, Vargha-Khadem, Watkins, Monaco, & Pembrey, 1998). So big brains and high intelligence do not automatically produce language.

Furthermore, consider **Williams syndrome,** *a genetic condition characterized by mental retardation in most regards but skillful use of language.* One 14-year-old with Williams syndrome could write good creative stories and both the music and words to songs, but in other ways she performed like a 5- to 7-year-old and could not be left alone without a baby-sitter. Another child with Williams syndrome, when asked to name as many animals as he could think of, started with "ibex, whale, bull, yak, zebra, puppy, kitten, tiger, koala, dragon . . ." Another child could sing more than 1000 songs in 22 languages (Bellugi & St. George, 2000). However, such children prefer 50 pennies to 5 dollars and, when asked to estimate the length of a bus, give answers such as "3 inches or 100 inches, maybe" (Bellugi, Lichtenberger, Jones, Lai,

& St. George, 2000). Again, the conclusion is that language ability is not synonymous with overall intelligence.

## Language Learning as a Specialized Capacity

Susan Carey (1978) calculated that children between the ages of 1½ and 6 learn an average of nine new words per day. Deciphering the meanings of words would seem to be an overwhelmingly difficult task (Markman, 1990). Suppose someone points to a pillow and says "makura." If you were a Japanese child, you would accept *makura* as the word for *pillow*. You would do the same if you were trying to learn Japanese as a second language. But how did you know that the word *makura* meant *pillow*? Logically, it could have meant "soft thing," "throwable thing," or any of countless other possibilities. More important, how did you know it meant anything at all? All you observed was that someone made a sound and held out an arm; you inferred the intention to communicate. That inference comes naturally to humans, unlike other species.

Noam Chomsky has argued that language is so easily learned in spite of enormous complexity that its development could not depend on ordinary learning. Children must begin, probably since birth, with some preconceptions. The simplest and perhaps most important is the idea that words *mean* something. Children also make essential distinctions, such as between actors and actions (i.e., nouns and verbs), actors and recipients of action, singular and plural, same and different, and so forth. They have to learn how to express those concepts in their particular language, but they do not have to learn the concepts themselves. Chomsky and his followers therefore suggest that people are born with a **language acquisition device** or "language instinct," *a built-in mechanism for acquiring language* (Pinker, 1994). In effect, we may even be born with a kind of grammar, although not a grammar like the detailed rules of English or Spanish.

Doubts and controversies remain, however, about exactly what is built in. Are we really born with concepts, distinctions, and a primitive grammar, or just with the ability to learn them? If we are born with a predisposition to learn language, what is the nature of that predisposition? The predisposition could be far removed from the details of language itself (Deacon, 1997; Seidenberg, 1997).

Is it possible that infants learn all the complexities of word meanings and grammar from the apparently meager information they receive? Perhaps the information is better than we imagined. Parents throughout the world simplify the language-learning task by speaking to their infants in "parentese." I am not talking about silly "goo-goo" baby talk, but a pattern of speech that emphasizes and prolongs the vowels, making clearer than usual the difference between words such as *cat* and *cot* (Kuhl et al., 1997). Infants listen more intently to parentese than to normal speech and learn more from it. We also speak slowly, distinctly, and in simple words to someone who just barely understands our language. To those who know the language well, we can speak rapidly, mumble, or speak in a noisy environment and still expect decent understanding (Calvin & Bickerton, 2000).

Several studies have found that even infants younger than 1 year old detect some of the rules and regularities of the language they hear (Marcus, Vijayan, Rao, & Vishton, 1999). For example, when adults speak they usually run all their words together without pausing between them—"Lookattheprettybaby." How does the infant even know where one word ends and another begins? The infant is evidently a better learner than we might have thought; it learns which sounds usually go together. For example, because "pretty" isn't always followed by "baby," an infant learns that "pretty" and "baby" are more common sounds than "ty-ba" (the end of pretty and the start of baby). Therefore, the infant reacts to "ty-ba" as a new, attention-getting sound, whereas it doesn't react that way to "pretty" or "baby" (Saffran, Aslin, & Newport, 1996). In short, infants learn a great deal from what they hear.

## Language and the Human Brain

What aspect of the human brain enables us to learn language so easily? Studies of brain-damaged people have long pointed to two brain areas as particularly important for language. People with damage in the frontal cortex, including *Broca's area* (Figure 8.31), develop **Broca's**

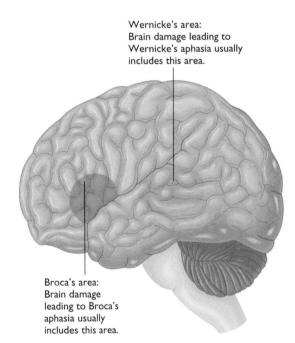

Wernicke's area: Brain damage leading to Wernicke's aphasia usually includes this area.

Broca's area: Brain damage leading to Broca's aphasia usually includes this area.

**FIGURE 8.31** Brain damage that produces major deficits in language usually includes the left-hemisphere areas shown here. However, the deficits are severe only if the damage is more extensive, including these areas but extending to others as well. Many areas of the human brain contribute to language comprehension and production.

**aphasia,** *a condition characterized by inarticulate speech and by difficulties with both using and understanding grammatical devices—prepositions, conjunctions, word endings, complex sentence structures, and so forth.* For example, one patient who was asked about a dental appointment slowly mumbled, "Yes . . . Monday . . . Dad and Dick . . . Wednesday nine o'clock . . . 10 o'clock . . . doctors . . . and . . . teeth" (Geschwind, 1979, p. 186). These people do not really lose all grammatical understanding; they merely find it much more difficult to use and understand language, much as undamaged people do when they are extremely distracted (Blackwell & Bates, 1995). People with damage in the temporal cortex, including *Wernicke's area* (Figure 8.31), develop **Wernicke's aphasia,** *a condition marked by difficulty recalling the names of objects and impaired comprehension of language.* Because these people do not remember names, their speech is nonsensical even when it is grammatical. For example, one patient responded to a question about his health, "I felt worse because I can no longer keep in mind from the mind of the minds to keep me from mind and up to the ear which can be to find among ourselves" (Brown, 1977).

However, language did not evolve simply by adding a language module to a chimpanzee brain. The human brain displays enormous expansion of the prefrontal cortex, increased connections among cortical areas, and numerous other specializations to facilitate language (Deacon, 1997). Brain damage that seriously impairs language always extends well beyond Broca's or Wernicke's area. Indeed, the nature of the language deficit varies from one person to another, and knowing whether the damage is primarily frontal or temporal does not always tell us what to expect. Perhaps each person's language cortex is organized somewhat differently from everyone else's. Furthermore, PET scans or other brain recordings show widespread activation during speech (Just, Carpenter, Keller, Eddy, & Thulborn, 1996). It is hardly an exaggeration to say that the whole human brain is specialized to make language possible.

## Stages of Language Development

Table 8.3 lists the average ages at which children reach various stages of language ability (Lenneberg, 1969; Moskowitz, 1978). Progression through these stages depends largely on maturation, not just extra experience (Lenneberg, 1967, 1969). Parents who expose their children to as much language as possible find that they can increase the children's vocabulary a bit, but they hardly affect the rate of progression through language stages (Figure 8.32). At the other extreme, hearing children of deaf parents are exposed to much less spoken language, but if they have periodic contact with speaking people, their language development progresses on schedule.

Deaf infants babble as much as hearing infants do for about the first 6 months and then start to decline. At first, hearing infants babble only haphazard sounds, but soon they start repeating the sounds that are common in the

**FIGURE 8.32** Some overeager parents try to teach their children language at a very early age. The child may enjoy the attention, but the activity is unlikely to accelerate the child's progress in language development.

**TABLE 8.3** Stages of Language Development

| Age | Typical Language Abilities (Much Individual Variation) |
|---|---|
| 3 months | Random vocalizations. |
| 6 months | More distinct babbling. |
| 1 year | Babbling that resembles the typical sounds of the family's language; probably one or more words including "mama"; language comprehension much better than production. |
| 1½ years | Can say some words (mean about 50), mostly nouns; no phrases. |
| 2 years | Speaks in two-word phrases. |
| 2½ years | Longer phrases and short sentences with some errors and unusual constructions. Can understand much more. |
| 3 years | Vocabulary of about 1000 words; longer sentences with fewer errors. |
| 4 years | Close to adult speech competence. |

language they have been hearing. Thus, 1-year-old French infants babble French sounds, Chinese infants babble Chinese sounds, and so forth (Locke, 1994).

By age 1 year, infants begin to understand language, and most can say at least a word or two. One of the first sounds they can make is *muh*, and *muh* or *muh-muh* has been adopted by most of the world's languages as the word for "mother." Infants also make the sounds *duh*, *puh*, and *buh*. In many languages the word for father is similar to *dada* or *papa*. *Baba* is the word for grandmother in several languages. In effect, infants tell their parents what words to use for certain concepts. Indeed, Deacon (1997) has made the point that languages evolve to be as easy as possible for children to learn.

By age 1½, most toddlers have a vocabulary of about 50 words, on the average, but they seldom link words together. Thus, a toddler will say "Daddy" and "bye-bye" but not "Bye-bye, Daddy." In context parents can usually discern considerable meaning in these single-word utterances. *Mama* might mean, "That's a picture of Mama," "Take me to Mama," "Mama went away and left me here," or "Mama, I'm hungry."

Some toddlers follow a different pattern of language development. Instead of speaking one word at a time, they speak poorly articulated, compressed phrases, such as "Do-it-again" or "I-like-read-Goodnight-Moon." At first, these expressions are poorly pronounced and hard to understand. Children who start off by generating these complex requests and phrases tend to continue doing so (Nelson, Baker, Denninger, Bonvillian, & Kaplan, 1985).

By age 2, children start producing "telegraphic" phrases of two or more words, including combinations such as "more page," "allgone sticky," and "allgone outside," to indicate "read some more," "my hands are now clean," and "someone has closed the door," respectively. Note the originality of such phrases; it is unlikely that the parents ever said "allgone sticky"!

By age 2½ to 3 years, most children are generating full sentences, though each child maintains a few peculiarities. For example, many young children have their own rules for forming negative sentences. A common one is to add *no* or *not* to the beginning or end of a sentence, such as, "No I want to go to bed!" One little girl formed her negatives just by saying something louder and at a higher pitch; for instance, if she shrieked, "I want to share my toys!" she really meant, "I do *not* want to share my toys." Presumably, she had learned this "rule" by remembering that people screamed at her when they told her not to do something. My son Sam made negatives for a while by adding the word *either* to the end of a sentence: "I want to eat lima beans either." Apparently, he had heard people say, "I don't want to do that either" and had decided that the word *either* at the end of the sentence made it an emphatic negative.

Young children act as if they were applying grammatical rules. (I say "as if" because they cannot state

the rules. By the same token, baseball players chasing a high fly ball act "as if" they understood calculus.) For example, a child may learn the word *feet* at an early age and then, after learning other plurals, abandon it in favor of *foots*. Later, the child begins to compromise by saying "feets," "footses," or "feetses" before eventually returning to "feet." Children at this stage say many things they have never heard anyone else say, such as "the womans goed and doed something." Clearly, they are applying rules for how to form plurals and past tenses, although they *overregularize* or *overgeneralize* those rules. My son David invented the word *shis* to mean "belonging to a female." (He had apparently generalized the rule "He–his, she–shis.") Note that all these inventions imply that children are learning rules, not just repeating word combinations.

## CONCEPT CHECK

13. At what age do children begin to string words into combinations that they have never heard before? Why do psychologists believe that even very young children learn some of the rules of grammar? (Check your answers on page 323.)

## Children Exposed to No Language or Two Languages

If children were exposed to no language at all, would they make up their own? In rare cases an infant who was accidentally separated from other people grew up in a forest without human contact until discovered years later. Such children not only fail to show a language of their own but also fail to learn much language after they are given the chance (Pinker, 1994). However, their development is so abnormal and their early life so unknown that we should hesitate to draw conclusions.

The best evidence comes from the unfortunate condition of some deaf children. Children who cannot hear well enough to learn speech and who are not taught sign language invent their own sign language, which they teach to other deaf children and so far as possible to their parents. As they grow older, they make the system more complex, linking signs together into sentences with fairly consistent word order and grammatical rules—for example, "Mother, twist open the jar, blow a bubble, so I can clap it" (Goldin-Meadow, McNeill, & Singleton, 1996; Goldin-Meadow & Mylander, 1998).

Although each deaf child invents a different system, most systems share some interesting similarities. For example, most include some sort of marker to indicate the difference between a subject that is doing something to an object ("the mouse eats the cheese") and a subject that is doing something without an object ("the mouse is moving"). The sign languages invented by children in Taiwan resemble those of children in the United States, even though the spoken languages of those countries—Chinese and English—have very different grammars (Goldin-Meadow & Mylander, 1998).

If a deaf child starts to invent a sign language and no one responds to it, because the child meets no other deaf children and the adults fail to or refuse to learn, the child gradually abandons it and becomes totally without language. If such a child is exposed to sign language much later, such as age 12, it is too late, and he or she never becomes adept at signing (Harley & Wang, 1997). This observation is our best evidence for a critical period of human language learning: Children are predisposed to learn language easily, and if they don't learn one while young, they will be much impaired at learning one later.

Some children grow up in a **bilingual** environment, *learning two languages about equally well.* Bilingualism is especially common among immigrant children, who are generally bicultural as well, learning both their parents' customs and those of their new country. The areas of brain activity during language are the same in bilingual people as in those with only one language (Paradis, 1990; Solin, 1989).

 If the brain representations are so similar, how do bilingual people keep their two languages separate? The answer is that they do not, at least not completely (Francis, 1999). For example, one study asked people to say aloud the ink color (in English) of various English and Spanish words. You can try this task yourself with the following display:

**YELLOW** GREEN **RED BLUE**
**VERDE AZUL AMARILLO** ROJO

If you speak only English, you probably had more trouble with the first four than with the second four. However, if you recognized *verde, azul, amarillo,* and *rojo* as the Spanish words for *green, blue, yellow,* and *red,* then you probably had difficulty with the second four also, demonstrating the *bilingual Stroop effect.* The better your knowledge of Spanish, the more difficult those last four items, even though you answered in English (Altarriba & Mathis, 1997).

Bilingualism has two disadvantages: Children take longer to master two languages than to master one (of course), and even adult bilinguals occasionally confuse words from the two languages. The primary advantage is obvious: If you learn a second language, you can communicate with more people. A second advantage is subtle: A bilingual person gains extra cognitive flexibility by learning that there are different ways of expressing the same idea. For example, children younger than 6 years old who speak only one language apparently

believe that every object has only one name. If an adult gestures toward a cup and a gyroscope and says, "Please bring me the gyroscope," a child who knows the word *cup* will immediately bring the gyroscope, assuming that if one object is the cup, the other one must be the gyroscope. But the child would also fetch the gyroscope if asked to bring the *vessel,* the *chalice,* or any other synonym for *cup.* A bilingual child, however, is more likely to hesitate or to ask for help, understanding that the unfamiliar word could refer to the cup just as easily as the other object (Davidson, Jergovic, Imami, & Theodos, 1997).

## CONCEPT CHECK

14. Suppose you know that someone understands both English and another language, and you want to determine what that language is without even asking. How could you do this using one of the tasks described in this section? (Check your answer on page 323.)

# Understanding Language

Making sense of language requires knowledge about the world. For example, consider the following sentences (from Just & Carpenter, 1987):

That store sells horse shoes.
That store sells alligator shoes.

You would not interpret the second sentence as referring to "shoes for alligators to wear" because alligators do not wear shoes. But that is a fact you had to know, not something you could discern from the structure of the sentence. Here is another example:

I'm going to buy a pet hamster at the store, if it's open.
I'm going to buy a pet hamster at the store, if it's healthy.

Nothing about the sentence structure told you that *it* refers to the store in the first sentence and the hamster in the second sentence. You understood because you know that stores but not hamsters can be open, whereas hamsters but not stores can be healthy.

Reading English has special difficulties because some English words have multiple meanings. For example, consider this sentence:

A pelican dove into the water and scared away the dove.

The word *dove* is ambiguous, but the context enables you to infer—so fast that you were unaware of what you were doing—that the first *dove* rhymes with *stove* and means "plunged"; the second *dove* rhymes with *love* and means a "pigeonlike bird." Now consider another sentence:

A flying fish jumped out of the water and scared the pigeon and dove away.

In this case the word *dove* is hopelessly ambiguous. The sentence might mean that the flying fish scared two birds (a pigeon and a dove) or that the fish scared the pigeon and then dove (plunged) away. Consider this confusing sentence from a student newspaper:

He said Harris told him she and Brothers told French that grades had been changed.

When good readers encounter such a sentence, they reread it until they resolve their confusion or give it up as hopeless. Poor readers do not slow down as much when they come to difficult sentences. That is, good readers read simple materials quickly and complicated materials slowly; poor readers read everything at about the same speed.

In short, language comprehension depends on assumptions that the speaker and the listener (or the writer and the reader) share. Sometimes we even have to remember that something has one meaning in the United States and another in Britain (Figure 8.33).

**FIGURE 8.33** In England a football coach is a bus full of soccer fans. In the United States it's the person who directs a team of American football players.

## Hearing a Word as a Whole

We customarily describe the word *cat* as being composed of three sounds, *kuh, ah,* and *tuh.* However, the first sound in *cat* is not quite the same as the consonant sound in *kuh;* the *a* and *t* sounds are changed also. Each letter changes its sound depending on the other sounds that precede and follow it.

One of the clearest demonstrations of this principle was an experiment in which students listened to a tape recording of a sentence with one sound missing (Warren, 1970). The sentence was, "The state governors met with their respective legislatures convening in the capital city." However, the sound of the first *s* in the word *legislatures,* along with part of the adjacent *i* and *l,* had been replaced by a cough or a tone. The students were asked to listen to

the recording and try to identify the location of the cough or tone. None of the 20 students identified the location correctly, and half thought the cough or tone interrupted one of the other words on the tape. They all claimed to have heard the *s* plainly. In fact, even those who had been told that the *s* sound was missing still insisted that they had heard the sound. Apparently, the brain uses the context to fill in the missing sound.

## Understanding Words in Context

Many words have different meanings in different contexts. *Rose* can refer to a flower, or it can be the past tense of the verb *to rise.* Consider the word *mean* in this sentence: "What did that mean old statistician mean by asking us to find the mean and mode of this distribution?"

Just as we hear the word *legislatures* as a whole, not as a string of separate letters, we interpret a sequence of words as a whole, not one at a time. For example, suppose you hear a tape-recorded word that is carefully engineered to sound halfway between *dent* and *tent.* If you simply hear it and are asked to say what you heard, you might reply "dent," "tent," or "something sort of intermediate between dent and tent." But now suppose you hear that same sound in context:

1. When the *ent in the fender was well camouflaged, we sold the car.
2. When the *ent in the forest was well camouflaged, we began our hike.

Most people who hear sentence 1 report the word *dent.* Most who hear sentence 2 report *tent.* Now consider two more sentences:

3. When the *ent was noticed in the fender, we sold the car.
4. When the *ent was noticed in the forest, we stopped to rest.

For sentences 3 and 4, the context comes too late to help. People are as likely to report hearing *dent* in one sentence as in the other (Connine, Blasko, & Hall, 1991). Think for a moment what this means: In the first two sentences, the fender or forest showed up three syllables after *ent. In the second pair, the fender or forest appeared six syllables later. Evidently, when you hear an ambiguous sound, you can hold it in a temporary "undecided" state for about three syllables for the context to help you understand it. Beyond that point it is too late; you hear it one way or the other and stick with your decision, regardless of the later context.

Although a long delayed context cannot help you hear an ambiguous word correctly, it can help you understand what it means. Consider the following sentence from Karl Lashley (1951):

Rapid righting with his uninjured hand saved from loss the contents of the capsized canoe.

**FIGURE 8.34** Most students preferred Kool-Aid made with sugar labeled "sugar" instead of sugar labeled "not cyanide," even though they had placed the labels themselves. Evidently, people do not fully believe the word "not." (Based on results of Rozin, Markwith, & Ross, 1990)

If you hear this sentence spoken aloud, so that spelling is not a clue, you are likely at first to interpret the second word as *writing,* until you reach the final two words of the sentence. Suddenly, the phrase *capsized canoe* changes the whole scenario; now we understand that *righting* meant "pushing with a paddle." In summary, only the immediate context can influence what you hear, but even a much delayed context can change the sentence's meaning.

## Understanding Negatives

Suppose you are trying to decide whether to buy a product at the supermarket. You notice on the package, "Contains no cyanide or rat pieces!" Does that notice encourage you to buy the product? Hardly! Just the mention of disgusting contaminants kills your interest, as if you did not fully believe the "no." (After all, why would the manufacturer even mention the absence of something unless there were some chance of its presence?) I was once on an airplane that turned around and returned to its departure city. The pilot kept reassuring us, "There is nothing to worry about . . . We have all been trained on this procedure . . ." The more times he told us not to worry, the more we worried.

Even if you had every reason to believe a denial, you still might act as though you doubted it. Students in one study watched as an experimenter poured sugar into two jars. The students were then told to identify whichever jar they chose with the label "sucrose, table sugar" and the other with the label "not sodium cyanide, not poison." Then the experimenter made two cups of Kool-Aid, one from each jar of sugar, and asked the students to choose one cup to drink (Figure 8.34). Almost half said they had no preference, but of those who did have a preference, 35 of 44 wanted Kool-Aid made from the jar marked "sucrose," not from the one that denied cyanide and poison (Rozin, Markwith, & Ross, 1990). They acted as though the label "not sodium cyanide, not poison" meant something was wrong.

People have particular trouble understanding double negatives, such as "she is not unfriendly." The state of Illinois gives the following instructions to the jurors in murder cases; note the four (!) negatives (emphasis added):

> If you do *not* unanimously find from your consideration of all the evidence that there are *no* mitigating factors sufficient to *preclude* the imposition of a death sentence, then you should sign the verdict requiring the court to impose a sentence *other than* death.

Does that sound clear to you? Do you think the author of these instructions was trying to make the point clear?

**CRITICAL THINKING**
### A STEP FURTHER
*Understanding Negatives*

In one of the U.S. presidential debates in 2000, the moderator said that candidate Al Gore had called candidate George W. Bush a "bumbler." At the start of the next debate, the moderator apologized, admitting that Gore had not called Bush a bumbler. Should Bush be happy about this retraction? Should Gore?

## Reading

As you will recall from earlier in this chapter, expertise achieved after 10 or so years of intensive practice enables one to recognize complex patterns at a glance. You have intensively practiced reading for more than the last 10 years, so in that regard you qualify as an expert reader. You may not think of yourself as an expert because we usually reserve the term *expert* for someone who is far more skilled than others. Nevertheless, your years of reading enable you to recognize words instantaneously, like an expert who recognizes chess patterns at a glance.

**FIGURE 8.35** A student watches either a word or a single letter flashed on a screen. An interfering pattern is then flashed on the screen and the student is asked, "Which was presented: *C* or *J*?" More students were able to identify the letter correctly when it was part of a word.

## Reading and Word Recognition

Consider the following experiment: The investigator flashes one letter on a screen for less than a quarter of a second and then shows an interfering pattern and asks, "What was the letter, C or J?" Then the experimenter flashes an entire word on the screen for the same length of time and asks, "Was the first letter of the word C or J?" (Figure 8.35). Which question do you think would be easier to answer? Most people can *identify the letter more accurately when it is part of a whole word than when it is presented by itself* (Reicher, 1969; Wheeler, 1970). This is known as the **word-superiority effect.**

In a follow-up experiment, James Johnston and James McClelland (1974) briefly flashed words on the screen and asked students to identify one letter (whose position was marked) in each word (Figure 8.36). On some trials the experimenters told the students to focus on the center of the area where the word would appear and to try to see the whole word. On other trials they showed the students exactly where the critical letter would appear on the screen and told them to focus on that spot and ignore the rest of the screen. Most students identified the critical letter more successfully when they looked at the whole word than when they focused on just the letter itself. This benefit occurs only with a real word, like COIN, not with a nonsense combination, like CXQF (Rumelhart & McClelland, 1982).

You may have experienced the word-superiority effect yourself. A common game on long car trips is to try to find every letter of the alphabet on the billboards along the way. Many people find it easier to spot a particular letter by reading whole words than by checking letter by letter.

What accounts for the word-superiority effect? According to one model (J. L. McClelland, 1988; Rumelhart, McClelland, & the PDP Research Group, 1986), our perceptions and memories are represented by vast numbers of connections among "units," presumably corresponding to sets of neurons. Each unit is connected to other units (Figure 8.37). Each unit, when activated, excites some of its neighbors and inhibits others. Suppose that, at a given moment, units corresponding to the letters C, O, I, and N are moderately active but not quite active enough for a firm identification of each letter. These units excite a higher-order unit corresponding to the word COIN. Although none of the four letter units sends a strong message by itself, the collective impact is strong (J. L. McClelland & Rumelhart, 1981). This higher-level perception COIN then feeds excitation back to the individual letter-identifying units and confirms their tentative decisions.

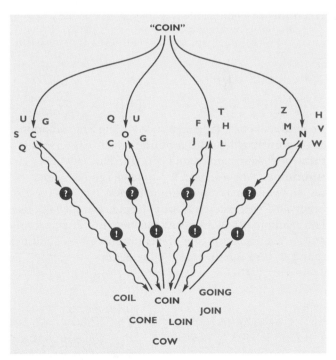

**FIGURE 8.37** According to one version of the connectionist model, a visual stimulus activates certain letter units, some more strongly than others. Those letter units then activate a word unit, which in turn strengthens the letter units that compose it. For this reason we recognize a whole word more easily than we recognize a single letter.

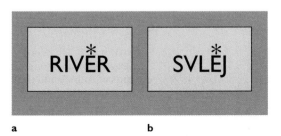

a                          b

**FIGURE 8.36** Students performed better at identifying an indicated letter when they focused on an entire word (a) than on a single letter in a designated spot among random letters (b).

Figure 8.38 is an example of the kind of phenomenon this model attempts to explain. Why do you see the top word in that figure as *RED* instead of *PFB*? After all, in the other words, those letters do look like *P, F,* and *B*. But in the top word, one ambiguous figure activates some *P* units and some *R* units; the next figure activates *E* and *F* units, and the third figure activates *D* and *B* units. All of those units in turn activate other more complex units corresponding to *RFB, PFB, PFD,* and *RED*. As you tentatively perceive the word as *RED* (the only English word among those choices), the feedback strengthens the activity of the *R, E,* and *D* units.

**FIGURE 8.38** The combination of possible letters enables us to identify a word; word recognition in turn helps to confirm the letter identifications. Although each of the letters in the top word is ambiguous, a whole word—RED—is perceived. (From Rumelhart, McClelland, & the PDP Research Group, 1986)

## Reading and Eye Movements

In an alphabetical language such as English, the printed page consists of letters that form familiar clusters that in turn form words and sentences. One kind of cluster is a **phoneme,** *a unit of sound.* A phoneme can be a single letter (such as *f*) or a combination of letters (such as *sh*). Another kind of cluster is a **morpheme,** *a unit of meaning.* For example, the word *thrills* has two morphemes (*thrill* and *s*). The final *s* is a unit of meaning because it indicates that the word is plural (see Figure 8.39).

# CONCEPT CHECK

**15.** How many phonemes are in the word *thoughtfully*? How many morphemes? (Check your answers on page 323.)

When we read, do we ordinarily read one letter, one phoneme, one morpheme, or one or more words at a time? And do we move our eyes in a steady or jerky fashion? The movements are so fast that introspection cannot answer the questions. Psychologists have arranged devices to monitor eye movements during reading. Their first discovery was that a reader's eyes move in a jerky fashion. You can move your eyes steadily when they are following a moving object, but when you are scanning a stationary object, such as a page of print, you alternate between *periods called* **fixations,** *when your eyes are stationary, and quick eye movements called* **saccades** (sa-KAHDS) *that take your eyes from one fixation point to another.*

 You read during your fixations but you are virtually blind during the saccades. To illustrate that point, try the following demonstration: Look at yourself in the mirror and focus on your left eye. Then move your focus to the right eye. Can you see your eyes moving in the mirror? (Go ahead; try it.) People generally agree that they do not see their eyes move.

"Oh, but wait," you say. "That movement in the mirror was simply too quick and too small to be seen." Wrong. Try again, but this time get someone else to look at your left eye and then shift his or her gaze to your right eye. Now you do see the other person's eye movement, so the movement itself is not too fast or too small to be seen. Go back and try your own eyes in the mirror again and observe the difference. You can see someone else's eyes moving, but you cannot see your own eyes moving in the mirror.

There are two explanations: First, certain areas in the parietal cortex monitor impending eye movements and send a message to the primary visual cortex, in effect telling the visual cortex, "The eyes are about to move, so shut down activity for a moment." Even if you are in total darkness, the visual cortex decreases its activity during saccadic eye movements (Burr, Morrone, & Ross, 1994; Paus, Marrett, Worsley, & Evans, 1995). Second, what you see at the end of a saccade interferes with what you saw during the saccade (Matin, Clymer, & Matin, 1972).

**FIGURE 8.39** The word *shamelessness* has nine phonemes (units of sound) and three morphemes (units of meaning).

Phonemes (units of sound):

Morphemes (units of meaning):

**SHAMELESSNESS**

That is, when you see a brief blur followed by a distinct stimulus, your brain concentrates on the distinct stimulus and ignores the blur.

The consequence is that we see during fixations and not during saccades. An average adult reading something of average complexity fixates on each point for about 200–250 milliseconds (ms). Good readers generally have briefer fixations than poor readers do, and everyone has briefer fixations on familiar words like *girl* than on harder words like *ghoul*. After each fixation, the saccade lasts 25–50 ms. Thus, most readers have about four fixations per second (Rayner, 1998).

(In the attentional blink experiments discussed earlier, a letter that is flashed on the screen interferes with another letter that is flashed 200 ms later. So why doesn't one fixation interfere with another one when you are reading? The main explanation is that the flashes are very brief in the attentional blink experiments. The other explanation relates to the word-superiority effect: It is easier to read whole words in a meaningful context than to identify isolated letters.)

 How much can a person read during one fixation? Many people believe they see quite a bit of the page at each instant. However, research indicates that we read only about 11 characters—one or two words—at a time. To demonstrate this limitation, focus on the letter *i* marked by an arrow (↓) in the two sentences below.

↓
**1.** This is a sentence with no misspelled words.
↓
**2.** Xboc tx zjg rxunce with no mijvgab zucn.

If you permit your eyes to wander back and forth, you quickly notice that sentence 2 is mostly gibberish. But as long as you dutifully keep your eyes on the fixation point, the sentence looks all right. You can read the letter on which you fixated plus about three or four characters (including spaces) to the left and about seven to the right. Therefore, you see —*ce with no m*—, or possibly —*nce with no mi*—.

 This limit of about 11 letters depends partly on the lighting; in faint light your span can decrease to as little as 1 or 2 letters, and your reading ability suffers accordingly (Legge, Ahn, Klitz, & Luebker, 1997). The limit also depends on attention. In the following display, again focus on the letter *i* in each sentence and check how many letters you can read to its left and right:

↓
This is a sentence with no misspelled words.
↓
This is a sentence with no misspelled words.
↓
is a sentence with no misspelled

If your reading span were limited just by how many letters can fit into the fovea of your retina, you should be able to read more letters in the top sentence and fewer as the letters get larger. In fact, you do at least as well, maybe even better, with a larger print sentence (up to a point).

What we can see at a glance also depends on our habits of reading. In Japanese, where each character conveys more information than English letters do, readers see fewer letters per fixation (Rayner, 1998). And in Hebrew and Farsi, which are written right to left, readers read more letters to the left of fixation and fewer to the right (Brysbaert, Vitu, & Schroyens, 1996; Faust, Kravetz, & Babkoff, 1993; Malamed & Zaidel, 1993).

Often, our 11-character window of reading includes one word plus a fragment of another. For example, suppose you have fixated on the point shown by an arrow in the following sentence:

↓
The government made serious mistakes.

Readers can see the word *serious* plus about the first three letters of *mistakes*. Three letters do not identify the word; from what the reader knows, the next word could be *misspellings, misbehavior, missiles, mishmash,* or any of a number of other *mis*-things that a government might make. Does the preview of the next word facilitate reading? Yes. In one study college students again read passages on a computer screen while a machine monitored their eye movements. The computer correctly displayed the word the student fixated on plus the next zero, three, or four letters. So the display might look like this:

↓
made
↓
serious
↓
mistakes.

or like this:

↓
made ser
↓
serious mis
↓
mistakes.

Students who could preview the first three or four letters of the next word read significantly faster than those who could not (Inhoff, 1989). Evidently, while we are reading one word, we are previewing the next.

You might wonder what speed-readers do differently from normal readers. An average adult reader has about four or five fixations per second with occasional backtracks, for an overall rate of about 200 words per minute. Speed-readers have briefer fixations with fewer backtracks. With practice people can double or triple their

■ Reading is a complex skill that includes many stages, from eye movements through understanding and using the material. Investigators find that they cannot separate these stages, though how well a reader understands the material influences the speed of the eye movements. By studying reading psychologists hope to improve methods of teaching reading.

reading speed with normal comprehension. Some claim that they see more than 11 characters per fixation, and unfortunately, researchers haven't done enough studies to test this possibility. However, unless they increase their span enormously, reading speed has some physical limits. Each saccadic eye movement lasts 25 to 50 ms, and reading does not occur during saccades. Thus, it would be impossible to exceed 20–40 fixations per second, even if each fixation lasted no time at all! If we make the generous estimate that people might be able to average 2 words per fixation, the theoretical maximum would be 20–80 words per second, or 1200–4800 words per minute. And remember, this calculation unrealistically assumes a fixation time of zero. Yet some people claim to read 5000 to 10,000 words per minute. In fact, they are fixating on some words and guessing the rest. A combination of reading and guessing can produce very fast reading and adequate comprehension of predictable content, like a James Bond novel. However, the speed-reader does miss details, and speed-readers who know they will be tested on the details do slow their reading (Just & Carpenter, 1987).

##  ONCEPT CHECK

16. Why can we sometimes read two or three short words at a time, whereas we need a saccade or two to read the same number of longer words?

17. If a word is longer than 11 letters, will a reader need more than one fixation to read it? (Check your answers on page 323.)

# *Language And Humanity*

At the start of this module, we considered the question, "If language is so extremely useful to humans, why haven't other species evolved at least a little of it?" None of the research directly answers this question, but we can speculate. Certain adaptations are much more useful on a large scale than on a small scale. For example, skunks survive because they are very stinky; it wouldn't help to be just a little bit stinky. Porcupines survive because they have long, sharp quills; having a few short quills might be slightly helpful, but not very. Similarly, a little language might be slightly helpful (like a little stink or a few short quills), but better developed language is so enormously useful that a little bit of language development is probably an unstable condition, evolutionarily speaking. Once a species such as humans had evolved a little language, those individuals with still better language abilities would have a huge selective advantage over the others.

## Summary

- **Language productivity.** Human languages enable us to create new words and phrases to express new ideas. (page 310)

- **Language training in nonhumans.** Bonobos, and to a lesser extent other chimpanzees, have shown an ability to learn certain aspects of language. Human evolution evidently elaborated on potentials found in our apelike ancestors but developed that potential well beyond the level it reached in other species. (page 310)

- **Rapid language learning in children.** Children learn language at such an amazing rate, considering the unsystematic training they receive, that many psychologists believe humans are born with a predisposition to learn language. However, exactly *what* we are born with is uncertain; we are quick to learn language, but surely we are not born with the grammar of our language. (page 313)

- **Brain organization and aphasia.** Brain damage, especially in the left hemisphere, can impair people's ability to understand or use language. However, many brain areas contribute to language in varied ways. (page 313)

- **Stages of language development.** Children advance through several stages of language development, probably reflecting maturation of brain structures necessary for language and not just the total amount of experience. From the start children's language is creative and shows an effort to understand and use rules of grammar. (page 314)

- **Children exposed to no language or two.** If deaf children of hearing parents are not exposed to language, they invent a sign language of their own. Children in a bilingual environment sometimes have trouble keeping the two languages separate but gain the ability to converse with many people and in certain ways show greater than usual cognitive flexibility. (page 315)
- **Understanding language.** Much of speech is ambiguous; we understand words and sentences in context by applying the knowledge we have about the world in general. (page 316)
- **Reading.** When we read, we have fixation periods separated by eye movements called saccades. We read during the fixations, not the saccades. Even good readers can read only about 11 letters per fixation; people increase their speed of reading by increasing the number of fixations per second. (page 318)

## Answers to Concept Checks

**12.** Start language learning when a child is young. Rely on imitation as much as possible, instead of providing direct reinforcements for correct responses. (page 312)

**13.** Children begin to string words into novel combinations as soon as they begin to speak two words at a time. We believe that they learn rules of grammar because they overgeneralize those rules, creating such words as *womans* and *goed*. (page 315)

**14.** Set up a Stroop task, asking the person to read off the color of the ink of all the words. Let the words be color names from many languages. The person should show some delay at naming the colors of ink for English words (*red, green,* and so forth) and for whatever other language he or she knows well. (page 316)

**15.** *thoughtfully* has seven phonemes: th-ough-t-f-u-ll-y. (A phoneme is a unit of sound, not necessarily a letter of the alphabet.) It has three morphemes: thought-fully. (Each morpheme has a distinct meaning.) (page 320)

**16.** Two or three short words can fall within the window of about 11 letters that we can fixate at one time. If the words are longer, it may be impossible to see them all at once. (page 322)

**17.** Sometimes but not always. Suppose your eyes fixate on the fourth letter of *memorization.* You should be able to see the three letters to its left and the seven to its right—in other words all except the final letter. Because there is only one English word that starts *memorizatio-,* you already know the word. (page 322)

# Key Terms and Activities

## Key Terms

**algorithm:** a mechanical, repetitive procedure for solving a problem (page 294)

**attentional blink:** a brief period after perceiving a stimulus, during which it is difficult to attend to another stimulus (page 285)

**attentive process:** a procedure that extracts information from one part of the visual field at a time (page 284)

**availability heuristic:** the strategy of assuming that how easily one can remember examples of some kind of event indicates how common the event actually is (page 302)

**base-rate information:** data about the frequency or probability of a given item (page 301)

**bilingual:** able to use two languages about equally well (page 316)

**Broca's aphasia:** a condition characterized by inarticulate speech and by difficulties with both using and understanding grammatical devices—prepositions, conjunctions, word endings, complex sentence structures, and so forth (page 313)

**cognition:** the processes of thinking, gaining knowledge, and dealing with knowledge (page 279)

**cognitive map:** a mental representation of a spatial arrangement (page 288)

**critical thinking:** the careful evaluation of evidence for and against any conclusion (page 298)

**fixation:** a period when the eyes are steady (page 320)

**framing effect:** the tendency to answer a question differently when it is framed (phrased) differently (page 303)

**functional fixedness:** the tendency to adhere to a single approach to a problem or a single way of using an item (page 300)

**heuristics:** strategies for simplifying a problem or for guiding an investigation (page 294)

**language acquisition device:** a built-in mechanism for acquiring language (page 313)

**morpheme:** a unit of meaning (page 320)

**negative priming:** phenomenon that someone who attends to one of two objects and ignores the other will find it temporarily difficult to identify the other (page 285)

**overconfidence:** belief that one's opinions or predictions are highly correct when in fact they are not (page 299)

**phoneme:** a unit of sound (page 320)

**preattentive process:** a procedure for extracting information automatically and simultaneously across a large portion of the visual field (page 283)

**productivity:** the ability to express new ideas (page 310)

**prototype:** a familiar or typical example of a category (page 279)

**representativeness heuristic:** the tendency to assume that, if an item is similar to members of a particular category, it is probably a member of that category itself (page 301)

**saccade:** a quick jump in the focus of the eyes from one point to another (page 320)

**spreading activation:** the process by which the activation of one concept also activates or primes other concepts that are linked to it (page 282)

**Stroop effect:** the tendency to read a word, especially if it is a color name, in spite of instructions to disregard the word and state the color of the ink in which it is printed (page 284)

**sunk cost effect:** the willingness to do something we wouldn't otherwise choose to do, because of money or effort already spent (page 304)

**transformational grammar:** a system for converting a deep structure into a surface structure (page 310)

**Wernicke's aphasia:** a condition marked by difficulty recalling the names of objects and impaired comprehension of language (page 314)

**Williams syndrome:** genetic condition characterized by mental retardation in most regards but skillful use of language (page 312)

**word-superiority effect:** identifying a letter with greater ease when it is part of a whole word than when it is presented by itself (page 319)

## Suggestions for Further Reading

Bransford, J. B., & Stein, B. S. (1984). *The ideal problem solver.* New York: Freeman. Advice about how to approach and solve both "mind-bender" problems and practical problems.

Calvin, W. H., & Bickerton, D. (2000). *Lingua ex machina.* Cambridge, MA: MIT Press. Insightful treatment of the psychology of language.

# Web/Technology Resources

## Preattentive Processes

**www.csc.ncsu.edu/faculty/healey/PP/Interfere.html**

A description of preattentive processes with interesting demonstrations.

## Creativity

**www2.shore.net/~sek/STCreativity.html**

Robert Sekuler and Randolph Blake, authors of *Star Trek on the Brain,* explore creativity and humans' limitations in creativity.

## Chimpanzee Language

**www.cwu.edu/~cwuchci/main.html**

Central Washington University offers information about chimpanzees that have learned to use American Sign Language to communicate.

## Human Language

**http://www.ilovelanguages.com**

This site has links to many sources of information about languages.

# Intelligence and Its Measurement

9

CHAPTER

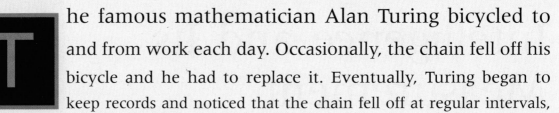

he famous mathematician Alan Turing bicycled to and from work each day. Occasionally, the chain fell off his bicycle and he had to replace it. Eventually, Turing began to keep records and noticed that the chain fell off at regular intervals, after exactly a certain number of turns of the front wheel. He then calculated that this number was an even multiple of the number of spokes in the front wheel, the number of links in the chain, and the number of cogs in the pedal. From these data he deduced that the chain came loose whenever a particular link in the chain came in contact with a particular bent spoke on the wheel. He identified that spoke, repaired it, and never again had trouble with his bicycle (I. Stewart, 1987).

Turing's solution to his problem qualifies as highly intelligent, but hold your applause. Your local bicycle mechanic could have solved the problem in just a few minutes without using any mathematics at all.

So, you might ask, what's my point? Was Turing unintelligent? Of course not. If I had a complicated, unfamiliar problem to solve, I would take it to someone like Turing, not to my local bicycle mechanic.

■ To repair a bicycle, you could use general problem-solving skills or specific expertise about bicycles. Either approach qualifies as a kind of intelligence.

The point is that intelligence is a combination of general abilities and practiced skills. The term *intelligence* can refer to the highly practiced skills shown by a good bicycle mechanic, a Micronesian sailor, a hunter-gatherer of the Serengeti Plain, or anyone else with extensive experience. *Intelligence* can also refer to the generalized problem-solving ability that Turing displayed in unfamiliar situations. But even that sort of ability develops gradually, reflecting the contributions of many kinds of experience.

# Intelligence and Intelligence Tests

*What do we mean by "intelligence"? Is there more than one kind of intelligence?*

Intelligence testing has a long history of controversy, partly because of misconceptions about its purpose. Consider this analogy: You have just been put in charge of choosing the members of your country's next Olympic team. However, the Olympic rules have been changed: Each country will send only 30 men and 30 women, and each athlete must compete in every event. Furthermore, all the events will be new ones, and the Olympic committee will not announce the rules for any of them until all the athletes have arrived at the Olympic site. Clearly, you cannot hold the usual kind of tryouts, but neither will you choose people at random. How will you proceed?

Your best bet would be to devise a test of "general athletic ability." You might measure the abilities of applicants to run, jump, change direction, maintain balance, throw and catch, kick, lift weights, respond rapidly to signals, and perform other athletic feats. Then you would choose the applicants with the best scores, confident that they will do reasonably well at almost any athletic event.

No doubt, your test would be imperfect. But if you want your team to do well, you must choose the athletes by some sort of test. So you go ahead with your test of general athletic ability. As time passes other people begin to use your test. Does its wide acceptance imply that athletic ability is a single quantity, like speed or weight? Not at all. You found it useful to act as if athletic ability were a single quantity, but you know that great basketball players are not necessarily great swimmers or gymnasts.

## What Is Intelligence?

Intelligence tests resemble our imaginary test of athletic ability. If you were in charge of choosing which applicants to admit to a school or college, you would want to select those who would profit most from the experience. Because students may be studying subjects that they have never studied before, it makes sense to measure their general ability to profit from education rather than any specific knowledge or ability.

Intelligence tests were developed for the practical function of selecting students for admission or placement in schools. The tests were not based on any theory of intelligence, and many test administrators have been content to define *intelligence* as the ability to do well in school. Given that definition, IQ tests do measure intelligence.

For theoretical purposes, however, that definition is hardly satisfactory. What would be a better definition? Here are some of the ways that psychologists have defined *intelligence* (Sternberg, 1997; Wolman, 1989):

- The mental abilities that enable one to adapt to, shape, or select one's environment.
- The ability to judge, comprehend, and reason.
- The ability to understand and deal with people, objects, and symbols.
- The ability to act purposefully, think rationally, and deal effectively with the environment.

Note that these definitions use such terms as *judge, comprehend, understand,* and *think rationally*—terms that are no better defined than *intelligence* itself. Psychologists would like to better organize this list of intelligent abilities. Just as all the objects in the world are composed of compounds of only 92 elements, most psychologists expect to find that all the various kinds of intelligence are compounds of a few basic abilities. They have proposed several models of how intelligence is organized.

## Spearman's Psychometric Approach and the g Factor

The **psychometric approach** to intelligence, pioneered by Charles Spearman (1904), features *the measurement (metric) of individual differences in behaviors and abilities*. Spearman began by measuring how well a variety of people performed various tasks, such as following complex directions, judging musical pitch, matching colors, and performing arithmetic calculations. He then found that performance on any single task correlated positively with performance on all the other tasks. He therefore deduced that all these tasks must have something in common. To perform well on any test of mental ability, Spearman argued, people need a certain *"general" ability,* which he called *g.* (The *g* is always italicized and always lowercase, like the terms *e* and *i* in mathematics.) Later researchers have confirmed that scores on virtually all kinds of cognitive tests correlate fairly strongly with one another, including tests that do not require any particular knowledge

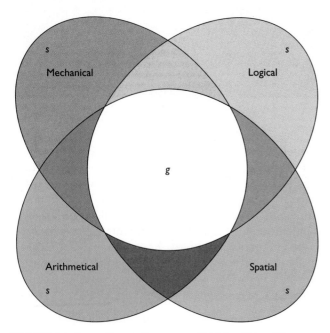

**FIGURE 9.1** According to Spearman (1904), all intelligent abilities have an area of overlap, which he called *g* (for "general"). Each ability also depends partly on an *s* (for "specific") factor.

or schooling. Consider, for example, the following task:

Either ⊓ or ⊓ is flashed on a screen for a fraction of a

second. Then ⊓ is flashed on the screen in the same location to serve as a "masking stimulus" (to make the task a bit more difficult). The observer's task is to say whether the left or right arm was longer on the first stimulus. The investigator varies the duration of the first stimulus to determine the briefest flash that still enables the observer to answer correctly. Performance on this perceptual task has a correlation of at least .4 to .5 with scores on a standard intelligence test (Deary & Stough, 1996). So intelligence tests are measuring some fairly general processes, not just factual knowledge.

To account for the fact that performance on various tasks does not correlate perfectly, Spearman suggested that each task requires the use of a *"specific" ability, s,* in addition to the general ability, *g,* that all tasks require (Figure 9.1). Thus, intelligence consists of a general ability plus an unknown number of specific abilities, such as mechanical, musical, arithmetical, logical, and spatial ability. The specific abilities probably depend more on practice than on any innate tendency; researchers have found evidence for a genetic contribution to *g* but no clear evidence for a genetic basis of any *s* ability (Petrill et al., 1998). Spearman called his theory a "monarchic" theory of intelligence because it included a dominant ability, or monarch (*g*), which ruled over the lesser abilities.

Psychologists do not entirely agree on what *g* represents. That is, the ability to do well on one task does cor-

relate with the ability to do well on another task, but that correlation could indicate either a single unitary process, such as the ability to perceive and manipulate relationships, or else the correlation could represent the fact that many separate processes depend on the same growth factors (Petrill, Luo, Thompson, & Detterman, 1996). Consider the following analogy:

First, consider the high correlation among the tasks shown in Figure 9.2: People who excel at running a 100-meter race also generally do well at the high jump and the long jump. A particular athlete might be a little better at one of these events than the others, but we can hardly imagine an outstanding high jumper who could not manage a decent long jump. The reason for this high correlation is that all three events depend on the same leg muscles. An injury that impaired performance on one event would impair performance on all three.

Second, consider the lengths of three body parts—the left leg, the right arm, and the left index finger—as illus-

**FIGURE 9.2** Measurements of sprinting, high jumping, and long jumping correlate with one another because they all depend on the same leg muscles. Similarly, the *g* factor that emerges in IQ testing could reflect a single ability that all tests tap.

trated in Figure 9.3: Within a normal population of people, these three measurements will correlate strongly with one another. That is, most people with a long left leg also have a long right arm and left index finger. Why? These measurements definitely do not measure the same thing. (Amputation of one of them would not affect the others.) Lengths of leg, arm, and finger correlate because the *causes* of growth are the same for all three—nutrition, health, age, and genetics.

Now which of these cases is more like intelligence? Do the various intellectual skills correlate with one another because they all measure a single underlying ability or because they all grow together, based on health, nutrition, education, genetics, and so forth?

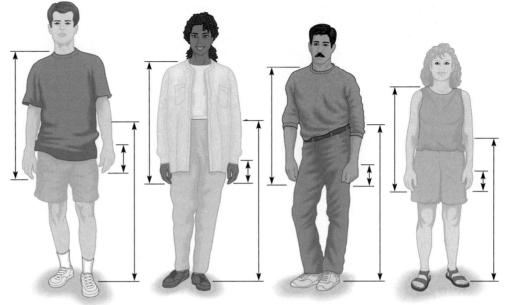

**FIGURE 9.3** Measurements of leg, arm, and finger length correlate with one another only because the genes, nutrition, and health factors that promote the growth of any one of these also promote the growth of the others. Similarly, the *g* factor that emerges in IQ testing could reflect that different intellectual abilities depend on the same nutritional, health, and educational influences.

The evidence supports both hypotheses. For example, intellectual tasks that correlate most highly with other intellectual tasks (and which are therefore said to "load highly on *g*") all activate the same areas of the frontal cortex (Duncan et al., 2000). Those brain areas are important for attention and working memory, important for almost any intellectual task. Thus, various intellectual abilities correlate with one another partly because they depend on some of the same underlying processes. However, as we have seen in previous chapters, some brain-damaged people lose a specific kind of memory or perceptual ability while retaining other abilities. That is, different intellectual functions require different brain areas, in addition to the frontal cortex that they all require. To a considerable degree, the sizes and activities of various brain areas correlate with one another because they all grow together, dependent on the same influences of health, nutrition, genetics, education, and so forth.

## Fluid Intelligence and Crystallized Intelligence

Raymond Cattell accepted Spearman's psychometric approach but proposed one important modification. According to Cattell (1987), the *g* factor has two components: fluid intelligence and crystallized intelligence. The analogy is to water: Fluid water can take any shape, whereas ice crystals are rigid. **Fluid intelligence** is *the power of reasoning and using information*. It includes the

ability to perceive relationships, solve unfamiliar problems, and gain new types of knowledge. Fluid intelligence mostly relates to the ability to process quickly large amounts of information in working memory (Fry & Hale, 1996). **Crystallized intelligence** consists of *acquired skills and knowledge and the application of that knowledge to the specific content of a person's experience*. For example, fluid intelligence is the ability to learn new skills in a new job, whereas crystallized intelligence includes the skills already learned and practiced by someone who has had the job for years.

Fluid intelligence, according to Cattell and his colleagues, reaches its peak before age 20 and then remains fairly steady throughout life, except for the effects of brain damage or disease (Horn, 1968). Crystallized intelligence, on the other hand, continues to increase as long as people are active and alert (Cattell, 1987; Horn & Donaldson, 1976). A 20-year-old may be more successful than a 65-year-old at solving a problem unfamiliar to both of them, but the 65-year-old will excel on problems in his or her area of specialization.

Although the distinction between crystallized and fluid intelligence is useful, it is not an absolute. Any task taps at least a little of both crystallized and fluid intelligence.

## CONCEPT CHECK

1. Was Alan Turing's solution to the slipping bicycle chain an example of fluid or crystallized intelligence? Would the solution provided by a bicycle mechanic be an example of fluid or crystallized intelligence? (Check your answers on page 339.)

■ According to Howard Gardner, we have many intelligences, including mathematical ability, artistic skill, muscle skills, and musical abilities.

## Gardner's Theory of Multiple Intelligences

The traditional defense of theories proposing a single kind of intelligence has rested on the concept of *g:* Tests of all kinds of intellectual abilities—mathematical, verbal, and others—correlate with one another and therefore support the idea of a single underlying ability called *g*. However, critics reply, the statistical emergence of *g* merely indicates that mathematics, language, and the other tested skills happen to be related. If we expand the concept of *intelligence* to include other skills that society values, the concept of *g* may fade away or even disappear.

In particular, Howard Gardner (1985) has claimed that people have **multiple intelligences**—*numerous unrelated forms of intelligence*. Gardner distinguishes language abilities, musical abilities, logical and mathematical reasoning, spatial reasoning, body movement skills, self-control and self-understanding, and sensitivity to other people's social signals. He points out that people can be outstanding in one type of intelligence but not in others. For example, an athlete can excel at body movement skills but lack musical abilities; an outstanding musician can be insensitive to other people; and so forth. Someone who seems very intelligent in certain regards may surprise us by doing something foolish in another setting.

Gardner certainly makes an important point: People do have a variety of socially valued abilities, and almost no one is strong or weak in all of them. However, to date we have little research on how independent the various intellectual skills really are. One example often cited is the *savant* (literally, "learned one"), an individual with outstanding performance in just one area. For example, some people of below-average overall intelligence can do phenomenal calendar calculations, such as "On what day of the week was the 10th of July, 1917?" One such person is 97% accurate for dates from 1772 to the year 819,206, answering with a delay that averaged less than 2 seconds (O'Connor, Cowan, & Samella, 2000). However, savant skills do not necessarily demonstrate the complete independence of different kinds of intelligence, as the best-developed savant skills occur in people of almost normal IQ (L. K. Miller, 1999).

A further question is whether we should use one word, *intelligence,* to refer to every valued skill from writing a novel to dribbling a basketball. If we do, then Gardner is correct that people have many unrelated kinds of intelligence. However, we have then changed the meaning of the word *intelligence*.

## Sternberg's Triarchic Theory of Intelligence

Spearman concluded that intelligence depends on one overall ability; Cattell suggested two kinds of ability, and Gardner suggested many. Still, the concept of ability tells us nothing about *how* a person processes information or engages in "intelligent" behavior (Das, 1992).

Robert Sternberg (1985) has offered one of the most influential attempts to specify in detail the processes of intelligent behavior. Sternberg's description is called a **triarchic theory** (in contrast to Spearman's monarchic theory) because Sternberg deals with *three aspects of intelligence: (a) the cognitive processes that occur within the individual, (b) the identification of situations that require intelligence, and (c) the ability to use intelligence in the external world.*

According to Sternberg, the first part of the triarchy—the cognitive processes within the individual—includes three components: learning the necessary information, planning an approach to a problem, and combining the knowledge with the plan to solve a problem.

Standard IQ tests do not try to measure the learning or planning components; they concentrate on the third component—how well someone solves a problem. For example, a test might ask you to complete an analogy, such as

Washington is to 1 as Lincoln is to:
(a) 5, (b) 10, (c) 20, (d) 50.

To solve this problem, you must have already learned a fair amount of relevant information, and you must develop a strategy for applying it to this question. Ultimately,

■ In Garrison Keillor's fictional *Lake Wobegon,* "all the children are above average." Although that description sounds impossible, in one sense it is true: Everyone is above average at something. A given individual may excel at mathematics, dancing, piano playing, juggling, poetry, cooking, or whatever. A single measurement of "intelligence" necessarily overlooks people's specialized skills.

if you are successful, you decide that the question must be referring to George Washington and the $1 bill and that the answer is a, because Abraham Lincoln's picture is on the $5 bill. This question is reasonable, as far as it goes, although we need to recognize that it measures only the final outcome, not the steps that led to it. An improved measure of intelligence might separate the learning and planning components from the performance component.

The second part of Sternberg's triarchy is the identification of situations that require intelligence. It is important to distinguish novel situations from repeated situations because they require different responses. In a novel situation, we must examine a problem in various ways until we find a successful approach. (Recall, for example, the insight problems of Chapter 8.) In a repeated situation, we profit by developing automatic habits so that we can quickly make a successful response.

The third part of the triarchy is the relationship between intelligence and the outside world. An intelligent person either adapts to the environment or tries to improve the environment, and if all else fails, escapes to a better environment. Sternberg (1985) and others (Weinberg, 1989) have tried to develop special tests of people's practical intelligence—for example, the ability of a young person to identify the steps that most likely lead to career advancement. Sternberg explicity recognizes that, because intelligent behavior must be practical, the term *intelligence* is meaningful only in a sociocultural context. For example, we cannot meaningfully compare the intelligence of a European city-dweller with that of someone living in the Amazon rain forests or the Serengeti Plain. What is important and practical for a member of one group may not be for members of other groups.

Sternberg's theory is admittedly complex. Probably the main points are that psychologists need to study intellectual processes, not just intellectual outcomes, and that what matters most is the application of intelligence to practical situations.

Table 9.1 summarizes four theories of intelligence.

**TABLE 9.1 Four Theories of Intelligence**

| Theory | Principal Theorist | Key Ideas and Terms | Examples |
|---|---|---|---|
| *Psychometric approach* | Charles Spearman | $g$ factor: general abstract reasoning ability common to various tasks | Perceiving and manipulating relationships |
| | | $s$ factor: specific ability required for a given task | Mechanical, verbal, spatial abilities |
| *Fluid and crystallized intelligence* | Raymond Cattell | Fluid intelligence: reasoning and using information; peaks in young adulthood | Finding a solution to an unfamiliar problem |
| | | Crystallized intelligence: acquired skills and knowledge; continues growing throughout life | Knowing how to play the piano, build a cabinet, write a novel, calculate a sales tax |
| *Multiple intelligences* | Howard Gardner | Intelligence includes all the abilities that one's society values | Music, social attentiveness, dancing, language skills, mathematics, etc. |
| *Triarchic theory* | Robert Sternberg | Cognitive mechanisms | Gaining knowledge, planning a strategy, solving a problem |
| | | Situations that require intelligence | Novel situations; repeated situations |
| | | Relationship to the environment | Adapting to one's environment, improving it, or escaping from it |

**2.** In Sternberg's theory novel situations call for creative problem solving, whereas repeated situations call for automatic habits. Using Cattell's terminology, which kind of situation calls for fluid intelligence and which calls for crystallized intelligence? (Check your answer on page 339.)

## Theories of Intelligence and Tests of Intelligence

The standard IQ tests, which we shall consider momentarily, were devised decades ago, before most of the discoveries about memory and cognition that we discussed in the last two chapters. Today, there are several theories about intelligence and a variety of intelligence tests, but these theories have little relationship to the tests.

Can we measure something—in this case intelligence—without fundamentally understanding what it is? Possibly so; physicists measured gravity and magnetism long before they understood them theoretically. Maybe psychologists can do the same with intelligence.

But then again, maybe not. Physicists of the past measured not only gravity and magnetism but also "phlogiston," a substance that they later discovered does not exist. Measurements of a poorly understood phenomenon are risky. Many psychologists are dissatisfied with the currently available intelligence tests, and some are working toward eventually producing a fundamentally better test. In the meantime the available tests have both strengths and weaknesses. Let's examine some of these tests.

## IQ Tests

It would be hard to estimate how much time you have already spent taking tests. Some need for testing is clear, even if educators sometimes overdo it. More students want to attend medical school than our medical schools could possibly accommodate, just as more people would like to play college basketball than their teams can include. We must somehow select among applicants.

Schools and colleges base their admissions decisions partly on students' grades and teachers' recommendations, but they know that the value of such information is limited. (Some schools are better than others, and some teachers grade more strictly than others.) To compare students from different schools, admissions officials check scores on standardized tests.

**Intelligence quotient (IQ)** tests attempt to *measure an individual's probable performance in school and similar settings.* (The term *quotient* dates from when IQ was determined by dividing mental age by chronological age and then multiplying by 100. For example, an 8-year-old who performed like an average 10-year-old would have a

mental age of 10, a chronological age of 8, and an IQ of $10/8 \times 100 = 125$. That method is now obsolete, but the term remains.) The first IQ tests were devised for a practical purpose by two French psychologists, Alfred Binet and Theophile Simon (1905). The French Ministry of Public Instruction wanted a fair way to identify children who had such serious intellectual deficiencies that they could not succeed in the public school system and who therefore should not be placed in the same classes with other students. The task of identifying such children had formerly been left to medical doctors, but the school system was seeking a fairer, more impartial test. Binet and Simon produced a test to measure the skills that children need for success in school, such as understanding and using language, computational skills, memory, and the ability to follow instructions.

Their test and others like it do make reasonably accurate predictions. But suppose that a test correctly predicts that one student will perform better than another in school. Can we then say that the first student did better in school *because of* a higher IQ score?

No. Consider this analogy: Suppose we ask why some basketball player misses so many of his shots. Someone answers, "Because he has a low shooting average." Clearly, that explains nothing. (The reason for his low shooting average is that he misses so many shots.) Similarly, saying that a student does poorly in school because of a low IQ score isn't much of an explanation; after all, the IQ test was designed to measure the very skills that schoolwork requires. An IQ score measures performance; it does not explain it.

## The Stanford-Binet Test

*The test that Binet and Simon designed was later modified for English speakers by Lewis Terman and other Stanford psychologists and published as the* **Stanford-Binet IQ test.** This test is administered to individual students by someone who has been carefully trained on how to present the items and score the answers. It contains items that range in difficulty, designated by age (see Table 9.2). An item designated as "age 8," for example, will be answered correctly by 60–90% of all 8-year-olds. (A higher percentage of older children answer it correctly and a lower percentage of younger children.) Those who take this test are asked only those items that are pegged at about their level of functioning. For example, the psychologist testing an 8-year-old might start with the items designated for 7-year-olds. Unless the child missed many of the 7-year-old items, the psychologist would simply give credit for all the 6-year-old items without testing them. If the child answered most of the 7-year-old items correctly, the psychologist would proceed to the items for 8-year-olds, 9-year-olds, and so forth, until the child began to miss item after item. At that point the psychologist would end the test without proceeding to the still more difficult items. (This method is known as *adaptive testing.*)

**TABLE 9.2 Examples of the Types of Items on the Stanford-Binet Test**

| Age | Sample Test Item |
|---|---|
| 2 | Test administrator points at pictures of everyday objects and asks, "What is this?" "Here are some pegs of different sizes and shapes. See whether you can put each one into the correct hole." |
| 4 | "Why do people live in houses?" "Birds fly in the air; fish swim in the ____." |
| 6 | "Here is a picutre of a horse. Do you see what part of the horse is missing?" "Here are some candies. Can you count how many there are?" |
| 8 | "What should you do if you find a lost puppy?" "Stephanie can't write today because she twisted her ankle. What is wrong with that?" |
| 10 | "Why should people be quiet in a library?" "Repeat after me: 4 8 3 7 1 4." |
| 12 | "What does *regret* mean?" "Here is a picture. Can you tell me what is wrong with it?" |
| 14 | "What is the similarity between high and low?" "Watch me fold this paper and cut it. Now, when I unfold it, how many holes will there be?" |
| Adult | "Make up a sentence using the words *celebrate, reverse,* and *appointment.*" "What do people mean when they say, 'People who live in glass houses should not throw stones' "? |

Source: Modified from Nietzel and Bernstein, 1987.

Ordinarily, the entire test lasts somewhat more than an hour. However, unlike most other IQ tests, the current edition of the Stanford-Binet imposes no time limit; people are allowed to proceed at their own pace (McCall, Yates, Hendricks, Turner, & McNabb, 1989).

Stanford-Binet IQ scores are computed from tables set up to ensure that a given IQ score will mean the same at different ages. The mean IQ at each age is 100. A 6-year-old with an IQ score of, say, 116, has performed better on the test than 84% of other 6-year-olds; similarly, an adult with an IQ score of 116 has performed better than 84% of other adults. The modern version of the Stanford-Binet also provides subscores reflecting crystallized intelligence, abstract visual reasoning, and short-term memory (Daniel, 1997; McCall et al., 1989).

In Table 9.2 note that the Stanford-Binet test includes questions designated for children who are only 2 years old. However, scores below age 4 or 5 fluctuate markedly (Honzik, 1974; Morrow & Morrow, 1974). Sometimes children that age will try very hard, but when they just don't feel like trying, they really don't try at all. You may have noticed that tendency in preschool children, if you

have spent any time with them. Consequently, their test scores are useful for research purposes, but they should not be weighed heavily when making placement decisions about individual children.

## The Wechsler Tests

*Two IQ tests devised by David Wechsler,* known as the **Wechsler Adult Intelligence Scale–Third Edition (WAIS–III)** and the **Wechsler Intelligence Scale for Children–Third Edition (WISC–III),** produce the same average, 100, and almost the same distribution of scores as the Stanford-Binet. The WISC is given to children up to age 16; the WAIS is for everyone older. As with the Stanford-Binet, the Wechsler tests are administered to one person at a time. A Wechsler test provides an overall score and scores in two major categories (verbal and performance), which are subdivided into component abilities. (Table 9.3 shows examples of test items, and Figure 9.4 shows one individual's test profile.) Thus, a Wechsler test provides a profile of someone's strengths and weaknesses. People who learned English as a second language, for example, ordinarily receive higher scores on the performance section than on the verbal section.

Each of the 12 parts of the WISC–III or the WAIS–III begins with the simplest questions and progresses to increasingly difficult ones. The six parts constituting the Performance Scale call for nonverbal answers (Figure 9.5). The other parts, constituting the Verbal Scale, require spoken or written answers.

The inclusion of questions that ask for factual information (e.g., "From what animal do we get milk?") has caused much controversy. Critics complain that such items measure knowledge, not ability. That is, the term *intelligence* should refer to something more than memorizing facts. Defenders reply as follows:

- "Intelligent" people tend to learn more facts than others do, even if they have had no more exposure to the information.
- As researchers in artificial intelligence have discovered, most of what we call intelligence requires a vast store of factual knowledge (Schank & Birnbaum, 1994). That is, factual knowledge is not *sufficient* to demonstrate intelligence, but it is *necessary.*
- The purpose of an IQ test is to predict performance in school, and in that respect it works. Students who already know a great many facts tend to do well in school.

We shall consider further criticism of intelligence tests in the second module of this chapter.

## Raven's Progressive Matrices

The Stanford-Binet and Wechsler tests, though useful for many purposes, have one major limitation: Because they require use and comprehension of the English language,

**TABLE 9.3 Examples of the Types of Items on the Wechsler Intelligence Scale for Children (WISC–III)**

| Test | Example |
|---|---|
| **Verbal Scale** | |
| Information | From what animal do we get milk?<br>(Either "cow" or "goat" is an acceptable answer.) |
| Similarities | How are a plum and a peach similar?<br>(Correct answer: "They are both fruits." Half credit is given for "Both are food." or "Both are round.") |
| Arithmetic | Count these blocks: ■ ■ ■ ■ ■ ■ ■ ■ ■ |
| Vocabulary | Define the word *letter*. |
| Comprehension | What should you do if you see a train approaching a broken track?<br>(A correct answer is "Stand safely out of the way and wave something to warn the train."<br>Half credit is given for "Tell someone at the railroad station."<br>No credit is given for "I would try to fix the track.") |
| Digit Span | Repeat these numbers after I say them: 3 6 2. |
| **Performance Scale** | |
| Picture completion | What is missing from this picture? |
| Coding | Here is a page full of shapes. Put a slash (/) through all the circles and an × through all the squares. |
| Picture arrangement | Here are some cards with a gardener on them.<br>Can you put them in order? |
| Block design | See how I have arranged these four blocks?<br>Here are four more blocks.<br>Can you arrange your blocks like mine? |
| Object assembly | Can you put these five puzzle pieces together to make a dog? |
| Mazes | Here is a maze. Start with your pencil here and trace a path to the other end of the maze without crossing any lines. |

Source: Based on Wechsler, 1991. Items shown are similar but not identical to those actually on the WISC–III.

they are unfair to immigrants, hearing-impaired people, and anyone else who does not speak English well. "Why not simply translate the tests into other languages, including sign language?" you might ask. Psychologists sometimes do, but it is difficult to equate the translation with the original. For example, one part of the Stanford-Binet presents certain words and asks for words that rhyme with them. Generating rhymes is moderately easy in English, even easier in Italian, but I am told it is virtually impossible in Zulu (M. W. Smith, 1974).

 To overcome such problems, psychologists have tried to devise a "culture-fair" or culture-reduced test that would make minimal use of language and not ask for any specific facts. *One example of a culture-reduced test* is the **Progressive Matrices** test

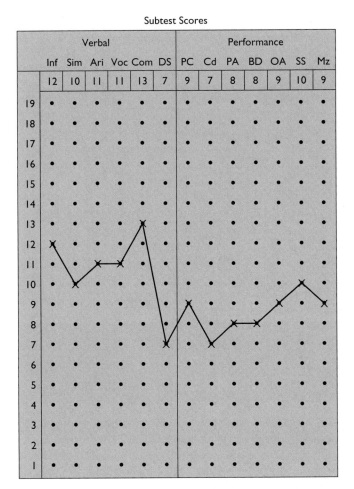

Subtest Scores

| | Verbal | | | | | | Performance | | | | | | |
|---|---|---|---|---|---|---|---|---|---|---|---|---|---|
| Inf | Sim | Ari | Voc | Com | DS | PC | Cd | PA | BD | OA | SS | Mz |
| 12 | 10 | 11 | 11 | 13 | 7 | 9 | 7 | 8 | 8 | 9 | 10 | 9 |

**FIGURE 9.4** A score profile for one child on the WISC–III IQ test. Each subtest score represents performance on one type of task compared with other children of the same age. Besides providing an overall IQ score, a profile such as this highlights an individual's strengths and weaknesses. Note that this child performed better on verbal tasks than on performance tasks. (Data courtesy of Patricia Collins)

**FIGURE 9.5** Much of the WAIS–III involves nonverbal tests in which a person is asked to perform certain tasks. Here, to evaluate visual-spatial organization, a woman arranges colored blocks according to a specified pattern while a psychologist times her.

devised by John C. Raven. These matrices, which *progress gradually from easy to difficult items,* attempt to measure abstract reasoning. To answer the questions, a person must generate hypotheses, test them, and infer rules (Carpenter, Just, & Shell, 1990). Figure 9.6 presents three matrices similar to those of this test. The first is relatively easy, the second is harder, and the third is harder still.

The Progressive Matrices test does not call for any verbal responses or specific information, and the instructions are simple. It therefore gives a non-English-speaker a better opportunity than most other IQ tests do. The main disadvantage is that this test provides only a single overall score, instead of also identifying an individual's strengths and weaknesses, as do other IQ tests.

How culture-fair, then, is the Progressive Matrices test? It requires less information than the Wechsler or Stanford-Binet tests, but it does assume familiarity with pencil-and-paper, multiple-choice tests, and several other

Western customs. For example, children from some cultures have been taught not to express their own opinions without first checking with their parents, or not to speak to unfamiliar adults, such as the person administering the test (Greenfield, 1997). In Western culture, if a child is asked to sort items into categories, the response considered "most intelligent" is to put all the metal tools in one category, all the foods in another, and so forth. But among the Kpelle people of Africa, the "intelligent" response would be to link objects that might be used together, such as placing a knife with a potato because one would use the knife to cut the potato (Greenfield, 1997). In short, no test is completely culture-free.

## *The Scholastic Assessment Test*

The test once known as the Scholastic Aptitude Test, *designed to measure a student's likelihood of doing well in college,* is now titled the **Scholastic Assessment Test (SAT).** The term *aptitude* means *ability;* the publishers of the test changed the name because the test does not and cannot measure innate ability. However, because the term *assessment* means *test,* the new title really means *school-based test test.* Many people call it the "SAT test," adding even more redundancy.

The Scholastic Assessment Test serves the same function as an IQ test: It predicts performance in school,

**FIGURE 9.6** Items similar to those in Raven's Progressive Matrices test. The instructions are: "Each pattern has a piece missing. From the eight choices provided, select the one that completes the pattern, both going across and going down." (You can check your answers against answer A on page 339.)

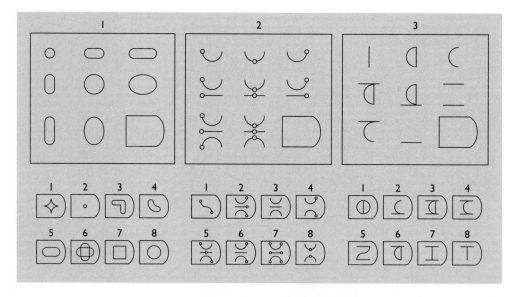

specifically in college. (Figure 9.7 shows the relationship between SAT scores and grade-point average during the freshman year in college at one university.) The SAT consists of multiple-choice items divided into two sets, verbal and quantitative. The SAT also offers subject tests in individual fields, such as history. Each test is scored on a scale from 200 to 800. The mean was originally set at 500. Over the years the mean gradually drifted downward, partly because a wider range of students were taking the test, instead of just the best. In 1995 the scoring system was readjusted to return the mean to 500. (Thus, scores reported before the readjustment do not mean the same thing as scores reported after the readjustment.)

Figure 9.8 presents examples of the types of items found on the SAT. If you are a college student in the United States, you are probably familiar with either the SAT or the similar American College Test (ACT).

**IN CLOSING**

## *Measuring Something We Don't Fully Understand*

The standard IQ tests and related tests have survived for decades, despite persistent criticism. These tests have both pluses and minuses. An IQ score is useful for certain practical purposes such as selecting students for special programs. It also relates roughly to some biological variables. For example, studies using modern methods such as MRI scans have found a moderate positive correlation between students' IQ scores and their brain volumes (Willerman, Schultz, Rutledge, & Bigler, 1991).

In a way the overall intelligence of an individual is like the gross national product of a country because both figures provide a summary that may be useful for certain purposes. However, if we want to understand the processes in any detail, we need to go beyond the

**FIGURE 9.7** In this scatter plot, each point represents one freshman student at a particular university. That student's SAT score is given on the *x* axis; the grade-point average is on the *y* axis. Note that SAT scores predict college grades moderately well, with a correlation of .3 for this sample. Also note the exceptions—students with high SAT scores but poor grades and students with low SAT scores but good grades.

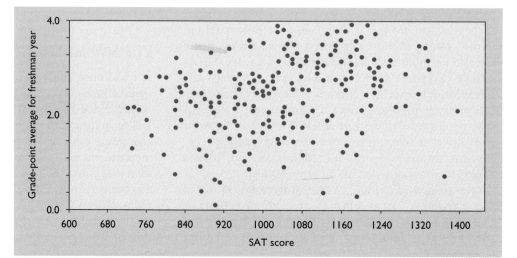

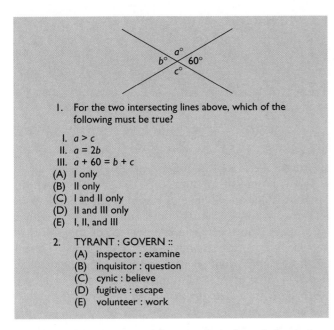

1. For the two intersecting lines above, which of the following must be true?

   I. $a > c$
   II. $a = 2b$
   III. $a + 60 = b + c$

   (A) I only
   (B) II only
   (C) I and II only
   (D) II and III only
   (E) I, II, and III

2. TYRANT : GOVERN ::
   (A) inspector : examine
   (B) inquisitor : question
   (C) cynic : believe
   (D) fugitive : escape
   (E) volunteer : work

**FIGURE 9.8** These two sample items from the Scholastic Assessment Test (SAT) reflect its two parts, which measure mathematical and verbal skills. (Check answer B on this page.) (From the College Entrance Examination Board and the Educational Testing Service)

summaries and explore the detailed components that underlie them.

Psychologists hope to develop new and better tests, but producing a significantly improved IQ test is not as easy as it may sound (Grigorenko & Sternberg, 1998). The current tests, even with their shortcomings, are the products of decades of research and effort. Devising a valid measure of more complex and varied abilities will require at least as much research.

In the next module of this chapter, we shall consider how psychologists evaluate tests, including the currently available IQ tests and any new tests that might someday be proposed to take their place. Psychologists have devised some clear criteria for evaluating tests and deciding which tests are better than others.

At this point let's simply stress that the value of an IQ test, like that of any tool, depends on how it is used. Just as a hammer can be used to build a door or to break one down, a test score can be used to open the doors of opportunity or to close them. A test score, if cautiously interpreted, can aid schools in making placement decisions. If the score is treated as an infallible guide, it can be seriously misleading.

## Summary

- **Defining intelligence.** The designers of the standard IQ tests defined intelligence simply as the ability to do well in school. Psychologists with a more theoretical interest have defined intelligence by listing the abilities that it includes. (page 329)

- **g factor.** Various "intelligent" abilities apparently share a common element known as the *g* factor, which is closely related to abstract reasoning. The *g* factor may arise either because various tests tap the same ability or because the health and educational factors that promote the growth of one intellectual ability also promote the development of other intellectual abilities. (page 329)

- **Fluid and crystallized intelligence.** Psychologists distinguish between fluid intelligence (a basic reasoning ability that can be applied to any problem, including unfamiliar ones) and crystallized intelligence (acquired abilities to solve familiar types of problems). (page 331)

- **Abilities that make up intelligence.** Psychologists have drawn up different lists of the abilities that make up intelligence. Some define intelligence fairly narrowly in terms of academic skills; others include such abilities as social attentiveness, musical abilities, and motor skills. According to the theory of multiple intelligences, people possess many independent types of intelligence. (page 332)

- **Triarchic theory.** According to Sternberg's triarchic theory, intelligence consists of three aspects: the cognitive mechanisms within the individual, the situations that require intelligence, and the ways that intelligent behavior relates to the environment. (page 332)

- **IQ tests.** The Stanford-Binet and other IQ tests were devised to predict the level of performance in school. (page 334)

- **Wechsler IQ tests.** The Wechsler IQ tests measure separate abilities, grouped into a Verbal Scale and a Performance Scale of six parts each. (page 335)

- **Culture-reduced tests.** Culture-reduced tests such as Raven's Progressive Matrices can be used to test people who are unfamiliar with English. (page 336)

- **SAT.** The Scholastic Assessment Test is similar to IQ tests because it predicts performance in school, specifically in college. (page 337)

## Answers to Concept Checks

1. Turing's solution reflected fluid intelligence, a generalized ability that could apply to any topic. The solution provided by a bicycle mechanic reflected crystallized intelligence, an ability developed in a particular area of experience. (page 331)

2. Using Cattell's terminology, a novel situation calls for fluid intelligence, whereas a repeated situation calls for crystallized intelligence. (page 334)

## Answers to Other Questions in the Module

**A.** 1. (8); 2. (2); 3. (4) (page 338)
**B.** 1. (D); 2. (B) (page 339)

# Evaluation of Intelligence Tests

*How accurate and fair are the IQ tests? Why do some groups score higher than others on the average?*

Edward Thorndike, a pioneer in the study of both animal and human learning, is often quoted as saying, "If something exists, it exists in some amount. If it exists in some amount, it can be measured." Douglas Detterman (1979) countered, "Anything which exists can be measured incorrectly."

Both quotes apply well to intelligence: If intelligence exists at all, it must be measurable, but it can also be measured incorrectly. One major task now facing researchers is to determine whether IQ tests measure what their designers claim they measure and whether they apply fairly to all groups. Because much is at stake here, the conclusions are often controversial.

## The Standardization of IQ Tests

To specify what various scores mean, those who devise a test must *standardize* it. **Standardization** is *the process of establishing rules for administering a test and interpreting the scores.* One of the main steps in standardization is to find the **norms,** which are *descriptions of how frequently various scores occur.*

Psychologists try to standardize a test on a large representative population. For example, if a test is to be used with children throughout the United States and Canada, psychologists need to measure the norms with a large random or representative sample of U.S. and Canadian children, not just with children of one group or region.

### The Distribution of IQ Scores

Binet, Wechsler, and the other pioneers who devised the first IQ tests chose items and arranged the scoring method to establish the mean score at 100, with a standard deviation of 15 for the Wechsler test, as Figure 9.9 shows, and 16 for the Stanford-Binet. (Recall from Chapter 2 that the standard deviation is a measure of the variability of performance. It is small if most scores are close to the mean and large if scores vary widely.) The scores of almost any population approximate a *normal distribution,* or bell-

shaped curve, as shown in Figure 9.9; the distribution is symmetrical and most scores are close to the mean.

In any normal distribution, 68% of all people fall within 1 standard deviation above or below the mean and about 95% are within 2 standard deviations. Someone with a score of 115 on the Wechsler test exceeds the scores of people within 1 standard deviation from the mean, plus all of those more than 1 standard deviation below the mean—a total of 84% of all people, as shown in Figure 9.9. We say that such a person is "in the 84th percentile." Someone with an IQ score of 130 is in the 98th percentile, with a score higher than those of 98% of others.

Psychologists sometimes refer to people more than 2 standard deviations above the mean as "gifted." The cutoff line is arbitrary, as a child with an IQ of 129 is virtually the same as one with an IQ of 130. Still, regardless of where we draw the line, some people do stand out as

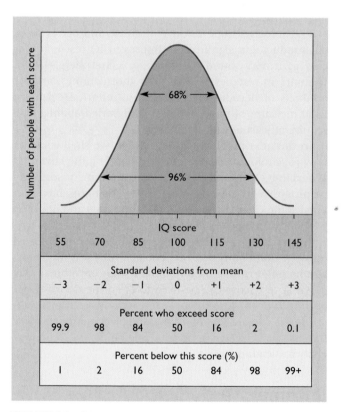

**FIGURE 9.9** The scores on an IQ test form an approximately bell-shaped curve. The curve shown here represents scores on the Wechsler IQ test, with a standard deviation of 15 (15 points above and below the mean, which is 100). The results on the Stanford-Binet test are very similar, except that the standard deviation is 16, so the spread is slightly wider.

exceptionally bright. They learn rapidly without needing much help; they show an intense drive to master knowledge; they ask deep philosophical questions; and they create and develop new ideas and products (Winner, 2000).

Psychologists classify people more than 2 standard deviations below the mean as "retarded." In the United States, the *Individuals with Disabilities Act* requires public schools to provide "free and appropriate" education for all children, regardless of their limitations. Children with severe mental or physical disabilities are placed in a special class, but those with milder disabilities are "mainstreamed" as much as possible—that is, placed in the same classes with other children but given special consideration. For example, a child with a mild hearing impairment might sit close to the front of the room or a child with limited hand coordination might be given extra time on tests. The results of mainstreaming have been mixed. On the plus side, some studies have found that children included in mainstream classes develop better language abilities than those in classes limited to disabled children (Laws, Byrne, & Buckley, 2000). However, most disabled children have few friends and they become increasingly isolated as they progress from early to later grades (Hall & McGregor, 2000). Some are victims of bullying (Llewellyn, 2000). Unfortunately, we do not know as much as we would like about how to educate people with special needs (Detterman & Thompson, 1997).

■ People with IQ scores at least 2 standard deviations below the mean are classified as "retarded." Many can be "mainstreamed" in regular classes; severely retarded children are taught in special classes.

## Restandardizations and the Flynn Effect

Over the years the standardization of any test eventually becomes obsolete. In 1920 a question that asked people to identify Mars was fairly difficult because most people knew little about the planets. Today, in an era of space exploration, the same question is much easier. Every part of the test needs to be restandardized periodically, not just those with factual content, to make sure the test is not becoming easier or harder.

Those who restandardized the IQ tests eventually realized that they were consistently having to make the questions more difficult to keep the mean from rising. That is, *decade by decade, generation by generation, people's raw scores on IQ tests have been gradually increasing, and test makers have had to make the tests harder to keep the mean score at 100.* This tendency is known as the **Flynn effect,** after the psychologist who first called attention to it (Flynn, 1984,

1999). The Flynn effect amounts to about 6 IQ points per 10 years. So if you took the same IQ test your parents did when they were your age, then (assuming your parents are about 25 years older than you) your score would be about 15 points higher than on today's test and 15 points higher than your parents' test scores. If you took an IQ test from your grandparents' era, not only you but also most other people your age would score in or near the gifted range.

What accounts for the Flynn effect? No one knows. Evolution is not a plausible explanation for such a rapid change. Improved health and nutrition are a possibility (Lynn, 1998). After all, people have been getting taller over the years, and that trend is assumed to reflect advances in health and nutrition. However, the improving IQ trends have continued during recent decades, even though researchers are not convinced that nutrition has continued to improve (Martorell, 1998). Another possible explanation is better education (Williams, 1998). However, the IQ gains have been greatest on Raven's Progressive Matrices (see page 338) and other tests of reasoning; they have been weak or nonexistent on vocabulary, knowledge, and arithmetic—the topics taught in school (Flynn, 1999). Another possibility is the beneficial influence of television and video games, which presumably stimulate some kinds of visual-spatial thinking (Neisser, 1997). The problem with that hypothesis is that IQ scores began rising in the early 1900s, well before the spread of television and electronic devices. One more hypothesis is that people simply have been getting better at taking tests. However, the improvement on test scores amounts to 30 IQ points over the last 50 years, and no amount of test-taking practice produces that much benefit. Besides, the IQ improvement is evident in 6-year-old children, who have not had extensive practice at taking tests.

The Flynn effect is difficult to explain because it has been so widespread and pervasive over time and place. The improvement on IQ test performance has been steady since the development of the first tests early in the 1900s, and it has been present in every country for which we have data: the United States, Canada, Britain, Australia, New Zealand, all of continental Europe, Israel, Japan, and urban areas of Brazil and China (Flynn, 1998). It is also present in all ethnic groups (Raven, 2000). If the effect occurred at some times and places but not others, we could try to determine what was true about those times and places. But if the effect occurs in all groups everywhere and always, finding the cause is difficult.

The other major problem is that although IQ test performance has been increasing, actual intelligence may not have been. It is possible to argue that young adults today are a bit smarter overall than young adults of previous generations (Howard, 1999; Schooler, 1998). However, a mean increase of 30 IQ points over 50 years is huge. If people really are that much smarter, teachers should have noticed that their classes are full of creative geniuses. Conversely, if the people of 50 years ago really were the equivalent of those with an IQ of 70 today, then most people back then could barely have taken care of themselves without supervision, and most would not have been able to understand the rules of a team sport. Flynn (1998) therefore argues that we have seen an increase in IQ scores, but not intelligence, over time. If so, what exactly do IQ scores mean?

# Evaluation of Tests

At some point in your academic career, you probably complained about an unfair test. Psychologists avoid simply arguing about whether an IQ test seems fair; they examine specific kinds of evidence to determine what the test achieves. The main ways of evaluating any test—of intelligence, personality, or anything else—are to check its reliability and validity.

## *Reliability*

The **reliability** of a test is defined as *the repeatability of its scores* (T. B. Rogers, 1995). A reliable test measures something consistently. To determine the reliability of a test, psychologists calculate a correlation coefficient. They may test the same people twice, either with the same test or with equivalent versions of it, and compare the two sets of scores. Or they may compare the scores on the first and second halves of the test or the scores on the test's odd-numbered and even-numbered items. If all items measure approximately the same abilities, one set of scores should correlate highly with the other set. As with any other correlation coefficient, the reliability of a test can (theoretically) range from +1 to −1. In the real world, however, reliability is always positive. (A negative reliability would mean that most of the people who score high on one set of items score low on the other set. That pattern simply never happens.) Figure 9.10 illustrates **test-retest reliability,** *the correlation between scores on a first test and a retest.*

If a test's reliability is perfect (+1), the person who scores the highest on the first test will also score highest on the retest, the person who scores second highest on the first test will also score second highest on the retest, and so forth. If the reliability is 0, scores vary randomly from one test to another. The reliability of the WISC–III has been measured at .96 (Wechsler, 1991), and the reli-

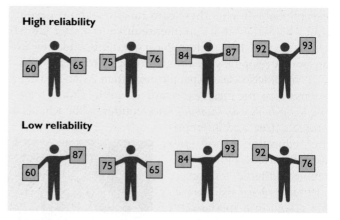

**High reliability**

**Low reliability**

**FIGURE 9.10** On a test with high reliability, people who score high the first time will score high when they take the test again. On a test with low reliability, scores fluctuate randomly.

abilities of the Stanford-Binet, Progressive Matrices, and SAT are similar. These figures indicate that the tests are measuring *something,* but they do not tell us what that something is. However, that something is stable over time. Many studies have found correlations over .9 for people taking the same test at two times 10 years apart, and one study found that IQ scores at age 11 correlate .63 with scores at age 77 (Deary, Whalley, Lemmon, Crawford, & Starr, 2000).

**A STEP FURTHER**
*Reliability*

Try to imagine a test with 0 reliability. What kind of questions would such a test include?

# CONCEPT CHECKS

3. I have just devised a new "intelligence test." I measure your intelligence by dividing the length of your head by its width and then multiplying by 100. Would that be a reliable test?
4. Most students find that their SAT scores increase the second time they take the test. Does that improvement indicate that the test is unreliable? (Check your answers on page 354.)

## *Validity*

A test's **validity** is *a determination of how well it measures what it claims to measure.* One type of validity is **content validity.** We say that a test has high content validity if *its items accurately represent the information that the test is meant to measure.* For example, a test for a driver's license has content validity if it includes important laws and regula-

In some countries test scores determine a student's future almost irrevocably. Students who perform well are almost assured of future success; those who perform poorly will have very limited opportunities.

tions that pertain to driving. A licensing examination for psychologists would have high content validity if it tested information that a practicing psychologist needs to know. If you took a test in class that concentrated mostly on material that your professor never mentioned, that test would have low content validity.

A second type of validity is **construct validity.** A test has construct validity if *what it measures corresponds to a theoretical construct.* For example, intelligence is a theoretical construct that should have certain properties, such as increasing as a child grows older. For an IQ test to have construct validity, older children should as a rule answer more questions correctly than younger children do. It should also have the property of being independent of eyesight and motor coordination; people with physical limitations should be able to get scores similar to other people. A test of anxiety would have construct validity if the scores increased in situations likely to make people nervous. In short, a test has good construct validity if the scores depend on factors we believe to be important and not on factors we regard as unimportant (Messick, 1995).

**Predictive validity,** a third type of validity, is *the ability of a test's scores to predict some real-world performance.* For example, an interest test that correctly predicts what courses a student will enjoy has predictive validity, as does an IQ test that correctly predicts how well a student will perform in school.

As with reliability, psychologists measure predictive validity by a correlation coefficient. To determine the predictive validity of an IQ test or the SAT, psychologists determine how well the scores predict students' grades. A validity of +1 would mean that the scores perfectly predicted performance, and a validity of 0 would mean that the scores were worthless as predictors. A problem is that the IQ tests are trying to predict school performance, and

our measure of school performance—grades—is itself an inaccurate, even sloppy measurement. The less reliable the grading system, the harder it is for anything else to correlate with it.

The predictive validities of most IQ tests and the SAT range from about .3 to .6, varying from one school to another (Anastasi, 1988; Siegler & Richards, 1982). As these figures suggest, success in school depends not only on students' academic skills, but also on their motivation, persistence, and other personality attributes that are hard to measure—as well as what courses they take and what standards their teachers use. Some law schools now use a complex method to evaluate applicants' college grades and test scores: Suppose you are applying and you have high grades and moderately high test scores. The law school compares your grades and scores to those of other applicants from your college. If the other applicants also had high test scores, the law school concludes that your college is a strong one with many good students. However, if the other applicants also had high grades, it concludes that your college gives out high grades easily. Your chance of admission is best if your grades were higher than those of the other applicants, but the other applicants did well on their standardized tests (Swets, Dawes, & Monahan, 2000).

## Validity of Test Scores for Selecting Among Job Applicants

Besides predicting school performance, IQ tests also have some validity for predicting success on a variety of jobs, and if combined with other information, such as a structured interview or a work sample, they produce a validity greater than .6 (Schmidt & Hunter, 1998). According to Frank Schmidt and John Hunter (1981, p. 1128), "Professionally developed cognitive ability tests are valid predictors of performance on the job . . . for all jobs . . . in all settings." That is probably an overstatement. (It could hardly be an understatement!) Also, a controversy continues about whether job performance is more accurately predicted by more or less standard cognitive test scores or by measures of specific competencies and practical skills (McClelland, 1998). Personality factors such as persistence and willingness to listen and learn would probably be excellent predictors also, if we had better ways to measure them (Wagner, 1997). Still, for many jobs, using some type of cognitive test score to select employees increases the chances that those who are hired will succeed at their jobs, and in many cases the cognitive test is the best measure available.

In some cases job applicants have challenged the right of an employer to deny them a job based on a test score or their education. Their claim is that those criteria create unnecessary barriers for people with little formal education who can nevertheless perform the job well. U.S. courts have ruled that an employer can use test scores to select employees only if the employer can demonstrate that the scores are valid predictors of performance on that particular job. In fact, employers may use almost any criterion that they demonstrate to be valid. If a police department wants to hire only tall police officers or an airline wants to hire only thin flight attendants, the courts ask a simple question (Hogan & Quigley, 1986): Can you demonstrate that people who meet this criterion do the job better than people who don't?

**Special Problems in Measuring Validity**
Measuring the validity of a test can be tricky. Consider data for the Graduate Record Examination (GRE), a test similar to the SAT. For predicting grades in the first year of graduate school, the verbal and quantitative parts of the GRE have the following predictive validities (Educational Testing Service, 1994):

|  | GRE verbal score | GRE quantitative score |
|---|---|---|
| Graduate students in physics | .19 | .13 |
| Graduate students in English | .23 | .29 |

Note that the verbal score is the better predictor of grades for physics students, whereas the quantitative score is a better predictor for English students! How can we explain these surprising results? Simply. Almost all graduate students in physics have about the same (very high) score on the quantitative test, and almost all English graduate students have the same (very high) score on the verbal test. When almost all the students in a department have practically the same score, that score cannot predict which students will be more successful. A test can have a high predictive validity only for a population whose scores vary over a substantial range.

**C**ONCEPT CHECK

5. Can a test have high reliability and low validity? Can a test have low reliability and high validity?
6. If physics graduate departments tried admitting some students with low quantitative scores on the GRE and English departments tried admitting some students with low verbal scores, what would happen to the predictive validity of the tests?

7. Would you expect the SAT scores to show higher predictive validity at a college with extremely competitive admissions standards, such as MIT, or at a college that admits almost every applicant? (Check your answers on page 354.)

## Utility

In addition to reliability and validity, a good test should have utility. **Utility** is defined as *usefulness for a practical purpose*. A test can be reliable and valid without being very useful.

For example, one study found that first-year grades at the University of Pennsylvania correlated positively with both SAT general test scores and SAT achievement test scores. That is, both general scores and achievement scores were valid. However, because the general test correlated highly with the achievement tests, there wasn't much advantage to having both. Investigators found that they could predict first-year grades just as well from achievement scores alone as they could from a combination of general and achievement scores (Baron & Norman, 1992). Those results may not apply to other colleges, and they are of course irrelevant for colleges that do not require the achievement tests. The point is that any institution should determine whether a given test has utility for its purposes.

Table 9.4 summarizes the criteria for evaluating intelligence tests.

## Interpreting Fluctuations in Scores

Suppose your score on the first test in your psychology course is 94% correct. On the second test (which was equally difficult), your score is only 88%. Does that score indicate that you studied harder for the first test than for the second test? Not necessarily. Whenever you take tests that are not perfectly reliable, your scores are likely to fluctuate. The lower the reliability, the greater the fluctuation.

When people lose sight of this fact, they sometimes offer complex explanations for random fluctuations in results. In

**TABLE 9.4** Evaluating Intelligence Tests

| Reliability | Validity | Utility | Bias |
|---|---|---|---|
| How consistent are the same person's scores? | How well does the test measure what it claims to measure? | How useful is the test for a particular purpose? | Do test scores make equally accurate predictions from all groups? |
| | Content: Do the test items represent the pertinent information? | | |
| | Construct: Do the results match theoretical expectations? | | |
| | Prediction: Do the test scores predict real-world performance? | | |

one well-known study, Harold M. Skeels (1966) tested infants in an orphanage and identified those with the lowest IQ scores. He then placed them in an institution that provided more personal attention. Several years later most of them showed major increases in their IQ scores. Should we conclude, as many psychologists did, that the extra attention improved the children's IQ performances? Not necessarily (Longstreth, 1981). IQ tests for infants have low reliability—in other words the scores fluctuate widely from one time to another. If someone selects infants with low IQ scores on a given day and retests them later, their mean IQ score is almost certain to improve simply because the scores had nowhere to go but up.

**A STEP FURTHER**
*Score Fluctuations*

What would be the proper control group for the study by Skeels?

# Group Differences in IQ Scores

Binet and the other pioneers in IQ testing discovered that girls tend to do better than boys on certain kinds of language tasks, especially verbal fluency. Boys, however, tend to do better than girls on visual-spatial rotations and certain kinds of mathematical reasoning. By loading the test with one type of item, they could have produced results showing that girls are smarter than boys or that boys are smarter than girls. Instead, they carefully balanced these two types of items to ensure that the mean score of both girls and boys would be 100.

Over the years studies have continued to demonstrate similar male–female differences in many countries and cultures (Halpern, 1997; Stumpf & Stanley, 1998). Note that these are differences between the *averages;* the differences within either group are large compared to the differences between the two groups:

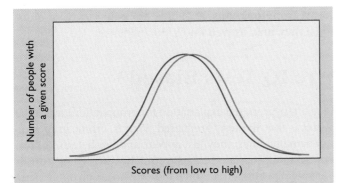

Males tend to show greater individual variability. Thus, the data on a variety of intellectual measures show a higher percentage of males than females at the very top of the range and also at the very bottom (Hedges & Nowell, 1995). For example, one finds more males than females among the top achievers in many fields but also among those with mental retardation, attention deficit disorder, and reading and speaking impairments (Halpern, 1997). (*Why* this is true, we do not know.)

Ethnic groups in the United States also differ in their mean performances on IQ tests (Herrnstein & Murray, 1994). One problem when dealing with these data is that any group—such as Black, or African American—refers to a diverse population who vary among themselves both genetically and environmentally. Ordinarily, researchers classify people simply by asking them how they classify themselves; therefore, these categories are only partly satisfactory (at best) from either a biological or sociological standpoint.

Nevertheless, here are the data, for whatever they are worth (Neisser et al., 1996; Suzuki & Valencia, 1997): The mean score of European Americans as a whole is about 100, with the Jewish subpopulation averaging a few points higher. The mean score for Latinos is in the 90s, but many of those people are first-generation immigrants to the United States who are hampered by language problems. The means for East Asians (those of Japanese, Chinese, or Korean descent) vary from one

■ Many immigrants to the United States settle in ethnic neighborhoods where they can use their original language. Most first-generation immigrants do not score highly on English-language intelligence tests; as a rule their children and grandchildren get higher scores.

sample to another, sometimes about 100 and sometimes a few points higher. The mean for African Americans used to be 85 but has risen over the last several decades to about 90. From about 1970 to 1990, African Americans' SAT scores, vocabulary scores, and other achievement scores increased dramatically, cutting the gap by about one third between African Americans and European Americans (Grissmer, Williamson, Kirby, & Berends, 1998; Hauser, 1998; Huang & Hauser, 1998). The reasons are unknown, but possibilities include improved socioeconomic status, better health and nutrition, better education of both children and their parents, smaller family size, and possibly decreased smoking and drinking by the mothers during pregnancy.

*Please bear in mind that all these data reflect the means for entire populations. Each ethnic group includes many individuals with extremely high and low scores. The data do not justify prejudices or assumptions about any given individual.*

Part of the group difference, although probably only a small part, is due to people's expectations of themselves and others. Claude Steele has discussed the influence of **stereotype threat,** *people's perceived risk that they might do something that supports an unfavorable stereotype about their group.* When African American students take an IQ test, they may fear not only that a poor score would reflect badly on themselves personally, but that it may support the prejudice that African Americans in general do poorly on those tests. They may become distracted and upset, or they may decide not even to try. In either case they would perform less well than they could. Studies have found that African Americans do slightly worse if they are told that a test measures intellectual ability and slightly better if they are told it has nothing to do with ability (Steele & Aronson, 1995). Two later studies found that calling the attention of Asian American women to their status as women slightly depressed their performance on a math test, presumably because of the stereotype that women do not do well at math. However, focusing their attention on being Asians (who stereotypically do well at math) improved their math performance in one study and depressed it in the other (Cheryan & Bodenhausen, 2000; Shih, Pittinsky, & Ambady, 1999).

In addition to the effects of stereotype threat, what else accounts for the observed differences among ethnic groups? In a controversial book, *The Bell Curve*, Richard Herrnstein and Charles Murray (1994) argued that the IQ differences are probably due partly to genetic differences. In response to this book and the ensuing controversy, a panel of distinguished investigators reviewed the evidence and issued a report (Neisser et al., 1996). The panel largely agreed with Herrnstein and Murray about the following points, although they had different phrasing and emphases:

1. IQ tests, imperfect as they are, reliably measure something, regardless of whether we choose to call it intelligence.

2. Whatever IQ tests measure is not all-important, but it is not trivial either. It correlates with school performance, the likelihood of getting and succeeding at certain jobs, and many other behavioral measures.
3. Measured differences among groups are not illusions that we can attribute to faulty tests.
4. IQ differences within the European American population reflect a combination of environmental and genetic differences. Not much is known about the genes that affect intelligence. Important environmental factors include the obvious ones such as education but also such factors as early nutrition, exposure to lead and other toxins, and whether the mother drank alcohol during pregnancy.
5. IQ differences among ethnic groups may also reflect a combination of environmental and genetic differences.

The first and second points simply say that IQ tests are reliable and valid for certain purposes, as mentioned earlier in this chapter. According to a consensus of 52 leading researchers in this area (Arvey et al., 1994), Herrnstein and Murray's third and fourth points also fit the data: The apparent group differences are not due to faulty testing or bias, and differences among European Americans are probably due to both genetic and environmental influences. The fifth point is the difficult one. If taken literally, it is so vague that one could hardly disagree with it: The ethnic differences *may* reflect some combination of environmental and genetic differences. (After all, they *must* reflect at least one or the other!) However, if the statement is taken as implying that genetic factors are an important part of the ethnic differences, then the evidence is too weak to establish a consensus one way or the other. With that preview in mind, let us proceed.

## *Should We Care?*

On such a politically charged question, it is risky to say anything at all. Even discussing the differences among ethnic groups calls extra attention to such matters and runs the risk of supporting prejudices against minority groups. No doubt most people look forward to the day when race and ethnicity are no longer a divisive issue and no one even cares about IQ differences among groups. However, that day has not yet arrived. Many people do care about why ethnic groups differ, and many people form strong opinions. If people are going to have opinions, they may as well know the evidence.

## **Are IQ Tests Biased?**

One often-proposed explanation for group differences in IQ scores is that the tests are biased. That is, ethnic groups do not actually differ; they just appear to differ because of unfair or inappropriate tests. Presumably, according to this viewpoint, a better test would indicate no group differences.

■ Women who return to school after age 25 usually get better grades than their test scores would predict. That is, the tests are "biased" against them in the technical sense of the term *bias*. Saying this does not mean the tests were designed to be unfair to them, just that the test scores underpredict their performance.

The first point to emphasize is that the existence of measurable group differences does not, by itself, demonstrate bias in the tests. If on the average one group scores higher than a second group, the tests might be biased, but possibly, the groups really do differ. For example, on the average, 20-year-olds answer more questions correctly on almost any information test than do 6-year-olds. This fact does not indicate that tests are biased against 6-year-olds; the 20-year-olds really are better informed, and the tests state that difference correctly.

To determine whether or not a test is **biased** against a group, psychologists determine *whether the test systematically underestimates group members' performance.* Consider two examples in which a test does show bias: First, the Stanford-Binet and Wechsler IQ tests *are* biased against non-English speaking immigrants to the United States. In the long run, after immigrants have learned the language, they usually succeed beyond what their initial test scores would indicate. That is, the test scores underestimate their eventual performance.

As a second example, women who enter college or graduate school after age 25 generally receive better grades than their test scores predict (Swinton, 1987). Therefore, the tests are biased against them, even though in fact their test scores are usually pretty good. When we say that the tests are biased against them, we are merely saying that a given test score means something different for a 30-year-old woman than for one who is 20. Why do women returning to school get better grades than their test scores predict? Here are three hypotheses: (a) Because they have been away from school for a while, their test-taking skills are rusty. (b) To return to school at all at that point, they must have strong motivation. (c) Their life experiences give them some advantages.

Repeating for emphasis: To determine whether a test is biased—against 30-year-old women, ethnic minorities, or whatever—psychologists must find out whether such individuals do better in school or college than the test scores predict. Psychologists try to identify bias both in individual test items and in the test as a whole.

## Evaluating Possible Bias in Single Test Items

To determine whether a single item on a test is biased, psychologists examine whether an item might be relatively easier for one group than another (Schmitt & Dorans, 1990). If *all* items are more difficult for one group

■ "Students will rise to your level of expectation," says Jaime Escalante (left), the high school teacher portrayed by Edward James Olmos (right) in *Stand and Deliver*. The movie chronicles Escalante's talent for inspiring average students to excel in calculus. School counselors warned that he asked too much of his students; parents said their kids didn't need calculus. And when his students first passed the advanced placement test, they were accused of cheating, a charge that seemed to reflect prejudice against the students, who were not European American, middle-class, college-prep types.

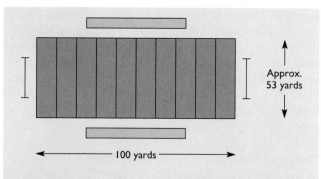

The diagram above represents a football field. What is the ratio of the distance between the goal lines to the distance between the sidelines?

a. 1.89
b. 1.53
c. 0.53
d. 5.3
e. 53

**FIGURE 9.11** This item was once included on the SAT, until psychologists determined that it was biased against women. Some women who did very well on the rest of the test did not know which were the goal lines and which were the sidelines.

than for another, we draw no conclusion about bias, but if some item is among the easiest for one group but relatively difficult for another group, then something is wrong.

Figure 9.11, an item that once appeared on the SAT, shows a diagram of an American football field and asks for the ratio of the distance between the goal lines to the distance between the sidelines. For men this was one of the easiest items on the test. Few men missed it, and those few did poorly on the rest of the test also. In contrast, many more women missed this item, including some of the very brightest women, who missed almost no other questions. The reason was that some women had no interest in football and did not even know which were the goal lines and which were the sidelines. The evidence indicated that the item was biased against women, and the publishers of the SAT removed the item from the test. Standardized tests such as the SAT are routinely purged of any items with demonstrable bias against a particular group.

### Evaluating Possible Bias in a Test as a Whole

By definition a biased test is one that systematically underestimates (underpredicts) the performance of a group. If an IQ test is indeed biased against African Americans, for example, then African Americans who score, say, 100 really have greater abilities than the score indicates and should do better in school than European Americans with the same score.

However, the evidence indicates that African American students with a given IQ score generally do about the

same in school as do European Americans with the same score (Jensen, 1980). The same is true for SAT scores (McCornack, 1983). The unpleasant fact is that on the average European American students get better grades in school than African Americans do. The IQ tests simply report that fact. In recent decades African American students have been doing somewhat better than before on the tests and getting better grades also. In short, the tests seem to be reporting the facts accurately, and it is wrong to blame the tests themselves for the difference between the groups.

Some critics have argued that African American students' performance is depressed because they are intimidated by a European American tester or because they are confused by the language of the test. However, research studies have found no consistent improvement in scores when the test is administered by an African American examiner using an African American dialect (Sattler & Gwynne, 1982). Furthermore, the difference between the groups is at least as large on the Raven's Progressive Matrices, a nonverbal test, as on the Wechsler or Stanford-Binet (Flynn, 1999).

Denying that IQ tests are biased, however, has nothing to do with whether the differences in scores depend on genetic or environmental influences. It merely means that whatever causes children to differ in school performance also causes them to differ in test performance. The cause of that difference is a separate question.

### CONCEPT CHECK

8. A test of driving skills includes items requiring people to describe what they see. People with visual impairments score lower than people with good vision. Is the test therefore biased against people with visual impairments?

9. Suppose that on some new IQ test tall people generally get higher scores than short people. How could we determine whether this test is biased against short people? (Check your answers on page 354.)

### How Do Heredity and Environment Affect IQ Scores?

The British scholar Francis Galton (1869/1978) was the first to argue that the differences in intelligence are hereditary. As evidence he simply pointed out that eminent and distinguished men—politicians, judges, and the like—generally had distinguished relatives. We no longer consider that evidence convincing because distinguished people and their relatives share their environment as well as their genes. Besides, becoming a distinguished person is only partly a result of intelligence.

The question of how heredity affects intelligence has persisted to this day and remains difficult to answer. Here are descriptions of the available kinds of evidence, with their strengths and limitations.

## Family Resemblances

Figure 9.12, based on a literature review by Thomas Bouchard and Matthew McGue (1981), shows the correlations of IQ scores for people with various degrees of genetic relationship. These data are based on European American families; we do not know how well the results apply to other ethnic groups.

Because no IQ test has perfect reliability, someone taking the test on two occasions will get slightly different scores, and the correlation between the two test scores will be close to .9. The scores of monozygotic (identical) twins correlate with each other almost as well (McGue & Bouchard,

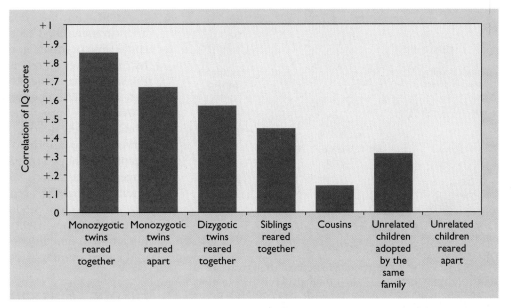

FIGURE 9.12 Mean correlations for the IQs of children with various degrees of genetic and environmental similarity. (Siblings are nontwin children in the same family.) (Adapted from Bouchard & McGue, 1981)

1998). Monozygotic twins resemble each other not only in overall IQ but also in individual tests of verbal ability, spatial ability, processing speed, and memory; they continue to resemble each other throughout life—even beyond age 80 in one study (Petrill et al., 1998). Fraternal twins and nontwin siblings also resemble each other, but not as closely as monozygotic twins. The greater similarity between monozygotic twins implies a probable genetic basis.

Note also in Figure 9.12 the positive correlation between unrelated children adopted into the same family. That correlation indicates a significant contribution from the environment. However, because this correlation is lower than the correlation between siblings (brothers or sisters), the resemblances among siblings must be due partly to genetics (or prenatal environment), not just to growing up together.

## Identical Twins Reared Apart

In Figure 9.12 note the high correlation between monozygotic twins reared apart. That is, identical twins who have been adopted by different parents and reared in separate environments strongly resemble each other in IQ scores (Bouchard & McGue, 1981; Farber, 1981). That resemblance implies a genetic contribution to IQ. Skeptics point out that the "separate" environments have often been similar (Farber, 1981; Kamin, 1974). In some cases the biological parents raised one twin, and close relatives or next-door neighbors raised the other twin. Yet, it is difficult to escape the suggestion of at least a small genetic contribution because it is unlikely that monozygotic twins reared apart would have *more* similar environments than dizygotic twins who grow up in the same household.

## Twins and Single Births

One final point about Figure 9.12: Dizygotic twins resemble each other more closely than single-birth siblings do. That finding, consistent across several studies, indicates an influence from being born at the same time, since the genetic similarity between dizygotic twins is the same as that between siblings. These results probably reflect the importance of prenatal and early postnatal environment. Twins share a prenatal environment and therefore get the same nutrition, body temperature, alcohol or tobacco effects, and so forth while the brain is developing (Devlin, Daniels, & Roeder, 1997). In fact, it is often difficult to distinguish between the role of genetics and that of prenatal environment.

## Adopted Children

Another line of evidence comes from studies of adopted children. Children who are reared by their biological parents generally have IQ scores similar to those of their parents (Figure 9.13). For adopted children IQ scores in early childhood are generally intermediate between those of their biological parents and those of their adoptive parents. As they grow older and become adolescents, their IQ scores gradually correlate more with those of their biological parents and less with those of their adoptive parents (Loehlin, Horn, & Willerman, 1989; Plomin, Fulker, Corley, & DeFries, 1997). Furthermore, related children who are adopted in separate families resemble each other in IQ more than do unrelated children adopted by one family (Teasdale & Owen, 1984).

There is one major problem, however: Low-IQ parents who put their children up for adoption probably do not

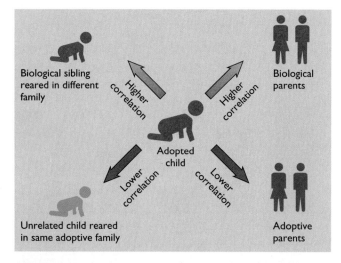

**FIGURE 9.13** The IQ scores of adopted children correlate more highly with those of their biological relatives than with those of their adoptive relatives. Such data point to a probable role of heredity.

provide the best prenatal care. The mother may be young, may not get good prenatal nutrition, may smoke and drink, and may in other ways put her infant at risk for low IQ for reasons other than genetics. In short, adoption data do not clearly distinguish between the contributions of genetics and prenatal environment.

## Gene Identification

The most direct kind of evidence is the identification of specific genes linked to intelligence. One set of investigators compared the chromosomes of children with very high IQ scores (mean 136) and those with average scores (mean 103). They found 1 gene of the 37 they examined that was significantly more common in the high-IQ group (Chorney et al., 1998). Because they had examined so many genes, they knew that a discrepancy in one gene could arise by accident, so they repeated their study with other populations, and again they found that the gene in question was more common in the high-IQ groups. For the combined populations, 46% of the high-IQ people and 23% of the low-IQ people had this gene. Obviously, this gene is neither necessary nor sufficient for high intelligence, but it may be one contributor.

Most researchers agree that hereditary and environmental factors both contribute to the observed variations in IQ scores, at least within the European American population (L. A. Thompson, Detterman, & Plomin, 1991; Turkheimer, 1991). (Few studies have been done on other populations.) The important question is no longer *do* heredity and environment contribute to IQ, but *how* do they contribute? (The one identified gene that appears to be linked to IQ controls a brain chemical whose functions are poorly understood.)

The heritability of variations in IQ scores does not mean that people are somehow limited by the abilities they had at birth. Obviously, if we gave every child either an extremely good or extremely bad environment, we could raise or lower all their IQ scores. Positive heritability of IQ scores merely means that if children grow up in the same environment, some do better than others, and part of that difference relates to genetics.

A variety of programs have attempted to take children from extremely deprived homes and give them special intervention to improve their intellectual development. People who hoped that a brief intervention might lead to huge long-term gains have been disappointed. However, intensive programs occupying many hours per week for several years do produce significant, lasting benefits (Ramey & Ramey, 1998). Again, the point is that conceding a role to heredity does not minimize the importance of the environment.

## Heredity, Environment, and Ethnic Differences

Is it likely that hereditary differences contribute to part of the observed differences in IQ scores among ethnic groups? People disagree on this issue, often with more confidence than the data would justify.

Those who believe that heredity is a likely contributor to ethnic differences offer the following simple proposition: Hereditary differences do appear to contribute to IQ differences among people of European ancestry, so they probably also contribute to the differences among ethnic groups. However, consider the following: Imagine that

■ If ethnic differences in IQ are largely the result of environmental differences, African American children adopted by middle-class European American families should score higher on average than similar children reared in African American homes. The results of research have been unimpressive and also hard to interpret because many of the children studied were adopted relatively late.

someone finds that the children in a certain city differ in their IQ scores, partly for genetic reasons. Now we take a random sample of the families and move them to a second city with worse health, nutrition, education, and overall opportunities. Before long the transported children would no doubt perform worse on the tests. If we compared children within one city or the other, *those* differences could be largely genetic, but the difference between cities would be entirely due to environment (see Figure 9.14).

People who argue that heredity could not contribute to ethnic differences in IQ argue as follows: The various human ethnic groups have diverged for only a brief evolutionary period. The great majority of human genes either show no variation at all among individuals or differ widely *within* each ethnic group. There are probably *no* genes that are present in all members of one group but none of another.

Granting all of that, the implications for the genetics of intelligence are still unclear. No one, or only the most ignorant person, believes that all members of one group have some gene that all members of the other group lack. However, a few genes do occur significantly more often in one population or the other. For example, more African Americans have the sickle-cell anemia gene, and more European Americans have the phenylketonuria gene. No one knows which genes or how many of them are critical for intelligence, but it is possible for certain genes to be more common in one group than another. Furthermore, just as different ethnic groups do share most of their genes, they also share a good deal of their environment, especially within a given country (Rowe, Vazsonyi, & Flannery, 1994). In short, we cannot find the cause of ethnic differences in IQ performance by arguing about likelihoods and probabilities. We need evidence.

## WHAT'S THE EVIDENCE?
### *Environmental Contributors to Ethnic Differences*

Many people have argued that the reason for the IQ differences is that most European American children grow

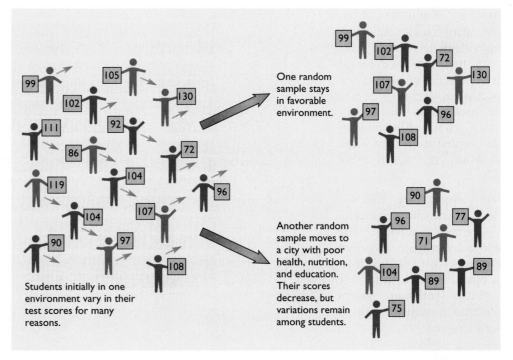

**FIGURE 9.14** If two sets of children grow up in very different circumstances, it is possible that the difference between the two groups is entirely due to environmental differences, even if the differences within each group are partly due to genetic factors.

up in wealthier homes than most African American children. However, if we compare African American children to European American children *of the same socioeconomic status,* the IQ differences remain. They decrease by about 2 or 3 points, but not enough to support the view that wealth is the deciding factor (Herrnstein & Murray, 1994). Still, there are other differences between African American and European American homes. Rather than try to identify the critical one, a simpler approach is to examine African American children who were adopted by upper-middle-class European American families. The idea is that those children should gain all the advantages of the European American families, whatever those advantages might be.

**HYPOTHESIS** If the IQ differences between groups is partly due to environmental differences, then African American children reared by European American families should perform well on IQ tests compared to other African American children.

**METHOD** Sandra Scarr and Richard Weinberg (1976) studied European American families in Minnesota that had adopted African American children (with two African American parents) or ethnically mixed children (one African American and one European American parent). Many of the adopting parents also had biological children of their own, and many had adopted other children of various ethnic backgrounds. The investigators tested the IQs of the children and the adopting parents and tested them again 10 years later (Scarr & Weinberg, 1976; Weinberg, Scarr, & Waldman, 1992).

**RESULTS** Figure 9.15 shows the mean scores for only those individuals who were tested both times. All the means were lower at the second test because of changes in the IQ test itself. (As mentioned earlier, psychologists restandardize the test every few years, generally making it more difficult.)

**INTERPRETATION** The key data are the mean scores for the adopted children. The adopted European American children scored higher than adopted children with one African American parent ("ethnically mixed"), who in turn scored higher than adopted children with two African American parents. However, the ethnically mixed adopted children scored near 100 (slightly higher on the

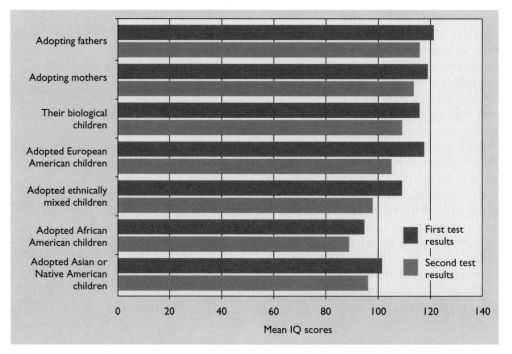

**FIGURE 9.15** During childhood African American children adopted by upper-middle-class European American families showed IQ scores well above the national average for African Americans, but 10 years later they showed only small benefits.

first test and slightly lower on the second). Adopted children with two African American parents scored a mean of 95 on the first test and 89 ten years later.

These results are not easy to interpret (e.g., Levin, 1994; Waldman, Weinberg, & Scarr, 1994). Raising African American children in upper-middle-class European American families may have raised their IQs a little, but not much. (The mean IQ for African American children in Minnesota at the time was about 88.)

If these data suggest a disappointingly small environmental influence, one possible reason is that many of the birth mothers of the adopted African American children may not have provided good prenatal nutrition and health care. Also, many of the adopted African American and ethnically mixed children lived in several foster homes of unknown quality before being adopted. In short, the results suggest that the home in which a child grows up may not have an enormous effect on IQ, but we do not know about possible effects of early environment, including prenatal environment. In short, this study, which was designed to demonstrate environmental influences, instead produced small and equivocal effects.

 **WHAT'S THE EVIDENCE?**
*Hereditary Contributors to Ethnic Differences*

In comparison let us now examine a study with the potential to show a strong hereditary contribution.

**HYPOTHESIS** Few U.S. African Americans have 100% African ancestry. If heredity is responsible for even part of the race difference in IQ performance, then African Americans with much European ancestry should obtain higher IQ scores than African Americans with less.

**METHOD** Determining the ethnic ancestry of an African American child is difficult. Most family trees do not go back far enough, and skin color is not a good indicator. (Even in Africa skin darkness varies greatly from one subpopulation to another.) Blood-typing, however, provides a somewhat better estimate.

The investigators (Scarr, Pakstis, Katz, & Barker, 1977) examined 362 African American children in Philadelphia, testing different blood factors such as the familiar ABO blood types, the Rh factor, the Duffy factor, and 11 others. Certain blood factors are more common in Europe than in Africa, and vice versa. For example, type B blood is present in only 9% of Europeans but in 21% of Africans. Few if any Europeans have Duffy type A– B– blood, whereas 94% of Africans do. By comparing each child's blood factors to the frequency of those blood factors in both Europe and Africa, the investigators estimated the degree of European ancestry for each child. Then the investigators correlated their estimates of European ancestry with the children's performances on Raven's Progressive Matrices and four other tests.

**RESULTS** The investigators tried several methods of weighting the importance of various blood factors to estimate European and African ancestry. Regardless of which method they used, however, they found virtually 0 cor-

■ Variations in skin darkness are an inaccurate indicator of degree of African ancestry. Blood-typing provides a somewhat better indicator, although it is also far from certain.

relation between estimates of European ancestry and measures of performance.

**INTERPRETATION**  If hereditary factors were a major contributor to ethnic differences in IQ scores, we would predict that the greater the amount of European ancestry, the higher the IQ scores. The absence of such a correlation indicates that heredity contributes either nothing to the ethnic differences or too little to measure by this method. Unfortunately, this is only one study, and no one has attempted to replicate it.

**IN CLOSING**

## Heredity and Environment

Where does all this information leave us with regard to ethnic differences in IQ scores? The best-designed study found no evidence for a role of genetics, but it is also true that no one has identified an environmental factor that convincingly explains the group differences. Nevertheless, as James Flynn (1999) has pointed out, people in general have improved their IQ test performance by about 30 points over the last 50 years, and we cannot explain that difference either. So we should not be too amazed that we have not yet explained the smaller differences among ethnic groups. Given the weakness of the evidence, the best recommendation is to withhold drawing any conclusion about why groups differ on IQ tests.

The studies just described concerning cross-racial adoptions and correlations with blood types are fairly old now, and no one has tried to replicate them. Frankly, this research area has not been popular. Some avoid it because they are afraid that their results might support racism or other undesirable ends (Reiss, 2000). Others avoid it simply because the research is difficult, and in

fact, I would not urge young psychologists to enter this field. However, a closely related topic deserves more attention: Given that environmental factors do contribute at least somewhat to differences in intelligence, which are the critical environmental factors? Simply growing up in an upper-middle-class home is apparently not a major factor. But what is? Prenatal health and nutrition, perhaps? Other factors in an infant's environment? If we could identify those factors, we might be able to accomplish something that would benefit everyone.

Finally, of course, this whole controversy centers around traditional IQ tests. As discussed in the first module, these tests overlook many kinds of intelligent behavior and measure only the outcomes of intelligence, not the processes behind them. Any advances that psychologists make toward a better understanding of intelligence itself is sure to have an impact on studies of how intelligence develops.

## Summary

- **Standardization.** To determine the meaning of a test's scores, the authors of a test determine the mean and the distribution of scores for a random or representative sample of the population. IQ tests are revised periodically. To keep the same mean, test authors make the tests more difficult from time to time. (page 340)

- **Distribution of IQ scores.** IQ tests have a mean of 100 and a standard deviation of about 15 or 16, depending on the test. Items are carefully selected so that performance on each item correlates positively with performance on the test as a whole. (page 340)

- **Reliability and validity.** Tests are evaluated in terms of reliability and validity. Reliability is a measure of the repeatability of a test's scores. Validity is a determination of how well a test measures what it claims to measure. (page 342)

- **Test bias.** Psychologists try to remove from a test any item that tends to be easy for one group of people to answer but difficult for another. They also try to evaluate the possible bias of a test as a whole. Bias is defined as a systematically incorrect estimation of how well a group will perform. By that definition IQ tests are biased against immigrants but apparently not against racial minorities; they predict the school performance of African Americans about as accurately as that of European Americans. (page 346)

- **Hereditary and environmental influences.** To determine the contribution of heredity to the variations in scores on IQ tests, investigators compare identical twins and fraternal twins, study identical twins reared apart, and compare adopted children with their biological and adoptive parents. For European American families (about whom we have the most information), both hereditary and environmental factors appear to contribute to observed differences in performance. (page 348)

- **The controversy concerning ethnic differences in IQ.** Ethnic groups differ on the average in IQ performance, although the group mean scores cannot tell us what to expect from each individual. Research designed to show environmental contributors to these ethnic differences have generally produced disappointingly small effects that are difficult to interpret. The best-designed study capable of demonstrating a hereditary contribution failed to show even marginal effects. At present the existing research evidence does not justify a confident conclusion about the origin of ethnic differences. (page 350)

## Answers to Concept Checks

3. Yes! To say that a test is "reliable" is simply to say that its scores are repeatable—that and only that. My test would give perfectly reliable (repeatable) measurements. True, they would be utterly useless, but usefulness is not the point. Reliability is not a measure of usefulness. (page 342)

4. No. An individual's score may be higher on the retest either because of practice at taking the test or because of additional months of education. But the rank order of scores does not change much. That is, if some people retake the test, all of them are likely to improve their scores, but those who had the highest scores the first time will probably still have the highest scores the second time. (page 342)

5. Yes, a test can have high reliability and low validity. A measure of intelligence determined by dividing head length by head width has high reliability (repeatability) but presumably no validity. A test with low reliability cannot have high validity, however. Low reliability means that the scores fluctuate randomly. If the test scores cannot even predict a later score on the same test, then they can hardly predict anything else. (page 344)

6. The predictive validity of the tests would increase. The predictive validity tends to be low when almost all students have practically the same score; it is higher when students' scores are highly variable. (page 344)

7. The predictive validity of SAT scores will be higher at the university that admits almost anyone. At the university with extremely competitive admissions standards, almost all students have nearly the same SAT scores, and the slight variation in scores cannot predict which students will get the best grades. (page 344)

8. No, this test is not biased against people with visual impairments. It correctly determines that they are likely to be poor drivers. (page 348)

9. We would need to determine whether the test accurately predicts the school performances of both short and tall people. If short people with, say, an IQ score of 100 perform better in school than tall people with an IQ score of 100, then the test is underpredicting the performances of short people, and we can thus conclude that this test is biased against them. (Merely that the test reports a difference between short people and tall people is not in itself evidence of test bias.) (page 348)

---

CHAPTER ENDING

# Key Terms and Activities

## Key Terms

**bias:** the tendency for test scores to exaggerate a difference between groups or to report a nonexistent difference (page 347)

**construct validity:** the correspondence of a test's measurements to a theoretical construct (page 343)

**content validity:** the similarity between the items in a test and the information that the test is meant to measure (page 342)

**crystallized intelligence:** acquired skills and knowledge and the application of that knowledge to the specific content of a person's experience (page 331)

**fluid intelligence:** the basic power of reasoning and using information, including the ability to perceive relationships, solve unfamiliar problems, and gain new types of knowledge (page 331)

**Flynn effect:** the tendency for people's performance on IQ tests to improve from one decade or generation to the next (page 341)

*g:* Spearman's "general" factor which all IQ tests and all parts of an IQ test are believed to have in common (page 329)

**intelligence quotient (IQ):** a measure of an individual's probable performance in school and in similar settings (page 334)

**multiple intelligences:** Gardner's theory that intelligence is composed of numerous unrelated forms of intelligent behavior (page 332)

**norms:** description of the frequencies of occurrence of particular scores (page 340)

**predictive validity:** the ability of a test's scores to predict some real-world performance (page 343)

**Progressive Matrices:** an IQ test that attempts to measure abstract reasoning without the use of language or recall of facts (page 336)

**psychometric approach:** the measurement of individual differences in abilities and behaviors (page 329)

**reliability:** the repeatability of a test's scores (page 342)

*s:* a "specific" factor that is more important for performance on some portions of an intelligence test than it is for others  (page 330)

**Scholastic Assessment Test (SAT):** a test designed to measure a student's likelihood of performing well in college  (page 337)

**standardization:** the process of establishing rules for administering a test and for interpreting the scores  (page 340)

**Stanford-Binet IQ test:** a test of intelligence, the first important IQ test in the English language  (page 334)

**stereotype threat:** people's perceived risk that they might do something that supports an unfavorable stereotype about their group  (page 346)

**test-retest reliability:** the correlation between scores on a first test and on a retest  (page 342)

**triarchic theory:** Sternberg's theory that intelligence has three aspects: the cognitive processes that occur within the individual, the situations that require intelligence, and how intelligence relates to the external world  (page 332)

**utility:** the usefulness of a test for a practical purpose  (page 344)

**validity:** the determination of how well a test measures what it claims to measure  (page 342)

**Wechsler Adult Intelligence Scale–Third Edition (WAIS–III):** an IQ test originally devised by David Wechsler, commonly used with adults  (page 335)

**Wechsler Intelligence Scale for Children–Third Edition (WISC–III):** an IQ test originally devised by David Wechsler, commonly used with children  (page 335)

## Suggestions for Further Reading

Ceci, S. J. (1990). *On intelligence . . . more or less.* Upper Saddle River, NJ: Prentice Hall. Perceptive critique of traditional assumptions about intelligence.

Neisser, U., et al. (1996). Intelligence: Knowns and unknowns. *American Psychologist, 51,* 77–101. Although much dispute surrounds the meaning of IQ scores and the reasons individuals differ, psychologists have also found areas of agreement. This article describes the consensus of most psychologists today, the evidence behind their conclusions, and the questions that still remain unanswered.

# Web/Technology Resources

## Sample IQ Tests

**2h.com/**

Take a variety of IQ and personality tests. Some are serious and some are obviously fake. None of these are the best established tests, and their reliability and validity are unknown; still, you might find them interesting.*

## The Flynn Effect

**sciam.com/1999/0199issue/0199profile.html**

**plaza.powersurfr.com/delajara/Locations.html**

The first of these describes James Flynn and his discovery of the effect that bears his name. The second presents data on the strength of the Flynn effect in many countries.

## The Bell Curve

**apa.org/journals/bell.html**

Two noted psychologists present reviews with very different conclusions concerning the controversial book, *The Bell Curve.*

## Multiple Intelligences

**http://edweb.gsn.org/edref.mi.hist.html**

Explore Howard Gardner's view of multiple intelligences and its contrast with other views of intelligence.

---

*Note: Any psychological test that is readily available to the public, while entertaining and possibly informative, should not be used to make important decisions. The most powerful, valid, and reliable psychological assessment devices are usually kept under the tight control of their creators or copyright holders.

# Human Development

**10**

CHAPTER

**S**uppose you buy a robot. When you get home, you discover that it does nothing useful. It cannot even maintain its balance. It makes irritating, high-pitched noises, moves its limbs haphazardly, and leaks. The store you bought it from refuses to take it back. And for some reason it is illegal to turn it off. So you are stuck with this useless machine.

A few years later, your robot can walk and talk, read and write, draw pictures, and do arithmetic. It follows your directions (usually) and sometimes even finds useful things to do without being told. It often beats you at checkers and almost always at memory games.

How did all this happen? After all, you knew nothing about how to program a robot. Did your robot have some sort of built-in programming that simply took a long time to phase in? Or was it programmed to learn all these skills?

Children are a great deal like that robot. Nearly every parent wonders, "How did my children get to be the way they are?" The goal of developmental psychology is to understand everything that influences human behavior "from womb to tomb."

■ As we grow older, we change in many ways—we gain in some ways and lose in others. Developmental psychologists seek to understand the changes in our behavior and the reasons behind these changes.

# The Study of Early Development

*What can infants think and do? How can we determine an infant's capacities?*

The artwork of young children is amazingly inventive and sometimes revealing. One toddler, 1½ years old, showed off a drawing that consisted only of dots on a sheet of paper. Puzzled adults did not understand the drawing. It is a rabbit, the child explained, while making more dots: "Look: hop, hop, hop . . . ." (Winner, 1986).

When my daughter, Robin, was 6 years old, she drew a picture of a boy and a girl drawing pictures (Figure 10.1). The overall drawing has features that may not be clear; for

Sometimes, as in this case, a child's drawing can tell us a great deal about the child's world-view. As children grow older, their art changes. Robin Kalat, now a college student, draws pictures with skill that I envy. Still, I sometimes miss the highly expressive drawings of her early childhood. The point is this: As we grow older, we gain many new abilities and skills. But we lose something, too.

Studying the abilities of infants and young children is extremely challenging. The very young are often capable of far more than we realize simply because they misunderstand our questions or we misunderstand their answers or because we assume that, if they cannot do very much, they probably don't think very much either. We also sometimes underestimate the abilities of the very old. Developmental psychologists have made much progress by devising increasingly careful and sensitive ways to measure behavioral abilities. We begin with physical development and then return to young children's thought processes.

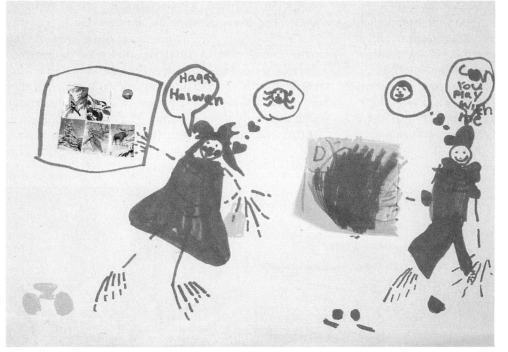

**FIGURE 10.1** A drawing of two children drawing pictures, courtesy of 6-year-old Robin Kalat.

example, both children are wearing Halloween costumes. For the little girl's drawing, Robin pasted on some wildlife photos. This array, she maintained, was what the little girl had drawn. Now look at the little boy's drawing, which is just a scribble. When I asked why the little girl's drawing was so much better than the little boy's, Robin replied, "Don't make fun of him, Daddy. He's doing the best he can."

## The Fetus and the Newborn

Behavioral development begins long before birth. During **prenatal development**—*development before birth*—everyone starts life as a *fertilized egg cell,* or **zygote.** That fertilized egg develops through several stages, known as *blastula, gastrula, embryo* (from about 2 to 8 weeks after conception in humans), and **fetus** (from about 8 weeks after conception until birth in humans). By about the 6th or 7th week of pregnancy, the hindbrain and midbrain are well enough developed to produce the first few movements. Those structures continue developing, and by the 36th week, they can produce head turns and eye movements in response to sounds, as well as waking, sleeping, and REM sleep (Joseph, 2000). None of this somewhat complex behavior requires any

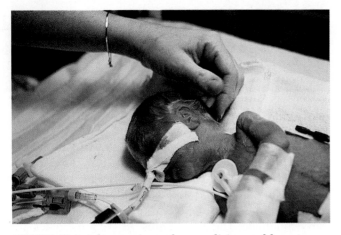

**FIGURE 10.2** Advances in modern medicine enable us to keep premature and very small babies alive. Low-birth-weight babies are susceptible to a variety of physical and behavioral difficulties later in life; however, we cannot be sure that low birthweight causes these problems. Many of these babies are born to mothers who are very young or impoverished, who take illegal drugs, or who fail to obtain good nutrition and care.

activity in the cerebral cortex, which is a much slower part of the brain to mature.

The growing body receives nutrition from the mother. If she eats little, the baby receives little nourishment. If she takes drugs, the baby gets them too. Undernourished mothers generally give birth to small babies (Figure 10.2), and investigators have long known that newborns weighing less than about 1750–2000 grams (4 pounds) are at high risk of dying in infancy (Kopp, 1990). Those that survive have an increased risk of conduct problems and poor academic performance (Taylor, Klein, Minich, & Hack, 2000). Those facts are beyond dispute, but their meaning is less certain.

The apparently obvious interpretation is that low birthweight leads to impaired brain development and thus to later academic and behavior problems. However, many low-birthweight babies are born with low birthweights for a reason: Their mothers were teenaged, unmarried, victims of family violence, poor, uneducated, unhealthy, poorly nourished, possibly smoking or drinking during pregnancy, not visiting a doctor for care and advice during pregnancy, and unable to provide a good home after delivering the baby (Garcia Coll, 1990; McCormick, 1985). In

short, many low-birthweight babies have other, probably more serious problems as well, which combine to increase the risk to the child (Brooks-Gunn & Furstenberg, 1989; Zeanah, Boris, & Larrieu, 1997).

One way to study the effect of low birthweight separately from other problems is to examine pairs of twins where one twin was born much heavier than the other. The twins differ in birthweight but have the same parents and nearly the same environment. In most cases the low-birthweight infant develops about as well as the heavier twin (Wilson, 1987). In short, low birthweight *by itself* is not necessarily a serious problem; it correlates with developmental difficulties partly because many low-birthweight babies have other disadvantages.

A more severe risk arises if the fetus is exposed to alcohol or other substances. *If the mother drinks alcohol during pregnancy,* the infant may develop signs of **fetal alcohol syndrome,** *a condition marked by stunted growth of the head and body; malformations of the face, heart, and ears; and nervous system damage, including seizures, hyperactivity, learning disabilities, and mental retardation* (Streissguth, Sampson, & Barr, 1989). In milder cases the child's appearance is normal, but he or she has impaired academic skills and moderate deficits in language, memory, and coordination (Mattson, Riley, Grambling, Delis, & Jones, 1998). The more alcohol the mother drinks and the longer she drinks during pregnancy, the greater the risk to the fetus (see Figure 10.3). The reason for the nervous-system damage is now understood: Developing neurons require persistent excitation to survive. Without it, they activate a self-destruct program. Alcohol facilitates the main inhibitory neurotransmitter of the brain (known as GABA) and interferes with the main excitatory neurotransmitter (glutamate). It therefore decreases the total

a
b

**FIGURE 10.3** (a) The more alcohol a woman drinks during pregnancy, the more likely her baby is to have anomalies of the head, face, and organs. (Based on data of Ernhart et al., 1987) (b) A child with fetal alcohol syndrome: Note especially the wide separation between the eyes, a common feature of this syndrome.

excitation of neurons and leads them to self-destruct (Ikonomidou et al., 2000). Now that we understand this mechanism, we can predict that similar damage would result from the use of other drugs with related brain effects. In other words pregnant women should minimize the use of tranquilizers, anesthetics, and antidepressant drugs because they all increase activity at inhibitory synapses.

Women who smoke during pregnancy have an increased probability that their babies will have health problems early in life. They also run an increased risk that their children, especially sons, eventually will develop *conduct disorder,* a condition marked by discipline problems both at school and at home and potentially even criminal behavior in adulthood. Conduct disorder has been found to correlate more strongly with the mother's smoking during pregnancy than with the father's antisocial behavior, the family's economic status, lack of supervision of the child, or excessive punishment (Wakschlag et al., 1997). To be safe, pregnant women should avoid alcohol and tobacco and should get a physician's advice before taking any medications.

Still, it is remarkable that an occasional "high-risk" child—small at birth, perhaps exposed to alcohol or other drugs before birth, perhaps from an impoverished or turbulent family—overcomes all odds and becomes a healthy, productive, outstanding person. Resilience (the ability to overcome obstacles) is poorly understood and difficult to study (Luthar, Cicchetti, & Becker, 2000). However, the more positive influences one has in life, the easier it is to overcome negative ones. That is, most people who overcome disadvantages have some special source of strength such as a close relationship with one or more supporting people, an effective school, a strong faith, some special skill, or just a naturally easygoing disposition (Masten & Coatsworth, 1998).

## CONCEPT CHECK

1. Why should a pregnant woman avoid taking large amounts of tranquilizers? (Check your answer on page 366.)

# Behavioral Capacities of the Newborn

A human newborn is a little like a computer that is not attached to a monitor: No matter how much information it processes, it cannot tell us about it. The challenge of studying the newborn is to figure out how to attach some sort of "monitor" to find out what is going on inside.

Newborns have little control of their muscles. At first they cannot keep their head from flopping over, and their arms and legs flail about aimlessly. They gradually gain more muscle control, partly through growth and matura-

tion of the muscles and nerves and partly from practice. For example, babies are much more persistent at waving their arms if they can see their arms than if they have to wave without watching (van der Meer, van der Weel, & Lee, 1995). Also, babies who are too young to support their own weight flail their arms and legs in varied and haphazard ways; as soon as they can support their weight, they quickly abandon most of their varied movement patterns and settle on the standard patterns and rhythms of human crawling (Freedland & Bertenthal, 1994).

About the only useful movements that newborns can make are eye and mouth movements, especially sucking. As the months pass, and as their control spreads from the head muscles downward, they are able to make progressively finer movements, eventually culminating in the ability to move a single finger at a time.

If we want to test infants' sensory and learning abilities, we must test the responses that the infants can control. For example, if we want to test what an infant can see, we should examine eye movements or head movements. If we try to train an infant to reach out and grab something, we will almost certainly underestimate the infant's capacities.

## Newborns' Vision

William James, a pioneer in American psychology, once said that as far as an infant can tell, the world is a "buzzing confusion," full of meaningless sights and sounds. Since James's time, psychologists have substantially increased their estimates of what an infant can see.

One research method is to record the infant's eye movements. In general, infants direct their eyes toward the same kinds of objects that attract adults' attention. For example, even 2-day-old infants spend more time looking at drawings of human faces than at other patterns with similar areas of light and dark (Fantz, 1963) (see Figure 10.4).

By the age of 5 months or so, infants have had extensive visual experience but almost no experience at crawling or reaching for objects. As they start to gain control of their arm and leg movements, they suddenly have to reach out to pick up toys, crawl around objects, avoid crawling off ledges, and in other ways coordinate what they see with what they do.

Apparently, infants must have some experience of controlling their own movements before they show a fear of heights. Infants who have learned to avoid falling from a sitting position do not show the same skill when they start to crawl, and they usually take a tumble or two before they develop a fear of heights (Adolph, 2000). Infants who crawl early develop a fear of heights early; infants who are late to crawl are also late to develop a fear of heights (Campos, Bertenthal, & Kermoian, 1992).

Although visual-motor coordination develops quickly, infants need practice to maintain and improve that coordination. Kittens are ideal for studies of visual-motor

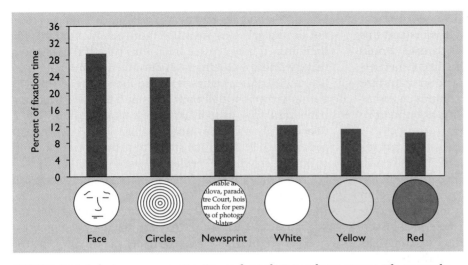

FIGURE 10.4 Infants pay more attention to faces than to other patterns. These results suggest that infants are born with certain visual preferences. (Based on Fantz, 1963)

## Newborns' Hearing

At first it might seem difficult to measure newborns' responses to sounds; after all, we cannot observe anything similar to eye movements. However, we can record the effects of sounds on an infant's sucking. Infants suck more vigorously when they are aroused, and certain sounds arouse them more than others do.

In one study the experimenters played a brief sound and noted how it affected the infant's sucking rate (Figure 10.6). On the first few occasions, the sound increased the sucking rate. After the sound had been played repeatedly, it produced less and less effect. We say that the infant became *habituated* to the sound.

**Habituation** is *decreased response to a repeated stimulus.* When the experimenters substituted a new sound, it produced a sharp increase in the sucking rate. Evidently, the infant was aroused because of the new unfamiliar sound. *When a change in a stimulus produces an increase in a previously habituated response,* we say that the stimulus has produced **dishabituation.**

Psychologists use this technique to determine whether infants hear a difference between two sounds. For example, an infant who has become habituated to the sound *ba* will increase the sucking rate in response to the sound *pa* (Eimas, Siqueland, Jusczyk, & Vigorito, 1971). Apparently, even month-old infants can tell the difference between *ba* and *pa,* an important distinction for

development because they can move about quite well by the time they first open their eyes. In one experiment kittens were permitted to walk around in a dark room for 21 hours a day (Held & Hein, 1963). For the other 3 hours, half of the kittens (the "active" group) were permitted to walk around in a well-lit cylindrical room, as Figure 10.5 shows. The other kittens (the "passive" group) were confined to boxes that were propelled around the room by the active kittens.

The active kittens gradually developed good paw-eye coordination, but the passive kittens lagged far behind. In fact, the passive kittens' coordination actually grew worse instead of better as the experiment continued. Evidently, kittens need to see and move at the same time in order to maintain and improve their visually guided behavior. The same is almost certainly true for humans as well.

FIGURE 10.5 As the kitten carousel experiment demonstrates, experience influences development. These two kittens see the same thing, but only one can correlate what it sees with its own movements. Only the active kitten develops normal paw-eye coordination. (Modified from Held & Hein, 1963)

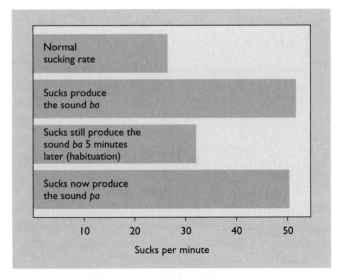

FIGURE 10.6 After 5 minutes of hearing a *ba* sound, the infant's sucking habituates. When a new sound, *pa,* follows, the sucking rate increases, an indication that infants do hear a difference between the two sounds. (Based on results of Eimas, Siqueland, Juscyk, & Vigorito, 1971)

later language comprehension. Similar studies have shown that infants who have habituated to hearing one language, such as Dutch, dishabituate when they hear a different language, such as Japanese, and this evidence was taken to indicate a predisposition of human children to pay special attention to language sounds. However, a later study found similar results with monkeys, so distinguishing Dutch from Japanese sounds apparently does not require a special language readiness of the brain (Ramus, Hauser, Miller, Morris, & Mehler, 2000).

## Infants' Learning and Memory

Infants certainly cannot describe their memories to us. But if they respond differently to a stimulus because of previous experience with it, we can infer some kind of memory.

Several studies have begun with the observation that infants learn to suck harder on a nipple if their sucking turns on a sound. Investigators then tried to determine whether infants will work harder to turn on certain sounds than they will for others. In one study 26 babies less than 3 days old could turn on a tape recording of their mother's voice by sucking on a nipple at certain times and at certain rates. By sucking at different times or at different rates, they could turn on a tape recording of another woman's voice. When their manner of sucking produced their own mother's voice, they sucked more frequently (DeCasper & Fifer, 1980). They did not suck much to produce a different voice. Apparently, even very young infants recognized their own mother's voice and preferred it to an unfamiliar voice. Because they showed this preference so early—in some cases on the day of their birth—developmental psychologists believe that the infants are displaying a memory of what they heard *before* birth.

## CONCEPT CHECK

2. Suppose that a newborn sucks to turn on a tape recording of its father's voice. Eventually, the baby habituates and the sucking frequency decreases. Now the experimenters substitute the recording of a different man's voice for the father's. What would you conclude if the sucking frequency increased? What if it remained the same? What if it decreased? (Check your answer on page 366.)

Using somewhat older infants, Carolyn Rovee-Collier (1997, 1999) demonstrated an ability to learn a response and remember it for days afterward. In one series of studies, she attached a ribbon to one ankle so that an infant could activate a mobile by kicking with one leg (Figure 10.7); 2-month-old infants quickly learned this response and generally kept the mobile going nonstop for a full 45-minute session. (I know I said infants cannot control their leg muscles, but they don't need much con-

**FIGURE 10.7** By the age of 8 weeks, infants can rapidly learn to kick to activate a mobile attached to their ankles with a ribbon. After a little practice, they can keep the mobile going for a full 45-minute session. They also remember how to activate the mobile from one session to the next. (From Rovee-Collier, 1984)

trol to keep the mobile going.) Once they have learned, they quickly remember what to do when the ribbon is reattached several days later—to the infants' evident delight.

In another series of studies, Rovee-Collier found that 9-month-olds can learn to press a lever to make a toy train go around a track. In both the mobile studies and the train studies, the youngest infants remembered well if they were tested a short time later, but older ones could remember over a longer delay (Hartshorn et al., 1998).

**WHAT'S THE EVIDENCE?**
*The Infant's Thought Processes About Object Permanence*

Measuring an infant's vision, hearing, and memory can be difficult enough. Inferring the infant's thoughts and knowledge is trickier yet, although researchers have found some clever ways to do just that. As you can imagine, however, these inferences must be made cautiously and tentatively.

Jean Piaget (pee-ah-ZHAY), whose theories we shall consider in more detail in the next module, inferred that infants in the first few months of life lack the concept of **object permanence,** *the idea that objects continue to exist even when we do not see or hear them.* How could he know? He drew the inference from observations of the following type: Place a toy in front of a 6-month-old infant, who reaches out and grabs it. Later place a toy in the same

**FIGURE 10.8** (a) A 6- to 9-month-old child will reach for a visible toy, but not one that is hidden behind a barrier (b) even if the child sees someone hide the toy. According to Piaget, this observation indicates that the child hasn't yet grasped the concept of object permanence.

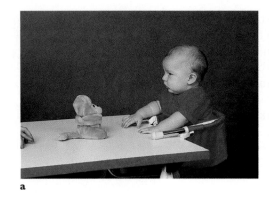

a

b

place, but before the infant has a chance to grab it, cover it with a clear glass. No problem; the infant removes the glass and takes the toy. Now you repeat that procedure, but this time you cover the toy with an opaque (nonclear) glass. The infant, who watched you place the glass over the toy, makes no effort to remove the glass and obtain the toy. Or you put the toy down and then place a thin barrier between the infant and the toy. The infant reaches for a toy that is partly visible but not for one that is completely hidden (Piaget, 1937/1954) (see Figure 10.8).

Why not? According to Piaget, the infant *does not know* that the hidden toy is there, and not until about the age of 9 months does he or she understand object permanence. Even at that age, a child who has repeatedly found a toy in one location will reach there again even after watching you hide it in a neighboring location. However, one can imagine other possible explanations for each of Piaget's results. For example, the child who has repeatedly found a toy in one location has developed a reaching habit that interferes with finding the toy in a new location. The behavior is not much different from an adult who sets out to drive to one location

and then absentmindedly turns in the wrong direction, driving home instead (L. B. Smith, Thelen, Titzer, & McLin, 1999).

A study by Renee Baillargeon (1986) suggests that infants do show signs of understanding object permanence when they are tested differently.

**HYPOTHESIS** An infant who sees an event that would be impossible (if objects are permanent) will be surprised and therefore will stare longer than will an infant that sees a similar but possible event.

**METHOD** Infants aged 6 or 8 months watched a series of events staged by the researcher. First, the child watched the experimenter raise a screen to show nothing behind it and then watched a toy car go down a slope and emerge on the other side, as shown in the drawing below. The researchers measured how long the child stared after the car went down the slope. They repeated the procedure until the child decreased his or her staring time for three trials in a row (showing habituation).

Then the experimenters presented two kinds of events, three times each:

**Possible event**

**Impossible event**

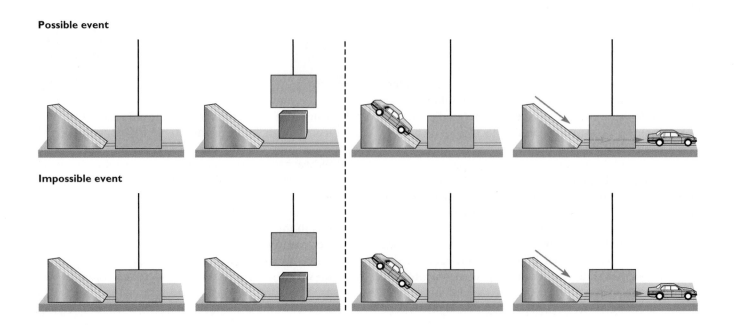

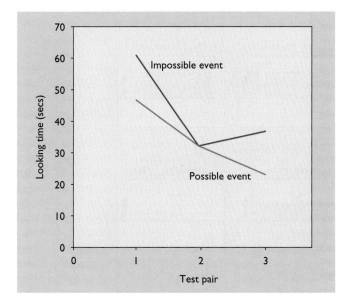

**FIGURE 10.9** Mean looking times of 6- and 8-month-old infants after they had watched either possible or impossible events. (From Baillargeon, 1986)

In a possible event, the raised screen showed a box that was behind the screen but not on the track. In an impossible event, the raised screen showed a box that was on the track, right where the car would pass. After the screen lowered, the car went down the slope and (for both possible and impossible events) emerged on the other side. (For impossible events the experimenters had pulled the box off the track after lowering the screen.) The experimenters measured each child's staring times after both kinds of events. They repeated both events two more times, randomizing the order of events.

**RESULTS** Figure 10.9 shows the mean looking times. Infants stared longer after seeing an impossible event than after seeing a possible event. They also stared longer during the first pair of events than after the second pair and longer after the second than the third (Baillargeon, 1986).

**INTERPRETATION** Why did the infants stare longer at the "impossible" event? The inference—and admittedly it is only an inference, not a certainty—is that the infants found the impossible event surprising. To be surprised, the infants had to expect that the box would continue to exist where it was hidden and that a car could not go through it. If this inference is correct, even 6-month-old infants have some understanding of the permanence of objects. A later study with a slightly different method again measured how long infants stared at possible and impossible events and demonstrated object permanence in infants as young as $3\frac{1}{2}$ months (Baillargeon, 1987).

Still, remember that 9-month-olds failed Piaget's object permanence task of reaching out to pick up a hidden object. Do infants have the concept of object permanence or do they lack it? Perhaps there is something wrong with the question. It is possible to have a concept but use it in some situations and not in others (Munakata, McClelland, Johnson, & Siegler, 1997). Even college students can pass a physics test and then fail to apply the laws of motion in a new situation, or they can state the rules of grammar and yet make grammatical errors.

The important point about research is this: When we are dealing with infants or anyone else whose thought processes are likely to be different from our own, we should be cautious about inferring what he or she can or cannot do. The results may vary depending on the exact procedures and tests.

## Further Capacities of the Infant

Using the technique of measuring infants' staring time, researchers have also made a surprising inference about infants' concept of number: Karen Wynn and W.-C. Chiang (1998) showed an infant an object, placed a curtain in front of it, and then placed another object behind the screen. Finally, the experimenter removed the screen, revealing either the correct, expected number of objects $(1 + 1 = 2)$ or an "impossible" total $(1 + 1 = 1)$, the other one having fallen through a trapdoor. Figure 10.10 shows these procedures. On the average, 8-month-old infants stared longer at an impossible total than at an expected total. Evidently, even young infants have a primitive concept that adding something should make the total more and subtracting should make it less. However, not all infants show this effect, especially if they are not alert or not paying attention (Wakely, Rivera, & Langer, 2000). Even the simplest aspects of numerical understanding develop gradually.

**IN CLOSING**

## Infants—Capable of So Little and So Much

Notice that the experiments just described enable psychologists to explore the thought and perception of infants too young to talk. As research methods have advanced, the trend has been a steady increase in our estimation of infants' capacities. Because of infants' poor control of their muscles, they are indeed like a computer with an unattached monitor: They have a lot more going on inside than they can easily show us.

## Summary

- **Prenatal development.** Behavioral development begins before birth. During prenatal development an individual is especially vulnerable to the damaging effects of alcohol and other drugs. Babies who are very

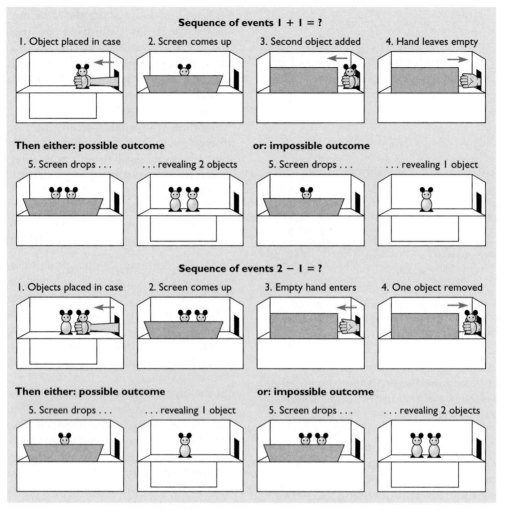

**FIGURE 10.10** Five-month-old infants stare longer at an impossible display than at the possible display. Evidently, even at this age children understand that adding or subtracting an object should change the number present.

small at birth have a high risk of later problems, mainly because they generally do not receive good care or stimulation later in life. (page 359)

- **Inferring infant capacities.** It is easy to underestimate the capacities of newborn human infants because they have so little control over their muscles. With careful testing procedures, we can demonstrate that newborns can see, hear, and remember more than we might have supposed. (page 361)

- **Inferring infant thought processes.** Infants behave differently from older children in many ways. For example, infants fail to reach for a toy after watching someone hide it within their reach, suggesting that they do not understand the concept of object permanence. However, they stare longer at an impossible event than a possible event, where the first event should seem impossible only if the infant understands that a hidden object continues to exist. In short, an infant can have a concept but show it in one testing method and not in another. (page 363)

## Answers to Concept Checks

1. Tranquilizers, like alcohol, increase activity at inhibitory synapses. Therefore, a mother who uses tranquilizers extensively during pregnancy risks subjecting her fetus to something similar to fetal alcohol syndrome. (page 361)

2. If the frequency increased, we would conclude that the infant recognizes the difference between the father's voice and the other voice. If the frequency remained the same, we would conclude that the infant did not notice a difference. If it decreased, we would assume that the infant preferred the sound of the father's voice for some reason. (page 363)

# The Development of Thinking and Reasoning

*How do children's thought processes differ from adults'?*

**CRITICAL THINKING**

**A STEP FURTHER**
*Children's Thinking*

Preschool children ask some profound questions: "Why is the sky blue? What makes ice cubes cold? If it's dangerous to look at the sun, why is it safe to look at a picture of the sun? Where does the sun go at night?" They are relentlessly curious about how things work and why. (Moreover, they never interrupt your answers to ask, "Is this going to be on the test?")

These same budding little scientists also believe in Santa Claus and the tooth fairy. Adults find it difficult to recapture what it is like to be a child. It is clear that children think differently from adults in a variety of ways, although it is not easy to specify those ways. Nevertheless, we try.

If children answer questions differently from adults, how could we know whether the difference was qualitative or quantitative? Consider: A modern computer differs from an old one from 1980 in purely quantitative ways—speed of processing and amount of memory. The basic principles of computing are the same. Yet the new computer can run programs that the old one cannot—an apparently qualitative difference in results. Could the differences between child and adult thinking be strictly a matter of speed of processing and amount of memory?

## Jean Piaget's Views of Development

Attending a rousing political rally can have a profound effect on a young adult, less effect on a preteen, and none at all on an infant. However, playing with a pile of blocks will be a more stimulating experience for a young child than for anyone older. The effect of any experience on anyone's thinking and knowledge depends on that person's maturity and previous experiences. The theorist who made this point most influentially was Jean Piaget (1896–1980) (see Figure 10.11).

Early in Piaget's career, he administered IQ tests to French-speaking children in Switzerland. He grew bored with the tests, but he was fascinated by children's consistently incorrect answers. For example, when asked, "If you mix some water at a temperature of 50 degrees with an equal amount of water at 70 degrees, what temperature will the mixture be?" most 9-year-olds answer, "120 degrees" (Jensen, 1980).

Unless someone was going around mischievously misinforming all the Swiss children, they must be reaching incorrect conclusions on their own. In other words, according to Piaget, children's thought processes are different from those of adults qualitatively as well as quantitatively. That is, the thought processes differ in both kind and amount. Piaget supported this conclusion with extensive studies of children, especially his own.

**FIGURE 10.11** Jean Piaget, the man on the left, demonstrated that children with different levels of maturity react differently to the same experience.

**FIGURE 10.12** (a) An infant assimilates new objects to the grasp schema, applying an established behavior to them. (b) However, the infant also accommodates the grasp schema, adjusting it to fit objects of different shapes and sizes.

a

b

## An Overview of Piaget's Theory

According to Piaget, a child's intellectual development is not merely an accumulation of experience or a maturational unfolding. Rather, the child constructs new mental processes as he or she interacts with the environment.

In Piaget's terminology behavior is based on schemata (the plural of *schema*). A **schema** is *an organized way of interacting with objects in the world.* For instance, infants have a grasping schema and a sucking schema. Older infants gradually add new schemata to their repertoire and adapt their old ones. The adaptation takes place through the processes of assimilation and accommodation.

With **assimilation,** a person *applies an old schema to new objects or problems*—for example, an infant may suck an unfamiliar object or use the grasp response when trying to manipulate it. With **accommodation,** a person *modifies an old schema to fit a new object or problem*—for example, an infant may suck a breast, a bottle, and a pacifier in different ways or modify the grasp response to accommodate the size or shape of a new toy (Figure 10.12). Older children modify thought processes as well as actions.

Infants shift back and forth from assimilation to accommodation. For example, an infant who tries to suck on a rubber ball (assimilating it to her sucking schema) may find that she cannot fit it into her mouth. First, she may try to accommodate her sucking schema to fit the ball; if that fails, she may try to shake the ball. She is assimilating the new object to her grasping schema, but she is also accommodating that schema—changing it—to fit the ball. **Equilibration** *is the establishment of harmony or balance between assimilation and accommodation,* and according to Piaget, equilibration is the key to intellectual growth. A disturbance or discrepancy occurs between what the child wants to do and can do, or between what the child wants to understand and can understand. That disturbance leads to assimilation and accommodation, and then to equilibration at a higher level of functioning.

Adults do much the same thing. When you are given a new mathematical problem to solve, you try several of the methods you have already learned until you hit upon one that works. In other words you assimilate the new problem to your old schema. However, if the new problem is different from any problem you have ever solved before, you modify (accommodate) your schema until you work out a solution. Through processes like these, said Piaget, intellectual growth occurs.

Piaget contended that children progress through four major stages of intellectual development:

1. *The sensorimotor stage* (from birth to about $1\frac{1}{2}$ years)
2. *The preoperational stage* (from about $1\frac{1}{2}$ to 7 years)
3. *The concrete operations stage* (from about 7 to 11 years)
4. *The formal operations stage* (from about 11 years onward)

The ages given here are approximate and culture dependent. People in some cultures, especially those with less education, progress through the stages more slowly (Rogoff & Chavajay, 1995). Piaget was rightly more interested in the sequence of stages than the exact age at which someone reaches a particular stage (Lourenço & Machado, 1996). Let us consider children's capacities at each stage.

## Sensorimotor Stage

Piaget called the first stage of intellectual development the **sensorimotor stage** because *at this early age (birth to $1\frac{1}{2}$ years) behavior consists mostly of simple motor responses to sensory stimuli*—for example, the grasp reflex and the sucking reflex. The fact that infants do not look for objects that they cannot see indicated to Piaget that infants respond only to what they see and hear rather than to what they might remember or imagine.

Infants do nevertheless notice relationships among their experiences. For example, even young infants can figure out which person in the room is talking, based on lip movements, age, and gender, and then look at the talking person (Lickliter & Bahrick, 2000). So they are actively discovering patterns in their experiences.

As children progress through the sensorimotor stage of development, they appear to gain some concept of self. The data are as follows: A mother puts a spot of unscented rouge on an infant's nose and then places the infant in front of a mirror. Infants younger than $1\frac{1}{2}$ years old either ignore the red spot they see on the baby in the mirror or else reach out to touch the red spot. At some point after age 1½ years, infants in the same situation will touch themselves on the nose, indicating that they recognize themselves in the mirror (Figure 10.13). Infants show this sign of self-recognition at varying ages; the age when they start to show self-recognition is also when they sometimes begin to act embarrassed (Lewis, Sullivan, Stanger, & Weiss, 1991). That is, they show a sense of self either in both situations or in neither.

## Preoperational Stage

By about age 1½, most children are learning to speak; within a few years, they will have nearly mastered their language. Nevertheless, they do not understand everything in the same way that adults do. For example, they have difficulty understanding that a mother can be someone else's daughter. A boy with one brother will assert that his brother has no brother. Piaget refers to this period as the **preoperational stage** because *the child lacks* **operations,** *which are reversible mental processes.* For example, for a boy to understand that his brother has a brother, he must be able to reverse the concept of "having a brother."

According to Piaget, preoperational children lack the concept of **conservation.** They fail *to understand that objects conserve such properties as number, length, volume, area, and mass after changes in the shape or arrangement of the objects.* They cannot perform the mental operations necessary to understand such transformations. (Table 10.1 shows some typical conservation tasks.)

For example, if we set up two glasses of the same size containing the same amount of water and then pour the contents of one glass into a taller, thinner glass, preoperational children will say that the second glass contains more water (Figure 10.14).

I once doubted whether children really believed what they were saying in such a situation. I thought perhaps the phrasing of the questions somehow tricks them into saying something they do not believe. If you have these same doubts, borrow someone's 6-year-old

**FIGURE 10.13** If someone places a bit of unscented rouge on a child's nose, a 2-year-old shows self-recognition by touching his or her own nose. A younger child ignores the red spot or points at the mirror.

**TABLE 10.1 Typical Tasks Used to Measure Conservation**

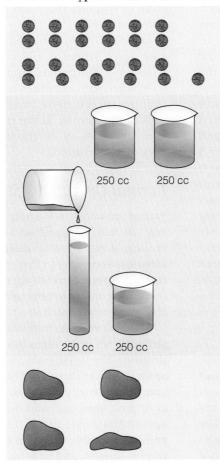

**Conservation of number**

Preoperational children say that these two rows contain the same number of pennies.

Preoperational children say that the second row has more pennies.

**Conservation of volume**

Preoperational children say that the two same-size containers have the same amount of water.

Preoperational children say that the taller, thinner container has more water.

**Conservation of mass**

Preoperational children say that the two same-size balls of clay have the same amount of clay.

Preoperational children say that a squashed ball of clay contains a different amount of clay than the same-size round ball of clay.

**FIGURE 10.14** Preoperational children, usually younger than age 7, don't understand that a property of a substance—such as the volume of water—remains constant despite changes in its appearance. During the transition from preoperational thinking to concrete operations at around age 7, conservation tasks seem difficult and confusing to the child.

child and try it yourself, with your own wording. Here's my own experience: One year when I was discussing Piaget in my introductory psychology class, I invited my son Sam, then 5½ years old, to take part in a class demonstration. I started with two glasses of water, which he agreed contained equal amounts of water. Then I poured the water from one glass into a wider glass, lowering the water level. When I asked Sam which glass contained more water, he confidently pointed to the tall, thin one.

After class he complained, "Daddy, why did you ask me such an easy question? Everyone could see that there was more water in that glass! You should have asked me something harder to show how smart I am!"

The following year I brought Sam to class again for the same demonstration. He was now 6½ years old, about the age when children make the transition from preoperational thinking to the next stage. I again poured the water from one of the tall glasses into a wider one and asked him which glass contained more water. He looked and paused. His face got red. Finally, he whispered, "Daddy, I don't know!" After class he complained, "Why did you ask me such a hard question? I'm never coming back to any of your classes again!" The question that was embarrassingly easy 1 year ago had in the interim become embarrassingly difficult.

The next year, when he was 7½, I tried again (at home). This time he answered confidently, "Both glasses have the same amount of water, of course. Why? Is this some sort of trick question?"

## Concrete Operations Stage

At about the age of 7, children enter the stage of concrete operations and begin to understand the conservation of physical properties. This transition is not sudden, however. The ability to understand the conservation of various properties emerges sequentially at different ages. For instance, a 6-year-old child may understand that squashing a ball of clay will not change its weight but may not

realize until years later that squashing the ball will not change the volume of water it displaces when it is dropped into a glass.

According to Piaget, during the **stage of concrete operations,** *children can perform mental operations on concrete objects but still have trouble with abstract or hypothetical ideas.* For example, ask this question: "How could you move a 4-mile-high mountain of whipped cream from one side of the city to the other?" Older children think of imaginative answers, but children in the concrete operations stage are likely to complain that the question is silly.

Or ask, "If you could have a third eye anywhere on your body, where would you put it?" Children in this stage generally respond immediately that they would put it right between the other two, on their foreheads. Older children suggest more imaginative ideas such as on the back of their heads, in the stomach (so they could watch food digesting), or on the tip of a finger (so they could peek around corners).

## Formal Operations Stage

*Formal operations* is Piaget's term for *the mental processes used to deal with abstract, hypothetical situations. Those processes demand logical, deductive reasoning and systematic planning.* According to Piaget, children reach the **stage of formal operations** at about age 11. Later researchers found that many people take longer to reach this stage, and some never reach it.

Suppose we ask three children, ages 6, 10, and 14, to arrange a set of 12 sticks in order from the longest to the shortest. The 6-year-old (preoperational) child fails to order the sticks correctly. The 10-year-old (concrete operations) eventually gets them in the right order, but only after prolonged trial and error. The 14-year-old (formal operations) holds the sticks upright with their bottom ends on the table and then removes the longest one, the second-longest, and so forth.

A second example: We set up five bottles of clear liquid and explain that it is possible to mix some combination of them to produce a yellow liquid. The task is to find that combination. Children in the concrete operations stage plunge right in with no plan. They try combining bottles A and B, then C and D, then perhaps A, C, and E. Soon they have forgotten which combinations they've already tried. If they do stumble onto the correct combination, it is mostly by luck.

Children in the formal operations stage approach the problem more systematically. They may first try all the two-bottle combinations: AB, AC, AD, AE, BC, and so forth. If those fail, they try three-bottle combinations: ABC, ABD, ABE, ACD, and so on. By trying every possible combination only once, they are sure to succeed.

Children do not reach the stage of formal operations any more suddenly than they reach the concrete operations stage. Reasoning logically about a particular problem requires some experience with it. A 9-year-old chess hobbyist reasons logically about chess problems and plans several moves ahead but reverts to concrete reasoning when faced with an unfamiliar problem.

Table 10.2 summarizes Piaget's four stages.

## CONCEPT CHECK

3. You are given the following information about four children. Assign each of them to one of Piaget's stages of intellectual development. (Check your answers on page 380.)
   a. Child has mastered the concept of conservation; still has trouble with abstract and hypothetical questions.
   b. Child performs well on tests of object permanence; still has trouble with conservation.
   c. Child has schemata; does not speak in complete sentences; fails tests of object permanence.
   d. Child performs well on tests of object permanence, conservation, and hypothetical questions.

## Are Piaget's Stages Distinct?

According to Piaget, the four stages of intellectual development are distinct, and each transition from one stage to the next requires a major reorganization of the child's way of thinking. He contended that children in the sensorimotor stage fail certain tasks because they lack the concept of object permanence and that children in the preoperational stage fail conservation tasks because they lack the necessary mental processes. In other words intellectual growth is marked by periods of revolutionary reorganization, as a child advances from one stage of thinking to another.

Later research has cast much doubt on this conclusion. If it were true, then a child in a given stage of development—say, the preoperational stage—should perform consistently at that level. In fact, a given child's performance fluctuates, especially depending on the difficulty of a task. For example, preschool children ordinarily fail conservation-of-number tasks, in which an investigator presents two rows of coins or candies with seven or more objects in each row and then spreads out one row and asks which row "has more." Preoperational children reply that the spread-out row has more. However, when Rochel Gelman (1982) presented two rows of only three objects each (Figure 10.15) and then spread out one of the rows, even 3- and 4-year-old children answered that the rows had the same number of items. After much practice with these short rows, most of the 3- and 4-year-olds also answered correctly that a spread-out row of eight items had the same number of items as the tightly packed row of eight.

In general, the progression from one stage of thinking to another appears to be gradual and not sudden (Siegler, 1994). That is, the difference between older children and younger children is not so much a matter of *having* an ability or of *lacking* it; the difference is between readily using the ability or using it only for simple

**TABLE 10.2  Summary of Piaget's Stages of Cognitive Development**

| Stage and Approximate Age | Achievements and Activities | Limitations |
|---|---|---|
| Sensorimotor (birth to $1\frac{1}{2}$ years) | Reacts to sensory stimuli through reflexes and other responses | Little use of language; seems not to understand object permanence in the early part of this stage |
| Preoperational ($1\frac{1}{2}$ to 7 years) | Develops language; can represent objects mentally by words and other symbols; can respond to objects that are remembered but not present | Lacks operations (reversible mental processes); lacks concept of conservation; focuses on one property at a time (such as length or width), not on both at once; still has trouble distinguishing appearance from reality |
| Concrete operations (7 to 11 years) | Understands conservation of mass, number, and volume; can reason logically with regard to concrete objects that can be seen or touched | Has trouble reasoning about abstract concepts and hypothetical situations |
| Formal operations (11 years onward) | Can reason logically about abstract and hypothetical concepts; develops strategies; plans actions in advance | None beyond the occasional irrationalities of all human thought |

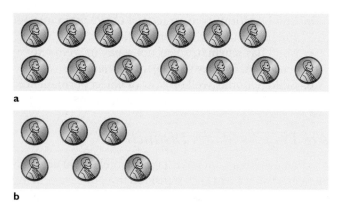

**FIGURE 10.15** (a) With the standard conservation-of-number task, preoperational children answer that the lower row has more items. (b) With a simplified task, the same children say that both rows have the same number of items.

■ Lev Vygotsky called attention to a child's zone of proximal development: the gap between what a child can do alone and what the child can do with help. Education within the zone of proximal development can advance a child's reasoning abilities.

tasks. As children develop, they use the ability for increasingly more complex tasks.

## Differing Views: Piaget and Vygotsky

One implication of Piaget's findings is that children must discover certain concepts, such as the concept of conservation, mainly on their own. Teaching a concept means directing children's attention to the key aspects and then letting them discover the concept for themselves.

Another implication frequently drawn from Piaget's work is that teachers should determine a child's level of functioning and then teach material appropriate to that level. For example, teachers should not try introducing abstract concepts to children who are at the concrete operations stage of development.

In contrast to this view, Russian psychologist Lev Vygotsky (1978) argued that education cannot simply wait for children to reach the next stage of development on their own. Indeed, Vygotsky argued, the one distinguishing characteristic of human thought is that it is based on language and symbols. We use language both to influence others and to control our own behavior (as when we tell ourselves what to do and what not to do). Children do sometimes discover ideas on their own, but it is inefficient and unrealistic to expect them to discover everything; adults should indeed teach them (Karpov & Haywood, 1998).

However, when Vygotsky said that adults should teach children, he did not necessarily mean to teach by lecturing, and he certainly did not mean that adults should ignore the child's developmental level. What he meant was this: Every child has a **zone of proximal development,** which is *the distance between what a child can do alone and what the child can do with the help of adults or other children.* Instruction should remain within that zone. For example, one should not try to teach a 4-year-old the concept of conservation of volume, and it would be a waste of time to try to teach it to an 8-year-old who understands it already. But

a child around 6 years old who does not yet understand the concept might learn it with help and guidance from an adult or older child. Similarly, children improve their recall of a story when adults provide appropriate hints and reminders, and they can solve more complicated math problems with help than they can solve alone. Vygotsky compared this help to *scaffolding,* the temporary supports builders use when constructing a new building: After the building is complete, the scaffolding is removed.

Good advice for an educator, therefore, is to be sensitive to a child's zone of proximal development and attempt to detect how much further the child can be pushed. In some cases the child may provide clues. For example, several preoperational children who are asked which beaker has more water may all point to the tall, thin one, but the children who could most easily learn conservation of volume describe the various beakers by using hand gestures that indicate both height and width (Goldin-Meadow, 1997). Children who use such gestures are more ready than the other children to learn the concept of conservation.

## CONCEPT CHECK

4. If a child does not yet understand the concept of conservation, what would be the opinions of Piaget and Vygotsky about the feasibility of teaching that concept? (Check your answer on page 380.)

## Difficulties of Inferring Children's Concepts

In the previous module, we considered the difficulty of deciding whether infants understand object permanence. Similar issues arise with understanding somewhat older children's thinking, and as you will see, the conclusions are similar: Children do not "have" or "fail to have" a concept. Concepts develop gradually and may appear with one method of testing and not another. We shall consider two examples.

## Distinguishing Appearance from Reality

Many psychologists have contended that children in the early preoperational stage do not distinguish clearly between appearance and reality. For example, a child who sees you put a white ball behind a blue filter will say that the ball is blue. When you ask, "Yes, I know the ball *looks* blue, but what color is it *really*?" the child replies that it really *is* blue (Flavell, 1986). Similarly, a 3-year-old who encounters a sponge that looks like a rock probably will say either that it really is a rock or that it not only *is* a sponge but also *looks like* a sponge. Children have to grow a year or two older before they can say that something looks like one thing but really is another.

However, other psychologists have argued that the 3-year-old's problem is more with use of the language than with understanding the appearance–reality distinction. (After all, 3-year-olds do play games of make-believe, so they sometimes do distinguish appearance from reality.) In one study psychologists showed 3-year-olds a sponge that looked like a rock and let them touch it. When the investigators asked what it looked like and what it was *really*, most of the children said either "rock" both times or "sponge" both times. However, if the investigators asked,

"Bring me something so I can wipe up some spilled water," the children brought the sponge. And when the investigators asked, "Bring me something so I can take a picture of a teddy bear with something that looks like a rock," they again brought the sponge. So evidently, they did understand that something could be a sponge and look like a rock, even if they couldn't say so (Sapp, Lee, & Muir, 2000).

Also consider the following experiment: A psychologist shows a child a playhouse room that is a scale model of a full-size room. Then the psychologist hides a tiny toy in the small room (while the child watches) and explains that a bigger toy just like it is "in the same place" in the bigger room. (For example, if the little toy was behind the sofa in the little room, the big toy would be behind the sofa in the big room.) Then the psychologist asks the child to find the big toy in the big room. Most 3-year-olds look in the correct place and find the toy immediately. Most $2\frac{1}{2}$-year-olds, however, search haphazardly (see Figure 10.16a). If the experimenter shows the child the big toy in the big room and asks the child to find the little toy "in the same place" in the little room, the results are the same: 3-year-olds find it but $2\frac{1}{2}$-year-olds cannot. It appears that 3-year-olds have an ability that $2\frac{1}{2}$-year-olds lack (DeLoache, 1989).

Before we speak too confidently about what a $2\frac{1}{2}$-year-old cannot do, however, consider this clever follow-up study: The psychologist hides a toy in the small

**a**  A $2\frac{1}{2}$-year-old is shown small room where stuffed animal is hidden.

Child is unable to find the stuffed animal in the larger room.

**b**  Child is shown small room where stuffed animal is hidden.

Child is told that the machine expands the room. Child stands out of the way during some noises and then returns.

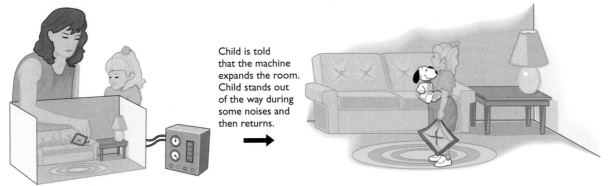

Child is able to find the stuffed animal in the "blown-up" room.

**FIGURE 10.16** If an experimenter hides a small toy in a small room and asks a child to find a larger toy "in the same place" in the larger room, a $2\frac{1}{2}$-year-old searches haphazardly. (a) However, the same child knows exactly where to look, if the experimenter says this is the same room as before, except that a machine has expanded it (b).

room while the child watches. Then they both step out of the room, and the psychologist shows the child a "machine that can make things bigger." The psychologist aims a beam from the machine at the room and takes the child out of the way. They hear some chunkata-chunkata-clunkata-clunkata sounds, and then the psychologist shows the full-sized "blown-up" room and asks the child to find the hidden toy. Even 2½-year-olds go immediately to the correct location (DeLoache, Miller, & Rosengren, 1997) (see Figure 10.16b). Evidently, they can use one room as a "map" of the other *if* they think of them as "the same room." (Incidentally, hardly any of the children showed any doubt that the machine had actually expanded the room, and many continued to believe it even after the psychologist tried to explain what had really happened!) The overall conclusion: A child can appear to have an ability or to lack it depending on the type of test.

## Understanding Other People's Thoughts

According to Piaget, young children's thought is **egocentric.** By this term Piaget did *not* mean that children are selfish; instead, he meant that *a child sees the world as centered around himself or herself and cannot easily take another person's perspective.* If you and a preschooler sit on opposite sides of a complicated pile of blocks and you ask the child to draw or describe what the blocks would look like from your side, the child draws or describes them as they look from the child's side.

Another example: Young children hear a story about a little girl, Lucy, who wants her old pair of red shoes. Part way through the story, Lucy's brother Linus comes into the room, and she asks him to bring her red shoes. He goes and brings back her new red shoes, and she is angry because she wanted the old red shoes. Young children are often surprised that he brought the wrong shoes because *they* knew which shoes she wanted (Keysar, Barr, & Horton, 1998).

Unfortunately, adults are often egocentric in a similar way. In one study adults heard a story in which Jane recommends a restaurant to David. He goes there and dislikes it. Later she asks him how he liked the restaurant, and he replies, ". . . it was marvelous, just marvelous." Adults who knew he disliked it are surprised that Jane didn't realize he was being sarcastic. Like the children, the adults were egocentric by assuming that what they knew other people would know also (Keysar et al., 1998).

## CONCEPT CHECK

5. Which of the following is the clearest example of egocentric thinking?
   a. A writer who uses someone else's words without giving credit.
   b. A politician who blames others for everything that goes wrong.
   c. A professor who gives the same complicated lecture to a freshman class that she gives to a convention of professionals. (Check your answer on page 380.)

To say that a child is egocentric is to say that he or she has trouble understanding what other people know and don't know. How can we know what a child thinks about other people's thoughts? Here is one example of a research effort.

**WHAT'S THE EVIDENCE?**
*Children's Understanding of Other People's Cognitions*

How and when do children first understand that other people have minds and knowledge? Researchers have developed some very clever experiments to answer this difficult question.

**HYPOTHESIS** A child who understands that other people have minds will distinguish between someone who is in a position to know something and someone who could not know it.

**METHOD** A 3- or 4-year-old child sat in front of four cups (Figure 10.17) and watched as one adult hid a candy or toy under one of the cups, although a screen prevented the child from seeing which cup. Then another adult entered the room. The "informed" adult pointed to one cup to show where he or she had just hidden the surprise; the "uninformed" adult pointed to one of the other cups. The child was then given an opportunity to look under one cup for the surprise.

This procedure was repeated ten times for each child. The two adults alternated roles, but on each trial one or the other hid the surprise while the other was absent. That is, one was in a position to know where the surprise was hidden and the other was not.

**RESULTS** Of the 4-year-olds, 10 of 20 consistently chose the correct cup (the one indicated by the informed adult). That is, many of the 4-year-olds showed that they understood who had the relevant knowledge and who did not. However, all of the 3-year-olds were just as likely to follow the lead of the uninformed adult as that of the informed adult (Povinelli & deBlois, 1992).

**INTERPRETATION** Evidently, some 4-year-olds have a greater understanding of other people's knowledge (or lack of it) than 3-year-olds have.

Other experiments, using a somewhat different procedure, have yielded similar results. For example, children in one study watched a dramatization where a girl who had a marble in her basket left the room temporarily.

During her absence a second girl moved the marble from the first girl's basket to her own basket. When the first girl returned to the room, the children were asked "Where is the marble?" and "Where will the first girl look for it?" Most 4-year-olds answered that she would look in her own basket, but younger children thought she would look in the second girl's basket (Wimmer & Perner, 1983). As in the previous study, 4-year-olds are better able than younger children to make inferences about what various people might or might not know.

Although these are important results, we should avoid concluding that children at some point suddenly understand that other people have minds. When children are tested on a range of items, many show an understanding of other people's minds on some items and not on others (Yirmiya, Erel, Shaked, & Solomonica-Levi, 1998). Even children 3 years old and younger show an understanding on simple tasks. As we have seen in previous cases in this chapter, gaining a concept is seldom an all-or-none process. Many children seem to understand a concept in one situation and not another.

# The Development of Moral Reasoning

As children develop their reasoning powers, they apply their new reasoning abilities to moral issues. Just as 11-year-olds reason differently from 5-year-olds about what happens when water is poured from one beaker into another, they also reason differently about issues of right and wrong.

## Kohlberg's Method of Evaluating Levels of Moral Reasoning

Psychologists once regarded morality as a set of arbitrary, learned rules with no logical basis. Lawrence Kohlberg (1969; Kohlberg & Hersh, 1977) rejected that view, arguing instead that moral reasoning is the result of a reasoning process that resembles Piaget's stages of intellectual development. Young children mostly equate "wrong" with "punished." Adults understand that certain acts are wrong even though they may never lead to punishment and that other acts are right even if they do lead to punishment. Children younger than about 6 years old think that accidentally breaking something valuable is worse than intentionally breaking something of less value; older children and adults give more regard to people's intentions.

**FIGURE 10.17** A child sits in front of a screen covering four cups and watches as one adult hides a surprise under one of the cups. Then that adult and another (who had not been present initially) point to one of the cups to signal where the surprise is hidden. Many 4-year-olds consistently follow the advice of the informed adult; 3-year-olds do not.

Kohlberg proposed that people pass through distinct stages as they develop moral reasoning. Although those stages are analogous to Piaget's stages, they do not follow the same time sequence. For example, an individual may progress rapidly through Piaget's stages but move more slowly through Kohlberg's stages.

Kohlberg suggested that moral reasoning should not be evaluated according to the decisions a person makes but according to the reasoning behind them. For example, do you think that designing nuclear bombs is a moral way to make a living? According to Kohlberg, whether that job shows good moral reasoning depends on one's reasons for taking it. Hugh Gusterson (1992) interviewed nuclear bomb designers at the Lawrence Livermore National Laboratory. When he asked them about the morality of their actions, nearly everyone said something like, "You're lucky you chose me to interview, because I, unlike all the others, think deeply about these matters." (Clearly, all of them were thinking about the moral issues but not discussing them.) The vast majority said they were confident that the weapons they designed would never be used and that their only function was to threaten and thereby to prevent wars. If you doubt that assumption, you might disagree with the morality of the bomb designers' *actions,* but nevertheless, they are operating at a high level of moral *reasoning* because they explained their actions in terms of the expected benefits to humanity.

Kohlberg believed that we all start with a low level of moral reasoning and mature through higher stages. To measure the maturity of a person's moral judgments, Kohlberg devised a series of **moral dilemmas**—*problems that pit one moral value against another.* Each dilemma is accompanied by a question, such as "What should this person do?" or "Did this person do the right thing?" Kohlberg was not concerned about the choice a person makes because the dilemmas pit one value against another, and well-meaning people do disagree on the right answer. More revealing than the answer itself is the explanation behind it. The respondent's explanations are then matched to one of Kohlberg's six stages, which are grouped into three levels (see Table 10.3). Because very few people operate consistently at stage 6, many authorities combine stages 5 and 6. To emphasize: In Kohlberg's scheme there are no moral or immoral decisions, only moral and immoral *reasons* for making a decision (see Figure 10.18).

**A STEP FURTHER**
*Kohlberg's Stages*

Suppose a military junta overthrows a democratic government and sets up a dictatorship. In which of Kohlberg's stages of moral reasoning would you classify the members of the junta? Would your answer depend on the reasons they gave for setting up their dictatorship?

People's responses to Kohlberg's moral dilemmas suggest the level of moral reasoning at which they *usually* operate. Few people are absolutely consistent in their moral reasoning, any more than they are consistent in any other kind of reasoning.

Kohlberg and others have found that people begin at the first stage and progress through the others in order, although few reach the highest stages. (The order of progression is an important point: If people were just as likely to progress in the order 3-5-4 as in the order 3-4-5, then we would have no justification for regarding stage 5 as more advanced than stage 4.) People seldom skip a stage or revert to an earlier stage after reaching a higher one. However, people do fluctuate. For example, someone who usually answers at stage 4 will also give some answers at higher or lower levels. Figure 10.19 shows that most 10-year-olds' judgments are at Kohlberg's first or second stage, but 13- and 16-year-olds progress to higher levels. Kohlberg suggests that this rather swift development of moral reasoning results from cognitive growth: 16-year-olds are capable of more mature reasoning than 10-year-olds.

## CONCEPT CHECK

6. For the moral dilemma described at the top of Table 10.3, suppose someone says that Heinz was wrong to steal the drug to save his wife's life. Which level of moral reasoning is characteristic of this judgment? (Check your answer on page 380.)

## Limitations of Kohlberg's Views

Kohlberg's theory is based on several uncertain assumptions. Let us consider two major issues: (a) justice versus caring orientations to morality and (b) the relationship between moral reasoning and moral behavior.

### Are There Other Types of Moral Reasoning?

Kohlberg concentrated on what we might call the "justice" orientation based on people's rights. Carol Gilligan (1977, 1979) pointed out a different orientation based on "caring"—that is, what would help or hurt other people. For example, consider a situation during the Vietnam War, when a group of soldiers were ordered to kill a group of unarmed civilians. One soldier, who regarded the order as immoral, refused to shoot. So in terms of "justice," he acted at a high moral level, following a "higher law" that required him not to kill. However, his actions made no difference, as the other soldiers killed all the civilians. In terms of "caring," he would have been more moral if he had found a way to hide a few of the victims (Linn & Gilligan, 1990).

Initially, Gilligan (1977, 1979) proposed that the "justice" and "caring" orientations represented a sex difference. Men, she said, focus mostly on rights and duties; women focus more on caring and relationships. For example, when asked about the ethics of abortion, many

**TABLE 10.3  Responses to One of Kohlberg's Moral Dilemmas by People at Six Levels of Moral Reasoning**

*The dilemma:* Heinz's wife was near death from cancer. A druggist had recently discovered a drug that might be able to save her. The druggist was charging $2000 for the drug, which cost him $200 to make. Heinz could not afford to pay for it, and he could borrow only $1000 from friends. He offered to pay the rest later. The druggist refused to sell the drug for less than the full price paid in advance: "I discovered the drug, and I'm going to make money from it." Late that night, Heinz broke into the store to steal the drug for his wife. Did Heinz do the right thing?

| Level/Stage | Typical Answer | Basis for Judging Right from Wrong | Description of Stage |
|---|---|---|---|
| **The Level of Preconventional Morality** | | | |
| 1. Punishment and obedience orientation | "No. If he steals the drug, he might go to jail." "Yes. If he can't afford the drug, he can't afford a funeral, either." | Wrong is equated with punishment. What is good is whatever is in the man's immediate self-interest. | Decisions are based on their immediate consequences. Whatever is rewarded is "good" and whatever is punished is "bad." If you break something and are punished, then what you did was bad. |
| 2. Instrumental relativist orientation | "He can steal the drug and save his wife, and he'll be with her when he gets out of jail." | Again, what is good is whatever is in the man's own best interests, but his interests include delayed benefits. | It is good to help other people, but only because they may one day return the favor: "You scratch my back and I'll scratch yours." |
| **The Level of Conventional Morality** | | | |
| 3. Interpersonal concordance, or "good boy/nice girl" orientation | "People will understand if you steal the drug to save your wife, but they'll think you're cruel and a coward if you don't." | Public opinion is the main basis for judging what is good. | The "right" thing to do is whatever pleases others, especially those in authority. Be a good person so others will think you are good. Conformity to the dictates of public opinion is important. |
| 4. "Law and order" orientation | "No, because stealing is illegal." "Yes. It is the husband's duty to save his wife even if he feels guilty afterward for stealing the drug." | Right and wrong can be determined by duty or by one's role in society. | You should respect the law— simply because it *is* the law— and work to strengthen the social order than enforces it. |
| **The Level of Postconventional or Principled Morality** | | | |
| 5. Social-contract legalistic orientation | "The husband has a right to the drug even if he can't pay now. If the druggist won't charge it, the government should look after it." | Laws are made for people's benefit. They should be flexible. If necessary, we may have to change certain laws or allow for exceptions to them. | The "right" thing to do is whatever people have agreed is the best thing for society. As in stage 4, you respect the law, but in addition recognize that a majority of the people can agree to change the rules. Anyone who makes a promise is obligated to keep the promise. |
| 6. Universal ethical principle orientation | "Although it is legally wrong to steal, the husband would be morally wrong not to steal to save his wife. A life is more precious than financial gain." | Right and wrong are based on absolute values such as human life. Sometimes these values take precedence over human laws. | In special cases it may be right to violate a law that conflicts with higher ethical principles, such as justice and respect for human life. Among those who have obeyed a "higher law" are Jesus, Mahatma Gandhi, and Martin Luther King, Jr. |

*Source:* Kohlberg, 1981.

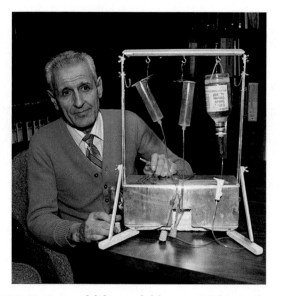

**FIGURE 10.18** A real-life moral dilemma: Michigan physician Jack Kevorkian developed a device to help terminally ill patients kill themselves painlessly. Is it morally right or wrong to aid in someone else's suicide? According to Kohlberg's viewpoint, the morality of an act does not depend on the act itself, but on the reasoning behind the act.

men give a yes or no answer and then state a general principle to support their answer. Either answer could get a high evaluation in Kohlberg's system if explained clearly. But many women say that the ethics of abortion depends on the details of the situation. An "it depends" answer seldom gets high marks in Kohlberg's system, even if it reflects a sympathetic, caring approach.

Gilligan therefore proposed alternative stages of moral development, as outlined in Table 10.4. The postconventional stage is the most mature; the preconventional stage is the least mature. Like Kohlberg, Gilligan concentrates on the reasons behind someone's moral decisions, not on the decisions themselves. But unlike Kohlberg, Gilligan emphasizes the "caring" aspect of the reasons: Will this action help or hurt the people it affects?

Later researchers have agreed with Gilligan that people have two ways of reasoning about moral issues—one based on justice and the other based on caring. The gender difference is small, however. Men are slightly more likely to answer in terms of abstract principles of justice, and women are slightly more likely to base their answers on a sympathetic, caring orientation (Jaffee & Hyde, 2000). But nearly everyone shows some concern with both justice and caring. Because those orientations are sometimes in conflict, moral decisions can be complicated (see Figure 10.20).

## How Does Moral Reasoning Relate to Behavior?

The movie *Schindler's List* portrays a German man who risked his life to save Jewish people from the Nazi Holocaust. We all agree he did the right thing. But if you or I had been non-Jewish Germans at the time, what would we have done? I don't know. Saying what is the right thing to do is not the same as doing it (see Figure 10.21).

Kohlberg's approach to morality has been criticized from two standpoints—that he overestimated people's moral behavior and that he underestimated their moral behavior. I shall present both arguments and let you draw your own conclusions.

The first argument goes as follows: Although many people give answers that qualify as stages 4, 5, and 6, moral *behavior* at those levels is uncommon, and we can understand why (Krebs, 2000). Behavior at stages 1, 2, and 3 benefits yourself: Seek rewards, avoid punishments, and cooperate with others who cooperate with you. ("You scratch my back and I'll scratch yours.") Natural selection would favor a tendency to act in those ways and so would reasoning based on enlightened self-interest. Behavior at stages 4, 5, and 6 benefits other people whom you will never meet, who will never repay the favor. The incentive to act in that way is weak. You want *other* people to behave in a way that benefits society as a whole, but why should *you* unless you get some benefit from it? How many people contribute much to charity anonymously and without getting a tax deduction? How

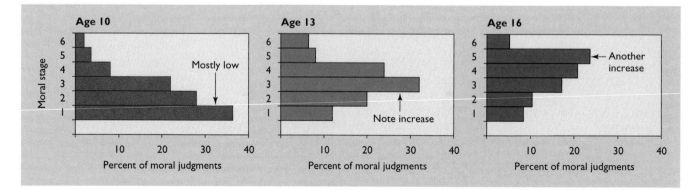

**FIGURE 10.19** Learning to distinguish right from wrong is the development of moral reasoning. Most younger adolescents give answers corresponding to Kohlberg's earlier moral stages. By age 16 most are at Kohlberg's fourth and fifth stages. (Based on Kohlberg, 1969)

**TABLE 10.4** Carol Gilligan's Stages of Moral Development

| Stage | Basis for Deciding Right from Wrong |
|---|---|
| Preconventional | What is helpful or harmful to myself? |
| Conventional | What is helpful or harmful to other people? |
| Postconventional | What is helpful or harmful to myself and others? |

**FIGURE 10.21** Critics of Kohlberg's approach point out that moral reasoning is not the same as moral action. This cadet at a Russian military academy (left) could probably explain why cheating is immoral, but he cheats nevertheless.

many companies voluntarily install expensive equipment to decrease the air pollution they cause?

On the other hand, maybe we are underestimating people's moral behavior. For example, young children who are asked why stealing is wrong reply "because you might get caught," and they are classified in Kohlberg's stage 1. But that answer, after all, is what they have been told: Don't steal or you'll be punished. However, if we ask the same children whether they would steal if they were sure they would not be caught, many say no. Apparently, they have some sense of right and wrong, even if they cannot state the idea clearly, and the research method may be underestimating children's reasoning, just like so many other research methods that we discussed earlier in this chapter.

In many cultures, such as the Hindu culture of India, almost all moral reasoning is stated in terms of natural principles of right and wrong, not in terms of the laws and social conventions that figure so heavily in Western thought. Most people's decisions are guided in terms of a sense of duty, not in terms of getting ahead in life or achieving personal happiness. That is, moral obligation may be a more widespread concept than Kohlberg thought, and the ideas of law and justice may be more culture specific than he thought (Shweder, Mahapatra, & Miller, 1987).

Furthermore, even in Western culture, the fact that most people say they are motivated by self-interest could be a consequence of the fact that we have repeatedly *told* each other that we are, or should be, motivated by self-interest (D. T. Miller, 1999). Many people do contribute extensively to charity and work to help people they don't know, and some act almost apologetic about it because they have been told that most people act solely for their own benefit. Charities find that they receive far more contributions if they offer something in return—a calendar, a magazine, perhaps a T-shirt—even if the object they offer has only slight value. The point of the reward is to give people an excuse to behave generously, as they really wanted to do.

**FIGURE 10.20** Sometimes the two "voices" of moral reasoning—justice and caring—are in conflict with each other. From a caring standpoint, you want to help someone in distress. From a justice standpoint, though, you may think it wrong to encourage begging. In many controversial situations, ranging from abortion to the death penalty to animal protection, well-meaning people disagree about what actions are moral.

## IN CLOSING

### *Developing Cognitive Abilities*

The universe is a complicated place, and even well-educated adults continue working throughout their lives to understand it. For a young child, this work is an enormous challenge, and we adults find it difficult to reconstruct what the world looks like through a child's eyes. In childhood, as throughout life, a person is constantly constructing one hypothesis after another, discarding old conceptions of the world to make way for new ones. However, children's hypotheses include some that adults would not take seriously. Young children have trouble with the distinction between appearance and reality and they have trouble understanding anyone else's viewpoint if it differs from their own. On the other hand, we sometimes underestimate children's thinking just because they cannot express themselves clearly. Developmental psychologists have made remarkable progress toward understanding the mind of a child, but enormous challenges remain.

## Summary

- **Piaget's view of children's thinking.** According to Jean Piaget, children's thought differs from adults' thought qualitatively as well as quantitatively. He believed children grew intellectually through accommodation and assimilation. (page 367)

- **Piaget's stages of development.** Children in the sensorimotor stage respond to what they see or otherwise sense at the moment. In the preoperational stage, according to Piaget, they lack reversible operations, such as the ability to understand that a mother could be someone else's daughter. In the concrete operations stage, children can reason about concrete problems but not abstractions. Adults and older children are in the formal operations stage, in which they can plan a strategy and can deal with hypothetical or abstract questions. (page 368)

- **Alternatives to Piaget.** Most psychologists now doubt that children go through distinct stages. Rather, one level of performance gradually blends into the next. According to Lev Vygotsky, children must learn new abilities from adults or older children; we cannot wait for them to make the discoveries by themselves. (page 372)

- **Appearance and reality.** Young children sometimes seem not to distinguish between appearance and reality. However, with a simpler task or different method of testing, they do distinguish. In many cases children do not fully have or lack a concept; they show the concept under some conditions and not others. (page 373)

- **Egocentric thinking.** Young children sometimes have trouble understanding other people's point of view. Before about age 4, children have trouble inferring what someone else knows. (page 373)

- **Kohlberg's view of moral reasoning.** Lawrence Kohlberg contended that moral reasoning can also be described in terms of stages. According to Kohlberg, a person's moral reasoning should be evaluated on the basis of the reasons the person gives for a decision rather than on the basis of the decision itself. (page 375)

- **Challenges to Kohlberg's views.** Kohlberg attended only to a "justice" orientation, ignoring a "caring" orientation that sometimes gives a conflicting view on morality. Moral reasoning, as measured by Kohlberg, often fails to translate into equally moral behavior. It has been argued both that people's actions are less moral than their answers to Kohlberg's questions and that their actions are in fact more moral than their answers imply. (page 376)

## Answers to Concept Checks

3. **a.** concrete operations stage; **b.** preoperational stage; **c.** sensorimotor stage; **d.** formal operations stage. (page 371)
4. Piaget would recommend waiting for the child to discover the concept by himself or herself. According to Vygotsky, the answer depends on the child's zone of proximal development. Some children could be taught the concept, and others are not yet ready for it. (page 372)
5. **c** is the clearest case of egocentric thought, a failure to recognize another person's point of view. It is not the same as selfishness. (page 374)
6. Not enough information is provided to answer this question. In Kohlberg's system any judgment can represent either a high or a low level of moral reasoning; we evaluate a person's moral reasoning entirely by the explanation for the judgment, not by the judgment itself. (page 376)

# Social and Emotional Development

*How do we change, socially and emotionally, as we grow older?*

You are a contestant on a new TV game show called *What's My Worry?* Behind the curtain is someone with an overriding concern. You are to identify that concern by questioning a psychologist who knows what it is. (You neither see nor hear the person.) You must ask questions that can be answered with a single word or a short phrase. If you identify the worry correctly, you can win as much as $50,000.

But there is one catch: The more questions you ask, the smaller the prize. If you guess correctly after only one question, you win $50,000. After two questions, you win $25,000 and so on. It would therefore be poor strategy to keep asking questions until you are sure; instead, you should ask one or two questions and then make an educated guess.

What would your first question be? Mine would be: "How old is this person?" The principal worries of teenagers are different from those of most 20-year-olds, which in turn differ from those of most 40-year-olds and 70-year-olds. Each age has its own characteristic concerns, opportunities, and pleasures.

## Research Designs for Studying Development

Comparing the psychology of people of different ages may sound easy, but details of the methods can change the results. Psychologists use either cross-sectional studies or longitudinal studies. A **cross-sectional study** *compares groups of individuals of different ages all at the same time*. For example, we could compare the drawing abilities of 6-year-olds, 8-year-olds, and 10-year-olds. The main weakness of cross-sectional studies is the difficulty of obtaining equivalent samples at different ages. For example, suppose you want to do a cross-sectional study comparing 20-year-olds and 60-year-olds. You study a sample of 20-year-olds from the local college, but how will you find a comparable group of 60-year-olds? The 60-year-olds you eventually select may have been less educated from the start, perhaps less wealthy, perhaps different in many other regards.

A **longitudinal study** *follows a single group of individuals as they develop*. For example, we could study a group of

■ As we grow older, we mature in our social and emotional behaviors. However, many revert quickly to childlike behaviors in situations where such behavior is acceptable.

6-year-olds and then study the same children again when they reach ages 9 and 12. Table 10.5 contrasts the two kinds of studies.

Longitudinal studies face practical difficulties. A longitudinal study of children from the ages of 6 to 12 requires 6 years to complete, and one from 6 to 60 would last longer than an investigator's career. To make matters worse, many of the children who begin in a study at, say, age 6 may move out of town or refuse to participate later. In a longitudinal study of the elderly, many people will die or become incapacitated before the end of the study. Furthermore, those who leave a study may be different in important ways from those who continue. For example, suppose a creature from outer space observes humans for the first time and discovers that about 50% of young adults are males but that only 10–20% of 90-year-olds are males. The creature concludes that, as human males grow older, most of them transform into females.

You can see why that conclusion is wrong. Males—with a few exceptions—do not change into females, but on the average they die earlier, leaving a greater percentage of older females. Similarly, in any longitudinal study, those who left a study may have been brighter or less bright, more motivated or less motivated, or different in

**TABLE 10.5 Cross-Sectional and Longitudinal Studies**

| | Description | Advantages | Disadvantages | Example |
|---|---|---|---|---|
| **Cross-sectional** 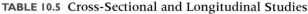 | Several groups of subjects of various ages studied at one time | 1. Quick<br>2. No risk of confusing age effects with effects of changes in society | 1. Risk of sampling error by getting different kinds of people at different ages<br>2. Risk of cohort effects | Compare memory abilities of 3-, 5-, and 7-year-olds |
| **Longi-tudinal** | One group of subjects studied repeatedly as the members grow older | 1. No risk of sampling differences<br>2. Can study effects of one experience on later development<br>3. Can study consistency within individuals over time | 1. Takes a long time<br>2. Some subjects quit<br>3. Sometimes hard to separate effects of age from changes in society | Study social and emotional behavior of children at time of parents' divorce and at various times afterward |

other ways from those who continued. If so, the differences between people at the beginning and end of the study are not really due to aging. **Selective attrition,** also known as *differential survival,* is *the tendency for some kinds of people to be more likely than others to drop out of a study.* Psychologists can partly reduce this problem by reporting the data only for the people who completed the study. That is, even when presenting the data for the early part of the study, they include results for only the participants who stayed to the end of the study.

A longitudinal study also faces the difficulty of separating the effects of age from the effects of changes in society. For example, suppose we found that a group of people who were 20 years old in 1970 became politically more conservative by age 50. We would not know whether these people became more conservative because of their age or because of changes in the political situation between 1970 and 2000.

Why, then, would investigators ever conduct a longitudinal study? One reason is that certain questions logically require a longitudinal study. For example, to study the effects of divorce on children, we can learn much by comparing how each child reacts at first with how that same child reacts later. To study whether happy children are likely to become happy adults, we would have to follow a single group of people over time.

Consider another contrast: On the average who knows more about the Vietnam War, current 20-year-olds or current 60-year-olds? Who knows more about computer programming, 20-year-olds or 60-year-olds? Presumably, you

answered *60-year-olds* to the first question and *20-year-olds* to the second. Neither of those questions depends on age itself, but on generations. People born in different eras develop different knowledge, interests, and skills. Psychologists call these differences *cohort effects* (Figure 10.22). A **cohort** is *a group of people born at a particular time or a group of people who entered an organization at a particular time.* Psychologists try to distinguish whether a difference among people of different ages is really due to age or whether it is a difference among cohorts. A longitudinal study eliminates cohort effects because it can study a group of people who are all in the same cohort.

## CONCEPT CHECK

7. Suppose you want to study the effect of age on artistic abilities, and you want to be sure that any apparent differences are due to age and not to cohort effects. Which should you use, a longitudinal study or a cross-sectional study?

8. Suppose you want to study the effect of age on choice of clothing. What problems would arise with either a longitudinal study or a cross-sectional study?

9. At Santa Enigma College, the average first-year student has a C-minus average, and the average senior has a B-plus average. An observer concludes that, as students progress through college, they improve their study habits. Based on the idea of selective attrition, propose another possible explanation. (Check your answers on page 392.)

FIGURE 10.22 Children of the 1920s, 1960s, and 1990s differed in their behavior because they grew up in different historical eras, with different options regarding education, nutrition, and health care. Differences among age groups based on such influences are called "cohort effects."

# Erikson's Ages of Human Development

Using a combination of cross-sectional and longitudinal studies, psychologists study changes in people's abilities and also changes in their life situations. To understand why people behave as they do, we need to know the decisions they are facing at the current stage of their lives.

Erik Erikson (Figure 10.23) divided the human life span into eight ages, each with its own social and emotional conflicts. First is *the age of the newborn infant,* whose main conflict is **basic trust versus mistrust.** The infant asks, in effect, *"Is my social world predictable and supportive?"* An infant whose early environment is supportive, nurturing, and loving will form a strong attachment to

FIGURE 10.23 Erik Erikson argued that each age group has its own special social and emotional conflicts.

the parents, and this will also positively influence future relationships with other people (Erikson, 1963).

Erikson's second age is *the age of the toddler,* 1–3 years old, whose main conflict is **autonomy versus shame and doubt.** The toddler faces the issue, *"Can I do things by myself or must I always rely on others?"* Experiencing independence for the first time, the toddler begins to walk and talk, to become toilet trained, to obey some instructions and defy others. Depending on how the parents react, children either develop a healthy feeling of autonomy (independence) or a self-critical sense of shame and the doubt that they can accomplish things on their own.

Erikson's third age is the age of *the preschool child,* whose main conflict is **initiative versus guilt.** At ages 3–6, as children begin to broaden their horizons, their boundless energy comes into conflict with parental restrictions. Sooner or later, the child breaks something or makes a big mess. The child then faces the question *"Am I good or bad?"* In contrast to the previous stage, when the concern was about what the child *can* do, at this stage the concern is about what the child *should* do.

In the fourth age, *preadolescence* (about ages 6–12), **industry versus inferiority** is the main conflict. The question is: *"Am I successful or worthless?"* Children widen their focus from the immediate family to society at large and begin to prepare for adult roles. They fantasize about the great successes ahead, and they begin to compete with their peers in an effort to excel in the activities popular with their age group. Children begin to develop a sense of either competence or inadequacy.

Erikson's fifth age is *adolescence (the early teens),* where the main conflict is **identity versus role confusion.** Adolescents begin to seek independence from their parents and try to answer the question *"Who am I?"* or *"Who will I be?"* They may eventually settle on a satisfactory answer—form an identity—or they may continue to experiment with goals and lifestyles—a state of role confusion.

Erikson's sixth age is *young adulthood,* in which **intimacy versus isolation** is the main conflict: *"Shall I share my life with another person or live alone?"* Young adults who marry or live with a friend find that they must adjust their habits to make the relationship succeed. Those who

**TABLE 10.6** Erikson's Ages of Human Development

| Age | Main Conflict | Typical Question |
|-----|---------------|------------------|
| *Infant* | Basic trust versus mistrust | Is my social world predictable and supportive? |
| *Toddler* (ages 1–3) | Autonomy versus shame and doubt | Can I do things by myself or must I always rely on others? |
| *Preschool child* (ages 3–6) | Initiative versus guilt | Am I good or bad? |
| *Preadolescent* (ages 6–12) | Industry versus inferiority | Am I successful or worthless? |
| *Adolescent* (early teens) | Identity versus role confusion | Who am I? |
| *Young adult* (late teens and early 20s) | Intimacy versus isolation | Shall I share my life with another person or live alone? |
| *Middle adult* (late 20s to retirement) | Generativity versus stagnation | Will I succeed in my life, both as a parent and as a worker? |
| *Older adult* (after retirement) | Ego integrity versus despair | Have I lived a full life or have I failed? |

choose to live alone may experience loneliness and pressure from their parents and friends to find a suitable partner.

Erikson's seventh age is *middle adulthood.* Here the major conflict is **generativity versus stagnation:** *"Will I produce something of real value? Will I succeed in my life, both as a parent and as a worker? Will I in some way give something back to society?"*

Finally comes *old age* (the years after retirement), where the main conflict is **ego integrity versus despair.** *"Have I lived a full life or have I failed?"* Integrity is a state of contentment about one's life, past, present, and future. Despair is a state of great disappointment about the past and the present, coupled with fear of the future. Table 10.6 summarizes Erikson's ages.

Is Erikson's view of development accurate? This question is unanswerable. Some psychologists find Erikson's description of development a useful way to organize our thinking about human life; others find it less useful, and it is not the kind of theory that one can test scientifically.

Now let's take a closer look at some of the major issues that confront people in their social and emotional development at different ages. Beyond the primary conflicts that Erikson highlighted, development is marked by a succession of other significant problems.

**A STEP FURTHER**
*Erikson's Ages*

Suppose you disagreed with Erikson's analysis; for example, suppose you believe that the main concern of young adults is not "intimacy versus isolation" but "earning money versus not earning money" or "finding meaning in life versus meaninglessness." How might you determine whether your theory or Erikson's is more accurate?

# Infancy and Childhood

Before the late 1950s, if someone asked, "What causes an infant to develop an attachment to the mother?" almost all psychologists replied, "Mother's milk." They were wrong.

## Studies of Attachment Among Monkeys

**Attachment**—*a long-term feeling of closeness between people, such as a child and a caregiver*—depends on more than just being fed. Attachment is part of trust, in Erikson's sense of "trust versus mistrust." Attachment depends on the emotional responses provoked by such acts as hugging.

Some highly influential evidence comes from an experiment that Harry Harlow conducted with monkeys. Harlow (1958) separated eight newborn rhesus monkeys from their mothers and isolated each of them in a room containing two artificial mothers. Four of the infant monkeys had a mother made of wire and equipped with a milk bottle in the breast position and a mother made of cloth with no bottle (Figure 10.24). The other four monkeys had a cloth mother with a bottle and a wire mother with no bottle. Harlow wanted to see how much time the baby monkeys would spend with the artificial mother that fed them.

Figure 10.25 shows the mean number of hours per day that the monkeys spent with the two kinds of mothers. Regardless of which mother had the milk, all the infants spent most of their time clinging to the cloth mother. Evidently,

**FIGURE 10.24** In Harlow's studies monkeys who got milk from the wire mother still clung to the cloth mother as much as they could.

their attachment depended mainly on *contact comfort*—comfortable skin sensations.

At first, Harlow thought that the cloth mothers were adequately serving the infants' emotional needs. He discovered, however, that the infants failed to develop normal social behaviors (Harlow, Harlow, & Suomi, 1971) (see Figure 10.26). When some of the females finally became pregnant, they proved to be woefully inadequate mothers, rejecting every approach their babies made. Clearly, the monkeys that had been reared by artificial mothers did not know how to react to other monkeys. With monkeys, as with humans, raising a child requires more than just being warm and cuddly.

The results of this study do *not* mean that an infant needs a mother's constant attention. They do mean that an infant needs social attention from *someone*. In other studies Harry Harlow and Margaret Harlow (1965) found that infant monkeys reared by artificial mothers could develop fairly normally if they had frequent opportunities to play with other infant monkeys.

## Early Attachment in Humans

Why do some infants form stronger attachments to their parents than others do? Which is better, a strong attachment to one person, such as the mother, or moderate attachments to several people? Does a good relationship with someone early in life make it easier to develop close bonds with other people later in life?

Before we can begin to answer such questions, we need a good way to measure attachment. One popular method has been the **Strange Situation** (usually capitalized), pioneered by Mary Ainsworth (1979). In this procedure *a mother and her infant* (typically 12 or 18 months old) *come into a room with many toys. Then a stranger enters the room. The mother leaves and then returns. A few minutes later both the stranger and the mother leave; then the stranger returns, and finally the mother returns.* Through a one-way mirror, a psychologist observes the infant's reactions to each of these events.

Observers classify infants' responses as follows:

- *Securely attached.* The infant uses the mother as a base of exploration, often showing her a toy, cooing at her, or making eye contact with her. The infant shows some distress when the mother leaves, but cries only a little, if at all. When she returns, the infant goes to her with apparent delight, cuddles for a while, and then returns to the toys.
- *Anxiously (or insecurely) attached.* Responses toward the mother fluctuate between happy and angry. The infant clings to the mother and cries profusely when she leaves, as if worried that she might not return. When she does return, the infant clings to her again.
- *Anxious and avoidant.* While the mother is present, the infant does not stay near her and does not interact much with her. The infant cries when she leaves but does not go to her when she returns.
- *Disorganized.* The infant seems not even to notice the mother or looks away while approaching her or covers his or her face or lies on the floor. In one way or another, the infant shows more fear than affection.

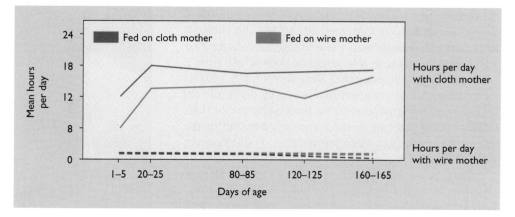

**FIGURE 10.25** All the baby monkeys preferred the cloth mothers, regardless of which artificial mother fed them. The two bottom lines show hours per day spent with the wire mothers.

FIGURE 10.26 Much of what we need and learn depends on interaction with others. This mother monkey reared in isolation ignores her baby.

The Strange Situation also can be used to evaluate the relationship between child and father (Belsky, 1996), child and grandparent, even pet dog and owner (Topál, Miklósi, Csàny, & Dóka, 1998). As a rule the quality of one relationship correlates with the quality of others. For example, most children who have a good relationship with the mother also have a good relationship with the father, and chances are the parents are happy with each other as well (Elicker, Englund, & Sroufe, 1992; Erel & Burman, 1995). Results of the Strange Situation seem to be tapping something important and long lasting. Most infants who have a secure relationship with their parents at age 12 months continue to have a close relationship with them years and even decades later (Waters, Merrick, Treboux, Crowell, & Albersheim, 2000).

Why do some children develop a more secure attachment than others do? Some children seem to be calmer and easier to please from the start, although temperament is not the whole explanation of attachment (Mangelsdorf & Frosch, 2000). Presumably, parental behavior is also an important factor, although measuring that factor is more difficult than it might sound. For example, we know that parents who are more affectionate with their children tend to have securely attached infants (Cox, Owen, Henderson, & Margand, 1992). But did their affectionate behavior influence the children, or did they act affectionately because the children started off with a calm, pleasant temperament? Very few studies address the cause-and-effect relationship. However, one study did find that teaching parents to be more sensitive to their infants' needs led to a more secure relationship in the infants' behavior (van IJzendoorn, Juffer, & Duyvesteyn, 1995).

Note that the interpretation of results in the Strange Situation is firmly linked to Western assumptions and values. In particular, Western society encourages children to go out and explore the world independently, to become assertive, and to develop a strong sense of self.

More collectivist cultures, such as Japan, China, and India, put greater emphasis on working with others and consider an assertive, self-oriented person immature and uncivilized. Typical Asian mothers hold their infants much of the day, keep them in bed with the parents at night, and do whatever they can to minimize stress in the infants. Many Asian mothers object to leaving their infants alone with a stranger, even for research purposes. If they are eventually persuaded to try it, the infants cry loud and long. By Western standards these children qualify as "anxiously attached," but the behavior really means something different in its cultural context (Rothbaum, Weisz, Pott, Miyake, & Morelli, 2000). One message is that we should be cautious about interpreting attachment results. Another is that we should be cautious about generalizing from one culture to another.

# CONCEPT CHECK

10. If a child in the Strange Situation clings tightly to the mother and cries furiously when she leaves, which kind of attachment does the child have? Does the child's culture affect the answer? (Check your answers on page 392.)

# Social Development in Childhood and Adolescence

The social and emotional development of children depends in part on how successful they are in forming friendships with other children (Figure 10.27). Some children are "popular" and have many friends and admirers. Others are "rejected" and avoided by most other children. Still others are "controversial" and liked by some but rejected by others. Controversial children generally have some social skills but an aggressive streak. In most cases a child's status as popular, rejected, or controversial is consistent from year to year (Coie & Dodge, 1983).

FIGURE 10.27 Children learn social skills by interacting with brothers, sisters, and friends close to their own age.

■ Adolescence is a Western state of mind. (a) American teenagers are financially dependent on their parents, but have the opportunity to spend much time in whatever way they choose. (b) In many non-technological societies, teenagers are expected to do adult work and accept adult responsibilities.

Adolescence begins when the body reaches *puberty,* the onset of sexual maturation. In North America the usual ages are around 9 to 13 in girls and about 10 to 16 in boys. The end of adolescence is harder to identify. Adolescence merges into adulthood, and adulthood is more a state of mind than a condition of the body. Some 12-year-olds act like adults, and some 30-year-olds act like adolescents.

Adolescence has sometimes been portrayed as a period of "storm and stress," characterized by moodiness, conflict with parents, and outbursts of risky behaviors. To some extent those trends reflect hormonal changes and brain maturation during adolescence. Even adolescent rats and other species show increased risk-taking and sensation-seeking behaviors (Spear, 2000). However, all this "storm and stress" also varies substantially among individuals, families, and cultures (Arnett, 1999). In many nontechnological societies, most teenagers are married and working. In effect they move directly from childhood into adulthood. In Western culture our excellent health and nutrition have gradually lowered the average age of puberty. However, for economic reasons we expect people to stay in school at least through their teenage years and probably well into their 20s, and we expect them to postpone marriage, family, and career until even later (Arnett, 2000). The consequence is a long period of physical maturity without adult status. Just imagine: Suppose our society decided that 4 years of college weren't nearly enough and people should stay in school until age 30, postponing marriage, children, and career decisions until even later. Would this policy bring out the best behavior in 25- to 30-year-olds?

In spite of it all, most adolescents survive and some even thrive. Not everyone will look back on the high school years as the best time of life, but most have a reasonably good adolescent experience.

## Identity Development

Adolescence is a time of "finding yourself," of determining "who am I?" or "who will I be?" It is when most people first construct a coherent "life story" of how they got to be the way they are and how one life event led to another (Habermas & Bluck, 2000).

In some societies most people are expected to enter the same occupation as their parents and to live in the same town. The parents may even choose their children's marriage partners. Western society offers young people far more choices: how much education to get, what job to seek, where to live, whether to marry and whom and when, what political and religious affiliation to adopt, and what standards to follow regarding sex, alcohol, and drugs. Remember from Chapter 8 that, even when people are given all the information they need to answer a question, they sometimes still rely on inappropriate heuristics and make illogical decisions. With regard to life's most important choices, people almost never have all the information. Having a great deal of freedom to choose a life path can be invigorating, but it can also be more than a little frightening.

An adolescent's *concern with decisions about the future and the quest for self-understanding* has been called an **identity crisis.** The term *crisis* implies more emotional turbulence than most adolescents actually experience. There are two major elements of identity development: whether one is actively exploring the issue and whether one has made any decisions (Marcia, 1980). We can diagram the possibilities using the following grid:

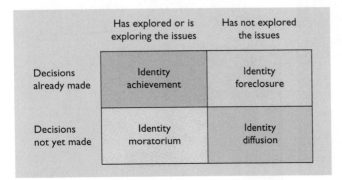

|  | Has explored or is exploring the issues | Has not explored the issues |
|---|---|---|
| Decisions already made | Identity achievement | Identity foreclosure |
| Decisions not yet made | Identity moratorium | Identity diffusion |

*Those who have not yet given any serious thought to making any decisions and who, in fact, have no clear sense of identity* are said to have **identity diffusion.** People in this stage are not actively concerned with their identity and are waiting until later to clarify the issues.

People in **identity moratorium** are *seriously considering the issues but have not yet made any decisions.* They experiment with various possibilities and imagine themselves in different roles before deciding which one is best.

**Identity foreclosure** is a state of *reaching firm decisions without having given them much thought.* For example, a young man might be told that he is expected to go into the family business with his father, or a young woman might be told that she is expected to marry and raise children. Decrees of that sort were once common in North America and Europe, and they are still common in many other societies today. Someone who accepts such decisions has little reason to explore the possibility of alternative identities.

Finally, **identity achievement** is *the outcome of having explored various possible identities and then making one's own decisions.* Identity achievement does not come all at once. For example, you might be fully decided about your career but not about marriage, or about marriage but not a career. It is also possible, even common, to reach identity achievement and then rethink some of those decisions years later.

## The "Personal Fable" of Teenagers

Answer the following items true or false:

- Other people may fail to realize their life ambitions, but I will realize mine.
- I understand love and sex in a way that my parents never did.
- Tragedy may strike other people, but probably not me.
- Almost everyone notices how I look and how I dress.

According to David Elkind (1984), teenagers are particularly likely to harbor such beliefs. Taken together, he calls

**FIGURE 10.28** Some teenagers seriously risk their health and safety. According to David Elkind, one reason for such risky behavior is the "personal fable," the secret belief that "nothing bad can happen to me."

them the "personal fable," the conviction that "I am special—what is true for everyone else is not true for me." Up to a point, this fable can help us to maintain a cheerful, optimistic outlook on life, but it becomes dangerous when it leads people to take foolish chances (see Figure 10.28).

For example, one study found that high school girls who were having sexual intercourse without contraception estimated that they had only a small chance of becoming pregnant through unprotected sex. Girls who were either having no sex or using contraception during sex estimated a much higher probability that unprotected sex would lead to pregnancy (Arnett, 1990). Because this was a correlational study, we do not know which came first—the girls' underestimation of the risk of pregnancy or their willingness to have unprotected sex. In either case the results illustrate the "it can't happen to me" attitude.

That attitude is hardly unique to teenagers, however. Middle-aged adults also overestimate their own chances of winning a lottery and regard themselves as more likely than other people to succeed on the job and as less likely than average to have an injury or a serious illness (Quadrel, Fischhoff, & Davis, 1993). That is, few people fully outgrow the "personal fable."

## Adulthood

From their 20s until retirement, the main concern of most adults is: "What will I achieve and contribute to society and my family? Will I be successful at the activities I have chosen?"

The young adult years begin with a flurry of major decisions about marriage, career, having children, where to live, and how to live. Whether middle age is a time of satisfaction and contentment or feeling stuck in a rut depends on the quality of those decisions.

## Job Satisfaction

Adults who are satisfied with their jobs are generally satisfied with their lives, and people who like their lives generally like their jobs (Keon & McDonald, 1982). Some adults manage to be happy even though they work at an unrewarding job, but the daily work routine is bound to influence their satisfaction with life.

How satisfied *are* most workers? The answer surely depends on the culture, but most research deals with the United States. The answer also depends on how the question is phrased. When pollsters simply ask, "Are you satisfied with your job?" most people say yes. But when pollsters ask, "If you could start over, would you seek the same job you have now?" most people say no (Weaver, 1980). Although most workers say they are "satisfied" with their jobs, they could easily imagine being *more* satisfied.

The level of satisfaction is lower on the average among young workers than among older workers (Pond & Geyer, 1991) (see Figure 10.29). One possible explanation is that older workers have better, higher-paying jobs. Another is that today's young people are harder to satisfy than past cohorts. Another possibility is that many young workers start in the wrong job and find a more suitable one later on. Still another is that many young people are still considering the possibility of changing jobs. By middle age most people have reconciled themselves to whatever jobs they have.

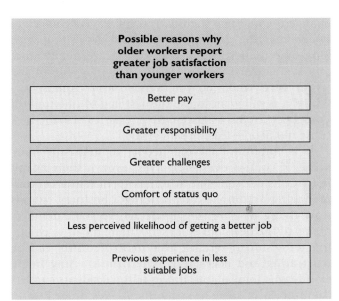

**FIGURE 10.29** Psychologists propose several reasons why most older workers report higher job satisfaction than younger workers do.

Your choice of career has a profound effect on the quality of your life. A student once told me that he found the courses in his major boring, but at least they were preparing him for a job. I cautioned him that he probably would find the job just as boring. Between the ages of 20 and 70, you will spend about half of your waking hours on the job—a long time to live with work you find unsatisfying.

## The Midlife Transition

No doubt you have heard people talk about a "midlife crisis." Few people experience enough disruption of life to qualify as a crisis, but many people do experience *a reassessment of personal goals,* which we call a **midlife transition.** As people realize that their lives are about half over, they talk less about their own futures. Many talk more about their children and take pride in their children's current and possible accomplishments (Rosenberg, Rosenberg, & Farrell, 1999).

Many middle-aged people also recontemplate their careers and other choices. Just as the adolescent identity crisis is a bigger issue in cultures that give young people many choices, the same is true for the midlife transition. If you lived in a society that dictated your role in life, you would have little reason to worry about the paths not taken because there *were* no other paths! People in Western society, however, have many choices and enter adulthood with high hopes. As they settle into a daily round of activities, they postpone some of their ambitions. While you are young, you dream of all the great things you will experience and accomplish. You plan to get an advanced degree, get a wonderful job, excel at it, marry a wonderful person, have marvelous children, become a leader in your community, run for political office, write a great novel, compose great music, travel the world. . . You know you are not working on all of your goals right now, but you can tell yourself, "I'll do it later." But at some point, perhaps around age 40, you realize that you are running out of "later." Even if some of your dreams are still achievable, time is passing: "What am I waiting for?"

People deal with their midlife transitions in many ways. Some abandon their unrealistic goals and set new goals more consistent with the direction their lives have taken. That is, they decide to do as well as possible at what they are already doing. Others decide that they have been ignoring dreams that they are not willing to abandon. They quit their unsatisfactory jobs and go back to school, set up a business of their own, or try something else they had always wanted to do. In one study middle-aged women who made major changes in their lives were happier and more successful than than those who didn't (Stewart & Ostrove, 1998). (Of course, we don't know whether the life changes made women happy and successful or whether happy and successful women are more likely than others to make changes.)

The least satisfactory outcome is to decide, "I can't abandon my dreams, but I can't do anything about them either. I can't take the risk of making a major change in my life, even though I am dissatisfied with it." People with that attitude become frustrated and discouraged.

The moral is clear: To increase your chances of feeling good in middle age and beyond, make the right decisions now. If there is something you really care about, such that you will feel sad if you don't at least try it, get started on it now. Take chances on yourself. If you fail, well, at least you won't always wonder what would have happened if you had tried. Besides, in the process of trying to do what you want, you might discover a related opportunity that you would not have found otherwise. And you never know: You just might succeed.

# CONCEPT CHECK

11. How does a midlife transition resemble an adolescent identity crisis? (Check your answer on page 392.)

# Old Age

People age in different ways. Some people, especially those with Alzheimer's disease or other serious ailments, deteriorate both intellectually and physically—in some cases quite rapidly. Other older people remain active and alert well into their 80s and 90s. The trend over the last few decades has been toward improved health, activity, and intellect in old age (Schaie, 1994).

One common concern of old age is to maintain a sense of dignity and self-esteem. Satisfaction in old age depends largely on how people lived when they were younger. Some older people can say, "I hope to continue living many more years, but even if I don't, I have lived my life well. I did everything that I really cared about." Others, unfortunately, say, "There is so much that I wanted to do but never did."

How well older people maintain their dignity also depends on how they are treated by their families, their communities, and their societies (Figure 10.30). Some cultures, including the people of Korea, observe a special ceremony to celebrate a person's retirement or 70th birthday (Damron-Rodriguez, 1991). African American and Native American families traditionally honor their elders, giving them a position of status in the family and calling on them for advice. Japanese families follow a similar tradition, at least publicly (Koyano, 1991). Dignity and self-esteem also depend on a feeling of having lived life well. To feel dignity in old age, spend your time wisely in your youth.

Older people make some different choices than young people, but their decisions are generally easy to understand. For example, suppose we ask young and

**FIGURE 10.30** In Tibet and many other cultures, children are taught to treat old people with respect and honor. Most older people say that maintaining a sense of dignity is very important to them.

old adults how they would prefer to spend this weekend, meeting interesting and exciting new people or visiting with friends they have known for years. Many young people opt for meeting the exciting stranger, but older people strongly prefer long-time friends. Why? You can probably identify with the older people if we change the question slightly. You still have a choice between meeting exciting new people or visiting with long-time friends, except that it is the weekend before you will move permanently to the other side of the world. Now whom do you want to visit? Almost certainly you will want to use this last opportunity to visit your best friends (Carstensen & Charles, 1998). In a sense old people feel the same way.

It is important for old people to maintain some sense of control over their lives, even if their health fails. Consider someone who has spent half a century managing a household or running a business, who is now living in a nursing home where staff members make all the decisions from scheduling meals to choosing television programs. This loss of control can be frustrating and degrading. When the nursing home staff leaves some of the choices to the residents and lets them perform some tasks by themselves, their health, alertness, and memory improve (Rodin, 1986; Rowe & Kahn, 1987).

# The Psychology of Facing Death

A man who has not found something he is willing to die for is not fit to live.

—MARTIN LUTHER KING, JR. (1964)

This is perhaps the greatest lesson we learned from our patients: LIVE, so you do not have to look back and say, "God, how I have wasted my life!"

—ELISABETH KÜBLER-ROSS (1975)

The worst thing about death is the fact that when a man is dead it's impossible any longer to undo the harm you have done him, or to do the good you haven't done him. They say: live in such a way as to be always ready to die. I would say: live in such a way that anyone can die without you having anything to regret.

—LEO TOLSTOY (1865/1978, p. 192)

We commonly associate death with older people, although people die at any age. Not only do we have trouble dealing with the prospect of our own death, but we also find it difficult to deal with the death of others. Each society provides standards and guidance for how people should deal with the death of a loved one, and Western society has changed its standards over the last century. In the 1800s the death of a spouse was expected to lead to a long-lasting, perhaps permanent grief. Today, society encourages people to return to normal functioning (Stroebe, Gergen, Gergen, & Stroebe, 1992). Most people need about a year to work through their grief, but bereavement varies greatly from one person to another.

If you like life, you don't want the people you care about to die, and you don't want to die yourself. In fact, just knowing that you will eventually die evokes distress bordering on terror. According to **terror-management theory,** *we cope with our fear of death by avoiding thinking about death and by affirming a world-view that provides self-esteem, hope, and value in life* (Pyszczynski, Greenberg, & Solomon, 2000). If someone simply reminds you that you are mortal, your probable reactions include self-assurances that you have many years to live, that your health is good, and that you will quit smoking, lose weight, or do something else to improve your health. You probably also will increase your ambitions temporarily, talking about the high salary you will earn and the exciting things you will do during the rest of your life (Kasser & Sheldon, 2000).

Still, even excellent health merely postpones death, so a reminder of death also redoubles people's efforts to defend a belief that life is part of something eternal. People with strong religious beliefs may believe in a continuation of their own lives after death. Others think in terms of how their lives contribute to their families, their countries, their professions, or something else that will last long after they are gone (Pyszczynski et al., 2000). In either case even a casual reference to death increases people's defenses of their beliefs, whatever those beliefs are.

IN CLOSING

## Social and Emotional Issues Through the Life Span

People confront crises and issues at different ages, but whatever you do at one age strongly affects your life at later ages. If you have bad experiences or make bad decisions at one age, you enter the next age with a backlog of problems. You could think of it as starting a new semester while trying to finish some incomplete courses from the previous semester. Don't wait until middle age to start deciding what is important or what you want to do with your life. Decide now and then live your life accordingly.

## Summary

■ Linda McCartney battled cancer for several years before her death in 1998. Many people with terminal illnesses come to a realistic acceptance of their coming death.

- **Cross-sectional and longitudinal studies.** Psychologists study development by means of cross-sectional studies, which examine people of different ages at the same time, and by means of longitudinal studies, which look at a single group of people at various times as they grow older. Each method has its advantages and disadvantages. (page 381)
- **Cohort effects.** In some cases a difference between young people and old people is not due to age itself but to a cohort effect: People born in one era differ from those born in a different era. (page 382)

- **Erikson's ages of development.** Erik Erikson described the human life span as a series of eight ages, each with its own social and emotional conflicts. (page 383)
- **Infant attachment.** Infants can develop several kinds of attachment to their mothers and other significant people in their lives, as measured in the Strange Situation. Different cultures have different values and assumptions about infant behavior, and the styles of attachment we discuss in Western society do not apply equally well in more collectivist societies. (page 384)
- **Adolescent identity crisis.** Adolescents have to deal with an identity crisis, the question "Who am I?" Many experiment with several identities before deciding which one seems right. (page 387)
- **Adults' concerns.** One of the main concerns of adults is balancing the competing demands of family and career. Many adults experience a midlife transition when they reevaluate their goals. (page 389)
- **Old age.** In old age maintaining dignity and independence is a key concern. (page 390)
- **Facing death.** People at all ages must face the anxieties associated with the inevitability of death. A reminder of death influences people to set higher goals and to defend their world views. (page 391)

# Answers to Concept Checks

7. Use a longitudinal study, which studies the same people repeatedly instead of comparing one cohort with another. (page 382)
8. With a longitudinal study, you would see clothing changes over time but you would not know whether the changes were due to age or to changes in society. A cross-sectional study would be better, but you would still have problems due to cohort effects. The older generation has probably always differed in its tastes from the current younger generation. (page 382)
9. Another possible explanation is that the first-year students who have the lowest grades (and therefore pull down the grade average for first-year students) do not stay in school long enough to become seniors. (page 382)
10. In the United States, this pattern would indicate an anxious or insecure attachment. In southeast Asia, however, this behavior is normal and we should beware of applying any of the labels that have been established for Western children. (page 386)
11. In both cases people examine their lives, goals, and possible directions for the future. (page 390)

# Temperament, Family, Gender, and Cultural Influences on Development

MODULE

10.4

*What factors influence development of personality and social behavior?*

If you had to describe yourself in as few words as possible, what would you write? You probably would mention your age, whether you are male or female, where you live, your family, where you work or go to school, and your main interests and activities. You might mention your political or religious affiliation and possibly your nationality or ethnic identity.

The point is this: You are a unique individual and you are also a member of various identifiable groups. Your group memberships mold some of what you think of yourself and how other people treat you. You are a complex product of both what you bring to a situation (your personality and temperament) and how a situation affects you. Let's begin with temperament.

## Temperament and Lifelong Development

People differ markedly in their **temperament**—their *tendency to be either active or inactive, outgoing or reserved,* and to respond vigorously or quietly to new stimuli. Would you rather go to a party where you will meet new people, or would you prefer to spend a quiet evening with a few old friends? Do you like to try a new, somewhat risky adventure, or would you prefer to watch while someone else tries it first? In general, are you more impulsive or more reserved than most of the people you know?

Now consider how you just described yourself: Is that the way you have always been, more or less? Or have

you changed considerably? Were you at one time a great deal more outgoing and adventurous, or more shy and reserved, than you are now?

According to the research, most people are fairly consistent in their temperament over long periods of time. We can begin to measure temperament even before birth. During the last 2 months before birth, infants differ substantially in the amount of kicking and other movements, and the ones that are most active before birth tend to remain the most active after birth (Eaton & Saudino, 1992).

Jerome Kagan and Nancy Snidman (1991) measured how often 4-month-old infants kicked, how often they cried, and how tense their hands were. A few months later, they examined the same infants' responses to mildly frightening situations. (For example, the experimenter might uncover a rotating toy, frown, and scream a nonsense phrase.) Infants who showed the most kicking, crying, and tension at the age of 4 months also tended to show the most fears at the ages of 9 and 14 months. That is, their temperaments were consistent from one test to the next.

## CONCEPT CHECK

12. Was Kagan and Snidman's study longitudinal or cross-sectional? (Check your answer on page 403.)

Infants who seldom kick, cry, or display fear are called "easy" or "uninhibited" (Thomas & Chess, 1980; Thomas, Chess, & Birch, 1968). Easy infants develop regular sleeping and eating habits, show interest in new people and new objects, and are easily comforted. The kicking, crying, highly fearful infants are, as you might guess, termed "difficult" or "inhibited." Their eating and sleeping habits are irregular, they show frequent signs of tension, and they are hard to comfort (Kagan, 1989). These infants are also more likely to contract various contagious diseases (Lewis, Thomas, & Worobey, 1990). Evidently, temperament is connected to all aspects of how the body functions. Children who are not especially easy or difficult can be classified as "average." Some children fit a special category called "slow to warm up": They withdraw from unfamiliar people and

■ Most people's temperaments remain fairly consistent over time. An outgoing, uninhibited child will probably continue to be outgoing and uninhibited for years, perhaps even into adulthood.

393

new experiences, but after repeated exposures they react positively. We could call them "shy."

How long do infant temperaments last? Infants identified as highly inhibited at the age of 21 months are more likely than others to end up as shy, quiet, nervous, and fearful 7½-year-olds (Kagan, Reznick, & Snidman, 1988). Similarly, many uninhibited infants develop into socially interactive, highly talkative 7½-year-olds. However, major changes occur, too; about 10% of *uninhibited* infants develop into shy 7½-year-olds (Kagan, 1989).

What causes differences in temperament? Both heredity and environment contribute. Monozygotic (identical) twins resemble each other in temperament more than dizygotic (fraternal) twins do (Matheny, 1989). Monozygotic twins reared in separate and apparently rather different environments still generally end up with similar temperaments (Bouchard, Lykken, McGue, Segal, & Tellegen, 1990). However, environmental factors obviously are important also; otherwise, monozygotic twins would always exactly match each other in temperament.

## CONCEPT CHECK

13. Why is it likely that temperament is one influence on behavior in the Strange Situation? (Check your answer on page 403.)

## The Family

Each of us starts life surrounded by family members, and in early childhood our parents and other relatives are the most important people in, our lives. How do those early family experiences mold our personality and social behavior?

### Birth Order and Family Size

You have no doubt heard people say that first-born children are more successful in schoolwork and career accomplishments than later borns. First borns also rate themselves as more ambitious, honest, and conscientious (e.g., Paulhus, Trapnell, & Chen, 1999). On the other hand, later-born children are said to be more popular, more independent, less conforming, less neurotic, and possibly more creative.

We have all heard those conclusions many times, and they are based on an enormous number of studies. However, nearly all of those studies have used flawed research methods (Ernst & Angst, 1983; Schooler, 1972), and an enormous number of flawed studies don't add up to a solid conclusion. The simplest and by far most common way to do the research is this: You ask some large number of people to tell you their birth order and something

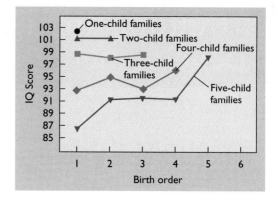

**FIGURE 10.31** Children from small families tend to score higher on IQ tests than children from large families. However, within a family of a given size, birth order is not related to IQ. If we combine results for families of different sizes, first borns have a higher mean score, but only because many of them come from small families. (Adapted from Rodgers et al., 2000)

else about themselves, such as their grade-point average in school. Then you measure the correlation between the two measurements. Do you see any possible problem here?

The problem is that many of the first borns come from families with *only* one child, whereas (of course) none of the third- or fourth-born children do. In general, high-IQ, highly ambitious parents are more likely to have only one child, whereas low-IQ parents are more likely to have larger families. Therefore, what appears to be a difference between first- and later-born children could really be a difference between small and large families.

The proper (but rare) way to do the study is to compare first- versus second-born children in only those families that had at least two children, first- versus third-born children in only those families with at least three children, and so forth. Figure 10.31 shows the results of one such study. As you can see, small families tend to have higher IQs than larger families. However, within a family of any given size, first borns do no better than later borns on the average (Rodgers, Cleveland, van den Oord, & Rowe, 2000). Similarly, if we look only at people from large enough families, we find no evidence that first borns have a different personality from the later borns.

"But wait," you may say. "The first born in my family does act different from the later borns, and most of the people I know agree that they see the same pattern in their own families." In a sense you are right: The first born takes more responsibility, identifies more with the parents, bosses the younger children around, and in many other ways acts differently from the later-born children *while at home*! However, the way people act at home is not necessarily the way they act among friends at school (Harris, 2000). A great deal of our behavior is specific to the situation, and the research finds no strong re-lationship between birth order and behavior outside the home.

 ONCEPT CHECK

14. Suppose someone found that last-born children (those with no younger brothers or sisters) do better in school than second-to-last borns. What would be one likely explanation? (Check your answer on page 403.)

## Effects of Parenting Styles

If and when you have children of your own, will you be loving and kind or strict and distant? Will you give them everything they want or make them work for rewards? Will you encourage their independence or keep them under your guidance as long as possible? Moreover, how much does your behavior matter?

Psychologists have done a great deal of research comparing parenting styles to the behavior and personality of the children. Much of this research is based on four parenting styles described by Diana Baumrind (1971):

**Authoritative parents:** These parents *set high standards and impose controls, but they are also warm and responsive*

■ Physical contact and cuddling are essential for the attachment that develops between parent and child. However, it is difficult to determine how much of attachment depends on the mother's behavior and how much depends on the infant's temperament.

*to the child's communications.* They encourage their children to set their own goals and to strive toward them. These parents set limits but adjust them appropriately as the child grows older.

**Authoritarian parents:** Like the *authoritative* parents, *authoritarian* parents set firm controls, but they tend to be *emotionally more distant from the child; they set rules without explaining why they are good rules.*

**Permissive parents:** Permissive parents are *warm and loving but undemanding.*

**Indifferent or uninvolved parents:** Some parents *spend little time with their children and do little more than provide them with food and shelter.*

Parenting styles are reasonably consistent within a family. For example, parents who are permissive with one child are usually permissive with their other children too (Holden & Miller, 1999). The research has found small but reasonably consistent links betweeen parenting style and children's behavior. For example, the children of authoritative parents are usually self-reliant, cooperate with others, and generally do well in school. Children of authoritarian parents tend to be law-abiding but distrustful and not very independent. Children of permissive parents are often socially irresponsible. Children of indifferent parents tend to be impulsive and undisciplined. However, although I said these results are "reasonably" consistent, they apply mostly to Americans of European ancestry. In other countries or ethnic groups, these parental behaviors link with somewhat different outcomes in the children (Darling & Steinberg, 1993).

Furthermore, the interpretation of the results is not as easy as it may appear. We can be tempted to draw cause-and-effect conclusions, and over the years many psychologists have. For example, we might assume that parental indifference *leads to* impulsive, out-of-control children. However, as Judith Rich Harris (1998) pointed out, other explanations are possible. Maybe impulsive, hard-to-control children cause their parents to withdraw into indifference. Or maybe the parents and children share genes that lead to uncooperative behaviors in both. Similarly, the kindly behaviors of authoritative parents could encourage well-mannered behaviors in their children, but it is also possible that these children were well behaved from the start, thereby encouraging kindly, understanding behaviors in their parents. The problem is that we cannot draw cause-and-effect conclusions from correlational studies between parents and children who share genetics as well as environment.

A better approach is to study adopted children, who are genetically unrelated to the parents rearing them. The results of such studies surprise most people: Most aspects of personality show almost no correlation at all between adoptive parents and their adopted children (Heath, Neale, Kessler, Eaves, & Kendler, 1992; Loehlin, 1992;

Viken, Rose, Kaprio, & Koskenvuo, 1994). For that reason Harris (1995, 1998) has argued that family life has little lasting influence on most aspects of personality (except for behaviors shown specifically at home). Much of personality variation depends on genetic differences, and the rest of the variation, she argues, might reflect peer influences—that is, the other children we grew up with and the neighborhood where we lived (Caspi, Taylor, Moffitt, & Plomin, 2000).

As you can imagine, Harris's argument did not immediately become widely popular. Psychologists who had spent a career studying parenting styles were not pleased to be told that their results were inconclusive. Parents were not pleased to be told that they had less influence on their children than they had thought.

Harris (2000), however, chose her words carefully. She certainly did not say that it makes no difference how you treat your children. For one thing, obviously, if you treat your children badly, they won't like you! Also, parents control where the children live and therefore influence their choice of peers, and parents influence some aspects of life that peers usually don't care about, such as religion, exposure to music lessons, and what spices to put on food. Parents have other influences too, even if they are statistically small, and indeed, Harris may have overstated her case (Vandell, 2000). What is clear, however, is that psychologists need to reconsider the conclusions they have long accepted about the influence of parents on their children's behavior.

FIGURE 10.32 In many cultures it has long been the custom for a mother to leave her infant for much of the day with friends, relatives, and other children.

 **C** ONCEPT CHECK

15. Why is a correlation between parents' behavior and children's behavior undecisive concerning how parents influence their children? Why would a correlation between adoptive parents' behavior and that of their adopted children provide more useful information? (Check your answer on page 403.)

## Parental Employment and Child Care

Many people assume that the "normal" way to rear infants is for the mother to stay with them full-time because that custom was prevalent in much of North America and Europe for many years. However, child-rearing customs vary greatly from one culture to another, one era to another, even one social class to another (see Figure 10.32). In many subsistence cultures, a mother returns to her usual tasks of gathering food and so forth shortly after giving birth, leaving her infant most of the day with other women, relatives, and older children (McGurk, Caplan, Hennessy, & Moss, 1993). For example, in the Efe culture of Africa, a mother stays with her infant only about half of the day, but the infant is seldom alone. Within the first few months, the infant will establish strong attachments

to several adults and children (Tronick, Morelli, & Ivey, 1992). In wealthy families in Europe, it has long been the custom for "nannies" (paid caregivers) to take care of the children for most of the day. In short, if we considered all the people who ever lived anywhere, what we consider the "traditional" way of rearing children might be a minority method.

Still, many psychologists in Europe and North America developed a theoretical belief that healthy emotional development required an infant to establish a strong attachment to a single caregiver—ordinarily, the mother. When more and more families began placing infants in day care so that both parents could return to work shortly after their infant's birth, a question arose about whether those children would be psychologically harmed.

Many studies have compared children who stayed with their mothers and those who entered day care early. The studies examined attachment (as measured by the Strange Situation or in other ways), adjustment and well-being, play with other children, social relations with other adults, and intellectual development. What results would you expect?

The mean results have indicated that children develop satisfactorily, both intellectually and socially, if they receive at least adequate day care (Scarr, 1998). According to most measures, the children in day care were virtually the same as those reared at home (Erel, Oberman, & Yirmiya, 2000). Probably most of us would have expected to see bigger differences, but the results haven't supported that prediction.

About the only difference that stands out in the data is a surprising one: Children who start day care after age 2½ show some insecure attachment behaviors, whereas those who start day care before age 1 show more favorable attachment reactions (Erel et al., 2000). We might have guessed that starting day care very early would be more of a problem, but it is not. Perhaps those who start day care early get used to it, whereas those who start later have more trouble adjusting to the change.

Undoubtedly, the quality of day care makes a difference to children's behavior, although most studies have not found a big difference except in cases where the child comes from a disadvantaged home. Evidently, development is satisfactory when either home life or day care is good; problems arise when both are bad. When children from disadvantaged homes experience good day care (with a consistent, affectionate staff and adequate facilities), they develop *better* than if they had stayed at home (McGurk et al., 1993; Scarr, Phillips, & McCartney, 1990). Children from deprived homes who experience poor day care, which is often all the parents can afford, are at a definite disadvantage.

## Nontraditional Families

Just as Western society has defined "traditional" child care as an infant staying with the mother, it considers a "traditional" family to be a mother, a father, and their children. A "nontraditional" family is, therefore, anything else.

Psychologists have studied the personalities of children who were reared by unmarried mothers (Weissman, Leaf, & Bruce, 1987), gay or lesbian couples (Patterson, 1994), and families where the mother works full-time and the father stays home with the children (Parke, 1995). Parenting styles do differ a bit; for example, fathers generally play with their children more, talk to them less, and tell them more facts with less praise (Leaper, Anderson, & Sanders, 1998). However, according to the available data, the number of caregivers, their gender, and their relationship to the child have little measurable effect on the child's ultimate personality development (Silverstein & Auerbach, 1999). What matters most is that the child have a stable, favorable emotional relationship with at least one adult. In cases where the children of a single parent do have emotional problems, the main cause of the problems usually is either poverty (common among single mothers) or the emotional turmoil associated with the parents' divorce.

By now you probably see a pattern: Children's personality development has little demonstrable relationship to the style of parenting, whether the child stays home in early life or goes to day care, or the number or gender or sexual orientation of the parents. Apparently, within a fairly wide range of experiences, children develop according to their own agendas, and the adults around them have less influence than we once imagined.

■  Many children today are reared by a single parent. Some are reared primarily by the father or grandparents. Some are reared by gay parents. The research says that who rears the child has little influence on long-term personality development, if the caretakers are loving and dependable.

## Parental Conflict and Divorce

At an earlier time in the United States, divorce was unusual and considered shameful. When Adlai Stevenson was defeated in the presidential campaign of 1952, one explanation was that American voters would never elect a divorced candidate as president. By 1980, when Ronald Reagan was elected president, hardly anyone was concerned about his divorce and remarriage. By then divorce was simply a fact of life.

An estimated 75% of African American children and 38% of European American children will experience the divorce of their parents before the children reach the age of 16. Most of those children show a variety of academic, social, and emotional problems compared to children in two-parent households. One reason is that the children of divorced families receive less attention and suffer greater economic hardship. The main reason, however, is that children in divorced families often endure the prolonged conflict and hostility between their parents (Amato & Keith, 1991). If the divorce takes place while the children are still too young to realize what is happening, the effects are milder (Tschann, Johnston, Kline, & Wallerstein, 1990).

Mavis Hetherington and her associates have conducted longitudinal studies of middle-class children and their families following a divorce (Hetherington, 1989). Compared to children in intact families, those in divorced families are more likely to have conflicts with their parents and with other children. They pout and seek attention, especially in the first year after a divorce. The boys in particular become aggressive, both at home and at school (Figure 10.33). Generally, distress was greatest if a mother who had not worked before the divorce took a job immediately afterward—often by economic necessity. The children in such families felt that they had lost both parents.

In families where the mother remarried, the daughters were often indifferent or hostile to the stepfather and showed poorer adjustment than children of mothers who did not remarry (Hetherington, Bridges, & Insabella, 1998). Many of the girls rejected every attempt by their stepfathers to establish a positive relationship until eventually the stepfather simply gave up (Hetherington, 1989).

"Complex" or "blended" stepfamilies are composed of a mother and her children from a previous marriage plus the father and his children from a previous marriage. Such families have some special problems and difficulties, and child–parent conflicts are common. Interestingly, the stepchildren within such families usually get along with one another fairly well. In fact, most children quarrel with their biological brothers and sisters more than with their stepsiblings (Hetherington, Henderson, & Reiss, 1999).

Hetherington's studies concentrated on European American middle-class children, and the results are different for other cultures. Divorce is more common in African American families, but in most cases it is more accepted and less stressful (Fine & Schwebel, 1987). Many African American families ease the burden of single parenthood by having a grandmother or other relative share the child care. As in European American families, the more upset the mother is by the divorce, the more upset the children are likely to be (R. T. Phillips & Alcebo, 1986).

Exceptions can be found to almost any generalization about the effects of divorce on children, however (Hetherington, Stanley-Hagan, & Anderson, 1989). Some children show emotional distress for 1 or 2 years and then gradually feel better. Others continue to act depressed 5 or 10 years after the divorce. A few seem to do well for a while and then show signs of distress years later, especially during adolescence. Other children are amazingly resilient throughout their parents' divorce and afterward. They keep their friends, they do all right in school, and they maintain good relationships with both parents. Generally, these children were well-adjusted before the divorce, and their parents displayed a minimum of hostility toward each other (Hetherington, 1989; Kline, Tschann, Johnston, & Wallerstein, 1989).

Given the emotional trauma commonly associated with divorce, should parents stay together for the children's sake? The answer depends on the parents' conflicts. Children do not fare well if their parents are constantly fighting. Indeed, most children (especially boys) begin to show signs of distress years *before* their parents divorce, perhaps in response to the parental conflict they already see (Cherlin et al., 1991).

**FIGURE 10.33** Many sons of divorced parents go through a period when they act out their frustrations by starting fights.

careers in mathematics, physical sciences, and engineering (Benbow, Lubinski, Shea, & Efekhari-Sanjani, 2000).

 You might try this task and compare results with your friends: Here is a drawing of a bottle half full of water and then the same bottle tilted. Draw the water level in the tilted bottle.

Most studies—although I have never been able to see this effect with my own students—report that most U.S. men draw the water level parallel to the ground, as shown below in the drawing on the left, whereas most women draw it partly or entirely parallel to the bottom of the bottle, as shown in the other two drawings (Vasta & Liben, 1996). (The one on the left is correct, of course.)

Many researchers have speculated that men evolved greater attention to spatial relationships because men in early hunter-gatherer societies had to find their way home from hunting, whereas women spent more time close to home (Silverman et al., 2000). However, we know little for sure about prehistoric human life. Also, male rats have been reported to have better spatial learning abilities than female rats (Williams, Barnett, & Meck, 1990), so the difference is probably not specific to humans or to anything about our early culture.

## Differences in Self-Esteem

Do you think highly of yourself, do you think of yourself as a loser, or as somewhere in between? According to a great many studies, men on the average report slightly higher self-esteem than women (Kling, Hyde, Showers, & Buswell, 1999). The difference is largest during adolescence.

What does this difference mean? The answer is uncertain. Part of the problem is that psychologists use many measurements of self-esteem, some of which have uncertain reliability and validity. Moreover, consider some example questions on self-esteem questionnaires (Blascovich & Tomaka, 1991):

• At times I think I'm no good at all.
• I'm a failure.

■ Although young children quickly become aware of the boy–girl distinction, their understanding of gender roles develops gradually. In their early years it is common for boys and girls to try on the clothes and participate in activities of the other gender.

# Gender Influences

How would you be different if you had been born female instead of male or male instead of female? On the average men fight more often than women and with less provocation. Men also swear more. Most women know more than men do about flowers. Men and women generally carry books and packages in different ways, men to the side and women in front. Men are generally more likely to help a stranger change a flat tire, but women are more likely to provide long-term nurturing support (Eagly & Crowley, 1986). As a rule the more pairs of shoes you own, the more likely you are female. The list of miscellaneous differences could go on and on. The more difficult question is why men and women differ. Is it because of biological influences, social and cultural differences, or both? On that question people have many firm opinions, but not much basis for certainty.

## Cognitive Differences

Two cognitive differences are reasonably consistent. First, beginning at an early age, females tend to perform better on certain aspects of language use, especially language fluency (Maccoby & Jacklin, 1974). Second, men generally do better on difficult mathematical and spatial tasks (Collins & Kimura, 1997) and are more likely to enter

■ Many studies report that teenage girls have low self-esteem. However, given the nature of those questionnaires, the results could be interpreted as indicating high goals and dissatisfaction with achieving anything less than the best.

- I feel that I have a number of good qualities.
- I am able to do things as well as most other people.

If you said "true" to the first two and "false" to the second two, I would agree that you had a low opinion of yourself. But now consider these items:

- There are lots of things about myself I'd change if I could.
- I'm often sorry for the things I do.
- I'm not doing as well in school as I'd like.
- I wish I could change my physical appearance.

A "true" answer on any of those items would count as a point toward low self-esteem. But do they really indicate low self-esteem, or high goals? Someone who says

"true" may be striving for self-improvement. In short, when teenage boys express higher self-esteem than girls, it is not clear whether we should try to help the girls improve their self-esteem or worry about boys who have set low goals for themselves!

## Differences in Social Situations

One idea you have encountered repeatedly in this chapter is that the results of any study depend on details of the method. The same is true for gender differences. If you watch boys and girls at a playground, you see large, consistent differences in their play. So you try to set up some laboratory test to measure those differences. You test boys and girls one at a time, and you are stunned to find almost no male–female difference. What is wrong with your test? Maybe nothing. Many of the differences between males and females emerge only in a social context (Maccoby, 1990). For example, boys get together with other boys and girls get together with other girls, and the social influence brings out behaviors you would not see when you examine each person individually (Figure 10.34).

Girls sometimes play competitive games, but they are more likely than boys to spend long times at quiet, cooperative play. They take turns; they present their desires as "suggestions" instead of demands; they exchange compliments; and they generally try to avoid hurting each other's feelings.

Meanwhile, boys compete with each other almost constantly, even when they are just talking: They shout orders, they interrupt, they make threats and boasts, and they exchange insults. When a group of elementary school boys play a game, sooner or later they have a dispute about the rules. Even after they work out a com-

**FIGURE 10.34** One girl tested alone behaves about the same as one boy tested alone. But when boys play together, they show off to one another and to other observers (a); girls play more cooperatively (b).

a

b

promise and resume the game, they continue screaming, "You cheater!"

What do you suppose happens when boys and girls play together? If they are working on a task that requires cooperation, few sex differences are evident (Powlishta & Maccoby, 1990). However, in unsupervised situations the boys often dominate and intimidate the girls. In some cases the boys take control and the girls simply watch (Maccoby, 1990).

When boys grow up, do they change their ways? Not entirely. Deborah Tannen (1990) reports one episode at a college basketball game: At the University of Michigan at the time, the custom was for students to ignore the seat numbers on their tickets and take seats on a first-come, first-served basis. One night several men from the visiting team, Michigan State, tried to go to the seats listed on their tickets, only to find University of Michigan students, both men and women, already seated there. The Michigan State students asked the others to leave; the University of Michigan men replied rudely, and the dispute quickly escalated to insults. The women were mortified with embarrassment.

Within a few minutes, however, the Michigan State men settled into neighboring seats, and soon the two groups of men were happily discussing basketball strategies. The women didn't understand why the men had screamed insults in the first place or how they had made friends so quickly afterward.

Do the differences between men and women reflect biological, possibly genetic, influences? Are they the product of the way we rear children and the social roles we assign men and women? If so, *why* does our culture rear children that way and assign those roles to men and women? The answers are undoubtedly complex (Bussey & Bandura, 1999). Biological influences combine with early experiences in ways that are almost impossible to untangle. One of the biggest social influences is the playground. Parents who try to rear their children in a nonsexist way find their efforts thwarted by the social influence of other children.

## *Male–Female Relationships*

When boys and girls become young men and women, romantic interests draw them together, but both are ill prepared to deal with the other sex. Men are used to demanding what they want; women are used to cooperating. Men worry about their status in relation to other men; women often fail to understand these status contests. When women discuss their problems, they expect their listeners to express sympathy; men often fail to understand this need. Here are examples of the resultant misunderstanding (Tannen, 1990):

• A man invites an out-of-town friend to spend the night in the guest bedroom. The man's wife is upset that her husband did not check with her before inviting his friend.

He replies that he would feel embarrassed to say, "I have to ask my wife first."

• A woman asks her husband to get their VCR to record a TV movie. The husband says this particular kind of VCR plays tapes but cannot record. The woman then asks their next-door neighbor to check the VCR. He too tells her the VCR cannot record. The husband resents his wife's implication that he was incompetent.

• A woman who has had breast surgery tells her husband she is unhappy about the scar left by the surgery. He replies, "You can have plastic surgery . . . ." She is upset by the implication that he doesn't like the way she looks. He replies that he doesn't care about the scar; he was trying to help because *she* said she was unhappy.

Are male–female relationhips always like this? Of course not. Differences *on the average* between men and women do not apply to every individual. For any behavior the distribution for men completely overlaps that for women, as in the following diagram. The averages are just guidlines and should never be taken as an excuse to form an opinion about some individual without first knowing that individual well.

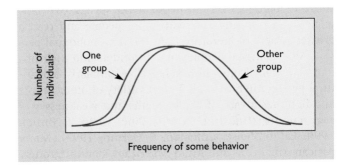

## Ethnic and Cultural Influences

Membership in a minority group molds a child's development in two major ways: First, the customs of the minority group may in fact differ from those of other groups. Second, members of a minority group are affected by the attitudes of other people, who may treat them differently or expect certain behaviors from them simply because they are members of that minority group.

Immigrants to the United States or any other country undergo a period of **acculturation,** *a transition from feeling part of the culture of their original country to the culture of the country they enter.* Acculturation is gradual; people sometimes require a generation or more before they or their descendants feel fully comfortable in a new culture. Most recent immigrants to the United States have come from Latin America or Asia, and most of the children have been highly motivated to learn English and to achieve beyond

■ Many immigrants are bicultural, having reasonable familiarity with two sets of customs. These immigrant children attend middle school in Michigan. Some immigrant children don't speak English and some have never attended a school anywhere.

the level of their parents. Delinquency, crime, and drug and alcohol abuse are less common in recent immigrants than in other U.S. residents (Fuligni, 1998).

Although most immigrant parents want their children to become successful members of their new culture, they also want them to maintain the best parts of their old cultures, such as values of hard work, cooperation, and generosity (Fuligni, 1998). The alternative to full assimilation is **biculturalism,** *the ability to alternate between membership in one culture and membership in another.* For example, people who settle in an Italian American community speak Italian and follow Italian customs in their home neighborhood but speak English and follow U.S. customs elsewhere. The advantages of biculturalism are similar to those of bilingualism: Someone who speaks two languages can communicate with more people and read a greater variety of literature than can a monolingual person. Also, bilingual people come to understand their primary language from a new perspective. Similarly, a bicultural person interacts with a great variety of other people and becomes aware of the strengths and weaknesses of each culture (Harrison, Wilson, Pine, Chan, & Buriel, 1990; LaFromboise, Coleman, & Gerton, 1993). Many African Americans and Asian Americans identify strongly with their ethnic groups, live in a neighborhood populated mostly by others of the same group, and rely on the help of an extended family, but also join the melting pot culture at school, on the job, and in other settings.

At least to a small extent, nearly all of us learn to function in a variety of subcultures. Unless you live in a small town where everyone has the same background, religion, and customs, you have to learn to adjust what you say and do in different settings and with different groups of people. However, the transitions are more noticeable and more intense for ethnic minorities.

## IN CLOSING
### Understanding and Accepting Many Ways of Life

Each of us can easily fall into the trap of thinking that our own way of growing up and relating to other people is the "right" or "normal" way. In fact, people differ substantially in their social development; we have examined some of

the major reasons for this difference—temperament, family influences, gender, and ethnic and cultural identity. As a society we are beginning to recognize and appreciate the resulting diversity of behavior that these influences create.

## Summary

- **Temperament.** Even infants who are only a few months old show clear differences in temperament, their own characteristic way of reacting to experiences. Temperament remains fairly consistent as a person grows older. (page 393)

- **Birth order.** Most studies comparing first-born versus later-born children confound the effects of birth order with the effects of family size. If we disregard families with only one child, first borns and later borns behave about the same way when they are outside the home. (page 394)

- **Parenting styles.** Parenting style correlates with the behavior of the children. For example, caring, understanding parents tend to have well-behaved children. However, most studies do not separate the effects of social influences from genetics. Adopted children usually do not resemble their adoptive parents' personalities. Judith Rich Harris has therefore argued that personality and social behavior depend mostly on genetics and peer influences, with little family influence in most cases. (page 395)

- **Nontraditional child care.** Children who spend much time early in day care develop about the same as those reared at home by a parent. A child's normal personality and social development require at least one caring adult, but the number of caregivers and their gender and sexual orientation apparently matter little. (page 396)

- **Effects of divorce.** Children of divorcing families often show signs of distress, sometimes even before the divorce. The distress is generally more marked in European American families than in African American families. (page 398)

- **Gender influences.** Women tend to do better than men on certain aspects of language, whereas men excel on difficult mathematical and spatial problems. Social differences between males and females are small on the average when people are tested one at a time. However, in social settings males tend to associate with other males while females associate with females. Males tend to be more competitive, sometimes aggressively so. All differences are on the average; individuals can differ greatly from the averages. (page 399)
- **Ethnic and cultural differences.** People also differ because of ethnic and cultural influences. Acculturation is the process of transition from one culture to another. Many people can function successfully as members of two or more cultures simultaneously. (page 401)

## Answers to Concept Checks

**12.** Kagan and Snidman's study was longitudinal; they studied the same children at different ages. (page 393)

**13.** Temperament is a measure of how people react to novel stimuli, and the Strange Situation is also a test of reaction to novel stimuli. The difference is that the Strange Situation focuses specifically on social stimuli, particularly the presence or absence of the mother or some other important person in a child's life. (page 394)

**14.** An only child is a last born as well as a first born. A large sample of last borns will include many children from single-child families, which are often characterized by high IQ and ambitions. Second-to-last borns necessarily come from larger families. (page 395)

**15.** Children can resemble their parents' behavior either because of genetics or social influences. Adoptive children do not necessarily resemble their adopted parents genetically, so any similarity in behavior would reflect environmental influences. Of course, the question would remain as to whether the parents influenced the children or the children influenced the parents. (page 396)

CHAPTER ENDING
## *Key Terms and Activities*

## Key Terms

**accommodation:** Piaget's term for the modification of an established schema to fit a new object or problem (page 368)

**acculturation:** a transition from feeling part of the culture of one's original country to the culture of the country that one enters (page 401)

**assimilation:** Piaget's term for the application of an established schema to new objects or problems (page 368)

**attachment:** a long-term feeling of closeness between people, such as a child and a caregiver (page 384)

**authoritarian parents:** those who exert firm controls on their children, generally without explaining the reasons for the rules and without providing much warmth (page 395)

**authoritative parents:** those who are demanding and impose firm controls, but who are also warm and responsive to the child's communications (page 395)

**autonomy versus shame and doubt:** the conflict between independence and doubt about one's abilities (page 383)

**basic trust versus mistrust:** the conflict between trusting and mistrusting that parents and other key figures will meet one's basic needs; the first conflict in Erikson's eight ages of human development (page 383)

**biculturalism:** the ability to alternate between membership in one culture and membership in another (page 402)

**cohort:** a group of people born at a particular time (as compared to people born at different times) (page 382)

**conservation:** the concept that objects retain their weight, volume, and certain other properties in spite of changes in their shape or arrangement (page 369)

**cross-sectional study:** a study of groups of individuals of different ages all at the same time (page 381)

**dishabituation:** an increase in a previously habituated response as a result of a change in the stimulus (page 362)

**ego integrity versus despair:** the conflict between satisfaction and dissatisfaction with one's life; the final conflict in Erikson's eight ages of human development (page 384)

**egocentric:** the inability to take the perspective of another person, a tendency to view the world as centered around oneself (page 373)

**equilibration:** the establishment of harmony or balance between assimilation and accommodation (page 368)

**fetal alcohol syndrome:** a condition marked by stunted growth of the head and body; malformations of the face, heart, and ears; and nervous system damage, including seizures, hyperactivity, learning disabilities, and mental retardation (page 360)

**fetus:** an organism more developed than an embryo but not yet born (from about 8 weeks after conception until birth, in humans) (page 359)

**generativity versus stagnation:** the conflict between a productive life and an unproductive one (page 384)

**habituation:** a decrease in a person's response to a stimulus after it has been presented repeatedly (page 362)

**identity achievement:** the outcome of having explored various possible identities and then making one's own decisions (page 388)

**identity crisis:** concerns with decisions about the future and the quest for self-understanding (page 387)

**identity diffusion:** the condition of having not yet given any serious thought to identity decisions and having no clear sense of identity (page 388)

**identity foreclosure:** the state of having made firm identity decisions without having thought much about them (page 388)

**identity moratorium:** the state of seriously considering one's identity without yet having made any decisions (page 388)

**identity versus role confusion:** the conflict of discovering who one is or will be (page 383)

**indifferent or uninvolved parents:** those who pay little attention to their children beyond doing what is necessary to feed and shelter them (page 395)

**industry versus inferiority:** the conflict between feelings of accomplishment and feelings of worthlessness (page 383)

**initiative versus guilt:** the conflict between independent behavior and behavior inhibited by guilt (page 383)

**intimacy versus isolation:** the conflict between spending one's life with a partner and living alone (page 383)

**longitudinal study:** a study of a single group of individuals over time (page 381)

**midlife transition:** a time of goal reassessment (page 389)

**moral dilemma:** a problem that pits one moral value against another (page 376)

**object permanence:** the concept that objects continue to exist even when one does not see, hear, or otherwise sense them (page 363)

**operation:** according to Piaget, a mental process that can be reversed (page 369)

**permissive parents:** those who are warm and loving but undemanding (page 395)

**prenatal development:** development before birth (page 359)

**preoperational stage:** according to Piaget, the second stage of intellectual development, in which children lack operations (page 369)

**schema** (pl.: **schemata**): an organized way of interacting with objects in the world (page 368)

**selective attrition:** the tendency of some kinds of people to be more likely than others to drop out of a study (page 382)

**sensorimotor stage:** according to Piaget, the first stage of intellectual development; an infant's behavior is limited to making simple motor responses to sensory stimuli (page 368)

**stage of concrete operations:** according to Piaget, the third stage of intellectual development; children can deal with the properties of concrete objects but cannot readily comprehend hypothetical or abstract questions (page 370)

**stage of formal operations:** according to Piaget, the fourth and final stage of intellectual development; in this stage, people deal with abstract, hypothetical situations, which demand logical, deductive reasoning and systematic planning (page 370)

**Strange Situation:** procedure in which a psychologist observes an infant's behavior in an unfamiliar room at various times as a stranger enters, leaves, and returns, and the mother enters, leaves, and returns (page 385)

**temperament:** people's tendency to be either active or inactive, outgoing or reserved, and to respond vigorously or quietly to new stimuli (page 393)

**terror-management theory:** proposal that we cope with our fear of death by avoiding thinking about death and by affirming a world-view that provides self-esteem, hope, and value in life (page 391)

**zone of proximal development:** the distance between what a child can do on his or her own and what the child can do with the help of adults or older children (page 372)

**zygote:** a fertilized egg cell (page 359)

## Suggestions for Further Reading

Elkind, D. (1984). *All grown up and no place to go.* Reading, MA: Addison-Wesley. An account of the problems that teenagers and young adults face.

Hobson, R. P. (1993). *Autism and the development of mind.* Hove, East Sussex, UK: Erlbaum. Despite the title, this book is only partly about autism; it is about how children come to understand other people and to communicate with them.

Kail, R. V., & Cavanaugh, J. C. (2000). *Human development* (2nd ed.). Belmont, CA: Wadsworth. A good textbook on all aspects of developmental psychology.

Tannen, D. (1990). *You just don't understand.* New York: William Morrow. A popular book that discusses the various reasons that men and women often fail to understand one another.

## Web/Technology Resources

American Demographics

**www.demographics.com/**

*American Demographics Magazine* uses U.S. Census Bureau statistics to describe consumer trends for business leaders. Search the archives using such terms as *divorce, diversity, personality, gender,* or whatever else is of interest to find articles about trends in these topics.

### The Child Psychologist

**www.childpsychology.com/**

Rene Thomas Folse's site focuses on "Specific Disorders and Other Reasons for Concern" about the behavior of children and on "Treatment, Resources, and Remediation." There are links to information about several specific diagnostic tests used with children.

### American Academy of Child and Adolescent Psychiatry

**http://www.aacap.org**

Check this site for information about common psychological disorders of children and teenagers.

### The Nurture Assumption

**home.att.net/~xchar/tna/**

Judith Rich Harris maintains this Web page about her controversial book on the importance of peers and the relative unimportance of parenting styles.

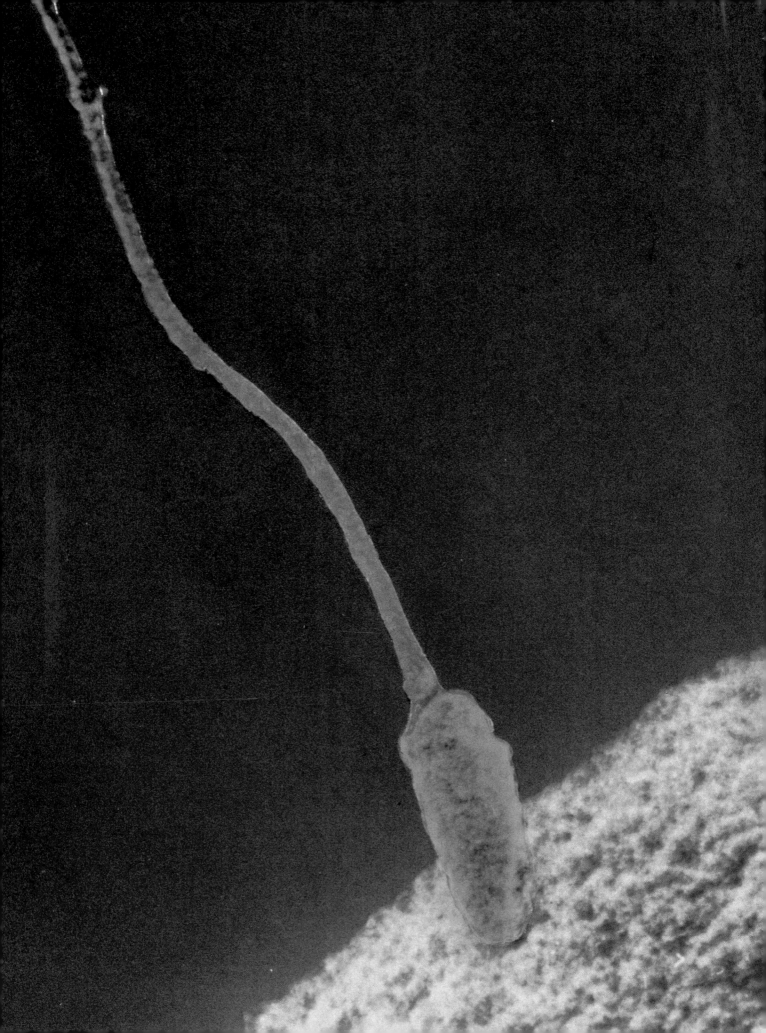

# Motivation

**11**
CHAPTER

uring the summer of 1996, the proprietors of London's Kew Gardens announced that they had a most unusual plant, native to Sumatra and rarely cultivated elsewhere, that was about to bloom for the first time since 1963. If you had been in London then, with enough time available, would you have made a point of visiting Kew Gardens to witness this rare event? No? What if I told you that it was a truly beautiful flower? With a lovely, sweet smell? Still no?

Then what if I told you the truth—that it has the nastiest, most obnoxious smell of any flower on Earth—that the name of the flower is the *stinking lily* because it smells like a huge, week-old carcass of rotting meat or fish and that one whiff of it can make a strong person retch. Now would you want to visit the flower? If so, you would have to wait in line. When Kew Gardens announced that the stinking lily was about to bloom, an enormous crowd gathered, forming a line that stretched to the length of a soccer field (MacQuitty, 1996). (The first day that the flower bloomed, it had hardly begun to stink. Disappointed visitors vowed to return later.)

Human motivations are surprising, puzzling, and often seemingly illogical. Psychologists have made progress in understanding complex motivated behaviors, but much still remains to be learned. We begin this chapter with an overview of some general principles of motivation. Then we shall explore hunger, sexual activity, and striving for achievement—three examples of motivations that are central to human life—and interesting examples that illustrate how our biology interacts with our social setting.

■ This flower is seldom cultivated outside its native Sumatra for good reasons. Would you stand in line to visit it?

# General Principles of Motivation

*What is motivation?*

*What is the difference between motivated and nonmotivated behaviors?*

You are sitting quietly, reading a book, when suddenly you hear a loud noise. You jump a little and gasp. Was your action motivated? "No," you say. "I jumped involuntarily." Now I tell you that I want to do a little experiment. As soon as you hear me tap my pencil, you should try to jump and gasp just as you did the first time. I tap my pencil, and sure enough, you jump and gasp. Was that action motivated? "Yes," you reply.

So, what appears to be approximately the same behavior can be motivated at one time and unmotivated at another time. Can we trust people to tell us whether their behavior was motivated or unmotivated? Not always. Someone accused of murder says, "I didn't mean to kill him. It was an accident." Your friend, who promised to drive you somewhere and then left without you, says, "I didn't do it on purpose. I just forgot." Maybe so and maybe not. How can we determine whether a behavior is motivated or accidental? Intentional or unintentional? We need a clear understanding of how motivated behaviors differ from unmotivated behaviors.

## Properties of Motivated Behavior

What, if anything, do various types of motivated behavior have in common? The foremost characteristic is that they are goal directed. Motivated individuals continue working until they reach their goals, if necessary setting up subgoals that they need to achieve on the way to their final goals (Austin & Vancouver, 1996). For example, if you were motivated to improve your house, you might make a list of the items that need repair and the tools you need.

Another characteristic of motivated behaviors is that they vary from time to time and from one individual to another under the influence of both internal (biological) and external (social) controls. For example, you wear different clothes from one day to the next, and you wear different clothes from your roommate.

To determine whether a particular behavior is motivated, as opposed to automatic or reflexive, an observer needs to watch someone in a variety of circumstances. If the individual varies the behavior and persists until reaching a goal, then the behavior is motivated, not reflexive.

All of this is good in principle. However, nearly all human behaviors depend on a combination of motivation and reflex. Even intentional acts such as walking depend on leg reflexes that maintain balance. Eating is motivated but requires reflexes of digestion. Fixating your eyes on a target is motivated but is also controlled by reflexive movements of eye muscles.

**A STEP FURTHER**
*Motivations and Reflexes*

A frog flicks its tongue at a passing insect, captures it, and swallows it. The behavior satisfies the frog's need for food, so we might guess that it is motivated. However, the behavior appears to be as constant as a reflex. How might you determine whether this behavior is motivated?

## Views of Motivation

What is motivation? Let's try some definitions: "Motivation is what activates and directs behavior." That description fits many examples well enough, but it also fits some nonmotivational phenomena. For example, light activates and directs the growth of plants, but we would hardly say that light motivates plants.

"Motivation is what makes our behavior more vigorous and energetic." The problem with that definition is that some people are strongly motivated to lie motionless for hours on end. Also, coffee can make you more energetic without changing your motives.

How about this: "Motivation is what changes one's preferences or choices"? The idea is right, but we would first have to define preference and choice.

Frankly, it is hard to state precisely what we mean by motivation, and psychologists have repeatedly altered their views. By considering one theory after another, they have seen the shortcomings of each and have in the process developed some idea of what motivation is and is not.

**409**

## Motivation as an Energy

*Motivation,* which comes from the same root as *motion,* is literally something that "moves" a person. So we might think of it as a type of energy. According to Konrad Lorenz (1950), a pioneer in the study of animal behavior, animals engage in instinctive acts when specific energies reach a critical level. For example, a male stickleback fish has no specific energy for mating outside the breeding season, so it will not respond sexually. At the start of the breeding season, it has a small amount of mating energy, and it will then court female stickleback fish and attack male stickleback fish. At the height of the breeding season, it has a great amount of mating energy, so it will court females vigorously; it may even respond sexually to a piece of wood painted to resemble a female of its species.

Figure 11.1 illustrates Lorenz's model. A specific kind of energy builds up in the reservoir and flows into the tray below. The outlets in that tray represent ways of releasing this energy. If conditions are right, the energy is released through the lowest outlet—for example, mating with a normal partner. If that outlet is blocked and energy continues to build up, the energy will spill through one of the higher, less preferred outlets. However, Lorenz's theories reflect an obsolete conception of how the nervous system works. He believed that every impulse to action had to be carried out so that if one response was blocked, the energy would activate something else. We now know that an individual can simply inhibit the impulses toward disadvantageous behavior.

## Drive Theories

Related to the instinctive energy theories are theories that describe motivation as a **drive,** *a state of unrest or irritation that energizes one behavior after another until one of them removes the irritation* (Hull, 1943). For example, when you get a splinter in your finger, the discomfort motivates you to try various actions until you remove the splinter.

According to the *drive-reduction theory* that was popular among psychologists of the 1940s and 1950s, animals including humans strive to reduce their needs and drives as much as possible. They eat to reduce their hunger, drink to reduce their thirst, have sexual activity to reduce their sex drive, and so forth. This view implies that we all strive for a state where all our needs have been met, at which time we would become inactive. The primary shortcoming of this view is that, in fact, most people seek variety and activity in life. We do not seek a condition of nonstimulation.

Another flaw in this drive theory is that it ignores the role of external stimulation. For example, your interest in food depends not only on hunger (an internal drive) but also on what foods are available. Similarly, interest in sex depends partly on an internal drive and partly on the presence of a suitable partner.

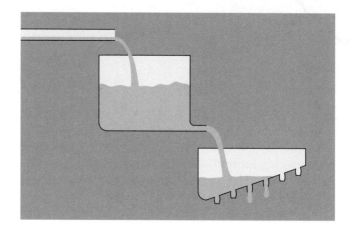

**FIGURE 11.1** According to Konrad Lorenz, energy (represented as a fluid) builds up in a "reservoir" in the brain and needs to be discharged. For example, you might build up a sexual-behavior–specific energy. If that energy cannot discharge through its normal outlets (because they are blocked), the energy builds up until it discharges through some less normal outlet. (After Lorenz, 1950)

## Homeostasis

One important advance upon the idea of drive reduction is the concept of **homeostasis,** *the maintenance of an optimum level of biological conditions within an organism* (Cannon, 1929). The idea of homeostasis recognizes that we are motivated to seek a state of equilibrium, which is not zero stimulation. For example, people maintain a nearly constant body temperature, fighting against both increases and decreases in temperature. We also work to maintain a fairly steady body weight, a nearly constant amount of water in the body, a moderate amount of sensory experience, and so on.

Unlike a rock, which remains static only because nothing is acting upon it, the homeostasis of the body is more like a spinning top; someone must apply additional energy from time to time to keep it spinning. For example, we maintain constant body temperature partly by shivering, sweating, and other involuntary physiological responses and partly by putting on extra clothing, taking off excess clothing, or finding a more comfortable location.

Human motivated behaviors differ from the actions of a thermostat in one important regard: Our behavior often anticipates future needs. For example, you might eat a large breakfast one morning even though you are not terribly hungry, just because you know you are going to be too busy to stop for lunch. If you are angry or frightened, you begin to sweat even before you begin the vigorous actions that might heat your body. (We call this phenomenon a "cold sweat.") Thus, a fruitful way of describing motivation is that it maintains current homeostasis and anticipates future needs to maintain future homeostasis (Appley, 1991).

Still, even that conception of motivation overlooks the power of new stimuli to arouse motivated behaviors. For example, nonhungry people may eat or drink just to be sociable or because someone has offered them something especially tasty.

## Incentive Theories

Why do people ride roller coasters? It is doubtful that they have any special need to go thundering down a steep decline. Or suppose you have just finished a big meal and someone offers you a slice of a very special cake. You might eat it but not because you need it. Evidently, motivation includes more than the internal forces that push us toward certain behaviors; it also includes **incentives**—*external stimuli that pull us toward certain actions.*

Most motivated behaviors are controlled by a combination of drives and incentives. You eat because you are hungry (a drive) and because you see appealing food in front of you (an incentive). You jump into a swimming pool on a hot day to cool your body (a drive) and because you will enjoy splashing around in the water with friends (an incentive).

## Intrinsic and Extrinsic Motivations

Similar to the distinction between drives and incentives, psychologists also distinguish between intrinsic and extrinsic motivations. An **intrinsic motivation** is *a motivation to do an act for its own sake;* an **extrinsic motivation** is *based on the reinforcements and punishments that the act may bring.* For example, if you eat because the food tastes good, you are following an intrinsic motivation; if you eat something just to please the cook, you are following an extrinsic motivation. Most behaviors follow a combination of both kinds of motivation. For instance, an artist paints for the joy of creation (intrinsic) and for the hope of profit (extrinsic). You read this book partly because

**FIGURE 11.2** Monkeys learned to remove the pin, hook, and hasp in that order to open this device. When they started receiving a raisin instead of opening it just for fun, their performance deteriorated.

you enjoy reading it (I hope), partly because you want to get a good grade in the course, partly because you know you will feel guilty if you spend a lot of money on a college education and then fail your courses, and partly because you saw your roommate studying a textbook and decided to follow the example. We seldom do anything for only one reason.

Does a combination of intrinsic and extrinsic motivations lead to more persistent and effective performance than, say, an intrinsic motivation alone? Not always. In a classic study, researchers let four monkeys play with a device like the one in Figure 11.2. To open it, a monkey had to remove the pin, lift the hook, and then lift the hasp in that order. The monkeys played with the device over a period of 10 days. They received no reinforcements; they played with it apparently just for the fun of it (an intrinsic motivation). Then the device was placed over a food well where the monkeys were accustomed to finding a raisin (an extrinsic motivation). If they opened the device, they could get the raisin. Suddenly, their ability to open the device deteriorated. Instead of patiently removing the pin, the hook, and the hasp as before, they attacked the hasp forcefully. They took longer to open the device for food than they had for play. Later, when they were offered the device by itself with no food available, they played with it less than before (Harlow, Harlow, & Meyer, 1950). Evidently, opening the device for food had made it work and not play.

Might the same principle apply to human behavior? In a typical experiment to test this idea, college students were asked to try to arrange seven plastic pieces with complex shapes to match figures in a drawing. At one point halfway through the experiment, students in the experimental group were paid $1 for each correct match. (Students in the control group did not know that the experimental group was being paid.) Then the experiment continued without pay for anyone. After pay was suspended, the experimental group decreased their efforts (Deci, 1971). Results such as these illustrate the **overjustification effect**: *When people are*

■  We eat because of intrinsic and extrinsic motivations. Even when hunger (an intrinsic motivation) is satisfied, we eat because of the taste and the desire to socialize (extrinsic motivations).

*given more extrinsic motivation than necessary to perform a task, their intrinsic motivation declines.* The same principle works for both rewards and punishments. That is, you could work harder than usual to get a reward or to avoid a punishment. In either case, after you finished what you had to do, you probably would stop working on the task, even if it was something you previously enjoyed (Ryan & Deci, 2000).

One explanation for the overjustification effect is that after working extra hard on a task, you are simply tired of it. However, even after a rest period, people still often show a decreased interest in the task. According to another explanation, people ask themselves, "Why am I doing this?" They then answer, "It's not because I enjoy the task. It's because I'm being paid." (Or "Because I'll be punished if I stop.") Therefore, they no longer do it for the sheer joy of it.

The overjustification effect, like various other psychological principles, applies under some conditions but not others, and it is sometimes a weak effect (Eisenberger & Cameron, 1996). Paying people with money, food, or other tangible rewards sometimes decreases their intrinsic motivation, but praising them does not (Deci, Koestner, & Ryan, 1999).

Table 11.1 summarizes four views of motivation.

## CONCEPT CHECK

1. Suppose you want to encourage your younger cousin to continue taking piano lessons. Based on the overjustification effect, would it be wise to pay him for practicing? (Check your answer on page 414.)

# Types of Motivation

How many motivations do people have? They are motivated to obtain food, water, shelter, and clothing; to have social contact with others; to smell the stinking lily in Kew Gardens . . . . The list could go on and on. Can we group these motivations into a few coherent categories?

## *Primary and Secondary Motivation*

One way to categorize motivations is to distinguish primary motivations from secondary motivations. **Primary motivations**—such as the search for food and water—are *processes based on biological needs.* **Secondary motivations** *develop as a result of specific learning experiences,* presumably because the secondary motivation has in the past led to the satisfaction of a primary motivation. Primary and secondary motivations are analogous to the unconditioned and conditioned reinforcers that we considered in Chapter 6.

Presumably, we learn secondary motivations because they help us to satisfy primary motivations. For example, we learn to have a desire for money (a secondary motivation) because it helps us to obtain food, water, and shelter (primary motivations). Often, however, a secondary motivation seems to develop a momentum of its own, thus becoming apparently independent of the original primary motivations associated with it. For example, many people start a coin or stamp collection because they think it might be worth something and eventually start spending money to add to the collection for its own sake. Some people try to perform spectacular feats to get into

**TABLE 11.1** Four Views of Motivation

| View | Basic Position | Major Weaknesses |
|---|---|---|
| **Instinct theories** According to instinct theories, motivation is a kind of energy that builds up until it finds a release. | Motivations are energies that accumulate; each energy specifies a preferred action, although it might spill over into a less preferred outlet. | Based on obsolete view of the nervous system. |
| **Drive theories** According to drive theories, motivation is an irritation that continues until we find a way to reduce it. | Motivations are based on needs or irritations that we try to reduce; they do not specify particular actions. | Implies that we always try to reduce stimulation, never to increase it. Also overlooks importance of external stimuli. |
| **Homeostasis (plus anticipation)** Homeostasis is the process of maintaining a variable such as body temperature within a set range. | Motivations tend to maintain body states near some optimum intermediate level. They may react to current needs and anticipate future needs. | Overlooks importance of external stimuli. |
| **Incentive theories** Incentives are external stimuli that attract us even if we have no biological need for them. | Motivations are responses to attractive stimuli. | Incomplete theory unless combined with drive or homeostasis. |

■ This man is trying to set the world record for being covered by bees. The desire for fame is an amazingly strong motivator.

the *Guinness Book of World Records*. Why? To achieve fame? In any case they sometimes lose sight of the fact that they are devoting more effort than the fame or any other reward is likely to be worth. One man holds the record for the longest fingernails, at 41.6 inches and still growing; another man has been growing his fingernails for 30 years in hopes of eventually catching up and surpassing the current champion. Other people have performed such feats as smoking 114 cigarettes in 3 minutes, push-

ing a pea with their nose for 3 miles, French-kissing snakes, and allowing their body to be covered with a record number of scorpions—all in failed attempts to get into the *Guinness* book (Spaeth, 1995). (The Guinness people refuse to publicize such records because they don't want to encourage self-destructive behaviors.)

## CONCEPT CHECK

**2.** Is your interest in graduating from college a primary motivation or a secondary motivation? (Check your answer on page 414.)

## Maslow's Hierarchy of Needs

Abraham Maslow (1970) attempted to bring some organization to the listing of human motivations, including both primary and secondary motivations. According to Maslow, our behavior is governed by a **hierarchy of needs,** *an organization from the most necessary and insistent to the ones that receive attention only when all others are under control.* The most basic are the physiological needs for food, drink, oxygen, and warmth, as shown at the bottom level of Figure 11.3. According to Maslow, these basic needs ordinarily take priority over all others (Figure 11.4). For example, people who are gasping for breath will not take time out to do something else until they have satisfied their need for oxygen. Once people have satisfied all of their physiological needs, they seek to satisfy their safety needs, such as security from attack and avoidance of pain. When those needs are satisfied, they proceed to the needs for love and belonging—making friends and socializing with them. Next come the needs for esteem, such as gaining prestige and a feeling of accomplishment. At the apex of Maslow's hierarchy is the need for **self-actualization,** *the need to achieve one's full potential.*

Maslow's theory is appealing because it recognizes that the various motivations are not equal. When they conflict, people will generally give priority to the tasks most necessary for survival. However, there is no evidence to support the idea that motivations fall into five distinct categories (Wahba & Bridwell, 1976). That is, the differences between the need for oxygen and the need for food (both basic physiological needs) are as great as the differences between the need for love and the need for self-esteem. Furthermore, people sometimes work to satisfy higher level needs before they satisfy lower level needs. Even when you are ravenously hungry, you might skip a meal to be with someone you love, to study for a test, or to accept an award. Martyrs have willingly sacrificed their lives to advance a political or religious cause. Depending on the circumstances, almost any motivation may take priority over the others, at least temporarily.

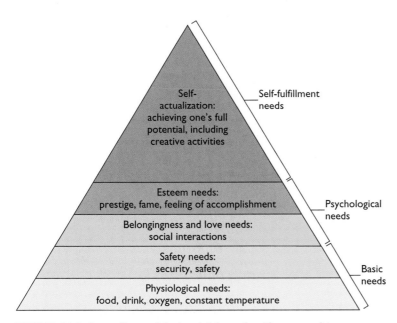

**FIGURE 11.3** According to Maslow's hierarchy, if you are thirsty, you will want to drink something to satisfy that basic need. If you fulfill all your basic needs, you move on to your psychological needs and then your self-fulfillment needs. However, some people do sacrifice their comfort, security, and even health to strive for artistic, athletic, or other accomplishments.

**FIGURE 11.4** According to Maslow's hierarchy, we concentrate first on the lowest level of needs until we meet them. Thus, an impoverished and homeless person is unlikely to devote much effort to creative endeavors. (Some exceptions to this rule do occur, however.)

## IN CLOSING

### *Many Types of Motivation*

People frequently puzzle over why a person did something. For example, why would someone stand in line for hours to smell a stinking lily? We almost exclusively puzzle over behaviors that contribute little or nothing to survival. That is, we do not bother to ask why someone gasps for breath, eats, drinks, or runs away from a tiger. For the unusual behaviors such as trying to smell a stinking lily, people seldom have one simple motivation. More often, it is a combination: curiosity, the desire to have something unusual to talk about with friends, perhaps even a desire for fame of a very local variety.

## Summary

- **Characteristics of motivated behaviors.** Motivated behaviors persist until the individual reaches the goal. They are controlled by internal and external forces and by biological and social forces. Motivated behaviors vary from time to time, from situation to situation, and from person to person. (page 409)
- **Motivation as energy or drive reduction.** Psychologists have sometimes viewed motivation as an energy that must be used up in one way or another or as a process that persists until all drives are reduced. Each of these views has serious limitations. (page 410)
- **Motivation as a way of maintaining homeostasis.** To a large degree, motivated behaviors tend to maintain body conditions and stimulation at a near-constant, or homeostatic, level. This view of motivation can account for much behavior, if we also assume that behaviors anticipate future needs instead of just

responding to current needs. However, the homeostatic view of motivation overlooks the role of external stimuli for arousing behavior. (page 410)
- **Motivation as incentive.** Motivations are partly under the control of incentives—external stimuli that pull us toward certain actions. Both drives and incentives control most motivated behaviors. (page 411)
- **Intrinsic and extrinsic motivations.** People and animals engage in some actions because the actions themselves are interesting or pleasing (intrinsic motivation). Providing a physical reinforcement (extrinsic motivation) for the actions sometimes backfires by reducing the interest or pleasure they provide. (page 411)
- **Types of motivations.** Psychologists have made several attempts to list or categorize various motivations. One prominent attempt, offered by Abraham Maslow, arranged needs in a hierarchy ranging from basic physiological needs at the bottom to the need for self-actualization at the top. His claim that people satisfy their lower needs before their higher needs does not apply in all cases, however. (page 412)

## Answers to Concept Checks

1. According to the overjustification effect, you should not pay him enough that he starts practicing just for the reward. However, verbal praise would be good. (page 412)
2. Your interest in graduating from college is a secondary motivation because it is something you had to learn to value. Such secondary motivations can become very strong. (page 413)

# Hunger Motivation

*How do we decide which foods to eat and how much to eat?*

Small birds eat only what they need at the moment, storing almost no fat at all. The advantage is that they remain light and fast enough to escape predators. The disadvantage is that they can starve to death if they have trouble finding food for even a short time. Bears follow a different strategy. When nuts and berries are in season, they find abundant food, but at other times they go days or even weeks with nothing to eat. Their evolved strategy is to eat as much as they can whenever they can and then live off their stored fat.

Few humans eat as gluttonously as bears, but we too have apparently evolved a strategy of eating more than we need at the moment in case food is scarce tomorrow. After all, famine has been a frequent occurrence in human history, and sometimes life has been "survival of the fattest." Today, however, prosperous countries have abundant, tasty food every day, and the result is that most of us overeat (Pinel, Assanand, & Lehman, 2000).

How much we eat and what and when we eat also depend on social motives (Figure 11.5). Imagine that you visit your boyfriend or girlfriend's family and you want to make a good impression. "Dinner's ready!" someone calls. You go into the dining room and find a huge meal spread out before you, which your hosts clearly expect you to enjoy. Do you explain that you are not hungry because you already made a pig of yourself at lunch? Probably not.

## Motives in Food Selection

Have you ever wondered how people first figured out which foods were edible? It was easy for you and me; our parents and other people told us what to eat, and we did not have to try all the weeds in the field to decide which ones were good. Our parents learned from their parents and they from their parents, but long ago somebody had to discover what was edible by trial and error. Moreover, people had to discover how to prepare many foods that are inedible when raw (Rozin, 1996). For example, cassava, a root native to South America, is poisonous unless someone washes and pounds it for 3 days. Can you imagine discovering that fact? Someone had to say, "Sure, everyone else who ever ate this plant died, but I bet that if I wash and pound it for 3 days, then it will be okay." Cashews are covered with a thin membrane that must be carefully removed; anyone who touches it will react as if he or she had touched poison ivy. American corn (maize) has a deficit of certain nutrients and beans are deficient in other nutrients, but corn and beans together make a good combination—as the Native Americans discovered long ago.

We learn our food choices largely by learning what *not* to eat. Toddlers around the age of 1½ will try to eat almost anything they can fit into their mouths (Figure 11.6). Up to age 7 or 8, about the only reason children give for refusing to eat something is that they think it would taste bad (Rozin, Fallon, & Augustoni-Ziskind, 1986). As they grow older, they cite more and more reasons for accepting certain foods and rejecting others. As with other motivations, food selection depends on a combination of physiological, social, and cognitive factors.

**FIGURE 11.5** Mealtime is more than just an opportunity to satisfy hunger: It is an occasion to bring the family and sometimes friends together, to share a pleasant experience, to discuss the events of the day, and even to pass on cultural traditions from one generation to the next. We expect family members to participate in these meals, even if they are not hungry.

**FIGURE 11.6** Infants and young children will try to eat almost anything. As they grow older, they learn to avoid foods for reasons other than just taste.

## Food Selection Based on Taste

Some taste preferences are present at birth. Infants readily consume sweet liquids but spit out anything bitter or sour. Humans and most other mammals like the taste and texture of fats (Schiffman, Graham, Sattely-Miller, & Warwick, 1998). People also have temporary taste cravings, most of which we cannot explain. For example, about one-fourth of women report a strong craving for sweets, especially chocolate, around the time of menstruation. We might guess the craving has something to do with hormones or discomfort, but hormonal treatments don't alter the craving and neither do tranquilizers (Michener, Rozin, Freeman, & Gale, 1999).

One craving that we can explain, at least in some cases, is the craving for salty tastes. Many years ago a young child showed a strong craving for salt. As an infant he licked the salt off crackers and bacon but refused to eat the food itself. One of the first words he learned was *salt*. He put a thick layer of salt on everything he ate, and sometimes he swallowed salt directly from the shaker. When deprived of salt, he ate almost nothing and began to waste away. At the age of 3½, he was taken to the hospital and fed the usual hospital fare. He soon died of salt deficiency (Wilkins & Richter, 1940).

The reason was that he had defective adrenal glands. These glands secrete hormones that enable the body to retain salt (Verrey & Beron, 1996). He craved salt because it was being excreted so rapidly from his body. (We are often told to limit our salt intake for health reasons, but too little salt can also be dangerous.)

Research on animals confirms that as soon as animals, including humans, become salt deficient, they show a heightened preference for salty tastes (Rozin & Kalat, 1971). People who have lost large quantities of salt as a result of bleeding or heavy sweating often express a craving for salt. Apparently, salty foods taste better to salt-deficient people and animals than they do to others (Jacobs, Mark, & Scott, 1988). In short, changes in body chemistry can alter a person's motivation to choose a particular food.

## Preference for Familiar Foods

People from different parts of the world have different taste preferences. Contrast, for example, Greek, Mexican, and Chinese cuisines. Do the different cultural food preferences relate in any way to differences in people's sense of taste? Evidently not. Taste buds are about the same throughout the world (Laing et al., 1993). People's food preferences depend mainly on familiarity (Rozin, 1996).

Cuisine is one of the most stable and defining features of any culture. In one study researchers interviewed Japanese high school and college students who had spent a year in another country as part of an exchange program. The researchers asked the students how much they enjoyed their experience. Their satisfaction had little relationship to the educational system, religion, family life, recreation, or dating customs of the host country. The main determinant was the food: Students who could sometimes eat Japanese food had a good time. Those who could not became unhappy and homesick (Furukawa, 1997).

## Learned Associations with Food

As mentioned in Chapter 6, animals associate foods with the gastrointestinal consequences of eating them. Humans do, too. When you eat something and later feel sick, you may form a strong aversion to the food, especially if it was unfamiliar. It doesn't matter whether you consciously think the food made you ill. If you eat something at an amusement park and then go on a wild ride and get sick, you may never again like that food (Figure 11.7). Even though you know the ride was at fault, an area deep in your brain still associates the food with the sickness.

People can also develop preferences by associating a food with another food that they already enjoy (Capaldi, 1996). For example, parents who want their child to learn to like broccoli might mix a little broccoli with cheese or some other food that the child already likes. Later they could gradually reduce the amount of cheese.

People also reject safe foods because of the very idea of what they are (Rozin & Fallon, 1987; Rozin, Millman, & Nemeroff, 1986). In the United States, most people refuse

FIGURE 11.7 People associate what they eat, especially unfamiliar foods, with the way they feel afterward. If you ate corn dogs and cotton candy and then got sick on a wild ride, something in your brain would blame the food, regardless of what you think consciously. Ordinarily, however, this kind of learning teaches us to avoid harmful substances.

to eat dog, cat, or horse meat. Many vegetarians consider any kind of meat disgusting and are distressed even to watch other people eat it. The longer people have been vegetarians, the more firmly they tend to regard meat-eating as not only undesirable but even immoral (Rozin, Markwith, & Stoess, 1997).

How would you like to try the tasty morsels described in Figure 11.8? Most people find the idea of eating insects

---

**Crispy Cajun Crickets**

Adapted from a recipe in the *Food Insects Newsletter*, March 1990

Tired of the same old snack food? Perk up your next party with Crispy Cajun Crickets ("pampered" house crickets, *Acheta domesticus*, available from Flucker's Cricket Farm, P.O. Box 378, Baton Rouge, LA 70821, 800-735-8537).

1  cup crickets
1  pinch oatmeal
4  ounces butter, melted
  Salt
  Garlic
  Cayenne

1. Put crickets in a clean, airy container with oatmeal for food. After one day, discard sick crickets and freeze the rest.
2. Wash frozen crickets in warm water and spread on a cookie sheet. Roast in a 250-degree oven until crunchy.
3. Meanwhile heat butter with remaining ingredients and sprinkle this sauce on crickets before serving.

Yield: 1 serving

FIGURE 11.8 People avoid some potential foods because they are disgusted by the very idea of eating them. For example, most Westerners would refuse to eat insects, despite assurances that most are nutritious and harmless.

 Different cultures have different taboos. Here is an assortment of insect and reptile dishes. (Yum, yum?)

repulsive, even if the insects were sterilized to kill all the germs (Rozin & Fallon, 1987). Would you be willing to drink a glass of apple juice after a dead cockroach had been dipped into it? What if the cockroach had been carefully sterilized? Many people not only refuse to drink that glass of apple juice but say they have lost their taste for apple juice in general (Rozin, Millman, & Nemeroff, 1986).

## CONCEPT CHECK

**3.** Why do many menstruating women crave potato chips? (Check your answer on page 428.)

# The Physiological Mechanisms of Hunger

Hunger is a partly homeostatic drive that keeps fuel available for the body. Specialized mechanisms in your brain monitor how much fuel is available; when supplies begin to drop, the brain triggers behaviors that lead to eating. But how does your brain know how much fuel is available and how much more you should eat?

The problem is more complex than keeping enough fuel in your car's gas tank. When the fuel gauge shows that the tank is running low, you fill it with gas. By contrast, keeping track of the fuel in your stomach does not tell you how much more you need. In addition to the fuel in your stomach and intestines, a fair amount of fuel is present in every cell of your body and more is circulating in your blood, ready to enter cells that need it. Still more fuel is stored in the fat cells, available to be converted into a form that can enter the bloodstream. If necessary, your body can break down muscle tissues to provide additional fuel. Your car will stop within seconds after it uses up all the fuel in the gas tank, whereas your body can keep going for days or weeks on an empty stomach.

How do you know how much to eat, considering that each meal has a different density of nutrients from any other? Fortunately, you don't have to get it exactly right. You have one set of mechanisms that control short-term changes in hunger and a separate set of long-term mechanisms that act as a correction if your short-term mechanisms cause you to eat too much or too little.

## Short-Term Regulation of Hunger

Under most circumstances the main factor responsible for ending a meal is distension of the stomach and intestines; we feel full because the digestive system is literally full (Seeley, Kaplan, & Grill, 1995). We also monitor how much we have eaten (Spiegel, 1973); with familiar foods we calibrate approximately how much nutrition we are getting per amount swallowed (Deutsch & Gonzalez, 1980), and we have receptors in the intestines that detect the sugars in the food (Lavin et al., 1996).

The main factor responsible for the onset of hunger and the start of a meal is a drop in how much glucose enters the cells, but the control of glucose is a complicated story (Figure 11.9). **Glucose,** *the most abundant sugar in your blood, is an important source of energy for all parts of the body and almost the only source for the brain.* The body can make glucose from almost any nutrient. Excess blood glucose can be converted into fats and other stored fuels, and stored fuels can be converted back into blood glucose when necessary. The flow of glucose to or from the blood depends on two hormones released by the pancreas: insulin and glucagon.

**Insulin** is *a hormone that increases the flow of glucose and several other nutrients into body cells.* At the beginning of a meal, before the nutrients have even started entering the blood, the brain sends messages to the pancreas to increase its secretion of insulin. Insulin promotes the

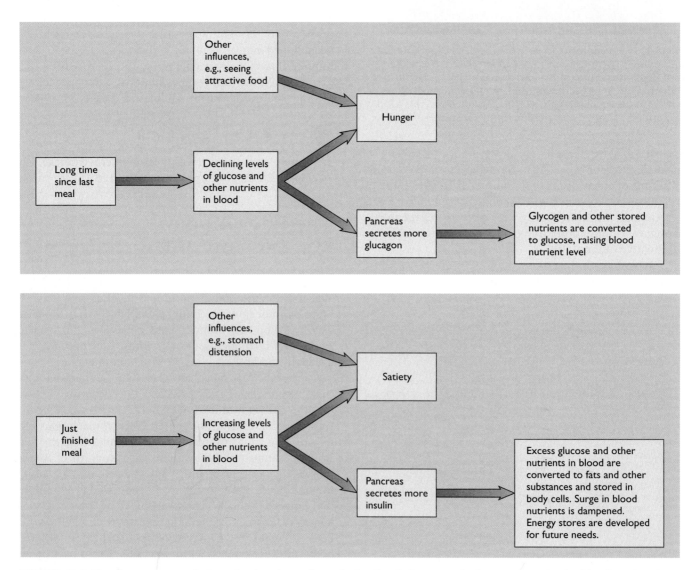

**FIGURE 11.9** The short-term regulation of eating depends on the levels of glucose and other nutrients in the blood; it also depends on the appearance and flavor of the food, social influences, and so forth. Varying secretions of the hormones insulin and glucagon help to keep the blood nutrient levels reasonably constant.

movement of glucose and other nutrients out of the blood and into both the cells that need fuel (such as muscles and neurons) and the cells that store the nutrients as fats and other supplies. As the meal continues, the digested food enters the blood, but almost as fast as it enters, insulin helps to move excess nutrients out of the blood and into the liver or fat cells. In that manner the insulin holds down the surge of glucose and other nutrients in the blood (Woods, 1991). Later, long after the meal, when the nutrient supply in the blood starts to drop, the pancreas reduces its secretion of insulin and increases

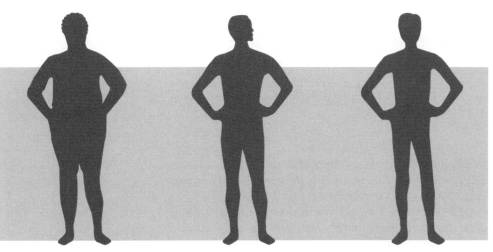

**High insulin**
Food is stored as fat. Little glucose in blood. Appetite increases. Weight increases.

**Lower insulin**
Fat supplies are converted to glucose. Appetite is lower.

**Very low insulin**
Glucose cannot enter cells. Appetite is high, but much of nutrition is excreted. Weight decreases.

**FIGURE 11.10** How insulin affects glucose, appetite, and weight.

its secretions of **glucagon,** *a hormone that helps to convert stored energy supplies back into blood glucose.*

However, consider what happens if insulin levels stay constantly high or low: When insulin levels are consistently low, as with the medical condition diabetes, nutrients enter the cells very slowly (Figure 11.10). People with untreated diabetes eat without satisfying their hunger because so little glucose enters the cells. It does not even enter the fat cells, so people with diabetes eat a great deal without gaining weight (Lindberg, Coburn, & Stricker, 1984). They simply excrete much of what they eat.

At the opposite extreme, if insulin levels are consistently high, nutrients enter the cells easily, but most of the glucose is converted to fats and stored in fat cells. Because the insulin level remains high, the food stored in fat cells simply stays there instead of being mobilized back into blood glucose. Consequently, blood glucose levels begin to decline again soon after each meal *(hypoglycemia)* and appetite increases. (Figure 11.11 shows the relationship between glucose level and food intake.) Note that if the insulin level is either consistently low or consistently high, the result will be an increased appetite; however, very low insulin levels lead to weight loss, whereas very high insulin levels lead to weight gain.

 ONCEPT CHECK

4. Insulin levels fluctuate cyclically over the course of a day. Would you guess that they are higher in the middle of the day, when people tend to be hungry, or late at night, when they are generally less hungry? (Check your answer on page 428.)

## Long-Term Regulation of Hunger

Stomach distension, intestinal distension, and the other mechanisms for ending a meal are far from perfect. Depending on the caloric density of your next meal, you may eat a bit more or less than you need to replenish your resources. If you misjudged in the same direction with every meal, you would soon have a problem.

However, you have long-term mechanisms to correct short-term errors. If you overeat for several meals, you will feel less hungry until you get back to about your normal weight. Conversely, if you undereat for a few meals, you will start feeling hungrier than usual until you get back to normal. Most people's weight fluctuates from one day to the next but remains remarkably stable from

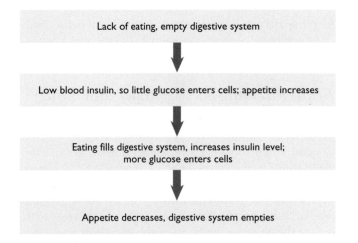

**FIGURE 11.11** A feedback system between eating and insulin levels maintains homeostatic control of nutrition.

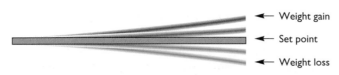

**FIGURE 11.12** For most people, weight fluctuates around a set point, the way a diving board bounces up and down from a central position.

month to month, even if they seldom check the scales. That mean weight is referred to as a **set point**—*a level that the body works to maintain* (Figure 11.12).

The mechanism for this correction is now partly understood (Friedman, 2000). *The body's fat cells produce a hormone called* **leptin** *in amounts proportional to the total amount of fat.* When the body gains fat, the extra leptin alters activity in parts of the hypothalamus (an area of the brain), causing meals to satisfy hunger faster. That is, leptin is your fat cells' way of telling the brain "you have enough fat cells already, so stop eating." Among the many other effects of leptin, it triggers the start of puberty: When the body reaches a certain size and weight, the increased leptin levels combine with other forces to induce the hormonal changes of puberty (Chehab, Mounzih, Lu, & Lim, 1997).

A very few people fail to produce leptin. As you might guess, they become obese. Their brains get no signals about their fat supplies, so they act as if they have no fat and are starving. These people also fail to enter puberty (Clément et al., 1998). For those few people, injections of leptin greatly reduce obesity. However, leptin is ineffective for most obese people. They in fact produce large amounts of it themselves, but apparently they are not very sensitive to it. Injections of even larger amounts can decrease their appetite somewhat, but only at the risk of inducing diabetes and other medical disorders (B. Cohen, Novick, & Rubinstein, 1996).

## CONCEPT CHECK

**5.** What are two hormones that influence appetite, and which body parts release them? (Check your answer on page 428.)

## Brain Mechanisms of Hunger and Satiety

The brain must somehow monitor information from the blood, cells, and digestive system to determine when to eat and when to stop eating. Several brain areas, especially those in the hypothalamus (Figure 11.13), are especially important in this process.

The **lateral hypothalamus** appears to be *a critical area for starting meals.* It modulates other brain areas to increase the taste of foods, increase salivation and digestion, and increase the reward value of food (Hernandez, Murzi, Schwartz, & Hoebel, 1992; van den Pol, 1999).

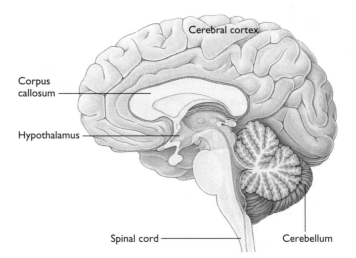

**FIGURE 11.13** The hypothalamus, a small area on the underside of the brain, contains several subareas that contribute in various ways to eating, drinking, sexual behavior, and other motivated activities.

Two areas of the hypothalamus are important for ending meals. One is the **ventromedial hypothalamus.** *After damage that includes the ventromedial hypothalamus and the axons that pass nearby, an individual digests food more rapidly than usual and secretes more insulin.* The high insulin level causes a disproportionate amount of each meal to be stored as fat. Because the food passes quickly through the digestive system and into the fat cells where it stays, the individual becomes hungry again shortly after each meal (Hoebel & Hernandez, 1993). Figure 11.14 shows a rat with this kind of brain damage. One woman with a tumor in this area gained an average of more than 10 kg (20 pounds) per month (Reeves & Plum, 1969).

Another area of the hypothalamus contributes to ending meals in a different way. *After damage to or chemical in-*

**FIGURE 11.14** An obese rat with a damaged ventromedial hypothalamus (left) can eat less than an ordinary rat (right) and still gain weight. This rat's excess fat prevents it from grooming its fur.

hibition of the **paraventricular hypothalamus,** *meals are of normal frequency but each individual meal is enormous* (Leibowitz & Alexander, 1991; Leibowitz, Hammer, & Chang, 1981). An individual with such brain damage continues eating until the stomach and intestines are about to burst.

## CONCEPT CHECK

**6.** Many young ballet dancers and other female athletes who exercise heavily and keep their weight low are slower to start puberty than most other girls. Why?

**7.** After damage to the ventromedial hypothalamus, an animal's weight eventually reaches a higher than usual level and then fluctuates around that amount. What has happened to the set point? (Check your answers on page 428.)

# Eating Too Much or Too Little

The mechanisms I have discussed so far enable most people to select a reasonable, well-balanced diet and to maintain their weight within normal limits. In some individuals, though, the motivational mechanisms go awry. They feel hungry all the time and eat too much, or they alternate between stuffing themselves and starving themselves, or they feel hungry but refuse to eat. Some of these disorders result from physiological abnormalities; others result from social and cognitive influences that are competing with the normal physiological mechanisms.

## Obesity

**Obesity** is *the excessive accumulation of body fat.* Physicians calculate a *body mass index,* which is defined as weight in kilograms divided by height in meters squared ($kg/m^2$). A ratio over 25 is considered overweight; over 30, obese; over 40, extremely obese (National Institutes of Health, 2000). Obesity increases the risk of diabetes, coronary heart disease, certain kinds of cancer, sleep apnea (difficulty breathing while asleep), and several other diseases (Kopelman, 2000). People become seriously overweight because they take in more calories than they use up. But *why* do they do that?

### The Limited Role of Emotional Disturbances
Are overweight people more likely than others to have psychological problems? One prevalent idea has been that anxiety, depression, or other emotional problems lead to overeating and weight gain. Another theory is that extreme weight gain leads to anxiety or depression. The research, however, fails to support either hypothesis. Anxiety, depression, and other psychological concerns are not unusually common among obese people (Wadden & Stunkard, 1987). Nevertheless, there may be a subpopulation of obese people who react strongly to the

unfavorable way in which they are treated. Because prejudices against the obese are so common, many obese people have a restricted social life and have trouble getting a good job. Dealing with such prejudices and barriers leads some obese people to psychological distress and low self-esteem (Friedman & Brownell, 1996).

Although emotional distress is not the cause of obesity, it can produce temporary fluctuations in eating and body weight for almost anyone. In one survey of 100 adults (Edelman, 1981), 40 said that they overeat three or more times per month when they feel nervous, tired, lonely, or sorry for themselves. The eating binge enables them to focus their attention on eating and away from their other concerns (Heatherton & Baumeister, 1991). Such eating binges are most frequent and most extreme with people who have been dieting to lose weight (Greeno & Wing, 1994). Evidently, dieters actively inhibit their desire to eat, until a stressful experience breaks these inhibitions and releases the pent-up desire to eat.

### Genetics
Obesity tends to run in families, and studies of twins and adopted children indicate a fairly high heritability for obesity (Comuzzie & Allison, 1998). In other words, other things being equal, certain genes increase the chances that someone will become overweight. This evidence does not mean that genetics fully explains obesity,

■ Although obesity is not significantly linked with either anxiety or depression, some obese people feel distressed and suffer from low self-esteem because of how other people react to them.

FIGURE 11.15 Most Pima Indians have a gene that leads to excess weight gain if they eat a standard U.S. diet. However, few were obese when they ate their traditional diet of desert plants, as shown at the left.

however. In particular, consider the fact that obesity is far more common in the United States today than it was in the early 1900s or earlier. The spread of obesity is obviously due to lifestyle changes, not genetics. (Evolution could not produce such a rapid effect.) Obesity has also spread in other countries as they became more influenced by Western culture, or as some people put it, "Coca-Colonized" (Friedman, 2000). Not that long ago, most of our ancestors spent most of the day in farming or manual labor. Today, many people drive to work, take an elevator instead of climbing stairs, and then sit all day in an office. Eating habits have also changed. Fast-food hamburger outlets provide inexpensive high-fat meals, restaurants with all-you-can-eat buffets encourage gluttony, and even grocery stores and supermarkets offer a large variety of tempting high-calorie convenience foods. Most obese people show a strong preference for foods that are rich in both fats and carbohydrates, such as cake frosting, and these foods are more readily available today than ever before (Drewnowski, 1996).

A strong illustration of the relationship between genetics and lifestyle for the onset of obesity comes from the Pima Indians of Arizona. Most Pima adults are severely obese, probably because of several genes (Norman et al., 1998), and most also have high blood pressure and diabetes. However, they were not obese until the 1940s. Previously, they ate only the fruits and vegetables that grow in the Sonoran Desert, such as the ones shown in Figure 11.15, and those were available only for brief seasons of the year. To survive, they had to eat as much as possible when food was available and conserve their energy as much as possible. Today, they live on about the same diet as other Americans, which

is available year-round. They still eat massive quantities and conserve their energy by being relatively inactive, and the result is weight gain. We see here a superb example of the combined influence of genetics and environment. The Pimas become obese because of their genes, but the genes have that effect only because of the environment, which includes an abundance of food.

### Decreased Energy Output

Many overweight people who claim to eat only normal amounts of food eat more than they admit, maybe even more than they admit to themselves. However, some really do eat only normal-sized meals (DeLuise, Blackburn, & Flier, 1980). Their overweight condition is not due to high energy intake but to low energy output. Not only do they fail to exercise, but they also have a low overall metabolic rate, presumably for genetic reasons.

One group of investigators compared the infants of twelve overweight mothers and six normal-weight mothers over their first year of life. All the babies weighed about the same at birth, but six of the babies of the overweight mothers had become overweight by the end of that first year. Those babies had also been relatively inactive since birth. During the first 3 months, they had expended about 20% less energy per day than the babies who maintained normal weight (Roberts, Savage, Coward, Chew, & Lucas, 1988).

Low energy expenditure is a good predictor of weight gain in adults as well. Eric Ravussin and his associates (1988) found that the adults with the lowest energy expenditure over a 24-hour period were the most likely to gain weight over the next 2 to 4 years.

## Losing Weight

If you talk to enough people about weight loss, some will tell you that it is almost impossible to lose weight and keep it off, but others will recount stories of people who succeeded. The reason we hear about more failures than successes is simple: Most of the people who lose weight and keep it off don't keep talking about it and don't keep seeking help (Schachter, 1982). Most of the people who show up at one weight-loss clinic after another have repeatedly failed to lose weight, and so the difficult patients seem disproportionately common.

For those who seek professional help in losing weight, a variety of approaches are available. Most therapists recommend starting with the simplest methods; if those methods fail, then consider trying more intensive methods (Friedman & Brownell, 1996):

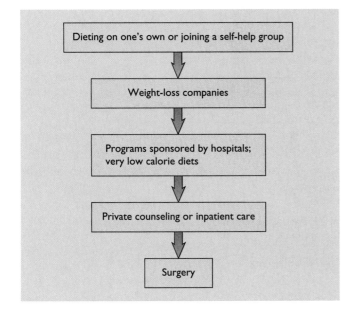

A survey of weight-loss experts found that they disagreed about much but did agree on a few recommendations (Schwartz & Brownell, 1995):

- Except for people with unusual medical problems, almost anyone who needs to lose weight should include increased exercise as part of the strategy. The best advice is to set realistic exercise goals and then stick to them: Someone who has hardly lifted a muscle in years should start with a modest goal and then gradually increase the activity instead of trying for too much all at once.
- The severity of the problem should dictate the approach. For example, only people with severe, life-threatening obesity should even consider surgical removal of fat.
- Programs such as Overeaters Anonymous (OA) are helpful to people who feel comfortable with the strong spiritual focus and the emphasis on overeating as an addiction or disease. However, not everyone feels comfortable with this approach.
- Private counseling is useful mostly for people with other psychological problems in addition to their weight problem.

The advisability of weight-loss drugs is controversial, but the variety of drugs has increased. Medications are now available or are being researched to weaken hunger signals to the brain, block absorption of fat in the intestines, and increase metabolism (Bray & Tartaglia, 2000).

## The Effect of Intentional Weight Loss on Appetite

Are you satisfied with your own weight? In the United States, almost everyone says "no." Women in particular are unlikely to be satisfied with their own appearance, and the percentage of women expressing dissatisfaction has increased gradually over decades. Recall from the last chapter that women report lower self-esteem than men on the average. The same principle applies to weight and body appearance: Even unattractive men are likely to say they are satisfied with their appearance and even attractive women say they are dissatisfied with their appearance (Feingold & Mazzella, 1998).

 Dissatisfaction about one's body often translates into worry about what one eats, especially in the United States. Before we proceed, try these questions. In each case circle one of the choices.

- *Ice cream* belongs best with:     delicious     fattening
- *Chocolate cake* belongs best with:     guilt     celebration
- *Heavy cream* belongs best with:     whipped     unhealthy
- *Fried eggs* belong best with:     breakfast     cholesterol

On questions like these, U.S. people, especially women, are more likely to circle *fattening, guilt, unhealthy,* and *cholesterol*—indicating worry about food—whereas people in Japan, Belgium, and France are more likely to circle *delicious, celebration, whipped,* and *breakfast.* On a wide range of questions, U.S. people indicate more interest in getting low-fat, low-salt, highly healthful foods, and yet when they are asked whether they eat a healthy diet, the Americans mostly say "no" while the French say "yes" (Rozin, Fischler, Imada, Sarubin, & Wrzesniewski, 1999). Furthermore, the French eat a high-fat diet, which Americans consider unhealthy, and yet they have *less* cardiovascular disease than Americans do. Several explanations have been offered for the French people's health, including small portion sizes and the benefits of drinking moderate amounts of

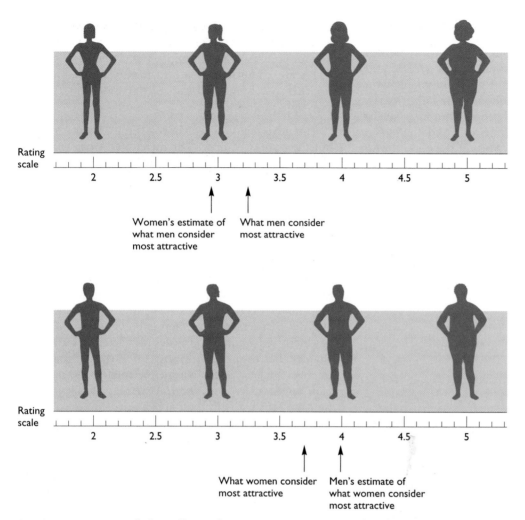

Rating scale

2  2.5  3  3.5  4  4.5  5

Women's estimate of what men consider most attractive

What men consider most attractive

Rating scale

2  2.5  3  3.5  4  4.5  5

What women consider most attractive

Men's estimate of what women consider most attractive

**FIGURE 11.16** In a study by Fallon and Rozin (1985), women and men were asked which figure they considered most attractive and which figure they believed the opposite sex considered most attractive. Each sex misestimated the other's preferences.

wine. In addition, Rozin and colleagues (1999) suggest that perhaps one reason for the French people's surprisingly good health is simply that they worry less!

In the United States and other Western countries, slenderness is fashionable, especially for women. April Fallon and Paul Rozin (1985) asked women to indicate on a diagram which body figure they thought men considered most attractive. The investigators also asked men which female figure *they* considered most attractive. As Figure 11.16 shows, women thought that men preferred thinner women than most men actually do. (The same study also found that men thought women preferred heavier men than most women actually do.)

Given the social pressure to be thin, many normal-weight people deprive themselves of food they would like to eat. Doing so apparently requires considerable mental effort. Here is a somewhat complicated experiment to illustrate this point.

 **WHAT'S THE EVIDENCE?**
*Dieting Requires Mental Energy*

In this study dieters were exposed to the temptation to snack and then, after they resisted the temptation, required to eat some ice cream in the second part of the study (Vohs & Heatherton, 2000).

**HYPOTHESIS** Dieters who have to fight a strong temptation to eat will be "mentally worn out" and therefore more likely to yield to the next temptation.

**METHOD** Chronic dieters and nondieters participated in a two-part study. First, they watched a video and answered some questions about it. During the video an array of snacks (cheese-flavored corn chips, candies, and salted peanuts) was either next to them or 3 meters (10 feet) away. Half of each group were told not to touch the snacks (because they were for people in another study), and the other half were told to help themselves. That is, the study had eight groups of participants:

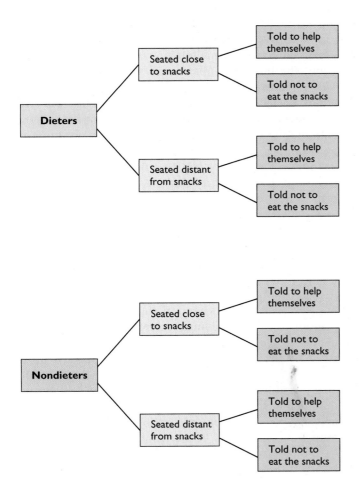

The key to the study was the results for dieters who were seated next to the snacks and told to help themselves. In fact, they did not eat any snacks (because they were on a diet), but presumably (and according to their own reports), they were strongly tempted. Those who were told not to eat the snacks had less temptation, as did those who were seated far from the snacks. But imagine yourself on a diet sitting right next to appealing snacks and being told to help yourself. You fight the urge, but the resistance is not easy.

Next, participants were taken to another room where their task was to sample ice cream from three large containers and rate the taste of each. The experimenter left the room, remarking, "Help yourself to any ice cream you want; we have tons in the freezer." During this part even the dieters had no choice but to eat, although they could control how much they ate.

**RESULTS** Of the eight groups in this study, the people who ate the most ice cream were the dieters who had been told "help yourself" to snacks in the first part of the study while being seated close to the snacks.

**INTERPRETATION** According to the researchers, these results suggest that people have limited resources for self-regulation. After you have resisted temptation for a while (using up some self-regulation resources), your ability to regulate your behavior again weakens, leaving you vulnerable to the next temptation.

The study has the interesting implication that you should try to avoid putting yourself into one tempting situation after another, especially within a short time. That conclusion probably applies to temptations other than hunger. The experiment is also interesting in showing that research procedures frequently require more than just an experimental group and a control group. Here we care about whether the results differ for dieters and nondieters, as well as the difference between various levels of temptations and kinds of instructions.

# CONCEPT CHECK

**8.** Which group in the experiment ate the most ice cream and why? (Check your answer on page 428.)

## *Anorexia Nervosa*

The Duchess of Windsor once said, "You can't be too rich or too thin." She may have been right about too rich, but she was definitely wrong about too thin. Some people are so strongly motivated to be thin (for social and cognitive reasons) that they manage to overrule their physiological drives almost completely.

Here is a case history: A somewhat chubby 11-year-old girl who weighed 118 pounds (53 kg) was told to watch her weight (Bachrach, Erwin, & Mohr, 1965). She did so all through her teens. Along the way she suffered certain hormonal difficulties, including menstrual irregularity, heavy menstrual bleeding, and deficient activity of her thyroid gland. At age 18 she still weighed 118 pounds, but with her taller frame, that weight was normal for her.

After she was married, she moved from her home in Virginia to her husband's area of employment in California. She immediately became homesick. Because the couple could afford only a small apartment with no cooking facilities, they ate most of their meals at a very inexpensive restaurant. Soon she began to lose weight and stopped menstruating. She found sexual relations painful and unpleasant. Her physician warned her that, if she did not start regaining some weight, he would be forced to send her home to her parents. He intended this as a threat, but she took it as a promise. By the time she visited the physician again, she had lost even more weight and soon went back to Virginia.

Even after returning to familiar surroundings and home cooking, however, she continued to lose weight. The weight loss seemed to have developed a momentum

■ While being treated at an anorexia clinic, this young woman was approached on an outing by someone who offered her a job as a model. Society's pressures on women to be ultra-thin are a probable source of the anorexia problem.

of its own, and she continued to get thinner, eventually reaching a weight of only 47 pounds (21 kg).

This is a case of **anorexia nervosa,** *a condition in which a person refuses to eat adequate food and steadily loses weight.* (*Anorexia* means "loss of appetite." *Nervosa* means "for reasons of the nerves," to distinguish it from disorders of the digestive system.) At the outset the person may have decided to lose weight for health reasons or to become a dancer or for some other reason. But the weight loss continues well beyond the original goal. Surprisingly, though, even when anorectic women are on the verge of starvation, they have unusually high energy levels (Falk, Halmi, & Tryon, 1985). They run long distances, compete at sports, work diligently on their school assignments, and sleep very little. As with other psychological conditions, anorexia nervosa comes in all degrees, but in its most severe form, it can lead to atrophy of the heart muscle and death.

Anorexia nervosa usually begins during the teenage years. Earlier onset is almost unheard of. Later onset is uncommon, although anorexia that begins during the teenage years can continue into later life. It occurs mostly in middle-class or upper-middle-class women, independent of their ethnic backgrounds (Mulholland & Mintz, 2001). It also occurs in men, although less commonly.

One of the major contributors to anorexia is societal pressure, especially on women, to be very thin. Anorexia is uncommon in cultures that tolerate or cherish a somewhat plumper look, such as Jamaica (D. E. Smith & Cogswell, 1994) or Europe in an earlier era (Figure 11.17).

In the Fiji Islands, women were mostly rather heavy but content with their bodies, until television arrived and they started watching programs featuring very thin women. Soon many of them started dieting, and a few even started forcing themselves to vomit (Becker & Burwell, 1999).

Some psychologists have tried to explain anorexia nervosa in terms of a malfunction of the lateral hypothalamus, the brain area that seems so central for hunger. That explanation is unlikely, however. Many people with anorexia enjoy preparing food, seem quite interested in food, and enjoy the taste, but they avoid food in far more extreme ways than people who are merely not hungry. For example, some people with anorexia even refuse to lick postage stamps for fear that the glue might contain some tiny fraction of a calorie. A mere lack of hunger could hardly explain such behavior.

A better description of anorexia nervosa is that it reflects a "pathological fear of fatness." Even when anorectic women become painfully thin, they often describe themselves as "looking fat" and "needing to lose weight" (Figure 11.18).

What motivates someone to become anorectic? No one knows. Many biochemical abnormalities have been demonstrated in the brains of anorexics, but those abnormalities could easily be the result of near-starvation instead of the cause (Ferguson & Pigott, 2000). Most anorectic women are highly perfectionist (Halmi et al., 2000), and many take pride in the extreme self-control they demonstrate by refusing to eat. The perfectionist personality is probably a contributor to anorexia, although it could hardly be the whole explanation.

**FIGURE 11.17** Beauty is in the eye of the beholder. Many cultures, including Europe in earlier centuries, have had a standard of female beauty that is noticeably plumper than that of Western society today.

**FIGURE 11.18** A fun house mirror causes a temporary distortion of everyone's appearance. People with anorexia nervosa report a similar distortion of body image at all times, describing themselves as much fatter than they really are.

## Bulimia

Other people, again mostly women, starve themselves at times but occasionally throw themselves into an eating binge. They may consume as many as 20,000 calories at a time (Schlesier-Stropp, 1984)—the equivalent of about 30 Big Macs, 10 helpings of French fries, and 10 chocolate milkshakes. Then they go back to eating almost nothing. Some either force themselves to vomit or use laxatives to increase their weight loss. People who *alternate between self-starvation and excessive eating* are said to suffer from **bulimia** (literally, "ox hunger"). In the United States, about 1–2% of adult women have bulimia and another 3% have occasional binge eating (Vogeltanz-Holm et al., 2000).

We might imagine that people who go on eating binges starve themselves for a while to make up for it. According to Janet Polivy and Peter Herman (1985), however, the causation goes in the other direction: It is the dieting that causes the binges. Bulimic people starve themselves for a while, fight their persistent feelings of hunger, and then go on an eating binge.

Most people with bulimia have low self-esteem, a tendency toward depression, a perfectionist personality, dissatisfaction with their body, and a history of growing up in a somewhat troubled family (Bardone, Vohs, Abramson, Heatherton, & Joiner, 2000; Fairburn, Welch, Doll,

Davies, & O'Connor, 1997). Of course, so do many other people who do not develop bulimia. Some people with bulimia are thin (as with anorexia), but others fluctuate around a normal or high body weight. One study of women who sought psychological help for bulimia found that, 6 years after the treatment, 60% no longer had an eating disorder, 30% still had a moderate problem, and 10% either had serious disorders or had died (Fichter & Quadflieg, 1997).

Eating disorders including anorexia and bulimia increased in the United States during the 1980s and 1990s, especially among women. Meanwhile, most surveys also found an increasing percentage of young women who report feeling dissatisfied with their appearance, especially those who think they are too heavy (Feingold & Mazzella, 1998). The pressure on women to try to look thin is probably a major contributor to both anorexia and bulimia.

---

**IN CLOSING**

## The Complexities of Hunger

The research on anorexia and bulimia underscores the idea that our motivations are controlled by a complex mixture of physiological, social, and cognitive forces. People become overweight (or falsely perceive themselves as overweight) for a variety of reasons, relating to everything from genetics to culture, and they then try to lose weight mostly for social reasons, such as trying to look attractive. Sometimes the physiological factors and the social factors collide, as when normal-weight people try to make themselves thinner and thinner.

The overall point is this: All our motivations interact and combine. How much we eat and what and when we eat depend not only on our need for food, but also on social needs and the need for self-esteem.

## Summary

* **Food selection.** Food preferences can be altered by changes in body chemistry, such as a deficiency of salt. Other things being equal, we tend to prefer familiar foods. We avoid foods that have been associated with something nauseating or repulsive and prefer foods previously associated with other good-tasting foods. (page 415)

* **Short-term regulation of hunger.** Meals are ended by several mechanisms, principally distension of the stomach and intestines. Hunger resumes when the cells begin to receive less glucose and other nutrients. The hormones insulin and glucagon regulate the flow of nutrients from the blood to storage and from there back into the blood. (page 418)

- **Long-term regulation of hunger.** An individual meal can be larger or smaller than necessary to provide the energy that the body needs. The body's fat cells secrete the hormone leptin in proportion to their mass; an increase of leptin decreases hunger, and a decrease of leptin increases hunger. (page 419)
- **Causes of being overweight.** People become overweight for many reasons, but emotional difficulties are rarely a major factor. Some people are predisposed to obesity for genetic reasons; whether they become obese or how obese they become depends on what kinds of food their culture provides. Among the mechanisms leading to obesity are low energy output and insensitivity to leptin. (page 421)
- **Weight-loss techniques.** People in our society resort to a variety of strategies to lose weight, ranging from dieting to surgery. Increased exercise is a good idea for almost anyone who needs to lose weight. Resisting the temptation to snack requires significant mental effort or resources. (page 423)
- **Anorexia nervosa and bulimia.** People suffering from anorexia nervosa deprive themselves of food, sometimes to the point of starvation. People suffering from bulimia alternate between periods of strict dieting and brief but spectacular eating binges. Causes of these disorders are not yet understood. (page 425)

# Answers to Concept Checks

3. It is possible to lose much blood and therefore salts during menstruation. The loss of salt triggers an increased preference for salty tastes, such as found with potato chips. (page 417)
4. Insulin levels are higher in the middle of the day (LeMagnen, 1981). As a result much of the food you eat is stored as fats, and you become hungry again soon. Late at night, when insulin levels are lower, some of your fat supplies are converted to glucose, which enters the blood. (page 419)
5. Leptin, released by fat cells, and insulin, released by the pancreas. (You could also mention glucagon, released by the pancreas.) (page 420)
6. By keeping their fat levels very low, they also keep their leptin levels low, and leptin is one of the triggers for puberty. (page 421)
7. The set point has increased. (page 421)
8. The group who were dieters seated next to the snacks in the first part of the study and told to "help yourself." These people had been more strongly tempted to snack than dieters who were seated far from the snacks or who were told not to eat them. Therefore, they had presumably exhausted much of their "self-restraint" reserves. (page 425)

# Sexual Motivation

*What do people do sexually? Why are some people's sexual interests different from others'?*

For most of us, sexual activity does not occupy a major fraction of the average day, but thinking about it does. If you have any doubts about people's interest in sex, take a look at television listings, popular books and magazines, and films. (In fact, one way that people can tell they are getting old is that they only think about sex most of the time . . . instead of all the time!)

Humans, unlike most other mammalian species, are interested in sex even at times when a woman is unlikely to get pregnant. In fact, people often take measures to prevent pregnancy. Worldwide, most couples stay together not only long enough to rear children but also long after the children are grown up. Sexual motivation binds people together in powerful and intimate relationships and can also drive them apart.

Sexual motivation, like hunger, depends on both a physiological drive and available incentives. Also like hunger, the sex drive increases during times of deprivation, at least up to a point, and it also can be inhibited for social and symbolic reasons, including religious ones.

■ Sexual customs vary sharply from one society to another. At a Hmong Festival, unmarried women toss tennis balls to potential suitors.

However, the sex drive differs from hunger in important ways. We do not need to be around food to feel hungry, but many people do need a partner to feel sexual arousal. Eating in public is normal; sexual intercourse in public is not.

## What Do People Do, and How Often?

Researchers have many reasons for inquiring about the frequency of various sexual behaviors. For example, if we want to predict how fast and how far AIDS is likely to spread in the population, it is important to know how many people are having unsafe sex and with how many partners.

In addition to the important scientific and medical reasons for studying sexual behavior, let's admit it: Most of us are curious about what other people do. Each of us would like to know, "Am I normal?"

The answer depends on what we mean by "normal." If that term means "reasonably common in the population," then it is hard to think of anything you might be doing—or not doing—that would make you abnormal. People vary enormously in their sexual behavior and interests.

### The Kinsey Survey

The first important survey of human sexual behavior was conducted by Alfred C. Kinsey (Figure 11.19), a shy insect biologist who once agreed to teach the biological portion of Indiana University's course on marriage. When he found that the library included very little information about human sexuality, he decided to conduct a survey. What he intended as a small-scale project for teaching purposes grew into a survey of 18,000 people.

Although Kinsey's sample was large, it was neither random nor representative. He obtained most of his interviews by going to organizations, ranging from fraternities to nunneries, and asking everyone in the organization to talk to him. As a result he interviewed mostly midwestern European Americans who belonged to organizations that agreed to cooperate, and his data do not provide a trustworthy assessment of the whole U.S. population. Nevertheless, he did document that human sexual behavior is extremely variable (Kinsey, Pomeroy, &

**FIGURE 11.19** Alfred C. Kinsey pioneered survey studies of sexual behavior. As an interviewer he was peerless—he always put people at ease so that they could speak freely, but he was also alert to probable lies. His results should be interpreted cautiously, however, because he did not obtain a random or representative sample of the U.S. population.

Martin, 1948; Kinsey, Pomeroy, Martin, & Gebhard, 1953). For example, he found some men and women who had rarely or never experienced orgasm. At the other extreme, he found one man who reported an average of four or five orgasms per day over the preceding 30 years (with a wide variety of male, female, and nonhuman partners) and several women who sometimes had 50 or more orgasms within 20 minutes.

Kinsey found that most people were unaware of the great variation in sexual behavior in the population at large. When he asked people whether they believed that "excessive masturbation" causes physical and mental illness, most said yes. (We now know it does not.) He then asked what would constitute "excessive." For each person, "excessive" meant a little more than what he or she did. One young man who masturbated about once per month said he thought three times per month would cause mental illness. A man who masturbated three times per day said he thought five times per day would be excessive. (In reaction to these findings, Kinsey once defined a *nymphomaniac* as "someone who wants sex more than you do.")

## Contemporary Surveys

Kinsey did not even try to interview a random sample of the population because he assumed that most people would refuse to cooperate and perhaps even take offense at being asked. He may have been right about people in the 1940s, but in the 1980s and 1990s, researchers identified random samples of the U.S. population and man-

aged to get cooperation from most of the people they approached (Fay, Turner, Klassen, & Gagnon, 1989; Laumann, Gagnon, Michael, & Michaels, 1994).

(Some advice if anyone ever asks you to participate in a sex survey: Do not cooperate until you know who the questioner is. Legitimate researchers are careful to present their credentials to show their affiliation with a research institute. They also take elaborate precautions to guarantee the confidentiality of people's responses. If "researchers" who want to ask you about your sex life fail to show their credentials or seem unconcerned about your confidentiality, do not trust them. Be especially wary of sex surveys by telephone. Although a few sex researchers do conduct research by telephone, most use a face-to-face interview. When in doubt, assume that the alleged survey is an obscene phone call in disguise.)

A survey of a random sample of almost 3500 U.S. adults (Laumann et al., 1994) has added greatly to our knowledge of U.S. sexual practices and customs. First, what would people *like* to be doing? Figure 11.20 shows the percentage of men and women who describe various sexual activities as "very appealing." The most popular sexual activity is vaginal intercourse, followed by watching one's partner undress and then by oral sex. Other possible options lag well behind. Note an ambiguity in people's responses: When 13% of men say they find group sex "very appealing," do they mean they have frequently enjoyed doing it or just that they have fantasies about it?

Note that more men than women report enjoying every activity on the graph. Besides the differences shown in Figure 11.20, men are much more likely than women to masturbate frequently and to look forward to opportunities for casual sex (Oliver & Hyde, 1993). In general, men also have stronger preferences for what activities they want to do, how often, and with how much variety. A woman who changes partners is more likely to accept the preferences of her new partner than a man is to alter his pattern to suit a new female partner (Baumeister, 2000). Why that is so remains uncertain.

Figure 11.21 shows the number of sex partners during the past year for people of various ages. Most people of all ages report either no partner or only one. The percentage of people having multiple partners is greatest in young adulthood and declines steadily with age.

The results in Figure 11.21 are cross-sectional, not longitudinal. That is, the 20-year-olds and 50-year-olds grew up in different eras. Figure 11.22 emphasizes these differences among cohorts. People were asked how many sex partners they had in their lifetime. As Figure 11.22 shows, people in their 40s were more likely to report a large number of partners than were people in their 50s. The reason is that people who were in their 40s at the time of the survey were young and unmarried during the 1970s, an era of sexual freedom. People in their 50s were young during a more restrictive era.

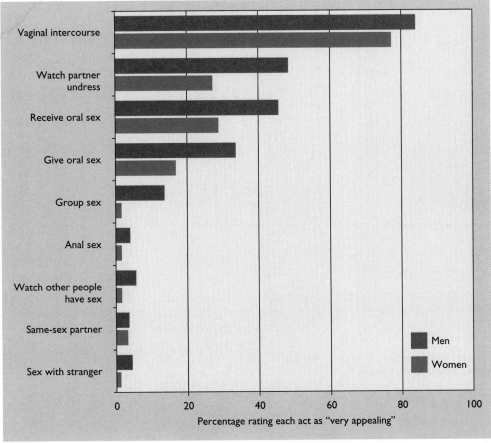

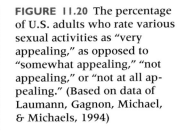

**FIGURE 11.20** The percentage of U.S. adults who rate various sexual activities as "very appealing," as opposed to "somewhat appealing," "not appealing," or "not at all appealing." (Based on data of Laumann, Gagnon, Michael, & Michaels, 1994)

In Figure 11.23 you can see differences in current sexual activity reported by people of different ages. The older respondents are less likely than the young ones to report having sex more than twice per week. That trend is probably a real effect of age, not a cohort effect. That is, most 50- to 60-year-olds agree that they are having sexual relations less often than when they were younger.

The frequencies of various sexual practices vary, of course, among cultures and historical eras. Certainly, a sex survey of the United States in 1992 does not apply to other locations or other times. Several studies have reported on the exotic sexual customs of people in certain non-Western cultures (Davenport, 1977). When we consider how difficult it has been to get reasonably accurate data about U.S. sexual practices, we should be skeptical about many reports from other cultures. Nevertheless, there are such striking differences in observable practices (e.g., dating, marriage, and public display of the human body) that clearly sexual behavior depends to a large extent on learned customs, not just biological drives.

**FIGURE 11.21** The number of sex partners in the previous 12 months by U.S. adults of various ages, both sexes combined. (Based on data of Laumann et al., 1994)

# CONCEPT CHECK

**9.** Why were Kinsey's results different from those of later surveys? (Check your answer on page 439.)

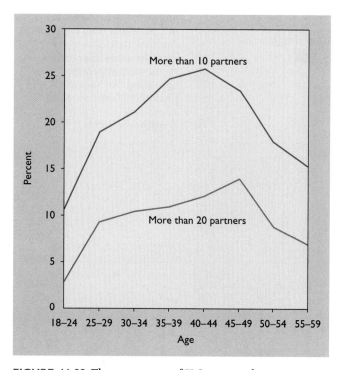

**FIGURE 11.22** The percentage of U.S. men and women reporting more than 10 or 20 sex partners in their lives. (Based on data of Laumann et al., 1994)

## Sexual Behavior in the Era of AIDS

During the 1980s a new factor entered into people's sexual motivations: the fear of **acquired immune deficiency syndrome (AIDS)**, *a sexually transmitted disease that gradually destroys the body's immune system.*

For HIV (human immunodeficiency virus)—the virus that causes AIDS—to spread from one person to another, it must enter the second person's blood. (The virus does not survive long outside body fluids.) The three common routes of transmission are transfusions of contaminated blood, sharing needles used for intravenous injections of illegal drugs, and sexual contact. Other contacts between people, even kissing, do not spread the virus (unless perhaps both people had a cut on the mouth that was actively bleeding at the time).

An infected male has an estimated 3% chance of transmitting the virus to a female during vaginal intercourse; an infected woman has no more than a 2% chance, probably much less, of transmitting it to a male (Kaplan, 1988). The likelihood of transmission increases if either partner has an open wound on the genitals or if the woman is menstruating. The probability of transmission during anal intercourse is higher, about 7–10%, because the lining of the rectum easily tears (Kaplan, 1988). These estimates are approximations, of course.

For generations people have known how to avoid contracting syphilis, gonorrhea, and other sexually transmitted diseases: Don't have sex with someone who might be infected, or when in doubt, use a condom. If people had con-

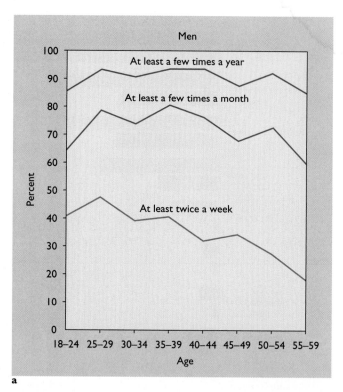

a

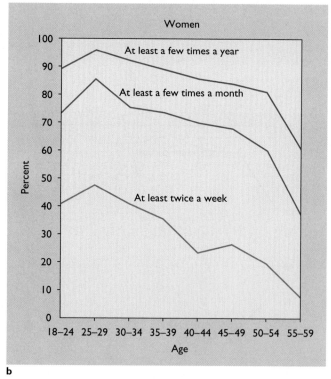

b

**FIGURE 11.23** The percentage of U.S. adults who have had sexual relations with a partner at varying frequencies in the previous year. (a) Results for men. (b) Results for women. (Based on data of Laumann et al., 1994)

sistently followed this advice, we could have eliminated those diseases long ago. The same advice is now offered to combat AIDS, and the amount of compliance varies. Among homosexual men who have anal intercourse, some

■ Different cultures have very different standards regarding public display of the human body, dating, marriage, and premarital sex.

use condoms almost always, some usually, and some only rarely. Their explanations vary (Adam, Sears, & Schellenberg, 2000). Men who already have the virus say they have nothing to lose because they are already infected. Some men who do not have the virus have a relationship with a single partner who is HIV-negative. Some believe they can surmise whether a new partner has the virus or not. Also, some men have unprotected sex when drunk, coerced by a partner, or just in a bad mood when they "don't want to think about AIDS or prevention."

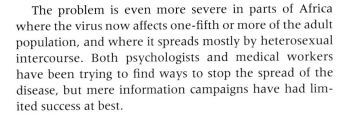

■ AIDS is a preventable disease. Use condoms during sex and don't share injection needles with other people, and you greatly decrease the probability of transmitting or receiving the AIDS virus. Advertisements such as this one have prompted many people to change their behavior.

The problem is even more severe in parts of Africa where the virus now affects one-fifth or more of the adult population, and where it spreads mostly by heterosexual intercourse. Both psychologists and medical workers have been trying to find ways to stop the spread of the disease, but mere information campaigns have had limited success at best.

## Sexual Arousal

Sexual motivation depends on both physiological and cognitive influences—that is, not just the "plumbing" of the body but also the presence of a suitable partner, a willingness to be aroused, and a lack of anxiety. William Masters and Virginia Johnson (1966), who pioneered the study of human sexual response, discovered that physiological arousal during the sex act is similar in men and women. They observed hundreds of people masturbating or having sexual intercourse in a laboratory and monitored their physiological responses, including heart rate, breathing, muscle tension, blood engorgement of the genitals and breasts, and nipple erection. Masters and Johnson identified four physiological stages in sexual arousal (Figure 11.24).

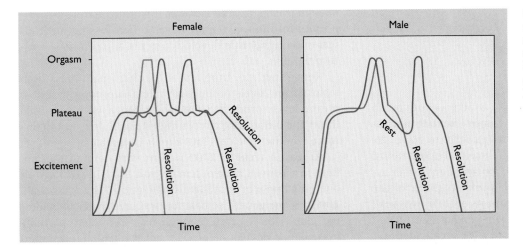

**FIGURE 11.24** Sexual arousal usually proceeds through four stages—excitement, plateau, orgasm, and resolution. Each line represents the response of a different individual. (After Masters & Johnson, 1966)

During the first stage, *excitement,* a man's penis becomes erect and a woman's vagina becomes lubricated. Breathing becomes rapid and deep. Heart rate and blood pressure increase. Many people experience a flush of the skin, which sometimes resembles a measles rash. Women's nipples become erect, and if women have never nursed a baby, their breasts swell slightly. Although this stage is referred to as excitement, it actually requires a kind of relaxation. Nervousness interferes with sexual excitement, as do stimulant drugs (even coffee). A man's erection requires relaxation of the smooth muscles controlling blood flow to the penis. The drug sildenafil (trade name Viagra) relaxes those muscles and thereby helps men get an erection if they were previously having difficulty (Rowland & Burnett, 2000).

During the second stage, called the *plateau,* excitement remains fairly constant. This stage lasts for varying lengths of time depending on the person's age and the intensity of the stimulation. During the third stage, excitement becomes intense and is followed by a sudden release of tension known as *climax* or *orgasm,* which is felt throughout the entire body. During the fourth and final stage, *resolution,* the person returns to an unaroused state.

As Figure 11.24 shows, the pattern of excitation varies from one person to another. During a given episode, a woman may experience either no orgasm at all, a single orgasm, or many. Men do not experience multiple consecutive orgasms, although they can achieve orgasm again following a rest (or refractory) period. Among individuals in both sexes, the intensity of the orgasm ranges from something like a sigh to an extremely intense experience.

At any rate that is the usual pattern. Some people are unable to complete the four stages of arousal. Some men cannot produce or maintain an erection. Others have premature ejaculations, advancing from excitement to orgasm sooner than they or their partners wish. Perhaps as many as 10% of women and a few men stay at the plateau stage without experiencing orgasm. Some sexual disorders can be traced to physiological causes, but usually the cause is unknown.

# Sexual Identity and Orientation

Just as hunger includes two major aspects—how much food to eat and which foods to choose—sexual motivation includes two aspects: how frequently to have sex and with whom. People vary in their sexual orientations, just as they do in their food preferences or any other aspect of life. Why do some people prefer partners of the opposite sex and others prefer partners of their own sex?

Psychologists distinguish between gender identity and sexual orientation. **Gender identity** (or sexual identity) is *the sex that a person regards him- or herself as being.* Ordi-

■ Attitudes toward homosexual relationships have varied among cultures and among historical eras.

narily, people with male genitals have a male identity and people with female genitals have a female identity, although exceptions occur. **Sexual orientation** is *a person's preference for male or female sex partners (or both or neither).* People who prefer partners of their own sex have a homosexual (gay or lesbian) orientation.

## Influences on Sexual Anatomy

In the earliest stages of development, the human fetus has a "unisex" appearance (Figure 11.25). One structure subsequently develops into either a penis or a clitoris; another structure develops into either a scrotum or labia. The direction this development takes depends on hormonal influences during prenatal development. Beginning in the seventh or eighth week after conception, genetic *male fetuses generally secrete higher levels of the hormone* **testosterone** *than do females* (although both sexes produce some), and over the next couple of months, the testosterone causes the tiny fetal structures to grow into a penis and a scrotum. In genetic female fetuses, with lower levels of testosterone, the structures develop into a clitoris and labia. Levels of *the hormone* **estrogen** *increase more in females than in males* at this time; estrogen is important for internal female development but has little effect on whether one develops a penis or a clitoris, a scrotum or labia.

Remember: In humans and other mammals, high testosterone levels produce a male anatomy; low testosterone levels produce a female anatomy. Within normal limits the amount of circulating estrogen does not determine whether one develops a male or female appearance.

At least 1 child in 2000 is born with genitals that are hard to classify as male or female, and 1 or 2 in 100 have an anatomy that is at least slightly ambiguous (Blackless et al., 2000). Some genetic female fetuses have overactive adrenal glands that secrete enough testosterone to partially masculinize development. The genetic female may then develop a sexual anatomy that looks intermediate between

**Undifferentiated before sixth week**

Genital tubercle
Urethral fold
Urethral groove
Genital fold
Anal pit

a

**Seventh to eighth week**

Male                    Female

Glans
Area where foreskin (prepuce) forms
Urethral fold
Urogenital groove
Genital fold (becomes
shaft of penis or labia minora)
Labioscrotal swelling
(becomes scrotum or labia majora)
Anus

b

**Fully developed by twelfth week**

Urethral          Male                    Female
opening
(meatus)
                    Prepuce
                    (Penis) Glans (Clitoris)
                    (Penis) Shaft (Clitoris)
                    Labia minora
                                              Urethral opening
                    Scrotum    Labia majora   (meatus)
                                              Vaginal
                                              opening
                    Anus

c

**FIGURE 11.25** The human genitals look the same in male and female fetuses for about the first 6 or 7 weeks after conception (a). Differences begin to emerge over the next couple of months (b) and are well developed at birth (c).

male and female (Money & Ehrhardt, 1972). In rarer cases a genetic male develops an intermediate appearance because of a gene that alters hormone receptors (Misrahi et al., 1997). *People with an anatomy that appears intermediate between male and female* are known as **intersexes** (Figure 11.26).

How should parents and others treat intersexes? The main question is how these people can be most successful and satisfied socially. For decades the standard medical recommendation has been, when in doubt, call the child female and perform surgery to make her anatomy look female. This surgery includes creating or lengthening a vagina and reducing the ambiguous penis/clitoris to the size of an average clitoris. In

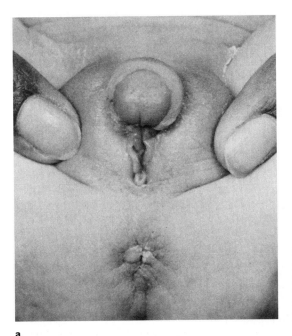

a

b

**FIGURE 11.26** (a) External genitals of a 3-month-old genetic female: This infant was masculinized before birth by excess androgens from the adrenal gland. (b) A group of intersex adults who have gathered to provide mutual support and protest against involuntary surgical intervention for intersexes. To emphasize that they do not consider intersexuality shameful, they have requested that their names be used. Left to right: Martha Coventry, Max Beck, David Vandertie, Kristi Bruse, and Angela Moreno.

many cases the initial surgery is unsatisfactory and additional operations are performed later. That is a lot of surgery, but most physicians think it is easier and produces a more normal appearance than any attempts to expand an ambiguous penis/clitoris to the size of a penis.

That recommendation has been based on the assumption that, if a child looks like a girl and is treated like a girl, she will develop psychologically as a girl. Physicians never had much evidence for that assumption, and some adult intersexes, in spite of their appearance and rearing, develop a male identity. Furthermore, a great many complain that genital surgery—reducing or removing the penis/clitoris—left them with greatly reduced sexual excitation and a feeling of mutilation. An artificial vagina may be satisfactory to a male partner, but it provides no sensation or pleasure to the woman, and it requires frequent attention to prevent scar tissue. Finally, intersexes object that, in many cases, physicians lied to them about the surgery they had performed and why. The standard, traditional approach in medicine is now being opposed by those who recommend complete honesty with intersexes and avoiding surgery until or unless such people request it themselves as adults (Dreger, 1998).

## CONCEPT CHECK

10. If a human fetus were exposed to very low levels of both testosterone and estrogen during prenatal development, how would the sexual anatomy appear?
11. If a human fetus were exposed to high levels of both testosterone and estrogen throughout prenatal development, how would the sexual anatomy appear? (Check your answers on page 439.)

## Influences on Sexual Orientation

How many people have a homosexual orientation? You may have heard people confidently assert "10%." That number is derived from Kinsey's report that about 13% of the men and 7% of the women he interviewed in the 1940s and 1950s stated a predominantly homosexual orientation. The often-quoted figure of 10% is simply the mean of Kinsey's results for men and women. However, Kinsey's data were based on a nonrandom sample of the population.

According to a survey of a random sample of 3500 U.S. adults, 2.8% of men and 1.4% of women describe themselves as having a homosexual (gay or lesbian) orientation (Laumann et al., 1994). More people describe a homosexual experience if they answer on a computer than if they fill out a piece of paper, presumably because the computer answer is more clearly anonymous (Turner et al., 1998). However, even with the greatest assurances of anonymity, the descriptions of homosexuality don't increase much.

As Figure 11.27 illustrates, heterosexuality versus homosexuality is a continuum. Of the 1–3% of people who regard themselves as gay or lesbian, most have had at least an experience or two with heterosexuality, and some alternate between considering themselves homosexual and bisexual (Diamond, 2000). Some people who consider themselves fully heterosexual report at least one adult homosexual experience, and if we expand the scope to include early adolescence, 9% of men report at least one homosexual experience (Laumann et al., 1994).

If you have frequently heard the prevalence of homosexual orientations estimated at 10%, you may be skeptical of the report that only 1–3% of people identify themselves as gay or lesbian. However, three other large surveys reported that 1–2%, 3%, or 6% of U.S. men were either gay or bisexual (Billy, Tanfer, Grady, & Klepinger, 1993; Cameron, Proctor, Coburn, & Forde, 1985; Fay et al., 1989). The study reporting the 6% figure had the least satisfactory sampling technique. Surveys in four other countries have reported similar or slightly lower percentages, as shown in Figure 11.28 (Izazola-Licea, Gortmaker, Tolbert, De Gruttola, & Mann, 2000; Sandfort, de Graaf, Bijl, & Schnabel, 2001; Spira et al., 1993; Wellings, Field, Johnson, & Wadsworth, 1994).

Society's attitudes toward homosexuality have changed

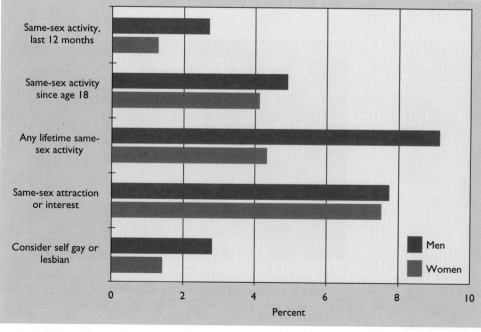

**FIGURE 11.27** The percentages of U.S. adults who report sexual activity or interest in sexual activity with people of their own sex. (Based on data of Laumann et al., 1994)

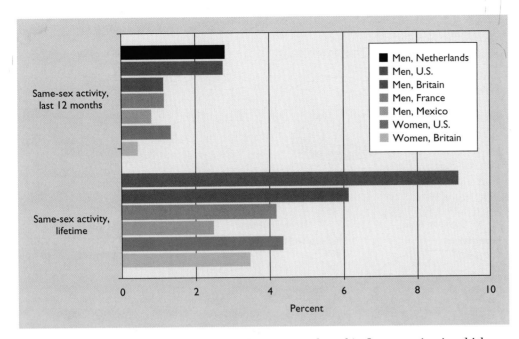

**FIGURE 11.28** Comparisons of the results of surveys conducted in five countries, in which people were asked whether they had had homosexual experiences. (Based on data of Izazola-Licea, Gortmaker, Tolbert, De Gruttola, & Mann, 2000; Laumann, Gagnon, Michael, & Michaels, 1994; Sandfort, de Graaf, Bijl, & Schnabel, 2001; Spira et al., 1993; Wellings, Field, Johnson, & Wadsworth, 1994)

could decide to be right-handed. What causes people to develop a heterosexual or a homosexual orientation?

Most of the available research deals with gay men. Lesbians are less numerous, and many are sufficiently private about their orientation that they become invisible to researchers. The research we do have suggests that genetic factors contribute toward sexual orientation for both men and women. Figure 11.29 shows the results of studies concerning homosexuality in twins and other relatives of adult gays and lesbians (Bailey & Pillard, 1991; Bailey, Pillard, Neale, & Agyei, 1993). Note that homosexuality is more prevalent in their monozygotic (identical) twins than in their dizygotic (fraternal) twins.

repeatedly over time. As far as we can determine, the ancient Greeks and Romans considered it fairly typical for men to engage in occasional sexual activities with each other as well as with women (Boswell, 1990). (The Greek and Roman writers had little to say about women's sexual interests.) During a later era, Europeans regarded male homosexuality as sinful or criminal. By the early 20th century, the "enlightened" view was that homosexuality was not sinful but "merely" a sign of disease or mental illness. The evidence, however, was based on a badly distorted sample: Psychiatrists and psychologists were acquainted with homosexual men who had sought help for psychological troubles. But homosexual men without psychological problems never consulted therapists, and therefore, the therapists did not know about them. Studies of broader samples have found that most homosexual people are mentally healthy and well adjusted (Siegelman, 1974), although a large minority of them have depression or alcohol abuse. For example, the lifetime depression rates are 39% among homosexual men and 48% among homosexual women—in each case two to three times the rate for heterosexuals (Sandfort et al., 2001). Because most homosexual people are mentally healthy, psychologists and psychiatrists today consider a homosexual orientation to be a natural variation in sexual motivation.

The origins and determinants of sexual orientation are not well understood. Adult homosexuals, especially males, often report that their sexual orientation was apparent to them from as young as they can remember. They did not choose it and they could not change it, even if they wanted to, any more easily than a left-hander

That trend suggests a genetic influence toward homosexuality, although a gene could hardly be the only factor. (If it were, then 100% of their monozygotic twins would have a homosexual orientation.) Note also that homosexuality is more common among the dizygotic twins of a homosexual person than among adopted brothers or sisters. That trend also suggests a genetic factor, although it could also indicate the influence of a factor in the prenatal environment shared by twins but not by boys who simply grow up in the same family.

If genes affect sexual orientation, they must do so by altering the development of some part of the body. The answer does *not* lie in adult hormone levels. On the average, adult homosexual people are similar to heterosexual people in their levels of testosterone and estrogen, and giving people testosterone or estrogen does not change their sexual orientation, although it can alter the strength of their sex drive (Tuiten et al., 2000).

It is possible, however, that sexual orientation is influenced by prenatal sex hormones (Lalumiére, Blanchard, & Zucker, 2000). For example, here is a structural difference between men and women that you probably never noticed: Compare the length of your index finger (the one next to the thumb) to the length of your ring finger. The ring finger is longer in most men, especially on the right hand, whereas in most women they are about the same length or the index finger is slightly longer. That difference is believed to represent the effects of prenatal testosterone. In most lesbians the ring finger is longer, as in men (Williams et al., 2000).

Presumably, if prenatal hormones influence sexual orientation, the main place to look for any anatomical

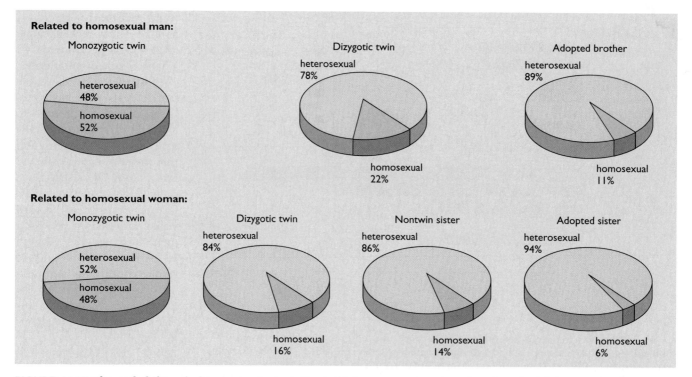

**FIGURE 11.29** The probability of a homosexual orientation is higher among monozygotic twins of adult homosexuals than among their dizygotic twins. The probability is higher among dizygotic twins than among adopted brothers or sisters who grew up in the same family. These data suggest a possible genetic role in the development of sexual orientation. (Based on results of Bailey & Pillard, 1991; Bailey, Pillard, Neale, & Agyei, 1993)

differences is in the brain. One widely quoted and often misunderstood study reported a small but measurable difference between the brains of homosexual and heterosexual men. Let's examine the evidence.

### WHAT'S THE EVIDENCE?
### *Sexual Orientation and Brain Anatomy*

Animal studies have demonstrated that one section of the anterior hypothalamus, known to neuroanatomists as INAH3 or the sexually dimorphic nucleus, is generally larger in males than in females. This brain area is necessary for the display of male-typical sexual activity in many mammalian species, and its size depends on prenatal hormones. Might it differ between homosexual and heterosexual men?

**HYPOTHESIS**  INAH3, a particular cluster of neurons in the anterior hypothalamus, will be larger on average in the brains of heterosexual men than in the brains of homosexual men or heterosexual women.

**METHOD**  Simon LeVay (1991) examined the brains of 41 adults who died at ages 26–59. AIDS was the cause of death for all 19 of the homosexual men in the study, 6 of the 16 heterosexual men, and 1 of the 6 heterosexual women. No brains of homosexual women were available

for study. LeVay measured the sizes of four clusters of neurons in the anterior hypothalamus, including two clusters for which sex differences are common and two that do not differ between the sexes.

**RESULTS**  LeVay found that three of the four neuron clusters did not consistently vary in size among the groups he studied. However, area INAH3 was on the average about twice as large in heterosexual men as it was in homosexual men and about the same size in homosexual men as it was in heterosexual women. Figure 11.30 shows results for two representative individuals. The size of this area was about the same in heterosexual men who died of AIDS as in heterosexual men who died of other causes, so AIDS probably did not control the size of this area.

**INTERPRETATION**  These results suggest that the size of the INAH3 area of the anterior hypothalamus may be related to heterosexual versus homosexual orientation, at least for some individuals. These results are consistent with the idea that genes or prenatal hormones guide brain development, thus altering the probabilities of developing various sexual orientations. However, like most studies, this one has its limitations: Possibly, a homosexual or heterosexual lifestyle might alter brain anatomy instead of brain anatomy predisposing an individual to a particular sexual orientation. (As mentioned in Chapter 3, extensive experience can modify some aspects of brain anatomy, even in adults.) Also, we do not know whether

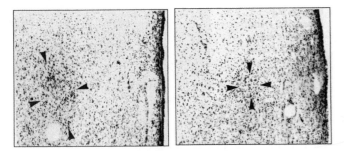

**FIGURE 11.30** One section of the anterior hypothalamus (marked by arrows) is larger on the average in the brains of heterosexual men (a) than in the brains of homosexual men (b) or heterosexual women (LeVay, 1991). Review Figure 11.13 for the location of the hypothalamus.

the people that LeVay studied were representative of other people; certainly, we must await replications on other samples. Finally, the variations in brain structure from one person to another indicate that brain anatomy does not completely control sexual orientation. (The INAH3 nucleus was fairly large in some homosexual men and fairly small in some heterosexual men.)

So, where do all these studies leave us? At this point the evidence suggest that certain genes and patterns of brain anatomy may predispose some people toward one sexual orientation or another. We know little, however, about how those biological predispositions combine with experience to produce sexual orientation, and we have no reason to assume that just one explanation will apply to all people. We need to await additional studies before we can draw any confident conclusions.

Uncertainty and tentative conclusions are not unusual in psychology. If you decide to become a psychologist, you will need to get used to the words *maybe* and *probably*. As I pointed out in Chapter 2, most psychologists avoid the word "prove"; they merely increase or decrease their confidence in a conclusion.

## CONCEPT CHECK

12. Most studies find that adult homosexual men have approximately the same levels of testosterone in their blood as heterosexual men of the same age. Do such results conflict with the suggestion that prenatal hormonal conditions can predispose certain men to homosexuality? (Check your answer on this page.)

### IN CLOSING
## *The Biology and Sociology of Sex*

Sexual motivation at any moment reflects an interplay of biological readiness and the availability of a suitable partner. Similarly, the development of sexual interest and

sexual orientation reflects a complex combination of biological predisposition and experiences. Researchers are making progress, but much remains to be learned.

## Summary

- **Variability in human sexual behavior.** Alfred Kinsey, who conducted the first extensive survey of human sexual behavior, found that sexual activity varies more widely than most people realize. (page 429)
- **Prevalence of sexual behaviors.** Modern surveys indicate that most U.S. adults have either one sex partner or none during a given year. Men express a greater interest than women do in varied sexual practices with varied partners. (page 430)
- **Sexual arousal.** Sexual arousal proceeds through four stages: excitement, plateau, orgasm, and resolution. (page 433)
- **Development of genitals.** In the early stages of development, the human fetus possesses anatomical structures that may develop into either male genitals (if testosterone levels are high enough) or female genitals (if testosterone levels are lower). (page 434)
- **Prevalence of homosexuality.** According to surveys in several countries, about 2–4% of adult men and about half that percentage of women regard themselves as primarily or exclusively homosexual. Sexual orientation varies in degree from exclusively homosexual to exclusively heterosexual, with many intermediate gradations. (page 436)
- **Origins of sexual orientation.** The reasons for different sexual orientations remain unclear. Genetic influences can apparently alter the probability of a homosexual orientation, although these influences alone cannot account for all variations in sexual orientation. On the average, heterosexual and homosexual men differ in the size of one structure in the hypothalamus that contributes to certain aspects of sexual behavior. (page 437)

## Answers to Concept Checks

9. Kinsey interviewed a nonrandom, nonrepresentative sample of people. (page 431)
10. A fetus exposed to very low levels of both testosterone and estrogen throughout prenatal development would develop a female appearance. (page 436)
11. A fetus exposed to high levels of both testosterone and estrogen would develop a male appearance. High levels of testosterone lead to male anatomy; low levels lead to female anatomy. The level of estrogen does not play a decisive role. (page 436)
12. Not necessarily. The suggestion is that prenatal hormones can alter early brain development. In adulthood hormone levels are normal, but certain aspects of brain development have already been determined. (page 439)

# 11.4 Achievement Motivation

*Why do some people try harder than others?*

Most people like to compete against others, at least if they think they have a chance of winning. Archeologists once excavated an ancient human civilization from about 1400 B.C., where they discovered, to their surprise, a ball court complete with nets (Hill, Blake, & Clark, 1998). No one knows the rules of the game, but clearly the idea of competitive sports dates back a long time.

People compete not only in sports but in just about anything. You could check a copy of the *Guinness Book of Records* to see a very miscellaneous list of acts at which people have competed. Even when we don't compete against others, we compete against ourselves to see whether we can do something better than we have done it before.

Most of us strive for the joy of accomplishment, some of us more than others. What occupation do you hope to enter after graduation? Have you chosen it because it is the surest way to earn a lot of money or because it will enable you to take pride in your achievements? Many people forgo better paying jobs to take one that will give a greater feeling of accomplishment.

## Measuring the Need for Achievement

The **need for achievement** is *a striving for accomplishment and excellence.* That definition sounds straightforward, but it confuses two types of motivation (D. C. McClelland, Koestner, & Weinberger, 1989). Usually, when people describe themselves as having a strong achievement motivation, they refer to an extrinsic motivation. That is, they are drawn by the rewards they have been receiving or expect to receive. However, as we saw

in the first module of this chapter, people also have a second, more intrinsic kind of motivation for achievement. People with this intrinsic need for achievement take pleasure in accomplishing goals for their own sake. They persist at a task for a long time and develop great skill at it. For example, people who spend every spare moment playing a video game may be driven by an intrinsic motivation to excel at it, even if they do not think of themselves as highly motivated toward achievement. (They may even say that they are wasting their time.) We shall concentrate here on the intrinsic need for achievement.

■ The need for achievement includes both extrinsic and intrinsic motivation. The artist who created this wooden cow probably hoped for recognition and money (an extrinsic motivation) but also must have enjoyed the creative process itself (an intrinsic motivation). The back of the cow folds out to reveal a desk.

The intrinsic need for achievement was first inferred from the performance of schoolchildren. Some children are more successful in school than others who seemingly have equal ability and equal interest in the rewards that good grades might bring. Also in athletics, business, and other aspects of life, some people simply try harder than others. If so, then we should be able to measure and study this tendency as a personality variable. But how?

If you wanted to determine which workers or schoolchildren were most highly motivated to achieve, what would you measure? You could not simply measure *how much* they achieve because you are trying to explain *why* some achieve more than others. You need to measure need for achievement separately from achievement itself.

Another way *not* to measure need for achievement is to ask people about their motivation for success. Many people say they are highly motivated because they believe

**440**

**FIGURE 11.31** In the Thematic Apperception Test, each person looks at a series of pictures similar to this and tells a story about each one. Psychologists count the number of achievement themes mentioned by each person to measure that person's need for achievement. They can measure other motivations by counting other kinds of themes.

they should be. Psychologists measure achievement motivation indirectly, without even telling people what they are measuring.

One of the most popular methods of measuring the need for achievement uses the *Thematic Apperception Test (TAT),* which we shall examine again in Chapter 13 (D. C. McClelland, Atkinson, Clark, & Lowell, 1953). Investigators show people pictures and ask them to tell a story about each.

 Before reading further, try it yourself: Examine the picture in Figure 11.31 and tell a story that includes what led up to this scene, what is happening now, and what will happen next. If you ever take the TAT, after you finish your stories about all the pictures, psychologists will count the number of times you mentioned various themes, including striving for goals and achievements. For example, this story would get a high score on need for achievement:

> This girl is taking an important test. First she went through the test and answered all the items she knew well. Now she is trying to remember the answer to one of the more difficult questions. She gazes off into the distance, trying to remember everything she has read about this topic. She finally remembers, writes down the correct answer, and gets a perfect score. Later she goes on to college, becomes a Rhodes scholar, and eventually becomes a famous inventor.

Contrast that story with this one:

> This girl is sitting through a boring class. She is looking at the page but thinking about the party she went to last weekend. As soon as class is over, she goes out and has a good time with her friends.

Such a story would rate zero on the need for achievement. (It might rate high on other motives, of course.) Your answer on any one picture is not decisive. For example, you might tell some stories that have nothing to do with achievement and other stories rich in achievement themes. What matters is the total.

How well does the Thematic Apperception Test measure need for achievement? The data suggest that it provides a moderately useful measure. Children who score high on the need for achievement generally work harder and get higher grades in school than do children with a lower need for achievement (Khalid, 1991). Similarly, adults with a high need for achievement are generally successful and highly paid. However, the correlation between achievement motivation and success in school or work is small (about .2), and one explanation is that people with high IQ scores tend to score high on need for achievement and also tend to succeed more than others do in school and on the job (Lilienfeld, Wood, & Garb, 2000). Thus, it is not clear how much need for achievement predicts beyond what IQ scores already predict.

## The Need for Achievement and Setting Goals

Suppose you have a choice of three video games to play. One game is easy; you know you can get a high score on it, but so could anyone else. The second game is more difficult; you are not sure how well you would do. The third is so difficult that you are sure you would lose quickly, as most people do. Which do you choose? Most people prefer the difficult but not impossible game, especially people with a strong need for achievement (Atkinson & Birch, 1978).

People sometimes prefer especially easy or especially difficult tasks if they are dominated by a **fear of failure,** *a concern with avoiding defeat as opposed to gaining victory.* When they try very easy tasks, they avoid failure, although they never achieve any remarkable success. When they try very difficult tasks, they provide themselves with an excuse for failure. Apparently, they would rather fail at an impossible task than run the risk of failing at a realistic task.

People with a strong fear of failure will make a normal effort, or even an extraordinary effort, when given an easy task or when in a relaxed, low-pressure situation. But if they are told, "This is an important test; you are going to be evaluated, so do your best," they expend less effort. In contrast, people with a strong need for achievement try much harder in a competitive situation when they expect to be evaluated (Nygard, 1982).

Suppose you take a test and get 82% correct. How would you react? If you have a strong need for achievement, you would say to yourself, "I can do better. I'll study harder for the next test." If you have a low need for achievement, you would say, "It looks like there is no chance of getting an A, and I'm sure to get a C anyway, so I'll put out less effort next time." Almost any feedback increases the efforts of people with a high need for achievement and lowers the efforts of those with a low need for achievement (Matsui, Okada, & Kakuyama, 1982).

## A STEP FURTHER
### Achievement Motivation

Some people have suggested that our society has become less ambitious and less motivated by achievement than it once was. How could we test this hypothesis?

## CONCEPT CHECK

13. The new basketball coach at Generic Tech has set up a game schedule for next year. The team will play only opponents that had about average records last year, winning as many as they lost. Does this coach have a high need for achievement or a high fear of failure? (Check your answer on page 446.)

## Effective and Ineffective Goals

High goals are somewhat effective in motivating most people, especially people with a strong need for achievement (see Figure 11.32). At the start of the college semester, four young women are asked to state their goals. One is aiming for a straight-A average. Another hopes to get at least a C average. A third plans to "do as well as I can." A fourth has set no goals. Which student will work hardest and get the best grades?

The student aiming for a straight-A average will do the best, under certain circumstances (Locke & Latham, 1991):

- She must have enough ability for the goal to be realistic. If she has previously struggled just to get passing grades, she will quickly become discouraged.
- She must take her goal seriously. If she casually decides she is aiming for straight As and then never thinks about it again, it will make no difference to her. She can increase her commitment to the goal by stating it publicly. The more people who know about her goal, the harder it will be for her to ignore it.
- She must get frequent feedback from test scores and assignments to tell her what topics she needs to study harder (Figure 11.33).

FIGURE 11.32 People with a high need for achievement prefer high goals. Research findings indicate that people work hardest when they set high goals for themselves, provided they think they have a realistic chance of succeeding.

- She will be most likely to pursue her goal diligently if she is *not* being paid to achieve it or if the payment does not require an extremely outstanding performance. If she needs all As to earn a reward, she will become discouraged if it appears that she might get even one B. At that point she may quit trying. An offer of money helps people achieve easy goals, but most people who pursue high goals have intrinsic motivations.

The same conditions hold for workers (Locke, Shaw, Saari, & Latham, 1981). A very high goal leads to the best performance, provided that the goal seems realistic. A vague "do your best" goal is meaningless, because you

**Setting goals leads to vigorous activity if:**

The goal is realistic.

A serious commitment is made, especially if it is made publicly.

Feedback is received.

FIGURE 11.33 Conditions for high activity toward achieving goals.

don't know whether you are achieving it. For a goal to be effective, workers must be committed to achieving it and must receive periodic feedback on their progress. Once they reach their goal, they must be rewarded; otherwise, they will be indifferent toward setting goals later on.

Ordinarily, people do set realistic goals, striving for whatever is possible under the circumstances. For example, someone fishing with a simple pole in a small pond will keep anything that is legal to catch, whereas someone in a large yacht on the ocean will throw back all but the biggest fish. People with great job skills will accept only an outstanding job offer; those with few skills accept whatever they can get. In Poland shoppers willingly bought inferior products before 1989, but after the fall of communism and the introduction of better consumer products, they became much more discriminating (Wieczorkowska & Burnstein, 1999).

■ Preschool children show delight in their successes, but no clear sign of discouragement after their failures. Perhaps they are ever-confident of their eventual success, or perhaps they simply do not yet understand the concept of failure.

ONCEPT CHECK

14. Under what conditions would people be most likely to keep their New Year's resolutions? (Check your answer on page 446.)

# Age and Sex Differences in Need for Achievement

Some people have such a strong need for achievement that they will devote every available moment to an ambitious task they have set for themselves. How does the need for achievement develop, and why does it become stronger in some people than in others?

## *Need for Achievement in Early Childhood*

Achievement and success mean different things to different people (Phalet & Claeys, 1993). In some cultures, and for some people within a given culture, the emphasis is on individual accomplishments, such as gaining wealth, fame, and influence. For others the emphasis is on identification with the group, such as serving one's country or helping one's family. The Japanese culture in particular stresses bringing honor to one's family.

Achievement also has different meanings for people of varying ages. For older people jobs and earnings become less important goals (Maehr & Kleiber, 1981); hobbies become more important, and even mere competence in taking care of one's own needs can be a source of feelings of accomplishment. Still, even within a sometimes restricted range, people strive for some kind of achievement.

In early childhood achievement also means something more like competence than prestige. Even children who are only 18 months old clearly show pride in their accomplishments, such as building a tall stack of blocks. By age 2½, they understand the idea of competition; they

show pleasure at outdoing someone else and disappointment at losing (Heckhausen, 1984).

Although preschoolers show great pleasure when they have completed a task, they seldom appear distressed by their inability to complete it. Heinz Heckhausen (1984) tried to find out how children younger than 4 years old would react to failure. He rigged up various contraptions so that a child's stack of blocks would topple or fall through a trapdoor. He often managed to arouse the children's curiosity, but never their discouragement. He could not find a way to make young children feel that they had failed.

Preschool children are highly optimistic about their own abilities. Even when they have failed a task repeatedly, they confidently announce that they will succeed the next time. An adult asks, "Who is going to win this game the next time we play?" Most preschoolers shout "me!" even if they have lost time after time in the past (Stipek, 1984). Perhaps optimism comes naturally to humans. We quickly learn how it feels to succeed; we learn more slowly what it means to fail.

## *Gender Differences in Need for Achievement*

Times change. In the United States prior to the 1960s, relatively few women sought long-term careers; most expected to quit work when they got married or when they had their first child. However, by the mid-1980s, most women, even mothers of preschoolers, had jobs outside the home (Matthews & Rodin, 1989). Even many older women, who had grown up in an earlier era with much less support for women's careers, reentered the job market (Clausen & Gilens, 1990). For women as well as for men, work provides an opportunity to gain a sense of accomplishment as well as a source of income.

Nevertheless, industrial/organizational psychologists find that most women still do not advance as rapidly as men do in business. Companies hire women about as frequently as men for their lower level management positions, but they tend to give men faster promotions and salary increases. When women do reach high levels of leadership, they are generally rated as about equally effective as men at the same level, except in a few settings such as the military (Eagly, Karau, & Makhijani, 1995).

Why? One possibility is that women place themselves at a disadvantage by interrupting their careers for child care or by refusing promotions that would require moving to another city. However, even women who accept transfers to other cities and who never interrupt their careers still fail to advance as rapidly as men on the average (Stroh, Brett, & Reilly, 1992).

The seemingly obvious conclusion is that companies continue to discriminate against women in spite of their claims that they try hard not to do so. Still, there is one more possibility: According to some reports, women on the average score lower than men do on need for achievement, as measured by the Thematic Apperception Test. That is, perhaps many women are simply content with a lower rate of advancement, or maybe more men are willing to sacrifice everything else to get ahead.

If men and women really do differ in need for achievement, the explanation must include the fact that society discourages girls and women from setting high goals. Many girls set high goals for themselves while they are in high school but lower their goals within the next few years (Farmer, 1983). In one study a group of adult women filled out a job-interest questionnaire. Their interests most frequently included secretary, elementary school teacher, home economics teacher, and dietitian. Two weeks later, they filled out the same questionnaire again, but this time they were given these instructions:

> I want you to pretend with me that men have come of age and that: (1) Men like intelligent women; (2) Men and women are promoted equally in business and the professions; and (3) Raising a family well is very possible for a career woman. (Farmer & Bohn, 1970, p. 229)

After hearing these instructions, the women expressed a significantly increased interest in becoming an author, psychologist, lawyer, insurance salesperson, or physician. They largely lost interest in becoming a secretary, teacher, or dietitian (Farmer & Bohn, 1970). Evidently, the results suggest that many women raise or lower their career ambitions depending on what they believe other people expect of them (Farmer, 1987).

## Jobs That Encourage or Discourage Achievement Motivation

Imagine that you are either starting up or reorganizing a company, and you must decide how to di-

vide the workload. Should you make the jobs challenging and interesting, at the risk of being difficult? Or should you make them simple and foolproof, at the risk of being boring?

Your answer will depend on what you assume about the workers and their motivations. *According to the* **scientific-management approach** to job design, also known as *Theory X, most employees are lazy, indifferent, and uncreative.* Therefore, employers should make the work as foolproof as possible and supervise the workers to make sure they are doing each task the right way, not only to save time but also to avoid injury (Figure 11.34). The employer leaves nothing to chance or to the worker's own initiative (McGregor, 1960).

*According to an alternative view,* the **human-relations approach** to job design, also known as *Theory Y, employees like to take responsibility for their work, to enjoy some variety in their job, and to feel a sense of accomplishment* (McGregor, 1960). In short, they have a need for achievement. According to this approach, employers should enrich the jobs, giving each employee responsibility for meaningful tasks. For example, a financial services corporation that followed the scientific-management approach would have one employee keep one kind of records, another keep another kind of records, and so on. The same company, reorganized according to the human-relations approach, would put each employee in charge of the services for particular clients, therefore keeping a variety of records, doing different things at various times, and seeing how all the pieces come together. Employees with enriched jobs generally report greater satisfaction (Campion & McClelland, 1991). From the employer's standpoint, the enriched jobs are beneficial in most ways, although they pose two possible disadvantages: It takes longer to train the workers than it would with simpler jobs, and the workers performing enriched jobs expect to be paid more than before!

So, which approach is better? Before you answer consider an analogy to education: Professor X tells students exactly what to read on which day, what facts to study

**FIGURE 11.34** Psychologists have conducted research to determine the best, safest, most efficient ways to perform even simple tasks. For example, the drawing on the left shows the right way to lift a brick, and the drawing on the right shows the wrong way, according to Gilbreth (1911).

for each test, and precisely what to do to get a good grade. (This course is analogous to the scientific-management approach; it leaves nothing to the students' initiative.) Professor Y outlines some general issues to be discussed in the course, provides a long list of suggested readings, lets the students control class discussion, and invites students to create their own ideas for projects instead of taking tests. (This course is analogous to the human-relations approach, though perhaps a little more extreme.) Which class would you like better?

My answer would be, "It depends." If I am extremely interested in the topic of the course and I would like to pursue some ideas of my own, then I would love Professor Y's course and I would consider Professor X's course tedious and insulting. But if I am just taking the course to satisfy a requirement with no enthusiasm for the topic, I might appreciate the precise structure of Professor X's class.

The same is true of jobs. Some workers, especially the younger and brighter ones, thrive on the challenge of an enriched job. Others, especially those who have been doing a simple job for many years, dislike the insecurity of learning new skills and solving problems on their own (Arnold & House, 1980; Campion & Thayer, 1985; Hackman & Lawler, 1971).

■   People who have already achieved much, such as author Stephen King, seldom rest on their successes. They set new goals and try to achieve even more.

## CONCEPT CHECK

**15.** "I want my employees to enjoy their work and to feel pride in their achievements." Does that statement reflect a belief in the human-relations approach or the scientific-management approach? (Check your answer on page 446.)

---

IN CLOSING

## *What Need for Achievement Says About Motivation*

Although we sometimes regard hunger as a "typical" motivation, it differs in some striking ways from the need for achievement. For example, people can satisfy their hunger but seldom satisfy their need for achievement. At the end of a big meal, you are quite uninterested in food. In contrast, no matter how marvelous people's achievements are, they seldom lose interest in further achievements. Anyone who reaches his or her life goal sets new, even higher goals (Cantor & Fleeson, 1994). The satisfaction comes partly from the attainment of goals but also partly from the striving itself.

## Summary

- **Measurement of need for achievement.** Some people work harder than others because of their strong need for achievement. Need for achievement is

sometimes measured by the stories a person tells when looking at pictures in the Thematic Apperception Test. (page 440)
- **Goal setting.** People with a strong need for achievement prefer to set goals that are high but realistic. Given such a goal, they will work as hard as possible. In contrast, people with a low need for achievement or a strong fear of failure prefer goals that are either easy to achieve or so difficult that they provide a ready excuse for failure. (page 441)
- **Effectiveness of goal setting.** Almost all of us are motivated to achieve a goal if the goal is realistic, if we make a serious commitment to achieving it, and if we get feedback on our efforts to reach the goal. (page 442)
- **Achievement motivation in children.** Children begin showing delight in their accomplishments by the age of 1½. Preschool children are highly optimistic about their own abilities. After they enter school, they learn the meaning of failure and start to show discouragement. (page 443)
- **Sex differences in need for achievement.** According to some reports, men have a stronger need for achievement than women have on the average, although some of the results are difficult to replicate. To some extent, women lower their aspirations because they fear that their success may displease men or because they believe that employers will not promote them fairly. (page 443)
- **Jobs that encourage or discourage need for achievement.** According to the scientific-management

approach, jobs should be made simple and foolproof. According to the human-management approach, jobs should be made interesting enough to give workers a sense of achievement. (page 444)

## Answers to Concept Checks

**13.** The answer depends on how good a team Generic Tech has. If they won most of their games last year and return most of their top players, then the coach has set a very low goal for them, and we can there-fore assume that the coach has more fear of failure than need for achievement. If, however, Generic Tech has a mediocre team, then the coach may have set a realistic challenge. We would then assume that the coach has a high need for achievement. (page 442)

**14.** A New Year's resolution is like any other goal: People are more likely to keep it if it is realistic, if they state the resolution publicly, and if they receive feedback on how well they are doing. (page 443)

**15.** It reflects the human-relations approach. (page 445)

CHAPTER ENDING
## Key Terms and Activities

## Key Terms

**acquired immune deficiency syndrome (AIDS):** a disease often transmitted sexually that gradually destroys the body's immune system (page 432)

**anorexia nervosa:** a psychological condition in which a person refuses to eat adequate food and steadily loses weight (page 426)

**bulimia:** a condition in which a person alternates between self-starvation and excessive eating (page 427)

**drive:** an internal state of unrest or irritation that energizes one behavior after another until one of them removes the irritation (page 410)

**estrogen:** a hormone present in higher quantities in females than in males (page 434)

**extrinsic motivation:** motivation based on the rewards and punishments that an act may bring (page 411)

**fear of failure:** a preoccupation with avoiding failure, rather than taking risks in order to succeed (page 441)

**gender identity:** the sex that a person regards him- or herself as being (page 434)

**glucagon:** a hormone that the pancreas releases to convert stored energy supplies back into blood glucose (page 419)

**glucose:** the most abundant sugar in the blood (page 418)

**hierarchy of needs:** Maslow's categorization of human motivations, ranging from basic physiological needs at the bottom to the need for self-actualization at the top (page 413)

**homeostasis:** the maintenance of biological conditions at an optimum level within an organism (page 410)

**human relations approach** (also known as Theory Y): view that employees like to take responsibility for their work, to enjoy some variety in their jobs, and to feel a sense of accomplishment (page 444)

**incentive:** an external stimulus that prompts an action to obtain the stimulus (page 411)

**insulin:** a hormone that the pancreas releases to increase the entry of glucose and other nutrients into the cells (page 418)

**intersexes:** people with an anatomy that appears intermediate between male and female (page 435)

**intrinsic motivation:** motivation to engage in an act for its own sake (page 411)

**lateral hypothalamus:** an area of the brain that contributes to the control of hunger (page 420)

**leptin:** a hormone released by fat cells; among other effects, it signals the brain to decrease meal size (page 420)

**need for achievement:** a striving for accomplishment and excellence (page 440)

**obesity:** the excessive accumulation of body fat (page 421)

**overjustification effect:** the tendency of people who are given more extrinsic motivation than necessary to perform a task to experience a decline in their intrinsic motivation (page 411)

**paraventricular hypothalamus:** an area of the brain in which damage leads to weight gain via an increase in the size of meals (page 421)

**primary motivation:** motivation that serves biological needs (page 412)

**scientific management approach** (also known as Theory X): view that most employees are lazy, indifferent, and uncreative, so jobs should be made simple and foolproof (page 444)

**secondary motivation:** motivation that serves no direct biological need but develops as a result of specific learning experiences (page 412)

**self-actualization:** the achievement of one's full potential (page 413)

**set point:** a level of some variable (such as weight) that the body works to maintain (page 420)

**sexual orientation:** a person's preference for either male or female sex partners (page 434)

**testosterone:** a hormone present in higher quantities in males than in females (page 434)

**ventromedial hypothalamus:** an area of the brain in which damage leads to weight gain via an increase in the frequency of meals (page 420)

# Suggestions for Further Reading

Capaldi, E. D. (Ed.). (1996). *Why we eat what we eat.* Washington, DC: American Psychological Association. A collection of articles about food selection and the regulation of hunger.

Dreger, A. D. (1998). *Hermaphrodites and the medical invention of sex.* Cambridge, MA: Harvard University Press. Fascinating history of the medical treatment and mistreatment of intersexes.

Logue, A. W. (1991). *The psychology of eating and drinking* (2nd ed.). New York: Freeman. Discusses normal and abnormal eating, including anorexia and bulimia.

# Web/Technology Resources

Autobiography of Konrad Lorenz

**www.nobel.se/medicine/laureates/1973/lorenz-autobio.html**

Konrad Lorenz is one of psychology's few Nobel Laureates. The 1973 Nobel Prize in Physiology or Medicine was jointly awarded to Konrad Lorenz and two other ethologists "for their discoveries concerning organization and elicitation of individual and social behaviour patterns." This site gives Lorenz's autobiography.

## Anorexia Nervosa

**www.mentalhealth.com/dis/p20-et01.html**

Check all kinds of information about this serious eating disorder.

## Sexual Behavior

**www.indiana.edu/~kinsey/**

See the latest research reports by the research institute that Kinsey founded.

## Intersexes

**www.isna.org/**

Information from a support group for people with ambiguous genitalia.

## Theories X and Y

**sol.brunel.ac.uk/~jarvis/bola/motivation/mcgregor.html**

Consider the assumptions and consequences of two theories of management and motivation: Which management style do you prefer?

# Emotions, Health Psychology, and Stress

12

CHAPTER

**S**uppose you are the first astronaut to land on a planet where the inhabitants experience no emotions at all (but who conveniently speak English). They gather around and ask you, their first visitor from Earth, what *emotion* is. What do you tell them?

"Well," you might say, "emotion is how you feel when something surprisingly good or surprisingly bad happens to you." "Wait a minute," they reply. "We don't understand these words *feel* and *surprisingly*."

"All right, how about this: Emotions are experiences like anger, fear, happiness, sadness . . ."

"*Anger, fear* . . . what do those terms mean?" they ask.

Could you explain those terms? Could you even explain how to measure emotions? (After all, you could show blind people how to measure color vision, even if they never had the experience themselves.) Probably you could not. Emotions are hard to define except by showing examples, and the examples will not mean anything to someone who does not experience emotions.

■ Would you make more intelligent decisions if you could thoroughly suppress your emotions, like the fictional character Spock? Observations of brain-damaged people indicate that people with impaired emotions make worse than average decisions.

In this chapter we shall consider what psychologists have learned so far about emotions, while leaving some major questions unanswered. We begin with general theories and principles. Later we turn to the role of emotions in health and how people cope with the emotions associated with stress.

# Emotional Behaviors

*What is the relationship between arousal and emotion?*

*How many kinds of emotions do people have?*

The philosopher Paul Griffiths (1997, p. 14) wrote, "My central conclusion is that the general concept of emotion is unlikely to be a useful concept in psychological theory." He compares the concept of emotion to ancient astronomy's concept of "superlunary objects," which referred to all objects beyond the orbit of the moon: The items that fit the concept are too diverse to form a useful category.

If you would like to defend the category *emotion,* first try to define it. When you find it difficult to define (as you will), you may object, "Even if I can't define it in so many words, I can recognize it when I see it." Can you? When you swat at a housefly and it flies away, is it frightened? If you poke at a beehive and the bees attack you, are they angry? If fear and anger refer only to the behaviors, then, yes, the fly is frightened and the bees are angry. But if emotions are experiences, like what you and I feel when we experience fear and anger, then it is difficult—maybe even impossible—to know whether insects have emotions.

Never mind insects; what about humans: Is boredom an emotion? Interest? Pain? Courage? Confidence? Sexual desire? How do we decide what is an emotion and what is not?

Emotion is often a slippery concept, difficult to define and difficult to measure. It is, nevertheless, so important that psychologists can hardly ignore it. The cautious approach is to anchor our discussion as carefully as possible in observable, measurable behaviors.

## Emotion, Decision Making, and Emotional Intelligence

When drawing conclusions, you are generally advised to look at the evidence "calmly, rationally, unemotionally." The *Star Trek* character Mr. Spock, the personification of this advice, is extremely logical and rarely emotional. If emotions only get in the way of intelligent decision making, why do we have them at all?

The answer is that emotions usually do not interfere with decision making. In fact, the capacity to feel emotion may even be necessary for good decisions. Antonio

Damasio (1994) described patients who suffered impoverished emotions following brain damage. One was the famous patient Phineas Gage, who survived an accident in 1848 in which an iron bar shot through his head. Nearly one-and-a-half centuries later, researchers examined his skull (which is still on display in a Boston museum) and reconstructed the route that the bar must have taken through his brain (Damasio, Grabowski, Frank, Galaburda, & Damasio, 1994). As you can see in Figure 12.1, the accident damaged part of his prefrontal cortex. As a result Gage showed little emotion and seemed to lose his former values, becoming unreliable in both his work and his personal habits. He made rude sexual advances and used profanities that people had not heard him say before. He followed each whim of the moment, unable to carry out any long-term plans.

A parallel case in more recent times is known to us as "Elliot" (Damasio, 1994). Elliot, too, suffered damage to his prefrontal cortex as a result of surgery to remove a brain tumor. After the operation he showed almost no emotional expression, no impatience, no frustration, no

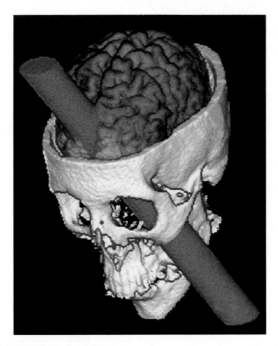

**FIGURE 12.1** In the 1990s researchers used modern technology to reconstruct the path that an iron bar must have made through the brain of Phineas Gage, who survived this injury in 1848. The damage impaired Gage's judgment and decision-making ability. (From Damasio, Grabowski, Frank, Galaburda, & Damasio, 1994.)

joy from music or art, and almost no anger. He describes his brain surgery and the resulting deterioration of his life with calm detachment, as if he were describing events that happened to a stranger. Besides his impaired emotions, he has great difficulty making or following any reasonable plans. If given an array of information, he can discuss the probable outcome of each possible decision, but after describing those outcomes, he still has trouble deciding. Or if he does announce a decision, he abandons it soon after. As a result Elliot cannot keep a job, cannot invest his money intelligently, and cannot maintain normal friendships.

According to Damasio (1994), Elliot has trouble making decisions because of his weak emotions. Ordinarily, when you or I consider possible decisions, we contemplate the possible outcomes and feel a brief "as if" emotion with each. For example, if you consider a job offer from a company that pollutes the environment, you get a feeling of revulsion, so you reject the offer. When you consider another offer from a company that recently fired your best friend, you imagine the unpleasant scene when you next face that friend, and again you reject the offer. You continue until you come to a job offer that will make you feel good if you accept it. Now imagine eliminating all those emotions, and you can see the value of emotions for making decisions. As Damasio (1999, p. 55) said, "Emotions are inseparable from the idea of good and evil." Good decisions make people happy and evil causes unhappiness. If you cannot even imagine happiness or unhappiness, you are likely to make terrible decisions.

Many psychologists speak of **emotional intelligence,** *the ability to perceive, imagine, and understand emotions and to use that information in decision making* (Mayer & Salovey, 1995, 1997). For example, imagine that you are standing in line for lunch but you have left a small gap between you and the next person. Someone else steps into the line in front of you. You have to judge whether this person was being rude or merely making an honest mistake by not realizing you were in line. Should you scream threats, calmly inform this person of the mistake, or ignore it altogether?

Now imagine a man who is trying to decide whether to tell a certain joke to a woman. He needs to gauge how she will probably respond: Will she enjoy it, or will she regard it as sexist and offensive? Suppose he tells it. Now she has to judge his intentions: Was he just trying to share some amusement, or was this joke the start of some sort of sexual harassment?

Emotional intelligence has other aspects as well. Some people are simply more aware of their own mood swings than others are (Swinkels & Giuliano, 1995). Also, some people are better than others at managing their emotions, expressing them in appropriate circumstances and restraining them in others (Mayer, 2001). For example, expressing anger is sometimes helpful and sometimes hurtful.

In short, we frequently need to make complicated judgments about our own and other people's emotions and the probable emotional outcomes of anything we might do. Who would you guess tends to be better at emotional intelligence, men or women? Women are, as you probably surmised. Even in early childhood, most girls are better than boys at interpreting people's facial expressions (McClure, 2000). One chain of U.S. stores ran into a problem when it required all employees to smile at all customers: Many male customers interpreted the female employees' smiles as sexual flirtation. No matter how hard the women tried to give a nonflirtatious smile, some men just didn't get the point.

## CONCEPT CHECK

1. In what way does prefrontal cortex damage impair emotional intelligence? (Check your answer on page 469.)

# Excitement and Physiological Arousal

Originally, the term *emotion* referred to any sort of turbulent motion. People used to describe thunder as an "emotion of the atmosphere." Eventually, the term came to refer only to vigorous body motions and their associated feelings, such as fear, anger, and joy.

We experience emotional arousal or excitement when we have a strong tendency to approach or avoid something. For example, love includes a strong drive to be close to someone. Anger includes an urge to charge and attack. Fear and disgust are associated with escape tendencies. Although anger, fear, and happiness feel very different, we can express any one of them by screams and frenzied activity.

■ Ordinarily, an emotional state elicits a tendency toward vigorous action, even if we suppress that tendency. Here a soldier disarms a mine during the war in the former Yugoslavia. No doubt he feels an intense desire to run away, and no doubt his heart is racing, but he manages to restrain himself from acting upon these impulses.

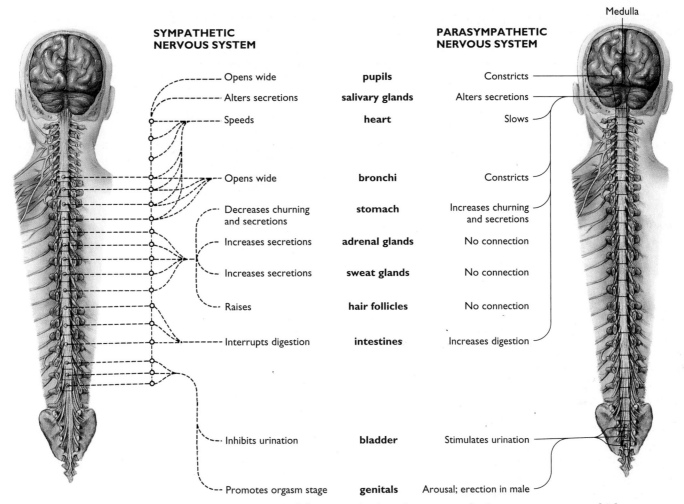

**SYMPATHETIC NERVOUS SYSTEM**

**PARASYMPATHETIC NERVOUS SYSTEM**

Medulla

| SYMPATHETIC | | PARASYMPATHETIC |
|---|---|---|
| Opens wide | **pupils** | Constricts |
| Alters secretions | **salivary glands** | Alters secretions |
| Speeds | **heart** | Slows |
| Opens wide | **bronchi** | Constricts |
| Decreases churning and secretions | **stomach** | Increases churning and secretions |
| Increases secretions | **adrenal glands** | No connection |
| Increases secretions | **sweat glands** | No connection |
| Raises | **hair follicles** | No connection |
| Interrupts digestion | **intestines** | Increases digestion |
| Inhibits urination | **bladder** | Stimulates urination |
| Promotes orgasm stage | **genitals** | Arousal; erection in male |

**FIGURE 12.2** The autonomic nervous system consists of the sympathetic and parasympathetic nervous systems, which sometimes act in opposing ways and sometimes cooperate. The sympathetic nervous system readies the body for emergency action; the parasympathetic nervous system supports digestive and other nonemergency functions.

"But wait," you say. "Sometimes when I feel highly emotional, I can hardly do anything at all. Like the time I borrowed a friend's car and wrecked it. When I had to explain, I could hardly speak." True, but even then your emotion was associated with an urge for vigorous action. While you were telling your friend about the wreck, you undoubtedly felt like running away. That urge expressed itself in your trembling voice and shaking hands.

## The Role of the Autonomic Nervous System

Any stimulus that arouses an emotion—such as a hug, a fire alarm, or a slap on the face—alters the activity of the **autonomic nervous system,** *the section of the nervous system that controls the functioning of the internal organs.* The word *autonomic* means independent; biologists once believed that the autonomic nervous system operated independently of the brain and the spinal cord. We now know that the brain and spinal cord send messages to alter the activity of the autonomic nervous system, but we continue to use the term *autonomic.*

The autonomic nervous system consists of the sympathetic and the parasympathetic nervous systems (Figure 12.2). *Two chains of neuron clusters just to the left and right of the spinal cord* make up the **sympathetic nervous system,** *which arouses the body for vigorous action* (see Figure 12.3). Traditionally, it has been called the "fight-or-flight" system, although some say that for women it should be called the "tend-and-befriend" system (Taylor, Klein, et al., 2000). That is, sympathetic nervous system response increases your heart rate, breathing rate, production of sweat, and flow of epinephrine (EP-i-NEF-rin; also known as adrenaline), thereby preparing you for intense activity. However, exactly which intense activity depends on the situation, your experiences, and your personality.

The **parasympathetic nervous system** consists of *neurons whose axons extend from the medulla* (Figure 12.2) *and the lower part of the spinal cord to neuron clusters near the internal organs. The parasympathetic nervous system decreases the heart rate, promotes digestion, and in general supports nonemergency functions.* Both the sympathetic and

FIGURE 12.3 The sympathetic nervous system prepares the body for a vigorous burst of activity.

parasympathetic systems send axons to the heart, the digestive system, and other organs. A few organs, such as the adrenal gland, receive input from only the sympathetic nervous system.

Both systems are constantly active. The alternation or shifting balance between them helps keep the body in homeostasis (see Chapter 11), but one system can temporarily dominate the other. An emergency that demands a vigorous response mostly activates the sympathetic system, whereas a restful situation mostly activates the parasympathetic system. Many situations activate parts of both systems at once (Berntson, Cacioppo, & Quigley, 1993). For example, a frightening situation may increase your heart rate and sweating (sympathetic responses) and also promote bowel and bladder evacuation (parasympathetic responses). Remember the last time you were seriously frightened. Chances are your heart was beating wildly, you found yourself gasping for breath, and you were afraid you were going to lose your bladder control. Both your sympathetic and parasympathetic nervous systems were responsible for those responses.

We do not voluntarily control autonomic responses, but we can learn to influence them indirectly. Imagine a golfer about to hit a ball or an archer or rifle expert about to shoot. Even a breath or a heartbeat could throw off the aim slightly. Expert golfers, archers, and shooters suppress their breathing and relax enough muscles to decrease their heart rate, improving their chance for accuracy (Robazza, Bortoli, & Nougier, 1998).

## The Opponent-Process Principle of Emotions

After the cessation of a stimulus that has excited sympathetic activity, the system "rebounds" with increased parasympathetic activity (Gellhorn, 1970) (see Figure 12.4). For example, while you are running away from an

attacker, your sympathetic nervous system increases your heart rate and your breathing rate. If the police suddenly intercept your attacker, your sympathetic arousal drops and your parasympathetic activity increases as a rebound. If the rebound is large enough, your heart rate may drop so low that you faint.

This tendency is related to the **opponent-process principle of emotions** (Solomon, 1980; Solomon & Corbit, 1974): *the removal of a stimulus that excites one emotion causes a swing to an opposite emotion* (Figure 12.5). This principle is similar to the opponent-process principle of color vision discussed in Chapter 4. Recall that if you stare at one color and then look away, you see its opposite. (After staring at yellow, you see blue.) Solomon and Corbit suggest that the same principle holds for emotions.

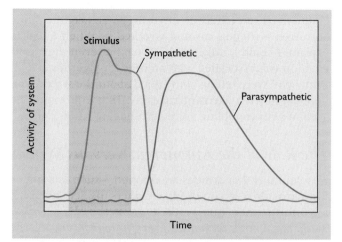

FIGURE 12.4 After the stimulus eliciting the sympathetic response is removed, that response is reduced, and the opposing parasympathetic response is enhanced. This is why people sometimes feel faint at the end of an exciting experience.

**FIGURE 12.5** According to the *opponent-process principle of the emotions,* removing the stimulus for one emotion elicits a rebound to the opposite emotion. A hiker who sees a snake may feel terrified. When the threat passes, the terror gives way to relief and elation.

For example, suppose you are making your first parachute jump. As you start your fall, you probably experience fright. As you continue to fall and your parachute opens, your terror begins to subside. When you land safely, your emotional state does not simply return to normal; it rebounds to relief and even elation for a brief time. Figure 12.6 shows these changes in emotional response over time. Solomon and Corbit refer to the initial emotion as the A state and the opposite, rebound emotion as the B state.

Here is another example: You hear on the radio that you have just won $1 million in the lottery, and you become elated. Later you discover that the winner was not you, but someone else with a similar name. Now you feel sad, even though you "lost" something you never really had.

Solomon and Corbit further propose that repetition of an experience strengthens the B state but not the A state. For example, after you have made several parachute jumps, your rebound pleasure becomes greater and starts to occur earlier and earlier. Eventually, you may not be aware of any initial fright at all; the entire experience becomes pleasant.

Figure 12.6 illustrates the changes in emotional response that occur when the experience-and-rebound cycle is repeated many times. Note that the A state has become weaker and the B state has become stronger and more prolonged.

## CONCEPT CHECKS

2. When you ride a roller coaster, does your heart rate increase or decrease? What happens after you get off the ride?

3. If we apply the opponent-process principle to the experiences that drugs produce, we can describe the initial "high" as the A state and the subsequent unpleasant withdrawal experience as the B state. If someone takes a drug repeatedly, how will the A state and the B state change? (Check your answers on page 469.)

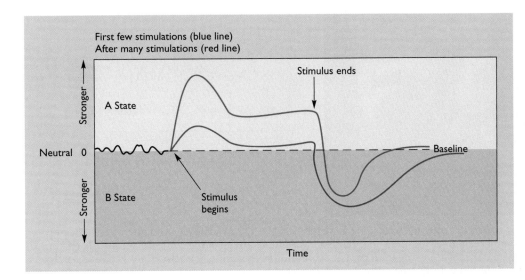

**FIGURE 12.6** According to the *opponent-process principle of emotions,* removing of the stimulus for one emotion (A state) induces the opposite emotion (B state). The blue line traces emotional responses to a stimulus that is introduced and then withdrawn. The red line traces emotional responses to a stimulus that has been introduced and withdrawn repeatedly. Note how the intensity of the response changes over time. (Based on Solomon & Corbit, 1974)

## The Sympathetic Nervous System and Lie Detection

Frequently, the police interview a suspect who denies any participation in a crime, or an employer interviews a prospective employee who claims to be skillful, honest, and trustworthy. In such cases the interviewer would like to know whether the person is telling the truth. Unfortunately, most of us are not very good at detecting lies. In one study a well-known British political commentator gave two consecutive interviews about his favorite films. In one he told the truth; in the other he lied on every question. Both interviews were broadcast on radio and television and printed in a newspaper. Members of the public were invited to guess which of the interviews was the honest one and which one was full of lies. Of the more than 41,000 people who responded, only 53% answered correctly (Wiseman, 1995). Curiously, the television viewers were less accurate than the radio listeners or newspaper readers.

For centuries people have tried to find a simple test to determine who is lying. One of the best-known attempts is the **polygraph,** *an instrument that simultaneously records several indications of sympathetic nervous system arousal, generally including blood pressure, heart rate, breathing rate, and electrical conduction of the skin* (Figure 12.7). (Slight sweating, a sympathetic nervous system response, increases electrical conduction of the skin.) The assumption is that when people lie, they feel nervous and therefore have increased sympathetic nervous system arousal.

The polygraph sometimes accomplishes its goal simply because an accused person hooked up to a polygraph confesses, "Oh, what's the use. You're going to figure it out now anyway, so I may as well tell you . . . ." But if people do not break down and confess, how effectively does a polygraph detect lying? Let's examine the evidence.

### WHAT'S THE EVIDENCE?
*The Effectiveness of a Polygraph in Detecting Lies*

**HYPOTHESIS** Polygraph administrators will identify guilty suspects as liars more often than they identify innocent suspects as liars.

**METHOD** To test this hypothesis, the investigators need a sample of people who are known to be guilty and another sample who are known to be innocent but who are otherwise similar to the guilty people. In one study the investigators selected 50 criminal cases where two suspects had taken a polygraph test and one suspect had later confessed to the crime (Kleinmuntz & Szucko, 1984). Thus, the investigators knew which 50 suspects were guilty, and they knew that the 50 innocent people were similar enough to have been plausible suspects. It is important to note that all suspects had denied their guilt at the time of the polygraph test.

During the administration of the polygraph, suspects were asked two kinds of questions: *Relevant* questions pertained to the crime itself; for example, "Did you steal $125 from the convenience store last Tuesday?" *Control* questions took the following form: "Have you ever taken anything of value that was not yours?" Theoretically, someone who robbed the convenience store should be more nervous about the first question; other people should be, if anything, more nervous about the second.

Six professional polygraph administrators examined all the polygraph results and judged which suspects were lying and which were telling the truth by comparing arousal on relevant and control questions.

**RESULTS** Figure 12.8 shows the results. The polygraph administrators did manage to identify 76% of the guilty

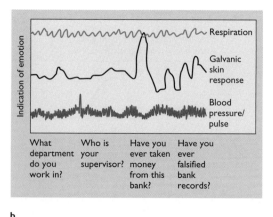

**FIGURE 12.7** The polygraph, a method for detecting nervous arousal, is the basis for the so-called "lie detector" test. The polygraph operator (a) asks a series of nonthreatening questions to establish base-line readings of the subject's autonomic responses (b), then asks questions relevant to an investigation. The underlying assumption is that an increase in arousal indicates nervousness, which in turn indicates lying. Unfortunately, a large percentage of innocent people become nervous and therefore appear to be lying.

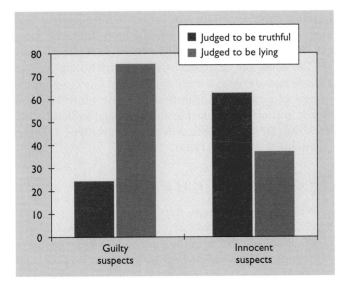

FIGURE 12.8 Polygraph examiners correctly identified 76% of guilty suspects as lying. However, they also identified 37% of innocent suspects as lying. (Based on data of Kleinmuntz & Szucko, 1984)

suspects as liars; however, they also classified 37% of the innocent suspects as liars.

**INTERPRETATION** Recall from the discussion of signal detection in Chapter 4 that, when a person is trying to determine whether something is present or absent, there are two possible correct decisions (green in the following diagram) and two possible errors (red).

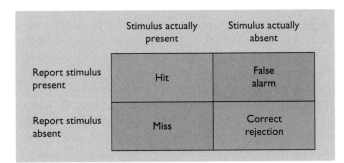

Polygraph administrators can also make two kinds of correct decisions and two kinds of errors:

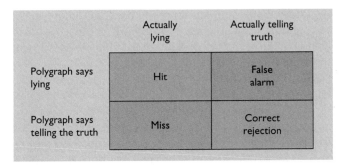

A polygraph user obtains many "hits" but also many "false alarms" (also known as "false positives")—falsely identifying innocent people as lying. Given the usual belief that we would prefer to let guilty people go free than to convict innocent people, these polygraph results are disturbing.

Other research on the polygraph has produced varying results, and most of the studies are scientifically poor. An ideal study is one in which the people are seriously worried about being convicted of some crime and in which the investigators eventually determine for certain who was guilty and who was innocent based on some evidence other than the polygraph itself. Such studies are difficult and rare (Iacono & Patrick, 1999).

When police investigators use the polygraph, they tend to identify many innocent people as liars. When government investigators use the polygraph with top-level CIA and FBI employees, they often make the opposite mistake, calling almost everyone innocent, including some guilty people (Iacono & Patrick, 1999). In other words it is probably impossible to reduce the number of "false alarm" errors on innocent people without increasing the number of "misses" on guilty people.

Although many police officers continue to believe in polygraph testing, most researchers either believe the accuracy is too low for making important decisions or regard the evidence as inconclusive one way or the other (Iacono & Patrick, 1999). Therefore, polygraph results are seldom admitted as evidence in court (Saxe & Ben-Shakhar, 1999). The U.S. Congress passed a law in 1988 prohibiting private employers from giving polygraph tests to employees or job applicants, except under special circumstances (Camara, 1988).

## An Alternative: The Guilty-Knowledge Test

The **guilty-knowledge test,** *a modified version of the polygraph test,* produces more accurate results by *asking questions that should be threatening only to someone who knows the facts of a crime that have not been publicized* (Lykken, 1979). Instead of asking, "Did you rob the gas station?" the interrogator asks, "Was the gas station robbed at 8 P.M.? At 10:30? At midnight? At 1:30 in the morning? Did the robber carry a gun? A knife? A club? Was the getaway car green? Red? Blue?" Someone who shows heightened arousal only in response to the correct details of the crime is presumed to have "guilty knowledge"—knowledge that only the guilty person or someone who had talked to the guilty person would possess. The guilty-knowledge test, when properly administered, identifies most guilty people and only rarely makes the mistake of classifying an innocent person as guilty (Iacono & Patrick, 1999). However, it is applicable only if the police know a number of facts about the crime that a falsely accused person would not know.

**A STEP FURTHER**
*The Guilty-Knowledge Test*

How might the results of the guilty-knowledge test be biased by a questioner who knows the correct details of the crime? How should the test be administered to minimize that bias?

## Pencil-and-Paper Integrity Tests

Suppose you are an employer who wants to know whether someone applying for a job is likely to be an honest worker. Giving a polygraph test is illegal and would not be very accurate anyway, and you can't give a guilty-knowledge test because no one can have guilty knowledge about a crime that has not yet occurred. So, what do you do?

One approach is to administer pencil-and-paper "integrity tests" that ask questions such as these:

- Have you ever stolen money or property from a previous employer?
- Do you think that most employees occasionally steal from their employers?
- On previous jobs have you ever left work early while claiming to work a full day?
- Have you sometimes come to work while under the influence of illegal drugs?
- If you were sure you wouldn't get caught, would you ever make personal long-distance phone calls and charge them to your employer?

You might imagine that anyone who has a history of dishonest dealings with previous employers would lie about it. Amazingly, many people fill out the questionnaire honestly, admitting a long history of past dishonesty. (Perhaps they assume the new employer will find out about this history anyway by checking with previous employers.) Research on such tests is limited, but it suggests that these tests manage to identify a good percentage of dishonest people (Camara & Schneider, 1994).

However, the integrity tests have two major problems. First, they misidentify some extremely ethical and scrupulous people who "confess" to being imperfect (Lilienfeld, Alliger, & Mitchell, 1995). For example, someone may read the question, "Have you ever stolen property from a previous employer?" and think, "Well, there was that one time when I used a business envelope to mail a personal letter, and technically that was stealing."

Second, if the tests become widely used, job applicants will surely learn how to pretend to be honest: They will say they have never stolen from an employer, they have never cheated their employer, they don't think most other people do either, and they think anyone who does should be punished. Test designers can then reword the questions to make their point less obvious by asking

questions about conscientiousness, impulse control, and other characteristics that correlate with honesty. They can also include *social desirability* items: People who say "no" to items like *Occasionally I overeat* or who say "yes" to *I donate money to every worthy charity that I know* can be suspected of answering dishonestly to the more relevant items. In short, it may be possible to design valid integrity tests, but at present we have no guarantees (Alliger, Lilienfeld, & Mitchell, 1996).

## CONCEPT CHECKS

4. What does a polygraph measure?
5. What is the main objection to polygraph tests?
6. What advantages does the guilty-knowledge test have over the polygraph? (Check your answers on page 469.)

# Emotion and Perceived Arousal

Psychologists generally agree that emotions are related to the activity of the autonomic nervous system and the activity of the body in general. But which comes first, the emotion or the arousal?

## The James-Lange Theory of Emotions

In 1884 William James and Carl Lange independently proposed a theory that immediately became highly influential and still remains highly influential, although psychologists have often misunderstood it (Ellsworth, 1994). Common sense suggests that you feel sad and therefore you cry; you become afraid and therefore you tremble; you feel angry and therefore your heart beats faster and your face turns red. James and Lange turned this concept around. According to the **James-Lange theory** (Figure 12.9), *a person's interpretation of a stimulus evokes the autonomic changes directly; the emotion is the perception of those changes.* You decide that you are sad *because* you cry, you feel afraid *because* you tremble, and you feel angry *because* your heart is racing and your face is turning red. Similarly, smiling brings happiness and frowning brings sadness. The body responses alone, James and Lange would agree, are not sufficient for emotions, but they are necessary. For example, trembling itself would not make you afraid. (You might be trembling because you are cold.) Nevertheless, if you did not tremble, you could not have the full experience of fear.

According to this theory, how would you know which emotion you are feeling? Actually, James was skeptical of separating emotion into different categories such as fear, anger, and disgust. He regarded emotions as endlessly varying, with no firm border between one and the next. Still, as far as it makes sense to label emotions, the James-Lange theory suggests that we distinguish our emotions

Schachter and
Singer's Theory
I'm scared because
of the situation.
My heart's pounding,
so I must be very scared.

James-Lange Theory
My heart's pounding,
so I must be scared.

**FIGURE 12.9** According to the James-Lange theory, physiological arousal determines the nature of an emotion. According to Schachter and Singer's theory, physiological arousal determines the intensity of an emotion, but not which emotion is experienced.

by observing our bodily responses, especially our autonomic responses. We sense one pattern of autonomic responses when we are angry, another pattern when happy, still another when frightened or sad. (Remember, according to this theory, an emotion is the *perception* of what is happening in the body, not the *cause* of that change.) But is the autonomic state associated with anger noticeably different from the state associated with anxiety or any other emotion? Most researchers find clear but small differences among the emotions in how they relate to heart rate, skin temperature, and other autonomic activities, but the differences are probably not large or consistent enough to identify one emotion from another (Lang, 1994). In fact, most people cannot accurately report even the intensity of their autonomic arousal. Furthermore, when people voluntarily suppress their expression of an emotion, such as disgust, they greatly alter their physiological reactions without any change in their subjective experience of the emotion (Gross & Levenson,

1993). However, if people have *no* autonomic arousal, as happens after certain rare kinds of brain damage, they feel very little emotion (Damasio, 1999).

 Here is a demonstration of how your perceptions of body changes contribute to your emotions, even if they are not the whole explanation: James Laird (1974) molded people's faces into a smile or a frown by telling them to contract first this muscle and then that one, without ever using the word *smile* or *frown*. He found that an induced smile made people more likely to feel happy and that an induced frown made them more likely to feel sad or angry. You might try this yourself: Smile for a while. Then frown for a while. Do you feel happier when you are smiling, even though it was a purely voluntary smile?

If you do, remember the problem of *demand characteristics:* Maybe you say you felt happier when you smiled only because you knew you were supposed to. Similarly, participants in an experiment often report what they think the experimenter expects them to report. Even though Laird never used the word *smile* or *frown,* the participants may have identified their expressions and guessed that they were supposed to be related to their mood.

In another study the experimenters found a clever way to conceal their purpose. They told participants that the experiment had to do with how people with disabilities learn to write after losing control of their arms. The participants were told to hold a pen either with their teeth or with their protruded lips, as Figure 12.10 shows. Then they were to use the pen in various ways, such as drawing lines between dots and making checkmarks to rate the funniness of cartoons. When they held the pen with their teeth, their face was forced into a near smile and they rated the cartoons as

a    b

**FIGURE 12.10** Facial expression can influence mood. When people hold a pen with their teeth (a), they rate cartoons as funnier than when they hold a pen with their protruded lips (b).

very funny. When they held the pen with protruded lips, they rated the cartoons as significantly less funny (Strack, Martin, & Stepper, 1988). Try holding a pen one way and then the other while reading newspaper cartoons. Do you notice any difference?

## Schachter and Singer's Theory of Emotions

Suppose we wire you to another person so that you share the other person's heart rate, breathing rate, skin temperature, and muscle tension. When the other person feels a particular emotion, will you feel it too? According to the James-Lange theory, you would.

We cannot perform that experiment with current technology. What we can do is to use a drug to induce nearly the same physiological state in two people and then see whether they both report the same emotion. To make things a little more interesting, we can put them in different situations. If emotion depends only on a person's physiological state, then both people will report the same emotion, even if they happen to be in different situations. Stanley Schachter and Jerome Singer (1962) put these ideas to the test in a now-famous experiment.

Schachter and Singer gave injections of the hormone epinephrine (adrenaline) to a group of college students who agreed to participate in the experiment. (Epinephrine mimics the effects of arousing the sympathetic nervous system.) The experimenters told some participants that the injections were vitamins, without warning of possible autonomic effects. Others were told to expect increased heart rate, butterflies in the stomach, and so forth. Therefore, when these people did have such experiences, they would attribute the effects to the injection, not to the situation.

Participants were then placed in different situations to elicit euphoria (excited happiness) or anger. Each student in the euphoria situation was asked to wait in a room with a very playful young man who flipped paper wads into a trash can, sailed paper airplanes, built a tower with manila folders, shot paper wads at the tower with a rubber band, and played with a Hula-Hoop. He encouraged the participant to join him in play.

Each participant in the anger situation was asked to fill out a questionnaire that included such insulting items as these:

Which member of your immediate family does not bathe or wash regularly?
With how many men (other than your father) has your mother had extramarital relationships?
4 or fewer          5–9          10 or more

Many students in the euphoria situation joined the playful partner (Figure 12.11), and some of them initiated play on their own. (One jumped up and down on the desk, and another opened a window and threw paper wads at passersby.) Some of the students in the anger situation muttered angry comments, and a few refused to complete the questionnaire.

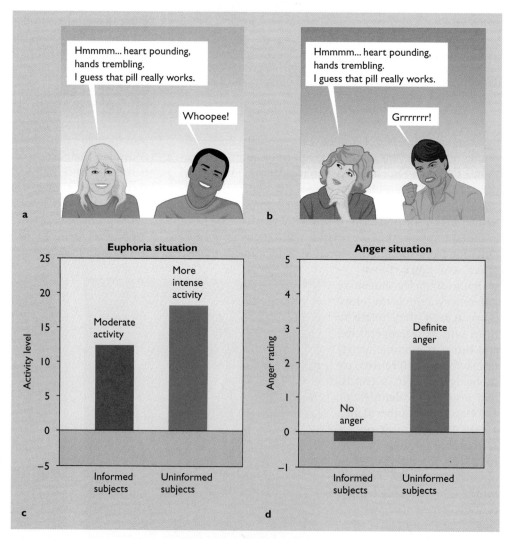

**FIGURE 12.11** In Schachter and Singer's experiment, people who were uninformed about the effects of epinephrine reported strong emotions appropriate to the situation. According to Schachter and Singer, autonomic arousal controls the strength of an emotion, but cognitive factors tell us which emotion we are experiencing.

**TABLE 12.1** Two Theories of Emotion

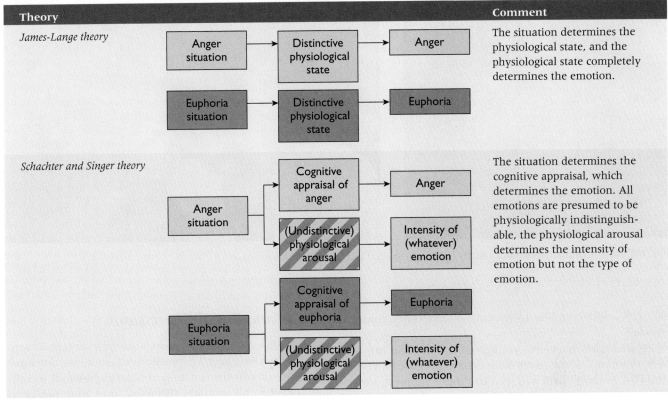

| Theory | | Comment |
|---|---|---|
| *James-Lange theory* | | The situation determines the physiological state, and the physiological state completely determines the emotion. |
| *Schachter and Singer theory* | | The situation determines the cognitive appraisal, which determines the emotion. All emotions are presumed to be physiologically indistinguishable, the physiological arousal determines the intensity of emotion but not the type of emotion. |

But another factor was important in this experiment. Some of the participants had been informed beforehand that the injections would produce certain autonomic effects, including hand tremors and increased heart rate. No matter which situation those participants were in, they showed only slight emotional responses. When they felt themselves sweating and their hands trembling, they said to themselves, "Aha! I'm getting the side effects, just as they said I would."

What can we conclude from this experiment? According to **Schachter and Singer's theory of emotions,** a physiological state is not the same as an emotion (see Figure 12.9). *The intensity of the physiological state—that is, the degree of sympathetic nervous system arousal—determines the intensity of the emotion, but not the type of emotion.* Depending on all the information people have about themselves and the situation, they can interpret a particular type of arousal as either anger, euphoria, or just an interesting side effect of a pill. That is, arousal intensifies an emotion, but cognitive appraisal of the situation tells us *which* emotion we are feeling. Table 12.1 contrasts Schachter and Singer's theory with the James-Lange theory.

Unfortunately, Schachter and Singer's conclusions neglect another group of participants—those whose results raise problems for their theory. These participants, who were given placebo injections instead of epinephrine, showed about as much euphoria in the euphoria situation and as much anger in the anger situation as did the participants injected with epinephrine. Therefore,

critics argue, the epinephrine injections probably had nothing to do with the results. If we accept that possibility, we are left with this summary of the results: People in a situation designed to induce euphoria act happy; people in an anger situation act angry. This result is not very interesting (Plutchik & Ax, 1967).

The overall questions related to the James-Lange and Schachter and Singer theories are complex and difficult to investigate. Most investigators today believe that a more fruitful strategy is to explore the nature of specific emotions and their causes and expressions. Perhaps some day, after we know enough about specific emotions, we can return to study the issue of emotions in general.

## CONCEPT CHECK

7. You are in a small boat far from shore, and you see a storm approaching. You feel frightened and start to tremble. According to the James-Lange theory, which came first—the fright or the trembling? According to Schachter and Singer's theory, which came first? (Check your answers on page 469.)

## The Range of Emotions

How many different emotions do humans experience? Do we perhaps have a few "basic" emotions that combine to form other emotional experiences, just as three

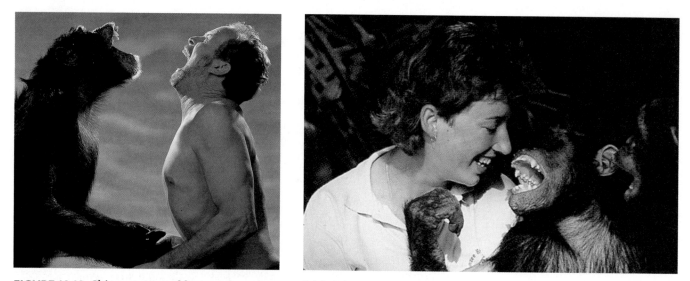

**FIGURE 12.12** Chimpanzees and humans have very special facial expressions.

primary colors combine to produce all the other colors we see?

Psychologists have not yet agreed on a single list of basic emotions. Some psychologists have proposed a very short list, such as "pain and pleasure" or "happiness, sadness, and anger." Most theorists who have tried to list the basic emotions have included happiness, sadness, anger, fear, disgust, surprise, contempt, and shame. However, many also include one or more other emotions, such as guilt, interest, hope, pride, relief, frustration, love, awe, boredom, jealousy, regret, or embarrassment (Keltner & Buswell, 1997). The Japanese list "the pleasant feeling of depending on someone else" as a separate emotion (Lazarus, Averill, & Opton, 1970), and Hindus include heroism, amusement, peace, and wonder (Hejmadi, Davidson, & Rozin, 2000). Still other theorists question whether it makes sense even to talk about basic emotions (e.g., Ortony & Turner, 1990).

How can we decide what is a basic emotion? The English language draws a distinction among shame, guilt, and embarrassment, but using different words does not guarantee that each is a distinct and basic emotion. English also distinguishes red, orange, and pink (as well as scarlet, crimson, and other variants), but we do not accept each of these as a basic color. Psychologists have generally accepted the following criteria for establishing a basic emotion:

- Basic emotions should emerge early in life, without requiring much experience. For example, fear and anger occur even in young children and are more likely to be basic emotions than nostalgia and pride, which emerge later (Lewis, 1995).
- The basic emotions should be similar across cultures.
- Each basic emotion should have its own biological basis and perhaps its own facial expression.

## Producing Facial Expressions

Does each emotion have its own special expression? And why do we have facial expressions of emotions, anyway?

Quite simply, the function of facial expressions is communication. All primates (humans, apes, and monkeys) communicate their emotional states through gestures and facial expressions (Redican, 1982) (see Figure 12.12). We humans can use spoken language as well, but we ordinarily rely on nonverbal expressions. You wink, nod, or smile to show a possible romantic interest; you withhold such expressions to indicate a lack of interest. (You could tell a stranger "I find you sexually attractive" or "please stay away from me," but facial expressions are at least as effective and much less risky.)

Facial expressions provide a kind of "truth in advertising." That is, your expression reflects your internal state—such as being happy, sad, or angry—and therefore tells other people whether you are likely to interact with them in a friendly or an uncooperative manner (Buck, 1994). Emotional expressions occur mostly in the presence of other people. For example, Olympic medal winners generally smile if they are waiting for the awards ceremony with others but not if they are waiting alone (Fernández-Dols & Ruiz-Belda, 1997). Even 10-month-old infants smile more when their mothers are watching than when their mothers are sitting nearby but reading a magazine (S. S. Jones, Collins, & Hong, 1991). Laughter occurs vastly more often in social settings than when people are alone, and it is highly contagious. That is, we laugh mostly when others are laughing. Robert Provine (2000) spent many hours in shopping malls and elsewhere recording who laughed and when. He found that people laughed almost entirely when they were with friends and mostly when they were talking, not when someone else said something. Most of the time they

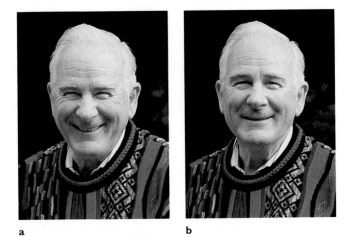

**a**                    **b**

**FIGURE 12.13** A spontaneous, happy smile (a) uses both the mouth muscles and the muscles surrounding the eyes. This expression is sometimes called the "Duchenne smile." A voluntary smile (b) ordinarily includes only the mouth muscles. Most people cannot voluntarily activate the eye muscles associated with the Duchenne smile.

laughed while saying something that wasn't even funny, such as "Can I join you?" or "It was nice meeting you too." The laughter seemed to be simply a way of expressing friendliness.

Voluntary smiles, frowns, and other facial expressions do not exactly match the appearance of spontaneous expressions (except with skilled actors). For example, the smile of a truly happy person includes movements of the mouth muscles and the muscles surrounding the eyes (Figure 12.13a). Voluntary smiles (Figure 12.13b) include the mouth movements but generally do not include the muscles around the eyes (Ekman & Davidson,

1993). *The full expression including the muscles around the eyes* is called the **Duchenne smile,** named after Duchenne de Boulogne, the first person to describe it. Because the Duchenne smile is hard to produce voluntarily, it is a good indicator of someone's true feelings. Researchers have found that women with a Duchenne smile in their college yearbooks were more likely than other women to have happy, long-lasting marriages (Keltner, Kring, & Bonanno, 1999) and to report feeling happy and competent decades after graduation from college (Harker & Keltner, 2001).

## Understanding Facial Expressions

Do we learn how to make appropriate facial expressions, or are they part of our biological heritage? One way to approach this question is through naturalistic observations. Charles Darwin (1872/1965) asked missionaries and other people stationed in remote parts of the world to describe the facial expressions of the people who lived there. He found that people everywhere had similar facial expressions, including expressions of grief, determination, anger, surprise, terror, and disgust.

A century later Irenäus Eibl-Eibesfeldt (1973, 1974) photographed people in different cultures, documenting the similarities in their facial expressions. He found smiling, frowning, laughing, and crying throughout the world, even in children who were born deaf and blind (Figures 12.14 and 12.15). Evidently, at least some of our facial expressions develop without any need for imitation. Eibl-Eibesfeldt also found that people everywhere

**FIGURE 12.14** This laughing girl was born deaf and blind. (From Eibl-Eibesfeldt, 1973)

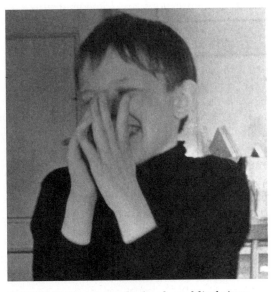

**FIGURE 12.15** A boy who has been blind since birth covers his face in embarrassment. He prevents others from seeing his face, even though he has never experienced sight himself. (From Eibl-Eibesfeldt, 1973)

expressed a friendly greeting by briefly raising their eyebrows (Figure 12.16). The mean duration of that expression is the same in all cultures: one third of a second from start to finish.

 To move beyond naturalistic observations, researchers typically use photos of people showing the presumed "basic" facial expressions, as shown in Figure 12.17. Look at each face and try to name its expression. (Please try now.)

Then look at each and match the expressions to the following labels (one face per label): anger, disgust, fear, happiness, sadness, and surprise.

Most people can match all six expressions to their labels. After researchers translated the labels into other languages, people in other cultures also matched them, though somewhat less accurately (Ekman, 1992). What should we conclude? Evidently, these facial expressions have approximately the same meaning throughout the world (Ekman, 1994). However, the results do not necessarily indicate that people have precisely six basic emotions (Russell, 1994). One problem is that most expressions are somewhat ambiguous. For example, in a matching task, if you know that one of them has to be surprise and one has to be fear, you probably guess that picture d in Figure 12.17 is surprise and f is fear. However, if you saw one of these faces by itself, you probably would have identified the expression correctly, but you would be less certain (Frank & Stennett, 2001). Ordinarily, we do not identify emotions by facial expression alone. We take into account gestures, changes in expression over time, and the social situation (Edwards, 1998; Russell, 1997).

Furthermore, why stop at six emotions? As mentioned earlier, Hindus identify some emotions that Americans do not, such as peace and heroism. When English-speaking people watched videotapes of Indians showing these emotions, most were able to identify them (Hejmadi et al., 2000). So if the ability to identify an ex-

pression is evidence for a basic emotion, our list should grow.

Finally, the fact that we can recognize a facial expression of something doesn't necessarily make it an emotion. For example, do you have any trouble recognizing the facial expression in Figure 12.18? Presumably not. However, even though sleepiness has an easily recognized facial expression, we do not regard it as an emotion. In that case how do we decide what is an emotion and what is not? For example, what evidence do we have that surprise is an emotion, as opposed to a state of alertness? This module began with a quote from Griffiths that emotion is a useless concept. Sooner or later we will either have better evidence or we will decide that he was right.

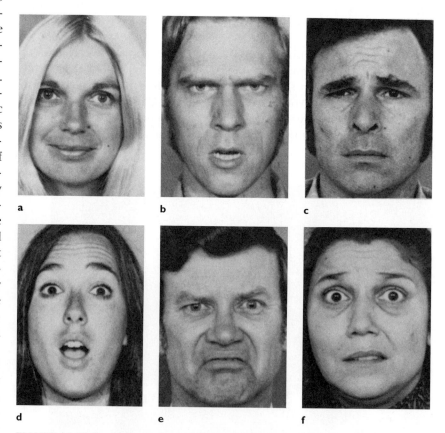

**FIGURE 12.17** Paul Ekman has used these faces in experiments testing people's ability to recognize emotional expressions. Can you identify anger, disgust, fear, happiness, sadness, and surprise? Check the answer on page 469. (From Ekman & Friesen, 1984)

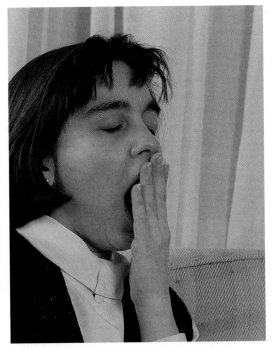

**FIGURE 12.18** Simple point: The fact that you can easily identify the meaning of a facial expression doesn't necessarily mean that what it expresses is an emotion.

8. What is meant by a "basic" emotion?
9. What evidence supports the idea that happiness, sadness, anger, fear, disgust, and surprise are basic emotions?
10. What are some criticisms of the idea that those six are humans' basic emotions? (Check your answers on page 469.)

## A Biological Approach to Identifying Basic Emotions

One way to seek better evidence about basic emotions, or even about the usefulness of the whole concept of emotion, is to study the relationship between emotions and brain activity. Does each emotion have its own special pattern of brain activity?

 Researchers have found evidence linking fear or anxiety to part of the amygdala, as shown in Figure 12.19. This figure shows a human brain, although much of the research has been conducted with rodents. Both rats and people with damage in this area still show fears, but they do not modulate it very well depending on the situation. For example, imagine yourself

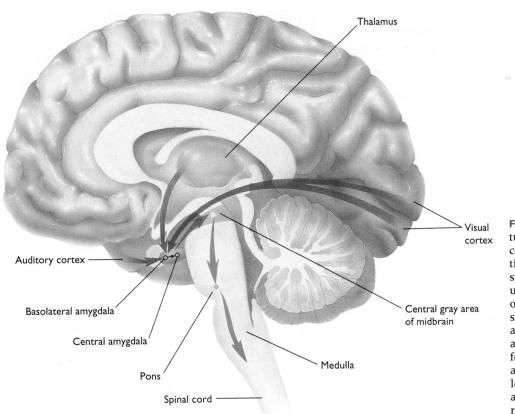

Thalamus

Visual cortex

Auditory cortex

Basolateral amygdala

Central amygdala

Pons

Spinal cord

Medulla

Central gray area of midbrain

**FIGURE 12.19** Certain structures in the pons and medulla control unlearned fear reactions, such as a startle response to a sudden unexpected loud sound. Another structure, the amygdala, sends information to the pons and medulla. Damage to the amygdala eliminates learned fears but does not affect the automatic startle response to a loud sound. This drawing is of a human brain, although the relevant experiments were conducted with rats.

walking alone in an unfamiliar part of town late at night. The only street lamp in the area goes out, leaving you in complete darkness. You wander on anyway . . . until suddenly you hear a loud noise! You will be frightened, right? People and rats with amygdala damage are startled by a loud noise too, but not much more in a dangerous situation than in familiar, comfortable circumstances (LaBar, LeDoux, Spencer, & Phelps, 1995; R. G. Phillips & LeDoux, 1992). Try this: "As the car was speeding down the mountain, Mike stepped down to find that he had no brakes." Rate Mike's fear on a scale from 0 (complete relaxation) to 9 (utter terror).

Almost every normal person rates Mike's fear at 9. If you are ever going to be terrified, this is as good an occasion as any. However, a woman with a damaged amygdala rated it only 6 (Adolphs, Russell, & Tranel, 1999). People with amygdala damage also have trouble recognizing other people's facial expressions of fear (Anderson & Phelps, 2000) and have trouble inferring other people's emotions from their tone of voice (Scott et al., 1997). However, their problems are not limited to depictions of fear or anxiety; they also have some trouble recognizing expressions of anger, disgust, and surprise. Researchers now think the amygdala is not specialized for fear, but for processing information relevant to several kinds of emotions (Whalen, 1998).

Research has also identified a brain area apparently associated with disgust. In one study people looked at photos of other people's facial expressions. Whenever they looked at photos showing disgust, activity increased in a brain area known as the anterior insular cortex (M. L. Phillips et al., 1997). That finding is particularly interesting because the anterior insular cortex is also known to respond strongly when people taste something offensive. Taste is also known as *gustation,* so *dis-gust* is literally *bad taste.* Our brains respond to disgusting things as if they tasted bad.

Overall these brain data do not answer the question about how many emotions we have and how distinct they are. However, they point the way to future studies that may clarify the picture more thoroughly.

# Happiness

Historically, psychologists have concentrated mostly on the "negative" (unpleasant) emotions such as fear, anger, and sadness. One reason is that the negative emotions are the business of clinical psychology; people come to therapists because they want to stop being frightened, angry, or sad. Another reason is that fear and anger have behavioral correlates. A laboratory researcher can study what makes a rat run away or attack. But how can you tell whether a rat is happy? In fact, how do you know when people are happy? Happiness doesn't necessarily make us *do* anything, except smile (sometimes) and take optimistic actions (Peterson,

2000). Most researchers have resorted simply to asking people how happy they are.

In spite of the measurement problem, Martin Seligman and others have called for greater attention to **positive psychology,** *the study of the features that enrich life, such as hope, creativity, courage, spirituality, and responsibility* (Seligman & Csikszentmihalyi, 2000). The meaning of an enriched life varies from one culture to another. For example, in Japan and several other Asian countries, the goal in life is to fulfill one's duty to family and society rather than to seek personal happiness, and the esteem of others is considered far more important than self-esteem (Heine, Lehman, Markus, & Kitayama, 1999). American researchers have concentrated largely on **subjective well-being,** *which is a self-evaluation of one's life as pleasant, interesting, and satisfying* (Diener, 2000). It is approximately what we mean by *happiness,* although it is more a state of contentment than elation or ecstasy.

 What factors influence happiness or subjective well-being? Answer these questions yourself or ask them to a few of your friends. You can ask everyone question 1, but for some people add just question 2 and for other people question 3. (Answering either question 2 or 3 alters people's answer to the other one.)

1. Rate your happiness on a scale where 0 means extremely unhappy and 10 means extremely happy.
2. What would make you happier than you are now?
3. What makes you happy?

On the first question, most people rate themselves on the positive side of the scale, calling themselves happy. A longer questionnaire produces a more reliable measurement (Pavot & Diener, 1993), but the point remains that most people consider themselves happy. That trend is found worldwide, except in countries overrun by poverty, war, or disease (Diener & Diener, 1996).

To the question of what would make you happier, most U.S. students mention money, a good job, more time to relax, or a boyfriend or girlfriend (or a "better" boyfriend or girlfriend). To the question of what makes you happy, common answers include relationships with friends and family, exercise, music, a sense of accomplishing something well, religious faith, and enjoyment of nature.

## Influence of Wealth

Note that many people say more money would make them happier, but few say their money does make them happy. How important is money for happiness?

The simplest approach is to survey rich people and poor people or people in rich and poor countries. Results have been consistent (Myers, 2000): Within a country, rich people on the average rate themselves only slightly happier than poor people, except in countries where the poor are diseased or starving. The results across countries differ in complex ways. Figure 12.20 shows a comparison across countries, comparing their average income to their average reported happiness (Inglehart, 1997). Note that the results fall into two clusters. People in the 19 most prosperous countries in the study rate themselves as relatively happy and those in the least prosperous countries rate themselves as less happy. However, within either cluster, wealth has virtually no relationship to happiness. That is, wealth does not explain why people in Poland are happier than those in Russia, or why people in Iceland are happier than those in Japan.

Whenever two variables have an unimpressive correlation (such as wealth and happiness), one possible explanation is that the relationship really is weak, but another is that one or both of the variables were poorly measured. (An unreliable measurement cannot correlate highly with anything else.) Consider the cross-cultural data. In some low-income countries, many of the people with no money have enough land to grow the food they need to feed their family. So having little money doesn't mean the same thing in Argentina as in the United States or Japan. Also, different cultures have different customary styles for answering questionnaires. Given a rating scale with almost any question, most Japanese answer closer to the middle of the scale than most Americans do. So a particular happiness rating may not mean exactly the same thing in Japan as in another country.

Now consider the comparisons between rich and poor within a country. If a rich person and a poor person both rate their happiness as 7, are they equally happy? Not necessarily. Consider this analogy: Some people have far more taste buds on their tongues than others. Those with the most taste buds ("supertasters") reject many foods as too bitter or too sweet, whereas people with the fewest taste buds ("nontasters") barely detect the bitterness and enjoy the sweetness (Bartoshuk, Duffy, Lucchina, Prutkin, & Fast, 1998). However, if supertasters and nontasters eat something and rate how strong it tastes on a 0 to 10 scale, on the average the nontasters rate it just as high as the supertasters. The reason is that when a nontaster rates something 10 it means "as strong as tastes ever get . . . in my experience." Similarly, 7 means "pretty close to being as strong as possible . . . in my experience." Nontasters don't

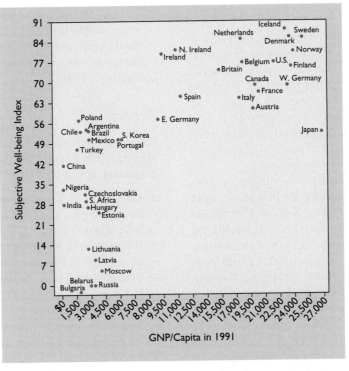

**FIGURE 12.20** Each dot shows the mean data for one country. Note that people in wealthier countries do not consistently regard themselves as happier than people in poorer countries. (From Inglehart, 1997)

get a very strong taste experience, but it's all they know (Bartoshuk, 2000). Therefore, we cannot assume that a particular rating means the same thing from one person to another.

The relationship to happiness surveys should be obvious. If rich and poor people rate themselves 7 on a 0 to 10 scale, we do not know that they are equally happy. They may be using the scale differently.

Another way to examine the effect of wealth on happiness is to interview people who recently gained much wealth. As you might guess, people who have just won a lottery call themselves very happy. As you might not guess, people who won a lottery a few months ago no longer rate themselves any happier than average (Diener, Suh, Lucas, & Smith, 1999; Myers, 2000). There are several possible reasons. First, maybe money really doesn't buy happiness. Second, even if wealth does increase happiness, lottery winners get used to a new level of happiness, so a 7 rating doesn't mean what it meant to them previously. Third, people are naturally greedy. One newspaper survey found that regardless of people's salaries, most said it would take about twice that much to make them happy (Csikszentmihalyi, 1999). Fourth, winning a lottery backfires for many people. Some lottery winners spend themselves into debt; many quit their jobs and lose all sense of accomplishment; and many encounter conflicts with relatives and friends who expect to share the lottery winnings.

The overall conclusion: Wealth does not have a big influence on happiness. Many poor people are happy and many rich people are depressed. However, because of difficulties in measuring happiness, we cannot say for sure how much influence wealth has on happiness.

# CONCEPT CHECK

11. According to one survey, most students in Michigan say they think they would be happier if they lived in a warmer climate, such as California, but on the average students in California rate themselves no happier than students in Michigan (Schkade & Kahneman, 1998). How could we explain these results? (Check your answer on page 469.)

## Other Influences

At this point, after I have emphasized how hard it is to measure happiness, you might be discouraged about finding anything that influences it. However, some factors do correlate fairly well with our rather unreliable measures of happiness. The more sloppily something is measured, the harder it is for anything else to correlate with it, so if one variable is measured inaccurately and something else correlates with it anyway, the correlation probably *underestimates* the true strength of the relationship.

One of the strongest influences is simply people's built-in temperament or personality. In one study more than 2000 twins in Minnesota rated their own happiness. Their ratings correlated only slightly with their wealth, education, job prestige, and so forth, but in most cases either both twins were happy, both were neutral, or both were unhappy (Lykken & Tellegen, 1996). Happiness is apparently part of someone's personality, more rooted in genetics or prenatal environment than in recent experiences. Some people tend to be gloomy and others tend to be cheerful, and most events shift the level of happiness only moderately or temporarily. In other words how happy you are now is a pretty good predictor of how happy you will be a few years from now (Pavot & Diener, 1993).

Many aspects of life correlate somewhat with happiness or subjective well-being. In the following list, remember that in each case the link is based on a correlation, and correlations do not demonstrate causation. For example, married people tend to be happier than unmarried people. That result could mean that marriage tends to make people happy (probably true). It could also mean that happy people are more likely to get married than unhappy people are (probably true also). Happiness also correlates with striving toward goals. Is that because goals provide meaning in life or because happy people set goals and unhappy people give up on their goals? For most of the following, you should be able to think of more than one explanation:

- Married people tend to be happier than unmarried people (DeNeve, 1999; Myers, 2000).
- Happy people are more likely than unhappy people to have a goal in life, such as advancing the cause of peace and justice or making some other great contribution to society. The only kind of goal *not* correlated with happiness is the goal of making money (Csikszentmihalyi, 1999; Diener et al., 1999).
- Generally, healthy people are happier than unhealthy people (DeNeve, 1999; Myers, 2000).
- People with religious faith are more likely to be happy than those without it (Myers, 2000).
- Happy people are more likely to trust others, to be emotionally stable, to be conscientious workers, and to enjoy being in control of a situation (DeNeve, 1999; DeNeve & Cooper, 1998).
- Finally, happy people are less likely than other people to be unhappy (!). This point is not as obvious as it

sounds. Psychologists considered the possibility that some people easily experience intense emotions of any kind, both pleasant and unpleasant. The research, however, disconfirmed that hypothesis (Russell & Carroll, 1999).

## Advice

Based on the research just described, psychologists have offered a few nuggets of advice, none of them especially surprising, about how to be happy:

- Choose your parents carefully. If you are related to happy people, you probably will be happy too (Lykken & Tellegen, 1996).
- If you want to be happy in the long run, think in terms of the future. For example, a teenager might find temporary happiness by watching television, playing video games, and hanging around with friends at the mall, but too much time spent pursuing temporary happiness limits the opportunities for adult happiness (Seligman & Csikszentmihalyi, 2000).
- Develop strong social relationships. Choose a mate similar to yourself, stay in close contact with your relatives, and develop close friendships (Buss, 2000).
- Participate in an activity that seems important. Remember, happiness isn't something that happens to you; it is something that you make happen (Csikszentmihalyi, 1999).

## IN CLOSING

## Determining the Range of Emotions

When psychologists debate how many basic emotions people have (if any), it may seem that the answer to this question is not terribly important. In a practical sense, it may not be, but it is part of a much larger issue. Similarly, in a practical sense, it may not matter whether there are 92 naturally occurring chemical elements or some other number, but when chemists established the number with confidence, they knew that they then understood something important about elements and that they were on the way to still greater understanding. Any field must start out by understanding its elements as clearly as possible. The psychology of emotions continues to be a difficult field simply because researchers are still searching for the answers to some basic questions.

## Summary

- **The usefulness of emotions.** We make many decisions by imagining the emotional consequences of the possible outcomes. Brain-damaged people who suffer a loss of emotions also have trouble making good decisions. (page 451)

- **Emotional intelligence.** In social situations people need special skills to judge other people's emotions and intentions and the probable emotional outcomes of their own possible behaviors. People who misjudge others' emotions can easily cause themselves trouble. (page 452)
- **Emotions and autonomic arousal.** Most emotions are associated with increased arousal of the sympathetic nervous system, although some parts of the parasympathetic nervous system increase their activity also. The sympathetic nervous system readies the body for emergency action. (page 453)
- **Opponent-process principle.** Removing the impetus for a given emotion instigates a sudden swing to the opposite emotion. For example, removing something that had made you happy would make you unhappy. (page 454)
- **Polygraph.** The polygraph measures the activity of the sympathetic nervous system through such variables as heart rate, breathing rate, blood pressure, and electrical conductance of the skin. The polygraph is sometimes used as a "lie detector," although it is not very accurate for that purpose. (page 456)
- **James-Lange theory.** According to the James-Lange theory of emotions, an emotion is the perception of a change in the body's physiological state. (page 458)
- **Schachter and Singer's theory.** According to Schachter and Singer's theory, autonomic arousal determines the intensity of an emotion but does not determine what that emotion will be. We identify an emotion on the basis of how we perceive the situation. (page 460)
- **Range of emotions.** Psychologists do not fully agree on which emotions, if any, are basic. Different cultures recognize different emotions. (page 461)
- **Facial expressions.** Many human facial expressions have similar meanings in cultures throughout the world. (page 462)
- **Happiness.** Most studies of happiness rely on questionnaires and self-ratings. Unfortunately, a given rating may mean something different to one person than another. Happiness level appears to be a fairly stable aspect of personality despite changes in people's lives. It correlates with marriage and friendships, health, goals other than wealth, religious faith, and several aspects of personality. (page 466)

## Answers to Concept Checks

1. People with prefrontal cortex damage feel little emotion themselves and have trouble imagining the emotional consequences of any decision, for themselves as well as others. (page 452)

2. When you ride a roller coaster, your heart rate increases (sympathetic activity). After you get off the ride, your heart rate falls to lower than usual (rebound increase in parasympathetic activity). (page 455)
3. After someone takes a drug repeatedly, the A state becomes weaker. (The weakening is called tolerance, as discussed in Chapter 6.) The B state (withdrawal) becomes stronger. (page 455)
4. The polygraph measures several aspects of sympathetic nervous system activity, such as heart rate, breathing rate, and sweating. (page 458)
5. A polygraph will too often identify an innocent person as lying. (page 458)
6. A guilty-knowledge test measures information that only a guilty person would know. If properly used, it should almost never call an innocent person guilty. (page 458)
7. According to the James-Lange theory, the trembling and shaking came first. Schachter and Singer's theory agrees. However, according to the James-Lange theory, your perception of the trembling and shaking produces the experience of fear. According to Schachter and Singer, you interpret your trembling on the basis of the situation: "Am I shaking because someone made me angry? Because I'm excited? Because I'm frightened? Because of a pill I took?" (page 461)
8. A basic emotion emerges early in life without needing to be learned. It is similar across cultures and it probably has its own special expression. (page 465)
9. People of different cultures can usually identify which facial expression goes with which named emotion, such as fear or anger. (page 465)
10. Emotions are named less accurately if the observer simply looks at one picture at a time and labels it, instead of matching a group of faces to a list of words. Several other cultures identify additional emotions, which even Americans can also identify, especially if given a sequence of pictures instead of one still. Also, the fact that we can identify a facial expression does not necessarily mean that what it expresses is an emotion. (page 465)
11. One possibility is that climate makes less difference to people's happiness than they think it will. The other is that a given happiness rating means something different in California than in Michigan. Students in each state rate themselves compared to how happy they usually are or think they could be. (page 467)

## Answers to Other Question in the Module

Figure 12.17, page 464. The faces express (a) happiness, (b) anger, (c) sadness, (d) surprise, (e) disgust, and (f) fear.

# Anger and Violence

During World War II—while nearly all the industrialized nations were at war, while the Nazis were exterminating the Jews, and while the United States was preparing a nuclear bomb that it later dropped on Japan—Mohandas K. Gandhi, the world's foremost advocate of nonviolence, was in jail for leading a protest march against British rule in India. The charge against Gandhi was, ironically, "disturbing the peace." Someone asked Gandhi what he thought of Western civilization. He replied that he thought it might be a good idea.

Human beings are capable of ghastly acts of cruelty, but also of nobility, heroism, and courageous opposition to violence. The struggle to understand violence is among the most important goals facing humanity in general and psychology in particular.

## Situations with Violence

Most people become angry far more often than they actually attack anyone. Participants in one study kept an "anger diary" for a week (Averill, 1983). Most of their experiences with anger were provoked by people they knew well, such as, "My roommate locked me out of the room when I went to the shower." The diaries also included descriptions of what people did in response to each event. Nearly all the replies were either, "I talked to the person who made me angry," "I talked to someone else about it," or "I did nothing about it." Very few admitted to issuing even threats of violence, much less actually attacking.

## Frustration and Aggression

If you try keeping track of your own anger experiences, you may find that you are often provoked when someone prevents you from doing something you wanted to do, such as if a person borrows something you needed without asking you. Psychologists have long spoken of the **frustration-aggression hypothesis,** *the idea that frustration—a failure to obtain something that one expected—leads to aggressive behavior* (Dollard, Miller, Doob, Mowrer, & Sears, 1939). However, this hypothesis has several limitations. First, frustration produces anger and the potential for aggression mainly when one attributes an intention to the person who caused the frustration. For example, if someone runs down the hall, bumps into you, and knocks you down, you might feel angry. But if someone slipped on a wet spot on the floor and knocked you down, you would probably not feel angry because you do not assess blame.

■ Violent behavior depends both on individuals' dispositions and their situations. When police confront nonviolent protesters, it would be easy for a nonviolent situation to explode into a violent one.

Second, even when frustration leads to anger, the anger will not usually lead to aggression. Finally, frustration is important only for emotional aggression, not for calm aggressive behaviors that people learn as strategies for getting what they want.

Leonard Berkowitz (1983, 1989) therefore proposed a more comprehensive theory: Any unpleasant event—frustration, pain, foul odors, a hot environment, frightening information, whatever—excites both the impulse to fight and the impulse to flee. Which impulse dominates depends on the circumstances, and one of the main circumstances is the expected result of an attack. If you have frequently struck people before, have won most of your fights, and have seldom been punished, and you think the person who just spilled coffee on you looks easy to beat, you may threaten this person or even strike. But if you have had mostly bad experiences in fights, or if the offending person looks large and ferocious, you will suppress your anger. And if the one who bumped into you is your boss, or the loan and scholarship officer at your college, you will most likely smile and apologize for being in the way.

Although any kind of frustration or disappointment can lead to anger, and potentially to violence, the likelihood is particularly strong in a sexual context. In most of the animal kingdom, who are more likely to fight with one another—males or females? Males. When do they fight the most? During the reproductive season. And what are they fighting about? Access to females. In some cases they are fighting for a position of dominance, but the main value of dominance is increased access to sexual partners. In humans as well, one of the leading causes of murder is sexual jealousy (Daly, Wilson, & Weghorst, 1982).

## After Violence: Reconciliation

For many years psychologists' and biologists' ideas about violence were shaped by their observations of birds in the wild. Birds of many species fight to protect breeding territories, and aggression serves the function of spreading out the population.

A problem arises, however, if we assume that fighting serves the same function in all species, including humans. Two male birds don't have much use for each other during the breeding season, and each would be pleased to drive the other as far away as possible. The same is not true for wolves, monkeys, humans, or any other species that lives in social groups. Very few humans would want to drive all other people as far away as possible.

Moreover, most fights break out between people who know each other well such as brothers or sisters, husband and wife, co-workers, perhaps roommates. After a fight they realize they must get along together and they cannot continue fighting. Therefore, they find some way to reconcile. They apologize, hug, shake hands, or signal in some other way that the fight is over and they will go back to cooperating.

We had always known about humans' habit of making up after a fight, but researchers paid little attention to it until they saw reconciliation among chimpanzees (de Waal, 2000). As in humans, most chimpanzee fights occur between individuals that know each other well and live in the same troop. After a fight two individuals *increase* the amount of time they spend together. They groom each other, hold hands, kiss, and sometimes even have sexual intercourse. After one of these reconciliation ceremonies, they become less likely to fight. If they don't reconcile quickly, one of the other chimpanzees literally drags them together.

## CONCEPT CHECK

12. Psychologists often study the causes of aggression by putting one person at a time in a laboratory and testing the effects of some experience on that person's willingness to flip a switch that supposedly shocks another person. Which aspect of aggression will that procedure probably overlook? (Check your answer on page 476.)

## Characteristics of Violent People

Can we identify the people who are most likely to commit violent acts? In one regard many psychologists were on the wrong track for a long time, assuming that people committed violence because of low self-esteem. According to that idea, people who thought little of themselves tried to build themselves up by tearing someone else down. Perhaps (but only perhaps) that hypothesis works in certain cases of group violence. Some outbreaks of ethnic violence have occurred when one group suffered defeats and humiliations and then blamed another group for their problems (Staub, 1996).

For individuals, however, the research finds little or no link between violence and low self-esteem. *Victims* certainly report low self-esteem, sometimes extremely low, but aggressors tend to be arrogant, egotistical, and self-confident. At most it may be that violence results when something threatens someone's high self-esteem, and that person then strikes out against someone to reaffirm a sense of superiority (Baumeister, Smart, & Boden, 1996).

One extensive study of Norwegian and Swedish bullies, ages 7 through 16, found that hardly any of them suffered from feelings of anxiety or insecurity. They were as a rule large, strong, impulsive, and indifferent to their victims. Why did they do it? They said it was fun. They enjoyed taking another child's money, forcing him to eat weeds, or leading him around as a pet with a string around his neck, and most important, they got away with it. Psychologists found they could reduce the bullying by increasing adult supervision, enforcing rules, and having

■ Throughout the animal kingdom, aggressive behavior is common among males when they are competing for the attention and affection of females.

serious talks with the offending children and their parents (Olweus, 1995). Telling the bullies that they are fine human beings, to try to raise their self-esteem, would be utterly pointless.

If low self-esteem is not a good predictor of violence, what is? Sometimes psychologists or other mental-health professionals are asked to predict how violent someone will be. For example, a judge may be trying to decide between a prison sentence and a period of probation for someone recently convicted of a crime. Or perhaps someone has been in prison and is now eligible for parole or has been in a hospital for mentally disordered criminal offenders and is now being considered for release.

Under such circumstances, how accurate would you guess that a psychologist's predictions are? Predictions based on interviews are a bit more accurate than flipping a coin, but not by much (Monahan, 1984). One reason for these mediocre results is that violent behavior is sporadic and situation-dependent. Even the most violence-prone people can be pleasant and charming while talking to a psychologist who will decide whether they belong in prison. The best basis for predicting violence is past behavior. People with a long history of violent acts are likely to commit more, whereas those who committed only a single violent act are less dangerous. From an examination of someone's past, it is possible to make moderately useful predictions, although it is still best to admit uncertainty, just as weather forecasters usually qualify their predictions, such as, "the chance of rain is 80% for Tuesday and 60% for Wednesday." Many psychologists prefer to say something like, "This defendant has a less than 25% risk of violence if he gets a job and a higher than 50% chance if he does not" (Borum, 1996; Grisso & Tomkins, 1996; Monahan & Steadman, 1996).

People who were physically abused as children and who witnessed violence between their parents are more likely than others to commit repeated acts of violence, including murder (Malinosky-Rummell & Hansen, 1993). The physical pain of being beaten may provoke future vi-

olence, and a violent parent provides a model for the child to imitate. (Recall the principles of social learning from Chapter 6.) Even this predictor is far from foolproof, however; only about one third of abused children become abusive parents (Widom, 1989).

Several other factors are associated with a tendency toward violent behavior (Davidson, Putnam, & Larson, 2000; Lewis et al., 1985; Lynam, 1996; Osofsky, 1995; Raine, Lencz, Bihrle, LaCasse, & Colletti, 2000):

* Frequent abuse of alcohol and other drugs
* A history of impulsive acts
* Growing up in a violent neighborhood
* Not feeling guilty after hurting someone
* Weaker-than-normal physiological responses to arousal
* Smaller-than-average prefrontal cortex and decreased release of serotonin to this area
* A history of suicide attempts
* Watching a great deal of violence on television

The probability of attack also depends on biological factors. In all cultures violent and criminal activities are more common in men than in women, and the probability of such activities increases sharply during puberty, when testosterone levels are increasing. Figure 12.21 shows the probability of arrest for robbery, burglary, and aggravated assault as a function of age in the United States. For each crime the age of the maximum number of arrests was set at 100%, so the graph does not show that burglary is more than three times more common than either of the other two crimes. Note that for each crime the rate of occurrence rises sharply during the teen years, reaches a peak at 17 to 21 years, and then declines steadily.

With humans as well as with other species, testosterone increases the probability of violence, although the correlation is not high (Bernhardt, 1997; Brooks & Reddon, 1996; Dabbs, Carr, Frady, & Riad, 1995). (Recall the link between violence and sexual jealousy.) A variety of

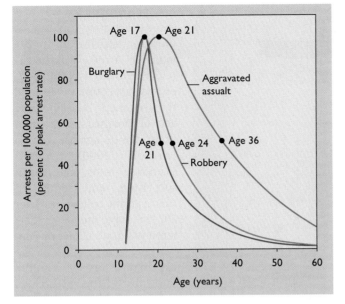

**FIGURE 12.21** Relative frequencies of arrest at different ages in the United States. For each crime the age of the maximum number of arrests was set at 100%. Note that the arrest rate rises for each crime until ages 17–21 and thereafter declines. (From data of the Federal Bureau of Investigation, 1984)

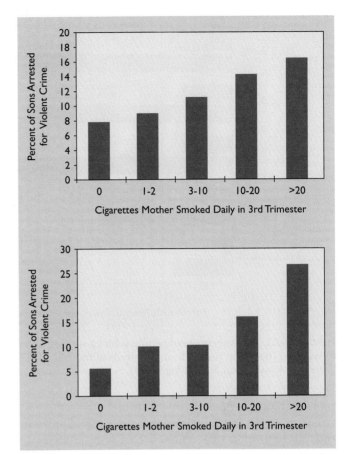

**FIGURE 12.22** The more cigarettes the mother of a male baby smoked during pregnancy, the more likely her son was to be arrested for a crime during late adolescence or early adulthood. The top graph shows results for all women; the bottom graph shows only those women who also had complications during delivery. (From Brennan, Grekin, & Mednick, 1999)

drugs, notably alcohol and tranquilizers, increase the probability of violent behavior (Bushman, 1993; Bushman & Cooper, 1990). Tranquilizers presumably increase violent behavior by decreasing people's fear of the possible retaliation by the person being attacked. Also, the probability of violent behavior is highest among adults with low activity of the neurotransmitter serotonin. Exactly how a deficit of serotonin activity could lead to violence is unknown, but measurements of serotonin metabolites in the blood or urine have provided moderately accurate predictors of several kinds of violent acts (Davidson et al., 2000).

Finally, two studies have found that the more cigarettes a woman smoked during pregnancy, the greater the probability that her son would be arrested for violent crimes in adolescence or early adulthood, especially if the woman also had complications during delivery (Brennan, Grekin, & Mednick, 1999; Fergusson, Woodward, & Horwood, 1998). Figure 12.22 shows the link between smoking in pregnancy and violent crimes by the woman's son decades later. These are correlational data, so as always we should beware of cause-and-effect conclusions. Some women who smoked during pregnancy may have provided poor care for their sons after birth.

## Violence and Psychiatric Disorders

Decades ago psychologists believed that people with psychiatric disorders were no more dangerous than anyone else and no more likely to commit crimes. However, there was a problem with their evidence. At the time most patients in mental hospitals stayed there indefi-

nitely, and only the best recovered and least dangerous ones were released. Today, nearly all such patients are released after brief stays.

The results vary from one study to another and depend greatly on the type of psychiatric disorder (Eronen, Hakola, & Tiihonen, 1996; Hodgins, Mednick, Brennan, Schulsinger, & Engberg, 1996; Teplin, Abram, & McClelland, 1996) (see Figure 12.23). The highest criminal risk is with people with *antisocial personality disorder* (Hodgins et al., 1996). However, the criteria for that diagnosis include repeatedly performing acts that are grounds for arrest (American Psychiatric Association, 1994), so its association with crime is hardly a surprise! The other psychiatric disorder highly associated with crime is drug and alcohol abuse (Hodgins et al., 1996; Monahan, 1992; Teplin et al., 1996). One unresolved question is whether drugs lead to violence or whether they just appear to because people prone to violence are also likely to use drugs. Curiously, one study found that giving methylphenidate (Ritalin), a stimulant drug, actually decreased troublesome behaviors by adolescents with conduct problems (Klein et al., 1997).

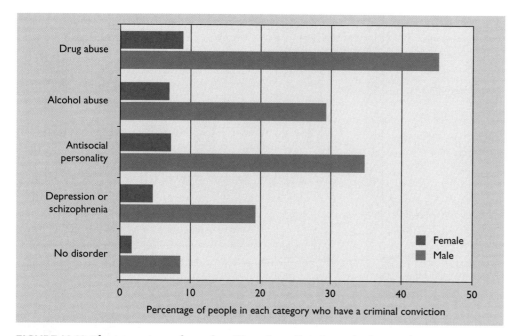

**FIGURE 12.23** The percentage of people with various disorders who have at least one criminal conviction. (Based on results from hundreds of thousands of Danes, from Hodgins, Mednick, Brennan, Schulsinger, & Engberg, 1996)

For most psychiatric disorders, including depression and schizophrenia, the crime rate is only moderately higher than for the population as a whole, and even that elevation is traceable mostly to patients who have drug and alcohol problems in addition to depression or schizophrenia. Most people with psychiatric disorders are not dangerous, and very few are dangerous to people they do not know.

Still, even though certain disorders are associated with an increased risk of violence, the task remains to predict which individuals with a given disorder are dangerous. As with anyone else, interviews and personality measures provide only weak predictors of violence (Bonta, Law, & Hanson, 1998). The best predictor is the person's past history of violent or criminal behavior. As shown in Figure 12.24, psychiatric patients with a past history of criminal arrests are likely to be arrested again; those with no previous arrests are likely to continue keeping a clean record (Cocozza, Melick, & Steadman, 1978).

# CONCEPT CHECK

13. What information provides the best predictor of someone's violent behavior? Is low self-esteem a good predictor? (Check your answer on page 476.)

## Sex-Related Violence

Most acts of violence occur between people who know each other well, and dating and married couples certainly know each other well. Many of the people brought to

hospital emergency wards—some estimate 25% or more—are victims of spouse violence. A review of the extensive research within heterosexual couples reported that women commit *more* acts of violence against men than men do against women (Archer, 2000). Almost everyone finds that result surprising, and some say they cannot believe it. After all, we have heard of battered women's clinics but not battered men's clinics. The explanation for the result is that most of the researchers defined violence extremely broadly. If a man on a date got too close to the woman and she shoved him away, or if he insulted her and she slapped him, those rather trivial acts counted as violence. The results are different if we define violence more narrowly: Men commit more serious attacks, inflict more injuries, and are certainly more likely to kill their partners than women are. Men who attack their wives or girlfriends vary in their degree and frequency of violence. Ordinarily, those with the most frequent

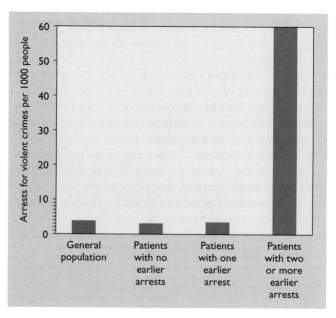

**FIGURE 12.24** The arrest rates for psychiatric patients and for members of the general public. Patients with a history of criminal offenses usually continue to be dangerous, but those without such a history are not. (After data of Cocozza, Melick, & Steadman, 1978)

and severe attacks also have a long history of criminal and violent behavior toward other people as well (Holtzworth-Munroe, 2000).

## *Rape*

**Rape** is *sexual contact obtained through violence or threats.* Although that definition sounds simple enough, in practice, offenses range on a continuum from forcible rape through ambiguous resistance. For example, 9% of the women surveyed at 32 colleges reported that they had been forced into unwanted sexual intercourse, and 25% said they had participated in unwanted intercourse in response to verbal coaxing or while under the influence of alcohol (Koss, Gidycz, & Wisniewski, 1987). At the same colleges, only 4.4% of the men said they had forced a woman to have sex (Koss & Dinero, 1988). Why the discrepancy? Perhaps some men are lying, and perhaps a small percentage of the men forced themselves sexually on a larger percentage of women. Another explanation relates to the wording of the questions. If a couple has had sex repeatedly in the past, and then one night the woman doesn't feel like having sex but the man talks her into it, she could say she "had unwanted intercourse in response to verbal coaxing," but probably the man would not say he "forced" her to have sex. Cases also occur in which the woman says no, but the man disbelieves or disregards her refusal. Preventing date rape is partly a matter of persuading men to respect a woman's refusal and partly a matter of advising women to express their refusal emphatically.

What kind of men commit rape? Unfortunately, most of our data are based on convicted rapists who committed violent attacks and who may not be representative of other rapists. Still, the best available evidence indicates that most men who commit sexual attacks have a history of hostility and violence against both men and women (Hanson, 2000). Unlike most men, rapists find the idea of forcible sex appealing, and in some cases that appeal can be traced to a history of watching violent pornography (Donnerstein & Malamuth, 1997). However, finding the idea appealing is not enough. The other element is extreme self-centeredness, or lack of concern for others' feelings (Dean & Malamuth, 1997).

Many rapists were abused children, though certainly not all. Low self-esteem is not related to a history of sex crimes. Many rapists (although, again, not all) express anger toward women and a need to dominate or control them. One survey of admitted date rapists found that they too reported anger against women and a wish to dominate them (Lisak & Roth, 1988). The probability of rape is also elevated when a man becomes so intoxicated from alcohol or other drugs that he sheds the inhibitions that would ordinarily prevent such an attack (Lisak & Roth, 1988).

What should a woman do if a stranger is trying to rape her? Some psychologists recommend fighting back; oth-

ers recommend trying to appeal to the would-be rapist's better nature; others recommend doing something to upset or offend the rapist, such as vomiting. However, none of these approaches is dependable. The best advice is to avoid attacks: Stay alert; don't walk alone at night; and conspicuously carry something that could be used for defense.

Most rapes, however, are by dates or other acquaintances. For those cases the advice is different, although again not guaranteed: Stay reasonably sober; avoid being totally alone with someone you don't know well; and make your refusal strong, clear, and quick. Some advice for men also: If you don't want to be a date rapist, listen to what your date is saying instead of assuming she does not really mean it. And avoid drinking too heavily, lest you lose control of your usual good sense.

> ### CRITICAL THINKING
> ### A STEP FURTHER
> *Pornography*
>
> Rapists and child molesters sometimes pore over sexually explicit magazines and watch videotapes just before committing an offense. Can we conclude that such materials lead to the offenses? (Remember, correlation does not mean causation.) What kind of evidence would we need to determine whether sexually explicit materials lead to sexual offenses?

## *Sexual Abuse of Children*

Finally, what do we know about sexual abuse of children and its effects? One article published on this topic became far more controversial than it deserved to be. Its authors observed that sexual abuse varies in intensity and frequency and that people vary in their resilience after an unpleasant experience. Thus, some people are traumatized by early sexual abuse but many are not (Rind, Tromovitch, & Bauserman, 1998). Some people who heard brief summaries of this article apparently thought the authors were saying that it is acceptable for adults to sexually molest children. The United States Congress even passed a resolution calling on the American Psychological Association to condemn the article. However, saying that many people recover from sexual abuse without being permanently traumatized is hardly the same as saying that sexual abuse is acceptable.

Part of the problem here is the definition of sexual abuse. Some people define it very broadly to include such events as once seeing an exhibitionist, and they conclude that sexual abuse is extremely widespread. Others define it narrowly, including such events as being repeatedly raped or molested by your father, and they conclude that sexual abuse is extremely traumatic. The severe kinds of sexual abuse do lead to long-term psychological problems, but those kinds are less common (although admittedly we don't know how uncommon). The point is that any study that lumps together major and minor kinds of abuse and then looks for the psychological consequences will have misleading, even meaningless, results (Haugaard, 2000).

Proper therapy for sexually abused children varies, again depending on the severity and frequency of the abuse. In many cases a single talk with a counselor is sufficient, but in other cases the children have severe anxieties and need long-term treatment (Saywitz, Mannarino, Berliner, & Cohen, 2000).

## IN CLOSING

### Controlling Violence

Most of us would like to believe that people are fundamentally good and that acts of violence and cruelty are an abnormality: If only we could get rid of poverty, injustice, ignorance, low self-esteem, and so forth, then people would stop being cruel to one another. The problem is that some perpetrators of unspeakable cruelty have had all the advantages of wealth and opportunity. Improvements in society can decrease violent crime—after all, the crime rate usually does go down when the economy improves—but we are unlikely to eliminate violence completely.

Is punishment therefore the answer? Only in part. Children are less likely to be bullies if they have enough adult supervision, and adults are also less likely to abuse others if they believe someone will retaliate against them. However, making punishments quicker and more certain is more effective than making them harsher. In fact, excessively painful punishment actually triggers aggressive behavior.

Finally, it is possible to help people control their aggressive tendencies, if they wish to receive help. People can be taught to accept frustration and to react to disappointments in less disruptive ways. Those who are accustomed to gaining attention or other reinforcements from violent outbursts can learn other ways to get what they want (Fehrenbach & Thelen, 1982). People are less likely to turn to violence, even as a last resort, if they can see other options.

## Summary

- **Anger.** People experience anger frequently, although it seldom leads to violent acts. Aggressive behavior often occurs in defense of territory or in competition for a mate. Frustration or other unpleasant experiences often prompt aggressive behavior. (page 470)
- **Predicting violence.** Psychologists and psychiatrists find it difficult to predict whether a particular prisoner would be dangerous if released. The best way to make such predictions is to review someone's past behavior, especially the history of violent behavior. Many other factors also correlate with violence, including drug and alcohol abuse, living in a violent neighborhood, a history of being abused as a child, several physiological indicators, and having a mother who smoked heavily during pregnancy. (page 471)
- **Violence by mental patients.** People with certain kinds of psychological disorders, especially substance abusers, are more likely than other people to commit violent acts. Still, the best predictor of violence among mental patients, as among other people, is their past behavior. (page 473)
- **Sex-related violence.** Most of the men who are convicted of violent rape have a history of other kinds of violent acts also. (page 474)
- **Sexual abuse of children.** Sexual abuse ranges from mild events, such as once seeing an exhibitionist, to less common and more severe events, such as rape or molestation. Children's reactions also vary accordingly, from mild distress to persisting trauma. (page 475)

## Answers to Concept Checks

**12.** It would overlook reconciliation. (page 471)
**13.** The best predictor of violent behavior is the person's history of previous violent behavior. Low self-esteem is not a good predictor. (page 474)

# Health Psychology

*What is stress and how does it affect health?*

Imagine you meet a man suffering from, say, multiple sclerosis. Would you say, "It's his own fault he's sick; he's being punished for his sins"? I presume you would neither say nor believe anything so cruel. However, in the Middle Ages and in ancient times, many people believed just that. We congratulate ourselves today on having advanced beyond that way of thinking; we know it is wrong to blame the victim.

Or do we? We may think that cigarette smokers are at least partly at fault if they develop lung cancer. We note that AIDS is usually contracted by people with a history of intravenous drug use or unsafe sex. If women drink alcohol during pregnancy, we hold them partly responsible if their infants have deformities or mental retardation. As we learn more and more about the causes of various illnesses, we expect people to accept more responsibility for their own health.

However, we can easily overstate how much people's behavior influences their health. Even if you are as careful as possible about your diet, exercise regularly, and have healthy habits, you could become ill anyway.

**Health psychology** *is concerned with how people's behavior can enhance health and prevent illness and how behavior contributes to recovery from illness.* It deals with such issues as why people smoke, why they sometimes ignore their physician's advice, and how to reduce pain. In this module we focus mainly on how stress and other emotional conditions affect health.

## Stress

Have you ever gone without sleep several nights in a row trying to meet a deadline? Or waited what seemed like forever for someone who was supposed to pick you up? Or had a close friend suddenly not want to see you anymore? Or tried to explain why you no longer want to date someone? An enormous variety of experiences can cause stress.

### Selye's Concept of Stress

According to Hans Selye (1979), an Austrian-born physician who worked at McGill University in Montreal, **stress** is *the nonspecific response of the body to any demand made upon it.* Every demand on the body evokes certain specific responses as well. The body responds in one way to the loss

■ The emotions we feel affect physiological processes and thereby influence health.

of blood and in another way to the lack of sleep. But all demands on the body evoke generalized responses such as increased response of the sympathetic nervous system, increased release of the hormone epinephrine, and impaired concentration.

When people say, "I've been under a lot of stress lately," they are generally referring to a string of unpleasant experiences. Selye's concept of stress is broader, including any experience that brings about change in a person's life. For example, getting married and being promoted are presumably pleasant experiences, but they also demand that you make changes in your life, so in Selye's sense, they produce stress. Note, however, that Selye's definition counts only *changes* in your life. Dealing with the effects of poverty, racism, or a lifelong disability would *not* count as a stress because they are unchanging over time. In that sense Selye's definition is simply wrong, or at least too limited. The experience of African Americans of being insulted, avoided, excluded from opportunities, and so on certainly appears to be stressful, is described as stressful, and produces or aggravates health problems (Clark, Anderson, Clark, & Williams, 1999; Contrada et al., 2000). Clearly, a long-lasting or permanent situation can be stressful.

Selye believed that the body goes through three stages in its response to a stressor: The first is **alarm,** *a brief period of high arousal of the sympathetic nervous system, readying the body for vigorous activity.* Some stressors last longer than the body can maintain this high state of arousal, however. If you have a high-stress job or live near the runway of a busy airport, you cannot overcome your problem with a brief burst of intense activity. You enter **resistance,** *a stage of prolonged but moderate arousal.* Your epinephrine levels remain at a high level day after day, week after week. Your adrenal cortex secretes cortisol, a hormone that elevates blood sugar and enhances metabolism. The increased fuel supply to the cells enables them to sustain a high, steady level of activity to endure prolonged stress. However, you no longer feel ready for vigorous activity; you feel withdrawn and inactive much of the time, your performance deteriorates, and you complain of a decreased quality of life (Evans, Bullinger, & Hygge, 1998). The body often treats prolonged, inescapable problems the same way it treats an illness: You develop a fever, become sleepier, lose your appetite, and lose much of your sex drive (Maier & Watkins, 1988). Also, the elevated cortisol level impairs memory retrieval (deQuervain, Roozendaal, Nitsch, McGaugh, & Hock, 2000).

With even more intense and long-lasting stress, the body enters the third stage, **exhaustion.** *As cortisol and other hormones shift energy toward increasing blood sugar and metabolism, they shift it away from synthesis of proteins, including the proteins necessary for the immune system.* In the short term, that shift may not be a problem; however, severe stress over months can leave an individual vulnerable to a variety of illnesses (S. Cohen, 1996). The end result is

characterized by weakness, fatigue, loss of appetite, and a general lack of interest.

## CONCEPT CHECK

14. According to Selye's definition of stress, would getting married be stressful? Would constant quarreling with your family be stressful? (Check your answers on page 483.)

## Posttraumatic Stress Disorder

Perhaps the most powerful demonstration of the effects of severe stress is **posttraumatic stress disorder (PTSD).** *People who have endured extreme stress feel prolonged anxiety and depression.* This condition has been recognized in postwar periods throughout history and given such names as "battle fatigue" or "shell shock." One nationwide survey reported posttraumatic stress disorder in 20% of the American veterans who were wounded in Vietnam (Helzer, Robins, & McEnvoy, 1987). It also occurs in rape or assault victims, torture victims, survivors of an airplane crash or a severe automobile crash, and witnesses to a murder.

However, people who have undergone apparently similar experiences can react differently, some developing PTSD and some not (McFarlane, 1997). Psychologists do not yet know why. The brains of PTSD victims differ in several ways from those of other people, but we do not know whether they differed before the traumatic event or only as a result of it (Stein, Hanna, Koverola, Torchia, & McClarty, 1997; Yehuda, 1997).

People with posttraumatic stress disorder suffer from frequent nightmares, outbursts of anger, unhappiness, and guilt. A brief reminder of the tragic experience can

■ This group of Vietnam vets met regularly for a year to work on problems related to posttraumatic stress. Since the group disbanded, one member has had an exhibition of his hand-colored photographs. (This portrait is a sample of his work.) Another has started his own company. Some members have created new careers; some have been in and out of substance-abuse programs. Most continue to experience vivid dreams full of war images.

■ The stressfulness of an event depends on how we interpret it, not just on the event itself. For example, most people would be delighted to finish second or third in an Olympic event, but someone who was expecting to finish first may consider any lesser result a defeat and a disappointment.

trigger a flashback that borders on panic. Many mundane events become stressful, even years after the original event (Solomon, Mikulincer, & Flum, 1988). In one study eight Vietnam veterans with PTSD watched a 15-minute videotape of dramatized combat. Watching the film elevated their endorphin levels just as people generally react to an actual injury (Pitman, van der Kolk, Orr, & Greenberg, 1990).

## Measuring Stress

Most investigators agree that severe stress can endanger a person's health. For example, people often become ill shortly after the death of a husband or wife. Also, people who experience severe stress on the job report frequent illnesses as well.

How much stress is injurious to one's health? Is it true that the more stress a person experiences, the more that person's health suffers? To answer such questions, we need to measure both stress and health. Measuring health is difficult enough; measuring stress is even more difficult. One approach is to give people a checklist of presumably stressful experiences. For example, the Social Readjustment Rating Scale lists 43 life-change events (Holmes & Rahe, 1967). The authors of this test asked a group of people to rate how stressful each event would be, and on that basis they assigned each event a certain number of points, such as 100 for death of a spouse and 11 for receiving a traffic ticket. If you answered this questionnaire, you would check each event you have experienced recently, and then the psychologist administering the test would total your points to determine how stressful your life has been.

Checklists like this have low reliability and validity (Brown, 1989). That is, people's answers vary from time

to time, and the scores correlate poorly with illness or anything else of interest. One reason is the ambiguity of many items. You can get 44 points for "change in health of a family member." You would certainly check that item if you discovered that your 5-year-old has diabetes and 44 points would underestimate the stress. Someone else might check that item because his aunt, whom he seldom sees, recovered nicely from a bout of influenza.

A further difficulty with any checklist is that a given event has different meanings for different people depending on how they interpret the event and what they can do about it (Lazarus, 1977). Becoming pregnant does not mean the same thing to a 27-year-old married woman as to an unmarried 16-year-old. Losing a job is a disaster to most 50-year-olds, a minor annoyance to a 17-year-old with a summer job, and a nonevent for an actor who works in many plays each year and never expects any one of them to last long.

According to Lazarus, *a stressful situation is one that someone regards as threatening and as possibly exceeding his or her resources* (Lazarus, 1977) (see Figure 12.25). For example, if you are bitten by a snake, you might remain calm if you recognize the snake as a harmless variety. If your boss criticizes your work, you might shrug off the insult if you know your boss had reason to be in a bad mood.

People can learn to deal with events actively instead of feeling threatened by them. Given this view the proper measure of stress would include not only the unpleasant events ("hassles") that we have to deal with but also the pleasant events ("uplifts") that brighten our day and help to cancel out the unpleasant events (Kanner, Coyne, Schaefer, & Lazarus, 1981). Table 12.2 presents one example of this approach.

Given that the stressfulness of an event depends on our interpretation of the event, our reaction to it, and the

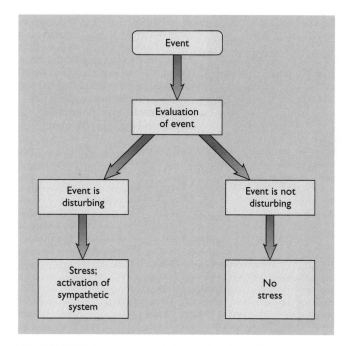

**FIGURE 12.25** Lazarus stated that evaluation of some kind, conscious or unconscious, always precedes emotion. Thus, a given event can be highly stressful for one person yet only slightly stressful or not at all for someone else.

**TABLE 12.2 Ten Most Frequent Hassles and Uplifts**

| Hassles | Uplifts |
|---|---|
| 1. Concerns about weight | 1. Relating well with your spouse or lover |
| 2. Health of a family member | 2. Relating well with friends |
| 3. Rising prices of common goods | 3. Completing task |
| 4. Home maintenance | 4. Feeling healthy |
| 5. Too many things to do | 5. Getting enough sleep |
| 6. Misplacing or losing things | 6. Eating out |
| 7. Yard work or outside home maintenance | 7. Meeting your responsibilities |
| 8. Property, investment, or taxes | 8. Visiting, phoning, or writing someone |
| 9. Crime | 9. Spending time with family |
| 10. Physical appearance | 10. Home (inside) pleasing to you |

Source: Kanner, Coyne, Schaefer, & Lazarus, 1981.

other events in our lives, the best way to measure someone's stress is through a careful, well-structured interview that can evaluate all the pluses and minuses (Brown, 1989). In short, stress research is difficult to do, or at least difficult to do well. Nevertheless, researchers can identify particular kinds of experiences that endanger health, as we shall explore in the next section.

## C ONCEPT CHECK

15. Why are checklists an unsatisfactory way to measure stress? (Check your answer on page 483.)

## Stress and Psychosomatic Illness

A **psychosomatic illness** is not an imagined or a feigned illness. Rather, it is *an illness that is influenced by someone's experiences—particularly stressful experiences—or by his or her reactions to those experiences.* That is, something about the person's behavior or way of life influenced the onset and progression of the disease. Most illnesses are partly psychosomatic in this sense.

Researchers do not assume that emotions lead directly to illness. One possible route is that people with emotional difficulties are likely to overeat, to smoke, or to have unsafe sex, and so forth. Prolonged stressful experiences can damage the immune system and increase a person's vulnerability to a variety of disorders, ranging

from minor infections to cancer (Maier & Watkins, 1998; Tingate, Lugg, Muller, Stowe, & Pierson, 1997).

Emotions can also impair health in strange, roundabout ways: Many years ago a midwife delivered three female babies on Friday the 13th and announced that all three were hexed and would die before their 23rd birthday. The first two did die young. As the third woman approached her 23rd birthday, she checked into a hospital and informed the staff of her fears. The staff noted that she dealt with her anxiety by extreme hyperventilation (deep breathing). Shortly before her birthday, she hyperventilated to death.

How did this happen? Ordinarily, when people do not breathe voluntarily, they breathe reflexively; the reflex is triggered by carbon dioxide in the blood. By extreme hyperventilation this woman had exhaled so much carbon dioxide that she did not have enough left to trigger reflexive breathing. When she stopped breathing voluntarily, she stopped breathing altogether ("Clinicopathologic conference," 1967). This is a clear example of a self-fulfilling prophecy: The fact that the woman believed the hex caused it to be fulfilled. This is also a clear example of the indirect influence of emotions on health.

### Heart Disease

An upholsterer repairing the chairs in a physician's waiting room once noticed that the fronts of the seats wore out before the backs. To figure out why, the physician began watching patients in the waiting room. He noticed that his heart patients habitually sat on the front edges of their seats, waiting impatiently to be called in for their appointments. This observation led the physician to hypothesize a link between heart disease and an impatient, success-driven personality, now known as the Type A personality (Friedman & Rosenman, 1974).

People with **Type A personality** are *highly competitive; they believe that they must always win. They are impatient, always in a hurry, and often angry and hostile.* By contrast, people with **a Type B personality** are *relatively easygoing, less hurried, and less hostile.* For example, Gary Schwartz (1987) described his observations of two men fishing: One (a Type B) slowly baited his hook, dropped his line into the water, and sat back watching the gulls and waiting for a bite. Another man (a Type A), fishing with two poles, spent much of his time rushing back and forth between the two poles, cursing when the two lines tangled with each other. When another fisher caught a large fish, this man pulled up his anchor in frustration and raced his boat off to another part of the bay. (Are you a Type A or a Type B? Test yourself by answering the questions in Figure 12.26.)

Statistically, a link does exist between heart disease and Type A behavior, especially with hostility. However, this is a relatively weak link compared to the effects of genetics, diet, exercise, and other factors (Jorgensen, Johnson, Kolodziej, & Schreer, 1996; T. Q. Miller, Smith, Turner, Guijarro, & Hallet, 1996). The strongest known psychological influence on heart disease is the power of social support. People with strong friendships and family ties usually take better care of themselves and keep their heart rate and blood pressure under control (Uchino, Cacioppo, & Kiecolt-Glaser, 1996).

Variations in the prevalence of heart disease across cultures may have behavioral influences (Levine, 1990). Some cultures have a hurried pace of life; people walk fast; they talk fast; almost everyone wears a watch; storekeepers pay prompt attention to their customers. Other cultures have a more relaxed pace of life; people are seldom in a rush; few people wear watches; the buses and trains seldom arrive on schedule but no one seems to care (Figure 12.27). As you might guess, the rate of

**FIGURE 12.27** People in some cultures (top) live at a frantic pace: People walk fast, talk fast, and push one another around. In other cultures (bottom), no one is sure what time it is and no one cares. The risk of heart disease is greatest in cultures and subcultures characterized by a hectic pace.

---

**Measuring the Type A Personality**

_____  1. Do you find it difficult to restrain yourself from hurrying others' speech (finishing their sentences for them)?

_____  2. Do you often try to do more than one thing at a time (such as eat and read simultaneously)?

_____  3. Do you often feel guilty if you use extra time to relax?

_____  4. Do you tend to get involved in a great number of projects at once?

_____  5. Do you find yourself racing through yellow lights when you drive?

_____  6. Do you need to win in order to derive enjoyment from games and sports?

_____  7. Do you generally move, walk, and eat rapidly?

_____  8. Do you agree to take on too many responsibilities?

_____  9. Do you detest waiting in lines?

_____ 10. Do you have an intense desire to better your position in life and impress others?

**FIGURE 12.26** If you answer "yes" to a majority of these items, Friedman and Rosenman (1974) would say that you probably have a Type A personality. But they would also take into account how you explain your answers, so this questionnaire gives only a rough estimate of your personality. Friedman and Rosenman classified everyone as either Type A or Type B, but most psychologists believe that people can exhibit various degrees of Type A traits.

heart disease is higher in countries with a hurried pace of life than it is in countries with a more relaxed pace. In the United States, the risk of heart attacks and the pace of life are generally highest in large northeastern cities; they are lowest in the small towns in the west and the south. Of course, these are correlational data; they do not demonstrate conclusively that a frantic pace of life causes heart problems. (For example, something about cultural differences in diet or climate might simultaneously influence people's activity levels and their heart muscles.)

## CONCEPT CHECK

16. People with a Type A personality are likely to develop stress-related heart disease. Yet, when they fill out a stress checklist like one of those mentioned earlier, their scores are often low. Why might that scale understate the stress levels of Type A people? (Check your answer on page 483.)

## Cancer

There are many kinds of cancer and many causes that are not yet well understood. Behavior can also influence the onset and spread of cancer, at least indirectly. For example, women who examine their breasts regularly can detect breast cancer at an early stage, when treatment is more likely to be successful. However, most women do not conduct regular, competent self-examinations, either because they do not know how, because they are fearful, or because they doubt that a checkup would help (S. M. Miller, Shoda & Hurley, 1996). Latina women in the United States have a higher rate of cervical cancer than other women, partly because they are less likely than other women to see doctors regularly for Pap smear tests (Meyerowitz, Richardson, Hudson, & Leedham, 1998). In many ways preventing or treating cancer requires behavioral as well as medical interventions.

Do our emotions contribute directly to cancer? Because the brain influences the immune system, which fights cancer, an emotional experience might lead to an impairment of the immune system and therefore to a greater risk of certain kinds of cancer.

The two emotional states most likely to lead to cancer are depression and stress. Many cancer patients are depressed (Weinstock, 1984), and many of them report that they were depressed, often following the death of a loved one, long before they knew they had cancer. Severe depression suppresses the activity of the immune system and leaves a person more vulnerable than usual to all sorts of infections and diseases, including the spread of certain types of tumors (Anisman & Zacharko, 1983; Baker, 1987).

While conducting research on the effects of stress in animals, investigators have found that stress increases the spread of cancer and shortens the animal's life span. But it is difficult to extrapolate from those results to humans. First, the results vary from one study to another depending on the duration and type of stress and the genetic makeup of the animals. Second, nearly all animal studies deal with cancers caused by viruses, and viruses cause fewer than 5% of human cancers (Fox, 1983).

Depression, stress, and severe emotional problems probably do increase the risk of cancer in humans. Still, their influence is minor; emotional factors are far less important in causing cancer than are genes and toxic substances (Anisman & Zacharko, 1983; Derogatis, 1986; Fox, 1983). Keeping a positive outlook on life may help to prevent cancer; still, many people suffering from serious, long-lasting depression manage to survive into old age (Stein, Miller, & Trestman, 1991).

Psychological factors exert a stronger influence on what happens after the onset of cancer. For many people the stress of dealing with cancer decreases the pleasures of life, impairs eating and sleeping, and directly or indirectly weakens the ability of the immune system to attack the cancer cells (B. L. Andersen, Kiecolt-Glaser, & Glaser, 1994). People who receive steady support from their family and friends, or from a psychotherapist or a self-help group, have a better chance of recovery and a better quality of life while they are fighting the disease (Fawzy, Fawzy, Arndt, & Pasnau, 1995).

## IN CLOSING

# Health is Both Psycho and Somatic

The important point to remember about health psychology is that personality, emotions, and behavior are just one aspect of health. A well-balanced diet, regular exercise, and quitting tobacco improve one's chances for good health; regular breast self-exams help to detect possible problems early; controlling hostility and other negative emotions decreases the risk of heart disease. Still, we should not set unrealistic expectations for behavioral strategies. No matter how much someone follows the best psychological advice, health is also subject to the influence of genetics, toxic substances in the environment, and other factors that are hard to control. So, yes, do what you can to improve your behavior and attitude, but if problems arise, don't expect attitude readjustment to take the place of medical help. And if you become ill, don't feel guilty that you just didn't have the right attitude. What happens to your health is partly under your control, but not entirely.

## Summary

- **Selye's concept of stress.** According to Hans Selye, stress is "the nonspecific response of the body to any demand made upon it." Any event, pleasant or unpleasant, that brings about change in a person's life produces some measure of stress. One problem with this definition is that it omits lifelong problems such as coping with racism.  (page 477)

- **Stages of response to stress.** The body goes through three stages in response to a stressful experience: alarm, resistance, and exhaustion. In the resistance and exhaustion stages, prolonged channeling of energy toward resisting stress can weaken the immune system.  (page 478)
- **Influence of past experiences.** The degree of stress that an event evokes depends not only on the event itself but also on the person's interpretation of that event. People with posttraumatic stress disorder react strongly to daily events because of their previous experiences with war, rape, or other deeply upsetting occurrences.  (page 478)
- **Difficulties of measuring stress.** Stress checklists have low reliability and validity because many items are ambiguous. Also, the stressfulness of an event depends on the person's interpretation of the event and ability to cope with it.  (page 479)
- **Psychosomatic illness.** Stress, hostility, and other emotional experiences may increase the probability of certain illnesses. A psychosomatic illness is somehow related to a person's experiences or to his or her reactions to those experiences.  (page 480)
- **Heart disease.** People with a Type A personality are competitive, impatient, and hostile. The hostility in-

creases the risk of heart disease, although that effect is small. Having the support of friends improves health and decreases the danger of heart disease.  (page 480)
- **Cancer.** Depression and stress can increase the risk of cancer, at least slightly. Social support improves people's chances of recovery from cancer and also improves their quality of life while fighting the disease.  (page 481)

## Answers to Concept Checks

**14.** By Selye's definition getting married produces stress because it requires a change in one's life. However, constant quarreling with one's family would not be stressful because it is not a change in one's life. (page 478)

**15.** Items on stress checklists are often ambiguous, and therefore, the results have low reliability and validity. Also, a given event can be more stressful for one person than another. (page 480)

**16.** The Social Readjustment Rating Scale measures events that change a person's life; it does not measure constant sources of stress such as the pressures of work. The scale also fails to measure people's reactions, such as impatience, competitiveness, and hostility. (page 482)

# 12.4 Coping with Stress

*What are some effective ways to combat stress?*

An eccentric millionaire whom you have never met before hands you a $10 bill for no apparent reason, no strings attached. How do you feel? Pleased, I assume.

Now let's change the circumstances a bit: The millionaire had been handing out $100 bills until it was your turn, but then said, "Sorry, I just ran out of $100 bills. So I'll give you a $10 bill instead." Now how do you feel? Disappointed? Sad? Angry? You may even feel *cheated,* even though you have just received something for nothing.

Just as your reaction to a gift of $10 depends on the circumstances, so does your reaction to bad news. How would you feel if you had studied hard for a test and then got a C−? Unhappy, I presume. But if you then discovered that everyone around you had failed the test, you would begin to feel much better about your C−.

How you feel about an event depends not just on the event itself but also on how you interpret it (Frijda, 1988; Lazarus, Averill, & Opton, 1970). Was it better or worse than you had expected? Better or worse than what happened to other people? Was it a one-time event, or did it carry a hint of what might happen in the future? How you feel about an event also depends on

your personality. Some people manage to keep their spirits high even in the face of tragedy; others are devastated by minor setbacks.

Coping with stress is the process of developing ways to decrease its effects and to get through difficult tasks despite the stress. Can we learn to cope more successfully?

## Coping Styles and Strategies

People cope with stress in a great many ways, but we can group most of them into two major categories: *monitoring* and *blunting.* In **monitoring** *one attends carefully to the stressful event and tries to take effective action.* In **blunting** *one tries to avoid the stressful event or at least avoid thinking about it.* Some people tend to rely more on one style than on the other, but it is best to vary one's strategy depending on circumstances (Heszen-Niejodek, 1997). In particular it is best to take action (monitoring) if you have any control over the situation. For example, if you have test-taking anxieties, you could try to relax and not think about the test, but if you instead spend time studying for the test, you will probably improve your grade and reduce your anxiety. Similarly, if you have troubles in your marriage or with your job, the best way to reduce the stress is to search for a solution to the problem.

However, suppose your stress comes from having to lie in a hospital bed awaiting an operation or recovering

■ Relaxation and exercise are among the strategies we use to manage our reactions to problems. People who devote a short time each day to deliberate relaxation report diminished stress; exercise can work off excess energy, allowing greater relaxation.

■ "Cabin fever," the distress associated with being cooped up and unable to leave, is largely due to the inability to predict or control events.

from one. Or sitting in a dentist's chair for some unpleasant procedure. Now you can't run away, attack, or do anything else to control the situation. You just have to sit there and endure it. In such cases you should turn to a blunting strategy.

# Monitoring Strategies

Whenever a stressful situation is at all controllable, people feel better if they take action. In fact, even an ineffective action makes them feel better, as long as they *think* it might be effective. Here we consider the importance of a sense of control and then discuss a few additional monitoring strategies.

## *The Importance of Predictability and Control*

Let's start by contrasting two hypothetical situations. First, imagine that some torturer is keeping you awake 24 hours per day. You have no way of escaping and no way of knowing how long the torture will last, but in fact, it lasts 3 days until someone finally liberates you. Contrast that experience with an experiment in which you agree to go without sleep for 3 days. You could quit if you wanted, but in fact, you don't.

Another comparison: A huge snowstorm has trapped you in a small cabin. You have enough food and fuel, but you have no idea how long you will be stuck. The snow melts 5 days later, enabling you to leave. Contrast a case where you decide to isolate yourself in a cabin for 5 days so you can finish a painting.

In both cases the physical circumstances are the same—3 days without sleep or 5 days without leaving a cabin. But if you are doing something voluntarily, you know what to expect and you know that you could quit. When hospital patients or nursing-home residents are told what to expect and are given the chance to make some decisions for themselves, they feel better and on the average live longer (D. H. Shapiro, Schwartz, & Astin, 1996). Many people find that religious faith helps them to cope with stress by giving them some sense of control over matters that are otherwise uncontrollable.

Why does a predictable or controllable event produce less stress than an unpredictable or uncontrollable event? One explanation is that we fear an unpredictable, uncontrollable event may grow so intense that it will eventually become unbearable. If we have some control, we tell ourselves that we can do something if the situation becomes unbearable.

A second explanation is that, when an event is predictable, we can prepare for it at the appropriate time and relax at other times. If you dread being called upon to answer questions in class and your professor calls on students at random, you have to remain tense and ready at all times. But if your professor calls on students in alphabetical order, you can relax until shortly before your turn.

People can gain a sense of control over a future problem by rehearsing it in their imagination. For example, you might imagine what someone else might say or do and then what you might say or do in response (Sanna, 2000). Of course, the better you can predict the situation, the more easily you can rehearse your responses to it. Many self-help books advise you to "visualize yourself succeeding" at something. The research says that visualizing yourself getting good grades, winning a prize, or receiving honors does little or no good. What does help is to visualize yourself doing the work that will achieve the prize. You might visualize yourself performing some athletic feat because visualizing the act is a kind of practice. As a student you might visualize yourself studying in the library or writing a long research paper. By imagining the work, you get started on it sooner, organize your time better, and finish sooner (Taylor, Pham, Rivkin, & Armor, 1998). You also gain a feeling of control, which makes the task less stressful.

# CONCEPT CHECK

17. Which would disrupt your studying more, your own radio or your roommate's radio? Why? (Check your answers on page 489.)

## *Inoculation*

A stressful experience is less disturbing if you know what to expect, but it is hard to know what to expect if you have not been through the experience before. Sometimes

■ Practicing self-defense serves as a kind of inoculation against fear. The thought of being attacked is less frightening when we have some idea of how to handle a situation.

a good solution is to get a small-scale preview of a stressful experience that you may face later. In other words you can "inoculate" or immunize yourself against stressful experiences.

One way to **inoculate** yourself against stressful events is *to expose yourself to smaller amounts of such events beforehand* (Janis, 1983; Meichenbaum, 1985; Meichenbaum & Cameron, 1983). For example, many armies have soldiers practice combat skills under realistic conditions, even under actual gunfire. Another way is through role-playing. A police trainee might pretend to intervene while two people act like a husband and wife engaged in a violent quarrel. If you are nervous about going to your landlord with a complaint, you might get a friend to play the part of the landlord and then practice what you plan to say.

Inoculation has proved successful with young people suffering from "dating anxiety." Some young people are so nervous about saying or doing the wrong thing that they avoid all opportunities to go out on a date. By means of role-playing, they can practice dating behaviors with assigned partners and thus feel less apprehensive about dating (Jaremko, 1983).

## CONCEPT CHECK

18. Suppose you are nervous about giving a speech before a group of 200 strangers. How could you inoculate yourself to reduce the stress? (Check your answer on page 489.)

## Social Support

Have you ever had a secret too shameful to tell? Have you stopped yourself from disclosing a personal experience because you thought others would think less of you? . . . Have you ever lied to yourself by claiming that a major upheaval in your life didn't affect you or, perhaps, didn't occur? If so you may be hurting yourself. Not because you have had a troubling experience but because you can't express it.
—James W. Pennebaker (1990)

A great many people have undergone a severely painful experience at one time or another. Perhaps you were beaten or sexually molested; perhaps you were responsible for someone else's injury; perhaps you attempted suicide; perhaps someone humiliated you in public. Whatever your experience, you may decide that it was too painful even to think about, much less talk about. Therefore, the pain builds up inside.

People who have had painful experiences report that they feel better after they have a chance to talk about them to someone or even just write about them. In one series of experiments, college students were randomly assigned to two groups. For about half an hour per day on 3–5 consecutive days, the experimental group was asked to write their deepest thoughts and feelings about an emotional issue that had affected them. For example, many wrote about the death of a loved one, a personal failure, or sexual or physical abuse. The psychologists conducting the study said nothing to them about what they had written and in fact kept no record of which student had written which essay. The control group spent

■ Simply writing about our deepest feelings or distressing experiences helps relieve tension by showing us that we can face and survive our pain.

the same amount of time writing about unemotional topics, such as how they budgeted their time in a typical day. The experimental group described the experience as extremely valuable, in spite of the fact that many of them had become very upset, even tearful, during the experiment. A follow-up measurement found that the experimental group members had better health over the next few months, got better grades, and drank less alcohol (Pennebaker, 1997). Evidently, just expressing their feelings reduced their stress and enabled them to relax and deal more effectively with life.

In many cases people gain the greatest support by talking with people who have lived through similar crises. People with strong friendships tend to be healthier than other people for a variety of reasons, including improved functioning of the immune system. Also, many people without friends don't even try to take good care of themselves (Uchino, Uno, & Holt-Lunstad, 1999).

Alcoholics Anonymous, composed of recovering alcoholics who try to help one another, is an excellent example of an organization that increases people's social support. An estimated 3 to 4% of the U.S. population participates in self-help groups of various sorts, especially for problems that people do not like to talk about publicly, such as alcoholism, AIDS, anorexia, and breast and prostate cancer (Davison, Pennebaker, & Dickerson, 2000). Computer-based on-line support groups are now becoming increasingly popular because they can bring together people with unusual problems who do not live near one another. Receiving social support, especially from sympathetic people who have endured similar problems, improves overall health and increases life expectancy (Uchino, Cacioppo, & Kiecolt-Glaser, 1996).

## *Beliefs as Coping Strategies*

- In the long run, I shall be more successful than most.
- Sure, I have my strengths and weaknesses, but my strengths are in areas that are important; my weaknesses are in areas that don't really matter.
- When I fail, it is because I didn't try hard enough or because I got some bad breaks—not because of any lack of ability.
- No matter how bad (or good) things are, they are going to get better.
- Right now I'm sad that my wife (husband) left me, but in the long run, I'll be better off without her (him).
- I lost my job, but in many ways it was a crummy job. The more I think about it, the happier I am about it. I can get a better one.

Any of these statements may be correct or incorrect for a given person at a given time. Remember the "personal fable" of adolescence from Chapter 10? Most normal, happy people nurture various versions of that fable throughout life. They emphasize their strengths, downplay their weaknesses, and distort bad news to make it seem not so bad, maybe even good (Taylor & Brown, 1988). To some extent, these beliefs can help people to deal with the difficult and stressful times of life.

If you had a life-threatening disease such as AIDS or cancer, would it be better to look at the facts realistically or to nurture an illusion that everything will be okay? The answer is not the same in all circumstances, but the research does find that people do better if they maintain hope, even if that hope is based on a certain degree of illusion. In one study men with AIDS answered a questionnaire about their attitudes toward the illness and death. Those who said "yes" to items like "I refuse to believe that this problem has happened" survived longer than those who endorsed items like "I prepare myself for the worst" (Taylor, Kemeny, Reed, Bower, & Gruenwald, 2000).

# Blunting Strategies

Blunting strategies do not attempt to solve the underlying problems, but they help us to manage our reactions to them. Three common examples are relaxation, exercise, and distraction.

## *Relaxation*

Sometimes people have a real problem, such as an impending medical operation, that they cannot control. At other times they get nervous even when they have no real problem (Manuck, Cohen, Rabin, Muldoon, & Bachen, 1991). In such situations it is helpful to try to relax. Here are some suggestions (Benson, 1985):

- Find a quiet place. Do not insist on absolute silence; just find a spot where the noise is least disturbing.
- Adopt a comfortable position, relaxing your muscles. If you are not sure how to do so, start with the opposite: *Tense* all your muscles so you become fully aware of how they feel. Then relax them one by one, starting from your toes and working systematically toward your head.
- Reduce sources of stimulation, including your own thoughts. Focus your eyes on a simple, unexciting object. Or repeat something over and over—a sentence, a phrase, a prayer, or even the Hindu syllable *om*—whatever feels comfortable to you.
- Don't worry about anything, not even about relaxing. If worrisome thoughts keep popping into your head, dismiss them with "oh, well."

Some people call this practice meditation. People who practice this technique daily report that they feel less stress. Many of them improve their overall health (Benson, 1977, 1985). One study found that people who went through a 12-week meditation program had a long-lasting decrease in anxiety and depression, as compared with a control group who spent the same amount of time listening to lectures about how to reduce stress (Sheppard, Staggers, & John, 1997).

Another step toward relaxation is to learn to interpret situations realistically. Some people fret forever about disasters that *might* happen or about a comment that *might* be taken as an insult. Psychologists encourage people to reinterpret situations and events in less threatening ways.

## Exercise

Exercise also can help to reduce stress. It may seem contradictory to say that both relaxation and exercise reduce stress, but exercise does help people relax (Mobily, 1982). Suppose you are tense about something that you have to do tomorrow. Your sympathetic nervous system becomes highly aroused but you cannot actually do anything. Under those conditions your best approach may be to work off some excess energy through exercise and then relax afterward.

Regular exercise also prepares people for the unexpected. People in good physical condition react less strongly than other people do to stressful events (Crews & Landers, 1987). An event that would elevate the heart rate enormously in other people elevates it only moderately in a person who has been exercising regularly.

## Distraction

Another powerful blunting strategy is distraction (Cioffi, 1991). For example, many people find that they can reduce dental or postsurgical pain by playing video games or by watching comedies on television. The Lamaze method teaches pregnant women to suppress the pain of childbirth by concentrating on breathing exercises.

The effectiveness of distraction depends partly on people's expectations. In one experiment college students were asked to hold their fingers in ice water until the sensation became too painful to endure (Melzack, Weisz, & Sprague, 1963). Some of them listened to music of their own choice and were told that listening to music would lessen the pain. Others also listened to music but were given no suggestion that it would ease the pain. Still others heard nothing but were told that a special "ultrasonic sound" was being transmitted that would lessen the pain. The group that heard music and expected it to lessen the pain tolerated the pain better than either of the other two groups. Evidently, neither the music nor the suggestion of reduced pain is as effective as both are together.

Distraction also helps us cope with nonpainful stress. People who are concentrating on a difficult task find it helpful to take a break once in a while. They may go to

a movie, read something entertaining, play a round of golf, or just daydream. Furthermore, trying to find the humor in a stressful situation often provides an effective distraction.

## CONCEPT CHECK

19. What is the difference between monitoring strategies and blunting strategies? (Check your answer on page 489.)

**CRITICAL THINKING**

**A STEP FURTHER**
*Placebos*

Many experiments report that a placebo alone serves as an effective painkiller for certain patients. Why might that be true?

**IN CLOSING**

## Does Coping Work?

In this module we have considered the ways people try to deal with stressful situations, but how well do these strategies work? The answer is that they work well for many people, but at a cost. The cost is that coping with serious stressors requires energy. You might recall the experiment in Chapter 11 that showed resisting the temptation of snacks at arm's reach took so much mental energy that people were likely to overeat afterward. People who have had to cope with more long-lasting stressors break their diets, resume smoking and drinking habits that they had abandoned long ago, and find it difficult to concentrate on difficult cognitive tasks (Muraven & Baumeister, 2000).

Still, in spite of the costs, an amazing number of people say that the experience of battling with a chronic illness, tending to a loved one with a severe illness, or dealing with other painful experiences has brought them personal strength and an enhanced feeling of meaning in life (Folkman & Moskowitz, 2000). They found positive moments even in the midst of fear and loss. Not everyone rises to the occasion, but we should respect and admire those who do.

## Summary

- **Coping styles.** People's strategies for dealing with stress fall into two major categories. Monitoring is an attempt to focus on the source of the problems; blunting is an attempt to distract oneself and to reduce the distress without addressing the problem. (page 484)

- **Prediction and control.** Events are generally less stressful when people think they can predict or control them. (page 485)
- **Inoculation.** Someone who has experienced a mildly stressful experience is less stressed than other people are by a later, more intense version of the same experience. (page 485)
- **Social support.** Support and encouragement from friends and family help to alleviate stress. Many people cope with problems by talking with other people who have dealt with similar problems, such as members of self-help groups. (page 486)
- **Beliefs.** A belief in one's capacity to succeed may help to reduce stress, even if this belief is not entirely accurate. (page 487)
- **Relaxation and exercise.** One way of coping with stress is to find a quiet place, relax the muscles, and eliminate distracting stimuli. Exercise can be a helpful way of channeling nervous energy and enabling oneself to relax. (page 487–488)
- **Distraction.** Distracting a person's attention from the source of stress helps to reduce the stress. (page 488)

## Answers to Concept Checks

17. Your roommate's radio would be more disruptive. You can turn your own radio on or off, switch stations, or reduce the volume. You have no such control over your roommate's radio (unless your roommate happens to be very cooperative). (page 485)
18. Practice giving your speech to a small group of friends. If possible, practice giving the speech in the room where you will ultimately deliver it. (page 486)
19. Monitoring strategies attack the cause of the problem and increase one's sense of control over it. Blunting strategies distract one from a presumably uncontrollable problem. (page 488)

CHAPTER ENDING

# Key Terms and Activities

## Key Terms

**alarm:** the first stage of response to stress, a brief period of high arousal of the sympathetic nervous system, readying the body for vigorous activity (page 478)

**autonomic nervous system:** a section of the nervous system that controls the functioning of the internal organs, such as the heart (page 453)

**blunting:** trying to avoid the stressful event or at least avoid thinking about it (page 484)

**Duchenne smile:** a spontaneous expression that includes movement of both the mouth muscles and certain muscles near the eyes (page 463)

**emotional intelligence:** the ability to perceive, imagine, and understand emotions and to use that information in decision-making (page 452)

**exhaustion:** the third stage of response to stress, when the body's prolonged response to stress decreases the synthesis of proteins, including the proteins necessary for activity of the immune system (page 478)

**frustration-aggression hypothesis:** the theory that frustration leads to aggressive behavior (page 470)

**guilty-knowledge test:** a test that uses the polygraph to measure whether a person has information that should be known only by someone guilty of a certain crime or someone who talked with the guilty person (page 457)

**health psychology:** a field of psychology concerned with how people's behavior can enhance health and prevent illness and how behavior contributes to recovery from illness (page 477)

**inoculation:** protection against the harmful effects of stress by earlier exposure to smaller amounts of it (page 486)

**James-Lange theory:** the theory that emotion is merely our perception of autonomic changes and movements evoked directly by various stimuli (page 458)

**monitoring:** attending carefully to the stressful event and one's reaction to it and trying to take effective action (page 484)

**opponent-process principle of emotions:** the principle that the removal of a stimulus that excites one emotion causes a swing to an opposite emotion (page 454)

**parasympathetic nervous system:** a system of neurons located in the medulla and the bottom of the spinal cord; these neurons send messages to the internal organs to prepare the body for digestion and related processes (page 453)

**polygraph:** a machine that simultaneously measures heart rate, breathing rate, blood pressure, and electrical conduction of the skin (page 456)

**positive psychology:** the study of the features that enrich life, such as hope, creativity, courage, spirituality, and responsibility (page 466)

**posttraumatic stress disorder (PTSD):** a condition in which people who have endured extreme stress feel prolonged anxiety and depression (page 478)

**psychosomatic illness:** an illness that is influenced by a person's experiences—particularly stressful experiences—or by his or her reactions to those experiences (page 480)

**rape:** sexual contact obtained through violence or threats (page 475)

**resistance:** (1) the second stage of response to stress, a stage of prolonged but moderate arousal (page 478) (2) according to psychoanalysts, continued repression that interferes with therapy (page 478)

**Schachter and Singer's theory of emotions:** the theory that the intensity of sympathetic arousal determines the intensity of an emotion but that cognitive factors determine the type of emotion (page 461)

**stress:** according to Hans Selye, the nonspecific response of the body to any demands made upon it; according to Lazarus, a situation that someone regards as threatening and as possibly exceeding his or her resources (page 477)

**subjective well-being:** a self-evaluation of one's life as pleasant, interesting, and satisfying (page 466)

**sympathetic nervous system:** a system composed of two chains of neuron clusters lying just to the left and right of the spinal cord; these neurons send messages to the internal organs to prepare them for a burst of vigorous activity (page 453)

**Type A personality:** a personality characterized by constant competitiveness, impatience, anger, and hostility (page 481)

**Type B personality:** a personality characterized by an easygoing attitude, with little hurry or hostility (page 481)

## Suggestions for Further Reading

Damasio, A. (1999). *The feeling of what happens.* New York: Harcourt Brace. Ambitious treatment of the role of emotions in thinking and consciousness.

LeDoux, J. E. (1996). *The emotional brain.* New York: Simon & Schuster. Discussion of the biological bases of emotion by a pioneering researcher.

Pennebaker, J. W. (1990). *Opening up.* New York: William Morrow. A description of the stress-relieving values of discussing your most painful experiences, either with other people or to yourself in writing.

Provine, R. (2000). *Laughter.* New York: Viking. Pioneering observations of who laughs, when, and why. Highly recommended.

Staub, E. (1989). *The roots of evil.* New York: Cambridge University Press. An inquiry into why people engage in extremely violent behavior.

## Web/Technology Resources

### Cross-Cultural Studies of Happiness

**www.eur.nl/fsw/research/happiness/index.htm**

This site presents survey results from many countries, as well as links to many other kinds of research on happiness.

### MINCAVA: Global Links on Violence

**www.mincava.umn.edu/index.asp**

The Minnesota Center Against Violence & Abuse (MINCAVA) maintains hundreds of links to sites that provide information about all forms of violence.

### Lifescan Health Risk Appraisal

**wellness.uwsp.edu/Health_Service/services/lifeScan.shtml**

Do you know what your *appraised health age* is? Answer a few health questions and find out. If possible, first check your blood pressure, total cholesterol, and HDL cholesterol levels.

### Stress Assess

**wellness.uwsp.edu/Health_Service/services/stress.shtml**

Evaluate your current stress sources, distress symptoms, and lifestyle behaviors. A personalized assessment includes strategies to counteract stress.*

### How to Fight and Conquer Stress

**www.coolware.com/health/medical_reporter/stress.html**

Material from the Rose Men's Health Resource defines stress, examines its positive and negative aspects, identifies some major life stressors, and provides tips on how to combat the negative effects of stress.

---

*Note: Any psychological test that is readily available to the public, while entertaining and possibly informative, should not be used to make important decisions about yourself or others. The most powerful, valid, and reliable psychological assessment devices are usually kept under the tight control of their creators or copyright holders.

# Personality

**13**

CHAPTER

S everal thousand people have the task of assembling the world's largest jigsaw puzzle, which contains more than a trillion pieces. Connie Conclusionjumper examines 20 pieces very closely, stares off into space, and announces, "When the puzzle is fully assembled, it will be a picture of the Sydney Opera House!" Prudence Plodder says, "Well, I don't know what the whole puzzle will look like, but I think I've found two little pieces that fit together."

Which of the two has made the greater contribution to completing the puzzle? We could argue either way. Clearly, the task requires an enormous number of little, unglamorous accomplishments like Prudence's. But if Connie is right, her flash of insight will be extremely valuable for assembling all the pieces. Of course, if the puzzle turns out to be a picture of a sailboat at sunset, then Connie will have made us waste time looking for nonexistent connections.

Some psychologists have offered grand theories about the nature of personality. Others have investigated why people with a certain type of personality act the way they do in a specific situation. In this chapter we shall explore several methods of approaching personality, ranging from large scale to small scale and from theoretical to descriptive. In the first module, we survey some of the most famous and influential theories of personality, such as

■ This three-dimensional jigsaw puzzle of the ocean liner Titanic consists of 26,000 pieces. Assembling all the pieces is an overwhelming task, but at least people know how the final product should look. Understanding personality is an even more complex puzzle, and we do not know the overall structure before we start investigaing.

that of Sigmund Freud. The second module concerns traits, which are descriptions of personality. To say that personality is composed of traits is, of course, a theory, but it is a different kind of theory that is not in competition with any of those in this module. The final module deals with measurements of personality.

# Personality Theories

*How can we best describe the overall structure of personality?*

Every individual is virtually an enemy of civilization. . . . Thus civilization has to be defended against the individual. . . . For the masses are lazy and unintelligent . . . and the individuals composing them support one another in giving free rein to their indiscipline.

—Sigmund Freud (1927/1961)

It has been my experience that persons have a basically positive direction. In my deepest contacts with individuals in therapy, even those whose troubles are most disturbing, whose behavior has been most anti-social, whose feelings seem most abnormal, I find this to be true.

—Carl Rogers (1961)

What makes us tick? What makes us the way we are? The 17th-century philosopher Thomas Hobbes argued that humans are by nature selfish. Life in a state of nature, he said, is "nasty, brutish, and short." If we are to protect ourselves from one another, we must be restrained by a watchful government. The 18th-century political philosopher Jean-Jacques Rousseau disagreed. He maintained that humans are basically good and that "civilized" governments are the problem, not the solution. Although he conceded that society could never return to "noble savagery," he believed that education and government should promote the freedom of the individual. Rational people acting freely, he maintained, would advance the welfare of all.

The debate between those two viewpoints survives in modern theories of personality (Figure 13.1). Some theorists, including Sigmund Freud, have held that people are born with sexual and destructive impulses that must be held in check if civilization is to survive. Others, including Carl Rogers, believed that people will achieve good and noble goals once they have been freed from unnecessary restraints.

Which point of view is correct? Way down deep, are we good, bad, both, or neither? How shall we go about trying to answer such questions? Are they even meaningful?

The term *personality* comes from the Latin word *persona*, meaning "mask." In the plays of ancient Greece and Rome, actors wore masks to indicate whether they were comic or tragic characters. Unlike a mask that one can either put on or take off, however, the term *personality*

implies something stable. **Personality** consists of *all the consistent ways in which the behavior of one person differs from that of others, especially in social situations.* (Differences among people in their learning, memory, or sensory functions are not generally considered part of personality.) Of course, any one aspect of your personality will resemble that of many other people. For example, you might be cheerful, and so are many others. Nevertheless, your particular combination of behavior tendencies is special and sets you apart from anyone else.

The ancient Greeks believed that personality depended on which of four different "humors" predominated in a person's body (Figure 13.2). A predominance of yellow bile made people hot tempered. A predominance of black bile made people depressed. An excess of phlegm made people sluggish and apathetic. An excess of blood made people courageous, hopeful, and amorous. The ancient Greek theory persists in the English language in such terms as *phlegmatic* and *melancholic* (literally, "black bile-ic").

Today, although we no longer believe in the four humors, we do believe that personality is influenced by other chemicals, such as hormones and neurotransmitters, as well as by our experiences. We no longer believe in four

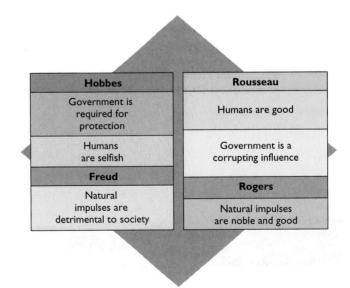

**FIGURE 13.1** Philosophers Thomas Hobbes and Jean-Jacques Rousseau held opposing views of human nature. Psychologists Sigmund Freud and Carl Rogers also held conflicting views. Freud, like Hobbes, stressed the more negative aspects of human nature; Rogers, like Rousseau, the more positive aspects.

a        b

c        d

FIGURE 13.2 According to the 2nd-century Greek physician Galen, personality depended on four humors. These were (a) sanguine (optimistic); (b) melancholic (depressive); (c) choleric (irritable); and (d) phlegmatic (calm). Galen's theory was influential throughout medieval Europe.

FIGURE 13.3 Sigmund Freud interpreted dreams, slips of the tongue, psychological disorders, and other behaviors that people had previously considered "random" or "unexplainable." According to Freud, even apparently purposeless behaviors reveal the influence of unconscious thoughts and motivations. Freud's theories have had an immense influence on many people, not only psychologists. Most psychological researchers, however, are skeptical of Freud's approach.

personality types, but we do believe in at least a few major dimensions along which personality can vary. Psychologists are not agreed on the fundamental organization of personality or even on whether personality has a fundamental organization. In this module we concentrate mostly on the theory of Sigmund Freud because the theory has been extremely influential outside psychology as well as within. You may decide not to take it very seriously, but you should know what the theory is and what evidence (or lack of evidence) supports it.

# Sigmund Freud and the Psychodynamic Approach

Sigmund Freud (1856–1939; Figure 13.3), an Austrian physician, developed the first psychodynamic theory. *A* **psychodynamic theory** *relates personality to the interplay of conflicting forces within the individual, including some that the individual may not consciously recognize.* That is, we are being pushed and pulled by internal forces that we do not fully understand.

Freud's influence on society is vast, extending into sociology, literature, art, even religion and politics (Figure 13.4). And yet, here we are, about three-fourths of the way through this text on psychology, and until now I have barely mentioned Freud. Why?

The reason is that Freud's influence within psychology is very much on the decline. According to one psychologist, Frederick Crews (1996, p. 63), "independent studies have begun to converge toward a verdict that was once considered a sign of extremism or even of neurosis: that there is literally nothing to be said, scientifically or therapeutically, to the advantage of the entire Freudian system or any of its constituent dogmas."

Think about that: *nothing* to be said in favor of *any* of Freud's theories. Needless to say, not everyone agrees with Crews. Still, the decline of Freud's influence is striking.

## Freud's Search for the Unconscious

Freud would have liked to become a professor of cultural history or anthropology; he wrote several books and articles about those topics in his later years. As a Jew in late 19th-century Austria, however, he knew that he had little chance of becoming a university professor. The only professional careers open to Jews in his time and place were in law, business, and medicine. Freud chose medicine, but without any deep commitment to healing people. His interests were almost purely theoretical.

Early in his career, Freud worked with the psychiatrist Josef Breuer, who had been treating a young woman with a fluctuating variety of physical complaints. As she talked with Breuer about her past, she recalled various traumatic, or emotionally damaging, experiences. Breuer, and later Freud also, said that recalling these experiences produced **catharsis,** *a release of pent-up emotional tension,* and thereby relieved her illness. However, later scholars who reexamined the medical records of the time found that this woman who was so famous in the history of psychoanalysis was not cured at all. She may not even have benefited from the

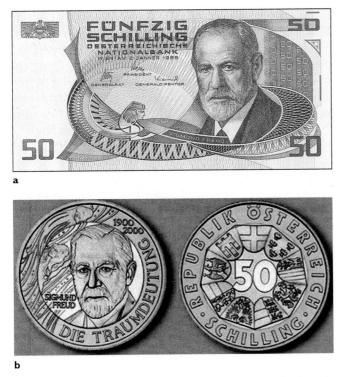

**a**

**b**

**FIGURE 13.4** The fame of Sigmund Freud far exceeds that of any other psychologist. His picture has even appeared on the Austrian 50-schilling bill and bimetal millenial coin.

treatment. She entered a hospital where she was treated with drugs. Eventually, she recovered, but the cause of her problems and the basis for her recovery remain unknown (Ellenberger, 1972).

Regardless of whether Breuer's "talking cure" had been successful, Freud began applying it to his own emotionally disturbed patients. He referred to *his method of explaining and dealing with personality, based on the interplay of conscious and unconscious forces,* as **psychoanalysis.** To this day psychoanalysts remain loyal to some version of Freud's methods and theories, although their views have of course evolved over the decades.

Psychoanalysis started out as a fairly simple theory: Each of us has an unconscious mind as well as a conscious mind (Figure 13.5). The **unconscious** is *the repository of memories, emotions, and thoughts, many of them illogical, that affect our behavior even though we cannot talk about them.* Traumatic experiences force thoughts and emotions into the unconscious, and the goal of psychoanalysts is to bring those memories back to consciousness. Doing so produces catharsis and enables the person to confront irrational and self-defeating impulses.

As Freud listened to his patients, however, he became convinced that the traumatic events they recalled were not sufficient to account for their abnormal behavior. Some patients reacted strongly to events that others took in stride. Why? At first, in the early 1890s, Freud attributed their overreactions to sexual difficulties (Macmillan, 1997). People with excessive anxiety, he said, were suffer-

ing from a lack of sexual gratification, and they could solve their problems by increased sexual activity. (For a while Freud claimed that increased sexual activity cured people's psychological problems, but he soon abandoned this view, and since then no one has found any reason to revive it.) People suffering from nervous exhaustion, he said, were suffering from the results of masturbation. His evidence for this idea was that all the patients who were suffering from nervous exhaustion had masturbated (!). You can see the problem: Freud was practicing long before Kinsey's survey of sexual behavior, and no one knew how common masturbation was. Freud boldly asserted that normal mentally healthy people do not masturbate. Suppose you were in his audience. Would you raise your hand and say, "Wait a minute, Dr. Freud, I think I'm mentally normal, and I masturbate . . ."? You probably wouldn't, and neither did anyone else, so Freud concluded that he was right.

A few years later, however, Freud abandoned these hypotheses and suggested instead that the ultimate cause of psychological disorders was traumatic sexual experiences from early childhood. In some of his writings, he attributed those experiences to seductions by other children; in later reports he said that the father or other adults had sexually abused the children. He had no evidence for these accusations. His patients did not even recall any such events, but Freud inferred that they must have happened nevertheless. He put together parts of the patients' dream reports, slips of the tongue, and so forth and claimed that these all pointed to early sexual abuse. At this point Freud's problems with evidence began to become serious. His ideas about inadequate sex or too much masturbation may sound ridiculous, but at least they were testable. But how was anyone to determine whether the events that Freud inferred from dreams and so forth had actually happened?

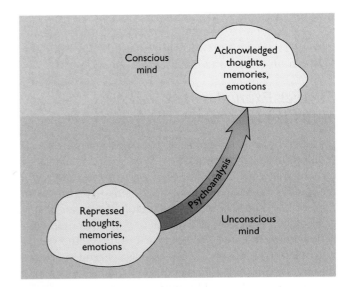

**FIGURE 13.5** Freud believed that psychoanalysis could bring parts of the unconscious into the conscious mind, where the client could deal with them.

A few years later, he backed down from saying that psychological disorders resulted from childhood sexual abuse. According to Freud's own description of these events, he realized that his patients had "misled" him into believing they had been sexually abused in early childhood, whereas in fact, Freud said, their claims of sexual contact with their parents were "wishful phantasies" (Freud, 1925). Although he never fully developed his views of girls' early sexual development, he was more explicit about boys: During early childhood every boy goes through an **Oedipus complex;** he *develops a sexual interest in his mother and competitive aggression toward his father.* (Oedipus—EHD-ah-puhs—a figure in an ancient Greek play by Sophocles, unknowingly murdered his father and married his mother.) In short, Freud said people become psychologically disturbed not because their parents sexually molested them, but because as children they wanted to have sex with their parents and couldn't.

Why did Freud switch from his idea about early sexual abuse to a theory about early sexual fantasies? According to one view (Masson, 1984), Freud was right the first time, and he simply lost the courage to defend his theory about childhood sexual abuse. According to other scholars, however, Freud never had any justification for either theory (Esterson, 1998; Powell & Boer, 1994; Schatzman, 1992). In his earliest writings, Freud inferred his patients' sexual abuse from their symptoms and dreams, despite their own denials of such sexual abuse. It was hardly fair, therefore, to complain that the patients had misled him into believing they had been sexually abused. When he switched to saying that the patients had had an Oedipus complex or other childhood sexual fantasies, he was again drawing inferences that his patients denied. (Freud considered his patients' protests to be signs of emotional resistance and therefore confirmation that his interpretations were correct.)

Apparently, Freud's main evidence for his interpretations was simply that he was able to construct a coherent story linking a patient's symptoms, dreams, and so forth to the sexual fantasies that Freud inferred must have occurred (Esterson, 1993). In short, he did not distinguish between his results and his interpretations.

## Further Examples of Casual Use of Evidence

Freud preferred complicated explanations to more parsimonious ones. At one point his friend Wilhelm Fliess performed a surgical operation on a woman's nose to try to relieve her stomach and menstrual pains—no, that's not a misprint—and absentmindedly left half a meter of surgical gauze in her nasal cavity after the operation. Her nose became infected and her face disfigured, and she almost bled to death. In a letter to Fliess, Freud suggested that the reason the woman continued to bleed for so long was that she had "an old wish to be loved in her illness" (Masson, 1985, Freud's letter of May 4, 1896).

Another patient, known as Dora, came to Freud at her father's insistence. Since about age 8, Dora had suffered from headaches, coughing, and shortness of breath, all of which Freud interpreted as psychological in nature. She had also avoided a certain friend of her father, Mr. K, ever since one episode when K grabbed Dora, then 14 years old, and kissed her on her lips. Freud wrote that Dora surely experienced sexual pleasure at this time because K's presumably erect penis must have rubbed up against her clitoris and excited it. Freud described Dora's reaction of disgust as "entirely and completely hysterical. I should without question consider a person hysterical in whom an occasion for sexual excitement elicited feelings that were preponderantly or exclusively unpleasurable" (Freud, 1905/1963, p. 44). He then proceeded to try to explain Dora's hysterical behavior, tracing it to her love for both K and her father and her homosexual attraction to Mrs. K. As one reads Freud's elaborate discussion, one wonders what was wrong with Dora's simpler explanation— that she really was repulsed by the sexual advances of this middle-aged man.

## Stages of Psychosexual Development in Freud's Theory of Personality

Right or wrong, Freud's theory is so well known that, as a student of psychology, you should know what his terms mean. One of his central points was that psychosexual interest and pleasure begin in infancy. He used the term **psychosexual pleasure** in a broad sense to include *all strong, pleasant excitement arising from body stimulation.* He maintained that how we deal with our psychosexual development influences nearly all aspects of our personality.

Freud proposed that young children have sexual tendencies like those of more primitive mammals. Just as nonhuman mammals respond sexually to sounds and smells that do not excite most adult humans, children respond sexually to stimulation of the mouth, the anus, and other body zones much more strongly than most adults do. Freud based his views on his patients' reconstructions of childhood; he did not systematically observe children himself.

According to Freud (1905/1925), people have a *psychosexual energy,* which he called **libido** (lih-BEE-doh), from a Latin word meaning "desire." Normally, libido is focused in an infant's mouth and "flows" to other parts of the body as the child grows older. Children go through five stages of psychosexual development, each with a characteristic sexual focus that leaves its mark on the adult personality. If normal sexual development is blocked or frustrated at any stage, Freud said, part of the libido becomes **fixated** at that stage; that is, it *continues to be preoccupied with the pleasure area associated with that stage.* Table 13.1 summarizes these stages.

**TABLE 13.1 Freud's Stages of Psychosexual Development**

| Stage (approximate ages) | Sexual Interests at This Stage | Effects of Fixation |
| --- | --- | --- |
| *Oral stage* (birth to 1 year) | Sucking, swallowing, biting | Lasting concerns with dependence and independence; pleasure from eating, drinking, and other oral activities |
| *Anal stage* (1 to 3 years) | Expelling feces, retaining feces | Orderliness, stinginess, stubbornness |
| *Phallic stage* (3 to 5 or 6 years) | Touching penis or clitoris; Oedipus complex | Difficulty feeling closeness. Males: fear of castration Females: penis envy |
| *Latency period* (5 or 6 to puberty) | Sexual interests suppressed | — |
| *Genital stage* (puberty onward) | Sexual contact with other people | — |

### The Oral Stage

In the **oral stage,** from birth through the first year or so (Freud was vague about the age limits of each stage), *the infant derives intense psychosexual pleasure from stimulation of the mouth, particularly while sucking at the mother's breast.* In the later part of the oral stage, the infant begins to bite as well as suck. A person fixated at this stage continues to receive great pleasure from eating, drinking, and smoking and may also have lasting concerns with dependence and independence.

### The Anal Stage

At about 1 to 3 years of age, children enter the **anal stage.** At this time *they get psychosexual pleasure from stimulation of the anal sphincter, the muscle that controls bowel movements.* A person fixated at this stage goes through life "holding things back"—being orderly, stingy, and stubborn—or, less commonly, may go to the opposite extreme and become wasteful, messy, and destructive.

### The Phallic Stage

Beginning at about age 3, in the **phallic stage,** children begin to *play with their genitals,* and according to Freud, become sexually attracted to the opposite-sex parent. Freud claimed that boys with a phallic fixation are afraid of being castrated; girls with such a fixation develop "penis envy." These ideas have always been controversial; developmental psychologists almost never observe castration fear or penis envy in children.

### The Latent Period

From about age 5 or 6 until adolescence, Freud said, most children enter a **latent period** in which they *suppress their psychosexual interest.* At this time they play mostly with peers of their own sex. The latent period is evidently a product of the culture and is not apparent in certain nonindustrialized societies.

### The Genital Stage

Beginning at puberty young people *take a strong sexual interest in other people.* This is known as the **genital stage.** According to Freud, anyone who has fixated a great deal of libido in an earlier stage has little libido left for the genital stage. But people who have successfully negotiated the earlier stages can now derive primary satisfaction from sexual intercourse.

### Evaluation of Freud's Stages

Freud's theory makes such vague predictions that it is difficult to test (Grünbaum, 1986; Popper, 1986). When it has been tested, the results have been mostly inconclusive. For

■ According to Freud, if normal sexual development is blocked at the oral stage, the child will seek pleasure from drinking and eating and later from kissing and smoking. Perhaps this pipe smoker's mother weaned him too quickly—or let him nurse too long. And perhaps such an explanation is incorrect. Like many of Freud's ideas, this one is difficult to test.

example, the characteristics of being orderly, stingy, and stubborn, which Freud described as due to anal fixation, tend to correlate with one another, suggesting that they are part of a single personality trait. However, we have no evidence that these attributes result from toilet training (Fisher & Greenberg, 1977).

## Freud's Description of the Structure of Personality

Personality, Freud claimed, consists of three aspects: id, ego, and superego. (Actually, he used German words that mean *it*, *I*, and *over-I*. A translator used Latin equivalents instead of English words.) The **id** consists of *all our biological drives*, such as sex and hunger, that demand immediate gratification. The **ego** is *the rational, decision-making aspect of the personality*. The **superego** contains *the memory of rules and prohibitions we learned from our parents and the rest of society*, such as, "Nice little boys and girls don't do that." Sometimes the id produces sexual or other motivations that the superego considers repugnant, thus evoking feelings of guilt. Conflict is especially likely with sexual and aggressive urges. The ego may side with either the id or the superego; if it sides with the superego, it tries to avoid even thinking about the id's unacceptable impulses. Most psychologists today find it difficult to imagine the mind in terms of three warring factions and therefore regard Freud's description as only a metaphor.

## CONCEPT CHECKS

1. If someone has persistent problems with independence and dependence, Freud would suggest a fixation at which psychosexual stage?
2. If someone is very neat and stingy, Freud would suggest a fixation at which psychosexual stage?
3. If someone is messy and wasteful, Freud would suggest a fixation at which psychosexual stage?
4. What kind of behavior would Freud expect of someone with a strong id and a weak superego? What behavior would you expect of someone with an unusually strong superego? (Check your answers on page 510.)

## Defense Mechanisms Against Anxiety

According to Freud, *the ego defends itself against conflicts and anxieties by relegating unpleasant thoughts and impulses to the unconscious.* Among the **defense mechanisms** that the ego employs are repression, denial, rationalization, displacement, regression, projection, reaction formation, and sublimation (Figure 13.6). Ordinarily, we are not aware of our own repressions, rationalizations, and so forth. Defense mechanisms are normal ways of suppressing anxiety

and are often adaptive, becoming a problem only when they prevent a person from effectively dealing with reality.

### Repression

The defense mechanism of **repression** is *motivated forgetting*—rejecting unacceptable thoughts, desires, and memories and banishing them to the unconscious. Repression is a central concept in Freud's theory.

One example of repression would be a woman who sees someone murdered and later cannot remember what she saw. Another example: A man gives a speech, several members of the audience raise serious objections to what he says, and later he forgets their objections.

Researchers have struggled to find clear evidence of repression. Investigators have exposed participants to various unpleasant or threatening experiences in the expectation that repression would interfere with their memories. However, whenever participants did have trouble remembering the events, we can see other possible explanations for their forgetting (Holmes, 1990). Outside the laboratory, repression is certainly not common in situations where we might expect it. As discussed in Chapter 7, most kidnapping victims, children who watched the death of their own parents, and others who endured similar misery remember the events intensely. If repression occurs, it occurs rarely and under circumstances we cannot yet define.

### Denial

*The refusal to believe information that provokes anxiety* ("This can't be happening") is called **denial.** Whereas repression is the motivated forgetting of certain information, denial is an assertion that the information is incorrect. For example, someone with a serious alcohol problem may insist, "I'm not an alcoholic. I can take it or leave it."

### Rationalization

When people *attempt to prove that their actions are rational and justifiable and thus worthy of approval*, they are using **rationalization.** For example, a student who wants to go to the movies instead of studying says, "More studying won't do me any good." Someone who misses a deadline to apply for a job says, "I didn't really want that job."

### Displacement

*By diverting a behavior or thought away from its natural target toward a less threatening target,* **displacement** lets people engage in the behavior they prefer without experiencing severe anxiety. For example, a man who is angry at his boss might come home and kick his dog. He really wants to kick his boss, but that would cause him too much anxiety. Or a student who is angry at her professor screams at her roommate.

### Regression

A *return to a more juvenile level of functioning,* **regression** is an effort to avoid the anxiety of facing one's current role in life. By adopting a childish role, a person can escape responsibility and return to an earlier, perhaps more secure, way of life. For example, after a new sibling is born, a 5-year-old child may start wetting the bed again. Following a divorce or a business setback, a man may resort to daydreaming, getting drunk, or other immature behaviors.

## Projection

*The attribution of one's own undesirable characteristics to other people* is known as **projection.** In theory, by suggesting that other people have those faults, the faults become more acceptable and less anxiety provoking. For example, someone who secretly enjoys pornography might accuse other people of enjoying it. However, the research finds that people using projection do not ordinarily decrease their anxiety or their awareness of their own faults (Holmes, 1978; Sherwood, 1981).

## Reaction Formation

To reduce anxiety and to keep undesirable characteristics repressed, people may use **reaction formation** to *present themselves as the opposite of what they really are to*

*hide the unpleasant truth either from themselves or others.* For example, a man troubled by doubts about his religious faith may try to convert others to the faith. Someone with unacceptable aggressive tendencies may join a group dedicated to preventing violence against babies or animals. (Not everyone who proselytizes for a faith has deep doubts about it, of course, and not everyone who tries to prevent violence is secretly a violent person. Different people have different reasons for the same actions.)

## Sublimation

*The transformation of sexual or aggressive energies into culturally acceptable, even admirable, behaviors is* **sublimation.** According to Freud, sublimation enables a person to express the impulse without admitting its existence. For example, painting and sculpture may represent a sublimation of sexual impulses. Someone with unacceptable aggressive impulses may sublimate them by becoming a surgeon. However, if the true motives of a painter are sexual, as Freud proposed, they are well hidden indeed. Sublimation is the one proposed defense mechanism that is associated with socially constructive behavior.

**FIGURE 13.6** The ego, or "rational I," has numerous ways of defending itself against anxiety, that apprehensive state named for the Latin word meaning "to strangle." We use defense mechanisms to avoid unpleasant realities. They are part of an internal battle that you fight against yourself.

# CONCEPT CHECK

5. Match the Freudian defense mechanisms in the top list with the situations in the list that follows:

   | | |
   |---|---|
   | Repression | Regression |
   | Denial | Projection |
   | Rationalization | Reaction formation |
   | Displacement | Sublimation |

   a. A man who is angry with his neighbor goes hunting and kills a deer.
   b. Someone with a smoking habit insists there is no convincing evidence that smoking impairs health.
   c. A woman with doubts about her religious faith tries to convert others to her religion.
   d. A man who beats his wife writes a book arguing that people have an instinctive need for aggressive behavior.
   e. A woman forgets a doctor's appointment for a test for cancer.
   f. Someone who has difficulty dealing with certain people resorts to pouting, crying, and throwing tantrums.
   g. A boss takes credit for a good idea suggested by an employee because "It's better for me to take the credit so that our department will look good and all the employees will benefit."
   h. Someone with an unacceptable impulse to shout obscenities becomes a writer of novels. (Check your answers on page 510.)

## Freud's Legacy

Undeniably, Freud was a great pioneer in identifying new questions. The validity of his answers is less certain, however. He based his conclusions on inferences he drew from what his patients said and did, and he had no sure

■ Freud's own couch is now part of our history. What is the future of the psychoanalytic couch? Psychoanalytic interpretations range from reasonable to doubtful; in any individual case, it is difficult or even impossible to judge the accuracy of an analyst's interpretation.

way of testing the validity of his inferences. A growing number of psychologists today contend that Freud imposed theories onto his data instead of drawing conclusions from the data.

It is possible, of course, for a visionary leader to derive correct theories from weak evidence, and Freud could have been right even if his methods were faulty. One reviewer of the literature (Westen, 1998) identifies the following ideas as among Freud's enduring contributions to psychology:

- Much of mental life is unconscious. We don't always know why we're doing something.
- People often have conflicting motives.
- Childhood experiences are important for the development of personality and social behavior.
- Our relationships with other people can resemble the relationships we had with other people in the past, such as our parents.
- People develop through stages of psychosexual interest and relationships with the social world.

However, a critic can reply that these comments are "damning with faint praise." That is, Freud thought he had found a way to probe people's unconscious thoughts and motives; he was not just looking for some vague generalizations about psychology. It is not much of a compliment to him to say that people have unconscious thoughts and motives. The research supports ideas such as implicit memory (Chapter 7), and concept priming (Chapter 8). These ideas do refer to unconscious processes, but they have little in common with the unconscious sexual motives that Freud inferred. Implicit memory occurs mainly for events to which we paid little attention when they happened, not for events that were emotionally traumatic. Similarly, the existence of conflicting motives or the importance of childhood is hardly a unique contribution of Freud. How much credit we should give Freud is a matter of opinion.

## Neo-Freudians

Some psychologists, known as **neo-Freudians,** *remained faithful to parts of Freud's theory while modifying other parts.* One of the most influential neo-Freudians was the German physician Karen Horney (HOR-nigh; 1885–1952; Figure 13.7), who believed that Freud exaggerated the role of the sex drive in human behavior and misunderstood the sexual motivations of women. She believed, for example, that the conflict between a child and parents was a reaction to parental hostility and intimidation, not a manifestation of sexual desires. Horney contended that Freud had slighted the importance of cultural influences on personality and that he neglected to help his patients work out practical solutions to their problems. Still, Horney's views were more a revision than a rejection of Freud's theories. Other theorists, including Carl Jung and Alfred Adler, broke more sharply with Freud. Although some psycholo-

**FIGURE 13.7** Karen Horney, a major neo-Freudian, revised some of Freud's theories and gave greater attention to cultural influences. She was a pioneer in the development of feminine psychology.

**FIGURE 13.8** Carl G. Jung rejected Freud's concept that dreams hide their meaning from the conscious mind: "To me dreams are a part of nature, which harbors no intention to deceive, but expresses something as best it can" (Jung, 1965).

gists call Jung and Adler neo-Freudians, the followers of Jung and Adler do not. Each offered a very different, distinctly non-Freudian view of personality.

# Carl Jung and the Collective Unconscious

Carl G. Jung (YOONG; 1875–1961; Figure 13.8), a Swiss physician, was an early member of Freud's inner circle. Freud regarded Jung like a son, the "heir apparent" or "crown prince" of the psychoanalytic movement, until their father–son relationship began to deteriorate (Alexander, 1982). At one point Freud and Jung agreed to analyze each other's dreams. Freud described one of his dreams, but then refused to provide the personal associations that would enable Jung to interpret it, insisting that "I cannot risk my authority."

Jung was more forthcoming. He described a dream in which he explored the upper stories of a house, then explored its basement, and finally discovering that the house had a subbasement, began to explore that. Jung thought the dream referred to his explorations of the mind. The top floor was the conscious mind; the basement was the unconscious; and the subbasement was a still deeper level of the unconscious, yet to be explored. Freud, however, insisted that the dream referred to Jung's personal experiences and frustrations (Hannah, 1976).

Jung's own theory of personality incorporated some of Freud's ideas but put greater emphasis on people's search for a spiritual meaning in life and on the continuity of human experience, past and present. Jung believed that every person has not only a conscious mind and a "personal unconscious" (equivalent to Freud's "unconscious") but also a collective unconscious. The personal unconscious represents a person's own experience. The **collective unconscious,** which is present at birth, represents *the cumulative experience of preceding generations.* Because all humans share a common ancestry, all have the same collective unconscious. The collective unconscious contains **archetypes,** which are *vague images that we all inherit from the experiences of our ancestors.* In other words almost all people would have practically the same collective unconscious. As evidence for this view, Jung pointed out that similar images emerge in the art of cul-

tures throughout the world (Figure 13.9) and that similar themes emerge in various religions, myths, and folklore. Those images and themes also appear in dreams and hallucinations. So, for example, if you dream about a beetle, Jung might relate your dream to the important role that beetles have played in human mythology dating back at least to the ancient Egyptians.

Given what biologists now know of genetics, Jung's ideas are hard to defend. Having an experience does not change one's genes, and even if we did somehow develop genes that represented common human experiences, those genes would certainly vary among people, as other genes do. Jung's alternative to a genetic explanation was that perhaps archetypes exist on their own, independent of time, space, and brains. That idea is difficult even to contemplate, much less test. In short, Jung's views of the collective unconscious and archetypes are vague and mystical (Neher, 1996).

### A STEP FURTHER
*Archetypes*

Jung believed that the similarities in artworks throughout the world—such as the drawings he called mandalas—indicated that people inherited images or archetypes for those shapes. Can you suggest a simpler, more parsimonious explanation?

## CONCEPT CHECK

**6.** How does Jung's idea of the collective unconscious differ from Freud's idea of the unconscious? (Check your answer on page 510.)

# Alfred Adler and Individual Psychology

Alfred Adler (1870–1937; Figure 13.10), an Austrian physician who, like Jung, had been one of Freud's early associates, broke with Freud because he believed Freud overemphasized the sex drive and neglected other more

**FIGURE 13.9** Carl Jung was fascinated that similar images appear in the artwork of different cultures. One recurring image is the circular mandala, a symbol of unity and wholeness. These mandalas are: (a) a Hindu painting from Bhutan; (b) a mosaic from Beth Alpha Synagogue, Israel; (c) a tie-dye tapestry created in California; and (d) a Navajo sand painting from the southwestern United States.

important influences on personality. They parted company in 1911, with Freud insisting that women experience "penis envy" and with Adler contending that women were more likely to envy men's status and power.

Adler founded a rival school of thought, which he called **individual psychology.** To Adler, this term did not mean "psychology of the individual." Rather, it meant *"indivisible psychology," a psychology of the person as a whole rather than a psychology of parts,* such as id, ego, and superego. Adler emphasized the importance of conscious,

goal-directed behavior and deemphasized (though he did not deny) unconscious influences.

## Adler's Description of Personality

Several of Adler's early patients were acrobats who had had an arm or a leg damaged by a childhood illness or injury. They were determined to overcome their disabilities, and they had worked hard to develop the needed strength and coordination to perform as acrobats. Per-

**FIGURE 13.10** Like Horney, Alfred Adler thought that Freud overemphasized the sex drive. Adler was very interested in feelings of self-esteem. According to Adler, the key to a healthy personality was not just freedom from disorders but "social interest," a desire for the welfare of other people.

haps, Adler surmised, people in general try to overcome their weaknesses and to transform them into strengths (Adler, 1932/1964).

As infants, Adler pointed out, we are small, dependent creatures who strive to overcome our inferiority. Normal experiences with failure goad people to try harder. However, persistent failures or overcritical parents and others can produce an **inferiority complex,** *an exaggerated feeling of weakness, inadequacy, and helplessness.*

According to Adler, everyone has a natural **striving for superiority,** *a desire to seek personal excellence and fulfillment.* Each person creates a **style of life,** or *master plan for achieving a sense of superiority.* That style of life may be directed toward success in business, sports, politics, or another competitive activity. People can also strive for other kinds of success. For example, someone who withdraws from life may gain a sense of accomplishment or superiority from being uncommonly self-sacrificing. Someone who constantly complains about real or imagined illnesses or disabilities may win a measure of control or superiority over friends and family. Or someone may commit crimes to savor the attention that they bring. People also sometimes get a feeling of superiority by making excuses for their lack of achievements. If you marry someone who is likely to thwart your ambitions, perhaps your underlying motivation is to maintain an illusion: "I could have been a great success if my husband/wife hadn't prevented me." Failure to study can have a similar motivation: "I could have done well on this test, but my friends talked me into going to a party the night before."

Adler recognized that people are not always aware of their own style of life and the assumptions behind it and may fail to understand that the real motive behind a word or action is to manipulate others. They may engage in self-defeating behavior because they have not admitted to themselves what their goals really are. Adler tried to determine people's real motives. For example, he would ask someone who complained of a backache, "How would your life be different if you could get rid of your backache?" Those who said they would become more active were presumably suffering from physical ailments that they were trying to overcome. Those who said they could not imagine how their life would change, or said only that they would get less sympathy from

others, were presumably suffering from psychologically caused ailments or, at least, were exaggerating their discomfort.

## CONCEPT CHECK

7. In Adler's theory what is the relationship between striving for superiority and style of life? (Check your answer on page 510.)

## *Adler's View of Psychological Disorders*

Any personality based on a selfish style of life is unhealthy, Adler (1928/1964) said. People's needs for one another require a **social interest,** *a sense of solidarity and identification with other people.* Note that social interest does not mean a desire to socialize; it means an interest in the welfare of society. People with a strong social interest strive for superiority and welfare of a large group of people or all of humanity. They want to cooperate with other people, not to compete. In equating mental health with a strong social interest, Adler saw mental health as a positive state, not just the absence of impairments.

In Adler's view people with psychological disorders are not suffering from an "illness." Rather, they have set immature goals, are following a faulty style of life, and show little social interest. Their response to new opportunity is "Yes, but . . ." (Adler, 1932/1964). They are striving for superiority in ways that are useless to themselves and others.

For example, one of Adler's patients was a man who lived in conflict with his wife because he was constantly trying to impress and dominate her (Adler, 1927). When discussing his problems, the man revealed that he had been very slow to mature physically and had not reached puberty until he was 17 years old. Other teenagers had ignored him and had treated him like a child. He was now a physically normal adult, but he was overcompensating for those years of feeling inferior by trying to seem bigger and more important than he really was.

Adler tried to get patients to understand their own style of life and to correct the faulty assumptions on which they had based their lives. He urged them to strengthen their social interest and to strive for superiority in ways that would benefit both themselves and others.

## *Adler's Legacy*

Adler's influence on psychology exceeds his fame. His concept of the "inferiority complex" has become part of the common culture. He was the first to talk about mental health as a positive state rather than as merely the absence of impairments. Many later forms of therapy drew upon Adler's emphasis on the assumptions underlying a patient's behavior. Many psychologists also followed Adler by urging people to take responsibility for their own behavior and for modifying their goals.

# The Learning Approach

How did you develop your personality? At least part of the answer surely depends on how you have learned to behave in certain situations. Indeed, some psychologists have argued that the whole concept of general personality is vastly overrated and that most of our personality is learned on a situation-by-situation basis (Mischel, 1973, 1981). For example, you might be honest about returning a lost wallet to its owner; yet you find yourself lying to your professor about why your paper is late. So how useful is it to say that you are an honest person or even that you are "more honest than 80% of other people"? It might be more useful to describe specific behaviors in particular situations (Mischel & Shoda, 1995). Presumably, these specific behaviors are learned, and different people learn different behaviors for a given situation. The fact that learning is specific to a situation helps explain both variations among individuals and variations among situations for a given individual.

The Social Learning section of Chapter 6 described some ways in which we learn our personality. We learn much by imitation or by vicarious reinforcement and punishment. That is, we copy behaviors that we know led to success for other people and avoid behaviors that led to failure for others. We behave like the people that we respect and want to resemble.

Let's illustrate this idea by applying this approach to masculine and feminine personality tendencies. Part of learning how we are expected to act is developing a **gender role,** *the pattern of behavior that each person is expected to follow because of being male or female.* A gender role is the psychological aspect of being male or female, as opposed to sex, which is the biological aspect. We know that gender role is at least partly learned because certain aspects of it vary strikingly among cultures (Figure 13.11). For example, some cultures define cooking as "women's work" and others define it as "men's work." Men wear their hair short in some cultures and long in others.

When we say that children learn their gender role, we do not necessarily mean that anyone teaches it to them deliberately or intentionally. More often people teach by example. Boys tend to imitate men, and girls tend to imitate women. In one experiment children watched adults choose between an apple and a banana. If all the men chose one fruit and all the women chose the other, the boys wanted what the men had and the girls wanted what the women had (Perry & Bussey, 1979). The choice

**FIGURE 13.11** Gender roles vary greatly from one culture to another and even from one time period to another within a single culture. Here a male Palestinian farmer near Jerusalem (a) and a woman in Vietnam (b) plow the fields. Men in Dhaka, Bangladesh, (c), and a Hmong woman in Thailand (d) do the wash.

**FIGURE 13.12** Children learn gender roles partly by imitating adults, but they probably learn more from other children.

havior has a cause) and in *reductionism* (the attempt to explain behavior in terms of its component elements). Humanistic psychologists avoid these attempts to explain behavior in terms of its parts or causes. They claim that people make deliberate, conscious decisions about what to do with their lives. People can decide to devote themselves to a great cause, to sacrifice their own well-being, and to risk their lives. To the humanistic psychologist, it is fruitless to ascribe such behavior to past rewards and punishments or to unconscious thought processes.

Humanistic psychologists generally study the special experiences of a given individual, as opposed to seeking means or medians for large representative groups. Their research consists mostly of recording narratives of individuals' lives, more like a biographer than like a scientist in the usual sense. Therefore, their data are qualitative, not quantitative.

They also study **peak experiences,** *moments in which a person feels truly fulfilled and content.* Some people report that they "feel at one with the universe" when they hear "thrilling" music, take part in an emotional religious ceremony, or achieve a great accomplishment.

of fruit is in itself trivial, but the study shows the potential for influence on more important behaviors. Even more powerfully, boys and girls learn their gender roles from older children (Figure 13.12).

In short, the learning approach focuses on specific behaviors and attempts to relate them to specific experiences. Some of these are the person's own experiences and some are those of others whom the person has imitated.

# Humanistic Psychology

Another general perspective on personality, **humanistic psychology,** *deals with consciousness, values, and abstract beliefs, including spiritual experiences and the beliefs that people live by and die for.* According to humanistic psychologists, personality depends on what people believe and how they perceive the world. If you *believe* that a particular experience was highly meaningful, then it *was* highly meaningful. A psychologist can understand your behavior only by asking you for your own evaluations and interpretations of the events in your life. (In theology a *humanist* glorifies humans, generally denying or at least paying little attention to a Supreme Being. The term *humanistic psychologist* implies nothing about an individual's religious beliefs.)

Humanistic psychology emerged in the 1950s and 1960s as a protest against both behaviorism and psychoanalysis, which were the dominant viewpoints in psychology at that time (Berlyne, 1981). Behaviorists and psychoanalysts often emphasize the less noble, or at least morally neutral, aspects of people's thoughts and actions, whereas humanistic psychologists see people as essentially good and striving toward perfection. Also, behaviorism and psychoanalysis, despite their many differences, are both rooted in *determinism* (the belief that every be-

## Carl Rogers and the Goal of Self-Actualization

Carl Rogers, an American psychologist, studied theology before turning to psychology, and the influence of those early studies is apparent in his view of human nature. Rogers (Figure 13.13) became probably the most influential humanistic psychologist.

**FIGURE 13.13** Carl Rogers maintained that people naturally strive toward positive goals and that they do not need special urging. He recommended that people relate to one another with "unconditional positive regard."

According to Rogers (1980), human nature is basically good. People have a natural drive toward **self-actualization,** which means *the achievement of one's full potential.* According to Rogers, it is as natural for people to strive for excellence as it is for a plant to grow. The drive for self-actualization is the basic drive behind the development of personality. (Rogers's concept of self-actualization is similar to Adler's concept of striving for superiority. Adler was a forerunner of humanistic psychology.)

Children evaluate themselves and their actions beginning at an early age. They learn that what they do is sometimes good and sometimes bad. They develop a **self-concept,** *an image of what they really are,* and an **ideal self,** *an image of what they would like to be.* Rogers measured a person's self-concept and ideal self by handing the person a stack of cards containing statements such as "I am honest" and "I am suspicious of others." The person would then sort the statements into piles representing *true of me* and *not true of me* or arrange them in a continuum from *most true of me* to *least true of me.* (This method is known as a *Q-sort.*) Then Rogers would provide an identical stack of cards and ask the person to sort them into two piles: *true of my ideal self* and *not true of my ideal self.* In this manner he could determine whether someone's self-concept was similar to his or her ideal self; people who perceive a great discrepancy between the two generally experience distress. Humanistic psychologists try to help people overcome this distress either by improving their self-concept or by changing their ideal self.

To promote human welfare, Rogers maintained that people should relate to one another with **unconditional positive regard,** a relationship that Thomas Harris (1967) described with the phrase "I'm OK—You're OK." Unconditional positive regard is *the complete, unqualified acceptance of another person as he or she is,* much like the love of a parent for a child. If someone expresses anger, or even a desire to kill, the listener should accept that as an understandable feeling, even while discouraging the person from taking certain possible actions. The listener must convey the message that the other person is inherently good, even though certain actions might be bad. This view resembles the Christian admonition to "hate the sin but love the sinner." The alternative is *conditional positive regard,* the attitude that "I shall like you only if . . . ." People who are treated this way may feel restrained about opening themselves to new ideas or behaviors for fear of losing someone else's esteem.

## Abraham Maslow and the Self-Actualized Personality

Abraham Maslow (Figure 13.14), another founder of humanistic psychology, proposed that people have a hierarchy of needs, an idea we considered in Chapter 11. The

FIGURE 13.14 Abraham Maslow, one of the founders of humanistic psychology, introduced the concept of a "self-actualized personality," a better than merely normal personality associated with high productivity and enjoyment of life.

highest of those needs is *self-actualization,* the fulfillment of a person's potential. What kind of person achieves self-actualization, and what is the result of achieving it? Maslow (1962, 1971) sought to describe the self-actualized personality. He complained that psychologists concentrate on disordered personalities, assuming that all personality is either "normal" (i.e., bland) or undesirable. Maslow insisted that personality can differ from the normal in positive, desirable ways.

To determine the characteristics of the self-actualized personality, Maslow made a list of people who in his opinion had achieved their full potential. His list included people he knew personally as well as figures from history (Figure 13.15). He then sought to discover what these people had in common.

FIGURE 13.15 Harriet Tubman, identified by Maslow as having a self-actualized personality, was a leader of the Underground Railroad, a system for helping slaves escape from the southern states before the Civil War. Maslow defined the self-actualized personality by first identifying highly productive and admirable people, such as Tubman, and then determining which personality features they had in common.

According to Maslow (1962, 1971), people with a self-actualized personality show the following characteristics:

- An accurate perception of reality: They perceive the world as it is, not as they would like it to be. They are willing to accept uncertainty and ambiguity when necessary.
- Independence, creativity, and spontaneity: They follow their own impulses.
- Acceptance of themselves and others: They treat people with unconditional positive regard.
- A problem-centered outlook rather than a self-centered outlook: They think about how best to solve a problem, not how to make themselves look good. They also concentrate on significant problems, such as philosophical or political issues, not just the petty issues of getting through the day.
- Enjoyment of life: They are open to positive experiences, including "peak experiences."
- A good sense of humor.

Critics have attacked Maslow's description on the ground that, because it is based on his own choice of examples, it may simply reflect the characteristics that he himself admired. That is, his reasoning was circular: He defined certain people as self-actualized and then inquired what they had in common to figure out what "self-actualized" means (Neher, 1991). In any case Maslow paved the way for other attempts to define a healthy personality as something more than a personality without disorder.

### CONCEPT CHECK

8. According to humanistic psychologists, is developing a self-actualized personality a way to achieve another person's unconditional positive regard? (Check your answer on page 510.)

---

**IN CLOSING**

## In Search of Human Nature

The three great comprehensive personality theories are generally agreed to be those of Freud, Jung, and Adler, who lived at the same place and time and knew each other well. It is noteworthy that many years later, even though most psychologists do not accept any of those three theories, no one seems to be trying to develop an alternative.

Recall from Chapter 1 that I said a good research question is interesting and answerable. Fundamental questions about human nature are extraordinarily interesting, but they may not be answerable, at least not all at once. Most researchers today try to answer smaller questions about specific aspects of behavior, such as why some people are more outgoing than others or how conscientiousness develops.

You have no doubt heard the parable of the blind people describing an elephant: One feels the tusks and says an elephant is like a smooth rock; another feels the tail and says an elephant is like a rope; and so forth. The full description of an elephant can emerge only from the combination of narratives. Similarly, a full description of personality emerges from a combination of research approaches.

## Summary

- **Personality theories as views of human nature.** Personality consists of all the stable, consistent ways that the behavior of one person differs from that of others. Theories of personality are closely related to conceptions of human nature. Some observers believe that human beings are basically hostile and need to be restrained (Hobbes, Freud). Others believe that humans are basically good and are hampered by restraints (Rousseau, Rogers). (page 495)
- **Psychodynamic theories.** Several historically influential theories have described personality as the outcome of internal forces of which people are not fully conscious. (page 496)
- **Freud.** Sigmund Freud, the founder of psychoanalysis, proposed that human behavior is greatly influenced by unconscious thoughts and motives and that much of what we do and say has hidden meanings. Many of his interpretations and theories did not follow clearly from his evidence. (page 496)
- **Freud's psychosexual stages.** Freud believed that many unconscious thoughts and motives are sexual in nature. He proposed that people progress through stages or periods of psychosexual development—oral, anal, phallic, latent, and genital—and that frustration at any one stage can lead to a lasting fixation of the libido at that stage. (page 498)
- **Jung.** Carl Jung believed that all people share a "collective unconscious" that represents the entire experience of humanity. (page 503)
- **Adler.** Alfred Adler proposed that people's primary motivation is a striving for superiority. Each person adopts his or her own "style of life," or method of striving. (page 503)
- **Adler's view of a healthy personality.** According to Adler, the healthiest style of life is one that emphasizes "social interest"—that is, concern for the welfare of others. (page 505)
- **The learning approach.** The behaviors that constitute personality can be learned through individual experience, or as social learning psychologists emphasize, they can be learned by imitation or vicarious reinforcement and punishment. Because people's experiences vary, they can behave different ways in different situations. (page 506)

- **Humanistic psychology.** Humanistic psychologists emphasize conscious, deliberate decision making; they oppose attempts to reduce behavior to its elements or to seek explanations in terms of unconscious influences. (page 507)

## Answers to Concept Checks

1. Freud would interpret this behavior as a fixation at the oral stage. (page 500)
2. Freud would interpret this behavior as a fixation at the anal stage. (page 500)
3. Freud would interpret this behavior as a fixation at the anal stage. Note that opposite behaviors—neat and stingy or messy and wasteful—can result from the same fixation in Freud's system. (page 500)
4. Someone with a strong id and a weak superego could be expected to give in to a variety of sexual and other impulses that other people would inhibit. Someone with an unusually strong superego would be unusually inhibited and dominated by feelings of guilt. (page 500)
5. **a.** displacement;
   **b.** denial;
   **c.** reaction formation;
   **d.** projection;
   **e.** repression;
   **f.** regression;
   **g.** rationalization;
   **h.** sublimation. (page 502)
6. Jung's collective unconscious is the same for all people and is present at birth. Freud believed the unconscious developed from repressed experiences. (page 503)
7. In Adler's theory a person's style of life is a method of striving for superiority. (page 505)
8. No. People strive for self-actualization because of their own intrinsic desire for it, not for any external reward. Unconditional positive regard is like the love of a parent for a child, independent of what the other person does. (page 509)

# Personality Traits

*What traits provide the best description of personality?*
*Why do people differ in their personalities?*

With regard to human personality, which would you say?

**a.** Every person is different from every other.
**b.** Way down deep, we're all the same.
**c.** It depends.

I vote for "it depends." The answer depends on our purposes. For analogy, in some ways every rock is different. If you want to know the fair market value of a rock, you cannot treat diamonds the same as granite, and if you want to predict how well a rock will conduct electricity or how easily you could break it, you need to know a good deal about the content of the rock. However, if you want to predict how fast a rock will fall if you drop it or what will happen when you throw it against a window, one kind of rock is about the same as another.

Similarly, people resemble one another in some ways but not in others. Psychologists study personalities in two ways, called the nomothetic and the idiographic approaches. The word *nomothetic* (NAHM-uh-THEHT-ick) comes from the Greek *nomothetes,* meaning "legislator," and the **nomothetic approach** *seeks general laws about how an aspect of personality affects behavior,* often based on statistical comparisons of large groups of people. For example, we might make the nomothetic statement that the more extraverted someone's personality, the more likely that person will introduce himself or herself to a stranger.

In contrast the word *idiographic* is based on the root *idio-,* meaning "individual." The **idiographic approach** concentrates on *intensive studies of individuals* (Allport, 1961). For example, psychologists have studied how people's life goals affect their moods and their reactions to various events. Because people have different goals, investigators draw carefully qualified conclusions about how people with a particular goal behave, and they would not expect that conclusion to apply to all people or even to a large number of people (Emmons, 1991).

## Personality Traits and States

Meteorologists distinguish between climate (the usual conditions) and weather (the current conditions). For example, the climate in Scotland is moister and cooler than the climate in Texas, but on a given day, the weather could be warm in Scotland and cool in Texas. Similarly, psychologists distinguish between long-lasting personality conditions and temporary fluctuations.

*A consistent, long-lasting tendency in behavior, such as shyness, hostility, or talkativeness,* is known as a **trait.** In contrast a **state** is *a temporary activation of a particular behavior.* For example, stage fright is a state; general nervousness is a trait. Being quiet in a library is a state; being quiet most of the time is a trait. A state depends on someone's motives, which vary from one time and situation to another (Winter, John, Steward, Klohnen, & Duncan, 1998). A trait is like a climate condition that manifests itself as an average over time, though not at every moment. Any brief observation of people's behavior could easily misjudge their personality traits, just as a brief observation of the weather could misstate the climate.

Note that both traits and states are descriptions of behavior, not explanations. To say that someone is nervous and quiet does not explain anything; it merely tells us what we are trying to explain.

■ Like this man playing the role of a woman in Japanese Kabuki theater, actors can present personalities that are very different from their private ones. All of us occasionally display temporary personalities that are different from our usual selves.

511

9. Suppose someone becomes nervous as soon as he sits down in a dentist's chair. Is this experience "trait anxiety" or "state anxiety"? (Check your answer on page 517.)

# The Search for Broad Personality Traits

The point of the **trait approach to personality** is the idea that *people have consistent personality characteristics that can be measured and studied*. Psychologists have described, studied, and measured a great many personality traits, such as honesty, friendliness, authoritarianism, and nervousness. Some of the research deals with traits that are not familiar descriptions in everyday life. For example, people who *believe they are largely in control of their lives* are said to have an **internal locus of control.** Those who *believe they are controlled mostly by external forces* are said to have an **external locus of control** (Rotter, 1966). Table 13.2 lists some items from a questionnaire designed to measure locus of control. After you complete these items, check answer A on page 517. Generally, people with an internal locus of control like to choose tasks where they believe they can control the outcome, and then they persist at these tasks. At the end they take the credit or blame for the outcome.

**TABLE 13.2 Sample Items from the Internal–External Scale**

| For each item, choose the statement you agree with more. |
|---|
| 1. a. Without the right breaks, one cannot be an effective leader. |
| b. Capable people who fail to become leaders have not taken advantage of their opportunities. |
| 2. a. Becoming a success is a matter of hard work; luck has little or nothing to do with it. |
| b. Getting a good job depends mainly on being in the right place at the right time. |
| 3. a. As far as world affairs are concerned, most of us are the victims of forces we can neither understand nor control. |
| b. By taking an active part in political and social affairs, people can control world events. |
| 4. a. Many times I feel that I have little influence over the things that happen to me. |
| b. It is impossible for me to believe that chance or luck plays an important role in my life. |

Source: Rotter, 1966, pp. 11–12.

10. Who would be more likely to buy lottery tickets—someone with an internal or external locus of control? (Check your answer on page 517.)

We could extend the list of personality traits indefinitely, but ultimately, we should aim for some order in the system so that we identify no more traits than necessary to describe and predict people's behavior. One way to begin is by examining our language. Many psychologists assume that any human language probably has a word for every important personality trait. Although this assumption is not a logical necessity, it seems reasonable considering how much attention people pay to other people's personalities.

Gordon Allport and H. S. Odbert (1936) plodded through an English dictionary and found almost 18,000 words that might be used to describe personality. They deleted from this list words that were merely evaluations, such as *pleasant* or *nasty*, and terms referring to temporary states, such as *confused*. (At least we hope that being confused is temporary.) In the remaining list, they looked for clusters of synonyms, such as *affectionate, warm*, and *loving*, and kept only one of these terms. When they found opposites, such as *honest* and *dishonest*, they also kept just one of the terms. (*Honesty* and *dishonesty* are different degrees of a single trait, not two separate traits.) After eliminating synonyms and antonyms, Raymond Cattell (1965) narrowed the original list down to 35 traits.

## The Big Five Personality Traits

Although some of the 35 personality traits that Cattell identified are not exactly synonyms or antonyms of one another, many of them overlapped enough to suggest that they were not independent traits. Furthermore, for practical purposes psychologists usually prefer to deal with a smaller number. Remember the principle of parsimony from Chapter 2: If we can explain most aspects of personality with, say, 5 or 10 traits, we do not need to measure 35.

To determine which traits correlate with one another, psychologists use a method called *factor analysis*. For example, if measurements of warmth, gregariousness, and assertiveness correlate strongly with one another, we can cluster them together as a single trait. But if this combined trait does not correlate highly with self-discipline, then self-discipline (and anything that correlates strongly with it) is a separate trait.

Using this approach researchers have found a few major clusters of personality traits, which they call the **big five personality traits:** *neuroticism, extraversion, agreeableness, conscientiousness, and openness to new experience* (McCrae & Costa, 1987). The case for these five traits is that (a) each correlates with many personality dimensions for which our language has a word and (b) none of these five traits correlates highly with any of the other five, so they are not measuring the same thing. The big five dimensions are described in the following list (Costa, McCrae, & Dye, 1991). Note that the first two, neuroticism and extraversion, are the "biggest" of the big five. Even psychologists who are skeptical of the big five model agree that neuroticism and extraversion are powerful traits that influence much of human behavior (Block, 1995).

**Neuroticism** is *a tendency to experience unpleasant emotions relatively easily.* Neuroticism correlates positively with anxiety, hostility, depression, and self-consciousness. It correlates negatively with emotional stability or self-control. In one study college students kept a diary in which they recorded the most stressful event of the day. Students who scored high on a neuroticism questionnaire were more likely than other students to identify their most stressful event as some conflict they had with another person. They were also more likely than other students to rate the experience as highly distressing, and they were less likely than others to deal effectively with their stressful events (Gunthert, Cohen, & Armeli, 1999).

**Extraversion** is *a tendency to seek stimulation and to enjoy the company of other people.* The opposite of extraversion is introversion. Extraversion is associated with warmth, gregariousness, assertiveness, impulsiveness, and a need for excitement. People high in extraversion enjoy meeting new people and tend to be happy under most circumstances (Francis, Brown, Lester, & Philipchalk, 1998). Research suggests that the core of extraversion is enjoyment of life. That is, extraverted people are generally happy, and the tendency to be happy leads to socializing with other people more than socializing with other people leads to happiness (Lucas, Diener, Grob, Suh, & Shao, 2000; Lucas & Fujita, 2000). Related to this enjoyment of life, extraverted people tend to be risk takers, and more extraverts than introverts have an alcohol problem (Martsh & Miller, 1997).

**Agreeableness** is *a tendency to be compassionate toward others and not antagonistic.* It implies a concern for the welfare of other people, closely related to Adler's concept of social interest. People high in agreeableness generally trust other people and expect other people to trust them.

**Conscientiousness** is *a tendency to show self-discipline, to be dutiful, and to strive for achievement and competence.* Research has shown that people high in conscientiousness tend to be good workers on almost any job (Barrick & Mount, 1991). They are likely to complete whatever task they say they will perform.

If you were giving a speech or making some other kind of performance, would you prefer to have your performance rated by someone high in agreeableness or conscientiousness? As you might guess, people high in conscientiousness generally give lower, presumably more honest, ratings, whereas people

■ The Japanese artist Morimura Yasumasa recreates famous paintings, substituting his own face for the original. Some people love his work; others dislike it or object to the whole idea. People high in "openness to experience" delight in new, unusual forms of art, literature, and music.

high in agreeableness give higher, more generous ratings (Bernardin, Cooke, & Villanova, 2000).

**Openness to experience,** the big five trait that is usually the least variable and hardest to observe, is *a tendency to enjoy new intellectual experiences and new ideas.* Someone high in this trait would be likely to enjoy modern art, unusual music, thought-provoking films and plays, and so forth. People open to experience enjoy meeting different kinds of people and exploring new ideas and opinions (McCrae, 1996).

## CONCEPT CHECK

11. Some psychologists suggest that we should divide extraversion into two traits—which they call *ambition* and *sociability*—changing the big five into the big six. How should psychologists determine whether to do so? (Check your answer on page 517.)

## *Criticisms of the Big Five Description*

You may already have thought about one criticism of the research discussed so far: The identification of the big five personality factors was based on a study of the English language, not on observations of actual behavior. We identify extraversion–introversion as a big factor, for example, because it relates to so many words in the English language—sociability, warmth, friendliness, adventuresomeness, gregariousness, happiness, and so forth. This method of identifying major personality traits could easily overlook important dimensions that do not have many synonyms. For example, some people are more religious than others, and I think most of us would regard those variations as important descriptions of personality. Religiousness does not correlate highly with any of the big five traits; the main reason researchers did not identify religiousness as a big personality trait is that we do not have many words for it. We have *religiousness, devoutness, piety, reverence,* and perhaps a few others, but not enough to emerge as a big cluster.

 Critics of the big five approach have identified nine overlooked personality dimensions that have few synonyms, and therefore do not emerge as big clusters, but which do not correlate strongly with any of the big five (Paunonen & Jackson, 2000). These nine are religiousness, manipulativeness, honesty, sexiness, thriftiness, conservativeness, masculinity–femininity, snobbishness, and sense of humor. We might debate some of these specific examples, and you might even want to add others to the list. If you do, however, first try to be sure that what you are suggesting does not correlate strongly with one of the other traits already listed. The main idea, however, is that the research method that identified the big five personality traits could easily have missed some important traits just because we do not have many words for them.

Other critics raise the opposite objection that five is more big traits than we need. Openness to experience has a modest positive correlation with extraversion, and conscientiousness correlates negatively with neuroticism, so perhaps we could get by with just three factors: neuroticism, extraversion, and agreeableness—or its opposite, hostility or "psychoticism" (Eysenck, 1992).

Cross-cultural studies offer partial, but only partial, support to the big five approach. Some studies have used translations of English words or an array of personality descriptions from other languages. Others have shown pictures of people in various activities and asked, "How likely would you be to do this?" The picture approach makes it easy to test people of various cultures without first thoroughly studying their language (Paunonen, Zeidner, Engvik, Oosterveld, & Maliphant, 2000). Many studies have found results approximately consistent with the big five model (McCrae & Costa, 1997). However, some studies did find important cross-cultural differences. For example, it is often difficult to demonstrate the openness to experience dimension (Saggino, 2000; Silverthorne, 2001). A study in China identified four big traits corresponding approximately to extraversion, neuroticism, conscientiousness, and "loyalty to Chinese traditions" (Cheung et al., 1996).

Overall, how should we evaluate the five-factor description? The answer depends on our purposes. If we are interested in a theoretical understanding of personality, it is premature at best to call the five-factor description a fact of nature (as some have done). The five-factor description accounts for enough of the variability in human behavior to be useful, although for some purposes three factors may be enough and for other purposes ten to fifteen may be necessary. It depends on how much precision we want in describing and predicting people's behavior.

# The Origins of Personality

A description of personality differences is not an explanation. The question is: What makes some people more extraverted, neurotic, agreeable, conscientious, or open to experience than other people are?

## *Heredity and Environment*

To measure the influences of heredity and environment, researchers have relied mostly on two kinds of data. First, they compare the similarities between monozygotic (identical) twins and dizygotic (fraternal) twins. As Figure 13.16 shows, five studies conducted in separate locations indicated much greater similarities in extraversion between monozygotic pairs than between dizygotic pairs (Loehlin, 1992). Studies in Australia and the United States found a similar pattern for neuroticism, with monozygotic twins resembling each other much more than dizygotic twins, who resembled each other no more than brothers or sisters born at different times (Lake, Eaves, Maes, Heath, & Martin, 2000). These results imply a strong genetic influence on personality, although they may slightly overstate that tendency, as dizygotic twins sometimes intentionally highlight the differences between them (Saudino, 1997).

Second, researchers compare the personalities of parents, their biological children, and their adopted children. As Figure 13.17 shows, parents' levels of extraversion correlate moderately with those of their biological children but hardly at all with those of their adopted children. Similarly, biologically related brothers or sisters growing up together resemble each other moderately, and unrelated children adopted into the same family do not develop similar personalities (Loehlin, 1992). The results shown in Figures 13.16 and 13.17 pertain to extraversion; similar studies provide a largely similar pattern for neuroticism and other personality traits (Heath, Neale, Kessler, Eaves, & Kendler, 1992; Loehlin, 1992; Viken, Rose, Kaprio, & Koskenvuo, 1994).

Overall, these results indicate a moderate influence of hereditary factors, although no one knows exactly how they contribute. One possibility is that genetically deter-

mined differences in neurotransmitter receptors influence how strongly people respond to new stimuli, thereby predisposing some people to be more sensation seeking or extraverted than others. However, the research so far has demonstrated only a weak relationship between neurotransmitter receptors and sensation-seeking behaviors (Goldman, Urbanek, Guenther, Robin, & Long, 1998; Noble et al., 1998).

The nongenetic contributors are less understood. Even children who grow up with their biological parents resemble their parents in personality only to a moderate degree (Bratko & Marušić, 1997), and the personalities correlations between adopted children and adoptive parents are even lower, sometimes even zero or negative. Evidently, children learn rather little of their personalities by imitating their parents. (Recall from Chapter 10 that Judith Harris made this same point.) Many researchers believe that much of the variation among people's personalities relates to the **unshared environment,** *the aspects of environment that differ from one individual to another, even within a family.* Unshared environment is, because of its idiosyncratic nature, difficult to investigate.

**C**ONCEPT CHECK

**12.** What evidence would indicate an important role of the *shared environment*—the influences that are the same for all children within a family? (Check your answer on page 517.)

## Age and Historical Era

Do you think your personality is similar now to what it was in childhood? Will your personality change much in the next few years?

According to the research, the older people get, the more consistent their personalities are over time. In childhood, answers on a personality questionnaire correlate only .34 between two tests given 6 or 7 years apart. By college age the correlation is .54. It increases to .64 at age 30 and .74 at age 60 (Roberts & DelVecchio, 2000). Why personality becomes more fixed as we grow older is not known, but you can probably imagine a few hypotheses.

The differences that occur over age are not large, but they are fairly predictable, and many of them are found cross-culturally. One clear trend is that as people grow older, they become more conscientious. In every culture that has been studied throughout the world, middle-aged people are more likely to be highly conscientious—that is, to do what they promise they will do—than are teenagers (McCrae et al., 2000). A simple explanation is that adults are forced, whether they like it or not, to hold a job, pay the bills, repair the house, care for children, and take responsibility in other ways.

As people age, they also tend to become less extraverted, especially less sensation seeking; again this trend is found cross-culturally (Labouvie-Vief, Diehl, Tarnowksi, & Shen, 2000). Older people also tend to be less neurotic—that is, less prone to anxieties and unpleasant mood swings—and slightly more agreeable (McCrae et al., 2000). In the United States, young people on the average score higher on openness to new experience than older people. This trend is no surprise; we see

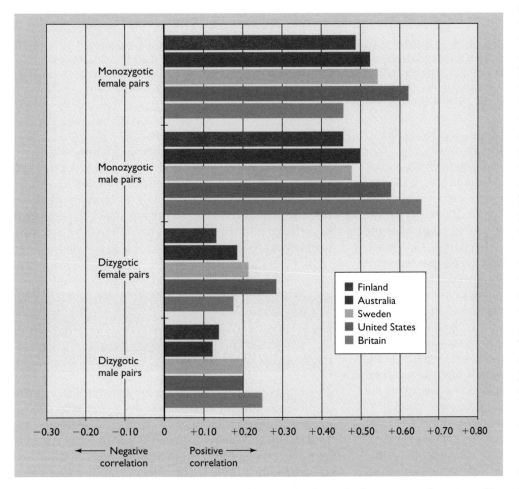

**FIGURE 13.16** Five studies—conducted in Great Britain, the United States, Sweden, Australia, and Finland—found larger correlations between the extraversion levels of monozygotic (MZ) twins than those of dizygotic (DZ) twins. (Based on data summarized by Loehlin, 1992)

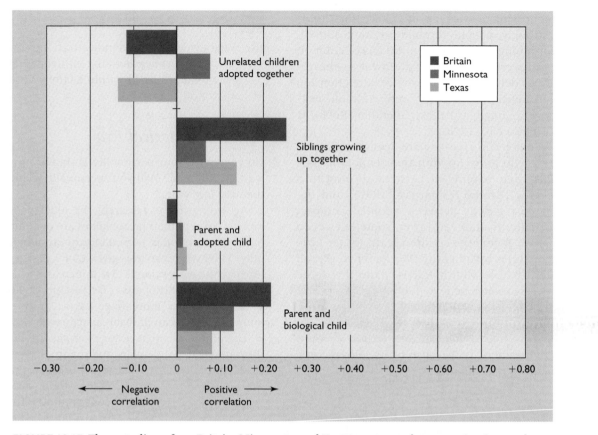

**FIGURE 13.17** Three studies—from Britain, Minnesota, and Texas—measured extraversion in members of hundreds of families. Each found moderate positive correlations between parents and their biological children and between pairs of biologically related brothers and sisters. However, all found low or even negative correlations between parents and adopted children and among adopted children living in the same family. (Based on data summarized by Loehlin, 1992)

that young people enjoy new types of music, new kinds of food, new styles of clothing, and so forth (Sapolsky, 1998), whereas older people stay with old habits. In some other cultures, however, openness to experience shows no clear trend over age (McCrae et al., 2000).

Finally, are there any changes in personality over the decades? Remember the Flynn effect from Chapter 9: Over the years people's performance on IQ tests has gradually increased so that each generation does better on the tests than the previous generation, for unknown reasons. Researchers looked for any similar trend in personality scores and found one. Over the years, beginning in the 1950s, measurements of anxiety have steadily increased (Twenge, 2000). On the Child Manifest Anxiety Scale, the mean score in the 1950s was 15.1, and the mean for children in mental hospitals was 20.1. By the 1980s the mean for *all* children was 23.3!

Do we really have that much more anxiety than in past generations? It is possible that people's answers do not mean exactly the same as what they used to so that the apparent difference is partly a measurement error. The more disturbing possibility is that we really do live in an age of anxiety, despite our increases in health and wealth and the decreased probability of nuclear war.

Compared to past generations, more children today have to live through their parents' divorce, and fewer live in a neighborhood with many friends and relatives. Might those social changes have raised the average anxiety level to what used to characterize the top 10%? The answer is uncertain, but now researchers need to worry about why people worry so much.

IN CLOSING
## The Challenges of Classifying Personality

As you have seen, personalities are difficult to categorize or measure. Researchers are not even sure whether we need five dimensions or more or fewer. Some are not convinced even that personality is a useful concept; perhaps we should be content to describe people's behaviors in various situations. The problem is not just that every person is different from every other. The larger problem is that human personalities change from one situation to another. As well as you know your closest friends and relatives, aren't you still sometimes surprised by how they act in a new situation? Aren't you sometimes surprised even at your own behavior? The complexities of human personality make this area of research particularly challenging.

## Summary

- **Nomothetic and idiographic laws.** Psychologists seek both nomothetic laws, which apply to all people, and idiographic laws, which apply to individual differences. (page 511)

- **Traits and states.** Traits are personality characteristics that persist over time; states are temporary changes in behavior in response to particular situations. (page 511)

- **Five major traits.** Psychologists seek a short list of traits that describes as much of behavior as possible. Much can be explained by these five traits: neuroticism, extraversion, openness to new experience, agreeableness, and conscientiousness. However, that classification is based more on studies of our language than actual behavior. Several other important dimensions may have been overlooked because our language has few synonyms for them. (page 512)

- **Determinants of personality.** Studies of twins and adopted children indicate that heredity contributes to part of the observed differences in personality. Family environment evidently contributes rather little. Much of the variation in personality may be due to unshared environment, the special experiences that vary from one person to another even within a family. (page 514)

- **Changes over time.** Compared to younger people, older people tend to be higher in conscientiousness and slightly higher in agreeableness. They are somewhat lower in extraversion and neuroticism. Openness to experience decreases with age in the United States, but several other countries do not show this trend. (page 515)

- **Changes over historical era.** Measurements of anxiety have gradually increased over the decades so that normal people are now showing anxiety levels that used to characterize people in mental hospitals. The reasons are not known. (page 516)

## Answers to Concept Checks

9. This nervousness is state anxiety because it is evoked by a particular situation. Trait anxiety is a strong tendency to become nervous in many situations. (page 512)

10. People with an external locus of control would be more likely to buy lottery tickets. Those with an internal locus of control prefer tasks where they can control the outcome. (page 512)

11. They should determine whether measures of ambition correlate strongly with measures of sociability. If they do, then ambition and sociability can be considered two aspects of a single trait, extraversion. If they do not correlate strongly, then they are indeed separate personality traits. (page 513)

12. If the personalities of adopted children within a family correlated highly with one another, we would conclude that the similarity reflected the shared environment. The weakness of such correlations is the main evidence for the importance of the unshared environment. (page 515)

## Answer to Other Question in the Module

A. Choices 1b, 2a, 3b, and 4b indicate internal locus of control; the other choices indicate external locus of control. Your answers to a longer list of such items could more accurately assess your locus of control. (page 512)

# Personality Assessment

*What inferences can we safely draw from the results of a personality test?*

A new P. T. Barnum Psychology Clinic has just opened at your local shopping mall and is offering a grand opening special on personality tests. You have always wanted to know more about yourself, so you sign up. Here is Barnum's true–false test:

---

**Questionnaire for Universal Assessment of Zealous Youth (QUAZY)**

1. I have never met a cannibal I didn't like.  T  F
2. Robbery is the only major felony I have ever committed.  T  F
3. I eat "funny mushrooms" less frequently than I used to.  T  F
4. I don't care what people say about my nose-picking habit.  T  F
5. Sex with vegetables no longer disgusts me.  T  F
6. This time I am quitting glue-sniffing for good.  T  F
7. I generally lie on questions like this one.  T  F
8. I spent much of my childhood sucking on telephone cords.  T  F
9. I find it impossible to sleep if I think my bed might be clean.  T  F
10. Naked bus drivers make me nervous.  T  F
11. Some of my friends don't know what a rotten person I am.  T  F
12. I usually find laxatives unsatisfying.  T  F
13. I spend my spare time playing strip solitaire.  T  F

---

You turn in your answers. A few minutes later, a computer prints out your individual personality profile:

You have a need for other people to like and admire you, and yet you tend to be critical of yourself. While you have some personality weaknesses, you are generally able to compensate for them. You have considerable unused capacity that you have not turned to your advantage. Disciplined and self-controlled on the outside, you tend to be worrisome and insecure on the inside. At times, you have serious doubts as to whether you have made the right decision or done the right thing. You prefer a certain amount of change and variety and become dissatisfied when hemmed in by restrictions and limitations. You also pride yourself as an independent thinker and do not accept others' statements without satisfactory proof. But you have found it unwise to be too frank in revealing yourself to others. At times you are extraverted, affable, and sociable, while at other times you are introverted, wary, and reserved. Some of your aspirations tend to be rather unrealistic. (Forer, 1949, p. 120)

Do you agree with this assessment?

Several experiments have been conducted along these lines with psychology classes (Forer, 1949; Marks & Kammann, 1980; Ulrich, Stachnik, & Stainton, 1963). Students started by filling out a questionnaire that looked fairly reasonable, not something as preposterous as the QUAZY. Several days later each student received a sealed envelope with his or her name on it. Inside was a "personality profile," supposedly based on the student's answers to the questionnaire. The students were asked, "How accurately does this profile describe you?" About 90% rated it as good or excellent. Some expressed amazement at its accuracy: "I didn't realize until now that psychology was an exact science." None of

■ People tend to accept almost any personality assessment that someone offers them, especially if it is stated in vague, general terms that each person can interpret to fit himself or herself.

them realized that everyone had received exactly the same personality profile—the same one you just read.

The students accepted this personality profile partly because it vaguely describes almost everyone, much like newspaper horoscopes do, and partly because people tend to accept almost *any* statement that a psychologist makes about them. Richard Kammann repeated this experiment but substituted a strange, unflattering personality profile that included statements like "your boundless energy is a little wearisome to your friends" and "you seem to find it impossible to work out a satisfactory adjustment to your problems." More than 20% of the students rated this unlikely assortment of statements a "good to excellent" description of their own personality (Marks & Kammann, 1980).

The conclusion: Psychological testing is tricky. If we want to know whether a particular test measures a particular person's personality, we cannot simply ask whether that person thinks it does. Even if a test is totally worthless, many people will describe its results as a "highly accurate" description of themselves. To devise a psychological test that not only *appears* to work but also actually *does* work, we need to follow some elaborate procedures to design the test carefully and to determine its reliability and validity.

## Standardized Personality Tests

Psychologists have devised a great variety of personality tests; they add new ones every year. A **standardized test** is *one that is administered according to specified rules and its scores are interpreted in a prescribed fashion.* One important step for standardizing a test is to determine the distribution of scores for a large number of people. We need to know the mean score and the range of scores for people in general and the mean and the range for various special populations, such as severely depressed people. Given such information, we can determine whether a given individual's score on the test is within the normal range or whether it is more typical of people with a particular disorder.

Most of the tests published in popular magazines have never been standardized. A magazine may herald an article: "Test Yourself: How Good Is Your Marriage?" or "Test Yourself: How Well Do You Control the Stress in Your Life?" After you take the test and compare your answers to the scoring key, the article may tell you that "if your score is greater than 80, you are doing very well . . . if it is below 20, you need to work on improving yourself!"—or some such nonsense. Unless the magazine states otherwise, you can safely assume that the author pulled the scoring norms out of thin air and never even

bothered to make sure that the test items were clear and unambiguous.

Over the years psychologists have developed an enormous variety of tests to measure both normal and abnormal personality. A great deal of research focused on trying to standardize their interpretation and measure their reliability and validity. We shall examine a few prominent examples and explore some creative possibilities for future personality measurement.

## Objective Personality Tests

Some of the most widely used personality tests are based on simple pencil-and-paper responses. We shall consider in detail the MMPI, the most widely used of all personality tests (Piotrowski & Keller, 1989).

### The Minnesota Multiphasic Personality Inventory

The **Minnesota Multiphasic Personality Inventory** (mercifully abbreviated **MMPI**) consists of *a series of true–false questions intended to measure certain personality dimensions and clinical conditions such as depression.* The original MMPI, developed in the 1940s and still in use, has 550 items; *the second edition,* **MMPI-2,** published in 1990, has 567. Typical items are "my mother never loved me" and "I think I would like the work of a pharmacist." (The items I mention in this text are rewordings of the actual items.)

The original MMPI was devised *empirically*—that is, by checking the evidence instead of relying on theory (Hathaway & McKinley, 1940). The authors developed hundreds of true–false questions that they thought might be useful for identifying personality dimensions. They put these questions to people who were known to be suffering from depression, paranoia, and other psychological disorders and to a group of hospital visitors, who were assumed to be psychologically normal. The researchers selected those items that most of the people in a given clinical group answered differently from most of the normal people. Their assumption was that, if you answer many questions as depressed people usually answer them, you probably are depressed too. The MMPI had ten scales—for reporting a depression score, a paranoia score, a schizophrenia score, and others. Later researchers found that they could use MMPI items to measure other dimensions of personality as well (Helmes & Reddon, 1993). The result was a test that worked, and still works, moderately well in practice. For example, most people with scores above a certain level on the Depression scale are in fact depressed.

Some of the items on the MMPI made sense theoretically; some did not. For example, some items on the Depression scale asked about feelings of helplessness or

**TABLE 13.3** The Ten MMPI-2 Clinical Scales

| Scale | Typical Item |
|---|---|
| Hypochondria (Hs) | I have chest pains several times a week. (T) |
| Depression (D) | I am glad that I am alive. (F) |
| Hysteria (Hy) | My heart frequently pounds so hard I can hear it. (T) |
| Psychopathic Deviation (Pd) | I get a fair deal from most people. (F) |
| Masculinity–Femininity (Mf) | I like to arrange flowers. (T = female) |
| Paranoia (Pa) | There are evil people trying to influence my mind. (T) |
| Psychasthenia (Obsessive–Compulsive) (Pt) | I save nearly everything I buy, even after I have no use for it. (T) |
| Schizophrenia (Sc) | I see, hear, and smell things that no one else knows about. (T) |
| Hypomania (Ma) | When things are dull I try to get some excitement started. (T) |
| Social Introversion (Si) | I have the time of my life at parties. (F) |

worthlessness, which are an important part of depression. But two other items were "I attend religious services frequently" and "occasionally I tease animals." If you answered *false* to either of those items, you would get a point on the Depression scale! These items were included simply because more depressed people than nondepressed people answered *false* to these items. Why they did is not obvious. (Perhaps depressed people do not tease animals because they do hardly anything just for fun.)

## Revisions of the Test

The MMPI was standardized in the 1940s. As time passed the meaning of certain items, or at least of certain answers, changed. For example, how would you respond to the following item?

I believe I am important.    T    F

In the 1940s fewer than 10% of all people marked this item *true*. At the time the word "important" meant about the same thing as "famous," and people who called themselves important were thought to have an inflated view of themselves. Today, we are more likely to say that every person is important.

What about this item?

I like to play drop the handkerchief.    T    F

Drop the handkerchief, a game similar to tag, dropped out of popularity in the 1950s. Most people born since then have never even heard of it, much less played it.

To bring the MMPI up to date, a group of psychologists rephrased some of the items, eliminated some, and added new ones to deal with drug abuse, suicidal ideas, Type A personality, and other issues that did not concern psychologists in the 1940s (Butcher, Graham, Williams, & Ben-Porath, 1990). Then they tried out the new MMPI-2 on 2600 people selected to resemble the

current mix of age, sex, race, and education in the United States. In other words they restandardized the test. (Any test must be restandardized periodically. You may recall the discussion in Chapter 9 about the need to restandardize IQ tests.) These psychologists also developed a new form, the MMPI-A, intended for use with adolescents.

The MMPI-2 has ten clinical scales, as shown in Table 13.3. The various scales have 32 to 78 items each, scattered throughout the test rather than clustered. Most people get at least a few points on each scale; a score above a certain level indicates a probable difficulty. Figure 13.18 shows how MMPI-2 scores are plotted.

## The Generalizability of the MMPI

Your personality is an integral part of who you are. Is it possible for one test to measure personality for all kinds of people? In particular, is the MMPI (or MMPI-2 or MMPI-A) a fair measure of personality for people of different ethnic and cultural backgrounds?

This is a difficult question to answer. In general, the means and ranges on each scale are about the same for many ethnic groups (Negy, Leal-Puente, Trainor, & Carlson, 1997). A few small differences in scores do occur, but they could reflect either real differences in personality or differences in interpreting what certain questions mean. Consequently, psychologists use the same norms for all groups, but they are slightly more cautious about interpreting the scores of racial minorities, especially people with the least education (Gynther, 1989).

## Detection of Deception on the MMPI and Other Tests

If you were taking the MMPI or another personality test, could you lie to make yourself look mentally healthier

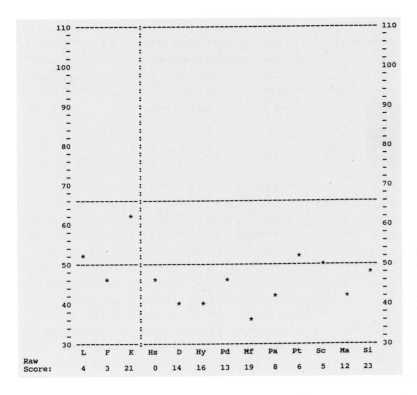

**FIGURE 13.18** For the MMPI-2's ten clinical scales, a score is plotted to profile an individual. This is the profile of a middle-aged man with no psychological problems. A person with a disorder such as hypochondria or paranoia would have scores in the range of 65 or higher on the Hypochondria or Paranoia scales. (Source: Minnesota Multiphasic Personality Inventory-2, © by the Regents of the University of Minnesota. Data courtesy of R.J. Huber.)

than you really are? Yes. Could someone catch your lies? Probably.

The designers of the MMPI and the MMPI-2 included certain items designed to identify lying (Woychyshyn, McElheran, & Romney, 1992). For example, consider the items "I like every person I have ever met" and "occasionally I get angry at someone." If you answer *true* to the first question and *false* to the second, you are either a saint or a liar. The test authors, convinced that there are more liars than saints, would give you 1 point for each of these answers on a special scale that counts probable lies. If you get too many points on that scale, a psychologist will distrust your answers to the other items. Strangely enough, some people lie on the test to try to make themselves look bad. The MMPI includes items to detect that kind of faking also.

A similar method can detect deception on other types of tests. For example, many employers ask job applicants to fill out a questionnaire that asks them about their experience with job-related skills. Suppose some employer's questionnaire asked you how much experience you have had at "matrixing solvency files." You're not sure what that means, but you really want the job. Do you claim to have had extensive experience? If so, your claimed expertise will count *against* you because "matrixing solvency files" doesn't mean anything. According to the results of one study, almost half of all job applicants claimed to have experience with one or more nonexistent tasks, such as the ones listed in Table 13.4 (Anderson, Warner, & Spencer, 1984). Most job applicants who claimed experience with nonexistent tasks also overstated their abilities on real tasks. The more

**TABLE 13.4** Part of an Employment Application Designed to Determine Whether Applicants Are Lying About Their Skills

| How much experience have you had at . . . | None | A Little | Much |
|---|---|---|---|
| Matrixing solvency files? | ☐ | ☐ | ☐ |
| Typing from audio-Fortran reports? | ☐ | ☐ | ☐ |
| Determining myopic weights for periodic tables? | ☐ | ☐ | ☐ |
| Resolving disputes by isometric analysis? | ☐ | ☐ | ☐ |
| Stocking solubility product constants? | ☐ | ☐ | ☐ |
| Planning basic entropy programs? | ☐ | ☐ | ☐ |
| Operating a matriculation machine? | ☐ | ☐ | ☐ |

skill an applicant claims to have on nonexistent tasks, the more the employer discounts that applicant's claims about real tasks.

## A STEP FURTHER
### *Assessing Honesty*

Could you use this strategy in other situations? Suppose a political candidate promises to increase aid to college students. You are skeptical. How could you use the candidate's statements on other issues to help you decide whether to believe this promise?

## Uses of the MMPI

The MMPI is useful to psychologists who want to measure personality for research purposes. For example, researchers have found that monozygotic twins give remarkably similar answers on the MMPI, even if they were adopted by separate families and reared apart. Dizygotic twins' answers do not correlate so strongly (DiLalla, Carey, Gottesman, & Bouchard, 1996). Therefore, much of personality appears to reflect genetic influences.

The MMPI is also useful to clinical psychologists who want to learn something about a client before beginning therapy or who want an independent measure of how much a client's personality has changed during the course of therapy. The MMPI has better reliability and validity than other widely used personality tests (Garb, Florio, & Grove, 1998).

How informative are the results to the client who takes the MMPI test? To the client, the results are usually not surprising. For example, suppose you gave the following answers:

| | |
|---|---|
| I doubt that I will ever be successful. | True |
| I am glad that I am alive. | False |
| I have thoughts about suicide. | True |
| I am helpless to control the important events in my life. | True |

A psychologist analyzes your answer sheet and tells you, "Your results show indications of depression." Yes, of course. You already knew that. But even in a case like this, the results can be useful—not just for telling you that you are depressed (which you already knew), but for measuring *how* depressed you are at this moment and comparing a later measurement to see whether you are improving.

## CONCEPT CHECKS

13. Suppose that a person thinks "True or false, black is my favorite color" would be a good item for the De-

pression scale of the MMPI. How would a researcher decide whether to include it?

14. Why does the MMPI include some items that ask about common flaws, such as, "Sometimes I think more about my own welfare than that of others"? (Check your answers on page 528.)

# Projective Techniques

The MMPI and similar personality tests are easy to score and easy to handle statistically, but they restrict how a person can respond to a question. In hopes of learning more, psychologists ask open-ended questions that permit an unlimited range of responses.

However, the inquiry "tell me about yourself" rarely evokes much information. In fact, most people find such invitations threatening. It is difficult to be fully honest with ourselves, much less with someone else.

Many people find it easier to discuss their problems in the abstract than in the first person. For instance, they might say, "I have a friend with this problem. Let me tell you my friend's problem and ask what my friend should do." They then describe their own problem. They are "projecting" their problem onto someone else, in Freud's sense of the word—attributing their own characteristics to someone else.

Rather than discouraging projection, psychologists often make use of it. They use **projective techniques,** which are *designed to encourage people to project their personality characteristics onto ambiguous stimuli*. This strategy helps people to reveal themselves more fully than they normally would to a stranger or even to themselves. Let's consider the best-known projective techniques: the Rorschach Inkblots and the Thematic Apperception Test.

## CONCEPT CHECK

15. Which of the following is a projective technique?
    **a.** A psychologist gives a child a set of puppets with instructions to act out a story about a family.
    **b.** A psychologist hands you a stack of cards, each containing one word, such as *tolerant*, with instructions to sort the cards into a stack of cards that apply to you and a stack of cards that do not. (Check your answers on page 528.)

## The Rorschach Inkblots

The **Rorschach Inkblots,** *a projective technique based on people's interpretations of ten ambiguous inkblots,* is the most famous and most widely used projective personality technique. It was created by Hermann Rorschach (ROARshock), a Swiss psychiatrist, who read a book in which Justinus Kerner made a series of random inkblots and wrote a poem about each one. Kerner believed that anything that happens at random reveals the influence of occult, supernatural forces.

Rorschach made his own inkblots but used them differently. He was familiar with a word-association test then in use where a person was given a word and asked to say the first word that came to mind. Combining this approach with his inkblots, Rorschach showed people an inkblot and then asked them to say whatever came to mind (Pichot, 1984).

After testing a series of inkblots on his patients, Rorschach was impressed that their interpretations of the blots differed from his own. In a book published in 1921 (English translation 1942), he presented the ten symmetrical inkblots that still constitute the Rorschach Inkblot Technique. (Originally, he had worked with a larger number, but the publisher insisted on cutting the number to ten to reduce printing costs.) As other psychiatrists and psychologists began using these blots, they gradually developed the Rorschach into the projective technique we know today.

## Administering the Rorschach

The Rorschach Inkblot Technique consists of cards similar to the one in Figure 13.19. There are five in black and white and five in color. A psychologist administering this procedure hands you a card and asks, "What might this be?" The instructions are intentionally vague on the assumption that everything you do in an ill-defined situation reveals something significant about your personality.

Sometimes people's answers reveal much, either immediately or in response to a psychologist's probes. Here is an example (Aronow, Reznikoff, & Moreland, 1995):

*(Card 5).* **CLIENT:** Some kind of insect; it's not pretty enough to be a butterfly.
**PSYCHOLOGIST:** Any association to that?
**CLIENT:** It's an ugly black butterfly, no colors.
**PSYCHOLOGIST:** What does that make you think of in your own life?
**CLIENT:** You probably want me to say "myself." Well, that's probably how I thought of myself when I was younger—I never thought of myself as attractive—my sister was the attractive one. I was the ugly duckling—I did get more attractive as I got older.

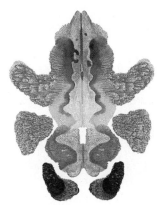

**FIGURE 13.19** In the Rorschach Inkblot Technique, people study an abstract pattern and say what it looks like to them. The underlying theory is that in an ambiguous situation personality will be revealed by anything that someone does and says.

## Evaluation of the Rorschach

It is true that personality makes a bigger difference in an ill-defined, ambiguous situation than in one where everyone is asked to do something specific. The question is how accurately a psychologist can interpret your responses in that ambiguous situation. When I look at a picture and describe what I see, I am myself aware of how my answer relates to some detail of my past experience. But would anyone else see the connection?

In the 1950s and 1960s, certain psychologists made exaggerated claims, even calling the Rorschach "an x-ray of the mind." Those claims provoked vigorous criticism. The main problem was that different psychologists drew different conclusions from the same answer depending on their theoretical bent or expectations about a particular client.

For example, a depressed man described one blot as, "It looks like a bat that has been squashed on the pavement under the heel of a giant's boot" (Dawes, 1994, p. 149). Psychologist Robyn Dawes initially was impressed with how the Rorschach had revealed the client's sense of being overwhelmed and crushed by powers beyond his control. However, Dawes later realized that he had already known the client was depressed and interpreted the response accordingly. If a client with a history of violence had made the same response, he would have focused on the aggressive nature of the giant's foot stomp. For a hallucinating or paranoid client, he would have made still other interpretations. That is, Rorschach interpretations depend on the psychologist's expectations at least as much as they do on what the client says. (Recall the need for double-blind procedures, as discussed in Chapter 2.)

James Exner (1986) developed methods for interpreting Rorschach responses that decrease, but don't eliminate, this problem. Using Exner's system, a psychologist counts the number of times a client mentions certain kinds of themes, such as aggression, how often the response refers to the whole blot or just part of it, and several other reasonably objective measurements. From comparison to standards that presumably represent normal people, a psychologist derives measures of certain kinds of mental disturbance.

However, some serious problems with the Rorschach remain (Lilienfeld, Wood, & Garb, 2000):

- Something must have been strange about the standardization sample because the test identifies a large percentage of normal people as having psychological disorders.
- People are asked to give as many answers as they wish on each blot, but psychologists count the *total number* of aggressive, depressive, or otherwise pathological answers. Highly intelligent or talkative people give more answers than other people do, and the more total answers you give, the more likely you are to say something that counts as "disturbed."

- Different ethnic groups have certain characteristic ways of responding that differ from the standardization group, and the test may be inappropriate for use with some groups.
- The interrater reliability of the test is only about .85. That is, different psychologists listening to the same answers do not fully agree on their counts of aggressive themes, depressive themes, and so forth. A reliability around .85 is acceptable for research purposes but is risky for making decisions about an individual.
- Many of the individual scales have doubtful validity. (Recall the distinction between reliability and validity from Chapter 9.) For example, some of the supposed measures of depression, anxiety, and hostility have low correlations with depressive, anxious, or hostile behavior.
- Finally and most important, the Rorschach only rarely gives information that could not be obtained more easily in other ways. For example, psychologists who are given biographical and MMPI information about someone usually make the same personality judgments as psychologists who are given the same biographical and MMPI information plus the Rorschach results. In fact, sometimes adding the Rorschach results makes their judgments *less* accurate.

Critics of the Rorschach stop short of calling it completely invalid. Their point is that it is not valid enough to make decisions about any individual and that it seldom provides information that someone could not get more easily in other ways. Many psychologists have serious qualms when their colleagues use Rorschach results to recommend that someone be committed to a mental hospital or to recommend for or against a prisoner's parole (Dawes, 1994).

In its defense some users of the Rorschach say they use it not for diagnosis or decisions, but only as a way of starting a conversation and getting clients to talk more freely about topics they might be reluctant to discuss (Aronow et al., 1995). Used in that way, the Rorschach is beyond criticism, but its limitations are clear.

## CONCEPT CHECK

16. Why are highly talkative people more likely than others to have their Rorschach answers considered disturbed? (Check your answer on page 528.)

## The Thematic Apperception Test

The **Thematic Apperception Test (TAT)** consists of pictures like the one shown in Figure 13.20. *The person is asked to make up a story for each picture, describing what is happening, what events led up to the scene, and what will happen in the future.* The test was devised by Christiana Mor-

gan and Henry Murray as a means of measuring people's needs; it was revised and published by Murray (1943) and later revised by others. There are 31 pictures in all, including some showing women, some showing men, some showing both or neither, and one that is totally blank. Originally, it was intended that a psychologist would select 20 cards for use with a given client, but in actual practice most psychologists use only 5 to 12 per person (Lilienfeld et al., 2000).

The assumption behind the TAT is that if you tell a story about a person in the drawing, you probably identify with the person and so the story is really about yourself. You might describe events and concerns in your own life, including some that you might be reluctant to discuss openly. For example, one young man told the following story about a picture of a man clinging to a rope:

> This man is escaping. Several months ago he was beat up and shanghaied and taken aboard ship. Since then, he has been mistreated and unhappy and has been looking for a way to escape. Now the ship is anchored near a tropical island and he is climbing down a rope to the water. He will get away successfully and swim to shore. When he gets there, he will be met by a group of beautiful native women with whom he will live the rest of his life in luxury and never tell anyone what happened. Sometimes he will feel that he should go back to his old life; but he will never do it. (Kimble & Garmezy, 1968, pp. 582–583)

This young man had entered divinity school, mainly to please his parents, but was quite unhappy there. He was wrestling with a secret desire to escape to a new life with greater worldly pleasures. In his story he described someone doing what he wanted to do but would not admit.

As mentioned in Chapter 11, psychologists use the TAT to measure people's need for achievement by counting all the times that they mention achievement. The same could be done for aggression, passivity, power, control of outside events, and so forth. The TAT is also used by clinicians to draw inferences about people's personalities and psychological problems.

**FIGURE 13.20** In the Thematic Apperception Test, people tell a story about what is going on in a picture such as this one. Most people include material that relates to current concerns in their lives. (From Murray, 1971)

Unfortunately, little about this procedure is systematic. Different therapists use different cards and different numbers of cards, and nearly all draw their conclusions based on "clinical judgment" instead of any clear rules. Therefore, it is difficult to conduct research on the reliability and validity of the test. If you took the TAT with two psychologists, they might reach different conclusions about you. As with the Rorschach, the interrater reliability is about .85—good enough for research purposes but not for making important decisions about an individual (Cramer, 1996). When someone retakes the test a few weeks later, the test-retest reliability is generally lower, usually less than .5 and sometimes much less than that (Cramer, 1996). Criticisms of the TAT for clinical use are the same as those for the Rorschach: Reliability and validity are low, the test identifies too many normal people as being disturbed, and the test seldom provides information that goes beyond what we could get in other ways (Lilienfeld et al., 2000).

## Less Common Projective Techniques

Based on the theory that your personality affects everything you do, some psychologists (and others) have tried analyzing people's handwriting. For example, perhaps people who dot their i's with a dash— *i* —are especially energetic, or perhaps people who draw large loops above the line—as in *allow* —are highly idealistic. Carefully collected data, however, show only random relationships between handwriting and personality (Tett & Palmer, 1997).

Another projective technique is to offer children dolls and invite them to act out a story. The dolls might be chosen, for example, to represent two parents and a child. The idea is that a child who cannot or will not describe physical or sexual abuse might act out a story in which the adults abuse the child. The problem is with the interpretation of results: If a child acts out sexual contact between two dolls, should we surmise that someone has sexually molested the child? Maybe not; the child may have discovered sex play with other children or may have watched late-night cable television shows. Doll play tells us nothing for certain about the child's own experiences (Ceci, 1995; Koocher et al., 1995).

## Research on Possible Implicit Personality Tests

Recall from Chapter 7 the distinction between explicit and implicit memory. If you listen to a list of words and then try to repeat them, what you recall is explicit memory. If you unintentionally use some words from that list in your later conversation, your use of those words con-

stitutes implicit memory. Implicit memory can occur even when you are not consciously aware of remembering something.

Many researchers are trying to develop an implicit personality test—that is, one that does not require you to describe your own personality, but measures some aspect of your personality without your awareness. No one knows yet whether these methods will become more effective than projective tests, but the research seems worth a try. We shall consider two examples: the Emotional Stroop Test and the Implicit Association Test.

### The Emotional Stroop Test

Recall the Stroop effect from Chapter 8: People are asked to look at a display like this and read the color of the ink instead of reading the words:

purple brown green blue yellow purple yellow red brown

 In the **Emotional Stroop Test,** *someone examines a list of words, some of which relate to a possible source of worry or concern to the person, and tries to* say the color of the ink of each word. For example, in the following display, say the color of the ink of each word as fast as possible:

cancer venom defeat hospital rattler failure fangs blood loser slither nurses bite jobless cobra inadequate disease

If you had a snake phobia, might you pause longer when you try to read the color of snake-related words— *venom, rattler, fangs, slither, bite, cobra?* Let's examine a representative study.

### WHAT'S THE EVIDENCE?
### *The Emotional Stroop Test and Suicidal Anxieties*

The Emotional Stroop Test is sometimes called the Personal Stroop Test because the items are individualized to concerns that some person might have. In this case the research dealt with people who had attempted suicide (Becker, Strohbach, & Rinck, 1999).

**HYPOTHESIS** It is always somewhat difficult to look at a word and say the color of ink instead of reading the word. It may be especially difficult if the word has a strong emotional meaning. In this case the hypothesis is that people who have attempted suicide may be more delayed than other people when they are looking at suicide-related words.

**METHOD** The experimenters asked 31 previous suicide attempters and 31 other people to look at a card with 12 words and say the color of ink for each word. One card had words with *positive* connotations, such as *talent* and *love.* Another card had words with *negative* connotations, such as *jail* and *stupidity.* A third card had words with *neutral* connotations, such as *ankle bone* and *square.* The final card had *suicide-related* words such as *grave, coldness,* and *darkness.* Different people looked at the cards in different orders. The experimenters timed how long each person took to say the ink colors of words on each card.

**RESULTS** Previous suicide attempters took slightly longer to read the suicide-related words. Other people took about equal times with all four cards. Here are the means for the two groups:

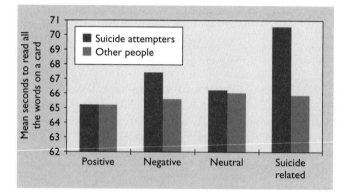

**INTERPRETATION** The previous suicide attempters apparently were distracted by the suicide-related words. The difference is not large, however. In its present form, this test is not accurate enough to make decisions about any individual.

Similar studies have shown that people worried about their health have long delays on the disease-related words, and people concerned about success and failure have long delays on words like *loser* and *jobless* (Williams, Mathews, & MacLeod, 1996). Elementary schoolchildren with few friends show extra delays on words like *lonely* and *hated* (Martin & Cole, 2000). Alcoholics and heroin addicts show extra delays for words related to alcohol or heroin (Franken, Kroon, Wiers, & Jansen, 2000; Stormark, Laberg, Nordby, & Hugdahl, 2000). Pain sufferers respond slowly for words related to pain (Crombez, Hermans, & Adriaensen, 2000). In each case, however, the differences between the troubled group and the normal group is small.

## The Implicit Association Test

Recall from Chapter 9 the idea of priming: Immediately after reading or hearing a word, such as *red,* you are quicker than usual to identify a related word, such as *cherry.* The fact that you are quicker indicates that you see the two words as related. Similarly, the **Implicit Association Test** *measures whether you respond faster to a category that combines some topic with pleasant words or with unpleasant words.*

To illustrate, imagine this example: You rest your left and right forefingers on a computer keyboard. When the experimenter reads a word, you are to press with your left finger if it is an unpleasant word, such as *blunder, fail,* or *shame,* and press with your right finger if it is a pleasant word, such as *joy, nice,* or *success.* Once you have mastered this procedure, we change the instructions. Now you should press the left key if you hear either an unpleasant word or a word relating to insects, and the right key if you hear either a pleasant word or one relating to flowers. Some other people have the reverse instructions: The left key means either an unpleasant word or a flower; the right key means either a pleasant word or an insect. Most people respond faster if they pair flowers with pleasant and insects with unpleasant than if they have to pair flowers with unpleasant and insects with pleasant. The conclusion is that most people like flowers and dislike insects.

This principle can be applied to people with different personalities. In one experiment people were asked to pair social words such as *date* and *chat* with either pleasant or unpleasant words. Most people responded faster if the social words were paired with pleasant words. However, people with social anxieties responded faster when social words were paired with unpleasant words, suggesting that they found social encounters unpleasant (de Jong, Pasman, Kindt, & van den Hout, 2001).

So far, the results indicate that implicit personality tests measure something, but not accurately enough for practical purposes. Research continues, however, because of some potential advantages: First, the results are not fakable. People can try to conceal their personalities in an interview or on the MMPI, but it is almost impossible to control reaction times on the Stroop test or an association test. Second, the results of these tests are sufficiently objective that they leave little room for the psychologist's preconceptions to alter the interpretation. Those potential advantages justify further research, even if current results are only modestly encouraging.

## CONCEPT CHECK

17. On the preceding sample items of an emotional Stroop test, if you had the greatest delay in naming the ink color for *cancer, hospital, blood, nurses,* and *disease,* what would these results imply about your emotions? (Check your answer on page 528.)

# Uses and Misuses of Personality Tests

Before any drug company can market a new drug in the United States, the Food and Drug Administration (FDA) requires that it be carefully tested. If the FDA finds the drug safe and effective, it approves the drug for certain purposes, with a warning label that lists precautions, such as that pregnant women should avoid it. After the drug is approved, however, the FDA cannot prevent a physician from prescribing it for unapproved purposes.

Personality tests are a little like prescription drugs: They ought to be used with caution and only for the purposes for which they have demonstrable usefulness. They are, at a minimum, helpful to psychologists as an interviewing technique to help "break the ice" and begin a good conversation. Tests can also be useful as an aid in personality assessment by a clinical psychologist. Note that I said "as an aid," *not* "as a sufficient method of personality assessment." For example, suppose someone has an MMPI personality profile that resembles the profile typical for schizophrenia. Identifying schizophrenia or any other unusual condition is a signal-detection problem, as we discussed in Chapter 4—a problem of reporting a stimulus when it is present without falsely reporting it when it is absent. Suppose (realistically) that people without schizophrenia outnumber people with schizophrenia by 100 to 1. Suppose further that a particular personality profile on the MMPI-2 is characteristic of 95% of people with schizophrenia and only 5% of other people. As Figure 13.21 shows, 5% of the normal population is a *larger* group than 95% of the schizophrenic population. Thus, if we labeled as "schizophrenic" everyone with a high score, we would be wrong more often than right. (Recall the representativeness heuristic and the issue of base-rate information, discussed in Chapter 8: Someone who seems "representative" of people in a rare category does not necessarily belong to that category.) Therefore, a conscientious psychologist will look for other evidence beyond the test score before drawing a firm conclusion. (The same, of course, should be said of any test, including IQ tests.) The rarer a personality problem, the stronger the evidence should be before a psychologist diagnoses it.

Some employers use personality tests to screen job applicants, selecting only those who have the "right" personality. The underlying idea is correct: What makes a good worker is at least as much a matter of personality as it is intelligence. A good worker is conscientious, cooperative with other workers, calm under pressure, persistent about achieving goals, responsive to the client's needs, and so forth—all personality traits. The difficulty is not that personality is unimportant but that many personality tests do not measure the right factors (Hogan, Hogan, & Roberts, 1996). For example, a personality test that claims to measure an "aggressive" personality may not measure the kind of aggressiveness that is presumably useful in a sales job. For ethical, legal, and practical reasons, employers should use a personality test *only* when they have clear evidence that the results help them to select among job applicants more accurately than they could without the test.

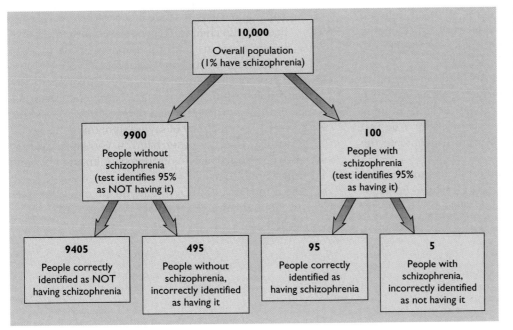

**FIGURE 13.21** Even the best personality tests are imperfect. A test for detecting an unusual condition will often identify normal people as having the condition. Here we assume that a certain profile occurs in 95% of people with schizophrenia and 5% of other people. If we relied entirely on this test, we would correctly identify 95 schizophrenic people, but we would also misidentify 495 normal people as schizophrenic.

## Trying to Measure Personality

As you have been reading about personality tests, you may have objected that no test could adequately describe the factors that make you the unique individual that you are. You are right. Just try to imagine how long it would take to measure everything that is worth knowing about your personality. After all, even family members who have known you all your life are sometimes surprised by what you say and do.

The goals of personality testing are more modest: to measure aspects of personality that are useful for certain purposes. But we need to remember what these purposes are and determine how well (or poorly) various tests can achieve them. Within their proper place tests can be useful; problems arise when people try to draw strong conclusions from weak data.

## Summary

- **People's tendency to accept personality test results.** Because most people are inclined to accept almost any interpretation of their personality based on a personality test, tests must be carefully scrutinized to ensure that they are measuring what they claim to measure. (page 518)
- **Standardized personality tests.** A standardized test is one that is administered according to explicit rules and its results are interpreted in a prescribed fashion. Standards are based on the scores of people who have already taken the test. (page 519)
- **The MMPI.** The MMPI, a widely used personality test, consists of a series of true–false questions selected in an effort to distinguish among various personality types. The MMPI-2 is a modernization of the version first developed in the 1940s. (page 519)
- **Detection of lying.** The MMPI and certain other tests guard against lying by including items on which nearly all honest people admit common faults or deny rare virtues. Any other answer is probably a lie. An unusual number of lying answers will invalidate the results. (page 520)
- **Projective techniques.** A projective technique, such as the Rorschach Inkblots or the Thematic Apperception Test, lets people describe their concerns indirectly while talking about the person in the picture or about other ambiguous stimuli. The results from projective techniques are difficult to interpret and have unimpressive validity for making decisions about any individual. (page 522)
- **Implicit personality tests.** The Emotional Stroop Test measures people's delays in naming the color of ink on the assumption that they will pause longer if the word has emotional meaning to them. The Implicit Association Test asks people to give one response to a particular combination of categories (e.g., social words and happy outcomes) and a different response to a different combination (e.g., nonsocial words and unhappy outcomes). The assumption is that people's emotions involuntarily control their response times. So far, the results are only mildly encouraging, but more research is needed. (page 525)
- **Uses and misuses of personality tests.** Personality tests can be used as an aid for assessing personality, but their results should be interpreted cautiously and in conjunction with other evidence. These tests should be used for job selection only when evidence clearly indicates that the results are valid for this purpose. (page 527)

## Answers to Concept Checks

13. Researchers would determine whether depressed people were more likely than other people to answer *true*. If so, the item could be included. If depressed people answer about the same as others, the item would be discarded. (page 522)
14. Such items are intended to detect lying. If you answered *false*, you would get a point on a lying scale. (page 522)
15. **a.** The puppet activity could be a projective technique because the child is likely to project his or her own family concerns onto the puppets, using them to enact various problems. (page 522)
16. The psychologist administering the test counts the total number of answers that are considered abnormal or disturbed. The more answers someone gives, the greater the probability of saying something that seems disturbed. (On the other hand, if you give very few answers, you will be considered unimaginative and dull-witted.) (page 524)
17. The results would suggest that you are especially worried about health-related matters. (page 526)

# Key Terms and Activities

## Key Terms

**agreeableness:** the tendency to be compassionate toward others and not antagonistic   (page 513)

**anal stage:** Freud's second stage of psychosexual development; here, psychosexual pleasure is focused on the anus   (page 499)

**archetypes:** according to Jung, vague images inherited from our ancestors and contained in the collective unconscious   (page 503)

**big five personality traits:** five traits that account for a great deal of human personality differences: neuroticism, extraversion, agreeableness, conscientiousness, and openness to new experience   (page 512)

**catharsis:** the release of pent-up emotions associated with unconscious thoughts and memories   (page 496)

**collective unconscious:** according to Jung, an inborn level of the unconscious that symbolizes the collective experience of the human species   (page 503)

**conscientiousness:** the tendency to show self-discipline, to be dutiful, and to strive for achievement and competence   (page 513)

**defense mechanism:** a method employed by the ego to protect itself against anxiety caused by the conflict between the id's demands and the superego's constraints   (page 500)

**denial:** the refusal to believe information that provokes anxiety   (page 500)

**displacement:** the diversion of a thought or behavior away from its natural target toward a less threatening target   (page 500)

**ego:** according to Freud, the rational, decision-making aspect of personality   (page 500)

**Emotional Stroop Test:** procedure in which someone tries to say the color of ink for a number of words, some of which might pertain to a source of worry or concern   (page 525)

**external locus of control:** the belief that external forces are largely in control of the events of one's life   (page 512)

**extraversion:** the tendency to seek stimulation and to enjoy the company of other people   (page 513)

**fixation:** in Freud's theory, a persisting preoccupation with an immature psychosexual interest as a result of frustration at that stage of psychosexual development   (page 498)

**gender role:** the pattern of behavior that each person is expected to follow because of being male or female   (page 506)

**genital stage:** Freud's final stage of psychosexual development, in which sexual pleasure is focused on sexual intimacy with others   (page 499)

**humanistic psychology:** a field that is concerned with consciousness, values, and abstract beliefs, including spiritual experiences and the beliefs that people live by and die for   (page 507)

**id:** according to Freud, the aspect of personality that consists of all our biological drives and demands for immediate gratification   (page 500)

**ideal self:** an image of what one would like to be   (page 508)

**idiographic approach:** an approach to the study of personality differences that concentrates on intensive studies of individuals   (page 511)

**Implicit Association Test:** procedure that measures how fast someone responds to a category that combines a topic with pleasant words or with unpleasant words   (page 526)

**individual psychology:** the psychology of the person as an indivisible whole, as formulated by Adler   (page 504)

**inferiority complex:** an exaggerated feeling of weakness, inadequacy, and helplessness   (page 505)

**internal locus of control:** the belief that one is largely in control of the events of one's life   (page 512)

**latent period:** according to Freud, a period in which psychosexual interest is suppressed or dormant   (page 499)

**libido:** in Freud's theory, psychosexual energy   (page 498)

**Minnesota Multiphasic Personality Inventory (MMPI):** a standardized test consisting of true–false items and intended to measure various personality dimensions and clinical conditions such as depression   (page 519)

**MMPI-2:** the modernized edition of the MMPI   (page 519)

**neo-Freudians:** personality theorists who have remained faithful to parts of Freud's theory while modifying other parts  (page 502)

**neuroticism:** the tendency to experience unpleasant emotions relatively easily  (page 513)

**nomothetic approach:** an approach to the study of individual differences that seeks general laws about how an aspect of personality affects behavior  (page 511)

**Oedipus complex:** according to Freud, a young boy's sexual interest in his mother accompanied by competitive aggression toward his father  (page 498)

**openness to experience:** the tendency to enjoy new intellectual experiences, the arts, fantasies, and anything that exposes a person to new ideas  (page 513)

**oral stage:** Freud's first stage of psychosexual development; here, psychosexual pleasure is focused on the mouth  (page 499)

**peak experiences:** moments in a person's life when he or she feels truly fulfilled and content  (page 507)

**personality:** all the consistent ways in which the behavior of one person differs from that of others, especially in social situations  (page 495)

**phallic stage:** Freud's third stage of psychosexual development; here, psychosexual interest is focused on the penis or clitoris  (page 499)

**projection:** the attribution of one's own undesirable characteristics to other people  (page 501)

**projective techniques:** procedures designed to encourage people to project their personality characteristics onto ambiguous stimuli  (page 522)

**psychoanalysis:** an approach to personality and psychotherapy developed by Sigmund Freud, based on identifying unconscious thoughts and emotions and bringing them to consciousness  (page 497)

**psychodynamic theory:** a system that relates personality to the interplay of conflicting forces within the individual, including some that the individual may not consciously recognize  (page 496)

**psychosexual pleasure:** according to Freud, any strong, pleasant enjoyment arising from body stimulation  (page 498)

**rationalization:** attempting to prove that one's actions are rational and justifiable and thus worthy of approval  (page 501)

**reaction formation:** presenting oneself as the opposite of what one really is, in an effort to reduce anxiety  (page 501)

**regression:** the return to a more juvenile level of functioning as a means of reducing anxiety or in response to emotionally trying circumstances  (page 500)

**repression:** according to Freudian theory, motivated forgetting, the process of moving an unacceptable memory, motivation, or emotion from the conscious mind to the unconscious mind  (page 500)

**Rorschach Inkblots:** a projective personality technique; people are shown ten inkblots and asked what each might be depicting  (page 522)

**self-actualization:** the achievement of one's full potential  (page 508)

**self-concept:** an image of what one really is  (page 508)

**social interest:** a sense of solidarity and identification with other people  (page 505)

**standardized test:** a test that is administered according to specified rules and its scores are interpreted in a prescribed fashion  (page 519)

**state:** a temporary activation of a particular behavior  (page 511)

**striving for superiority:** according to Adler, a universal desire to seek personal excellence and fulfillment  (page 505)

**style of life:** according to Adler, a person's master plan for achieving a sense of superiority  (page 505)

**sublimation:** the transformation of sexual or aggressive energies into culturally acceptable, even admirable, behaviors  (page 501)

**superego:** according to Freud, the aspect of personality that consists of memories of rules put forth by one's parents  (page 500)

**Thematic Apperception Test (TAT):** a projective personality technique; a person is asked to tell a story about each of 20 pictures  (page 524)

**trait:** a consistent, long-lasting tendency in behavior  (page 511)

**trait approach to personality:** the study and measure of consistent personality characteristics  (page 512)

**unconditional positive regard:** the complete, unqualified acceptance of another person as he or she is  (page 508)

**unconscious:** according to Freud, the repository of memories, emotions, and thoughts—often illogical thoughts—that affect our behavior even though we cannot talk about them  (page 497)

**unshared environment:** the aspects of environment that differ from one individual to another, even within a family  (page 515)

# Suggestions for Further Reading

Crews, F. C. (1998). *Unauthorized Freud.* New York: Viking. Devastating criticisms of Sigmund Freud's use and misuse of evidence.

Freud, S. (1924). *Introductory lectures on psychoanalysis.* New York: Boni and Liveright. Read Freud's own words and form your own opinion.

Rogers, C. R. (1961). *On becoming a person.* Boston: Houghton Mifflin. A good statement of the goals and assumptions of humanistic psychology.

# Web/Technology Resources

## The Jung Index

**www.jungindex.net/**

This detailed introduction to Jung's theory includes a glossary of Jungian terms, a newsletter, and other valuable features.

## Alfred Adler Institute of San Francisco

**ourworld.compuserve.com/homepages/hstein/**

The definitive Adler site includes dozens of articles about classical Adlerian psychology, how to become an Adlerian therapist, biographical sketches of Adler and prominent Adlerian therapists, and more.

## Personality Measures and the Big Five

**personality-project.org/personality.html**

This site offers a wealth of information about personality traits and research.

## Barbarian's Online Test Page

**www.iglobal.net/psman/personality.html**

The Barbarian provides links to dozens of sites that feature personality tests, including the Kiersey Temperament Sorter, the Enneagram Test, the Type A Personality Test, and the Locus of Control Test. Additional tests can be found in the *Other Online Tests* section.[*]

---

*Note: Any psychological test that is readily available to the public, while entertaining and possibly informative, should not be used to make important decisions about yourself or others. The most powerful, valid, and reliable psychological assessment devices are usually kept under the tight control of their creators or copyright holders.

# Social Psychology

**14**

**CHAPTER**

**I**n the *Communist Manifesto*, Karl Marx and Friedrich Engels wrote, "Mankind are more disposed to suffer, while evils are sufferable, than to right themselves by abolishing the forms to which they are accustomed. But when a long train of abuses and usurpations, pursuing invariably the same object, evinces a design to reduce them under absolute despotism, it is their right, it is their duty, to throw off such government." Fidel Castro wrote, "A little rebellion, now and then, is a good thing."

Do you agree with those statements? Why or why not? Can you think of anything that would change your mind?

Oh, pardon me. . . . That first statement is not from the *Communist Manifesto*. It is from the United States' Declaration of Independence. Sorry. And that second statement is a quotation from Thomas Jefferson, not Castro.

Do you agree more with these statements now that you know they came from democratic revolutionaries instead of communist revolutionaries? What kinds of influences alter your opinions? This question is one example of the issues that interest **social psychologists**—*the psychologists who study social behavior and how individuals influence other people and are influenced by other people.* Social psychology is a broad, diverse field that extends to the study of attitudes, persuasion, self-understanding, and almost all everyday behaviors of relatively normal people in their relationships with others.

■ Social psychologists find that influence depends not only on what someone says but also on who says it and on what the listeners think of that person.

*What factors influence our judgments of others?*

*How can we measure stereotypes that people do not want to admit?*

*How do we explain the behaviors of ourselves and others?*

Shortly after a massacre in Lebanon in 1982, several audiences were polled concerning their reactions to the television news coverage. Pro-Israeli audiences were angry about the news programs' anti-Israeli bias, whereas pro-Arab audiences were angry about the *same* programs' anti-Arab bias (Vallone, Ross, & Lepper, 1985).

We inevitably form attitudes about other people and groups of people—whether good, bad, or indifferent. Once we have formed such attitudes, they alter the way we perceive new information. **Social perception and cognition** are *the processes we use to gather and remember information about others and to make inferences based on that information.* Social perception and cognition resemble the general principles of perception and cognition that we examined in earlier chapters in that our expectations influence our observations, memory, and thinking.

## First Impressions

Other things being equal, *the first information we learn about someone influences us more than later information does* (Belmore, 1987; E. E. Jones & Goethals, 1972). This tendency is known as the **primacy effect.** For example, if a professor seems energetic and engaging on the first day of class, you will start with a favorable attitude and thus probably forgive his or her lackluster performance later in the semester. A professor who seems dull at first will have a hard time impressing you favorably later. Similarly, your professors' early impressions of you can have lasting effects.

Why are first impressions so influential? If our first impression of someone is unfavorable, we may not spend enough time with that person to form an alternative view. Also, once we have formed an impression, it alters our interpretation of later experiences. Suppose that your first impression of someone is that he talks about himself too much. Later, when he talks about himself again, even in an appropriate way, you take his comments as support

for your initial impression. Anything he says about someone else will merely seem like an exception to the rule.

Our first impressions can become self-fulfilling prophecies. Suppose a psychologist hands you a telephone receiver and asks you to have a conversation with someone, while handing you a photo that supposedly shows that person. It is not actually a photo of that person at all. Unknown to you and to the person you are talking to, the psychologist hands some people a photo of a very attractive member of the opposite sex and hands other people a photo of someone whose appearance is best described as "unfortunate." Not surprisingly, you would act friendlier to someone you regarded as attractive. More interesting, if you think you are talking to someone attractive, that person himself or herself becomes more cheerful and more talkative. In short, your first impression of someone changes how you act and may influence the other person to live up to (or down to) your first impression (Snyder, Tanke, & Berscheid, 1977).

■ If you were a new patient of Dr. Balamurali Ambati, the world's youngest doctor (at age 17), what would your first impression probably be? A first impression based only on his youthful appearance could be greatly mistaken.

536 Chapter 14 Social Psychology

**A STEP FURTHER**
*First Impressions*

In a criminal trial, the prosecution presents its evidence first. Might that give the jury an unfavorable first impression of the defendant and increase the probability of a conviction?

ONCEPT CHECK

1. Why do some professors avoid looking at students' names when they grade essay exams? Why is it more important for them to avoid looking at the names on tests given later in the semester than on the first test? (Check your answers on page 543.)

# Stereotypes and Prejudices

A **stereotype** is *a generalized belief or expectation about a group of people.* It is possible to develop false stereotypes because of our tendency to remember the unusual. If we see an unusual person doing something unusual, the event is doubly memorable. For example, you might remember being cheated by a left-handed redhead and then form a false stereotype about left-handed redheads—an illusory correlation, as discussed in Chapter 2.

Stereotypes can also be based on an exaggeration of a correct observation. In particular, people tend to perceive and describe their political opponents as being far more extreme than they really are (Keltner & Robinson, 1996). Some English-literature professors in the United States have been arguing for a revision of the curriculum to include more feminist and non-Western writers. When defenders of the standard curriculum (Shakespeare, Chaucer, etc.) were asked to guess what the revisionists really wanted, most guessed that the revisionists wanted students to read *only* feminist and multicultural authors. In fact, the revisionists wanted a mixture of such authors along with some traditional choices (Robinson & Keltner, 1996).

Researchers have, however, also discovered that some stereotypes are correct. For example, who do you think gets into more fistfights on the average—men or women? If you answered "men," you are expressing a stereotype, but you are correct. Similarly, who do you think is more likely to be sensitive to the subtle social

■ If you have stereotypes of young people as active and old people as inactive, your stereotypes are correct on the average. However, many individuals are exceptions and we need to treat people as they are, not according to the stereotypes.

connotations of what people say—a liberal-arts major or an engineering major? Again, if you said "liberal-arts major," you are endorsing a stereotype, but the research supports you (Ottati & Lee, 1995).

Indeed, whenever we say that members of two cultures behave differently, we are endorsing a stereotype. In some cases members of both cultures agree on those stereotypes, although they express them in different words. For example, many Americans describe the Chinese as "inhibited," whereas Chinese call themselves "self-controlled." U.S. businesspeople complain that Mexicans "don't show up on time and don't keep schedules," whereas Mexicans complain that people in the United States "are always in a rush" and "act like robots" (Lee & Duenas, 1995). In short, it may be wrong to try to eliminate all stereotypes. If a stereotype is correct, we should accept the differences as part of the enjoyable diversity of human life.

However, agreeing that stereotypes are sometimes correct summaries of groups does not mean we should treat individuals according to the stereotypes (Banaji & Bhaskar, 2000). For example, most 80-year-olds are less athletic than most 20-year-olds, but some 80-year-olds are in amazingly good shape and some 20-year-olds are in amazingly poor shape. We have to treat people as they are individually, not just as group members.

## Aversive Racism

A **prejudice** is *an unfavorable attitude toward a group of people,* such as a dislike of some group. It is usually associated with **discrimination,** which is *unequal treatment of different groups.* Decades ago many Americans admitted their prejudices openly. Today, most prejudices are so subtle that people may not even be aware of them. Researchers describe unconscious racial prejudice and discrimination as **aversive racism:** *consciously expressing the idea that all people are equal, but nevertheless unintentionally discriminating against some groups.* It is called "aversive" because it is unpleasant to the person who acts this way.

Here is an example of a study that demonstrates aversive racism (Dovidio & Gaertner, 2000): Each of many White college students was given a folder for one person who was supposedly applying for a job as a peer counselor. Each was asked whether he or she would recommend hiring this person. One third of the applications described strong experience and qualifications for the job, whereas others described marginal or weak qualifications. Of each kind of application (strong, marginal, or weak), half mentioned membership in a nearly all-White fraternity and the other half mentioned membership in the Black Student Union. So each student read what appeared to be a strong White, strong Black, marginal White, marginal Black, weak

White, or weak Black application. The following graph shows the mean results:

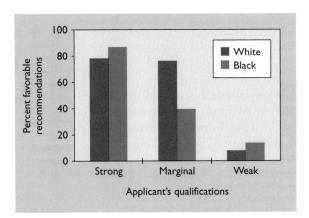

Note that the students were slightly more generous with well-qualified Black applicants than with equally well-qualified Whites. Several other studies have reported that same trend (Hass, Katz, Rizzo, Bailey, & Eisenstadt, 1991). They were also slightly more generous with weak Black than weak White applications. The big difference, however, was for the marginal applications. The students favorably recommended 77% of the marginal White applicants but only 40% of the equally marginal Black applicants (Dovidio & Gaertner, 2000). Without realizing it, the students evaluated the ambiguous qualifications more positively if they thought they applied to White applicants.

## Implicit Measures of Stereotypes and Prejudice

Prejudice that is subtle, unintentional, and unconscious is difficult to measure. When people are asked how much racism they think occurs in the United States, most say they perceive "some" or "much" racism. But if asked whether they themselves are racist, almost everyone says "no." Similarly, many people deny having any biases about differences between men and women. We all believe in fair treatment for everyone, or so we say. But if no one is racist or sexist and no one holds any other prejudices, where do all the racism, sexism, and so forth come from?

Psychologists can measure stereotypes in subtle ways. For example, suppose you watch a videotape of several young men who are talking loudly, although you cannot determine exactly what they are saying. After a while one of them pushes another. Now you are asked whether you think the push was aggressive or playful. Do you think your decision would be influenced by whether the men were Black or White? Many people *are* influenced,

**FIGURE 14.1** Procedures for an Implicit Association Test to measure prejudices.

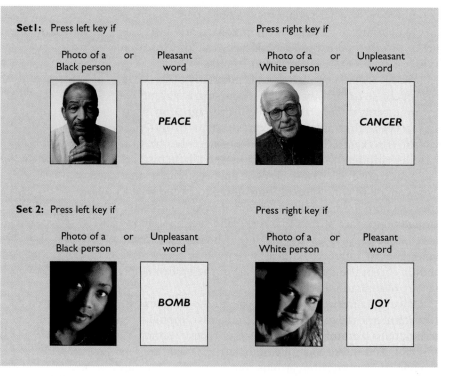

even if they think they would not be. If the man doing the pushing is either White or a well-dressed Black man, most people guess "playful," but if he is Black and not neatly dressed, most guess "aggressive" (Banaji & Greenwald, 1994; Kunda & Thagard, 1996). The more confusing the events on the videotape, the more likely people are to be influenced by their stereotypes (Sherman & Bessenoff, 1999).

Currently, the best way to measure prejudices is by the Implicit Association Test, already described in Chapter 13. Recall the idea: A participant might be asked to press the left key after hearing either a pleasant word or the name of a flower and to press the right key after either an unpleasant word or the name of an insect. At another time the participant might be asked to press the left key for pleasant or insect and the right key for unpleasant or flower. The fact that "unpleasant or insect" is easier than "pleasant or insect" indicates that most people find insects unpleasant. The effect is not huge, but it has some advantages over just asking people what they like and dislike. (People sometimes say what they think they are supposed to say instead of what they really think.)

The same strategy can be used for measuring prejudices. Imagine yourself in the following experiment: You are seated in front of a computer screen that will sometimes show a photo of some person and sometimes show a word. If it is a photo of a Black person or a pleasant word (e.g., *peace, joy,* or *love*), press the left key. If it is a photo of a White person or an unpleasant word (e.g., *cancer, bomb,* or *devil*), press the right key. After you have done it that way for a while, the rule will switch and you will press the left key for a Black person or unpleasant word and the right key for a White person or pleasant word.

Figure 14.1 summarizes the procedures and Figure 14.2 summarizes the results. Note that most people responded faster if the responses were for *Black or unpleasant* and *White or pleasant*. They responded slower if the responses were for *Black or pleasant* and *White or unpleasant*. That is, even though most of the White college students in this study claimed to have no racial stereotypes or prejudices, they evaluated White faces more favorably than Black faces (Phelps et al., 2000). A similar study found that White students found it easier to pair pleasant words with

White names, such as *Andrew* and *Brandon*, and unpleasant words with Black names, such as *Lamar* and *Jamal* (Dasgupta, McGhee, Greenwald, & Banaji, 2000).

So, what's my point? Is it, "See, way down deep these people really are nasty racists"? Not at all. Most were well-meaning people who would be embarrassed to discover that they exhibited signs of stereotypes or prejudice. The point is that racism, sexism, and all the other -isms can operate without our awareness (Greenwald & Banaji, 1995). Many people insist that we should evaluate

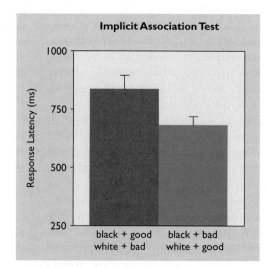

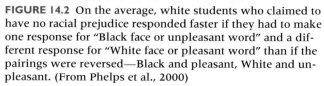

**FIGURE 14.2** On the average, white students who claimed to have no racial prejudice responded faster if they had to make one response for "Black face or unpleasant word" and a different response for "White face or pleasant word" than if the pairings were reversed—Black and pleasant, White and unpleasant. (From Phelps et al., 2000)

people, such as job applicants, "entirely on the basis of their qualifications." The problem is that we may be influenced by stereotypes and prejudices that we do not even consciously recognize. Perhaps it is better to recognize that we have stereotypes and try to fight them instead of convincing ourselves that we do not have them at all.

## CONCEPT CHECKS

**2.** What is aversive racism?
**3.** What is the advantage of the Implicit Association Test over simply asking people about their racial prejudices? (Check your answers on page 543.)

### *Overcoming Prejudice*

After prejudices and hostility have arisen between two groups, what can anyone do to break down those barriers? Simply getting to know each other better sometimes helps, but not dependably. A more effective technique is to get the two groups to work toward a common goal, to think of themselves as part of a larger, combined group (Dovidio & Gaertner, 1999).

Many years ago psychologists demonstrated the power of this technique using two arbitrarily chosen groups, not different races (Sherif, 1966). At a summer camp at Robbers' Cave, Oklahoma, 11- to 12-year-old boys were divided into two groups in separate cabins. The groups competed for prizes in sports, treasure hunts, and other activities. With each competition the antagonism between the two groups grew more intense. The boys made threatening posters, shouted insults, and engaged in food fights. Each group had clearly developed prejudice and hostility toward the other.

Up to a point, the "counselors" (the experimenters) allowed the hostility to take its course, neither encouraging nor prohibiting it. Then, they tried to reverse it by stop-

■ People who work together for a common goal can overcome prejudices that initially divide them.

ping the competitions and setting common goals. First, they asked the two groups to work together to find and repair a leak in the water pipe that supplied the camp. Later, they had the two groups pool their treasuries to rent a movie that both groups wanted to see. Still later, they had the boys pull together to get a truck out of a rut. Gradually, hostility turned into friendship—except for a few holdouts who nursed their hatred to the bitter end! The point of this study is that competition leads to hostility; cooperation leads to friendship.

# Attribution

We often try to figure out why the people we observe behave as they do. Yesterday you won $1 million in the state lottery, and today some classmates who hardly noticed you before want to be your friends. You draw some inferences about their reasons. When we observe any behavior that seems at all out of the ordinary, we *attribute* causes that seem appropriate. **Attribution** is *the set of thought processes we use to assign causes to our own behavior and to the behavior of others.*

### *Internal Causes Versus External Causes*

Fritz Heider, the founder of attribution theory, maintained that people often try to decide whether someone's behavior is the result of internal or external causes (Heider, 1958). **Internal attributions** are *explanations based on someone's individual characteristics, such as attitudes, personality traits, or abilities.* **External attributions** are *explanations based on the current situation, including events that presumably would influence almost anyone.* For example, your brother decides to walk to work this morning instead of drive. An example of an internal attribution is "he likes the exercise." A possible external attribution is "his car is broken." Internal attributions are also known as *dispositional* (that is, something about the person's disposition led to the behavior); external attributions are also known as *situational* (that is, something about the situation led to the behavior).

You make internal attributions when someone does something that you think most people would not do. For example, if I tell you I would like to visit Hawaii, you probably draw no conclusions about me. However, if I say I would like to visit northern Norway in midwinter, you would seek an attribution in terms of my personality or interests (Krull & Anderson, 1997).

This tendency sometimes leads to misunderstandings between members of different cultures. Each person views the other's behavior as "something I would not have done" and therefore as grounds for making an attribution about the other individual's personality. In fact, such behavior may actually be what the other person's culture dictates. For example, some cultures expect people to cry loudly at funerals, whereas other cultures expect

 We are sometimes surprised by people's behavior and attribute an internal cause when in fact the people are acting in accord with the customs of their culture. In the United States a funeral usually calls for reserved behavior; in many other places the opposite is true.

people to be more restrained. People who are unfamiliar with other cultures may attribute a behavior to someone's personality and overlook the culturally determined response to that situation.

Harold Kelley (1967) proposed that we rely on three types of information when deciding whether to make an internal or an external attribution for someone's behavior:

• **Consensus information** *(how the person's behavior compares with other people's behavior).* If someone behaves the same way you believe other people would in the same situation, then you make an external attribution. If someone's behavior seems unusual, you look for an internal attribution pertaining to something about the person instead of the situation. (Note that you can easily be wrong if you misunderstand the situation.)

• **Consistency information** *(how the person's behavior varies from one time to the next).* If someone almost always seems friendly, for example, you would make an internal attribution ("a friendly person"). If someone's friendliness varies, you look for an external attribution, such as some event that put the person in a bad or good mood.

• **Distinctiveness** *(how the person's behavior varies from one situation to another).* For example, if your friend is pleasant to most people but consistently unfriendly to one particular person, you make an external attribution. You assume that person has done something to irritate your friend.

## CONCEPT CHECKS

4. Classify the following as either internal or external attributions:
   a. She contributed money to charity because she is generous.

   b. She contributed money to charity because she wanted to impress her boss, who was watching.
   c. She contributed money to charity because she owed a favor to the man who was asking for contributions.
5. Juanita returns from watching *The Return of the Son of Sequel Strikes Back Again Part 2* and says it was excellent. Most other people that you know disliked the movie. Will you make an internal or external attribution for Juanita's opinion? Why? (Distinctiveness, consensus, or consistency?) (Check your answers on page 543.)

## The Fundamental Attribution Error

One of the most common errors of attribution is *to make internal attributions for people's behavior even when we see evidence for an external influence on behavior.* That tendency is known as the **fundamental attribution error** (Ross, 1977). It is also known as the *correspondence bias,* meaning a tendency to assume a strong similarity between someone's current actions and his or her dispositions.

 Imagine yourself in a classic study demonstrating this phenomenon. You are told that U.S. college students were randomly assigned to write essays praising or condemning Fidel Castro, the Communist leader of Cuba. You read an essay like this one:

Castro has been treated unfairly by the American press. He has been in power since 1959! Does that sound like someone who is hated by his people? Sure, life in Cuba is bad, but it was even worse before he came to power. Castro has given his country strong law enforcement and one of the strongest economies in the Caribbean. It wouldn't be fair to compare its economy to Europe or the United States. Castro's government doesn't give the citizens much freedom, but it isn't as corrupt as many other governments. It has free medical care for all citizens . . .

Now what's your guess about the actual attitude of the student who wrote this essay?

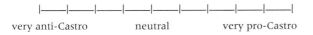

very anti-Castro          neutral          very pro-Castro

Most U.S. students in one study guessed that the author of a pro-Castro essay was at least mildly pro-Castro, even though they were informed, as you were, that the author had been told to praise Castro (E. E. Jones & Harris, 1967). In a later study, experimenters explained that one student in a creative writing class had been assigned to write a pro-Castro essay and an anti-Castro essay at different times in the course. Then the participants read the two essays and estimated the writer's true beliefs. Most thought that the writer had changed attitudes between the two essays (Allison, Mackie, Muller, & Worth, 1993). That is, even when people are told of a powerful external reason for someone's behavior, they apparently believe the person must have had internal reasons as well (McClure, 1998).

 This tendency, the fundamental attribution error, is easy to demonstrate in the United States, but sometimes weaker in cross-cultural studies. When people in China, India, Japan, and Korea were told that someone was told to do something, they attributed the behavior mainly to the situation without adding attributions about the person's personality dispositions (Choi, Nisbett, & Norenzayan, 1999; Norenzayan & Nisbett, 2000). In contrast to Western society, the cultures of Japan, India, Korea, and China often explain behavior more in terms of the situation. To illustrate, consider the fish designated with an arrow in this drawing. Describe what it is doing and why.

Americans are more likely to say this fish is leading the others (an internal attribution), whereas many southeast Asians say the other fish are chasing it (an external attribution). In one study Hong Kong students who had spent the last few minutes thinking about symbols of American culture (e.g., Mickey Mouse) were more likely to say the front fish was leading, whereas their classmates who had been thinking about symbols of Chinese culture (e.g., a

Chinese dragon) generally said the front fish was being chased (Hong, Morris, Chiu, & Benet-Martinez, 2000). That is, it is possible to shift people temporarily toward more internal or external attributions by emphasizing certain cultural influences.

## CONCEPT CHECK

6. Would people who believe they control their own destinies in life be more likely or less likely than others to make the fundamental attribution error? (Check your answer on page 543.)

### The Actor-Observer Effect

Here is another common bias related to the fundamental attribution error: *People are more likely to make internal attributions for other people's behavior and more likely to make external attributions for their own* (E. E. Jones & Nisbett, 1972). This tendency is called the **actor-observer effect.** You are an "actor" when you try to explain the causes of your own behavior and an "observer" when you try to explain someone else's behavior.

In one study Richard Nisbett and his colleagues (1973) asked college students to rate themselves, their fathers, their best friends, and Walter Cronkite (a television news announcer at the time) on several personality traits. For each trait (e.g., "leniency"), the participants were given three choices: (a) the person possesses the trait, (b) the person possesses the opposite trait, and (c) the person's behavior "depends on the situation." Participants checked "depends on the situation"—an external attribution—most frequently when they were rating themselves, less frequently when they were rating their fathers and friends, and least often when they were rating Walter Cronkite. Figure 14.3 shows the results.

Why do we tend to explain our own behavior differently from that of others? First, we are aware of how our own behavior varies from one situation to another. (Recall Kelley's theory: You make external attributions when someone's behavior varies across time and across situations.) The less well we know someone else, the less aware we are of variations from situation to situation.

Second, we tend to attribute unexpected, surprising behavior to internal causes. Our own behavior seldom surprises us, so we do not attribute it to internal causes.

The third reason is perceptual. We do not see ourselves as objects because our eyes look outward and focus on our environment. We see other people, however, as objects in our visual field.

The perceptual explanation for the actor-observer effect has an interesting implication: If you could somehow become an object in your own visual field, then you might explain your own behavior in terms of internal traits, just as you tend to explain the behavior of others. In one innovative study, Michael Storms (1973) videotaped several participants in a conversation. Before

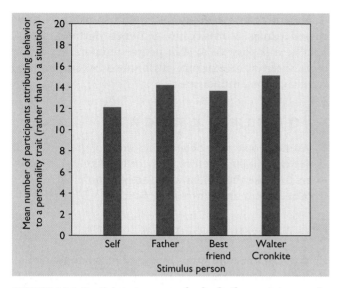

**FIGURE 14.3** Participants were asked whether certain people had certain traits, such as "leniency," the opposite traits, such as "firmness," or whether "it depended on the situation." They were most likely to say that their own behavior depended on the situation and least likely to say "it depends" for Walter Cronkite, the person they knew the least. (Based on data of Nisbett, Caputo, Legant, & Marecek, 1973)

showing them the videotape, he asked the reasons behind what they said and what the other people said. Most participants attributed their own remarks to external causes ("I was responding to what the other person said") and attributed other people's comments to internal causes ("he was showing off"). Then Storms showed them the videotape and asked the same questions. This time many participants attributed their own behavior more often to internal causes ("I was being smart-alecky. . . . I was trying to act friendly"). That is, when people watched themselves, they interpreted their behavior like that of other people, making mostly internal attributions.

**A STEP FURTHER**
*Attributions*

Try to explain these examples of behavior:

- Why did you choose to go to the college you are attending?
- Why did your roommate choose this college?
- Why are you reading this book right now?
- Why does your roommate study so much (or so little)?

Did you attribute internal causes or external causes for these behaviors? Did you rely more on external causes to explain other people's behavior or to explain your own?

## Using Attributions to Control Perceptions of Ourselves

Although we generally attribute our own behavior largely to external causes, we vary our attributions to try to present ourselves in a favorable light. For example, you may credit your intelligence for your good grades (an internal attribution) and blame unfair tests for your bad grades (an external attribution). *Attributions that we adopt to maximize our credit for our success and minimize our blame for our failure* are called **self-serving biases** (D. T. Miller & Ross, 1975; van der Pligt & Eiser, 1983).

People can also protect their images by adopting **self-handicapping strategies,** in which they *intentionally put themselves at a disadvantage to provide an excuse for an expected failure.* Suppose you expect to do poorly on a test. You go to a party the night before and stay out until three in the morning. Now you can blame your low score on your lack of sleep and avoid having to admit even to yourself that you might have done poorly anyway.

In an experiment on self-handicapping strategies, Steven Berglas and Edward Jones (1978) asked some college students to work on solvable problems and asked others to work on a mixture of solvable and unsolvable problems. (The students of course did not know that some of the problems were impossible.) Then the experimenters told all the students that they had done well. The students who had been given solvable problems (and had solved them) felt good about their success. Those who had worked on many unsolvable problems were unsure in what way they had "done well." They certainly had no confidence that they could continue to do well.

Next the experimenters told the participants that the purpose of the experiment was to investigate the effects of drugs on problem solving and that they were now going to hand out another set of problems. The participants could choose between taking a drug that supposedly impaired problem-solving abilities and another drug that supposedly improved them. The participants who had worked on unsolvable problems the first time were more likely than the others to choose the drug that supposedly impaired performance. Because they did not expect to do well on the second set of problems anyway, they chose to provide themselves with a convenient excuse.

**IN CLOSING**
## How Social Perceptions Affect Behavior

We are seldom fully aware of the reasons for our own behavior, much less someone else's, but we make our best guesses. If someone you know passes by without saying hello, you might attribute that person's behavior to either absent-mindedness, indifference, or outright hostility. If someone acts unusually friendly, you might attribute that response to your own personal charm, the other person's extraverted personality, or that person's devious and manipulative personality. Whatever attributions you make are sure to influence your own social behaviors.

## Summary

- **First impressions.** Other things being equal, we pay more attention to the first information we learn about someone than to later information. (page 535)
- **Stereotypes.** Stereotypes are generalized beliefs about groups of people. They are sometimes illusory correlations that arise from people's tendency to remember unusual actions clearly, especially unusual actions by members of minority groups. However, some stereotypes are also correct or partly correct. (page 536)
- **Prejudice.** A prejudice is an unfavorable stereotype. Many people will not admit, even to themselves, that they have prejudices. Through indirect measures, researchers have found ways to demonstrate subtle effects of stereotypes and prejudices even in people who deny having them. (page 537)
- **Attribution.** Attribution is the set of thought processes by which we assign causes to behavior. We attribute behavior either to internal causes or to external causes. According to Harold Kelley, we are likely to attribute behavior to an internal cause if it is consistent over time, different from most other people's behavior, and directed toward a variety of other people or objects. (page 539)
- **Fundamental attribution error.** People frequently attribute people's behavior to internal causes, even when they see evidence of external influences. (page 540)

- **Actor-observer effect.** We are more likely to attribute internal causes to other people's behavior than to our own. (page 541)
- **Self-serving bias and self-handicapping.** People sometimes try to protect their self-esteem by attributing their successes to skill and their failures to outside influences. They can also intentionally place themselves at a disadvantage to provide an excuse for their expected failure. (page 542)

## Answers to Concept Checks

1. They want to avoid being biased by their first impressions of the students. This procedure is less important with the first test because they have not yet formed strong impressions of the students. (page 536)
2. Aversive racism is unintentional discrimination against some group by someone who consciously expresses a lack of stereotypes and prejudice. (page 539)
3. The advantage is that the Implicit Association Test can reveal prejudices that people don't want to admit, perhaps even to themselves. (page 539)
4. **a.** internal; **b.** and **c.** external. An internal attribution relates to a stable aspect of personality or attitudes; an external attribution relates to the current situation. (page 540)
5. You probably will make an internal attribution for Juanita's enjoyment. The reason is *consensus*. When one person's behavior differs from others', we make an internal attribution. (page 540)
6. They would be more likely to make the fundamental attribution error because they tend to attribute behaviors to internal causes instead of situations. (page 541)

# Attitudes and Persuasion

*What are some effective ways of influencing people's attitudes?*

"If you want to change people's behavior, you have to change their attitudes first." Do you agree?

Suppose you say "yes." Now answer two more questions: (a) What is your attitude about paying higher taxes? (b) If the government raises taxes, will you pay the higher taxes?

If you're like most people, you will say that your attitude about paying higher taxes is unfavorable, but if the taxes are raised, you will pay them. In other words, by changing the law, the government can change your behavior without changing your attitude.

So what effects do attitudes have on behavior? And what leads people to change their attitudes?

## Attitudes and Their Influence

An **attitude** is *a like or dislike that influences our behavior toward a person or thing* (Allport, 1935; Petty & Cacioppo, 1981). Your attitudes include an evaluative or emotional component (how you feel about something), a cognitive component (what you know or believe), and a behavioral component (what you are likely to do). *Persuasion* is an attempt to alter your attitudes or behavior.

One common way of measuring attitudes (and thus the effectiveness of persuasion) is through the use of attitude scales, such as Likert scales, also known as summated rating scales (Dawes & Smith, 1985). On a Likert scale (named after psychologist Rensis Likert), a person checks a point along a line ranging from 1, meaning "strongly disagree," to 7, meaning "strongly agree," for each of several statements about a topic, as shown in Figure 14.4.

The attitudes that people report on pencil-and-paper scales sometimes relate closely to their behaviors but surprisingly often do not. People sometimes report attitudes about cigarettes, alcohol, safe sex, wearing seat belts in a car, studying hard for tests, and so forth that are quite different from their actual behavior. Why? I shall mention three reasons, but you could probably think of others.

One reason is that people sometimes answer attitude questionnaires impulsively, especially on questions that are not important to them (van der Pligt, de Vries, Manstead, & van Harreveld, 2000). Recall that the same idea arose in Chapter 2 concerning surveys: People reported on one survey that they didn't believe there was intelligent life in outer space but also that they believed the U.S. government was hiding evidence of intelligent life in outer space.

Indicate your level of agreement with the items below, using the following scale:

| | Strongly disagree | | | Neutral | | | Strongly agree |
|---|---|---|---|---|---|---|---|
| 1. Labor unions are necessary to protect the rights of workers. | 1 | 2 | 3 | 4 | 5 | 6 | 7 |
| 2. Labor union leaders have too much power. | 1 | 2 | 3 | 4 | 5 | 6 | 7 |
| 3. If I worked for a company with a union, I would join the union. | 1 | 2 | 3 | 4 | 5 | 6 | 7 |
| 4. I would never cross a picket line of striking workers. | 1 | 2 | 3 | 4 | 5 | 6 | 7 |
| 5. Striking workers hurt their company and unfairly raise prices for the consumer. | 1 | 2 | 3 | 4 | 5 | 6 | 7 |
| 6. Labor unions should not be permitted to engage in political activity. | 1 | 2 | 3 | 4 | 5 | 6 | 7 |
| 7. America is a better place for today's workers because of the efforts by labor unions in the past. | 1 | 2 | 3 | 4 | 5 | 6 | 7 |

*Note: Items 2, 5, and 6 are scored the opposite of 1, 3, 4, and 7.*

**FIGURE 14.4** Likert scales, such as this one assessing attitudes toward labor unions, are commonly used in attitude research. Subjects rate the degree to which they agree or disagree with items that measure various aspects of a particular attitude.

People answer researchers' questions, but they don't always think about their answers very carefully.

A second reason is that people's answers to an attitude question depend on exactly how they think about that question (Lord & Lepper, 1999). For example, what is your attitude toward politicians on a scale from 1 (very unfavorable) to 7 (very favorable)? If you are thinking about the public servants you admire most, you might rate politicians very favorably. At a later time, however, you might be thinking about corrupt or incompetent politicians, and you would answer differently.

A third reason, which overlaps the other two, is that people sometimes maintain mixed or contradictory attitudes (T. D. Wilson, Lindsey, & Schooler, 2000). For example, you might have long held an unfavorable attitude toward homosexuals. More recently you have been persuaded that this attitude was unfair, and you now express a more positive attitude. You state your new explicit attitude on questionnaires, but your old attitude may emerge in your nonverbal behaviors and emotional reactions.

## CONCEPT CHECK

**7.** What method mentioned in the first module of this chapter could demonstrate mixed or contradictory attitudes? (Check your answer on page 553.)

# Two Routes of Attitude Change and Persuasion

Sometimes people ponder the evidence carefully and develop a carefully reasoned attitude, and sometimes they form attitudes with only a flimsy, superficial basis. Richard Petty and John Cacioppo (1981, 1986) proposed the fol-

■ Most political candidates will try both the central and peripheral routes to persuasion, depending on the situation. In debates and interviews, they try to impress with their knowledge and logic. In brief campaign appearances, they are more concerned with presenting an image, such as that of a "regular person just like you."

lowing distinction: *When people take a decision seriously, they invest the necessary time and effort to carefully evaluate the evidence and logic behind each message.* Petty and Caciopp call this logical approach the **central route to persuasion.** In contrast, *when people listen to a message on a topic of little importance to them, they pay more attention to such factors as the speaker's appearance and reputation or the sheer number of arguments presented, regardless of their quality.* This superficial approach is the **peripheral route to persuasion.**

## CONCEPT CHECK

**8.** You are listening to someone who is trying to persuade you to change your major from astrology to psychology. Your future success may depend on making the right decision. You also listen to someone explain why a trip to the Bahamas is better than a trip to the Fiji Islands. You had no intention of going to either place. In which case will you follow the central route to persuasion? (Check your answer on page 553.)

## *Highly Resistant Attitudes*

Most people's attitudes fall along a continuum: You know much and care deeply about a few topics; regarding these you have firm, well-informed attitudes that you would change only by solid evidence and logic—the central route. At the other end of the continuum, many topics hardly interest you at all; you might express an opinion if asked, but you have little basis for that opinion, so you could change it easily, even by the peripheral route.

On a few topics, however, many people form strong, unshakable attitudes based on hardly any information at all. One such topic is the death penalty. In the United States, about 60–75% say that they support the death penalty, whereas 20–30% oppose it, and the others are undecided. The percentages vary a bit from year to year, but unlike most other topics, the answers do not depend much on how the question is worded (Ellsworth & Gross, 1994).

 Before we continue, answer the following questions:

**Knowledge Items**

**1.** The death penalty has been abolished by a majority of Western European nations.
   True        I don't know        False

**2.** Over the years states which have had the death penalty have shown lower murder rates than neighboring states which did not have the death penalty.
   True        I don't know        False

**3.** Studies have shown that the rate of murder usually drops in the weeks following a publicized execution.
   True        I don't know        False

**4.** Poor people who commit murder are more likely to be sentenced to death than rich people.
   True        I don't know        False

**5.** After the U.S. Supreme Court struck down the death penalty in 1972, the murder rate in the United States showed a sharp upturn.

    True      I don't know      False

**6.** On the average the death penalty costs the taxpayers less than life imprisonment.

    True      I don't know      False

**Reasons for Support or Opposition**

**1.** We need capital punishment to provide support and protection for the police.

    Agree      I don't know      Disagree

**2.** Even when a murderer gets a life sentence, he usually gets out on parole, so it is better to execute him.

    Agree      I don't know      Disagree

**3.** We need capital punishment to show criminals that we mean business about wiping out crime in this country.

    Agree      I don't know      Disagree

**4.** Society has a right to get revenge when a very serious crime like murder has been committed.

    Agree      I don't know      Disagree

**5.** Sometimes I have felt a sense of personal outrage when a convicted murderer was sentenced to a penalty less than death.

    Agree      I don't know      Disagree

**6.** One problem with the death penalty is that only the poor and unfortunate are likely to be executed.

    Agree      I don't know      Disagree

**7.** There is too much danger of executing an innocent man.

    Agree      I don't know      Disagree

**8.** Executions set a violent example which may even encourage violence and killing in our society.

    Agree      I don't know      Disagree

**9.** It is immoral for society to take a life regardless of the crime the individual has committed.

    Agree      I don't know      Disagree

**10.** Any execution would make me sad regardless of the crime the individual has committed.

    Agree      I don't know      Disagree

For the knowledge items, the correct answers are: (1) true, (2) false, (3) false, (4) true, (5) false, and (6) false. When these questions were asked of 500 Californians, the average person said "uncertain" to 1.5 of 6 items and answered 2.4 correctly and 2.0 incorrectly (Ellsworth & Ross, 1983). However, most said that even if their guesses on these items and others were wrong, they couldn't imagine any facts that would change their attitude. Regarding the reasons for support or opposition, many people agreed with all or almost all of the reasons supporting their attitude and none of those against it.

You can see the difficulties of trying to persuade people, or even to arrange a compromise, on highly divisive issues such as the death penalty or abortion. People adopt a position and then accept any argument that favors it, and they reject or ignore any contrary information or argument.

Much is at stake here. In U.S. states that have instituted the death penalty, anyone who says, "I could never vote for the death penalty under any circumstances" is excluded from jury service on a murder trial because he or she cannot abide by the laws stating that a jury should consider the death penalty under certain circumstances. Because many opponents of the death penalty say that they are opposed under *all* circumstances, trial juries in murder cases are composed almost entirely of death-penalty supporters—who are more often White than Black, male than female, old than young, and more sympathetic to the prosecution than to the defense (Cowan, Thompson, & Ellsworth, 1984; Fitzgerald & Ellsworth, 1984).

## Delayed Influence of Messages

In certain cases a message may have no apparent influence on you when you hear it, but an important effect later. There are several reasons a message can have a delayed effect; we shall consider two examples.

### The Sleeper Effect

Suppose you reject a message because of peripheral route influences. For example, you reject a new idea without giving it much thought because you have a low opinion of the person who suggested it. If the idea is a good one, it may have a delayed effect. Weeks or months later, you may forget where you heard the idea and remember only the idea itself; at that time you can evaluate it on its merits (Hovland & Weiss, 1951; Pratkanis, Greenwald, Leippe, & Baumgardner, 1988). Psychologists use the term **sleeper effect** to describe *delayed persuasion by an initially rejected message.*

### Minority Influence

Delayed influence also occurs when a minority group, especially one that is not widely respected, proposes a worthwhile idea: The majority may reject the idea at first but adopt it later in some form. By "minority group," I do not necessarily mean an ethnic minority; the minority may be a political minority or any other outnumbered group.

If a minority group continually repeats a single simple message and if its members seem united, it has a good chance of eventually influencing the majority's decision. The minority's united, uncompromising stance forces the majority to wonder, "Why won't these people conform? Maybe their idea is better than we thought." The minority's influence often increases gradually, even if the majority hesitates to admit that the minority has swayed them (Wood, Lundgren, Ouellette, Busceme, & Blackstone, 1994). A minority, by expressing its views, can also prompt the majority to generate new ideas of its own (Nemeth, 1986). That is, by demonstrating the possibility of disagreement, the minority opens the way for other people to offer new suggestions

■   Julia Butterfly Hill camped out in a California redwood tree she named Luna. She remained in the tree for two years to protect it and to protest the logging of old-growth trees.

different from the original views of both the majority and the minority.

One powerful example of minority influence is that of the Socialist party of the United States, which ran candidates for elective offices from 1900 through the 1950s. The party never received more than 6% of the vote in any presidential election. No Socialist candidate was ever elected senator or governor, and only a few were elected to the House of Representatives (Shannon, 1955). Beginning in the 1930s, the party's membership and support began to dwindle, until eventually the party stopped nominating candidates.

Was that because the Socialists had failed? No. It was because they had already accomplished most of their goals! Most of the major points in the party's 1900 platform had been enacted into law (see Table 14.1). Of course, the Democrats and Republicans who voted for these changes claimed credit for the ideas. Still, the Socialist party, though always a minority, had exerted an enormous influence.

## CONCEPT CHECK

9. At a meeting of your student government, you suggest a new method of testing and grading students. The other members immediately reject your plan. Should you become discouraged and give up? If not, what should you do? (Check your answer on page 553.)

**TABLE 14.1  The Political Platform of the U.S. Socialist Party, 1900**

| Proposal | Eventual Fate of Proposal |
| --- | --- |
| Women's right to vote | Established by 19th Amendment to U.S. Constitution; ratified in 1920 |
| Old-age pensions | Included in the Social Security Act of 1935 |
| Unemployment insurance | Included in the Social Security Act of 1935; also guaranteed by the other state and federal legislation |
| Health and accident insurance | Included in part in the Social Security Act of 1935 and in the Medicare Act of 1965 |
| Increased wages, including minimum wage | First minimum-wage law passed in 1938; periodically updated since then |
| Reduction of working hours | Maximum 40-hour workweek (with exceptions) established by the Fair Labor Standards Act of 1938 |
| Public ownership of electric, gas, and other utilities and of the means of transportation and communication | Utilities not owned by government but heavily regulated by federal and state government since the 1930s |
| Initiative, referendum, and recall (mechanisms for private citizens to push for changes in legislation and for removal of elected officials) | Adopted by most state governments |

Sources: Foster, 1968; and Leuchtenburg, 1963.

## Ways of Presenting Persuasive Messages

Most persuasive messages fall into one of two categories: (a) do this to make something good happen and (b) do this to prevent something bad. Either one can be effective depending on the circumstances. Figure 14.5 shows a chain letter that has been circulated widely throughout the world over several decades. It has been called a "mind virus" because it inspires people to duplicate and spread the letter (Goodenough & Dawkins, 1994). Many people who receive this letter cannot resist its command to make copies and send them to others, even if they regard its message as a silly superstition. The letter claims to be offering "good luck" and "love," but it follows those promises with an implied threat: Allegedly, people who have failed to follow the instructions have been victims of terrible events. (They lost their job, lost a loved one, died, or had car problems!) The threat makes people feel nervous and uneasy if they decline to follow the instructions.

Fear messages are effective in some cases, as in the St. Jude letter, but not always. Appeals for money are often accompanied by implied threats, such as "If you don't send enough money to support our cause, then our political opponents will gain power and do terrible things." According to the research, messages that appeal to fear are effective only if they can convince people that the danger is real (Leventhal, 1970). People tend to disbelieve an organization that exaggerates the threats or sends "emergency" appeals too often.

Moreover, a fear message is most effective if people believe they can do something to reduce the danger, especially if they need to act only on rare occasions. For example, most people will visit a physician for an immunization against a contagious disease or for an x-ray to test for cancer. Many people will also change their sex habits to avoid herpes or AIDS, but not everyone remains consistent in these practices. Even fewer people consistently change their behavior to conserve natural resources or to avoid damaging the world's climate because most people doubt that their behavior will exert a major influence.

## Audience Variables

Some people are more easily persuaded than others are, and an individual may be more easily influenced at some times than at others. The ease of persuading someone depends on both person variables and situation variables.

### Person Variables

Who would you guess would be persuaded more easily—highly intelligent or less intelligent people? Actually, the answer depends on the message. Other things being equal, the peripheral route to persuasion is generally more effective with less intelligent people, who are more likely to accept an illogical or poorly supported idea (Eagly & Warren, 1976). The central route to persuasion is generally more effective with highly intelligent people, who are better able to understand complicated evidence and more likely to devote the energy necessary to evaluate it.

However, the effectiveness of the central or peripheral route depends not only on the listener's intelligence but also his or her level of interest. Suppose you listen to a debate about raising the tuition at Santa Enigma Junior College to pay for new buildings and equipment. You have never heard of the college, and you pay little attention. A neatly dressed, smooth-talking speaker can probably persuade you, using the peripheral route, even though you are an intelligent, well-educated person. But now imagine that you listen to a debate about raising tuition at your own college. The speaker could be the same, stating the same evidence and arguments, but you will now evaluate the arguments much more carefully, and the central route to persuasion will be more effective for you.

You also change depending on your mood. Which would you guess: Would you pay more attention to the logic of an argument when you are in a good mood or in a bad mood? Perhaps surprisingly, when people feel sad they are more likely to evaluate the evidence logically. Happy people seem to lower their guard and follow their impulses (Park & Banaji, 2000; Schwartz, Bless, & Bohner, 1991).

### Situation Variables

Other things being equal, a persuasive message is more effective if the speaker conveys the message, "I am similar to you" or "my message is right for people like you." We like people who resemble ourselves in almost any way. In one striking illustration of this tendency, students were asked to read a very unflattering description of Grigory Rasputin, the "mad monk of Russia," and then rate Rasputin's personality on several scales such as

**With Love All Things Are Possible.**

This paper has been sent to you for Luck. The original is in New England. It has been sent around the world. The Luck has been sent to you. You will receive good luck within 4 days of receiving this letter pending in turn you send it on. This is no joke. You will receive good luck in the mail. Send no money. Send copies to people you think need good luck. Do not send money cause faith has no price. Do not keep this letter. It must leave your hands within 96 hrs. An A.R.P. officer Joe Elliot received $40,000,000. George Welch lost his wife 5 days after this letter. However before her death he received $7,775,000. Please send copies and see what happens after 4 days. The chain comes from Venezula and was written by Saul Anthony Degnas, a missionary from S.America. Since that copy must tour the World. You must make 20 copies and send them to friends and associates after a few days you will get a surprise. This is love even if you are not superstitious. Do Note the following: Contonare Dias received this letter in 1903. He asked his Sec'y. to make copies and send them out. A few days later he won a lottery of 20 million dollars. Carl Dobbitt, an office employee received the letter - forgot it had to leave his hands within 96 hrs. He lost his job. After finding the letter again he made copies and mailed 20 copies. A few days later he got a better job. Dolan Fairchild received the letter and not believing he threw it away. 9 days later he died. In 1987 the letter was received by a young woman in Calif. It was faded and hardly readable. She promised her self she would recype the letter and send it on but, she put it aside to do later. She was plagued with various problems, including expensive car problems. This letter did not leave her hands in 96 hrs. She finally typed the letter as promised and got a new car. Remember send no money. Do not ignor this - it works.

St. Jude

**FIGURE 14.5** If you received a copy of this chain letter, would you copy it and send it on to other people, as it requests? Why or why not?

■ Grigory Rasputin was a contemptible person. However, people who are told he resembled them, even in trivial ways, soften their criticisms.

pleasant to unpleasant, effective to ineffective, and strong to weak. All students read the same description except for Rasputin's birth date: In some cases Rasputin's birth date had been changed to match the student's own birth date. Students who thought Rasputin had the same birth date as their own liked him better than other students did. Nobody thought he was "pleasant," but many did rate him as "strong" and "effective" (Finch & Cialdini, 1989).

You have probably heard speakers who begin by stressing their resemblance to the audience: "I remember when I was a student like you." "I grew up in a town similar to this one." "I believe in family values, and I'm sure you do too."

### People with Heightened Resistance
Psychologists long assumed that people avoided reading or listening to arguments with which they disagree. Researchers have found, however, that people do expose themselves to ideas they dislike, and they remember the arguments surprisingly well. However, they argue against them and resist any major change in their attitudes (Eagly, Kulesa, Chen, & Chaiken, 2001). *Simply informing participants a few minutes ahead of time that they are about to hear a persuasive speech activates their resistance and weakens the effect of the talk on their attitudes* (Petty & Cacioppo, 1977). This tendency is called the **forewarning effect.**

With the **inoculation effect,** *people first hear a weak argument and then a stronger argument supporting the same conclusion.* After they have rejected the first argument, they are likely to reject the second one also. In one ex-

periment people listened to speeches *against* brushing their teeth after every meal. Some of them heard just a strong argument (e.g., "Brushing your teeth too frequently wears away tooth enamel, leading to serious disease"). Others first heard a weak argument and then the strong argument 2 days later. Still others first heard an argument *for* toothbrushing and then the strong argument against it. Only the people who heard the weak antibrushing argument before the strong one resisted its influence; the other two groups found it highly persuasive (McGuire & Papageorgis, 1961). So if you want to convince someone, present your best evidence first; don't start with evidence that he or she may consider faulty.

### C O N C E P T   C H E C K

**10.** If you want your children to preserve the beliefs and attitudes you try to teach them, should you give them only arguments that support those beliefs or should you also expose them to attacks on those beliefs? Why? (Check your answers on page 553.)

## Strategies of Persuasion

People representing anything from worthless products to noble charities will sometimes ask you to give more of your time or money than you would rationally choose to spend. You should understand several of their techniques so that you can resist these appeals.

*One technique is to make a modest request at first and then to follow it with a larger request.* This procedure is called the **foot-in-the-door technique.** When Jonathan Freedman and Scott Fraser (1966) asked suburban residents in Palo Alto, California, to put a small "Drive Safely" sign in their windows, most of them agreed to do so. A couple of weeks later, other researchers asked the same residents to let them set up a large, unsightly "Drive Safely" billboard in their front yards for 10 days. They also made the request to some residents that had not been approached by the first researchers. Of those who had already agreed to display the small sign, 76% agreed to the billboard. Only 17% of the others agreed. Even agreeing to make as small a commitment as signing a petition to support a cause significantly increases the probability that people will later donate money to that cause (Schwarzwald, Bizman, & Raz, 1983).

In another approach, called the **door-in-the-face technique** (Cialdini et al., 1975), *someone follows an outrageous initial request with a much more reasonable second one,* implying that if you refused the first request, you should compromise by agreeing to the second. For example, I once received a telephone call from a college alumni association asking me to show my loyalty by contributing $1000. When I apologetically declined, the caller acted sympathetic (as if to say, "It's too bad you don't have a high-paying job like all our other alumni . . .") and then asked whether I could contribute $500. And if not $500, how about $200? And so forth. The implication was that, if I had refused the original request, I should "compromise" by donating a smaller amount.

Robert Cialdini and his colleagues (1975) demonstrated the power of the door-in-the-face technique with a clever experiment. They asked one group of college students, chosen randomly, whether they would be willing to chaperone a group from the juvenile detention center on a trip to the zoo. Only 17% said they would. They asked other students to spend 2 hours per week for 2 years working as counselors with juvenile delinquents. Not surprisingly, all of them refused. But then the researchers asked them, "If you won't do that, would you chaperone a group from the juvenile detention center on one trip to the zoo?" Half of them said they would. Apparently, they felt that the researchers were conceding a great deal and that it was only fair to meet them halfway.

Someone using the **bait-and-switch technique** *first offers an extremely favorable deal and then makes additional demands after the other person has committed to the deal.* Alternatively, the person might offer a product at a very low price to get customers to the store but then claim to be out of the product and try to sell them something else. For example, a car dealer offers you an exceptionally good price on a new car and a most generous price for the trade-in of your old car. You weren't sure you wanted this make of car, but the deal is too good to resist. After you have committed yourself to buying this car, the dealer checks with the boss, who rejects the deal. Your salesperson comes back saying, "I'm so sorry. I forgot that this car has some special features that raise the value. If we sold it for the price I originally quoted, we'd lose money." So you agree to a higher price. Then the company's used car specialist looks at your old car and "corrects" the trade-in value to a lower amount. Still, you have already committed yourself, so you don't back out. Eventually, you leave with a deal that you would not have accepted at the start.

In the **that's-not-all technique,** *someone makes an offer and then improves the offer before anyone has a chance to reply.* The television announcer says, "Here's your chance to buy this amazing combination paper shredder and coffeemaker for only $39.95. But wait, there's more! We'll throw in a can of dog deodorant! And this handy windshield wiper cleaner and a subscription to *Modern Lobotomist*! And if you act now, you can get this amazing offer, which usually costs $39.95, for only $19.95! Call this number!" People who hear the first offer and then the "improved" offer are more likely to comply than are people who first hear the "improved" offer (Burger, 1986).

 **C** ONCEPT CHECK

11. Identify each of the following as an example of the foot-in-the-door technique, the door-in-the-face technique, or the that's-not-all technique.
    a. Your boss says, "We need to cut costs drastically

around here. I'm afraid I'm going to have to cut your salary in half." You protest vigorously. Your boss replies, "Well, I suppose we could cut expenses some other way. Maybe I can give you just a 5% cut." "Thanks," you reply. "I can live with that."
    b. A store marks its prices "25% off" and then scratches that out and marks them "50% off!" Though the prices are now about the same as at competing stores, customers flock into the store.
    c. A friend asks you to help carry some supplies over to the elementary school for an afternoon tutoring program. When you get there, the principal says that one of the tutors is late and asks whether you could take her place until she arrives. You agree and spend the rest of the afternoon tutoring. The principal then talks you into coming back every week as a tutor. (Check your answers on page 553.)

# Cognitive Dissonance

On page 544 we considered whether a change in people's attitudes will change their behavior. The theory of cognitive dissonance reverses the direction: It holds that, when people's behavior changes, their attitudes will change (Festinger, 1957).

**Cognitive dissonance** is *a state of unpleasant tension that people experience when they hold contradictory attitudes or when their behavior is inconsistent with their attitudes, especially if they are displeased about this inconsistency.* For example, if you pride yourself on honesty and find yourself saying something you do not believe, you feel tension. You can reduce that tension in three ways: You can change what you are saying to match your attitudes, change your attitude to match what you are saying, or adopt an explanation that justifies your behavior under the circumstances (Wicklund & Brehm, 1976) (see Figure 14.6). Although you might adopt any of these options, most of the existing research has focused on how cognitive dissonance changes people's attitudes.

## Evidence Favoring the Cognitive Dissonance Theory

Leon Festinger and J. Merrill Carlsmith (1959) carried out the following classic experiment on cognitive dissonance. Imagine yourself as one of the participants. The experimenters explain that they are studying motor behavior. They show you a board full of pegs. Your task is to take each peg out of the board, rotate it one-fourth of a turn, and return it to the board. When you finish all the pegs, you start over from the top, rotating all the pegs again as quickly and accurately as possible for an hour. As you proceed an experimenter silently takes notes. You find your task tedious and boring.

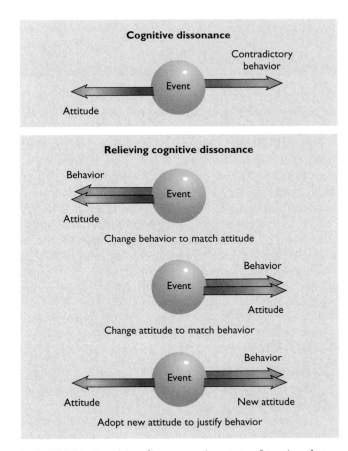

**FIGURE 14.6** Cognitive dissonance is a state of tension that arises when people perceive that their attitudes do not match their behavior. Theoretically, they could resolve this discrepancy by changing either their attitudes or their behavior or by developing a new attitude or excuse to explain the discrepancy. Most of the research, however, has focused on how cognitive dissonance leads to a change of attitude.

At the end of the hour, the experimenter thanks you for participating and "explains" to you (falsely) that the study's purpose was to determine whether people's performances are influenced by their attitudes toward the task. You were in the neutral-attitude group, but those in the positive-attitude group are told before they start that this will be an enjoyable, interesting experience. In fact, the experimenter continues, right now the research assistant is supposed to give that instruction to the next participant, a young woman waiting in the next room. The experimenter excuses himself to find the research assistant and then returns distraught. The assistant is nowhere to be found, he says. He turns to you and asks, "Would you be willing to tell the next participant that you thought this was an interesting, enjoyable experiment? If so, I will pay you."

Assume that you consent, as most students in the study did. After you tell that woman in the next room that you enjoyed the study, what would you actually think of the study, assuming the experimenter paid you $1? What if he paid you $20? (This study occurred in the 1950s, before decades of inflation. In today's money that $20 would be worth more than $100.)

In this study, after participants told the woman how much fun the experiment was, they left, believing the study was over. As they walked down the hall, they were met by a representative of the psychology department who explained that the department wanted to find out what kinds of experiments were being conducted and whether they were educationally worthwhile. (The answers to these questions were the real point of the experiment.) Participants were asked how enjoyable they considered the experiment and whether they would be willing to participate in a similar experiment later.

The students who received $20 said they thought the experiment was boring and that they wanted nothing to do with another such experiment. However, contrary to what you might guess, those who received $1 said they enjoyed the experiment and would be willing to participate again (Figure 14.7).

Why? According to the theory of cognitive dissonance, those who accepted $20 to tell a lie experienced little conflict. They knew they were lying, but they also knew why: for the $20. They had no reason to change their original low opinion of the experiment. However, the students who had told a lie for only $1 felt a conflict between their true attitude and what they had said about

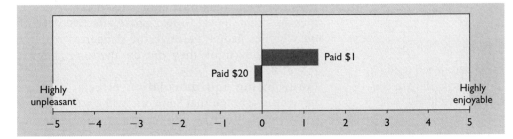

**FIGURE 14.7** In a classic experiment demonstrating cognitive dissonance, participants were paid either $1 or $20 for telling another subject that they enjoyed an experiment (which was actually boring). Later they were asked for their real opinions. Those participants who were paid the smaller amount said that they enjoyed the study more than the others. (Based on data from Festinger & Carlsmith, 1959)

the experiment. The small payment provided little reason for lying, so they experienced cognitive dissonance—an unpleasant tension. They did not want to feel bad about telling a lie, so the only way they could reduce their tension was to change their attitude by deciding that the experiment really had been interesting after all. ("I learned a lot of interesting things about myself, like . . . uh . . . how good I am at rotating pegs.")

The idea of cognitive dissonance attracted much attention and inspired a great deal of research (Aronson, 1997). Here are two representative examples:

• An experimenter left a child in a room with toys but forbade the child to play with one particular toy. If the experimenter threatened the child with severe punishment for playing with the toy, the child avoided it but still regarded it as desirable. However, if the experimenter merely said that he or she would be unhappy or disappointed if the child played with that toy, the child avoided the toy and said (even weeks later) that it was not a good toy (Aronson & Carlsmith, 1963).

• The experimenter asked college students to write an essay defending a position that the experimenter knew, from previous information, was contrary to the students' beliefs. For example, college students who favored freer access to alcohol might be asked to write essays on why the college should increase restrictions on alcohol. Those who were told they must write the essays did not change their views significantly, but those who were asked to "please" write the essay and were also reminded that they did so voluntarily generally came to agree with what they wrote (Croyle & Cooper, 1983).

The general principle is that, if you entice people to do something by means of a minimum reward or a tiny threat so that they are acting voluntarily or almost voluntarily, they will change their attitudes to defend what they are doing and reduce cognitive dissonance. This procedure is a powerful way of changing attitudes because people are actively participating, not just quietly listening to someone. This module began with the statement, "If you want to change people's behavior, you have to change their attitudes first." The results of cognitive dissonance experiments tell us quite the opposite: If you start by changing people's behavior, their attitudes will change too.

## CONCEPT CHECKS

12. Suppose your parents pay you to get a good grade in a course that you consider boring. According to cognitive dissonance theory, are you more likely to develop a positive attitude toward your studies if your parents pay you $10 or $100?
13. The effort to avoid cognitive dissonance leads to consistency in behavior. Use that principle to explain the foot-in-the-door technique. (Check your answers on page 553.)

## IN CLOSING
### Persuasion and Manipulation

When you are forming an attitude about something of little consequence to you, it is understandable that you will follow the peripheral route, paying little attention to the complexities of the evidence. When you are dealing with important matters, however, such as how you will spend your time and money or who to choose for your partner in life, you will almost certainly follow the central route, examining the facts as carefully as you can. It is important to be alert to some of the influences that might throw you off course, such as the foot-in-the-door technique, bait-and-switch, and cognitive dissonance. Advertisers, politicians, and vast numbers of others try to polish their techniques of persuasion, and not everyone has your best interest at heart.

## Summary

• **Attitudes.** An attitude is a like or dislike of something or somebody that influences our behavior toward that thing or person. (page 544)
• **Two routes to persuasion.** When people consider a topic of little importance to them, they are easily persuaded by the speaker's appearance and other superficial factors, regardless of the strength or weakness of the evidence. When people care about the topic, they pay more attention to logic and to the quality of the evidence. (page 545)
• **Resistant attitudes.** On a few topics, such as the death penalty, many people form entrenched attitudes that are based on little real information. (page 545)
• **Sleeper effect.** When people reject a message because of their low regard for the person who proposed it, they sometimes forget where they heard the idea and later come to accept it. (page 546)
• **Minority influence.** Although a minority may have little influence at first, it can, through persistent repetition of its message, eventually persuade the majority to adopt its position or to consider other alternatives. (page 547)
• **Influence of fear-inducing messages.** Whether messages that appeal to fear prove effective depends on whether people perceive the danger as real and whether they think they can do anything about it. (page 548)
• **Forewarning and inoculation effects.** If people have been warned that someone will try to persuade them of something, or if they have previously heard a weak version of the persuasive argument, they tend to resist the argument more strongly than they otherwise would have. (page 549)
• **Strategies of persuasion.** Several procedures can influence people to do something they would not have

done otherwise. These include starting with a tiny request and then increasing it, starting with an enormous request and offering to compromise, offering a generous deal and then demanding more, and offering a moderate deal and then adding inducements. (page 549)

- **Cognitive dissonance.** Cognitive dissonance is a state of unpleasant tension that arises from contradictory attitudes or from behavior that conflicts with a person's attitudes. When people's behavior does not match their attitudes, they try to eliminate the inconsistency by changing either their behavior or their attitudes. (page 550)

## Answers to Concept Checks

7. Some people express one attitude openly but demonstrate another attitude on the Implicit Attitudes Test. (page 545)

8. You will pay more attention to the evidence and logic, following the central route to persuasion, for the decision about your major. (page 545)

9. The fact that your idea was overwhelmingly rejected does not mean that you should give up. If you and a few allies continue to present this plan in a simple way, showing apparent agreement among yourselves, the majority may eventually endorse a similar plan—but probably without giving you credit for suggesting the idea. (page 547)

10. You should expose them to weak attacks on their beliefs so that they will learn how to resist such attacks. Otherwise, they will be like children who grow up in a germ-free environment: They will develop no "immunity" and will thus be vulnerable when their beliefs are attacked. (page 549)

11. **a.** door-in-the-face technique; **b.** that's-not-all technique; **c.** foot-in-the-door technique. (page 550)

12. You will come to like your studies more if you are paid $10 than if you are paid $100. If you are paid only $10, you won't be able to tell yourself that you are studying harder only for the money. Instead, you will tell yourself that you must be really interested. The theory of intrinsic and extrinsic motivation leads to the same prediction: If you study hard in the absence of any strong external reason, you will perceive that you have internal reasons for studying. (page 552)

13. Once you have agreed to a small request, you can maintain consistency (decrease dissonance) by agreeing to similar requests in the future. (page 552)

# Interpersonal Attraction

*How do we choose our partners? Do men and women choose on the same basis?*

William Proxmire, a former U.S. senator, used to give Golden Fleece Awards to those who, in his opinion, most flagrantly wasted the taxpayers' money. He once bestowed an award on some psychologists who had received a federal grant to study how people fall in love. According to Proxmire, the research was pointless because people do not want to understand love. They prefer, he said, to let such matters remain a mystery.

This module presents the information Senator Proxmire thought you did not want to know.

## Establishing Lasting Relationships

Of all the people you meet, how do you choose those few who become your friends? Here we shall consider factors relevant to both friendships and dating relationships; later we shall specifically discuss dating and marriage.

### Proximity and Familiarity

**Proximity** means *closeness*. (It comes from the same root as *approximate*.) Not surprisingly, *we are most likely to become friends with people who live or work in close proximity and who become familiar to us.* At the start of a school year, Robert Hays (1985) asked college students to name two other students with whom they thought they might become friends. After 3 months he found that more of the potential friends who lived close together had become friends than had those who lived farther apart.

Proximity increases the probability that two people will become friends or lovers, partly by giving them more opportunities to meet and talk and partly by just making them familiar with each other. Other things being equal, *the more often we come in contact with someone—or with an inanimate object such as a food or a painting—the more we tend to like that person or object* (Saegert, Swap, & Zajonc, 1973; Zajonc, 1968). This tendency is known as the **mere exposure effect.** The exception is that repeated exposure to someone or something we hate will not increase our liking.

### Similarity

Here's another finding that will hardly surprise you: Most close friends resemble one another in age, physical attractiveness, political and religious beliefs, intelligence, academic interests, religion, and attitudes (Laumann, 1969). Most people also date and eventually marry people who closely resemble themselves in many ways. Couples who marry in spite of major differences in personality are likely to have troubled marriages (Russell & Wells, 1991).

Choice of friends raises a different issue for members of racial or ethnic minorities. Members of minority groups often have many friends with whom they have little in common, except for being members of the same minority group. That tendency is especially strong for a badly outnumbered group: If you can find only a few members of your group, you may stick together even if you have few interests in common. Friendships between members of different ethnic groups are, as you would guess, usually based on similar interests and activities (Hamm, 2000).

Do you like people better when you learn that their beliefs and attitudes are similar to yours? That question

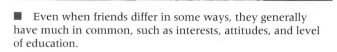

■ Even when friends differ in some ways, they generally have much in common, such as interests, attitudes, and level of education.

turns out to be a little trickier than it sounds at first. You probably like most of the people you meet until you have a reason to alter your judgment. If you think at all about a new acquaintance's beliefs and attitudes, you probably assume that he or she shares your own beliefs and attitudes . . . because most people do, don't they? After all, your opinions and actions are normal and correct, so of course most other people share them (Alicke & Largo, 1995). Therefore, finding a disagreement with someone *lowers* your regard for them more than finding an agreement *increases* your regard (Rosenbaum, 1986).

## Confirmation of Self-Concept

You might well be saying, "Big deal. People make friends with others who live nearby and resemble them. Psychologists needed research to demonstrate *that?*"

Occasionally, it is worthwhile to test the obvious in case it might be wrong. For example, suppose you are in a research study. First you are asked to describe yourself. Then two other people tell you how they reacted. The first person says, "You seem a pleasant, honest person. You're intelligent and you have some interesting ideas and a nice sense of humor."

The second says, "I hate to be rude, but frankly you seem superficial. You're trying to make a good impression, but for me, you're failing. You drift aimlessly from one topic to another; you can't even organize your thoughts."

Which one would you choose to spend time with? The obvious answer is the first one. However, many people with very low self-esteem choose the person who gave them a low evaluation (Swann, 1997). Evidently, people seek the company of someone who confirms their self-evaluation. Some who think little of themselves find it satisfying to be with others who share that low evaluation.

You can see the harmful consequences of this tendency. Someone with a low self-evaluation chooses friends and perhaps even a husband or wife who constantly criticizes. The result of all that criticizing is even lower self-esteem.

## The Equity Principle

According to **exchange** or **equity theories,** *social relationships are transactions in which partners exchange goods and services.* In some cases the businesslike nature of a romantic relationship is fairly blatant. In the "Singles' Ads" sections of many newspapers, those seeking a relationship describe what they have to offer ("35-year-old divorced male, 6' 1", business executive, athletic . . .") and what they want in return ("seeks warm, caring, attractive woman, age 27–33 . . ."). The ads resemble the "asked" and "bid" columns for the stock exchange (Kenrick & Trost, 1989). People run ads for nonromantic friendships less often, but the same principle applies: A good friendship has a balance of giving and taking.

As in business, a friendship or romantic relationship is most stable if both partners believe the deal is fair. It is easiest to establish a fair deal if the partners are about equally attractive and intelligent, contribute about equally to the finances and the chores, and so forth. With some couples one partner is wealthier but the other is more attractive, or one is more intelligent but the other is very kind and considerate, or some other kind of compensation exists. Those arrangements can also seem fair, although it is more difficult to be sure.

## CONCEPT CHECK

14. A person your own age from another country moves next door. Neither of you speaks the other's language. Are you likely to become friends? What factors will tend to strengthen the likelihood of your becoming friends? What factors will tend to weaken it? (Check your answers on page 561.)

# Special Concerns in Selecting a Mate

Choosing a partner for marriage (or the equivalent of marriage) is not the same as choosing other kinds of friends, mostly because of the extra dimension of raising children. Yes, I know, not everyone wants to get married, not all married couples plan to have children, and many unmarried people rear children. What I shall describe does not apply to everyone. Still, it applies to those who hope to marry and have children.

## Physical Attractiveness

What characteristics do you look for in a person you date and perhaps eventually marry? You probably reply that you want "someone who is intelligent, honest, easy to talk to, with a good sense of humor."

Now imagine a friend says, "Hey, you're not doing anything this weekend, right? How about going on a blind date with my cousin who is visiting for the weekend?"

"Well, I don't know. Tell me about your cousin."

"My cousin is intelligent, honest, easy to talk to, and has a good sense of humor."

Are you eager to date this person? Probably not. Your friend did not even mention the cousin's appearance, so you assume the worst. Were you being dishonest when you said you wanted someone intelligent, honest, and easy to talk to? Not really. You did not mention appearance because you assumed that people would take that for granted. (You also didn't say that you hope your date speaks English and doesn't have a prison record. You don't need to mention the obvious.)

In one study social psychologists arranged blind dates for 332 freshman couples for a dance before the start of classes. They asked participants to fill out lengthy questionnaires, but the experimenters actually paired students at random. Midway through the dance, the experimenters separated the men and women and asked them to rate how much they liked their dates. The only factor that influenced the ratings was appearance (Walster, Aronson, Abrahams, & Rottman, 1966). Similarities of attitudes, personality, and intelligence counted for almost nothing. Surprising? Hardly. During the brief time they had spent together at the dance, the couples had little opportunity to learn about each other. Intelligence, honesty, and other character values do become important in a lasting relationship, but usually not in the first hour or two.

On the average, attractive people are judged more favorably than other people. They have more friends and they are treated better. In turn they behave in friendlier and more outgoing ways (Langlois et al., 2000). Exceptions are plentiful, of course, but the usual result is a self-fulfilling prophecy: Because people expect to like attractive people, they treat them better, and the attractive people therefore become more likable.

## The Possible Biological Value of Attractiveness

Why is physical appearance so important in a romantic relationship? We take its importance so much for granted that we don't even understand why there is a question, so for a moment let's look in a more detached way at other species. In many bird species, early in the mating season, females shop around among the unmated males of their species and choose one that is brilliantly colored and singing vigorously from the treetops. In a few species, a female also prefers a male with an especially long tail (Figure 14.8). From an evolutionary standpoint, aren't these choices foolish? Females are choosing males that devoted enormous energy to feather color. (It takes more energy to produce bright colors than dull ones.) Singing loudly from the treetops is practically an invitation to hawks and eagles. If he has a long tail, it may look pretty, but it interferes with his flying. Why should the female prefer a mate who wastes his energies and endangers his life?

**FIGURE 14.8** In a few bird species, males with very long tails attract more mates. However, they pay a price: The long tail impairs their flying abilities. Only healthy males can afford this handicap.

Biologists eventually decided that wasting energy and risking life were precisely the point (Zahavi & Zahavi, 1997). Only a healthy, vigorous male can afford to spend that much energy on colorful feathers or a long tail or risk predation by singing from an exposed perch. A weak or sickly male who spent his energies in those ways would probably die young. In effect, a colorful, singing male is screaming, "Look at me! I am so vigorous that I can afford to take crazy risks, and I have so much energy to spare that I can afford to waste it. You will certainly want me as the father of your children!" The female, we presume, does not understand why she is attracted to colorful, loudly singing males. She just is because throughout her evolutionary history, females who chose colorful, loudly singing males generally had energetic partners who provided them with plenty of food while they were sitting on the nest and probably also provided the babies with good genes.

So it would seem, theoretically. The problem has been that a male's bright colors, vigorous singing, and even health are mainly due to his luck in finding a good feeding place. So far, researchers haven't found much evidence that a male bird's (or fish's) attractiveness indicates much about good genes (Brooks, 2000; Cunningham & Russell, 2000).

Now back to humans: Is attractiveness in humans a valid indicator of health, fertility, and other favorable characteristics? Theoretically, it should be. Certainly, many illnesses decrease people's attractiveness. Also, *good-looking* is in many regards similar to *normal*. A computer can take photographs of a large number of moderately similar people, all sitting in the same position and looking in the same direction, and average their faces. Most people regard the resulting averaged face as more attractive than most of the original faces (Langlois & Roggman, 1990; Langlois, Roggman, & Musselman, 1994; Rhodes, Sumich, & Byatt, 1999) (see Figure 14.9). In other words a highly attractive face has an average nose, about an average mouth, about an average distance between the eyes, and so forth. If we note anything "unusual" about an attractive face, it is the absence of irregularities—no crooked teeth, no skin blemishes, no asymmetries or peculiarities.

Why is normal attractive? One hypothesis is that a normal face is probably a healthy face. Presumably, the genes for an average face have spread in the population because they are linked to success. Any face that departs much from the average is risky because it might indicate a genetic mutation. A competing hypothesis, however, is that we like the normal, average face because it is familiar, and we like anything that is familiar. Research has found that people tend to think that "average-looking" dogs, birds, and wristwatches are attractive (Halberstadt & Rhodes, 2000). So our preference for normal faces might have nothing to do with healthy genes. Still, in defense of the evolutionary view, researchers have found that judgments of facial attractiveness are similar across

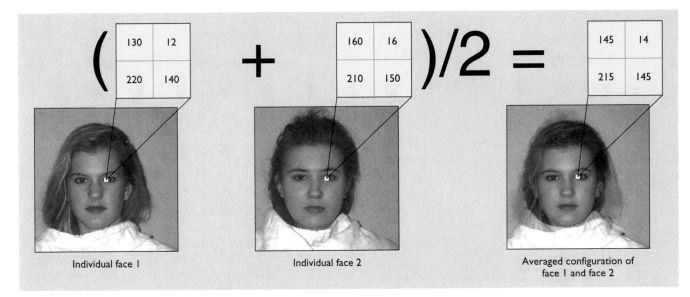

| | | | | | | |
|---|---|---|---|---|---|---|
| 130 | 12 | | 160 | 16 | | 145 | 14 |
| 220 | 140 | | 210 | 150 | | 215 | 145 |

Individual face 1       Individual face 2       Averaged configuration of face 1 and face 2

**FIGURE 14.9**  A computer averaged a set of faces by measuring the gray value of each point on each picture and then producing a new picture with the average of the grays at each point. This set of photos illustrates the procedure for two original faces. The numbers are for illustrative purposes only. Especially when a large number of faces have been averaged, most people rate the resulting "average" face more attractive than most of the originals. (From Langlois, Roggman, & Musselman, 1994)

cultures and that even young infants prefer to look at the same faces that adults consider attractive (Berry, 2000).

The best way to settle this issue is to test whether attractive people tend to be healthier or more fertile than others. In one study researchers obtained photos of hundreds of teenagers from long ago. They asked other people to rate the faces for attractiveness; they also obtained extensive medical records for the people in the photos. The ratings of attractiveness did not correlate reliably with health, either for adolescence or later life. People who were rated attractive were more likely to marry, and especially to marry early, but unattractive people who did marry were just as likely to have children as the more attractive people (Kalick, Zebrowitz, Langlois, & Johnson, 1998). Evidently, at least for this sample, attractiveness had nothing to do with health or fertility.

 If facial attractiveness is a poor cue to health, what about the rest of the body? According to one theory, men should prefer women with a narrow waist and wide hips—a waist-to-hip ratio of about 0.7—because medical researchers believe women with that ratio are most likely to be healthy and fertile. Examine the drawings of women's figures in Figure 14.10. Which one do you consider most attractive? The mean preferences are close to 0.7 for many cultures, but exceptions do occur. In the United States, both men and women rated even thinner women as the most attractive (Tassinary & Hansen, 1998). In non-Westernized cultures of Tanzania and southeastern Peru, most men regarded heavier women (with a high waist-to-hip ratio) as the most attractive (Marlowe & Wetsman, 2001; Yu & Shepard, 1998). In short, preferences for female shape

vary somewhat across cultures and do not necessarily match what the medical profession states is healthy or fertile.

Where do all these studies leave us? Theoretically, it would make sense to be attracted to healthy mates with good genes, and we can imagine how good genes should lead to a good physical appearance. That is, good appearance should represent "truthful advertising." However, so far researchers have not found a strong link between good appearance and healthy genes for either humans or nonhumans. On the one hand, we should not cling to a theory not supported by the evidence. On the other hand, we should not abandon an appealing theory too quickly. Maybe we just have not yet found the best way to test it. For example, maybe attractiveness is a good cue to health in human societies with poor nutrition and medical care. The results might differ for less prosperous societies. Until we have more extensive research, we cannot be sure.

## CONCEPT CHECK

**15.** According to the evolutionary theory, attractiveness is a sign of good health. Why would it be difficult for an unhealthy individual to produce "counterfeit" attractiveness? (Check your answer on page 561.)

## Men's and Women's Preferences

 Imagine that two people have expressed a desire to date you, and there is reason to believe that if the date goes well it could lead to a

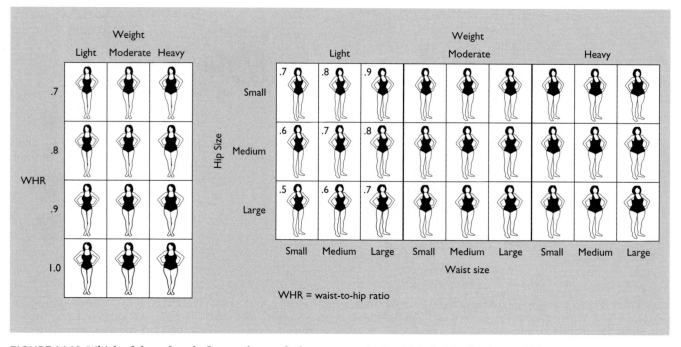

FIGURE 14.10 Which of these female figures do you find most attractive? Which do you think would be most likely to have babies successfully? In one study most men and women picked one of the thinner women as most attractive but one of the heavier women as most likely to be fertile, thereby failing to support the theory that attractive means fertile. (From Tassinary & Hansen, 1998)

long-term relationship and eventual marriage. You have to choose between the two; you cannot date both. Here are the descriptions:

The choice for women: Man A is extraordinarily good-looking. He works as a waiter at a small restaurant and has no ambition to do anything more. Man B is about average looking. He patented an invention and sold it for a fortune. He was recently accepted to a prestigious medical school, and he is said to have an outstanding career ahead as a medical researcher.

The choice for men: Woman A is extraordinarily good-looking. She works as a waitress at a small restaurant and has no ambition to do anything more. Woman B is about average looking. She patented an invention and sold it for a fortune. She was recently accepted to a prestigious medical school, and she is said to have an outstanding career ahead as a medical researcher.

I have offered these choices to my own classes, and I think you can guess the results: Most of the women choose man B, and most of the men choose woman A. (Curiously, secret ballots give very different results from a show of hands, but the trend is in the same direction.)

The most interesting point about these trends is that they are present in all cultures for which we have data (Buss, 2000a). Men everywhere want a young, attractive wife, and women everywhere prefer a husband who can be a good provider. Another trend found worldwide is that many men will accept almost partner for a short-term sexual relationship, whereas most women either refuse any short-term sexual relationship or accept only a

very appealing partner (Buss, 2000a). Still another trend pertains to jealousy: In most cultures men insist that women be sexually faithful more than women require fidelity from men. In some cultures, such as China, men and women are equally insistent on the other's sexual fidelity, and in Sweden both are equally unconcerned. However, in no culture are women more insistent than men on their partners' sexual fidelity. On the other hand, women are generally more upset than men are if their partners become emotionally close to someone else (Buss, Larsen, Westen, & Semmelroth, 1992; Buunk, Angleitner, Oubaid, & Buss, 1996).

All of those trends are well confirmed, but the question is why. One explanation is that we have evolved to be that way. The argument goes as follows. First, for men (Buss, 2000a; Geary, 2000): A man who mates with as many women as possible has some chance of spreading his genes if he makes some of them pregnant and they manage to rear the children successfully, with or without his help. So if a quick sexual relationship requires little investment on his part, he has almost nothing to lose. His other strategy is to marry and then devote his energies to keeping the woman and her children healthy. However, marriage spreads his genes only if she is fertile. A young woman will be fertile for a long time and an attractive woman is (perhaps) more likely to be fertile. So men increase their probable contribution to the gene pool if they marry young, attractive women. Furthermore, if a man is going to pair with just one woman for life and help rear her children, he should make sure that she is sexually faithful; otherwise, he devotes his energies to rearing another man's children.

Now for women (Bjorklund & Shackelford, 1999; Gangestad, 2000): A woman can become pregnant no more than once every 9 months, and having sex with many partners cannot give her more babies than sex with one partner. Given that she will have limited mobility during late pregnancy and during the early months of child care, she should prefer a man who can provide food and other resources. If her husband has a brief sexual affair with some other woman, it is not necessarily a disaster. (A woman doesn't have to worry about whether she is the mother of her child as a man has to worry about whether he is the father.) However, if her husband becomes emotionally close to another woman, the threat is that he might devote his resources to that other woman.

According to theorists of evolutionary psychology, the differences in men's and women's investments in mating and child care have led our species to evolve these tendencies in behavior. The alternative view is that people throughout the world have learned these preferences (Eagly & Wood, 1999). The fact that certain tendencies occur in all cultures does not necessarily mean that they are built in and genetically controlled. As an analogy, people throughout the world believe that 2 + 2 = 4, but not because we have a gene for that belief. In all cultures people aim an arrow higher if they want it to go farther, but not because we share a gene for that tendency. We all learn similar rules by living in the same world.

Furthermore, although women throughout the world do prefer financially secure men who can provide resources, the strength of that preference varies by cultures. As you might guess, it is strongest in cultures where women have the least opportunity to get an education, hold a job, or accumulate property of their own (Kasser & Sharma, 1999).

Finally, is it really true that women gain nothing from having sex with multiple partners? Sarah Hrdy (2000) has pointed out a number of potential benefits, including the following:

- Her husband might be infertile.
- Another man might have better genes than her husband and give her better children.
- The other man may provide her with additional resources and protection. (In effect she trades sex for resources.)
- She might be able to "trade up," leaving her husband and joining the new partner.
- If she has sex with many men, all of them may provide a modest amount of care and protection for her children. (After all, any of them might be the father.)

An important point here is that we cannot reconstruct the social life of our ancestors with great confidence. Mating customs vary from one human culture to another, and even from one chimpanzee troop to another (Parish & deWaal, 2000).

What would count as decisive evidence for or against the evolutionary theory of men's and women's partner preferences? Theoretically, one could find a gene that influences partner choice. (If so, then men who had mutations in that gene might prefer old, ugly women, and women with a mutation would seek impoverished men!) A more feasible strategy would be to examine cultural differences more closely or to study how partner preferences develop in childhood and early adolescence. Theories about how human behavior evolved can be plausible, but they are hard to test.

## CONCEPT CHECK

16. Suppose astronauts discover humanlike beings on another planet, whose biology and culture resemble ours except that all men have exactly the same wealth and women remain fertile all their lives instead of losing their fertility at menopause. What would you predict about the mate preferences of men and women on this planet? (Check your answer on page 561.)

# Marriage

A couple that decides to marry pledges that they will stay together as long as they both shall live, and yet a distressing percentage of marriages end in divorce. What went wrong?

Sometimes people change in ways they could not have foreseen, but in many cases the problem is that people simply marry the wrong partners. The Western custom of dating is well adapted for determining whether two people enjoy the same kinds of entertainment but not for determining the factors that are critical for long-term family life. Questionnaire studies have found that, as couples continue to date, their estimates of each other's sexual histories, activity preferences, and so forth become more *confident*, but not more *accurate* (Swann & Gill, 1997).

 Answer the following questions, first for yourself and second *as you think your dating partner would answer them*. (Several of these questions assume a heterosexual relationship; disregard any items that do not apply to you.)

1. After you marry or establish another long-term relationship, how often would you want to visit your parents? Your in-laws?
2. How many children do you want to have? How soon?
3. How do you want to raise your children? Should one partner stay home with the children full-time while they are young? Should both partners share the responsibility for child care? Should the children be placed in a day-care center as soon as possible?
4. Suppose one of you is offered a good job in one city and the other is offered a good job in a city 100 miles

away. Neither of you can find a satisfactory job in the other's city. How would you decide where to live?

5. Suppose a sudden financial crisis strikes. Where would you cut expenses to balance the budget? Clothes? Food? Housing? Entertainment?

6. How often do you plan to attend religious services?

7. How and where do you like to spend your vacations?

8. How often would you expect to spend an evening with friends, apart from your partner?

Were you uncertain about how your dating partner would answer any of these questions? If so, you are in the majority. Disagreements about such questions are common reasons for conflict in marriage or equivalent relationships. I am not suggesting that you should ask every person you date to fill out this questionnaire. However, before you get far enough into a relationship that love and marriage become a realistic possibility, you should discuss anything that is important to you. If you care about having children, find out what your partner thinks. If you want your eventual husband or wife to share your religious beliefs (or lack of them), discuss religion and your deepest values.

## Marriages That Last

When you hear about the high percentage of marriages that end in divorce, it is easy to despair, but many marriages still remain strong for a lifetime. Most characteristics of successful marriages are what you would probably expect (Karney & Bradbury, 1995):

- The husband and wife have similar attitudes and personalities.
- Both find sexual satisfaction in the relationship.
- The couple has an adequate income.

■ In a mature, lasting relationship, a couple can count on each other for care and affection through both good and bad times.

- The husband has a good enough job to maintain self-respect.
- The wife was not pregnant before they married.
- The couple's parents also had successful marriages.

A successful marriage changes over the years, just as individual lives do. At first the couple has the intense excitement of learning about each other and doing new things together. Over time, the excitement fades, as described by the opponent-process theory of emotions in Chapter 12. Years later the two have worked out a complex system of shared work and understandings. Although they do not arouse each other's emotions as intensely as before (Berscheid, 1983), they still love each other, perhaps even more deeply. If one of them becomes ill or dies, the emotion inherent in the mature relationship becomes vividly apparent.

## Trying to Save a Marriage

Many couples who know their marriage is in trouble seek help from a marriage counselor. The results of marriage counseling are, unfortunately, not very encouraging. Of the couples receiving help, only about one-third improve their relationship during treatment, and nearly half of those will deteriorate later, leaving only about a 15–20% long-term success rate for marriage counseling (Gottman, 1999). One reason, of course, is that it takes two to save a marriage, and in many cases one partner has already given up before meeting the marriage counselor.

Another reason, however, is that many marriage counselors have offered well-meaning advice that doesn't work (Gottman, 1999). For example, many counselors work hard on increasing open communication. The problem is that if someone feels hostility, open communication expresses intense hostility. Another bit of well-meaning bad advice is to keep track of what you do for your partner and what your partner does for you to make sure you give as much as you receive. People in successful marriages never act that way; they simply give unconditionally without counting what they receive in return.

John Gottman's (1999) advice to marriage counselors is to break up couples' name-calling and expressions of contempt, much as one might stop a large child from bullying a smaller one. Then get the couple to cope with their emotions without inflicting pain. Perhaps his main insight is that almost every marriage has problems. The key to a successful marriage is to repair the problems quickly.

IN CLOSING
## Choosing Your Partners Carefully

Few people enjoy living as a hermit, isolated from others. In prisons one of the harshest forms of punishment is solitary confinement. Almost any social contact is better than none at all. However, many people may choose their friends and their spouses poorly.

Life is like a roller-coaster ride in the dark: It has lots of ups and downs, and you never know what is going to happen next. Be sure you are riding with someone you like and trust.

## Summary

- **Friendship choices.** People generally choose friends and romantic partners who live near them, resemble them, and confirm their self-esteem. Relationships are most likely to survive and grow if each person believes that he or she is getting about as good a deal as the other person is. (page 554)
- **Marriage and similar attachments.** People have special considerations when choosing a potential marriage partner because marriage usually implies a commitment to rearing children together. (page 555)
- **Physical attractiveness.** In many nonhuman species, physical attractiveness is a reliable cue to the individual's health, vigor, and therefore desirability as a mate. In humans attractiveness is a powerful determinant of mate choice but has not been demonstrably linked to health or other biologically useful functions. (page 555)
- **Men's and women's preferences in marriage partners.** In every human culture, men prefer young, attractive women and women prefer men who are good providers. Men tend to be more upset about possible sexual infidelity by their wives, whereas women tend to be more upset about their husbands' becoming emotionally close to another woman. Evolutionary theorists believe humans evolved to have

these preferences, which help each person to increase his or her chances of reproducing. However, it is also plausible that people in different societies have learned these preferences. (page 557)
- **Marriage.** Marriage and similar relationships often break up because the partners chose each other for the wrong reasons, without learning about the values and attitudes that are important for daily life and rearing a family. Marriages are successful when the partners have much in common and find ways to satisfy each other's needs. They are unsuccessful if the partners express too much hostility and if they fail to repair problems when they arise. (page 559)

## Answers to Concept Checks

14. Proximity and familiarity will strengthen the likelihood of your becoming friends. The similarity principle will weaken it. Because of the difference in languages, you will have little chance, at least at first, to discover any similarities in interests or attitudes. In fact, proximity will probably not be a potent force because it serves largely as a means of enabling people to discover what they have in common. (page 555)
15. Attractive features such as bright feathers in a bird or large muscles in a man require much energy. It would be difficult for an unhealthy individual to devote enough energy to produce such features. (page 557)
16. If all men are equally wealthy, women would select men on some other basis, such as appearance. If women's fertility lasts as late in life as men's does, then the men on this planet should not have a strong preference for younger women. (page 559)

# Interpersonal Influence

*How are we influenced by other people's actions or inactions?*

During the Gulf War of 1991, U.S. and allied soldiers were told to prepare for biological or chemical weapons that Iraq's forces might use against them. Many were vaccinated against anthrax and botulism toxoid. They were given gas masks and pills that might protect them against certain poisonous gases. They endured high temperatures, poor food, disease-carrying flies, and other circumstances conducive to bad health. When they returned after the war, thousands began complaining of vague medical problems that became known as Gulf War syndrome—nausea, headaches, depression, rashes, joint and muscle pain, fatigue, numbness and tingling, balance problems, chest pains, bowel and bladder problems, sleep and memory problems, and so forth. Ten years of research yielded no explanation. The symptoms vary enormously from one ex-soldier to another, with no relationship to where the soldiers were stationed during the war—not even to whether they actually served in battle.

Many researchers now doubt that Gulf War syndrome has just one explanation, and many believe the causes are partly psychological (Ferguson & Cassaday, 1999). They do not by any means imply that the sufferers are imagining or pretending their illnesses. However, their immune systems and overall health could have been compromised by the powerful expectation that they would become sick. That is, the expectation of illness became a self-fulfilling prophecy. Impaired immune responses could even be a conditioned response to sights and sounds that resemble Gulf War experiences.

In short, we can be influenced in huge ways by what other people lead us to expect. We live in an ambiguous world, and when we do not know what to do or what to expect, we take our cues from other people.

Other people influence us in two major ways: First, they provide us with *information* (or misinformation). For example, if almost everyone else is flocking toward or away from something, they probably have a reason (e.g., if they are all taking massive precautions against chemical and biological weapons, the danger is probably great). Second, people set *norms* that define what we are expected to do. In much of our social behavior, we follow rules of politeness, such as "do not interrupt," "raise your hand if you want to speak," and "wait in line." Here we shall encounter many examples of both informational and normative influences.

## Conformity

**Conformity** means *maintaining or changing one's behavior to match the behavior or expectations of others.* The pressure to conform sometimes exerts an overwhelming normative influence. Koversada, on the coast of the Adriatic Sea, is a small, totally nudist city (although people do sometimes dress for dinner at an elegant restaurant). If a first-time visitor walks around the city wearing clothes, other people stop and stare, sometimes shaking their heads with disapproval. The visitor begins to feel awkward, out of place, and just as self-conscious as a naked person would be in a city of fully clothed people. Most visitors quickly undress (Newman, 1988).

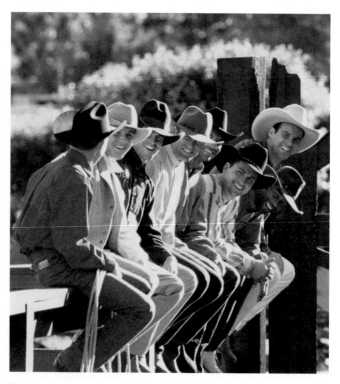

■ People conform to one another in their clothing and many other customs. Conformity in such matters can be helpful or at least not harmful.

Conformity can also serve informational functions, especially when we are not quite sure what we are seeing or hearing. One example is an illusion known as the **autokinetic effect:** *If you sit in a darkened room and stare at a small, stationary point of light, the point will eventually seem to move,* partly because of small involuntary eye movements that we all make all the time. If someone says, "I see it moving in a zigzag manner" or "I see it moving slowly in a counterclockwise direction," you are likely to perceive it the same way. You will perceive some movement on your own, but other people's suggestions greatly alter the apparent speed and direction of the movement.

Early research suggested that people are most likely to conform their opinions in ambiguous situations that make it difficult for people to be sure of their own judgment (Sherif, 1935). For example, there are no absolutely right or wrong styles of clothing. In matters such as politics, religion, or the movement of a single point of light in a darkened room, we do not have enough information to be sure of our own opinions. In the autokinetic effect, we see the light apparently moving, but we are not sure how much. Consequently, we rely on other people's opinions to help form our own.

Would we also conform to the opinions or behaviors of others if we were sure they were wrong? To answer that question, Solomon Asch (1951, 1956) carried out a now-famous series of experiments.

Asch assembled groups of students and asked them to look at a vertical bar, as shown in Figure 14.11, which was defined as the model. He also showed them three other vertical bars (right half of Figure 14.11) and asked them which bar was the same length as the model. As you can see, the task is simple. Asch asked the students to give their answers aloud. He repeated the procedure with 18 sets of bars.

Only one student in each group was a real participant. All the others were confederates who had been instructed to give incorrect answers on 12 of the 18 trials. Asch arranged for the real participant to be the next-to-the-last person in the group to announce his answer so that he would hear most of the confederates' incorrect responses before giving his own (Figure 14.12). Would he go along with the crowd?

FIGURE 14.12 Three of the eight participants in one of Asch's experiments on conformity. The one in the middle is the real participant; the others are the experimenter's confederates. (From Asch, 1951)

To Asch's surprise, 37 of the 50 participants conformed to the majority at least once, and 14 conformed on more than half of the trials. When faced with a unanimous wrong answer by the other group members, the mean participant conformed on 4 of the 12 trials. Asch was disturbed by these results: "That we have found the tendency to conformity in our society so strong . . . is a matter of concern. It raises questions about our ways of education and about the values that guide our conduct" (Asch, 1955, p. 34).

Why did people conform so readily? When they were interviewed after the experiment, some said they thought the rest of the group was correct or they guessed that an optical illusion was influencing the appearance of the bars. Others said they knew their "conforming" answers were wrong but went along with the group for fear of being ridiculed. That is, they were subject to a normative influence even when there was no informational influence. Reactions of the nonconformers were interesting, too. Some were very nervous but felt duty bound to say how the bars looked to them. A few seemed socially withdrawn, as if they paid no attention to anyone else. Still others were supremely self-confident, as if to say, "I'm right and everyone else is wrong. It happens all the time."

Asch (1951, 1955) found that the amount of conforming influence depended on the size of the opposing majority. In a series of studies, he varied the number of confederates who gave incorrect answers from 1 to 15. He found that people conformed to a group of 3 or 4 just as readily as they did to a larger group (Figure 14.13). However, a participant conformed much less if he or she had an "ally." Being a minority of one is painful, but being in a minority of two is not as bad (Figure 14.14).

Over the years since Asch's experiments, similar studies have been conducted many times in many countries. In the United States, most studies show a slight decrease in the amount of conformity since the 1950s. In cultures that emphasize collectivist values, such as most Asian cultures, the percentage of conforming answers tends to

FIGURE 14.11 In Asch's conformity studies, subjects were asked to match one line with one of three other lines on another card. They were surrounded by people who gave obviously wrong answers.

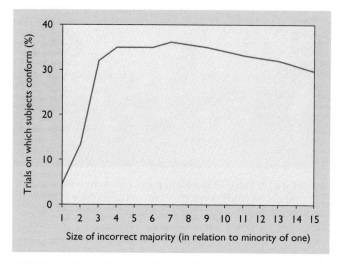

FIGURE 14.13 Asch (1955) found that conformity became more frequent as group size increased to about three, and then it leveled off.

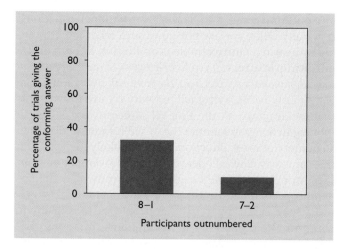

FIGURE 14.14 In Asch's experiments participants who were faced with a unanimous majority giving wrong answers conformed to the majority view on 32% of trials. Participants who had one "ally" giving the correct answer were less likely to conform. Evidently, it is less difficult to be in a minority of two.

be relatively high. However, in those collectivist cultures, people seem to be motivated mostly by politeness and not wishing to embarrass the others by correcting them (Bond & Smith, 1996). That is, when researchers use what appears to be the same task in a different culture, they may not be testing the same psychological processes.

## CONCEPT CHECK

17. Are you more likely to conform to a group when you are outnumbered 5 to 1, 10 to 1, or 10 to 2? (Check your answer on page 568.)

# Accepting or Denying Responsibility Toward Others

Other people can encourage us to do something we would not have done on our own, as in Asch's studies. Other people can also inhibit us from doing something that we would have done on our own. We look around to see what others are doing—or *not* doing—and we say, "Okay, I'll do that too. I'll do my fair share—no more, no less." Why do people sometimes work together to help one another and sometimes ignore the needs of others?

## Bystander Helpfulness and Apathy

Suppose, while you are waiting at a bus stop, you see me trip and fall down, just 10 meters away from you. I am not screaming in agony, but I don't get up right away either, so you are not sure whether I need help. Would you come over and offer to help? Or would you stand there and ignore me? Before you answer, try imagining the situation in two ways: First, you and I are the only people in sight. Second, there are many other people nearby,

none of whom is rushing to my aid. Does the presence of those other people make any difference in your response? (Note that it doesn't change *my* predicament. I am in the same amount of pain, regardless of whether one person or many people ignore me.)

Late one night in March 1964, Kitty Genovese was stabbed to death near her apartment in Queens, New York. For 30 minutes, 38 of her neighbors listened to her screams. A few stood at their windows watching, but none called the police or helped in any other way.

In 1998 a man confessed twice to his Internet self-help chat group that he deliberately set fire to his house to murder his 5-year-old daughter. Although 200 people read his message—and many later said they had been very upset about it—only 3 of them notified the police. Are we less likely to act just because we know that another person could act on the same information?

Bibb Latané and John Darley (1969) proposed that being in a crowd decreases our probability of action because of **diffusion of responsibility:** *We tend to feel less responsibility for being helpful when other people are around because the others are equally able to act.* Latané and Darley suggested that people ignored Kitty Genovese's distress because everyone knew that many other people *could* help her.

In an experiment designed to test this hypothesis, a young woman ushered either one or two students into a room and asked them to wait for the start of a market research study (Latané & Darley, 1968, 1969). She then went into the next room, closing the door behind her. There she played a tape recording that made it sound as though she had climbed onto a chair and had fallen off. For about 2 minutes, she could be heard crying and moaning, "Oh . . . my foot . . . I can't move it. Oh . . . my ankle . . ." Of the participants who were waiting alone,

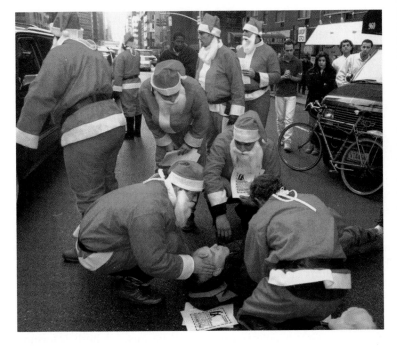

70% went next door and offered to help. Of the participants who were waiting with someone else, only 13% offered to help.

In a more recent study, investigators entered 400 Internet chat groups of different sizes and in each one asked, "Can anyone tell me how to look at someone's profile?" (That is, how can I check the biographical sketch that each chat room user posts?) The researchers found that the more people in a chat room at the time, the longer the wait before anyone answered the question. In large groups the researchers sometimes had to post the same question repeatedly (Markey, 2000).

Diffusion of responsibility is one possible explanation. Each person thinks, "It's not my responsibility to help any more than it is someone else's." A second possible explanation is that the presence of other people who are also doing nothing provides information (or misinformation). At first the situation is ambiguous: "Do I need to act or not?" Other people's inaction implies that the situation requires no action. In fact, the others are just as uncertain as you are, and they are drawing conclusions from *your* inaction. Social psychologists use the term **pluralistic ignorance** to describe *a situation in which people say nothing and each person falsely assumes that everyone else has a different, perhaps better informed, opinion.* Notice that the presence of other people exerts both normative and informational influences: Their inactivity implies that doing nothing is acceptable (a norm) and that the situation is not an emergency (information).

## Social Loafing

When you take a test, you are required to work alone, and your success depends entirely on your own effort. In many other cases, however, you work with other people as part

■ People watch other people's responses to help decide how they should respond. When a group of sidewalk Santas—who had gathered in Manhattan to promote a back-rub business—came to the aid of an injured cyclist, a few Santas made the first move and then the others decided to follow suit.

of a team. For example, if you work for a company that gives workers a share of the profits, your rewards depend on other workers' productivity as well as your own. Do you work as hard when the rewards depend on the group's productivity as you do when they depend on your own efforts alone?

In many cases the answer is "no." In one experiment students were told to scream and clap and try to make as much noise as possible, like cheerleaders at a sports event. Sometimes each student screamed and clapped alone; sometimes students acted in groups of two to six; and sometimes they acted alone but *thought* that other people were screaming and clapping too. (They wore headphones so they could not hear anyone else.) As a rule, students who screamed and clapped alone made more noise than students who were or thought they were part of a group (Latané, Williams, & Harkins, 1979). Social psychologists call this phenomenon **social loafing**—*the tendency to "loaf" (or work less hard) when sharing work with other people.* Social loafing has been demonstrated in many situations. For example, suppose you were asked to "name all the uses you can think of for a brick" (e.g., crack nuts, anchor a boat, or use as a doorstop) and write each one on a card. You would probably use many cards by yourself, but fewer if you were tossing cards into a pile along with other people's suggestions to be evaluated as a group (Harkins & Jackson, 1985). You probably wouldn't bother writing out ideas that you assume other people had already suggested.

At this point you may be thinking, "Wait a minute. When I'm playing on a basketball team, I try as hard as I can. I don't think I loaf just because others are working together." And you are right; social loafing is rare in team sports. The reason is that observers, including teammates, can easily see how hard you are trying. People work hard in groups if they expect other people to notice their effort or if they think they can contribute something that other group members cannot (Shepperd, 1993; Williams & Karau, 1991). In one study college students worked on math problems, and some of them thought they had a partner who was working on the same problems. On the average they worked harder if they thought they had a female partner than if they thought they had a male partner (Plaks & Higgins, 2000). This study demonstrated stereotypes and social loafing at the same time: People who thought they had a female partner guessed she might not be good at math, so they had to work hard. Those who thought they had a male partner felt they could loaf and let their partner do more of the work.

**FIGURE 14.15** During a catastrophe people abandon their usual tendencies toward bystander apathy and social loafing. Just after an earthquake in Los Angeles, people pitched in to serve soup to those whose homes were damaged.

Social loafing occurs most prominently when people consider the task unimportant and not when they believe much is at stake (see Figure 14.15). It is more common in Western cultures than in Asian cultures, which stress the value of helping one's group (Karau & Williams, 1995). Japanese people scorn anyone who does not do a fair share of a group effort. If some people continue to loaf, the ones who had been working generally quit. That is, in Japanese society either everyone works or no one does (Shepperd, 1995).

## CONCEPT CHECKS

18. Given what we have learned about social loafing, why are most people unlikely to work hard to clean the environment?
19. Suppose the head of a large library wants the staff to pay more attention to shelving all the books into their correct locations. Currently, many of the books are misplaced, and the staff seem to be "loafing" at rearranging them. What could be done to encourage greater efforts? (Check your answers on page 568.)

## Group Decision Making

An organization that needs to reach a decision will frequently set up a committee to look into the issues and make recommendations. We prefer a committee to an individual because the committee has more time, more total information, and fewer peculiarities and biases than any individual has. Research finds that a group generally makes better decisions than the average individual. However, the advantage of a group over an individual is often not as great as we might expect (Sorkin, Hays, & West, 2001). Groups sometimes rush through a decision without exploring everyone's opinion. Also, social loafing oc-

curs in many groups. Some individuals conform to the majority opinion and discard their own, possibly better, opinions.

## Group Polarization

*If nearly all the people who compose a group lean in the same direction on a particular issue, the group as a whole will tend to move even further in that direction after they discuss that issue.* This phenomenon is known as **group polarization.** Note that in this case *polarization* does not mean that the group breaks up into fragments favoring different positions. Rather, it means that, after discussing the issues, the members of a group move *together* toward one pole (extreme position) or the other. For example, a group of people who are opposed to abortion or in favor of animal rights or opposed to gun regulations will, after discussing the issue among themselves, generally become more extreme in their views than they had been at the start (Lamm & Myers, 1978).

Group polarization occurs because of both informational and normative influences (Isenberg, 1986). During the group discussion, the members become aware of new arguments and new information. If most of the members were leaning in one direction at the start, they hear many new arguments favoring that side of the issue and few or none for the opposition. The lack of balance between positive and negative arguments is essential for group polarization (Kuhn & Lao, 1996). Also, as the members of the group become aware of the consensus during the discussion, they feel pressure to conform, especially those who feel that they are not fully accepted by the rest of the group (Noel, Wann, & Branscombe, 1995).

## CONCEPT CHECK

20. Is a jury more likely to reach a biased or extreme decision than a single individual would be? (Check your answer on page 568.)

## Groupthink

One extreme form of group polarization is known as **groupthink,** when *the members of a group suppress their doubts about a group's poorly thought-out decision for fear of making a bad impression or disrupting the harmony of the group* (Janis, 1972, 1985). In some cases dominant members of the group ask dissenters to be quiet; more often, dissenters silence themselves.

One dramatic example of groupthink led to the Bay of Pigs fiasco of 1962. President John F. Kennedy and his advisers were considering a plan to support a small-scale invasion of Cuba at the Bay of Pigs. They assumed that a small group of Cuban exiles could overwhelm the Cuban army and trigger a spontaneous rebellion of the Cuban people against their government. Most of the advisers who doubted this assumption felt pressured to keep

■ Many organizations try to resist the tendency toward groupthink, which stifles dissenting views and proceeds to a possibly disastrous decision. During the Renaissance, European kings sometimes called on a "fool" (or court jester) to describe some proposal in a fresh and possibly amusing light. In a court composed largely of yes-men, the fool sometimes was the only one who could openly point out the folly of a proposed action without fear of reprisals.

quiet. The one who did express his doubts was told that he should loyally support the president, who had already made up his mind. Within a few hours after the invasion began, all the invaders were killed or captured. The decision makers themselves wondered how they could have made such a stupid decision.

Another example of groupthink was NASA's ill-fated decision to launch the space shuttle *Challenger* on a cold morning in 1986. The top decision makers let it be known that they had strong economic and public-relations reasons for launching the shuttle on schedule. Project engineers who knew the rocket booster was unsafe at low temperatures dutifully kept quiet and hoped for the best. Then, 73 seconds after the launch, the *Challenger* exploded because an O-ring could not function at low temperatures.

In both of these examples, group members who doubted the wisdom of the decision kept quiet and thus created an illusion of unanimous support. Originally, psychologists believed that groupthink occurs mostly in highly cohesive groups, such as fraternal or religious organizations, where the members think that it would be rude to criticize one another. Later research has found that almost all groups, not just cohesive ones, exert pressure to conform (Aldag & Fuller, 1993).

How can a group minimize the groupthink pressure? Some people have suggested designating someone as a "devil's advocate," who is supposed to raise objections.

However, when people know that someone is required to raise objections, they discount those objections and solidify their original opinions (Nemeth, Connell, Rogers, & Brown, 2001). A better strategy is for a leader to consult the advisers individually so they are not influenced by what they hear other advisers saying. In any case group members who entertain doubts about a leader's decision should remember the lessons of the Bay of Pigs and the *Challenger:* When much is at stake, it is better to risk angering one's partners than to go along with a possibly disastrous decision.

## IN CLOSING
### *To Conform or Not?*

Conforming to what others do is not, in itself, a bad idea. When I drive on the right side of the road, I am rather relieved that other people are being conformists and driving on the same side. Problems arise when we are surrounded by people who are expressing an extreme and possibly wrong opinion (as in group polarization) or by people who are doing nothing when something needs to be done (as in bystander apathy). We should conform when conformity is helpful or harmless but resist when it is dangerous.

## Summary

- **Types of social influence.** People influence our behavior by offering information (right or wrong) and by setting norms that they enforce by providing or withholding their approval. (page 562)
- **Conformity.** Many people conform to the majority view even when they are confident that the majority is wrong. An individual is as likely to conform to a group of three as to a larger group, but an individual who has an ally is less likely to conform to the majority. (page 562)
- **Diffusion of responsibility.** People in groups are less likely than an isolated individual to come to the aid of another because they experience a diffusion of responsibility. (page 564)
- **Social loafing.** People working together on a task tend to exert less effort than people working independently. However, people will work just as hard on the group task if they are evaluated on the basis of their individual performances or if they believe their contributions will make a big difference to the group's success. (page 565)
- **Group polarization.** Groups of people who lean mostly in the same direction on a given issue often make decisions that are more extreme than the decisions that most individuals would have made on their own. (page 566)

- **Groupthink.** Groupthink occurs when members of a cohesive group fail to express their opposition to a decision for fear of making a bad impression or harming the cohesive spirit of the group. (page 566)

## Answers to Concept Checks

**17.** You would be about equally likely to conform when outnumbered 5 to 1 or 10 to 1. Any group of 3 or more produces about the same urge to conform. However, having even one ally decreases the pressure, so you would be less likely to conform when outnumbered 10 to 2. (page 564)

**18.** For the task of protecting the environment, each person is part of a group containing billions of other people. Social loafing is likely because many one-person contributions, such as picking up litter, would not earn individual credit or recognition. Also, each person thinks, "What good could one person do with such a gigantic problem?" (page 566)

**19.** One approach would be to make the contributions of each staff member more apparent (because social loafing is common when people do not see that their own efforts make much difference). For example, assign each person a different set of shelves and report which shelves have shown the greatest improvement in orderliness. (page 566)

**20.** If a jury were almost unanimous, group polarization would probably move the group toward a unanimous verdict. However, a jury that starts out divided would not experience group polarization. Most research has found that juries and similar groups are no more extreme than the average individual (Kerr, MacCoun, & Kramer, 1996). (page 566)

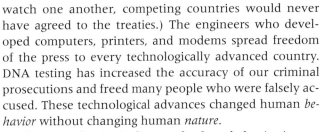
In the 1960s world problems seemed to threaten the very future of civilization. The Vietnam War seemed to go on forever, the nations of the world were preparing for global nuclear war, racial injustice was widespread, and we were beginning to recognize how terribly people were damaging the environment. As a high school and college student at the time, I had grandiose dreams of saving the world. I wasn't sure how, but I thought psychological research was a possibility. I hoped to somehow change human nature so that people would stop being so cruel and selfish.

Decades later I reflect on the people who really did make the world a better place. Some made their impact through moral leadership—Martin Luther King, Jr., Mother Teresa, Alexander Solzhenitsyn, Nelson Mandela, and others. However, many advanced the causes of peace and justice through technology—a route that I never even contemplated during my youthful "save the world" fantasies. For example, the engineers who devised spy satellites made possible the international treaties banning tests of nuclear weapons. (Without the capacity to watch one another, competing countries would never have agreed to the treaties.) The engineers who developed computers, printers, and modems spread freedom of the press to every technologically advanced country. DNA testing has increased the accuracy of our criminal prosecutions and freed many people who were falsely accused. These technological advances changed human *behavior* without changing human *nature*.

The general point is that much of our behavior is controlled by the situation—sometimes the technological situation, sometimes the social situation. A situation can almost compel us to behave either in constructive ways or in uncooperative and self-defeating ways. We need to recognize the power of these situations so that we can avoid or change the most harmful ones.

What would you think of a person who knowingly paid a great deal more for something than it was worth? Or an individual who confessed to a crime even though the police admitted they did not have enough evidence for a conviction? Or someone who used up all the available resources at once instead of saving some for later? You would probably question that person's intelligence or sanity. And yet, under certain circumstances, you would probably do the same. Sometimes we fall into a **behavior trap**—*a situation that coerces us into self-defeating behaviors.* We call such situations "traps" because people wander into them without realizing the danger. A simple example is being in a crowded theater when someone shouts "fire!" We all know we should file out calmly because a panic would jam the exits and no one could escape. In a real situation, though, we might see that it will be difficult for everyone to get out in time. We might also realize that if there is going to be panic, it is better to be among the first to panic and try to escape than to be among the last to panic! In some situations panic is almost sure to occur, no matter how rational and well-meaning the people are (Helbing, Farkes, & Vicsek, 2000).

We shall consider four situations: escalation of conflict, the prisoner's dilemma, the commons dilemma, and obedience to authority.

## Escalation of Conflict

Imagine that you, I, and a few other people are at an auction. The auctioneer explains that the next item up for bids is a dollar bill, to be sold to the highest bidder, even if the highest bid is only a

■ A crowd of rock music fans can trample one another while trying to get close to the stage. Sometimes a situation becomes dangerous before people recognize the risk.

few cents. There is one catch, however; at the end, when someone finally buys the dollar bill, the second highest bidder must pay his or her bid to the auctioneer also, receiving nothing in return. So, for example, if I bid 5 cents, you bid 10 cents, and the bidding stops there, you would buy the dollar bill for 10 cents and I would simply lose my 5 cents.

Suppose we plunge right in. I bid 5 cents, you bid 10, I bid 15, and so forth. Eventually, you bid 90 cents and I bid 95. Now what do you do? If you let me have the dollar bill for 95 cents, you lose 90 cents. So you bid $1, hoping to break even. What do I do? If I stop bidding, I lose 95 cents, but if I can buy the dollar for $1.05, I sustain a net loss of only 5 cents. So I bid $1.05. Then you bid $1.10 because you would rather lose 10 cents than lose a whole dollar. The bidding continues. After a while, we start to lose track of the economics and begin to get angry with each other. After all, as soon as one of us quits bidding, the other one will "win."

Psychologists have repeatedly set up such situations to see what would happen. They have usually managed to sell their dollar bills in the range of $3 to $5 and once for $25 (Brockner & Rubin, 1985). As soon as the bidding went over $1, bidders became increasingly distressed—sweating, trembling, sometimes even crying. (At the end of the experiment, the psychologists always returned the money that the bidders paid them, although they had not promised to do so.)

The point of this study is *not:* "Here's a good scam you can use to work your way through college." The point is that, once anyone gets into a situation of this kind, it is hard to escape. Similar situations do arise in real life. The arms race between the United States and the Soviet Union was a classic example: From the end of World War II until 1991 when the Soviet Union collapsed, the two countries devoted enormous sums of money to weapons. Critics often wondered whether those expenditures made sense. The reply was, "Having spent as much as we have already, we may as well spend a little more to be sure that we have more weapons than the other side."

Such situations are common, though not easy to recognize (Staw & Ross, 1989). Someone who has invested in a stock that lost money may hold onto the stock rather than sell it and admit that buying it was a mistake. A manager who has already spent a fortune developing and advertising a product feels a need to continue developing the product, even though it appears to be a sure loser, because quitting would mean that the whole investment was wasted (Lant & Hurley, 1999). Perhaps you can think of additional examples. Note also the similarity of these examples to the sunk cost effect, mentioned in Chapter 8.

# The Prisoner's Dilemma

In some situations you have a choice between an action that seems best for you and one that seems best for your group. If everyone in the group chooses the action that seems best for himself or herself, everyone will suffer.

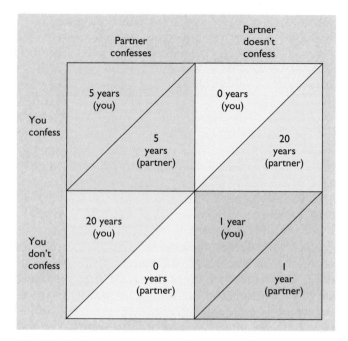

**FIGURE 14.16** In the prisoner's dilemma, each person considering the choice alone finds it beneficial to confess. But when both people confess, they suffer worse consequences than if both had refused to confess.

The most widely studied example is the **prisoner's dilemma,** *a situation where people must choose between a cooperative act and an act that could benefit only themselves while hurting others.* There are many versions of this dilemma, but let's start with the original: You and a partner are arrested and charged with armed robbery. The police take each of you into separate rooms and ask you to confess. If neither of you confesses, the police do not have enough evidence to convict you of armed robbery, but they can convict you of a lesser offense with a sentence of 1 year in prison. If either of you confesses and testifies against the other, the confessor goes free and the other gets 20 years in prison. If you both confess, you each get 5 years in prison. Each of you knows that the other person has the same options. Figure 14.16 illustrates your choices.

If your partner does not confess, it is to your own advantage to confess because you will go free. (Your partner will get 20 years in prison, but let's assume you care mostly about yourself.) If your partner does confess, it is still to your advantage to confess, because you will get only 5 years in prison instead of 20. So, you confess. Your partner, reasoning the same way, also confesses, and you both get 5 years in prison. If you had both kept quiet, you would each have served only 1 year in prison. The situation led you both to uncooperative, self-defeating behavior.

If you and your partner could have discussed your strategy, you would have agreed not to confess. Then, when the police took you to separate rooms, you would each hope that the other would keep the bargain. If your friend did keep the bargain, what should you do? Confess, of course! We're back where we started.

The two of you are likely to cooperate only if you can stay in constant communication with each other (Nemeth, 1972). If each can listen to everything the other one says, you know that, if one confesses, the other will retaliate immediately. Indeed, many self-defeating behaviors arise because of poor communication (Thompson & Hrebec, 1996).

The prisoner's dilemma can also be stated in terms of gains instead of losses. Suppose you and another person have a choice between two moves, which we call *cooperate* and *compete*. Depending on what each of you choose, here are the payoffs:

|  | Other person cooperates | Other person competes |
|---|---|---|
| You cooperate | Both win $1 | Other person gains $2; you lose $2 |
| You compete | You gain $2; other person loses $2 | Both lose $1 |

Suppose you are playing this game only once. The other person is answering by telephone, and the two of you will never meet. Which move do you choose? If the other person cooperates, your winning choice is *compete* because you will get $2 instead of $1. If the other person competes, again you gain by competing because you will lose just $1 instead of $2. Logically, you should choose to compete, and so should the other person, and you both lose $1. Here we encounter a classic behavior trap in which the situation logically leads people into self-defeating behaviors (Axelrod & Dion, 1988).

The strategy changes drastically if the two of you are going to play repeatedly. Unless you know what the other person will do, the recommended strategy is "tit-for-tat": Start with the *cooperate* move. If the other person cooperates too, then cooperate again on the next move and so on. But if the other person makes a *compete* move, retaliate with a *compete* move on your next turn. (Your retaliation should teach the other person not to try to take advantage of you.) Furthermore, if you know that some other person makes mostly *compete* moves, you should refuse to play the game with him or her (Wilson, Near, & Miller, 1996).

This game is much more than a laboratory curiosity. First, it is a pretty good model of what happens in business deals, in which each person has to cooperate with the agreement or the other person will retaliate. Second, it has implications for how human social behavior evolved. From a strictly biological standpoint, why should you ever help someone else who is unrelated to you? A reasonable answer is **reciprocal altruism:** *You help someone and the other person may eventually help you.* Reciprocal altruism works only if you can keep track of who returns your favors and who "cheats" by accepting help and then not helping in return. Therefore, reciprocal altruism, and in general any cooperative social behavior among nonrelatives, requires individual recognition. If

we could not recognize people from one time to the next, we could not distinguish between cooperators and cheaters. As it is, we not only remember who cooperates (or doesn't) with us, but we also notice who cooperates (or doesn't) with other people. People develop a reputation for cooperating or cheating, and that reputation guides everyone's behavior toward them (Nowak, Page, & Sigmund, 2000; Wedekind & Milinski, 2000). In species that cannot recognize individuals, theoretically, reciprocal altruism should not evolve. In fact, altruism is rare in nonhuman animals.

## CONCEPT CHECK

**21.** Suppose you have been playing the prisoner's dilemma game as just described, using the tit-for-tat strategy, and the other person has been cooperating on every move. When you get to the last move (so there will be no further chance to retaliate), what move would be best? Why? (Check your answers on page 575.)

## The Commons Dilemma

Here is another case where people hurt themselves and others by considering only their own short-term interests (Hardin, 1968): In the **commons dilemma,** *people who share a common resource tend to overuse it and therefore make it unavailable in the long run.* The commons dilemma takes its name from this parable: You are a shepherd in a small village. There is a piece of land, called the commons, that everyone is free to share. Most of the time, your sheep graze on your own land, but when a few of them need a little extra grass, you are free to take them to the commons. There are 50 shepherds in the village, and the commons can support about 50 sheep a day. So if each shepherd takes an average of one sheep per day to the commons, everything works out. Suppose a few shepherds decide to take several sheep per day to the commons to save the grass on their own land. Not to be outdone, other shepherds do the same. Soon the commons is barren and useless to all.

Social psychologists have simulated the commons dilemma in laboratory games. In one study college students were asked to sit around a bowl that contained ten nuts (Edney, 1979). They were told that they could take as many nuts as they wanted anytime they chose. Every 10 seconds the number of nuts remaining in the bowl would double. The object of the game was to collect as many nuts as possible. The rational strategy is to let the nuts double every 10 seconds for a while and then let each participant occasionally harvest some. But most of the groups never made it past the first 10 seconds. The students simply plunged in and grabbed as many nuts as they could, immediately exhausting the resources.

Some people do cooperate, however. Consider this scenario: You are in the fishing business. The numbers of fish have been declining, and the government has asked you and the other fishing companies to reduce your annual catch. You know the government cannot enforce this regulation, so you can still catch more than your assigned share without penalty. What do you do? About half of the college students who were asked this question said they would cooperate and limit their catch (Baron, 1997). If they were actually depending on fishing to make a living, they might decide differently (Figure 14.17). Still, the reasons they gave were interesting. Students said that they wanted to do their part to make the world a better place, and they thought their cooperation would influence others to cooperate and thus benefit everyone in the long run.

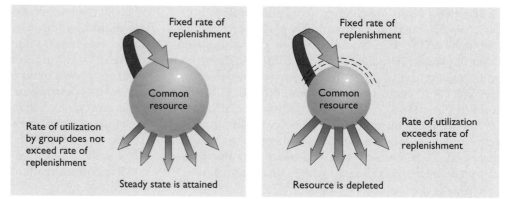

FIGURE 14.17 The commons dilemma: Unless the users agree to moderate their use of a common resource, it will soon be used up. For example, years of overfishing off the coast of Newfoundland so thoroughly depleted the fish population that the Canadian government finally had to ban commercial fishing.

# Obedience to Authority

One final example of a self-defeating situation arises when people obey an authority who gives bad orders. Ordinarily, if someone you hardly know says that "you *have* to do this," you probably would refuse. Sometimes, however, you may be in a situation where you feel obligated to obey unreasonable orders. We might have thought that only people with a rigid, authority-worshipping personality would follow objectionable orders, but evidence has shown that some situations build up powerful pressures that influence almost anyone.

Research on this topic was inspired by reports of atrocities in the Nazi concentration camps during World War II. Those who had committed the atrocities defended themselves by saying that they were only obeying orders. International courts rejected that defense, and outraged people throughout the world told themselves, "If I had been there, I would have refused to follow such orders" and "It couldn't happen here." What do you think? Could it happen here?

 **WHAT'S THE EVIDENCE?**
*The Milgram Experiment*

Stanley Milgram (1974) set up an experiment to discover whether a carefully designed situation could trap people into obeying apparently dangerous orders. Milgram's experiment quickly became one of the most famous studies in psychology.

**HYPOTHESIS** When an authority figure gives normal people instructions to do something that might hurt another person, at least some of them will obey, under carefully designed circumstances.

**METHOD** Two adult male participants arrived at the experimental room—the real participant and a confederate of the experimenter pretending to be a participant. (They were not college students. The experimenters wanted results that would generalize to a broad population. They also wanted to minimize the risk that the participants would guess the true purpose of the experiment.) The experimenter told the participants that this experiment dealt with learning and that one participant would be the "teacher" and the other the "learner." The teacher would read lists of words through a microphone to the learner, who would sit in a nearby room. The teacher would then test the learner's memory for the words. Whenever the learner made a mistake, the teacher was to deliver an electric shock as punishment.

The experiment was rigged so that the participant was always the teacher and the confederate was always the learner. The teacher watched as the learner was strapped into the shock device from which there was no escape (Figure 14.18). The learner never received any shocks, but the teacher was led to believe that he did. In fact, before the start of the study, the experimenter also had the teacher feel a "sample shock" from the machine, demonstrating that the machine really worked.

At the start of the experiment, the teacher read the words and the learner made many mistakes. The teacher sat at a shock generator that had levers to deliver shocks ranging from 15 volts up to 450 volts in 15-volt increments (Figure 14.19). The experimenter instructed the teacher to deliver a shock every time the learner made a mistake, beginning with the 15-volt switch and raising the voltage by 15 volts for each successive mistake. As the voltage went up, the learner in the next room cried out in pain and even kicked the wall.

**FIGURE 14.18** In Milgram's experiment a rigged drawing selected a confederate of the experimenter to be the "learner." Here the learner is strapped to a device that supposedly delivers shocks.

In one version of the experiment, the learner complained that he had a heart condition. If a teacher asked who would take responsibility for any harm done to the learner, the experimenter replied that he, the experimenter, would take responsibility but insisted that "while the shocks may be painful, they are not dangerous." When the shocks reached 150 volts, the learner called out in pain and begged to be let out of the experiment, complaining that his heart was bothering him. Beginning at 270 volts, he responded to shocks with agonized screams. At 300 volts, he shouted that he would no longer answer any questions. After 330 volts, he made no response at all. Still, the experimenter ordered the teacher to continue asking questions and delivering shocks. (Remember, the learner was not really being shocked. The screams of pain came from a tape recording.)

**RESULTS** Of 40 participants, 25 continued to deliver shocks all the way up to 450 volts. The people who did so were not sadists, but normal adults recruited from the community through newspaper ads. They were paid a few dollars for their services, and those who asked were

told that they could keep the money even if they quit. (Not many asked.) People from all walks of life obeyed the experimenter's orders, including blue-collar workers, white-collar workers, and professionals. Most of them grew quite upset and agitated while they were supposedly delivering shocks to the screaming learner, but they kept right on.

**INTERPRETATION** The level of obedience Milgram observed depended on certain factors that he injected into the situation. One was that the experimenter agreed to take responsibility. (Remember the diffusion of responsibility principle.) Another influence was that the experimenter started with a small request, asking the participant to press the lever for a 15-volt shock, and then gradually progressed to stronger shocks.

Figures 14.20 and 14.21 illustrate the results of a few variations in procedure that Milgram tried. For example, participants were more obedient to an experimenter who remained in the same room than to one who left. They were less obedient if they needed to force the learner's hand back onto the shock plate. If additional "teachers" divided the task—the other "teachers" also being confederates of the experimenter—a participant was very likely to obey if the others obeyed, but unlikely to obey if the others disobeyed.

Still, the remarkable conclusion remains that, under a variety of conditions, many normal people followed orders from an experimenter they had just met, even though they thought they might hurt or even kill someone. Imagine how much stronger the pressure to obey orders from a government or military leader would be.

**ETHICAL ISSUES** Milgram's experiment told us something about ourselves that we did not want to hear. No longer could we say, "What happened in Nazi Germany could never happen here." We found that most of us do follow orders, even quite offensive orders. We are indebted

**FIGURE 14.19** The "teacher" in Milgram's experiment flipped switches on this box, apparently delivering stronger and stronger shocks for each successive error that the "learner" made. The situation was designed to appear realistic, although the device did not shock the learner.

**FIGURE 14.20** In one variation of Milgram's standard procedure, he asked the teacher to hold the learner's hand on the shock electrode. This close contact with the learner decreased obedience to less than half its usual level; still, some teachers continued following orders to deliver shocks. (From Milgram's 1965 film, *Obedience*)

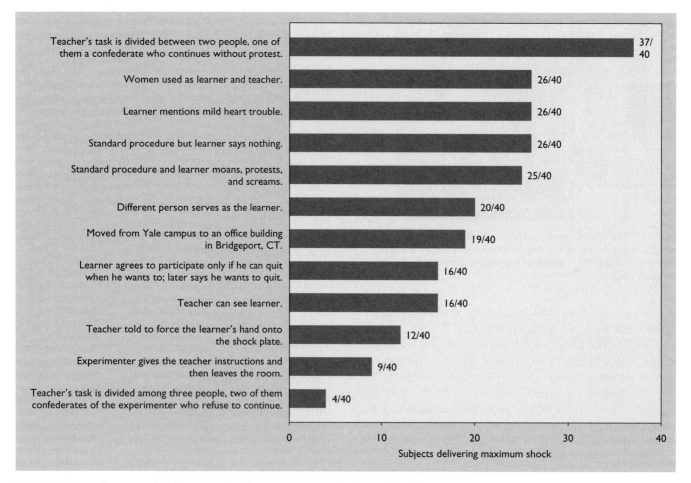

Teacher's task is divided between two people, one of them a confederate who continues without protest. — 37/40

Women used as learner and teacher. — 26/40

Learner mentions mild heart trouble. — 26/40

Standard procedure but learner says nothing. — 26/40

Standard procedure and learner moans, protests, and screams. — 25/40

Different person serves as the learner. — 20/40

Moved from Yale campus to an office building in Bridgeport, CT. — 19/40

Learner agrees to participate only if he can quit when he wants to; later says he wants to quit. — 16/40

Teacher can see learner. — 16/40

Teacher told to force the learner's hand onto the shock plate. — 12/40

Experimenter gives the teacher instructions and then leaves the room. — 9/40

Teacher's task is divided among three people, two of them confederates of the experimenter who refuse to continue. — 4/40

*Subjects delivering maximum shock*

**FIGURE 14.21** Milgram varied his procedure in many ways to find out what elements promoted or inhibited obedience. Division of responsibility increased obedience; an implication of personal responsibility decreased obedience.

to Milgram's study for this important, if unwelcome, information. However, although I am glad to know about Milgram's results, I doubt that I would have enjoyed being in his experiment. Most people were emotionally drained by the experience, and some were visibly upset to discover how readily they had obeyed orders to deliver dangerous shocks to another person.

Milgram's study prompted psychology researchers to establish much clearer and stricter rules about what an experimenter can ethically ask someone to do. Today, before the start of any psychological experiment—even the simplest and most innocuous—the experimenter is required to submit a plan to an institutional committee that must either approve or reject the ethics of the experiment.

If anyone today submitted a proposal to conduct research similar to Milgram's study, the local institutional committee would almost certainly refuse permission. However, if the same procedures had been in place *at the time of Milgram's study,* would a committee have permitted his study? Possibly. Before Milgram's research, very few people expected his results to turn out as they did.

Milgram asked various psychologists and psychiatrists to predict the results, and nearly all replied that only a rare psychopathic weirdo would press levers to deliver severe shocks. A committee that shared this expectation might have foreseen little ethical difficulty with Milgram's study. The unforeseen ethical problem underscores just how surprising Milgram's results were.

# CONCEPT CHECK

22. In what way did the obedience in Milgram's experiment resemble the foot-in-the-door procedure? How did it resemble Skinner's shaping procedure? (Check your answers on page 575.)

**A STEP FURTHER**
*Modifying Obedience*

Here is one version of the experiment that Milgram never tried: At the start of the experiment, we announce that the teacher and the learner will trade places halfway through the experiment so that the previous learner will start delivering shocks to the teacher. How do you think the teachers would behave then? What other changes in procedure can you imagine that might influence the degree of obedience?

## Fix the Situation, Not Human Nature

If we want to prevent people from panicking when a fire breaks out in a crowded theater, the best solution is not to teach cooperation but to build more exits. Similarly, it is difficult to teach people to behave productively in any of the behavior traps presented in this chapter; the best advice is to avoid those situations. The best time to quit is before the situation gets started. In short, instead of just finding the right action to take in each situation, it is important to choose one's situations.

## Summary

- **Behavior traps.** Certain situations pressure even intelligent people into self-defeating behaviors. (page 569)
- **The dollar auction.** In the dollar auction, the second highest bidder must pay the amount bid and receives

nothing in return. If two people start bidding, it is difficult to stop. (page 569)
- **The prisoner's dilemma.** In the prisoner's dilemma, two people can choose to cooperate or compete. The *compete* move seems best from the individual's point of view, but it is harmful to the group. (page 570)
- **The commons dilemma.** If people can withdraw resources from a common pool while saving their individual resources, it is tempting to take as much as possible and therefore ruin the common pool. (page 571)
- **Obedience.** Many people obey the orders of a person in authority even if they believe their actions will injure someone else. They are less likely to obey if they can see the person who would be injured. They are more likely to obey if other people are following orders without protest. (page 572)

## Answers to Concept Checks

**21.** If your identity is completely anonymous, you have something to gain and nothing to lose by choosing to *compete* on the final move—leaving aside issues of morality. However, if anyone will know your identity, it may be better to cooperate in order to protect your reputation as a cooperator. That reputation could help you the next time you play. (page 571)

**22.** In all three cases—Milgram's experiment, the foot-in-the-door procedure, and Skinner's shaping procedure—someone starts with a small, hard-to-refuse request and gradually builds up to bigger requests. (page 574)

## Key Terms and Activities

## Key Terms

**actor-observer effect:** the tendency to attribute internal causes more often for other people's behavior and external attributions more often for one's own behavior (page 541)

**attitude:** a like or dislike that influences our behavior toward a person or thing (page 544)

**attribution:** the set of thought processes we use to assign causes to our own behavior and to the behavior of others (page 539)

**autokinetic effect:** the illusory perception that a point of light in a darkened room is in motion (page 563)

**aversive racism:** consciously expressing the idea that all people are equal, but nevertheless unintentionally discriminating against some groups (page 537)

**bait-and-switch technique:** the procedure of first offering an extremely favorable deal and then making

additional demands after the other person has committed to the deal (page 550)

**behavior trap:** a situation that almost forces people into self-defeating behaviors (page 569)

**central route to persuasion:** a method of persuasion based on careful evaluation of evidence and logic (page 545)

**cognitive dissonance:** a state of unpleasant tension that people experience when they hold contradictory attitudes or when their behavior is inconsistent with their attitudes, especially if they are displeased with this inconsistency (page 550)

**commons dilemma:** a situation where people who share a common resource tend to overuse it and therefore make it unavailable in the long run (page 571)

**conformity:** maintaining or changing one's behavior to match the behavior or expectations of others (page 562)

**consensus information:** comparisons of one person's behavior with that of others (page 540)

**consistency information:** observations of how a person's behavior varies from one time to another (page 540)

**diffusion of responsibility:** the tendency to feel less responsibility for helping when other people are around than when we know that no one else can help (page 564)

**discrimination:** in social behavior, unequal treatment of different groups of people (page 337)

**distinctiveness:** observations of how a person's behavior varies from one object or social partner to another (page 540)

**door-in-the-face technique:** a method of eliciting compliance by first making an outrageous request and then replying to the refusal with a more reasonable request (page 549)

**exchange** (or **equity**) **theories:** theories maintaining that social relationships are transactions in which partners exchange goods and services (page 555)

**external attribution:** an explanation for someone's behavior based on the current situation, including events that presumably would influence almost anyone (page 539)

**foot-in-the-door technique:** a method of eliciting compliance by first making a modest request and then following it with a larger request (page 549)

**forewarning effect:** the tendency of a brief preview of a message to decrease its persuasiveness (page 549)

**fundamental attribution error:** the tendency to make internal attributions for people's behavior, even when an observer sees evidence for an external influence (page 540)

**group polarization:** the tendency of a group whose members lean in the same direction on a particular issue to become more extreme in its views after discussing the issue as a group (page 566)

**groupthink:** a process by which the members of a group suppress their doubts about a group's poorly thought-out decision, for fear of making a bad impression or disrupting the harmony of the group (page 566)

**inoculation effect:** the tendency of a persuasive message to be weakened if people first hear a weak argument supporting the same conclusion (page 549)

**internal attribution:** an explanation based on someone's individual characteristics, such as attitudes, personality traits, or abilities (page 539)

**mere exposure effect:** the tendency to increase our liking for everything and everyone that has become familiar (page 554)

**peripheral route to persuasion:** a method of persuasion based on such superficial factors as the speaker's appearance and reputation or the sheer number of arguments presented, regardless of their quality (page 545)

**pluralistic ignorance:** a situation where people say nothing and each person falsely assumes that everyone else has a different, perhaps better informed opinion. (page 565)

**prejudice:** an unfavorable stereotype; a negative attitude toward a group of people (page 337)

**primacy effect:** the tendency to be more influenced by the first information learned about someone than by later information about the same person (page 335)

**prisoner's dilemma:** a situation where people must choose between an act that is beneficial to themselves but harmful to others and an act that is moderately beneficial to all (page 570)

**proximity:** in social psychology, the tendency to choose as friends people with whom we come in frequent contact (page 554)

**reciprocal altruism:** helping someone in the expectation that the other person will eventually repay the favor (page 571)

**self-handicapping strategies:** techniques for intentionally putting oneself at a disadvantage to provide an excuse for an expected failure (page 542)

**self-serving biases:** attributions that people adopt to maximize their credit for their successes and to minimize their blame for their failures (page 542)

**sleeper effect:** delayed persuasion by an initially rejected message (page 547)

**social loafing:** the tendency to "loaf" (or work less hard) when sharing work with other people (page 565)

**social perception and cognition:** the process of gathering and remembering information about others and making inferences based on that information (page 335)

**social psychologists:** the psychologists who study social behavior and how individuals influence other people and are influenced by other people (page 334)

**stereotypes:** overgeneralization of either positive or negative attitudes toward a group of people (page 336)

**that's-not-all technique:** a method of eliciting compliance whereby someone makes an offer and then improves the offer before anyone has a chance to reply (page 550)

## Suggestions for Further Reading

Cialdini, R. B. (1993). *Influence: Science and practice* (Rev. ed.). New York: William Morrow. One of the most enjoyable and entertaining books in psychology. Buy a copy and take it with you on vacation.

Milgram, S. (1975). *Obedience to authority.* New York: Harper & Row. Describes Milgram's classic experiments on obedience.

Miller, G. (2000). *The mating mind: How sexual choice shaped the evolution of human nature.* New York: Doubleday. Discusses the evolutionary approach to explaining human mate choice.

# Web/Technology Resources

## Implicit Association Test

**buster.cs.yale.edu/implicit/research/research01/intro.shtml**

Test your own responses on the Implicit Association Test.

## Physical Attraction

**miavx1.muohio.edu/~psybersite/attraction/**

Four students in an advanced social psychology course developed this tutorial examining physical attraction and how it is affected by attributions and gender; it provides some cross-cultural comparisons and a quiz.

## Groupthink: Theoretical Framework

**choo.fis.utoronto.ca/FIS/Courses/LIS2149/Groupthink.html**

This three-page series by Chun Wei Choo of the University of Toronto begins with an elaborate diagram showing the antecedent conditions and observable consequences of groupthink; pages 2 and 3 provide steps to minimize its development.

## Social Psychology Network

**www.socialpsychology.org/**

This huge database includes more than 5,000 links to resources about social behavior.

## Cross-Cultural Psychology

**www.vanguard.edu/psychology/webculture.html**

This page contains links to worldwide studies of cultural influences and culture differences.

## Interpersonal Perception

**nw3.nai.net/~dakenny/interp.htm**

David A. Kenny of the University of Connecticut, author of *Interpersonal Perception: A Social Relations Analysis,* offers an outstanding tutorial on the judgments that one person makes about another.

## Prisoner's Dilemma

**serendip.brynmawr.edu/bb/pd.html**

Play the prisoner's dilemma game with a computer opponent. Win as much as you can!

# Abnormality, Therapy, and Social Issues

**15**

CHAPTER

■ Peculiar behavior was once explained as demon possession. Here St. Zenobius exorcises devils, seen fleeing from the mouths of the possessed. At the time of this late 15th-century work, attributed to Botticelli, the priest Savonarola was exorcising the city with public burnings of luxury goods.

ver the past 4 months, George has struck and injured several dozen people, most of whom he hardly knew. Two of them had to be sent to the hospital. George expresses no guilt, no regrets. He says he would attack every one of them again if he got the chance. What should society do with George?

1. Send him to jail.
2. Commit him to a mental hospital.
3. Give him an award for being the best defensive player in the league.

You cannot answer the question unless you know the context of George's behavior. Behavior that seems normal at a party might seem bizarre in a business meeting. Behavior that earns millions for a rock singer might earn a trip to the mental hospital for a college professor. Behavior that is routine in one culture might be criminal in another.

■ A protestor who spends years of his life picketing the White House in search of peace is statistically abnormal and puts himself at risk of harm. Still, most of us would not call him psychologically abnormal. Abnormality is hard to define.

Even knowing the context of someone's behavior may not tell us whether it is normal. Suppose your rich Aunt Tillie starts to pass out money to strangers on the street corner and vows that she will continue until she has exhausted her fortune. Should the court commit her to a mental hospital and make you the trustee of her estate?

A man claims to be Jesus Christ and asks permission to appear before the United Nations to announce God's message to the world. A psychiatrist is sure that he can relieve this man of his disordered thinking by giving him antipsychotic drugs, but the man insists that he is perfectly sane. Should we force him to take the drugs, ignore him, or place his address on the agenda of the United Nations?

# Abnormal Behavior: An Overview

*What do we mean by "abnormal" behavior and how can we distinguish it from normal?*

Students in medical school often contract what is known as "medical students' disease." Imagine that you are just beginning your training in medicine. One of your textbooks describes "Cryptic Ruminating Umbilicus Disorder":

"The symptoms are hardly noticeable until the condition becomes hopeless. The first symptom is a pale tongue." (You go to the mirror. You can't remember what your tongue is supposed to look like, but it *does* look a little pale.) "Later a hard spot forms in the neck." (You feel your neck. "Wait! I never felt *this* before! I think it's something hard!") "Just before the arms and legs fall off, there is shortness of breath, increased heart rate, and sweating." (Already distressed, you *do* have shortness of breath, your heart *is* racing, and you *are* sweating profusely.)

Sooner or later most medical students misunderstand the description of some disease and confuse it with their own normal condition. When my brother was in medical school, he diagnosed himself as having a rare, fatal ill-ness, checked himself into a hospital, and wrote out his will. (He finished medical school and is still doing fine today, decades later.)

"Medical students' disease" is even more common among students of psychological disorders. As you read this chapter and the next one, you may decide that you are suffering from one of the disorders you read about. Perhaps you are, but recognizing a little of yourself in the description of a psychological disorder does not mean that you have the disorder. All of us feel sad, nervous, or angry occasionally, and many of us have mood swings, bad habits, or beliefs that strike other people as odd. *A diagnosis of a psychological disorder should be reserved for people with problems that seriously interfere with their lives.*

## Defining Abnormal Behavior

How should we define abnormal behavior? To try to be completely objective, we might define *abnormal* as any behavior that differs very much from the average. However, by that definition, unusually happy or successful people are abnormal, and severe depression would be normal if it became common enough. When we say "abnormal," we mean something other than "different."

a

b

■ What we consider normal or abnormal depends on the context. (a) People dressed as witches ski down a mountain as part of an annual festival in Belalp, Switzerland, in which dressing as witches is supposed to chase away evil spirits. (b) A Malaysian boy kisses a deadly king cobra as part of a competition to win $2000 for performing various feats with three species of snakes.

The American Psychiatric Association (1994) has defined as abnormal any behavior that leads to distress (pain), disability (impaired functioning), or an increased risk of death, pain, or loss of freedom. We can question this definition as well. For example, when Martin Luther King, Jr., fought for the rights of African Americans, he risked death, pain, and loss of freedom, but we regard his acts as heroic, not abnormal.

Another way to define abnormal would be to let people decide for themselves whether they are troubled. For example, someone might say, "Everyone thinks I'm doing fine, but inside I feel miserable." According to a definition that focuses on distress, anyone who thinks he has a psychological problem does have a problem (Figure 15.1).

Fair enough, but what about people who insist that they do *not* have a problem? Imagine a woman who babbles incoherently, urinates and defecates in the street, insults strangers, begs for $1 bills and then sets fire to them, while claiming to be obeying messages from another planet. She reports feeling no distress and refuses all offers of help. If we call her abnormal or disordered, then what we mean by "abnormal" does not require a feeling of distress. Perhaps, when we say "abnormal," we inevitably imply that the condition is somehow undesirable.

**A STEP FURTHER**
*What Is Abnormal?*

How would *you* define abnormal behavior?

## Cultural Influences on Abnormality

Each time and place has interpreted abnormal behavior according to its own world-view. People in the Middle Ages, for example, regarded peculiar behavior as a sign of demon possession that needed treatment with religious rituals.

In one culture in Sudan some years ago, women had low status and very limited rights; if a woman's husband mistreated her, she had no defense. However, people in this society believed that a woman could be possessed by a demon, who caused her to lose control and scream all sorts of "crazy" things that she "could not possibly believe," including insults against her own husband (!). Her husband could not scold or punish her because, after all, it was not really she, but only the demon who was speaking. The standard way to remove the demon was to provide the woman with luxurious food, new clothing, an opportunity to spend much time with other women, and almost anything else she demanded until the demon departed. You can guess how common demon possession became (Constantinides, 1977).

More examples: *Brain fag syndrome* is a psychiatric condition with headache, eye fatigue, and inability to concentrate—a common complaint among West African students just before exams. You might try explaining to your own professor that you cannot take a test tomorrow because you have brain fag syndrome, but unless you live in West Africa, I doubt that your explanation will do you much good.

You have probably heard the expression "to run amok." *Running amok* is a type of abnormal behavior recognized in parts of Southeast Asia, where someone (usually a young man) runs around engaging in indiscriminate violent behavior (Berry, Poortinga, Segal, & Dasen, 1992). Such behavior is considered an understandable reaction to psychological stress, not a criminal

**FIGURE 15.1** Munch, Edvard (1864–1944), *Self Portrait, The Night Wanderer*, 1923–24, Munch Museum, Oslo, Norway. In this self-portrait, Munch reveals sides of his life that most other people wish to keep hidden; anxiety and restlessness are a result of loneliness. The uncurtained windows and the bare room emphasize the feeling of loneliness and isolation.

offense. Does running amok remind you of anything common in North America or Europe? How about the celebrations that occur after a sports team wins a major championship? (see Figure 15.2) Like running amok, we regard such wild displays as temporary excusable responses to overwhelming emotion.

I do not mean to imply that brain fag, running amok, or demon possession is pretended mental illness. Chances are those people really do have stresses and problems in their lives. The point is that their way of reacting to those problems was modeled on suggestions they had received from others. One Australian psychiatrist found that three mental patients had cut off one of their ears. Assuming that this behavior must be a common but previously unpublicized symptom of mental illness, he contacted other psychiatrists throughout Australia and New Zealand to ask how often they had

FIGURE 15.2 After a victory in a major sports event, the home-town fans often celebrate with a destructive rampage. Under other circumstances such acts would be considered criminal or insane; under these circumstances we are more tolerant.

observed the same thing. Only one of them ever had, and he had seen it only once. Apparently, one patient cut off his ear and the other two copied (Alroe & Gunda, 1995). (Why they copied is, of course, an interesting question.)

Suggestion is probably also a major influence in **dissociative identity disorder (DID),** previously known as **multiple personality disorder,** in which *a person alternates among two or more distinct personalities, each with its own behavioral patterns, memories, and even name, almost as if each personality were really a different person.* Note that alternating among different personalities is *not* schizophrenia, although the media often misdescribe it as such. We consider schizophrenia in Chapter 16. Dissociative identity disorder was extremely rare before the 1950s, when a few cases received much publicity. Chris Costner White Sizemore was featured in the book and movie *The Three Faces of Eve,* written by her psychiatrists (Thigpen & Cleckley, 1957). Sizemore ("Eve") eventually told her own story, which was very different from her psychiatrists' version (Sizemore & Huber, 1988; Sizemore & Pittillo, 1977) (see Figure 15.3). A few other people with dissociative identity disorder also received extensive publicity, such as the celebrated case *Sybil,* and by the early 1990s, some therapists were reporting many such cases. Why has the apparent prevalence increased so much? Some observers have charged that dissociative identity disorder does not even exist, and people are imagining or pretending their symptoms. Researchers have assembled convincing evidence against that hypothesis; people are unlikely to choose dis-

sociative identity disorder voluntarily (Eich, Macaulay, Loewenstein, & Dihle, 1997; Gleaves, 1996). A more plausible hypothesis is that overeager therapists notice minor symptoms and then through well-meaning questions, sometimes with the individual under hypnosis, suggest that the person might have an additional personality. At first, the person may have had only a small tendency toward different personalities at different times, but after a few therapy sessions, the dissociation becomes more severe (Lilienfeld et al., 1999). As mentioned in the last chapter, people often conform to the expectations of others, and an expectation of abnormal behavior can produce that abnormality in vulnerable people.

In Western cultures today, the predominant view is the **biopsychosocial model,** which emphasizes that *abnormal behavior has three major aspects: biological, psychological, and sociological.* Many researchers and therapists focus more on one aspect than another, but few would deny that all three are important.

The *biological* roots of abnormal behavior include genetic factors, which can lead to abnormal brain development, excesses or deficiencies in the activity of various neurotransmitters or hormones, and so forth. Behavior can also be affected by brain damage, infectious diseases,

FIGURE 15.3 Chris Sizemore, whose story was told in *The Three Faces of Eve,* exhibited a total of 22 personalities, including her final, permanent identity. Films, television, and other media often mistakenly refer to dissociative identity disorder (DID) as "schizophrenia." People with schizophrenia have only one personality; that personality, however, is abnormal in serious ways.

brain tumors, poor nutrition, inadequate sleep, and the overuse of drugs, including nonprescription medications.

The *psychological* component of abnormality includes a person's vulnerability to stressful events. For example, people who are known to have been physically or sexually abused in childhood are more likely than others to develop psychological problems in adulthood (Johnson, Cohen, Brown, Smailes, & Bernstein, 1999). Of course, almost anyone can develop problems if the difficulties of current life are severe enough.

Finally, the behavior must be understood in a *social* and *cultural* context. People are greatly influenced by how other people act toward them and what other people expect of them. When someone acts strange, in many cases that person is part of a disordered family or social network, and the others are acting just as strange or even worse.

Unfortunately, the agreement that abnormality depends on biological, psychological, and social influences doesn't tell us much about an individual case. For example, suppose you are a therapist and you meet someone who cries almost constantly. Before you begin treatment for depression, you need to rule out other possibilities, ranging from the recent death of a loved one to the presence of a brain tumor. Different people with apparently the same symptoms can have different underlying problems.

## CONCEPT CHECK

I. Of the three aspects of the biopsychosocial model, which one would be most prominent in explanations of brain fag syndrome and running amok? (Check your answer on page 588.)

# Classifying Psychological Disorders

Any scientific study must be based on agreed standards for classifying information. If several psychologists conducted research on the causes or treatment of depression but each defined depression differently, chaos would result.

That kind of chaos *has* often occurred in psychology, and as a result, psychologists have worked hard to establish uniform definitions and standards for diagnosis. The result of that effort is *a reference book called* the **Diagnostic and Statistical Manual of Mental Disorders (DSM)**—now in its fourth edition and therefore known as **DSM-IV**—which *lists the acceptable labels for all psychological disorders* (alcohol intoxication, exhibitionism, pathological gambling, anorexia nervosa, sleepwalking disorder, stuttering, and hundreds of others), with a description of each disorder and an explanation of how to distinguish it from similar disorders.

■ Almost everyone has an unpleasant mood or behaves strangely once in a while. Many people who qualify for a *DSM-IV* diagnosis are not very different from anyone else.

## DSM-IV *Classifications*

The clinicians and researchers who use *DSM-IV* classify each client along five separate *axes* (lists). A person may have one or more disorders on a given axis—for example, alcohol abuse and depression—or none at all. The axis that gets the most attention is *Axis I, clinical disorders.* Table 15.1 lists the major categories of disorder on Axis I. Every disorder on Axis I has its onset at some time after infancy and thus represents a deterioration of functioning. That is, the person is doing worse now than at some point in the past. Axis I conditions include the most common psychological disorders—anxiety disorders, substance abuse, and depression. They also include schizophrenia, a condition that can be extremely disabling. (In Chapter 16 we shall explore these disorders in detail.) Axis I also includes eating disorders, sleep disorders, and impulse control disorders, which have all been mentioned in previous chapters, as well as several others.

*Axis II, personality disorders and mental retardation*, lists disorders that generally persist throughout life (see Table 15.2). These conditions seem to be an integral part of the self rather than something that a person acquires. A **personality disorder** is *a maladaptive, inflexible way of dealing with the environment and other people*, such as antisocial behavior or avoidance of other people. Many other psychological disorders resemble medical diseases to some extent, whereas personality disorders are an integral part of the person, like being tall, left-handed, or red-headed. People with personality disorders seldom complain about their condition and seldom seek treatment, except at the insistence of family, acquaintances, or an employer. Even when they do seek treatment, substantial improvement is uncommon.

*Axis III, general medical conditions*, lists physical disorders, such as diabetes or alcoholic cirrhosis of the liver. A psychotherapist does not provide treatment for Axis III

**TABLE 15.1** Some Major Categories of Psychological Disorders According to Axis I of *DSM-IV*

| Category | Examples and Descriptions |
| --- | --- |
| *Disorder usually first evident in childhood* | *Attention deficit hyperactivity disorder:* impulsivity, impaired attention<br>*Tourette's disorder:* repetitive movements such as blinking, twitching, chanting sounds or words<br>*Elimination disorders:* bedwetting, urinating or defecating in one's clothes<br>*Stuttering:* frequent repetition or prolongation of sounds while trying to speak |
| *Substance-related disorders* | *Abuse of alcohol, cocaine, opiates, or other drugs* |
| *Schizophrenia* | Deterioration of daily functioning along with a combination of hallucinations, delusions, or other symptoms |
| *Delusional (paranoid) disorder* | Unjustifiable beliefs, such as "everyone is talking about me behind my back" |
| *Mood disorders* | *Major depressive disorder:* Repeated episodes of depressed mood and lack of energy<br>*Bipolar disorder:* Alternation between periods of depression and mania |
| *Anxiety disorders* | *Panic disorder:* Repeated attacks of intense terror<br>*Phobia:* Severe anxiety and avoidance of a particular object or situation |
| *Somatoform disorders* | *Conversion disorder:* Physical ailments caused partly by psychological factors but not faked<br>*Hypochondriasis:* Exaggerated complaints of illness<br>*Somatization disorder:* Complaints of pain or other ailments without any physical disorder |
| *Dissociative disorders* | Loss of personal identity or memory without brain damage |
| *Sexual disorders* | *Pedophilia:* Sexual attraction to children<br>*Voyeurism:* Sexual arousal primarily from watching others undress or have sexual relations<br>*Exhibitionism:* Sexual arousal from exposing one's genitals in public |
| *Eating disorders* | *Anorexia nervosa:* Refusal to eat, fear of fatness<br>*Bulimia nervosa:* Binge eating alternating with severe dieting |
| *Sleep disorders* | *Sleep terror disorder:* Repeated sudden awakenings in a state of panic<br>*Insomnia:* Frequently not getting enough sleep to feel well rested the next day |
| *Impulse control disorders* | Frequently acting on impulses that others would inhibit, such as stealing, gambling foolishly, or hitting people |

disorders but needs to know about them because they influence behavior.

*Axis IV, psychosocial and environmental problems,* indicates how much stress the person has had to endure, on a scale from 0 (almost none) to 6 (the equivalent of experiencing the death of a child). Stress can intensify a psychological disorder and thus affect the course of treatment.

*Axis V, global assessment of functioning,* evaluates a person's overall level of functioning, on a scale from 1 (serious attempt at suicide or complete inability to take care of oneself) to 90 (happy, productive, with many interests). Some

people with a psychological disorder are able to proceed with their normal work and social activities; others are not.

## The Importance of Differential Diagnosis

In abnormal psychology, as in medicine, any diagnosis (identification) of a disorder requires ruling out other possibilities. For example, suppose someone says, "I feel unenergetic and pessimistic; I have trouble sleeping at nights; I don't have much appetite; and nothing brings me pleasure anymore." That description sounds very

**TABLE 15.2 Some Major Categories of Psychological Disorders According to Axis II of** *DSM-IV*

| Category | Examples and Descriptions |
|---|---|
| *Mental retardation* | Intellectual functioning significantly below average; inability to function effectively and independently |
| *Personality disorders* | *Paranoid personality disorder:* Suspiciousness, habitual interpretation of others' acts as threatening |
| | *Schizotypal personality disorder:* Poor relationships with other people; odd thinking; neglect of normal grooming. Similar to schizophrenia but less severe. |
| | *Antisocial personality disorder:* Lack of affection for others; high probability of harming others without feeling guilty |
| | *Borderline personality disorder:* Lack of stable self-image; trouble establishing lasting relationships or maintaining lasting decisions; repeated self-endangering behaviors |
| | *Histrionic personality disorder:* Excessive emotionality and attention seeking |
| | *Narcissistic personality disorder:* Exaggerated opinion of one's own importance and disregard for others. (Narcissus was a figure in Greek mythology who fell in love with his own image.) |
| | *Avoidant personality disorder:* Avoidance of social contact; lack of friends |
| | *Dependent personality disorder:* Preference for letting other people make decisions; lack of initiative and self-confidence |

much like depression, but the same symptoms could be the result of a malfunctioning thyroid gland, a stroke, the side effects from taking certain medications, withdrawal effects after quitting cocaine, a grief reaction following the death of a loved one, nutritional deficiencies, or fatigue. Psychiatrists and clinical psychologists must learn to make a **differential diagnosis**—that is, *a determination of what problem a person has in contrast to all the other possible problems that might produce similar symptoms.* Only a therapist who understands the problem well can choose the best treatment.

## Criticisms of DSM-IV

*DSM-IV* has helped standardize psychiatric diagnoses, but even its loyalest defenders admit it is far from perfect. Problems include the difficulty of distinguishing normal from abnormal and the question of whether *DSM-IV* is treating adjustment problems as if they were mental illnesses.

### Distinguishing Normal from Abnormal

Consider the sexual disorders such as *pedophilia* (sexual interest in children), *voyeurism* (sexual excitement from secretly watching others undress or have sexual relations), and *sexual masochism* (sexual pleasure from receiving pain). *DSM-IV* classifies each of these as a mental illness if it continues for at least 6 months. Obviously, it is arbitrary to say that 5 months of pedophilia is not a disorder but 6 months is. A more difficult question is whether everyone who has unacceptable sexual desires is

mentally ill. We do not assume that all murderers are mentally ill, for example. Frankly, no one knows how to decide whether a socially unacceptable sexual desire is or is not a product of mental illness (Widiger & Clark, 2000).

Furthermore, every disorder varies in degree from mild to severe. Psychologists and psychiatrists do their best to make consistent diagnoses, but marginal cases call for difficult judgments. Therefore, any statistics about the prevalence of psychological disorders are somewhat uncertain. In one survey of a random sample of about 20,000 people in three U.S. cities, trained interviewers reported that about one-fifth of all adults were suffering from a psychological disorder of some sort (as defined by *DSM*) and that close to one-third had suffered from such a disorder at some point (Myers et al., 1984; Robins et al., 1984). A similar study conducted 10 years later estimated that about one-half of all people endure a psychological disorder at some point in their lives (Kessler et al., 1994). According to both surveys, the most common psychological disorders are anxiety disorders, alcohol or drug abuse, and mood disorders (including depression), as shown in Figure 15.4. Is it believable that half of all people are psychologically disordered at some point in life? Depending on how we classify marginal cases, the percentage could be lower or even higher.

A related issue is that many people do not fit neatly into any single category. For example, many have combinations of depression, anxiety, alcohol abuse, and other disorders. *DSM-IV* lists these as separate disorders, but in the real world, they overlap heavily (Widiger & Clark, 2000).

### Is Abnormal Behavior in the Person or the Situation?

Another major criticism is that *DSM-IV* classifies adjustment problems as if they were mental illnesses (Kutchins & Kirk, 1997). Health insurance companies are more likely to reimburse psychotherapy for people with diagnosed disorders than for sessions with people who just want to talk about life's difficulties. Suppose a child who is frequently bullied starts protesting vehemently against going to school, sometimes even vomiting on school

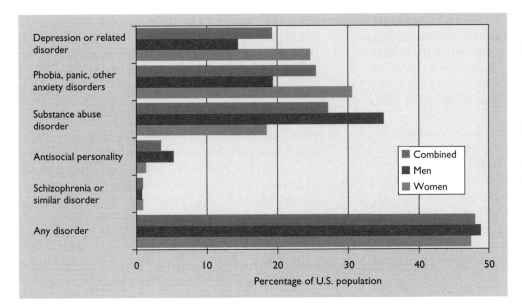

**FIGURE 15.4** According to one extensive survey, about half the people in the United States will suffer at least one psychological disorder at some time. (The figures for the individual conditions do not add up to the total percentage for "any disorder" because some people have more than one disorder.) However, the exact percentages depend on where one draws the dividing line between "normal" and "abnormal." (Based on data of Kessler et al., 1994)

mornings. Imagine a woman who has left an abusive relationship and is trying to restore her damaged self-esteem. If a therapist diagnoses them as having an anxiety disorder, the insurance company will pay for the treatment. Therefore, the authors of *DSM-IV* broadened the definitions of many disorders and described new disorders so that if you go to a therapist for almost any problem, you can receive a psychiatric diagnosis and have your insurance company pay for at least a few sessions of treatment.

The disadvantage is that you will have the stigma of being diagnosed with a psychological disorder. Also, the diagnosis implies that the problem is in you, whereas in reality the problem may be in the social situation. After all, almost anyone would balk at going to school and being bullied, and almost anyone would have trouble recovering from an abusive relationship.

### CONCEPT CHECKS

2. If a new psychological disorder is discovered, how would we decide whether to list it on Axis I or Axis II of *DSM-IV*?
3. Why should we be somewhat skeptical of all statistics about the prevalence of psychological disorders? (Check your answers on page 588.)

### IN CLOSING
### *Is Anyone Normal?*

Being diagnosed with a psychological disorder still has a stigma. Almost any synonym for mental illness is considered an insult. Nevertheless, according to one study described in this module, about one-half of all people in the

United States will have a *DSM-IV* disorder at some point in life. If that statistic is even close to accurate, the implication is obvious: Most of the people who qualify for a psychological diagnosis are not very different from everyone else. At some point in your life, you may have a bout of depression or anxiety or suffer from substance abuse or other psychological distress. If so, remember that you have plenty of company.

## Summary

- **Normal and abnormal behavior.** Although psychologists and psychiatrists try to be objective and scientific when identifying abnormal behavior, some assessments are necessarily difficult and dependent on value judgments. To avoid tyrannical subjugation of eccentric people, we should be cautious about applying psychiatric labels. (page 581)
- **Cultural influences on abnormality.** Every culture provides examples not only of how to behave normally but also of how to behave abnormally. (page 582)
- **Multiple causes of abnormal behavior.** Abnormal behavior is the result of various combinations of biological factors, early experiences, and learned responses to a stressful or unsupportive environment. (page 583)
- **The *Diagnostic and Statistical Manual.*** Psychological disorders are classified in the *Diagnostic and Statistical Manual of Mental Disorders, Fourth Edition (DSM-IV)*. This manual classifies disorders along five axes. Axes I and II contain psychological disorders; Axis III lists physical ailments that can affect behavior; Axes IV and V provide the means of evaluating a person's stress level and overall functioning. (page 584)
- **Axis I, disorders that affect part of a person's life.** Axis I of *DSM-IV* lists disorders that usually begin after

588 Chapter 15 Abnormality, Therapy, and Social Issues

infancy and that have at least some likelihood of recovery. Three common disorders of this sort are anxiety disorders, substance abuse, and depression. (page 584)

- **Axis II, lifelong disorders.** Axis II of *DSM-IV* lists conditions that arise early and persist throughout a lifetime, such as mental retardation and personality disorders. (page 584)
- **Personality disorders.** Personality disorders are stable characteristics that impair a person's effectiveness or ability to get along with others. Examples of personality disorders are excessive dependence on others and excessive self-centeredness. (page 584)
- **Differential diagnosis.** Psychiatrists and clinical psychologists need to learn to consider all the possible diagnoses of a given set of symptoms and to identify the correct one by eliminating all the other possibilities. (page 585)
- **Criticisms of *DSM-IV*.** In spite of the efforts of *DSM-IV* to provide clear guidelines, it remains difficult to

distinguish between normal and abnormal. Also, *DSM-IV* has been criticized for labeling many people as psychologically disordered, when in fact they are reacting normally to an abnormal situation. (page 586)

## Answers to Concept Checks

1. The social aspect would certainly be prominent because these disorders occur only in cultures that have made them seem like options. However, the people showing these symptoms may have biological and psychological problems as well. (page 584)
2. If it begins early in life and lasts a lifetime, it belongs on Axis II. If it begins later in life and has some prospect of being relieved, it belongs on Axis I. (page 587)
3. Each disorder occurs in varying degrees, and psychologists can disagree about their diagnosis for many mild or marginal cases. (page 587)

# Psychotherapy: An Overview

*What methods are used to combat psychological disorders, and how effective are they?*

Observation
If I don't drive around the park,
I'm pretty sure to make my mark.
If I'm in bed each night by ten,
I may get back my looks again.
If I abstain from fun and such,
I'll probably amount to much.
But I shall stay the way I am,
Because I do not give a damn.
—Dorothy Parker (1944)

**Psychotherapy** is *a treatment of psychological disorders by methods that include a personal relationship between a trained therapist and a client.* But psychotherapy does little good unless the client gives the proverbial damn.

Psychotherapy is used for many well-defined disorders that are listed in *DSM-IV* and also for adjustment and coping problems. Some psychotherapy clients are virtually incapacitated by their problems, but others are reasonably happy, successful people who would like to function even more successfully.

Before World War II, almost all psychotherapists were psychiatrists, and most of them used Freudian methods.

■ A psychotherapist, like this military psychologist in a Haitian refugee camp, tries to help people overcome problems or, better yet, to help themselves.

Today, psychotherapy is available from clinical psychologists, social workers, counseling psychologists, and others, using hundreds of methods and approaches that differ markedly. A therapist might argue with a client or just sit and listen sympathetically. A therapist might try to trace the client's problem to past experiences or just concentrate on the present. The goal might be to understand the meaning behind a behavior or just to change the behavior. Nevertheless, as you will see, the various forms of therapy have major similarities as well as differences.

## Psychoanalysis

**Psychodynamic therapies** *attempt to relate personality to the interplay of conflicting forces within the individual, including some that the individual may not consciously recognize.* For example, both Sigmund Freud's procedure (looking for sexual motives) and Alfred Adler's procedure (looking for power and superiority motives) are considered psychodynamic, despite the differences between them. Here we shall focus on the procedure developed by Freud, although its practitioners have modified and developed it further since Freud's time.

**Psychoanalysis,** the first of the "talk" therapies, is *a method based on identifying unconscious thoughts and emotions and bringing them to consciousness to help people understand their thoughts and actions.* Psychoanalysis is therefore described as an "insight-oriented therapy" in contrast to therapies that focus on changing thoughts and behaviors (Figure 15.5).

Freud believed that psychological problems are the result of unconscious thought processes and that the only way to control self-defeating behavior is to make those processes conscious. Bringing them to consciousness, he thought, would produce **catharsis,** *a release of pent-up emotions associated with unconscious thoughts and memories.* Among Freud's methods of bringing unconscious material to consciousness were free association and transference. He also used dream analysis, as discussed in Chapter 5.

### Free Association

Free association is a method that Freud and his patients developed together. (Actually, a more accurate translation of the original German expression is "free intrusion.") In **free association** the client *starts thinking about a particular symptom or problem and then reports everything*

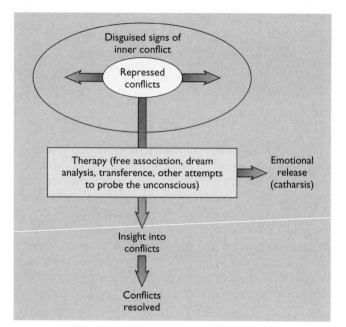

**FIGURE 15.5** The goal of psychoanalysis is to resolve psychological problems by bringing to awareness the unconscious thought processes that created the difficulty. *Analysis* literally means "to loosen or break up, to look at the parts."

*that comes to mind—a word, a phrase, a visual image.* The client is instructed not to omit or censor anything or even try to speak in complete sentences.

The psychoanalyst listens for links and themes that might tie the patient's fragmentary remarks together. The assumption is that all behavior is determined, that nothing happens without a cause. (Recall from Chapter 6 that behaviorists make the same assumption, although they look for a different kind of cause.) Every jump from one thought to another reveals a relationship between them.

Here is a paraphrased excerpt from a free-association session:

A man begins by describing a conference he had with his boss the previous day. He did not like the boss's policy, but he was in no position to contradict the boss. He had had a dream. It was something about an ironing board, but that was all he remembered of the dream. He comments that his wife has been complaining about the way their maid irons. He thinks his wife is being unfair; he hopes she does not fire the maid. He complains that his boss did not give him credit for some work he did recently. He recalls a childhood episode: He jumped off a cupboard and bounced off his mother's behind while she was leaning over to do some ironing. She told his father, who gave him a spanking. His father never let him explain; he was always too strict. (Munroe, 1955, p. 39)

To a psychoanalyst, the links in this story suggest that the man is associating his wife with his mother. His wife was unfair to the maid about the ironing, just as his mother had been unfair to him. Moreover, his boss is like his father, never giving him a chance to explain his errors and never giving him credit for what he did well.

## Transference

Some clients show either exaggerated love or hatred for their therapist, which seems inappropriate under the circumstances. Psychoanalysts call this reaction **transference;** they mean that clients are *transferring onto the therapist the behaviors and feelings they originally established toward their father or mother or another important figure.* Transference often provides clues to the client's feelings about that person.

Psychoanalysts offer **interpretations** of what the client says—that is, they *explain the underlying meaning*—and may even argue with the client about interpretations. They may regard the client's disagreement as **resistance,** *continued repression that interferes with therapy.* Resistance can take many forms; for example, a client who has begun to touch on an extremely anxiety-provoking topic may turn the conversation to something trivial or may simply "forget" to come to the next session.

Psychoanalysts today modify Freud's approach in many ways (Karon & Widener, 1995). The goal is still to bring about a major reorganization of the personality, changing a person from the inside out, by helping people understand the hidden reasons behind their actions.

# Behavior Therapy

Behavior therapists assume that human behavior is learned and that it can be unlearned. They identify the behavior that needs to be changed, such as a phobia or an addiction or a nervous twitch, and then set about changing it through reinforcement, punishment, and other principles of learning. They may try to understand the causes of the behavior as a first step toward changing it, but unlike psychoanalysts, they are more interested in changing behaviors than in understanding their hidden meanings.

**Behavior therapy** *begins with clear, well-defined behavioral goals, such as eliminating test anxiety or breaking a bad habit, and then attempts to achieve those goals through learning.* Setting clear goals enables the therapist to judge whether the therapy is succeeding. If the client shows no improvement after a few sessions, the therapist tries a different procedure.

One example of behavior therapy is for children who wet the bed long after the usual age of toilet training. Most of them outgrow the problem, but it occasionally lingers to age 5, 10, or even into the teens. We now know that many bedwetters have small bladders and thus have difficulty getting through the night without urinating. We also know that many are unusually deep sleepers who do not wake up when they need to urinate (Stegat, 1975).

The most effective procedure uses classical conditioning to train the child to wake up at night when the bladder is full (Houts, Berman, & Abramson, 1994). A small battery-powered device is attached to the child's under-

**FIGURE 15.6** A small device called a Potty Pager fits into a child's underwear and produces a vibration when it becomes moist. This awakens the child, who then learns to awaken when the bladder is full. (Photo courtesy of Ideas for Living, Inc., Boulder, CO)

wear at night (Figure 15.6). When the child urinates, the device detects the moisture and produces a pulsing vibration that awakens the child. (Alternative devices work on the same principle but produce loud noises.)

The vibration acts as an unconditioned stimulus (UCS) that evokes the unconditioned response (UCR) of waking up. In this instance the body itself generates the conditioned stimulus (CS): the sensation produced by a full bladder (Figure 15.7). Whenever that sensation is present, it serves as a signal that the vibration is imminent. After a few pairings (or more), the sensation of a full bladder is enough to wake the child.

Actually, the situation is a little more complicated because the child is positively reinforced with praise for waking up to use the toilet. Thus, the process includes both classical and operant conditioning. Training by use of an alarm or vibration eliminates bedwetting in most children, though not all, and is sometimes effective after as little as one night.

# Therapies That Focus on Thoughts and Beliefs

Someone says to you, "Look how messy your room is! Don't you ever clean it?" How do you react? You might say, "Big deal. Maybe I'll clean it tomorrow." Or you might feel worried, angry, or even depressed. If you get upset, it may not be because you were criticized but because you want everyone to believe that you are scrupulously clean and tidy. Some therapists focus on the thoughts and beliefs that underlie emotional reactions. Unlike psychoanalysts, these therapists are more concerned about what their clients are thinking right now than about the early experiences that led to these thoughts.

## Cognitive and Rational-Emotive Therapies

**Cognitive therapy** *seeks to improve people's psychological well-being by changing their thoughts and beliefs—their cognitions* (Beck, 1976; Hollon & Beck, 1979). For example, someone who has undergone an extremely stressful experience, such as being raped or witnessing a fatal accident, may harbor irrational and harmful beliefs such as "it was my fault" or "it will happen to me again" (Marks, Lovell, Noshirvani, Livanou, & Thrasher, 1998). A cognitive therapist tries to identify these thoughts and encourages the client to explore the evidence behind them. Usually, the client discovers that the beliefs are unjustified and eventually learns to identify and challenge the disruptive thoughts. (We shall discuss cognitive therapy for depression in Chapter 16.)

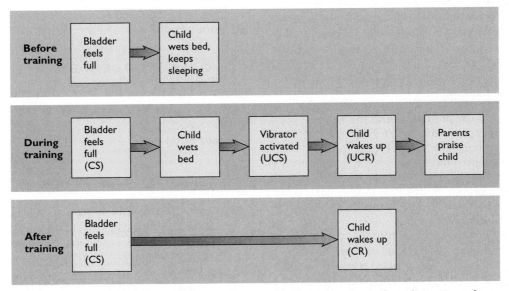

**FIGURE 15.7** A child can be trained not to wet the bed by using classical conditioning techniques. At first, the sensation of a full bladder (the CS) produces no response, and the child wets the bed. This causes a vibration or other alarm (the UCS), and the child wakes up (the UCR). By associating the sensation of a full bladder with a vibration, the child soon begins waking up to the sensation of a full bladder alone and will not wet the bed.

a                                                      b

■ (a) The explosion of the space shuttle *Challenger* in 1986 killed six astronauts and a school teacher, and was deeply upsetting to a great many people. (b) Fictional tragedies in films, like the one in *Con Air*, are far less disturbing. The impact of any event depends not just on the event itself but also on its context and how we interpret it.

A related approach, **rational-emotive therapy,** *assumes that thoughts (rationality) lead to emotions. The problem therefore is not the unpleasant emotions themselves, but the irrational thoughts that lead to them.*

Rational-emotive therapists believe that abnormal behavior often results from irrational "internal sentences" such as these (Ellis, 1987):

- I must perform certain tasks successfully.
- I must perform well at all times.
- I must have the approval of certain people at all times.
- Others must treat me fairly and with consideration.
- I must live under easy, gratifying conditions.

The word *must* makes these beliefs irrational. Rational-emotive therapists try to identify irrational beliefs (which people may never have verbalized) and then contradict them. They urge clients to substitute other more realistic internal sentences. Here is an excerpt from a rational-emotive therapy session with a 25-year-old physicist:

**CLIENT:** The whole trouble is that I am really a phony. I am living under false pretenses. And the longer it goes on, the more people praise me and make a fuss over my accomplishments, the worse I feel.

**THERAPIST:** What do you mean you are a phony? I thought that you told me, during our last session, that your work has been examined at another laboratory and that some of the people there think your ideas are of revolutionary importance.

**CLIENT:** But I have wasted so much time. I could be doing very much better. . . . Remember that book I told you I was writing . . . it's been three weeks now since I've spent any time on it. And this is simple stuff that I should be able to do with my left hand while I am writing a technical paper with my right. I have heard Bob Oppenheimer reel off stuff extemporaneously to a bunch of newspaper reporters that is twice as good as what I am mightily laboring on in this damned book!

**THERAPIST:** Perhaps so. And perhaps you're not quite as good—yet—as Oppenheimer or a few other outstanding people in your field. But the real point, it seems to me, is that . . . here you are, at just twenty-five, with a Ph.D. in a most difficult field, with an excellent job, much good work in process, and what well may be a fine professional paper and a good popular book also in progress. And just because you're not another Oppenheimer or Einstein quite yet, you're savagely berating yourself.

**CLIENT:** Well, shouldn't I be doing much better than I am?

**THERAPIST:** No, why the devil should you? As far as I can see, you are not doing badly at all. But your major difficulty—the main cause of your present unhappiness—is your utterly perfectionistic criteria for judging your performance. (Ellis & Harper, 1961, pp. 99–100)

## CONCEPT CHECK

4. How does the concept behind rational-emotive therapy compare to the James-Lange theory of emotions discussed in Chapter 12? (Check your answer on page 601.)

## Cognitive-Behavior Therapy

Many therapists combine important features of both behavior therapy and cognitive therapy to form **cognitive-behavior therapy.** Cognitive-behavior therapists *set explicit goals for changing people's behavior, but they place more emphasis than most behavior therapists do on changing people's interpretation of their situation.* For example, most of us become very upset if we see a video news report showing a fatal automobile accident; we would be much less upset if someone told us that the film was a special-effects simulation (Meichenbaum, 1995). Similarly, cognitive-behavior therapists try to help clients distinguish between serious problems and imagined or exaggerated problems. They help clients change their interpretations of past events, current concerns, and future possibilities. Cognitive-behavior therapy has become one of the most widespread forms of therapy in the United States.

# Humanistic Therapy

As we saw in Chapter 13, humanistic psychologists believe that people can decide consciously and deliberately what kind of person to be and that we naturally strive to achieve our full potential. However, people sometimes learn to dislike themselves because others criticize and reject them. They become distressed by the **incongruence** *(mismatch) between their self-concept and their ideal self.* According to humanistic therapists, once people are freed from the inhibiting influences of a rejecting society, they can solve their own problems.

The best-known version of humanistic therapy is **person-centered therapy,** pioneered by Carl Rogers, which is also known as *nondirective* or *client-centered* therapy. *The therapist listens to the client sympathetically, with total acceptance and unconditional positive regard.* Most of the time, the therapist restates what the client has said to clarify it, thus conveying the message, "I'm trying to understand your experience from your point of view." The therapist strives to be genuine, empathic, and caring, rarely offering any interpretation or advice. Here is an example (shortened from Rogers, 1951, pp. 46–47):

**CLIENT:** I've never said this before to anyone. This is a terrible thing to say, but if I could just find some glorious cause that I could give my life for I would be happy. I guess maybe I haven't the guts—or the strength—to kill myself—and I just don't want to live.

**COUNSELOR:** At the present time things look so black to you that you can't see much point in living.

**CLIENT:** Yes. I wish people hated me, because then I could turn away from them and could blame them. But no, it is all in my hands. I either fight whatever it is that holds me in this terrible conflict, or retreat clear back to the security of my dream world where I could do things, have clever friends, be a pretty wonderful sort of person.

**COUNSELOR:** It's really a tough struggle, digging into this like you are, and at times the shelter of your dream world looks more attractive and comfortable.

**CLIENT:** My dream world or suicide.

**COUNSELOR:** Your dream world or something more permanent than dreams.

**CLIENT:** Yes. (A long pause. Complete change of voice.) So I don't see why I should waste your time. I'm not worth it. What do you think?

**COUNSELOR:** It's up to you, Gil. It isn't wasting my time. I'd be glad to see you, whenever you come, but it's how you feel about it. If you want to come twice a week, once a week, it's up to you.

**CLIENT:** You're not going to suggest that I come in oftener? You're not alarmed and think I ought to come in every day until I get out of this?

**COUNSELOR:** I believe you are able to make your own decision. I'll see you whenever you want to come.

**CLIENT:** I don't believe you are alarmed about . . . I see. I may be afraid of myself, but you aren't afraid for me.

The therapist provides an atmosphere in which the client can freely explore feelings of guilt, anxiety, and hostility. By accepting the client's feelings, the therapist conveys the message, "You can make your own decisions. Now that you are more aware of certain problems, you can deal with them constructively yourself."

## CONCEPT CHECK

5. Answer the following questions with reference to psychoanalysis, cognitive or rational-emotive therapy, humanistic therapy, and behavior therapy.
   a. With which type of therapy is the therapist least likely to offer advice and interpretations of behavior?
   b. Which type focuses more on changing what people do than on exploring what they think?
   c. Which two types of therapy try to change what people think? (Check your answers on page 601.)

# Family Systems Therapy

In **family systems therapy,** *the guiding assumptions are that most people's problems develop in a family setting and that the best way to deal with them is to improve family relationships and communication.* Family systems therapy is not exactly an alternative to other forms of therapy; a family therapist can use behavior therapy, cognitive therapy, or other techniques. What distinguishes family therapists is that they prefer to talk with two or more members of a family together. Even when they do talk with just one member of a family, they focus on how that individual fits into the family and how other members of the family have learned to react to him or her. Solving the problem requires changing the family dynamics as well as the individual behavior (Clarkin & Carpenter, 1995; Rohrbaugh, Shoham, Spungen, & Steinglass, 1995).

For example, a young woman with anorexia nervosa (as described in Chapter 10) may have parents who are excessively demanding or may have other difficulties within the family. Providing treatment to only the woman with anorexia would be pointless. It is necessary to enlist her parents' help in monitoring her eating, but without blame, criticism, or dominance (Eisler et al., 2000).

For another example, a young man who had been caught stealing a car was taken to a family therapist who asked to talk with the parents as well. As it turned out, the father had been a heavy drinker until his boss pressured

■ Family therapists treat anorexia nervosa by trying to get the parents to supervise the patient's feeding, but without criticism or blame.

him to quit drinking and join Alcoholics Anonymous. Until that time the mother had made most of the family decisions in close consultation with her son, who had become almost a substitute husband. When the father quit drinking, he began to assume more authority over the family, and his son came to resent him. The mother felt less needed and grew depressed. Each member of the family had problems that they could not resolve separately. The therapist worked to help the father improve his relationship with both his son and his wife and to help all three find satisfying roles within the family (Foley, 1984).

## Other Trends in Psychotherapy

Hundreds of types of therapy are available, including some that are quite different from the five discussed thus far (see Table 15.3). About half of all U.S. psychotherapists profess no strong allegiance to any single form of therapy. Instead, they practice **eclectic therapy,** meaning that they *use a combination of methods and approaches.* An eclectic therapist might use behavior therapy with one client and rational-emotive therapy with another or else start with one therapy and then shift to another if the

**TABLE 15.3** Comparison of Five Types of Psychotherapy

| Type of Psychotherapy | Theory of What Causes Psychological Disorders | Goal of Treatment | Therapeutic Methods | Role of Therapist |
|---|---|---|---|---|
| *Psychoanalysis* | Unconscious thoughts and motivations | To bring unconscious thoughts to consciousness to achieve insight | Free association, dream analysis, and other methods of probing the unconscious mind | To interpret associations |
| *Cognitive therapies* | Irrational beliefs and unrealistic goals | To establish realistic goals, expectations, and interpretations of a situation | Dialog with the therapist | To help the client reexamine assumptions |
| *Humanistic (person-centered) therapy* | Reactions to a rejecting society; incongruence between self-concept and ideal self | To enable client to make personal decisions; to promote self-acceptance | Client-centered interviews | To focus the client's attention; to provide unconditional positive regard |
| *Behavior therapy* | Learned inappropriate maladaptive behaviors | To change behaviors | Positive reinforcement and other learning techniques | To develop, direct, and evaluate the behavior therapy program |
| *Family system therapy* | Distorted communication and confused roles within a family | To improve the life of each individual by improving functioning of the family | Counseling sessions with the whole family or with the individual talking about life in the family | To promote better family communication and understanding |

first is ineffective. The therapist might also borrow insights from several approaches. Today, most therapists regard themselves as eclectic (Wachtel, 2000).

The early practitioners of psychotherapy insisted on seeing each client one at a time, frequently, and on a long-term basis. Over the years psychotherapists have found ways to make their services less costly, less time-consuming, and therefore available to more people. We shall now consider the alternatives of brief therapy, group therapy, and self-help groups.

## Brief Therapy

Psychotherapy can require a major commitment of time and money. An individual psychotherapy session usually lasts about 50 minutes; depending on the therapist and the nature of the client's problems, the sessions are generally scheduled once per week but can be as often as every day. If the therapy begins with an open-ended plan to continue "as long as necessary," it can easily drag on for years. Indeed, many therapists, especially psychoanalysts, have assumed that frequent sessions conducted over a long period of time are essential for a successful outcome, and they regarded any client who quit after a few sessions as a dropout, a failure.

Eventually, therapists realized that some of the apparent failures were really "premature successes" who did not need further treatment. In fact, about half of all people who enter psychotherapy show significant improvement within 8 sessions, and three-fourths show improvement within 26 sessions (Howard, Kopta, Krause, & Orlinsky, 1986).

As a result many therapists began to place limits on the duration of therapy. At the start of **brief therapy,** or *time-limited therapy, the therapist and the client reach an agreement about what they can expect from each other and how long the treatment will last*—such as once per week for 2 months (Koss & Butcher, 1986). As the deadline approaches, both the therapist and the client are strongly motivated to bring the therapy to a successful conclusion. (How hard would you work on a term paper if you had no deadline to meet? How would a professor conduct the class if a course were scheduled to continue "as long as necessary"? Without deadlines, few of us would apply ourselves diligently.)

Moreover, with a deadline that's agreed on in advance, clients do not feel deserted or rejected when the therapy ends. They may return for an occasional extra session months later, but for a time they must get along without help. Any client who fails to make progress by the deadline should consider going to a different therapist. Many clients, probably most, prefer brief therapy to an indefinitely long commitment, and most clients with mild problems respond well to it.

Unfortunately, however, recent economic trends have created pressure for therapy to be extremely brief, sometimes too brief. People who receive health care through health maintenance organizations (HMOs) pay a fixed amount per month and then receive whatever medical care they need from the staff of the organization. Most HMOs include brief therapy or "crisis intervention" in their services. Anyone who belongs to such an HMO can get a few psychotherapy sessions (typically 3–20, depending on the HMO) without any extra payment or with a small copayment. The advantage is that many people who could not otherwise afford psychotherapy can get help during a time of distress (Hoyt & Austad, 1992). The disadvantage is that the HMO saves money by minimizing services and therefore authorizes only brief therapy even for people with more extensive problems. Any client who needs more than the allotted amount of treatment is either given a prescription for drugs instead of psychotherapy or is encouraged to see a therapist outside the HMO at the client's own expense (Karon, 1995).

Economically speaking, it is impossible to maximize the quality of care and minimize the cost at the same time. The goal of HMOs, to provide good yet inexpensive therapy, is understandable; however, some HMOs provide simply too little. Working out a cost-effective solution is a serious challenge.

## Group Therapy

The pioneers of psychotherapy saw their clients individually. Individual psychotherapy has advantages—most of all, privacy. But for many purposes, it is helpful to treat clients in groups. **Group therapy** *is administered to a group of people all at once.* It first became popular as a method of providing help to people who could not afford to pay for individual sessions. (Spreading the costs of a session among five to ten group members reduces the cost for each.) Eventually, therapists found that group therapy has other advantages as well. Just meeting other people grappling with similar problems can be reassuring. People learn, "I am not so odd after all." Also, many clients seek help because of failed relationships or because they have trouble dealing with other people. A group therapy session enables them to examine how they relate to others, to practice better social skills, and to receive feedback from a variety of people (Ballinger & Yalom, 1995).

## Self-Help Groups

A **self-help group,** such as Alcoholics Anonymous, *operates much like group therapy sessions, except that it does not include a therapist.* Each participant both gives and receives help. People who have experienced a particular problem themselves can offer special insights to others with the same problem. They are especially well prepared for someone who says, "You just don't understand." They reply, "Oh, yes, we do!" Self-help groups

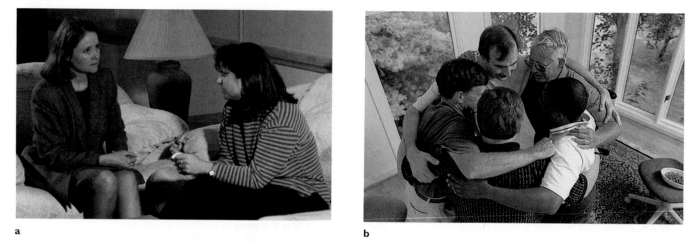

a       b

■ (a) Individual therapy offers complete privacy and the opportunity to pursue individual problems in depth. (b) In group therapy participants can explore their ways of relating to other people.

have another advantage: The members are available whenever someone needs help—often or seldom, without an appointment, and without charge.

Some self-help groups are composed of current or former mental patients. The members feel a need to talk to others who have gone through a similar experience, either in addition to or instead of seeing a therapist. The Mental Patients' Association in Canada was organized by former patients who were frustrated and angry about the treatment they had received (or not received), especially in mental hospitals (Chamberlin, 1978). In similar organizations in the United States and Europe, former patients share experiences, provide support, and work together to defend the rights and welfare of mental patients.

The ultimate in self-help is to deal with problems yourself, without any therapist or group. In a series of studies, James Pennebaker and his colleagues have found that people with mild problems can do themselves an amazing amount of good just by organizing their thoughts about their emotional difficulties. People have been randomly assigned to two groups. One group writes about their most intense and difficult emotional experiences for 15 minutes on 3 or more days; the other group spends the same time writing about unemotional events. The people writing about their emotions consistently show improved mental and physical health over the next few months (Pennebaker & Seagal, 1999). Apparently, writing about a difficult experience helps people to make sense of it and eventually put it behind them. In some cases writing about emotions prompts people to make decisions and change their way of life. In short, for mild problems you might be a good therapist for yourself.

## CONCEPT CHECK

**6.** Brief therapy is a goal or policy for many therapists. Why would it be less important in self-help groups? (Check your answer on page 601.)

## WHAT'S THE EVIDENCE?
### *How Effective Is Psychotherapy?*

The rise of HMOs and other insurance programs heightened interest in measuring the effectiveness of psychotherapy. If you want to pay your own money to talk to someone five times a week for the next 10 years, that decision is yours. However, if you want an insurance company to pay for your sessions, then the company and the other policyholders want to know whether your benefits are worth the cost.

It is easy to demonstrate that most people feel better at the end of treatment than at the start, but we cannot assume that the treatment caused all of the improvement. Hans Eysenck (1952) pointed out that most of the people who receive no therapy nevertheless improve in a year or two. (Most psychological crises are temporary.) *Improvement without therapy* is called **spontaneous remission.** To measure the effectiveness of psychotherapy, an investigator must compare the improvement of psychotherapy clients to the spontaneous remission rate.

In other chapters each What's the Evidence? section has highlighted a particular study. Here I want to describe a general research approach. Hundreds of research studies similar to this have been conducted, although they vary in their details (Kazdin, 1995).

**HYPOTHESIS** Psychologically troubled people who receive psychotherapy will show greater improvements in their condition than similar people who do not receive therapy.

**METHOD** For the results to be meaningful, participants must be assigned at random to the therapy and nontherapy groups. (Comparing people who sought therapy to those who did not seek it would be unfair because the two groups might differ in the severity of their problems

a                                          b

■ Because everyone's moods and effectiveness fluctuate over time, an apparent improvement between (a) the start of therapy and (b) the end is hard to interpret. How much of the improvement is due to the therapy and how much would have occurred even without it? Adequate research on this issue requires a control group.

or their motivation for overcoming them.) In the best studies, people who contact a clinic about receiving therapy are all given a preliminary examination and are then randomly assigned to receive therapy at once or to be placed on a waiting list for therapy at a later time. A few months later, the investigators compare the amount of improvement shown by the therapy group and the waiting-list group.

How should the investigators measure the amount of improvement? Researchers cannot rely on the judgments of the therapists; after all, they want to demonstrate the effectiveness of their procedures. For similar reasons they cannot ask the clients for an unbiased opinion about how much they have improved. Therefore, the researchers may ask a "blind" observer (see Chapter 2) to evaluate each client, without knowing who has received therapy and who has been on the waiting list. Or they may ask each person to take a standardized personality test, such as the MMPI. None of these measures are perfect, of course, and it is possible that they overlook some kinds of improvement.

Many experiments simply compare a group that received therapy to a control group that was on the waiting list. Other experiments, however, have compared groups receiving different kinds of therapy or different frequencies of therapy.

**RESULTS**  Here we are not interested in the results of any single study. Most experiments have included only a modest number of people, such as 10 or 20 receiving therapy and a similar number on the waiting list. To draw a conclusion, we need to pool the results from a great many similar experiments. Psychologists use a method called **meta-analysis,** *taking the results of many experiments, weighting each one in proportion to the number of participants, and determining the overall average effect.* According to one meta-analysis that pooled the results of 475 experiments, the average person in therapy shows greater improvement than 80% of similarly troubled people who

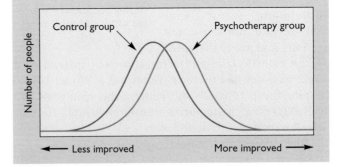

**FIGURE 15.8** According to one review of 475 studies, the average person receiving psychotherapy shows more improvement than do 80% of similar, randomly assigned people who are not in therapy. Note that both groups show substantial variation; some untreated people progress better than some treated people. This comparison lumps together all kinds of therapy and people with all kinds of trouble. (From Smith, Glass, & Miller, 1980)

are not receiving therapy (M. L. Smith, Glass, & Miller, 1980). Figure 15.8 illustrates this effect.

**INTERPRETATION**  One could easily complain that investigators have invested a great deal of effort for rather little payoff. After 475 experiments, we can confidently say that therapy is usually better than no therapy. This conclusion is like saying that, if you are ill, some medicine is better than no medicine. However, even if this conclusion seems unimpressive, it does pave the way for further, more detailed studies about which kinds of therapy are best, how therapy produces its benefits, and so forth.

## CONCEPT CHECK

7. Although well-designed experiments on psychotherapy use a blind observer to rate clients' mental health, double-blind studies are virtually impossible. Why? (Check your answer on page 601.)

# Comparing Therapies and Therapists

Next, of course, we want to know which kinds of therapy are most effective for which disorders. The practical problem for researchers is that therapists have identified hundreds of psychological disorders and have developed hundreds of types of therapy. To test each form of therapy on each possible disorder would require tens of thousands of experiments, each using as many participants as possible. Furthermore, many clients have several problems, not just one, and many therapists

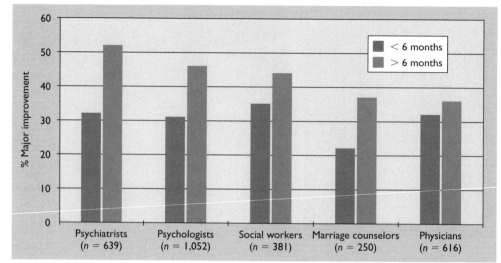

FIGURE 15.9 The percentage of *Consumer Reports* respondents who said they experienced great improvement in the problem that led them to treatment. For those who visited therapists for less than 6 months, the reported improvements were the same after seeing psychiatrists, psychologists, social workers, or family physicians. Marriage counselors, who deal with different kinds of problems, had somewhat lower ratings. (From Seligman, 1995)

use an eclectic trial-and-error approach instead of a single well-defined therapy (Goldfried & Wolfe, 1996). Despite these research difficulties, the results of the available research support a stunningly simple conclusion: For many kinds of disorders, all the common mainstream forms of therapy are approximately equal in effectiveness (Lipsey & Wilson, 1993; Stiles, Shapiro, & Elliott, 1986; Wampold et al., 1997). This finding is surprising, given that psychoanalysis, behavior therapy, person-centered therapy, and the others differ so sharply in their assumptions, methods, and goals. If all treatments succeed almost equally well, they must resemble one another more than we had thought.

Researchers have also compared the effectiveness of therapists with different kinds of training. The U.S. magazine *Consumer Reports* (1995) surveyed its readers about their mental health and their contact with psychotherapy. Of the thousands who said they had sought help for a mental-health problem within the previous 3 years, most said they were satisfied with the treatment and thought it had helped them. For measuring the effectiveness of psychotherapy, this study has some obvious problems: the lack of a random sample, the lack of a control group, and reliance on clients to evaluate their own im-

■ Just talking to a sympathetic listener, even someone without training, is helpful for many people with mild to moderate problems.

provement (Jacobson & Christensen, 1996). Nevertheless, the results indicated that people reported about equal satisfaction and benefits from talking with a psychiatrist, a psychologist, or a social worker (Seligman, 1995). They reported somewhat less satisfaction from consulting a marriage counselor. As mentioned in Chapter 14, marriage counseling is particularly difficult (see Figure 15.9). People also reported somewhat less satisfaction with talking to general-practice physicians if the treatment continued long-term.

The same general pattern emerged in a variety of other studies that used more traditional experimental methods, though with smaller samples of people: Therapy generally helps, but the type of therapist is less critical. In fact, studies have even compared the results for clients who were randomly assigned to talk with either an experienced therapist or a caring individual who had no formal training in psychology. Most clients gained about as much from consulting a nonprofessional as an experienced therapist. In short, we have no concrete evidence that the extensive experience or training of a therapist is essential for the effectiveness of psychotherapy (Christensen & Jacobson, 1994; Dawes, 1994).

Is the conclusion, then, that if you are psychologically troubled, you may as well talk to your next-door neighbor instead of a psychotherapist? No, for several reasons:

- The study comparing nonprofessionals to experienced therapists dealt with clients who had mild problems. We cannot assume that the same results would hold true for other clients.
- Few of us know someone with enough patience to listen to hours of personal ramblings and occasional outbursts of anger.
- Conversation with a professional psychotherapist is completely confidential. You cannot be sure that a friend will keep your secrets.
- A well-trained psychotherapist can recognize symptoms of a brain tumor or other medical disorder and can refer you to an appropriate medical specialist.
- Clinical psychologists know enough about therapy research that they are less likely than other people to follow untested "fad" treatments (Maki & Syman, 1997).

In short, although you would probably benefit by talking to almost any sympathetic listener, there are important advantages to seeing a professional psychotherapist (Strupp, 1996).

## Is More Treatment Better?

If it helps to meet with a therapist once per week for 3 months, would meeting for 6 months help even more? Would meeting twice per week for a year help even more? How much is the right amount?

Respondents in the *Consumer Reports* (1995) study were asked how much treatment they received and how much it helped them. Generally, those who received longer treatment reported that it helped them more. However, this was not an experimental study, and people were not randomly assigned to groups receiving different amounts of treatment. It may well be that the people who stayed in treatment the longest were those with the greatest problems at the start and therefore had the greatest room for improvement.

A somewhat better research design examines a single group of clients repeatedly as all progress through a given number of therapy sessions. Figure 15.10 shows the results of one such study. According to both the researchers and the clients themselves, most clients showed fairly rapid progress at first and then gradual progress that continued over 2 years (Howard et al., 1986). Evidently, prolonged treatment is at least somewhat more beneficial than brief treatment on the average.

The most elaborate study of this issue so far is a 5-year study conducted at Fort Bragg, North Carolina. A government-supported program provided free clinical services for every teenager or child who needed psychological help and who had a parent in the military. Each client had a case manager who determined what treatment plan was best, made sure that the client received every necessary type of help, and coordinated all the service providers to make sure that each one knew what the others were doing for the client. The goal was to demonstrate that a well-planned, integrated program would be more effective than the usual forms of treatment and that it might even be less expensive because there would be less waste and overlap of services. Results were compared to those in a similar community that offered the usual less-coordinated services. The result? The integrated program at Fort Bragg was no more beneficial. It was just more expensive (Bickman, 1996). We should not draw too strong a conclusion from this study or from any other single study. Still, most people had expected the integrated program to show some advantages, and the results do seem to imply that more therapy is not always better.

## Similarities Among Psychotherapeutic Methods

Because all the common forms of psychotherapy have been shown to be almost equally effective, they presumably share some important features. One feature is that all rely on the "therapeutic alliance"—a relationship between therapist and client that is characterized by acceptance, caring, respect, and attention. This relationship provides the social support that helps clients deal with their problems and acquire social skills that they can apply to other relationships (Krupnick et al., 1994).

Moreover, in nearly all forms of therapy, clients talk openly and honestly about their beliefs and emotions, relationships with family members, and other issues that people ordinarily keep secret. They examine aspects of

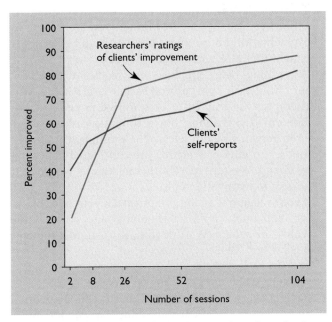

**FIGURE 15.10** The relationship of the number of psychotherapy sessions to the percentage of clients who improved. (From Howard et al., 1986)

themselves that they usually take for granted; in so doing they gain self-understanding. Because of the expectation of self-disclosure, psychotherapy as practiced in North America and Europe does not transplant readily into other cultures. For example, most Chinese would consider it shameful to discuss personal or family matters with a stranger (Bond, 1991).

The mere fact of entering therapy, whatever the method used, improves clients' morale. The therapist conveys the message "you are going to get better." Clients thus begin to think of themselves as people who can cope with their problems and overcome them. The expectation of improvement can lead to improvement.

Finally, every form of therapy requires clients to commit themselves to making some sort of change in their lifestyle. Simply by coming to the therapy session, they are reaffirming their commitment—to drink less, to feel less depressed, or to overcome their fears. They are also obliged to work on that change between sessions so that they can come to the next session and report, "I've been doing a little better lately." Improvement may depend at least as much on what clients do between sessions as on what happens in the sessions themselves.

## Advice for Potential Clients

At some point you or someone close to you may be interested in seeing a psychotherapist. If so, here are some points to remember:

- Consulting a therapist does not mean that something is wrong with you. Many people with no diagnosable disorder merely want to talk with someone.
- If you live in the United States, you can look in the white pages of your telephone directory for the Mental Health Association. Call and ask for a recommendation. You can specify how much you are willing to pay, what kind of problem you have, and even what kind of therapist you prefer.
- Other things being equal, you may do best with a therapist from your own cultural background (Sue, 1998). Therapists are trained to be sensitive to people from different backgrounds, but a communication barrier often remains nevertheless. For example, certain responses to grief or fear that are considered abnormal by many Western psychotherapists are considered normal in many other cultures.
- If your religion is an important part of your outlook on life, you might prefer a therapist who sympathizes with your beliefs (Worthington, Kurusu, McCullough & Sandage, 1996). Conversely, of course, if you are not devoutly religious, you might want to avoid a therapist who wants to focus on religion.
- Be skeptical of any therapist who seems overconfident. Clinical experience does not give anyone quick access to your private thoughts.

- Expect at least the start of improvement within 6 to 8 weeks. If you do not seem to be making progress, ask your therapist why. If you do not receive a convincing answer, consider seeing someone else.

## IN CLOSING
## Finding the Best Therapy

The research indicates that various kinds of therapy are about equally effective for the average client and that psychiatrists, psychologists, and social workers are about equally effective therapists on the average. These results do not mean, however, that any therapist is just as good as any other.

Although no one has done the research, chances are that one could also find that, on the average, professors using a lecture approach are about equally as effective as those using mostly discussion. And yet you know from extensive experience that some lecturers are excellent and others are poor and that some discussion leaders are better than others. Also, a professor who meets the needs of one student may be unsatisfactory for another. The same is true for psychotherapists. No one way of doing therapy is right for every client; the challenge is to find a good match between client and therapist.

## Summary

- **Psychoanalysis.** Psychoanalysts try to uncover the unconscious reasons behind self-defeating behaviors. To bring the unconscious to consciousness, they rely on free association, dream analysis, and transference. (page 589)
- **Behavior therapy.** Behavior therapists set specific goals for changing a client's behavior and use learning techniques to help a client achieve those goals. (page 590)
- **Cognitive therapies.** Cognitive therapists try to get clients to give up their irrational beliefs and unrealistic goals and to replace defeatist thinking with more favorable views of themselves and the world. Many therapists combine features of behavior therapy and cognitive therapy, attempting to change people's behaviors by altering how they interpret the situation. (page 591)
- **Humanistic therapy.** Humanistic therapists, including person-centered therapists, assume that, if people accept themselves as they are, they can solve their own problems. Person-centered therapists listen with unconditional positive regard but seldom offer interpretations or advice. (page 593)
- **Family systems therapy.** In many cases an individual's problem is part of an overall disorder of family

communications and expectations. Family systems therapists try to work with a whole family. (page 593)

- **Eclectic therapy.** About half of all psychotherapists today call themselves "eclectic." That is, they use a combination of methods depending on the circumstances. (page 594)
- **Brief therapy.** Many therapists set a time limit for the treatment, usually ranging from 2–6 months. Brief therapy is usually about as successful as long-term therapy if the goals are limited. (page 595)
- **Group therapies and self-help groups.** Psychotherapy is sometimes provided to people in groups, often composed of individuals with similar problems. Self-help groups provide sessions similar to group therapy but without a therapist. (page 595)
- **Effectiveness of psychotherapy.** The average troubled person in therapy improves more than at least 80% of the troubled people who are not in therapy. On the average each of the common forms of therapy provides approximately equal benefits for the disorders that have been extensively tested. Psychiatrists, psychologists, and social workers also provide approximately equal benefits on the average. (page 596)
- **Similarities among therapies.** A wide variety of therapies share certain features: All rely on a caring relationship between therapist and client. All promote self-understanding. All improve clients' morale. And all require a commitment by clients to try to make changes in their lives. (page 598)

## Answers to Concept Checks

4. Rational-emotive therapy assumes that many thoughts lead to emotions. This assumption is the reverse of the James-Lange theory, which argues that emotion-related changes in the body give rise to thoughts. (page 592)
5. **a.** humanistic therapy;
   **b.** behavior therapy;
   **c.** psychoanalysis and cognitive therapy. (page 593)
6. One of the advantages of brief therapy is that it limits the expense. Expense is not an issue for self-help groups because they charge nothing other than a voluntary contribution toward rental of the facilities. (page 596)
7. A double-blind design requires that neither the subjects nor the observers know which subjects received the experimental treatment and which ones were in the control group. It is not possible to prevent subjects from knowing whether they have received psychotherapy. (page 597)

# Social and Legal Aspects of Treatment

*How should we as a society deal with psychological disorders?*

A group of nearsighted people, lost in the woods, were trying to find their way home. One of the few who wore glasses said, "I think I know the way. Follow me." The others burst into laughter. "That's ridiculous," said one. "How could anybody who needs glasses be our leader?"

In 1972 the Democratic party nominated Senator Thomas Eagleton for vice president of the United States. Shortly after his nomination, he revealed that he had once received psychiatric treatment for depression. He was ridiculed mercilessly: "How could anybody who needed a psychiatrist be our leader?"

A great many people suffer from psychological disorders at some point in life. Unfortunately, many people in our society consider it shameful to seek help for a psychological disorder. They struggle along on their own, like a nearsighted person who refuses to wear glasses, rather than admit that they need help.

As a citizen and a voter, you should be aware of issues relating to psychological disorders and therapies: Who, if anyone, should receive psychiatric treatment involuntarily? Should mental patients have the right to refuse treatment? Under what circumstances, if any, should a criminal defendant be acquitted because of "insanity"? Can society as a whole take steps to prevent psychological disorders from developing?

## Deinstitutionalization

In the United States until the 1950s, people with severe psychological disturbances were generally confined in large mental hospitals supported by their state or county. Most of these hospitals were understaffed, poorly funded, prisonlike institutions that kept patients alive and out of other people's way but provided little if any psychiatric care (Okin, 1983). Hospital attendants cooked the food, washed the laundry, and generally cared for the patients but did not try to teach them the skills they would need if they were ever to leave. After all, few patients ever left. Some hospitals were better than others, but most were very grim.

With the advent of antidepressant and antischizophrenic drugs, advances in psychotherapy, and changes

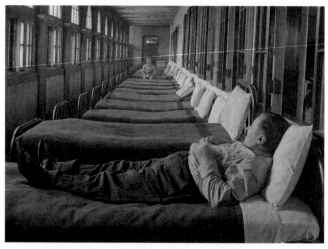

Mental hospitals of the 1950s were unpleasant warehouses where people received minimal care. Many stayed for years; some for the rest of their lives.

in the commitment laws, the number of long-term mental patients declined steadily. Today, the number of hospital beds reserved for psychiatric patients is one-fifth of what it was in 1955. A given patient may be admitted to a hospital repeatedly, but most stays are brief (Appleby et al., 1993).

Studies have consistently found that community mental-health centers are less expensive than large mental hospitals and at least as effective in restoring people to independent living (Fenton, Mosher, Herrell, & Blyler, 1998). Such research prompted a movement toward **deinstitutionalization,** *the removal of patients from mental hospitals,* to give them the least restrictive care possible. Hospital stays would be brief, except for people who were dangerous to themselves or others. Instead, people would live in or near their own communities and continue to receive outpatient care as needed.

Several alternatives to hospitalization are available. Many cities have homes staffed and organized to treat people with psychiatric problems. Another alternative is a community mental-health center, where some patients reside and others visit during the day. The idea behind these various forms of care is that patients should receive appropriate supervision and treatment but should also have as much contact as possible with the outside world.

Unfortunately, under deinstitutionalization most states discharged great numbers of patients from their mental hospitals without planning adequate alternatives for their care and housing. Many of the people who

■ Deinstitutionalization moved people out of mental hospitals, but many received little or no treatment after their release. Some became unemployed and homeless.

might once have been in a mental hospital are now homeless, especially those who have lost contact with their relatives and those with substance-abuse problems (Odell & Commander, 2000). Some of the others are in nursing homes or prisons.

# Involuntary Commitment and Treatment

In a democratic society, we treasure both freedom and security. Sometimes these values are in conflict. For example, the right of a psychologically disordered person to be free may conflict with the right of other people to feel safe and secure.

Suppose Charles mutters incoherently, cannot keep a job, does not pay his bills or take care of his personal hygiene, and bothers his neighbors. His family wants to commit him to a mental hospital, and the psychiatrist wants to give him drugs. But he refuses both courses, claiming that his family is "out to get him." Should he be permitted to refuse treatment?

We can argue this question either way. On the one hand, some of the most seriously disordered people fail to recognize that there is anything wrong with them. On the other hand, some families have been known to commit annoying relatives to mental hospitals just to get them out of the way, and some psychiatrists have given drugs to people with only minor problems, doing them more harm than good.

Unfortunately, it is difficult to determine who really needs help and who doesn't. Who, if anyone, should be

unwillingly confined to a mental hospital? In the United States, laws vary from state to state, but in all cases a judge holds a hearing and makes the final decision (Weiner & Wettstein, 1993). In some states a court can commit patients to a mental hospital only if they are suffering from a mental disorder and are dangerous to themselves or others. Even where the law does require a ruling of dangerousness, however, courts sometimes declare an apparently incompetent person to be dangerous simply because of one or two ambiguous, possibly threatening statements (Durham, 1996). Involuntary commitment is generally applied only for people with long-term, severe problems (Watson, Bowers, & Anderson, 2000).

After people have been committed to a mental hospital, voluntarily or involuntarily, they still have the right to refuse treatment (Appelbaum, 1988). According to their psychiatrists, most of the people who refuse treatment are hostile, emotionally withdrawn, and prone to disorganized thinking (Marder et al., 1983). According to the patients themselves, they have good reason to be hostile and withdrawn; the hospital staff is trying to force them to submit to unnecessary and dangerous treatments. Figure 15.11 compares patients with schizophrenia who refused drug treatment and patients who agreed to drug treatment. Understandably, it can be very difficult to make decisions about enforced treatment.

**A STEP FURTHER**
*Involuntary Treatment*

Thomas Szasz (1982) proposed that psychologically "normal" people write a "psychiatric will," specifying what treatments to give them, and what treatments to avoid, if they ever develop a severe psychological disorder. If you wrote such a will, what would you include? Or would you prefer to trust your judgment later, at the onset of the disorder?

# The Duty to Protect

Suppose someone tells his psychotherapist that he is planning to kill his former girlfriend. The therapist talks with the client and, by the end of the session, believes that the client has changed his mind. However, a few days later, the client does kill his ex-girlfriend. Should the therapist have notified the police and warned the woman of the danger? Should the woman's family be able to sue the therapist and collect damages?

Before you answer "yes," consider the following: First, psychotherapy is based on a trusting relationship in which the therapist promises to keep secret anything that the client says. Second, therapists are seldom certain

**FIGURE 15.11** People with schizophrenia who refuse drug therapy impress their physicians as being seriously disturbed. Patients who refuse drugs rate themselves as dissatisfied with their physicians and their treatments. (a) Physicians' ratings of their patients. High scores indicate greater disturbance. Those refusing treatment showed greater indications of disturbance on most scales. (b) Patients' self-ratings. The higher scores of patients who agreed to drug treatment indicate their higher levels of satisfaction with their treatment. (Based on data from Marder et al., 1983)

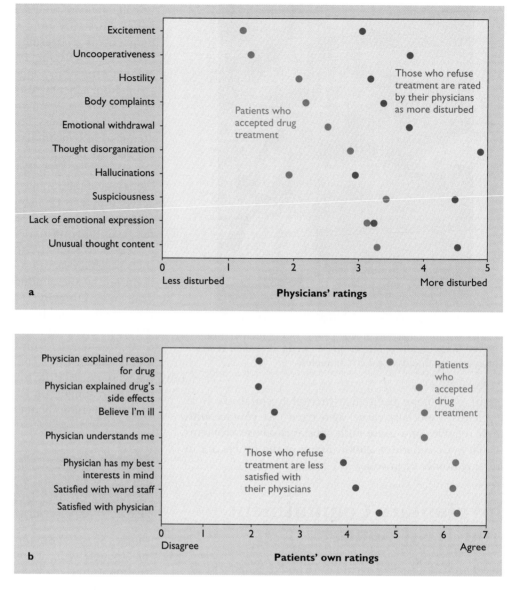

about which clients are really dangerous (Monahan, 1993). Suppose you are a therapist. Over the course of a day, you see eight patients, and three of them say they are so angry they could kill somebody. How do you decide which ones, if any, to take seriously? (Have you ever made a threatening statement yourself?)

In 1976 a California court ruled in the **Tarasoff** case that *a therapist who knew, or who should have known, that a client was dangerous is obligated to break the pledge of confidentiality and warn the endangered person* (Weiner & Wettstein, 1993). In 1991 a Canadian court made a similar ruling in the case of *Wenden v. Trikha* (Truscott & Crook, 1993). However, applying this rule in practice is difficult because of the uncertainty in judging dangerousness. The courts have also ruled that the duty to inform applies only to an identifiable endangered individual. If the client is, for example, an alcohol- and drug-abusing airplane pilot, countless people are endangered, but the therapist is not

obligated to inform anyone. In fact, the rules on confidentiality prohibit the therapist from informing the pilot's employer (Felthous, 1993). One can sympathize with therapists who wonder what to do, short of keeping a legal consultant available. So far, the courts have been reluctant to hold therapists legally accountable.

## The Insanity Defense

Suppose that, in the midst of an epileptic seizure, you flail your arms about and accidentally knock someone down the stairs, who dies from the fall. Should you be convicted of murder? Of course not. Now suppose that, in the midst of severely disordered thinking and perception, you attack and kill what appears to be a giant insect, but is in fact a human being. You didn't even realize you were attacking a person. Should you be convicted of murder?

■ Occasionally a disturbed person does something harmful, such as ramming a truck into the state capitol building. However, most people—even those who make threats—are harmless. Therapists face a difficult decision about whether to warn anyone about a possibly dangerous patient.

The tradition dating back to Roman times has been that you would be "not guilty by reason of insanity." Most people agree with that principle for extreme cases. The problem is where to draw the line. Under what conditions should someone be judged legally insane? *Insanity* is a legal term, not a psychological or medical one, and its definition is based on politics more than on science.

One point of broad agreement is that the crime itself, no matter how atrocious, does not demonstrate insanity. In Chapter 5 we considered the Hillside Strangler who committed a long series of rapes and murders but who was eventually ruled sane and sentenced to prison. The same decision was made for Jeffrey Dahmer, who was arrested in 1991 after murdering and cannibalizing several men. Theodore Kaczynski, arrested as the Unabomber who had mailed bombs for decades, refused to plead insanity and probably would not have been ruled insane anyway. Bizarre crimes do

not, in themselves, demonstrate insanity. In fact, each of these murderers knew what he was doing and took steps to avoid getting caught.

In many cases, however, a decision about sanity or insanity is difficult; lawyers, physicians, and psychologists have long struggled to establish a clear and acceptable definition of *insanity*. Probably the most famous definition, the **M'Naghten rule,** written in Great Britain in 1843, states:

> To establish a defense on the ground of insanity, it must be clearly proved that, at the time of the committing of the act, the party accused was laboring under such a defect of reason, from disease of the mind, as not to know the nature and quality of the act he was doing; or if he did know it, that he did not know he was doing what was wrong. (Shapiro, 1985)

In other words, *to be regarded as insane under the M'Naghten rule, people must be so disordered that they do not understand what they are doing.* Presumably, they would continue the act even if a police officer were standing nearby. Many observers have considered that rule too narrow and would like to broaden the definition of insanity to include "irresistible impulses"—acts similar to sneezing or hiccuping, which people could not inhibit for long, no matter how hard they tried. Under the **Durham rule,** established in 1954 in the case of a man named Durham, a U.S. court held that *a defendant is not criminally responsible if the activity was "a product of mental disease or defect."* That rule confused more than it clarified and is no longer used. (Is ignorance a mental defect? What about sleepiness? Grouchiness? Almost any criminal act is the product of some sort of mental defect, broadly defined.)

The **Model Penal Code,** written by the American Law Institute in the 1950s, is stricter than the Durham rule but less rigid than the M'Naghten rule. According to this rule, *someone is not responsible for criminal conduct if a mental disease or defect deprived the person of substantial capacity to*

■ Theodore Kaczynski (a) a brilliant mathematician who once had a promising career, became (b) a recluse who over the course of 17 years mailed bombs to people, killing 3 and injuring 23 others. However, merely being "strange" or committing bizarre acts of violence does not qualify a person as legally insane.

a                              b

*recognize that the act was wrong, or to act in accordance with the law* (Simon, 1994).

Under this rule a jury still needs to make a difficult judgment about the defendant's state of mind at the time of the act. When the defendant's sanity is in question, psychologists and psychiatrists are called as "expert witnesses" to evaluate the defendant's state of mind. If all the experts agree that the defendant is insane, the prosecution almost always accepts the insanity plea. If they agree the defendant is not insane, the defense almost always abandons the plea. Therefore, the only insanity cases that come to a jury trial are the difficult cases in which the experts disagree. Those cases are rare. In the United States, fewer than 1% of accused felons plead insanity, and of those, only about one-fourth are found not guilty (Lymburner & Roesch, 1999). However, those few cases generally receive much media attention, and because people hear about them, they assume such cases are common. (Remember the availability heuristic from Chapter 8). The insanity defense is just as rare in other countries.

Another common misconception is that defendants found not guilty by reason of insanity simply go free, where they are apt to commit further attacks. People found not guilty by reason of insanity are almost always committed to a mental hospital, and their average stay in the hospital is at least equal to the time they would have spent in prison (Silver, 1995).

Several states in the United States have experimented with allowing a verdict of "guilty but mentally ill," intended as a compromise between guilty and not guilty. However, the defendant actually receives the same sentence as if he or she had been simply found guilty and is no more likely to receive psychiatric care in prison than any other convicted person (Lymburner & Roesch, 1999). In short, the guilty but mentally ill verdict is the same as a guilty verdict. An appealing alternative proposal is to specify that anyone found not guilty by reason of insanity must be temporarily hospitalized and, when eventually released, must abide by many conditions and restrictions, similar to those of a released prisoner on parole (Linhorst & Dirks-Linhorst, 1999).

## CONCEPT CHECK

8. Someone who has been involuntarily committed to a mental hospital escapes and commits a murder. Will this person be judged not guilty by reason of insanity? (Check your answer on page 607.)

## Preventing Mental Illness

Traditionally, psychotherapy has been a method to relieve psychological distress. More recently, certain psychologists, especially community psychologists, are making efforts at prevention. **Community psychologists** *focus on the needs of large groups rather than those of individu-*

*als.* They distinguish between **primary prevention,** *preventing a disorder from starting,* and **secondary prevention,** *identifying a disorder in its early stages and preventing it from becoming more serious.*

Just as our society puts fluoride into drinking water to prevent tooth decay and immunizes people against contagious diseases, it can take action to prevent certain types of psychological disorders (Albee, 1986; Goldston, 1986; Long, 1986; Yoshikawa, 1994). For example, we could take the following steps:

- **Ban toxins.** The sale of lead-based paint has been banned because children who eat flakes of it sustain brain damage. Other toxins in the air and water have yet to be controlled.
- **Educate pregnant women about prenatal care.** For example, women need to be informed that the use of alcohol or other drugs during pregnancy can cause brain damage to the fetus and that contracting bacterial and viral infections during pregnancy can impair fetal brain development and increase the risk of psychological disorders in the child.
- **Help people get jobs.** People who lose their jobs lose self-esteem and increase their risk of depression and substance abuse.
- **Provide child care.** Providing better day-care facilities would contribute to the psychological health of both parents and children.
- **Improve educational opportunities.** Programs that get young people interested in their schoolwork have made notable progress in decreasing juvenile delinquency.

These techniques are aimed at primary prevention for the entire community. Secondary prevention techniques can be targeted at specific individuals who are beginning to show symptoms of a particular disorder. For example, psychologists identified fifth- and sixth-grade children prone to distress and then for 12 weeks taught them how to avoid negative beliefs about themselves. Those children showed fewer signs of depression over the next 2 years compared to a similarly distressed group who did not receive this training (Gillham, Reivich, Jaycox, & Seligman, 1995).

Unfortunately, prevention is often more difficult than it might seem. Many programs designed to teach young people to avoid illegal drugs have produced no measurable benefits. Attempts have been made to combat suicide, especially teenage suicide, by television programs about suicide and the pain it causes to friends and relatives. Those programs have never decreased the suicide rate; in fact, the research controversy is about how much those programs *increase* the suicide rate (Joiner, 1999). One study compared suicidal patients receiving brief crisis intervention to others receiving more prolonged therapy. Those receiving more help had a *higher* rate of suicide (Moller, 1992). The general point is that we cannot take it for granted that a procedure intended to help actually will. Developing good prevention requires research.

## The Science and Politics of Mental Illness

Suppose you are a storekeeper. Someone dressed as Batman stands outside your store every day shouting gibberish at anyone who comes by. Your once-thriving business draws fewer and fewer customers each day. The disturbing man outside does not seem to be breaking any laws, but you would like to have him removed from the area. Should he be taken to a mental hospital and treated, even though he insists that he is normal? It is a difficult decision. How disordered is he? What treatment would help him, and how much is it likely to help? And if nothing is done, what happens to your rights as a storekeeper?

Similarly, the insanity defense and all the other issues in this module are complicated questions that require political decisions by society as a whole, not just the opinions of psychologists or psychiatrists. Regardless of what career you enter, you will be a voter and potential juror, and you will have much to say about these issues. The decisions deserve serious, informed consideration.

## Summary

* **Mental hospitals and deinstitutionalization.** Today, few patients stay very long in mental hospitals. However, many states have released patients from mental hospitals without providing adequate community mental-health facilities. (page 602)

* **Involuntary commitment.** Laws on involuntary commitment to mental hospitals vary. In some states people can be committed only if they are dangerous; in other states people can be committed if they are judged incompetent to make decisions about their own treatment. It is difficult to frame laws that ensure treatment for those who need it while also protecting the rights of those who have good reasons for refusing it. (page 603)

* **Duty to warn.** The courts have ruled that a therapist who is convinced that a client is dangerous should warn the endangered person. Applying this rule in practice is difficult, however. (page 603)

* **The insanity defense.** Some defendants accused of a crime are acquitted for reasons of insanity, which is a legal rather than a medical or psychological concept. The criteria for establishing insanity are vague and controversial. (page 605)

* **Prevention of psychological disorders.** Psychologists and psychiatrists are increasingly concerned about preventing psychological disorders. Many preventive measures require the cooperation of society as a whole. Methods of prevention based on good intentions do not always succeed; solid research is necessary. (page 606)

## Answer to Concept Check

8. Not necessarily. Having a psychological disorder, even a severe one, does not automatically qualify a person as insane in the legal sense. The judge or jury must also find that the psychological disorder prevented the person from knowing what he or she was doing or made law-abiding behavior impossible. (page 608)

## Key Terms and Activities

## Key Terms

**behavior therapy:** treatment that begins with clear, well-defined behavioral goals, such as eliminating test anxiety, and then attempts to achieve those goals through learning (page 590)

**biopsychosocial model:** the concept that abnormal behavior has three major aspects—biological, psychological, and sociological (page 583)

**brief therapy:** (or time-limited therapy) treatment that begins with an agreement about what the therapist and the client can expect from each other and how long the treatment will last (page 595)

**catharsis:** the release of pent-up emotions associated with unconscious thoughts and memories (page 589)

**cognitive therapy:** treatment that seeks to improve people's psychological well-being by changing their cognitions (page 591)

**cognitive-behavior therapy:** treatment that combines important features of both behavior therapy and cognitive therapy, attempting to change people's behavior by changing their interpretation of their situation (page 592)

**community psychologist:** a psychologist who focuses on the needs of large groups rather than those of individuals (page 606)

**deinstitutionalization:** the removal of patients from mental hospitals (page 602)

***Diagnostic and Statistical Manual of Mental Disorders, Fourth Edition (DSM-IV):*** a book that lists the acceptable labels for all psychological disorders, with a description of each and guidelines on how to distinguish it from similar disorders (page 584)

**differential diagnosis:** a determination of what problem a person has, in contrast to all the other possible problems that might produce similar symptoms (page 586)

**dissociative identity disorder:** a rare condition in which the personality separates into several identities; also known as multiple personality disorder (page 583)

**Durham rule:** the rule that a defendant is not criminally responsible if the activity was "a product of mental disease or defect" (page 605)

**eclectic therapy:** treatment that uses a combination of methods and approaches (page 594)

**family systems therapy:** treatment based on the assumptions that most people's problems develop in a family setting and that the best way to deal with them is to improve family relationships and communication (page 593)

**free association:** a procedure where a client lies on a couch, starts thinking about a particular symptom or problem and then reports everything that comes to mind (page 589)

**group therapy:** treatment administered to a group of people all at once (page 595)

**incongruence:** a mismatch between someone's self-concept and ideal self (page 593)

**interpretation:** a therapist's explanation of the underlying meaning of what a client says (page 590)

**meta-analysis:** a method of taking the results of many experiments, weighting each one in proportion to the number of participants, and determining the overall average effect (page 597)

**M'Naghten rule:** the rule that a defendant is not criminally responsible if, at the time of committing an unlawful act, the person was laboring under such a defect of reason, from disease of the mind, as not to know the nature and quality of the act he was doing; or if he did know it, that he did not know he was doing wrong (page 605)

**Model Penal Code:** the rule that a person is not responsible for criminal conduct if, at the time of such conduct and as a result of mental disease or defect, he or she lacks substantial capacity either to appreciate the criminality (wrongfulness) of this conduct or to conform his or her conduct to the requirements of law (page 605)

**person-centered therapy:** (also known as nondirective or client-centered therapy) a procedure in which a therapist listens to the client sympathetically, provides unconditional positive regard, and offers little interpretation or advice (page 593)

**personality disorder:** a maladaptive, inflexible way of dealing with the environment and other people (page 584)

**primary prevention:** preventing a disorder from starting (page 606)

**psychoanalysis:** an approach to personality and psychotherapy developed by Sigmund Freud, based on

identifying unconscious thoughts and emotions and bringing them to consciousness (page 589)

**psychodynamic therapies:** treatment that attempts to uncover people's underlying drives and motivations (page 589)

**psychotherapy:** the treatment of psychological disorders by methods that include a personal relationship between a trained therapist and a client (page 589)

**rational-emotive therapy:** treatment based on the assumption that thoughts (rationality) lead to emotions, and that problems arise not from the unpleasant emotions themselves, but the irrational thoughts that lead to them (page 592)

**resistance:** according to psychoanalysts, continued repression that interferes with therapy (page 590)

**secondary prevention:** identifying a disorder in its early stages and preventing it from becoming more serious (page 606)

**self-help group:** assembly of people with similar problems, who operate much like group therapy but without a therapist (page 595)

**spontaneous remission:** improvement of a psychological condition without therapy (page 596)

*Tarasoff:* the rule that a therapist who knew, or who should have known, that a client was dangerous is obligated to break the pledge of confidentiality and warn the endangered person (page 604)

**transference:** the extension of a client's feelings toward a parent or other important figure onto the therapist (page 590)

## Suggestions for Further Reading

Dawes, R. M. (1994). *House of cards: Psychology and psychotherapy built on myth.* New York: Free Press. A harsh criticism of psychotherapists who rely on their intuition and experience instead of scientific evidence.

Holmes, D. S. (2000). *Abnormal psychology* (4th ed.). Needham Heights, MA: Allyn & Bacon. An outstanding textbook.

Seligman, M. E. P. (1993). *What you can change . . . and what you can't.* New York: Fawcett Columbine. Description of both the possibilities and the limitations of psychotherapy.

Sheehan, S. (1982). *Is there no place on earth for me?* Boston: Houghton Mifflin. The story of a young woman with schizophrenia and her life in and out of mental hospitals.

Simon, R. I. (1994). The law and psychiatry. In R. E. Hales, S. C. Yudofsky, & J. A. Talbott (Eds.), *Textbook of psychiatry* (2nd ed., pp. 1297–1340). Washington, DC: American Psychiatric Press. A survey of many of the legal issues related to mental illness.

# Web/Technology Resources

## Research on Prevention and Treatment

**Journals.apa.org/prevention/**

The free on-line journal *Prevention and Treatment* features research studies and commentaries on that research.

## Health Center: Therapy

**www.health-center.com/english/brain/therapy/**

This site includes definitions of therapy, descriptions of several major kinds of therapy, and suggestions on how to go about seeing a therapist.

## Landmark Cases in Forensic Psychiatry

**bama.ua.edu/~jhooper/tableofc.html**

In his excellent Forensic Psychiatry Resource Page, James Hooper offers brief summaries of almost 100 criminal cases that involve the insanity defense and civil cases that involve mental disorders. You can view the cases chronologically, alphabetically, or in a Java™ file.

## Journal of Psychotherapy Practice and Research

**http://jppr.psychiatryonline.org**

You can view abstracts of research articles for free, or pay for full articles. The research deals with advances in psychotherapy.

# Specific Disorders and Treatments

**16**
CHAPTER

■ Abnormal behavior can result from biological predisposition, stressful experience, or a combination of both. In Shakespeare's *Hamlet*, Ophelia became "mad" and drowned herself after Hamlet's behavior changed from loving to cruel and he murdered her father.

n the 1700s and 1800s, medical science was very primitive by today's standards. Physicians seldom distinguished one illness from another, and in fact, most did not even try. Regardless of the symptoms, physicians recommended general all-purpose "tonics," suggested bed rest, sometimes applied leeches to withdraw blood, and so forth. Medical progress since then has been marked by an increasing ability to distinguish among disorders and apply different treatments.

Similarly, much of the progress in abnormal psychology has come from making appropriate distinctions among disorders and developing treatments aimed at specific disorders. The first three modules discuss the most commonly diagnosed psychological disorders: anxiety disorders, substance abuse, and depression. The final module is about schizophrenia, which is less common but sometimes extremely disabling.

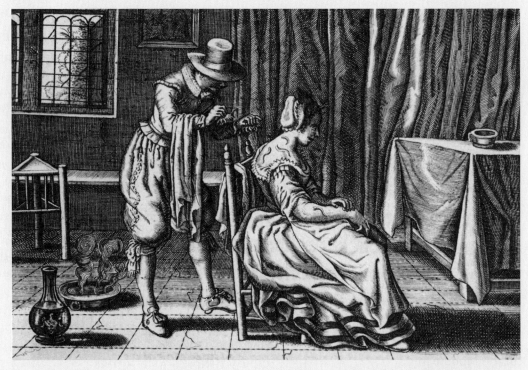

■ In the early days of medicine, physicians provided the same treatments for all diseases (such as applying leeches as a means of letting blood, as shown). Progress depended on differentiating particular disorders and developing individual treatments for each. Clinical psychology, likewise, is trying to determine the right treatment for different types of psychological disorders.

# Anxiety and Avoidance Disorders

*Why do some people develop exaggerated fears?*

*Why do some people develop strange habits of thought and action?*

You go to the beach, looking forward to an afternoon of swimming and surfing. Will you go in the water if someone tells you that a shark attacked two swimmers yesterday? What if the shark attack occurred a month ago? What if no shark has attacked anyone in this area, but someone saw a small shark a few days ago?

■ Many situations evoke temporary anxiety or tension in almost anyone. Anxiety becomes a problem only if it is frequently more intense than the situation justifies.

How much fear and caution are normal? Staying out of the water because you see a large shark is perfectly reasonable. Staying out because a small shark was present a few days ago is less sensible. If you refuse even to look at photographs of the ocean because they might *remind* you of sharks, you have a serious problem indeed. Excessive fear and caution are linked to some common psychological disorders.

## Disorders Characterized by Excessive Anxiety

Many psychological disorders are marked by anxiety and attempts to avoid anxiety. Anxiety, unlike fear, is not generally associated with a specific situation. You might be afraid of a growling dog, but your fear subsides when you get away from the dog. Anxiety is an apprehensive feeling that something might go wrong. We also talk of anxieties about dying or anxieties about some personal deficiency. The key is that you cannot escape from anxieties as easily as you could from the growling dog.

Some degree of anxiety is normal; anxiety becomes a problem only when it interferes with our ability to cope with everyday life. The people most prone to severe anxiety are those who feel helpless to control the major events of their lives (Chorpita & Barlow, 1998). Recall from Chapter 12 that shock, noise, and all sorts of other unpleasant events are more stressful when people cannot predict or control them.

### Generalized Anxiety Disorder (GAD)

People with **generalized anxiety disorder** (GAD) are *almost constantly plagued by exaggerated worries.* They worry that "I might get sick," "My daughter might get sick," "I might lose my job," or "I might not be able to pay my bills." Although these people have no more reason for such worries than anyone else, they grow so tense, irritable, and fatigued that they have trouble working at their jobs or enjoying life. About 5% of all people experience generalized anxiety disorder at some point in life, often in conjunction with depression, panic disorder, or other psychological problems (Wittchen, Zhao, Kessler, & Eaton, 1994).

GAD is frequently *comorbid* with depression. That is, people who have one of them are likely to have the other one also. Unsurprisingly, GAD responds fairly well to antidepressant drugs (Rivas-Vazquez, 2001). Another effective treatment is relaxation training, in which people are taught how to relax their muscles quickly in stressful situations (Öst & Breitholtz, 2000). The drug treatment shows benefits more quickly, but the relaxation training is more likely to produce long-lasting benefits.

### Panic Disorder (PD)

People with **panic disorder** (PD) *have frequent periods of anxiety and occasional attacks of panic—rapid breathing, increased heart rate, chest pains, sweating, faintness, and trembling.* A panic attack usually lasts only a few minutes, although it can last an hour or more. During an attack, people worry about fainting, having a heart attack, dying, or going crazy. Panic disorder occurs in 1–3% of adults at some time during their lives in many cultures throughout

**613**

the world. It is more common in women than men (Weissman, Warner, Wickramaratne, Moreau, & Olfson, 1997).

Researchers have made some progress toward understanding panic disorder. First, the key symptom seems to be **hyperventilation,** *rapid deep breathing.* Almost anything that causes hyperventilation makes the body react as if it were suffocating, thereby triggering other sympathetic nervous system responses such as sweating and increased heart rate (Coplan et al., 1998; Klein, 1993). If this arousal occurs after exercise, people do not react emotionally. However, sometimes people experience increased breathing rate, heart rate, and sweating without understanding why. (The reason could be nervous tension, something they ate, a high level of carbon dioxide in the room, or some other temporary problem.) When people are surprised by their suddenly high arousal, their interpretation of it becomes critical.

Many people have one of these episodes but relax as soon as it is over. They had a panic attack but did not develop panic disorder. Other people, however, worry that they are having a heart attack. Even after the period of high arousal ends and they are assured that it was not a heart attack, they worry that it will happen again. If so, will it turn into an actual heart attack? Will it embarrass them in public? What if they have an attack while driving a car?

The result of these worries is almost constant anxiety. Anxiety is not the same as panic, but it increases the probability of a panic attack. After several such episodes, people start to associate them with places, events, activities, or even internal states. That is, a situation that resembles that of a previous panic attack may trigger a new panic attack as a conditioned response (Bouton, Mineka, & Barlow, 2001). Also, whenever these individuals begin to breathe heavily, they interpret their hyperventilation as the start of a panic attack, and their worry about it makes it happen (Battaglia, Bertella, Ogliari, Bellodi, & Smeraldi, 2001; Gorman et al., 2001). Figure 16.1 summarizes the processes of panic attack.

Panic attack has been treated with psychotherapy as well as antidepressant drugs with varying degrees of benefit. Because the fear is a learned response, it can be unlearned, and behavior therapy is often an effective strategy. Part of any treatment is based on rather simple advice: Don't worry about having panic attacks. If you do have one, it is not going to kill you, and it probably won't last very long. If you feel an attack coming on, say, "Excuse me, but I feel a breathing problem starting." Sit down, wait it out, and then go back to your activities. Of course, it is not always easy to take that advice.

Many people with panic disorder also have **social phobia,** *a severe avoidance of other people and a fear of doing anything in public,* where they might become embarrassed. Common types of social phobia include fear of

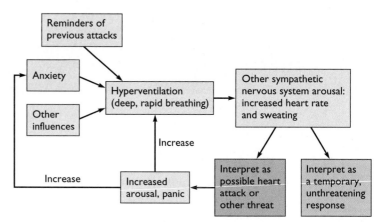

**FIGURE 16.1** Many people experience an episode of hyperventilation leading to increased arousal. If they interpret it as nonthreatening, the episode passes. However, if they interpret it as threatening, their worry heightens the arousal, magnifies the symptoms, and increases the constant anxiety level.

talking to strangers or large groups and fear of feeling rejected or ridiculed by others (Stein, Torgrud, & Walker, 2000). Many also have **agoraphobia** (from *agora,* the Greek word for "marketplace"), *an excessive fear of open or public places,* although it is also possible to have agoraphobia without panic disorder (Wittchen, Reed, & Kessler, 1998). Most psychologists believe that people with panic disorder develop their social phobia or agoraphobia because they are afraid of being incapacitated or embarrassed by a panic attack in a public place. In a sense they are afraid of their own fear (McNally, 1990). To avoid the prospect of a public panic attack, they stay home as much as possible and seldom go out alone.

## CONCEPT CHECK

1. Some psychologists advise people with panic attacks to stop worrying about their attacks and to adopt the attitude, "If it happens, it happens." Why would they make this recommendation? (Check your answer on page 623.)

# Disorders Characterized by Exaggerated Avoidance

People learn to avoid punishment, as we saw in Chapter 6. In some cases their efforts become so extreme and persistent that they interfere with daily activities.

Let's begin with some general observations on avoidance learning, which is relevant to the later discussion of phobias (extreme fears) and compulsions (rituals designed to avoid unpleasant thoughts or events). If you learn to do something for positive reinforcement, you will extinguish your response soon after you stop receiving reinforcements. Avoidance behaviors are different,

■ Many people who watched the famous shower scene in the movie *Psycho* became afraid to take showers. Actress Janet Leigh, who portrayed the woman killed in that shower scene, was herself so terrified that she subsequently avoided showers.

however. Suppose you learn to press a lever to avoid electric shocks. Soon you are responding steadily and you receive no shocks. Now the experimenter disconnects the shock generator without telling you. The extinction procedure has begun; you no longer need to press the lever. What will you do? You will continue pressing it, of course. As far as you can tell, nothing has changed; the response still works. *Avoidance behaviors are highly resistant to extinction;* once someone learns a response to avoid mishap, the response continues long after it ceases to be necessary.

You can see how this tendency would support superstitions. Suppose you believe that Friday the 13th is dangerous. Every Friday the 13th, you are very cautious, but occasionally a misfortune happens anyway. The misfortune confirms your belief that Friday the 13th is dangerous. The next Friday the 13th, nothing goes wrong. You conclude, "I was cautious all day long, so I avoided bad luck." In other words, as long as you continue an avoidance behavior, you can never find out whether it is useful or not.

 ONCEPT CHECK

**2.** Suppose you are an experimenter, and you have trained someone to press a lever to avoid shocks. Now you disconnect the shock generator. Other than telling the person what you have done, what procedure could you use to facilitate extinction of the lever pressing? (Check your answer on page 623.)

## Phobias

Terror is the only thing that comes close to how I feel when I think of moths. Their willowy, see-through wings always seem filthy. I remember being stuck in a car with a huge moth and my date, not knowing how terrified I was of moths, thought I was kidding when I told him I was afraid. It was terrible! I can feel it right now . . . feeling trapped and the moth with its ugly body flitting around so quickly, I couldn't anticipate where it would go next. Finally that

creature hit me in the arm and I screamed—it felt dirty and sleazy and then it hit me in the face and I began to scream uncontrollably. I had the terrible feeling it was going to fly into my mouth while I was screaming, but I couldn't stop. (Duke & Nowicki, 1979, p. 244)

A **phobia** is best defined as *a strong, persistent fear of a specific object, extreme enough to interfere with normal living.* It is often described as an unreasonable or irrational fear, but in most cases the fear itself is not irrational. For example, fearing snakes is not irrational, because snakes can be dangerous. What is irrational is the excessive degree of the fear, which leads to avoidance behaviors—avoiding the object itself (e.g., a snake), places where the object might be lurking, and even reminders of the object.

Confronting the object of a phobia can lead to sweating, trembling, and rapid breathing and heart rate. In most cases people with phobias are not so much afraid of the object itself but of their own reactions (Beck & Emery, 1985). They fear that they will have a heart attack or that they will embarrass themselves by trembling or fainting. In many ways phobias are like panic disorder, but phobias are aroused by a specific object or event, whereas panic attacks occur less predictably.

Because most people with phobias are well aware that their fears are exaggerated, it does no good to tell them not to be afraid. In fact, informational attempts to reduce phobias sometimes backfire. One city tried to combat elevator phobias by posting signs on elevators throughout the city: "There is no reason to be afraid of elevators. There is almost no chance at all that the cable will break or that you will suffocate." The signs (of course!) *increased* the fear of elevators.

### The Prevalence of Phobias

According to an extensive study of U.S. adults, about 11% of people suffer a phobia at some time in life, and 5–6% have a phobia at any given time (Magee, Eaton, Wittchen, McGonagle, & Kessler, 1996). However, as with many other psychological disorders, phobias vary in degree from mild to extreme, and their apparent prevalence

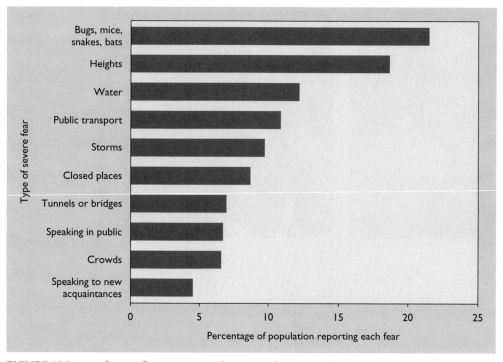

**FIGURE 16.2** Prevalence of some commonly reported extreme fears. (Not all extreme fears qualify as phobias.)

increases or decreases depending on how many marginal cases one includes. Figure 16.2 shows the prevalence of some frequently reported extreme fears. Figure 16.3 shows the prevalence of phobias by age. Note the early onset and gradual decline in prevalence with age (Burke, Burke, Regier, & Rae, 1990).

## Acquiring a Phobia

Like almost everything else in psychology, phobias show a genetic predisposition, and the more closely related you are to someone with a phobia, the more likely you are to

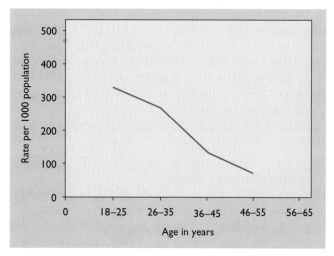

**FIGURE 16.3** Most phobias do not last a lifetime. Young people with phobias often lose them by middle age.

develop one yourself (Kendler, Myers, Prescott, & Neale, 2001). However, no one is born with a phobia. People seem to be born with a few fears, such as a fear of sudden loud noises, but most fears are learned, and so are phobias. Indeed, some phobias can be traced to a specific event; for example, one child got locked in a trunk and developed a phobia of closed spaces. Another person developed a phobia of water by diving into a lake and discovering a corpse (Kendler et al., 1995).

John B. Watson, one of the founders of behaviorism, was the first to demonstrate the possibility that people learn fears (Watson & Rayner, 1920). Today, we would consider it unethical to try to create a fear, especially in humans, but in 1920 researchers felt less restraint. Watson and Rosalie Rayner studied an 11-month-old child, "Albert B.," who had previously shown no fear of white rats or other animals (Figure 16.4). They set a white rat down in front of Albert, and then, just behind him, they struck a large steel bar with a hammer. The sudden sound made Albert whimper and cover his face. After a few repetitions the mere sight of the rat would make Albert cry and crawl away. Watson and Rayner declared that they had created a strong fear and that phobias in general might develop along similar lines. (Unfortunately, they made no attempt to extinguish Albert's fear.)

Watson and Rayner's explanation of phobias failed to answer some important questions: Why do people develop phobias toward objects that have never injured them? Why are some phobias much more common than others? And why are phobias so persistent? Although

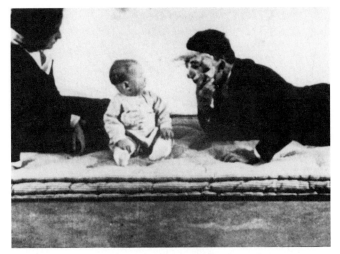

**FIGURE 16.4** John B. Watson argued that most fears are learned, including phobias. Watson first demonstrated that Little Albert showed little fear of small animals. Then Watson paired the presentation of a white rat with a loud, frightening noise. Little Albert became afraid of the white rat; he also began showing fears of other small animals, odd-looking masks, and other objects he had not previously feared. (Courtesy of Professor Benjamin Harris)

Watson and Rayner's study was unsatisfactory in many ways (B. Harris, 1979; Samelson, 1980), it led the way for later studies of phobias as learned responses.

 **ONCEPT CHECK**

**3.** In classical conditioning terms, what was the CS in Watson and Rayner's experiment? The UCS? The CR? The UCR? (Check your answers on page 623.)

**WHAT'S THE EVIDENCE?**
*Learning Fear by Observation*

Contrary to Watson and Rayner's explanation, almost half of all people with phobias have never had a painful experience with the object they fear (Öst & Hugdahl, 1981). For example, many people have phobias, or at least intense fears, of snakes, spiders, or sharks, even though they have never been hurt by them. However, we have all heard about people who were injured or killed by such animals. As noted in the discussion of social learning in Chapter 6, we learn many things by watching or listening to others. Perhaps we learn our fears and phobias from other people.

That hypothesis is probably correct, but how can we demonstrate it? Susan Mineka and her colleagues demonstrated that monkeys learn fears by observing other monkeys (Mineka, 1987; Mineka, Davidson, Cook, & Keir, 1984). Her experiments show how animal studies can shed light on important human issues.

**EXPERIMENT 1**

**HYPOTHESIS** Monkeys that have seen other monkeys show fear of a snake will develop such a fear themselves.

**METHOD** Monkeys that live in the wild generally develop a strong fear of snakes; however, monkeys reared in a laboratory do not. Mineka put a laboratory-reared monkey together with a wild-born monkey and let them both see a snake (Figure 16.5a). The lab monkey watched the wild monkey show signs of fear. Later Mineka tested the lab monkey by itself to see whether it had acquired a fear of snakes.

**RESULTS** When the lab monkey saw how frightened its partner was of the snake, it became frightened too (Figure 16.5b). It continued to be afraid of the snake when tested by itself, even months later.

| Wild-reared monkey | Lab-reared monkey |
|---|---|

 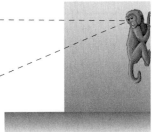

a  Wild-reared monkey shows fear of snake.  Lab-reared monkey shows no fear of snake.

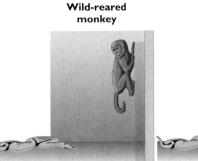 

b  Lab-reared monkey learns fear of snake by observing wild-reared monkey and snake.

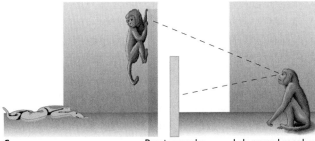

c  Barrier masks snake from view of lab-reared monkey.  Lab-reared monkey does not learn fear when snake is not visible.

**FIGURE 16.5** A lab-reared monkey learns to fear snakes from the reactions of a wild-reared monkey. But if the snake is not visible, the lab-reared monkey fails to learn any fear.

**INTERPRETATION** The lab monkey may have learned a fear of snakes because it saw that its partner was afraid of snakes. But Mineka considered another possible, though less likely, interpretation: The lab monkey may have become fearful simply because it observed the other monkey's fear. That is, maybe it did not matter *what* the wild monkey was afraid of. To test this possibility, Mineka conducted a second experiment.

**EXPERIMENT 2**

**HYPOTHESIS** A monkey that does not see the object that another monkey fears will not develop a fear itself.

**METHOD** A monkey reared in a lab watched a monkey reared in the wild through a plate-glass window. The wild monkey could look through another window, where it saw a snake. Thus, when the wild monkey shrieked and ran away from the snake, the lab monkey saw the wild monkey's fear but did not know what it was afraid of. Later the lab monkey was placed close to a snake to see whether it would show fear.

**RESULTS** The lab monkey showed no fear of the snake.

**INTERPRETATION** To develop a fear of snakes, the observer monkey needed to see that the other monkey was frightened of snakes, not just that it was frightened (Figure 16.5c).

Note that, although the observer monkey had to see *what* the other monkey was afraid of, it did not have to see *why* it was afraid. Just seeing the other monkey's fear of the snake in Experiment 1 was enough. Humans not only observe other people's fears but can also tell one another what we are afraid of and why.

## Why Some Phobias Are More Common Than Others

 Imagine that you survey your friends. (You can actually survey them, if you like, but in this case it's pretty easy to imagine the results.) You ask them:

- Are you afraid of snakes?
- Are you afraid of cars?
- Have you ever been bitten by a snake or seen someone else get bitten?
- Have you ever been injured in a car accident or seen someone else get injured?

I think you know what results to expect. A fair number of people will admit being afraid of snakes, even though very few have any firsthand experience of snakebites. Hardly anyone is afraid of cars, even though almost everyone has experienced or witnessed a car accident in which someone was injured. So why do people develop some fears more readily than others?

Common phobias include open spaces, closed spaces, heights, lightning and thunder, animals, and illness. In

■ Phobias are usually associated with danger that we can neither predict nor control or with events that are occasionally unpleasant and never safe or pleasant. Many people are afraid of extreme heights.

contrast, few people have phobias of cars, guns, tools, or electricity—even though they produce many injuries. When my son Sam was a toddler, at least three times he stuck his finger into an electric outlet. He even had a name for it: "Smoky got me again." I worried about him! But he never developed a fear of electricity or gadgets. One explanation is that, as Martin Seligman (1971) put it, people may be inherently "prepared" to learn certain phobias. For millions of years, people who quickly learned to avoid snakes, heights, and lightning probably improved their chance to survive and to transmit their genes. We have not had enough time to evolve a tendency to fear cars and electricity.

We have evidence to support this view from both monkey and human studies. Monkeys who watch a videotape of another monkey running away from a snake learn to fear snakes; monkeys who watch another monkey running away from a flower show no fear of flowers (Mineka, 1987). People who receive electric shocks paired with pictures of snakes quickly develop a strong and persistent response to snake pictures; people who receive shocks paired with pictures of houses show a much weaker response (Öhman, Eriksson, & Olofsson, 1975).

There may be other reasons some phobias are more common than others. One is that we have many safe experiences with cars and tools that outweigh any bad experiences. Most people have few experiences with snakes or spiders, and few experiences—certainly no safe experiences—of falling from high places. One study found that people who had extensive experiences with tarantulas lost their fears and sometimes even developed an interest in tarantulas as a hobby (Kleinknecht, 1982).

Another possible explanation is that people generally develop phobias of objects that they cannot predict or control. If you are afraid of spiders, for example, you must be constantly on the alert for those tiny, unpredictable critters. Because you never know where they might be or when they might bite, you can never completely relax.

Lightning is also unpredictable and uncontrollable. In contrast, electric outlets can also be dangerous, but you don't have to worry that they will take you by surprise. You must be on the alert for cars when you are near a road, but not at other times.

## Behavior Therapy for Phobias

Well-established phobias can last a lifetime. Remembering the discussion about avoidance learning, you can see why phobias are so difficult to extinguish: If you have learned to press a lever to avoid shock, you may not stop pressing long enough to find out that such a response is no longer necessary. Similarly, if you stay away from snakes or heights or closed places, you will never learn that your fear is exaggerated. In other words you will not extinguish your fear.

Recall the concept of behavior therapy from Chapter 15: A therapist sets a specific goal and uses learning techniques to help the client achieve that goal. One common and usually very successful behavioral treatment for phobia is **systematic desensitization,** *a method of reducing fear by gradually exposing people to the object of their fear* (Wolpe, 1961). Someone with a phobia of snakes, for example, is first trained in relaxation methods. Then the client is asked to lie on a comfortable couch with relaxing music playing in the background and with the therapist nearby. The therapist first asks the client to imagine a small black-and-white photo of a snake, then to imagine a color photo, and then to imagine a real snake. After the client has successfully visualized all of those images, the same sequence is repeated with real photos and eventually with a real snake (Figure 16.6).

The process resembles Skinner's shaping procedure (see Chapter 6). The person is given time to master each step before going on to the next. The client can say "stop"

if the distress becomes threatening; the therapist then goes back several steps and repeats the sequence. Some people complete the whole procedure in a single 1-hour session; others need weekly sessions for a couple of months. Systematic desensitization can easily be combined with social learning: The person with a phobia watches other people who display a fearless response to the object.

Some therapists use a high-tech approach (Rothbaum et al., 1995): The client is equipped with a helmet that displays a virtual-reality scene, as shown in Figure 16.7. Then, without even leaving the office, the therapist can expose the client to the feared object or situation. For example, a client with a phobia of heights can go up a glass elevator in a hotel or walk across a narrow bridge over a chasm (Rothbaum et al., 1995). This technology gives the therapist excellent control of the situation, including the option of turning off the display and removing the helmet if the client becomes too fearful.

**Flooding** or **implosion** is *a treatment that exposes the person to the object of the phobia suddenly rather than gradually* (Hogan & Kirchner, 1967; Rachman, 1969). (This treatment is called *flooding* because the patient is flooded with fear.) If you had a phobia of rats, for example, you might be told to imagine that you were locked in a room full of rats crawling all over you and viciously attacking you. The image arouses your sympathetic nervous system enormously, and your heart and breathing rates soar (Lande, 1982).

The human sympathetic nervous system is not capable of maintaining extreme arousal for very long, however, so within a few minutes your heart and breathing rates begin to decline. A little later you report that you feel more relaxed, even though the therapist continues to suggest gory images of what rats are doing to you. Once you have reached this point, the battle is half won. The main problem of people with phobias is their fear

**FIGURE 16.6** Systematic desensitization is one of the most effective therapies for phobia. A therapist gradually exposes a client to the object of the phobia, first in imagination and later in reality. Exposure therapy is a similar procedure. The therapist demonstrates fearlessness in the presence of the object and encourages the client to do the same.

**FIGURE 16.7** Some therapists use virtual reality to let a patient with a phobia of heights experience heights under carefully controlled conditions.

that they will have a heart attack or other catastrophic reaction. When they learn that they can withstand even the most frightening experience, they become less afraid of their own responses.

### Drug Therapies for Phobias and Anxiety Disorders

Tranquilizers are among the most widely prescribed drugs in the United States. The most common tranquilizers are the *benzodiazepines* (BEN-zo-die-AZ-uh-peens), including drugs with the trade names Valium, Librium, and Xanax. Benzodiazepines relieve anxiety, relax the muscles, induce sleep, and inhibit epileptic seizures. They act by facilitating activity at synapses using the transmitter GABA (Macdonald, Weddle, & Gross, 1986). These drugs can serve as a means of relieving an occasional episode of anxiety or as a sleeping pill. One disadvantage is that they can be habit-forming; another is that they suppress symptoms only temporarily. For example, someone who takes pills to combat panic disorder is likely to find that the attacks resume after the person discontinues the pills (Wiborg & Dahl, 1996). In many cases therapists treat anxiety disorders more effectively with antidepressant drugs, which we shall discuss later in this chapter.

## CONCEPT CHECKS

4. How does systematic desensitization resemble extinction of a learned shock-avoidance response?
5. How is the flooding procedure related to the James-Lange theory of emotions that was discussed in Chapter 12?
6. Alcohol facilitates transmission at GABA synapses. What effect should we expect if someone took both alcohol and a benzodiazepine tranquilizer? (Check your answers on page 623.)

## *Obsessive-Compulsive Disorder*

People with **obsessive-compulsive disorder** have two kinds of problems. An **obsession** is a *repetitive, unwelcome stream of thought.* For example, such people might find themselves constantly imagining gruesome scenes, worrying that they are about to kill someone, dwelling on doubts about their religion, or thinking "I hate my sister. I hate my sister." A **compulsion** is a *repetitive, almost irresistible action.* Obsessions generally lead to compulsions, as an itching sensation leads to scratching.

About 2–3% of all people in the United States suffer from obsessive-compulsive disorder at some time in life (Karno, Golding, Sorenson, & Burnam, 1988). The disorder occurs most frequently among hardworking, perfectionist people of average or above-average intelligence. It can develop either suddenly or gradually, usually beginning between the ages of 10 and 25. Nearly all people with obsessive-compulsive disorder have some insight into their own behavior and realize that their rituals are inappropriate. However, that realization does not stop the rituals.

Obsessive-compulsive disorder tends to run in families, suggesting a possible genetic basis. Many of the relatives who do not have obsessive-compulsive disorder have other anxiety disorders (Black, Noyes, Goldstein, & Blum, 1992).

 People with obsessive-compulsive disorder feel a combination of guilt and anxiety over persistent frightening impulses—perhaps an impulse to engage in a sexual act that they consider shameful, an impulse to hurt someone they love, or an impulse to commit suicide. They decide, "Oh, what a terrible thought. I don't want to think that ever again." And so they resolve to shut the thought or impulse out of their consciousness. However, the harder one tries to block out a thought, the more intrusive it becomes. As a child, the Russian novelist Leo Tolstoy once organized a club with a most unusual qualification for membership: A prospective member had to stand alone in a corner *without thinking about a white bear* (Simmons, 1949). If you think that sounds easy, try it. Ordinarily, you go months at a time between thoughts about polar bears, but when you try *not* to think about them, you can think of little else.

In one experiment college students were asked to tape-record everything that came to mind during 5 minutes but to try *not* to think about white bears. If they did, they were to mention it and ring a bell. Participants reported thinking about bears a mean of more than six times during the 5 minutes (Wegner, Schneider, Carter, & White, 1987). Afterward, they reported that almost everything in the room reminded them of white bears. Evidently, attempts to suppress a thought are likely to backfire, even with an emotionally trivial thought about something such as white bears. You can imagine how hard it must be with severely upsetting thoughts.

■ Most people seldom think about polar bears. But if you try to avoid thinking about them, you can think of little else but polar bears. Many attempts to block obsessive thinking backfire in a similar way.

People with obsessive-compulsive disorder have any of several kinds of compulsions. Some collect things. (One man collected newspapers under his bed until they raised the bed so high it almost touched the ceiling.) Others have odd habits, such as touching everything they see, trying to arrange objects in a completely symmetrical manner, or walking back and forth through a doorway nine times before leaving a building. One obsessive-compulsive person could not go to sleep at night until he had counted the corners of every object in the room to make sure that the total number of corners was evenly divisible by 16. If it was not, he would add or remove objects until the room had an acceptable total of corners. (The Obsessive-Compulsive Foundation produces a button that reads, "Every Member Counts"!) The most common compulsions are cleaning and checking.

## Cleaning Compulsion

Obsessive-compulsive cleaning is similar to a phobia of dirt. Here is a description of a severe cleaning compulsion (Nagera, 1976):

"R.," a 12-year-old boy, had a longstanding habit of prolonged bathing and hand washing, dating from a film about germs he had seen in the second grade. At about age 12, he started to complain about "being dirty" and having "bad thoughts," but he would not elaborate. His hand washing and bathing became longer and more frequent. When he bathed, he carefully washed himself with soap and washcloth all over, including the inside of his mouth and the inside of each nostril. He even opened his eyes in the soapy water and carefully washed his eyeballs. The only part he did not wash was his penis, which he covered with a washcloth as soon as he entered the tub.

Coupled with R.'s strange bathing habits, he developed some original superstitions. Whenever he did anything with one hand, he immediately did the same thing with the other hand. Whenever anyone mentioned a member of R.'s family, he would mention the corresponding member of the other person's family. He always walked to school by the same route, being careful never to step on any spot he had ever stepped on before. (After a while, this habit seriously strained his memory.) At school he would wipe the palm of his hand on his pants after any "good" thought; at home he would wipe his hand on his pants after any "bad" thought.

R.'s problems were traced to a single event. Just before the onset of his exaggerated behaviors, R. and another boy had pulled down their pants and looked at each other. Afterward, he felt guilty and full of anxiety that he might do the same thing again. The constant bathing was apparently an attempt to wash away his feelings of "dirtiness." The superstitious rituals were an attempt to impose rigid self-control. His underlying reasoning could be described as: "If I can keep myself under perfect control at all times, even following these rigid and pointless rules, I will never again lose control and do something shameful."

## Checking Compulsion

An obsessive-compulsive checker "double-checks" everything. Before going to bed at night, he or she makes sure that all the doors and windows are locked and that all the water faucets and gas outlets are turned off. But then the question arises, "Did I *really* check them all, or did I only imagine it?" So everything has to be checked again. And again. "After all, maybe I accidentally unlocked one of the doors while I was checking it." Obsessive-compulsive checkers can never decide when to stop checking; they may go on for hours and even then not be satisfied.

Obsessive-compulsive checkers have been known to check every door they pass to see whether anyone has been locked in, to check trash containers and bushes to see whether anyone has abandoned a baby, to call the police every day to ask whether they have committed a crime that they have forgotten, and to drive back and forth along a street to see whether they ran over any pedestrians the last time through (Pollak, 1979; Rachman & Hodgson, 1980).

Why do they go on checking? Part of the explanation is that they do not trust their own memory. In one study obsessive-compulsive patients and other people took a memory test and estimated how many questions they answered correctly. The normal people on the average estimated they had 76.4% correct, and in fact, they had 76.6% correct. The obsessive-compulsive people answered 75.6% correct—almost the same as the normals—but estimated they had only 60.4% correct (Dar, Rish, Hermish, Taub, & Fux, 2000). So perhaps one reason the obsessive-compulsive patients continue checking is they do not trust their memory that they have already checked.

 Table 16.1 summarizes key differences between obsessive-compulsive cleaners and checkers. Table 16.2 lists some items from a questionnaire on obsessive-compulsive tendencies (Rachman & Hodgson, 1980). Try answering these questions yourself, or try guessing how an obsessive-compulsive person would answer them. (The few items listed here are not sufficient to diagnose someone as obsessive-compulsive. So don't obsess about it if you agreed with all the obsessive-compulsive answers.)

## Therapies for Obsessive-Compulsive Disorder

Most people with obsessive-compulsive disorder improve over time, with or without treatment, and about half will become normal or nearly normal (Skoog & Skoog, 1999). Still, no one wants to wait years for spontaneous improvement if a treatment can hasten matters. One effective treatment is *exposure therapy*, which resembles systematic desensitization for phobias: The obsessive-compulsive person is exposed to the situation in which he or she ordinarily performs certain rituals and is then prevented from performing them. For example, an obsessive-compulsive cleaner would be prevented from

**TABLE 16.1 Obsessive-Compulsive Cleaners and Checkers**

|  | Cleaners | Checkers |
|---|---|---|
| *Sex distribution* | Mostly female | About equally male and female |
| *Dominant emotion* | Anxiety, similar to phobia | Guilt, shame |
| *Speed of onset* | Usually rapid | More often gradual |
| *Life disruption* | Dominates life | Usually does not disrupt job and family life |
| *Ritual length* | Less than 1 hour at a time | Some go on indefinitely |
| *Feel better after rituals?* | Yes | Usually not |

SOURCE: Rachman & Hodgson, 1980.

**TABLE 16.2 Obsessive-Compulsive Tendencies**

| | | |
|---|---|---|
| **1.** I avoid public telephones because of possible contamination. | T | F |
| **2.** I frequently get nasty thoughts and have difficulty getting rid of them. | T | F |
| **3.** I usually have serious thoughts about the simple everyday things I do. | T | F |
| **4.** Neither of my parents was very strict during my childhood. | T | F |
| **5.** I do not take a long time to dress in the morning. | T | F |
| **6.** One of my major problems is that I pay too much attention to detail. | T | F |
| **7.** I do not stick to a very strict routine when doing ordinary things. | T | F |
| **8.** I do not usually count when doing a routine task. | T | F |
| **9.** Even when I do something very carefully, I often feel that it is not quite right. | T | F |

SOURCE: Rachman & Hodgson, 1980. (Check typical answers on page 623.)

cleaning, or someone who ordinarily spends hours checking the doors and windows before going to sleep would be prevented from making the rounds. The point is to demonstrate that nothing catastrophic occurs if one leaves a little mess in the house or runs a slight risk of leaving a door unlocked.

The drug clomipramine (Anafranil) and related drugs are also helpful for at least half of obsessive-compulsive patients (Greist, Jefferson, Kobak, Katzelnick, & Serlin, 1995). Clomipramine prolongs the effects of the neurotransmitter serotonin by preventing the presynaptic neuron from reabsorbing it. That is, after an axon releases serotonin from its terminal button, clomipramine causes the serotonin to remain longer than usual in the synapse, reexciting the postsynaptic neuron. Researchers do not yet understand why prolonging serotonin activity should relieve obsessive-compulsive disorder.

## IN CLOSING
## *Emotions and Avoidance*

Phobia and obsessive-compulsive disorder illustrate some of the possible links between emotions and cognitions. At the risk of seriously oversimplifying, we could say that people with phobias experience emotional attacks because of their cognitions about a particular object, whereas people with obsessive-compulsive disorder experience repetitive cognitions for emotional reasons. In both conditions most people are cognitively aware that their reactions are exaggerated, but mere awareness of the problem does not correct it. Dealing with such conditions requires attention to emotions, cognitions, and the links between them.

## Summary

- **Anxiety disorder and panic disorder.** People with generalized anxiety disorder or panic disorder experience extreme anxiety. Panic disorder is characterized by episodes of disabling anxiety. People have periods of hyperventilation leading to high heart and breathing rates, then interpret the episode as threatening, and panic. (page 613)

- **Persistence of avoidance behaviors.** Once an individual has learned a shock-avoidance response, the response can persist long after the possibility of shock has been removed. As with shock-avoidance responses, phobias and obsessive-compulsive disorder persist because people do not discover that their avoidance behaviors are unnecessary. (page 614)

- **Phobia.** A phobia is a fear so extreme that it interferes with normal living. Phobias are learned through observation as well as through experience. (page 615)
- **Common phobias.** People are more likely to develop phobias of certain objects than of others; for example, snake phobias are more common than car phobias. The objects of the most common phobias have menaced humans throughout evolutionary history. They pose dangers that are difficult to predict or control, and they are generally objects with which we have had few safe experiences. (page 618)
- **Systematic desensitization of phobias.** A common therapy for phobia is systematic desensitization. The patient is taught to relax and is then gradually exposed to the object of the phobia. Flooding is similar, but the person is exposed to the object suddenly. (page 619)
- **Tranquilizers.** Drugs that facilitate activity at GABA synapses help to relieve anxiety. (page 620)
- **Obsessive-compulsive disorder.** People with obsessive-compulsive disorder try to avoid certain thoughts or impulses that cause anxiety or guilt. They also perform repetitive behaviors. (page 620)
- **Types of obsessive-compulsive disorder.** Two common types of compulsion are cleaning and checking. Cleaners try to avoid any type of contamination. Checkers constantly double-check themselves and invent elaborate rituals. (page 621)

## Answers to Concept Checks

1. Worrying about anything—even panic attacks themselves—often prompts these people to hyperventilate, and hyperventilation can in turn lead to another panic attack. (page 614)

2. Temporarily prevent the person from pressing the lever. Only by ceasing to press it does the person discover that pressing is not necessary. (page 615)
3. The CS was the white rat. The UCS was the loud noise. The CR and the UCR were a combination of crying and other reactions of fear. (page 617)
4. The method of extinguishing a learned shock-avoidance response is to prevent the response so that the individual learns that the failure to respond is not followed by shock. Similarly, with systematic desensitization the patient is prevented from fleeing the feared stimulus; he or she therefore learns that the danger is not as great as imagined. (page 620)
5. The flooding procedure is compatible with the James-Lange theory of emotions, which holds that emotions follow from perceptions of body arousal. In flooding, as arousal of the autonomic nervous system decreases, the person perceives, "I am calming down. I must not be as frightened of this situation as I thought I was." (page 620)
6. The combined effect of alcohol and a benzodiazepine tranquilizer would decrease anxiety, relax the muscles, and induce sleep more effectively than either alcohol or a benzodiazepine by itself. In fact, the combined effect can be so strong as to be dangerous, even fatal. People given prescriptions for benzodiazepine tranquilizers are warned not to take them in conjunction with alcohol. (page 620)

## Answers to Other Questions in the Module

Typical answers for obsessive-compulsive people (page 622):
1. T; 2. T; 3. T; 4. F; 5. F; 6. T; 7. F; 8. F; 9. T

# Substance-Related Disorders

*Why do people sometimes abuse alcohol or other drugs, and what can be done to help them?*

How would you like to volunteer for a little experiment? I want to implant a brain device into your head—something that will automatically lift your mood. There are still a few kinks in it, but most people who have tried say that it makes them feel good at least some of the time, and some people say it makes them feel very happy.

I should tell you about the possible risks. My device will endanger your health and will reduce your life expectancy by, oh, 10 years or so. Some people believe it may cause permanent brain damage, but they haven't proved that charge, so I don't think you should worry about it. Your behavior will change a good bit, though. You may have difficulty concentrating, for example. The device affects some people more than others. If you happen to be one of those who are strongly affected, you will have difficulty completing your education, getting or keeping a job, and carrying on a satisfactory personal life. But if you are lucky, you can avoid all that. Anyway, you can quit the experiment anytime you want to. You should know, though, that the longer the device remains in your brain, the harder it is to remove.

I cannot pay you for taking part in this experiment. In fact, *you* will have to pay *me*. But I'll give you a bargain

rate: only $5 for the first week and then a little more each week as time passes. One other thing: Technically speaking, this experiment is illegal. We probably won't get caught, but if we do, we could both go to jail.

What do you say? Is it a deal? I presume you will say "no." I get very few volunteers. And yet, if I change the term *brain device* to *drug* and change *experimenter* to *drug peddler*, it is amazing how many volunteers come forward.

For some people using alcohol or other drugs is apparently a harmless pleasure. For others it is extremely destructive. In Chapter 5 we examined the effects of several drugs on behavior. Instead of reviewing all of those drugs again here, we shall focus on abuse of alcohol and opiates, with a few comments about nicotine.

## Substance Dependence (Addiction)

We think of opiate drugs, such as morphine and heroin, as highly addictive. However, when patients recovering from surgery are given morphine or similar drugs to decrease their pain, virtually none of them develop an addiction. Why not? One reason is the dosage; hospital patients get only as much of the drug as they need to control the pain. Another is the social setting; taking a drug in a hospital room is not the same as at a party.

The main point is that simply taking a drug does not automatically produce addiction. Even people who take a drug such as morphine or heroin illegally do not all become addicted. A major question for researchers is what causes occasional drug use to develop into an overwhelming craving that dominates a person's life.

People who *find it difficult or impossible to quit a self-destructive habit* are said to have a **dependence** on it or an **addiction** to it. Addictions vary in many ways, and it is easy for people to convince themselves that they are not addicted because they are still able to function. In fact, many alcoholics or drug addicts keep their jobs and even work well at times; many of them also sometimes go days or weeks without using the substance at all. To decide whether you are addicted, ask, "Does the substance cause troubles in my life, and do I often take more than I had decided I would?"

### What Makes a Substance Addictive?

Nearly all the drugs that commonly produce addictions stimulate dopamine receptors in the *nucleus accumbens,* a

■ Addiction is in the user, not in the drug. Some people will continue using drugs even though they know the substances endanger their health, limit their opportunities, and provide them with little pleasure.

small area in the forebrain (Koob & LeMoal, 1997). For that reason both researchers and news reporters have described those dopamine synapses as "pleasure receptors." That characterization is probably wrong, as the same synapses are also activated by painful stimuli (Young, Joseph, & Gray, 1993). Activation of those dopamine synapses apparently pertains to attention more than to pleasure. Indeed, it is probably more helpful to think of drug addiction as something that monopolizes people's attention than as something that gives great pleasure (Robinson & Berridge, 2000).

Moreover, it is probably not helpful to imagine that something becomes addictive because it stimulates the nucleus accumbens. If anything, we might say that it stimulates the nucleus accumbens because it has become addictive. Gambling and even video game playing stimulate the nucleus accumbens in people who have developed strong habits (Koepp et al., 1998). That is, addiction or dependence is not an inherent property of any substance; it is a habit that depends on the person.

As discussed in Chapters 5 and 6, a drug addiction includes tolerance (decreased effect of a given dose) and withdrawal symptoms (disagreeable sensations while abstaining from the drug). Many psychologists have proposed that the withdrawal symptoms are a major reason for the addiction; that is, addicted people take the drug to escape the withdrawal symptoms. Withdrawal symptoms are certainly part of the problem, but not necessarily the main basis (Robinson & Berridge, 2000). An addict who quits a drug may continue to crave it months or even years later, long after the end of the withdrawal symptoms (Piasecki, Kenford, Smith, Fiore, & Baker, 1997). Also, withdrawal from tranquilizers produces stronger withdrawal symptoms than withdrawal from stimulants, but stimulants produce stronger addictions. Finally, some people develop powerful addictions to gambling, and sometimes even to video game playing, even though these addictions include no "substance" and should not produce any withdrawal symptoms at all (Griffiths & Wood, 2000).

Almost any substance can be addictive under certain circumstances. In a hospital ward where alcoholics were being treated, one of the patients moved his bed into the men's room (Cummings, 1979). At first, the hospital staff ignored this curious behavior. Then, one by one, other patients moved their beds into the men's room. Eventually, the staff discovered what was happening. These men, deprived of alcohol, had discovered that they could get a feeling similar to drunkenness by drinking enormous amounts of water! By drinking about 30 liters (7.5 gallons) of water per day and urinating the same amount (which was why they moved into the men's room), they managed to alter the acid-to-base balance of their blood enough to produce a sensation that resembled drunkenness. Is water addictive? Evidently, it can be. Addiction is in the person, not in the drug.

## Is Substance Dependence a Disease?

You have no doubt heard people say that alcoholism or drug dependence is a disease. It is hard to confirm or deny that statement, however, unless someone specifies exactly what *disease* means. (The medical profession assigns it no precise meaning, and the term has a wide variety of connotations.) When people call alcoholism or drug dependence a disease, they apparently mean that alcoholics and drug abusers should feel no guiltier about their condition than they would feel about having pneumonia.

Although the "disease" label is more constructive than thinking of substance dependence as a sign of moral weakness, the concept has some implications that the data do not support. For example, it implies an all or none distinction between those who have the disease and those who do not. The current trend among psychologists favors a continuum from people with no problem to those with a severe problem (W. R. Miller & Brown, 1997; Polcin, 1997).

Also, "disease" implies that alcoholism or drug dependence becomes inevitably worse over time. In fact, the long-term outcome for alcoholics and drug abusers varies enormously (Hser, Anglin, & Powers, 1993; Vaillant, 1983). Some individuals deteriorate rapidly and severely, some reach a steady level of abuse, and still others show a gradual improvement in their condition.

Furthermore, to regard substance dependence strictly as a disease seems to imply a need for medical intervention and downplays the importance of environmental factors. One of the most effective treatments for alcoholism or drug dependence is family therapy (Stanton & Shadish, 1997). By improving the person's family life, possibly improving the job situation, and helping the person to develop new interests, family therapy decreases the person's compulsion for alcohol or drug use.

## Nicotine Dependence

You have no doubt learned that the cigarette smoking habit is based largely on the nicotine. One type of evidence supporting this conclusion is that some people find it easier to quit smoking cigarettes if they have a replacement source of nicotine, such as a nicotine patch, nicotine chewing gum, or nicotine nasal spray (Rose, 1996). "If so," you may have wondered, "why have so many smokers switched to low-tar, low-nicotine cigarette brands? Wouldn't those brands fail to satisfy a nicotine craving?" Yes, they would, *if* they delivered low nicotine! Most low-tar, low-nicotine cigarettes have the same kind of tobacco as other cigarettes but a different filter, which contains a row of little air holes, as shown at the top of Figure 16.8. The theory is that air entering these holes will dilute the tobacco smoke coming through the barrel of the cigarette. However, many smokers wrap their fingers around the air holes, either accidentally or intentionally. Some even wrap tape over the holes. Regardless of whether people cover the holes, those who switch to

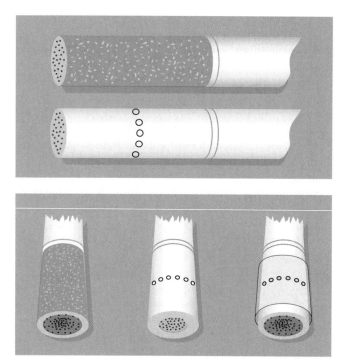

**FIGURE 16.8** "Low-nicotine" cigarettes have a row of small holes in the filter; room air is supposed to enter through those holes when the smoker inhales and therefore dilute the tobacco smoke. If people smoke such cigarettes without covering the air holes, little tar and nicotine pass through the cigarette, as we see from the relatively clean filter tip. However, if people cover the holes with their fingers or tape, they will receive about as much tar and nicotine as they would from any other filtered cigarette.

low-nicotine cigarettes generally inhale more deeply than they did when smoking regular cigarettes, and they smoke more cigarettes per day. As a result of all these changes in their smoking behavior, people smoking low-nicotine cigarettes inhale about as much tar and nicotine per day as do people smoking regular cigarettes (Benowitz, 1986; Kozlowski, Frecker, Khouw, & Pope, 1980).

**A STEP FURTHER**
*Addictions*

Are any addictive behaviors beneficial? (If a behavior is beneficial, can we call it *addictive*?)

**C**ONCEPT CHECK

7. Suppose we try to combat drug abuse with yet another drug. This new drug decreases the responsiveness of dopamine synapses in the nucleus accumbens. Will that drug decrease drug cravings and abuse? (Check your answer on page 631.)

# Alcoholism

Why do some people and not others develop addictions? The issue is particularly relevant to **alcoholism,** *the habitual overuse of alcohol.* If we wait until someone has become a chronic alcoholic, treatment is very difficult. If we could identify alcoholism at a very early stage, or identify young people who are at great risk for alcoholism, perhaps treatment would be more effective. At least psychologists would like to try.

## *Genetics and Family Background*

People differ in their genetic predisposition to addiction in general. Comparisons of twins indicate that the probability of occasionally trying drugs, including illegal drugs, depends on your family background. That is, you are likely to resemble your parents and siblings, but you would not resemble an identical twin any more than the rest of your family. However, your probability of addiction, as opposed to casual use, depends on your genes. If you had an identical twin, you and your twin would be very likely to have the same pattern of drug abuse or lack of it. Twin studies indicate a strong genetic basis for habitual cigarette smoking (Kendler, Thornton, & Pedersen, 2000), heavy use or dependence on illegal drugs (Kendler, Karkowski, Neale, & Prescott, 2000), and habitual gambling (Slutske et al., 2000). Because many people have more than one addiction, the likely interpretation is that some genes predispose people to excessive or addictive behaviors of many types.

A genetic predisposition is also a contributor specifically for alcoholism, or at least for early-onset alcoholism. Late-onset, or **Type I alcoholism,** *develops gradually over the years, affects about as many women as men, is generally less severe, and depends more on life experiences than genetics.* Early-onset, or **Type II alcoholism,** *develops rapidly, usually by age 25, is much more common in men than women, is usually more severe, and shows a strong genetic basis* (Devor, Abell, Hoffman, Tabakoff, & Cloninger, 1994; McGue, 1999). Table 16.3 summarizes this distinction. Naturally,

Italian and Jewish cultures, which stress moderation, have a fair amount of alcohol use but relatively little alcohol abuse.

**TABLE 16.3** Type I and Type II Alcoholism

| | Severity | Gender Distribution | Genetics Basis | Onset |
|---|---|---|---|---|
| *Type I* (or Type A) | Generally less severe; better long-term outcome | Both males and females | Weaker genetic contribution | Gradual onset later in life |
| *Type II* (or Type B) | More severe, more likely to be associated with aggressive behavior and antisocial personality | Almost exclusively males | Strong evidence for genetic contribution | Rapid onset in teens or early 20s |

not every alcoholic fits neatly into one category or the other, but the distinction accounts for most cases. Biological children of alcoholic parents have an increased risk of Type I alcoholism, even if they are adopted by nonalcoholics (Cloninger, Bohman, & Sigvardsson, 1981; Vaillant & Milofsky, 1982). However, no one is totally safe; even people with no family history of alcoholism sometimes develop an alcohol problem.

The incidence of alcoholism—either Type I or Type II—is greater than average among people who grew up in families marked by conflict between parents, poor relationships between parents and children, and inadequate parental supervision of the children (Schulsinger, Knop, Goodwin, Teasdale, & Mikkelsen, 1986; Zucker & Gomberg, 1986). Women who were sexually abused in childhood have an increased probability of alcohol abuse later in life. Ordinarily, one problem with data of this type is that most sexually abused children grew up in strife-torn families where sexual abuse was hardly the only problem. One study, however, found a number of pairs of twin girls in which only one had been sexually abused. The sexually abused girl was more likely than her twin to develop alcoholism and other problems in adulthood, so in this case the conclusion seems stronger than usual that sexual abuse led to the later problems (Kendler, Bulik, et al., 2000).

Culture also plays an important role. For example, most Jewish families emphasize drinking in moderation, and relatively few Jews become alcoholics (Cahalan, 1978). The same conclusion holds true for Italians as well. By contrast, alcoholism is more prevalent in the Irish culture, which tolerates it more (Vaillant & Milofsky, 1982).

Still, individuals differ. Not all children of alcoholic parents become alcoholics themselves, and not all children who grow up in a culture that tolerates heavy drinking become alcoholics. Can we identify people who are highly vulnerable to alcoholism?

 **WHAT'S THE EVIDENCE?** *Ways of Predicting Alcoholism*

Perhaps people's early behavior might indicate who is more likely to become an alcoholic. One way to find such clues would be to record the presence or absence of vari-

ous behaviors in hundreds of young people; many years later we could find out which of them have become alcoholics and determine which early behaviors might have predicted those outcomes. However, such a study would take long to complete. Moreover, finding all the participants after all that time, especially the alcoholics, might be difficult.

A more feasible approach is to compare children of an alcoholic parent with children of parents who are not alcoholics. From previous studies, we know that more children of alcoholics will become alcoholics. Therefore, behaviors that are significantly more prevalent among the children of alcoholics may predict vulnerability to alcoholism.

In the first of the following studies, experimenters tested whether alcohol might be more rewarding to the sons of alcoholics than to the sons of nonalcoholics (Levenson, Oyama, & Meek, 1987). (The study focused on men because alcoholism is more common in men than women.) Alcohol is known to help people relax when nervous (Swendsen et al., 2000); the question is whether it helps some people more than others.

**EXPERIMENT 1**

**HYPOTHESIS** When people are placed in a stressful situation, drinking alcohol will reduce stress for almost everyone. It will have a greater effect on the adult sons of an alcoholic parent than on other men of the same age.

**METHOD** The experiment was conducted on young men, half of them sons of alcoholic fathers and half the sons of nonalcoholics. The men were told that, at a certain time, they would receive an electric shock and, at another time, they would have to give a 3-minute speech entitled "What I Like and Dislike About My Body." They watched a clock tick off the waiting time. Half of each group were given alcohol to drink at the start of the waiting period, and everyone who was offered alcohol drank it.

**RESULTS** All of the men showed considerable stress, as measured by heart rate, restlessness, and self-reports of emotions. All of those who drank alcohol showed a lower heart rate and reported less anxiety. The easing of stress was more pronounced in those who had an alcoholic father (Figure 16.9).

**INTERPRETATION** Men who are genetically vulnerable to alcoholism experience greater stress-reducing effects

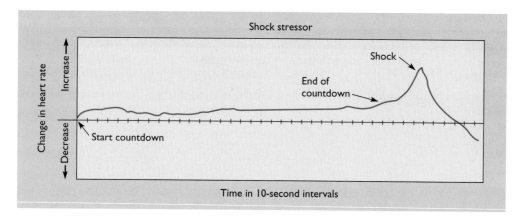

FIGURE 16.9 Changes in stress over time for a typical subject: The line goes up to indicate an increase in heart rate. Note that heart rate increased as soon as the countdown began and then remained stable. It rose toward the end of the countdown and again at the time of the shock or speech. Alcohol suppressed these signs of stress, especially for the sons of alcoholics. (From Levenson, Oyama, & Meek, 1987)

from alcohol than other men of the same age. Why that is true, we do not know, but we can examine the stress-reducing effects as a predictor of who might be vulnerable to alcoholism.

Several other studies tested and confirmed the hypothesis that young men who are vulnerable to alcoholism might have difficulty estimating their own degree of intoxication. The following study tested whether young drinkers who underestimate their degree of intoxication are more likely than others to become alcoholics later in life (Schuckit & Smith, 1997).

**EXPERIMENT 2**

**HYPOTHESIS** Men who underestimate how intoxicated they are after moderate drinking will be more likely than others to become alcoholics later.

**METHOD** This study was limited to 18- to 25-year-old men who had a close relative who was alcoholic. All of them drank a fixed amount of alcohol and were then asked to walk and to describe how intoxicated they felt. Experimenters noted how much the men staggered or swayed when they walked. Ten years later, the experimenters located as many of these men as possible, interviewed them, and determined whether they had become alcoholics.

**RESULTS** Of those who either did not sway much when walking or stated that they did not feel intoxicated, 51 of 81 (63%) became alcoholics within 10 years. Of those who clearly swayed and reported that they felt intoxicated, only 9 of 52 (17%) became alcoholics.

**INTERPRETATION** Men who neither act nor feel intoxicated after a moderate amount of drinking are likely to continue drinking and to become alcoholics. By watching and interviewing young drinkers, psychologists may be able to identify a high-risk population.

Any research study has limitations, and one limitation of these studies is clear: They examined only men. Considering that more men than women become alcoholics, the research strategy was reasonable; however, someone should repeat the studies with women.

## Treatments for Alcoholism

My mind is a dark place, and I should not be left alone there at night.

—Participant at Alcoholics Anonymous Meeting

Of all the people who try to quit alcohol or other drugs on their own, an estimated 10–20% manage to succeed (S. Cohen et al., 1989), though not necessarily on the first try. Some people quit and relapse and quit and relapse many times before eventually succeeding. In many cases, however, people with a substance-abuse problem find that they cannot quit on their own. Eventually, they "hit bottom," discovering that they have damaged their health, their ability to hold a job, and their relationships with friends and family. At that point they turn to others for help—either a mental-health professional or a self-help group such as Alcoholics Anonymous.

People who seek professional help improve their likelihood of long-term abstention, although there are no guarantees. Addicts who check into a hospital for treatment can be supervised 24 hours a day to ensure full abstinence. **Detoxification** refers to *a supervised period to remove drugs from the body.* In the long run, however, most addicts respond just as well to outpatient treatment as they do to hospital treatment (W. R. Miller & Hester, 1986).

Combating alcoholism is difficult but not hopeless. Let's consider several approaches and controversies.

### Alcoholics Anonymous

The most widespread treatment for alcoholism in North America is **Alcoholics Anonymous (AA),** *a self-help group of people who are trying to abstain from alcohol use and to help others do the same.* AA meetings are held regularly in community halls, church basements, and other available spaces. The meeting format varies but often includes study of the book *Alcoholics Anonymous* (Anonymous, 1955) and discussions of participants' individual problems. Some meetings feature an invited speaker. The group has a strong spiritual focus, including a reliance on "a Power greater than ourselves," but no affiliation with any particular religion. Although AA imposes no requirements on its members other than making an effort to give up drinking alcohol, new members are strongly encouraged to attend 90 meetings during the first 90 days. (Those who miss a day can compensate by attending two or more meetings another day.) The idea of doing so is to make a strong commitment. From then on, members attend as often as they like.

Millions of people have participated in the AA program in the United States and elsewhere around the world. One reason for its appeal is that all its members have gone through similar experiences. If someone tries to make an excuse for drinking, saying "you just don't understand how I feel" others can retort, "oh, yes we do!" A member who feels the urge to take a drink or who has already had one, can call a fellow member day or night for support. There is no charge for attendance at meetings; members simply contribute what they can toward the cost of renting the meeting place. AA has inspired other "anonymous" self-help groups whose purpose is to help drug addicts, compulsive gamblers, compulsive eaters, and so forth.

Although AA members themselves have confidence in the value of the program, research on its effectiveness has been scarce. One reason is that the organization is serious about its members' anonymity; it does not provide a list of members, and many of its meetings are closed to nonmembers. One further problem is that people cannot be assigned randomly to an AA group and a control group; AA participants are simply those who wish to participate, and they undoubtedly differ in many ways from those who choose not to participate.

### Antabuse

In addition to or instead of attendance at AA meetings, some alcoholics seek medical treatment. Many years ago investigators noticed that the workers in a certain rubber manufacturing plant drank very little alcohol. The investigators eventually linked this behavior to *disulfiram,* a chemical that was used in the manufacturing process. Ordinarily, the liver converts alcohol into a toxic substance, *acetaldehyde* (ASS-eh-TAL-de-HIDE), and then converts acetaldehyde into a harmless substance, *acetic acid.* Disulfiram, however, blocks the conversion of acetaldehyde to acetic acid. Whenever the workers drank alcohol, however, they accumulated acetaldehyde and became ill. Over time they learned to avoid all use of alcohol.

Disulfiram, available under the trade name **Antabuse,** is now sometimes used in the treatment of alcoholism, for which it is regarded as only moderately effective (Hughes & Cook, 1997). *Alcoholics who take a daily Antabuse pill become very sick whenever they have a drink.* They develop a sensation of heat in the face, headache, nausea, blurred vision, and anxiety. The threat of sickness is probably more effective than the sickness itself (Fuller & Roth, 1979). By taking a daily Antabuse pill, a recovering alcoholic renews the decision not to drink. Those who do take a drink in spite of the threat become quite ill, at which point they decide either not to drink again or not to take the pill again!

## CONCEPT CHECK

**8.** About 50% of Southeast Asians have a gene that makes them unable to convert acetaldehyde to acetic acid. Would such people be more likely or less likely than others to become alcoholics? (Check your answer on page 631.)

### Controlled Drinking

Most physicians agree with Alcoholics Anonymous that the only hope for an alcoholic is total abstinence. Drinking in moderation, they insist, is out of the question.

A few psychologists, however, are not convinced that abstinence is the best advice for *all* alcoholics (Peele, 1998). A few alcoholics repeatedly fail to learn abstention but do manage to reduce their drinking somewhat. This is not to say that alcoholics can simply decide to drink in moderation; if they could, they would not have become alcoholics in the first place. Rather, the point is that a few people who fail to stick to an abstention program can learn (with difficulty) to drink less than they have been, to stay out of legal trouble, and in general to do themselves less damage.

Psychologists have established several programs to try to teach alcoholics "controlled drinking," with at least occasional success (Rosenberg, 1993). Similarly, the **harm reduction** approach to drug abuse *concentrates on decreasing the frequency of drug use and minimizing the harmful consequences to health and well-being,* even if the person does not quit altogether (MacCoun, 1998). Critics charge that the controlled drinking and harm reduction approaches may discourage people from making a serious effort at quitting completely. Defenders reply that when people find that they cannot quit, we should not give up on helping them. This controversy is not likely to end soon.

### Contingency Management

Another treatment approach for alcoholism or any other kind of substance abuse is a form of behavior therapy known as *contingency management.* Practitioners carefully monitor alcohol use by a Breathalyzer or other drugs by urine samples. Whenever the test shows no alcohol or drugs, an immediate reinforcement is given. For example, teenagers might receive a few dollars, a movie pass, or a voucher for a hamburger or pizza (Kaminer, 2000). A major strength of this approach is that many people who are not motivated to try other approaches do agree to receive rewards for being free of alcohol and drugs. In a way the effectiveness of contingency management is surprising, as the rewards are small. That is, people could have abstained from alcohol and drugs and then used the money they saved to give themselves the same rewards or greater. Evidently, there is something powerful about testing negative for drugs and then receiving an immediate reinforcement.

# Opiate Dependence

Prior to 1900 opiate drugs such as morphine and heroin were considered far less dangerous than alcohol (Siegel, 1987). In fact, many doctors urged their alcoholic patients to switch from alcohol to morphine. Then, around 1900, using opiates became illegal in the United States, except by prescription to control pain. Since then research on opiate use has been limited by the fact that only lawbreakers now use opiates.

Opiates are widely used as painkillers, and even people who use them illegally do not necessarily develop a dependence. However, opiate dependence when it does occur often has a very rapid onset. People sometimes become dependent after using opiates only once or twice, in contrast to alcohol and tobacco dependence, which develop much more gradually. Like alcoholism, opiate abuse shows a hereditary tendency; that is, the closer your genetic relationship to an opiate abuser, the higher your probability of developing the same problem (Kendler, Karkowski, Neale, & Prescott, 2000).

## Treatments for Opiate Dependence

Some users of heroin and other opiates try to break their habit by going "cold turkey"—abstaining completely and suddenly, sometimes under medical supervision. Many people, however, experience a recurring urge to take the drug, even long after the withdrawal symptoms have subsided. To combat that urge, they can turn to self-help groups, contingency management, and other treatments, which are sometimes but not always successful. For those who cannot quit, researchers have sought to find a nonaddictive substitute that would satisfy the craving for opiates without harmful side effects. (Heroin was originally introduced as a substitute for morphine, before physicians discovered that it is even more addictive and troublesome!)

■ Heroin withdrawal resembles a severe bout of the flu, with aching limbs, intense chills, vomiting, and diarrhea; it takes a week on average to go cold turkey. Unfortunately, even after people have suffered through withdrawal, they are likely to experience periods of craving for the drug.

Today, the drug **methadone** (METH-uh-don) *is commonly offered as a less dangerous substitute for opiates.* Methadone is chemically similar to both morphine and heroin and can itself be addictive. (Table 16.4 compares methadone and morphine.) When methadone is taken in pill form, however, it enters the bloodstream gradually and also departs gradually (Dole, 1980). (If morphine or heroin is taken as a pill, much of the drug is broken down in the digestive system and never reaches the brain.) Thus, methadone does not produce the "rush" associated with intravenous injections of opiates, nor does it produce rapid withdrawal symptoms. Although methadone satisfies the craving for opiates without seriously disrupting the user's behavior, it does not eliminate the addiction itself. If the dosage is reduced, the craving returns.

Many addicts who stick to a methadone maintenance program hold jobs and commit fewer crimes than they did when they were using heroin or morphine. After discovering that they can no longer get high from opiates, some turn instead to a nonopiate drug such as cocaine (Kosten, Rounsaville, & Kleber, 1987). In other words methadone maintenance programs do not eliminate addictive behaviors. They do, however, provide harm reduction for an addiction that is very difficult to break (Kreek, 2000).

**TABLE 16.4 Comparison of Methadone with Morphine**

|  | Morphine | Methadone By Injection | Methadone Taken Orally |
|---|---|---|---|
| *Addictive?* | Yes | Yes | Weakly |
| *Onset* | Rapid | Rapid | Slow |
| *"Rush"?* | Yes | Yes | No |
| *Relieves craving?* | Yes | Yes | Yes |
| *Rapid withdrawal symptoms?* | Yes | Yes | No |

## Substances, the Individual, and Society

Substance dependence is costly to society as well as to the individual. The United States and many other countries have tried to control the problem by issuing stiff prison sentences for those who use or sell certain drugs. The result? Hard to say; drug use continues to be widespread, but we do not know how much worse it might be without the legal prohibitions. However, we do know that law enforcement itself is costly; prisons are crowded with those whose only offense was drug related and nonviolent, and many drug users turn to theft or violence as a way of getting drugs. The Netherlands has experimented with greatly decreased penalties against the use and sale of drugs, especially marijuana. The results are in some ways favorable, but in other ways unfavorable; overall, it is impossible to generalize about what might happen if other countries tried the same approach (MacCoun & Reuter, 1997). As a voter, you will have to help our society make decisions about how to deal with substance dependence, a problem that shows no signs of becoming less difficult.

## Summary

- **Substance dependence.** People who find it difficult or impossible to stop using a substance are said to be dependent on it or addicted to it. (page 624)
- **Addictive substances.** Nearly all addictive substances stimulate dopamine synapses in one part of the brain. That area is apparently associated more with attention than with pleasure. Most addictions are associated with tolerance and withdrawal symptoms. However, the intensity of the withdrawal is not closely related to the addiction, and cravings continue long after the end of withdrawal. Gambling and video game playing can be addictive, even though they do not include any substance. Therefore, to understand addictions, we need to understand the person using it, not just the drug itself. (page 624)
- **The disease concept.** Whether or not substance abuse is considered a disease depends on what we

mean by disease. The long-term course varies among different alcoholics or drug abusers. One of the most effective treatments for substance abuse is family therapy, which takes a nonmedical approach. (page 625)
- **Predisposition to alcoholism.** Some people may be predisposed to become alcoholics for genetic or other reasons. People at risk for alcoholism find that alcohol relieves their stress more than it does for other people. People who underestimate their level of intoxication are more likely than others to become alcoholics later. (page 626)
- **Alcoholics Anonymous.** The most common treatment for alcoholism in North America is provided by the self-help group Alcoholics Anonymous. (page 628)
- **Antabuse.** Some alcoholics are treated with Antabuse, a prescription drug that makes them ill if they drink alcohol. (page 629)
- **The controlled drinking controversy.** Whether certain alcoholics can be trained to drink in moderation is a controversial question. A similar controversy pertains to whether it is wise to help drug users decrease the harm to their lives without necessarily quitting the drugs altogether. (page 629)
- **Opiate abuse.** Some opiate users quit using opiates, suffer through the withdrawal symptoms, and manage to abstain from further use. Others substitute methadone under medical supervision. Although methadone has fewer destructive effects than morphine or heroin, it does not eliminate the underlying dependence. (page 630)

## Answers to Concept Checks

**7.** Possibly, but the other outcome is that the addicted person may use even more of the drug to try to increase the stimulation. Prolonged use of cigarettes, for example, is known to decrease responsiveness of those dopamine synapses, but the effect is greater dependence on cigarettes, not less. (page 626)
**8.** They are less likely than others to become alcoholics. This gene is considered the probable reason that relatively few Asians become alcoholics (Harada, Agarwal, Goedde, Tagaki, & Ishikawa, 1982; Reed, 1985). (page 629)

# Mood Disorders

*Why do people have severe mood swings, and what can be done to help them?*

For most of us, most of the time, our moods match the events of our lives. We feel happy when life is going well and sad when we experience disappointments. Some people, however, feel extremely good or extremely bad for long periods of time, regardless of the events in their lives. Why?

## Depression

When people say "I'm depressed," they often mean "I'm sad. Life isn't going very well for me right now." In psychology **major depression** is a much more *extreme condition, persisting most of each day for a period of months, in which the person experiences little interest in anything, little pleasure, and little motivation for any productive activity.* Aaron Beck (1973) described one depressed woman who stood in front of an elevator for 15 minutes because she did not have enough desire to press the button.

Sad people are unhappy at the moment, whereas depressed people cannot even imagine something that would make them happy. They have trouble concentrating. They lose interest in food and sex. They feel worthless, fearful, guilty, and powerless to control what happens to them. Most severely depressed people consider suicide, and many attempt it. As with any other psychological disorder, depression varies in severity from one person to another and from one time to another (Flett, Vredenburg, & Krames, 1997).

Nearly all depressed people experience sleep abnormalities (Carroll, 1980; Healy & Williams, 1988) (see Figure 16.10). They enter REM sleep less than 45 minutes after falling asleep (an unusually short time for most people). Most depressed people wake up too early and cannot get back to sleep. When morning comes, they feel poorly rested. In fact, they usually feel most depressed early in the morning. During much of the day, they feel a little sleepy.

Depression is common from adolescence through old age. Regardless of the age at diagnosis, most people say they had been somewhat depressed for years before the condition became severe enough for them to visit a therapist (Eaton et al., 1997). Some reports indicate that depression has been growing more common over the decades, but the research is mixed on this point (Murphy, Laird, Monson, Sobol, & Leighton, 2000). It is difficult, of course, to determine whether a condition has been increasing in prevalence or whether psychiatrists have changed their standards of diagnosis.

The good news is that very few people remain constantly and permanently depressed. Typically, people have an episode of depression that lasts a few months (less commonly for years), then recover for months or years, and then experience another episode of depression. On the average earlier depressed episodes last longer than later ones (Solomon et al., 1997).

People with a special variety of depression known as **seasonal affective disorder (SAD),** or **depression with a seasonal pattern** (Figure 16.11), *consistently become depressed during a particular season of the year.* It is common in areas of the world that have little sunlight in winter, such as Scandinavia. Although annual winter depressions have received the most publicity, annual summer depressions also occur (Faedda et al., 1993). Unlike most other depressed patients, people with seasonal affective disorder tend to sleep and eat excessively during

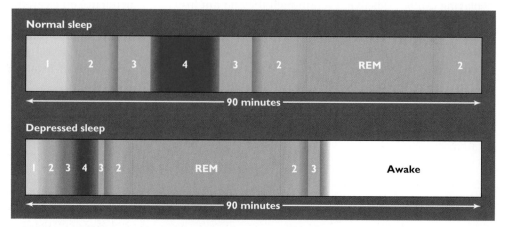

**FIGURE 16.10** When most people go to sleep at their usual time, they progress slowly to stage 4 and then back through stages 3 and 2, reaching REM sleep toward the end of their first 90-minute cycle. Depressed people, however, reach REM more rapidly, generally in less than 45 minutes. They also tend to awaken frequently during the night.

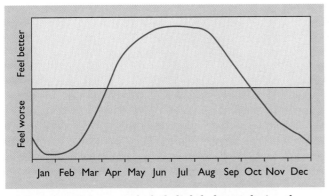

**FIGURE 16.11** Most people feel slightly better during the summer (when the sun is out most of the day) than during the winter (when there are fewer hours of sunlight). People with seasonal affective disorder (SAD) feel good in the summer and seriously depressed in the winter (or good in the winter and depressed in the summer). Seasonal affective disorder is commonest in far northern locations such as Scandinavia, where the summer days are very long and bright and the winter days are very short and dark. The disorder is unheard-of in tropical locations such as Hawaii, where the amount of sunlight per day varies only slightly between summer and winter.

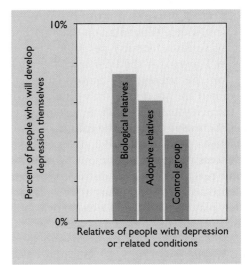

**FIGURE 16.12** Blood relatives of depressed people, substance-dependent people, and suicidal people are more likely to suffer depression themselves when compared with incidences of depression in the general public, which is 5–10%. Adopted relatives share some of this same tendency. (Based on data of Weissman, Kidd, & Prusoff, 1982)

their depressed periods (Jacobsen, Sack, Wehr, Rogers, & Rosenthal, 1987). Also, they tend to fall asleep late and awaken late, in contrast to other depressed patients who generally get sleepy early and wake up early (Teicher et al., 1997).

Seasonal affective disorder of the winter variety can be relieved by sitting for a few hours each day in front of a bright light, preferably in the morning. The morning light shifts the circadian rhythm forward so that the person wakes earlier and feels sleepy earlier. A strong shift in the circadian rhythm is essential to the antidepressant effect, but why that shift helps depression remains uncertain (Terman, Terman, Lo, & Cooper, 2001).

Although the effects of light therapy are poorly understood, they are consistently more powerful and more reliable than either antidepressant drugs or psychotherapy. Furthermore, light therapy costs little and has no side effects. Some therapists recommend research on whether it could relieve other kinds of depression in addition to seasonal affective disorder (Wirz-Justice, 1998).

**Bipolar disorder,** previously known as *manic-depressive disorder,* is a related condition in which a *person alternates between periods of depression and periods of mania, which are opposite extremes.* We shall consider bipolar disorder in more detail later.

## Genetic Predisposition to Depression

Your probability of becoming depressed is increased if you have close biological relatives with depression. It is also increased, but not as much, if you have adoptive relatives with depression (see Figure 16.12). Those findings imply that depression depends on both hereditary and

family influences. Your probability of depression is especially high if you have biological relatives who became severely depressed before age 30 (Kendler, Gardner, & Prescott, 1999; Lyons et al., 1998). In that regard depression fits the same pattern as many other disorders, including Parkinson's disease, Alzheimer's disease, alcoholism, and schizophrenia: If someone shows the condition early in life, the genetic influence is probably strong. The later the onset, the less likely the person is to have close relatives with the same disorder.

Researchers have tried to locate a gene that leads to depression but so far have not succeeded (Faraone, Kremen, & Tsuang, 1990; McQuillin, Lawrence, Kalsi, Chen, & Gurling, 1999). It is likely that several genes can increase the likelihood of depression, not just one. It is also nearly certain that no gene *causes* depression; rather, genes alter people's temperament in ways that alter their responses to events.

## The Gender Difference in Depression

Depression is uncommon before adolescence, but at that age it occurs about equally in boys and girls. From adolescence onward it is about twice as common in women as in men, and the ratio is even higher for severe depression. Women experience depression more than men in all cultures for which we have data (Culberson, 1997; Cyranowski, Frank, Young, & Shear, 2000; Silberg et al., 1999).

Why is depression more common in women than it is in men? One possibility is that hormonal changes as a result of menstrual cycles, pregnancy, childbirth, or menopause trigger episodes of depression. For example, *shortly after giving birth, a time of massive hormonal changes, some women enter a* **postpartum depression.** Frequency estimates vary widely depending on whether one counts only the severe cases (about 1 per 1000), the moderate cases (about 1 in 10), or the mild cases (about 3 in 10). However, on the average the hormonal levels of depressed women are not significantly different from those of other women (Roca, Schmidt, & Rubinow, 1999), so hormones themselves are not the culprit.

Susan Nolen-Hoeksema (1990, 1991) has suggested that the excess of depression among women relates to how people react to emotional distress: When men start to feel depressed, they generally try to distract themselves. They play basketball or watch a movie or do something else instead of thinking about how they feel. Women are more likely to ruminate—to think about why they are depressed, to talk with others about their feelings, even to have a long cry. According to Nolen-Hoeksema, ruminating about depression only makes it worse. The ruminative thoughts interfere with useful problem solving and bias a person toward a pessimistic appraisal of the situation. This explanation has the advantage of suggesting ways to help women (and men) avoid or minimize their depression.

It does not, however, address the question of *why* women ruminate more and distract themselves less than men do. It also faces a difficulty of interpretation: Do the thoughts *lead to* depression? Or are they just an early symptom of depression? The research so far does not clearly distinguish between these possibilities, and of course, both could be true.

## Events That Precipitate Depression

As a rule people become depressed when bad things happen to them. For example, most people are clearly depressed after the death of a spouse (L. W. Thompson, Gallagher-Thompson, Futterman, Gilewski, & Peterson, 1991). However, the severity of an unpleasant event is a poor predictor of how long or how intensely someone will feel depressed.

One study followed some students at a California university who had happened to answer a questionnaire about their mental health 2 weeks before a major earthquake in 1989. Psychologists asked the same students to fill out the same questionnaires again 10 days and 7 weeks after the earthquake. The results were that students who were already somewhat depressed before the earthquake became very depressed and remained depressed; students who were not depressed earlier suffered some distress but in most cases recovered rapidly (Nolen-Hoeksema & Morrow, 1991). In other words a stressful event makes anyone feel bad, but it has its strongest effects on people who were already mildly depressed.

So, what makes some people more vulnerable than others? One explanation is that severe losses early in life make people more vulnerable to later depression. For example, adolescents who lose a parent through death or

■ Depression is most common among people who have little social support.

divorce are likely to react strongly to other losses later in life, even to routine events such as breaking up with a boyfriend or girlfriend (Roy, 1985).

People with poor social support also tend to be vulnerable to depression. As we saw in Chapter 12, social support helps people cope with stress. People who are happily married or who have close friends are less likely to become or remain depressed than people without close friends or people who fail to make use of the emotional support that their friends offer (Rivera, Rose, Futterman, Lovett, & Gallagher-Thompson, 1991).

Depression depends less on the events that transpire than on how people interpret them. For example, a trivial event such as not being invited to a party might contribute toward depression for someone who regarded the noninvitation as evidence of rejection by other people (Johnson & Roberts, 1995). To understand who becomes depressed and why, we need to understand how people think.

## Cognitive Aspects of Depression

Most people believe that every cloud has a silver lining. Depressed people believe that every silver lining has a cloud. Perhaps their thought patterns lead to their depression.

 Suppose you fail a test. How would you probably explain your failure?

- The test was extremely difficult. Most other students probably did badly too.
- I had a weaker background from my previous education than most other students in the class.
- I was sick and didn't get a chance to study.
- I'm just stupid. I always do badly, no matter how hard I try.

**FIGURE 16.13** During the Gulf War in 1991, U.S. President George Bush and Iraqi leader Saddam Hussein tended to make bold, risky decisions during periods when their speeches were optimistic; both were passive and cautious during periods when their speeches were pessimistic. Of course, the data do not tell us whether optimism changed the decisions, the decisions changed the optimism level, or world events influenced both the decisions and the optimism level. (Satterfield & Seligman, 1994)

Using any of the first three explanations, you probably wouldn't feel very depressed. You would be attributing your failure to a temporary, specific, or correctable situation. However, the fourth attribution applies to you at all times in all situations. If you make that attribution—and if your grades are important to you—you are likely to feel depressed about your failure (Abramson, Seligman, & Teasdale, 1978; C. Peterson, Bettes, & Seligman, 1985). The more often you make similar attributions in other situations, the more likely you are to be depressed.

In a given situation, such as a low grade on a test, you might have a good reason for one attribution or another. For example, perhaps you really are the only one in this French class who did not take high school French. Still, everyone has an **explanatory style,** *a tendency to accept one kind of explanation for success or failure more often than others.* Recall from Chapter 14 that an *internal attribution* cites a cause within the person. ("I failed the test because I studied poorly.") An *external attribution* identifies a causes outside the person. ("I failed the test because it was extremely hard.") Most people are not very consistent about how they explain their successes, but most are quite consistent, even over decades, in how they explain their failures. People who take the blame for their failures today will probably continue blaming themselves 30 or 40 years from now (Burns & Seligman, 1989).

Blaming yourself isn't always wrong; if you make mistakes, you should look for ways to improve. However, consistently taking the blame even when the problem is not your fault constitutes a *pessimistic* explanatory style, especially if your explanations for failure are global (consistent over situations) and stable (consistent over time). For example, "I failed the test because I'm stupid" is global and stable; it applies to everything you do at all times.

Although pessimism is hardly the same as depression, people with a pessimistic style are more likely than others to have been depressed in the past, and they are more likely to become depressed in the future (Alloy et al.,

1999). Indeed, according to Aaron Beck (1973, 1987), depressed people consistently put unfavorable interpretations on the events of their lives. If someone walks by without comment, their likely response is, "See, people ignore me. They don't like me." After any kind of defeat, "I'm a loser. I'm hopeless." After any kind of win, "That was just luck. I had nothing to do with it." Depressed people exaggerate their failures, minimize their successes, and give themselves a very low evaluation. Given this explanatory style, almost any event can trigger depression.

Researchers have also gauged the explanatory styles of famous people, even dead people, by reading their speeches and writings to see what explanations they offered for successes and failures. Using this method psychologists have found that pessimistic political leaders tend to be cautious, indecisive, and inactive. Leaders with an optimistic explanatory style take bold, even risky actions (Satterfield & Seligman, 1994; Zullow, Oettingen, Peterson, & Seligman, 1988) (see Figure 16.13). Athletes with a pessimistic style tend to give up and try less after a defeat. Athletes with a more optimistic style try harder after a defeat because, after all, they believe they can overcome their defeats if they work hard enough (Seligman, Nolen-Hoeksema, Thornton, & Thornton, 1990). (How do you react after you try something and fail? Do you try harder or do you give up?)

## CONCEPT CHECK

**9.** Would depressed people be more or less likely than nondepressed people to buy a lottery ticket? (Check your answer on page 642.)

## *Treatments for Depression*

Depression can be severe, even incapacitating, but it often responds well to treatment. Both psychotherapy and drug therapy are effective.

## Cognitive Therapy

According to Aaron Beck, a pioneer in cognitive therapy, depressed people are guided by certain thoughts or assumptions of which they are only dimly aware. He refers to the "negative cognitive triad of depression":

- I am deprived or defeated.
- The world is full of obstacles.
- The future is devoid of hope.

Based on these assumptions, which Beck calls "automatic thoughts," depressed people interpret ambiguous situations to their own disadvantage. When something goes wrong, they blame themselves: "I'm worthless, and I can't do anything right." When someone walks past without smiling, they think, "She doesn't like me." They do not even consider alternative interpretations (Beck, 1991).

The task of a cognitive therapist is to help depressed people to substitute favorable beliefs. Cognitive therapists try to motivate their clients to make discoveries for themselves. The therapist focuses on a belief, such as "no one likes me," points out that it is a hypothesis, and invites the client to test the hypothesis as a scientist would:

**THERAPIST:** What evidence do you have for this hypothesis?

**CLIENT:** Well, when I arrive at work in the morning, hardly anyone says hello.

**THERAPIST:** Is there any other way of looking at that evidence?

**CLIENT:** Hmm. . . . I suppose it's possible that the others are busy.

**THERAPIST:** Does anyone ever seem happy to see you?

**CLIENT:** Well, maybe. I'm not sure.

**THERAPIST:** Then let's find out. For the next week, keep a notebook with you and record every time that anyone smiles or seems happy to see you. The next time I see you, we'll discuss what you've discovered.

The therapist's goal is to encourage depressed clients to discover that their automatic thoughts are incorrect, that things are not nearly as bad as they seem, and that the future is not hopeless. If one of the client's thoughts does turn out to be accurate—for example, "my boyfriend is interested in someone else"—then the therapist asks, "Even if it's true, is that the end of the world?"

Cognitive therapy can also be used to prevent depression. In one study 231 college students with a pessimistic explanatory style were randomly assigned to no treatment or a series of eight 2-hour group workshops devoted to teaching them how to combat negative thoughts about themselves. Those who were given the workshops reported fewer episodes of anxiety and depression over the next 3 years (Seligman, Schulman, DeRubeis, & Hollon, 1999).

## Antidepressant Drugs

The common antidepressants include tricyclics, serotonin reuptake inhibitors, and monoamine oxidase inhibitors. **Tricyclic drugs** (e.g., imipramine, trade name Tofranil) *block the reabsorption of the neurotransmitters dopamine, norepinephrine, and serotonin after they are released by an axon's terminal* (Figure 16.14). Thus, tricyclics prolong the effect of these neurotransmitters on the receptors of the postsynaptic cell. Although they are effective for most people, they produce unpleasant side effects, including dry mouth, difficulty urinating, heart irregularities, and drowsiness (Horst & Preskorn, 1998). Many people quit taking the drugs because of their side effects.

**Selective serotonin reuptake inhibitors (SSRIs)** (e.g., fluoxetine, trade name Prozac) are similar to tricyclic drugs but more specific in their effects. They *block the reuptake of the neurotransmitter serotonin.* Their side effects are usually limited to mild nausea or headache (Feighner et al., 1991), and consequently, many people can take them in larger doses than the tricyclics. However, the selective

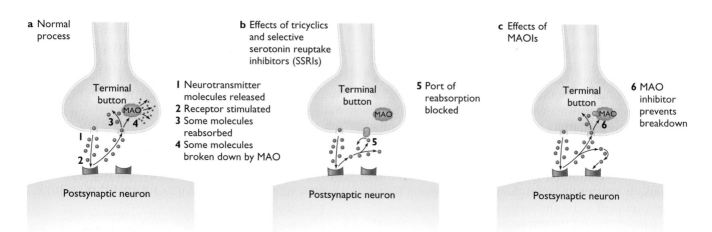

**FIGURE 16.14** Antidepressant drugs prolong the activity of the neurotransmitters dopamine, norepinephrine, and serotonin. (a) Ordinarily, after the release of one of the neurotransmitters, some of the molecules are reabsorbed by the terminal button, and other molecules are broken down by the enzyme monoamine oxidase (MAO). (b) Selective serotonin reuptake inhibitors (SSRIs) prevent reabsorption of serotonin. Tricyclic drugs prevent reabsorption of dopamine, norepinephrine, and serotonin. (c) MAO inhibitors (MAOIs) block the enzyme monoamine oxidase and thereby prolong the effects of the neurotransmitters.

serotonin reuptake blockers sometimes produce nervousness, and they are not recommended for people with both depression and anxiety. Other common drugs in this category are sertraline (Zoloft), fluvoxamine (Luvox), citalopram (Celexa), and paroxetine (Paxil or Seroxat).

**Monoamine** (MAHN-oh-ah-MEEN) **oxidase inhibitors (MAOIs)** (e.g., phenelzine, trade name Nardil) *block the metabolic breakdown of released dopamine, norepinephrine, and serotonin* by the enzyme monoamine oxidase (MAO) (Figure 16.14c). Thus, MAOIs also prolong the ability of released neurotransmitters to stimulate the postsynaptic cell. MAOIs are less effective than the other antidepressant drugs for most people, but they help some people who failed to respond to the other drugs (Thase, Trivedi, & Rush, 1995).

Another group of antidepressant drugs is not really a group; they have little in common with each other except that they fail to fit into any of the first three groups. These **atypical antidepressants** *are helpful to some patients who did not respond to the other antidepressant drugs and generally produce only mild side effects.* The most common of these, buproprion (Wellbutrin) acts mainly by blocking the reuptake of dopamine (Horst & Preskorn, 1998).

You have probably heard about **St. John's wort,** *an herb with antidepressant effects.* It contains several chemicals that block the reuptake of dopamine and serotonin, as other antidepressant drugs do. Because St. John's wort is a naturally occurring substance, it is fairly inexpensive and available without a doctor's prescription. It is one of many nonprescription treatments that have become popular means of fighting depression, including relaxation techniques, large doses of vitamins, massage, spiritual healing, self-help groups, and aroma therapy (Kessler et al., 2001). St. John's wort is about as effective as other antidepressant drugs, but it has drawbacks. First, because the Food and Drug Administration does not regulate the sale of herbs, the purity varies from one bottle to another. Second, it has side effects, including gastrointestinal distress, drowsiness, and painful sensitivity to light (Wong, Smith, & Boon, 1998). Third, it has an additional very interesting side effect: It activates a liver enzyme that breaks down a wide variety of toxic plant chemicals. Helping to break down toxins sounds like a benefit, and indeed it can be. However, that enzyme also breaks down most medications. Therefore, taking St. John's wort decreases the effectiveness of cancer drugs, AIDS drugs, and even birth-control pills (Moore et al., 2000). How much it impairs those other drugs varies from one person to another. Thus, the advice is that depressed people should consider trying St. John's wort only if they take *no* other medications.

 **C**ONCEPT CHECKS

10. Which type of antidepressant drug has effects similar to methylphenidate (Ritalin), discussed in Chapter 5?

11. If someone takes prescription antidepressant drugs, would it help to take St. John's wort also? (Check your answers on page 642.)

The effects of antidepressant drugs build up gradually. Some depressed people report feeling better within the first week or two of use. The early benefit is almost always a *placebo effect;* that is, it depends on the person's expectation of feeling better and not on the drug itself. People who report quick benefits can be switched to an inactive substance such as sugar tablets without any loss of benefit (Stewart et al., 1998). The drug itself begins to show effects after 2 to 3 weeks of use, and the effects increase over the following 4 to 5 weeks (Blaine, Prien, & Levine, 1983). Even then, part of what appears to be a drug effect is also a placebo effect or an effect of the passage of time. That is, people taking the drugs usually improve, but many people taking no drug or an ineffective drug would also improve to some extent over the same time (Kirsch & Sapirstein, 1998).

The fact that antidepressant drugs alter synaptic activity within an hour or so but need weeks to improve a patient's mood tells us that the explanation in terms of synapses must be incomplete. Prolonging the effects of dopamine and serotonin at the synaptic receptors sets in motion a series of events, and it is not obvious which of those is the key to success. Currently, investigators focus on how the drugs facilitate cell growth. Stressful events can cause the shrinkage and death of neurons, and several brain areas are smaller in depressed people than in most others. Prolonged use of antidepressants leads to expansion of cell bodies, growth of dendrites, and even the maturation of new neurons in the hippocampus (Duman, Heninger, & Nestler, 1997; Jacobs, van Praag, & Gage, 2000).

### Choosing Between Psychotherapy and Antidepressant Drugs

Cognitive therapy helps some depressed people who do not respond well to drug therapy (Paykel et al., 1999) and produces no side effects. Also, its benefits generally persist longer after the end of therapy (Robinson, Berman, & Neimeyer, 1990). That is, people who quit taking antidepressant drugs are likely to relapse into another depressive episode months or years later; people who have completed psychotherapy are less likely to relapse into another episode. Nevertheless, the use of antidepressant drugs has been increasing (Olfson et al., 1998). You might wonder why.

Two reasons are convenience and cost. The cost of psychotherapy varies depending on the therapist and the geographical region, but let's use $100 (U.S.) per hour as an approximation. If a depressed person has enough time and either enough money or a generous insurance program that will pay for many visits, then psychotherapy is a good idea. However, someone who cannot afford the time or money might be tempted by some relatively inexpensive pills.

Double-blind studies have consistently found that about two-thirds of the adults who take antidepressant drugs experience improvements in their moods. Similarly, talk-based psychotherapy produces benefits for about two-thirds to three-fourths of patients. Taking a placebo or waiting a few months helps one-third to one-half. Would a combination of drugs and psychotherapy help more than either one alone? Combining them is helpful only for patients with severe depressions. For people with mild to moderate depression, either one alone is as good as the combination (Thase et al., 1997). Apparently, some people's depressions are easy to lift and others' are not, regardless of methods.

### A STEP FURTHER
#### Drugs and Psychotherapy

If the combination of drugs plus psychotherapy helps about the same percentage of people as either one alone, what inference can we draw about whether drugs help the same people who would have responded to psychotherapy?

### Electroconvulsive Shock Therapy (ECT)

Another well-known but controversial treatment for depression is **electroconvulsive therapy (ECT)** (Figure 16.15): *A brief electrical shock is administered across the patient's head to induce a convulsion similar to epilepsy.* ECT was first used in the 1930s and became popular in the 1940s and 1950s as a treatment for schizophrenia, depression, and many other psychiatric disorders. It then fell out of

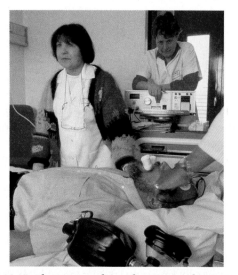

**FIGURE 16.15** Electroconvulsive therapy is administered today only with the patient's informed consent. ECT is given in conjunction with muscle relaxants and anesthetics to minimize discomfort.

favor, partly because antidepressant drugs and other therapeutic methods had become available and partly because ECT had been widely abused. Some patients were subjected to ECT hundreds of times without their consent, and in many cases ECT was used as a threat to enforce patients' cooperation.

Beginning in the 1970s, ECT has made a comeback in modified form, mostly for severely depressed people who fail to respond to antidepressant drugs, whose thinking is seriously disordered, or who have strong suicidal tendencies (Scovern & Kilmann, 1980). For suicidal patients, ECT has the advantage of taking effect rapidly, generally within 1 week. When a life is at stake, rapid relief is important.

ECT is now used only with patients who have given their informed consent. The shock is less intense than it used to be, and the patient is given muscle relaxants and anesthetics to prevent injury and to reduce discomfort. As a rule the procedure is applied every other day for about 2 weeks. Then the psychiatrist evaluates the progress and either stops the treatment or decides to repeat it a few more times.

How ECT works is uncertain (Fink, 2000). Some have suggested that it relieves depression by causing people to forget certain depressing thoughts and memories. However, the data do not support that suggestion. Although ECT usually does impair memory, if it is administered to just the frontal part of the brain or to only the right hemisphere at high intensity, it is as effective as the usual whole-brain ECT, but with little or no memory loss (Lisanby, Maddox, Prudic, Devanand, & Sackeim, 2000; Sackeim et al., 2000). Another option is to apply powerful magnetic fields over the scalp, temporarily disabling all the neurons under the magnet (George et al., 1997). That procedure has effects very similar to those of ECT, but there is no electric shock.

Although ECT is effective for most depressed patients and produces fewer side effects than drugs, its benefits are generally temporary. About half of those who show a good response will relapse into depression within 6 months unless they receive some other therapy to prevent it (Riddle & Scott, 1995).

## Bipolar Disorder

People with bipolar disorder (formerly known as manic-depressive disorder) alternate between the extremes of mania and depression. In many respects **mania** is the *opposite of depression.* When people with bipolar disorder are in the depressed phase, they are slow, inactive, and inhibited. When they are in the manic phase, they are *constantly active and uninhibited.* For example, mental hospitals do not install fire alarms in certain wards because manic patients cannot resist the impulse to pull the alarm. People during a depressed phase feel helpless, guilt-ridden, and sad. When they are manic, they are either *happy* or *irritable.* Typically, episodes of depression alternate with briefer episodes of mania. Although most people's episodes last months, episodes as short as a day are possible.

Psychologists distinguish two types of bipolar disorder. People with **bipolar I disorder** *have had at least one episode of mania.* People with **bipolar II disorder** *have had episodes of major depression and hypomania, which is a milder degree of mania.* In some cases the hypomanic phases do not seem troubling to the patient, although others may regard the behavior as erratic or odd.

In the past about 1% of all adults in the United States have been diagnosed with bipolar disorder (Robins et al., 1984). However, the diagnosis is difficult. Many people have some not very prominent symptoms of bipolar disorder plus symptoms of attention deficits, anxiety, or even hallucinations or delusions (Hilty, Brady, & Hales, 1999). For people with multiple or mixed symptoms, therapists today are more likely than those of the past to diagnose bipolar disorder. Studies of twins and adopted children indicate a strong hereditary influence on bipolar disorder (Craddock & Jones, 1999).

The rambling speech of a manic person has been described as a "flight of ideas." The person starts talking about one topic, which suggests another, which in turn suggests another. Here is a quote from a manic patient:

> I like playing pool a lot, that's one of my releases, that I play pool a lot. Oh, what else? Bartend, bartend on the side, it's kind of fun to, if you're a bartender you can, you can see how people reacted, amounts of alcohol and different guys around, different chicks around, and different situations, if it's snowing outside, if it's cold outside, the weather conditions, all types of different types of environments and types of different types of people you'll usually find in a bar. (Hoffman, Stopek, & Andreasen, 1986, p. 835)

Some people experience a constant, mild degree of mania ("hypomania"). They are productive, popular, extraverted, life-of-the-party types. Many artists, writers, and composers have suffered from bipolar disorder. To test whether creative skills increase or decrease over various phases of the bipolar cycle, Robert Weisberg (1994) examined the works of the classical composer Robert Schumann, who is known to have had bipolar disorder. He found that Schumann produced more works during his manic phases than during his depressed phases. However, the compositions written during his depressed phases have been performed and recorded just as often as those written during his manic phases, on average. That is, the works that he composed during his depressed phases have been about as popular as those during his manic phases.

## Self-Report

Mania can become so serious, however, that it makes normal life impossible. The theatrical director Joshua Logan has described his own experiences with depression and mania. A few excerpts follow.

### Depressive Phase

First, Logan describes life in his depressed phase.

> I had no faith in the work I was doing or the people I was working with. . . . It was a great burden to get up in the morning and I couldn't wait to go to bed at night, even though I started not sleeping well. . . . I thought I was well but feeling low because of a hidden personal discouragement of some sort—something I couldn't quite put my finger on. . . . I just forced myself to live through a dreary, hopeless existence that lasted for months on end. . . .
>
> My depressions actually began around the age of thirty-two. I remember I was working on a play, and I was forcing myself to work. . . . I can remember that I sat in some sort of aggravated agony as it was read aloud for the first time by the cast. It sounded so awful that I didn't want to direct it. I didn't even want to see it. I remember feeling so depressed that I wished that I were dead without having to go through the shame and defeat of suicide. I couldn't sleep well at all, and sleep meant, for me, oblivion, and that's what I longed for and couldn't get. I didn't know what to do and I felt very, very lost. (Fieve, 1975, pp. 42–43)

### Manic Phase

Here Logan describes his manic experiences:

> Finally, as time passed, the depression gradually wore off and turned into something else, which I didn't understand either. But it was a much pleasanter thing to go through, at least at first. Instead of hating everything, I started liking things—liking them too much, perhaps. . . . I put out a thousand ideas a minute: things to do, plays to write, plots to write stories about. . . .
>
> I decided to get married on the spur of the moment. . . . I practically forced her to say yes. Suddenly we had a loveless marriage and that had to be broken up overnight. . . .
>
> I can only remember that I worked constantly, day and night, never even seeming to need more than a few hours of sleep. I always had a new idea or another conference. . . . It was an exhilarating time for me.
>
> It finally went too far. In the end I went over the bounds of reality, or law and order, so to say. I don't mean that I committed any crimes, but I could easily have done so if anyone had crossed me. I flew into rages if contradicted. I began to be irritable with everyone. Should a man, friend or foe, object to anything I did or said, it was quite possible that I could poke him in the jaw. I was eventually persuaded by the doctors that I was desperately ill and should go into the hospital. But it was not, even then, convincing to me that I was ill.
>
> There I was, on the sixth floor of a New York building that had special iron bars around it and an iron gate that had slid into place and locked me away from the rest of the world. . . . I looked about and saw that there was an open window. I leaped up on the sill and climbed out of the window on the ledge on the sixth floor and said, "Unless you open the door, I'm going to climb down the outside of this building." At the time, I remember feeling so powerful that I might actually be able to scale the building. . . . They immediately opened the steel door, and I climbed back in. That's where manic elation can take you. (Fieve, 1975, pp. 43–45)

## CONCEPT CHECK

12. What are the similarities and differences between seasonal affective disorder and bipolar disorder? (Check your answer on page 642.)

### Drug Therapies for Bipolar Disorder

Many years ago researcher J. F. Cade proposed that uric acid might be effective for treating mania. To dissolve uric acid in water, he mixed it with lithium salts. The resulting mixture proved effective, but researchers eventually discovered that the benefits depended on the lithium salts, not the uric acid.

Lithium salts were soon adopted for use in the Scandinavian countries, but they were slow to be accepted in the United States. One reason was that drug manufacturers had no interest in marketing lithium pills. (Lithium is a natural substance and cannot be patented.) A second reason was that the lithium dosage must be carefully monitored. A dose slightly too low does no good, and one slightly too high produces nausea, blurred vision, and tremors.

Properly regulated dosages of lithium became a common and effective treatment for bipolar disorder (Baldessarini & Tondo, 2000). Lithium reduces mania and prevents the pendulum from swinging into depression. It does not provide a permanent cure, so the patient must take lithium pills daily. However, people can take the recommended doses of lithium for years without suffering unfavorable consequences (Schou, 1997). At this point no one is certain how lithium relieves bipolar disorder. Many researchers believe that it works primarily on chemical pathways within the neurons, not on transmission at a particular kind of synapse (Manji, Potter, & Lenox, 1995). The other kind of medication often used for bipolar disorder is valproate (Depakene, Depacote) and other anticonvulsant drugs, which are about equal to lithium in effectiveness (Hilty et al., 1999). Counseling helps the person cope with life difficulties that stem from bipolar disorder, but treatment for the symptoms themselves relies on the drugs.

## Mood Disorders and Suicide

Most severely depressed people and people with bipolar disorder consider suicide, and many attempt it. Suicides also occur for other reasons, though. Some people commit suicide because of feelings of guilt or disgrace. Some commit suicide because a cult leader assures them that death is the route to salvation (Maris, 1997). Others have a painful terminal illness and wish to hasten the end, sometimes with a physician's assistance. However, some people who request a physician's assistance in dying suffer from treatable depression or insufficiently controlled pain (Farberman, 1997; Muskin, 1998).

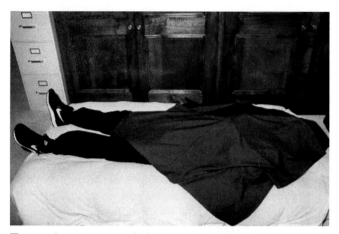

■ People commit suicide for a great many reasons. Members of the Heaven's Gate cult in San Diego committed mass suicide in 1997 because their leader assured them that death was the route to being rescued from Earth by an alien spacecraft that tailed the comet Hale-Bopp.

Records on suicide cannot be fully accurate because some people disguise their suicides to look like accidents and because many physicians, when in doubt, record the cause of death as something other than suicide. One survey in the United States reported that more than 13% of adults had considered suicide and more than 4% had survived a suicide attempt (Kessler, Borges, & Walters, 1999). Figure 16.16 shows the recorded deaths by suicide for three countries in 1988 (Lester, 1996). Note the major differences in the suicide rate as a function of age, country, and gender. Across cultures women make more suicide attempts, but more men die by suicide (Canetto & Sakinofsky, 1998; Cross & Hirschfeld, 1986). Most men who attempt suicide use guns or other violent means. Women are more likely to try poison, drugs, or other nonviolent methods that are less certain to be fatal (Rich, Ricketts, Fowler, & Young, 1988). Many people, especially women, who injure themselves in suicide attempts are believed to be crying out for help and not really intending to kill themselves. Unfortunately, some of them die, and others become disabled for life.

Suicide has no dependable pattern. Many people who attempt it give warning signals well in advance, but some do not. One study found that more than half of the people who made a serious suicide attempt decided to try it within 24 hours before the attempt (Peterson, Peterson, O'Shanick, & Swann, 1985). However, anyone working with troubled people should be aware of the warning signals and risk factors listed in Table 16.5. The same patterns have been found in the United States and China, so they are apparently not culture-specific (Cheng, 1995).

If you suspect that someone you know is thinking about suicide, what should you do? Treat the person like a normal human being. Anyone contemplating suicide needs social support and friendship. Don't assume that he or she is so fragile that one wrong word will be disastrous. Don't be afraid to ask a person whether he or she

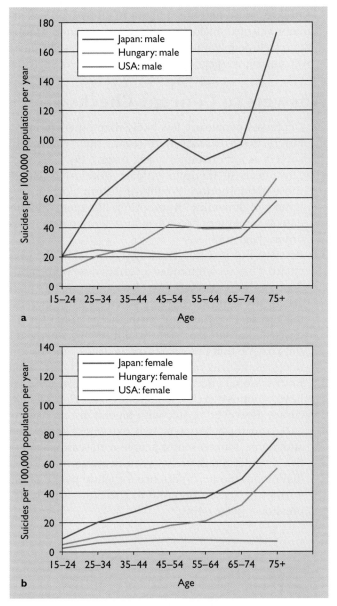

**FIGURE 16.16** Suicide rates differ as a function of age, gender, and culture. The rates shown here are for 1988; the rate has dropped since then for Hungary, presumably because of economic and social changes within the country. (Based on data of Lester, 1996)

**TABLE 16.5** People Most Likely to Attempt Suicide

- Depressed people, especially those with feelings of hopelessness (Beck, Steer, Beck, & Newman, 1993)
- People who have made previous suicide attempts (Beck, Steer, & Brown, 1993)
- People who have untreated psychological disorders (Brent et al. 1988), especially drug or alcohol abuse (Beck & Steer, 1989)
- People who have recently suffered the death of a spouse and men who have recently been divorced or separated, especially those who have little social support from friends and family (Blumenthal & Kupfer, 1986)
- People who, during their childhood or adolescence, lost a parent through death or divorce (Adam, 1986)
- People with guns in their home, particularly those with a history of violent attacks on others (Brent et al., 1988)
- People whose relatives have committed suicide (Blumenthal & Kupfer, 1986)
- People with low serotonin activity in the brain (Roy, Dejong, & Linnoila, 1989)

normal emotions, distorting all experiences to fit the prevailing mood. Mood disorders are like a monster, and we need a wide arsenal of weapons to fight them.

## Summary

- **Symptoms of depression.** A depressed person finds little interest or pleasure in life, feels worthless, powerless, and guilty, and may consider suicide. Such a person has trouble sleeping, loses interest in sex and food, and cannot concentrate. (page 632)
- **Seasonal affective disorder.** Seasonal affective disorder is a condition in which people become depressed during one season of the year. Bright light in the morning is a highly effective treatment for this disorder. (page 632)
- **Predispositions.** Growing up among depressed adoptive relatives increases one's risk of depression, but growing up among depressed biological relatives increases it even more. Evidently, both genetic and family influences contribute to one's vulnerability to depression. (page 633)
- **Sex differences.** Psychologists are uncertain why more women than men suffer depression. One hypothesis is that women are more likely to ruminate about their depression, and therefore aggravate and prolong it, whereas men are more likely to find some way of distracting themselves from their depression. (page 633)
- **Cognitive factors in depression.** People with a pessimistic explanatory style tend to blame themselves for

has been contemplating suicide. The person may be relieved to find that you are willing to discuss it.

IN CLOSING
## Mood and Mood Disorders

The capacity to feel emotions is important. If you never felt sad, regardless of what misfortunes befell you, you might make disastrous decisions, and a lack of happiness would be equally disastrous. Mood disorders go beyond

their failures more than the evidence actually warrants. Depressed people almost invariably have a pessimistic explanatory style, seeing evidence of their own failures in almost everything that happens. (page 634)

- **Cognitive therapy.** A frequently effective form of psychotherapy is to help depressed people reinterpret their experiences in a more favorable manner. (page 634)
- **Effects of antidepressant drugs.** Several kinds of drugs help relieve depression by prolonging the activity of dopamine or serotonin at synaptic receptors. The drugs produce varying side effects that sometimes limit a patient's dosage. Although the drugs affect the synapses within an hour or so, their behavioral effects begin after 2 or 3 weeks of treatment. The benefits may depend on stimulating the growth of existing neurons or the maturation of additional neurons. (page 636)
- **Advantages and disadvantages.** Psychotherapy is more likely to produce long-lasting benefits, but antidepressant drugs remain popular because of their convenience and lower cost. (page 637)
- **Electroconvulsive therapy.** Electroconvulsive therapy (ECT) has a long history of abuse; in modified form ECT has made a comeback and is now helpful to some depressed people who fail to respond to antidepressant drugs. (page 638)
- **Bipolar disorder.** People with bipolar disorder alternate between periods of depression and periods of mania, when they engage in constant, driven, uninhibited activity. Lithium salts are an effective treatment for bipolar disorder, as are certain anticonvulsant drugs. (page 638)

- **Suicide.** Although it is difficult to know who will attempt suicide, suicidal attempts are common among depressed people and people who show certain other warning signs. (page 640)

## Answers to Concept Checks

9. Depressed people are less likely than others to buy a lottery ticket because they regard their chances of success as remote on any task. (page 635)
10. The effects of methylphenidate (Ritalin) resemble those of buproprion (Wellbutrin). Both block the reuptake of dopamine. Buproprion, like methylphenidate, is sometimes prescribed for attention deficit disorder. (page 637)
11. Possibly, but it would be risky. Presumably, the psychiatrist has recommended a certain dose of the antidepressant drug for a reason. Because St. John's wort acts by the same mechanism, adding it is like increasing the dose of the drug, with the potential for increased side effects. Also, St. John's wort activates the enzyme that inactivates many drugs, and the antidepressant drug might be one of them. (page 637)
12. Both seasonal affective disorder and bipolar disorder have repetitive cycles, sometimes with clocklike accuracy. However, people with bipolar disorder swing back and forth between two extremes, depression and mania, whereas most people with seasonal affective disorder alternate between depression and normal mood. (Some experience a slightly manic phase during the season opposite to the time of their depression.) (page 640)

# Schizophrenia

*What is schizophrenia? What causes it and what can be done about it?*

How would you like to live in a world all your own? You can be the supreme ruler, and no one will ever criticize you or tell you what to do. You can tell other people—and even inanimate objects—what to do, and they will immediately obey. Your fantasies become realities.

Perhaps that world sounds like heaven to you. I suspect it soon would be more like hell. Most of us enjoy the give and take of interactions with other people; we enjoy struggling to achieve our fantasies more than we would enjoy their immediate fulfillment.

Some people with schizophrenia live practically in a world of their own, confusing fantasy with reality. They have trouble understanding what others say and experience difficulty making themselves understood. Eventually, they may retreat into a private existence and pay little attention to others.

## The Symptoms of Schizophrenia

The widely misunderstood term *schizophrenia* is based on Greek roots meaning "split mind." However, the term does *not* refer to a split into two minds or personalities. Many people use the term *schizophrenia* when they really mean *dissociative identity disorder* or *multiple personality.* People with dissociative identity disorder have several personalities, any one of which might be considered normal if the person had only that one personality.

The "split" in the schizophrenic "split mind" is not a split between two personalities, but a split between the intellectual and emotional aspects of one personality, as if the intellect were no longer in contact with the emotions (Figure 16.17). A person suffering from schizophrenia may seem happy or sad for no apparent reason or may fail to show emotion in a situation that should evoke it. This separation of intellect and emotions is no longer considered the key feature of schizophrenia, but it does occur.

To be diagnosed with **schizophrenia,** according to *DSM-IV, a person must exhibit a deterioration of daily activities, including work, social relations, and self-care. He or she must* also exhibit at least two of the following: hallucinations, delusions, incoherent speech, grossly disorganized behavior, certain thought disorders, or a loss of normal emotional responses and social behaviors (American Psychiatric Association, 1994). An exception is if someone's hallucinations or delusions are sufficiently severe. Then no other symptoms are necessary. Finally, before assigning a diagnosis of schizophrenia, a psychologist or psychiatrist must rule out other conditions that produce similar symptoms, including depression, bipolar illness, drug abuse, brain damage, the early stages of Huntington's disease, niacin deficiency, and food allergies.

## Positive and Negative Symptoms

The definition of schizophrenia called for "two or more" symptoms from a list of six. Consequently, it is possible for two or three people diagnosed with schizophrenia to have no symptoms in common with one another (Andreasen, 1999). What we have traditionally lumped together as one disorder, schizophrenia, may consist of two, three, or more separate conditions with different causes and different responses to treatment.

One way of trying to separate different types of schizophrenia is to distinguish between positive and negative symptoms. In this case *positive* means *present* and *negative* means *absent;* they do not mean *good* and *bad.* **Positive symptoms** are *behaviors that are notable because of their*

**FIGURE 16.17** Although the term *schizophrenia* is derived from Greek roots meaning "split personality," it does not refer to cases where people alternate among different personalities. Rather, the term originally indicated a split between the intellectual and emotional aspects of a single personality.

Intellect

Emotions

*presence,* such as hallucinations, delusions, and thought disorder. **Negative symptoms** are *behaviors that are notable by their absence,* including a lack of emotional expression, both in the face and in tone of voice, a deficit of speech, a lack of ability to feel pleasure, and a general inability to take care of oneself.

Patients with mostly negative symptoms may be different from those with mostly positive or a mixture of positive and negative symptoms (Kirkpatrick, Buchanan, Ross, & Carpenter, 2001). Their symptoms tend to be more consistent over time and more difficult to treat (Arndt, Andreasen, Flaum, Miller, & Nopoulos, 1995). People with many negative symptoms have an earlier onset of the disorder and worse performance in school and on the job (Andreasen, Flaum, Swayze, Tyrrell, & Arndt, 1990). They also have different kinds of brain abnormalities (Palmer et al., 1997).

We now consider some of the common positive symptoms in more detail.

## Hallucinations

**Hallucinations** are *sensory experiences that do not correspond to anything in the objective world.* A common hallucination is to hear voices and other sounds that no one else hears. Not all schizophrenic people hear voices, but most people who hear them suffer from schizophrenia. The voices may speak nonsense, or they may direct the person to do something. Hallucinating people may think the voices are real, they may know the voices are coming from within their own head, or they may not be sure (Junginger & Frame, 1985). Auditory hallucinations occur at the same time as spontaneous activity in the auditory cortex and several related brain areas (Shergill, Brammer, Williams, Murray, & McGuire, 2000).

Visual hallucinations are less common with schizophrenia, although some people have distorted or exaggerated visual experiences (Figure 16.18). Strong visual hallucinations are usually symptoms of drug abuse.

## Delusions

**Delusions** are *unfounded beliefs.* Three common types are delusions of persecution, grandeur, and reference. A **delusion of persecution** is *a belief that one is being persecuted,* that "people are out to get me." A **delusion of grandeur** is *a belief that one is unusually important,* perhaps a special messenger from God or a person of central importance to the future of the world. A **delusion of reference** is *a tendency to interpret all sorts of messages as if they were meant for oneself.* Someone with a delusion of reference may interpret a headline in the morning newspaper as a coded message or take a television announcer's comments as personal insults.

In some cases it is fairly easy to identify a belief as delusional. For example, if someone who can hardly

**FIGURE 16.18** These portraits graphically illustrate an artist's progressive psychological deterioration. When well-known animal artist Louis Wain (1860–1939) began suffering delusions of persecution, his drawings showed a schizophrenic's disturbing distortions in perception.

put together a complete sentence claims to be a messenger from the planet Zipton, chances are the belief is a delusion. But what about someone who constantly sees evidence of government conspiracies in everyday events? Is that belief a delusion or merely an unusual opinion? Members of religious and political minorities have many beliefs that other people regard as wrong, but unpopular views are not necessarily products of delusional thinking.

Furthermore, consider the following: During the Vietnam War, one U.S. Army unit massacred hundreds of unarmed women and children at the village of My Lai. One horrified soldier refused to participate. After the war he told a social worker about his recurring nightmares and his fear that the other soldiers might kill him to prevent him from telling. When the social worker told her colleagues about this client, most of them labeled his story a delusion and suggested a diagnosis of schizophrenia. The story, however, was true (Scott, 1990).

In short, one should be cautious about diagnosing anyone as schizophrenic when the only symptom is an apparently delusional belief. (If the truth be known, don't most of us have a belief or two that someone else might consider strange and unjustifiable?)

## Disordered Thinking

Some people with schizophrenia have normal or above-average intelligence, but even they have difficulty with tasks requiring selective attention, or "executive functions," as described in Chapter 7 (Weickert et al., 2000). For example, the Wisconsin Card Sorting Task asks people to sort a stack of cards by one rule (e.g., putting them into piles according to color) and then shift to a different rule (e.g., number or shape). People with schizophrenia have trouble with this task, as do people with frontal cortex damage.

The impaired attention may relate to the tendency of schizophrenic patients to loose and idiosyncratic associations, somewhat like the illogical leaps that occur in dreams. For example, one man used the words *Jesus, cigar,* and *sex* as synonyms. When asked to explain, he said they were all the same because Jesus has a halo around his head, a cigar has a band around it, and during sex people put their arms around each other.

Another characteristic of schizophrenic thought is difficulty using abstract concepts. For instance, many people with schizophrenia have trouble sorting objects into categories. Many also give strictly literal responses when asked to interpret the meaning of proverbs. Here are some examples (Krueger, 1978, pp. 196–197):

*Proverb:* People who live in glass houses shouldn't throw stones.
*Interpretation:* "It would break the glass."
*Proverb:* All that glitters is not gold.
*Interpretation:* "It might be brass."
*Proverb:* A stitch in time saves nine.
*Interpretation:* "If you take one stitch for a small tear now, it will save nine later."

People with schizophrenic thought disorder often misunderstand simple statements because of their tendency to interpret everything literally. Upon being taken to the admitting office of a hospital, one person said, "Oh, is this where people go to admit their faults?"

Many schizophrenic people also use many words to say very little, as in this excerpt from a letter one man wrote to his mother:

I am writing on paper. The pen which I am using is from a factory called "Perry & Co." This factory is in England. I assume this. Behind the name of Perry & Co. the city of London is inscribed; but not the city. The city of London is in England. I know this from my school-days. Then, I always liked geography. My last teacher in that subject was Professor August A. He was a man with black eyes. I also like black eyes. There are also blue and gray eyes and other sorts, too. I have heard it said that snakes have green eyes. All people have eyes. There are some, too, who are blind. These blind people are led about by a boy. It must be very terrible not to be able to see. There are people who can't see and, in addition, can't hear. I know some who hear too much. (Bleuler, 1911/1950, p. 17)

# Types and Prevalence of Schizophrenia

Depending on which symptoms are most prominent, psychiatrists and psychologists distinguish four major types of schizophrenia. These distinctions are useful for descriptive purposes, although they do not identify the underlying causes.

## Four Types of Schizophrenia

**Undifferentiated schizophrenia** is characterized by the *basic symptoms—deterioration of daily functioning plus some combination of hallucinations, delusions, inappropriate emotions, thought disorders, and so forth.* However, none of these symptoms is unusually pronounced or bizarre.

**Catatonic schizophrenia** is characterized by a *prominent movement disorder, including either rigid inactivity or excessive activity.* In either case the person's movement pattern seems to be unrelated to events in the outside world. Periods of extremely rapid, mostly repetitive activity may alternate with periods of total inactivity. During the inactive periods, he or she may hold a given posture without moving and may resist attempts to alter that posture (Figure 16.19). Despite the inactivity, the brain is alert and the person may complain later about something an individual said during one of the periods of catatonia. Catatonic schizophrenia is rare.

**Disorganized schizophrenia** is characterized by *incoherent speech, extreme lack of social relationships, and "silly" or odd behavior.* For example, one man gift wrapped one of

FIGURE 16.19 A person suffering from catatonic schizophrenia can hold a bizarre posture for hours and alternate this rigid stupor with equally purposeless excited activity. Such people may stubbornly resist attempts to change their behavior, but they need supervision to avoid hurting themselves or others. Catatonic schizophrenia is uncommon.

his bowel movements and proudly presented it to his therapist. Here is a conversation with someone suffering from disorganized schizophrenia (Duke & Nowicki, 1979, p. 162):

**INTERVIEWER:** How does it feel to have your problems?

**PATIENT:** Who can tell me the name of my song? I don't know, but it won't be long. It won't be short, tall, none at all. My head hurts, my knees hurt—my nephew, his uncle, my aunt. My God, I'm happy . . . not a care in the world. My hair's been curled, the flag's unfurled. This is my country, land that I love, this is the country, land that I love.

**INTERVIEWER:** How do you feel?

**PATIENT:** Happy! Don't you hear me? Why do you talk to me? (barks like a dog).

**Paranoid schizophrenia** is characterized by *strong or elaborate hallucinations and delusions, especially delusions of persecution and delusions of grandeur.* Many people with paranoid schizophrenia are more cognitively intact than most people with other forms of schizophrenia. They can generally take care of themselves well enough to get through the activities of the day, and some manage to complete college work and take good jobs.

Many people fall on the margin between two or more types of schizophrenia, perhaps switching back and forth between them. Switching is especially common between undifferentiated schizophrenia and one of the other types (Kendler, Gruenberg, & Tsuang, 1985).

 **CONCEPT CHECK**

13. Why are people more likely to switch between undifferentiated schizophrenia and one of the other types than, say, between disorganized schizophrenia and one of the other types? (Check your answer on page 651.)

## Prevalence

About 1% of Americans are afflicted with schizophrenia at some point in life (Kendler, Gallagher, Abelson, & Kessler, 1996). Some sources cite higher or lower figures, depending on how many marginal cases they include. However, regardless of the cutoff point, the prevalence of schizophrenia has been gradually declining since the mid-1900s in many countries (Suvisaari, Haukka, Tanskanen, & Lönnqvist, 1999). The reason for that decline is unknown, but the fact of the decline implies that schizophrenia is not under tight genetic control.

Schizophrenia occurs in all ethnic groups, but it is uncommon in Third World countries (Torrey, 1986). It is more common in crowded cities than in small towns and farms (Torrey, Bowler, & Clark, 1997). One explanation is that mentally ill people move from small towns and farms to big cities where they can get more help. Another is that certain aspects of life in crowded and technologi-

cally advanced countries may increase the risk of schizophrenia. Still another possibility is that people in small towns and Third World countries live close to many relatives and friends who provide social support and thereby decrease the severity of schizophrenia.

Schizophrenia is most frequently diagnosed in young adults in their teens or 20s. Generally, men are diagnosed with schizophrenia earlier than women. A first diagnosis is uncommon after age 30, but some women have an onset of schizophrenia at menopause, around age 45–50. One hypothesis is that estrogen protects against schizophrenia and a decline in estrogen releases a suppressed tendency (Häfner et al., 1998).

Schizophrenia's onset can be sudden but is usually gradual. Most people with schizophrenia are described as having been strange children who had a short attention span, made few friends, and often disrupted their class (Arboleda & Holzman, 1985; Parnas, Schulsinger, Schulsinger, Mednick, & Teasdale, 1982).

**A STEP FURTHER**
*Retrospective Accounts*

If you try to recall the childhood behavior of someone who later developed schizophrenia, what kinds of memory errors are you likely to make and why? (Recall the issues raised in Chapters 7 and 8.)

## Causes

The predominant view is that schizophrenia depends on a genetic predisposition that is aggravated by some sort of environmental influence. Sound vague? Unfortunately, the details are not yet clear about either the genetics or the environmental influences. We shall examine what researchers currently understand about the causes of schizophrenia, but bear in mind that our understanding is tentative.

### Genetics

The evidence of a genetic basis rests primarily on studies of adopted children and comparisons of twins. With adopted children who eventually develop schizophrenia, it is more common among their biological relatives than among their adoptive relatives (Kety et al., 1994). If one member of a pair of monozygotic (identical) twins develops schizophrenia, there is an almost 50% chance that the other will develop it too (Cardno et al., 1999; Gottesman, 1991) (see Figure 16.20).

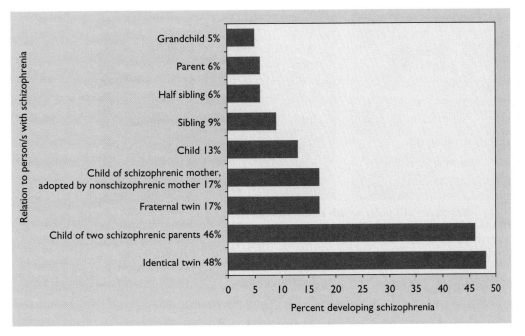

**FIGURE 16.20** The relatives of a schizophrenic person have an increased probability of developing schizophrenia themselves. Note that children of a schizophrenic mother have a 17% risk of schizophrenia even if adopted by a family with no schizophrenic members. (Based on data from Gottesman, 1991)

However, most of the research is subject to an alternative interpretation. For example, consider the fact that an adopted child is more likely to have biological than adoptive parents with schizophrenia. The biological mother can influence her baby's brain development not only through genes but also through prenatal environment. Schizophrenic women (and women who mate with schizophrenic men) tend to be impoverished and poorly educated. Many smoke and drink during pregnancy and fail to eat a good diet. Therefore, if her child eventually develops schizophrenia, we cannot assume that the reason was genetic.

The most persuasive evidence would be a demonstration linking schizophrenia to a specific gene. Using current biotechnology techniques, researchers have located genes for many diseases, and several groups have tried to do the same for schizophrenia. So far the results have been disappointing. Identifiable genetic abnormalities have been found for childhood schizophrenia, an uncommon condition that differs from adult-onset schizophrenia in several regards, including its link to severe brain abnormalities (Burgess et al., 1998; Nopoulos, Giedd, Andreasen, & Rapoport, 1998). Also, research on some families, all of Celtic ancestry and all of which included many schizophrenic relatives, found evidence pointing to a gene in one approximate location on chromosome #1 (Brzustowica, Hodgkinson, Chow, Honer, & Bassett, 2000). However, two large-scale studies comparing schizophrenic and nonschizophrenic patients failed to locate any gene strongly linked to schizophrenia (Blouin et al., 1998; Levinson et al., 1998). Schizophrenia does not appear to be a one-gene disorder. Evidently, several genes contribute, and probably, some people develop schizophrenia without a genetic basis.

**A STEP FURTHER**
*Genetics of Schizophrenia*

People with schizophrenia, especially men, are less likely than others to have children. So it is difficult to imagine how a gene that leads to schizophrenia could spread enough to affect 1% of the population. Can you imagine a possible explanation, assuming that schizophrenia is largely influenced by genetics?

## Brain Damage

Much evidence points to mild brain abnormalities in many, though not all, people with schizophrenia. Brain damage is, of course, not an alternative to genetics; brain damage could occur for either genetic or nongenetic reasons. Brain scans indicate that the hippocampus and several areas of the cerebral cortex are a few percent smaller than normal in people with schizophrenia, especially those with the greatest behavioral deficits (Velakoulis et al., 1999; Wright et al., 2000). The cerebral ventricles, which are fluid-filled cavities in the brain, are larger than normal in schizophrenic people (Wolkin et al., 1998; Wright et al., 2000). Figure 16.21 shows an example of enlarged cerebral ventricles.

People with schizophrenia also show smaller than average neurons (Weinberger, 1999) and fewer than the normal number of synapses on the average, especially in the prefrontal cortex (Glantz & Lewis, 1997, 2000). Indications of brain abnormalities have been reported in patients in cultures as different as the United States and

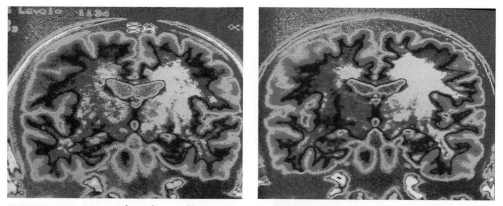

**FIGURE 16.21** Many (though not all) people with schizophrenia show signs of mild loss of neurons in the brain. Here we see views of the brains of twins. The twin on the left has schizophrenia; the twin on the right does not. Note that the ventricles (near the center of each brain) are larger in the twin with schizophrenia. The ventricles are fluid-filled cavities; an enlargement of the ventricles implies a loss of brain tissue. (Photos courtesy of E. F. Torrey & M. F. Casanova / NIMH)

Nigeria (Ohaeri, Adeyinka, & Osuntokun, 1995). One area of the cortex that is consistently reduced (the dorsolateral prefrontal cortex) is theoretically interesting: It is important for those aspects of working memory that are consistently impaired in schizophrenia, and it is one of the slowest areas of the brain to mature. Therefore, its malformation supports the view that schizophrenia is related to impaired brain maturation (Gur et al., 2000; Pearlson, Petty, Ross, & Tien, 1996; Sowell, Thompson, Holmes, Jernigan, & Toga, 1999).

Although the causes of these brain abnormalities are uncertain, most studies indicate that the abnormalities develop early in life, either before birth or early after birth, and do not grow worse over time. People with schizophrenia do not show signs of progressive brain damage, and they do not gradually deteriorate on tests sensitive to brain damage (Benes, 1995; Heaton et al., 2001).

## CONCEPT CHECK

14. Following a stroke, a patient shows symptoms similar to schizophrenia. Where is the brain damage probably located? (Check your answer on page 651.)

## The Neurodevelopmental Hypothesis

Most researchers now concentrate on the **neurodevelopmental hypothesis,** *the idea that schizophrenia originates with nervous system impairments that develop before or around the time of birth, possibly but not necessarily for genetic reasons.* For example, the probability of schizophrenia is higher than normal following these events relating to early brain development:

- The patient's mother had a very difficult pregnancy, labor, or delivery (Hultman, Öhman, Cnattingius, Wieselgren, & Lindström, 1997).

- The mother was poorly nourished during pregnancy (Dalman, Allebeck, Cullberg, Grunewald, & Köstler, 1999; Susser et al., 1996).
- The patient was unusually small at birth (Wahlbeck, Forsén, Osmond, Barker, & Eriksson, 2001).
- The mother had an Rh-negative blood type and her baby was Rh-positive. The risk of schizophrenia is more than 2% for her second and later Rh-positive children, especially boys (Hollister, Laing, & Mednick, 1996).

Furthermore, *a person born in the winter months is slightly more likely to develop schizophrenia than a person born at any other time* (Bradbury & Miller, 1985). Investigators have clearly demonstrated this **season-of-birth effect** only in the northern climates, not near the equator. Evidently, something about the weather contributes to some people's vulnerability to schizophrenia. No other psychological disorder has this characteristic.

One possible explanation is that influenza and other epidemics are most common in the fall, especially in northern climates. If a woman catches influenza or other infection during the second trimester of pregnancy, her illness can impair critical stages of brain development in her fetus at that time. A virus does not cross the placenta into the fetus (Taller et al., 1996), so the problem is not the virus itself but probably the mother's fever, which can impair the development of fetal neurons (Laburn, 1996).

You might ask, "If brain damage occurs before or near the time of birth, why do the symptoms emerge so much later?" One possible answer is that certain parts of the brain, especially the prefrontal cortex, go through a critical stage of development during the second trimester of pregnancy but do not become fully functional until adolescence. As the brain begins to rely more and more on those areas, the effects of damage become more evident (Weinberger, 1987).

■  Schizophrenia is slightly more common in people who were born in winter than in those born at other times. The critical factor is probably the weather during the second trimester of pregnancy. Those born in winter were in the second trimester during fall, the main time for viral and bacterial epidemics.

# Therapies for Schizophrenia

Before the discovery of effective drugs to combat schizophrenia, the outlook for people with the disorder was bleak. Usually, people underwent gradual deterioration, interrupted by periods of partial recovery. Many spent virtually their entire adult lives in mental hospitals. Matters are better now, although there is still enormous room for improvement.

## Drug Therapies

During the 1950s researchers discovered the first effective antischizophrenic drug: chlorpromazine (klor-PRAHM-uh-ZEEN, trade name Thorazine). *Drugs that relieve schizophrenia* are known as **antipsychotic drugs** or *neuroleptic drugs.* Chlorpromazine and other antipsychotic drugs, including haloperidol (HAHL-o-PAIR-ih-dol, trade name Haldol), have enabled many schizophrenic people to escape lifelong confinement in mental hospitals. Although these drugs do not cure the disorder, a daily dosage does help to control it, much as daily insulin shots control diabetes. Since the 1950s a majority of people with schizophrenia have improved enough to leave mental hospitals or to avoid ever entering one (Harding, Brooks, Ashikaga, Straus, and Breier, 1987).

Antipsychotic drugs take effect gradually and produce variable degrees of recovery. As a rule antipsychotic drugs produce their clearest effects if treatment begins shortly after a sudden onset of schizophrenia. The greater someone's deterioration before drug treatment begins, the less the recovery will be. Most of the recovery that will ever take place emerges gradually during the first month (Szymanski, Simon, & Gutterman, 1983). Beyond that

point the drugs merely maintain behavior but do not improve it. When affected people stop taking the drugs, the symptoms return and in most cases worsen (Figure 16.22).

All antipsychotic drugs share one characteristic: They block dopamine synapses in the brain. In fact, their therapeutic effectiveness is nearly proportional to their ability to block those synapses (Seeman & Lee, 1975). Furthermore, large doses of amphetamines, cocaine, or other drugs that stimulate dopamine activity can induce a temporary state that resembles schizophrenia. These phenomena have led to the **dopamine hypothesis of schizophrenia,** which holds that *the underlying cause of schizophrenia is excessive stimulation of certain types of dopamine synapses.*

However, measurements from blood and other body fluids have generally found nearly normal levels of dopamine and its metabolic breakdown products (Jaskiw & Weinberger, 1992). According to an alternative view, the **glutamate hypothesis of schizophrenia,** *the underlying problem causing schizophrenia is deficient stimulation of certain glutamate synapses.* In many brain areas, dopamine inhibits glutamate activity, so drugs that block dopamine synapses would increase the activity of glutamate synapses. The glutamate hypothesis is supported by the fact that prolonged use of the drug *phencyclidine* ("angel

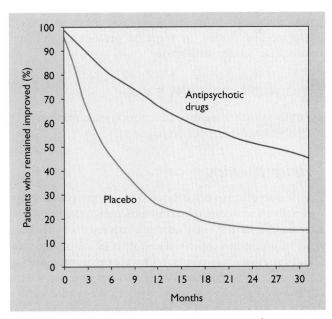

**FIGURE 16.22** This graph indicates that during 2½ years following apparent recovery from schizophrenia, the percentage of schizophrenic patients who remained improved is higher in the group that received continuing drug treatment than in the placebo group. But the graph also shows that antipsychotic drugs do not always prevent relapse. (Based on Baldessarini, 1984)

dust"), which inhibits glutamate receptors, produces symptoms that match schizophrenia even more closely than do cocaine and amphetamines, which stimulate dopamine synapses (Olney & Farger, 1995).

## Side Effects of Drugs

Antipsychotic drugs produce unwelcome side effects in many people. The most serious, **tardive dyskinesia** (TAHRD-eev DIS-ki-NEE-zhuh), *a condition characterized by tremors and involuntary movements,* develops gradually after years of taking antipsychotic drugs, especially with people who take large dosages (Kiriakakis, Bhatia, Quinn, & Marsden, 1998). Presumably, tardive dyskinesia relates to the fact that antipsychotic drugs alter activity at dopamine synapses, some of which control movement.

Researchers have sought new drugs that can combat schizophrenia without causing tardive dyskinesia. **Atypical antipsychotic drugs** *relieve schizophrenia without causing tardive dyskinesia.* Two such drugs are *clozapine* and *risperidone,* which combine moderate effects on dopamine synapses with additional effects on serotonin synapses. These drugs have shown significant promise for relieving schizophrenia with only minimal risk of tardive dyskinesia; they also relieve the negative symptoms of schizophrenia (e.g., social withdrawal) that other antipsychotic drugs fail to address (Carpenter, 1995; Meltzer, 1995). Unfortunately, they produce serious side effects of their own, including an impaired immune system. People taking these drugs spend less time in mental hospitals but more time in regular hospitals for laboratory tests and other procedures to keep their immune systems functioning (Essock, Frisman, Covell, & Hargreaves, 2000). In short, at present no antipsychotic drug is fully satisfactory.

## CONCEPT CHECK

15. Why is early diagnosis of schizophrenia important? (Check your answer on page 651.)

## Family Therapy

The degree of recovery produced by antipsychotic drugs varies. Even someone who responds well to the drugs and appears to be living fairly normally can have a sudden relapse of symptoms. Much of this fluctuation in outcome reflects stressors in the person's family environment.

If you had a brother, sister, son, or daughter with schizophrenia, how would you react? We would all like to think that we would be 100% supportive and sympathetic to this troubled person. However, family members are human beings, too, and after years of dealing with someone who says and does strange things and requires extensive attention to get through normal daily activities, even the most saintly of relatives occasionally loses

patience and makes *hostile or critical comments,* known as **expressed emotion.** Researchers have found that the more frequently a person is exposed to expressed emotion, the greater the probability of a relapse into severe schizophrenic symptoms (Butzlaff & Hooley, 1998). In several studies family members were taught to reduce their expressed emotion; the result has been fewer relapses into schizophrenia, as compared to control groups where families received no such training (de Jesus Mari & Streiner, 1994).

The results regarding expressed emotion suggest an explanation for some cross-cultural differences: Compared to North America and western Europe, schizophrenia in India and the Arab countries tends to be less severe and marked by fewer relapses. In these cultures troubled people are generally cared for by a large extended family, including cousins, aunts and uncles, and so forth, and not just by the immediate family. By sharing care these families decrease the amount of strain on each individual, while increasing the care for the suffering person. Relatives can thus maintain their patience and good spirits; they show far fewer expressed emotions than their U.S. counterparts (El-Islam, 1982; Leff et al., 1987; Wig et al., 1987).

## IN CLOSING

### The Elusiveness of Schizophrenia

You could meet two people both diagnosed with schizophrenia who nevertheless had relatively little in common. One has hallucinations and delusions; the other has a thought disorder and a lack of emotional expression. One has relatives with schizophrenia; the other doesn't. One has evidence of brain abnormalities; the other doesn't. As you can imagine, it is difficult to draw generalizations that apply to all people with schizophrenia; thus, many researchers still wonder whether we are dealing with one disorder or several. We need more research to understand the disorder itself as well as its causes and treatment.

## Summary

- **Symptoms of schizophrenia.** A person with schizophrenia is someone whose everyday functioning has deteriorated over a period of at least 6 months and who shows at least two of the following symptoms: hallucinations (mostly auditory), delusions, incoherent speech, disorganized behavior, thought disorders, and loss of normal emotional responses and social behaviors. (page 643)
- **Positive and negative symptoms.** Positive symptoms are behaviors that attract attention by their presence, such as hallucinations and delusions. Negative symptoms are behaviors that are noteworthy by

their absence, such as impaired emotional expression. (page 643)

- **Thought disorder of schizophrenia.** The thought disorder of schizophrenia is characterized by loose associations, impaired use of abstract concepts, and vague, wandering speech that conveys little information. (page 645)
- **Types of schizophrenia.** What we call *schizophrenia* may in fact consist of two or more separate conditions with overlapping symptoms. Psychologists distinguish four types of schizophrenia: undifferentiated, catatonic, disorganized, and paranoid. (page 645)
- **Genetic influences.** Much evidence indicates that it is possible to inherit a predisposition toward schizophrenia, although little is known about how the genes exert their influence. (page 646)
- **Brain abnormalities.** Many people with schizophrenia show indications of mild brain abnormalities, especially in the prefrontal cortex, The abnormalities apparently develop early in life and do not grow worse over time. (page 647)
- **Neurodevelopmental hypothesis.** Many researchers believe that schizophrenia originates with abnormal brain development before or around the time of birth, sometimes for genetic reasons but sometimes for other reasons, such as mother's fever during pregnancy. (page 648)
- **Antipsychotic drugs.** Drugs that alleviate schizophrenia block dopamine synapses. Results are best if treatment begins before the person has suffered serious deterioration. (page 649)
- **Neurotransmitters.** The effectiveness of dopamine blockers in alleviating schizophrenia has suggested that

the underlying problem might be excessive dopamine activity. However, people with schizophrenia appear to have normal dopamine levels. An alternative hypothesis is that the underlying problem is a deficiency of glutamate, a neurotransmitter inhibited by dopamine. (page 649)
- **Family therapy.** The family's hostile comments (expressed emotion) toward someone with schizophrenia increase the risk of renewed symptoms. Reducing the family's expressed emotion improves the patient's chances for lasting recovery. (page 650)

## Answers to Concept Checks

13. With any disorder, symptoms are more severe at some times than at others. Whenever any of the special symptoms of catatonic, disorganized, or paranoid schizophrenia become less severe, the person is left with undifferentiated schizophrenia. To shift between any two of the other types, a person would have to lose the symptoms of one type and gain the symptoms of the other type. (page 646)
14. The damage is probably located in the frontal or temporal lobes of the cerebral cortex, the areas that are generally damaged in people with schizophrenia. (page 648)
15. Antipsychotics are more helpful to people in the early stages of schizophrenia than to those who have deteriorated severely. However, psychiatrists do not want to administer antipsychotics to people who do not need them because of the risk of tardive dyskinesia. Consequently, early and accurate diagnosis of schizophrenia is helpful. (page 650)

## CHAPTER ENDING
## *Key Terms and Activities*

## Key Terms

**agoraphobia:** an excessive fear of open places or public places  (page 614)

**Alcoholics Anonymous (AA):** a self-help group of people who are trying to abstain from alcohol use and to help others do the same  (page 628)

**alcoholism:** habitual overuse of alcohol  (page 626)

**Antabuse:** the trade name for disulfiram, a drug used in the treatment of alcoholism  (page 629)

**antipsychotic drugs:** drugs that relieve schizophrenia  (page 649)

**atypical antidepressants:** drugs that relieve depression for some patients who do not respond to other antidepressants, generally with only mild side effects  (page 637)

**atypical antipsychotic drugs:** drugs such as clozapine and risperidone, which relieve schizophrenia without causing tardive dyskinesia  (page 650)

**bipolar disorder:** a condition in which a person alternates between periods of depression and periods of mania  (page 633)

**bipolar I disorder:** disorder condition characterized by at least one episode of mania  (page 639)

**bipolar II disorder:** disorder condition characterized by episodes of major depression and  hypomania, which is a milder degree of mania  (page 639)

**catatonic schizophrenia:** a type of schizophrenia characterized by the basic symptoms plus prominent movement disorders  (page 645)

**compulsion:** a repetitive, almost irresistible action  (page 620)

**delusion:** unfounded belief (page 644)

**delusion of grandeur:** the belief that one is unusually important (page 644)

**delusion of persecution:** the belief that one is being persecuted (page 644)

**delusion of reference:** the tendency to interpret all sorts of messages as if they were meant for oneself (page 644)

**dependence (or addiction):** a self-destructive habit that someone finds difficult or impossible to quit (page 624)

**detoxification:** a supervised period for removing drugs from the body (page 628)

**disorganized schizophrenia:** a type of schizophrenia characterized by incoherent speech, extreme lack of social relationships, and "silly" or odd behavior (page 645)

**dopamine hypothesis of schizophrenia:** the theory that the underlying cause of schizophrenia is excessive stimulation of certain types of dopamine synapses (page 649)

**electroconvulsive therapy (ECT):** a treatment using a brief electrical shock that is administered across the patient's head to induce a convulsion similar to epilepsy, sometimes used as a treatment for certain types of depression (page 638)

**explanatory style:** a tendency to accept one kind of explanation for success or failure more often than others (page 635)

**expressed emotion:** hostile or critical comments directed toward a person with a psychiatric disorder such as schizophrenia (page 650)

**flooding (or implosion):** a treatment for phobia in which the person is suddenly exposed to the object of the phobia (page 619)

**generalized anxiety disorder (GAD):** a disorder in which people are almost constantly plagued by exaggerated worries (page 613)

**glutamate hypothesis of schizophrenia:** the view that the underlying problem causing schizophrenia is deficient stimulation of certain glutamate synapses (page 649)

**hallucinations:** a sensory experience not corresponding to reality, such as seeing or hearing something that is not present or failing to see or hear something that is present (page 644)

**harm reduction:** approach to drug abuse that concentrates on decreasing the frequency of drug use and minimizing the harmful consequences to health and well-being (page 629)

**hyperventilate:** breathe deeply and frequently (page 614)

**major depression:** a condition lasting most of the day, day after day, with a loss of interest and pleasure and a lack of productive activity (page 632)

**mania:** a condition in which people are constantly active, uninhibited, and either happy or irritable (page 638)

**methadone:** a drug commonly offered as a less dangerous substitute for opiates (page 630)

**monoamine oxidase inhibitors (MAOIs):** drugs that block the metabolic breakdown of released dopamine, norepinephrine, and serotonin, thus prolonging the effects of these neurotransmitters on the receptors of the postsynaptic cell (page 637)

**negative symptoms:** symptoms that are present in other people—such as the ability to take care of themselves—but absent in schizophrenic people (page 644)

**neurodevelopmental hypothesis:** the idea that schizophrenia originates with impaired development of the nervous system before or around the time of birth, possibly but not necessarily for genetic reasons (page 648)

**obsession:** a repetitive, unwelcome stream of thought (page 620)

**obsessive-compulsive disorder:** a condition with repetitive thoughts and actions (page 620)

**panic disorder (PD):** a disorder characterized by frequent bouts of moderate anxiety and occasional attacks of sudden increased heart rate, chest pains, difficulty breathing, sweating, faintness, and trembling (page 613)

**paranoid schizophrenia:** a type of schizophrenia characterized by the basic symptoms plus strong or elaborate hallucinations and delusions (page 646)

**phobia:** a strong, persistent fear of a specific object, extreme enough to interfere with normal living (page 615)

**positive symptoms:** characteristics present in people with schizophrenia and absent in others—such as hallucinations, delusions, abnormal movements, and thought disorder (page 643)

**postpartum depression:** a period of depression that some women experience shortly after giving birth (page 634)

**schizophrenia:** a condition marked by deterioration of daily activities over a period of at least 6 months, plus hallucinations, delusions, flat or inappropriate emotions, certain movement disorders, or thought disorders (page 643)

**season-of-birth effect:** the tendency for people born in the winter months to be slightly more likely than other people are to develop schizophrenia (page 648)

**seasonal affective disorder (SAD):** a condition in which people become seriously depressed in one season of the year, such as winter (page 632)

**selective serotonin reuptake inhibitors (SSRIs):** drugs that block the reuptake of the neurotransmitter serotonin by the terminal bouton (page 636)

**social phobia:** a severe avoidance of other people and an especially strong fear of doing anything in public (page 614)

**St. John's wort:** wort an herb with antidepressant effects (page 637)

**systematic desensitization:** a method of reducing fear by gradually exposing people to the object of their fear (page 619)

**tardive dyskinesia:** a disorder characterized by tremors and involuntary movements (page 650)

**tricyclic drugs:** drugs that block the reabsorption of the neurotransmitters dopamine, norepinephrine, and serotonin, after they are released by the terminal button, thus prolonging the effect of these neurotransmitters on the receptors of the postsynaptic cell (page 636)

**Type I (or Type A) alcoholism:** the type that is generally less severe, equally common in men and women, less dependent on genetics, and likely to develop gradually, presumably in response to the difficulties of life (page 626)

**Type II (or Type B) alcoholism:** the type that is generally more severe, more common in men, more often associated with aggressive or antisocial behavior, more dependent on genetics, and likely to begin early in life (page 626)

**undifferentiated schizophrenia:** a type of schizophrenia characterized by the basic symptoms but no unusual or especially prominent symptoms (page 645)

## Suggestions for Further Reading

Andreasen, N. C. (1994). *Schizophrenia: From mind to molecule.* Washington, DC: American Psychiatric Press. Review of schizophrenia by one of the leading researchers.

Beers, C. W. (1948). *A mind that found itself.* Garden City, NY: Doubleday. (Original work published in 1908) An autobiography of a man who recovered from a severe case of bipolar disorder.

de Silva, P., & Rachman, S. (1998). *Obsessive-compulsive disorder: The facts* (2nd ed.). Oxford, England: Oxford University Press. Concise overview of the symptoms and treatments for obsessive-compulsive disorder.

Jamison, K. R. (1997). *An unquiet mind.* New York: Random House. A psychiatrist describes her own lifelong battle with bipolar disorder.

Marlatt, G. A., & VandenBos, G. R. (Eds.). (1997). *Addictive behaviors: Readings on etiology, prevention, and treatment.* Washington, DC: American Psychological Association. A collection of research articles on the nature of addiction and the methods of treatment.

Whybrow, P. C. (1997). *A mood apart.* New York: HarperCollins. A nontechnical description of the various forms of depression and their treatment.

## Web/Technology Resources

### Psychological Disorders and More

**www.psych.org/**

The American Psychiatric Association offers facts about various disorders, drug therapies, how to choose a therapist, and much more.

### National Clearinghouse for Alcohol and Drug Information

**www.health.org/**

Here is comprehensive information for those who want to overcome a drug problem.

### Harbor of Refuge

**www.Harbor-of-Refuge.org/**

Postings by people with bipolar disorder for others with the same problem.

### The Experience of Schizophrenia

**http://www.chovil.com**

This the the personal site of Ian Chovil, who began struggling with schizophrenia in late adolescence and suffered greatly until he began taking medication in 1990. He tells his own story in unsparing detail. He describes the biology of schizophrenia, recommends books and movies on the subject, and provides many links.

### Walkers in Darkness

**http://www.walkers.org/**

This long-established and award-winning site is dedicated to helping people with schizophrenia, bipolar illness, and related mood disorders. Included are descriptions of each disorder, information on medication and therapy, links to a variety of resources, forums, chat rooms, and mailing lists.

# Epilogue

Here we are at the end of the book. As I have been writing and revising, I have imagined you sitting there reading. I have imagined a student somewhat like I was in college, reading about psychology for the first time and often growing excited about it. I remember periodically telling my roommate or a relative, "Guess what I just learned about psychology! Isn't this interesting?" (I still do the same today.) I also remember occasionally thinking, "Hmm. The book says such-and-so, but I'm not convinced. I wonder whether psychologists ever considered a different explanation . . . ." I started thinking about research I might do if I ever became a psychologist.

I hope that you have had similar experiences yourself. I hope you have occasionally become so excited about something you read that you thought about it and told other people about it. In fact, I hope you told your roommate so much about psychology that you started to become annoying. I also hope you have sometimes doubted a conclusion, imagining a research project that might test it or improve on it.

Now, as I picture you reaching the end of the course, I'm not sure how you will react. You might be thinking, "Wow, I sure have learned a lot!" Or you might be thinking, "Is that *all?*" Maybe you are reacting both ways: "Yes, I learned a lot. But it seems like there ought to be more. I still don't understand what conscious experience is all about, and I don't understand why I react the way I do

sometimes. And this book—*wonderful as it is*—hardly mentioned certain topics. Why do we laugh? How do we sense the passage of time? Why do people like to watch sports? Why are some people religious and others not? Why do I feel like yawning whenever I see someone else yawn?"

I have two good reasons for not answering all your questions. One is that this is an introductory text. If you want to learn more, you should take other psychology courses or do some additional reading. The other reason is that psychologists do not know all the answers.

Perhaps someday you will become a researcher yourself and add to the sum of our knowledge. If not, you can try to keep up to date on current developments in psychology by reading good books and newspaper and magazine articles. One of my main goals has been to prepare you to continue learning about psychology in that fashion. Try to read critically: Is it based on good evidence? If you read about a survey, were the questions worded clearly? If someone draws a cause-and-effect conclusion, was the evidence based on experiments or only correlations? No matter what the evidence, can you think of a more reasonable, more parsimonious explanation than the one the author suggests?

Above all, remember that nearly all our conclusions are tentative. Psychological researchers seldom use the word *prove;* their conclusions are almost always tentative and guarded. I once suggested to my editor, half-

■ Many fairly simple aspects of behavior remain little investigated and not well understood. For example, why do we yawn? Why do we laugh? Why are both yawning and laughter so contagious? If you decide to become a psychological researcher, you will find no shortage of topics that deserve more investigation.

seriously, that we should include in the index to this book the entry "*maybe*—see pages 1–677." We did not include such an entry, partly because I doubt anyone would have noticed the humor, and partly because our understanding of psychology is not really that bad. Still, be leery of anyone who seems a little too certain about a great new insight in psychology. The route from *maybe* to *definitely* is long and arduous.

# References

Numbers in parentheses indicate the chapter in which a source is cited.

Abramson, L. Y., Seligman, M. E. P., & Teasdale, J. D. (1978). Learned helplessness in humans: Critique and reformulation. *Journal of Abnormal Psychology, 87,* 49–74. (16)

Adam, B. D., Sears, A., & Schellenberg, E. G. (2000). Accounting for unsafe sex: Interviews with men who have sex with men. *Journal of Sex Research, 37,* 24–36. (11)

Adam, K. S. (1986). Early family influences on suicidal behavior. *Annals of the New York Academy of Sciences, 487,* 63–76. (16)

Adler, A. (1927). *Understanding human nature.* New York: Greenberg. (13)

Adler, A. (1964). Brief comments on reason, intelligence, and feeble-mindedness. In H. L. Ansbacher & R. R. Ansbacher (Eds.), *Superiority and social interest* (pp. 41–49). New York: Viking Press. (Original work published 1928) (13)

Adler, A. (1964). The structure of neurosis. In H. L. Ansbacher & R. R. Ansbacher (Eds.), *Superiority and social interest* (pp. 83–95). New York: Viking. (Original work published 1932) (13)

Adolph, K. E. (2000). Specificity of learning: Why infants fall over a veritable cliff. *Psychological Science, 11,* 290–295. (10)

Adolphs, R., Russell, J. A., & Tranel, D. (1999). A role for the human amygdala in recognizing emotional arousal from unpleasant stimuli. *Psychological Science, 10,* 167–171. (12)

Adolphs, R., Tranel, D., Damasio, H., & Damasio, A. (1994). Impaired recognition of emotion in facial expressions following bilateral damage to the human amygdala. *Nature, 372,* 669–672. (3)

Adolphs, R., Tranel, D., Damasio, H., & Damasio, A. (1995). Fear and the human amygdala. *Journal of Neuroscience, 15,* 5879–5891. (3)

Ainsworth, M. D. S. (1979). Attachment as related to mother-infant interaction. In J. S. Rosenblatt, R. A. Hinde, C. Beer, & M. Busnel (Eds.), *Advances in the study of behavior* (Vol. 9, pp. 1–51). New York: Academic Press. (10)

Albee, G. W. (1986). Toward a just society: Lessons from observations on the primary prevention of psychopathology. *American Psychologist, 41,* 891–898. (15)

Aldag, R. J., & Fuller, S. R. (1993). Beyond fiasco: A reappraisal of the groupthink phenomenon and a new model of group decision processes. *Psychological Bulletin, 113,* 533–552. (14)

Alexander, I. E. (1982). The Freud-Jung relationship—the other side of Oedipus and countertransference. *American Psychologist, 37,* 1009–1018. (13)

Alicke, M. D., & Largo, E. (1995). The role of the self in the false consensus effect. *Journal of Experimental Social Psychology, 31,* 28–47. (14)

Alliger, G. M., Lilienfeld, S. O., & Mitchell, K. E. (1996). The susceptibility of overt and covert integrity tests to coaching and faking. *Psychological Science, 7,* 32–39. (12)

Allison, S. T., Mackie, D. M., Muller, M. M., & Worth, L. T. (1993). Sequential correspondence biases and perceptions of change: The Castro studies revisited. *Personality and Social Psychology Bulletin, 19,* 151–157. (14)

Alloy, L. B., Abramson, L. Y., Whitehouse, W. G., Hogan, M. E., Tashman, N. A., Steinberg, D. L., Rose, D. T., & Donovan, P. (1999). Depressogenic cognitive styles: Predictive validity, information processing and personality characteristics, and developmental origins. *Behaviour Research and Therapy, 37,* 503–531. (16)

Allport, G. W. (1935). Attitudes. In C. Murchison (Ed.), *A handbook of social psychology* (pp. 798–844). Worcester, MA: Clark University Press. (14)

Allport, G. W. (1961). *Pattern and growth in personality.* New York: Holt, Rinehart & Winston. (13)

Allport, G. W., & Odbert, H. S. (1936). Trait-names: A psycholexical study. *Psychological Monographs, 47*(Whole No. 211). (13)

Alroe, C. J., & Gunda, V. (1995). Self-amputation of the ear. *Australian and New Zealand Journal of Psychiatry, 29,* 508–512. (15)

Altarriba, J., & Mathis, K. M. (1997). Conceptual and lexical development in second language acquisition. *Journal of Memory and Language, 36,* 550–568. (8)

Amato, P. R., & Keith, B. (1991). Parental divorce and the well-being of children: A meta-analysis. *Psychological Bulletin, 110,* 26–46. (10)

American Medical Association. (1986). Council report: Scientific status of refreshing recollection by the use of hypnosis. *International Journal of Clinical and Experimental Hypnosis, 34,* 1–12. (5)

American Psychiatric Association (1994*). Diagnostic and statistical manual of mental disorders* (4th ed.). Washington, DC: Author. (12, 15, 16)

American Psychological Association. (1982). *Ethical principles in the conduct of research with human participants.* Washington, DC: Author. (2)

Amzica, F., & Steriade, M. (1996). Progressive cortical synchronization of ponto-geniculo-occipital potentials during rapid eye movement sleep. *Neuroscience, 72,* 309–314. (5)

Anastasi, A. (1988). *Psychological testing* (6th ed.). New York: Macmillan. (9)

Anderson, A., & Phelps, E. A. (2000). Expression without recognition: Contributions of the human amygdala to emotional communication. *Psychological Science, 11,* 106–111. (12)

Andersen, B. L. (1983). Primary orgasmic dysfunction: Diagnostic considerations and review of treatment. *Psychological Bulletin, 93,* 105–136. (11)

Andersen, B. L., Kiecolt-Glaser, J. K., & Glaser, R. (1994). A biobehavioral model of cancer stress and disease course. *American Psychologist, 49,* 389–404. (12)

Anderson, C. A., Benjamin, A. J., Jr., & Bartholow, B. D. (1998). Does the gun pull the trigger? Automatic priming effects of weapon pictures and weapon names. *Psychological Science, 9,* 308–314. (8)

Anderson, C. D., Warner, J. L., & Spencer, C. C. (1984). Inflation bias in self-assessment examinations: Implications for valid employee selection. *Journal of Applied Psychology, 69,* 574–580. (13)

Andreasen, N. C. (1999). A unitary model of schizophrenia. *Archives of General Psychiatry, 56,* 781–787. (16)

Andreasen, N. C., Arndt, S., Alliger, R., Miller, D., & Flaum, M. (1995). Symptoms of schizophrenia: Methods, meanings, and mechanisms. *Archives of General Psychiatry, 52,* 341–351. (16)

Andreasen, N. C., Flaum, M. Swayze, V. W., II, Tyrrell, G., & Arndt, S. (1990). Positive and negative symptoms in schizophrenia. *Archives of General Psychiatry, 47,* 615–621. (16)

Anglin, D., Spears, K. L., & Hutson, H. R. (1997). Flunitrazepam and its involvement in date or acquaintance rape. *Academy of Emergency Medicine, 4,* 323–326. (5)

Anisman, H., & Zacharko, R. M. (1983). Stress and neoplasia: Speculations and caveats. *Behavioral Medicine Update, 5,* 27–35. (12)

Anonymous. (1955). *Alcoholics anonymous* (2nd ed.). New York: Alcoholics Anonymous World Services. (16)

Appelbaum, P. S. (1988). The new preventive detention: Psychiatry's problematic responsibility for the control of violence. *American Journal of Psychiatry, 145,* 779–785. (15)

Appleby, L., Desai, P. N., Luchins, D. J., Gibbons, R. D., & Hedeker, D. R. (1993). Length of stay and recidivism in schizophrenia: A study of public psychiatric hospital patients. *American Journal of Psychiatry, 150,* 72–76. (15)

Appley, M. H. (1991). Motivation, equilibration, and stress. In R. Dienstbier (Ed.), *Nebraska Symposium on Motivation 1990* (pp. 1–67). Lincoln: University of Nebraska Press. (11)

Arandea, R. C., Kini, A. D., & Firestein, S. (2000). The molecular receptive range of an odorant receptor. *Nature Neuroscience, 3,* 1248–1255. (4)

Arboleda, C., & Holzman, P. S. (1985). Thought disorder in children at risk for psychosis. *Archives of General Psychiatry, 42,* 1004–1013. (16)

Archer, J. (2000). Sex differences in aggression between heterosexual partners: A meta-analytic review. *Psychological Bulletin, 126,* 651–680. (12)

Arkes, H. R., & Ayton, P. (1999). The sunk cost and Concorde effects: Are humans less rational than lower animals? *Psychological Bulletin, 125,* 591–600. (8)

Arndt, S., Andreasen, N. C., Flaum, M., Miller, D., & Nopoulos, P. (1995). A longitudinal study of symptom dimensions in schizophrenia. *Archives of General Psychiatry, 52,* 352–360. (16)

Arnett, J. (1990). Contraceptive use, sensation seeking, and adolescent egocentrism. *Journal of Youth and Adolescence, 19,* 171–180. (10)

Arnett, J. J. (1999). Adolescent storm and stress reconsidered. *American Psychologist, 54,* 317–326. (10)

Arnett, J. J. (2000). Emerging adulthood: A theory of development from the late teens through the twenties. *American Psychologist, 55,* 469–480. (10)

Arnold, H. J., & House, R. J. (1980). Methodological and substantive extensions to the job characteristics model of motivation. *Organizational Behavior and Human Performance, 25,* 161–183. (11)

Aronow, E., Reznikoff, M., & Moreland, K. L. (1995). The Rorschach: Projective technique or psychometric test? *Journal of Personality Assessment, 64,* 213–228. (13)

Aronson, E. (1997). The theory of cognitive dissonance: The evolution and vicissitudes of an idea. In C. McGarty & S. A. Haslam (Eds.), *The message of social psychology* (pp. 20–35). Cambridge, MA: Blackwell. (14)

Aronson, E., & Carlsmith, J. M. (1963). Effect of the severity of threat on the devaluation of forbidden behavior. *Journal of Abnormal and Social Psychology, 66,* 584–588. (14)

Arrigo, J. M., & Pezdek, K. (1997). Lessons from the study of psychogenic amnesia. *Current Directions in Psychological Science, 6,* 148–152. (7)

Arvey, R. D., & 51 others. (1994, December 13). Mainstream science on intelligence. *Wall Street Journal,* p. A18. (9)

Asch, S. E. (1951). Effects of group pressure upon the modification and distortion of judgments. In H. Guetzkow (Ed.), *Groups, leadership, and men* (pp. 177–190). Pittsburgh, PA: Carnegie Press. (14)

Asch, S. E. (1955, November). Opinions and social pressure. *Scientific American, 193*(5), 31–35. (14)

Asch, S. E. (1956). Studies of independence and conformity: I. A minority of one against a unanimous majority. *Psychological Monographs, 70* (9, Whole No. 416). (14)

Ash, R. (1986, August). An anecdote submitted by Ron Ash. *The Industrial-Organizational Psychologist, 23*(4), 8. (6)

Atkinson, J. W., & Birch, D. (1978). *Introduction to motivation* (2nd ed.). New York: D. Van Nostrand. (11)

Atkinson, R. C., & Shiffrin, R. M. (1968). Human memory: A proposed system and its control. In K. W. Spence & J. T. Spence (Eds.), *The psychology of learning and motivation* (Vol. 2, pp. 89–105). New York: Academic Press. (7)

Austin, J. T., & Vancouver, J. B. (1996). Goal constructs in psychology: Structure, process, and content. *Psychological Bulletin, 120,* 338–375. (11)

Averill, J. R. (1983). Studies on anger and aggression: Implications for theories of emotion. *American Psychologist, 38,* 1145–1160. (12)

Axelrod, R., & Dion, D. (1988). The further evolution of cooperation. *Science, 242,* 1385–1390. (14)

Azrin, N. H., & Nunn, R. G. (1973). Habit-reversal: A method of eliminating nervous habits and tics. *Behaviour Research and Therapy, 11,* 619–628. (6)

Babcock, R. L. & Salthouse, T. A. (1990). Effects of increased processing demands on age differences in working memory. *Psychology & Aging, 5,* 421–428. (7)

Babkoff, H., Caspy, T., Mikulincer, M., & Sing, H. C. (1991). Monotonic and rhythmic influences: A challenge for sleep deprivation research. *Psychological Bulletin, 109,* 411–428. (5)

Bachrach, A. J., Erwin, W. J., & Mohr, J. P. (1965). The control of eating behavior in an anoretic by operant conditioning techniques. In L. P. Ullmann & L. Krasner (Eds.), *Case studies in behavior modification* (pp. 153–163). New York: Holt, Rinehart & Winston. (11)

Baddeley, A., Gathercole, S., & Papagno, C. (1998). The phonological loop as a language learning device. *Psychological Review, 105,* 158–173. (7)

Baddeley, A. D., & Hitch, G. (1974). Working memory. In G. H. Bower (Ed.), *Psychology of learning and motivation* (Vol. 8, pp. 47–89). New York: Academic Press. (7)

Baddeley, A., & Hitch, G. J. (1994). Developments in the concept of working memory. *Neuropsychology, 8,* 485–493. (7)

Bahrick, H. (1984). Semantic memory content in permastore: 50 years of memory for Spanish learned in school. *Journal of Experimental Psychology: General, 113,* 1–29. (7)

Bahrick, H. P., Bahrick, L. E., Bahrick, A. S., & Bahrick, P. E. (1993). Maintenance of foreign language vocabulary and the spacing effect. *Psychological Science, 4,* 316–321. (7)

Bahrick, H. P., Hall, L. K., & Berger, S. A. (1996). Accuracy and distortion in memory for high school grades. *Psychological Science, 7,* 265–271. (8)

Bailey, J. M., & Pillard, R. C. (1991). A genetic study of male sexual orientation. *Archives of General Psychiatry, 48,* 1089–1096. (11)

Bailey, J. M., Pillard, R. C., Neale, M. C., & Agyei, Y. (1993) Heritable factors influence sexual orientation in women. *Archives of General Psychiatry, 50,* 217–223. (11).

Baillargeon, R. (1986). Representing the existence and the location of hidden objects: Object permanence in 6- and 8-month-old infants. *Cognition, 23,* 21–41. (10)

Baillargeon, R. (1987). Object permanence in 3 $^1/_2$- and 4 $^1/_2$-month-old infants. *Developmental Psychology, 23,* 655–664. (10)

Baird, J. C. (1982). The moon illusion: A reference theory. *Journal of Experimental Psychology: General, 111,* 304–315. (4)

Baker, G. H. B. (1987). Invited review: Psychological factors and immunity. *Journal of Psychosomatic Research, 31,* 1–10. (12)

Baker, T. B., & Tiffany, S. T. (1985). Morphine tolerance as habituation. *Psychological Bulletin, 92,* 78–108. (5)

Baker-Ward, L., Gordon, B. N., Ornstein, P. A., Larus, D. M., & Clubb, P. A. (1993)., Young children's long-term retention of a pediatric examination. *Child Development, 64,* 1519–1533. (7)

Baldessarini, R. J. (1984). Antipsychotic drugs. In T. B. Karasu (Ed.), *The psychiatric therapies: I. The somatic therapies* (pp. 119–170). Washington, DC: American Psychiatric Press. (16)

Baldessarini, R. J., & Tondo, L. (2000). Does lithium treatment still work? *Archives of General Psychiatry, 57,* 187–190. (16)

Ballinger, B., & Yalom, I. (1995). Group therapy in practice. In B. Bongar & L. E. Beutler (Eds.), *Comprehensive textbook of psychotherapy: Theory and practice* (pp. 189–204). Oxford, England: Oxford University Press. (15)

Banaji, M. R., & Bhaskar, R. (2000). Implicit stereotypes and memory: The bounded rationality of social beliefs. In D. L. Schacter & E. Scarry (Eds.), *Memory, brain, and belief* (pp. 139–175). Cambridge, MA: Harvard University Press. (14)

Banaji, M. R., & Greenwald, A. G. (1994). Implicit stereotyping and prejudice. In M. P. Zanna & J. M. Olson (Eds.), *The psychology of prejudice: The Ontario Symposium Volume 7* (pp. 55–76). Hillsdale, NJ: Erlbaum. (16)

Bandura, A. (1977). *Social learning theory.* Upper Saddle River, NJ: Prentice Hall. (6)

Bandura, A. (1986). *Social foundations of thought and action.* Upper Saddle River, NJ: Prentice Hall. (6)

Bandura, A. (2000). Exercise of human agency through collective efficacy. *Current Directions in Psychological Science, 9,* 75–78. (6)

Bandura, A., Ross, D., & Ross, S. A. (1963). Imitation of film-mediated aggressive models. *Journal of Abnormal and Social Psychology, 66,* 3–11. (6)

Banich, M. T. (1998). Integration of information between the cerebral hemispheres. *Current Directions in Psychological Science, 7,* 32–37. (3)

Baptista, L. F., & Petrinovich, L. (1984). Social interaction, sensitive phases and the song template hypothesis in the white-crowned sparrow. *Animal Behaviour, 32,* 172–181. (6)

Bar, M., & Biederman, I. (1998). Subliminal visual priming. *Psychological Science, 9,* 464–469. (4)

Bardone, A. M., Vohs, K. D., Abramson, L. Y., Heatherton, T. F., & Joiner, T. E., Jr. (2000). The confluence of perfectionism, body dissatisfaction, and low self-esteem predicts bulimic symptoms: Clinical implications. *Behavior Therapy, 31,* 265–280. (11)

Bargh, J. A., & Chartrand, T. L. (1999). The unbearable automaticity of being. *American Psychologist, 54,* 462–479. (8)

Barnier, A. J., & McConkey, K. M. (1998). Posthypnotic responding away from the hypnotic setting. *Psychological Science, 9,* 256–262. (5)

Baron, J. (1997). The illusion of morality as self-interest: A reason to cooperate in social dilemmas. *Psychological Science, 8,* 330–335. (14)

Baron, J., & Norman, M. F. (1992). SATs, achievement tests, and high-school class rank as predictors of college performance. *Educational and Psychological Measurement, 52,* 1047–1055. (9)

Barrick, M. R., & Mount, M. K. (1991). The big five personality dimensions and job performance: A meta-analysis. *Personnel Psychology, 44,* 1–26. (13)

Bartoshuk, L. M. (1991). Taste, smell, and pleasure. In R. C. Bolles (Ed.), *The hedonics of taste* (pp. 5–28). Hillsdale, NJ: Erlbaum. (4)

Bartoshuk, L. M. (2000). Psychophysical advances aid the study of genetic variation in taste. *Appetite, 34,* 105. (12)

Bartoshuk, L. M., Duffy, V. B., Lucchina, L. B., Prutkin, J., & Fast, K. (1998). PROP (6-n-propyl-thiouracil) supertasters and the saltiness of NaCl. *Annals of the New York Academy of Sciences, 855,* 793–796. (4, 12)

Bassetti, C., & Aldrich, M. S. (1997). Idiopathic hypersomnia: A series of 42 patients. *Brain, 120,* 1423–1435. (5)

Battaglia, M., Bertella, S., Ogliari, A., Bellodi, L., & Smeraldi, E. (2001). Modulation by muscarinic antagonists of the response to carbon dioxide challenge in panic disorder. *Archives of General Psychiatry, 58,* 114–119. (16)

Bauer, P. J. (1996). What do infants recall of their lives? *American Psychologist, 51,* 29–41. (7)

Baumeister, R. F. (2000). Gender differences in erotic plasticity: The female sex drive as socially flexible and responsive. *Psychological Bulletin, 126,* 347–374. (11)

Baumeister, R. F., Smart, L., & Boden, J. M. (1996). Relation of threatened egotism to violence and aggression: The dark side of high self-esteem. *Psychological Review, 103,* 5–33. (12)

Baumrind, D. (1971). Current patterns of parental authority. *Developmental Psychology Monographs, 4* (1, Pt. 2). (10)

Beck, A. T. (1973). *The diagnosis and management of depression.* Philadelphia: University of Pennsylvania Press. (16)

Beck, A. T. (1976). *Cognitive therapy and the emotional disorders.* New York: New American Library. (15)

Beck, A. T. (1987). Cognitive models of depression. *Journal of Cognitive Psychotherapy: An International Quarterly, 1,* 5–37. (16)

Beck, A. T. (1991). Cognitive therapy: A 30-year retrospective. *American Psychologist, 46,* 368–375. (16)

Beck, A. T., & Emery, G. (1985). *Anxiety disorders and phobias.* New York: Basic Books. (16)

Beck, A. T., & Steer, R. A. (1989). Clinical predictors of eventual suicide: A 5- to 10-year prospective study of suicide attempters. *Journal of Affective Disorders, 17,* 203–209. (16)

Beck, A. T., Steer, R. A., Beck, J. S., & Newman, C. F. (1993). Hopelessness, depression, suicidal ideation, and clinical diagnosis of depression. *Suicide and Life-Threatening Behavior, 23,* 139–145. (16)

Beck, A. T., Steer, R. A., & Brown, G. (1993). Dysfunctional attitudes and suicidal ideation in psychiatric outpatients. *Suicide and Life-Threatening Behavior, 23,* 11–20. (16)

Becker, A. E., & Burwell, R. A. (1999). *Acculturation and disordered eating in Fiji.* Paper presented at the meeting of the American Psychiatric Association. (11)

Becker, E. S., Strohbach, D., & Rinck, M. (1999). A specific attentional bias in suicide attempters. *Journal of Nervous and Mental Disease, 187,* 730–735. (13)

Beeman, M. J., & Chiarello, C. (1998). Complementary right- and left-hemisphere language comprehension. *Current Directions in Psychological Science, 7,* 2–8. (3)

Bellugi, U., Lichtenberger, L., Jones, W., Lai, Z., & St. George, M. (2000). I. The neurocognitive profile of Williams syndrome: A complex pattern of strengths and weaknesses. *Journal of Cognitive Neuroscience, 12*(Suppl.), 7–29. (8)

Bellugi, U., & St. George, M. (2000). Preface. *Journal of Cognitive Neuroscience, 12*(Suppl.), 1–6. (8)

Bellugi, U., Wang, P. P., & Jernigan, T. L. (1994). Williams syndrome: An unusual neuropsychological profile. In S. H. Broman & J. Grafman (Eds.), *Atypical cognitive deficits in developmental disorders* (pp. 23–56). Hillsdale, NJ: Erlbaum. (2)

Belmore, S. M. (1987). Determinants of attention during impression formation. *Journal of Experimental Psychology: Learning, Memory, and Cognition, 13,* 480–489. (14)

Belsky, J. (1996). Parent, infant, and social-contextual antecedents of father-son attachment security. *Developmental Psychology, 32,* 905–913. (10)

Bem, D. J., & Honorton, C. (1994). Does psi exist? Replicable evidence for an anomalous process of information transfer. *Psychological Bulletin, 115,* 4–18. (2)

Bem, S. L. (1985). Androgyny and gender schema theory: A conceptual and empirical integration. In T. B. Sonderegger (Ed.), *Nebraska Symposium on Motivation, 1984: Psychology and gender* (pp. 179–226). Lincoln: University of Nebraska Press. (11)

Benbow, C. P., Lubinski, D., Shea, D. L., & Efekhari-Sanjani, H. (2000). Sex differences in mathematical reasoning at age 13: Their status 20 years later. *Psychological Science, 11,* 474–480. (10)

Benes, F. M. (1995). Is there a neuroanatomic basis for schizophrenia? An old question revisited. *The Neuroscientist, 1,* 104–115. (16)

Benowitz, N. L. (1986). The human pharmacology of nicotine. *Research Advances in Alcohol and Drug Problems, 9,* 1–52. (16)

Benson, H. (1977). Systemic hypertension and the relaxation response. *New England Journal of Medicine, 296,* 1152–1156. (12)

Benson, H. (1985). Stress, health, and the relaxation response. In W. D. Gentry, H. Benson, & C. J. de Wolff (Eds.), *Behavioral medicine: Work, stress and health* (pp. 15–32). Dordrecht, Netherlands: Martinus Nijhoff. (12)

Berger, R. J., & Phillips, N. H. (1995). Energy conservation and sleep. *Behavioural Brain Research, 69,* 65–73. (5)

Berglas, S., & Jones, E. E. (1978). Drug choice as a self-handicapping strategy in response to noncontingent success. *Journal of Personality and Social Psychology, 36,* 405–417. (14)

Berkowitz, L. (1983). Aversively stimulated aggression: Some parallels and differences in research with animals and humans. *American Psychologist, 38,* 1135–1144. (12)

Berkowitz, L. (1989). Frustration-aggression hypothesis: Examination and reformulation. *Psychological Bulletin, 106,* 59–73. (12)

Berlyne, D. E. (1981). Humanistic psychology as a protest movement. In J. R. Royce & L. P. Mos (Eds.), *Humanistic psychology: Concepts and criticisms* (pp. 261–293). New York: Plenum. (13)

Bernardin, H. J., Cooke, D. K., & Villanova, P. (2000). Conscientiousness and agreeableness as predictors of rating leniency. *Journal of Applied Psychology, 85,* 232–234. (13)

Berndt, T. J., & Heller, K. A. (1986). Gender stereotypes and social inferences: A developmental study. *Journal of Personality and Social Psychology, 50,* 889–898. (11)

Bernhardt, P. C. (1997). Influences of serotonin and testosterone in aggression and dominance: Convergence with social psychology. *Current Directions in Psychological Science, 6,* 44–48. (12)

Berntson, G. G., Cacioppo, J. T., & Quigley, K. S. (1993). Cardiac psychophysiology and autonomic space in humans: Empirical perspectives and conceptual implications. *Psychological Bulletin, 114,* 296–322. (12)

Berridge, K. C., & Robinson, T. E. (1995). The mind of an addicted brain: Neural sensitization of wanting versus liking. *Current Directions in Psychological Science, 4,* 71–76. (6)

Berridge, K. C., & Robinson, T. E. (1998). What is the role of dopamine in reward: Hedonic impact, reward learning, or incentive salience? *Brain Research Reviews, 28,* 309–369. (5)

Berry, D. S. (2000). Attractiveness, attraction, and sexual selection: Evolutionary perspectives on the form and function of physical attractiveness. *Advances in Experimental Social Psychology, 32,* 273–342. (14)

Berry, J. W., Poortinga, Y. H., Segal, H., & Dasen, P. R. (1992). *Cross-cultural psychology.* Cambridge, England: Cambridge University Press. (15)

Berscheid, E. (1983). Emotion. In H. H. Kelley, E. Berscheid, A. Christensen, J. H. Harvey, T. L. Huston, G. Levinger, E. McClintock, L. A. Peplau, & D. R. Peterson (Eds.), *Close relationships* (pp. 110–168). New York: W. H. Freeman. (14)

Bettencourt, B. A., & Miller, N. (1996). Gender differences in aggression as a function of provocation: A meta-analysis. *Psychological Bulletin, 119,* 422–447. (2)

Bickman, L. (1996). A continuum of care: More is not always better. *American Psychologist, 51,* 689–701. (15)

Billy, J. O. G., Tanfer, K., Grady, W. R., & Klepinger, D. H. (1993, March/April). The sexual behavior of men in the United States. *Family Planning Perspectives, 25,* 52–60. (11)

Binet, A., & Simon, T. (1905). Méthodes nouvelles pour le diagnostic du niveau intellectuel des anormaux [New methods for the measurement of the intellectual level of the abnormal]. *L'Année Psychologique, 11,* 191–244. (9)

Birnbaum, M. H. (1999). Testing critical properties of decision making on the Internet. *Psychological Science, 10,* 399–407. (8)

Bjorklund, D. F., & Shackelford, T. K. (1999). Differences in parental investment contribute to important differences between men and women. *Current Directions in Psychological Science, 8,* 86–92. (14)

Black, D. W., Noyes, R., Jr., Goldstein, R. B., & Blum, N. (1992). A family study of obsessive-compulsive disorder. *Archives of General Psychiatry, 49,* 362–368. (16)

Blackless, M., Charuvastra, A., Derryck, A., Fausto-Sterling, A., Lauzanne, K., & Lee, E. (2000). How sexually dimorphic are we? Review and synthesis. *American Journal of Human Biology, 12,* 151–166. (11)

Blackwell, A., & Bates, E. (1995). Inducing agrammatic profiles in normals: Evidence for the selective vulnerability of morphology under cognitive resource limitation. *Journal of Cognitive Neuroscience, 7,* 228–257. (8)

Blaine, J. D., Prien, R. F., & Levine, J. (1983). The role of antidepressants in the treatment of affective disorders. *American Journal of Psychotherapy, 37,* 502–520. (16)

Blakemore, C., & Sutton, P. (1969). Size adaptation: A new aftereffect. *Science, 166,* 245–247. (4)

Blascovich, J., & Tomaka, J. (1991). Measures of self-esteem. In J. P. Robinson, R. R. Shaver, & L. S. Wrightsman (Eds.), *Measures of personality and social psychological attitudes* (Vol. 1, pp. 115–160). San Diego, CA: Academic Press. (10)

Bleuler, E. (1950). *Dementia praecox, or the group of schizophrenias* (J. Zinkin, Trans.). New York: International Universities Press. (Original work published 1911) (16)

Block, J. (1995). A contrarian view of the five-factor approach to personality description. *Psychological Bulletin, 117,* 187–215. (13)

Blouin, J.-L., Dombroski, B. A., Nath, S. K., Lasseter, V. K., Wolyniec, P. S., Nestadt, G., Thornquist, M., Ullrich, G., McGrath, J., Kasch, L., Lamacz, M., Thomas, M. G., Gehrig, C., Radhakrishna, U., Snyder, S. E., Balk, S. E., Neufeld, K., Swartz, K. L., DeMarchi, N., Papadimitriou, G. N., Dikeos, D. G., Stefanis, C. N., Chakravarti, A., Childs, B., Housman, E. D., Kazazian, H. H., Antonarakis, S. E., & Pulver, A. E. (1998). Schizophrenia susceptibility loci on chromosomes 13q32 and 8p21. *Nature Genetics, 20,* 70–73. (16)

Blum, D. (1994). *The monkey wars.* New York: Oxford University Press. (1)

Blum, G. S., & Barbour, J. S. (1979). Selective inattention to anxiety-linked stimuli. *Journal of Experimental Psychology: General, 108,* 182–224. (4)

Blumenthal, S. J., & Kupfer, D. J. (1986). Generalizable treatment strategies for suicidal behavior. *Annals of the New York Academy of Sciences, 487,* 327–340. (16)

Bond, M. H. (1991). *Beyond the Chinese face.* New York: Oxford University Press. (15)

Bond, R., & Smith, P. B. (1996). Culture and conformity: A meta-analysis of studies using Asch's (1952b, 1956) line judgment task. *Psychological Bulletin, 119,* 111–137. (14)

Bonnet, M. H., & Arand, D. L. (1996). The consequences of a week of insomnia. *Sleep, 19,* 453–461. (5)

Bonnie, R. J. (1997). Research with cognitively impaired subjects: Unfinished business in the regulation of human research. *Archives of General Psychiatry, 54,* 105–111. (2)

Bonta, J., Law, M., & Hanson, K. (1998). The prediction of criminal and violent recidivism among mentally disordered offenders: A meta-analysis. *Psychological Bulletin, 123,* 123–142. (12)

Borden, V. M. H., & Rajecki, D. W. (2000). First-year employment outcomes of psychology baccalaureates: Relatedness, preparedness, and prospects. *Teaching of Psychology, 27,* 164–168. (1)

Boring, E. G. (1930). A new ambiguous figure. *American Journal of Psychology, 42,* 444–445. (4)

Bornstein, R. F. (1989). Subliminal techniques as propaganda tools: Review and critique. *Journal of Mind and Behavior, 10,* 231–262. (4)

Borum, R. (1996). Improving the clinical practice of violence risk assessment: Technology, guidelines, and training. *American Psychologist, 51,* 945–956. (12)

Boswell, J. (1990). Sexual and ethical categories in premodern Europe. In D. P. McWhirter, S. A. Sanders, & J. M. Reinisch (Eds.), *Homosexuality/heterosexuality* (pp. 15–31). New York: Oxford University Press. (11)

Bouchard, T. J., Lykken, D. T., McGue, M., Segal, N. L., & Tellegen, A. (1990). Sources of psychological differences: The Minnesota study of twins reared apart. *Science, 250,* 223–228. (10)

Bouchard, T. J., Jr., & McGue, M. (1981). Familial studies of intelligence: A review. *Science, 212,* 1055–1059. (9)

Bouton, M. E. (1994). Context, ambiguity, and classical conditioning. *Current Directions in Psychological Science, 3,* 49–53. (6)

Bouton, M. E., Mineka, S., & Barlow, D. H. (2001). A modern learning theory perspective on the etiology of panic disorder. *Psychological Review, 108,* 4–32. (16)

Bouton, M. E., Nelson, J. B., & Rosas, J. M. (1999). Stimulus generalization, context change, and forgetting. *Psychological Bulletin, 125,* 171–186. (7)

Bower, G. (1994). Temporary emotional states act like multiple personalities. In R. M. Klein & B. K. Doane (Eds.), *Psychological concepts and dissociative disorders* (pp. 207–234). Hillsdale, NJ: Erlbaum. (7)

Bowers, K. S., Regehr, G., Balthazard, C., & Parker, K. (1990). Intuition in the context of discovery. *Cognitive Psychology, 22,* 72–110. (8)

Bowmaker, J. K., & Dartnall, H. J. A. (1980). Visual pigments of rods and cones in a human retina. *Journal of Physiology* (London), *298,* 501–511. (4)

Boynton, R. M. (1988). Color vision. *Annual Review of Psychology, 39,* 69–100. (4)

Bradbury, T. N., & Miller, G. A. (1985). Season of birth in schizophrenia: A review of evidence, methodology, and etiology. *Psychological Bulletin, 98,* 569–594. (16)

Braffman, W., & Kirsch, I. (1999). Imaginative suggestibility and hypnotizability: An empirical analysis. *Journal of Personality and Social Psychology, 77,* 578–587. (5)

Brainard, M. S., & Doupe, A. J. (2000). Auditory feedback in learning and maintenance of vocal behaviour. *Nature Reviews Neuroscience, 1,* 31–40. (6)

Brandt, S. A., & Stark, L. W. (1997). Spontaneous eye movements during visual imagery reflect the content of the visual scene. *Journal of Cognitive Neuroscience, 9,* 27–38. (8)

Bransford, J. D., & Stein, B. S. (1984). *The ideal problem solver.* New York: W. H. Freeman. (8)

Bratko, D., & Marusic, I. (1997). Family study of the big five personality dimensions. *Personality and Individual Differences, 23,* 365–369. (13)

Braun, A. R., Balkin, T. J., Wesensten, N. J., Gwadry, F., Carson, R. E., Varga, M., Baldwin, P., Belenky, G., & Herscovitch, P. (1998). Dissociated pattern of activity in visual cortices and their projections during human rapid eye movement sleep. *Science, 279,* 91–95. (5)

Bray, G. A., & Tartaglia, L. A. (2000). Medicinal strategies in the treatment of obesity. *Nature, 404,* 672–677. (11)

Bregman, A. S. (1981). Asking the "what for" question in auditory perception. In M. Kubovy & J. R. Pomerantz (Eds.), *Perceptual organization* (pp. 99–118). Hillsdale, NJ: Erlbaum. (4)

Bremner, J. D., Shobe, K. K., & Kihlstrom, J. F. (2000). False memories in women with self-reported childhood sexual abuse: An empirical study. *Psychological Science, 11,* 333–337. (7)

Brennan, P. A., Grekin, E. R., & Mednick, S. A. (1999). Maternal smoking during pregnancy and adult male criminal outcomes. *Archives of General Psychiatry, 56,* 215–219. (12)

Brent, D. A., Perper, J. A., Goldstein, C. E., Kolko, D. J., Allan, M. J., Allman, C. J., & Zelenak, J. P. (1988). Risk factors for adolescent suicide. *Archives of General Psychiatry, 45,* 581–588. (16)

Brinkmann, R. R., Mezei, M. M., Theilmann, J., Almqvist, E., & Hayden, M. R. (1997). The likelihood of being affected with Huntington's disease by a particular age, for a specific CAG size. *American Journal of Human Genetics, 60,* 1202–1210. (3)

Brockner, J., & Rubin, J. Z. (1985). *Entrapment in escalating conflicts.* New York: Springer-Verlag. (14)

Brooks, J. H., & Reddon, J. R. (1996). Serum testosterone in violent and nonviolent young offenders. *Journal of Clinical Psychology, 52,* 475–483. (12)

Brooks, R. (2000). Negative genetic correlation between male sexual attractiveness and survival. *Nature, 406,* 67–70. (14)

Brooks-Gunn, J., & Furstenberg, F. F., Jr. (1989). Adolescent sexual behavior. *American Psychologist, 44,* 249–257. (10)

Brophy, J. (1987). Socializing students' motivation to learn. *Advances in Motivation and Achievement, 5,* 181–210. (11)

Brower, K. J., & Anglin, M. D. (1987). Adolescent cocaine use: Epidemiology, risk factors, and prevention. *Journal of Drug Education, 17,* 163–180. (5)

Brown, G. W. (1989). Life events and measurement. In G. W. Brown & T. O. Harris (Eds.), *Life events and illness* (pp. 3–45). New York: Guilford Press. (12)

Brown, J. (1977). *Mind, brain, and consciousness.* New York: Academic Press. (8)

Bruce, D., Dolan, A., & Phillips-Grant, K. (2000). On the transition from childhood amnesia to the recall of personal memories. *Psychological Science, 11,* 360–364. (7)

Bruck, M., Cavanagh, P., & Ceci, S. J. (1991). Fortysomething: Recognizing faces at one's 25th reunion. *Memory & Cognition, 19,* 221–228. (4)

Bruner, J. S., & Potter, M. C. (1964). Interference in visual recognition. *Science, 144,* 424–425. (8)

Brysbaert, M., Vitu, F., & Schroyens, W. (1996). The right visual field advantage and the optimal viewing position effect: On the relation between foveal and parafoveal word recognition. *Neuropsychology, 10,* 385–395. (8)

Brzustowica, L. M., Hodgkinson, K. A., Chow, E. W. C., Honer, W. G., & Bassett, A. S. (2000). Location of a major susceptibility locus for familial schizophrenia on chromosome 1q21-q22. *Science, 288,* 678–682. (16)

Buck, L., & Axel, R. (1991). A novel multigene family may encode odorant receptors: A molecular basis for odor recognition. *Cell, 65,* 175–187. (4)

Buck, R. (1994). Social and emotional functions in facial expression and communication: the readout hypothesis. *Biological Psychology, 38,* 95–115. (12)

Burger, J. M. (1986). Increasing compliance by improving the deal: The that's-not-all technique. *Journal of Personality and Social Psychology, 51,* 277–283. (14)

Burgess, C. E., Lindblad, K., Sigransky, E., Yuan, Q.-P., Long, R. T., Breschel, T., Ross, C. A., McInnis, M., Lee, P., Ginns, E., Lenane, M., Kumra, S., Jacobsen, L., Rapoport, J., & Schalling, M. (1998). Large CAG/CTG repeats are associated with childhood-onset schizophrenia. *Molecular Psychiatry, 3,* 321–327. (16)

Burke, K. C., Burke, J. D., Jr., Regier, D. A., & Rae, D. S. (1990). Age at onset of selected mental disorders in five community populations. *Archives of General Psychiatry, 47,* 511–518. (16)

Burns, M. O., & Seligman, M. E. P. (1989). Explanatory style across the life span: Evidence for stability over 52 years. *Journal of Personality and Social Psychology, 56,* 471–477. (16)

Burr, D. C., Morrone, M. C., & Ross, J. (1994). Selective suppression of the magnocellular visual pathway during saccadic eye movements. *Nature, 371,* 511–513. (8)

Bushman, B. J. (1993). Human aggression while under the influence of alcohol and other drugs: An integrative research review. *Current Directions in Psychological Science, 2,* 148–152. (12)

Bushman, B. J., & Cooper, H. M. (1990). Effects of alcohol on human aggression: An integrative research review. *Psychological Bulletin, 107,* 341–354. (12)

Buss, D. M. (1994). The strategies of human mating. *American Scientist, 82,* 238–249. (3)

Buss, D. M., Larsen, R. J., Westen, D., & Semmelroth, J. (1992). Sex differences in jealousy: Evolution, physiology, and psychology. *Psychological Science, 3,* 251–255. (14)

Buss, D. M. (2000a). Desires in human mating. *Annals of the New York Academy of Sciences, 907,* 39–49. (14)

Buss, D. M. (2000b). Evolution of happiness. *American Psychologist, 55,* 15–23. (12)

Bussey, K., & Bandura, A. (1999). Social cognitive theory of gender development and differentiation. *Psychological Review, 106,* 676–713. (10)

Butcher, J. N., Graham, J. R., Williams, C. L., & Ben-Porath, Y. S. (1990). *Development and use of the MMPI-2 content scales.* Minneapolis: University of Minnesota Press. (13)

Butzlaff, R. L., & Hooley, J. M. (1998). Expressed emotion and psychiatric relapse. *Archives of General Psychiatry, 55,* 547–552. (16)

Buunk, B. P., Angleitner, A., Oubaid, V., & Buss, D. M. (1996). Sex differences in jealousy in evolutionary and cultural perspective: Tests from the Netherlands, Germany, and the United States. *Psychological Science, 7,* 359–363. (14)

Cahalan, D. (1978). Subcultural differences in drinking behavior in U.S. national surveys and selected European studies. In P. E. Nathan, G. A. Marlatt, & T. Løberg (Eds.), *Alcoholism: New directions in behavioral research and treatment* (pp. 235–253). New York: Plenum. (16)

Cahill, L., Babinsky, R., Markowitsch, H. J., & McGaugh, J. L. (1995). The amygdala and emotional memory. *Nature, 377,* 295–296. (3)

Cahill, L., & McGaugh, J. L. (1998). Mechanisms of emotional arousal and lasting declarative memory. *Trends in Neurosciences, 21,* 294–299. (7)

Calvin, W. H., & Bickerton, D. (2000). *Lingua ex machina.* Cambridge, MA: MIT Press. (8)

Camara, W. J. (1988). Reagan signs ban of polygraph testing for job applicants. *The Industrial-Organizational Psychologist, 26,* 39–41. (12)

Camara, W. J., & Schneider, D. L. (1994). Integrity tests: Facts and unresolved issues. *American Psychologist, 49,* 112–119. (12)

Cameron, P., Proctor, K., Coburn, W., & Forde, N. (1985). Sexual orientation and sexually transmitted disease. *Nebraska Medical Journal, 70,* 292–299. (11)

Campbell, S. S., & Tobler, I. (1984). Animal sleep: A review of sleep duration across phylogeny. *Neuroscience & Biobehavioral Reviews, 8,* 269–300. (5)

Campbell, S. (2000). Is there an intrinsic period of the circadian clock? *Science, 288,* 1174. (5)

Campion, M. A., & McClelland, C. L. (1991). Interdisciplinary examination of the costs and benefits of enlarged jobs: A job design quasi-experiment. *Journal of Applied Psychology, 76,* 186–198. (11)

Campion, M. A., & Thayer, P. W. (1985). Development and field evaluation of an interdisciplinary measure of job design. *Journal of Applied Psychology, 70,* 29–43. (1, 11)

Campion, M. A., & Thayer, P. W. (1989). How do you design a job? *Personnel Journal, 68,* 43–46. (1)

Campos, J. J., Bertenthal, B. I., & Kermoian, R. (1992). Early experience and emotional development. *Psychological Science, 3,* 61–64. (10)

Canetto, S. S., & Sakinofsky, I. (1998). The gender paradox in suicide. *Suicide and Life-Threatening Behavior, 28,* 1–23. (16)

Cannon, W. B. (1929). Organization for physiological homeostasis. *Physiological Reviews, 9,* 399–431. (11)

Cantor, N., & Fleeson, W. (1994). Social intelligence and intelligent goal pursuit: A cognitive slice of motivation. In W. D. Spaulding (Ed.), *Integrative views of motivation, cognition, and emotion* (pp. 125–179). Lincoln: University of Nebraska Press. (11)

Capaldi, E. D. (1996). Conditioned food preferences. In E. D. Capaldi (Ed.), *Why we eat what we eat* (pp. 53–80). Washington, DC: American Psychological Association. (11)

Cardno, A. G., Marshall, E. J., Coid, B., Macdonald, A. M., Ribchester, T. R., Davies, N. J., Venturi, P., Jones, L. A., Lewis, S. W., Sham, P. C., Gottesman, I. I., Farmer, A. E., McGuffin, P., Reveley, A. M., & Murray, R. M. (1999). Heritability estimates for psychotic disorders. *Archives of General Psychiatry, 56,* 162–168. (16)

Carey, S. (1978). The child as word learner. In M. Halle, J. Bresnan, & G. A. Miller (Eds.), *Linguistic theory and psychological reality* (pp. 264–293). Cambridge, MA: MIT Press. (8)

Carlsson, K., Petrovic, P., Skare, S., Petersson, K. M., & Ingvar, M. (2000). Tickling expectations: Neural processing in anticipation of a sensory stimulus. *Journal of Cognitive Neuroscience, 12,* 691–703. (4)

Carney, R. N., & Levin, J. R. (1998). Coming to terms with the keyword method in introductory psychology: A "neuromnemonic" example. *Teaching of Psychology, 25,* 132–134. (7)

Carpenter, P. A., Just, M. A., & Shell, P. (1990). What one intelligence test measures: A theoretical account of the processing in the Raven Progressive Matrices test. *Psychological Review, 97,* 404–431. (9)

Carpenter, W. T. (1995). Serotonin-dopamine antagonists and treatment of negative symptoms. *Journal of Clinical Psychopharmacology, 15*(Suppl. 1), S30–S35. (16)

Carroll, B. J. (1980). Implications of biological research for the diagnosis of depression. In J. Mendlewicz (Ed.), *New advances in the diagnosis and treatment of depressive illness* (pp. 85–107). Amsterdam: Excerpta Medica. (16)

Carstensen, L. L., & Charles, S. T. (1998). Emotion in the second half of life. *Current Directions in Psychological Science, 7,* 144–149. (10)

Carvell, C., Inglis, N. F. J., Mace, G. M., & Purvis, A. (1998). How Diana climbed the ratings at the zoo. *Nature, 395,* 213. (2)

Caspi, A., Taylor, A., Moffitt, T. E., & Plomin, R. (2000). Neighborhood deprivation affects children's mental health. *Psychological Science, 11,* 338–342. (10)

Caterina, M. J., Rosen, T. A., Tominaga, M., Brake, A. J., & Julius, D. (1999). A capsaicin-receptor homologue with a high threshold for noxious heat. *Nature, 398,* 436–441. (4)

Cattell, R. B. (1965). *The scientific analysis of personality.* Chicago: Aldine. (13)

Cattell, R. B. (1987). *Intelligence: Its structure, growth and action.* Amsterdam: North-Holland. (9)

Cavell, T. A., & Woehr, D. J. (1994). Predicting introductory psychology test scores: An engaging and useful topic. *Teaching of Psychology, 21,* 108–110. (2)

Ceci, S. J. (1995). False beliefs: Some developmental and clinical considerations. In D. L. Schacter (Ed.), *Memory distortion* (pp. 91–125). Cambridge, MA: Harvard University Press. (7, 13)

Ceci, S. J., & Bruck, M. (1993). Suggestibility of the child witness: A historical review and synthesis. *Psychological Bulletin, 113,* 403–439. (7)

Chabris, C. F. (1999). Prelude or requiem for the 'Mozart effect'? *Nature, 400,* 826-827. (2)

Chamberlin, J. (1978). *On our own.* New York: Hawthorn. (15)

Chamberlin, J. (2000, February). Where are all these students coming from? *Monitor on Psychology, 31*(2), 32–34. (1)

Charlton, S. G. (1983). Differential conditionability: Reinforcing grooming in golden hamsters. *Animal Learning & Behavior, 11,* 27–34. (6)

Charness, N., & Gerchak, Y. (1996). Participation rates and maximal performance: A log-linear explanation for group differences, such as Russian and male dominance in chess. *Psychological Science, 7,* 46–51. (8)

Chaudhari, N., Landin, A. M., & Roper, S. D. (2000). A metabotropic glutamate receptor variant functions as a taste receptor. *Nature Neuroscience, 3,* 113–119. (4)

Cheetham, E. (1973). *The prophecies of Nostradamus.* New York: Putnam's. (2)

Chehab, F. F., Mounzih, K., Lu, R., & Lim, M. E. (1997). Early onset of reproductive function in normal female mice treated with leptin. *Science, 275,* 88–90. (11)

Chemelli, R. M., Willie, J. T., Sinton, C. M., Elmquist, J. K., Scammell, T., Lee, C., Richardson, J. A., Williams, S. C., Xiong, Y., Kisanuki, Y., Fitch, T. E., Nakazato, M. J., Hammer, R. E., Saper, C. B., & Yanagisawa, M. (1999). Narcolepsy in orexin knockout mice: Molecular genetics of sleep regulation. *Cell, 98,* 437–451. (5)

Cheng, A. T. A. (1995). Mental illness and suicide. *Archives of General Psychiatry, 52,* 594–603. (16)

Cherlin, A. J., Furstenberg, F. F., Jr., Chase-Lansdale, P. L., Kiernan, K. E., Robins, P. K., Morrison, D. R., & Teitler, J. O. (1991). Longitudinal studies of effects of divorce on children in Great Britain and the United States. *Science, 252,* 1386–1389. (10)

Cheryan, S., & Bodenhausen, G. V. (2000). When positive stereotypes threaten intellectual performance: The psychological hazards of "model minority" status. *Psychological Science, 11,* 399–402. (9)

Cheung, F. M., Leung, K., Fang, R. M., Song, W. Z., Zhang, J. X., & Zhang, J. P. (1996). Development of the Chinese Personality Assessment Inventory (CPAI). *Journal of Cross-Cultural Psychology, 27,* 181–199. (13)

Choi, I., Nisbett, R. E., & Norenzayan, A. (1999). Causal attribution: Variation and universality. *Psychological Bulletin, 125,* 47–63. (14)

Chomsky, N. (1980). *Rules and representations.* New York: Columbia University Press. (8)

Chorney, M. J., Chorney, K., Seese, N., Owen, M. J., Daniels, J., McGuffin, P., Thompson, L. A., Detterman, D. K., Benbow, C., Lubinski, D., Eley, T., & Plomin, R. (1998). A quantitative trait locus associated with cognitive ability in children. *Psychological Science, 9,* 159–166. (9)

Chorpita, B. F., & Barlow, D. H. (1998). The development of anxiety: The role of control in the early environment. *Psychological Bulletin, 124,* 3–21. (16)

Christensen, A., & Jacobson, N. S. (1994). Who (or what) can do psychotherapy: The status and challenge of nonprofessional therapies. *Psychological Science, 5,* 8–14. (15)

Cialdini, R. B. (1993). *Influence: The psychology of persuasion* (Rev. ed.). New York: Morrow. (6)

Cialdini, R. B., Vincent, J. E., Lewis, S. K., Catalan, J., Wheeler, D., & Darby, B. L. (1975). Reciprocal concessions procedure for inducing compliance: The door-in-the-face technique. *Journal of Personality and Social Psychology, 31,* 206–215. (14)

Cioffi, D. (1991). Beyond attentional strategies: A cognitive-perceptual model of somatic interpretation. *Psychological Bulletin, 109,* 25–41. (12)

Clancy, S. A., Schacter, D. L., McNally, R. J., & Pitman, R. K. (2000). False recognition in women reporting recovered memories of sexual abuse. *Psychological Science, 11,* 26–31. (7)

Clark, R., Anderson, N. B., Clark, V. R., & Williams, D. R. (1999). Racism as a stressor for African Americans. *American Psychologist, 54,* 805–816. (12)

Clark, R. E., & Squire, L. R. (1999). Human eyeblink classical conditioning: Effects of manipulating awareness of the stimulus contingencies. *Psychological Science, 10,* 14–18. (6)

Clarkin, J. F., & Carpenter, D. (1995). Family therapy in historical perspective. In B. Bongar & L. E. Beutler (Eds.), *Comprehensive textbook of psychotherapy: Theory and practice* (pp. 205–227). Oxford, England: Oxford University Press. (15)

Clausen, J. A., & Gilens, M. (1990). Personality and labor force participation across the life course: A longitudinal study of women's careers. *Sociological Forum, 5,* 595–618. (11)

Clément, K., Vaisse, C., Lahlou, N., Cabrol, S., Pelloux, V., Cassuto, D., Gourmelen, M., Dina, C., Chambaz, J., Lacorte, J.-M., Basdevant, A., Bougnères, P., Lebouc, Y., Groguel, P., & Guy-Grand, B. (1998). A mutation in the human leptin receptor gene causes obesity and pituitary dysfunction. *Nature, 392,* 398–401. (11)

"Clinicopathologic conference." (1967). *Johns Hopkins Medical Journal, 120,* 186–199. (12)

Cloninger, C. R., Bohman, M., & Sigvardsson, S. (1981). Inheritance of alcohol abuse: Cross-fostering analysis of adopted men. *Archives of General Psychiatry, 38,* 861–868. (16)

Cocozza, J., Melick, M., & Steadman, H. (1978). Trends in violent crime among ex-mental patients. *Criminology, 16,* 317–334. (12)

Cohen, B., Novick, D., & Rubinstein, M. (1996). Modulation of insulin activities by leptin. *Science, 274,* 1185–1188. (11)

Cohen, J. D., Noll, D. C., & Schneider, W. (1993). Functional magnetic resonance imaging: Overview and methods for psychological research. *Behavior Research Methods, Instruments, & Computers, 25,* 101–113. (3)

Cohen, J. D., & Schooler, J. W. (1997). Science and sentience: Some questions regarding the scientific investigation of consciousness. In J. D. Cohen & J. W. Schooler (Eds.), *Scientific approaches to consciousness* (pp. 3–10). Mahwah, NJ: Erlbaum. (5)

Cohen, N. J., Eichenbaum, H., Deacedo, B. S., & Corkin, S. (1985). Different memory systems underlying acquisition of procedural and declarative knowledge. *Annals of the New York Academy of Sciences, 444,* 54–71. (7)

Cohen, N. J., & Squire, L. R. (1980). Preserved learning and retention of pattern-analyzing skill in amnesia: Dissociation of knowing how and knowing that. *Science, 210,* 207–211. (7)

Cohen, S. (1996). Psychological stress, immunity, and upper respiratory infections. *Current Directions in Psychological Science, 5,* 86–90. (12)

Cohen, S., Lichtenstein, E., Prochaska, J. O., Rossi, J. S., Gritz, E. R., Carr, C. R., Orleans, C. T., Schoenbach, V. J., Biener, L., Abrams, D., DiClemente, C., Curry, S., Marlatt, G. A., Cummings, K. M., Emont, S. L., Giovino, G., & Ossip-Klein, D. (1989). Debunking myths about self-quitting: Evidence from 10 prospective studies of persons who attempt to quit smoking by themselves. *American Psychologist, 44,* 1355–1365. (16)

Coie, J. D., & Dodge, K. (1983). Continuities and change in children's social status: A five-year longitudinal study. *Merrill-Palmer Quarterly, 29,* 261–282. (10)

Collins, A. M., & Loftus, E. F. (1975). A spreading-activation theory of semantic processing. *Psychological Review, 82,* 407–428. (8)

Collins, A. M., & Quillian, M. R. (1969). Retrieval time from semantic memory. *Journal of Verbal Learning and Verbal Behavior, 8,* 240–247. (8)

Collins, A. M., & Quillian, M. R. (1970). Does category size affect categorization time? *Journal of Verbal Learning and Verbal Behavior, 9,* 432–438. (8)

Collins, D. W., & Kimura, D. (1997). A large sex difference on a two-dimensional mental rotation task. *Behavioral Neuroscience, 111,* 845–849. (10)

Collins, W. A., & Gunnar, M. R. (1990). Social and personality development. *Annual Review of Psychology, 41,* 387–416. (10)

Colwill, R. M. (1993). An associative analysis of instrumental learning. *Current Directions in Psychological Science, 2,* 111–116. (6)

Comings, D. E., & Amromin, G. D. (1974). Autosomal dominant insensitivity to pain with hyperplastic myelinopathy and autosomal dominant indifference to pain. *Neurology, 24,* 838–848. (4)

Comuzzie, A. G., & Allison, D. B. (1998). The search for human obesity genes. *Science, 280,* 1374–1377. (11)

Connine, C. M., Blasko, D. G., & Hall, M. (1991). Effects of subsequent sentence context in auditory word recognition: Temporal and linguistic constraints. *Journal of Memory and Language, 30,* 234–250. (8)

Constantinides, P. (1977). Ill at ease and sick at heart: Symbolic behavior in a Sudanese healing cult. In I. Wilson (Ed.), *Symbols and sentiments* (pp. 61–84). New York: Academic Press. (15)

*Consumer Reports.* (1995, November). Mental health: Does therapy help? *Consumer Reports,* pp. 734–739. (15)

Contrada, R. J., Ashmore, R. D., Gary, M. L., Coups, E., Egeth, J. D., Sewell, A., Ewell, K., Goyal, T. M., & Chasse, V. (2000). Ethnicity-related sources of stress and their effects on well-being. *Current Directions in Psychological Science, 9,* 136–139. (12)

Coplan, J. D., Goetz, R., Klein, D. F., Papp, L. A., Fyer, A. J., Leibowitz, M. R., Davies, S. O., & Gorman, J. M. (1998). Plasma cortisol concentrations preceding lactate-induced panic. *Archives of General Psychiatry, 55,* 130–136. (16)

Corkin, S. (1984). Lasting consequences of bilateral medial temporal lobectomy: Clinical course and experimental findings in H. M. *Seminars in Neurology, 4,* 249–259. (7)

Costa, P. T., Jr., McCrae, R. R., & Dye, D. A. (1991). Facet scales for agreeableness and conscientiousness: A revision of the NEO personality inventory. *Personality and Individual Differences, 12,* 887–898. (13)

Cowan, C. L., Thompson, W. C., & Ellsworth, P. C. (1984). The effects of death qualification on jurors' predisposition to convict and on the quality of deliberation. *Law and Human Behavior, 8,* 53–79. (14)

Cox, M. J., Owen, M. T., Henderson, V. K., & Margand, N. A. (1992). Prediction of infant-father and infant-mother attachment. *Developmental Psychology, 28,* 474–483. (10)

Craddock, N., & Jones, I. (1999). Genetics of bipolar disorder. *Journal of Medical Genetics, 36,* 585–594. (16)

Craig, A. D., Bushnell, M. C., Zhang, E. -T., & Blomqvist, A. (1994). A thalamic nucleus specific for pain and temperature sensation. *Nature, 372,* 770–773. (4)

Craik, F. I. M., & Lockhart, R. S. (1972). Levels of processing: A framework for memory research. *Journal of Verbal Learning and Verbal Behavior, 11,* 671–684. (7)

Cramer, P. (1996). *Storytelling, narrative, and the Thematic Apperception Test.* New York: Guilford Press. (13)

Crews, D. J., & Landers, D. M. (1987). A meta-analytic review of aerobic fitness and reactivity to psychosocial stressors. *Medicine & Science in Sports & Exercise, 19,* S114–S120. (12)

Crews, F. (1996). The verdict on Freud. *Psychological Science, 7,* 63–68. (13)

Crombez, G., Hermans, D., & Adriaensen, H. (2000). The emotional Stroop task and chronic pain: What is threatening for chronic pain sufferers? *European Journal of Pain (London), 4,* 37–44. (13)

Cross, C. K., & Hirschfeld, R. M. A. (1986). Psychosocial factors and suicidal behavior. *Annals of the New York Academy of Sciences, 487,* 77–89. (16)

Croyle, R. T., & Cooper, J. (1983). Dissonance arousal: Physiological evidence. *Journal of Personality and Social Psychology, 45,* 782–791. (14)

Csikszentmihalyi, M. (1999). If we are so rich, why aren't we happy? *American Psychologist, 54,* 821–827. (12)

Culbertson, F. M. (1997). Depression and gender. *American Psychologist, 52,* 25–31. (16)

Cummings, N. A. (1979). Turning bread into stones: Our modern antimiracle. *American Psychologist, 34,* 1119–1129. (16)

Cunningham, E. J. A., & Russell, A. F. (2000). Egg investment is influenced by male attractiveness in the mallard. *Nature, 404,* 74–77. (14)

Cyranowski, J. M., Frank, E., Young, E., & Shear, K. (2000). Adolescent onset of the gender difference in lifetime rates of major depression. *Archives of General Psychiatry, 57,* 21–27. (16)

Czeisler, C. A., Duffy, J. F., Shanahan, T. L., Brown, E. N., Mitchell, J. F., Rimmer, D. W., Ronda, J. M., Silva, E. J., Allan, J. S., Emens, J. S., Dijk, D.-J., & Kronauer, R. E. (1999). Stability, precision, and near-24-hour period of the human circadian pacemaker. *Science, 284,* 2177–2181. (5)

Czeisler, C. A., Johnson, M. P., Duffy, J. F., Brown, E. N., Ronda, J. M., & Kronauer, R. E. (1990). Exposure to bright light and darkness to treat physiologic maladaptation to night work. *New England Journal of Medicine, 322,* 1353–1359. (5)

Czeisler, C. A., Moore-Ede, M. C., & Coleman, R. M. (1982). Rotating shift work schedules that disrupt sleep are improved by applying circadian principles. *Science, 217,* 460–463. (5)

Dabbs, J. M., Jr., Carr, T. S., Frady, R. L., & Riad, J. K. (1995). Testosterone, crime, and misbehavior among 692 male prison inmates. *Personality and Individual Differences, 18,* 627–633. (12)

Dackis, C. A., Pottash, A. L. C., Annitto, W., & Gold, M. S. (1982). Persistence of urinary marijuana levels after supervised abstinence. *American Journal of Psychiatry, 139,* 1196–1198. (5)

Dadds, M. R., Bovbjerg, D. H., Redd, W. H., & Cutmore, T. R. H. (1997). Imagery in human classical conditioning. *Psychological Bulletin, 122,* 89–103. (6)

Dallenbach, K. M. (1951). A puzzle picture with a new principle of concealment. *American Journal of Psychology, 64,* 431–433. (4)

Dalman, C., Allebeck, P., Cullberg, J., Grunewald, C., & Köstler, M. (1999). Obstetric complications and the risk of schizophrenia. *Archives of General Psychiatry, 56,* 234–240. (16)

Daly, M., Wilson, M., & Weghorst, S. J. (1982). Male sexual jealousy. *Ethology & Sociobiology, 3,* 11–27. (12)

Damaser, E. C., Shor, R. E., & Orne, M. E. (1963). Physiological effects during hypnotically requested emotions. *Psychosomatic Medicine, 25,* 334–343. (5)

Damasio, A. R. (1994). *Descartes' error: Emotion, reason, and the human brain.* New York: G. P. Putnam's Sons. (12)

Damasio, A. (1999). *The feeling of what happens.* New York: Harcourt Brace. (5, 12)

Damasio, H., Grabowski, T., Frank, R., Galaburda, A. M., & Damasio, A. R. (1994). The return of Phineas Gage: The skull of a famous patient yields clues about the brain. *Science, 264,* 1102–1105. (12)

Damron-Rodriguez, J. (1991). Commentary: Multicultural aspects of aging in the U.S.: Implications for health and human services. *Journal of Cross-Cultural Gerontology, 6,* 135–143. (10)

Daniel, M. H. (1997). Intelligence testing: Status and trends. *American Psychologist, 52,* 1038–1045. (9)

Dar, R., Rish, S., Hermish, H., Taub, M., & Fux, M. (2000). Realism of confidence in obsessive-compulsive checkers. *Journal of Abnormal Psychology, 109,* 673–678. (16)

Darling, N., & Steinberg, L. (1993). Parenting style as context: An integrative model. *Psychological Bulletin, 113,* 487–496. (10)

Darwin, C. (1859). *On the origin of species by means of natural selection.* New York: D. Appleton. (1, 3)

Darwin, C. (1871). *The descent of man.* New York: D. Appleton. (1)

Darwin, C. (1965). *The expression of emotions in man and animals.* Chicago: University of Chicago Press. (Original work published 1872) (12)

Das, J. P. (1992). Beyond a unidimensional scale of merit. *Intelligence, 16,* 137–149. (9)

Dasgupta, N., McGhee, D. E., Greenwald, A. G., & Banaji, M. R. (2000). Automatic preference for White Americans: Eliminating the familiarity explanation. *Journal of Experimental Social Psychology, 36,* 316–328. (14)

Davenport, D., & Foley, J. M. (1979). Fringe benefits of cataract surgery. *Science, 204,* 454–457. (4)

Davenport, W. H. (1977). Sex in cross-cultural perspective. In F. A. Beach (Ed.), *Human sexuality in four perspectives* (pp. 62–86). Baltimore, MD: Johns Hopkins University Press. (11)

David, D., Brown, R., Pojoga, C., & David, A. (2000). Impact of posthypnotic amnesia and directed forgetting on implicit and explicit memory: New insights from a modified process dissociation procedure. *International Journal of Clinical and Experimental Hypnosis, 48,* 267–289. (5)

Davidson, D., Jergovic, D., Imami, Z., & Theodos, V. (1997). Monolingual and bilingual children's use of the mutual exclusivity constraint. *Journal of Child Language, 24,* 3–24. (8)

Davidson, R. J., Putnam, K. M., & Larson, C. L. (2000). Dysfunction in the neural circuitry of emotion regulation—A possible prelude to violence. *Science, 289,* 591–594. (12)

Davison, K. P., Pennebaker, J. W., & Dickerson, S. S. (2000). Who talks? The social psychology of illness support groups. *American Psychologist, 55,* 205–217. (12)

Dawes, R. M. (1994). *House of cards: Psychology and psychotherapy.* New York: Free Press. (15)

Dawes, R. M., & Smith, T. L. (1985). Attitude and opinion measurement. In G. Lindzey & E. Aronson (Eds.), *Handbook of social psychology* (Vol. 1, pp. 509–566). New York: Random House. (14)

Dawson, D., & Reid, K. (1997). Fatigue, alcohol, and performance impairment. *Nature, 388,* 235. (5)

Day, R. H. (1972). Visual spatial illusions: A general explanation. *Science, 175,* 1335–1340. (4)

Day, W. F., Jr., & Moore, J. (1995). On certain relations between contemporary philosophy and radical behaviorism. In J. T. Todd & E. K. Morris (Eds.), *Modern perspectives on B. F. Skinner and contemporary behaviorism* (pp. 75–84). Westport, CT: Greenwood Press. (6)

Deacon, S., & Arendt, J. (1996). Adapting to phase shifts: II. Effects of melatonin and conflicting light treatment. *Physiology & Behavior, 59,* 675–682. (5)

Deacon, T. W. (1997). *The symbolic species.* New York: Norton. (8)

Dean, K. E., & Malamuth, N. M. (1997). Characteristics of men who aggress sexually and of men who imagine aggressing: Risk and moderating variables. *Journal of Personality and Social Psychology, 72,* 449–455. (12)

Deary, I. J., & Stough, C. (1996). Intelligence and inspection time. *American Psychologist, 51,* 599–608. (9)

Deary, I. J., Whalley, L. J., Lemmon, H., Crawford, J. R., & Starr, J. M. (2000). The stability of individual differences in mental ability from childhood to old age: Follow-up of the 1932 Scottish mental survey. *Intelligence, 28,* 49–55. (9)

DeCasper, A. J., & Fifer, W. P. (1980). Of human bonding: Newborns prefer their mothers' voices. *Science, 208,* 1174–1177. (10)

Deci, E. L. (1971). Effects of externally mediated rewards on intrinsic motivation. *Journal of Personality and Social Psychology, 18,* 105–115. (11)

Deci, E. L., Koestner, R., & Ryan, R. M. (1999). A meta-analytic review of experiments examining the effects of extrinsic rewards on intrinsic motivation. *Psychological Bulletin, 125,* 627–668. (11)

Deese, J. (1959). On the prediction of occurrence of particular verbal intrusions in immediate recall. *Journal of Experimental Psychology, 58,* 17–22. (7)

DeFelipe, C., Herrero, J. F., O'Brien, J. A., Palmer, J. A., Doyle, C. A., Smith, A. J. H., Laird, J. M. A., Belmonte, C., Cervero, F., & Hunt, S. P. (1998). Altered nociception, analgesia and aggression in mice lacking the receptor for substance P. *Nature, 392,* 394–397. (4)

de Groot, A. D. (1966). Perception and memory versus thought: Some old ideas and recent findings. In B. Kleinmuntz (Ed.), *Problem solving* (pp. 19–50). New York: Wiley. (8)

DeGrandpre, R. J. (2000). A science of meaning: Can behaviorism bring meaning to psychological science? *American Psychologist, 55,* 721–739. (6)

Dehue, T. (2000). From deception trials to control agents. *American Psychologist, 55,* 264–268. (2)

de Jesus Mari, J., & Streiner, D. L. (1994). An overview of family interventions and relapse on schizophrenia: Meta-analysis of research findings. *Psychological Medicine, 24,* 565–578. (16)

de Jong, P. J., Pasman, W., Kindt, M., & van den Hout, M. A. (2001). A reaction time paradigm to assess (implicit) complaint-specific dysfunctional beliefs. *Behaviour Research and Therapy, 39,* 101–113. (13)

DeLoache, J. S. (1989). The development of representation in young children. *Advances in Child Development and Behavior, 22,* 1–39. (10)

DeLoache, J. S., Miller, K. F., & Rosengren, K. S. (1997). The credible shrinking room: Very young children's performance with symbolic and nonsymbolic relations. *Psychological Science, 8,* 308–313. (10)

DeLuise, M., Blackburn, G. L., & Flier, J. S. (1980). Reduced activity of the red-cell sodium-potassium pump in human obesity. *New England Journal of Medicine, 303,* 1017–1022. (11)

Dement, W. (1960). The effect of dream deprivation. *Science, 131,* 1705–1707. (5)

Dement, W. C. (1972). *Some must watch while some must sleep.* Stanford, CA: Stanford Alumni Association. (5)

Dement, W., & Kleitman, N. (1957a). Cyclic variations in EEG during sleep and their relation to eye movements, body motility, and dreaming. *Electroencephalography and Clinical Neurophysiology, 9,* 673–690. (5)

Dement, W., & Kleitman, N. (1957b). The relation of eye movements during sleep to dream activity: An objective method for the study of dreaming. *Journal of Experimental Psychology, 53,* 339–346. (5)

Dement, W. C., & Vaughan, C. (1999). *The promise of sleep.* New York: Dell. (5)

Dement, W., & Wolpert, E. A. (1958). The relation of eye movements, body motility, and external stimuli to dream content. *Journal of Experimental Psychology, 55,* 543–553. (5)

DeNeve, K. M. (1999). Happy as an extraverted clam? The role of personality for subjective well-being. *Current Directions in Psychological Science, 8,* 141–144. (12)

DeNeve, K. M., & Cooper, H. (1998). The happy personality: A meta-analysis of 137 personality traits and subjective well-being. *Psychological Bulletin, 124,* 197–229. (12)

Dennett, D. C. (1991). *Consciousness explained.* Boston: Little, Brown. (1)

Dennis, P. M. (1998). Chills and thrills: Does radio harm our children? The controversy over program violence during the age of radio. *Journal of the History of the Behavioral Sciences, 34,* 33–50. (2)

Denniston, J. C., Miller, R. R., & Matute, H. (1996). Biological significance as a determinant of cue competition. *Psychological Science, 7,* 325–331. (6)

deQuervain, D. J.-F., Roozendaal, B., Nitsch, R. M., McGaugh, J. L., & Hock, C. (2000). Acute cortisone administration impairs retrieval of long-term declarative memory in humans. *Nature Neuroscience, 3,* 313–314. (12)

Derogatis, L. (1986). Psychology in cancer medicine: A perspective and overview. *Journal of Consulting and Clinical Psychology, 54,* 632–638. (12)

Detterman, D. K. (1979). Detterman's laws of individual differences research. In R. J. Sternberg & D. K. Detterman (Eds.), *Human intelligence* (pp. 165–175). Norwood, NJ: Ablex. (9)

Detterman, D. K., & Thompson, L. A. (1997). What is so special about special education? *American Psychologist, 52,* 1082–1090. (9)

Deutsch, J. A., & Gonzalez, M. F. (1980). Gastric nutrient content signals satiety. *Behavioral and Neural Biology, 30,* 113–116. (11)

DeValois, R. L., & Jacobs, G. H. (1968). Primate color vision. *Science, 162,* 533–540. (4)

Devane, W. A., Hanu£, L., Breuer, A., Pertwee, R. G., Stevenson, L. A., Griffin, G., Gibson, D., Mandelbaum, A., Etinger, A., & Mechoulam, R. (1992). Isolation and structure of a brain constituent that binds to the cannabinoid receptor. *Science, 258,* 1946–1949. (3, 5)

Devlin, B., Daniels, M., & Roeder, K. (1997). The heritability of IQ. *Nature, 388,* 468–471. (3, 9)

Devor, E. J., Abell, C. W., Hoffman, P. L., Tabakoff, B., & Cloninger, C. R. (1994). Platelet MAO activity in Type I and Type II alcoholism. *Annals of the New York Academy of Sciences, 708,* 119–128. (16)

Devor, M. (1996). Pain mechanisms. *The Neuroscientist, 2,* 233–244. (4)

de Waal, F. B. M. (2000). Primates—A natural heritage of conflict resolution. *Science, 289,* 586–590. (12)

Dewsbury, D. A. (1998). Celebrating E. L. Thorndike a century after *Animal Intelligence. American Psychologist, 53,* 1121–1124. (6)

Dewsbury, D. A. (2000a). Introduction: Snapshots of psychology circa 1900. *American Psychologist, 55,* 255–259. (1)

Dewsbury, D. A. (2000b). Issues in comparative psychology at the dawn of the 20th century. *American Psychologist, 55,* 750–753. (6)

Diamond, L. M. (2000). Sexual identity, attractions, and behavior among young sexual-minority women over a 2-year period. *Developmental Psychology, 36,* 241–250. (11)

Diener, E. (2000). Subjective well-being. *American Psychologist, 55,* 34–43. (12)

Diener, E., & Diener, C. (1996). Most people are happy. *Psychological Science, 7,* 181–185. (12)

Diener, E., Suh, E. M., Lucas, R. E., & Smith, H. L. (1999). Subjective well-being: Three decades of progress. *Psychological Bulletin, 125,* 276–302. (12)

DiLalla, D. L., Carey, G., Gottesman, I. I., & Bouchard, T. J., Jr. (1996). Heritability of MMPI personality indicators of psychopathology in twins reared apart. *Journal of Abnormal Psychology, 105,* 491–499. (3, 13)

Dimberg, U., Thunberg, M., & Elmehed, K. (2000). Unconscious facial reactions to emotional facial expressions. *Psychological Science, 11,* 86–89. (4)

diTomaso, E., Beltramo, M., & Piomelli, D. (1996). Brain cannabinoids in chocolate. *Nature, 382,* 677–678. (5)

Dixon, A., Ross, D., O'Malley, S. L. C., & Burke, T. (1994). Paternal investment inversely related to degree of extrapair paternity in the reed bunting. *Nature, 371,* 698–700. (3)

Dobelle, W. H. (2000). Artificial vision for the blind by connecting a television camera to the visual cortex. *ASAIO Journal, 46,* 3–9. (4)

Dobrzecka, C., Szwejkowska, G., & Konorski, J. (1966). Qualitative versus directional cues in two forms of differentiation. *Science, 153,* 87–89. (6)

Dole, V. P. (1980). Addictive behavior. *Scientific American, 243*(6), 138–154. (16)

Dollard, J., Miller, N. E., Doob, L. W., Mowrer, O. H., & Sears, R. R. (1939). *Frustration and aggression.* New Haven, CT: Yale University Press. (12)

Domhoff, G. W. (1996). *Finding meaning in dreams: A quantitative approach.* New York: Plenum. (5)

Domhoff, G. W. (1999). Drawing theoretical implications from descriptive empirical findings on dream content. *Dreaming, 9,* 201–210. (5)

Domhoff, G. W. (2000). The misinterpretation of dreams. *American Scientist, 88,* 175–178. (5)

Domhoff, G. W. (2001). A new neurocognitive theory of dreams. *Dreaming, 11,* 13–33. (5)

Donnerstein, E., & Malamuth, N. (1997). Pornography: Its consequences on the observer. In L. B. Schlesinger & E. Revitch (Eds.), *Sexual dynamics of anti-social behavior* (2nd ed., pp. 30–49). Springfield, IL: Charles C Thomas. (12)

Dovidio, J. F., & Gaertner, S. L. (1999). Reducing prejudice: Combating intergroup biases. *Current Directions in Psychological Science, 8,* 101–105. (14)

Dovidio, J. F., & Gaertner, S. L. (2000). Aversive racism and selection decisions: 1989 and 1999. *Psychological Science, 11,* 315–319. (14)

Dragoi, V., & Staddon, J. E. R. (1999). The dynamics of operant conditioning. *Psychological Review, 106,* 20–61. (6)

Dreger, A. D. (1998). *Hermaphrodites and the medical invention of sex.* Cambridge, MA: Harvard University Press. (11)

Drewnowski, A. (1996). The behavioral phenotype in human obesity. In E. D. Capaldi (Ed.), *Why we eat what we eat* (pp. 291–308). Washington, DC: American Psychological Association. (11)

Drewnowski, A., Henderson, S. A., Shore, A. B., & Barratt-Fornell, A. (1998). Sensory responses to 6-n-propylthiouracil (PROP) or sucrose solutions and food preferences in young women. *Annals of the New York Academy of Sciences, 855,* 797–801. (4)

Duke, M., & Nowicki, S., Jr. (1979). *Abnormal psychology: Perspectives on being different.* Monterey, CA: Brooks/Cole. (16)

Duman, R. S., Heninger, G. R., & Nestler, E. J. (1997). A molecular and cellular theory of depression. *Archives of General Psychiatry, 54,* 597–606. (16)

Duncan, J., Seitz, R. J., Kolodny, J., Bor, D., Herzog, H., Ahmed, A., Newell, F. N., & Emslie, H. (2000). A neural basis for general intelligence. *Science, 289,* 457–460. (9)

Duncan, J., Ward, R., & Shapiro, K. (1994). Direct measurement of attentional dwell time in human vision. *Nature, 369,* 313–315. (8)

Dunne, M. P., Martin, N. G., Statham, D. J., Slutske, W. S., Dinwiddie, S. H., Bucholz, K. K., Madden, P. A. F., & Heath, A. C. (1997). Genetic and environmental contributions to variance in age at first sexual intercourse. *Psychological Science, 8,* 211–216. (3)

Durgin, F. H. (2000). The reverse Stroop effect. *Psychonomic Bulletin & Review, 7,* 121–125. (8)

Durham, M. L. (1996). Civil commitment of the mentally ill: Research, policy, and practice. In B. D. Sales & S. A. Shah (Eds.), *Mental health and law* (pp. 17–40). Durham, NC: Carolina Academic Press. (15)

Dywan, J., & Bowers, K. (1983). The use of hypnosis to enhance recall. *Science, 22,* 184–185. (5)

Eagly, A. H., & Crowley, M. (1986). Gender and helping behavior: A meta-analytic review of the social psychological literature. *Psychological Bulletin, 100,* 283–308. (10)

Eagly, A. H., Karau, S. J., & Makhigani, M. G. (1995). Gender and the effectiveness of leaders: A meta-analysis. *Psychological Bulletin, 117,* 125–145. (11)

Eagly, A. H., Kulesa, P., Chen, S., & Chaiken, S. (2001). Do attitudes affect memory? Tests of the congeniality hypothesis. *Current Directions in Psychological Science, 10,* 5–9. (14)

Eagly, A. H., & Warren, R. (1976). Intelligence, comprehension, and opinion change. *Journal of Personality, 44,* 226–242. (14)

Eagly, A. H., & Wood, W. (1999). The origins of sex differences in human behavior. *American Psychologist, 54,* 408–423. (14)

Earnest, D. J., Liang, F.-Q., Ratcliff, M., & Cassone, V. M. (1999). Immortal time: Circadian clock properties of rat suprachiasmatic cell lines. *Science, 283,* 693–695. (5)

Eaton, W. O., & Saudino, K. J. (1992). Prenatal activity level as a temperament dimension? Individual differences and developmental functions in fetal movement. *Infant Behavior & Development 15,* 57–70. (10)

Eaton, W. W., Anthony, J. C., Gallo, J., Cai, G., Tien, A., Romanoski, A., Lyketsos, C., & Chen, L.-S. (1997). Natural history of diagnostic interview schedule/*DSM-IV* major depression. *Archives of General Psychiatry, 54,* 993–999. (16)

Ebbinghaus, H. (1913). *Memory.* New York: Teachers College Press. (Original work published 1885) (7)

Edelman, B. (1981). Binge eating in normal weight and overweight individuals. *Psychological Reports, 49,* 739–746. (11)

Edney, J. H. (1979). The nuts game: A concise commons dilemma analog. *Environmental Psychology and Nonverbal Behavior, 3,* 252–254. (14)

Educational Testing Service. (1994). *GRE 1994–95 guide.* Princeton, NJ: Author. (9)

Edwards, K. (1998). The face of time: Temporal cues in facial expressions of emotion. *Psychological Science, 9,* 270–276. (12)

Eibl-Eibesfeldt, I. (1973). *Der vorprogrammierte Mensch* [The preprogrammed human]. Vienna: Verlag Fritz Molden. (12)

Eibl-Eibesfeldt, I. (1974). *Love and hate.* New York: Schocken. (12)

Eich, E., & Macaulay, D. (2000). Are real moods required to reveal mood-congruent and mood-dependent memory? *Psychological Science, 11,* 244–248. (7)

Eich, E., Macaulay, D., Loewenstein, R. J., & Dihle, P. H. (1997). Memory, amnesia, and dissociative identity disorder. *Psychological Science, 8,* 417–422. (15)

Eimas, P. D., Siqueland, E. R., Jusczyk, P., & Vigorito, J. (1971). Speech perception in infants. *Science, 171,* 303–306. (10)

Einstein, G. O., & Hunt, R. R. (1980). Levels of processing and organization: Additive effects of individual item and relational processing. *Journal of Experimental Psychology: Human Learning and Memory, 6,* 588–598. (7)

Einstein, G. O., McDaniel, M. A., Smith, R. E., & Shaw, P. (1998). Habitual prospective memory and aging: Remembering intentions and forgetting actions. *Psychological Science, 9,* 284–288. (7)

Eisenberger, R., & Cameron, J. (1996). Detrimental effects of reward: Reality or myth? *American Psychologist, 51,* 1153–1166. (11)

Eisler, I., Dare, C., Hodes, M., Russell, G., Dodge, E., & LeGrange, D. (2000). Family therapy for adolescent anorexia nervosa: The results of a controlled comparison of two family interventions. *Journal of Child Psychology and Psychiatry and Allied Disciplines, 41,* 727–736. (15)

Ekman, P. (1992). Facial expressions of emotion: New findings, new questions. *Psychological Science, 3,* 34–38. (12)

Ekman, P. (1994). Strong evidence for universals in facial expressions: A reply to Russell's mistaken critique. *Psychological Science, 3,* 34–38. (12)

Ekman, P., & Davidson, R. J. (1993). Voluntary smiling changes regional brain activity. *Psychological Science, 4,* 342–345. (12)

Ekman, P., & Friesen, W. V. (1984). *Unmasking the face* (2nd ed.). Palo Alto, CA: Consulting Psychologists Press. (12)

El-Islam, M. F. (1982). Rehabilitation of schizophrenics by the extended family. *Acta Psychiatrica Scandinavica, 65,* 112–119. (16)

Elbert, T., Pantev, C., Wienbruch, C., Rockstroh, B., & Taub, E. (1995). Increased cortical representation of the fingers of the left hand in string players. *Science, 270,* 305–307. (3)

Elicker, J., Englund, M., & Sroufe, L. A. (1992). Predicting peer competence and peer relationships in childhood from early parent-child relationships. In R. D. Parke & G. W. Ladd (Eds.), *Family-peer relationships* (pp. 77–106). Hillsdale, NJ: Erlbaum. (10)

Elkind, D. (1984). *All grown up and no place to go.* Reading, MA: Addison-Wesley. (10)

Ellenberger, H. F. (1972). The story of "Anna O": A critical review with new data. *Journal of the History of the Behavioral Sciences, 8,* 267–279. (13)

Elliott, C. (1997). Caring about risks: Are severely depressed patients competent to consent to research? *Archives of General Psychiatry, 54,* 113–116. (2)

Ellis, A. (1987). The impossibility of achieving consistently good mental health. *American Psychologist, 42,* 364–375. (15)

Ellis, A., & Harper, R. A. (1961). *A guide to rational living.* Upper Saddle River, NJ: Prentice Hall. (15)

Ellis, N. C., & Hennelley, R. A. (1980). A bilingual word-length effect: Implications for intelligence testing and the relative ease of mental calculation in Welsh and English. *British Journal of Psychology, 71,* 43–52. (7)

Ellsworth, P. C. (1994). William James and emotion: Is a century of fame worth a century of misunderstanding? *Psychological Review, 101,* 222–229. (12)

Ellsworth, P. C., & Gross, S. R. (1994). Hardening of the attitudes: Americans' views on the death penalty. *Journal of Social Issues, 50*(2), 19–52. (14)

Ellsworth, P. C., & Ross, L. (1983, January). Public opinion and capital punishment: A close examination of the views of abolitionists and retentionists. *Crime & Delinquency, 29,* 116–169. (14)

Emery, C. E., Jr. (1997, November/December). UFO survey yields conflicting conclusions. *Skeptical Inquirer, 21,* 9. (2)

Emmons, R. A. (1991). Personal strivings, daily life events, and psychological and physical well-being. *Journal of Personality, 59,* 453–472. (13)

Engel, S. A. (1999). Using neuroimaging to measure mental representations: Finding color-opponent neurons in visual cortex. *Current Directions in Psychological Science, 8,* 23–27. (4)

Engle, R. W., Tuholski, S. W., Laughlin, J. E., & Conway, A. R. A. (1999). Working memory, short-term memory, and general fluid intelligence: A latent-variable approach. *Journal of Experimental Psychology: General, 128,* 309–331. (7)

Erel, O., & Burman, B. (1995). Interrelatedness of marital relations and parent-child relations: A meta-analytic review. *Psychological Bulletin, 118,* 108–132. (10)

Erel, O., Oberman, Y., & Yirmiya, N. (2000). Maternal versus nonmaternal care and seven domains of children's development. *Psychological Bulletin, 126,* 727–747. (10)

Erev, I., Wallsten, T. S., & Budescu, D. V. (1994). Simultaneous over- and underconfidence: The role of error in judgment processes. *Psychological Review, 101,* 519–527. (8)

Ericsson, K. A., & Charness, N. (1994). Expert performance: Its structure and acquisition. *American Psychologist, 49,* 725–747. (8)

Ericsson, K. A., Chase, W. G., & Faloon, S. (1980). Acquisition of a memory skill. *Science, 208,* 1181–1182. (7)

Ericsson, K. A., Krampe, R. T., & Tesch-Römer, C. (1993). The role of deliberate practice in the acquisition of expert performance. *Psychological Review, 100,* 363–406. (8)

Erikson, E. H. (1963). *Childhood and society* (2nd ed.). New York: Norton. (10)

Eriksson, P. S., Perfilieva, E., Björk-Eriksson, T., Alborn, A.-M., Nordborg, C., Peterson, D. A., & Gage, F. H. (1998). Neurogenesis in the adult human hippocampus. *Nature Medicine, 4,* 1313–1317. (3)

Ernhart, C. B., Sokol, R. J., Martier, S., Moron, P., Nadler, D., Ager, J. W., & Wolf, A. (1987). Alcohol teratogenicity in the human: A detailed assessment of specificity, critical period, and threshold. *American Journal of Obstetrics and Gynecology, 156,* 33–39. (10)

Ernst, C., & Angst, J. (1983). *Birth order: Its influence on personality.* New York: Springer-Verlag. (10)

Eronen, M., Hakola, P., & Tiihonen, J. (1996). Mental disorders and homicidal behavior in Finland. *Archives of General Psychiatry, 53,* 497–501. (12)

Essock, S. M., Frisman, L. K., Covell, N. H., & Hargreaves, W. A. (2000). Cost-effectiveness of clozapine compared with conventional antipsychotic medication for patients in state hospitals. *Archives of General Psychiatry, 57,* 987–994. (16)

Esterson, A. (1993). *Seductive mirage.* Chicago: Open Court. (5)

Esterson, A. (1998). Jeffrey Masson and Freud's seduction theory: A new fable based on old myths. *History of the Human Sciences, 11,* 1–21. (13)

Etcoff, N. L., Ekman, P., Magee, J. J., & Frank, M. G. (2000). Lie detection and language comprehension. *Nature, 405,* 139. (3)

Evans, G. W., Bullinger, M., & Hygge, S. (1998). Chronic noise exposure and physiological response: A prospective study of children living under environmental stress. *Psychological Science, 9,* 75–77. (12)

Everson, C. A. (1995). Functional consequences of sustained sleep deprivation in the rat. *Behavioural Brain Research, 69,* 43–54. (5)

Exner, J. E., Jr. (1986). *The Rorschach: A comprehensive system* (2nd ed.). New York: Wiley. (13)

Eysenck, H. J. (1952). The effects of psychotherapy: An evaluation. *Journal of Consulting Psychology, 16,* 319–324. (15)

Eysenck, H. J. (1992). Four ways five factors are not basic. *Personality and Individual Differences, 13,* 667–673. (13)

Faedda, G. L., Tondo, L., Teicher, M. H., Baldessarini, R. J., Gelbard, H. A., & Floris, G. F. (1993). Seasonal mood disorders: patterns of seasonal recurrence in mania and depression. *Archives of General Psychiatry, 50,* 17–23. (16)

Fairburn, C. G., Welch, S. L., Doll, H. A., Davies, B. A., & O'Connor, M. E. (1997). Risk factors for bulimia nervosa. *Archives of General Psychiatry, 54,* 509–517. (11)

Falk, J. R., Halmi, K. A., & Tryon, W. W. (1985). Activity measures in anorexia nervosa. *Archives of General Psychiatry, 42,* 811–814. (11)

Fallon, A. E., & Rozin, P. (1985). Sex differences in perceptions of desirable body shape. *Journal of Abnormal Psychology, 94,* 102–105. (11)

Fantz, R. L. (1963). Pattern vision in newborn infants. *Science, 140,* 296–297. (10)

Farah, M. J. (1992). Is an object an object an object? Cognitive and neuropsychological investigations of domain specificity in visual object recognition. *Current Directions in Psychological Science, 1,* 164–169. (4)

Farah, M. J., Wilson, K. D., Drain, M., & Tanaka, J. N. (1998). What is "special" about face perception? *Psychological Review, 105,* 482–498. (3)

Faraone, S. V., & Biederman, J. (1998). Neurobiology of attention-deficit hyperactivity disorder. *Biological Psychiatry, 44,* 951–958. (3)

Faraone, S. V., Kremen, W. S., & Tsuang, M. T. (1990). Genetic transmission of major affective disorders: Quantitative models and linkage analyses. *Psychological Bulletin, 108,* 109–127. (16)

Farber, S. L. (1981). *Identical twins reared apart: A reanalysis.* New York: Basic Books. (9)

Farberman, R. K. (1997). Terminal illness and hastened death requests: The important role of the mental health professional. *Professional Psychology: Research and Practice, 28,* 544–547. (16)

Farmer, H. (1983). Career and homemaking plans for high school youth. *Journal of Counseling Psychology, 30,* 40–45. (11)

Farmer, H. S. (1987). Female motivation and achievement: Implications for interventions. *Advances in Motivation and Achievement, 5,* 51–97. (11)

Farmer, H., & Bohn, M. (1970). Home-career conflict reduction and the level of career interest in women. *Journal of Counseling Psychology, 17,* 228–232. (11)

Farmer-Dougan, V. (1998). A disequilibrium analysis of incidental teaching. *Behavior Modification, 22,* 78–95. (6)

Faust, M., Kravetz, S., & Babkoff, H. (1993). Hemispheric specialization or reading habits: Evidence from lexical decision research with Hebrew words and sentences. *Brain and Language, 44,* 254–263. (8)

Fawzy, F. I., Fawzy, N. W., Arndt, L. A., & Pasnau, R. O. (1995). Critical review of psychosocial interventions in cancer care. *Archives of General Psychiatry, 52,* 100–113. (12)

Fay, R. E., Turner, C. F., Klassen, A. D., & Gagnon, J. H. (1989). Prevalence and patterns of same-gender sexual contact among men. *Science, 243,* 338–348. (11)

Feeney, D. M. (1987). Human rights and animal welfare. *American Psychologist, 42,* 593–599. (2)

Fehrenbach, P. A., & Thelen, M. H. (1982). Behavioral approaches to the treatment of aggressive disorders. *Behavior Modification, 6,* 465–497. (12)

Feighner, J. P., Gardner, E. A., Johnston, J. A., Batey, S. R., Khayrallah, M. A., Ascher, J. A., & Lineberry, C. G. (1991). Double-blind comparison of buproprion and fluoxetine in depressed outpatients. *Journal of Clinical Psychiatry, 52,* 329–335. (16)

Feingold, A., & Mazzella, R. (1998). Gender differences in body image are increasing. *Psychological Science, 9,* 190–195. (11)

Felson, R. B. (1996). Mass media effects on violent behavior. *Annual Review of Sociology, 22,* 103–128. (2)

Felthous, A. R. (1993). Substance abuse and the duty to protect. *Bulletin of the American Academy of Psychiatry and the Law, 21,* 419–426. (15)

Fenton, W. S., Mosher, L. R., Herrell, J. M., & Blyler, C. R. (1998). Randomized trial of general hospital and residential alternative care for patients with severe and persistent mental illness. *American Journal of Psychiatry, 155,* 516–522. (15)

Ferguson, C. P., & Pigott, T. A. (2000). Anorexia and bulimia nervosa: Neurobiology and pharmacotherapy. *Behavior Therapy, 31,* 237–263. (11)

Ferguson, E., & Cassaday, H. J. (1999). The Gulf War and illness by association. *British Journal of Psychology, 90,* 459–475. (14)

Fergusson, D. M., Woodward, L. J., & Horwood, J. (1998). Maternal smoking during pregnancy and psychiatric adjustment in late adolescence. *Archives of General Psychiatry, 55,* 721–727. (12)

Fernald, D. (1984). *The Hans legacy: A story of science.* Hillsdale, NJ: Erlbaum. (2)

Fernández-Dols, J. M., & Ruiz-Belda, M. -A. (1997). Spontaneous facial behavior during intense emotional episodes: Artistic truth and optical truth. In J. A. Russell & J. M. Fernández-Dols (Eds.), *The psychology of facial expression* (pp. 255–274). Cambridge, England: Cambridge University Press. (12)

Fernandez, E., & Turk, D. C. (1992). Sensory and affective components of pain: Separation and synthesis. *Psychological Bulletin, 112,* 205–217. (4)

Fernandes, M. A., & Moscovitch, M. (2000). Divided attention and memory: Evidence of substantial interference effects at retrieval and encoding. *Journal of Experimental Psychology: General, 129,* 155–176. (7)

Festinger, L. (1957). *A theory of cognitive dissonance.* Stanford, CA: Stanford University Press. (14)

Festinger, L., & Carlsmith, J. M. (1959). Cognitive consequences of forced compliance. *Journal of Abnormal and Social Psychology, 58,* 203–210. (14)

Fichter, M. M., & Quadflieg, N. (1997). Six-year course of bulimia nervosa. *International Journal of Eating Disorders, 22,* 361–384. (11)

Fieve, R. R. (1975). *Moodswing.* New York: Morrow. (16)

Finch, J. F., & Cialdini, R. B. (1989). Another indirect tactic of (self-) image imagement: Boosting. *Personality and Social Psychology Bulletin, 15,* 222–232. (14)

Fine, M. A., & Schwebel, A. I. (1987). An emergent explanation of differing racial reactions to single parenthood. *Journal of Divorce, 11,* 1–15. (10)

Fink, M. (2000). Electroshock revisited. *American Scientist, 88,* 162–167. (16)

Fischhoff, B. (1975). Hindsight ≠ foresight: The effect of outcome knowledge on judgment under uncertainty. *Journal of Experimental Psychology: Human Perception and Performance, 1,* 288–299. (7)

Fischhoff, B. (1992). Giving advice: Decision theory perspectives on sexual assault. *American Psychologist, 47,* 577–588. (12)

Fisher, S., & Greenberg, R. P. (1977). *The scientific credibility of Freud's theories and therapy.* New York: Basic Books. (13)

Fisher, S. E., Vargha-Khadem, F., Watkins, K. E., Monaco, A. P., & Pembrey, M. E. (1998). Localisation of a gene implicated in a severe speech and language disorder. *Nature Genetics, 18,* 168–170. (8)

Fitzgerald, R., & Ellsworth, P. C. (1984). Due process vs. crime control: Death qualification and jury attitudes. *Law and Human Behavior, 8,* 31–51. (14)

Flatz, G. (1987). Genetics of lactose digestion in humans. *Advances in Human Genetics, 16,* 1–77. (3)

Flavell, J. (1986). The development of children's knowledge about the appearance-reality distinction. *American Psychologist, 41,* 418–425. (10)

Fletcher, R., & Voke, J. (1985). *Defective colour vision.* Bristol, England: Hilger. (4)

Flett, G. L., Vredenburg, K., & Krames, L. (1997). The continuity of depression in clinical and nonclinical samples. *Psychological Bulletin, 121,* 395–416. (16)

Fligstein, D., Barabasz, A., Barabasz, M., Trevisan, M. S., & Warner, D. (1998). Hypnosis enhances recall memory: A test of forced and non-forced conditions. *American Journal of Clinical Hypnosis, 40,* 297–305. (5)

Flor, H., Elbert, T., Knecht, S., Wienbruch, C., Pantev, C., Birbaumer, N., Larbig, W., & Taub, E. (1995). Phantom-limb pain as a perceptual correlate of cortical reorganization following arm amputation. *Nature, 375,* 482–484. (4)

Flynn, J. R. (1984). The mean IQ of Americans: Massive gains 1932 to 1978. *Psychological Bulletin, 95,* 29–51. (9)

Flynn, J. R. (1987). Massive IQ gains in 14 nations: What IQ tests really measure. *Psychological Bulletin, 101,* 171–191. (9)

Flynn, J. R. (1998). IQ gains over time: Toward finding the causes. In U. Neisser (Ed.), *The rising curve* (pp. 25–66). Washington, DC: American Psychological Association. (9)

Flynn, J. R. (1999). Searching for justice: The discovery of IQ gains over time. *American Psychologist, 54*, 5–20. (9)

Fodor, J. (1998). When is a dog a DOG? *Nature, 396*, 325–327. (8)

Foley, V. D. (1984). Family therapy. In R. J. Corini (Ed.), *Current psychotherapies* (3rd ed., pp. 447–490). Itasca, IL: F. E. Peacock. (15)

Folkman, S., & Moskowitz, J. T. (2000). Positive affect and the other side of coping. *American Psychologist, 55*, 647–654. (12)

Forer, B. R. (1949). The fallacy of personal validation: A classroom demonstration of gullibility. *Journal of Abnormal and Social Psychology, 44*, 118–123. (13)

Foster, W. Z. (1968). *History of the Communist party of the United States.* New York: Greenwood Press. (16)

Foulkes, D. (1999). *Children's dreaming and the development of consciousness.* Cambridge, MA: Harvard University Press. (5)

Fox, B. H. (1983). Current theory of psychogenic effects on cancer incidence and prognosis. *Journal of Psychosocial Oncology, 1*, 17–31. (12)

Francis, L. J., Brown, L. B., Lester, D., & Philipchalk, R. (1998). Happiness as stable extraversion: A cross-cultural examination of the reliability and validity of the Oxford Happiness Inventory among students in the U.K., U.S.A., Australia, and Canada. *Personality and Individual Differences, 24*, 167–171. (13)

Francis, W. S. (1999). Cognitive integration of language and memory in bilinguals: Semantic representation. *Psychological Bulletin, 125*, 193–222. (8)

Frank, M. G., & Stennett, J. (2000). The forced-choice paradigm and the perception of facial expressions of emotion. *Journal of Personality and Social Psychology, 80*, 75–85. (12)

Franken, I. H. A., Kroon, L. Y., Wiers, R. W., & Jansen, A. (2000). Selective cognitive processing of drug cues in heroin dependence. *Journal of Psychopharmacology, 14*, 395–400. (13)

Franz, E. A., Waldie, K. E., & Smith, M. J. (2000). The effect of callosotomy on novel versus familiar bimanual actions: A neural dissociation between controlled and automatic processes? *Psychological Science, 11*, 82–85. (3)

Freedland, R. L., & Bertenthal, B. I. (1994). Developmental changes in interlimb coordination: Transition to hands-and-knees crawling. *Psychological Science, 5*, 26–32. (10)

Freedman, J. L., & Fraser, S. C. (1966). Compliance without pressure: The foot in the door technique. *Journal of Personality and Social Psychology, 4*, 195–202. (14)

French, A. R. (1988). The patterns of mammalian hibernation. *American Scientist, 76*, 568–575. (5)

Freud, S. (1925). An autobiographical study. In J. Strachey, A. Freud, A. Strachey, & A. Tyson (Eds.), *The standard edition of the complete psychological works of Sigmund Freud* (Vol. XX, pp. 7–70). London: Hogarth Press and the Institute of Psycho-Analysis. (13)

Freud, S. (1925). *Three contributions to the theory of sex* (A. A. Brill, Trans.). New York: Nervous and Mental Disease Publishing (Original work published 1905) (13)

Freud, S. (1961). *The future of an illusion* (J. Strachey, Trans.). New York: Norton. (Original work published 1927) (13)

Freud, S. (1955). The interpretation of dreams (J. Strachey, Trans.). New York: Basic Books. (Original work published 1900) (5)

Freud, S. (1963). *Dora: An analysis of a case of hysteria.* New York: Collier Books. (Original work published 1905) (13)

Friedman, J. M. (2000). Obesity in the new millennium. *Nature, 404*, 632–634. (11)

Friedman, M., & Rosenman, R. H. (1974). *Type-A behavior and your heart.* New York: Knopf. (12)

Friedman, M. A., & Brownell, K. D. (1996). A comprehensive treatment manual for the management of obesity. In V. B. Van Hasselt & M. Hersen (Eds.), *Sourcebook of psychological treatment manuals for adult disorders* (pp. 375–422). New York: Plenum. (11)

Friedman, W. J., & Huttenlocher, J. (1997). Memory for the time of "60 minutes" stories and news events. *Journal of Experimental Psychology: Learning, Memory, and Cognition, 23*, 560–569. (7)

Frijda, N. H. (1988). The laws of emotion. *American Psychologist, 45*, 349–358. (12)

Fry, A. F., & Hale, S. (1996). Processing speed, working memory, and fluid intelligence: Evidence for a developmental cascade. *Psychological Science, 7*, 237–241. (9)

Fuligni, A. J. (1998). The adjustment of children from immigrant families. *Current Directions in Psychological Science, 7*, 99–103. (10)

Fuller, R. K., & Roth, H. P. (1979). Disulfiram for the treatment of alcoholism: An evaluation in 128 men. *Annals of Internal Medicine, 90*, 901–904. (16)

Furukawa, T. (1997). Cultural distance and its relationship to psychological adjustment of international exchange students. *Psychiatry and Clinical Neurosciences, 51*, 87–91. (11)

Gabrieli, J. D. E., Cohen, N. J., & Corkin, S. (1988). The impaired learning of semantic knowledge following bilateral medial temporal-lobe resection. *Brain and Cognition, 7*, 157–177. (7)

Galef, B. G., Jr. (1998). Edward Thorndike: Revolutionary psychologist, ambiguous biologist. *American Psychologist, 53*, 1128–1134. (6)

Gallistel, C. R., & Gibbon, J. (2000). Time, rate, and conditioning. *Psychological Review, 107*, 289–344. (6)

Galton, F. (1978). *Hereditary genius.* New York: St. Martin's Press. (Original work published 1869) (1, 9)

Galuske, R. A. W., Schlote, W., Bratzke, H., & Singer, W. (2000). Interhemispheric asymmetries of the modular structure in human temporal cortex. *Science, 289*, 1946–1949. (3)

Gangestad, S. W. (2000). Human sexual selection, good genes, and special design. *Annals of the New York Academy of Sciences, 907*, 50–61. (14)

Garb, H. N., Florio, C. M., & Grove, W. M. (1998). The validity of the Rorschach and the Minnesota Multiphasic Personality Inventory: Results from meta-analyses. *Psychological Science, 9*, 402–404. (13)

Garcia, J. (1990). Learning without memory. *Journal of Cognitive Neuroscience, 2*, 287–305. (6)

Garcia, J., Ervin, F. R., & Koelling, R. A. (1966). Learning with prolonged delay of reinforcement. *Psychonomic Science, 5*, 121–122. (6)

Garcia, J., & Koelling, R. A. (1966). Relation of cue to consequence in avoidance learning. *Psychonomic Science, 4*, 123–124. (6)

Garcia-Andrade, C., Wall, T. L., & Ehlers, C. L. (1997). The fire-water myth and response to alcohol in Mission Indians. *American Journal of Psychiatry, 154*, 983–988. (5)

Garcia Coll, C. T. (1990). Developmental outcome of minority infants: A process-oriented look into our beginnings. *Child Development, 61*, 270–289. (10)

Gardner, H. (1985). *Frames of mind.* New York: Basic Books. (9)

Gardner, H. (1993). *Creating minds.* New York: Basic Books. (8)

Gardner, H. (1995). Why would anyone become an expert? *American Psychologist, 50*, 802–803. (8)

Gardner, M. (1978). Mathematical games. *Scientific American, 239*(5), 22–32. (8)

Gardner, M. (1994). Notes of a fringe watcher: The tragedies of false memories. *Skeptical Inquirer, 18*, 464–470. (7)

Gardner, R. A., & Gardner, B. T. (1969). Teaching sign language to a chimpanzee. *Science, 165*, 664–672. (8)

Gawin, F. H. (1991). Cocaine addiction: Psychology and neuro-physiology. *Science, 251*, 1580–1586. (5)

Geary, D. C. (2000). Evolution and proximate expression of human paternal investment. *Psychological Bulletin, 126*, 55–77. (14)

Gellhorn, E. (1970). The emotions and the ergotropic and trophotropic systems. *Psychologische Forschung, 34*, 48–94. (12)

Gelman, R. (1982). Accessing one-to-one correspondence: Still another paper about conservation. *British Journal of Psychology, 73*, 209–220. (10)

George, M. S., Wasserman, E. M., Kimbrell, T. A., Little, J. T., Williams, W. E., Danielson, A. L., Greenberg, B. D., Hallett, M., & Post, R. M. (1997). Mood improvement following daily left prefrontal repetitive transcranial magnetic stimulation in patients with depression: A placebo-controlled crossover trial. *American Journal of Psychiatry, 154*, 1752–1756. (16)

Geschwind, N. (1970). The organization of language and the brain. *Science, 170*, 940–944. (3)

Geschwind, N. (1979). Specializations of the human brain. In *Scientific American* (Ed.), *The brain: A Scientific American book.* San Francisco: W. H. Freeman. (3, 8)

Gibson, J. J. (1968). What gives rise to the perception of movement? *Psychological Review, 75*, 335–346. (4)

Gick, M. L., & Holyoak, K. J. (1980). Analogical problem solving. *Cognitive Psychology, 12*, 306–355. (8)

Gick, M. L., & Holyoak, K. J. (1983). Schema induction and analogical transfer. *Cognitive Psychology, 15*, 1–38. (8)

Giebel, H. D. (1958). Visuelles Lernvermögen bei Einhufern [Visual learning capacity in hoofed animals]. *Zoologische Jahrbücher Abteilung für Allgemeine Zoologie, 67*, 487–520. (1)

Gilbreth, F. B. (1911). *Motion study.* London: Constable. (11)

Gillham, J. E., Reivich, K. J., Jaycox, L. H., & Seligman, M. E. P. (1995). Prevention of depressive symptoms in schoolchildren: Two year follow-up. *Psychological Science, 6*, 343–351. (15)

Gilligan, C. (1977). In a different voice: Women's conceptions of self and morality. *Harvard Educational Review, 47*, 481–517. (10)

Gilligan, C. (1979). Woman's place in man's life cycle. *Harvard Educational Review, 49*, 431–446. (10)

Giros, B., Jaber, M., Jones, S. R., Wightman, R. M., & Caron, M. G. (1996). Hyperlocomotion and indifference to cocaine and amphetamine in mice lacking the dopamine transporter. *Nature, 379*, 606–612. (3, 5)

Glantz, L. A., & Lewis, D. A. (1997). Reduction of synaptophysin immunoreactivity in the prefrontal cortex of subjects with schizophrenia. *Archives of General Psychiatry, 54*, 660–669. (16)

Glantz, L. A., & Lewis, D. A. (2000). Decreased dendritic spine density on prefrontal cortical pyramidal neurons in schizophrenia. *Archives of General Psychiatry, 57*, 65–73. (16)

Gleaves, D. H. (1996). The sociocognitive model of dissociative identity disorder: A reexamination of the evidence. *Psychological Bulletin, 120*, 42–59. (15)

Gobet, F., & Simon, H. A. (1996). The roles of recognition processes and look-ahead search in time-constrained expert problem solving. *Psychological Science, 7*, 52–55. (8)

Goldfield, G. S., Kalakanis, L. E., Ernst, M. M., & Epstein, L. H. (2000). Open-loop feedback to increase physical activity in obese children. *International Journal of Obesity, 24*, 888–892. (6)

Goldfried, M. R., & Wolfe, B. E. (1996). Psychotherapy practice and research: Repairing a strained alliance. *American Psychologist, 51*, 1007–1016. (15)

Goldin-Meadow, S. (1997). When gestures and words speak differently. *Current Directions in Psychological Science, 6*, 138–143. (10)

Goldin-Meadow, S., McNeill, D., & Singleton, J. (1996). Silence is liberating: Removing the handcuffs on grammatical expression in the manual modality. *Psychological Review, 103*, 34–55. (8)

Goldin-Meadow, S., & Mylander, C. (1998). Spontaneous sign systems created by deaf children in two cultures. *Nature, 391*, 279–281. (8)

Goldstein, A. (1980). Thrills in response to music and other stimuli. *Physiological Psychology, 8*, 126–129. (4)

Goldstein, E. B. (1989). *Sensation and perception* (3rd ed.). Belmont, CA: Wadsworth. (4)

Goldstein, M. D., Hopkins, J. R., & Strube, M. J. (1994). "The eye of the beholder": A classroom demonstration of observer bias. *Teaching of Psychology, 21*, 154–157. (2)

Goldston, S. E. (1986). Primary prevention. *American Psychologist, 41*, 453–460. (15)

Goodall, J. (1971). *In the shadow of man.* Boston: Houghton Mifflin. (2)

Goodenough, O. R., & Dawkins, R. (1994). The 'St Jude' mind virus. *Nature, 371*, 23–24. (14)

Goodwin, C. J. (1991). Misportraying Pavlov's apparatus. *American Journal of Psychology, 104*, 135–141. (6)

Gorman, J. M., Kent, J., Martinez, J., Browne, S., Coplan, J., & Papp, L. A. (2001). Physiological changes during carbon dioxide inhalation in patients with panic disorder, major depression, and premenstrual dysphoric disorder. *Archives of General Psychiatry, 58*, 125–131. (16)

Gottesman, I. I. (1991). *Schizophrenia genesis.* New York: W. H. Freeman. (16)

Gottlieb, G. (2000). Environmental and behavioral influences on gene activity. *Current Directions in Psychological Science, 9*, 93–97. (3)

Gottman, J. M. (1999). *The marriage clinic.* New York: Norton. (14)

Graf, P., & Mandler, G. (1984). Activation makes words more accessible, but not necessarily more retrievable. *Journal of Verbal Learning and Verbal Behavior, 23*, 553–568. (7)

Green, D. M., & Swets, J. A. (1966). *Signal detection theory and psychophysics.* New York: Wiley. (4)

Green, L., Myerson, J., & Ostraszewski, P. (1999). Discounting of delayed rewards across the life span: Age differences in individual discounting functions. *Behavioural Processes, 46,* 89–96. (6)

Greenfield, P. M. (1997). You can't take it with you: Why ability assessments don't cross cultures. *American Psychologist, 52,* 1115–1124. (9)

Greenhoot, A. F., Ornstein, P. A., Gordon, B. N., & Baker-Ward, L. (1999). Acting out the details of a pediatric check-up: The impact of interview condition and behavioral style on children's memory reports. *Child Development, 70,* 363–380. (7)

Greeno, C. G., & Wing, R. R. (1994). Stress-induced eating. *Psychological Bulletin, 115,* 444–464. (11)

Greenough, W. T. (1975). Experiential modification of the developing brain. *American Scientist, 63,* 37–46. (3)

Greenwald, A. G., & Banaji, M. R. (1995). Implicit social cognition: Attitudes, self-esteem, and stereotypes. *Psychological Review, 102,* 4–27. (14)

Greenwald, A. G., & Draine, S. C. (1997). Do subliminal stimuli enter the brain unnoticed? Tests with a new method. In J. D. Cohen & J. W. Schooler (Eds.), *Scientific approaches to consciousness* (pp. 83–108). Mahwah, NJ: Erlbaum. (4)

Greenwald, A. G., Spangenberg, E. R., Pratkanis, A. R., & Eskanazi, J. (1991). Double-blind tests of subliminal self-help audiotapes. *Psychological Science, 2,* 119–122. (4)

Greist, J. H., Jefferson, J. W., Kobak, K. A., Katzelnick, D. J., & Serlin, R. C. (1995). Efficacy and tolerability of serotonin transport inhibitors in obsessive-compulsive disorder. *Archives of General Psychiatry, 52,* 53–60. (16)

Griffiths, M., & Wood, R. T. A. (2000). Risk factors in adolescence: The case of gambling, videogame playing, and the Internet. *Journal of Gambling Studies, 16,* 199–225. (16)

Griffiths, P. E. (1997). *What emotions really are.* Chicago: University of Chicago Press. (12)

Grigorenko, E. L., & Sternberg, R. J. (1998). Dynamic testing. *Psychological Bulletin, 124,* 75–111. (9)

Grissmer, D. W., Williamson, S., Kirby, S. N., & Berends, M. (1998). Exploring the rapid rise in the Black achievement scores in the United States (1970-1990). In U. Neisser (Ed.), *The rising curve* (pp. 251–285). Washington, DC: American Psychological Association. (9)

Grisso, T., & Tomkins, A. J. (1996). Communicating violence risk assessments. *American Psychologist, 51,* 928–930. (12)

Grünbaum, A. (1986). Précis of The Foundations of Psychoanalysis: A philosophical critique. *Behavioral and Brain Sciences, 9,* 217–284. (13)

Gross, J. J., & Levenson, R. W. (1993). Emotional suppression: Physiology, self-report, and expressive behavior. *Journal of Personality and Social Psychology, 64,* 970–986. (12)

Guilleminault, C., Heinzer, R., Mignot, E., & Black, J. (1998). Investigations into the neurologic basis of narcolepsy. *Neurology, 50*(Suppl. 1), S8–S15. (5)

Gunthert, K. C., Cohen, L. H., & Armeli, S. (1999). The role of neuroticism in daily stress and coping. *Journal of Personality and Social Psychology, 77,* 1087–1100. (13)

Gur, R. E., Cowell, P. E., Latshaw, A., Turetsky, B. I., Grossman, R. I., Arnold, S. E., Bilker, W. B., & Gur, R. C. (2000). Reduced dorsal and orbital prefrontal gray matter volumes in schizophrenia. *Archives of General Psychiatry, 57,* 761–768. (16)

Gusterson, H. (1992, May/June). Coming of age in a weapons lab. *The Sciences, 32,* 16–22. (10)

Gynther, M. D. (1989). MMPI comparisons of Blacks and Whites: A review and commentary. *Journal of Clinical Psychology, 45,* 878–883. (13)

Haarmeier, T., Thier, P., Repnow, M., & Petersen, D. (1997). False perception of motion in a patient who cannot compensate for eye movements. *Nature, 389,* 849–852. (4)

Habermas, T., & Bluck, S. (2000). Getting a life: The emergence of the life story in adolescence. *Psychological Bulletin, 126,* 748–769. (10)

Hackman, J. R., & Lawler, E. E., III (1971). Employee reactions to job characteristics. *Journal of Applied Psychology, 55,* 259–286. (11)

Häfner, H., an der Heiden, W., Behrens, S., Gattaz, W. F., Hambrecht, M., Löffler, W., Maurer, K., Munk-Jørgensen, P., Nowotny, B., Riecher-Rössler, A., & Stein, A. (1998). Causes and consequences of the gender difference in age of onset of schizophrenia. *Schizophrenia Bulletin, 24,* 99–113. (16)

Hagenzieker, M. P., Bijleveld, F. D., & Davidse, R. J. (1997). Effects of incentive programs to stimulate safety belt use: A meta-analysis. *Accident Analysis and Prevention, 29,* 759–777. (6)

Halberstadt, J., & Rhodes, G. (2000). The attractiveness of non-face averages: Implications for an evolutionary explanation of the attractiveness of average faces. *Psychological Science, 11,* 285–289. (14)

Hale, S., Myerson, J., Rhee, S. H., Weiss, C. S., & Abrams, R. A. (1996). Selective interference with the maintenance of location information in working memory. *Neuropsychology, 10,* 228–240. (7)

Hall, C. S., & Van de Castle, R. L. (1966). *The content analysis of dreams.* New York: Appleton-Century-Crofts. (5)

Hall, L. J., & McGregor, J. A. (2000). A follow-up study of the peer relationships of children with disabilities in an inclusive school. *Journal of Special Education, 34,* 114–126. (9)

Halmi, K. A., Sunday, S. R., Strober, M., Kaplan, A., Woodside, D. B., Fichter, M., Treasure, J., Berrettini, W. H., & Kaye, W. H. (2000). Perfectionism in anorexia nervosa: Variation by clinical subtype, obsessionality, and pathological eating behavior. *American Journal of Psychiatry, 157,* 1799–1805. (11)

Halpern, D. F. (1997). Sex differences in intelligence. *American Psychologist, 52,* 1091–1102. (9)

Hamann, S. B., & Squire, L. R. (1997). Intact perceptual memory in the absence of conscious memory. *Behavioral Neuroscience, 111,* 850–854. (7)

Hamm, J. V. (2000). Do birds of a feather flock together? The variable bases for African American, Asian American, and European American adolescents' selection of similar friends. *Developmental Psychology, 36,* 209–219. (14)

Hannah, B. (1976). *Jung: His life and work.* New York: Putnam's. (13)

Hanson, R. K. (2000). Will they do it again? Predicting sex-offense recidivism. *Current Directions in Psychological Science, 9,* 106–109. (12)

Harada, S., Agarwal, D. P. Goedde, H. W., Tagaki, S., & Ishikawa, B. (1982). Possible protective role against alcoholism for aldehyde dehydrogenase isozyme deficiency in Japan. *Lancet, ii,* 827. (16)

Hardin, G. (1968). The tragedy of the commons. *Science, 162,* 1243–1248. (14)

Harding, C. M., Brooks, G. W., Ashikaga, T., Straus, J. S., & Breier, A. (1987). The Vermont longitudinal study of persons with severe mental illness. II: Long-term outcome of subjects who retrospectively met *DSM-III* criteria for schizophrenia. *American Journal of Psychiatry, 144,* 727–735. (16)

Harker, L. A., & Keltner, D. (2001). Expressions of positive emotion in women's college yearbook pictures and their relationship to personality and life outcomes across adulthood. *Journal of Personality and Social Psychology, 80,* 112–124. (12)

Harkins, S. G., & Jackson, J. M. (1985). The role of evaluation in eliminating social loafing. *Journal of Personality and Social Psychology, 11,* 457–465. (14)

Harley, B., & Wang, W. (1997). The critical period hypothesis: Where are we now? In A. M. B. deGroot & J. F. Knoll (Eds.), *Tutorials in bilingualism* (pp. 19–51). Mahwah, NJ: Erlbaum. (8)

Harlow, H. F. (1958). The nature of love. *American Psychologist, 13,* 673–685. (10)

Harlow, H. F., & Harlow, M. K. (1965). The affectional systems. In A. M. Schrier, H. F. Harlow, & F. Stollnitz (Eds.), *Behavior of nonhuman primates* (Vol. 2, pp. 287–334). New York: Academic Press. (10)

Harlow, H. F., Harlow, M. K., & Meyer, D. R. (1950). Learning motivated by a manipulative drive. *Journal of Experimental Psychology, 40,* 228–234. (11)

Harlow, H. F., Harlow, M. K., & Suomi, S. J. (1971). From thought to therapy: Lessons from a primate laboratory. *American Scientist, 59,* 538–549. (10)

Harris, B. (1979). What ever happened to Little Albert? *American Psychologist, 34,* 151–160. (16)

Harris, J. R. (1995). Where is the child's environment? A group socialization theory of development. *Psychological Review, 102,* 458–489. (10)

Harris, J. R. (1998). *The nurture assumption.* New York: Free Press. (10)

Harris, J. R. (2000). Context-specific learning, personality, and birth order. *Current Directions in Psychological Science, 9,* 174–177. (10)

Harris, R. J., Schoen, L. M., & Hensley, D. L. (1992). A cross-cultural study of story memory. *Journal of Cross-Cultural Psychology, 23,* 133–147. (7)

Harris, T. (1967). *I'm OK—You're OK.* New York: Avon. (13)

Harrison, A. O., Wilson, M. N., Pine, C. J., Chan, S. Q., & Buriel, R. (1990). Family ecologies of ethnic minority children. *Child Development, 61,* 347–362. (10)

Hartshorn, K., Rovee-Collier, C., Gerhardstein, P., Bhatt, R. S., Klein, P. J., Aaron, F., Wondolski, T. L., & Wurtzel, N. (1998). Developmental changes in the specificity of memory over the first year of life. *Developmental Psychobiology, 33,* 61–78. (10)

Hass, R. G., Katz, I., Rizzo, N., Bailey, J., & Eisenstadt, D. (1991). Cross-racial appraisal as related to attitude ambivalence and cognitive complexity. *Journal of Personality and Social Psychology, 17,* 83–92. (14)

Hathaway, S. R., & McKinley, J. C. (1940). A multiphasic personality schedule (Minnesota): I. Construction of the schedule. *Journal of Psychology, 10,* 249–254. (13)

Haugaard, J. J. (2000). The challenge of defining child sexual abuse. *American Psychologist, 55,* 1036–1039. (12)

Hauri, P. (1982). *The sleep disorders.* Kalamazoo, MI: Upjohn. (5)

Hauser, R. M. (1998). Trends in Black-White test-score differentials: I. Uses and misuses of NAEP/SAT data. In U. Neisser (Ed.), *The rising curve* (pp. 219–249). Washington, DC: American Psychological Association. (9)

Hayes, S. C., & Helby, E. (1996). Psychology's drug problem: Do we need a fix or should we just say no? *American Psychologist, 51,* 198–206. (1)

Hays, R. B. (1985). A longitudinal study of friendship development. *Journal of Personality and Social Psychology, 48,* 909–924. (14)

He, S., Cavanagh, P., & Intiligator, J. (1996). Attentional resolution and the locus of visual awareness. *Nature, 383,* 334–337. (4)

Healy, D., & Williams, J. M. G. (1988). Dysrhythmia, dysphoria, and depression: The interaction of learned helplessness and circadian dysrhythmia in the pathogenesis of depression. *Psychological Bulletin, 103,* 163–178. (16)

Heath, A. C., Neale, M. C., Kessler, R. C., Eaves, L. J., & Kendler, K. S. (1992). Evidence for genetic influences on personality from self-reports and informant ratings. *Journal of Personality and Social Psychology, 63,* 85–96. (10, 13)

Heatherton, T. G., & Baumeister, R. F. (1991). Binge eating as escape from self-awareness. *Psychological Bulletin, 110,* 86–108. (11)

Heaton, R. K., Gladsjo, J. A., Palmer, B. W., Kuck, J., Marcotte, T. D., & Jeste, D. V. (2001). Stability and course of neuropsychological deficits in schizophrenia. *Archives of General Psychiatry, 58,* 24–32. (16)

Heckhausen, H. (1984). Emergent achievement behavior: Some early developments. *Advances in Motivation and Achievement, 3,* 1–32. (11)

Hedges, L. V., & Nowell, A. (1995). Sex differences in mental test scores, variability, and numbers of high-scoring individuals. *Science, 269,* 41–45. (9)

Heider, E. R. (1972). Universals in color naming and memory. *Journal of Experimental Psychology, 93,* 10–20. (8)

Heider, F. (1958). *The psychology of interpersonal relations.* New York: Wiley. (14)

Heilman, K. M. (1979). Neglect and related disorders. In K. M. Heilman & E. Valenstein (Eds.), *Clinical neuropsychology* (pp. 268–307). New York: Oxford University Press. (3)

Heine, S. J., Lehman, D. R., Markus, H. R., & Kitayama, S. (1999). Is there a universal need for positive self-regard? *Psychological Review, 106,* 766–794. (12)

Heit, E. (1993). Modeling the effects of expectations on recognition memory. *Psychological Science, 4,* 244–251. (7)

Hejmadi, A., Davidson, R. J., & Rozin, P. (2000). Exploring Hindu Indian emotion expressions. *Psychological Science, 11,* 183–187. (12)

Helbing, D., Farkes, I., & Vicsek, T. (2000). Simulating dynamical features of escape panic. *Nature, 407,* 487–490. (14)

Held, R., & Hein, A. (1963). Movement-produced stimulation in the development of visually guided behavior. *Journal of Comparative and Physiological Psychology, 56,* 872–876. (10)

Heller, M. A. (1989). Picture and pattern perception in the sighted and the blind: The advantage of the late blind. *Perception, 18,* 379–389. (4)

Helmes, E., & Reddon, J. R. (1993). A perspective on developments in assessing psychopathology: A critical review of the MMPI and MMPI-2. *Psychological Bulletin, 113,* 453–471. (13)

Helzer, J. E., Robins, L. N., & McEnvoy, L. (1987). Post-traumatic stress disorder in the general population. *New England Journal of Medicine, 317,* 1630–1634. (12)

Hergenhahn, B. R. (1992). *An introduction to the history of psychology* (2nd ed.). Belmont, CA: Wadsworth. (1)

Herkenham, M., Lynn, A. B., deCosta, B. R., & Richfield, E. K. (1991). Neuronal localization of cannabinoid receptors in the basal ganglia of the rat. *Brain Research, 547,* 267–274. (5)

Herkenham, M., Lynn, A. B., Little, M. D., Johnson, M. R., Melvin, L. S., deCosta, B. R., & Rice, K. C. (1990). Cannabinoid receptor localization in brain. *Proceedings of the National Academy of Sciences, 87,* 1932–1936. (5)

Herman, J., Roffwarg, H., & Tauber, E. S. (1968). Color and other perceptual qualities of REM and NREM sleep. *Psychophysiology, 5,* 223. (5)

Hernandez, L., Murzi, E., Schwartz, D. H., & Hoebel, B. G. (1992). Electrophysiological and neurochemical approach to a hierarchical feeding organization. In P. Bjorntorp & B. N. Brodoff (Eds.), *Obesity* (pp. 171–183). Philadelphia, PA: Lippincott. (11)

Herrnstein, R. J., & Murray, C. (1994). *The bell curve.* New York: Free Press. (9)

Hess, T. M., Donley, J., & Vandermaas, M. O. (1989). Aging-related changes in the processing and retention of script information. *Experimental Aging Research, 15,* 89–96. (7)

Heszen-Niejodek, I. (1997). Coping style and its role in coping with stressful encounters. *European Psychologist, 2,* 342–351. (12)

Hetherington, E. M. (1989). Coping with family transitions. Winners, losers, and survivors. *Child Development, 60,* 1–14. (10)

Hetherington, E. M., Bridges, M., & Insabella, G. M. (1998). What matters? What does not? *American Psychologist, 53,* 167–184. (10)

Hetherington, E. M., Henderson, S. H., & Reiss, D. (1999). Adolescent siblings in stepfamilies: Family functioning and adolescent adjustment. *Monographs of the Society for Research in Child Development* (Serial No. 259). (10)

Hetherington, E. M., Stanley-Hagan, M., & Anderson, E. R. (1989). Marital transitions: A child's perspective. *American Psychologist, 44,* 303–312. (10)

Hilgard, E. R. (1971). Hypnotic phenomena: The struggle for scientific acceptance. *American Scientist, 59,* 567–577. (5)

Hilgard, E. R. (1973). A neodissociation interpretation of pain reduction in hypnosis. *Psychological Review, 80,* 396–411. (5)

Hill, W. D., Blake, M., & Clark, J. E. (1998). Ball court design dates back 3,400 years. *Nature, 392,* 878–879. (11)

Hilty, D. M., Brady, K. T., & Hales, R. E. (1999). A review of bipolar disorder among adults. *Psychiatric Services, 50,* 201–213. (16)

Hinton, G. (1979). Some demonstrations of the effects of structural descriptions in mental imagery. *Cognitive Science, 3,* 231–250. (8)

Hobson, J. A., & McCarley, R. W. (1977). The brain as a dream state generator: An activation-synthesis hypothesis of the dream process. *American Journal of Psychiatry, 134,* 1335–1348. (5)

Hodgins, S., Mednick, S. A., Brennan, P. A., Schulsinger, F., & Engberg, M. (1996). Mental disorder and crime. *Archives of General Psychiatry, 53,* 489–496. (12)

Hoebel, B. G., & Hernandez, L. (1993). Basic neural mechanisms of feeding and weight regulation. In A. J. Stunkard & T. A. Wadden (Eds.), *Obesity: Theory and therapy* (2nd ed., pp. 43–62). New York: Raven. (11)

Hoffman, R. E., Stopek, S., & Andreasen, N. C. (1986). A comparative study of manic vs. schizophrenic speech disorganization. *Archives of General Psychiatry, 43,* 831–838. (16)

Hoffrage, U., Hertwig, R., & Gigerenzer, G. (2000). Hindsight bias: A by-product of knowledge updating? *Journal of Experimental Psychology: Learning, Memory, and Cognition, 26,* 566–581. (7)

Hogan, J., & Quigley, A. M. (1986). Physical standards for employment and the courts. *American Psychologist, 11,* 1193–1217. (9)

Hogan, R., Hogan, J., & Roberts, B. W. (1996). Personality measurement and employment decisions. *American Psychologist, 51,* 469–477. (13)

Hogan, R. A., & Kirchner, J. H. (1967). Preliminary report of the extinction of learned fears via short-term implosive therapy. *Journal of Abnormal Psychology, 72,* 106–109. (16)

Holden, G. W., & Miller, P. C. (1999). Enduring and different: A meta-analysis of the similarity in parents' child rearing. *Psychological Bulletin, 125,* 223–254. (10)

Hollister, J. M., Laing, P., & Mednick, S. A. (1996). Rhesus incompatibility as a risk factor for schizophrenia in male adults. *Archives of General Psychiatry, 53,* 19–24. (16)

Hollon, S. D., & Beck, A. T. (1979). Cognitive therapy of depression. In P. C. Kendall & S. D. Hollon (Eds.), *Cognitive-behavioral interventions* (pp. 153–203). New York: Academic Press. (15)

Holmes, D. S. (1978). Projection as a defense mechanism. *Psychological Bulletin, 85,* 677–688. (13)

Holmes, D. S. (1987). The influence of meditation versus rest on physiological arousal: A second examination. In M. A. West (Ed.), *The psychology of meditation* (pp. 81–103). Oxford, England: Clarendon Press. (5)

Holmes, D. S. (1990). The evidence for repression: An examination of sixty years of research. In J. L. Singer (Ed.), *Repression and dissociation* (pp. 85–102). New York: Wiley. (7, 13)

Holmes, T., & Rahe, R. (1967). The social readjustment rating scale. *Journal of Psychosomatic Research, 11,* 213–218. (12)

Holtzworth-Munroe, A. (2000). A typology of men who are violent toward their female partners: Making sense of the heterogeneity in husband violence. *Current Directions in Psychological Science, 9,* 140–143. (12)

Hong, Y., Morris, M. W., Chiu, C., & Benet-Martinez, V. (2000). Multicultural minds: A dynamic constructivist approach to culture and cognition. *American Psychologist, 55,* 709–720. (14)

Honzik, M. P. (1974). The development of intelligence. In B. B. Wolman (Ed.), *Handbook of general psychology* (pp. 644–655). Upper Saddle River, NJ: Prentice Hall. (9)

Horn, J. L. (1968). Organization of abilities and the development of intelligence. *Psychological Review, 75,* 242–259. (9)

Horn, J. L., & Donaldson, G. (1976). On the myth of intellectual decline in adulthood. *American Psychologist, 31,* 701–719. (9)

Horne, J. A. (1988). *Why we sleep.* Oxford, England: Oxford University Press. (5)

Horne, J. A., Brass, C. G., & Pettitt, A. N. (1980). Circadian performance differences between morning and evening 'types.' *Ergonomics, 23,* 29–36. (5)

Horne, J. A., & Minard, A. (1985). Sleep and sleepiness following a behaviorally "active" day. *Ergonomics, 28,* 567–575. (5)

Horst, W. D., & Preskorn, S. H. (1998). Mechanisms of action and clinical characteristics of three atypical antidepressants: Venlafaxine, nefazodone, buproprion. *Journal of Affective Disorders, 51,* 237–254. (16)

Houts, A. C., Berman, J. S., & Abramson, H. (1994). Effectiveness of psychological and pharmacological treatments for nocturnal enuresis. *Journal of Consulting & Clinical Psychology, 62,* 737–745. (15)

Hovland, C. I., & Weiss, W. (1951). The influences of source credibility on communication effectiveness. *Public Opinion Quarterly, 15,* 635–650. (14)

Howard, G. S. (2000). Adapting human lifestyles for the 21st century. *American Psychologist, 55,* 509–515. (1)

Howard, K. I., Cornille, T. A., Lyons, J. S., Vessey, J. T., Lueger, R. J., & Saunders, S. M. (1996). Patterns of mental health service utilization. *Archives of General Psychiatry, 53,* 696–703. (1)

Howard, K. I., Kopta, S. M., Krause, M. S., & Orlinsky, D. E. (1986). The dose-effect relationship in psychotherapy. *American Psychologist, 41,* 159–164. (15)

Howard, R. W. (1999). Preliminary real-world evidence that average human intelligence really is rising. *Intelligence, 27,* 235–250. (9)

Howe, M. L., & Courage, M. L. (1993). On resolving the enigma of infantile amnesia. *Psychological Bulletin, 113,* 305–326. (7)

Howe, M. L., & Courage, M. L. (1997). The emergence and early development of autobiographical memory. *Psychological Review, 104,* 499–523. (7)

Hoyt, M. F., & Austad, C. S. (1992). Psychotherapy in a staff model health maintenance organization: Providing and assuring quality care in the future. *Psychotherapy, 29,* 119–129. (15)

Hrdy, S. B. (2000). The optimal number of fathers. *Annals of the New York Academy of Sciences, 907,* 75–96. (14)

Hser, Y. -I., Anglin, M. D., & Powers, K. (1993). A 24-year follow-up of California narcotics addicts. *Archives of General Psychiatry, 50,* 577–584. (16)

Huang, M.-H., & Hauser, R. M. (1998). Trends in Black-White test-score differentials: II. The WORDSUM vocabulary test. In U. Neisser (Ed.), *The rising curve* (pp. 303–332). Washington, DC: American Psychological Association. (9)

Hubel, D. H., & Wiesel, T. N. (1968). Receptive fields and functional architecture of monkey striate cortex. *Journal of Physiology* (London), *195,* 215–243. (4)

Hudson, W. (1960). Pictorial depth perception in sub-cultural groups in Africa. *Journal of Social Psychology, 52,* 183–208. (4)

Huff, D. (1954). *How to lie with statistics.* New York: Norton. (2)

Hughes, H. C., Nozawa, G., & Kitterle, F. (1996). Global precedence, spatial frequency channels, and the statistics of natural images. *Journal of Cognitive Neuroscience, 8,* 197–230. (4)

Hughes, J. C., & Cook, C. C. H. (1997). The efficacy of disulfiram: A review of outcome studies. *Addiction, 92,* 381–395. (16)

Hughes, J., Smith, T. W., Kosterlitz, H. W., Fothergill, L. A., Morgan, B. A., & Morris, H. R. (1975). Identification of two related pentapeptides from the brain with potent opiate antagonist activity. *Nature, 258,* 577–579. (5)

Hull, C. L. (1932). The goal gradient hypothesis and maze learning. *Psychological Review, 39,* 25–43. (1)

Hull, C. L. (1943). *Principles of behavior: An introduction to behavior theory.* New York: D. Appleton. (11)

Hultman, C. M., Öhman, A., Cnattingius, S., Wieselgren, I. -M., & Lindström, L. H. (1997). Prenatal and neonatal risk factors for schizophrenia. *British Journal of Psychiatry, 170,* 128–133. (16)

Hunter, J. E. (1997). Needed: A ban on the significance test. *Psychological Science, 8,* 3–7. (2)

Hur, Y.-M., Bouchard, T. J., Jr., & Eckert, E. (1998). Genetic and environmental influences on self-reported diet: A reared-apart twin study. *Physiology & Behavior, 64,* 629–636. (3)

Hur, Y.-M., Bouchard, T. J., Jr., & Lykken, D. T. (1998). Genetic and environmental influence on morningness-eveningness. *Personality and Individual Differences, 25,* 917–925. (3)

Hurovitz, C. S., Dunn, S., Domhoff, G. W., & Fiss, H. (1999). The dreams of blind men and women: A replication and extension of previous findings. *Dreaming, 9,* 183–193. (5)

Iacono, W. G., & Patrick, C. J. (1999). Polygraph ("lie detector") testing: The state of the art. In A. K. Hess & I. B. Weiner (Eds.), *The handbook of forensic psychology* (pp. 440–473). New York: Wiley. (12)

Iggo, A., & Andres, K. H. (1982). Morphology of cutaneous receptors. *Annual Review of Neuroscience, 5,* 1–31. (4)

Ikonomidou, C., Bittigau, P., Ishimaru, M. J., Wozniak, D. F., Koch, C., Genz, K., Price, M. T., Stefovska, V., Hörster, F., Tenkova, T., Dikranian, K., & Olney, J. W. (2000). Ethanol-induced apoptotic neurodegeneration and fetal alcohol syndrome. *Science, 287,* 1056–1060. (10)

Imhoff, M. C., & Baker-Ward, L. (1999). Preschoolers' suggestibility: Effects of developmentally appropriate language and interviewer supportiveness. *Journal of Applied Developmental Psychology, 20,* 407–429. (7)

Inglehart, R. (1997). *Modernization and postmodernization.* Princeton, NJ: Princeton University Press. (12)

Inhoff, A. W. (1989). Lexical access during eye fixations in sentence reading: Are word access codes used to integrate lexical information across interword fixations? *Journal of Memory and Language, 28,* 444–461. (8)

Inouye, S. T., & Kawamura, H. (1979). Persistence of circadian rhythmicity in a mammalian hypothalamic "island" containing the suprachiasmatic nucleus. *Proceedings of the National Academy of Sciences, U.S.A., 76,* 5962–5966. (5)

Isaacs, E. A., & Clark, H. H. (1987). References in conversation between experts and novices. *Journal of Experimental Psychology: General, 116,* 26–37. (1)

Isenberg, D. J. (1986). Group polarization: A critical review and meta-analysis. *Journal of Personality and Social Psychology, 50,* 1141–1151. (14)

Ivry, R. B., & Diener, H. C. (1991). Impaired velocity perception in patients with lesions of the cerebellum. *Journal of Cognitive Neuroscience, 3,* 355–366. (3)

Izazola-Licea, J. A., Gortmaker, S. L., Tolbert, K., De Gruttola, V., & Mann, J. (2000). Prevalence of same-gender sexual behavior and HIV in a probability household survey of Mexican men. *Journal of Sex Research, 37,* 37–43. (11)

Jacobs, B., Schall, M., & Scheibel, A. B. (1993). A quantitative dendritic analysis of Wernicke's area in humans: II. Gender, hemispheric, and environmental factors. *Journal of Comparative Neurology, 327,* 97–111. (3)

Jacobs, B. L. (1987). How hallucinogenic drugs work. *American Scientist, 75,* 386–392. (5)

Jacobs, B. L., van Praag, H., & Gage, F. H. (2000). Depression and the birth and death of brain cells. *American Scientist, 88,* 340–345. (16)

Jacobs, K. M., Mark, G. P., & Scott, T. R. (1988). Taste responses in the nucleus tractus solitarius of sodium-deprived rats. *Journal of Physiology, 406,* 393–410. (11)

Jacobsen, F. M., Sack, D. A., Wehr, T. A., Rogers, S., & Rosenthal, N. E. (1987). Neuroendocrine 5-hydroxytryptophan in seasonal affective disorder. *Archives of General Psychiatry, 44,* 1086–1091. (16)

Jacobson, N. S., & Christensen, A. (1996). Studying the effectiveness of psychotherapy: How well can clinical trials do the job? *American Psychologist, 51,* 1031–1039. (15)

Jaffee, S., & Hyde, J. S. (2000). Gender differences in moral orientation: A meta-analysis. *Psychological Bulletin, 126,* 703–726. (10)

James, W. (1884). What is an emotion? *Mind, 9,* 188–205. (12)

James, W. (1890). *The principles of psychology.* New York: Henry Holt. (1)

James, W. (1961). *Psychology: The briefer course.* New York: Harper. (Original work published 1892) (5)

Janis, I. L. (1972). *Victims of groupthink.* Boston: Houghton Mifflin. (14)

Janis, I. L. (1983). Stress inoculation in health care. In D. Meichenbaum & M. E. Jaremko (Eds.), *Stress reduction and prevention* (pp. 67–99). New York: Plenum. (12)

Janis, I. L. (1985). Sources of error in strategic decision making. In J. M. Pennings and associates (Eds.), *Organizational strategy and change* (pp. 157–197). San Francisco: Jossey-Bass. (14)

Jaremko, M. E. (1983). Stress inoculation training for social anxiety, with emphasis on dating anxiety. In D. Meichenbaum & M. E. Jaremko (Eds.), *Stress reduction and prevention* (pp. 419–450). New York: Plenum. (12)

Jaskiw, G. E., & Weinberger, D. R. (1992) Dopamine and schizophrenia—a cortically corrective perspective. *Seminars in the Neurosciences, 4,* 179–188. (16)

Jensen, A. R. (1980). *Bias in mental testing.* New York: Free Press. (9, 10)

Johnson, J. G., Cohen, P., Brown, J., Smailes, E. M., & Bernstein, D. P. (1999). Childhood maltreatment increases risk for personality disorders during early adulthood. *Archives of General Psychiatry, 56,* 600–606. (15)

Johnson, M. K., Hashtroudi, S., & Lindsay, D. S. (1993). Source monitoring. *Psychological Bulletin, 114,* 3–28. (7)

Johnson, S. L., & Roberts, J. E. (1995). Life events and bipolar disorders: Implications from biological theories. *Psychological Bulletin, 117,* 434–449. (16)

Johnston, J. C., & McClelland, J. L. (1974). Perception of letters in words: Seek not and ye shall find. *Science, 184,* 1192–1194. (8)

Johnston, J. J. (1975). Sticking with first responses on multiple-choice exams: For better or for worse? *Teaching of Psychology, 2,* 178–179. (Preface)

Joiner, T. E., Jr. (1999). The clustering and contagion of suicide. *Current Directions in Psychological Science, 8,* 89–92. (15)

Jones, E. E., & Goethals, G. R. (1972). Order effects in impression formation: Attribution context and the nature of the entity. In E. Jones, D. Kanouse, H. Kelley, R. Nisbett, S. Valins, & B. Wiener (Eds.), *Attribution: Perceiving the causes of behavior* (pp. 27–46). Morristown, NJ: General Learning Press. (14)

Jones, E. E., & Harris, V. A. (1967). The attribution of attitudes. *Journal of Experimental Social Psychology, 13,* 1–24. (14)

Jones, E. E., & Nisbett, R. E. (1972). The actor and the observer: Divergent perception of the causes of behavior. In E. Jones, D. Kanouse, H. Kelley, R. Nisbett, S. Valins, & B. Wiener (Eds.), *Attribution: Perceiving the causes of behavior* (pp. 79–94). Morristown, NJ: General Learning Press. (14)

Jones, S. S., Collins, K., & Hong, H. -W. (1991). An audience effect on smile production in 10-month-old infants. *Psychological Science, 2,* 45–49. (12)

Jorgensen, R. S., Johnson, B. T., Kolodziej, M. E., & Schreer, G. E. (1996). Elevated blood pressure and personality: A meta-analytic review. *Psychological Bulletin, 120,* 293–320. (12)

Joseph, R. (2000). Fetal brain behavior and cognitive development. *Developmental Review, 20,* 81–98. (10)

Jouvet, M., Michel, F., & Courjon, J. (1959). Sur un stade d'activité électrique cérébrale rapide au cours du sommeil physiologique [On a state of rapid electrical cerebral activity during physiological sleep]. *Comptes Rendus des Séances de la Société de Biologie, 153,* 1024–1028. (5)

Jung, C. G. (1965). *Memories, dreams, reflections* (A. Jaffe, Ed.). New York: Random House. (13)

Junginger, J., & Frame, C. L. (1985). Self-report of the frequency and phenomenology of verbal hallucinations. *Journal of Nervous and Mental Disease, 173,* 149–155. (16)

Juslin, P., Winman, A., & Olsson, H. (2000). Naive empiricism and dogmatism in confidence research: A critical examination of the hard–easy effect. *Psychological Review, 107,* 384–396. (8)

Just, M. A., & Carpenter, P. A. (1987). *The psychology of reading and language comprehension.* Boston: Allyn & Bacon. (8)

Just, M. A., Carpenter, P. A., Keller, T. A., Eddy, W. F., & Thulborn, K. R. (1996). Brain activation modulated by sentence comprehension. *Science, 274,* 114–116. (8)

Kagan, J. (1989). Temperamental contributions to social behavior. *American Psychologist, 44,* 668–674. (10)

Kagan, J., Reznick, J. S., & Snidman, N. (1988). Biological bases of childhood shyness. *Science, 240,* 167–171. (10)

Kagan, J., & Snidman, N. (1991). Infant predictors of inhibited and uninhibited profiles. *Psychological Science, 2,* 40–44. (10)

Kahneman, D., & Tversky, A. (1973). On the psychology of prediction. *Psychological Review, 80,* 237–251. (8)

Kaiser, M. K., Jonides, J., & Alexander, J. (1986). Intuitive reasoning about abstract and familiar physics problems. *Memory & Cognition, 14,* 308–312. (8)

Kales, A., Scharf, M. B., & Kales, J. D. (1978). Rebound insomnia: A new clinical syndrome. *Science, 201,* 1039–1041. (5)

Kales, A., Soldatos, C. R., Bixler, E. O., & Kales, J. D. (1983). Early morning insomnia with rapidly eliminated benzodiazepines. *Science, 220,* 95–97. (5)

Kalick, S. M., Zebrowitz, L. A., Langlois, J. H., & Johnson, R. M. (1998). Does human facial attractiveness honestly advertise health? *Psychological Science, 9,* 8–13. (14)

Kamin, L. J. (1969). Predictability, surprise, attention, and conditioning. In B. A. Campbell & R. M. Church (Eds.), *Punishment and aversive behavior* (pp. 279–296). New York: Appleton-Century-Crofts. (6)

Kamin, L. J. (1974). *The science and politics of IQ.* New York: Wiley. (9)

Kaminer, Y. (2000). Contingency management reinforcement procedures for adolescent substance abuse. *Journal of the American Academy of Child & Adolescent Psychiatry, 39,* 1324–1326. (16)

Kane, M. J., & Engle, R. W. (2000). Working-memory capacity, proactive interference, and divided attention: Limits on long-term memory retrieval. *Journal of Experimental Psychology: Learning, Memory, and Cognition, 26,* 336–358. (7)

Kanizsa, G. (1979). *Organization in vision.* New York: Praeger. (4)

Kanizsa, G. (1985). Seeing and thinking. *Acta Psychologia, 59,* 23–33. (4)

Kanner, A. D., Coyne, J. C., Schaefer, C., & Lazarus, R. S. (1981). Comparison of two modes of stress measurement: Daily hassles and uplifts versus major life events. *Journal of Behavioral Medicine, 4,* 1–39. (12)

Kanwisher, N. (2000). Domain specificity in face perception. *Nature Neuroscience, 3,* 759–763. (4)

Kaplan, E. H. (1988). Crisis? A brief critique of Masters, Johnson and Kolodny. *Journal of Sex Research, 25,* 317–322. (11)

Karau, S. J., & Williams, K. D. (1995). Social loafing: Research findings, implications, and future directions. *Current Directions in Psychological Science, 4,* 134–140. (14)

Karlin, R. A. (1997). Illusory safeguards: Legitimizing distortion in recall with guidelines for forensic hypnosis—two case reports. *International Journal of Clinical and Experimental Hypnosis, 45,* 18–40. (5)

Karney, B. R., & Bradbury, T. N. (1995). The longitudinal course of marital quality and stability: A review of theory, method, and research. *Psychological Review, 118,* 3–34. (14)

Karno, M., Golding, J. M., Sorenson, S. B., & Burnam, A. (1988). The epidemiology of obsessive-compulsive disorder in five U.S. communities. *Archives of General Psychiatry, 45,* 1094–1099. (16)

Karon, B. P. (1995). Provision of psychotherapy under managed health care: A growing crisis and national nightmare. *Professional Psychology: Research and Practice, 26,* 5–9. (15)

Karon, B. P., & Widener, A. J. (1995). Psychodynamic therapies in historical perspective: "Nothing human do I consider alien to me." In B. Bongar & L. E. Beutler (Eds.), *Comprehensive textbook of psychotherapy: Theory and practice* (pp. 24–47). Oxford, England: Oxford University Press. (15)

Karpov, Y. V., & Haywood, H. C. (1998). Two ways to elaborate Vygotsky's concept of mediation. *American Psychologist, 53,* 27–36. (10)

Kasser, T., & Sharma, Y. S. (1999). Reproductive freedom, educational equality, and females' preference for resource-acquisition characteristics in mates. *Psychological Science, 10,* 374–377. (14)

Kasser, T., & Sheldon, K. M. (2000). Of wealth and death. Materialism, mortality salience, and consumption behavior. *Psychological Science, 11,* 348–351. (10)

Kaufman, L., & Rock, I. (1989). The moon illusion thirty years later. In M. Hershenson (Ed.), *The moon illusion* (pp. 193–234). Hillsdale, NJ: Erlbaum. (4)

Kazdin, A. E. (1995). Methods of psychotherapy research. In B. Bongar & L. E. Beutler (Eds.), *Comprehensive textbook of psychotherapy: Theory and practice* (pp. 405–433). Oxford, England: Oxford University Press. (15)

Keele, S. W., & Ivry, R. B. (1990). Does the cerebellum provide a common computation for diverse tasks? *Annals of the New York Academy of Sciences, 608,* 179–207. (3)

Kelley, H. H. (1967). Attribution theory in social psychology. In D. Levine (Ed.), *Nebraska Symposium on Motivation* (Vol. 15, pp. 192–238). Lincoln: University of Nebraska Press. (14)

Keltner, D., & Buswell, B. N. (1997). Embarrassment: Its distinct form and appeasement functions. *Psychological Bulletin, 122,* 250–270. (12)

Keltner, D., Kring, A. M., & Bonanno, G. A. (1999). Fleeting signs of the course of life: Facial expression and personal adjustment. *Current Directions in Psychological Science, 8,* 18–22. (12)

Keltner, D., & Robinson, R. J. (1996). Extremism, power, and the imagined basis of social conflict. *Current Directions in Psychological Science, 5,* 101–105. (14)

Kendler, K. S., Bulik, C. M., Silberg, J., Hettema, J. M., Myers, J., & Prescott, C. A. (2000). Childhood sexual abuse and adult psychiatric and substance abuse disorders in women. *Archives of General Psychiatry, 57,* 953–959. (16)

Kendler, K. S., Gallagher, T. J., Abelson, J. M., & Kessler, R. C. (1996). Lifetime prevalence, demographic risk factors, and diagnostic validity of nonaffective psychosis as assessed in a U.S. community sample. *Archives of General Psychiatry, 53,* 1022–1031. (16)

Kendler, K. S., Gardner, C. O., & Prescott, C. A. (1999). Clinical characteristics of major depression that predict risk of depression in relatives. *Archives of General Psychiatry, 56,* 322–327. (16)

Kendler, K. S., Gruenberg, A. M., & Tsuang, M. T. (1985). Subtype stability in schizophrenia. *American Journal of Psychiatry, 142,* 827–832. (16)

Kendler, K. S., Karkowski, L. M., Neale, M. C., & Prescott, C. A. (2000). Illicit psychoactive substance use, heavy use, abuse, and dependence in a US population-based sample of male twins. *Archives of General Psychiatry, 57,* 261–269. (16)

Kendler, K. S., Myers, J., Prescott, C. A., & Neale, M. C. (2001). The genetic epidemiology of irrational fears and phobias in men. *Archives of General Psychiatry, 58,* 257–265. (16)

Kendler, K. S., Thornton, L. M., & Pedersen, N. L. (2000). Tobacco consumption in Swedish twins reared apart and reared together. *Archives of General Psychiatry, 57,* 886–892. (16)

Kendler, K. S., Walters, E. E., Neale, M. C., Kessler, R. C., Heath, A. C., & Eaves, L. J. (1995). The structure of the genetic and environmental risk factors for six major psychiatric disorders in women. *Archives of General Psychiatry, 52,* 374–383. (16)

Kenrick, D. T., & Trost, M. R. (1989). A reproductive exchange model of heterosexual relationships. In C. Hendick (Ed.), *Close relationships* (pp. 92–118). Newbury Park, CA: Sage. (14)

Keon, T. L., & McDonald, B. (1982). Job satisfaction and life satisfaction: An empirical evaluation of their interrelationship. *Human Relations, 35,* 167–180. (10)

Keppel, G., & Underwood, B. J. (1962). Proactive inhibition in short-term retention of single items. *Journal of Verbal Learning and Verbal Behavior, 1,* 153–161. (7)

Kerr, N. L., MacCoun, R. J., & Kramer, G. P. (1996). Bias in judgment: Comparing individuals and groups. *Psychological Review, 103,* 687–719. (14)

Kessler, R. C., Borges, G., & Walters, E. E. (1999). Prevalence of and risk factors for lifetime suicide attempts in the national comorbidity survey. *Archives of General Psychiatry, 56,* 617–626. (16)

Kessler, R. C., McGonagle, K. A., Zhao, S., Nelson, C. B., Hughes, E., Eshleman, S., Wittchen, H. -U., & Kendler, K. S. (1994). Lifetime and 12-month prevalence of *DSM-III-R* psychiatric disorders in the United States. *Archives of General Psychiatry, 51,* 8–19. (15)

Kessler, R. C., Soukup, J., Davis, R. B., Foster, D. F., Wilkey, S. A., Van Rompay, M. I., & Eisenberg, D. M. (2001). The use of complementary and alternative therapies to treat anxiety and depression in the United States. *American Journal of Psychiatry, 158,* 289–294. (16)

Kety, S. S., Wendler, P. H., Jacobsen, B., Ingraham, L. J., Jansson, L., Faber, B., & Kinney, D. K. (1994). Mental illness in the biological and adoptive relatives of schizophrenic adoptees. *Archives of General Psychiatry, 51,* 442–455. (16)

Keysar, B., Barr, D. J., & Horton, W. S. (1998). The egocentric basis of language use: Insights from a processing approach. *Current Directions in Psychological Science, 7,* 46–50. (10)

Khalid, R. (1991). Personality and academic achievement: A thematic apperception perspective. *British Journal of Projective Psychology, 36,* 25–34. (11)

Kihlstrom, J. F. (1979). Hypnosis and psychopathology: Retrospect and prospect. *Journal of Abnormal Psychology, 88,* 459–473. (5)

Kihlstrom, J. F., Barnhardt, T. M., & Tataryn, D. J. (1992). The psychological unconscious. *American Psychologist, 47,* 788–791. (8)

Kim, S. (1989). *Inversions.* San Francisco: W. H. Freeman. (4)

Kimble, G. A. (1961). *Hilgard and Marquis' Conditioning and Learning* (2nd ed.). New York: Appleton-Century-Crofts. (6)

Kimble, G. A. (1993). A modest proposal for a minor revolution in the language of psychology. *Psychological Science, 4,* 253–255. (6)

Kimble, G. A., & Garmezy, N. (1968). *Principles of general psychology* (3rd ed.). New York: Ronald. (13)

King, M. L., Jr. (1964, November 13). Speech at Duke University, Durham, NC. (10)

Kinsey, A. C., Pomeroy, W. B., & Martin, C. E. (1948). *Sexual behavior in the human male.* Philadelphia, PA: Saunders. (11)

Kinsey, A. C., Pomeroy, W. B., Martin, C. E., & Gebhard, P. H. (1953). *Sexual behavior in the human female.* Philadelphia, PA: Saunders. (11)

Kiriakakis, V., Bhatia, K. P., Quinn, N. P., & Marsden, C. D. (1998). The natural history of tardive dyskinesia: A long-term follow-up of 107 cases. *Brain, 121,* 2053–2066. (16)

Kirkpatrick, B., Buchanan, R. W., Ross, D. E., & Carpenter, W. T., Jr. (2001). A separate disease within the syndrome of schizophrenia. *Archives of General Psychiatry, 58,* 165–171. (16)

Kirsch, I., & Lynn, S. J. (1998). Dissociation theories of hypnosis. *Psychological Bulletin, 123,* 100–115. (5)

Kirsch, I., & Sapirstein, G. (1998). Listening to Prozac but hearing placebo: A meta-analysis of antidepressant medication. *Prevention and Treatment, 1,* article 2a. (16)

Klein, D. F. (1993). False suffocation alarms, spontaneous panics, and related conditions. *Archives of General Psychiatry, 50,* 306–317. (16)

Klein, R. G., Abikoff, H., Klass, E., Ganeles, D., Seese, L. M., & Pollack, S. (1997). Clinical efficacy of methylphenidate in conduct disorder with and without attention deficit hyperactivity disorder. *Archives of General Psychiatry, 54,* 1073–1080. (12)

Kleinknecht, R. A. (1982). The origins and remission of fear in a group of tarantula enthusiasts. *Behaviour Research & Therapy, 20,* 437–443. (16)

Kleinmuntz, B., & Szucko, J. J. (1984). A field study of the fallibility of polygraphic lie detection. *Nature, 308,* 449–450. (12)

Kleitman, N. (1963). *Sleep and wakefulness* (Rev. and enlarged ed.). Chicago: University of Chicago Press. (5)

Kline, M., Tschann, J. M., Johnston, J. R., & Wallerstein, J. S. (1989). Children's adjustment in joint and sole physical custody families. *Developmental Psychology, 25,* 430–438. (10)

Kling, K. C., Hyde, J. S., Showers, C. J., & Buswell, B. N. (1999). Gender differences in self-esteem: A meta-analysis. *Psychological Bulletin, 125,* 470–500. (10)

Koepp, M. J., Gunn, R. N., Lawrence, A. D., Cunningham, V. J., Dagher, A., Jones, T., Brooks, D. J., Bench, C. J., & Grasby, P. M. (1998). Evidence for striatal dopamine release during a video game. *Nature, 393,* 266–268. (5, 16)

Kohlberg, L. (1969). Stage and sequence: The cognitive-developmental approach to socialization. In D. A. Goslin (Ed.), *Handbook of socialization theory and research.* Chicago: Rand McNally (10)

Kohlberg, L., & Hersh, R. H. (1977). Moral development: A review of the theory. *Theory into Practice, 16,* 53–59. (10)

Koob, G. F., & LeMoal, M. (1997). Drug abuse: Hedonic homeostatic dysregulation. *Science, 278,* 52–58. (16)

Koocher, G. P., Goodman, G. S., White, C. S., Friedrich, W. N., Sivan, A. B., & Reynolds, C. R. (1995). Psychological science and the use of anatomically detailed dolls in child sexual-abuse assessments. *Psychological Bulletin, 118,* 199–222. (13)

Kopelman, P. G. (2000). Obesity as a medical problem. *Nature, 404,* 635–643. (11)

Kopp, C. B. (1990). Risks in infancy: Appraising the research. *Merrill-Palmer Quarterly, 36,* 117–139. (10)

Koppenaal, R. J. (1963). Time changes in the strengths of A-B, A-C lists: Spontaneous recovery? *Journal of Verbal Learning and Verbal Behavior, 2,* 310–319. (7)

Koss, M. P., & Butcher, J. N. (1986). Research on brief psychotherapy. In S. L. Garfield & A. E. Bergin (Eds.), *Handbook of psychotherapy and behavior change* (pp. 627–670). New York: Wiley. (15)

Koss, M. P., & Dinero, T. E. (1988). Predictors of sexual aggression among a national sample of male college students. *Annals of the New York Academy of Sciences, 528,* 133–147. (12)

Koss, M. P., Gidycz, C. A., & Wisniewski, N. (1987). The scope of rape: Incidence and prevalence of sexual aggression and victimization in a national sample of higher education students. *Journal of Consulting and Clinical Psychology, 55,* 162–170. (12)

Kosten, T. R., Rounsaville, B. J., & Kleber, H. D. (1987). A 2.5-year follow-up of cocaine use among treated opioid addicts. *Archives of General Psychiatry, 44,* 281–284. (16)

Koyano, W. (1991). Japanese attitudes toward the elderly: A review of research findings. *Journal of Cross-Cultural Gerontology, 4,* 335–345. (10)

Kozel, N. J., & Adams, E. H. (1986). Epidemiology of drug abuse: An overview. *Science, 234,* 970–974. (5)

Kozlowski, L. T., Frecker, R. C., Khouw, V., & Pope, M. A. (1980). The misuse of ìless hazardousî cigarettes and its detection: Hole blocking of ventilated filters. *American Journal of Public Health, 70,* 1202–1203. (16)

Krebs, D. L. (2000). The evolution of moral dispositions in the human species. *Annals of the New York Academy of Sciences, 907,* 132–148. (10)

Kreek, M. J. (2000). Methadone-related opioid agonist pharmacotherapy for heroin addiction. *Annals of the New York Academy of Sciences, 909,* 186–216. (16)

Kreiman, G., Koch, C., & Fried, I. (2000). Imagery neurons in the human brain. *Nature, 408,* 357–361. (8)

Kreskin. (1991). *Secrets of The Amazing Kreskin.* Buffalo, NY: Prometheus. (2)

Krueger, D. W. (1978). The differential diagnosis of proverb interpretation. In W. E. Fann, I. Karacan, A. D. Pokorny, & R. L. Williams (Eds.), *Phenomenology and treatment of schizophrenia* (pp. 193–201). New York: Spectrum. (16)

Krull, D. S., & Anderson, C. A. (1997). The process of explanation. *Current Directions in Psychological Science, 6,* 1–5. (14)

Krupnick, J. L., Elkin, I., Collins, J., Simmens, S., Sotsky, S. M., Pilkonis, P. A., & Watkins, J. T. (1994). Therapeutic alliance and clinical outcome in the NIMH Treatment of Depression Collaborative Research Program: Preliminary findings. *Psychotherapy, 31,* 28–35. (15)

Kübler-Ross, E. (1969). *On death and dying.* New York: Macmillan. (10)

Kuhl, P. K., Andruski, J. E., Chistovich, I. A., Chistovich, L. A., Kozhevnikova, E. V., Ryskina, V. L., Stolyarova, E. I., Sundberg, U., & Lacerda, F. (1997). Cross-language analysis of phonetic units in language addressed to infants. *Science, 277,* 684–686. (8)

Kuhn, D., & Lao, J. (1996). Effects of evidence on attitudes: Is polarization the norm? *Psychological Science, 7,* 115–120. (14)

Kunda, Z., & Thagard, P. (1996). Forming impressions from stereotypes, traits, and behaviors: A parallel-constraint-satisfaction theory. *Psychological Review, 103,* 284–308. (14)

Kurihara, K., & Kashiwayanagi, M. (1998). Introductory remarks on umami taste. *Annals of the New York Academy of Sciences, 855,* 393–397. (4)

Kutchins, H., & Kirk, S. A. (1997). *Making us crazy.* New York: Free Press. (15)

LaBar, K. S., LeDoux, J. E., Spencer, D. D., & Phelps, E. A. (1995). Impaired fear conditioning following unilateral temporal lobectomy in humans. *Journal of Neuroscience, 15,* 6846–6855. (3, 12)

LaBar, K. S., & Phelps, E. A. (1998). Arousal-mediated memory consolidation: Role of the medial temporal lobe in humans. *Psychological Science, 9,* 490–493. (7)

Labouvie-Vief, G., Diehl, M., Tarnowski, A., & Shen, J. (2000). Age differences in adult personality: Findings from the United States and China. *Journal of Gerontology: Psychological Sciences, 55B,* P4–P17. (13)

Laburn, H. P. (1996). How does the fetus cope with thermal challenges? *News in Physiological Sciences, 11,* 96–100. (16)

Lackner, J. R. (1993). Orientation and movement in unusual force environments. *Psychological Science, 4,* 134–142. (4)

LaFromboise, T., Coleman, H. L. K., & Gerton, J. (1993). Psychological impact of biculturalism: Evidence and theory. *Psychological Bulletin, 114,* 395–412. (10)

Laing, D. G., Prescott, J., Bell, G. A., Gillmore, R., James, C., Best, D. J., Allen, S., Yoshida, M., & Yamazaki, K. (1993). A cross-cultural study of taste discrimination with Australians and Japanese. *Chemical Senses, 18,* 161–168. (11)

Laird, J. D. (1974). Self-attribution of emotion: The effects of expressive behavior on the quality of emotional experience. *Journal of Personality and Social Psychology, 29,* 475–486. (12)

Lake, R. I. E., Eaves, L. J., Maes, H. H. M., Heath, A. C., & Martin, N. G. (2000). Further evidence against the environmental transmission of individual differences in neuroticism from a collaborative study of 45,850 twins and relatives on two continents. *Behavior Genetics, 30,* 223–233. (13)

Lalumière, M. L., Blanchard, R., & Zucker, K. J. (2000). Sexual orientation and handedness in men and women: A meta-analysis. *Psychological Bulletin, 126,* 575–592. (11)

Lamm, H., & Myers, D. G. (1978). Group-induced polarization of attitudes and behavior. *Advances in Experimental Social Psychology, 11,* 145–195. (14)

Land, E. H., Hubel, D. H., Livingstone, M. S., Perry, S. H., & Burns, M. M. (1983). Colour-generating interactions across the corpus callosum. *Nature, 303,* 616–618. (4)

Land, E. H., & McCann, J. J. (1971). Lightness and retinex theory. *Journal of the Optical Society of America, 61,* 1–11. (4)

Lande, S. D. (1982). Physiological and subjective measures of anxiety during flooding. *Behaviour Research and Therapy, 20,* 81–88. (16)

Lang, P. J. (1994). The varieties of emotional experience: A meditation on James-Lange theory. *Psychological Review, 101,* 211–221. (12)

Langer, E. J. (1975). The illusion of control. *Journal of Personality and Social Psychology, 32,* 311–328. (8)

Langlois, J. H., Kalakanis, L., Rubenstein, A. J., Larson, A., Hallam, M., & Smoot, M. (2000). Maxims or myths of beauty? A meta-analytic and theoretical review. *Psychological Bulletin, 126,* 390–423. (14)

Langlois, J. H., & Roggman, L. A. (1990). Attractive faces are only average. *Psychological Science, 1,* 115–121. (14)

Langlois, J. H., Roggman, L. A., & Musselman, L. (1994). What is average and what is not average about average faces? *Psychological Science, 5,* 214–220. (14)

Langworthy, R. A., & Jennings, J. W. (1972). Oddball, abstract olfactory learning in laboratory rats. *Psychological Record, 22,* 487–490. (1)

Lant, T. K., & Hurley, A. E. (1999). A contingency model of response to performance feedback. *Group & Organization Management, 24,* 421–437. (14)

Larson, S. J., & Siegel, S. (1998). Learning and tolerance to the ataxic effect of ethanol. *Pharmacology Biochemistry and Behavior, 61,* 131–142. (6)

Lashley, K. S. (1951). The problem of serial order in behavior. In L. A. Jeffress (Ed.), *Cerebral mechanisms in behavior* (pp. 112–146). New York: Wiley. (8)

Latané, B., & Darley, J. M. (1968). Group inhibition of bystander intervention in emergencies. *Journal of Personality and Social Psychology, 10,* 215–221. (14)

Latané, B., & Darley, J. M. (1969). Bystander "apathy." *American Scientist, 57,* 244–268. (14)

Latané, B., Williams, K., & Harkins, S. (1979). Many hands make light the work: The causes and consequences of social loafing. *Journal of Personality and Social Psychology, 37,* 823–832. (14)

Laumann, E. O. (1969). Friends of urban men: An assessment of accuracy in reporting their socio-economic attributes, mutual choice, and attitude development. *Sociometry, 32,* 54–69. (14)

Laumann, E. O., Gagnon, J. H., Michael, R. T., & Michaels, S. (1994). *The social organization of sexuality: Sexual practices in the United States.* Chicago: University of Chicago Press. (11)

Lavin, J. H., Wittert, G., Sun, W. -M., Horowitz, M., Morley, J. E., & Read, N. W. (1996). Appetite regulation by carbohydrate: Role of blood glucose and gastrointestinal hormones. *American Journal of Physiology, 271,* E209–E214. (11)

Laws, G., Byrne, A., & Buckley, S. (2000). Language and memory development in children with Down syndrome at mainstream schools and special schools: A comparison. *Educational Psychology, 20,* 447–457. (9)

Lazarus, R. S. (1977). Cognitive and coping processes in emotion. In A. Monat & R. S. Lazarus (Eds.), *Stress and coping* (pp. 145–158). New York: Columbia University Press. (12)

Lazarus, R. S., Averill, J. R., & Opton, E. M., Jr. (1970). Towards a cognitive theory of emotion. In M. B. Arnold (Ed.), *Feelings and emotions* (pp. 207–232). New York: Academic Press. (12)

Leaper, C., Anderson, K. J., & Sanders, P. (1998). Moderators of gender effects on parents' talk to their children: A meta-analysis. *Developmental Psychology, 34,* 3–27. (10)

Lee, Y. -T., & Duenas, G. (1995). Stereotype accuracy in multicultural business. In Y.-T. Lee, L. J. Jussim, & C. R. McCauley (Eds.), *Stereotype accuracy* (pp. 157–186). Washington, DC: American Psychological Association. (14)

Leff, J., Wig, N. N., Ghosh, A., Bedi, H., Menon, D. K., Kuipers, L., Korten, A., Ernberg, G., Day, R., Sartorius, N., & Jablensky, A. (1987). Expressed emotion and schizophrenia in North India: III. Influence of relatives' expressed emotion on the course of schizophrenia in Changigarh. *British Journal of Psychiatry, 151,* 166–173. (16)

Legge, G. E., Ahn, S. J., Klitz, T. S., & Luebker, A. (1997). Psychophysics of reading: XVI. The visual span in normal and low vision. *Vision Research, 37,* 1999–2010. (8)

Leibowitz, S. F., & Alexander, J. T. (1991). Analysis of neuropeptide Y-induced feeding: Dissociation of Y1 and Y2 receptor effects on natural meal patterns. *Peptides, 12,* 1251–1260. (11)

Leibowitz, S. F., Hammer, N. J., & Chang, K. (1981). Hypothalamic paraventricular nucleus lesions produce overeating and obesity in the rat. *Physiology & Behavior, 27,* 1031–1040. (11)

Leinders-Zufall, T., Lane, A. P., Puche, A. C., Ma, W., Novotny, M. V., Shipley, M. T., & Zufall, F. (2000). Ultrasensitive pheromone detection by mammalian vomeronasal neurons. *Nature, 405,* 792–796. (4)

LeMagnen, J. (1981). The metabolic basis of dual periodicity of feeding in rats. *Behavioral and Brain Sciences, 4,* 561–607. (11)

Lenneberg, E. H. (1967). *Biological foundations of language.* New York: Wiley. (8)

Lenneberg, E. H. (1969). On explaining language. *Science, 164,* 635–643. (8)

Lester, D. (1996). *Patterns of suicide and homicide in the world.* Commack, NY: Nova Science. (16)

Leuchtenburg, W. E. (1963). *Franklin D. Roosevelt and the New Deal 1932–1940.* New York: Harper & Row. (14)

LeVay, S. (1991). A difference in hypothalamic structure between heterosexual and homosexual men. *Science, 253,* 1034–1037. (11)

Levenson, R. W., Oyama, O. N., & Meek, P. S. (1987). Greater reinforcement from alcohol for those at risk: Parental risk, personality risk, and sex. *Journal of Abnormal Psychology, 96,* 242–253. (16)

Leventhal, H. (1970). Findings and theory in the study of fear communication. In L. Berkowitz (Ed.), *Advances in experimental social psychology* (Vol. 5, pp. 119–186). New York: Academic Press. (14)

Levin, M. (1994). Comment on the Minnesota transracial adoption study. *Intelligence, 19,* 13–20. (9)

Levine, R. V. (1990). The pace of life. *American Scientist, 78,* 450–459. (12)

Levinson, D. F., Mahtani, M. M., Nancarrow, D. J., Brown, D. M., Kruglyak, L., Kirby, A., Hayward, N. K., Crowe, R. R., Andreasen, N. C., Black, D. W., Silverman, J. M., Endicott, J., Sharpe, L., Mohs, R. C., Siever, L. J., Walters, M. K., Lennon, D. P., Jones, H. L., Nertney, D. A., Daly, M. J., Gladis, M., Mowry, B. J. (1998). Genome scan of schizophrenia. *American Journal of Psychiatry, 155,* 741–750. (16)

Lewis, D. O., Moy, E., Jackson, L. D., Aaronson, R., Restifo, N., Serra, S., & Simos, A. (1985). Biopsychosocial characteristics of children who later murder: A prospective study. *American Journal of Psychiatry, 142,* 1161–1167. (12)

Lewis, M. (1995). Self-conscious emotions. *American Scientist, 83,* 68–78. (12)

Lewis, M., Sullivan, M. W., Stanger, C., & Weiss, M. (1991). Self development and self-conscious emotions. In S. Chess & M. E. Hertzig (Eds.), *Annual progress in child psychiatry and child development 1990* (pp. 34–51). New York: Brunner/Mazel. (10)

Lewis, M., Thomas, D. A., & Worobey, J. (1990). Developmental organization, stress, and illness. *Psychological Science, 1,* 316–318. (10)

Lickliter, R., & Bahrick, L. E. (2000). The development of infant intersensory perception: Advantages of a comparative convergent-operations approach. *Psychological Bulletin, 126,* 260–280. (10)

Lilie, J. K., & Rosenberg, R. P. (1990). Behavioral treatment of insomnia. *Progress in Behavior Modification, 25,* 152–177. (5)

Lilienfeld, S. O., Alliger, G., & Mitchell, K. (1995). Why integrity testing remains controversial. *American Psychologist, 50,* 457–458. (12)

Lilienfeld, S. O., Lynn, S. J., Kirsch, I., Chaves, J. F., Sarbin, T. R., Ganaway, G. K., & Powell, R. A. (1999). Dissociative identity disorder and the sociocognitive model: Recalling the lessons of the past. *Psychological Bulletin, 125,* 507–523. (15)

Lilienfeld, S. O., Wood, J. M., & Garb, H. N. (2000). The scientific status of projective tests. *Psychological Science in the Public Interest, 1,* 27–66. (11, 13)

Lin, L., Faraco, J., Li, R., Kadotani, H., Rogers, W., Lin, X., Qiu, X., de Jong, P. J., Nishino, S., & Mignot, E. (1999). The sleep disorder canine narcolepsy is caused by a mutation in the hypocretin (orexin) receptor 2 gene. *Cell, 98,* 365–376. (5)

Lindberg, N. O., Coburn, C., & Stricker, E. M. (1984). Increased feeding by rats after subdiabetogenic streptozotocin treatment: A role for insulin in satiety. *Behavioral Neuroscience, 98,* 138–145. (11)

Lindemann, B. (1996). Taste reception. *Physiological Reviews, 76,* 719–766. (4)

Lindsay, D. S., & Read, J. D. (1994). Psychotherapy and memories of childhood sexual abuse: A cognitive perspective. *Applied Cognitive Psychology, 8,* 281–338. (7)

Linhorst, D. M., & Dirks-Linhorst, P. A. (1999). A critical assessment of disposition options for mentally ill offenders. *Social Science Review, 73,* 65–81. (15)

Linn, R., & Gilligan, C. (1990). One action, two moral orientations—The tension between justice and care voices in Israeli selective conscientious objectors. *New Ideas in Psychology, 8,* 189–203. (10)

Lipsey, M. W., & Wilson, D. B. (1993). The efficacy of psychological, educational, and behavioral treatment. *American Psychologist, 48,* 1181–1209. (15)

Lisak, D., & Roth, S. (1988). Motivational factors in nonincarcerated sexually aggressive men. *Journal of Personality and Social Psychology, 55,* 795–802. (12)

Lisanby, S. H., Maddox, J. H., Prudic, J., Devanand, D. P., & Sackeim, H. A. (2000). The effects of electroconvulsive therapy on memory of autobiographical and public events. *Archives of General Psychiatry, 57,* 581–590. (16)

Llewellyn, A. (2000). Perceptions of mainstreaming: A systems approach. *Developmental Medicine and Child Neurology, 42,* 106–115. (9)

Locke, E. A., & Latham, G. P. (1991). The fallacies of common sense "truths": A reply to Lamal. *Psychological Science, 2,* 131–132. (11)

Locke, E. A., Shaw, K. N., Saari, L. M., & Latham, G. P. (1981). Goal setting and task performance: 1969–1980. *Psychological Bulletin, 90,* 125–152. (11)

Locke, J. L. (1994). Phases in the child's development of language. *American Scientist, 82,* 436–445. (8)

Loeb, J. (1973). *Forced movements, tropisms, and animal conduct.* New York: Dover. (Original work published 1918) (6)

Loehlin, J. C. (1992). *Genes and environment in personality development.* Newbury Park, CA: Sage. (10)

Loehlin, J. C., Horn, J. M., & Willerman, L. (1989). Modeling IQ change: Evidence from the Texas adoption project. *Child Development, 60,* 993–1004. (9)

Loewi, O. (1960). An autobiographic sketch. *Perspectives in Biology, 4,* 3–25. (3)

Loftus, E. F. (1975). Leading questions and the eyewitness report. *Cognitive Psychology, 7,* 560–572. (7)

Loftus, E. F. (1993). The reality of repressed memories. *American Psychologist, 48,* 518–537. (7)

Loftus, E. F., Feldman, J., & Dashiell, R. (1995). The reality of illusory memories. In D. L. Schacter (Ed.) *Memory distortion* (pp. 47–68). Cambridge, MA: Harvard University Press. (7)

Loftus, G. R. (1996). Psychology will be a much better science when we change the way we analyze data. *Current Directions in Psychological Science, 5,* 161–171. (2)

Logothetis, N. K., Leopold, D. A., & Sheinberg, D. L. (1996). What is rivalling during binocular rivalry? *Nature, 380,* 621–624. (4)

London, E. D., Cascella, N. G., Wong, D. F., Phillips, R. L., Dannals, R. F., Links, J. M., Herning, R., Grayson, R., Jaffe, J. H., & Wagner, H. N. (1990). Cocaine-induced reduction of utilization in human brain. *Archives of General Psychiatry, 47,* 567–574. (5)

Long, B. B. (1986). The prevention of mental-emotional disabilities. *American Psychologist, 41,* 825–829. (15)

Longstreth, L. E. (1981). Revisiting Skeels' final study: A critique. *Developmental Psychology, 17,* 620–625. (9)

Lord, C. G., & Lepper, M. R. (1999). Attitude representation theory. *Advances in Experimental Social Psychology, 31,* 265–343. (14)

Lorenz, K. (1950). The comparative method in studying innate behaviour patterns. *Symposia of the Society for Experimental Biology, 4,* 221–268. (11)

Lotto, R. B., & Purves, D. (1999). The effects of color on brightness. *Nature Neuroscience, 2,* 1010–1014. (4)

Lotze, M., Grodd, W., Birbaumer, N., Erb, M., Huse, E., & Flor, H. (1999). Does use of a myoelectric prosthesis prevent cortical reorganization and phantom limb pain? *Nature Neuroscience, 2,* 501–502. (4)

Lourenço, O., & Machado, A. (1996). In defense of Piaget's theory: A reply to 10 common criticisms. *Psychological Review, 103,* 143–164. (10)

Lowe, M. R. (1993). The effects of dieting on eating behavior: A three-factor model. *Psychological Bulletin, 114,* 100–121. (11)

Lubinski, D., & Benbow, C. P. (1992). Gender differences in abilities and preferences among the gifted: Implications for the math-science pipeline. *Current Directions in Psychological Science, 1,* 61–66. (9)

Lucas, R. E., Diener, E., Grob, A., Suh, E. M., & Shao, L. (2000). Cross-cultural evidence for the fundamental features of extraversion. *Journal of Personality and Social Psychology, 79,* 452–468. (13)

Lucas, R. E., & Fujita, F. (2000). Factors influencing the relation between extraversion and pleasant affect. *Journal of Personality and Social Psychology, 79,* 1039–1056. (13)

Luck, S. J., & Vogel, E. K. (1997). The capacity of visual working memory for features and conjunctions. *Nature, 390,* 279–281. (7)

Lüer, G., Becker, D., Lass, U., Yunqiu, F., Guopeng, C., & Zhongming, W. (1998). Memory span in German and Chinese: Evidence for the phonological loop. *European Psychologist, 3,* 102–112. (7)

Luthar, S. S., Cicchetti, D., & Becker, B. (2000). The construct of resilience: A critical evaluation and guidelines for future work. *Child Development, 71,* 543–562. (10)

Lykken, D. T. (1979). The detection of deception. *Psychological Bulletin, 86,* 47–53. (12)

Lykken, D. T., Bouchard, T. J., Jr., McGue, M., & Tellegen, A. (1993). Heritability of interests: A twin study. *Journal of Applied Psychology, 78,* 649–661. (3)

Lykken, D. T., McGue, M., Tellegen, A., & Bouchard, T. J. (1992). Emergenesis: Genetic traits that may not run in families. *American Psychologist, 47,* 1565–1577. (3)

Lykken, D., & Tellegen, A. (1996). Happiness is a stochastic phenomenon. *Psychological Science, 7,* 186–189. (12)

Lymburner, J. A., & Roesch, R. (1999). The insanity defense: Five years of research (1993–1999). *International Journal of Law and Psychiatry, 22,* 213–240. (15)

Lynam, D. R. (1996). Early identification of chronic offenders: Who is the fledgling psychopath? *Psychological Bulletin, 120,* 209–234. (12)

Lynn, R. (1998). In support of the nutrition theory. In U. Neisser (Ed.), *The rising curve* (pp. 207–215). Washington, DC: American Psychological Association. (9)

Lyons, M. J., Eisen, S. A., Goldberg, J., True, W., Lin, N., Meyer, J. M., Toomey, R., Faraone, S. V., Merla-Ramos, M., & Tsuang, M. T. (1998). A registry-based twin study of depression in men. *Archives of General Psychiatry, 55,* 468–472. (16)

Maccoby, E. E. (1990). Gender and relationships. *American Psychologist, 45,* 513–520. (10)

Maccoby, E. E., & Jacklin, C. N. (1974). *The psychology of sex differences.* Stanford, CA: Stanford University Press. (10)

MacCoun, R. J. (1998). Toward a psychology of harm reduction. *American Psychologist, 53,* 1199–1208. (16)

MacCoun, R., & Reuter, P. (1997). Interpreting Dutch cannabis policy: Reasoning by analogy in the legalization debate. *Science, 278,* 47–52. (16)

Macdonald, R. L., Weddle, M. G., & Gross, R. A. (1986). Benzodiazepine, beta-carboline, and barbiturate actions on GABA responses. *Advances in Biochemical Psychopharmacology, 41*, 67–78. (16)

Macmillan, M. (1997). *Freud evaluated.* Cambridge, MA: MIT Press. (13)

MacNeilage, R. F., & Davis, B. L. (2000). On the origin of internal structure of word forms. *Science, 288*, 527–531. (8)

MacQuitty, J. (1996, August 1). Lily the stink loses its 33-year reputation by a nose. *The Times* (London), pp. 1–2. (11)

Maehr, M. L., & Kleiber, D. A. (1981). The graying of achievement motivation. *American Psychologist, 36*, 787–793. (11)

Magavi, S. S., Leavitt, B. R., & Macklis, J. D. (2000). Induction of neurogenesis in the neocortex of adult mice. *Nature, 405*, 951–955. (3)

Magee, W. J., Eaton, W. W., Wittchen, H. -U., McGonagle, K. A., & Kessler, R. C. (1996). Agoraphobia, simple phobia, and social phobia in the National Comorbidity Survey. *Archives of General Psychiatry, 53*, 159–168. (16)

Maguire, E. A., Gadian, D. G., Johnsrude, I. S., Good, C. D., Ashburner, J., Frackowiak, R. S. J., & Firth, C. D. (2000). Navigation-related structural change in the hippocampi of taxi drivers. *Proceedings of the National Academy of Sciences, 97*, 4398–4403. (3)

Maki, R. H. (1990). Memory for script actions: Effects of relevance and detail expectancy. *Memory & Cognition, 18*, 5–14. (7)

Maier, S. F., & Watkins, L. R. (1998). Cytokines for psychologists: Implications of bidirectional immune-to-brain communication for understanding behavior, mood, and cognition. *Psychological Review, 105*, 83–107. (12)

Maki, R. H., & Serra, M. (1992). The basis of test predictions for text material. *Journal of Experimental Psychology: Learning, Memory, and Cognition, 18*, 116–126. (7)

Maki, R. H., & Syman, E. M. (1997). Teaching of controversial and empirically validated treatments in APA-accredited clinical and counseling psychology programs. *Psychotherapy, 34*, 44–57. (15)

Malamed, F., & Zaidel, E. (1993). Language and task effects on lateralized word recognition. *Brain and Language, 45*, 70–85. (8)

Maldonado, R., Saiardi, A., Valverde, O., Samad, T. A., Roques, B. P., & Borrelli, E. (1997). Absence of opiate rewarding effects in mice lacking dopamine D2 receptors. *Nature, 388*, 586–589. (5)

Malinosky-Rummell, R., & Hansen, D. J. (1993). Long-term consequences of childhood physical abuse. *Psychological Bulletin, 114*, 68–79. (12)

Malmberg, A. B., Chen, C., Tonegawa, S., & Basbaum, A. I. (1997). Preserved acute pain and reduced neuropathic pain in mice lacking **PKC** . *Science, 278*, 179–283. (4)

Malmquist, C. P. (1986). Children who witness parental murder: Posttraumatic aspects. *Journal of the American Academy of Child Psychiatry, 25*, 320–325. (7)

Mangelsdorf, S. C., & Frosch, C. A. (2000). Temperament and attachment: One construct or two? *Advances in Child Development and Behavior, 27*, 181–220. (10)

Manji, H. K., Potter, W. Z., & Lenox, R. H. (1995). Signal transduction pathways. *Archives of General Psychiatry, 52*, 532–543. (16)

Mansky, P. A. (1978). Opiates: Human psychopharmacology. In L. L. Iversen, S. D. Iversen, & S. H. Snyder (Eds.), *Handbook of psychopharmacology: Vol. 12. Drugs of abuse* (pp. 95–185). New York: Plenum. (5)

Manuck, S. B., Cohen, S., Rabin, B. S., Muldoon, M. F., & Bachen, E. A. (1991). Individual differences in cellular immune response to stress. *Psychological Science, 2*, 111–115. (12)

Maquet, P., Laureys, S., Peigneux, P., Fuchs, S., Petiau, C., Phillips, C., Aerts, J., DelFiore, G., Degueldre, C., Meulemans, T., Luxen, A., Frank, G., Van Der Linden, M., Smith, C., & Cleeremans, A. (2000). Experience-dependent changes in cerebral activation during human REM sleep. *Nature Neuroscience, 3*, 831–836. (5)

Maquet, P., Peters, J. -M., Aerts, J., Delfiore, G., Degueldre, C., Luxen, A., & Franck, G. (1996). Functional neuroanatomy of human rapid-eye-movement sleep and dreaming. *Nature, 383*, 163–166. (5)

Marcar, V. L., Zihl, J., & Cowey, A. (1997). Comparing the visual deficits of a motion blind patient with the visual deficits of monkeys with area MT removed. *Neuropsychologia, 35*, 1459–1465. (3)

Marcia, J. E. (1980). Identity in adolescence. In J. Adelson (Ed.), *Handbook of adolescent psychology* (pp. 159–187). New York: Wiley. (10)

Marcus, G. F., Vijayan, S., Rao, S. B., & Vishton, P. M. (1999). Rule learning by seven-month-old infants. *Science, 283*, 77–80. (8)

Marder, S. R., Mebane, A., Chien, C., Winslade, W. J., Swann, E., & Van Putten, T. (1983). A comparison of patients who refuse and consent to neuroleptic treatment. *American Journal of Psychiatry, 140*, 470–472. (15)

Marian, V., & Neisser, U. (2000). Language-dependent recall of autobiographical memories. *Journal of Experimental Psychology: General, 129*, 361–368. (7)

Marin, R. H., Perez, M. F., Duero, D. G., & Ramirez, O. A. (1999). Preexposure to drug administration context blocks the development of tolerance to sedative effects of diazepam. *Pharmacology Biochemistry and Behavior, 64*, 473–477. (6)

Maris, R. W. (1997). Social suicide. *Suicide and Life-Threatening Behavior, 27*, 41–49. (16)

Markey, P. M. (2000). Bystander intervention in computer-mediated intervention. *Computers in Human Behavior, 16*, 183–188. (14)

Markman, E. M. (1990). Constraints children place on word meanings. *Cognitive Science, 14*, 57–77. (8)

Marks, D., & Kammann, R. (1980). *The psychology of the psychic.* Buffalo, NY: Prometheus. (2, 13)

Marks, I., Lovell, K., Noshirvani, H., Livanou, M., & Thrasher, S. (1998). Treatment of posttraumatic stress disorder by exposure and/or cognitive restructuring. *Archives of General Psychiatry, 55*, 317–325. (15)

Marler, P. (1997). Three models of song learning: Evidence from behavior. *Journal of Neurobiology, 33*, 501–516. (6)

Marler, P., & Peters, S. (1981). Sparrows learn adult song and more from memory. *Science, 213*, 780–782. (6)

Marler, P., & Peters, S. (1982). Long-term storage of learned birdsongs prior to production. *Animal Behaviour, 30*, 479–482. (6)

Marler, P., & Peters, S. (1987). A sensitive period for song acquisition in the song sparrow, *Melospiza melodia*: A case of age-limited learning. *Ethology, 76*, 89–100. (6)

Marler, P., & Peters, S. (1988). Sensitive periods for song acquisition from tape recordings and live tutors in the swamp sparrow, *Melospiza georgiana. Ethology, 77*, 76–84. (6)

Marlowe, F., & Wetsman, A. (2001). Preferred waist-to-hip ratio and ecology. *Personality and Individual Differences, 30*, 481–489. (14)

Marriott, F. H. C. (1976). Abnormal colour vision. In H. Davson (Ed.), *The eye* (2nd ed., pp. 533–547). New York: Academic Press. (4)

Marsh, R. L., Landau, J. D., & Hicks, J. L. (1997). Contributions of inadequate source monitoring to unconscious plagiarism during idea generation. *Journal of Experimental Psychology: Learning, Memory, and Cognition, 23*, 886–897. (7)

Martin, J. M., & Cole, D. A. (2000). Using the Personal Stroop to detect children's awareness of social rejection by peers. *Cognition and Emotion, 14*, 241–260. (13)

Martorell, R. (1998). Nutrition and the worldwide rise in IQ scores. In U. Neisser (Ed.), *The rising curve* (pp. 183–206). Washington, DC: American Psychological Association. (9)

Martsh, C. T., & Miller, W. R. (1997). Extraversion predicts heavy drinking in college students. *Personality and Individual Differences, 23*, 153–155. (13)

Masling, J. M., Bornstein, R. F., Poynton, F. G., Reid, S., & Katkin, E. S. (1991). Perception without awareness and electrodermal responding: A strong test of subliminal psychodynamic activation effects. *Journal of Mind and Behavior, 12*, 33–48. (4)

Maslow, A. H. (1962). *Toward a psychology of being.* Princeton, NJ: Van Nostrand. (13)

Maslow, A. H. (1970). *Motivation and personality* (2nd ed.). New York: Harper & Row. (11)

Maslow, A. H. (1971). *The farther reaches of human nature.* New York: Viking. (13)

Masson, J. M. (1984). *The assault on truth.* New York: Farrar, Straus and Giroux. (13)

Masson, J. M. (1985). *The complete letters of Sigmund Freud to Wilhelm Fliess 1887–1904.* Cambridge, MA: Harvard University Press. (13)

Masten, A. S., & Coatsworth, J. D. (1998). The development of competence in favorable and unfavorable environments. *American Psychologist, 53*, 205–220. (10)

Masters, W. H., & Johnson, V. E. (1966). *Human sexual response.* Boston: Little, Brown. (11)

Matheny, A. P., Jr. (1989). Children's behavioral inhibition over age and across situations: Genetic similarity for a trait to change. *Journal of Personality, 57*, 215–235. (10)

Mather, M., Shafir, E., & Johnson, M. K. (2000). Misremembrance of options past: Source monitoring and choice. *Psychological Science, 11*, 132–138. (7)

Matin, E., Clymer, A. B., & Matin, L. (1972). Metacontrast and saccadic suppression. *Science, 178*, 179–182. (8)

Matsui, T., Okada, A., & Kakuyama, T. (1982). Influence of goal setting, performance, and feedback effectiveness. *Journal of Applied Psychology, 67*, 645–648. (11)

Matsunami, H., Montmayeur, J.-P., & Buck, L. B. (2000). A family of candidate taste receptors in human and mouse. *Nature, 404*, 601–604. (4)

Matthews, K. A., & Rodin, J. (1989). Women's changing work roles. *American Psychologist, 44*, 1389–1393. (11)

Matsumoto, D. (1994). *People: Psychology from a cultural perspective.* Pacific Grove, CA: Brooks/Cole. (2)

Mattson, S. N., Riley, E. P., Grambling, L., Delis, D. C., & Jones, K. L. (1998). Neuropsychological comparison of alcohol-exposed children with or without physical features of fetal alcohol syndrome. *Neuropsychology, 12*, 146–153. (10)

Matute, H. (1996). Illusion of control: Detecting response-outcome independence in analytic but not in naturalistic conditions. *Psychological Science, 7*, 289–293. (8)

Maurice, D. M. (1998). The Von Sallman lecture of 1996: An ophthalmological explanation of REM sleep. *Experimental Eye Research, 66*, 139–145. (5)

May, C. P., Hasher, L., & Stoltzfus, E. R. (1993). Optimal time of day and the magnitude of age differences in memory. *Psychological Science, 4*, 326–330. (5)

May, M. (1999, January/February). Speed demons. *The Sciences, 39*(1), 16–18. (8)

Mayer, J. D. (2001). Emotion, intelligence, and emotional intelligence. In J. P. Forgas (Ed.), *Handbook of affect and social cognition* (pp. 410–431). Mahwah, NJ: Erlbaum. (12)

Mayer, J. D., & Salovey, P. (1995). Emotional intelligence and the construction and regulation of feelings. *Applied & Preventive Psychology, 4*, 197–208. (12)

Mayer, J. D., & Salovey, P. (1997). What is emotional intelligence? In P. Salovey & D. J. Sluyter (Eds.). *Emotional development and emotional intelligence* (pp. 3–34). New York: Basic Books. (12)

McCann, U. D., Lowe, K. A., & Ricaurte, G. A. (1997). Long-lasting effects of recreational drugs of abuse on the central nervous system. *The Neuroscientist, 3*, 399–411. (5)

McClelland, D. C. (1998). Identifying competencies with behavioral-event interviews. *Psychological Science, 9*, 331–339. (9)

McClelland, D. C., Atkinson, J. W., Clark, R. A., & Lowell, E. L. (1953). *The achievement motive.* New York: Appleton-Century-Crofts. (11)

McClelland, D. C., Koestner, R., & Weinberger, J. (1989). How do self-attributed and implicit motives differ? *Psychological Review, 96*, 690–702. (11)

McClelland, J. L. (1988). Connectionist models and psychological evidence. *Journal of Memory and Language, 27*, 107–123. (8)

McClelland, J. L., & Rumelhart, D. E. (1981). An interactive activation model of context effects in letter perception: Part 1. An account of basic findings. *Psychological Review, 88*, 375–407. (8)

McClintock, M. K. (1971). Menstrual synchrony and suppression. *Nature, 229*, 244–245. (4)

McClure, J. (1998). Discounting causes of behavior: Are two reasons better than one? *Journal of Personality and Social Psychology, 74*, 7–20. (14)

McClure, E. B. (2000). A meta-analytic review of sex differences in facial expression processing and their development in infants, children, and adolescents. *Psychological Bulletin, 126*, 424–453. (12)

McCormick, M. C. (1985). The contribution of low birth weight to infant mortality and childhood morbidity. *New England Journal of Medicine, 312*, 82–90. (10)

McCornack, R. L. (1983). Bias in the validity of predicted college grades in four ethnic minority groups. *Educational & Psychological Measurement, 43*, 517–522. (9)

McCourt, K., Bouchard, T. J., Jr., Lykken, D. T., Tellegen, A., & Keyes, M. (1999). Authoritarianism revisited: Genetic and environmental influences examined in twins reared apart and together. *Personality and Individual Differences, 27,* 985–1014. (3)

McCrae, R. R. (1996). Social consequences of experiential openness. *Psychological Bulletin, 120,* 323–337. (13)

McCrae, R. R., & Costa, P. T., Jr. (1987). Validation of the five-factor model of personality across instruments and observers. *Journal of Personality and Social Psychology, 52,* 81–90. (13)

McCrae, R. R., & Costa, P. T., Jr. (1994). The stability of personality: Observations and evaluations. *Current Directions in Psychological Science, 3,* 173–175. (13)

McCrae, R. R., & Costa, P. T., Jr. (1997). Personality trait structure as a human universal. *American Psychologist, 52,* 509–516. (13)

McCrae, R. R., Costa, P. T., Jr., Ostendorf, F., Angleitner, A., **Hrebícková,** M., Avia, M. D., Sanz, J., Sánchez-Bernardos, M. L., Kusdil, M. E., Woodfield, R., Saunders, P. R., & Smith, D. B. (2000). Nature over nurture: Temperament, personality, and life span development. *Journal of Personality and Social Psychology, 78,* 173–186. (13)

McDaniel, M. A., Einstein, G. O., & Lollis, T. (1988). Qualitative and quantitative considerations in encoding difficulty effects. *Memory & Cognition, 16,* 8–14. (7)

McFarlane, A. C. (1997). The prevalence and longitudinal course of PTSD. *Annals of the New York Academy of Sciences, 821,* 10–23. (12)

McGovern, P. E., Glusker, D. L., Exner, L. J., & Voigt, M. M. (1996). Neolithic resinated wine. *Nature, 381,* 480–481. (5)

McGregor, D. M. (1960). *The human side of enterprise.* New York: McGraw-Hill. (11)

McGue, M. (1999). The behavioral genetics of alcoholism. *Current Directions in Psychological Science, 8,* 109–115. (16)

McGue, M., & Bouchard, T. J., Jr. (1998). Genetic and environmental influences on human behavioral differences. *Annual Review of Neuroscience, 21,* 1–24. (9)

McGuire, W. J., & Papageorgis, D. (1961). The relative efficacy of various types of prior belief-defense in producing immunity against persuasion. *Journal of Abnormal and Social Psychology, 62,* 327–337. (14)

McGurk, H., Caplan, M., Hennessy, E., & Moss, P. (1993). Controversy, theory, and social context in contemporary day care research. *Journal of Child Psychology, 34,* 3–23. (10)

McMurtry, P. L., & Mershon, D. H. (1985). Auditory distance judgments in noise, with and without hearing protection. *Proceedings of the Human Factors Society* (Baltimore, MD), pp. 811–813. (4)

McNally, R. J. (1990). Psychological approaches to panic disorder: A review. *Psychological Bulletin, 108,* 403–419. (16)

McQuillin, A., Lawrence, J., Kalsi, G., Chen, A., & Gurling, H. (1999). No allelic association between bipolar affective disorder and the tryptophan hydroxylase gene. *Archives of General Psychiatry, 56,* 99–100. (16)

Mechner, D. A. (1998, January/February). All systems go. *The Sciences, 38*(1), 32–37. (8)

Meddis, R., Pearson, A. J. D., & Langford, G. (1973). An extreme case of healthy insomnia. *EEG and Clinical Neurophysiology, 35,* 213–214. (5)

Meichenbaum, D. (1985). *Stress inoculation training.* New York: Pergamon. (12)

Meichenbaum, D., & Cameron, R. (1983). Stress inoculation training. In D. Meichenbaum & M. E. Jaremko (Eds.), *Stress*

reduction and prevention* (pp. 115–154). New York: Plenum. (12)

Meichenbaum, D. H. (1995). Cognitive-behavioral therapy in historical perspective. In B. Bongar & L. E. Beutler (Eds.), *Comprehensive textbook of psychotherapy: Theory and practice* (pp. 140–158). Oxford, England: Oxford University Press. (15)

Meichenbaum, D. H., & Goodman, J. (1971). Training impulsive children to talk to themselves: A means of developing self-control. *Journal of Abnormal Psychology, 77,* 115–126. (6)

Mellers, B. A., Schwartz, A., Ho, K., & Ritov, I. (1997). Decision affect theory: Emotional reactions to the outcomes of risky options. *Psychological Science, 8,* 423–429. (8)

Mello, N. K., & Mendelson, J. H. (1978). Behavioral pharmacology of human alcohol, heroin and marihuana use. In J. Fishman (Ed.), *The bases of addiction* (pp. 133–158). Berlin, Germany: Dahlem Konferenzen. (5)

Meltzer, H. Y. (1995). The role of serotonin in schizophrenia and the place of serotonin-dopamine antagonist antipsychotics. *Journal of Clinical Psychopharmacology, 15*(Suppl. 1), S2–S3. (16)

Melzack, R., & Wall, P. D. (1965). Pain mechanisms: A new theory. *Science, 150,* 971–979. (4)

Melzack, R., Weisz, A. Z., & Sprague, L. T. (1963). Stratagems for controlling pain: Contributions of auditory stimulation and suggestion. *Experimental Neurology, 8,* 239–247. (12)

Mershon, D. H., Desaulniers, D. H., Kiefer, S. A., Amerson, T. L., Jr., & Mills, J. T. (1981). Perceived loudness and visually determined auditory distance. *Perception, 10,* 531–543. (4)

Mershon, D. H., & King, L. E. (1975). Intensity and reverberation as factors in the auditory perception of egocentric distance. *Perception and Psychophysics, 18,* 409–415. (4)

Mesmer, F. A. (1980). *Mesmerism: A translation of the original medical and scientific writings of F. A. Mesmer.* Los Altos, CA: Kaufmann. (5)

Messick, S. (1995). Validity of psychological assessment. *American Psychologist, 50,* 741–749. (9)

Metcalfe, J., & Wiebe, D. (1987). Intuition in insight and noninsight problem solving. *Memory & Cognition, 15,* 238–246. (8)

Meyerowitz, B. E., Richardson, J., Hudson, S., & Leedham, B. (1998). Ethnicity and cancer outcomes: Behavioral and psychosocial considerations. *Psychological Bulletin, 123,* 47–70. (12)

Mezzanotte, W. S., Tangel, D. J., & White, D. P. (1992). Waking genioglossal electromyogram in sleep apnea patients versus normal controls (a neuromuscular compensatory mechanism). *Journal of Clinical Investigation, 89,* 1571–1579. (5)

Michener, W., Rozin, P., Freeman, E., & Gale, L. (1999). The role of low progesterone and tension as triggers of perimenstrual chocolate and sweets cravings: Some negative experimental evidence. *Physiology & Behavior, 67,* 417–420. (11)

Milar, K. S. (2000). The first generation of women psychologists and the psychology of women. *American Psychologist, 55,* 616–619. (1)

Milgram, S. (1974). *Obedience to authority.* New York: Harper & Row. (14)

Miller, D. T. (1999). The norm of self-interest. *American Psychologist, 54,* 1053–1060. (10)

Miller, D. T., & Ross, M. (1975). Self-serving biases in the attribution of causality: Fact or fiction? *Psychological Bulletin, 82,* 213–225. (14)

Miller, G. A. (1956). The magical number seven, plus or minus two: Some limits on our capacity for processing information. *Psychological Review, 63,* 81–97. (7)

Miller, L. C., & Fishkin, S. A. (1997). On the dynamics of human bonding and reproductive success: Seeking windows on the adapted-for human-environmental interface. In J. A. Simpson & D. T. Kenrick (Eds.), *Evolutionary social psychology* (pp. 197–235). Mahwah, NJ: Erlbaum. (2)

Miller, L. K. (1999). The savant syndrome: Intellectual impairment and exceptional skill. *Psychological Bulletin, 125,* 31–46. (9)

Miller, L. L., & Branconnier, R. J. (1983). Cannabis: Effects on memory and the cholinergic limbic system. *Psychological Bulletin, 93,* 441–456. (5)

Miller, R. J., Hennessy, R. T., & Leibowitz, H. W. (1973). The effect of hypnotic ablation of the background on the magnitude of the Ponzo perspective illusion. *International Journal of Clinical and Experimental Hypnosis, 21,* 180–191. (5)

Miller, S. M., Shoda, Y., & Hurley, K. (1996). Applying cognitive-social theory to health-protective behavior: Breast self-examination in cancer screening. *Psychological Bulletin, 119,* 70–94. (12)

Miller, T. Q., Smith, T. W., Turner, C. W., Guijarro, M. L., & Hallet, A. J. (1996). A meta-analytic review of research on hostility and physical health. *Psychological Bulletin, 119,* 322–348. (12)

Miller, W. R., & Brown, S. A. (1997). Why psychologists should treat alcohol and drug problems. *American Psychologist, 52,* 1269–1279. (16)

Miller, W. R., & Hester, R. K. (1986). Inpatient alcohol treatment: Who benefits? *American Psychologist, 41,* 794–805. (16)

Milliken, B., Joorderns, S., Merikle, P. M., & Seiffert, A. E. (1998). Selective attention: A reevaluation of the implications of negative priming. *Psychological Review, 105,* 203–229. (8)

Milner, B. (1959). The memory defect in bilateral hippocampal lesions. *Psychiatric Research Reports, 11,* 43–52. (7)

Milton, J., & Wiseman, R. (1999). Does psi exist? Lack of replication of an anomalous process of information. *Psychological Bulletin, 125,* 387–391. (2)

Mineka, S. (1987). A primate model of phobic fears. In H. Eysenck & I. Martin (Eds.), *Theoretical foundations of behavior therapy* (pp. 81–111). New York: Plenum. (16)

Mineka, S., Davidson, M., Cook, M., & Keir, R. (1984). Observational conditioning of snake fear in rhesus monkeys. *Journal of Abnormal Psychology, 93,* 355–372. (16)

Mischel, W. (1973). Toward a cognitive social learning reconceptualization of personality. *Psychological Review, 80,* 252–283. (13)

Mischel, W. (1981). Current issues and challenges in personality. In L. T. Benjamin, Jr. (Ed.), *The G. Stanley Hall Lecture Series* (Vol. 1, pp. 81–99). Washington, DC: American Psychological Association. (13)

Mischel, W., & Shoda, Y. (1995). A cognitive-affective system theory of personality: Reconceptualizing situations, dispositions, dynamics, and invariance in personality structure. *Psychological Review, 102,* 246–268. (13)

Misrahi, M., Meduri, G., Pissard, S., Bouvattier, C. Beau, I., Loosfelt, H., Jolivet, A., Rappaport, R., Milgrom, E., & Bougneres, P. (1997). *Journal of Clinical Endocrinology and Metabolism, 82,* 2159–2165. (11)

Moar, I., & Bower, G. H. (1983). Inconsistency in spatial knowledge. *Memory & Cognition, 11,* 107–113. (8)

Mobily, K. (1982). Using physical therapy activity and recreation to cope with stress and anxiety: A review. *American Corrective Therapy Journal, 36,* 77–81. (12)

Moller, H. J. (1992). Attempted suicide: Efficacy of different aftercare strategies. *International Clinical Psychopharmacology, 6*(Suppl. 6), 58–59. (15)

Mombaerts, P. (1999). Seven-trans-membrane proteins as odorant and chemosensory receptors. *Science, 286,* 707–711. (4)

Monahan, J. (1984). The prediction of violent behavior: Toward a second generation of theory and policy. *American Journal of Psychiatry, 141,* 10–15. (12)

Monahan, J. (1992). Mental disorder and violent behavior. *American Psychologist, 47,* 511–521. (12)

Monahan, J. (1993). Limiting therapist exposure to *Tarasoff* liability: Guidelines for risk containment. *American Psychologist, 48,* 242–250. (15)

Monahan, J., & Steadman, H. J. (1996). Violent storms and violent people. *American Psychologist, 51,* 931–938. (12)

Money, J., & Ehrhardt, A. A. (1972). *Man and woman, boy and girl.* Baltimore, MD: Johns Hopkins University Press. (11)

Montello, D. R. (1995). How significant are cultural differences in spatial cognition? In A. U. Frank & W. Kuhn (Eds.), *Spatial information theory* (pp. 485–500). Berlin, Germany: Springer Verlag. (4)

Monti-Bloch, L., Jennings-White, C., Dolberg, D. S., & Berliner, D. L. (1994). The human vomeronasal system. *Psychoneuroendocrinology, 19,* 673–686. (4)

Montgomery, G., & Kirsch, I. (1996). Mechanisms of placebo pain reduction: An empirical investigation. *Psychological Science, 7,* 174–176. (4)

Moorcroft, W. (1993). *Sleep, dreaming, and sleep disorders: An introduction* (2nd ed.). Lanham, MD: University Press of America. (5)

Moore, B. C. J. (1989). *An introduction to the psychology of hearing* (3rd ed.). London: Academic Press. (4)

Moore, J. (1995). Some historical and conceptual relations among logical positivism, behaviorism, and cognitive psychology. In J. T. Todd & E. K. Morris (Eds.), *Modern perspectives on B. F. Skinner and contemporary behaviorism* (pp. 51–74). Westport, CT: Greenwood Press. (6)

Moore, L. B., Goodwin, B., Jones, S. A., Wisely, G. B., Serabjit-Singh, C. J., Willson, T. M., Collins, J. L., & Kliewer, S. A. (2000). St. John's wort induces hepatic drug metabolism through activation of the pregnane X receptor. *Proceedings of the National Academy of Sciences (U.S.A.), 97,* 7500–7502. (16)

Morrow, R. S., & Morrow, S. (1974). The measurement of intelligence. In B. B. Wolman (Ed.), *Handbook of general psychology* (pp. 656–670). Upper Saddle River, NJ: Prentice Hall. (9)

Moscovitch, M. (1985). Memory from infancy to old age: Implications for theories of normal and pathological memory. *Annals of the New York Academy of Sciences, 444,* 78–96. (7)

Moscovitch, M. (1989). Confabulation and the frontal systems: Strategic versus associative retrieval in neuropsychological theories of memory. In H. L. Roediger, III, & F. I. M. Craik (Eds.), *Varieties of memory and consciousness: Essays in honour of Endel Tulving* (pp. 133–160). Hillsdale, NJ: Erlbaum. (7)

Moscovitch, M. (1992). Memory and working-with-memory: A component process model based on modules and central systems. *Journal of Cognitive Neuroscience, 4,* 257–267. (7)

Moscovitch, M. (1995). Confabulation. In D. L. Schacter (Ed.), *Memory distortion* (pp. 226–251). Cambridge, MA: Harvard University Press. (7)

Moscovitch, M., & Behrmann, M. (1994). Coding of spatial information in the somatosensory system: Evidence from patients with neglect following parietal lobe damage. *Journal of Cognitive Neuroscience, 6,* 151–155. (3)

Moscovitch, M., Winocur, G., & Behrmann, M. (1997). What is special about face recognition? Nineteen experiments on a person with visual object agnosia and dyslexia but normal face recognition. *Journal of Cognitive Neuroscience, 9,* 555–604. (4)

Moskowitz, B. A. (1978). The acquisition of language. *Scientific American, 239*(5), 92–108. (8)

Mulholland, A. M., & Mintz, L. B. (2001). Prevalence of eating disorders among African American women. *Journal of Counseling Psychology, 48,* 111–116. (11)

Munakata, Y., McClelland, J. L., Johnson, M. H., & Siegler, R. S. (1997). Rethinking infant knowledge: Toward an adaptive process account of successes and failures in object permanence tasks. *Psychological Review, 104,* 686–713. (10)

Munroe, R. (1955). *Schools of psychoanalytic thought.* New York: Dryden. (15)

Muraven, M., & Baumeister, R. F. (2000). Self-regulation and depletion of limited resources: Does self-control resemble a muscle? *Psychological Bulletin, 126,* 247–259. (12)

Murphy, G. L., & Medin, D. L. (1985). The role of theories in conceptual coherence. *Psychological Review, 92,* 289–316. (8)

Murphy, J. M., Laird, N. M., Monson, R. R., Sobol, A. M., & Leighton, A. H. (2000). A 40-year perspective on the prevalence of depression. *Archives of General Psychiatry, 57,* 209–215. (16)

Murray, H. A. (1943). *Thematic Apperception Test manual.* Cambridge, MA: Harvard University Press. (13)

Murray, J. P. (1998). Studying television violence. A research agenda for the 21st century. In J. K. Asamen & G. L. Berry (Eds.), *Research paradigms, television, and social behavior* (pp. 369–410). Thousand Oaks, CA: Sage. (2)

Muskin, P. R. (1998). The request to die: Role for a psychodynamic perspective on physician-assisted suicide. *Journal of the American Medical Association, 279,* 323–328. (16)

Myers, D. G. (2000). The funds, friends, and faith of happy people. *American Psychologist, 55,* 56–67. (12)

Myers, J. K., Weissman, M. M., Tischler, G. L., Holzer, C. E., III, Leaf, P. J., Orvaschel, H., Anthony, J. C., Boyd, J. H., Burke, J. D., Jr., Kramer, M., & Stoltzman, R. (1984). Six-month prevalence of psychiatric disorders in three communities. *Archives of General Psychiatry, 41,* 959–967. (15)

Nagera, H. (1976). *Obsessional neuroses.* New York: Aronson. (16)

Nakajima, S., Hayashi, H., & Kato, T. (2000). Taste aversion induced by confinement in a running wheel. *Behavioural Processes, 49,* 35–42. (6)

Nantais, K. M., & Schellenberg, E. G. (1999). The Mozart effect: An artifact of preference. *Psychological Science, 10,* 370–373. (2)

Nash, M. (1987). What, if anything, is regressed about hypnotic age regression? A review of the empirical literature. *Psychological Bulletin, 102,* 42–52. (5)

Nash, M. R., Johnson, L. S., & Tipton, R. D. (1979). Hypnotic age regression and the occurrence of transitional object relationships. *Journal of Abnormal Psychology, 88,* 547–555. (5)

National Institute of Mental Health. (1982). *Television and behavior: Ten years of scientific progress and implications for the eighties.* Rockville, MD: Author. (2)

National Institutes of Health. (2000). *The practical guide: Identification, evaluation, and treatment of overweight and obesity in adults* (NIH Publication No. 00-4084). Washington, DC: Author. (11)

Nebes, R. D. (1974). Hemispheric specialization in commissurotomized man. *Psychological Bulletin, 81,* 1–14. (3)

Negy, C., Leal-Puente, L., Trainor, D. J., & Carlson, R. (1997). Mexican American adolescents' performance on the MMPI-A. *Journal of Personality Assessment, 69,* 205–214. (13)

Neher, A. (1996). Jung's theory of archetypes: A critique. *Journal of Humanistic Psychology, 36,* 61–91. (13)

Neisser, U. (1997). Rising scores on intelligence tests. *American Scientist, 85,* 440–447. (9)

Neisser, U. (chair), Boodoo, G., Bouchard, T. J., Jr., Boykin, A. W., Brody, N., Ceci, S. J., Halpern, D. F., Loehlin, J. C., Perloff, R., Sternberg, R. J., & Urbina, S. (1996). Intelligence: Knowns and unknowns. *American Psychologist, 51,* 77–101. (9)

Nelson, K. E., Baker, N. D., Denninger, M., Bonvillian, J. D., & Kaplan, B. J. (1985). Cookie versus Do-it-again: Imitative-referential and personal-social-syntactic-initiating language styles in young children. *Linguistics, 23,* 433–454. (8)

Nelson, T. O., & Leonesio, R. J. (1988). Allocation of self-paced study time and the "labor-in-vain effect." *Journal of Experimental Psychology: Learning, Memory, and Cognition, 14,* 676–686. (7)

Nemeth, C. (1972). A critical analysis of research utilizing the prisoner's dilemma paradigm for the study of bargaining. In L. Berkowitz (Ed.), *Advances in experimental social psychology* (Vol. 6, pp. 203–234). New York: Academic Press. (14)

Nemeth, C. J. (1986). Differential contributions of majority and minority influence. *Psychological Review, 93,* 23–32. (14)

Nemeth, C. J., Connell, J. B., Rogers, J. D., & Brown, K. S. (2001). Improving decision making by means of dissent. *Journal of Applied Social Psychology, 31,* 48–58. (14)

Newman, B. (1988, September 9). Dressing for dinner remains an issue in the naked city. *Wall Street Journal,* p. 1. (14)

Newstead, S. E., & Makinen, S. (1997). Psychology teaching in Europe. *European Psychologist, 2,* 3–10. (1)

Nickerson, R. S., & Adams, M. J. (1979). Long-term memory for a common object. *Cognitive Psychology, 11,* 287–307. (7)

Nietzel, M. T., & Bernstein, D. A. (1987). *Introduction to clinical psychology.* Upper Saddle River, NJ: Prentice Hall. (9)

Nikles, C. D. II, Brecht, D. L., Klinger, E., & Bursell, A. L. (1998). The effects of current-concern- and nonconcern-related waking suggestions on nocturnal dream content. *Journal of Personality and Social Psychology, 75,* 242–255. (5)

Nisbett, R. E., Caputo, C., Legant, P., & Marecek, J. (1973). Behavior as seen by the actor and as seen by the observer. *Journal of Personality and Social Psychology, 27,* 154–164. (14)

Nisbett, R. E., Fong, G. T., Lehman, D. R., & Cheng, P. W. (1987). Teaching reasoning. *Science, 238,* 625–631. (8)

Noble, E. P., Ozkaragoz, T. Z., Ritchie, T. L., Zhang, X., Belin, T. R., & Sparkes, R. S. (1998). D2 and D4 dopamine receptor polymorphisms and personality. *American Journal of Medical Genetics, 81,* 257–267. (13)

Noel, J. G., Wann, D. L., & Branscombe, N. R. (1995). Peripheral ingroup membership status and public negativity toward outgroups. *Journal of Personality and Social Psychology, 68,* 127–137. (14)

Nolen-Hoeksema, S. (1990). *Sex differences in depression.* Stanford, CA: Stanford University Press. (16)

Nolen-Hoeksema, S. (1991). Responses to depression and their effects on the duration of depressive episodes. *Journal of Abnormal Psychology, 100,* 569–582. (16)

Nolen-Hoeksema, S., & Morrow, J. (1991). A prospective study of depression and posttraumatic stress symptoms after a natural disaster: The Loma Prieta earthquake. *Journal of Personality and Social Psychology, 61,* 115–121. (16)

Nopoulos, P. C., Giedd, J. N., Andreasen, N. C., & Rapoport, J. L. (1998). Frequency and severity of enlarged cavum septi pellucidi in childhood-onset schizophrenia. *American Journal of Psychiatry, 155,* 1074–1079. (16)

Norenzayan, A., & Nisbett, R. E. (2000). Culture and causal cognition. *Current Directions in Psychological Science, 9,* 132–135. (14)

Norman, D. A. (1988). *The psychology of everyday things.* New York: Basic Books. (1)

Norman, R. A., Tataranni, P. A., Pratley, R., Thompson, D. B., Hanson, R. L., Prochazka, M., Baier, L., Ehm, M. G., Sakul, H., Foroud, T., Garvey, W. T., Burns, D., Knowler, W. C. Bennett, P. H., Bogardus, C., & Ravussin, E. (1998). Autosomal genomic scan for loci linked to obesity and energy metabolism in Pima Indians. *American Journal of Human Genetics, 62,* 659–668. (11)

North, R. A. (1992). Cellular actions of opiates and cocaine. *Annals of the New York Academy of Sciences, 654,* 1–6. (5)

Nowak, M. A., Page, K. M., & Sigmund, K. (2000). Fairness versus reason in the ultimatum game. *Science, 289,* 1773–1775. (14)

Nygard, R. (1982). Achievement motives and individual differences in situational specificity of behavior. *Journal of Personality and Social Psychology, 43,* 319–327. (11)

O'Connor, N., Cowan, R., & Samella, K. (2000). Calendrical calculation and intelligence. *Intelligence, 28,* 31–48. (9)

Odell, S. M., & Commander, M. J. (2000). Risk factors for homelessness among people with psychotic disorders. *Social Psychiatry and Psychiatric Epidemiology, 35,* 396–401. (15)

O'Donohue, W., & Kitchener, R. F. (1999). Introduction: The behaviorisms. In W. O'Donohue & R. Kitchener (Eds.), *Handbook of behaviorism* (pp. 1–13). San Diego, CA: Academic Press. (6)

Ohaeri, J. U., Adeyinka, A. O., & Osuntokun, B. O. (1995). Computed tomographic density changes in schizophrenic and manic Nigerian subjects. *Behavioural Neurology, 8,* 31–37. (16)

Ohayon, M. M. (1997). Prevalence of *DSM-IV* diagnostic criteria of insomnia: Distinguishing insomnia related to mental disorders from sleep disorders. *Journal of Psychiatric Research, 31,* 333–346. (5)

Öhman, A., Eriksson, A., & Olofsson, C. (1975). One-trial learning and superior resistance to extinction of autonomic responses conditioned to potentially phobic objects. *Journal of Comparative and Physiological Psychology, 88,* 619–627. (16)

Okin, R. L. (1983). The future of state hospitals: Should there be one? *American Journal of Psychiatry, 140,* 577–581. (15)

Olfson, M., Marcus, S. C., Pincus, H. A., Zito, J. M., Thompson, J. W., & Zarin, D. A. (1998). Antidepressant prescribing practices of outpatient psychiatrists. *Archives of General Psychiatry, 55,* 310–316. (16)

Oliver, M. B., & Hyde, J. S. (1993). Gender differences in sexuality: A meta-analysis. *Psychological Bulletin, 114,* 29–51. (11)

Olney, J. W., & Farger, N. B. (1995). Glutamate receptor dysfunction and schizophrenia. *Archives of General Psychiatry, 52,* 998–1007. (16)

Olweus, D. (1995). Bullying or peer abuse at school: Facts and intervention. *Current Directions in Psychological Science, 4,* 196–200. (12)

O'Neill, H. (2000, September 24). Her testimony sent man to prison, but was he the one who raped her? *Daily Press* (Newport News-Hampton, VA), pp. A1, A14, A15. (7)

Orne, M. T. (1951). The mechanisms of hypnotic age regression: An experimental study. *Journal of Abnormal and Social Psychology, 46,* 213–225. (5)

Orne, M. T. (1959). The nature of hypnosis: Artifact and essence. *Journal of Abnormal and Social Psychology, 58,* 277–299. (5)

Orne, M. T. (1969). Demand characteristics and the concept of quasi-controls. In R. Rosenthal & R. L. Rosnow (Eds.), *Artifact in behavioral research* (pp. 143–179). (2)

Orne, M. T. (1979). On the simulating subject as a quasi-control group in hypnosis research: What, why, and how. In E. Fromm & R. E. Shor (Eds.), *Hypnosis: Developments in research and new perspectives* (2nd ed., pp. 519–565). New York: Aldine. (5)

Orne, M. T., Dinges, D. F., & Orne, E. C. (1984). On the differential diagnosis of multiple personality in the forensic context. *International Journal of Clinical and Experimental Hypnosis, 32,* 118–169. (5)

Orne, M. T., & Evans, F. J. (1965). Social control in the psychological experiment: Antisocial behavior and hypnosis. *Journal of Personality and Social Psychology, 1,* 189–200. (5)

Orne, M. T., & Scheibe, K. E. (1964). The contribution of nondeprivation factors in the production of sensory deprivation effects: The psychology of the "panic button." *Journal of Abnormal and Social Psychology, 68,* 3–12. (2)

Ornstein, P. A., Merritt, K. A., Baker-Ward, L., Furtado, E., Gordon, B., & Principe, G. (1998). Children's knowledge, expectation, and long-term retention. *Applied Cognitive Psychology, 12,* 387–405. (7)

Ortony, A., & Turner, T. J. (1990). What's basic about basic emotions? *Psychological Review, 97,* 315–331. (12)

Osofsky, J. D. (1995). The effects of exposure to violence on young children. *American Psychologist, 50,* 782–788. (12)

Öst, L.-G., & Breitholtz, E. (2000). Applied relaxation vs. cognitive therapy in the treatment of generalized anxiety disorder. *Behaviour Research and Therapy, 38,* 777–790. (16)

Öst, L. -G., & Hugdahl, K. (1981). Acquisition of phobias and anxiety response patterns in clinical patients. *Behaviour Research and Therapy, 19,* 439–447. (16)

Ottati, V., & Lee, Y. -T. (1995). Accuracy: A neglected component of stereotype research. In Y. -T. Lee, L. J. Jussim, & C. R. McCauley (Eds.), *Stereotype accuracy* (pp. 29–59). Washington, DC: American Psychological Association. (14)

Overman, W. H., Pate, B. J., Moore, K., & Peuster, A. (1996). Ontogeny of place learning in children as measured in the radial arm maze, Morris search task, and open field task. *Behavioral Neuroscience, 110,* 1205–1228. (7)

Padgham, C. A. (1975). Colours experienced in dreams. *British Journal of Psychology, 66,* 25–28. (5)

Palmer, B. W., Heaton, R. K., Paulsen, J. S., Kuck, J., Braff, D., Harris, M. J., Zissook, S., & Jeste, D. V. (1997). Is it possible to be schizophrenic yet neuropsychologically normal? *Neuropsychology, 11,* 437–446. (16)

Papini, M. R., & Bitterman, M. E. (1990). The role of contingency in classical conditioning. *Psychological Review, 97,* 396–403. (6)

Paradis, M. (1990). Language lateralization in bilinguals: Enough already! *Brain and Language, 39,* 576–586. (8)

Parish, A. R., & deWaal, F. B. M. (2000). The other "closest living relative." *Annals of the New York Academy of Sciences, 907,* 97–113. (14)

Park, J., & Banaji, M. R. (2000). Mood and heuristics: The influence of happy and sad states on sensitivity and bias in stereotyping. *Journal of Personality and Social Psychology, 78,* 1005–1023. (14)

Parke, R. D. (1995). Fathers and families. In M. H. Bornstein (Ed.), *Handbook of parenting* (Vol. 3, pp. 27–63). Mahwah, NJ: Erlbaum. (10)

Parke, R. D., Berkowitz, L., Leyens, J. P., West, S. G., & Sebastian, R. J. (1977). Some effects of violent and nonviolent movies on the behavior of juvenile delinquents. In L. Berkowitz (Ed.), *Advances in experimental social psychology* (Vol. 10, pp. 135–172). New York: Academic Press. (2)

Parker, D. (1944). *The portable Dorothy Parker.* New York: Viking. (15)

Parmeggiani, P. L. (1982). Regulation of physiological functions during sleep in mammals. *Experientia, 38,* 1405–1408. (5)

Parnas, J., Schulsinger, F., Schulsinger, H., Mednick, S. A., & Teasdale, T. W. (1982). Behavioral precursors of schizophrenia spectrum. *Archives of General Psychiatry, 39,* 658–664. (16)

Parra, C., Esteves, F., Flykt, A., & Öhman, A. (1997). Pavlovian conditioning to social stimuli: Backward masking and the dissociation of implicit and explicit cognitive processes. *European Psychologist, 2,* 106–117. (6)

Parrott, A. C. (1999). Does cigarette smoking cause stress? *American Psychologist, 54,* 817–820. (5)

Pashler, H. (1994). Dual-task interference in simple tasks: Data and theory. *Psychological Bulletin, 116,* 220–244. (8)

Pate, J. L., & Rumbaugh, D. M. (1983). The language-like behavior of Lana chimpanzee: Is it merely discrimination and paired-associate learning? *Animal Learning & Behavior, 11,* 134–138. (8)

Patterson, C. J. (1994). Lesbian and gay families. *Current Directions in Psychological Science, 3,* 62–64. (10)

Paulhus, D. L., Trapnell, P. D., & Chen, D. (1999). Birth order effects on personality and achievement within families. *Psychological Science, 10,* 482–488. (10)

Paunonen, S. V., & Jackson, D. N. (2000). What is beyond the big five? Plenty! *Journal of Personality, 68,* 821–835. (13)

Paunonen, S. V., Zeidner, M., Engvik, H. A., Oosterveld, P., & Maliphant, R. (2000). The nonverbal assessment of personality in five cultures. *Journal of Cross-Cultural Psychology, 31,* 220–239. (13)

Paus, T., Marrett, S., Worsley, K. J., & Evans, A. C. (1995). Extraretinal modulation of cerebral blood flow in the human visual cortex: Implications for saccadic suppression. *Journal of Neurophysiology, 74,* 2179–2183. (8)

Pavlov, I. P. (1960). *Conditioned reflexes.* New York: Dover. (Original work published 1927) (6)

Pavot, W., & Diener, E. (1993). Review of the satisfaction with life scale. *Psychological Assessment, 5,* 164–172. (12)

Paykel, E. S., Scott, J., Teasdale, J. D., Johnson, A. L., Garland, A., Moore, R., Jenaway, A., Cornwall, P. L., Hayhurst, H., Abbott, R., & Pope, M. (1999). Prevention of relapse in residual depression by cognitive therapy. *Archives of General Psychiatry, 56,* 829–835. (16)

Pearce, J. M. (1994). Similarity and discrimination: A selective review and a connectionist model. *Psychological Review, 101,* 587–607. (6)

Pearlson, G. D., Petty, R. G., Ross, C. A., & Tien, A. Y. (1996). Schizophrenia—a disease of heteromodal association cortex. *Neuropsychopharmacology, 14,* 1–17. (16)

Peck, C. P. (1986). A public mental health issue: Risk-taking behavior and compulsive gambling. *American Psychologist, 41,* 461–465. (8)

Peele, S. (1998, March/April). All wet. *The Sciences, 38*(2), 17–21. (16)

Penfield, W., & Rasmussen, T. (1950). *The cerebral cortex of man.* New York: Macmillan. (3)

Pennebaker, J. W. (1990). *Opening up.* New York: Morrow. (12)

Pennebaker, J. W. (1997). Writing about emotional experiences as a therapeutic process. *Psychological Science, 8,* 162–166. (12)

Pennebaker, J. W., & Seagal, J. D. (1999). Forming a story: The health benefits of narrative. *Journal of Clinical Psychology, 55,* 1243–1254. (15)

Perez, E. A. (1995). Review of the preclinical pharmacology and comparative efficacy of 5-hydroxytryptamine-3 receptor antagonists for chemotherapy-induced emesis. *Journal of Clinical Oncology, 13,* 1036–1043. (3)

Perry, D. G., & Bussey, K. (1979). The social learning theory of sex differences: Imitation is alive and well. *Journal of Personality and Social Psychology, 37,* 1699–1712. (13)

Pert, C. B., & Snyder, S. H. (1973). The opiate receptor: Demonstration in nervous tissue. *Science, 179,* 1011–1014. (4, 5)

Peterson, C. (2000). The future of optimism. *American Psychologist, 55,* 44–55. (12)

Peterson, C., Bettes, B. A., & Seligman, M. E. P. (1985). Depressive symptoms and unprompted causal attributions: Content analysis. *Behaviour Research and Therapy, 23,* 379–382. (16)

Peterson, L. G., Peterson, M., O'Shanick, G. J., & Swann, A. (1985). Self-inflicted gunshot wounds: Lethality of method versus intent. *American Journal of Psychiatry, 142,* 228–231. (16)

Peterson, L. R., & Peterson, M. J. (1959). Short-term retention of individual verbal items. *Journal of Experimental Psychology, 58,* 193–198. (7)

Petrie, K. J., & Dawson, A. G. (1997). Symptoms of fatigue and coping strategies in international pilots. *International Journal of Aviation Psychology, 7,* 251–258. (5)

Petrill, S. A., Luo, D., Thompson, L. A., & Detterman, D. K. (1996). The independent prediction of general intelligence by elementary cognitive tasks: Genetic and environmental influences. *Behavior Genetics, 26,* 135–147. (9)

Petrill, S. A., Plomin, R., Berg, S., Johansson, B., Pedersen, N. L., Ahern, F., & McClearn, G. E. (1998). The genetic and environmental relationship between general and specific cognitive abilities in twins age 80 and older. *Psychological Science, 9,* 183–189. (9)

Petty, R. E., & Cacioppo, J. T. (1977). Effects of forewarning of persuasive intent and involvement on cognitive responses and persuasion. *Personality and Social Psychology Bulletin, 5,* 173–176. (14)

Petty, R. E., & Cacioppo, J. T. (1981). *Attitudes and persuasion: Classic and contemporary approaches.* Dubuque, IA: William C. Brown. (14)

Petty, R. E., & Cacioppo, J. T. (1986). *Communication and persuasion: Central and peripheral routes to attitude change.* New York: Springer-Verlag. (14)

Pezdek, K., Finger, K., & Hodge, D. (1997). Planting false childhood memories: The role of event plausibility. *Psychological Science, 8,* 437–441. (7)

Pfungst, O. (1911). *Clever Hans.* New York: Holt. (2)

Phalet, K., & Claeys, W. (1993). A comparative study of Turkish and Belgian youth. *Journal of Cross-Cultural Psychology, 24,* 319–343. (11)

Phelps, E. A., O'Connor, K. J., Cunningham, W. A., Funayama, E. S., Gatenby, J. C., Gore, J. C., & Banaji, M. R. (2000). Performance on indirect measures of race evaluation predicts amygdala activation. *Journal of Cognitive Neuroscience, 12,* 729–738. (14)

Phelps, J. A., Davis, J. O., & Schwartz, K. M. (1997). Nature, nurture, and twin research strategies. *Current Directions in Psychological Science, 6,* 117–121. (3)

Phelps, M. E., & Mazziotta, J. C. (1985). Positron emission tomography: Human brain function and biochemistry. *Science, 228,* 799–809. (1, 3)

Phillips, M. L., Young, A. W., Senior, C., Brammer, M., Andrew, C., Calder, A. J., Bullmore, E. T., Perrett, D. I., Rowland, D., Williams, S. C. R., Gray, J. A., & David, A. S. (1997). A specific neural substrate for perceiving facial expressions of disgust. *Nature, 389,* 495–498. (12)

Phillips, R. G., & LeDoux, J. E. (1992). Differential contribution of amygdala and hippocampus to cued and contextual fear conditioning. *Behavioral Neuroscience, 106,* 274–285. (12)

Phillips, R. T., & Alcebo, A. M. (1986). The effects of divorce on Black children and adolescents. *American Journal of Social Psychology, 6,* 69–73. (10)

Piaget, J. (1954). *The construction of reality in the child* (M. Cook, Trans.). New York: Basic Books. (Original work published 1937) (10)

Piasecki, T. M., Kenford, S. L., Smith, S. S., Fiore, M. C., & Baker, T. B. (1997). Listening to nicotine: Negative affect and the smoking withdrawal conundrum. *Psychological Science, 8,* 184–189. (16)

Pich, E. M., Pagliusi, S. R., Tessari, M., Talabot-Ayer, D., van Huijsduijnen, R. H., & Chiamuera, C. (1997). Common neural substrates for the addictive properties of nicotine and cocaine. *Science, 275,* 83–86. (5)

Pichot, P. (1984). Centenary of the birth of Hermann Rorschach. *Journal of Personality Assessment, 48,* 591–596. (13)

Pinel, J. P. J., Assanand, S., & Lehman, D. R. (2000). Hunger, eating, and ill health. *American Psychologist, 55,* 1105–1116. (11)

Pinker, S. (1994). *The language instinct.* New York: Morrow. (8)

Piotrowski, C., & Keller, J. W. (1989). Psychological testing in outpatient mental health facilities: A national study. *Professional Psychology: Research and Practice, 20,* 423–425. (13)

Pitman, R. K., van der Kolk, B. A., Orr, S. P., & Greenberg, M. S. (1990). Naloxone-reversible analgesic response to combat-related stimuli in posttraumatic stress disorder. *Archives of General Psychiatry, 47,* 541–544. (12)

Plaks, J. E., & Higgins, E. T. (2000). Pragmatic use of stereotyping in teamwork: Social loafing and compensation as a function of inferred partner-situation fit. *Journal of Personality and Social Psychology, 79,* 962–974. (14)

Plaut, D. C., & Booth, J. R. (2000). Individual and developmental differences in semantic priming: Empirical and computational support for a single-mechanism account of lexical priming. *Psychological Review, 107,* 786–823. (8)

Plihal, W., & Born, J. (1997). Effects of early and late nocturnal sleep on declarative and procedural memory. *Journal of Cognitive Neuroscience, 9,* 534–547. (5)

Ploghaus, A., Tracey, I., Gati, J. S., Clare, S., Menon, R. S., Matthews, P. M., & Rawlins, J. N. P. (1999). Dissociating pain from its anticipation in the human brain. *Science, 284,* 1979–1981. (4)

Plomin, R., Corley, R., DeFries, J. C., & Fulker, D. W. (1990). Individual differences in television viewing in early childhood: Nature as well as nurture. *Psychological Science, 1,* 371–377. (3)

Plomin, R., Fulker, D. W., Corley, R., & DeFries, J. C. (1997). Nature, nurture, and cognitive development from 1 to 16 years: A parent-offspring adoption study. *Psychological Science, 8,* 442–447. (9)

Plous, S. (1993). *The psychology of judgment and decision making.* Philadelphia, PA: Temple University Press. (8)

Plous, S. (1996). Attitudes toward the use of animals in psychological research and education. *American Psychologist, 51,* 1167–1180. (2)

Plutchik, R., & Ax, A. F. (1967). A critique of "determinants of emotional state" by Schachter and Singer (1962). *Psychophysiology, 4,* 79–82. (12)

Polcin, D. L. (1997). The etiology and diagnosis of alcohol dependence: Differences in the professional literature. *Psychotherapy, 34,* 297–306. (16)

Polivy, J., & Herman, C. P. (1985). Dieting and binging: A causal analysis. *American Psychologist, 40,* 193–201. (11)

Pollak, J. M. (1979). Obsessive-compulsive personality: A review. *Psychological Bulletin, 86,* 225–241. (16)

Polya, G. (1957). *How to solve it.* Garden City, NY: Doubleday Anchor. (8)

Pond, S. B., III, & Geyer, P. D. (1991). Differences in the relation between job satisfaction and perceived work alternatives among older and younger blue-collar workers. *Journal of Vocational Behavior, 39,* 251–262. (10)

Poole, D. A., & White, L. T. (1995). Tell me again and again: Stability and change in the repeated testimonies of children and adults. In M. S. Zaragoza, J. R. Graham, G. C. N. Hall, R. Hirschman, & Y. S. Ben-Porath (Eds.), *Memory and testimony in the child witness* (pp. 24–43). Thousand Oaks, CA: Sage. (7)

Pope, H. G., Jr., Hudson, J. I., Bodkin, J. A., & Oliva, P. (1998). Questionable validity of 'dissociative amnesia' in trauma victims. *British Journal of Psychology, 172,* 210–215. (7)

Pope, K. S. (1996). Memory, abuse, and science: Questioning claims about the false memory syndrome epidemic. *American Psychologist, 51,* 957–974. (7)

Popper, K. (1986). Predicting overt behavior versus predicting hidden states. *Behavioral and Brain Sciences, 9,* 254–255. (13)

Povinelli, D. J., & deBlois, S. (1992). Young children's *(Homo sapiens)* understanding of knowledge formation in themselves and others. *Journal of Comparative Psychology, 106,* 228–238. (10)

Powell, R. A., & Boer, D. P. (1994). Did Freud mislead patients to confabulate memories of abuse? *Psychological Reports, 74,* 1283–1298. (13)

Powlishta, K. K., & Maccoby, E. E. (1990). Resource utilization in mixed-sex dyads: The influence of adult presence and task type. *Sex Roles, 23,* 223–240. (10)

Pratkanis, A. R., Greenwald, A. G., Leippe, M. R., & Baumgardner, M. H. (1988). In search of reliable persuasion effects: III. The sleeper effect is dead. Long live the sleeper effect. *Journal of Personality and Social Psychology, 54,* 203–218. (14)

Premack, A. J., & Premack, D. (1972). Teaching language to an ape. *Scientific American, 227*(4), 92–99. (8)

Premack, D. (1965). Reinforcement theory. In D. Levine (Ed.), *Nebraska Symposium on Motivation* (pp. 123–188). Lincoln: University of Nebraska Press. (6)

Proffitt, J. B., Coley, J. D., & Medin, D. L. (2000). Expertise and category-based induction. *Journal of Experimental Psychology: Learning, Memory, and Cognition, 26,* 811–828. (8)

Prohaska, V. (1994). "I know I'll get an A": Confident overestimation of final course grades. *Teaching of Psychology, 21,* 141–143. (8)

Provine, R. (2000). *Laughter.* New York: Viking. (12)

Pyszczynski, T., Greenberg, J., & Solomon, S. (2000). Proximal and distal defense: A new perspective on unconscious motivation. *Current Directions in Psychological Science, 9,* 156–160. (10)

Quadrel, M. J., Fischhoff, B., & Davis, W. (1993). Adolescent (in)vulnerability. *American Psychologist, 48,* 102–116. (10)

Rachlin, H. (1990). Why do people gamble and keep gambling despite heavy losses? *Psychological Science, 1,* 294–297. (8)

Rachlin, H., Siegel, E., & Cross, D. (1994). Lotteries and the time horizon. *Psychological Science, 5,* 390–393. (8)

Rachman, S. (1969). Treatment by prolonged exposure to high intensity stimulation. *Behaviour Research and Therapy, 7,* 295–302. (16)

Rachman, S. J., & Hodgson, R. J. (1980). *Obsessions and compulsions.* Upper Saddle River, NJ: Prentice Hall. (16)

Raine, A., Lencz, T., Bihrle, S., LaCasse, L., & Colletti, P. (2000). Reduced prefrontal gray matter volume and reduced autonomic activity in antisocial personality disorder. *Archives of General Psychiatry, 57,* 119–127. (12)

Rainville, P., Duncan, G. H., Price, D. D., Carrier, B., & Bushnell, M. C. (1997). Pain affect encoded in human anterior cingulate but not somatosensory cortex. *Science, 277,* 968–971. (5)

Rainville, P., Hofbauer, R. K., Paus, T., Duncan, G. H., Bushnell, M. C., & Price, D. D. (1999). Cerebral mechanisms of hypnotic induction and suggestion. *Journal of Cognitive Neuroscience, 11,* 110–125. (5)

Ramachandran, V. S., & Blakeslee, S. (1998). *Phantoms in the brain.* New York: Morrow. (4)

Ramachandran, V. S., & Hirstein, W. (1998). The perception of phantom limbs: The D. O. Hebb lecture. *Brain, 121,* 1603–1630. (4)

Ramus, F., Hauser, M. D., Miller, C., Morris, D., & Mehler, J. (2000). Language discrimination by human newborn and by cotton-top tamarin monkeys. *Science, 288,* 349–351. (10)

Rattenborg, N. C., Lima, S. L., & Amlaner, C. J. (1999). Half-awake to the risk of predation. *Nature, 397,* 397–398. (5)

Rauscher, F. H., Shaw, G. L., & Ky, K. N. (1993). Music and spatial task performance. *Nature, 365,* 611. (2)

Raven, J. (2000). The Raven's Progressive Matrices: Change and stability over culture and time. *Cognitive Psychology, 41,* 1–48. (9)

Ravussin, E., Lillioja, S., Knowler, W. C., Christin, L., Freymona, D., Abbott, W. G. H., Boyce, V., Howard, B. V., & Bogardus, C. (1988). Reduced rate of energy expenditure as a risk factor for body-weight gain. *New England Journal of Medicine, 318,* 467–472. (11)

Rayner, K. (1998). Eye movements in reading and information processing: 20 years of research. *Psychological Bulletin, 124,* 372–422. (8)

Reber, A. S. (1997). How to differentiate implicit and explicit modes of acquisition. In J. D. Cohen & J. W. Schooler (Eds.), *Scientific approaches to consciousness* (pp. 137–159). Mahwah, NJ: Erlbaum. (7)

Rechtschaffen, A., & Bergmann, B. M. (1995). Sleep deprivation in the rat by the disk-over-water method. *Behavioural Brain Research, 69,* 55–63. (5)

Redican, W. K. (1982). An evolutionary perspective on human facial displays. In P. Ekman (Ed.), *Emotion in the human face* (pp. 212–280). Cambridge, England: Cambridge University Press. (12)

Reed, J. M., & Squire, L. R. (1999). Impaired transverse patterning in human amnesia is a special case of impaired memory for two-choice discrimination tasks. *Behavioral Neuroscience, 113,* 3–9. (7)

Reed, T. E. (1985). Ethnic differences in alcohol use, abuse, and sensitivity: A review with genetic interpretation. *Social Biology, 32,* 195–209. (16)

Reeves, A. G., & Plum, F. (1969). Hyperphagia, rage, and dementia accompanying a ventromedial hypothalamic neoplasm. *Archives of Neurology, 20,* 616–624. (11)

Reicher, G. M. (1969). Perceptual recognition as a function of meaningfulness of stimulus material. *Journal of Experimental Psychology, 81,* 275–280. (8)

Reichling, D. B., Kwiat, G. C., & Basbaum, A. I. (1988). Anatomy, physiology, and pharmacology of the periaqueductal gray contribution to antinociceptive controls. In H. L. Fields & J.-M. Besson (Eds.), *Progress in brain research* (Vol. 77, pp. 31–46). Amsterdam: Elsevier. (4)

Reiss, M. J. (2000). The ethics of genetic research on intelligence. *Bioethics, 14,* 1–15. (9)

Rescorla, R. A. (1968). Probability of shock in the presence and absence of CS in fear conditioning. *Journal of Comparative and Physiological Psychology, 66,* 1–5. (6)

Rescorla, R. A. (1988). Pavlovian conditioning: It's not what you think it is. *American Psychologist, 43,* 151–160. (6)

Restle, F. (1970). Moon illusion explained on the basis of relative size. *Science, 167,* 1092–1096. (4)

Rhodes, G., Sumich, A., & Byatt, G. (1999). Are average facial configurations attractive only because of their symmetry? *Psychological Science, 10,* 52–58. (14)

Riccio, D. C. (1994). Memory: When less is more. *American Psychologist, 49,* 917–926. (7)

Rich, C. L., Ricketts, J. E., Fowler, R. C., & Young, D. (1988). Some differences between men and women who commit suicide. *American Journal of Psychiatry, 145,* 718–722. (16)

Richter, W., Somorjai, R., Summers, R., Jarmasz, M., Messon, R. S., Gati, J. S., Georgopoulos, A. P., Tegeler, C., Ugurbil, K., & Kim, S.-G. (2000). Motor area activity during mental rotation studied by time-resolved single-trial fMRI. *Journal of Cognitive Neuroscience, 12,* 310–320. (8)

Riddle, W. J. R., & Scott, A. I. F. (1995). Relapse after successful electroconvulsive therapy: The use and impact of continuation antidepressant drug treatment. *Human Psychopharmacology, 10,* 201–205. (16)

Rind, B., Tromovitch, P., & Bauserman, R. (1998). A meta-analytic examination of assumed properties of child sexual abuse using college samples. *Psychological Bulletin, 124,* 22–53. (12)

Rivas-Vazquez, R. A. (2001). Antidepressants as first-line agents in the current pharmacotherapy of anxiety disorders. *Professional Psychology: Research and Practice, 32,* 101–104. (16)

Rivera, P. A., Rose, J. M., Futterman, A., Lovett, S. B., & Gallagher-Thompson, D. (1991). Dimensions of perceived social support in clinically depressed and nondepressed female caregivers. *Psychology and Aging, 6,* 232–237. (16)

Rivers, P. C. (1994). *Alcohol and human behavior.* Upper Saddle River, NJ: Prentice Hall. (5)

Robazza, C., Bortoli, L., & Nougier, V. (1998). Physiological arousal and performance in elite archers: A field study. *European Psychologist, 3,* 263–270. (12)

Roberson, D., Davies, I., & Davidoff, J. (2000). Color categories are not universal: Replications and new evidence from a Stone-Age culture. *Journal of Experimental Psychology: General, 129,* 369–398. (8)

Roberts, B. W., & DelVecchio, W. F. (2000). The rank-order consistency of personality traits from childhood to old age: A quantitative review of longitudinal studies. *Psychological Bulletin, 126,* 3–25. (13)

Roberts, S. B., Savage, J., Coward, W. A., Chew, B., & Lucas, A. (1988). Energy expenditure and intake in infants born to lean and overweight mothers. *New England Journal of Medicine, 318,* 461–466. (11)

Robins, L. N., Helzer, J. E., Weissman, M. M., Orvaschel, H., Gruenberg, E., Burke, J. D., Jr., & Regier, D. A. (1984). Lifetime prevalence of specific psychiatric disorders in three sites. *Archives of General Psychiatry, 41,* 949–958. (15, 16)

Robins, R. W., Gosling, S. D., & Craik, K. H. (1999). An empirical analysis of trends in psychology. *American Psychologist, 54,* 117–128. (1)

Robinson, L. A., Berman, J. S., & Neimeyer, R. A. (1990). Psychotherapy for the treatment of depression: A comprehensive review of controlled outcome research. *Psychological Bulletin, 108,* 30–49. (16)

Robinson, R. J., & Keltner, D. (1996). Much ado about nothing? Revisionists and traditionalists choose an introductory English syllabus. *Psychological Science, 7,* 18–24. (14)

Robinson, T. E., & Berridge, K. C. (2000). The psychology and neurobiology of addiction: An incentive-sensitization view. *Addiction, 95*(Suppl. 2), S91–S117. (16)

Roca, C. A., Schmidt, P. J., & Rubinow, D. R. (1999). Gonadal steroids and affective illness. *Neuroscientist, 5,* 227–237. (16)

Rock, I., & Kaufman, L. (1962). The moon illusion, II. *Science, 136,* 1023–1031. (4)

Rodgers, J. L., Cleveland, H. H., van den Oord, E., & Rowe, D. C. (2000). Resolving the debate over birth order, family size, and intelligence. *American Psychologist, 55,* 599–612. (10)

Rodin, J. (1986). Aging and health: Effects of the sense of control. *Science, 233,* 1271–1276. (10)

Rodriguez, E., George, N., Lachaux, J.-P., Martinerie, J., Renault, B., & Varela, F. J. (1999). Perception's shadow: Long-distance synchronization of human brain activity. *Nature, 397,* 430–433. (3)

Roediger, H. L., III, & McDermott, K. B. (2000). Tricks of memory. *Current Directions in Psychological Science, 9,* 123–127. (7)

Roelfsema, P. R., Engel, A. K., König, P., & Singer, W. (1997). Visuomotor integration is associated with zero time-lag synchronization among cortical areas. *Nature, 385,* 157–161. (3)

Rogers, C. R. (1951). *Client-centered therapy.* Boston: Houghton Mifflin. (15)

Rogers, C. R. (1961). *On becoming a person.* Boston: Houghton Mifflin. (13)

Rogers, C. R. (1980). *A way of being.* Boston: Houghton Mifflin. (13)

Rogers, T. B. (1995). *The psychological testing enterprise: An introduction.* Pacific Grove, CA: Brooks/Cole. (9)

Rogoff, B., & Chavajay, P. (1995). What's become of research on the cultural basis of cognitive development? *American Psychologist, 50,* 859–877. (10)

Rohrbaugh, M., Shoham, V., Spungen, C., & Steinglass, P. (1995). Family systems therapy in practice: A systemic couples therapy for problem drinking. In B. Bongar & L. E. Beutler (Eds.), *Comprehensive textbook of psychotherapy: Theory and practice* (pp. 228–253). Oxford, England: Oxford University Press. (15)

Rollman, G. B. (1991). Pain responsiveness. In M. Heller & W. Schiff (Eds.), *The psychology of touch* (pp. 91–118). Hillsdale, NJ: Erlbaum. (4)

Rolls, E. T. (1997). Taste and olfactory processing in the brain and its relation to the control of eating. *Critical Reviews in Neurobiology, 11,* 263–287. (4)

Rosch, E. (1978). Principles of categorization. In E. Rosch & B. B. Lloyd (Eds.), *Cognition and categorization* (pp. 27–48). Hillsdale, NJ: Erlbaum. (8)

Rosch, E., & Mervis, C. B. (1975). Family resemblances: Studies in the internal structure of categories. *Cognitive Psychology, 7,* 573–605. (8)

Rose, J. E. (1996). Nicotine addiction and treatment. *Annual Review of Medicine, 47,* 493–507. (16)

Rosen, V. M., & Engle, R. W. (1997). The role of working memory capacity in retrieval. *Journal of Experimental Psychology: General, 126,* 211–227. (7)

Rosenbaum, M. E. (1986). The repulsion hypothesis: on the nondevelopment of relationships. *Journal of Personality and Social Psychology, 51,* 1156–1166. (14)

Rosenbaum, R. S., Priselac, S., Köhler, S., Black, S. E., Gao, F., Nadel, L., & Moscovitch, M. (2000). Remote spatial memory in an amnesic person with extensive bilateral hippocampal lesions. *Nature Neuroscience, 3,* 1044–1048. (7)

Rosenberg, H. (1993). Prediction of controlled drinking by alcoholics and problem drinkers. *Psychological Bulletin, 113,* 129–139. (16)

Rosenberg, S. D., Rosenberg, H. J., & Farrell, M. P. (1999). The midlife crisis revisited. In S. L. Willis & J. D. Reid (Eds.), *Life in the middle* (pp. 47–73). San Diego, CA: Academic Press. (10)

Ross, L. (1977). The intuitive psychologist and his shortcomings: Distortions in the attribution process. In L. Berkowitz (Ed.), *Advances in experimental social psychology* (Vol. 10, pp. 173–220). New York: Academic Press. (14)

Roth, B. L., Lopez, E., & Kroeze, W. K. (2000). The multiplicity of serotonin receptors: Uselessly diverse molecules or an embarrassment of riches? *The Neuroscientist, 6,* 252–262. (3)

Rothbaum, B. O., Hodges, L. F., Kooper, R., Opdyke, D., Williford, J. S., & North, M. (1995). Effectiveness of computer-generated (virtual reality) graded exposure in the treatment of acrophobia. *American Journal of Psychiatry, 152,* 626–628. (16)

Rothbaum, F., Weisz, J., Pott, M., Miyake, K., & Morelli, G. (2000). Attachment and culture: Security in the United States and Japan. *American Psychologist, 55,* 1093–1104. (10)

Rothman, A. J., & Salovey, P. (1997). Shaping perceptions to motivate healthy behavior: The role of message framing. *Psychological Bulletin, 121,* 3–19. (8)

Rotter, J. B. (1966). Generalized expectancies for internal versus external control of reinforcement. *Psychological Monographs, 80*(Whole No. 603). (13)

Rotton, J., & Kelly, I. W. (1985). Much ado about the full moon: A meta-analysis of lunar-lunacy research. *Psychological Bulletin, 97,* 286–306. (2)

Routh, D. K. (2000). Clinical psychology training: A history of ideas and practices prior to 1946. *American Psychologist, 55,* 236–241. (1)

Rovee-Collier, C. (1984). The ontogeny of learning and memory in human infancy. In R. Kail & N. E. Spear (Eds.), *Comparative perspectives on the development of memory* (pp. 103–134). Hillsdale, NJ: Erlbaum. (10)

Rovee-Collier, C. (1997). Dissociations in infant memory: Rethinking the development of explicit and implicit memory. *Psychological Review, 104,* 467–498. (10)

Rovee-Collier, C. (1999). The development of infant memory. *Current Directions in Psychological Science, 8,* 80–85. (10)

Rowe, D. C., Vazsonyi, A. T., & Flannery, D. J. (1994). No more than skin deep: Ethnic and racial similarity in developmental process. *Psychological Review, 101,* 396–413. (9)

Rowe, J. B., Toni, I., Josephs, O., Frackowiak, R. S. J., & Passingham, R. E. (2000). The prefrontal cortex: Response selection or maintenance within working memory? *Science, 288,* 1656–1660. (3)

Rowe, J. W., & Kahn, R. L. (1987). Human aging: Usual and successful. *Science, 237,* 143–149. (10)

Rowland, D. L., & Burnett, A. L. (2000). Pharmacotherapy in the treatment of male sexual dysfunction. *Journal of Sex Research, 37,* 226–243. (11)

Roy, A. (1985). Early parental separation and adult depression. *Archives of General Psychiatry, 42,* 987–991. (16)

Roy, A., DeJong, J., & Linnoila, M. (1989). Cerebrospinal fluid monoamine metabolites and suicidal behavior in depressed patients. *Archives of General Psychiatry, 46,* 609–612. (16)

Rozin, P. (1996). Sociocultural influences on human food selection. In E. D. Capaldi (Ed.), *Why we eat what we eat* (pp. 233–263). Washington, DC: American Psychological Association. (11)

Rozin, P., & Fallon, A. E. (1987). A perspective on disgust. *Psychological Review, 94,* 23–41. (11)

Rozin, P., Fallon, A., & Augustoni-Ziskind, M. L. (1986). The child's conception of food: The development of categories of acceptable and rejected substances. *Journal of Nutrition Education, 18,* 75–81. (11)

Rozin, P., Fischler, C., Imada, S., Sarubin, A., & Wrzesniewski, A. (1999). Attitudes to food and the role of food in life in the U.S.A., Japan, Flemish Belgium and France: Possible

implications for the diet-health debate. *Appetite, 33,* 163–180. (11)

Rozin, P., & Kalat, J. W. (1971). Specific hungers and poison avoidance as adaptive specializations of learning. *Psychological Review, 78,* 459–486. (6, 11)

Rozin, P., Markwith, M., & Ross, B. (1990). The sympathetic magical law of similarity, nominal realism and neglect of negatives in response to negative labels. *Psychological Science, 1,* 383–384. (8)

Rozin, P., Markwith, M., & Stoess, C. (1997). Moralization and becoming a vegetarian: The transformation of preferences into values and the recruitment of disgust. *Psychological Science, 8,* 67–73. (11)

Rozin, P., Millman, L., & Nemeroff, C. (1986). Operation of the laws of sympathetic magic in disgust and other domains. *Journal of Personality and Social Psychology, 50,* 703–712. (11)

Rozin, P., & Pelchat, M. L. (1988). Memories of mammaries: Adaptations to weaning from milk. *Progress in Psychobiology and Physiological Psychology, 13,* 1–29. (3)

Rubenstein, R., & Newman, R. (1954). The living out of "future" experiences under hypnosis. *Science, 119,* 472–473. (5)

Rubin, D. C., & Wenzel, A. E. (1996). One hundred years of forgetting: A quantitative description of retention. *Psychological Review, 103,* 734–760. (7)

Ruch, J. (1984). *Psychology: The personal science.* Belmont, CA: Wadsworth. (3)

Rumelhart, D. E., & McClelland, J. L. (1982). An interactive activation model of context effects in letter perception: Part 2. The contextual enhancement effect and some tests and extensions of the model. *Psychological Review, 89,* 60–94. (8)

Rumelhart, D. E., McClelland, J. L., & the PDP Research Group. (1986). *Parallel distributed processing.* Cambridge, MA: MIT Press. (8)

Rusak, B. (1977). The role of the suprachiasmatic nuclei in the generation of circadian rhythms in the golden hamster, *Mesocricetus auratus. Journal of Comparative Physiology A, 118,* 145–164. (5)

Ruscio, J. (2000, March/April). Risky business: Vividness, availability, and the media paradox. *Skeptical Inquirer, 24*(2), 22–26. (8)

Russell, J. A. (1994). Is there universal recognition of emotion from facial expression? A review of the cross-cultural studies. *Psychological Bulletin, 115,* 102–141. (12)

Russell, J. A. (1997). Reading emotions from and into faces: Resurrecting a dimensional-contextual perspective. In J. A. Russell & J. M. Fernández-Dols (Eds.), *The psychology of facial expression* (pp. 295–320). Cambridge, England: Cambridge University Press. (12)

Russell, J. A., & Carroll, J. M. (1999). On the bipolarity of positive and negative affect. *Psychological Bulletin, 125,* 3–30. (12)

Russell, R. J. H., & Wells, P. A. (1991). Personality similarity and quality of marriage. *Personality and Individual Differences, 12,* 407–412. (14)

Ryan, R. M., & Deci, E. L. (2000). Self-determination theory and the facilitation of intrinsic motivation, social development, and well-being. *American Psychologist, 55,* 68–78. (11)

Sackeim, H. A., Prudic, J., Devanand, D. P., Nobler, M. S., Lisanby, S. H., Peyser, S., Fitzsimons, L., Moody, B. J., & Clark, J. (2000). A prospective, randomized, double-blind comparison of bilateral and right unilateral electroconvulsive therapy at different stimulus intensities. *Archives of General Psychiatry, 57,* 425–434. (16)

Saegert, S., Swap, W., & Zajonc, R. B. (1973). Exposure, context, and interpersonal attraction. *Journal of Personality and Social Psychology, 25,* 234–242. (14)

Saelens, B. E., & Epstein, L. H. (1999). The rate of sedentary activities determines the reinforcing value of physical activity. *Health Psychology, 18,* 655–659. (6)

Saffran, J. R., Aslin, R. N., & Newport, E. L. (1996). Statistical learning by 8-month-old infants. *Science, 274,* 1926–1928. (8)

Saggino, A. (2000). The big three or the big five? A replication study. *Personality and Individual Differences, 28,* 879–886. (13)

Salthouse, T. A., Mitchell, D. R., Skovronek, E., & Babcock, R. L. (1989). Effects of adult age and working memory on reasoning and spatial abilities. *Journal of Experimental Psychology: Learning, Memory, and Cognition, 15,* 507–516. (7)

Salzarulo, P., & Chevalier, A. (1983). Sleep problems in children and their relationship with early disturbances of the waking-sleeping rhythms. *Sleep, 6,* 47–51. (5)

Samelson, F. (1980). J. B. Watson's Little Albert, Cyril Burt's twins, and the need for a critical science. *American Scientist, 35,* 619–625. (16)

Sanderson, A., & Dugoni, B. (1999). *Summary report 1997: Doctorate recipients from United States institutions.* Chicago: National Opinion Research Council. (1)

Sandfort, T. G. M., de Graaf, R., Bijl, R. V., & Schnabel, P. (2001). Same-sex sexual behavior and psychiatric disorders. *Archives of General Psychiatry, 58,* 85–91. (11)

Sanna, L. J. (2000). Mental simulation, affect, and personality: A conceptual framework. *Current Directions in Psychological Science, 9,* 168–173. (12)

Sapolsky, R. M. (1998, March 30). Open season. *The New Yorker, 74*(6), 57–58, 71–72. (13)

Sapp, F., Lee, K., & Muir, D. (2000). Three-year-olds' difficulty with the appearance-reality distinction: Is it real or is it apparent? *Developmental Psychology, 36,* 547–560. (10)

Satterfield, J. M., & Seligman, M. E. P. (1994). Military aggression and risk predicted by explanatory style. *Psychological Science, 5,* 77–82. (16)

Sattler, J. M., & Gwynne, J. (1982). White examiners generally do not impede the intelligence test performance of Black children: To debunk a myth. *Journal of Consulting and Clinical Psychology, 50,* 196–208. (9)

Saudino, K. J. (1997). Moving beyond the heritability question: New directions in behavioral genetic studies of personality. *Current Directions in Psychological Science, 6,* 86–90. (13)

Savage-Rumbaugh, E. S. (1990). Language acquisition in a nonhuman species: Implications for the innateness debate. *Developmental Psychology, 23,* 599–620. (8)

Savage-Rumbaugh, E. S., Sevcik, R. A., Brakke, K. E., & Rumbaugh, D. M. (1992). Symbols: Their communicative use, communication, and combination by bonobos *(Pan paniscus).* In L. P. Lipsitt & C. Rovee-Collier (Eds.), *Advances in infancy research* (Vol. 7, pp. 221–278). Norwood, NJ: Ablex. (8)

Saxe, L., & Ben-Shakhar, G. (1999). Admissibility of polygraph tests: The application of scientific standards post-Daubert. *Psychology, Public Policy and Law, 5,* 203–223. (12)

Saywitz, K. J., Mannarino, A. P., Berliner, L., & Cohen, J. A. (2000). Treatment for sexually abused children and adolescents. *American Psychologist, 55,* 1040–1049. (12)

Scarborough, E., & Furomoto, L. (1987). *Untold lives: The first generation of American women psychologists.* New York: Columbia University Press. (1)

Scarr, S. (1997). Rules of evidence: A larger context for the statistical debate. *Psychological Science, 8,* 16–17. (2)

Scarr, S. (1998). American child care today. *American Psychologist, 53,* 95–108. (10)

Scarr, S., Pakstis, A. J., Katz, S. H., & Barker, W. B. (1977). The absence of a relationship between degree of White ancestry and intellectual skills within a Black population. *Human Genetics, 39,* 69–86. (9)

Scarr, S., Phillips, D., & McCartney, K. (1990). Facts, fantasies and the future of child care in the United States. *Psychological Science, 1,* 26–35. (10)

Scarr, S., & Weinberg, R. A. (1976). IQ test performance of Black children adopted by White families. *American Psychologist, 31,* 726–739. (9)

Schachter, D. L. (1987). Implicit memory: History and current status. *Journal of Experimental Psychology: Learning, Memory, and Cognition, 13,* 501–518. (7)

Schacter, D. L. (1999). The seven sins of memory. *American Psychologist, 54,* 182–203. (7)

Schacter, D. L., Verfaellie, M., Anes, M. D., & Racine, C. (1998). When true recognition suppresses false recognition: Evidence from amnesic patients. *Journal of Cognitive Neuroscience, 10,* 668–679. (7)

Schachter, S. (1982). Recidivism and self-cure of smoking and obesity. *American Psychologist, 37,* 436–444. (11)

Schachter, S., & Singer, J. (1962). Cognitive, social, and physiological determinants of emotional state. *Psychological Review, 69,* 379–399. (12)

Schaie, K. W. (1994). The course of adult intellectual development. *American Psychologist, 49,* 304–313. (7, 10)

Schank, R., & Birnbaum, L. (1994). Enhancing intelligence. In J. Khalfa (Ed.), *What is intelligence?* (pp. 72–106). Cambridge, England: Cambridge University Press. (9)

Schatzman, M. (1992, March 21). Freud: Who seduced whom? *New Scientist,* pp. 34–37. (13)

Schenck, C. H., & Mahowald, M. W. (1996). Long-term, nightly benzodiazepine treatment of injurious parasomnias and other disorders of disrupted nocturnal sleep in 170 adults. *American Journal of Medicine, 100,* 333–337. (5)

Schiffman, S. S., & Erickson, R. P. (1971). A psychophysical model for gustatory quality. *Physiology & Behavior, 7,* 617–633. (4)

Schiffman, S. S., Graham, B. G., Sattely-Miller, E. A., & Warwick, Z. S. (1998). Orosensory perception of dietary fat. *Current Directions in Psychological Science, 7,* 137–143. (11)

Schkade, D. A., & Kahneman, D. (1998). Does living in California make people happy? *Psychological Science, 9,* 340–346. (12)

Schlaug, G., Jäncke, L., Huang, Y., & Steinmetz, H. (1995). In vivo evidence of structural brain asymmetry in musicians. *Science, 267,* 699–701. (3)

Schlesier-Stropp, B. (1984). Bulimia: A review of the literature. *Psychological Review, 95,* 247–257. (11)

Schmidt, F. L., & Hunter, J. E. (1981). Employment testing: Old theories and new research findings. *American Psychologist, 36,* 1128–1137. (9)

Schmidt, F. L., & Hunter, J. E. (1998). The validity and utility of selection methods in personnel psychology: Practical and theoretical implications of 85 years of research findings. *Psychological Bulletin, 124,* 262–274. (9)

Schmidt, R. A., & Bjork, R. A. (1992). New conceptualizations of practice: Common principles in three paradigms suggest new concepts for training. *Psychological Science, 3,* 207–217. (7)

Schmitt, A. P., & Dorans, N. J. (1990). Differential item functioning for minority examinees on the SAT. *Journal of Educational Measurement, 27,* 67–81. (9)

Schmolck, H., Buffalo, E. A., & Squire, L. R. (2000). Memory distortions develop over time. *Psychological Science, 11,* 39–45. (7)

Schooler, C. (1972). Birth order effects: Not here, not now! *Psychological Bulletin, 78,* 161–175. (10)

Schooler, C. (1998). Environmental complexity and the Flynn effect. In U. Neisser (Ed.), *The rising curve* (pp. 67–79). Washington, DC: American Psychological Association. (9)

Schou, M. (1997). Forty years of lithium treatment. *Archives of General Psychiatry, 54,* 9–13. (16)

Schredl, M. (2000). Continuity between waking life and dreaming: Are all waking activities reflected equally often in dreams? *Perceptual and Motor Skills, 90,* 844–846. (5)

Schuckit, M. C., & Smith, T. L. (1997). Assessing the risk for alcoholism among sons of alcoholics. *Journal of Studies on Alcohol, 58,* 141–145. (16)

Schulsinger, F., Knop, J., Goodwin, D. W., Teasdale, T. W., & Mikkelsen, U. (1986). A prospective study of young men at high risk for alcoholism. *Archives of General Psychiatry, 43,* 755–760. (16)

Schultz, R. T., Gauthier, I., Klin, A., Fulbright, R. K., Anderson, A. W., Volkmar, F., Skudlarski, P., Lacadie, C., Cohen, D. J., & Gore, J. C. (2000). Abnormal ventral temporal cortical activity during face discrimination among individuals with autism and Asperger syndrome. *Archives of General Psychiatry, 57,* 331–340. (4)

Schwartz, G. E. (1987). Personality and health: An integrative health science approach. *The G. Stanley Hall Lecture Series, 7,* 125–157. (12)

Schwartz, M. B., & Brownell, K. D. (1995). Matching individuals to weight loss treatments: A survey of obesity experts. *Journal of Consulting and Clinical Psychology, 63,* 149–153. (11)

Schwarz, N. (1999). Self-reports: How the questions shape the answers. *American Psychologist, 54,* 93–105. (2)

Schwartz, N., Bless, H., & Bohner, G. (1991). Mood and persuasion: Affective states influence the processing of persuasive messages. *Advances in Experimental Social Psychology, 24,* 161–199. (14)

Schwarzwald, J., Bizman, A., & Raz, M. (1983). The foot-in-the-door paradigm: Effects of second request size on donation probability and donor generosity. *Personality and Social Psychology Bulletin, 9,* 443–450. (14)

Scott, S. K., Young, A. W., Calder, A. J., Hellawell, D. J., Aggleton, J. P., & Johnson, M. (1997). Impaired auditory recognition of fear and anger following bilateral amygdala lesions. *Nature, 385,* 254–257. (12)

Scott, W. J. (1990). PTSD in *DSM-III:* A case in the politics of diagnosis and disease. *Social Problems, 37,* 294–310. (16)

Scovern, A. W., & Kilmann, P. R. (1980). Status of electroconvulsive therapy: Review of the outcome literature. *Psychological Bulletin, 87,* 260–303. (16)

Scribner, S. (1974). Developmental aspects of categorized recall in a west African society. *Cognitive Psychology, 6,* 475–494.

(7)

Scripture, E. W. (1907). *Thinking, feeling, doing* (2nd ed.). New York: G. P. Putnam's Sons. (1)

Seeley, R. J., Kaplan, J. M., & Grill, H. J. (1995). Effect of occluding the pylorus on intraoral intake: A test of the gastric hypothesis of meal termination. *Physiology & Behavior, 58,* 245–249. (11)

Seeman, P., & Lee, T. (1975). Antipsychotic drugs: Direct correlation between clinical potency and presynaptic action on dopamine neurons. *Science, 188,* 1217–1219. (16)

Segal, M. H., Lonner, W. J., & Berry, J. W. (1998). Cross-cultural psychology as a scholarly discipline. *American Psychologist, 53,* 1101–1110. (1)

Segal, N. (1993). Twin, sibling, and adoption methods: Tests of evolutionary hypotheses. *American Psychologist, 48,* 943–956. (3)

Segall, M. H., Campbell, D. T., & Herskovits, M. J. (1966). *The influence of culture on visual perception.* Indianapolis, IN: Bobbs-Merrill. (4)

Seidenberg, M. S. (1997). Language acquisition and use: Learning and applying probabilistic constraints. *Science, 275,* 1599–1603. (8)

Seife, C. (1994, May/June). Studies from life: Mathemagician. *The Sciences, 34*(3), 12–15. (7)

Seligman, M. E. P. (1970). On the generality of the laws of learning. *Psychological Review, 77,* 406–418. (6)

Seligman, M. E. P. (1971). Phobias and preparedness. *Behavior Therapy, 2,* 307–320. (16)

Seligman, M. E. P. (1995). The effectiveness of psychotherapy: The *Consumer Reports* study. *American Psychologist, 50,* 965–974. (15)

Seligman, M. E. P., & Csikszentmihalyi, M. (2000). Positive psychology. *American Psychologist, 55,* 5–14. (12)

Seligman, M. E. P., Nolen-Hoeksema, S., Thornton, N., & Thornton, K. M. (1990). Explanatory style as a mechanism of disappointing athletic performance. *Psychological Science, 1,* 143–146. (16)

Seligman, M. E. P., Schulman, P., DeRubeis, R. J., & Hollon, S. D. (1999). The prevention of depression and anxiety. *Prevention and Treatment, 2,* article 8. (16)

Selye, H. (1979). Stress, cancer, and the mind. In J. Taché, H. Selye, & S. B. Day (Eds.), *Cancer, stress, and death* (pp. 11–27). New York: Plenum. (12)

Serizawa, S., Ishii, T., Nakatani, H., Tsuboi, A., Nagawa, F., Asano, M., Sudo, K., Sakagami, J., Sakano, H., Ijiri, T., Matsuda, Y., Suzuki, M., Yamamori, T., Iwakura, Y., & Sakano, H. (2000). Mutually exclusive expression of odorant receptor transgenes. *Nature Neuroscience, 3,* 687–693. (4)

Shafir, E. B., Smith, E. E., & Osheron, D. N. (1990). Typicality and reasoning fallacies. *Memory & Cognition, 18,* 229–239. (8)

Shafto, M., & MacKay, D. G. (2000). The Moses, mega-Moses, and Armstrong illusions: Integrating language comprehension and semantic memory. *Psychological Science, 11,* 372–378. (8)

Shannon, D. A. (1955). *The Socialist party of America.* New York: Macmillan. (14)

Shapiro, D. H., Jr., Schwartz, C. E., & Astin, J. A. (1996). Controlling ourselves, controlling our world. *American Psychologist, 51,* 1213–1230. (12)

Shapiro, D. L. (1985). Insanity and the assessment of criminal responsibility. In C. P. Ewing (Ed.), *Psychology, psychiatry, and the law: A clinical and forensic handbook* (pp. 67–94). Sarasota, FL: Professional Resource Exchange. (15)

Shapiro, K. L., Caldwell, J., & Sorensen, R. E. (1997). Personal names and the attentional blink: A visual "cocktail party" effect. *Journal of Experimental Psychology: Human Perception and Performance, 23,* 504–514. (8)

Shepard, R. N., & Metzler, J. N. (1971). Mental rotation of three-dimensional objects. *Science, 171,* 701–703. (8)

Sheppard, W. D., II, Staggers, F. J., Jr., & John, L. (1997). The effects of a stress management program in a high security government agency. *Anxiety, Stress, and Coping, 10,* 341–350. (12)

Shepperd, J. A. (1993). Productivity loss in performance groups: A motivation analysis. *Psychological Bulletin, 113,* 67–81. (14)

Shepperd, J. A. (1995). Remedying motivation and productivity loss in social settings. *Current Directions in Psychological Science, 4,* 131–134. (14)

Shergill, S. S., Brammer, M. J., Williams, S. C. R., Murray, R. M., & McGuire, P. K. (2000). Mapping auditory hallucinations in schizophrenia using functional magnetic resonance imaging. *Archives of General Psychiatry, 57,* 1033–1038. (16)

Sherif, M. (1935). A study of some social factors in perception. *Archives of Psychology, 27,* 1–60. (14)

Sherif, M. (1966). In common predicament. Boston: Houghton Mifflin. (14)

Sherman, J. W., & Bessenoff, G. R. (1999). Stereotypes as source-monitoring cues: On the interaction between episodes and semantic memory. *Psychological Science, 10,* 106–110. (14)

Sherwood, G. G. (1981). Self-serving biases in person perception: A reexamination of projection as a mechanism of defense. *Psychological Bulletin, 90,* 445–459. (13)

Shih, M., Pittinsky, T. L., & Ambady, N. (1999). Stereotype susceptibility: Identity salience and shifts in quantitative performance. *Psychological Science, 10,* 80–83. (9)

Shimamura, A. P., Berry, J. M., Mangels, J. A., Rusting, C. L., & Jurica, P. J. (1995). Memory and cognitive abilities in university professors. *Psychological Science, 6,* 271–277. (7)

Shimamura, A. P., Janowsky, J. S., & Squire, L. R. (1990). Memory for the temporal order of events in patients with frontal lobe lesions and amnesic patients. *Neuropsychologia, 28,* 803–813. (7)

Shimaya, A. (1997). Perception of complex line drawings. *Journal of Experimental Psychology: Human Perception and Performance, 23,* 25–50. (4)

Shogren, E. (1993, June 2). Survey finds 4 in 5 suffer sex harassment at school. *Los Angeles Times,* p. A10. (2)

Shweder, R., Mahapatra, M., & Miller, J. G. (1987). Culture and moral development. In J. Kagan & S. Lamb (Eds.), *The emergence of morality in young children* (pp. 1–83). Chicago: University of Chicago Press. (10)

Siegel, S. (1977). Morphine tolerance as an associative process. *Journal of Experimental Psychology: Animal Behavior Processes, 3,* 1–13. (6)

Siegel, S. (1983). Classical conditioning, drug tolerance, and drug dependence. *Research Advances in Alcohol and Drug Problems, 7,* 207–246. (6)

Siegel, S. (1987). Alcohol and opiate dependence: Reevaluation of the Victorian perspective. *Research Advances in Alcohol and Drug Problems, 9,* 279–314. (16)

Siegelman, M. (1974). Parental background of male homosexuals and heterosexuals. *Archives of Sexual Behavior, 3,* 3–18. (11)

Siegler, R. S. (2000). Unconscious insights. *Current Directions in Psychological Science, 9,* 79–83. (8)

Siegler, R. S., & Richards, D. D. (1982). The development of intelligence. In R. J. Sternberg (Ed.), *Handbook of human intelligence* (pp. 897–971). Cambridge, England: Cambridge University Press. (9)

Silberg, J., Pickles, A., Rutter, M., Hewitt, J., Simonoff, E., Maes, H., Carbonneau, R., Murrelle, L., Foley, D., & Eaves, L. (1999). The influence of genetic factors and life stress on depression among adolescent girls. *Archives of General Psychiatry, 56,* 225–232. (16)

Silver, E. (1995). Punishment or treatment? Comparing the lengths of confinement of successful and unsuccessful insanity defendants. *Law and Human Behavior, 19,* 375–388. (15)

Silverman, I., Choi, J., Mackewn, A., Fisher, M., Moro, J., & Olshansky, E. (2000). Evolved mechanisms underlying wayfinding: Further studies on the hunter-gatherer theory of spatial sex differences. *Evolution and Human Behavior, 21,* 201–213. (10)

Silverstein, L. B., & Auerbach, C. F. (1999). Deconstructing the essential father. *American Psychologist, 54,* 397–407. (10)

Silverthorne, C. (2001). Leadership effectiveness and personality: A crosscultural evaluation. *Personality and Individual Differences, 30,* 303–309. (13)

Simmons, E. J. (1949). *Leo Tolstoy.* London: Lehmann. (16)

Simon, R. I. (1994). The law and psychiatry, In R. E. Hales, S. C. Yudofsky, & J. A. Talbott (Eds.), *Textbook of psychiatry* (2nd ed.) (pp. 1297–1340). Washington, DC: American Psychiatric Press. (15)

Simonton, D. K. (1977). Eminence, creativity, and geographical marginality: A recursive structural equation model. *Journal of Personality and Social Psychology, 35,* 805–816. (2)

Simonton, D. K. (1997). Creative productivity: A predictive and explanatory model of career trajectories and landmarks. *Psychological Review, 104,* 66–89. (8)

Simonton, D. K. (2000a). Creative development as acquired expertise: Theoretical issues and an empirical test. *Developmental Review, 20,* 283–318. (8)

Simonton, D. K. (2000b). Creativity: Cognitive, personal, developmental, and social aspects. *American Psychologist, 55,* 151–158. (8)

Simpson, C. A., & Vuchinich, R. E. (2000). Reliability of a measure of temporal discounting. *Psychological Record, 50,* 3–16. (6)

Singh, M., Hoffman, D. D., & Albert, M. K. (1999). Contour completion and relative depth: Petter's rule and support ratio. *Psychological Science, 10,* 423–428. (4)

Sinha, P., & Poggio, T. (1996). I think I know that face . . . *Nature, 384,* 404. (4)

Sizemore, C. C., & Huber, R. J. (1988). The twenty-two faces of Eve. *Individual Psychology, 44,* 53–62. (15)

Sizemore, C. C., & Pittillo, E. S. (1977). *I'm Eve.* Garden City, NY: Doubleday. (15)

Skeels, H. M. (1966). Adult status of children with contrasting early life experiences. *Monographs of the Society for Research in Child Development, 31,* 1–65. (9)

Skinner, B. F. (1938). *The behavior of organisms.* New York: D. Appleton-Century. (6)

Skinner, B. F. (1960). Pigeons in a pelican. *American Psychologist, 15*, 28–37. (6)

Skinner, B. F. (1990). Can psychology be a science of mind? *American Psychologist, 45*, 1206–1210. (6)

Skoog, G., & Skoog, I. (1999). A 40-year follow-up of patients with obsessive-compulsive disorder. *Archives of General Psychiatry, 56*, 121–127. (16)

Slutske, W. S., Eisen, S., True, W. R., Lyons, M. J., Goldberg, J., & Tsuang, M. (2000). Common genetic vulnerability for pathological gambling and alcohol dependence in men. *Archives of General Psychiatry, 57*, 666–673. (16)

Smith, D. E., & Cogswell, C. (1994). A cross-cultural perspective on adolescent girls' body perception. *Perceptual and Motor Skills, 78*, 744–746. (11)

Smith, L. B., Thelen, E., Titzer, R., & McLin, D. (1999). Knowing in the context of acting: The task dynamics of the A-not-B error. *Psychological Review, 106*, 235–260. (10)

Smith, L. D. (1995). Inquiry nearer the source: Bacon, Mach, and *The Behavior of Organisms*. In J. T. Todd & E. K. Morris (Eds.), *Modern perspectives on B. F. Skinner and contemporary behaviorism* (pp. 39–50). Westport, CT: Greenwood Press. (6)

Smith, M. L. (1988). Recall of spatial location by the amnesic patient H. M. *Brain and Cognition, 7*, 178–183. (7)

Smith, M. L., Glass, G. V., & Miller, T. I. (1980). *The benefits of psychotherapy*. Baltimore, MD: Johns Hopkins University Press. (15)

Smith, M. W. (1974). Alfred Binet's remarkable questions: A cross-national and cross-temporal analysis of the cultural biases built into the Stanford-Binet intelligence scale and other Binet tests. *Genetic Psychology Monographs, 89*, 307–334. (9)

Snyder, M., Tanke, E. D., & Berscheid, E. (1977). Social perception and interpersonal behavior: On the self-fulfilling nature of social stereotypes. *Journal of Personality and Social Psychology, 35*, 656–666. (14)

Snyder, S. (1991). Movies and juvenile delinquency: An overview. *Adolescence, 26*, 121–132. (6)

Solin, D. (1989). The systematic misrepresentation of bilingual-crossed aphasia data and its consequences. *Brain and Language, 36*, 92–116. (8)

Solms, M. (1997). *The neuropsychology of dreams*. Mahwah, NJ: Erlbaum. (5)

Solms, M. (2000). Dreaming and REM sleep are controlled by different brain mechanisms. *Behavioral and Brain Sciences, 23*, iii–iii. (5)

Solomon, D. A., Keller, M. B., Leon, A. C., Mueller, T. I., Shea, T., Warshaw, M., Maser, J. D., Coryell, W., & Endicott, J. (1997). Recovery from major depression. *Archives of General Psychiatry, 54*, 1001–1006. (16)

Solomon, R. L. (1980). The opponent-process theory of acquired motivation. *American Psychologist, 35*, 691–712. (12)

Solomon, R. L., & Corbit, J. D. (1974). An opponent-process theory of motivation: I. Temporal dynamics of affect. *Psychological Review, 81*, 119–145. (12)

Solomon, Z., Mikulincer, M., & Flum, H. (1988). Negative life events, coping responses, and combat-related psychopathology: A prospective study. *Journal of Abnormal Psychology, 97*, 302–307. (12)

Sorkin, R. D., Hays, C. J., & West, R. (2001). Signal-detection analysis of group decision making. *Psychological Review, 108*, 183–203. (14)

Sowell, E. R., Thompson, P. M., Holmes, C. J., Jernigan, T. L., & Toga, A. W. (1999). *In vivo* evidence for post-adolescent brain maturation in frontal and striatal regions. *Nature Neuroscience, 2*, 859–861. (16)

Spaeth, A. (1995, August). Going for the Guinness. *World Press Review*, pp. 18–20. (11)

Spanos, N. P. (1987–88). Past-life hypnotic regression: A critical view. *Skeptical Inquirer, 12*, 174–180. (5)

Spear, L. P. (2000). Neurobehavioral changes in adolescence. *Current Directions in Psychological Science, 9*, 111–114. (10)

Spearman, C. (1904). "General intelligence," objectively determined and measured. *American Journal of Psychology, 15*, 201–293. (9)

Speer, J. R. (1989). Detection of plastic explosives. *Science, 243*, 1651. (8)

Sperling, G. (1960). The information available in brief visual presentations. *Psychological Monographs, 74*(11, Whole No. 498). (7)

Sperry, R. W. (1967). Split-brain approach to learning problems. In G. C. Quarton, T. Melnechuk, & F. O. Schmitt (Eds.), *The neurosciences: A study program* (pp. 714–722). New York: Rockefeller University Press. (3)

Spiegel, D., Frischholz, E. J., Fleiss, J. L., & Spiegel, H. (1993). Predictors of smoking abstinence following a single-session restructuring intervention with self-hypnosis. *American Journal of Psychiatry, 150*, 1090–1097. (5)

Spiegel, T. A. (1973). Caloric regulation of food intake in man. *Journal of Comparative and Physiological Psychology, 85*, 24–37. (11)

Spira, A., et al. (1993). *Les comportements sexuels en France*. Paris: La documentation Française. (11)

Squire, L. R., Amaral, D. G., & Press, G. A. (1990). Magnetic resonance imaging of the hippocampal formation and mammillary nuclei distinguish medial temporal lobe and diencephalic amnesia. *Journal of Neuroscience, 10*, 3106–3117. (7)

Squire, L. R., Haist, F., & Shimamura, A. P. (1989). The neurology of memory: Quantitative assessment of retrograde amnesia in two groups of amnesic patients. *Journal of Neuroscience, 9*, 828–839. (7)

Stanton, M. D., & Shadish, W. R. (1997). Outcome, attrition, and family-couples treatment for drug abuse: a meta-analysis and review of the controlled, comparative studies. *Psychological Bulletin, 122*, 170–191. (16)

Staddon, J. (1993). *Behaviorism*. London: Duckworth. (6)

Staddon, J. E. R. (1999). Theoretical behaviorism. In W. O'Donohue & R. Kitchener (Eds.), *Handbook of behaviorism* (pp. 217–241). San Diego, CA: Academic Press. (6)

Stajkovic, A. D., & Luthans, F. (1998). Self-efficacy and work-related performance: A meta-analysis. *Psychological Bulletin, 124*, 240–261. (6)

Starr, C., & Taggart, R. (1992). *Biology: The unity and diversity of life* (6th ed.). Belmont, CA: Wadsworth. (3)

Staub, E. (1996). Cultural-societal roots of violence. *American Psychologist, 51*, 117–132. (12)

Staw, B. M., & Ross, J. (1989). Understanding behavior in escalation situations. *Science, 246*, 216–220. (14)

Ste-Marie, D. M. (1999). Expert–novice differences in gymnastic judging: An information-processing perspective. *Applied Cognitive Psychology, 13*, 269–281. (8)

Steblay, N. M., & Bothwell, R. K. (1994). Evidence for hypnotically refreshed testimony. *Law and Human Behavior, 18*, 635–651. (5)

Steele, C. M., & Aronson, J. (1995). Stereotype threat and the intellectual test performance of African Americans. *Journal of Personality and Social Psychology, 69*, 797–811. (9)

Steele, K. M., Bass, K. E., & Crook, M. D. (1999). The mystery of the Mozart effect: Failure to replicate. *Psychological Science, 10*, 366–369. (2)

Stegat, H. (1975). Die Verhaltenstherapie der Enuresis und Enkopresis [Behavior therapy for enuresis and encopresis]. *Zeitschrift für Kinder- und Jugend-psychiatrie, 3*, 149–173. (15)

Stein, M. B., Hanna, C., Koverola, C., Torchia, M., & McClarty, B. (1997). Structural brain changes in PTSD. *Annals of the New York Academy of Sciences, 821*, 76–82. (12)

Stein, M., Miller, A. H., & Trestman, R. L. (1991). Depression, the immune system, and health and illness. *Archives of General Psychiatry, 48*, 171–177. (12)

Stein, M. B., Torgrud, L. J., & Walker, J. R. (2000). Social phobia symptoms, subtypes, and severity. *Archives of General Psychiatry, 57*, 1046–1052. (16)

Stella, N., Schweitzer, P., & Piomelli, D. (1997). A second endogenous cannabinoid that modulates long-term potentiation. *Nature, 382*, 677–678. (5)

Sternberg, R. J. (1985). *Beyond IQ.* Cambridge, England: Cambridge University Press. (9)

Sternberg, R. J. (1997). The concept of intelligence and its role in lifelong learning and success. *American Psychologist, 52*, 1030–1037. (9)

Stevens, A., & Coupe, P. (1978). Distortions in judged spatial relations. *Cognitive Psychology, 10*, 422–437. (8)

Stevens, S. S. (1961). To honor Fechner and repeal his law. *Science, 133*, 80–86. (1)

Stewart, A. J., & Ostrove, J. M. (1998). Women's personality in middle age. *American Psychologist, 53*, 1185–1194. (10)

Stewart, I. (1987). Are mathematicians logical? *Nature, 325*, 386–387. (9)

Stewart, J. W., Quitkin, F. M., McGrath, P. J., Amsterdam, J., Fava, M., Fawcett, J., Reimherr, F., Rosenbaum, J., Beasley, C., & Roback, P. (1998). Use of pattern analysis to predict differential relapse of remitted patients with major depression during 1 year of treatment with fluoxetine or placebo. *Archives of General Psychiatry, 55*, 334–343. (16)

Stewart, V. M. (1973). Tests of the "carpentered world" hypothesis by race and environment in America and Zambia. *International Journal of Psychology, 8*, 83–94. (4)

Stickgold, R., James, L., & Hobson, J. A. (2000). Visual discrimination learning requires sleep after training. *Nature Neuroscience, 3*, 1237–1238. (5)

Stickgold, R., Malia, A., Maguire, D., Roddenberry, D., & O'-Connor, M. (2000). Replaying the game: Hypnagogic images in normals and amnesics. *Science, 290*, 350–353. (7)

Stickgold, R., Whidbee, D., Schirmer, B., Patel, V., & Hobson, J. A. (2000). Visual discrimination task improvement: A multi-step process occurring during sleep. *Journal of Cognitive Neuroscience, 12*, 246–254. (5)

Stiles, W. B., Shapiro, D. A., & Elliott, R. (1986). "Are all psychotherapies equivalent?" *American Psychologist, 41*, 165–180. (15)

Stipek, D. J. (1984). Young children's performance expectations: Logical analysis or wishful thinking? *Advances in Motivation and Achievement, 3*, 33–56. (11)

Stone, V. E., Nisenson, L., Eliassen, J. C., & Gazzaniga, M. S. (1996). Left hemisphere representations of emotional facial expressions. *Neuropsychologia, 34*, 23–29. (3)

Stoolmiller, M. (1999). Implications of the restricted range of family environments for estimates of heritability and non-shared environment in behavior-genetic adoption studies. *Psychological Bulletin, 125*, 392–409. (3)

Stormark, K. M., Laberg, J. C., Nordby, H., & Hugdahl, K. (2000). Alcoholics' selective attention to alcohol stimuli: Automated processing? *Journal of Studies on Alcohol, 61*, 18–23. (13)

Storms, M. D. (1973). Videotape and the attribution process: Reversing actors' and observers' points of view. *Journal of Personality and Social Psychology, 27*, 165–175. (14)

Strack, F., Martin, L. L., & Stepper, S. (1988). Inhibiting and facilitating conditions of the human smile: A nonobtrusive test of the facial feedback hypothesis. *Journal of Personality and Social Psychology, 54*, 768–777. (12)

Strauch, I., & Lederbogen, S. (1999). The home dreams and waking fantasies of boys and girls between ages 9 and 15: A longitudinal study. *Dreaming, 9*, 153–161. (9)

Streissguth, A. P., Sampson, P. D., & Barr, H. M. (1989). Neurobehavioral dose-response effects of prenatal alcohol exposure in humans from infancy to adulthood. *Annals of the New York Academy of Sciences, 562*, 145–158. (10)

Stroebe, M., Gergen, M. M., Gergen, K. J., & Stroebe, W. (1992). Broken hearts or broken bonds: Love and death in historical perspective. *American Psychologist, 47*, 1205–1212. (10)

Stroh, L. K., Brett, J. M., & Reilly, A. H. (1992). All the right stuff: A comparison of female and male managers' career progression. *Journal of Applied Psychology, 77*, 251–260. (11)

Strupp, H. H. (1996). The tripartite model and the *Consumer Reports* study. *American Psychologist, 51*, 1017–1024. (15)

Stumpf, H., & Stanley, J. C. (1998). Stability and change in gender-related differences on the College Board Advanced Placement and Achievement Tests. *Current Directions in Psychological Science, 7*, 192–196. (9)

Stuss, D. T., Alexander, M. P., Palumbo, C. L., Buckle, L., Sayer, L., & Pogue, J. (1994). Organizational strategies of patients with unilateral or bilateral frontal lobe injury in word list learning tasks. *Neuropsychology, 8*, 355–373. (7)

Sudzak, P. D., Glowa, J. R., Crawley, J. N., Schwartz, R. D., Skolnick, P., & Paul, S. M. (1986). A selective imidazobenzodiazepine antagonist of ethanol in the rat. *Science, 234*, 1243–1247. (5)

Sue, S. (1998). In search of cultural competence in psychotherapy and counseling. *American Psychologist, 53*, 440–448. (15)

Susser, E., Neugebauer, R., Hoek, H. W., Brown, A. S., Lin, S., Labovitz, D., & Gorman, J. M. (1996). Schizophrenia after prenatal famine. *Archives of General Psychiatry, 53*, 25–31. (16)

Suvisaari, J. M., Haukka, J. K., Tanskanen, A. J., & Lönnqvist, J. K. (1999). Decline in the incidence of schizophrenia in Finnish cohorts born from 1954 to 1965. *Archives of General Psychiatry, 56*, 733–740. (16)

Suzuki, L. A., & Valencia, R. R. (1997). Race-ethnicity and measured intelligence. *American Psychologist, 52*, 1103–1114. (9)

Swann, W. B., Jr. (1997). The trouble with change: Self-verification and allegiance to the self. *Psychological Science, 8*, 177–180. (14)

Swann, W. B., Jr., & Gill, M. J. (1997). Confidence and accuracy in person perception: Do we know what we think we know about our relationship partners? *Journal of Personality and Social Psychology, 73,* 747–757. (14)

Swanson, J. M., Flodman, P., Kennedy, J., Spence, M. A., Moyzis, R., Schuck, S., Murias, M., Moriarty, J. Barr, C., Smith, M., & Posner, M. (2000). Dopamine genes and ADHD. *Neuroscience and Biobehavioral Reviews, 24,* 21–25. (3)

Swendsen, J. D., Tennen, H., Carney, M. A., Affleck, G., Willard, A., & Hromi, A. (2000). Mood and alcohol consumption: An experience sampling test of the self-medication hypothesis. *Journal of Abnormal Psychology, 109,* 198–204. (16)

Swets, J. A., Dawes, R. M., & Monahan, J. (2000). Psychological science can improve diagnostic decisions. *Psychological Science in the Public Interest, 1,* 1–26. (8, 9)

Swinkels, A., & Giuliano, T. A. (1995). The measurement and conceptualization of mood awareness: Monitoring and labeling one's mood states. *Personality and Social Psychology Bulletin, 21,* 934–949. (12)

Swinton, S. S. (1987). *The predictive validity of the restructured GRE with particular attention to older students* (GRE Board Professional Report No. 83-25P. ETS Research Report 87-22). Princeton, NJ: Educational Testing Service. (9)

Symons, C. S., & Johnson, B. T. (1997). The self-reference effect in memory: A meta-analysis. *Psychological Bulletin, 121,* 371–394. (7)

Szasz, T. S. (1982). The psychiatric will. *American Psychologist, 37,* 762–770. (15)

Szechtman, H., Woody, E., Bowers, K. S., & Nahmias, C. (1998). Where the imagined appears real: A positron emission tomography study of auditory hallucinations. *Proceedings of the National Academy of Sciences, U.S.A., 95,* 1956–1960. (5)

Szymanski, H. V., Simon, J. C., & Gutterman, N. (1983). Recovery from schizophrenic psychosis. *American Journal of Psychiatry, 140,* 335–338. (16)

Takeuchi, A. H., & Hulse, S. H. (1993). Absolute pitch. *Psychological Bulletin, 113,* 345–361. (3)

Taller, A. M., Asher, D. M., Pomeroy, K. L., Eldadah, B. A., Godec, M. S., Falkai, P. G., Bogert, B., Kleinman, J. E., Stevens, J. R., & Torrey, E. F. (1996). Search for viral nucleic acid sequences in brain tissues of patients with schizophrenia using nested polymerase chain reaction. *Archives of General Psychiatry, 53,* 32–40. (16)

Tannen, D. (1990). *You just don't understand.* New York: Morrow. (10)

Tarr, M. J., & Gauthier, I. (2000). FFA: A flexible fusiform area for subordinate-level visual processing automatized by experience. *Nature Neuroscience, 3,* 764–769. (3)

Tassinary, L. G., & Hansen, K. A. (1998). A critical test of the waist-to-hip-ratio hypothesis of female physical attractiveness. *Psychological Science, 9,* 150–155. (14)

Taylor, E. (2000). Psychotherapeutics and the problematic origins of clinical psychology in America. *American Psychologist, 55,* 1029–1033. (1)

Taylor, H. G., Klein, N., Minich, N. M., & Hack, M. (2000). Middle-school age outcomes in children with very low birthweight. *Child Development, 71,* 1495–1511. (10)

Taylor, S. E., & Brown, J. D. (1988). Illusion and well-being: A social psychological perspective on mental health. *Psychological Bulletin, 103,* 193–210. (12)

Taylor, S. E., Kemeny, M. E., Reed, G. M., Bower, J. E., & Gruenwald, T. L. (2000). Psychological resources, positive illusions, and health. *American Psychologist, 55,* 99–109. (12)

Taylor, S. E., Klein, L. C., Lewis, B. P., Gruenwald, T. L., Gurung, R. A. R., & Updegraff, J. A. (2000). Biobehavioral responses to stress in females: Tend-and-befriend, not fight-or-flight. *Psychological Review, 107,* 411–429. (12)

Taylor, S. E., Pham, L. B., Rivkin, I. D., & Armor, D. A. (1998). Harnessing the imagination: Mental simulation, self-regulation, and coping. *American Psychologist, 53,* 429–439. (12)

Teasdale, T. W., & Owen, D. R. (1984). Heredity and familial environment in intelligence and educational level: A sibling study. *Nature, 309,* 620–622. (9)

Teicher, M. H., Glod, C. A., Magnus, E., Harper, D., Benson, G., Krueger, K., & McGreenery, C. E. (1997). Circadian rest-activity disturbances in seasonal affective disorder. *Archives of General Psychiatry, 54,* 124–130. (16)

Teplin, L. A., Abram, K. M., & McClelland, G. M. (1996). Prevalence of psychiatric disorders among incarcerated women. *Archives of General Psychiatry, 53,* 505–512. (12)

Terman, J. S., Terman, M., Lo, E.-S., & Cooper, T. B. (2001). Circadian time of morning light administration and therapeutic response in winter depression. *Archives of General Psychiatry, 58,* 69–75. (16)

Terr, L. (1988). What happens to early memories of trauma? A study of twenty children under age five at the time of documented traumatic events. *Journal of the American Academy of Child and Adolescent Psychiatry, 27,* 96–104. (7)

Terrace, H. S., Petitto, L. A., Sanders, R. J., & Bever, T. G. (1979). Can an ape create a sentence? *Science, 206,* 891–902. (8)

Tetlock, P. E. (1994, July 2). *Good judgment in world politics: Who gets what right, when and why?* Address presented at the sixth annual convention of the American Psychological Society. (8)

Tett, R. P., & Palmer, C. A. (1997). The validity of handwriting elements in relation to self-report personality trait measures. *Personality and Individual Differences, 22,* 11–18. (13)

Thase, M. E., Greenhouse, J. B., Frank, E., Reynolds, C. F., III, Pilkonis, P. A., Hurley, K., Grochocinski, V., & Kupfer, D. J. (1997). Treatment of major depression with psychotherapy or psychotherapy-pharmacotherapy combinations. *Archives of General Psychiatry, 54,* 1009–1015. (16)

Thase, M. E., Trivedi, M. H., & Rush, A. J. (1995). MAOIs in the contemporary treatment of depression. *Neuropsychopharmacology, 12,* 185–219. (16)

Thieman, T. J. (1984). A classroom demonstration of encoding specificity. *Teaching of Psychology, 11,* 101–102. (7)

Thigpen, C., & Cleckley, H. (1957). *The three faces of Eve.* New York: McGraw-Hill. (15)

Thomas, A., & Chess, S. (1980). *The dynamics of psychological development.* New York: Brunner/Mazel. (10)

Thomas, A., Chess, S., & Birch, H. G. (1968). *Temperament and behavior disorders in children.* New York: New York University Press. (10)

Thompson, C. R., & Church, R. M. (1980). An explanation of the language of a chimpanzee. *Science, 208,* 313–314. (8)

Thompson, L., & Hrebec, D. (1996). Lose-lose agreements in interdependent decision making. *Psychological Bulletin, 120,* 396–409. (14)

Thompson, L. A., Detterman, D. K., & Plomin, R. (1991). Associations between cognitive abilities and scholastic achievement: Genetic overlap but environmental differences. *Psychological Science, 2*, 158–165. (9)

Thompson, L. W., Gallagher-Thompson, D., Futterman, A., Gilewski, M. J., & Peterson, J. (1991). The effects of late-life spousal bereavement over a 30-month interval. *Psychology and Aging, 6*, 434–441. (16)

Thompson, S. C., Armstrong, W., & Thomas, C. (1998). Illusions of control, underestimations, and accuracy: A control heuristic explanation. *Psychological Bulletin, 123*, 143–161. (8)

Thorndike, E. L. (1970). *Animal intelligence.* Darien, CT: Hafner. (Original work published 1911) (6)

Timberlake, W., & Farmer-Dougan, V. A. (1991). Reinforcement in applied settings: Figuring out ahead of time what will work. *Psychological Bulletin, 110*, 379–391. (6)

Tinbergen, N. (1958). *Curious naturalists.* New York: Basic Books. (3)

Tingate, T. R., Lugg, D. J., Muller, H. K., Stowe, R. P., & Pierson, D. L. (1997). Antarctic isolation: Immune and viral studies. *Immunology and Cell Biology, 75*, 275–283. (12)

Tipper, S. P. (1985). The negative priming effect: Inhibitory priming by ignored objects. *Quarterly Journal of Experimental Psychology, 37A*, 571–590. (8)

Titchener, E. B. (1910). *A textbook of psychology.* New York: Macmillan. (1)

Todes, D. P. (1997). From the machine to the ghost within. *American Psychologist, 52*, 947–955. (6)

Tolman, E. C. (1932). *Purposive behavior in animals and men.* New York: Century. (6)

Tolman, E. C., & Honzik, C. H. (1930). Introduction and removal of reward, and maze performance in rats. *University of California Publications in Psychology, 4*, 257–275. (6)

Tolstoy, L. (1978). *Tolstoy's letters: Vol. I: 1828–1879.* New York: Charles Scribner's Sons. (Original works written 1828–1879) (10)

Tombaugh, C. W. (1980). *Out of the darkness, the planet Pluto.* Harrisburg, PA: Stackpole. (4)

Topál, J., Miklósi, A., Csàny, V., & Dóka, A. (1998). Attachment behavior in dogs *(Canis familiaris):* A new application of Ainsworth's (1969) Strange Situation test. *Journal of Comparative Psychology, 112*, 219–229. (10)

Torrey, E. F. (1986). Geographic variations in schizophrenia. In C. Shagass, R. C. Josiassen, W. H. Bridger, K. J. Weiss, D. Stoff, & G. M. Simpson (Eds.), *Biological psychiatry 1985* (pp. 1080–1082). New York: Elsevier. (16)

Torrey, E. F., Bowler, A. E., & Clark, K. (1997). Urban birth and residence as risk factors for psychoses: An analysis of 1880 data. *Schizophrenia Research, 28*, 1–38. (16)

Townsend, J., Courchesne, E., Covington, J., Westerfield, M., Harris, N. S., Lyden, P., Lowry, T. P., & Press, G. A. (1999). Spatial attention deficits in patients with acquired or developmental cerebellar abnormality. *Journal of Neuroscience, 19*, 5632–5643. (3)

Tracy, J. A., Thompson, J. K., Krupa, D. J., & Thompson, R. F. (1998). Evidence of plasticity in the pontocerebellar conditioned stimulus pathway during classical conditioning of the eyeblink response in the rabbit. *Behavioral Neuroscience, 112*, 267–285. (6)

Travis, F., & Wallace, R. K. (1999). Autonomic and EEG patterns during eyes-closed rest and transcendental meditation (TM) practice: The basis for a neural model of TM practice. *Consciousness and Cognition, 8*, 302–318. (5)

Treisman, A., & Souther, J. (1985). Search asymmetry: A diagnostic for preattentive processing of separable features. *Journal of Experimental Psychology: General, 114*, 285–310. (8)

Tronick, E. Z., Morelli, G. A., & Ivey, P. K. (1992). The Efe forager infant and toddler's pattern of social relationships: Multiple and simultaneous. *Developmental Psychology, 28*, 568–577. (10)

Truscott, D., & Crook, K. H. (1993). Tarasoff in the Canadian context: Wenden and the duty to protect. *Canadian Journal of Psychiatry, 38*, 84–89. (15)

Tschann, J. M., Johnston, J. R., Kline, M., & Wallerstein, J. S. (1990). Conflict, loss, change and parent-child relationships: Predicting children's adjustment during divorce. *Journal of Divorce, 13*, 1–22. (10)

Tuiten, A., Van Honk, J., Koppeschaar, H., Bernaards, C., Thijssen, J., & Verbaten, R. (2000). Time course of effects of testosterone administration on sexual arousal in women. *Archives of General Psychiatry, 57*, 149–153. (11)

Tulving, E. (1989). Remembering and knowing the past. *American Scientist, 77*, 361–367. (7)

Tulving, E., & Thomson, D. M. (1973). Encoding specificity and retrieval processes in episodic memory. *Psychological Review, 80*, 352–373. (7)

Turkheimer, E. (1991). Individual and group differences in adoption studies of IQ. *Psychological Bulletin, 110*, 392–405. (9)

Turner, C. F., Ku, L., Rogers, S. M., Lindberg, L. D., Pleck, J. H., & Sonenstein, F. L. (1998). Adolescent sexual behavior, drug use, and violence: Increased reporting with computer survey technology. *Science, 280*, 867–873. (11)

Tversky, A., & Kahneman, D. (1981). The framing of decisions and the psychology of choice. *Science, 211*, 453–458. (8)

Tversky, A., & Kahneman, D. (1983). Extensional versus intuitive reasoning: The conjunctional fallacy in probability judgment. *Psychological Review, 90*, 293–315. (8)

Tversky, B. (1981). Distortions in memory for maps. *Cognitive Psychology, 13*, 407–433. (8)

Twenge, J. M. (2000). The age of anxiety? Birth cohort change in anxiety and neuroticism, 1952–1993. *Journal of Personality and Social Psychology, 79*, 1007–1021. (13)

Uchino, B. N., Cacioppo, J. T., & Kiecolt-Glaser, J. K. (1996). The relationship betweeen social support and physiological processes: A review with emphasis on underlying mechanisms and implications for health. *Psychological Bulletin, 119*, 488–531. (12)

Uchino, B. N., Uno, D., & Holt-Lunstad, J. (1999). Social support, physiological processes, and health. *Current Directions in Psychological Science, 8*, 145–148. (12)

Udolf, R. (1981). *Handbook of hypnosis for professionals.* New York: Van Nostrand Reinhold. (5)

Ulrich, R. E., Stachnik, T. J., & Stainton, N. R. (1963). Student acceptance of generalized personality interpretations. *Psychological Reports, 13*, 831–834. (13)

Ulrich, R. S. (1984). View through a window may influence recovery from surgery. *Science, 224*, 420–421. (4)

Vaillant, G. E. (1983). *The natural history of alcoholism.* Cambridge, MA: Harvard University Press. (16)

Vaillant, G. E., & Milofsky, E. S. (1982). The etiology of alcoholism: A prospective viewpoint. *American Psychologist, 37*, 494–503. (16)

Vallone, R. P., Ross, L., & Lepper, M. R. (1985). The hostile media phenomenon: Biased perception and perceptions of media bias in coverage of the "Beirut Massacre." *Journal of Personality and Social Psychology, 49,* 577–585. (14)

van den Pol, A. N. (1999). Hypothalamic hypocretin (orexin): Robust innervation of the spinal cord. *Journal of Neuroscience, 19,* 3171–3182. (11)

van der Meer, A. L. H., van der Weel, F. R., & Lee, D. N. (1995). The functional significance of arm movements in neonates. *Science, 267,* 693–695. (10)

van der Pligt, J., de Vries, N. K., Manstead, A. S. R., & van Harreveld, F. (2000). The importance of being selective: Weighing the role of attribute importance in attitudinal judgment. *Advances in Experimental Social Psychology, 32,* 135–200. (14)

van der Pligt, J., & Eiser, J. R. (1983). Actors' and observers' attributions, self-serving bias, and positivity. *European Journal of Social Psychology, 13,* 95–104. (14)

van IJzendoorn, M. H., Juffer, F., & Duyvesteyn, M. G. C. (1995). Breaking the intergenerational cycle of insecure attachment: A review of the effects of attachment-based interventions on maternal sensitivity and infant security. *Journal of Child Psychology and Psychiatry, 36,* 225–248. (10)

Vandell, D. L. (2000). Parents, peer groups, and other socializing influences. *Developmental Psychology, 36,* 699–710. (10)

Vasta, R., & Liben, L. S. (1996). The water-level task: An intriguing puzzle. *Current Directions in Psychological Science, 5,* 171–177. (10)

Velakoulis, D., Pantelis, C., McGorry, P. D., Dudgeon, P., Brewer, W., Cook, M., Desmond, P., Bridle, N., Tierney, P., Murrie, V., Singh, B., & Copolov, D. (1999). Hippocampal volume in first-episode psychoses and chronic schizophrenia. *Archives of General Psychiatry, 56,* 133–140. (16)

Velluti, R. A. (1997). Interactions between sleep and sensory physiology. *Journal of Sleep Research, 6,* 61–77. (5)

Verrey, F., & Beron, J. (1996). Activation and supply of channels and pumps by aldosterone. *News in Physiological Sciences, 11,* 126–133. (11)

Viken, R. J., Rose, R. J., Kaprio, J., & Koskenvuo, M. (1994). A developmental genetic analysis of adult personality: Extraversion and neuroticism from 18 to 59 years of age. *Journal of Personality and Social Psychology, 66,* 722–730. (10)

Visser, T. A. W., Bischof, W. F., & DiLollo, V. (1999). Attentional switching in spatial and nonspatial domains: Evidence from the attentional blink. *Psychological Bulletin, 125,* 458–469. (8)

Vogeltanz-Holm, N. D., Wonderlich, S. A., Lewis, B. A., Wilsnack, S. C., Harris, T. R., Wilsnack, R. W., & Kristjanson, A. F. (2000). Longitudinal predictors of binge eating, intense dieting, and weight concerns in a national sample of women. *Behavior Therapy, 31,* 221–235. (11)

Vohs, K. D., & Heatherton, T. F. (2000). Self-regulatory failure: A resource-depletion approach. *Psychological Science, 11,* 249–254. (11)

Vokey, J. R., & Read, J. D. (1985). Subliminal messages: Between the devil and the media. *American Psychologist, 40,* 1231–1239. (4)

Volkow, N. D., Wang, G.-J., & Fowler, J. S. (1997). Imaging studies of cocaine in the human brain and studies of the cocaine addict. *Annals of the New York Academy of Sciences, 820,* 41–55. (5)

Volkow, N. D., Wang, G.-J., Fowler, J., Gatley, S. J., Logan, J., Ding, Y.-S., Hitzemann, R., & Pappas, N. (1998). Dopamine transporter occupancies in the human brain induced by therapeutic doses of oral methylphenidate. *American Journal of Psychiatry, 155,* 1325–1331. (3, 5)

von Restorff, H. (1933). Analyse von Vorgängen im Spurenfeld. I. Über die Wirkung von Bereichsbildungen im Spurenfeld [Analysis of the events in memory. I. Concerning the effect of domain learning in the memory field].*J. Psychologische Forschung, 18,* 299–342. (7)

Vygotsky, L. S. (1978). *Mind in society.* Cambridge, MA: Harvard University Press. (10)

Wachtel, P. L. (2000). Psychotherapy in the twenty-first century. *American Journal of Psychotherapy, 54,* 441–450. (15)

Wadden, T. A., & Stunkard, A. J. (1987). Psychopathology and obesity. *Annals of the New York Academy of Sciences, 499,* 55–65. (11)

Wagner, A. D., Desmond, J. E., Demb, J. B., Glover, G. H., & Gabrieli, J. D. E. (1997). Semantic repetition priming for verbal and pictorial knowledge: A functional MRI study of left inferior prefrontal cortex. *Journal of Cognitive Neuroscience, 9,* 714–726. (3)

Wagner, R. K. (1997). Intelligence, training, and employment. *American Psychologist, 52,* 1059–1069. (9)

Wahba, M. A., & Bridwell, L. G. (1976). Maslow reconsidered: A review of research on the need hierarchy theory. *Organizational Behavior & Human Performance, 15,* 212–240. (11)

Wahlbeck, K., Forsén, T., Osmond, C., Barker, D. J. P., & Eriksson, J. G. (2001). Association of schizophrenia with low maternal body mass index, small size at birth, and thinness during childhood. *Archives of General Psychiatry, 58,* 48–52. (16)

Wakely, A., Rivera, S., & Langer, J. (2000). Can young infants add and subtract? *Child Development, 71,* 1525–1534. (10)

Wakschlag, L. S., Lahey, B. B., Loeber, R., Green, S. M., Gordon, R. A., & Leventhal, B. L. (1997). Maternal smoking during pregnancy and the risk of conduct disorder in boys. *Archives of General Psychiatry, 54,* 670–676. (10)

Wald, G. (1968). Molecular basis of visual excitation. *Science, 162,* 230–239. (4)

Waldman, I. D., Weinberg, R. A., & Scarr, S. (1994). Racial-group differences in IQ in the Minnesota transracial adoption study: A reply to Levin and Lynn. *Intelligence, 19,* 29–44. (9)

Waller, N. G., Kojetin, B. A., Bouchard, T. J., Jr., Lykken, D. T., & Tellegen, A. (1990). Genetic and environmental influences on religious interests, attitudes, and values: A study of twins reared apart and together. *Psychological Science, 1,* 138–142. (3)

Walster, E., Aronson, E., Abrahams, D., & Rottman, L. (1966). Importance of physical attractiveness in dating behavior. *Journal of Personality and Social Psychology, 4,* 508–516. (14)

Wampold, B. E., Mondin, G. W., Moody, M., Stich, F., Benson, K., & Ahn, H. (1997). A meta-analysis of outcome studies comparing bona fide psychotherapies: Empirically, "All must have prizes." *Psychological Bulletin, 122,* 203–215. (15)

Warren, R. M. (1970). Perceptual restoration of missing speech sounds. *Science, 167,* 392–393. (8)

Warren, R. M. (1999). *Auditory perception.* Cambridge, England: Cambridge University Press. (4)

Washburn, M. F. (1908). *The animal mind.* New York: Macmillan. (1)

Wason, P. C. (1960). On the failure to eliminate hypotheses in a conceptual task. *Quarterly Journal of Experimental Psychology, 12,* 129–140. (8)

Waters, E., Merrick, S., Treboux, D., Crowell, J., & Albersheim, L. (2000). Attachment security in infancy and early adulthood: A twenty-year longitudinal study. *Child Development, 71,* 684–689. (10)

Watson, J. B. (1913). Psychology as the behaviorist views it. *Psychological Review, 20,* 158–177. (1)

Watson, J. B. (1919). *Psychology from the standpoint of a behaviorist.* Philadelphia, PA: Lippincott. (1)

Watson, J. B. (1925). *Behaviorism.* New York: Norton. (1, 6)

Watson, J. B., & Rayner, R. (1920). Conditioned emotional reactions. *Journal of Experimental Psychology, 3,* 1–14. (16)

Watson, T. L., Bowers, W. A., & Anderson, A. E. (2000). Involuntary treatment of eating disorders. *American Journal of Psychiatry, 157,* 1806–1810. (15)

Weaver, C. A., III, & Kelemen, W. L. (1997). Judgments of learning at delays: Shifts in response patterns or increased metamemory accuracy? *Psychological Science, 8,* 318–321. (7)

Weaver, C. N. (1980). Job satisfaction in the United States in the 1970s. *Journal of Applied Psychology, 65,* 364–367. (10)

Webb, W. B. (1979). Theories of sleep functions and some clinical implications. In R. Drucker-Colín, M. Shkurovich, & M. B. Sterman (Eds.), *The functions of sleep* (pp. 19–35). New York: Academic Press. (5)

Wechsler, D. (1991). *Wechsler Intelligence Scale for Children-III.* San Antonio, TX: Psychological Corporation. (9)

Wedekind, C., & Milinski, M. (2000). Cooperation through image scoring in humans. *Science, 288,* 850–852. (14)

Wegner, D. M., Schneider, D. J., Carter, S. R., III, & White, T. L. (1987). Paradoxical effects of thought suppression. *Journal of Personality and Social Psychology, 53,* 5–13. (16)

Weickert, T. W., Goldberg, T. E., Gold, J. M., Bigelow, L. B., Egan, M. F., & Weinberger, D. R. (2000). Cognitive impairments in patients with schizophrenia displaying preserved and compromised intellect. *Archives of General Psychiatry, 57,* 907–913. (16)

Weil, A. T., Zinberg, N. E., & Nelson, J. M. (1968). Clinical and psychological effects of marihuana in man. *Science, 162,* 1234–1242. (5)

Weinberg, R. A. (1989). Intelligence and IQ: Landmark issues and great debates. *American Psychologist, 44,* 98–104. (9)

Weinberg, R. A., Scarr, S., & Waldman, I. D. (1992). The Minnesota transracial adoption study: A follow-up of IQ test performances at adolescence. *Intelligence, 16,* 117–135. (9)

Weinberger, D. R. (1987). Implications of normal brain development for the pathogenesis of schizophrenia. *Archives of General Psychiatry, 44,* 660–669. (16)

Weinberger, D. R. (1999). Cell biology of the hippocampal formation in schizophrenia. *Biological Psychiatry, 45,* 395–402. (16)

Weiner, B. A., & Wettstein, R. M. (1993). *Legal issues in mental health care.* New York: Plenum. (15)

Weiner, J. (1994). *The beak of the finch.* New York: Knopf. (3)

Weinstock, C. (1984). Further evidence on psychobiological aspects of cancer. *International Journal of Psychosomatics, 31,* 20–22. (12)

Weisberg, R. W. (1994). Genius and madness: A quasi-experimental test of the hypothesis that manic-depression increases creativity. *Psychological Science, 5,* 361–367. (16)

Weissman, M. M., Bland, R. C., Canino, G. J., Faravelli, C., Greenwald, S., Hwu, H. -G., Joyce, P. R., Karan, E. G., Lee, C. -K., Lellouch, J., Lépine, J. -P., Newman, S. C., Oakley-Browne, M. A., Rubio-Stipec, M., Wells, J. E., Wickmaratne, P. J., Wittchen, H. -U., & Yeh, E. -K. (1997). The cross-national epidemiology of panic disorder. *Archives of General Psychiatry, 54,* 305–309. (16)

Weissman, M. M., Kidd, K. K., & Prusoff, B. A. (1982). Variability in rates of affective disorders in relatives of depressed and normal probands. *Archives of General Psychiatry, 39,* 1397–1403. (16)

Weissman, M. M., Leaf, P. J., & Bruce, M. L. (1987). Single parent women: A community study. *Social Psychiatry, 22,* 29–36. (10)

Weissman, M. M., Warner, V., Wickramaratne, P., Moreau, D., & Olfson, M. (1997). Offspring of depressed parents. *Archives of General Psychiatry, 54,* 932–940. (16)

Weller, A., & Weller, L. (1997). Menstrual synchrony under optimal conditions: Bedouin families. *Journal of Comparative Psychology, 111,* 143–151. (4)

Wellings, K., Field, J., Johnson, A., & Wadsworth, J. (1994). *Sexual behavior in Britain: The national survey of sexual attitudes and lifestyles.* New York: Penguin. (11)

Wells, G. L., & Bradford, A. L. (1999). Distortions in eyewitnesses' recollections: Can the postidentification-feedback effect be moderated? *Psychological Science, 10,* 138–144. (7)

Wells, G. L., Malpass, R. S., Lindsay, R. C. L., Fisher, R. P., Turtle, J. W., & Fulero, S. M. (2000). From the lab to the police station. *American Psychologist, 55,* 581–598. (7)

Wenger, J. R., Tiffany, T. M., Bombardier, C., Nicholls, K., & Woods, S. C. (1981). Ethanol tolerance in the rat is learned. *Science, 213,* 575–576. (5)

Whalen, P. J. (1998). Fear, vigilance, and ambiguity: Initial neuroimaging studies of the human amygdala. *Current Directions in Psychological Science, 7,* 177–188. (12)

Wheeler, D. D. (1970). Processes in word recognition. *Cognitive Psychology, 1,* 59–85. (8)

Wiborg, I. M., & Dahl, A. A. (1996). Does brief dynamic psychotherapy reduce the relapse rate of panic disorder? *Archives of General Psychiatry, 53,* 689–694. (16)

Wicklund, R. A., & Brehm, J. W. (1976). *Perspectives on cognitive dissonance.* Hillsdale, NJ: Erlbaum. (14)

Widiger, T. A., & Clark, L. A. (2000). Toward *DSM-V* and the classification of psychopathology. *Psychological Bulletin, 126,* 946–963. (15)

Widom, C. S. (1989). Does violence beget violence? A critical examination of the literature. *Psychological Bulletin, 106,* 3–28. (12)

Wieczorkowska, G., & Burnstein, E. (1999). Adapting to the transition from socialism to capitalism in Poland: The role of screening strategies in social change. *Psychological Science, 10,* 98–105. (11)

Wig, N. N., Menon, D. K., Bedi, H., Leff, J., Kuipers, L., Ghosh, A., Day, R., Koretn, A., Ernberg, G., Sartorius, N., & Jablensky, A. (1987). Expressed emotion and schizophrenia in North India: II. Distribution of expressed emotion components among relatives of schizophrenic patients in Aarhus and Chandigarh. *British Journal of Psychiatry, 151,* 160–165. (16)

Wilkins, L., & Richter, C. P. (1940). A great craving for salt by a child with corticoadrenal insufficiency. *Journal of the American Medical Association, 114,* 866–868. (11)

Willerman, L., Schultz, R., Rutledge, J. N., & Bigler, E. D. (1991). In vivo brain size and intelligence. *Intelligence, 15,* 223–228. (9)

Williams, C. L., Men, D., Clayton, E. C., & Gold, P. E. (1998). Norepinephrine release in the amygdala after systemic injection of epinephrine or escapable footshock: Contribution of the nucleus of the solitary tract. *Behavioral Neuroscience, 122,* 1414–1422. (7)

Williams, J. M. G., Mathews, A., & MacLeod, C. (1996). The emotional Stroop task and psychopathology. *Psychological Bulletin, 120,* 3–24. (13)

Williams, K. D., & Karau, S. J. (1991). Social loafing and social compensation: The effects of expectations of co-worker performance. *Journal of Personality and Social Psychology, 61,* 570–581. (14)

Williams, L. M. (1994). Recall of childhood trauma: A prospective study of women's memories of child sexual abuse. *Journal of Consulting and Clinical Psychology, 61,* 1167–1176. (7)

Williams, R. W., & Herrup, K. (1988). The control of neuron number. *Annual Review of Neuroscience, 11,* 423–453. (3)

Williams, T. J., Pepitone, M. E., Christensen, S. E., Cooke, B. M., Huberman, A. D., Breedlove, N. J., Breedlove, T. J., & Jordan, C. L. (2000). Finger-length ratios and sexual orientation. *Nature, 404,* 455–456. (11)

Williams, W. M. (1998). Are we raising smarter children today? School- and home-related influences on IQ. In U. Neisser (Ed.), *The rising curve* (pp. 125–154). Washington, DC: American Psychological Association. (9)

Willingham, D. B., & Goedert-Eschmann, K. (1999). The relation betweeen implicit and explicit learning: Evidence for parallel development. *Psychological Science, 10,* 531–534. (7)

Wilson, D. S., Near, D., & Miller, R. R. (1996). Machiavellianism: A synthesis of the evolutionary and psychological literatures. *Psychological Bulletin, 119,* 285–299. (14)

Wilson, E. O. (1975). *Sociobiology: The new synthesis.* Cambridge, England: Belknap. (3)

Wilson, J. R., & the editors of *Life.* (1964). *The mind.* New York: Time. (4)

Wilson, R. S. (1987). Risk and resilience in early mental development. In S. Chess & A. Thomas (Eds.), *Annual progress in child psychiatry and child development 1986* (pp. 69–85). New York: Brunner/Mazel. (10)

Wilson, T. D., Lindsey, S., & Schooler, T. Y. (2000). A model of dual attitudes. *Psychological Review, 107,* 101–126. (14)

Wimmer, H., & Perner, J. (1983). Beliefs about beliefs: Representation and constraining function of wrong beliefs in young children's understanding of deception. *Cognition, 13,* 103–128. (10)

Winer, G. A., & Cottrell, J. E. (1996). Does anything leave the eye when we see? Extramission beliefs of children and adults. *Current Directions in Psychological Science, 5,* 137–142. (4)

Winner, E. (1986, August). Where pelicans kiss seals. *Psychology Today,* 24–35. (10)

Winner, E. (2000). Giftedness: Current theory and research. *Current Directions in Psychological Science, 9,* 153–156. (9)

Winocur, G., & Hasher, L. (1999). Aging and time-of-day effects on cognition in rats. *Behavioral Neuroscience, 113,* 991–997. (5)

Winter, D. G., John, O. P., Stewart, A. J., Klohnen, E. C., & Duncan, L. E. (1998). Traits and motives: Toward an integration of two traditions in personality research. *Psychological Review, 105,* 230–250. (13)

Wirz-Justice, A. (1998). Beginning to see the light. *Archives of General Psychiatry, 55,* 861–862. (16)

Wiseman, R. (1995). The megalab truth test. *Nature, 373,* 391. (12)

Wittchen, H.-U., Reed, V., & Kessler, R. C. (1998). The relationship of agoraphobia and panic in a community sample of adolescents and young adults. *Archives of General Psychiatry, 55,* 1017–1024. (16)

Wittchen, H.-U., Zhao, S., Kessler, R. C., & Eaton, W. W. (1994). *DSM-III-R* generalized anxiety disorder in the National Comorbidity Survey. *Archives of General Psychiatry, 51,* 355–364. (16)

Wolkin, A., Rusinek, H., Vaid, G., Arena, L., Lafargue, T., Sanfilipo, M., Loneragan, C., Lautin, A., & Rotrosen, J. (1998). Structural magnetic resonance image averaging in schizophrenia. *American Journal of Psychiatry, 155,* 1064–1073. (16)

Wolman, B. B. (1989). *Dictionary of behavioral science* (2nd ed.). San Diego, CA: Academic Press. (9)

Wolpe, J. (1961). The systematic desensitization treatment of neuroses. *Journal of Nervous and Mental Disease, 132,* 189–203. (16)

Wong, A. H. C., Smith, M., & Boon, H. S. (1998). Herbal remedies in psychiatric practice. *Archives of General Psychiatry, 55,* 1033–1044. (16)

Wood, W., Lundgren, S., Ouellette, J. A., Busceme, S., & Blackstone, T. (1994). Minority influence: A meta-analytic review of social influence processes. *Psychological Bulletin, 115,* 323–345. (14)

Woodruff-Pak, D. S., Papka, M., & Ivry, R. B. (1996). Cerebellar involvement in eyeblink classical conditioning in humans. *Neuropsychology, 10,* 443–458. (6)

Woods, J. H., & Winger, G. (1997). Abuse liability of flunitrazepam. *Journal of Clinical Psychopharmacology, 17*(Suppl. 3), S1–S57. (5)

Woods, S. C. (1991). The eating paradox: How we tolerate food. *Psychological Review, 98,* 488–505. (11)

Woodward, E. L. (1938). *The age of reform.* London: Oxford University Press. (7)

Woodworth, R. S. (1934). *Psychology* (3rd ed.). New York: Henry Holt. (1)

Woolf, N. J., Zinnerman, M. D., & Johnson, G. V. W. (1999). Hippocampal microtubule-associated protein-2 alterations with contextual memory. *Brain Research, 821,* 241–249. (3)

Worthington, E. L., Jr., Kurusu, T. A., McCullough, M. E., & Sandage, S. J. (1996). Empirical research on religion and psychotherapeutic processes and outcomes: A 10-year review and research prospectus. *Psychological Bulletin, 119,* 448–487. (15)

Woychyshyn, C. A., McElheran, W. G., & Romney, D. M. (1992). MMPI validity measures: A comparative study of original with alternative indices. *Journal of Personality Assessment, 58,* 138–148. (13)

Wright, D. B. (1993). Recall of the Hillsborough disaster over time: systematic biases in 'flashbulb' memories. *Applied Cognitive Psychology, 7,* 129–138. (7)

Wright, I. C., Rabe-Hesketh, S., Woodruff, P. W. R., David, A. S., Murray, R. M., & Bullmore, E. T. (2000). Meta-analysis of regional brain volumes in schizophrenia. *American Journal of Psychiatry, 157,* 16–25. (16)

Wright, L. (1994). *Remembering Satan.* New York: Knopf. (7)

Wundt, W. (1902). *Outlines of psychology* (C. H. Judd, Trans.). New York: Gustav Sechert. (Original work published 1896) (1)

Wundt, W. (1961). Contributions to the theory of sensory perception. In T. Shipley (Ed.), *Classics in psychology* (pp. 51–78).

New York: Philosophical Library. (Original work published 1862) (1)

Wynn, K., & Chiang, W.-C. (1998). Limits to infants' knowledge of objects: The case of magical appearance. *Psychological Science, 9,* 448–455. (10)

Yarsh, T. L., Farb, D. H., Leeman, S. E., & Jessell, T. M. (1979). Intrathecal capsaicin depletes substance P in the rat spinal cord and produces prolonged thermal analgesia. *Science, 206,* 481–483. (4)

Yip, P. S. F. (1998). Age, sex, marital status, and suicide: An empirical study of East and West. *Psychological Reports, 82,* 311–322. (1)

Yirmiya, N., Erel, O., Shaked, M., & Solomonica-Levi, D. (1998). Meta-analyses comparing theory of mind abilities of individuals with autism, individuals with mental retardation, and normally developing individuals. *Psychological Bulletin, 124,* 283–307. (10)

Yoshikawa, H. (1994). Prevention as cumulative protection: Effects of early family support and education on chronic delinquency and its risks. *Psychological Bulletin, 115,* 28–54. (15)

Young, A. M. J., Joseph, M. H., & Gray, J. A. (1993). Latent inhibition of conditioned dopamine release in rat nucleus accumbens. *Neuroscience, 54,* 5–9. (16)

Young, C. W., & Supa, M. (1941). Mnemic inhibition as a factor in the limitation of the memory span. *American Journal of Psychology, 54,* 546–552. (7)

Young, G. B., & Pigott, S. E. (1999). Neurobiological basis of consciousness. *Archives of Neurology, 56,* 153–157. (3)

Yu, D. W., & Shepard, G. H., Jr. (1998). Is beauty in the eye of the beholder? *Nature, 396,* 321–322. (14)

Zadra, A. L., Nielsen, T. A., & Donderi, D. C. (1998). Prevalence of auditory, olfactory, and gustatory experiences in home dreams. *Perceptual and Motor Skills, 87,* 819–826. (5)

Zahavi, A., & Zahavi, A. (1997). *The handicap principle.* New York: Oxford University Press. (14)

Zahn, T. P. Rapoport, J. L., & Thompson, C. L. (1980). Autonomic and behavioral effects of dextroamphetamine and placebo in normal and hyperactive prepubertal boys. *Journal of Abnormal Child Psychology, 8,* 145–160. (3)

Zajonc, R. B. (1968). Attitudinal effects of mere exposure. *Journal of Personality and Social Psychology, 9*(Monograph Suppl. 2, Pt. 2). (14)

Zaragoza, M. S., & Mitchell, K. J. (1996). Repeated exposure to suggestions and the creation of false memories. *Psychological Science, 7,* 294–300. (7)

Zeanah, C. H., Boris, N. W., & Larrieu, J. A. (1997). Infant development and developmental risk: A review of the past 10 years. *Journal of the American Academy of Child & Adolescent Psychiatry, 36,* 165–178. (10)

Zehr, D. (2000). Portrayals of Wundt and Titchener in introductory psychology texts: A context analysis. *Teaching of Psychology, 27,* 122–126. (1)

Zeki, S. (1980). The representation of colours in the cerebral cortex. *Nature, 284,* 412–418. (3)

Zeki, S. (1983). Colour coding in the cerebral cortex: The responses of wavelength-selective and colour-coded cells in monkey visual cortex to changes in wavelength composition. *Neuroscience, 9,* 767–781. (3)

Zeki, S. (1993). *A vision of the brain.* Oxford, England: Blackwell Scientific Publications. (4)

Zeki, S., McKeefry, D. J., Bartels, A., & Frackowiak, R. S. J. (1998). Has a new color area been discovered? *Nature Neuroscience, 1,* 335. (4)

Zepelin, H., & Rechtschaffen, A. (1974). Mammalian sleep, longevity, and energy metabolism. *Brain, Behavior, and Evolution, 10,* 425–470. (5)

Zihl, J., von Cramon, D., & Mai, N. (1983). Selective disturbance of movement vision after bilateral brain damage. *Brain, 106,* 313–340. (4)

Zucker, R. A., & Gomberg, E. S. L. (1986). Etiology of alcoholism reconsidered. *American Psychologist, 41,* 783–793. (16)

Zullow, H. M., Oettingen, G., Peterson, C., & Seligman, M. E. P. (1988). Pessimistic explanatory style in the historical record. *American Psychologist, 43,* 673–682. (16)

Zuriff, G. E. (1995). Continuity over change within the experimental analysis of behavior. In J. T. Todd & E. K. Morris (Eds.), *Modern perspectives on B. F. Skinner and contemporary behaviorism* (pp. 171–178). Westport, CT: Greenwood Press. (6)

# Credits

This page constitutes an extension of the copyright page. We have made every effort to trace the ownership of all copyrighted material and to secure permission from copyright holders. In the event of any question arising as to the use of any material, we will be pleased to make the necessary corrections in future printings. Thanks are due to the following authors, publishers, and agents for permission to use the material indicated.

## Text Credits

**Chapter 1:** **16:** Figure 1.6 from National Science Foundation, SRS, Science and Engineering Doctorate Awards: 1999.

**Chapter 3:** **93:** Figure 3.34 adapted from *The Cerebral Cortex of Man,* by W. Penfield and T. Rasmussen. Copyright © 1950 Macmillan Publishing Co., Inc. Renewed 1978 by Theodore Rasmussen. Reprinted by permission. **93:** Figure 3.35 from *Clinical Neuropsychology,* 3rd ed., edited by Kenneth M. Heilman & E. Valenstein. Copyright © 1993 by Oxford University Press, Inc. Used by permission of Oxford University Press, Inc.

**Chapter 4:** **119, 120:** Figures 4.19 & 4.20 reproduced from *Ishihara's Test for Colour Blindness,* Kanehara & Co., Ltd., Tokyo, Japan. A test for color blindness cannot be conducted with this material. For accurate testing, the original plate should be used. Reprinted by permission. **127:** Figure 4.27 from "Picture and Pattern Perception in the Sighted and the Blind: The Advantage of the Late Blind," by M. A. Heller, *Perception,* 1989, *18,* 379–389. Reprinted by permission from Pion, London. **141:** Figure 4.43b from *Inversions,* by S. Kim. Copyright © 1989 by Scott Kim. Used with permission of W. H. Freeman and Company. **143:** Figure 4.46 from *Organization in Vision: Essays on Gestalt Perception,* by Gaetano Kanizsa, pp. 7–9. Copyright © 1979 by Gaetano Kanizsa. Reproduced with permission of Greenwood Publishing Group, Westport, CT. **144:** Figure 4.49b from "A Puzzle Picture with A New Principle of Concealment," by K. M. Dallenbach, *American Journal of Psychology,* 1951, *54,* 431–433. Copyright © by The Board of Trustees of the University of Illinois. **144:** Figure 4.50c from *Mind Sights* by Roger Shepard © 1990 by Roger N. Shepard. Used with permission of W. H. Freeman and Company. **146:** Figure 4.52 from "Contour Completion and Relative Depth: Petter's Rule and Support Ratio," by M. Singh, D. D. Hoffman and M. K. Albert, *Psychological Science,* 1999, *10,* 423-428. Copyright © 1999 Blackwell Publishers Ltd. Reprinted by permission.

**Chapter 5:** **162:** Figure 5.2 from "Monotonic and Rhythmic Influences: A Challenge for Sleep Deprivation Research," by H. Babkoff, T. Caspy, M. Mikulincer, and H. C. Sing, *Psychological Bulletin,* 1991, *109,* 411–428. Copyright © 1991by the American Psychological Association. Reprinted by permission. **168:** Figure 5.11 courtesy of T. E. Le Vere **173:** Cartoon reprinted by permission of Jesse Reklaw. **180:** Figure 5.19 reprinted

with permission from "The Use of Hypnosis to Aid Recall," by J. Dywan & K. Bowers, *Science,* 1983, *222,* 184–185. Copyright © 1983 American Association for the Advancement of Science.

**Chapter 7:** **246:** Figure 7.11 reprinted with permission from "Acquisition of a Memory Skill," by K. A. Ericsson, W. G. Chase, and S. Faloon, *Science,* 1980, *208,* 1181–1182. Copyright © 1980 American Association for the Advancement of Science. **246:** Figure 7.12 from "Semantic Memory Content in Permastore: Fifty Years of Memory for Spanish Learned in School," by H. P. Bahrick, *Journal of Experimental Psychology: General,* 1984, *113,* 1–29. Copyright © 1984 by the American Psychological Association. Reprinted by permission of the author. **252:** Figure 7.15 from "Long-Term Memory for a Common Object," by R. S. Nickerson and M. J. Adams, *Cognitive Psychology,* 1979, *11,* 287–307. Copyright © 1979 Academic Press. Reprinted by permission. **273:** Lyrics from I REMEMBER IT WELL, by Alan Jay Lerner and Frederick Loewe. © 1957, 1958 (Copyrights renewed) Chappell & Co. All rights reserved. Used by permission of WARNER BROS. PUBLICATIONS U.S. INC., Miami, FL 33014.

**Chapter 8:** **282:** Figure 8.3 from "A Spreading-Activation Theory of Semantic Processing," by A. M. Collins and E. F. Loftus, *Psychological Review,* 1975, *82,* 407–428. Copyright © 1975 by the American Psychological Association. Reprinted by permission of the author. **286:** Figure 8.8 from "Direct Measurement of Attentional Dwell Time in Human Vision," by J. Duncan, R. Ward and K. Shapiro, *Nature,* 1994, *369,* 313–315. Copyright © 1994 Macmillan Magazines Ltd. Reprinted by permission. **288:** Figure 8.11 reprinted with permission from "Mental Rotation of Three-Dimensional Objects," by R. N. Shepard and J. N. Metzler, *Science,* 1971, *171,* 701–703. Copyright © 1980 American Association for the Advancement of Science. **320:** Figure 8.38 from "Parallel Distributed Processing Explorations in the Microstructure of Cognition," Vol. 1: *Foundations,* by David E. Rumelhart et al., p. 8, figure 2. (Series in Computational Models of Cognition and Perception.) Copyright 1986 by MIT Press. Used by permission of the publisher.

**Chapter 9:** **337:** Figure 9.4 from the *Wechsler Intelligence Scale for Children,* 3rd Ed. Copyright © 1990 by The Psychological Corporation. Reproduced by permission. All rights reserved. **339:** Figure 9.8 from SAT materials selected from *10 Real SATs,* College Entrance Examination Board, 1997. Reprinted by permission of Educational Testing Service and the College Entrance Examination Board, the copyright owners. Permission to reprint SAT test materials does not constitute review or endorsement by Educational Testing Service or the College Board of this publication as a whole or of any other questions or testing information it may contain. **349:** Figure 9.12 reprinted with permission from "Familial Studies of Intelligence: A Review," by T. Bouchard and M. McGue, *Science,* 1981, *212,* 1055–1059. Copyright © 1981 American Association for the Advancement of Science.

**Chapter 10:** **359:** Figure 10.1 courtesy of Robin Kalat. **362:** Figure 10.5 adapted from "Movement Produced Stimulation in the Development of Visually Guided Behavior," by R. Held and A. Hein, *Journal of Comparative Physiological Psychology*, 1963, *56*, 872–873. Copyright © 1963 by the American Psychological Association. Reprinted by permission of the author. **366:** Figure 10.10 reprinted with permission from "Addition and Subtraction by Human Infants," by K. Wynn, *Nature*, 1992, *358*, 749–750. Copyright © 1992 Macmillan Magazines Limited. **394:** Figure 10.31 from "Resolving the Debate Over Birth Order, Family Size, and Intelligence," by J. L. Rodgers, *American Psychologist*, 2000, 55(6), 599–612. Copyright © 2000 by the American Psychological Association. Adapted by permission of the author.

**Chapter 11:** **417:** Figure 11.8 reprinted by permission of Gene DeFoliart from *The Food Insects Newsletter,* March 1990.

**Chapter 12:** **455:** Figure 12.6 from "An Opponent-Process Theory of Motivation: I. Temporal Dynamics of Affect," by R. L. Solomon and J. D. Corbit, *Psychological Review*, 1974, *81*, 119–146. Copyright © 1974 by the American Psychological Association. Reprinted by permission of the author. **467:** Figure 12.20 from Modernization and Postmodernization, by R. Inglehart 1997. Copyright © 1997 by R. Inglehart. Reprinted by permission of Princeton University Press. **474:** Figure 12.22 from "Maternal Smoking During Pregnancy and Adult Male Criminal Outcomes," by P. A. Brennan, E. R. Grekin, & S. A. Mednick, *Archives of General Psychiatry*, 1999, *56*, 215–219. Copyright © 1999 American Medical Association. Reprinted by permission. **480:** Table 12.2 adapted from "Comparison of Two Modes of Stress Measurement: Daily Hassles and Uplifts Versus Major Life Events," by A. D. Kanner, J. C. Coyne, C. Schaefer, and R. S. Lazarus, *Journal of Behavioral Medicine*, 1981, *4*, 14. Copyright © 1981 Plenum Publishing Corporation. Reprinted by permission. **481:** Figure 12.26 from *Type A Behavior and Your Heart*, by Meyer Friedman and Ray H. Rosenman. Copyright © 1974 by Meyer Friedman. Reprinted by permission of Alfred A. Knopf, Inc.

**Chapter 13:** **521:** Figure 13.18 from Minnesota Multiphasic Personality Inventory-2. Copyright © by the Regents of the University of Minnesota 1942, 1943 (renewed 1970), 1989. This profile from 1989. All rights reserved. **524:** Figure 13.20 reprinted by permission of the publisher from Henry A. Murray, Thematic Apperception Test, Cambridge, Mass.: Harvard University Press, Copyright © 1943 by the President and Fellows of Harvard College, © 1971 by Henry A. Murray.

**Chapter 14:** **538:** Figure 14.2 from "Performance on Indirect Measures of Race Evaluation Predicts Amygdala Activation," by E. A. Phelps, K. J. O'Connor, W. A. Cunningham, E. S. Funayama, J. C. Gatenby, J. C. Gore & M. R. Banaji, *Journal of Cognitive Neuroscience*, 2000, *12*, 729–738. Copyright © 2000 MIT Press. Reprinted by permission. **558:** Figure 14.10 from "A Critical Test of the Waist-to-Hip-Ratio Hypothesis of Female Physical Attractiveness," by L. G. Tassinary & K. A. Hansen, *Psychological Science*, 1998, *9*, 150–155. Copyright © 1998 Blackwell Publishers. Reprinted by permission. **564:** Figure 14.13 adapted from "Opinion and Social Pressure," by Solomon Asch, *Scientific American*, November 1955. Copyright © 1955 by Scientific American, Inc. All rights reserved.

**Chapter 15:** **589:** Quote from "Observation" by Dorothy Parker, copyright 1928, renewed © 1956 by Dorothy Parker from The Portable Dorothy Parker, by Dorothy Parker, introduction by Brendan Gill. Used by permission of Viking Penguin, a division of Penguin Books USA Inc. **597:** Figure 15.8 from *The Benefits of Psychotherapy*, by M. L. Smith, G. V. Glass and T. I. Miller. Copyright © 1980 The Johns Hopkins University Press. Reprinted by permission. **598:** Figure 15.9 from "The Effectiveness of Psychotherapy: The Consumer Reports Study," by M. E. P. Seligman, *American Psychologist*, 1995, *50*, 965–974. Copyright © 1995 by the American Psychological Association. Reprinted by permission. **599:** Figure 15.10 from "The Dose-Effect Relationship in Psychotherapy," by K. I. Howard et al., *American Psychologist*, 1986, *41*, 159–164. Copyright © 1986 by the American Psychological Association. Reprinted by permission of the author.

**Chapter 16:** **622:** Table 16.1, 16.2 from *Obsessions and Compulsions*, by Stanley J. Rachman and Ray J. Hodgson. Copyright © 1980 by Prentice-Hall, Inc. Reprinted by permission. **628:** Figure 16.9 from "Greater Reinforcement from Alcohol for Those at Risk: Parental Risk, Personality Risk, and Sex," by Levenson et al, *Journal of Abnormal Psychology*, 1987, *96*, 242–253. Copyright © 1987 by the American Psychological Association. Reprinted by permission of the author. **639:** Excerpts from Joshua Logan in *Moodswing* by Ronald R. Fieve. Copyright © 1975 by Ronald R. Fieve. Published by William R. Morrow & Co.

## Photo Credits

**Chapter 1:** **2:** © Mark Downey/Lucid Images/PictureQuest. **4:** (top left) © Galen Rowell/Corbis. (top right) © Mitchell Gerber/Corbis. (center far left) © Francoise deMulder/Corbis. (center far right) © Richard Ellis/NEWSMAKERS/Liaison. (bottom left) AP/Wide World Photos. (bottom right) AP/Wide World Photos. **7:** © Rick Doyle/Corbis. **8:** Courtesy of Michael E. Phelps and John C. Mazziotta, University of California Los Angeles School of Medicine. **9:** (left) © Tom Rosenthal/SuperStock. (right) © David Young-Wolff/Photo Edit. **11:** © Michael Heron/Woodfin Camp & Associates. **13:** © Fred J. Maroon/Photo Researchers. **15:** Wellesley College Archives & Notman. **18:** (top right) © The Walt Disney Company. **19:** © Tom Rosenthal/SuperStock. **20:** © Glenn Rileyno. **23:** © Dario Perla/International Stock. **24:** (left) © Bob Daemmrich/Stock Boston. (right) © Kerstin Geier, Gallo Images/Corbis.

**Chapter 2:** **28:** © Gale Zucker/Stock Boston. **30:** © Frans Lanting/Minden Pictures. **35:** After Pfungst, 1911, in Fernald, 1984. **36:** (above) AP/Wide World Photos. (below) © Palace of Versailles, France/ET Archive, London/SuperStock. **38:** © 1994 Center for Inquiry. **42:** (left) © Paul Chesley/Tony Stone. (right) © Tannen Maury/The Image Works. **43:** © Breese/Liaison Agency. **47:** © Herman Eisenmeiss/Photo Researchers. **50:** © Dave Schaefer/The Picture Cube. **53:** © 1995 David Madison.

**Chapter 3:** **64:** © Alfred Pasteka/Science Photo Library/ Photo Researchers. **66:** © T. Dickinson/The Image Works. **67:** © Enrico Ferorelli. **68:** (above) © Science Photo

Library/Photo Researchers. (bottom left) © Gordon & Cathy Illg/Animals Animals. (bottom center) © Tom & Pat Leeson/Photo Researchers. (bottom right) © Maslowski Wildlife Productions. **70:** (above) © ZEFA/The Stock Market. (below) From Ruch, 1984. **75:** © Dan Buravich/Photo Researchers. **79:** (above) © Custom Medical Stock Photos. (below) © Manfred Kage/Peter Arnold. **82:** © Custom Medical Stock Photos. **85:** (left) © Bettmann/Corbis. (right) © Reuters NewMedia/Corbis. **91:** (both) © Dr. Colin Chumbley/Science Photo Library/Photo Researchers. **92:** (left) Courtesy of Dana Copeland. (right) © Manfred Kage/Peter Arnold. **94:** (above) © Michael Rosenfeld/Tony Stone. (below) © Alfred Pasteka/Science Photo Library/Photo Researchers. **95:** (top left) © Wellcome Dept. of Cognitive Neurology/Science Photo Library/Photo Researchers. (top right) © Wagner, Desmond, Demp, Glover & Gabrielli 1997. (below) Courtesy of Drs. Scott T. Grafton and John D. Van Horn, Dartmouth Brain Imaging Center, Dartmouth College. **97:** © Bettmann/Corbis.

**Chapter 4:** **106:** © B&C Alexander/Photo Researchers. **108:** © A. Gragera/Latin Stock/Photo Researchers. **111:** (above) (both) © Glenn Rileyno; (below) E.R. Lewis, F.S. Werb, & Y.Y. Zeevi. **112:** © Swift Photography/Chase Swift. **115:** © Reuters NewMedia Inc/Corbis. 117: © Musée de Louvre, Paris/SuperStock. **118:** (all) ZEFA/Klaus Benser. **124:** © San Francisco Chronicle/Lea Zuzukino. **125:** © Julie Lemberger/Corbis. **130:** © Richard T. Nowitz/Photo Researchers. **133:** © Louis Psihoyos/Contact Press Images/Colorific!. **135:** © Louis Psihoyos/Contact Press Images/Colorific! **139:** From Lotto & Purves, 1999. **140:** (above) M. Bruck, P. Cavanagh & S.J. Ceci "Fortysomething: Recognizing Faces at One's 25th Reunion," in Memory & Cognition, 19:221–228. 1991. Reprinted by permission of M. Bruck. (below) D. Halstead/Liaison Agency. **141:** (both) San Francisco Exploratorium. **144:** Courtesy of McDonnell Douglas. **146:** © Stock Market/Globus Bros./ZEFA. **148:** (left) © Lowell Observatory, photo by Clyde Tumbaugh. (right) © Richard T. Nowitz/Photo Researchers. **149:** © Steve McGurry/Magnum Photos, Inc. **151:** (above) © Andrew Brilliant. (below) The Exploratorium/S. Schwartzenberg. **153:** (both) © Mark Antman/The Image Works. **155:** San Francisco Exploratorium.

**Chapter 5:** **158:** © Trois JM/Explorer/Photo Researchers. **160:** © Craig Aurness/Corbis. **161:** © Jeff Greenberg/The Image Works **165:** San Diego Historical Society. **166:** (top) © Cliff Frith/Bruce Coleman Inc. (Center) © Wayne Lankinen/Bruce Coleman Inc. (below) © Photodisc. **167:** © Richard Nowitz/Black Star. **173:** (both) Slow Wave © 1996 Nick Munford & Jesse Recklaw. **174:** © Patrick Ramsey/International Stock. **176:** © David Young-Wolff/Photo Edit. **177:** Mary Evans Picture Library. **178:** (both) AP/Wide World Photos. **180:** AP/Wide World Photos. **182:** © Michael A. Schwartz/The Image Works. **184:** (above) © R.L. Oliver/Los Angeles Times. (below) © Nevada Wier/Corbis. **188:** (left) E.D. London et al, Archives of General Psychiatry 47:567–574, 1990. (right) © Tannenbaum/Corbis Sygma. **189:** © University of Pennsylvania Museum. **190:** © Ted Soqui/Corbis Sygma. **191:** © Archives for Research in Archetypal symbolism, San Francisco.

**Chapter 6:** **196:** © Richard A. Cooke/Corbis. **198:** © Mark Stack/Tom Stack & Associates. **200:** (above) © Owen Franken/Corbis. (below) © Warnher Krutein/Liaison Agency. **201:** © Peter Turnley/Corbis. **203:** © Sovfoto/Eastfoto. **216:** © Time, Inc./Nina Leen, *Life Magazine.* **217:** © Time Inc./Robert Kelly, *Life Magazine.* **219:** © Ales Fevzer/Corbis. **220:** (top left) © Russell D. Curtis/Photo Researchers. (top right) © Michael Justice/The Image Works. **221:** © R. Derek Smith/Image Bank. **223:** (left) © L. Marescot/Liaison Agency. (right) © Jose Azel/Aurora. **227:** Photo © Stuart Ellins. **229:** © Joe McDonald/Corbis. **230:** (top right) © Sonda Dawes/The Image Works. (left) © Robb Kendrick/Aurora. **231:** Courtesy of Dr. Albert Bandura. **232:** (top left) © Jeff Christensen/Liaison Agency. (top right) © Tommy Hindley/Professional Sport/Topham/The Image Works. (below) © Eric A. Wessman/Stock Boston.

**Chapter 7:** **236:** © Lawrence Migdale/Photo Researchers. **238:** AP/Wide World Photos. **239:** Courtesy of Professor John Horton Conway. **240:** Wellcome Institute Library, London. **242:** Courtesy of James Kalat. **243:** © Joe McDonald/Corbis. **245:** (above) © Ann Dowie. (below) © H. Gans/The Image Works. **248:** © Frans Lanting/Minden Pictures. **251:** © John chumack/Galactic Images/Photo Researchers. **252:** © Spencer Grant/Stock Boston. **253:** © Paul A. Souders/Corbis. **258:** (above) © UPI/Corbis/Bettmann. (below) © Remi Benali/Liaison Agency. **259:** © Suzanne Corkin, Psychology Dept., MIT. **263:** (above) Courtesy of Blue Planet Software, Inc. Tetris © Elorg 1987–2002. (below) © Anthea Sieveking/Matrix International, Inc. **266:** (both) AP/Wide World Photos.

**Chapter 8:** **276:** © Anthony Howarth/Woodfin Camp & Associates. **278:** © Owen Franken/Corbis. **287:** © GPU Nuclear Corp. **290:** © Glenn Riley. **291:** © David Burnett/Contact Press Images. **292:** © Chip Hires/Liaison Agency. **293:** (both) © Anne Dowie. **294:** (top left) AP/Wide World Photos. (top right) © Porterfield/Chickering/Photo Researchers. (below) © Stephen McBrady. **295:** © Jim Sugar Photography/Corbis. **296:** (left) © Steve Cole/PhotoDisc. (right) HP Museum. **297:** (above) © Glenn Riley. (below) © Bettmann/Corbis. **298:** (left) © Hulton-Deutsch Collection/Corbis. (right) © UPI Bettmann/Corbis. 303: (both) © Susan Ashukian. **305:** (above) © Susan Ashukian. (below) © Jeff Greenberg/The Image Works. **306:** AP/Wide World Photos. **307:** © Jonathan Blair/Corbis. **311:** (all) Courtesy of Ann Premack. **312:** Elizabeth Rubert, Language Research Center, Georgia State University. **314:** © Stephen Rapley. **317:** James Kalat. **322:** © Paula Lerner/Woodfin Camp & Associates.

**Chapter 9:** **326:** © Tom Wurl/Stock Boston. **328:** © Reuters/George Mulala/Archive Photos. **332:** (far left) © Bob Daemmrich/The Image Works. (near left) © Bob Daemmrich/Stock Boston. (near right) © Richard Hamilton/Corbis. (far right) © Derick A. Thomas/Corbis. **337:** © W. & D. McIntyre/Photo Researchers. **341:** © Bob Daemmrich/The Image Works. **343:** © Fujifotos/The Image Works. **345:** © John Nordell/The Image Works. **347:** (above) AP/Wide World Photos. (bottom left) © Shelly Gazin/Corbis. (bottom right) © Liaison Agency. **350:** © Eric Futran Photography, Chicago. **353:** © Joseph Sohm, ChromoSohm Inc./Corbis.

**Chapter 10:** **356:** © William Hubbell/Woodfin Camp & Associates. **358:** © David Gifford/Science Photo Library/Photo Researchers. **360:** (above) © G. Gardner/The Image Works.

(below) © George Steinmetz. **363:** © Dr. Carolyn Rovee-Collier, Dept. of Psychology, Rutgers University, Busch Campus. **364:** (both) © Doug Goodman/Monkmeyer Press. **367:** © Yves de Braine/Black Star. **368:** (both) © Stephen Rapley. **369:** © Ann Dowie. **370:** (all) © Ann Dowie. 372: © Elizabeth Crews. **378:** © Pugliano/Liaison Agency. **379:** (above) © Rick Smolan. (below) © Reuters/Str/A/Archive Photos. 381: © Myrleen Ferguson Cate/Photo Edit. **383:** (top, all) © UPI Corbis/Bettmann (below) © Ted Streshinsky/Corbis. **385:** Harlow Primate Laboratory, University of Wisconsin. **386:** (above) Harlow Primate Laboratory, University of Wisconsin. (below) © Doug Menuez/PhotoDisc. **387:** (left) © Sepp Seitz/Woodfin Camp & Associates. (right) © Jeremy Horner/Corbis. **388:** © Patrick Ward/Stock Boston. **390:** © Galen Rowell/Mountain Light Photography. 391: © Stephane Cardinale/Corbis Sygma. **393:** (all) © Sally & Richard Greenhill. **395:** © Joel Simon. **396:** ©Jeremy Horner/Corbis. **397:** (left) © Reuters/Collin McPherson/Archive Photos. (right) © Michael Newman/Photo Edit. **398:** © C. Glassman/The Image Works. **399:** Courtesy of Ludmilla Chordas. **400:** (above) © David Young-Wolff/Photo Edit. (bottom left) © Tim Thompson/Corbis. (bottom right) © Stephanie Maze/Corbis. **402:** AP/Wide World Photos.

**Chapter 11:** **406:** © D.W. Fawcett/Photo Researchers. **408:** © Reuters/Colin Braley/Archive Photos. **411:** © Benn Mitchell/Image Bank. **413:** AP/Wide World Photos. **414:** © Mike Maple/Woodfin Camp & Associates. **415:** © Annie Griffiths Belt/Corbis. **416:** © Sally & Richard Greenhill. **417:** (left) © Niel Rabinowitz/Corbis (right) © Peter Menzel/Stock Boston. **421:** © Bob Daemmrich/The Image Works. **422:** (left,all) © Scott Vlaun. (right) © Stephen Trimble. **426:** (above) © Archive Photos/Express Newspapers. (below) © Museo del Prado, Madrid, Spain/Giraudon, Paris/Superstock. **427:** © Tony Freeman/Photo Edit. **429:** © Jonathan Nourok/Photo Edit. **430:** Reproduced by permission of the Kinsey Institute for Research in Sex, Gender and Reproduction Inc. **433:** (left) © Thierry Mayer/Photo Researchers. (Center) © Owen Franken/Corbis. (right) © Robert Holmes/Corbis. (below) Courtesy of San Francisco AIDS Foundation. **434:** (left) © Musée de Louvre, Paris/Lauros-Giraudon, Paris/Superstock. (right) AP/Wide World Photos. **435:** (left) "Man-Woman-Boy-Girl," 1972/John Money & Enke Erhardt, Baltimore/Johns Hopkins University Press. (right) Courtesy of Intersex Society of North America. **439:** From S. LeVay, 1991, A difference in hypothalamic structure between heterosexual and homosexual men, *Science* 253, 2034–1037. **440:** (both) © Michael Speaker. **441:** © Elizabeth Crews. **442:** © Karl Weatherly/Corbis. **443:** © Elizabeth Crews/The Image Works. **445:** AP/Wide World Photos.

**Chapter 12:** **448:** AP/Wide World Photos. **450:** © 1994 Paramount Pictures/Liaison. **451:** Reprinted with permission from the Association for the Advancement of Science, "The return of Phineas Gage: Clues about the brain from the skull of a famous patient," by H Damasio, T. Grabowski, R. Frank, A.M. Galabu & A.R. Damasio, *Science* 264, 1994. **452:** Petar Kujundzic/Reuters/Bettmann/Corbis. **454:** (left) © Tom Brakefield/Corbis. (right) © Phil Schermeister/Corbis. **456:** © Richard Nowitz/Corbis. **459:** (both) © Ann Dowie. **462:** (both) © Ron Kimball. **463:** (above, both) © John Boykin. (bottom, both) © Eibl-Eibesfeldt. **464:** (above) © Eibl-

Eibesfeldt. (below) © P. Ekman & W. Friesen, from *Unmasking the Face,* 2nd Edition 1984. Used by permission of P. Ekman. **465:** © Mark C. Burnett/Stock Boston. **470:** AP/Wide World Photos. **472:** (left) © Louise Gubb/The Image Works. (right) © "The Young Racers," an American International Picture/Movie Still Archives. **477:** © Bob Daemmrich/The Image Works. **478:** © Frankee (Jim Lenoir). **479:** © Wally Macnamee/Corbis. **481:** (top) © Paul Chesley/Tony Stone. (bottom) © Bill Horsman/Stock Boston. **484:** (left) AP/Wide World Photos. (right) © Bob Daemmrich/Stock Boston. **485:** © Bob Winsett/Corbis. **486:** (above) © Cindy Charles/Liaison Agency. (below) © Owen Franken/Corbis.

**Chapter 13:** **492:** © Ed Young/Science Photo Library/Photo Researchers. **494:** AP/Wide World Photos. **496:** (left) © The Granger Collection, New York. (right) © Archive/Photo Researchers. **497:** (below) Courtesy of Wolfgang Schuster. **499:** (left) © Kindra Clineff/The Picture Cube. (right) © Carol Palmer/The Picture Cube. **502:** © The Freud Museum. **503:** (left) © Corbis/Bettmann. (right) © Culver Pictures. **504:** (top left) © Silvio Fiore/Superstock. (top right) © Archive for Research in Archetypal Symbolism. (bottom left) © Christine Garrigan. (bottom right) © Pat Berrett. **505:** © UPI/Bettmann/Corbis. **506:** (top left) © Paul A. Souders/Corbis. (top right) © Jeremy Horner/Corbis. (bottom left) © Roger Woods/Corbis. (bottom right) © Jeremy Horner/Corbis **507:** (top left) © Nancy Richmond/The Image Works. (top right) © Mary Kate Denny/Photo Edit. (below) © Bettmann/Corbis. **508:** (above) © Bettmann/Corbis. (below) © Corbis. **511:** © Fujifotos/The Image Works. **513:** Courtesy of Morimura Yasumasa. **518:** © Glenn Riley. **524:** From Thematic Apperception Test by Henry A. Murray, Harvard University Press, Cambridge, MA, Photo by Henry A. Murray © 1971 by the President and Fellows of Harvard College.

**Chapter 14:** **532:** © Raghu Rai/Magnum Photos. **534:** AP/Wide World Photos **535:** © Bettmann/Corbis. **536:** (left) © N.H. Cheatham/Photo Researchers. (right) © Bob Daemmrich/Stock Boston. **538:** (top left) © Kevin Peterson/PhotoDisc/PictureQuest. (bottom left) © Rubberball Productions 1998/PictureQuest. (top right) © Kevin Peterson/PhotoDisc/PictureQuest. (bottom right) © Rubberball Productions 1998/PictureQuest. **539:** © James Wilson/Woodfin Camp & Associates. **540:** (left) © Michael Newman/Photo Edit. (right) © David Turnley/Corbis. **545:** © Reuters/Rick Wilking/Archive Photos. **547:** © Gerard J. Burkhart/Liaison. **548:** © Glenn Riley. **549:** © Hulton-Deutsch Collection/Corbis. **554:** © Richard Hume/PhotoDisc. **557:** Langlois, Roggman & Musselman, "Averaging Faces,"*Psychological Science*, Vol. 5, no. 4. 560: © PhotoDisc. **562:** © Steve Thornton/Corbis. **563:** © William Vandivert. **565:** AP/Wide World Photos. **566:** © Spencer Grant/Photo Edit. **567:** © Ali Meyer/Corbis. **569:** © Reuters/Joe Trave/Archive Photos. **573:** (all) © Stanley Milgram, from the film "Obedience," distributed by Pennsylvania State University Audio Visual Services.

**Chapter 15:** **578:** © National Gallery Collection: by kind permission of the Trustees of the National Gallery, London/Corbis. **580:** © Jay Mallin. **581:** (left) © Rene Ritler/AP Photo/Keystone. (right) AP/Wide World Photos. **582:** © 2002 The Munch Museum/Munch Wllingsen Group. Artists Rights Society (ARS) NY/Erich Lessing/Art Resource, NY. **583:** (above) ©

Brian Barr/Allsport. (below) AP/Wide World Photos. **584:** © Bob Daemmrich/The Image Works. **589:** © Cindy Karp/NYT Pictures. **591:** Courtesy of Ideas For Living, Inc. **592:** (left) © NASA/Corbis. (right) © Paramount Still Library. **594:** © Express Newspapers/Archive Photos. **596:** (left) © Richard T. Nowitz/Corbis. (right) © Will & Deni McIntyre/Photo Researchers. **597:** (left) © Zigy Kaluzny/Tony Stone Images. (right) © Ken Fisher/Tony Stone Images. **598:** © Bob Daemmrich/Stock Boston. **602:** © Jerry Cooke/Corbis. **603:** © P.F. Bentley/Black Star. **605:** (top) © Reuters NewMedia/Corbis. (bottom left) © Scott Manchester/Corbis Sygma. (bottom right) © S. O'Sullivan/Corbis Sygma.

**Chapter 16: 610:** Reunion des Musées Nationaux/Art Resource, NY. **612:** © Hulton Getty Collection/Liaison Agency.

**613:** AP/Wide World Photos. **615:** (left) © Alfred Hitchcock/Bettmann Archive/Corbis. (right) © Los Angeles Times. **617:** Courtesy of Professor Benjamin Harris. **618:** © Todd Gipstein/Corbis. **619:** (left) © Andrew Sacks. (right) Courtesy of Virtuality Better, Inc. **620:** © Dan Guravich/Corbis. **624:** © Katsuyoshi Tanaka/Woodfin Camp & Associates. **626:** © Owen Franken/Corbis. **630:** © Ed Kashi/Corbis. **634:** National Museum of American Art, Washington, D.C./Art Resource, N.Y. **635:** (both) AP/Wide World Photos. **638:** © 1994 B.S.I.P./Custom Medical Stock Photo. **640:** AP/Wide World Photos. **644:** © Guttman-Macley Collection/The Bethlem Royal Hospital and the Maudsley Hospital. **645:** © Grunnitos/Monkmeyer. **648:** (both) Courtesy of E.F. Torrey & M.F. Casanova/NIMH. **649:** © Lowell Georgia/Corbis.

# Name Index

# Subject Index

visual, 109–121
Web resources on, 157
*See also* Perception
**Sensitive period** a time early in life during which some kind of learning occurs most readily, 229
**Sensorimotor stage** according to Piaget, the first stage of intellectual development; an infant's behavior is limited to making simple motor responses to sensory stimuli, 368–369, *369*
**Sensory neuron** a neuron that carries information about touch, pain, and other senses from the periphery of the body to the spinal cord, 88
**Sensory store** a very brief storage of sensory information, 243–244, *244*
**Sensory threshold** the intensity at which a given individual can detect a sensory stimulus 50% of the time; a low threshold indicates the ability to detect faint stimuli, 135–136, *135*, *136*
**Serial-order effect** the tendency to remember the items near the beginning and end of a list better than those in the middle, 253
Serotonin, 84, 473
**Set point** a level of some variable (e.g., weight) that the body works to maintain, 420, *420*
**Sex chromosomes** the pair of chromosomes that determine whether an individual will develop as a female or as a male, 70, *70*
**Sex-limited gene** a gene that affects one sex more strongly than the other, even though both sexes have the gene, 70
**Sex-linked gene** a gene located on the X chromosome, 70
Sexual abuse, 475–476
 false memories of, 272
 recovered memories of, 269–270
 repressed memories of, 270
Sexual anatomy, 434–436, *435*
Sexual arousal, 433–434, *433*
Sexual assault, 474–475
Sexual behavior, 429–439
 AIDS and, 432–433, *433*
 contemporary surveys of, 430–431, *431*, *432*
 cultural differences in, *429*, *433*
 Kinsey survey on, 429–430
 violence and, 474–476
 Web resources on, 447
Sexual identity. *See* Gender identity
**Sexual orientation** a person's preference for either male or female sex partners, 434, 436–439
 brain anatomy and, 438–439, *439*
 results of surveys on, 436, *436*, *437*
 twin studies on, 437, *438*
Shape constancy, 146, *147*
**Shaping** a technique for establishing a new response by reinforcing successive approximations, 217
Shift workers, 163, *163*
**Short-term memory** a temporary storage of a limited amount of information, 244–247
 capacity of, 244–246, *245*, *246*
 decay of, 246–247, *247*
 long-term memory and, 247, *247*
 working memory and, 247–248
Side effects of antipsychotic drugs, 650

**Signal-detection theory** the study of people's tendencies to make hits, correct rejections, misses, and false alarms, 136–137, *136*
Sign language, 315–316
**Similarity** in Gestalt psychology, the tendency to perceive objects that resemble each other as belonging to a group, 145, *145*
**Single-blind study** a study in which either the observer or the participants are unaware of which participants received which treatment, 43, *43*
Situational factors, 569–575
 abnormal behavior and, 586–587
 commons dilemma and, 571–572, *572*
 escalation of conflict and, 569–570
 obedience to authority and, 572–574, *573*, *574*
 prisoner's dilemma and, 570–571, *570*
 *See also* Environment
Size constancy, 146, *147*
Size perception, 150–152, *150*, *151*
**Skeletal responses** movements of the muscles that move the limbs, trunk, and head, 214
Skinner box, 216, *216*
Skin senses, 126–130
Sleep, 161–176
 abnormalities of, 172–176
 circadian rhythms and, 161–164
 depression and, 632, *632*
 deprivation of, 162, *162*
 dreaming and, 167, 170–172
 evolutionary (or energy-conservation) theory of, 165–166, *166*
 monitoring cycles of, 167, *167*, *168∠169*
 repair and restoration theory of, 164–165
 shift workers and, 163, *163*
 stages of, 166–170
 strategies for, 175, *176*
 Web resources on, 195
**Sleep apnea** a condition causing a person to have trouble breathing while asleep, 174
**Sleeper effect** delayed persuasion by an initially rejected message, 249, 546
Sleep talking, 175
Sleepwalking, 175
Smell, sense of, 131–133, *132*
Smoking
 dependence on, 625–626
 hypnosis and, 179
 nicotine and, *187*, 189, 625–626, *626*
 operant conditioning and, 225, *225*
 pregnancy and, 361, 473, *473*
Social development, 386–388
 gender differences in, 400–401
 identity and, 387–388
**Social interest** a sense of solidarity and identification with other people, 505
Socialist party, 547, *547*
**Social-learning approach** the view that people learn by observing and imitating the behavior of others and by imagining the consequences of their own behavior, 230–233
 modeling and imitation, 230–231, *230*, *231*
 self-efficacy, 231–232, *232*